Thurgood Marshall High School
5000 Truesdale Ave.
Baltimore, Maryland 21206
410-396-5938

Call to FREEDOM

1865 to the Present

Sterling Stuckey ■ Linda Kerrigan Salvucci

HOLT, RINEHART AND WINSTON

A Harcourt Classroom Education Company

Austin • New York • Orlando • Atlanta • San Francisco • Boston • Dallas • Toronto • London

About the Authors

Sterling Stuckey is Professor of History and holds the President's Chair at the University of California, Riverside. Dr. Stuckey is the author of *Slave Culture: Nationalist Theory and the Foundations of Black America* and *Going Through the Storm: The Influence of African American Art in History*.

Linda Kerrigan Salvucci is Associate Professor of History at Trinity University, San Antonio, Texas. Dr. Salvucci is currently working on a book entitled *Ironies of Empire: The United States–Cuba Trade Under Spanish Rule*.

Editorial
Sue Miller, *Director*
Steven L. Hayes,
 Executive Editor
Robert Wehnke,
 Managing Editor
Hadley Lewis Watson,
 Senior Editor

Pupil's Edition
Suzanne Hurley,
 Associate Editor
Doug Sims, *Associate Editor*
Julie Beckman,
 Administrative Assistant

Teacher's Edition
Joni Wackwitz, *Editor*
Deborah Gronich Tate,
 Associate Editor

Ancillaries
Deborah Gronich Tate,
 Associate Editor
Dwonna N. Goldstone,
 Associate Editor

Fact Checking
Bob Fullilove, *Editor*
Vaishali Jhaveri, *Assistant Editor*
Annette Saunders,
 Assistant Editor

Copy Editing
Merillat Frost, *Copy Editor*

Editorial Permissions
Ann B. Farrar,
 Senior Permissions Editor

Art, Design and Photo
Book Design
Diane Motz, *Senior Art Director*
Candace Moore,
 Senior Designer
Robin Bouvette, *Designer II*
Sally Bess, *Designer*
Jane Dixon, *Image Designer*
Ed Diaz, *Design Associate*

Image Acquisitions
Joe London,
 Image Acquisitions Director
Tim Taylor,
 Photo Research Supervisor
Terry Janecek,
 Photo Researcher
Lyndol Descant,
 Assistant Photo Researcher
Jackie Berger,
 Assistant Photo Researcher
Elinor Strot,
 Photo Coordinator

Michelle Rumpf,
 Art Buyer, Supervisor
CoCo Weir, *Art Buyer*

Cover Design
Decode, Inc.

Design Implementation
rosa+wesley design

New Media Design
Ed Blake, *Design Manager*
Czeslaw Sornat, *Designer*
Mike Rinella, *Design Assistant*

New Media
Kate Bennett,
 Associate Director
Debra Dorman,
 Senior Project Manager II
Ken Whiteside,
 Senior Project Manager II
Lydia Doty,
 Senior Project Manager
Stacy Doolittle,
 Project Manager
Armin Gutzmer,
 Manager Training and Technical Support
Cathy Kuhles,
 Technical Assistant
Nina Degollado,
 Technical Assistant

Henry Clark,
 Technology Project Associate

Production
Gene Rumann,
 Production Manager
Leanna Ford,
 Production Coordinator

Electronic Publishing
Carol Martin,
 EP Senior Manager
Heather Jernt, *EP Senior Project Administrator*
JoAnn Brown, Lana Kaupp, Indira Konanur, Christopher Lucas, Rina Ouellette, Nanda Patel, Sally Williams, *EP Staff*

Media Production
Kim Anderson-Scott,
 Sr. Production Manager
Kadonna Knape,
 Production Coordinator
Susan Mussey,
 Production Supervisor

Manufacturing
Jevara Jackson,
 Manufacturing Coordinator

Cover photo: National Aeronautics and Space Administration

ISBN 0-03-052458-X

3 4 5 6 7 8 9 48 01

COVER: *On September 16, 1994, astronaut Mark C. Lee tested a new space system 130 nautical miles above Earth.*

Call to FREEDOM
1865 to the Present

CONTENTS

U.S. symbol, the bald eagle

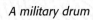
A military drum

A school for freedpeople

Song about
Ellis Island

ELLIS ISLAND BLUES

BY
HENRY SANTREY
BENTON LEY
AND
LEE DAVID

M.WITMARK & SONS
NEW YORK

Children working in a cannery

The Granger Collection, New York

Theodore Roosevelt campaign items

Trench warfare during World War I

The good times of the 1920s came to a screeching halt when the stock market crashed in October 1929.

Flappers during the 1920s

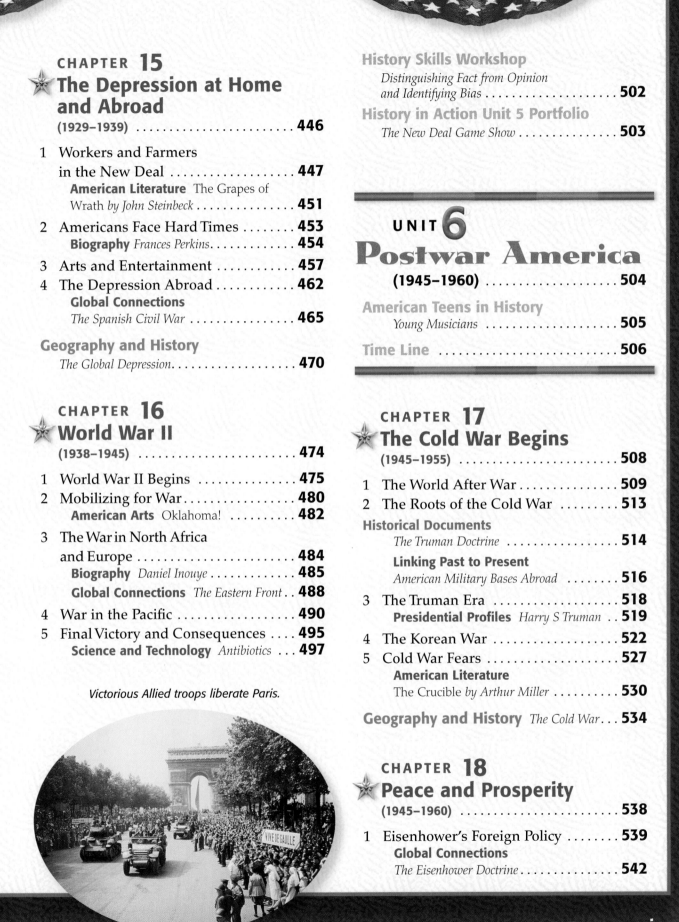

Victorious Allied troops liberate Paris.

A suburban family takes to the open road in the 1950s.

UNIT **7**

Searching for Solutions

CHAPTER 19
The Sixties

CHAPTER 20
The Search for Equal Rights

Martin Luther King Jr.

The Vietnam Veterans Memorial

*President Reagan and
Soviet leader Gorbachev*

NATO celebrates its 50th anniversary.

CHARTS

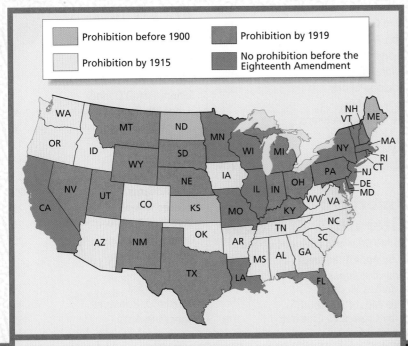

Prohibition before 1900
Prohibition by 1915
Prohibition by 1919
No prohibition before the
Eighteenth Amendment

Dry States, 1890–1919

Causes and Effects of World War II

Long-Term Causes
Treaty of Versailles
Debts from World War I
Global and local economic problems
Totalitarian governments
Repeated acts of aggression

Immediate Causes
Germany's invasion of Poland
Japanese aggression in Asia
Japanese attack on Pearl Harbor

World War II

Effects
Millions of deaths and widespread destruction in Europe and Asia
The Holocaust
The emergence of the United States as a superpower

FEATURES

◼ American Arts

◼ American Literature

◼ American Teens in History

◼ Biographies and Presidential Profiles

The Granger Collection, New York

I WANT YOU FOR U.S. ARMY
NEAREST RECRUITING STATION

Themes in American History

Call to Freedom begins every chapter with a set of theme questions. These questions are drawn from seven broad themes central to American history: Global Relations, Constitutional Heritage, Citizenship and Democracy, Technology and Society, Cultural Diversity, Geographic Diversity, and Economic Development. These themes provide a framework for the historical events in each chapter. This framework will help you understand the connections between historical events and see how past events relate to the social, political, and economic challenges our nation faces today.

As you begin each chapter, examine the theme questions and answer them based on your own experiences or prior knowledge. As you read the chapter, explore how the theme questions relate to the issues and events discussed. By tracing the themes through the book, you will be able to see how each theme has developed over time.

Global Relations

Since the first Asian nomads crossed a land bridge to the continent thousands of years ago, America has been involved in global events. The Global Relations theme invites you to trace ways in which our nation's political, social, and economic development has affected—and been affected by—other countries and their people.

An Inca knife

Constitutional Heritage

No study of American history would be complete without examining the U.S. Constitution, the document that provides the legal framework for our democratic government. The Constitutional Heritage theme will help you understand the Constitution's origins and how it has evolved through constitutional amendments, Supreme Court rulings, and congressional actions. This theme also explores how individuals and different groups in the nation's history have influenced the Constitution and have been affected by it. Finally, this theme asks you to consider how the relationship between Americans and their government has changed over time.

Citizenship and Democracy

The seal of the U.S. Congress

Throughout our history, Americans have struggled to define, possess, and protect individual rights and personal freedoms, such as the freedom of speech and religion, the right to vote, and the right to privacy. Americans have also worked to uphold the responsibilities of citizenship that accompany membership in our democracy. The Citizenship and Democracy theme explores how changing social, economic, and political conditions have influenced the theory and practices of these rights, freedoms, and responsibilities. This theme also examines the many conflicts that have arisen over these democratic values, and Americans' attempts to resolve these conflicts.

Technology and Society

From the building of the transcontinental railroad and the construction of skyscrapers during the Second Industrial Revolution to the computers that help you with your school assignments and personal projects today, technology has influenced every aspect of our culture and society. The Technology and Society theme explores technological developments and their influence on the U.S. economy and life.

Cultural Diversity

Our nation's rich and unique culture comes from its many ethnic, racial, and religious groups. The Cultural Diversity theme examines America's experience in dealing with diverse culture groups from the time of the Spanish explorers to recent immigration from around the world.

Geographic Diversity

The Geographic Diversity theme explores ways in which the nation's vast and diverse geography has played an important role in American history. The theme examines how the development of the nation's resources has helped shape its economy, society, and politics. In addition, the Geographic Diversity theme traces how public and government attitudes about resources and the environment have changed over time.

Economic Development

President Calvin Coolidge said in 1925 that "the business of America is business." The Economic Development theme asks you to explore the relationship between history and economics in the United States. The theme traces the changing relationship between government, business, and labor in America. It examines how the growth of a strong national economy has influenced the country's domestic and global politics, as well as individual lives and American society.

The Granger Collection, New York

Advertisement for barbed wire

★ Geography Themes ★

History and geography share many elements. History describes important events that have taken place from ancient times until the present day. Geography describes how physical environments affect human events. It also examines how people's actions influence the environment around them. To describe a series of events without placing them in their physical settings is to tell only part of the story. Geography themes include:

Location describes a site's position. It is the spot on the earth where something is found, often expressed in terms of its position in relation to other places.

Place refers to the physical features and the human influences that define a site and make it different from other sites. Physical features include landscape, climate, and vegetation. Human influences include land use, architecture, and population size.

Region is the common cultural or physical features of an area that distinguish it from other areas. One region may be different from another area because of physical characteristics, such as landforms or climate, or because of cultural features, such as dominant languages or religions.

Movement describes the way people interact as they travel, communicate, and trade goods and services. Movement includes human migration as well as the exchange of goods and ideas.

Human-Environment Interaction deals with the ways in which people interact with their natural environments, such as clearing forests, irrigating the land, and building cities. This theme is particularly important to the study of history in that it shows how people shape and are shaped by their surroundings.

Critical Thinking and the Study of History

Throughout *Call to Freedom*, you are asked to think critically about the events and issues that have shaped U.S. history. Critical thinking is the reasoned judgment of information and ideas. People who think critically study information to determine its accuracy. They evaluate arguments and analyze conclusions before accepting them. Critical thinkers are able to recognize and define problems and develop strategies for resolving them.

The development of critical thinking skills is essential to effective citizenship. Such skills empower you to exercise your civic rights and responsibilities. For example, critical thinking skills equip you to judge the messages of candidates for office and to evaluate news reports.

Helping you develop critical thinking skills is an important goal of *Call to Freedom*. The following eight critical thinking skills appear in the section reviews and chapter reviews.

Identifying Cause and Effect is part of interpreting the relationships between historical events. A cause is any action that leads to an event; the outcome of that action is an effect. Historians often point out multiple causes and effects for historical events. For example, economic and political problems caused the Soviet Union to break apart. This break-up ended the Cold War between the United States and the Soviet Union. This event in turn had many far-reaching effects.

A piece of the Berlin Wall

Evaluating is assessing the significance or overall importance of something, such as the success of a reform movement, the actions of a president, or the results of a major conflict. You should base your judgment on standards that others will understand and are likely to share. For example, you might consider the outcome of the Vietnam War and evaluate its effect on U.S. foreign policy. You could also evaluate the way in which debate over the war shaped domestic events in the United States.

Vietnam Service Medal

Synthesizing Information involves combining information and ideas from several sources or points in time to gain a new understanding of a topic or event. Much of the narrative writing in *Call to Freedom* is a synthesis. It pulls together historical data from many sources and perspectives from many people into a chronological story about our nation. Synthesizing information is important to understanding how many individual stories add up to create the big picture of events. Synthesizing the history of the Second Industrial Revolution, for example, might involve studying descriptions or images of factories and cities from the late 1800s, together with population and economic statistics. You could

Corliss engine

also examine the writings of industrial workers, business owners, immigrants, inventors, and others who lived during the period.

■ Drawing Conclusions is forming a possible explanation for an event, a situation, or a problem. This explanation should be an educated guess based on available evidence. Often you must be prepared to test your conclusions against new evidence or arguments. For example, a historian might conclude that the gains African Americans made because of the civil rights movement in the 1950s and 1960s inspired other groups to struggle for their rights. The historian would then organize the evidence needed to support this conclusion and challenge other explanations of the origins.

■ Determining the Strength of an Argument involves understanding the main points of an argument and determining if the argument is logical, well organized, and based on factual information. You should look for flaws in reasoning as well as possible errors in the conclusions of an argument. In addition, you need to consider whether the statements that the argument uses to support its points are accurate. For example, a historian might examine the Truman Doctrine and ask whether President Truman had a strong justification for telling the nations of the world that the United States would oppose the spread of communism.

■ Making Comparisons is examining events, situations, or points of view for their similarities and differences. *Comparing* focuses on both the similarities and the differences. *Contrasting* focuses only on the differences. For example, a comparison between the years immediately following World Wars I and II would note that both postwar economies had to adjust to decreased defense spending and the job requirements of returning veterans. In contrast, the United States was more involved in international politics

after World War II. Other factors to compare and contrast could include domestic reactions to communism following each war.

■ Identifying Generalizations and Stereotypes means viewing historical events and situations in ways that are fair to all cultural groups affected. Determining whether statements about a given group are consistent with each other and with the available facts helps you identify bias and unfair generalizations. Understanding how individuals and groups are sometimes inaccurately stereotyped by factors such as age, gender, religion, race, political views, and economic status broadens your knowledge of American history. For example, learning about American Indian cultures in the West before the arrival of American settlers helps you understand that settlers did not move into an empty western landscape. They encountered a land already settled by people with rich cultures.

■ Supporting a Point of View involves choosing a viewpoint on a particular event or issue and persuasively arguing for that position. Your argument should be well organized and based on specific evidence that supports the point of view you have chosen. Supporting a point of view often involves working with controversial or emotional issues. For example, you might consider the points of view surrounding the New Deal legislation of the 1930s. Whether you choose a position in favor of the agencies and programs created by the New Deal or against them, you would state your opinion clearly and give reasons to defend it.

New Deal poster

The Granger Collection, New York

ATLAS

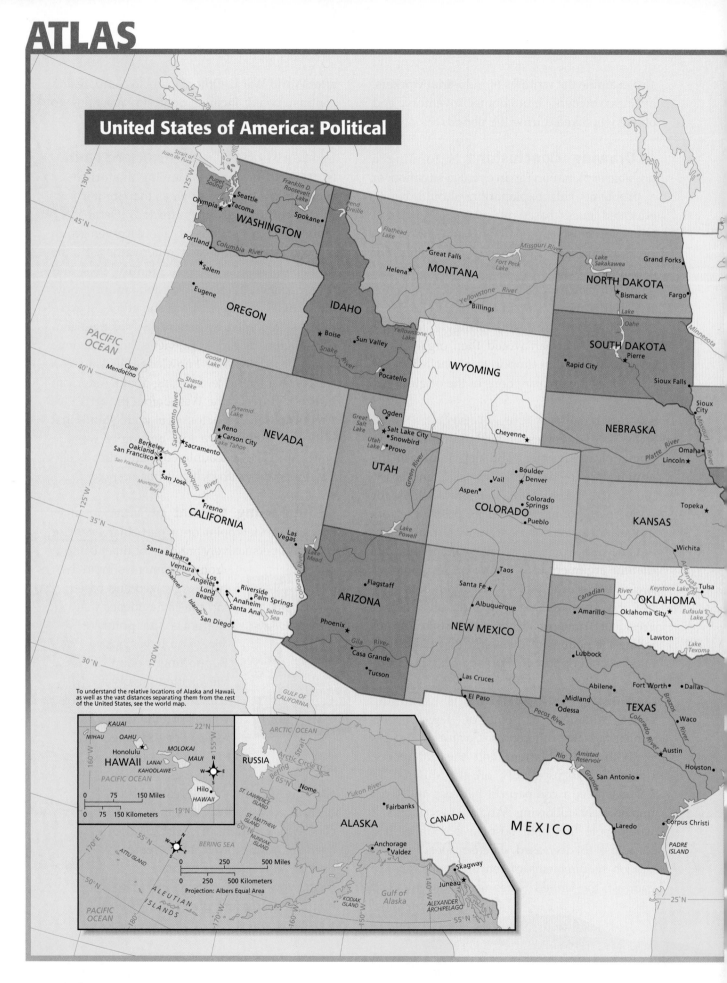

United States of America: Political

To understand the relative locations of Alaska and Hawaii, as well as the vast distances separating them from the rest of the United States, see the world map.

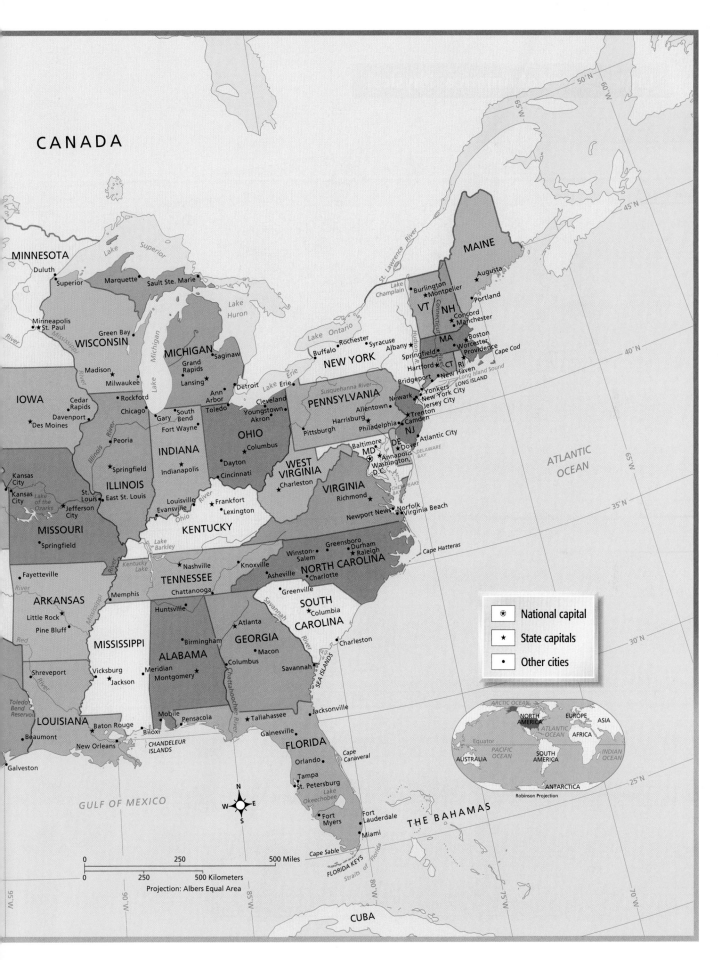

CANADA

MINNESOTA
Duluth
Superior
Marquette
Sault Ste. Marie
Lake Superior

Minneapolis
St. Paul
Green Bay
WISCONSIN
Madison
Milwaukee
Lake Michigan
MICHIGAN
Grand Rapids
Saginaw
Lansing
Lake Huron

IOWA
Cedar Rapids
Rockford
Davenport
Des Moines
Chicago
Gary
South Bend
Fort Wayne
Ann Arbor
Detroit
Lake Erie
Peoria
Springfield
INDIANA
Indianapolis
Dayton
Cincinnati
OHIO
Columbus
Toledo
Cleveland
Youngstown
Akron

Kansas City
Kansas City
Lake of the Ozarks
St. Louis
East St. Louis
ILLINOIS
Louisville
Evansville
Frankfort
Lexington
Ohio River
Jefferson City
MISSOURI
Springfield
KENTUCKY
Lake Barkley

Fayetteville
Kentucky Lake
Nashville
Knoxville
Asheville
TENNESSEE
Memphis
Chattanooga
Greenville

ARKANSAS
Little Rock
Pine Bluff
Red River
Huntsville
MISSISSIPPI
Birmingham
ALABAMA
Montgomery
Meridian
Jackson
Vicksburg
Shreveport
Mobile
Pensacola
GEORGIA
Macon
Columbus
Savannah
SOUTH CAROLINA
Columbia
Charleston
Chattahoochee River
Savannah River
Greenville
SEA ISLANDS

Toledo Bend Reservoir
LOUISIANA
Baton Rouge
Beaumont
New Orleans
Biloxi
CHANDELEUR ISLANDS
Tallahassee
Jacksonville
Gainesville
Galveston
GULF OF MEXICO
FLORIDA
Orlando
Cape Canaveral
Tampa
St. Petersburg
Lake Okeechobee
Fort Myers
Fort Lauderdale
Miami
Cape Sable
FLORIDA KEYS
Straits of Florida
THE BAHAMAS

CUBA

NEW YORK
Buffalo
Rochester
Syracuse
Albany
Lake Ontario
St. Lawrence River
MAINE
Augusta
Burlington
Montpelier
Portland
VT
NH
Concord
Manchester
Lake Champlain
Connecticut River
Hudson River
MA
Springfield
Worcester
Boston
Providence
Hartford
CT
RI
New Haven
Bridgeport
Cape Cod
Yonkers
New York City
LONG ISLAND
Long Island Sound
Newark
Jersey City
PENNSYLVANIA
Allentown
Harrisburg
Trenton
Camden
NJ
Pittsburgh
Philadelphia
Atlantic City
Susquehanna River
Baltimore
DE
Dover
MD
Annapolis
Washington, D.C.
DELAWARE BAY
WEST VIRGINIA
Charleston
VIRGINIA
Richmond
CHESAPEAKE BAY
Norfolk
Newport News
Virginia Beach
Cape Hatteras

Winston-Salem
Greensboro
Durham
Raleigh
NORTH CAROLINA
Charlotte
Cape Hatteras

ATLANTIC OCEAN

National capital ⊛
State capitals ★
Other cities •

ARCTIC OCEAN
NORTH AMERICA
EUROPE
ASIA
ATLANTIC OCEAN
AFRICA
Equator
PACIFIC OCEAN
SOUTH AMERICA
INDIAN OCEAN
AUSTRALIA
ANTARCTICA
Robinson Projection

N
W E
S

0   250   500 Miles
0   250   500 Kilometers
Projection: Albers Equal Area

50°N
60°W
65°W
45°N
40°N
65°W
35°N
30°N
75°W
25°N
70°W
80°W
85°W
90°W
95°W

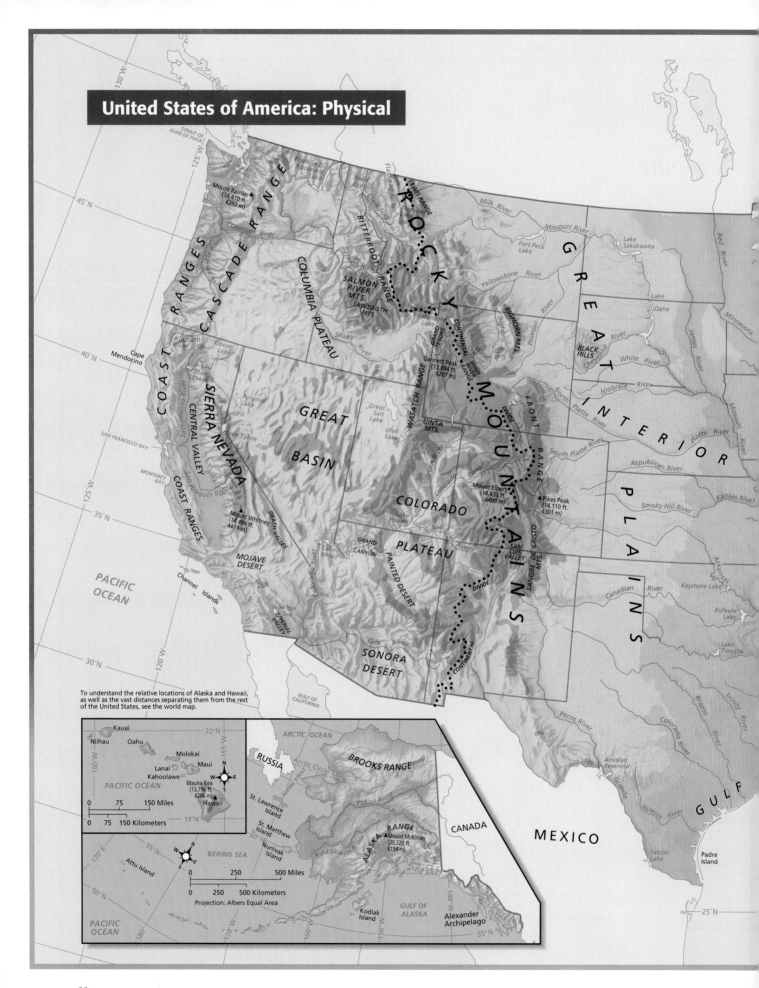

United States of America: Physical

STRAIT OF JUAN DE FUCA

130°W

125°W

45°N

Mount Rainier
(14,410 ft.
4392 m)

Franklin D. Roosevelt Lake

Pend Oreille

Flathead Lake

LEWIS RANGE

Milk River

Fort Peck Lake

Missouri River

Lake Sakakawea

COLUMBIA RIVER

Clark Fork

BITTERROOT RANGE

Yellowstone River

R O C K Y

G
R
E
A
T

Lake Oahe

Minnesota

COAST RANGES

CASCADE RANGE

COLUMBIA PLATEAU

SALMON RIVER MTS.

SAWTOOTH MTS.

Yellowstone Lake

CONTINENTAL DIVIDE

Wind River

GRAND TETON

WIND RIVER RANGE

BIGHORN MTS.

Powder River

James River

White River

BLACK HILLS

Cheyenne

River

Klamath River

Goose Lake

Snake River

40°N

Cape Mendocino

Shasta Lake

WASATCH RANGE

Gannett Peak
(13,804 ft.
4207 m)

Niobrara River

Missouri

M

O
U
N
T
A
I
N
S

I
N
T
E
R
I
O
R

Sacramento River

Pyramid Lake

GREAT

Great Salt Lake

UINTA MTS.

Green River

FRONT RANGE

North Platte River

SAN FRANCISCO BAY

SIERRA NEVADA

Lake Tahoe

BASIN

Utah Lake

DIVIDE

South Platte River

Republican River

CENTRAL VALLEY

Colorado River

Mount Elbert
(14,433 ft.
4400 m)

Pikes Peak
(14,110 ft.
4301 m)

P
L
A
I
N
S

35°N

MONTEREY BAY

COAST RANGES

San Joaquin River

Mount Whitney
(14,494 ft.
4419 m)

DEATH VALLEY

Lake Powell

COLORADO

Lake Mead

San Juan River

Smoky Hill River

Kansas River

120°W

125°W

Channel Islands

MOJAVE DESERT

GRAND CANYON

PLATEAU

SANGRE DE CRISTO MTS.

SAN LUIS VALLEY

Arkansas River

Keystone Lake

PACIFIC OCEAN

Salton Sea

IMPERIAL VALLEY

Colorado River

PAINTED DESERT

DIVIDE

Canadian River

Eufaula Lake

30°N

Gila River

SONORA DESERT

CONTINENTAL

Pecos River

Lake Texoma

To understand the relative locations of Alaska and Hawaii, as well as the vast distances separating them from the rest of the United States, see the world map.

GULF OF CALIFORNIA

Colorado River

Brazos River

Trinity River

Amistad Reservoir

Río Grande

Nueces River

G
U
L
F

25°N

Kauai

22°N

155°W

ARCTIC OCEAN

Falcon Lake

Padre Island

Niihau

Oahu

Molokai

RUSSIA

Arctic Circle

BROOKS RANGE

MEXICO

Lanai

Maui

N

Bering Strait

Yukon River

Kahoolawe

PACIFIC OCEAN

Mauna Kea
(13,796 ft.
4206 m)

Hawaii

19°N

160°W

0   75   150 Miles

0   75   150 Kilometers

St. Lawrence Island

St. Matthew Island

Nunivak Island

Kuskokwim River

ALASKA RANGE

Yukon River

CANADA

Mount McKinley
(20,320 ft.
6194 m)

140°W

170°E

55°N

50°N

180°

BERING SEA

0   250   500 Miles

0   250   500 Kilometers

Projection: Albers Equal Area

Attu Island

PACIFIC OCEAN

60°N

Kodiak Island

GULF OF ALASKA

Alexander Archipelago

55°N

CANADA

MESABI RANGE

Isle
Royale

Lake Superior

Lake Huron

Lake Michigan

Lake Ontario

St. Lawrence River

St. Lawrence Seaway

Lake Champlain

ADIRONDACK
MTS.

GREEN
MTS.

WHITE
MTS.

LONGFELLOW MTS.

St. John River

Penobscot River

Connecticut River

Cape Cod

LONG ISLAND SOUND

Long Island

P L A T E A U

A P P A L A C H I A N   M O U N T A I N S

Finger Lakes

CATSKILL
MTS.

Hudson R.

Delaware R.

ALLEGHENY PLATEAU

Allegheny River

Susquehanna River

Monongahela R.

Potomac River

DELAWARE
BAY

CHESAPEAKE
BAY

Kanawha River

James River

Roanoke River

PAMLICO
SOUND

Cape
Hatteras

Lake Erie

Scioto River

Ohio River

Wabash River

Illinois River

Mississippi River

Wisconsin River

Des Moines River

P L A I N S

Lake
of the
Ozarks

OZARK PLATEAU

OUACHITA
MTS.

White River

Red River

Kentucky Lake

Lake Barkley

Cumberland River

CUMBERLAND PLATEAU

GREAT SMOKY
MTS.

BLUE RIDGE MOUNTAINS

Tennessee River

P I E D M O N T

A T L A N T I C   C O A S T A L   P L A I N

Savannah River

Oconee River

Altamaha River

Sea Islands

Coosa River

Alabama R.

Tombigbee River

Chattahoochee River

Okefenokee
Swamp

Pearl River

Mississippi
Delta

Chandeleur
Islands

Sabine River

Toledo
Bend
Reservoir

C O A S T A L   P L A I N

GULF OF MEXICO

FLORIDA PENINSULA

Cape
Canaveral

Lake
Okeechobee

The
Everglades

Cape Sable

Florida Keys

STRAITS OF FLORIDA

THE BAHAMAS

CUBA

ATLANTIC
OCEAN

50°N

45°N

40°N

35°N

30°N

25°N

60°W

65°W

70°W

75°W

80°W

85°W

90°W

Elevation

Feet		Meters
13,120		4,000
6,560		2,000
1,640		500
656		200
(Sea level) 0		0 (Sea level)
Below sea level		Below sea level

Ice cap

ARCTIC OCEAN

NORTH
AMERICA

EUROPE

ASIA

ATLANTIC
OCEAN

AFRICA

Equator

PACIFIC
OCEAN

SOUTH
AMERICA

INDIAN
OCEAN

AUSTRALIA

ANTARCTICA

Robinson Projection

N
W E
S

0   250   500 Miles

0   250   500 Kilometers

Projection: Albers Equal Area

Atlas **xxiii**

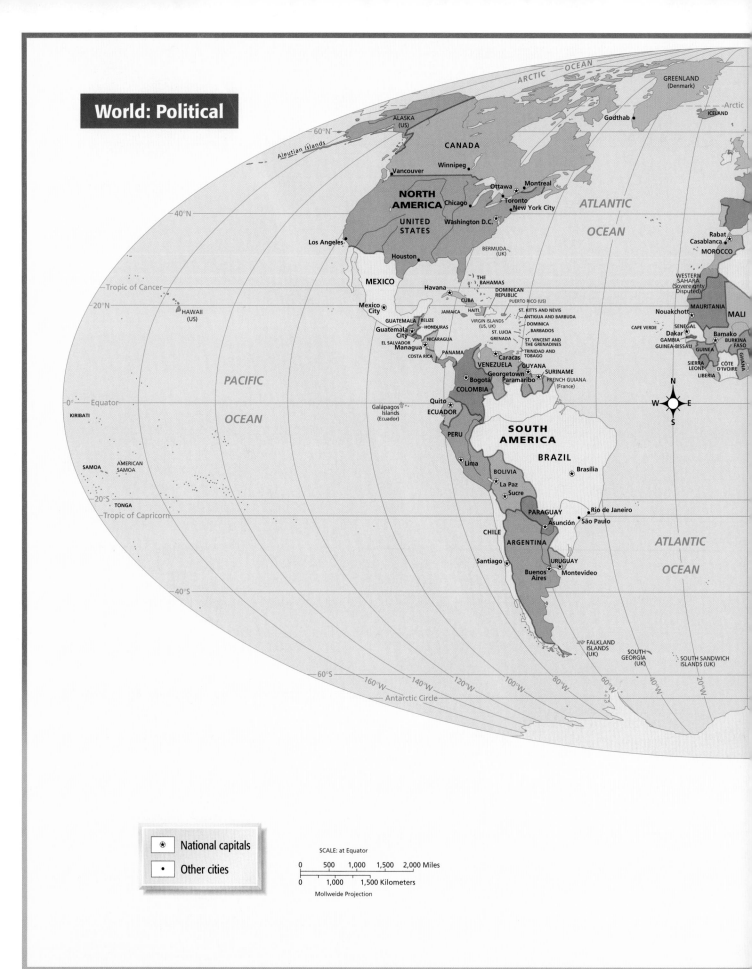

World: Political

ARCTIC OCEAN

GREENLAND (Denmark)

ICELAND

Godthab

Arctic

ALASKA (US)

60°N

Aleutian Islands

CANADA

Vancouver

Winnipeg

Ottawa
Montreal
Toronto
New York City

NORTH
AMERICA

Chicago

UNITED
STATES

40°N

Washington D.C.

ATLANTIC

OCEAN

Los Angeles

Rabat
Casablanca
MOROCCO

Houston

BERMUDA (UK)

MEXICO

Tropic of Cancer

Havana

THE
BAHAMAS

WESTERN
SAHARA
(Sovereignty
Disputed)

20°N

Mexico
City

CUBA

DOMINICAN
REPUBLIC

PUERTO RICO (US)

Nouakchott

MAURITANIA

MALI

HAITI

GUATEMALA

BELIZE

JAMAICA

VIRGIN ISLANDS
(US, UK)

ST. KITTS AND NEVIS
ANTIGUA AND BARBUDA

CAPE VERDE

SENEGAL

Dakar

Bamako

BURKINA
FASO

HAWAII
(US)

Guatemala
City

HONDURAS

DOMINICA

GAMBIA

GUINEA-BISSAU

GUINEA

GHANA

EL SALVADOR

NICARAGUA

ST. LUCIA
GRENADA

BARBADOS

SIERRA
LEONE

CÔTE
D'IVOIRE

Managua

ST. VINCENT AND
THE GRENADINES

LIBERIA

COSTA RICA

PANAMA

TRINIDAD AND
TOBAGO

VENEZUELA

Caracas

GUYANA

N

KIRIBATI

PACIFIC

Bogotá

COLOMBIA

Georgetown
Paramaribo

SURINAME

FRENCH GUIANA
(France)

W
E

0°

Equator

Quito

S

ECUADOR

Galápagos
Islands
(Ecuador)

OCEAN

PERU

SOUTH
AMERICA

SAMOA

AMERICAN
SAMOA

BRAZIL

Lima

Brasília

BOLIVIA

20°S

TONGA

La Paz
Sucre

Rio de Janeiro

Tropic of Capricorn

PARAGUAY

São Paulo

CHILE

Asunción

ATLANTIC

ARGENTINA

URUGUAY

OCEAN

40°S

Santiago

Buenos
Aires

Montevideo

FALKLAND
ISLANDS
(UK)

SOUTH
GEORGIA
(UK)

SOUTH SANDWICH
ISLANDS (UK)

60°S

160°W
140°W
120°W
100°W
80°W
60°W
40°W
20°W

Antarctic Circle

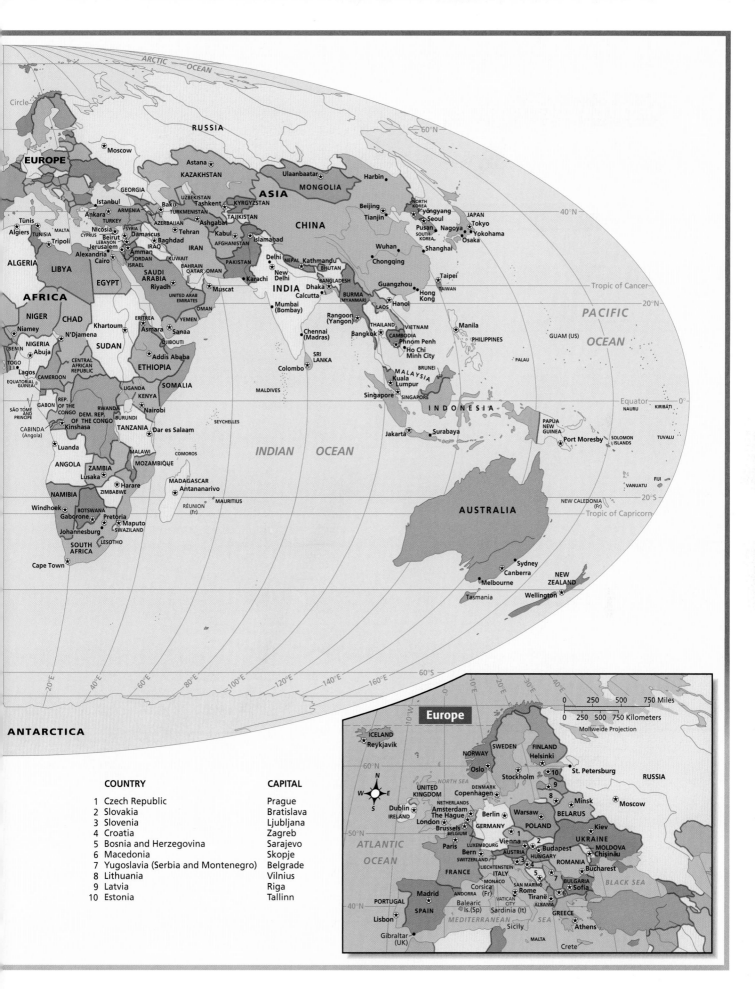

ARCTIC OCEAN

Circle

RUSSIA

EUROPE

Moscow

Astana

KAZAKHSTAN

Ulaanbaatar

MONGOLIA

Harbin

ASIA

GEORGIA

Istanbul

Ankara

ARMENIA

TURKEY

Baku

AZERBAIJAN

Tashkent

UZBEKISTAN

KYRGYZSTAN

TAJIKISTAN

Ashgabat

TURKMENISTAN

Beijing

Tianjin

NORTH KOREA

P'yŏngyang

Seoul

JAPAN

Tokyo

Nagoya

Yokohama

Osaka

SOUTH KOREA

Pusan

Tünis

TUNISIA

MALTA

Algiers

Tripoli

Nicosia

CYPRUS

Damascus

SYRIA

LEBANON

Beirut

Jerusalem

ISRAEL

Baghdad

IRAQ

Tehran

IRAN

Kabul

AFGHANISTAN

Islamabad

CHINA

Wuhan

Shanghai

Chongqing

ALGERIA

LIBYA

Alexandria

Cairo

EGYPT

Amman

JORDAN

KUWAIT

SAUDI ARABIA

Riyadh

BAHRAIN

QATAR

OMAN

UNITED ARAB EMIRATES

Muscat

PAKISTAN

Karachi

Delhi

New Delhi

NEPAL

Kathmandu

BHUTAN

INDIA

Calcutta

BANGLADESH

Dhaka

BURMA (MYANMAR)

Guangzhou

Taipei

TAIWAN

Hong Kong

Tropic of Cancer

PACIFIC OCEAN

AFRICA

NIGER

CHAD

Khartoum

SUDAN

ERITREA

Asmara

Sanaa

YEMEN

DJIBOUTI

Addis Ababa

ETHIOPIA

Mumbai (Bombay)

Chennai (Madras)

Rangoon (Yangon)

Bangkok

THAILAND

LAOS

Hanoi

VIETNAM

CAMBODIA

Phnom Penh

Ho Chi Minh City

Manila

PHILIPPINES

GUAM (US)

20°N

Niamey

BENIN

NIGERIA

Abuja

TOGO

Lagos

CAMEROON

EQUATORIAL GUINEA

N'Djamena

CENTRAL AFRICAN REPUBLIC

UGANDA

KENYA

SOMALIA

SRI LANKA

Colombo

MALDIVES

BRUNEI

MALAYSIA

Kuala Lumpur

PALAU

SÃO TOMÉ AND PRINCIPE

GABON

REP. OF THE CONGO

RWANDA

BURUNDI

DEM. REP. OF THE CONGO

Kinshasa

TANZANIA

Nairobi

Dar es Salaam

SEYCHELLES

Singapore

SINGAPORE

INDONESIA

Equator

NAURU

KIRIBATI

0°

CABINDA (Angola)

Luanda

ANGOLA

ZAMBIA

Lusaka

MALAWI

MOZAMBIQUE

COMOROS

Jakarta

Surabaya

PAPUA NEW GUINEA

Port Moresby

SOLOMON ISLANDS

TUVALU

NAMIBIA

Windhoek

BOTSWANA

Gaborone

Harare

ZIMBABWE

Antananarivo

MADAGASCAR

RÉUNION (Fr)

MAURITIUS

INDIAN OCEAN

FIJI

VANUATU

NEW CALEDONIA (Fr)

20°S

Tropic of Capricorn

Pretoria

Johannesburg

Maputo

SWAZILAND

LESOTHO

SOUTH AFRICA

Cape Town

AUSTRALIA

Sydney

Canberra

Melbourne

NEW ZEALAND

Tasmania

Wellington

ANTARCTICA

60°S

60°N

40°N

20°N

Equator

0°

20°S

60°S

COUNTRY	CAPITAL
1 Czech Republic	Prague
2 Slovakia	Bratislava
3 Slovenia	Ljubljana
4 Croatia	Zagreb
5 Bosnia and Herzegovina	Sarajevo
6 Macedonia	Skopje
7 Yugoslavia (Serbia and Montenegro)	Belgrade
8 Lithuania	Vilnius
9 Latvia	Riga
10 Estonia	Tallinn

Europe

0 250 500 750 Miles

0 250 500 750 Kilometers

Mollweide Projection

ICELAND

Reykjavik

NORWAY

SWEDEN

FINLAND

Helsinki

60°N

NORTH SEA

Oslo

Stockholm

10

St. Petersburg

RUSSIA

DENMARK

Copenhagen

9

8

Minsk

Moscow

N

W E

S

UNITED KINGDOM

NETHERLANDS

Amsterdam

The Hague

Berlin

Warsaw

BELARUS

Dublin

London

GERMANY

POLAND

Kiev

IRELAND

Brussels

BELGIUM

1

Vienna

2

Budapest

UKRAINE

MOLDOVA

Chişinău

50°N

Paris

LUXEMBOURG

AUSTRIA

3

4

HUNGARY

ROMANIA

Bucharest

ATLANTIC OCEAN

FRANCE

SWITZERLAND

LIECHTENSTEIN

ITALY

5

7

BLACK SEA

MONACO

San Marino

Rome

BULGARIA

Sofia

6

Corsica (Fr)

VATICAN CITY

ANDORRA

Tiranë

ALBANIA

GREECE

Madrid

SPAIN

Sardinia (It)

Balearic Is.(Sp)

40°N

PORTUGAL

Lisbon

Gibraltar (UK)

MEDITERRANEAN SEA

Sicily

MALTA

Athens

Crete

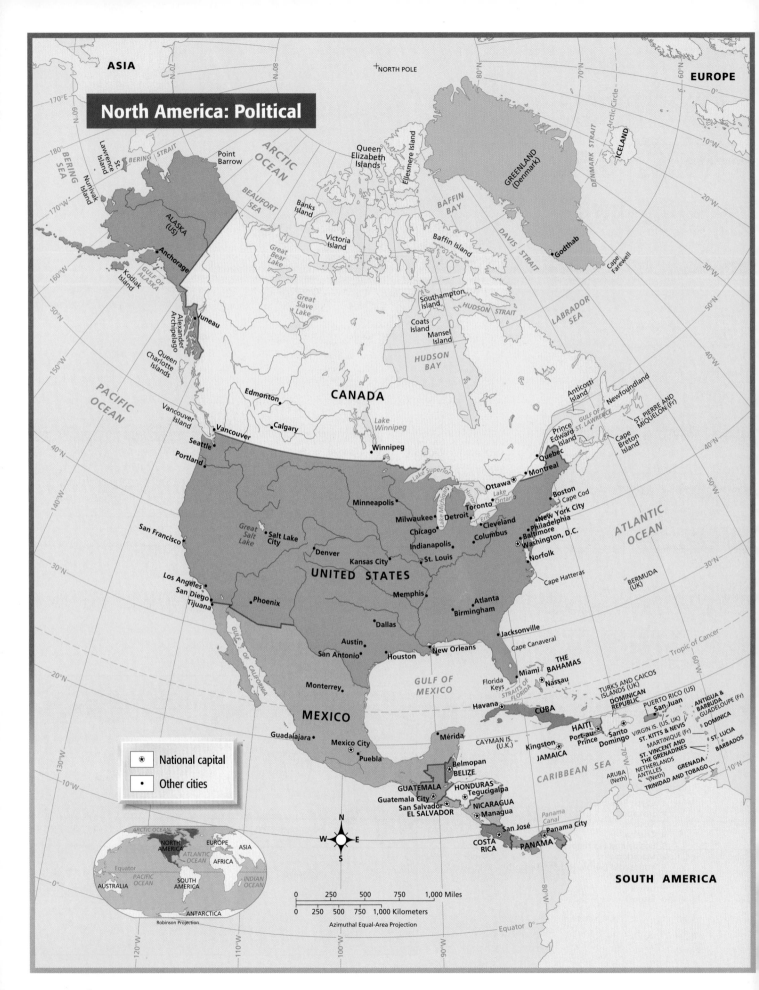

North America: Political

ASIA

EUROPE

†NORTH POLE

ARCTIC OCEAN

BERING STRAIT

St. Lawrence Island

Point Barrow

Queen Elizabeth Islands

Ellesmere Island

GREENLAND (Denmark)

ICELAND

Nunivak Island

BEAUFORT SEA

Banks Island

BAFFIN BAY

DENMARK STRAIT

ALASKA (US)

Anchorage

Victoria Island

Baffin Island

Godthab

DAVIS STRAIT

Cape Farewell

Kodiak Island

GULF OF ALASKA

Juneau

Great Bear Lake

Southampton Island

HUDSON STRAIT

LABRADOR SEA

Alexander Archipelago

Great Slave Lake

Coats Island

Mansel Island

Queen Charlotte Islands

HUDSON BAY

Vancouver Island

Edmonton

CANADA

Anticosti Island

Newfoundland

GULF OF ST. LAWRENCE

ST. PIERRE AND MIQUELON (Fr)

Vancouver

Calgary

Lake Winnipeg

Prince Edward Island

Cape Breton Island

Seattle

Winnipeg

Quebec

Portland

Lake Superior

Montreal

Ottawa

Lake Huron

Boston

Cape Cod

PACIFIC OCEAN

Minneapolis

Toronto

Lake Ontario

New York City

Milwaukee

Detroit

Lake Erie

Philadelphia

ATLANTIC OCEAN

San Francisco

Great Salt Lake

Salt Lake City

Chicago

Cleveland

Baltimore

Columbus

Washington, D.C.

Denver

Indianapolis

UNITED STATES

St. Louis

Kansas City

Norfolk

Los Angeles

Phoenix

Memphis

Cape Hatteras

BERMUDA (UK)

San Diego

Tijuana

Atlanta

Birmingham

Dallas

Jacksonville

Cape Canaveral

Austin

Houston

New Orleans

Tropic of Cancer

San Antonio

THE BAHAMAS

Monterrey

GULF OF MEXICO

Florida Keys

STRAITS OF FLORIDA

Nassau

TURKS AND CAICOS ISLANDS (UK)

MEXICO

Havana

CUBA

DOMINICAN REPUBLIC

PUERTO RICO (US)

San Juan

ANTIGUA & BARBUDA

GUADELOUPE (Fr)

Guadalajara

Mexico City

Puebla

Mérida

CAYMAN IS. (U.K.)

Kingston

JAMAICA

HAITI

Port-au-Prince

Santo Domingo

VIRGIN IS. (US, UK)

ST. KITTS & NEVIS

MARTINIQUE (Fr)

DOMINICA

ST. LUCIA

BELIZE

Belmopan

ST. VINCENT AND THE GRENADINES

BARBADOS

GUATEMALA

HONDURAS

Tegucigalpa

CARIBBEAN SEA

ARUBA (Neth)

NETHERLANDS ANTILLES (Neth)

GRENADA

TRINIDAD AND TOBAGO

Guatemala City

San Salvador

EL SALVADOR

NICARAGUA

Managua

Panama Canal

San José

Panama City

COSTA RICA

PANAMA

SOUTH AMERICA

| National capital ⊛ |
| Other cities • |

ARCTIC OCEAN

NORTH AMERICA

EUROPE

ASIA

ATLANTIC OCEAN

AFRICA

Equator

PACIFIC OCEAN

SOUTH AMERICA

INDIAN OCEAN

AUSTRALIA

ANTARCTICA

Robinson Projection

N W E S

0   250   500   750   1,000 Miles

0   250   500   750   1,000 Kilometers

Azimuthal Equal-Area Projection

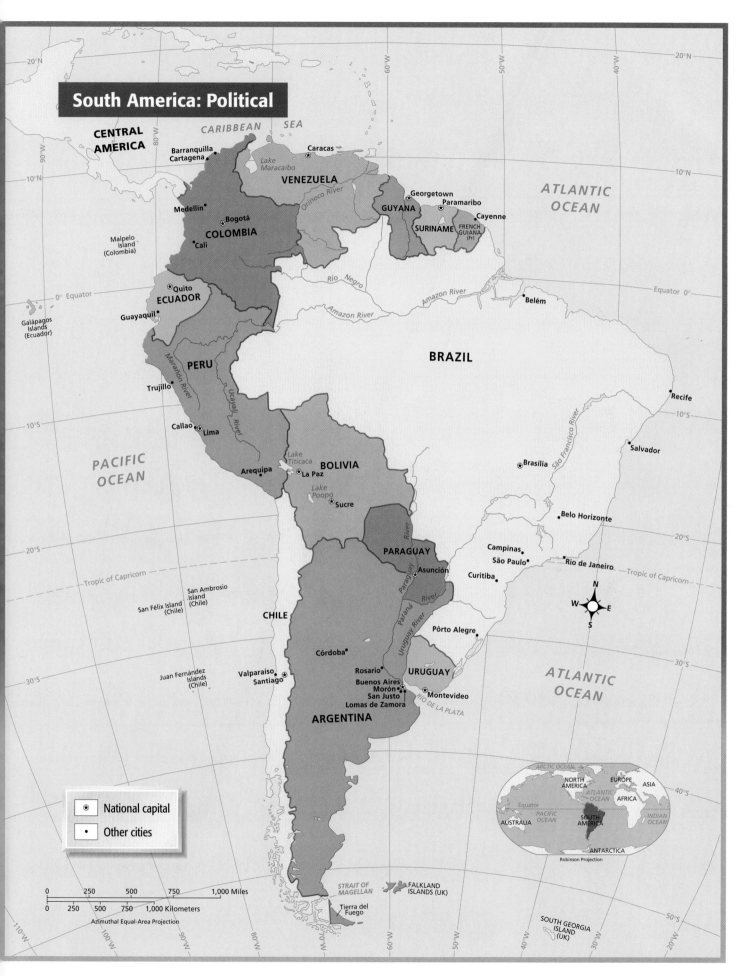

South America: Political

CENTRAL
AMERICA

CARIBBEAN SEA

Barranquilla
Cartagena

Caracas

VENEZUELA

Orinoco River

ATLANTIC
OCEAN

Lake
Maracaibo

Medellin

Bogotá

COLOMBIA

Georgetown
Paramaribo
Cayenne

GUYANA

SURINAME

FRENCH
GUIANA
(Fr)

Malpelo
Island
(Colombia)

Cali

Quito

Rio Negro

ECUADOR

Equator

Amazon River

Equator 0°

Galápagos
Islands
(Ecuador)

Guayaquil

Amazon River

Belém

BRAZIL

Marañón River

PERU

Trujillo

Ucayali River

Recife

Callao
Lima

10°S

Arequipa

Lake
Titicaca

BOLIVIA

Salvador

PACIFIC
OCEAN

La Paz

Brasília

São Francisco River

Lake
Poopó

Sucre

Belo Horizonte

River

Campinas

PARAGUAY

20°S

São Paulo

Rio de Janeiro

Paraguay River

Asunción

Curitiba

Tropic of Capricorn

San Ambrosio
Island
(Chile)

San Félix Island
(Chile)

CHILE

Paraná River

Uruguay River

N

W   E

S

Pôrto Alegre

Juan Fernández
Islands
(Chile)

Córdoba

Rosario

URUGUAY

Valparaíso
Santiago

Buenos Aires
Morón
San Justo
Lomas de Zamora

Montevideo

RIO DE LA PLATA

ATLANTIC
OCEAN

ARGENTINA

National capital

Other cities

ARCTIC OCEAN

NORTH
AMERICA

EUROPE

ASIA

ATLANTIC
OCEAN

AFRICA

PACIFIC
OCEAN

SOUTH
AMERICA

INDIAN
OCEAN

AUSTRALIA

ANTARCTICA

Robinson Projection

0   250   500   750   1,000 Miles

0   250   500   750   1,000 Kilometers

Azimuthal Equal-Area Projection

STRAIT OF
MAGELLAN

FALKLAND
ISLANDS (UK)

Tierra del
Fuego

SOUTH GEORGIA
ISLAND
(UK)

Europe: Political

ASIA

URAL MOUNTAINS

RUSSIA

Nizhny Novgorod

Moscow

BARENTS SEA

WHITE SEA

St. Petersburg

Helsinki

FINLAND

GULF OF BOTHNIA

Tallinn

ESTONIA

LATVIA

Riga

LITHUANIA

Vilnius

RUSSIA

Minsk

BELARUS

Kiev

UKRAINE

Don River

Volga River

Ural River

CASPIAN SEA

SOUTHWEST ASIA

BLACK SEA

Dnieper River

MOLDOVA

Chișinău

Odesa

Bucharest

ROMANIA

Danube River

YUGOSLAVIA

Belgrade

SERBIA

BULGARIA

Sofia

Skopje

MACEDONIA

ALBANIA

Tirana

Thessaloniki

GREECE

Athens

AEGEAN SEA

Rhodes

Crete

NORTH CAPE

Arctic Circle

ARCTIC OCEAN

SWEDEN

Stockholm

Göteborg

NORWAY

Oslo

Bergen

BALTIC SEA

Warsaw

POLAND

Łódź

Krakow

SLOVAKIA

Bratislava

HUNGARY

Budapest

Vienna

AUSTRIA

CZECH REPUBLIC

Prague

SLOVENIA

Ljubljana

Zagreb

CROATIA

BOSNIA & HERZEGOVINA

Sarajevo

MONTENEGRO

ADRIATIC SEA

SAN MARINO

San Marino

ITALY

Rome

VATICAN CITY

Naples

Palermo

Sicily

MALTA

Valletta

MEDITERRANEAN SEA

DENMARK

Copenhagen

Hamburg

Berlin

Leipzig

Dresden

GERMANY

Cologne

Bonn

Elbe River

Munich

LIECHTENSTEIN

Vaduz

Bern

SWITZERLAND

Lake Geneva

Milan

Turin

MONACO

Monaco

Corsica (France)

Sardinia (Italy)

Rhine River

Danube River

Po River

ALPS

FRANCE

Lyon

Marseille

Rhône River

Seine River

Loire River

BAY OF BISCAY

PYRENEES

ANDORRA

Andorra la Vella

Barcelona

Balearic Islands (Spain)

Valencia

SPAIN

Madrid

Seville

Gibraltar (UK)

STRAIT OF GIBRALTAR

PORTUGAL

Lisbon

Tagus River

AFRICA

NETHERLANDS

The Hague

Amsterdam

Rotterdam

Antwerp

BELGIUM

Brussels

LUXEMBOURG

Luxembourg

Paris

ENGLISH CHANNEL

Channel Islands (UK)

UNITED KINGDOM

SCOTLAND

Glasgow

Edinburgh

NORTHERN IRELAND

Belfast

IRELAND

Dublin

Manchester

Leeds

Sheffield

Liverpool

Birmingham

ENGLAND

WALES

London

British Isles

Shetland Islands

FAEROE ISLANDS (Denmark)

NORTH SEA

ICELAND

Reykjavik

ATLANTIC OCEAN

500 Miles

500 Kilometers

250

250

0

0

Azimuthal Equal-Area Projection

N E S W

EUROPE

ASIA

AFRICA

NORTH AMERICA

SOUTH AMERICA

ANTARCTICA

AUSTRALIA

PACIFIC OCEAN

ATLANTIC OCEAN

INDIAN OCEAN

ARCTIC OCEAN

Equator

Robinson Projection

Asia: Political

National capital ⊛
Other cities •

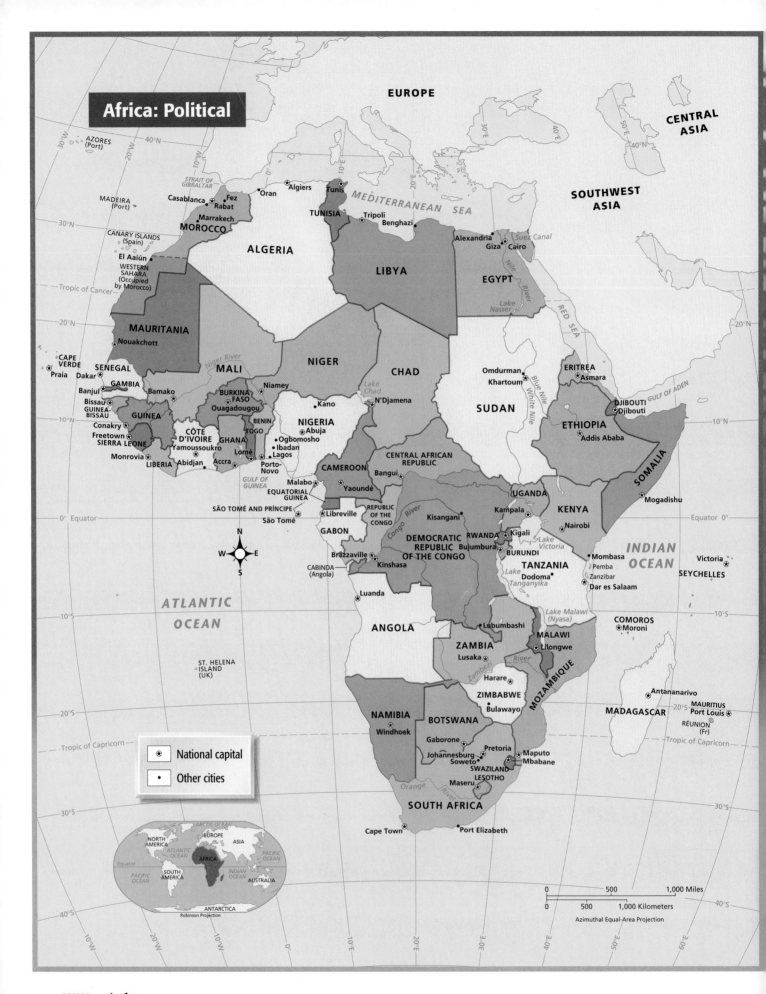

Africa: Political

EUROPE

CENTRAL ASIA

SOUTHWEST ASIA

AZORES (Port)

MEDITERRANEAN SEA

STRAIT OF GIBRALTAR

Algiers
Oran
Tunis
TUNISIA
Tripoli
Benghazi

Casablanca
Fez
Rabat
Marrakech
MOROCCO

MADEIRA (Port)

CANARY ISLANDS (Spain)

El Aaiún
WESTERN SAHARA (Occupied by Morocco)

Tropic of Cancer

ALGERIA

LIBYA

EGYPT

Alexandria
Giza
Cairo
Suez Canal

Lake Nasser

RED SEA

MAURITANIA

Nouakchott

NIGER

CHAD

SUDAN

Omdurman
Khartoum

ERITREA
Asmara

Blue Nile
White Nile

DJIBOUTI
Djibouti
GULF OF ADEN

CAPE VERDE
Praia

SENEGAL
Dakar
GAMBIA
Banjul
Bissau
GUINEA-BISSAU
Conakry
GUINEA
Freetown
SIERRA LEONE
Monrovia
LIBERIA

Niger River

MALI
Bamako

BURKINA FASO
Ouagadougou

CÔTE D'IVOIRE
Yamoussoukro
Abidjan

Niamey

Lake Chad

Kano
N'Djamena

NIGERIA
Abuja

BENIN
TOGO
GHANA
Lomé
Accra

Ogbomosho
Ibadan
Lagos
Porto-Novo

Malabo
EQUATORIAL GUINEA

CAMEROON
Yaoundé

CENTRAL AFRICAN REPUBLIC
Bangui

ETHIOPIA
Addis Ababa

SOMALIA
Mogadishu

SÃO TOMÉ AND PRÍNCIPE
São Tomé

Libreville
GABON

REPUBLIC OF THE CONGO

Congo River

Kisangani

DEMOCRATIC REPUBLIC OF THE CONGO

UGANDA
Kampala

RWANDA
Kigali
Bujumbura
BURUNDI

KENYA
Nairobi

Lake Victoria

Equator

GULF OF GUINEA

Brazzaville
Kinshasa

CABINDA (Angola)

Luanda

Lake Tanganyika

TANZANIA
Dodoma
Zanzibar
Dar es Salaam

Mombasa
Pemba

INDIAN OCEAN

Victoria
SEYCHELLES

ATLANTIC OCEAN

ANGOLA

Lubumbashi

ZAMBIA
Lusaka

Lake Malawi (Nyasa)

MALAWI
Lilongwe

COMOROS
Moroni

ST. HELENA ISLAND (UK)

Zambezi River

Harare

ZIMBABWE
Bulawayo

MOZAMBIQUE

Antananarivo
MADAGASCAR

MAURITIUS
Port Louis
RÉUNION (Fr)

Tropic of Capricorn

NAMIBIA
Windhoek

BOTSWANA
Gaborone

Johannesburg
Soweto
Pretoria
SWAZILAND
Mbabane
Maputo

Orange River

LESOTHO
Maseru

SOUTH AFRICA

Cape Town
Port Elizabeth

N
W E
S

* National capital
• Other cities

ARCTIC OCEAN
NORTH AMERICA
EUROPE
ASIA
ATLANTIC OCEAN
Equator
AFRICA
PACIFIC OCEAN
SOUTH AMERICA
INDIAN OCEAN
PACIFIC OCEAN
AUSTRALIA
ANTARCTICA
Robinson Projection

0   500   1,000 Miles
0   500   1,000 Kilometers
Azimuthal Equal-Area Projection

Pacific Islands: Political

NORTH AMERICA

ASIA

AUSTRALIA

NEW ZEALAND

INDONESIA

NORTH PACIFIC OCEAN

SOUTH PACIFIC OCEAN

PHILIPPINE SEA

SOUTH CHINA SEA

TIMOR SEA

ARAFURA SEA

CORAL SEA

TASMAN SEA

INDIAN OCEAN

International Date Line

Tropic of Cancer

Equator 0°

Tropic of Cancer

M I C R O N E S I A

P O L Y N E S I A

M E L A N E S I A

K I R I B A T I

BONIN ISLANDS (Japan)

VOLCANO ISLANDS (Japan)

NORTHERN MARIANAS (US)

GUAM (US) •Agăna

Koror⊛ PALAU

FEDERATED STATES OF MICRONESIA

Truk Is.

Palikir

New Guinea

PAPUA NEW GUINEA
Port Moresby⊛

Bismarck Archipelago

WAKE ISLAND (US)

MARSHALL ISLANDS

Eniwetok I.

Kwajalein Island ⊛ Majuro

Gilbert Islands ⊛ Tarawa

Yaren ⊛
NAURU

Guadalcanal Island

SOLOMON ISLANDS
Honiara⊛

TUVALU
Funafuti ⊛

FIJI
Suva•

Espiritu Santo I.

VANUATU
Malekula I.
Port-Vila⊛

NEW CALEDONIA (Fr)
Noumea•

Loyalty Islands (Fr)

NORFOLK ISLAND (Aust)

MIDWAY ISLAND (US)

JOHNSTON ISLAND (US)

Hawaiian Islands

HAWAII (US)

KINGMAN REEF (US)

PALMYRA ISLAND (US)

Teraina

Tabuaeran

JARVIS I. (US)

HOWLAND ISLAND (US)

BAKER ISLAND (US)

McKean I.

Gardner I.

Phoenix Islands

TOKELAU (NZ)

SAMOA
Apia⊛

AMERICAN SAMOA
•Pago Pago

WALLIS & FUTUNA (Fr)

TONGA
⊛ Nuku'alofa

NIUE (NZ)

Starbuck Island

COOK ISLANDS (NZ)

Manihiki Island

Rarotonga Island

Society Islands (Fr)

Marquesas Islands (Fr)

Tuamotu Archipelago (Fr)

FRENCH POLYNESIA

Papeete•
Tahiti (Fr)

Tubuai Islands (Fr)

Rapa Island (Fr)

PITCAIRN (UK)

Pitcairn Island

Ducie Island

Easter Island (Chile)

Kermadec Islands (NZ)

Chatham Islands (NZ)

Bounty Islands (NZ)

Auckland Islands (NZ)

Scale At Equator

1,000 Miles
500
0

1,000 Kilometers
500
0

Miller Cylindrical Projection

Robinson Projection

ARCTIC OCEAN
ATLANTIC OCEAN
PACIFIC OCEAN
INDIAN OCEAN
NORTH AMERICA
SOUTH AMERICA
EUROPE
ASIA
AFRICA
AUSTRALIA
ANTARCTICA
Equator

National capital   ⊛

Other cities   •

N E W S

UNIT 1
American Beginnings
(Beginnings–1865)

American Teens

IN HISTORY

Young Pioneers

Early colonists saw America as the land of opportunity, a place to succeed and build a better future. As settlers struggled to build towns and start farms, they often relied on contributions from family members. By the mid-1800s, good farming land along the Atlantic coast was scarce. Many families headed west, looking for land to cultivate.

Once the pioneers reached their destination, children and teenagers spent countless hours doing much of the essential work of western settlement. Children aged 7 to 12 helped feed their families. They gathered edible wild plants, which they called "vegetables out of place."

Teenagers had different responsibilities. Both boys and girls hunted wild animals. Boys worked in the fields with their fathers. Girls usually worked in the home and garden beside their mothers. Teenage girls might work in the fields if the farm was new or if there were no boys in the family. One teenager, Susie Crocket, helped plant the fields and trap animals on her family's farm in Oklahoma. Crocket recalled, "I hated to see Ma come in with a big batch of sewing, for I knew it meant many long hours sitting by her side sewing

Typically, teenage boys did the hard work of plowing the fields.

seams." Crocket believed that as a girl she was treated differently. "I could help the boys with the plowing or trapping, but they would never help me with sewing."

Edna Matthews Clifton grew up on a Texas frontier farm. She attended family celebrations and had good times at play and school. What she remembered most, however, was the work. Clifton cut wood, gardened, gathered, harvested, hunted, made soap, mopped, washed, and weeded. She particularly dreaded picking time. On summer mornings with the sun shining brightly, she saw the fields standing "like a monster." She wrote, "Sometimes I would lie down on my sack. . . . Sometimes they would pour water over my head to relieve me." Clifton understood "that *work was necessary*. Everybody worked; it was a part of life, for there was no life without it."

In this unit you will learn more about the people who helped create and expand the United States. The young nation faced many challenges, but it also offered its citizens many new opportunities.

LEFT PAGE: *George Caleb Bingham's painting* Daniel Boone Escorting Pioneers

American Beginnings

The *Niña,* the *Pinta,*
and the *Santa María*

Maize

UNITED STATES

c. 1000 B.C.
Maize, or corn, agriculture becomes an important source of food for Native Americans in the Southwest.

A.D. 1492
Italian sailor Christopher Columbus leaves Europe, headed for the Indies. Instead, he reaches the Americas.

1542
Spanish explorer Álvar Núñez Cabeza de Vaca publishes an account of his travels in North America.

50,000 B.C.	3000 B.C.	1000 B.C.	A.D. 1000	A.D. 1500	1550

WORLD

c. 50,000–10,000 B.C.
Paleo-Indians migrate to the Americas.

c. 2600 B.C.
The Great Pyramid is built in Giza, Egypt, as the tomb for the pharaoh Cheops.

A.D. 868
The Chinese produce the world's first printed book.

1192
The Kamakura shoguns begin their rule in Japan.

1508
Italian artist Michelangelo Buonarroti begins painting the Sistine Chapel in the Vatican in Rome.

Detail from *The Creation of Adam* from the Sistine Chapel

Paleo-Indian arrowheads

The Great Sphinx and the Pyramids of Giza

A colonial bed

Thomas Jefferson is the main author of the Declaration of Independence.

A Civil War uniform and sword

1607
English colonists establish a settlement at Jamestown in Virginia.

1776
The thirteen colonies issue the Declaration of Independence and break away from Great Britain.

1804
Lewis and Clark begin their journey to explore the American West.

1865
General Lee surrenders at Appomattox Courthouse, ending the Civil War.

| **1600** | **1650** | **1700** | **1750** | **1800** | **1850** |

1608
Samuel de Champlain founds Quebec in present-day Canada.

1652
The Dutch establish a colony near the Cape of Good Hope in Africa.

1703
Peter the Great of Russia lays the foundation stone for the city of St. Petersburg.

1811
Simón Bolívar leads an independence movement in Venezuela.

An African mask from the 1600s

Altar cross created for Peter the Great

Painting of Simón Bolívar on a jewel box

USING THE TIME LINE

1. Which events shown on the time line have to do with the founding of the United States?

2. How many years passed between Columbus's arrival in the Americas and the independence of the thirteen colonies?

3. Where did Europeans establish colonies in the 1600s?

Activity Identify the time line entries that relate to exploration. Create a chart of these journeys. Provide information on who led the explorations and where and when they took place. You might need to do some research using the library, your textbook, or other sources to find some additional information for your chart.

The Granger Collection, New York

▪ CHAPTER 1 ▪
The Founding of the Nation
(Beginnings–1791)

"The land of Liberty! how sweet the sound!" declared Eliza Wilkinson in 1782. Just a few years earlier Wilkinson—a young widow from Charleston, South Carolina—had shown little interest in politics. Soon, however, she was swept up in a movement against British rule. By 1782 Wilkinson—the once loyal British subject—was among many people proudly calling themselves Americans.

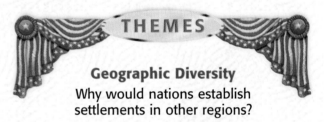

THEMES

Geographic Diversity
Why would nations establish settlements in other regions?

Citizenship and Democracy
What does it mean for a country to be founded on the idea of liberty?

Constitutional Heritage
What might a nation do to prevent its government from misusing power?

| 50,000 B.C. | 8000 B.C. | A.D. 1000 | 1200 | 1400 | 1600 |

50,000–10,000 B.C. Paleo-Indians migrate to the Americas.

C. A.D. 1000 The Vikings land in North America.

1492 Christopher Columbus and his crew land in the Bahamas.

1607 English colonists establish the Jamestown settlement.

The World Before the Opening of the Atlantic

Reading Focus

Where did the first Americans come from, and how did the environment influence Native Americans?

What was Europe like during the Middle Ages?

How did trade affect different regions of Africa, Asia, and the Mediterranean?

Key Terms

artifacts

Paleo-Indians

migration

societies

culture

Iroquois League

Middle Ages

feudalism

Crusades

Silk Road

ACCORDING TO SOME *northwestern Native American tribes, when the world was young there were only "the trees, the moon, the sun, water, and a few animals." In this emptiness, the lonely Raven walked along the beach and wished for companions. To Raven's surprise, a clam emerged from the sand and released a crowd of tiny people. Raven "sang a beautiful song of great joy," say the northwestern storytellers, for "he had brought the first people to the world." This story represents one of the many different ways that people explain how the first humans arrived in the Americas.*

The character of the Raven appears in many Native American stories.

IMAGE ON LEFT PAGE: *The Battle of Lexington*

1760 1765 1770 1775 1780 1785 1790

1763 Pontiac's Rebellion starts.

1775 Fighting at Lexington and Concord marks the beginning of the Revolutionary War.

1776 The Declaration of Independence is approved.

1781 The British surrender at Yorktown.

1787 Delegates sign the U.S. Constitution.

1791 The Bill of Rights becomes part of the Constitution.

★ The First Americans

Many scientists believe that people first arrived in North America during the last Ice Age, when glaciers covered much of Earth's surface. As the ocean levels dropped, a land bridge called Beringia was exposed between northeastern Asia and present-day Alaska. **Artifacts**, or remains of objects made by humans, indicate that **Paleo-Indians**, or the first Americans, crossed Beringia into Alaska sometime between 50,000 and 10,000 B.C. This **migration**, or movement of people from one region to another, occurred over a long time. Most Paleo-Indians traveled through Alaska and migrated south.

Paleo-Indians were hunter-gatherers, people who hunt animals and gather wild plants to provide for their needs. In time, these Native Americans began practicing agriculture, which provided stability and allowed complex **societies** to develop. A society is a group that has a common **culture**—shared values and traditions, such as language, government, and family relationships.

The earliest civilizations in the Americas developed in Mesoamerica—present-day Mexico and portions of Central America—and South America. The largest civilizations in Mesoamerica were the Olmec, Maya, Toltec, and Aztec. In South America the Inca civilization was the largest. Its empire stretched from present-day Colombia to central Chile.

An Inca knife

North America produced several complex farming cultures. The Mogollon and Hohokam were two of the first groups in the present-day southwestern United States to develop agriculture. Another southwestern group, the Anasazi (ahn-uh-SAHZ-ee), built large pueblos and developed irrigation systems in mesas and canyons. The Mississippian culture, Adena, and Hopewell developed in the Mississippi, Missouri, and Ohio River valleys. These cultures built large burial and religious mounds. The Adena were primarily hunter-gatherers, while the Hopewell and the Mississippian culture supported their large populations with agriculture and trade.

★ North American Culture Areas

In North America many different Native American culture areas developed. In the far North, the Inuit and the Aleut hunted large mammals and fished in the frozen Arctic, using dogsleds and kayaks for transportation. The Inuit sometimes used blocks of ice to build igloos for housing. In the Subarctic, Native Americans were nomadic, following the seasonal migrations of the caribou.

The Northwest Coast culture area stretched along the 2,000-mile shoreline from southern Alaska to northern California. A mild climate and rich food supplies allowed large, nonagricultural populations to develop. People in the Northwest fished for salmon and hunted whale. They also used trees to build houses and to carve images of totems—ancestor or animal spirits—on tall poles.

Farther south the California region included deserts, forests, and river-filled valleys. Native Americans there lived in isolated family groups or small villages. In the Columbia Plateau, Native Americans lived in permanent villages near rivers. They fished for salmon, hunted small game, and gathered plants. In the desertlike Great Basin, most people lived in small hunter-gatherer groups.

Native Americans of the Southwest also lived in a dry environment. They practiced irrigation to

Southwestern Native American tribes built cliff dwellings, like this one in Mesa Verde, Colorado, to protect themselves from weather and attacks.

Legend:
- Arctic
- Subarctic
- Northwest Coast
- Plateau
- Great Plains
- Northeast
- Great Basin
- California
- Southwest
- Southeast
- Mesoamerica
- Circum-Caribbean

Aztec, Maya, and Inca Empires
- Aztec
- Maya
- Inca

Tenochtitlán
Valley of Mexico
Tikal
Copán
Machu Picchu
Cuzco
ANDES
Amazon River
SOUTH AMERICA
PACIFIC OCEAN
ATLANTIC OCEAN
Equator
0   1,000   2,000 Miles
0   1,000   2,000 Kilometers
Lambert Equal-Area Projection

ASIA
ARCTIC OCEAN
PACIFIC OCEAN
NORTH AMERICA
Hudson Bay
Great Lakes
ATLANTIC OCEAN
Gulf of Mexico
CARIBBEAN SEA
MESOAMERICA
SOUTH AMERICA
Yucatán Peninsula

0   500   1,000 Miles
0   500   1,000 Kilometers
Azimuthal Equal-Area Projection

(inset globe) ARCTIC OCEAN, NORTH AMERICA, EUROPE, ASIA, ATLANTIC OCEAN, AFRICA, PACIFIC OCEAN, SOUTH AMERICA, INDIAN OCEAN, AUSTRALIA, ANTARCTICA, Equator, Robinson Projection

UNINHABITED LAND

Native American Culture Areas

Learning from Maps Various Native American cultures inhabited the Americas. These cultures adapted to a wide range of climatic and geographic regions.

Human-Environment Interaction How might the geography and climate of an area influence the culture that develops there?

grow crops such as maize. Some tribes, including the Navajo and Apache, hunted game, gathered food plants, and raided the villages of agricultural groups such as the Pueblo.

Millions of buffalo grazed on the grassland of the Great Plains, which stretch from Canada to the Rio Grande and lie between the Mississippi River and the Rocky Mountains. Native Americans in the Plains grew crops, gathered plants, and hunted buffalo on foot.

The East was primarily wooded and rich in resources. Southeastern tribes lived and farmed in villages along river valleys. Northeastern tribes lived in an area stretching west from the Atlantic to the Mississippi Valley and south from the Great Lakes to present-day Virginia and North Carolina. The Algonquian in the colder north were semi-nomadic, while tribes living farther south farmed and built permanent villages. The Iroquois were an agricultural people. They developed the **Iroquois League**, a political confederation of the Cayuga, Mohawk, Oneida, Onondaga, and Seneca tribes.

 ## The Middle Ages

The first Europeans known to have had contact with Native Americans were the Vikings from

Peasants like these tended the manor fields.

Scandinavia. These seafaring people had settled Iceland and Greenland. Around the year A.D. 1000 Leif Eriksson sailed farther west. He eventually landed in Labrador and Newfoundland, Canada. The Vikings explored along the coast and established a colony that lasted for a few years.

Feudal Europe

The Vikings were the only Europeans to explore the Americas during Europe's **Middle Ages**. This era started with the collapse of the Roman Empire in the late A.D. 400s and began to end around 1350. During this time Europe experienced political disorder, and many trade networks broke down. Some city populations declined as people moved to the countryside.

The early Middle Ages saw the rise of **feudalism**—a system of government in which people pledge loyalty to a lord in exchange for protection. A person's birth often determined his or her economic and social position in the feudal system. Monarchs and nobles defended their kingdoms and manors, or large estates, with the help of vassals. Vassals were knights and lords who gave their services in exchange for land. Peasant tenants, serfs, and slaves farmed the manor land. Manors provided most of the necessities for their inhabitants. Nobles ruled their manors without interference because there was little central government. The Catholic Church was the center of most social and religious life.

Nobles gradually lost power as monarchs expanded their control over vast areas. These growing kingdoms were called nations and included England and France. In 1215 English nobles forced King John to accept Magna Carta, or the Great Charter. The charter gave certain rights to the nobles and established that English monarchs must observe the law.

Trade also increased in the early 1200s. Merchants in Italian coastal cities traded regularly with countries around the Mediterranean Sea. As trade increased, Europeans built new towns and expanded existing cities. Towns and populations grew even faster as improved farming methods led to increased food production. Such changes in technology, trade, and political power marked the decline of Europe's Middle Ages.

Trade Across Continents

During the Middle Ages, Muslims made military conquests and built trade networks around the Mediterranean. Along with Christians and Jews, Muslims proved their religious devotion by visiting the Holy Land, which included the city of Jerusalem. Fearing that Muslim rulers would forbid Christians to enter Jerusalem, Pope Urban II called on Christians to fight a crusade, or holy war:

Statue of a trader in the Middle Ages

"Jerusalem . . . is now held captive by the enemies of Christ. . . . When an armed attack is made upon the enemy, let this one cry be raised by all the soldiers of God: it is the will of God!"

With these words, Christians launched the **Crusades**, five wars fought between 1096 and 1221 for possession of the Holy Land. The Crusades brought Europeans into closer contact with the East and increased their interest in trade with Asia and Africa.

Meanwhile, Genghis Khan was leading the Mongols, nomadic warriors from Central Asia, in an invasion of China. By 1279 his grandson Kublai Khan (KOO-bluh KAHN) ruled an empire that stretched 4,000 miles across Asia's central plains.

Kublai Khan used his powerful navy to open vast trading networks with present-day southern India, Sri Lanka, and Sumatra. Merchants also used the **Silk Road**, an overland trade route that stretched several thousand miles from China to the Black Sea.

In 1368 the Ming dynasty overthrew the Mongol Empire. In the early 1400s China sponsored several long ocean voyages.

Some Chinese merchants traveled to East African kingdoms, where thriving port cities traded goods such as ivory and gold. Berbers—nomads from North Africa—used camels to carry goods across the Sahara Desert. They brought salt south and gold north. People used salt to prevent food from spoiling too quickly.

In West Africa, Ghana (GAHN-uh) gained wealth trading gold, which Arab merchants carried to the Mediterranean. Mali emerged in the early 1200s after Ghana's collapse. In the late 1200s North African traders brought Islam to Mali and parts of Sudan. The Songhay (SAWNG-hy) Empire also had great influence in the area. Songhay's Muslim rulers helped spread Islamic culture throughout their vast territory.

SECTION 1 REVIEW

Identify and explain the significance of the following:
- artifacts
- Paleo-Indians
- migration
- societies
- culture
- Iroquois League
- Leif Eriksson
- Middle Ages
- feudalism
- Crusades
- Kublai Khan
- Silk Road

Reading for Content Understanding

1 **Main Idea** How were European societies organized during the Middle Ages?

2 **Main Idea** What influence did trade have within different empires in Africa, Asia, and the Mediterranean?

3 **Geographic Diversity** *Human-Environment Interaction* From where did the first people to reach North America come, and how did the environment affect Native American cultures?

4 **Writing** *Classifying* Write a paragraph explaining both the positive and the negative aspects of trade among various peoples or kingdoms during the Middle Ages.

5 **Critical Thinking** *Drawing Conclusions* Why do you think that Native Americans who practiced agriculture were more likely than hunter-gatherers to establish permanent settlements?

The Age of Exploration

Reading Focus

Why did Europeans set out on voyages of exploration?

How did the Protestant Reformation affect Europe and the Americas?

Why were Europeans interested in colonizing North America?

Key Terms

Commercial Revolution

monopoly

Columbian Exchange

Northwest Passage

Protestant Reformation

Spanish Armada

charter

IN 1299 THE CITY OF ARRAS in present-day France was famous for its wealthy merchants. The local Crespin family was so rich that it loaned money to cities, bishops, and even monarchs. The rise to power of the Crespins and other merchants worried some Europeans. "Money is too much worshipped here," wrote poet Adam de la Halle. Others, however, welcomed the changing economy because it provided opportunities for workers to make money and improve their social status.

European moneylenders and borrowers in the 1300s

 Economic Growth

In the 1400s Europe experienced the **Commercial Revolution**, a period of economic development that improved business practices. During this time a network of merchants, bankers, and traders brought prized goods to Europe's markets. Gold, ivory, slaves, and salt came from Africa, while silk and spices came from Asia. Traders used long and difficult overland routes, such as the Silk Road, to reach the Mediterranean Sea. From there, goods were shipped to Europe. Italian city-states, particularly Venice, had a **monopoly**, or economic control, in Europe of this profitable trade. Some

European countries looked for a sea route to Africa and Asia so they could establish direct trade.

Portugal became one of the leaders in exploration. Hoping to gain wealth and territory and to spread Christianity, Prince Henry the Navigator paid for expeditions to explore the west coast of Africa. In his 1487–88 voyage, Bartolomeu Dias sailed past the southern tip of Africa, which he called the Cape of Good Hope "for the promise it gave of the finding of India." Dias then returned home. Portugal built posts along Africa's coast, trading with local rulers for gold, ivory, and slaves. Enslaved Africans in Portugal's colonies endured hard labor and harsh living conditions.

★ Columbus's Bold Idea

Christopher Columbus, an Italian sailor from Genoa, hoped to find a sea route to Asia by sailing west across the Atlantic Ocean. King Ferdinand and Queen Isabella of Spain funded Columbus's fleet. The *Niña,* the *Pinta,* and the *Santa María* set sail on August 3, 1492. The crew became uneasy as time passed with no sight of land. Then on October 12, 1492, a lookout cried "Land! Land!" Columbus had reached one of the islands in the Bahamas. When Columbus explored other islands, he met the Taino (TY-noh). He called them Indians, believing that he was in the Indies, or Asia.

When the *Santa María* struck a coral reef and sank, Columbus built a small colony for its crew called *La Navidad.* He then set sail for Spain.

After a stormy voyage he arrived before Ferdinand and Isabella with gold nuggets, exotic treasures, and some Taino captives. The monarchs appointed Columbus a royal admiral and governor of the new Spanish territories.

When he returned to *La Navidad,* Columbus found that the colony had been destroyed. He created new settlements. On his next voyage he became the first European to see South America. Soon, poor conditions in the Caribbean colonies led to rebellion. Ferdinand and Isabella removed Columbus as governor.

The Metropolitan Museum of Art

Christopher Columbus

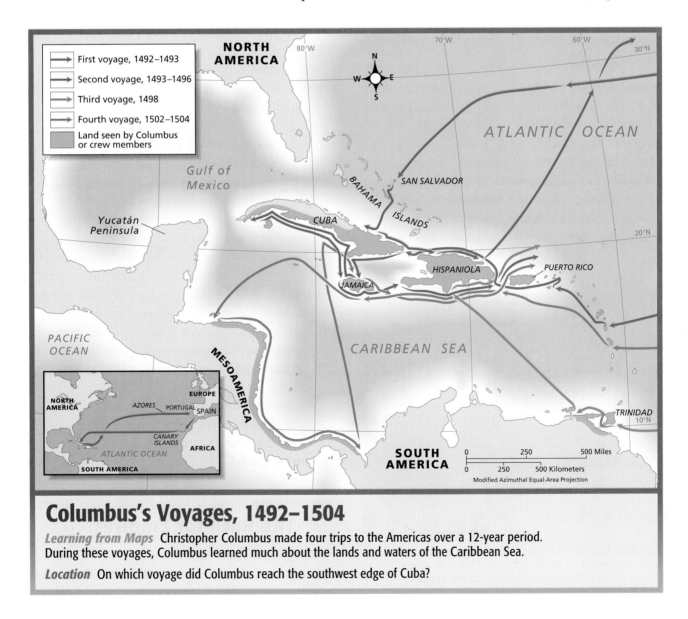

Columbus's Voyages, 1492–1504

Learning from Maps Christopher Columbus made four trips to the Americas over a 12-year period. During these voyages, Columbus learned much about the lands and waters of the Caribbean Sea.

Location On which voyage did Columbus reach the southwest edge of Cuba?

The Founding of the Nation **11**

Columbus's fourth voyage to the Americas ended in shipwreck. After being rescued, Columbus returned to Spain a broken man. He died in 1506, still believing that he had found a route to Asia.

Some Europeans who doubted that Columbus had reached the Indies continued to search for a water route to Asia. Sponsored by England, Italian sailor John Cabot reached the North American coast in 1497. Following Bartolomeu Dias's general route, Vasco da Gama sailed around the Cape of Good Hope and across the Indian Ocean. He arrived in India in 1498, thus winning for Portugal the race to Asia. In 1501 Italian Amerigo Vespucci (ve-SPOO-chee) sailed to South America. He noted, "We arrived at a new land which . . . we observed to be a continent." Europeans began calling the continents North and South America in his honor.

★ Spanish America

Spain continued to search for a western route to Asia. In 1513 Vasco Núñez de Balboa crossed present-day Panama on foot and reached the Pacific Ocean. Spain hoped to sail to Asia by way of this ocean. Ferdinand Magellan (muh-JEL-uhn) set sail with five ships in 1519 to find a waterway to the Pacific. Near the southern tip of South America, Magellan found a narrow sea passage to the Pacific. He crossed the ocean and reached

This map from the 1540s shows French explorations and settlements in North America. This map was drawn upside-down, so Canada is at the bottom and Florida is in the upper-right corner.

islands off the coast of Asia, where he was killed. Juan Sebastián de Elcano captained the one ship that returned to Spain in 1522. The 18 surviving sailors were the first people to circumnavigate, or sail completely around, Earth.

In the process of exploration, plants, animals, and diseases were transferred between the "Old World"—Europe, Asia, and Africa—and the "New World" of the Americas. This transfer has become known as the **Columbian Exchange**. Explorers brought American plants, such as corn, tomatoes, and potatoes, to Europe. They took wheat, horses, and cattle to the Americas. Explorers also carried diseases such as smallpox, measles, and typhus.

With no resistance to these diseases, American Indians died in huge numbers. The remaining Indians were thus vulnerable to conquest. In 1519 Hernán Cortés began his conquest of the Aztec Empire. In the 1530s Francisco Pizarro (puh-ZAHR-oh) conquered the Inca Empire.

Juan Ponce de León, Pánfilo de Narváez, and Hernando de Soto each led expeditions to Florida, looking for gold. All failed to find riches. Francisco Vásquez de Coronado's expedition reached the Grand Canyon, while Juan Rodríguez Cabrillo (kah-BREE-yoh) sailed up the California coast. These explorations gave Spain vast territories that had great mineral wealth. Using the labor of American Indians and enslaved Africans, Spain mined the wealth of the Americas to fill the royal treasury.

Spain created the Council of the Indies to oversee its American empire. Pueblos, or towns, served as trading posts and as centers of local government. Presidios, or military bases, protected towns in remote frontier areas. Priests established missions to convert local Indians to Catholicism. King Philip II of Spain issued an order stating that

preaching the holy gospel . . . is the principal purpose for which we order new discoveries and settlements to be made."

★ The Race for Empires

While Spain built its empire, other European nations searched for a **Northwest Passage**— a waterway in North America that would connect the Atlantic to the Pacific. In the 1530s Jacques Cartier sailed to Canada and claimed land for France. Around 75 years later Samuel de Champlain explored the Great Lakes region and founded the French colony of Quebec. He noted that by exploring:

Queen Elizabeth I

"we gain knowledge of different countries, regions and kingdoms; through it we attract and bring into our countries all kinds of riches; through it . . . Christianity [is spread] in all parts of the earth."

In 1609 English captain Henry Hudson sailed for the Dutch to present-day New York. The next year, while sailing for England, he reached present-day Hudson Bay. Although explorers failed to find a Northwest Passage, their voyages were the basis for European land claims in North America.

The Reformation

While Europeans explored the Americas, events in Europe were challenging Spain's power. In 1517 a priest named Martin Luther started the **Protestant Reformation**, a religious movement that began as an effort to reform the Catholic Church. Luther and other reformers became known as Protestants because they protested some of the church's

practices. Throughout Europe fighting broke out between Catholics and Protestants. King Philip II of Spain assembled a huge naval fleet—the **Spanish Armada**—to invade England and overthrow its Protestant queen, Elizabeth I. In 1588 the smaller English fleet defeated the Armada.

New Colonies in North America

With the Spanish navy weakened, other nations challenged Spain's power overseas. France established trading posts and fishing villages in Canada. In the late 1600s René-Robert de La Salle explored the Mississippi River valley. France called its North American territory New France.

In 1624 about 30 Dutch families settled in New Netherland. In 1638 the Swedish founded New Sweden near the Dutch colony. The Dutch seized New Sweden in 1655, claiming that it intruded upon their lands and fur trade.

England's Queen Elizabeth gave Sir Walter Raleigh a **charter**, a document granting permission to establish a colony. In 1585 he sent an expedition to Roanoke Island, part of present-day North Carolina. John White resettled Roanoke in 1587 and then went back to England. In 1590 he returned to find the colony deserted. Despite search efforts, White noted, "never any of them [were] found, nor seen to this day."

SECTION 2 REVIEW

Identify and explain the significance of the following:
- **Commercial Revolution**
- **monopoly**
- **Christopher Columbus**
- **Columbian Exchange**
- **Northwest Passage**
- **Martin Luther**
- **Protestant Reformation**
- **Spanish Armada**
- **Queen Elizabeth I**
- **charter**

Reading for Content Understanding

1 **Main Idea** What motivated Europeans to explore?

2 **Main Idea** How did the Protestant Reformation affect political power in Europe and North America?

3 **Economic Development** How did European countries benefit from establishing colonies in North America?

4 **Writing** *Describing* Imagine that you are an explorer. Write a journal entry describing the people you encounter.

5 **Critical Thinking** *Drawing Conclusions* Do you think Columbus's voyages were a success or a failure? Explain your answer.

The English Colonies

Reading Focus

What role did religion play in colonial life?

What was the economic relationship between the colonies and England?

How did the colonies differ from one another economically and politically?

Key Terms

Bacon's Rebellion

Mayflower Compact

town meetings

House of Burgesses

Parliament

bicameral legislature

Dominion of New England

imports

exports

Navigation Acts

Middle Passage

Great Awakening

N 1605 A GROUP *of English merchants asked the Crown for a charter to found a settlement and search for gold in North America. The area they wanted to settle was part of the region called Virginia, which at the time extended from present-day Maine to South Carolina. King James I granted the request, promising the London Company the rights to "all the lands, woods, soils, grounds, . . . ports, rivers, mines, minerals, . . . [and] commodities" along a section of the Virginia coast. The company's efforts, wrote King James, "may in time bring . . . a settled and quiet government."*

London Company advertisement

The Settlement of Virginia

The failure of Roanoke led the London Company to take a different approach to settlement. Instead of relying on the wealth of one person, investors formed a joint-stock company, so that several people shared the costs and risks.

On April 26, 1607, the first three ships sent by the London Company arrived in Virginia. The 105 male colonists established Jamestown, named after the king. Instead of building sturdy shelters or planting crops, they searched for gold. By the time winter arrived, two thirds of the colonists were dead, and the rest were starving and sick. In 1608 Captain John Smith gained control of the colony. He forced the settlers to plant crops and build better housing. About 400 more colonists arrived the next year. Smith returned to England, and that winter, disease and starvation struck the colony. By the summer of 1610, only 60 colonists were still alive.

The Powhatan Confederacy—a powerful alliance of Algonquian Indians—taught the colonists how to grow North American crops such as corn. However, the relationship between the two groups was rarely peaceful. In 1622 fighting broke out between the colonists and the Powhatan, beginning a war that lasted for the next 20 years. In one attack, the Powhatan killed about 350 colonists. In 1624 the colony's problems convinced England to cancel the London Company's charter and to make Virginia a royal colony.

The colony encouraged immigration because the high death rate had led to labor shortages. Many poor colonists signed an indenture, or contract, to work for several years for those who paid their ship fare to Virginia. Large numbers of these indentured servants died because of poor living conditions and disease. Some Africans came to Virginia as indentured servants, but by the late 1600s many were being kept in slavery. Slaves worked on the developing tobacco plantations.

Indentured servants often struggled to make a living after their contracts ended. They sometimes built farms on American Indian land. In 1676 Nathaniel Bacon led a group of poor colonists in an attack against some Indians. Bacon and his followers then attacked and burned Jamestown during **Bacon's Rebellion**. After Bacon died, the rebellion ended. Fearing another revolt by former indentured servants, many farmers began to use more slave labor in the Virginia colony.

⭐ The Founding of Plymouth

While Jamestown was being settled, religious tension was increasing in England. A Protestant group called the Puritans wanted to reform, or purify, the Church of England. One sect, or religious group, of Puritans wanted to separate from the Church of England entirely. English authorities often persecuted these Separatists.

One Separatist sect that emigrated to escape such persecution became known as the Pilgrims. On September 16, 1620, the *Mayflower* sailed from England with more than 100 men, women, and children as passengers. The Pilgrims drew up a basic agreement to govern their colony in the **Mayflower Compact**, creating

❝such just and equal laws . . . as shall be thought most meet [fitting] and

Biography

John Smith

Captain John Smith was a man of great physical and mental strength. Smith was born in 1580 in England to a farming family. At the age of 17, he entered the military, serving with English troops in the Netherlands. He fought in many military campaigns across Europe. These experiences helped prepare Smith for the difficulties he and the other colonists faced in Virginia.

After helping save Jamestown, Smith explored and mapped the Chesapeake Bay region. He also led an expedition exploring New England, from which he returned with a cargo of fish and furs. Smith later published books about his adventures in North America, including *The Generall Historie of Virginia* and *A Description of New England*.

convenient for the general good of the colony.❞

The Pilgrims chose to land in present-day Massachusetts, where they established the colony of Plymouth. Nearly half the Pilgrims died from sickness during the first winter. For some time, the Pilgrims met no American Indians. However, in the spring the Pilgrims met two English-speaking Indians, Samoset and Squanto. William Bradford, the Pilgrim leader, noted that Squanto showed

The Thirteen Colonies

Learning from Maps The thirteen colonies stretched for more than 1,200 miles along the coast of North America.

Region Which group of colonies is the largest in land area?

them "how to set [plant] their corn, [and] where to take [catch] fish." He also helped the Pilgrims establish peaceful relations with the Wampanoag Indians. To celebrate their harvest and their first year at Plymouth, the Pilgrims invited about 90 Wampanoag as guests to what became known as the first Thanksgiving.

A Pilgrim boy's leather shoes

Courtesy Peabody Essex Museum, Salem, Massachusetts

 The New England Colonies

In England, Puritans were persecuted for being dissenters—people who disagree with official religious or political opinions. In 1629 King Charles I granted some Puritans a charter to establish a colony in New England. The next year a fleet set sail. These Puritans believed that they had a covenant, or sacred agreement, with God to build an ideal Christian community. Aboard the *Arbella*, John Winthrop, the colony's governor, wrote that "we must consider that we shall be like a City upon a Hill; the eyes of all people are on us." By the end of 1630, about 1,000 more colonists had come to the Massachusetts Bay Colony.

While most colonists in Virginia were men, Puritan colonists tended to come in family groups that usually had some money and skills. The Puritans established several towns, including Boston, the colony's capital. Colonists also settled to the north, in present-day New Hampshire, which became a royal colony in 1680.

In its charter, Massachusetts had the right to govern itself, giving it more independence than Virginia, a royal colony. The Massachusetts General Court, which had representatives from each town, elected the governor. Settlements decided local issues in gatherings known as **town meetings**. Politics and religion were closely linked in Massachusetts—only church members could vote.

Ministers were highly respected members of the community. Religion also shaped everyday life. On most Sundays, colonists heard a morning and an afternoon sermon. In 1636 Harvard College was founded to teach ministers. In 1647 Massachusetts passed a law requiring towns with 50 or more households to appoint someone to teach children to read and write so they could read the Bible. This was one of the first public education laws in Europe or the Americas.

In the 1630s several important Puritans left Massachusetts because of their dissenting views. In 1636 minister Thomas Hooker left and helped found Connecticut. Roger Williams, another minister, said that the General Court had no authority in spiritual matters and should pay for American Indian land that it took. In response, Puritan authorities banished Williams. In 1636 he moved

N	NOAH did view The old world & new
O	Young OBADIAS, DAVID, JOSIAS All were pious.
P	PETER deny'd His Lord and cry'd.
Q	Queen ESTHER fues And faves the Jews.
R	Young pious RUTH. Left all for Truth.
S	Young SAM'L dear The Lord did fear.

A page from the New England Primer, *an early schoolbook*

south and established a settlement called Providence, which later became part of Rhode Island. Williams tried to establish fair dealings with the local Indians and supported religious tolerance. Anne Hutchinson also questioned Puritan authority. She was put on trial for her beliefs and banished from Massachusetts.

Community and religious conflicts peaked in New England with the Salem witch trials of 1692. More than 100 colonists were accused of witchcraft, and 19 people were executed. By the next year, some of the officials and clergymen involved in the witchcraft trials had come to regret their participation.

★ New Southern Colonies

The Puritans were not the only religious group to come to America to escape persecution. Maryland was founded as a haven for Catholics. It was a proprietary colony, which meant that the proprietor, or owner, controlled the government. Proprietor Cecilius Calvert, the second Lord Baltimore, sent 200 colonists to Maryland in 1634, most of whom were men. Having learned from the Jamestown experience, settlers in Maryland planted food crops before starting to grow tobacco for profit. When religious conflicts arose as Protestants began moving to the colony, Maryland passed the Toleration Act of 1649, which stated:

> **No person . . . professing [claiming] to believe in Jesus Christ shall . . . be . . . molested [persecuted], or . . . any way compelled [forced] to the belief or exercise of any other religion.**

American Literature

"To My Dear and Loving Husband"
Anne Bradstreet

When John Winthrop's flagship, the Arbella, *set sail for Boston in 1630, the Bradstreet family was on board. Twenty years later, Anne Bradstreet became the first published American poet with her collection* The Tenth Muse Lately Sprung Up in America. *Despite the demands of living in a new settlement and raising eight children, she continued writing and producing some of her finest poetry, including the following poem to her husband, Simon Bradstreet.*

If ever two were one, then surely we.
If ever man were loved by wife, then thee;
If ever wife was happy in a man,
Compare with me, ye women, if you can.
    I prize thy love more than whole
      mines of gold

Or all the riches the East doth hold.
My love is such that rivers cannot quench,
Nor ought but love from thee,
    give recompense.
Thy love is such I can no way repay,
The heavens reward thee manifold I pray.
Then while we live, in love let's so
    persevere
That when we live no more, we may
    live ever.

Understanding Literature

1. What value does Anne Bradstreet place on her marriage?

2. What words in the poem hint at Bradstreet's feelings toward her husband?

In 1663 Charles II gave land south of Virginia to eight of his supporters. This land, called Carolina, had two areas of settlement, each with its own governor. In 1729 the English government purchased Carolina and divided it into two separate royal colonies—North and South Carolina.

Most colonists in North Carolina were poor farmers from Virginia, and there were few towns until the early 1700s. Settlement in South Carolina began in 1700, when about 100 colonists arrived. They founded Charles Town, which was later called Charleston. The colony attracted many settlers, and wealthy people received large land grants. Records suggest that African laborers taught the colonists how to raise rice in the 1690s. Plantation owners used slaves to do the hard work involved in rice production.

In 1732 King George II granted a charter to found a colony for poor English people, such as those who had been jailed for debt. The king also hoped that this new colony—Georgia—would be a buffer between South Carolina and Spanish Florida. In 1733 James Oglethorpe founded the town of Savannah. The settlers there became unhappy with Oglethorpe's rules, which limited the size of land grants and outlawed slavery. Eventually, the colony eliminated these rules. In 1752 the trustees gave up their charter, and Georgia became a royal colony. Rice plantations worked by slaves soon dotted Georgia's fertile coast, while inland farmers struggled to survive.

⭐ The Middle Colonies

In 1664 the English challenged the Dutch claim to the territory occupied by New Netherland. Charles II's brother, the Duke of York, organized an English fleet that arrived in the harbor of New Amsterdam, the capital of New Netherland. The colony surrendered without any shots being fired. When New Netherland became the English colony of New York, most Dutch settlers remained there.

Shortly after the conquest of New Netherland, the Duke of York granted lands between the Hudson and Delaware Rivers to Sir George Carteret and Lord John Berkeley. These proprietors divided the land into East and West Jersey, which were made into the single royal colony of New Jersey in 1702. The Society of Friends, or the Quakers, made up one of the largest groups in New Jersey. The Quakers were a Protestant sect that believed in the equality of the sexes before God, religious tolerance for all peoples, and nonviolence. The Quakers were often persecuted for their beliefs.

One proprietor of the East Jersey colony was a Quaker named William Penn, whose father had loaned money to King Charles II. In 1681 the king paid his debts by granting Penn a charter for a colony that became known as Pennsylvania. Penn advertised throughout Europe for colonists, offering land grants and religious freedom to all Christians. Many of these settlers became farmers.

Penn visited his colony and treated local American Indians with respect. He also designed the colony's capital, which he named Philadelphia, or City of Brotherly Love. In 1682 he acquired a region that was called Delaware. Pennsylvania and Delaware shared the same governor until Delaware became a separate colony in 1776.

Colonial Quakers in Pennsylvania attend a meeting.

Life in the Thirteen Colonies

In England the Privy Council, a group of royal advisers, set policy for all thirteen colonies. Each colony had either an appointed or an elected governor, who served as the head of government. There were also colonial courts. In some cases, colonists elected representatives to an assembly that made laws. Virginia's **House of Burgesses** was the first colonial assembly. The assemblies were modeled on England's **Parliament**, or legislature. Parliament consists of a **bicameral legislature**—a lawmaking body that is made up of two houses, or groups.

Beginning in 1619, two representatives from every town in the Virginia colony met in Jamestown as the House of Burgesses.

When the Duke of York became King James II, he began suspending colonial charters and united the New England colonies under the **Dominion of New England** in 1686. A royal council and Governor Sir Edmund Andros ruled the Dominion. The king's attempts to centralize power made him unpopular in both England and the colonies. Parliament asked James's daughter Mary and her Dutch husband, William, to jointly rule England. When William landed in England with his army in the fall of 1688, James fled the country. When the colonists learned of this Glorious Revolution, they removed Andros and formed new assemblies. In time, the monarchs issued new colonial charters.

The Navigation Acts

One of England's main interests in its colonies was economic profit. Like other European nations, England practiced mercantilism—creating and maintaining wealth by controlling trade. England wanted to establish a favorable balance of trade by decreasing its **imports**, items purchased from other countries, and increasing its **exports**, items sold to other countries.

Between 1650 and 1696, Parliament passed a series of **Navigation Acts** to control colonial trade. The acts required colonists to use English ships to transport

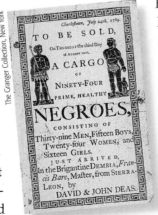

Slave auction poster

goods. All trade goods had to pass through English ports, where duties, or import taxes, were added to the items. Parliament also forbade colonists from trading "enumerated articles," or specified items, with any country other than England. These goods included sugar, tobacco, and cotton. However, customs officials often failed to enforce such regulations, and colonial trade networks developed.

One important part of the trade networks was the slave trade, which involved the transportation of more than 10 million Africans across the Atlantic Ocean to be sold as slaves in the Americas. This often deadly voyage was called the **Middle Passage**. Olaudah Equiano described his experiences in the Middle Passage: "The shrieks of the women, and the groans of the dying, rendered [made] the whole a scene of horror almost inconceivable [unbelievable]." Despite the human cost, the slave trade and slave labor became an important part of the colonial economy.

The Colonial Economies

The colonial economies varied from region to region. The South relied on agriculture and raw materials, such as timber and furs, for its economic base. With a warm climate and long growing season, the South produced cash crops—crops grown mainly to be sold for profit. The main cash crops—tobacco, rice, and indigo—required a large labor force. By the 1700s enslaved Africans did most of the work on plantations. To control slaves, most colonies passed slave codes, or laws.

New England had a more diverse economy. With a harsh climate and rocky soil, few New England farms could grow cash crops. Most families used their own labor, and not slave labor, to farm. Rich fishing waters and abundant lumber made fishing and shipbuilding two leading industries in New England, while Boston was a leader in colonial commerce.

With a good growing season and plenty of fertile land, the middle colonies produced surpluses of foodstuffs and livestock for export. Indentured servants performed much of the labor. Merchants in Philadelphia and New York City exported colonial goods to Europe and the West Indies. These cities became two of the largest and most important colonial cities.

A Revival of Faith

While the colonies had different economies, they shared some experiences. During the 1730s and 1740s, many colonists from New England to Georgia experienced what historians have called a "great awakening" in their religious lives. This

Colonial woman spinning wool for local use

Great Awakening was an unorganized but widespread movement of evangelical Christian revivals, or large church gatherings. Jonathan Edwards, George Whitefield, and other ministers preached that all people, regardless of their social status, were born sinners. They also said that everyone had an equal chance to be saved. Such messages of spiritual equality may have eventually encouraged some colonists to demand greater political equality.

SECTION 3 REVIEW

Identify and explain the significance of the following:
- Bacon's Rebellion
- Mayflower Compact
- town meetings
- House of Burgesses
- Parliament
- bicameral legislature
- Dominion of New England
- imports
- exports
- Navigation Acts
- Middle Passage
- Great Awakening

Reading for Content Understanding

1 **Main Idea** How did religion affect the colonies and colonial life?

2 **Main Idea** What economic ties existed between England and the colonies?

3 **Geographic Diversity** *Region* What effect did the environment have on the economies that developed in the New England, middle, and southern colonies?

4 **Writing** *Classifying* Imagine that you are a colonist in the late 1600s. Write a letter to a cousin in England telling him or her how the colonies differ from each other economically and politically.

5 **Critical Thinking** *Making Comparisons* How were the experiences of the Pilgrims similar to those of the Jamestown settlers?

The American Revolution

Reading Focus

Why did Britain impose new taxes on the colonies, and how did the colonists respond?

What events led the First Continental Congress to break away from Britain?

What events ended the American Revolution?

Key Terms

Pontiac's Rebellion

Stamp Act

Townshend Acts

Boston Massacre

Intolerable Acts

Battle of Bunker Hill

Declaration of Independence

Battle of Saratoga

Battle of Yorktown

Treaty of Paris of 1783

*I*N 1748 SWEDISH SCIENTIST *Peter Kalm traveled through the British colonies, which he said "have increased so much in their number of inhabitants, and in their riches, that they almost vie [compete] with Old England." Kalm also noted that the colonists were very independent, and that British trade laws caused them "to grow less tender for their mother country." The tensions that Kalm saw increased as the colonies and Great Britain grew further apart.*

The Granger Collection, New York

King George III

 ## Conflicts in the Colonies

From 1689 to 1763, France and England fought a series of wars to become the world's most powerful nation. The fighting ended with the British victory in the French and Indian War. As a result, France lost its lands in North America. Britain gained Canada, French lands east of the Mississippi River, and Florida. Spain, which had allied with Britain, received French Louisiana.

As the fighting ended, more settlers crossed the Appalachian Mountains onto American Indian land. In 1763 Chief Pontiac led Indians in **Pontiac's Rebellion**. They destroyed many British forts before Pontiac surrendered. To prevent more conflict, Britain issued the Proclamation of 1763, banning settlement west of the Appalachians.

Colonial conflicts were costly. To raise money, in 1764 Parliament passed the Sugar Act, which set duties on molasses and sugar. Some colonists argued that Britain did not have the right to tax them because there were no colonial representatives in Parliament. The colonists protested, "No taxation without representation." Samuel Adams of Boston voiced his opposition to the tax:

❝ **For if our trade may be taxed, why not our lands? Why not the produce of our lands and, in short, everything we possess or make use of?** ❞

Merchants in Massachusetts and New York agreed to boycott, or not buy, certain British goods until Parliament removed the duties.

In response, Prime Minister George Grenville proposed the **Stamp Act** in 1765. This act required colonists to pay for an official stamp, or seal, when they bought paper items such as newspapers and legal documents. Many colonists protested this tax on everyday items produced in the colonies. Some colonists formed secret societies called the Sons of Liberty, which sometimes used violence to frighten tax collectors. In October, delegates from nine colonies met and issued a declaration that the Stamp Act violated their rights and liberties. They asked Parliament to repeal, or abolish, the act. Parliament repealed the act in 1766, but asserted its authority to make laws for the colonies.

In 1767 Parliament passed the **Townshend Acts**, which required new import duties. The colonists responded with another boycott. When the Massachusetts legislature protested the acts, the British governor disbanded it. British soldiers arrived in Boston in 1768. On March 5, 1770, British troops fired into a mob, killing five people in the **Boston Massacre**.

Paul Revere's engraving of the Boston Massacre

Parliament repealed the Townshend duties but left the tax on tea. Colonists were further angered when Parliament passed the Tea Act in 1773. On December 16, a group of colonists crept onto three ships in Boston Harbor and dumped chests of tea overboard. To punish Massachusetts for this Boston Tea Party, Parliament passed four laws in 1774 that colonists called the **Intolerable Acts**. These acts included closing Boston Harbor and canceling the colony's charter.

★ The Revolutionary War Begins

In September 1774, colonial delegates met in Philadelphia for the First Continental Congress. The delegates discussed the crisis and recommended boycotting British goods and arming colonial militias. They also sent King George III a list of their rights. In response, British leaders ordered the colonists' weapons seized. General Thomas Gage targeted the militia weapons stored in Concord, about 20 miles from Boston. On April 18, 1775, colonists Paul Revere and William Dawes rode across the countryside warning, "The British are coming!"

The next morning, the militia met a large force of British troops at Lexington, near Concord. The colonial leader shouted to his men, "Don't fire unless fired upon. But if they mean to have a war, let it begin here!" Suddenly, a shot rang out. To this day, no one knows who fired this "shot heard round the world." The short battle that followed resulted in 18 colonial casualties. The British next marched to Concord, where they met more militia. After some British troops set fire to a few buildings, they retreated back to Boston. The militia fired upon them, inflicting many casualties.

Word of the fighting spread, and representatives from the colonies met in Philadelphia in May for the Second Continental Congress. The delegates organized the Continental Army and chose Virginian George Washington, a well-respected veteran of the French and Indian War, as commander. The Congress also sent the king a petition asking for a peaceful resolution.

After the battle at Concord, the colonial forces held Boston under siege—a military blockade of a

A soldier in the Continental Army

city or fort. Warned of a British plan to secure Charlestown, which overlooks Boston, colonial soldiers took up defensive positions atop nearby Bunker Hill and Breed's Hill. By the next morning, June 17, the colonial forces had secured the hills. The British then mounted a frontal assault. The colonial commander ordered his troops, who were low on gunpowder, not to fire on the British soldiers "until you see the whites of their eyes." The colonists finally retreated after running out of ammunition during the **Battle of Bunker Hill**.

In March 1776 General Washington's army positioned cannons on a hill overlooking Boston and fired on the British troops. On March 7 General William Howe ordered the British to retreat. Boston, the birthplace of the Revolution, was back in colonial hands.

★ Fighting for Independence

In January 1776 Thomas Paine published *Common Sense*, a pamphlet in which he argued that countries should be ruled by laws created by the people instead of by a monarchy. Many colonists agreed with Paine's ideas. In June the Continental Congress decided to break away from Britain. Thomas Jefferson, a delegate from Virginia, was the main author of the **Declaration of Independence**. This document defined the colonists' rights, listed their complaints against Britain, and declared the colonies free and independent.

On July 4, 1776, the Continental Congress approved the Declaration of Independence, creating the United States of America.

The signers of the Declaration of Independence drew inspiration from the Enlightenment, an intellectual movement that applied reason and logic to political behavior. Enlightenment philosophers believed that government was a social contract between people and their ruler. English philosopher John Locke agreed and added that people had a natural right to overthrow a corrupt government.

The Fight for Independence, 1776–1781

Learning from Maps The Revolutionary War was fought across the vast area of the thirteen colonies. British troops could be transported on ships of the British fleet, while the American army had to move on foot.

Region Where did most of the later battles of the war take place?

The Founding of the Nation **23**

Early Battles

The colonists were now in revolt against Britain, which had a large army and the world's most powerful navy. In contrast, the colonists had poorly trained local militias. However, the colonists were fighting for a cause they supported, while the British army faced a largely hostile civilian population. Colonists known as Patriots supported independence. Loyalists, or Tories, were loyal to Britain. More than 50,000 Loyalists fled the colonies during the Revolution.

Some Patriots wanted to fight a defensive war, while other military leaders wanted to invade Canada. The Patriots had taken Fort Ticonderoga, which controlled access to Lake Champlain, a waterway into Canada. In November 1775, Patriot troops captured Montreal. When the Patriots advanced on the city of Quebec on New Year's Eve, they suffered a crushing defeat.

Farther south, General Washington had moved his troops to New York. On June 29, 1776, Patriots spotted British ships approaching New York Bay. Led by General Howe, the British battered the Patriots until late August. Washington's troops retreated to avoid complete destruction.

Patriot Victories

General Howe sent troops to secure New Jersey in November 1776. Deciding to establish a winter base for his troops, Howe settled in New York City.

Washington Crossing the Delaware, *by German-born American Emanuel Leutze*

Washington decided to attack some British forces left in Trenton, New Jersey. On Christmas night, Washington's forces crossed the icy Delaware River. On December 26, the Patriots launched a surprise attack. The battle at Trenton lasted less than an hour before the British surrendered. Washington next attacked nearby Princeton, driving back the British forces. These victories boosted the spirits of the colonial troops.

 ## Hard Times and Victory

In the spring of 1777, British military leaders proposed a campaign to cut New England off from the rest of the colonies. The plan called for General John Burgoyne's troops in Canada to retake Fort Ticonderoga, then march south. Meanwhile, a second British force would march east from western New York, and General Howe's troops in New York City would move north. All three forces would combine near Albany, New York.

Burgoyne took Fort Ticonderoga by early July and began marching south. However, Howe moved to attack Philadelphia, instead of marching to Albany as planned. On September 11, 1777, his forces battled General Washington's troops at Brandywine Creek. The Patriots suffered heavy losses and retreated. Meanwhile, Burgoyne's troops were badly outnumbered when they clashed with Patriot soldiers at the **Battle of Saratoga**. On October 17, 1777, Burgoyne surrendered, marking the Patriots' greatest victory in the war up to that point.

After Saratoga, the French formally declared their support for the Patriots. The Marquis de Lafayette, who had already been fighting for the Patriots, believed that "the welfare of America is closely bound up with the welfare of mankind." Spain also helped the Patriots.

The entry of foreign allies into the war came at a critical time. After the victory at Saratoga, Washington settled his troops at Valley Forge,

Pennsylvania. Over the harsh winter of 1777–78, about one fourth of the soldiers stationed there died of disease and malnutrition. The troops grew restless and frustrated. In February 1778 an experienced Prussian army officer named Baron Friedrich von Steuben came to Washington's aid. He began training the troops and soon turned the Continental Army into a stronger fighting force.

By early 1781 British forces were in control of most of the South. British general Charles Cornwallis then moved his troops into Yorktown, Virginia.

Washington and the Comte de Rochambeau (raw-shahm-boh), a French general, moved their troops south. They surrounded the British and lay siege to Yorktown in September. The French fleet kept British ships from providing aid. Badly outnumbered, Cornwallis surrendered on October 19, 1781. A witness to the **Battle of Yorktown** described the surrender:

66 **The British officers rode right on before the army, who marched out beating and playing** a melancholy [sad] tune, their drums covered with black handkerchiefs. 99

The **Treaty of Paris of 1783** formally ended the war. Washington disbanded the army, noting, "The citizens of America are . . . acknowledged to be possessed of absolute freedom and independency."

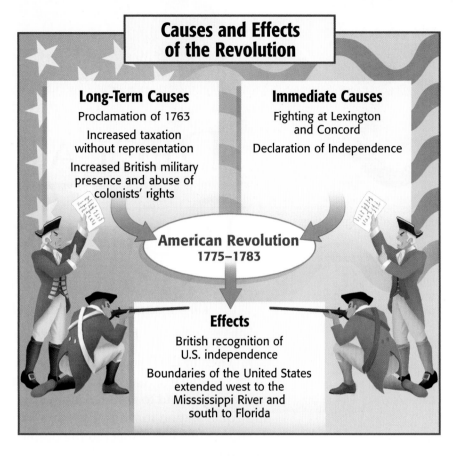

Causes and Effects of the Revolution

Long-Term Causes
Proclamation of 1763
Increased taxation without representation
Increased British military presence and abuse of colonists' rights

Immediate Causes
Fighting at Lexington and Concord
Declaration of Independence

American Revolution
1775–1783

Effects
British recognition of U.S. independence
Boundaries of the United States extended west to the Misssissippi River and south to Florida

SECTION 4 REVIEW

Identify and explain the significance of the following:
- **Pontiac's Rebellion**
- **Stamp Act**
- **Townshend Acts**
- **Boston Massacre**
- **Intolerable Acts**
- **Battle of Bunker Hill**
- **Declaration of Independence**
- **Battle of Saratoga**
- **Battle of Yorktown**
- **Treaty of Paris of 1783**

Reading for Content Understanding

1 **Main Idea** Why did Britain attempt to raise money from the colonies, and how did the colonists respond to new taxes?

2 **Main Idea** What events marked the beginning of the Revolutionary War?

3 **Citizenship and Democracy** How did Enlightenment ideas influence the signers of the Declaration of Independence?

4 **Writing** *Creating* Make a pamphlet listing the events leading to the war's end and the signing of the Treaty of Paris of 1783.

5 **Critical Thinking** *Determining the Strength of an Argument* Do you think the British were justified in their taxation policies? Explain your answer.

1776

Thomas Jefferson wrote the first draft of the Declaration in a little more than two weeks.

In the first paragraph, the signers state that it is important to justify why the colonists must break their political ties with Britain.

impel: force

endowed: provided

"Laws of Nature" and "Nature's God" refer to the belief common during the Scientific Revolution that certain patterns are constant and predictable and that they come from a supreme being. Natural or "unalienable" rights (the rights to life, liberty, and the pursuit of happiness) cannot be taken away. English philosopher John Locke had argued that people created governments to protect their natural rights. If a government abuses its powers, it is the right as well as the duty of the people to do away with that government.

usurpations: wrongful seizures of power

despotism: unlimited power

THE
DECLARATION
of
INDEPENDENCE

In Congress, July 4, 1776
The unanimous Declaration of the thirteen
united States of America,

When in the Course of human events, it becomes necessary for one people to dissolve the political bands which have connected them with another, and to assume among the Powers of the earth, the separate and equal station to which the Laws of Nature and of Nature's God entitle them, a decent respect to the opinions of mankind requires that they should declare the causes which impel them to the separation.

Natural Rights

We hold these truths to be self-evident, that all men are created equal, that they are endowed by their Creator with certain unalienable Rights, that among these are Life, Liberty, and the pursuit of Happiness. That to secure these rights, Governments are instituted among Men, deriving their just powers from the consent of the governed,

That whenever any Form of Government becomes destructive of these ends, it is the Right of the People to alter or to abolish it, and to institute new Government, laying its foundation on such principles and organizing its powers in such form, as to them shall seem most likely to effect their Safety and Happiness. Prudence, indeed, will dictate that Governments long established should not be changed for light and transient causes; and accordingly all experience hath shown, that mankind are more disposed to suffer, while evils are sufferable, than to right themselves by abolishing the forms to which they are accustomed. But when a long train of abuses and usurpations, pursuing invariably the same Object evinces a design to reduce them under absolute Despotism, it is their right, it is their duty, to throw off such Government, and to provide new Guards for their future security.—

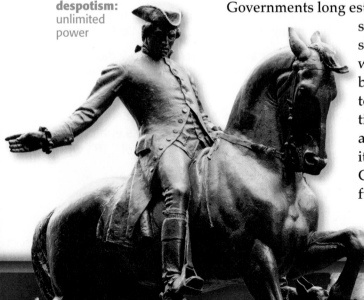

LEFT: *Revolutionary War hero Paul Revere*

Colonists' Complaints Against the King

Such has been the patient sufferance of these Colonies; and such is now the necessity which constrains them to alter their former Systems of Government. The history of the present King of Great Britain is a history of repeated injuries and usurpations, all having in direct object the establishment of an absolute Tyranny over these States. To prove this, let Facts be submitted to a candid world.

He has refused his Assent to Laws, the most wholesome and necessary for the public good.

He has forbidden his Governors to pass Laws of immediate and pressing importance, unless suspended in their operation till his Assent should be obtained; and when so suspended, he has utterly neglected to attend to them.

He has refused to pass other Laws for the accommodation of large districts of people, unless those people would relinquish the right of Representation in the Legislature, a right inestimable to them and formidable to tyrants only.

He has called together legislative bodies at places unusual, uncomfortable, and distant from the depository of their Public Records, for the sole purpose of fatiguing them into compliance with his measures.

He has dissolved Representative Houses repeatedly, for opposing with manly firmness his invasions on the rights of the people.

He has refused for a long time, after such dissolutions, to cause others to be elected; whereby the Legislative Powers, incapable of Annihilation, have returned to the People at large for their exercise; the State remaining in the mean time exposed to all the dangers of invasion from without, and convulsions within.

He has endeavored to prevent the population of these States; for that purpose obstructing the Laws of Naturalization of Foreigners; refusing to pass others to encourage their migration hither, and raising the conditions of new Appropriations of Lands.

He has obstructed the Administration of Justice, by refusing his Assent to Laws for establishing Judiciary Powers.

He has made Judges dependent on his Will alone, for the tenure of their offices, and the amount and payment of their salaries.

He has erected a multitude of New Offices, and sent hither swarms of Officers to harass our people, and eat out their substance.

He has kept among us, in times of peace, Standing Armies without the Consent of our legislature.

He has affected to render the Military independent of and superior to the Civil Power.

He has combined with others to subject us to a jurisdiction foreign to our constitution, and unacknowledged by our laws; giving his Assent to their Acts of pretended legislation:

tyranny: oppressive power exerted by a government or ruler

candid: fair

Here the Declaration lists the charges that the colonists had against King George III. How might the language in the list appeal to people's emotions?

relinquish: release, yield
inestimable: priceless
formidable: causing dread

Why do you think the king had his colonial legislatures meet in places that were hard to reach?

annihilation: destruction

convulsions: violent disturbances

naturalization of foreigners: the process by which foreign-born persons become citizens

appropriations of land: setting aside land for settlement

tenure: term

a multitude of: many

Name five acts that the Declaration states have been committed by the king and the British Parliament.

For quartering large bodies of armed troops among us:

For protecting them, by a mock Trial, from Punishment for any Murders which they should commit on the Inhabitants of these States:

For cutting off our Trade with all parts of the world:

For imposing taxes on us without our Consent:

For depriving us in many cases, of the benefits of Trial by Jury:

For transporting us beyond Seas to be tried for pretended offences:

For abolishing the free System of English Laws in a neighboring Province, establishing therein an Arbitrary government, and enlarging its Boundaries so as to render it at once an example and fit instrument for introducing the same absolute rule into these Colonies:

For taking away our Charters, abolishing our most valuable Laws, and altering fundamentally the Forms of our Governments:

For suspending our own Legislature, and declaring themselves invested with Power to legislate for us in all cases whatsoever.

He has abdicated Government here, by declaring us out of his Protection and waging War against us.

He has plundered our seas, ravaged our Coasts, burnt our towns, and destroyed the lives of our people.

He is at this time transporting large armies of foreign mercenaries to complete the works of death, desolation and tyranny, already begun with circumstances of Cruelty & perfidy scarcely paralleled in the most barbarous ages, and totally unworthy the Head of a civilized nation.

He has constrained our fellow Citizens taken Captive on the high Seas to bear Arms against their Country, to become the executioners of their friends and Brethren, or to fall themselves by their Hands.

He has excited domestic insurrections amongst us, and has endeavored to bring on the inhabitants of our frontiers, the merciless Indian Savages, whose known rule of warfare, is an undistinguished destruction of all ages, sexes and conditions.

In every stage of these Oppressions We have Petitioned for Redress in the most humble terms: Our repeated Petitions have been answered only by repeated injury. A Prince, whose character is thus marked by every act which may define a Tyrant, is unfit to be the ruler of a free People.

Nor have We been wanting in attention to our British brethren. We have warned them from time to time of attempts by their legislature to extend an unwarrantable jurisdiction over us. We have reminded them of the circumstances of our emigration and settlement here. We have appealed to their native justice and magnanimity, and we have conjured them by the ties of our common kindred to disavow these usurpations, which, would inevitably interrupt our connections and correspondence. They too have been deaf to the voice of justice and of consanguinity. We must, therefore, acquiesce in the necessity, which denounces our

quartering: lodging, housing

What was the colonists' rallying cry to protest the king's tax policies?

The "neighboring Province" that is referred to here is Canada.

arbitrary: not based on law

render: make

abdicated: given up

foreign mercenaries: soldiers hired to fight for a country not their own

perfidy: violation of trust

insurrections: rebellions

petitioned for redress: asked formally for a correction of wrongs

Notice that the Declaration has 18 paragraphs beginning with "He has" or "He is." What is the effect of this repetition?

unwarrantable jurisdiction: unjustified authority

magnanimity: generous spirit

conjured: urgently called upon

consanguinity: common ancestry

acquiesce: consent to

Separation, and hold them, as we hold the rest of mankind, Enemies in War, in Peace Friends.

An Independent United States

We, therefore, the Representatives of the united States of America, in General Congress, Assembled, appealing to the Supreme Judge of the world for the rectitude of our intentions, do, in the Name, and by Authority of the good People of these Colonies, solemnly publish and declare, That these United Colonies are, and of Right ought to be Free and Independent States; that they are Absolved from all Allegiance to the British Crown, and that all political connection between them and the State of Great Britain, is and ought to be totally dissolved; and that as Free and Independent States, they have full Power to levy War, conclude Peace, contract Alliances, establish Commerce, and to do all other Acts and Things which Independent States may of right do. And for the support of this Declaration, with a firm reliance on the Protection of Divine Providence, we mutually pledge to each other our Lives, our Fortunes and our sacred Honor.

rectitude: rightness

In this paragraph, the signers state their actual declaration of independence. What rights would the new United States of America now have as an independent nation?

John Hancock
President of
Massachusetts

GEORGIA
Button Gwinnett
Lyman Hall
George Walton

NORTH CAROLINA
William Hooper
Joseph Hewes
John Penn

SOUTH CAROLINA
Edward Rutledge
Thomas Heyward, Jr.
Thomas Lynch, Jr.
Arthur Middleton

MARYLAND
Samuel Chase
William Paca
Thomas Stone
Charles Carroll of
Carrollton

VIRGINIA
George Wythe
Richard Henry Lee

Thomas Jefferson
Benjamin Harrison
Thomas Nelson, Jr.
Francis Lightfoot Lee
Carter Braxton

PENNSYLVANIA
Robert Morris
Benjamin Rush
Benjamin Franklin
John Morton
George Clymer
James Smith
George Taylor
James Wilson
George Ross

DELAWARE
Caesar Rodney
George Read
Thomas McKean

NEW YORK
William Floyd
Phillip Livingston
Francis Lewis
Lewis Morris

NEW JERSEY
Richard Stockton
John Witherspoon
Francis Hopkinson
John Hart
Abraham Clark

NEW HAMPSHIRE
Josiah Bartlett
William Whipple
Matthew Thornton

MASSACHUSETTS
Samuel Adams
John Adams
Robert Treat Paine
Elbridge Gerry

RHODE ISLAND
Stephen Hopkins
William Ellery

CONNECTICUT
Roger Sherman
Samuel Huntington
William Williams
Oliver Wolcott

Congress adopted the final draft of the Declaration of Independence on July 4, 1776. A formal copy, written on parchment paper, was signed on August 2, 1776.

The following is part of a passage that the Congress took out of Jefferson's original draft: "He has waged cruel war against human nature itself, violating its most sacred rights of life and liberty in the persons of a distant people who never offended him, captivating and carrying them into slavery in another hemisphere, or to incur miserable death in their transportation thither." Why do you think the Congress might have wanted to delete this passage?

Forming a Nation

Reading Focus

What problems arose under the Articles of Confederation?

What were some of the main issues debated at the Constitutional Convention?

Why did some people oppose the new Constitution, and how were their concerns addressed?

Key Terms

Articles of Confederation

Constitutional Convention

Great Compromise

Three-Fifths Compromise

federalism

legislative branch

executive branch

judicial branch

checks and balances

amendments

Bill of Rights

I*N THE FIRST YEAR of the Revolutionary War, a young professor moved to New Hampshire, where he began teaching at Dartmouth College. Soon after, without revealing his name, he published a short essay calling for the newly independent states to establish representative governments. However, he warned that the American people needed to take great care when building their new governments. "They [the people] are now planting a seed, which will arise" with tree branches "extended to shelter the liberty of succeeding ages," he stated.*

The bald eagle, symbol of the United States

 Forming a New Government

Many states created their own constitution—a set of basic principles and laws that determines the powers and duties of the government. Most state constitutions began with a bill of rights—a document describing the civil liberties, or individual rights, that a government promises its citizens.

The Articles of Confederation

On November 15, 1777, the Second Continental Congress approved the **Articles of Confederation**, which created a national government with limited powers. In March 1781 the last state ratified, or formally approved, the Articles. The first permanent national government of the United States was thus in effect.

This new national government consisted of the Confederation Congress, in which each state had one vote. The Congress could coin and borrow money, negotiate treaties, and resolve conflicts between states. The Congress could not force states to contribute money or soldiers. There was no federal executive, such as a president, or a national court system.

Problems with the Articles

The new Congress had several issues to address, such as raising money to pay its war debts. Because Congress's ability to obtain money from the states was limited, it decided to raise revenue by selling its western lands. Congress passed the Land Ordinance of 1785 to organize surveys and division of these public lands. Congress also passed the Northwest Ordinance of 1787 to establish a political structure for the Northwest Territory. This region included present-day Illinois, Indiana, Michigan, Ohio, and Wisconsin.

The nation's economic problems worsened when Spain closed the lower Mississippi River to U.S. shipping in 1784. This action cut off western farmers' only effective way to transport goods to and from the East. Attempts to negotiate a treaty with Spain failed. In 1783 Britain closed many of its ports to U.S. ships and forced American merchants to pay tariffs—taxes on imports or exports—on goods sent to Britain. While U.S. exports declined, British goods flowed freely into the United States. This trade imbalance created serious economic problems.

Congress was powerless to fix the problem. It had no authority to establish tariffs or to regulate interstate commerce—trade conducted between two or more states. States adopted trade policies that were beneficial to their own interests rather than cooperating to improve the nation's trade position. In 1785 a British magazine playfully referred to the new nation as the "Dis-United States."

The states had other economic problems. Massachusetts was in a depression—a steep drop in economic activity. Many farmers who could not pay their land taxes had their property taken away. Daniel Shays, a poor farmer and veteran of the Revolutionary War, led a farmers' uprising in September 1786 known as Shays's Rebellion. The farmers hoped to stop the foreclosures on their farms, but state militia troops soon defeated the rebels. The national government, however, proved powerless to help put down the rebellion.

The Constitutional Convention

Alarmed by the nation's problems, Congress invited each of the 13 states to send delegates to a **Constitutional Convention** to be held in Philadelphia in May 1787. The invitation noted that the delegates were to revise the Articles of Confederation and

> 66 **to render [make] the federal constitution adequate to the exigencies [needs] of government, and the preservation of the Union.** 99

Rhode Island refused to attend, but the other 12 states sent a total of 55 delegates.

Several issues divided the delegates. The smaller states objected to the larger states' plan for a national legislature with representatives chosen in proportion to state populations. After deadlocking over the issue, delegates formed a special committee, which proposed the **Great Compromise**. It proposed that every state, regardless of its size, would receive two votes in the upper house of the legislature. In the lower house, each state would have representation according to its population.

Southerners wanted slaves to be counted as part of their state populations so that they would have more representatives. Northerners wanted slaves to be counted in deciding a state's taxes but

Virginia Museum of Fine Arts, Richmond, VA. Detail of *Washington Addressing the Constitutional Convention* by Junius Brutus Stearns. Gift of Edgar William and Bernice Chrysler Garbisch. Photo: Ron Jennings. ©2000 Virginia Museum of Fine Arts.

The delegates elected George Washington president of the Constitutional Convention. Virginian James Madison also played a crucial role.

The Articles of Confederation and the Constitution

ARTICLES	CONSTITUTION
EXECUTIVE BRANCH	
No executive to administer and enforce legislation; Congress has sole authority to govern. Executive committee to oversee government when Congress is out of session	President administers and enforces federal laws.
LEGISLATIVE BRANCH	
A unicameral (one-house) legislature Each state had one vote, regardless of population. Nine votes (of the original 13) to enact legislation	A bicameral (two-house) legislature Each state has equal representation in the Senate; each state is represented according to population in the House of Representatives. Simple majority to enact legislation
JUDICIAL BRANCH	
No national court system Congress to establish temporary courts to hear cases of piracy	National court system, headed by the Supreme Court Courts to hear cases involving national laws, treaties, and the Constitution as well as cases between states, between citizens of different states, or between a state and citizen of another state
OTHER MATTERS	
Admission to the Confederation by 9 votes (of 13) Amendment of the Articles by unanimous vote The states retained independence.	Congress to admit new states; all must have a republican form of government Amendment of the Constitution by two-thirds vote of both houses of Congress or by national convention, followed by ratification by three fourths of the states The states accept the Constitution as the supreme law of the land.

not its representatives. The delegates accepted the **Three-Fifths Compromise**. It provided that three fifths of the slaves in each state be counted as part of that state's population when allotting representatives to the lower house.

 ## The Living Constitution

The delegates to the Constitutional Convention created a balanced government based on the idea of **federalism**. Federalism is the distribution of governmental power within a nation between a central authority and the states or provinces that make up the nation.

The federal government is organized under three branches. The **legislative branch**, or Congress, is responsible for proposing bills and passing them into laws. Congress is made up of two houses. The Senate, or upper house, is composed of two members from each state. In the House of Representatives, or lower house, each state is represented according to its population. The **executive branch** includes the president and the administrative departments of the government. The **judicial branch** is made up of all the national courts. This branch is responsible for interpreting laws, punishing criminals, and settling disputes between states. (For the full text of the Constitution, see page 44.)

The framers of the Constitution established **checks and balances**, a system to prevent any branch of government from becoming too powerful. For example, the framers gave Congress the power to propose and pass bills into law, but also gave the president the power to veto congressional legislation. In later years, the Supreme Court established that it had the power to determine whether laws passed by Congress are unconstitutional.

An early printed copy of the Constitution

According to the Constitution, the laws of the federal government have authority over state laws. The federal government can enforce its laws through the use of troops under the president's command. However, the Constitution also allows states to keep control over many functions, such as local government and education.

In September 1787, after 16 weeks of debate, delegates signed a final draft of the Constitution and sent it to Congress. Congress then sent the document to the states for ratification. The Constitution would go into effect as soon as nine states ratified it.

★ The Ratification Fight

When the Constitution was made public, it sparked a heated debate. Some Americans feared that the new national government would take too much power away from the states and would not protect the rights of individual citizens. People who opposed the Constitution were called Antifederalists. Supporters of the Constitution, called Federalists, believed that it provided a good balance of power. One of the strongest defenses of the Constitution appeared in the *Federalist Papers,* a series of essays written by Alexander Hamilton, James Madison, and John Jay.

In December 1787 Delaware became the first state to ratify the Constitution. The Constitution went into effect in June 1788, after New Hampshire became the ninth state to ratify it. The next month, Congress declared the Constitution ratified and arranged for the first presidential and congressional elections under the new government of the United States.

Several states had ratified the Constitution only after the assurance that a bill of rights would be added as **amendments**—official changes, corrections, or additions. By December 1791 the states had ratified the first 10 amendments to the Constitution, known as the **Bill of Rights**. (For a full discussion of the Bill of Rights, see Chapter 2.) The Bill of Rights has helped the U.S. Constitution to survive as the oldest functioning written national constitution in the world.

SECTION 5 REVIEW

Identify and explain the significance of the following:
- **Articles of Confederation**
- **Constitutional Convention**
- **Great Compromise**
- **Three-Fifths Compromise**
- **federalism**
- **legislative branch**
- **executive branch**
- **judicial branch**
- **checks and balances**
- **amendments**
- **Bill of Rights**

Reading for Content Understanding

1 **Main Idea** What problems plagued the new nation under the Articles of Confederation?

2 **Main Idea** What issues did delegates debate at the Constitutional Convention?

3 **Constitutional Heritage** Why did some people insist that a bill of rights be added to the Constitution?

4 **Writing** *Describing* Write a paragraph describing how the federal government is organized.

5 **Critical Thinking** *Determining the Strength of an Argument* If you had been a citizen during the ratification process, would you have been a Federalist or an Antifederalist? Explain your answer.

CHAPTER 1 REVIEW

Chapter Summary

Trade with Africa and Asia motivated Europeans to explore the world. After Columbus's voyages, Europeans colonized the Americas—often with devastating results for American Indians. English colonists protested when Britain imposed new taxes, and in 1776 the colonies declared their independence. The Revolutionary War lasted from 1775 to 1783. The U.S. Constitution was signed in 1787, and the Bill of Rights was added later. ◼

On a separate sheet of paper, complete the following activities.

Identifying People and Ideas

Describe the historical significance of the following:

1. monopoly
2. amendments
3. Christopher Columbus
4. House of Burgesses
5. bicameral legislature
6. Constitutional Convention
7. Middle Passage
8. migration
9. Battle of Yorktown
10. Bill of Rights

go.hrw.com
SB1 Revolutionary War

Internet Activity

Imagine that you are a travel agent planning an educational tour. Search the Internet through the HRW Web site for information on important battlefields of the Revolutionary War. Put together a one-page travel brochure describing the sites that your clients could visit on their tour.

Understanding Main Ideas

1. How did the environment influence the development of Native American culture groups?
2. Why were Europeans interested in finding a sea route to Asia?
3. What were the differences and similarities between the Jamestown and Plymouth settlements?
4. How were the thirteen colonies governed before King James II came to power?
5. What events led to the outbreak of the Revolutionary War?
6. What were the terms of the Great Compromise?
7. How is the federal government organized under the Constitution?

Reviewing Themes

1. **Geographic Diversity** What motivated Europeans to explore and colonize the Americas?

Using the Time Line

Number your paper from 1 to 6. Match the letters on the time line below with the following events.

1. **Leif Eriksson lands in North America.**
2. **Paleo-Indians cross Beringia into Alaska.**
3. **Delegates sign a final draft of the Constitution.**
4. **Christopher Columbus and his crew land in the Americas.**
5. **Thomas Jefferson drafts the Declaration of Independence.**
6. **A small group of English settlers establishes the Jamestown colony.**

| 50,000 B.C. | A.D. 1000 | 1300 | 1600 | 1700 | 1730 | 1760 | 1790 |
| a | b | c | d | | | e | f |

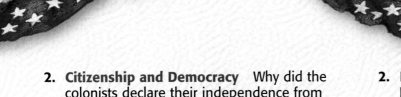

2. **Citizenship and Democracy**   Why did the colonists declare their independence from Britain, and what are some important ideas in the Declaration of Independence?

3. **Constitutional Heritage**   How does the Constitution guard against the misuse of power?

Thinking Critically

1. **Drawing Conclusions**   How did the Protestant Reformation affect European colonization of North America?

2. **Making Comparisons**   Compare and contrast the New England, middle, and southern colonies.

Writing About History

1. **Creating**   Make a poster supporting or opposing the ratification of the Constitution. Include specific reasons for your position.

Building Your Portfolio

American History

Complete the following activities individually or in groups.

1. **Trade Today**   Use the textbook or your library to research and compile a list of 10 goods that the United States imports and 10 goods that it exports. Then prepare a map of the world that shows trade patterns between the United States and other countries. Draw symbols on the map to show the goods that the United States imports and exports.

2. **Settling a New Land**   The first Jamestown settlers—many of whom were goldsmiths and jewelers—lacked the skills necessary for survival. Imagine that you are putting together a group of colonists to settle in North America. Decide how many people to take with you, what kinds of occupations they should have, and where to settle. Make sure you explain the reasons for each choice. Then write a short play about your first month in the colony. You may wish to perform your play for the class.

2. **Expressing**   Imagine that you are a Loyalist or a Patriot. Write a letter to a friend explaining your choice.

Linking Geography and History

1. **Human-Environment Interaction**   How did the Columbian Exchange affect American Indians and Europeans?

2. **Region**   How did geography and climate influence the economic development of the New England, middle, and southern colonies?

History Skills Workshop

Reading Maps   Study the map below, which shows early settlements in North America. Then answer the following questions: (a) In what present-day state was New Amsterdam located? (b) What river connected Fort Orange and the New Amsterdam settlement? (c) How far was Quebec from Montreal?

Early European Settlements

■ CHAPTER 2 ■
Citizenship and the Constitution
(1787–Present)

Thomas Jefferson admired the ideas of ancient Greek philosophers such as Aristotle. "Liberty and equality," wrote Aristotle, "will be best attained [reached] when all persons alike share in the government." Some 2,000 years after Aristotle, U.S. leaders began the process of creating a democratic system of government. Today most Americans can participate in the political process.

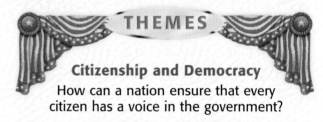

THEMES

Citizenship and Democracy
How can a nation ensure that every citizen has a voice in the government?

Constitutional Heritage
How does a government's organization affect the distribution of power?

Cultural Diversity
What contributions have different groups and individuals made to the nation's formation and government?

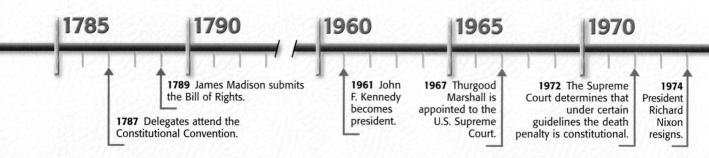

| 1785 | 1790 | // | 1960 | 1965 | 1970 |

1789 James Madison submits the Bill of Rights.

1787 Delegates attend the Constitutional Convention.

1961 John F. Kennedy becomes president.

1967 Thurgood Marshall is appointed to the U.S. Supreme Court.

1972 The Supreme Court determines that under certain guidelines the death penalty is constitutional.

1974 President Richard Nixon resigns.

SECTION 1

Understanding the Constitution

Reading Focus

How did the framers of the Constitution address concerns about the balance of state and federal powers?

What are the three branches of the federal government?

How is power divided among the three branches of government?

Key Terms

delegated powers

elastic clause

reserved powers

concurrent powers

representative democracy

apportionment

impeach

veto

executive orders

pardons

cabinet

TODAY A SIGN on the Justice Department building in Washington, D.C., reads, "No Free Government Can Survive That Is Not Based on the Supremacy of Law." This idea is central to the U.S. Constitution. Antifederalists opposed the Constitution for fear that the government it created would be too powerful and thus endanger the rights of the people. Federalists such as James Madison assured them that a system grounded in law was the best safeguard of the people.

The Constitution

The Granger Collection, New York

IMAGE ON LEFT PAGE: *Students view historic artwork in Washington, D.C.*

| 1975 | 1980 | 1985 | 1990 | 1995 |

1981 Sandra Day O'Connor is appointed to the U.S. Supreme Court.

1984 Geraldine Ferraro runs for vice president.

1997 Colin Powell launches a campaign to promote volunteerism.

The Federal System

The Antifederalists opposed the Constitution because they wanted a limited national government—one that would not have too much power. To address Antifederalist concerns, in 1787 the writers of the Constitution established the separation of powers between the states and the federal government.

Delegated powers, those granted to the federal government, include coining money, running the country's postal system, regulating interstate and international trade, providing for the nation's defense, declaring war, and conducting diplomacy. These powers allow the national government to protect citizens and to assure a more uniform economic system throughout the country.

The seal of the U.S. Congress

The **elastic clause** of the Constitution, found in Article I, Section 8, allows Congress to stretch its delegated powers to address issues that the nation's founders could not have foreseen. For example, the Constitution gives the federal government the power to run the postal system, which was the main form of long-distance communication when the Constitution was written. Today the government also regulates modern forms of long-distance communication technology, such as telephones and computers.

The powers retained by the state governments or by citizens are **reserved powers**. These powers include conducting elections, regulating trade within each state, establishing local governments, and regulating education. The federal and state governments also share powers. These **concurrent powers** include taxing, borrowing money, enforcing laws, and providing for citizens' welfare.

The Legislative Branch

The legislative branch makes the nation's laws. "Members of Congress are the human connection between the citizen and . . . government," noted one member of Congress. The founders discussed the legislative branch in Article I of the Constitution to emphasize that the United States would be a **representative democracy**, or government by representatives of the people.

The House and Senate

The House of Representatives is the larger of the two houses of Congress. Currently it has 435 members (originally it had 65). To maintain the current total, Congress decided that no state can gain a representative unless another state loses one. The number of representatives for each state is based on the U.S. census, a population count taken every 10 years. Congress examines changes in the population to determine the **apportionment**, or distribution, of representatives. After the 1990 census, for example, Texas gained three additional seats in the House while New York lost three.

House members represent a particular district of voters in a state. House members must be at least 25 years old, U.S. citizens for seven or more years, and residents of the state from which they are elected. They do not have to live in the district they represent, however.

Senators represent their entire state. They must be at least 30 years old, U.S. citizens for nine or more years, and residents of the state they represent. Each state has two senators. The one who has served longer is the state's senior senator.

The term for a House member is two years and for a Senate member is six years. No law limits the number of times someone may be elected to Congress. However, in recent years many Americans have supported imposing term limits to restrict the number of terms a member can serve.

Organization

Congress holds regular sessions, or meetings, every year beginning on January 3. During a time of national emergency the president may call a congressional meeting after the regular session has already ended. For example, President Abraham

Newt Gingrich became Speaker of the House in 1995.

American Literature

Federalist Paper "No. 51"
James Madison

During the debates over the ratification of the Constitution, New York newspapers printed a series of essays supporting ratification and countering Antifederalist arguments. The Federalist Papers *were written by Alexander Hamilton, John Jay, and James Madison. In this excerpt from essay "No. 51," Madison discusses the means by which the separation of powers among the various branches of government would be preserved.*

In order to lay a due [proper] foundation for . . . the different powers of government, . . . it is evident that each department should have a will of its own; and should be so constituted [set up] that the members of each should have as little agency [power] as possible in the appointment of the members of the others. Were this principle rigorously adhered to [strictly followed], it would require that all the appointments for the supreme executive, legislative, and judiciary magistracies [offices] should be drawn from the same fountain of authority, the people, through channels having no communication . . . with one another. . . . But the great security against a gradual concentration of the several powers in the same department consists in giving to those who administer each department the necessary constitutional means and personal motives to resist encroachments [advances] of the others. The provision for defense must . . . be made commensurate [equal] to the danger of attack. . . . It may be a reflection on human nature that such devices should be necessary to control the abuses of government. But what is government itself but the greatest of all reflections on human nature? If men were angels, no government would be necessary. If angels were to govern men, neither external nor internal controls on government would be necessary. In framing a government which is to be administered by men over men, the great difficulty lies in this: you must first enable the government to control the governed; and in the next place oblige [force] it to control itself.

Understanding Literature

1. What is the "fountain of authority"?
2. According to the excerpt, who should the government govern?

Lincoln called Congress into a special session during the Civil War.

The political party with the most members in each house of Congress is called the majority party. The party with fewer members is the minority party of that house. The leader of the House of Representatives is the Speaker of the House. House members select the Speaker, who is usually from the majority party. The vice president of the United States serves as the president of the Senate.

The vice president does not join in Senate debates and can cast a vote only if there is a tie. When the vice president is absent, the president *pro tempore,* usually the longest-serving senator of the majority party, leads the Senate.

Congress carries out most of its work in committees that examine every proposed bill. Currently the Senate has 16 standing, or permanent, committees and the House has 19. Each committee specializes in certain types of legislation.

For example, all bills relating to taxes originate in the House Ways and Means Committee.

★ The Executive Branch

Article II of the Constitution specifies the powers of the executive branch, which is responsible for enforcing the laws approved by Congress. The president, as head of the executive branch, is the most powerful elected official in the country.

Becoming President

To become president, one must be a native-born U.S. citizen, at least 35 years old, and have been a resident of the United States for at least 14 years. All presidents have been white men. In recent years, candidates have become more diverse, with African Americans such as Jesse Jackson seeking the presidency. Geraldine Ferraro became the first woman on the ticket of a major party when she was the Democratic nominee for vice president in 1984. No non-Christian has yet been president. When John F. Kennedy took office in 1961, he became the first Roman Catholic president.

Americans elect a president and vice president every four years. The president determines the vice president's responsibilities, which often include representing the president at official functions. Franklin D. Roosevelt, who won four presidential elections, has been the only president to serve more than two terms. The Twenty-second Amendment, ratified in 1951, prevents anyone from serving more than two terms as president. If the president dies, resigns, or is removed from office, the vice president becomes president.

The House of Representatives has the authority to **impeach**, or bring charges against, a president suspected of committing a crime or violating the essential presidential duties. The Senate tries all impeachment cases. If a president is found guilty, Congress can remove him or her from office. In 1868 Andrew Johnson became the first president to be impeached. President Bill Clinton was impeached in 1998. In each case the Senate tried the president and found him not guilty. In 1974 President Richard Nixon resigned to avoid possible impeachment.

Presidential Duties

The president has many duties, which involve overseeing all aspects of the government. The system of checks and balances often sets the president against Congress, particularly when the president's party is different from that of the majority party in Congress. First Lady Eleanor Roosevelt once noted, "It isn't really possible under our system, I fear, for the Executive and the Legislative to get along well."

Despite their differences, the executive and legislative branches must cooperate for the system to work. As President Lyndon Johnson observed:

> ❝ **What a President says and thinks is not worth five cents unless he has the people and Congress behind him. Without the Congress I'm just a six-feet-four Texan. With Congress I'm President of the United States in the fullest sense.** ❞

Although Congress passes laws, the president can influence legislation by encouraging members to approve or reject certain bills. The president also has the power to **veto**, or cancel, legislation. Congress can override a president's veto, but doing so is very difficult because it requires a two-thirds majority vote.

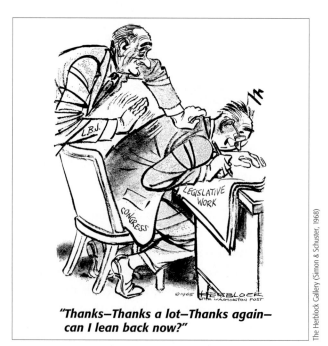

"Thanks—Thanks a lot—Thanks again— can I lean back now?"

The Herblock Gallery (Simon & Schuster, 1968)

President Lyndon Johnson was famous for praising members of Congress, or patting them on the back, so that they would pass his legislation.

The Executive Departments

DEPARTMENT OF STATE
• conducts foreign relations
• protects U.S. citizens abroad
• issues passports and visas

DEPARTMENT OF THE TREASURY
• mints coins and issues money
• collects taxes and pays bills
• manages government funds

DEPARTMENT OF JUSTICE
• investigates violations of federal laws
• prosecutes cases before courts
• administers naturalization laws
• enforces immigration laws

DEPARTMENT OF THE INTERIOR
• controls public lands
• maintains public parks
• supervises American Indian reservations
• controls water resources

DEPARTMENT OF AGRICULTURE
• conducts studies to help farmers
• manages food stamp and school
  lunch programs
• helps farmers raise and market crops
• directs soil conservation programs

DEPARTMENT OF COMMERCE
• sets standards for weights and measures
• encourages and regulates foreign trade
• publishes reports on business and trade

DEPARTMENT OF LABOR
• determines standards of labor
• publishes employment information
• directs public employment services

DEPARTMENT OF DEFENSE
• maintains U.S. armed services
• conducts military studies
• operates military bases

**DEPARTMENT OF HEALTH
AND HUMAN SERVICES**
• directs public health services
• sees that foods and medicines are safe

**DEPARTMENT OF HOUSING
AND URBAN DEVELOPMENT**
• helps urban-housing programs
• helps cities plan traffic control
• helps cities plan mass transportation
• cooperates with metropolitan-area planners

DEPARTMENT OF TRANSPORTATION
• helps develop the nation's transportation
  policy
• supervises federal-aid highway programs
• promotes transportation safety

DEPARTMENT OF ENERGY
• helps develop the nation's energy policy
• promotes conservation of energy
• regulates energy resources

DEPARTMENT OF EDUCATION
• sets guidelines for granting financial
  aid to schools
• conducts research on educational subjects
• administers federally sponsored
  educational programs

DEPARTMENT OF VETERANS AFFAIRS
• administers medical and disability benefits
  to veterans and their families
• provides pensions and death benefits
  for veterans

After Congress passes a law, federal agencies and departments usually determine how to put it into effect. To carry out laws that affect administrative matters or executive policy, the president sometimes issues **executive orders**, nonlegislative directives that have the force of law. In an emergency the president may issue an executive order that stretches the definition of laws enacted by Congress.

The president, although a civilian, is also commander in chief of the armed forces. Although the president can send U.S. troops into emergency situations, only Congress can declare war. The president's many other responsibilities include carrying out foreign relations through both diplomatic ties and the negotiation of treaties. The president also has the power to grant **pardons**, or freedom from punishment, for persons convicted of federal crimes or who are facing criminal charges.

Executive Departments

Numerous departments carry out most of the work of the executive branch. Currently there are 14 executive departments. The heads of these departments make up the **cabinet**, which advises

Sandra Day O'Connor

Sandra Day O'Connor was born in El Paso, Texas, in 1930. She attended college and law school at Stanford University in California. She began her legal career working as a deputy county attorney in California. Later she moved to Arizona, where she served as the assistant state attorney general and then as a state legislator. In 1973 she became the majority leader for the Arizona state senate before being appointed a judge on the state's second-highest court.

In 1981 President Ronald Reagan appointed O'Connor to the Supreme Court. Although she was appointed by a Republican president, O'Connor has at times opposed Republican policies when deciding cases. Her decisions illustrate how Supreme Court justices often can be free from party politics once appointed. When asked how she hoped to be remembered, O'Connor replied that she would like her tombstone to read simply, "Here lies a good judge."

the president. Some departments, such as the State Department, handle foreign-policy issues. Others, such as the Department of Education, focus on domestic issues.

 The Judicial Branch

The third branch of the government is the judicial branch, which consists of a series of federal courts headed by the U.S. Supreme Court. Article III of the Constitution defines the duties of the courts.

The Federal Court System

The president appoints all judges on each level of the federal court system for life. Each of these judges receives the appointment for life to ensure that he or she will make decisions free from the influence of a particular party. Federal judge Shirley Wohl Kram explains her duties, "It is the judge's role to resolve grievances and the role of the legislature to supply the answers for the social and economic problems facing the community."

The lower courts in the federal system are divided according to the types of cases over which they have jurisdiction, or authority. Each state has at least one district court to handle federal cases.

States with large populations usually have more than one district court. Currently there are 94 U.S. district courts.

Above the lower courts are 13 courts of appeals, which make sure that cases are tried properly in the lower courts. Someone convicted of a crime who believes that his or her rights were violated in the original trial can appeal the case to the higher court.

The courts of appeals do not use juries. Instead, a panel of judges decides whether the lower court handled the original case properly. If the judges uphold, or accept, the lower court's decision, then the case's original outcome remains. If they believe that the case was handled improperly, they usually send it back to the lower court for a new trial. The courts of appeals have the final say in most of the cases they review. Sometimes, however, the U.S. Supreme Court chooses to review decisions of the courts of appeals.

The Supreme Court

Most cases presented to the Supreme Court originate in lower courts. However, some cases—such as those that involve international diplomats or disputes between states—go directly to the Supreme Court.

Congress determines how many justices sit on the Court; typically that number is fixed at nine. The chief justice of the United States leads the Supreme Court. Unlike for the president and members of Congress, the Constitution sets no specific requirements for being a Court justice. So far, however, every justice has been an attorney. William Howard Taft is the only person to have been both president (1909–13) and a Supreme Court chief justice (1921–30).

In the past 50 years the Supreme Court has become more diverse. In 1967 Thurgood Marshall became the first African American justice; the second was Clarence Thomas in 1991. Currently two women sit on the high court—Ruth Bader Ginsburg and Sandra Day O'Connor, who became the first female Court justice after her 1981 appointment by President Ronald Reagan. Each justice contributes greatly to the Court. As O'Connor explained:

Supreme Court Justice Ruth Bader Ginsburg speaks to a group of students.

66 **The Court benefits from broad and diverse experiences of its members. My own experience in all three branches of state government gave me a background which differed from a majority of my colleagues. It undoubtedly has helped me understand and appreciate the** importance and value of the federal system designed by the Framers of the Constitution. 99

O'Connor and other Supreme Court justices have time to review around 100 of the thousands of cases appealed to them each year. The justices carefully choose which cases to hear. Generally, cases heard by the Court must involve an important constitutional or public interest issue. If the Court refuses to hear a case, the decision of the court of appeals is final. If the Court finds a law unconstitutional and Congress disagrees with the ruling, lawmakers can begin the process of amending the Constitution.

SECTION 1 REVIEW

Identify and explain the significance of the following:

- delegated powers
- elastic clause
- reserved powers
- concurrent powers
- representative democracy
- apportionment
- impeach
- veto

- executive orders
- pardons
- cabinet
- Sandra Day O'Connor

Reading for Content Understanding

1 **Main Idea** How are the state and federal powers balanced in the Constitution?

2 **Main Idea** List the three branches of the federal government, and explain how power is divided among them.

3 **Citizenship and Democracy** How does a state's population affect that state's representation in the House and Senate?

4 **Writing** *Describing* Write a two-paragraph essay that explains how the judicial system is structured.

5 **Critical Thinking** *Synthesizing Information* Do you think the three branches of government share power equally? If not, which branch do you think has the most power, and why?

THE CONSTITUTION

" *WE THE PEOPLE OF THE UNITED STATES, IN ORDER TO FORM A MORE PERFECT UNION, ESTABLISH JUSTICE, INSURE DOMESTIC TRANQUILITY, PROVIDE FOR THE COMMON DEFENCE, PROMOTE THE GENERAL WELFARE, AND SECURE THE BLESSINGS OF LIBERTY TO OURSELVES AND OUR POSTERITY, DO ORDAIN AND ESTABLISH THIS CONSTITUTION FOR THE UNITED STATES OF AMERICA.* "

Parts of the Constitution that have been ruled through are no longer in force or no longer apply because of later amendments.

Preamble
The short and dignified Preamble explains the goals of the new government under the Constitution.

LEFT: Independence Hall, Philadelphia

ARTICLE I

Section 1. All legislative Powers herein granted shall be vested in a Congress of the United States, which shall consist of a Senate and House of Representatives.

Section 2. The House of Representatives shall be composed of Members chosen every second Year by the People of the several States, and the Electors in each State shall have the Qualifications requisite for Electors of the most numerous Branch of the State Legislature.

No Person shall be a Representative who shall not have attained to the Age of twenty five Years, and been seven Years a Citizen of the United States, and who shall not, when elected, be an Inhabitant of that State in which he shall be chosen.

Representatives and direct Taxes shall be apportioned among the several States which may be included within this Union, according to their respective Numbers, which shall be determined by adding to the whole Number of free Persons, including those bound to Service for a Term of Years, and excluding Indians not taxed, three fifths of all other Persons. The actual Enumeration shall be made within three Years after the first Meeting of the Congress of the United States, and within every subsequent Term of ten Years, in such Manner as they shall by Law direct. The Number of Representatives shall not exceed one for every thirty Thousand, but each State shall have at Least one Representative; and until such enumeration shall be made, the State of New Hampshire shall be entitled to chuse three; Massachusetts eight; Rhode Island and Providence Plantations one; Connecticut five; New York six; New Jersey four; Pennsylvania eight; Delaware one; Maryland six; Virginia ten; North Carolina five; South Carolina five; and Georgia three.

When vacancies happen in the Representation from any State, the Executive Authority thereof shall issue Writs of Election to fill such Vacancies.

The House of Representatives shall chuse their Speaker and other Officers; and shall have the sole Power of Impeachment.

Section 3. The Senate of the United States shall be composed of two Senators from each State, chosen by the Legislature thereof, for six Years; and each Senator shall have one Vote.

Immediately after they shall be assembled in Consequence of the first Election, they shall be divided as equally as may be into three Classes. The Seats of the Senators of the first Class shall be vacated at the Expiration of the second Year, of the second Class at the Expiration of the fourth Year, and of the third Class at the Expiration of the sixth Year, so that one third may be chosen every second Year; and if Vacancies happen by

---

Legislative Branch

Article I explains how the legislative branch, called Congress, is organized. The chief purpose of the legislative branch is to make the laws. Congress is made up of the Senate and the House of Representatives. The decision to have two bodies of government solved a difficult problem during the Constitutional Convention. The large states wanted the membership of Congress to be based entirely on population. The small states wanted every state to have an equal vote. The solution to the problem of how the states were to be represented in Congress became known as the Great Compromise.

The number of members each state has in the House is based on the population of the individual state. Each state has at least one representative. In 1929 Congress permanently fixed the size of the House at 435 members. Today, if each member of the House were to represent only 30,000 Americans, the House would have more than 8,600 members.

Every state has two senators. Senators serve a six-year term. Every two years, one third of the senators reach the end of their terms. In any election, at least two thirds of the senators stay in office. This system ensures that there are experienced senators in office at all times.

~~Resignation, or otherwise, during the Recess of the Legislature of any State, the Executive thereof may make temporary Appointments until the next Meeting of the Legislature, which shall then fill such Vacancies.~~

No Person shall be a Senator who shall not have attained to the Age of thirty Years, and been nine Years a Citizen of the United States, and who shall not, when elected, be an Inhabitant of that State for which he shall be chosen.

The Vice President of the United States shall be President of the Senate, but shall have no Vote, unless they be equally divided.

The Senate shall chuse their other Officers, and also a President pro tempore, in the Absence of the Vice President, or when he shall exercise the Office of President of the United States.

The Senate shall have the sole Power to try all Impeachments. When sitting for that Purpose, they shall be on Oath or Affirmation. When the President of the United States is tried, the Chief Justice shall preside: And no Person shall be convicted without the Concurrence of two thirds of the Members present.

Judgment in Cases of Impeachment shall not extend further than to removal from Office, and disqualification to hold and enjoy any Office of honor, Trust or Profit under the United States: but the Party convicted shall nevertheless be liable and subject to Indictment, Trial, Judgment and Punishment, according to Law.

Section 4. The Times, Places and Manner of holding Elections for Senators and Representatives, shall be prescribed in each State by the Legislature thereof; but the Congress may at any time by Law make or alter such Regulations, except as to the Places of chusing Senators.

~~The Congress shall assemble at least once in every Year, and such Meeting shall be on the first Monday in December, unless they shall by Law appoint a different Day.~~

Section 5. Each House shall be the Judge of the Elections, Returns and Qualifications of its own Members, and a Majority of each shall constitute a Quorum to do Business; but a smaller Number may adjourn from day to day, and may be authorized to compel the Attendance of absent Members, in such Manner, and under such Penalties as each House may provide.

Each House may determine the Rules of its Proceedings, punish its Members for disorderly Behaviour, and, with the Concurrence of two thirds, expel a Member.

Each House shall keep a Journal of its Proceedings, and from time to time publish the same, excepting such Parts as may in their Judgment require Secrecy; and the Yeas and Nays of the Members of either House on any question shall, at the Desire of one fifth of those Present, be entered on the Journal.

The only duty that the Constitution assigns to the vice president is to preside over meetings of the Senate. Modern presidents have usually given their vice presidents more responsibilities.

The House charges a government official with wrongdoing, and the Senate acts as a court to decide if the official is guilty.

Congress decided that elections will be held on the Tuesday following the first Monday in November of even-numbered years. The Twentieth Amendment states that Congress shall meet in regular session on January 3 of each year. The president may call a special session of Congress whenever it is necessary.

Congress makes most of its own rules of conduct. The Senate and the House each have a code of ethics that members must follow. It is the task of each house of Congress to discipline its own members. Each house keeps a journal, and a daily, unofficial publication called the *Congressional Record* details what happens in congressional sessions. The general public can learn how their representatives voted on bills by reading the *Congressional Record*.

Neither House, during the Session of Congress, shall, without the Consent of the other, adjourn for more than three days, nor to any other Place than that in which the two Houses shall be sitting.

Section 6. The Senators and Representatives shall receive a Compensation for their Services, to be ascertained by Law, and paid out of the Treasury of the United States. They shall in all Cases, except Treason, Felony and Breach of the Peace, be privileged from Arrest during their Attendance at the Session of their respective Houses, and in going to and returning from the same; and for any Speech or Debate in either House, they shall not be questioned in any other Place.

No Senator or Representative shall, during the Time for which he was elected, be appointed to any civil Office under the Authority of the United States, which shall have been created, or the Emoluments whereof shall have been encreased during such time; and no Person holding any Office under the United States, shall be a Member of either House during his Continuance in Office.

Section 7. All Bills for raising Revenue shall originate in the House of Representatives; but the Senate may propose or concur with Amendments as on other Bills.

Every Bill which shall have passed the House of Representatives and the Senate, shall, before it become a Law, be presented to the President of the United States; If he approve he shall sign it, but if not he shall return it, with his Objections to that House in which it shall have originated, who shall enter the Objections at large on their Journal, and proceed to reconsider it. If after such Reconsideration two thirds of that House shall agree to pass the Bill, it shall be sent, together with the Objections, to the other House, by which it shall likewise be reconsidered, and if approved by two thirds of that House, it shall become a Law. But in all such Cases the Votes of both Houses shall be determined by yeas and Nays, and the Names of the Persons voting for and against the Bill shall be entered on the Journal of each House respectively. If any Bill shall not be returned by the President within ten Days (Sundays excepted) after it shall have been presented to him, the Same shall be a Law, in like Manner as if he had signed it, unless the Congress by their Adjournment prevent its Return, in which Case it shall not be a Law.

Every Order, Resolution, or Vote to which the Concurrence of the Senate and House of Representatives may be necessary (except on a question of Adjournment) shall be presented to the President of the United States; and before the Same shall take Effect, shall be approved by him, or being disapproved by him, shall be repassed by two thirds of the Senate and House of Representatives, according to the Rules and Limitations prescribed in the Case of a Bill.

The framers of the Constitution wanted to protect members of Congress from being arrested on false charges by political enemies who did not want them to attend important meetings. The framers also wanted to protect members of Congress from being taken to court for something they said in a speech or in a debate.

The power of taxing is the responsibility of the House of Representatives. The framers felt that because members of the House are elected every two years, representatives would listen to the public and seek its approval before passing taxes.

The veto power of the president and the ability of Congress to override a presidential veto are two of the important checks and balances in the Constitution.

The framers of the Constitution wanted a national government that was strong enough to be effective. This section lists the powers given to Congress. The last sentence in Section 8 contains the famous "elastic clause"—so called because it has been stretched (like elastic) to fit many different circumstances. The clause was first disputed when Alexander Hamilton proposed a national bank. Thomas Jefferson said that because the Constitution did not specifically give Congress the power to establish a bank, it could not do so. Hamilton argued that the bank was "necessary and proper" in order to carry out other powers of Congress, such as borrowing money and regulating currency. This argument was tested in the courts in 1819 in the case of *McCulloch v. Maryland,* when Chief Justice Marshall ruled in favor of the federal government. Powers given to the government by the elastic clause are called implied powers.

Section 8. The Congress shall have Power To lay and collect Taxes, Duties, Imposts and Excises, to pay the Debts and provide for the common Defence and general Welfare of the United States; but all Duties, Imposts and Excises shall be uniform throughout the United States;

To borrow Money on the credit of the United States;

To regulate Commerce with foreign Nations, and among the several States, and with the Indian Tribes;

To establish an uniform Rule of Naturalization, and uniform Laws on the subject of Bankruptcies throughout the United States;

To coin Money, regulate the Value thereof, and of foreign Coin, and fix the Standard of Weights and Measures;

To provide for the Punishment of counterfeiting the Securities and current Coin of the United States;

To establish Post Offices and post Roads;

To promote the Progress of Science and useful Arts, by securing for limited Times to Authors and Inventors the exclusive Right to their respective Writings and Discoveries;

To constitute Tribunals inferior to the supreme Court;

To define and punish Piracies and Felonies committed on the high Seas, and Offences against the Law of Nations;

To declare War, grant Letters of Marque and Reprisal, and make Rules concerning Captures on Land and Water;

To raise and support Armies, but no Appropriation of Money to that Use shall be for a longer Term than two Years;

To provide and maintain a Navy;

To make Rules for the Government and Regulation of the land and naval Forces;

To provide for calling forth the Militia to execute the Laws of the Union, suppress Insurrections and repel Invasions;

To provide for organizing, arming, and disciplining, the Militia, and for governing such Part of them as may be employed in the Service of the United States, reserving to the States respectively, the Appointment of the Officers, and the Authority of training the Militia according to the discipline prescribed by Congress;

To exercise exclusive Legislation in all Cases whatsoever, over such District (not exceeding ten Miles square) as may, by Cession of particular States, and the Acceptance of Congress, become the Seat of the Government of the United States, and to exercise like Authority over all Places purchased by the Consent of the Legislature of the State in which the Same shall be, for the Erection of Forts, Magazines, Arsenals, dock-Yards, and other needful Buildings;—And

To make all Laws which shall be necessary and proper for carrying into Execution the foregoing Powers, and all other Powers vested by this

Constitution in the Government of the United States, or in any Department or Officer thereof.

Section 9. ~~The Migration or Importation of such Persons as any of the States now existing shall think proper to admit, shall not be prohibited by the Congress prior to the Year one thousand eight hundred and eight, but a Tax or duty may be imposed on such Importation, not exceeding ten dollars for each Person.~~

The Privilege of the Writ of Habeas Corpus shall not be suspended, unless when in Cases of Rebellion or Invasion the public Safety may require it.

No Bill of Attainder or ex post facto Law shall be passed.

No Capitation, or other direct, Tax shall be laid, unless in Proportion to the Census or Enumeration herein before directed to be taken.

No Tax or Duty shall be laid on Articles exported from any State.

No Preference shall be given by any Regulation of Commerce or Revenue to the Ports of one State over those of another: nor shall Vessels bound to, or from, one State, be obliged to enter, clear, or pay Duties in another.

No Money shall be drawn from the Treasury, but in Consequence of Appropriations made by Law; and a regular Statement and Account of the Receipts and Expenditures of all public Money shall be published from time to time.

No Title of Nobility shall be granted by the United States: And no Person holding any Office of Profit or Trust under them, shall, without the Consent of the Congress, accept of any present, Emolument, Office, or Title, of any kind whatever, from any King, Prince, or foreign State.

Section 10. No State shall enter into any Treaty, Alliance, or Confederation; grant Letters of Marque and Reprisal; coin Money; emit Bills of Credit; make any Thing but gold and silver Coin a Tender in Payment of Debts; pass any Bill of Attainder, ex post facto Law, or law impairing the Obligation of Contracts, or grant any Title of Nobility.

No State shall, without the Consent of the Congress, lay any Imposts or Duties on Imports or Exports, except what may be absolutely necessary for executing its inspection Laws: and the net Produce of all Duties and Imposts, laid by any State on Imports or Exports, shall be for the Use of the Treasury of the United States; and all such Laws shall be subject to the Revision and Controul of the Congress.

No State shall, without the Consent of Congress, lay any Duty of Tonnage, keep Troops, or Ships of War in time of Peace, enter into any Agreement or Compact with another State, or with a foreign Power, or engage in War, unless actually invaded, or in such imminent Danger as will not admit of delay.

Although Congress has implied powers, there are also limits to its powers. Section 9 lists powers that are denied to the federal government. Several of the clauses protect the people of the United States from unjust treatment. For example, Section 9 guarantees the writ of *habeas corpus* and prohibits bills of attainder and *ex post facto* laws.

Section 10 lists the powers that are denied to the states. In our system of federalism, the state and federal governments have separate powers, share some powers, and are each denied other powers.

ARTICLE II

Section 1. The executive Power shall be vested in a President of the United States of America. He shall hold his Office during the Term of four Years, and, together with the Vice President, chosen for the same Term, be elected, as follows.

Each State shall appoint, in such Manner as the Legislature thereof may direct, a Number of Electors, equal to the whole Number of Senators and Representatives to which the State may be entitled in the Congress: but no Senator or Representative, or Person holding an Office of Trust or Profit under the United States, shall be appointed an Elector.

~~The Electors shall meet in their respective States, and vote by Ballot for two Persons, of whom one at least shall not be an Inhabitant of the same State with themselves. And they shall make a List of all the Persons voted for, and of the Number of Votes for each; which List they shall sign and certify, and transmit sealed to the Seat of the Government of the United States, directed to the President of the Senate. The President of the Senate shall, in the Presence of the Senate and House of Representatives, open all the Certificates, and the Votes shall then be counted. The Person having the greatest Number of Votes shall be the President, if such Number be a Majority of the whole Number of Electors appointed; and if there be more than one who have such Majority, and have an equal Number of Votes, then the House of Representatives shall immediately chuse by Ballot one of them for President; and if no Person have a Majority, then from the five highest on the List the said House shall in like Manner chuse the President. But in chusing the President, the Votes shall be taken by States, the Representation from each State having one Vote; A quorum for this Purpose shall consist of a Member or Members from two thirds of the States, and a Majority of all the States shall be necessary to a Choice. In every Case, after the Choice of the President, the Person having the greatest Number of Votes of the Electors shall be the Vice President. But if there should remain two or more who have equal Votes, the Senate shall chuse from them by Ballot the Vice President.~~

The Congress may determine the Time of chusing the Electors, and the Day on which they shall give their Votes; which Day shall be the same throughout the United States.

No Person except a natural born Citizen, ~~or a Citizen of the United States, at the time of the Adoption of this Constitution,~~ shall be eligible to the Office of President; neither shall any Person be eligible to that Office who shall not have attained to the Age of thirty five Years, and been fourteen Years a Resident within the United States.

In Case of the Removal of the President from Office, or of his Death, Resignation, or Inability to discharge the Powers and Duties of the said Office, the Same shall devolve on the Vice President, and the Congress

Executive Branch
The president is the chief of the executive branch. It is the job of the president to enforce the laws. The framers wanted the president's and vice president's term of office and manner of selection to be different from those of members of Congress. They decided on four-year terms, but they had a difficult time agreeing on how to select the president and vice president. The framers finally set up an electoral system, which varies greatly from our electoral process today. The Twelfth Amendment changed the process by requiring that separate ballots be cast for president and vice president. The rise of political parties has since changed the process even more.

In 1845 Congress set the Tuesday following the first Monday in November of every fourth year as the general election date for selecting presidential electors.

The youngest elected president was John F. Kennedy; he was 43 years old when he was inaugurated. (Theodore Roosevelt was 42 when he assumed office after the assassination of McKinley.) The oldest elected president was Ronald Reagan; he was 69 years old when he was inaugurated.

may by Law provide for the Case of Removal, Death, Resignation or Inability, both of the President and Vice President, declaring what Officer shall then act as President, and such Officer shall act accordingly, until the Disability be removed, or a President shall be elected.

The President shall, at stated Times, receive for his Services, a Compensation, which shall neither be increased nor diminished during the period for which he shall have been elected, and he shall not receive within that Period any other Emolument from the United States, or any of them.

Before he enter on the Execution of his Office, he shall take the following Oath or Affirmation:—"I do solemnly swear (or affirm) that I will faithfully execute the Office of President of the United States, and will to the best of my Ability, preserve, protect and defend the Constitution of the United States."

Section 2. The President shall be Commander in Chief of the Army and Navy of the United States, and of the Militia of the several States, when called into the actual Service of the United States; he may require the Opinion, in writing, of the principal Officer in each of the executive Departments, upon any Subject relating to the Duties of their respective Offices, and he shall have Power to grant Reprieves and Pardons for Offenses against the United States, except in Cases of Impeachment.

He shall have Power, by and with the Advice and Consent of the Senate, to make Treaties, provided two thirds of the Senators present concur; and he shall nominate, and by and with the Advice and Consent of the Senate, shall appoint Ambassadors, other public Ministers and Consuls, Judges of the supreme Court, and all other Officers of the United States, whose Appointments are not herein otherwise provided for, and which shall be established by Law: but the Congress may by Law vest the Appointment of such inferior Officers, as they think proper, in the President alone, in the Courts of Law, or in the Heads of Departments.

The President shall have Power to fill up all Vacancies that may happen during the Recess of the Senate, by granting Commissions which shall expire at the End of their next Session.

Section 3. He shall from time to time give to the Congress Information of the State of the Union, and recommend to their Consideration such Measures as he shall judge necessary and expedient; he may, on extraordinary Occasions, convene both Houses, or either of them, and in Case of Disagreement between them, with Respect to the Time of Adjournment, he may adjourn them to such Time as he shall think proper; he shall receive Ambassadors and other public Ministers; he shall take Care that the Laws be faithfully executed, and shall Commission all the Officers of the United States.

Emolument means "salary, or payment." In 1969 Congress set the president's salary at $200,000 per year. The president also receives an expense account of $50,000 per year. The president must pay taxes on both.

The oath of office is administered to the president by the chief justice of the U.S. Supreme Court. Washington added "So help me, God." All succeeding presidents have followed this practice.

The framers wanted to make sure that an elected representative of the people controlled the nation's military. Today, the president is in charge of the army, navy, air force, marines, and coast guard. Only Congress, however, can decide if the United States will declare war. This section also contains the basis for the formation of the president's cabinet. Every president, starting with George Washington, has appointed a cabinet.

Most of the president's appointments to office must be approved by the Senate.

Every year the president presents to Congress a State of the Union message. In this message, the president introduces and explains a legislative plan for the coming year. This clause states that one of the president's duties is to enforce the laws.

Section 4. The President, Vice President and all civil Officers of the United States, shall be removed from Office on Impeachment for, and Conviction of, Treason, Bribery, or other high Crimes and Misdemeanors.

ARTICLE III

Section 1. The judicial Power of the United States, shall be vested in one supreme Court, and in such inferior Courts as the Congress may from time to time ordain and establish. The Judges, both of the supreme and inferior Courts, shall hold their Offices during good Behaviour, and shall, at stated Times, receive for their Services, a Compensation, which shall not be diminished during their Continuance in Office.

Section 2. The judicial Power shall extend to all Cases, in Law and Equity, arising under this Constitution, the Laws of the United States, and Treaties made, or which shall be made, under their Authority;—to all Cases affecting Ambassadors, other public Ministers and Consuls;—to all Cases of admiralty and maritime Jurisdiction;—to Controversies to which the United States shall be a Party;—to Controversies between two or more States;— ~~between a State and Citizens of another State~~;— between Citizens of different States;—between Citizens of the same State claiming Lands under Grants of different States~~, and between a State, or the Citizens thereof, and foreign States, Citizens or Subjects~~.

In all Cases affecting Ambassadors, other public Ministers and Consuls, and those in which a State shall be Party, the supreme Court shall have original Jurisdiction. In all the other Cases before mentioned, the supreme Court shall have appellate Jurisdiction, both as to Law and fact, with such Exceptions, and under such Regulations as the Congress shall make.

The Trial of all Crimes, except in Cases of Impeachment, shall be by Jury; and such Trial shall be held in the State where the said Crimes shall have been committed; but when not committed within any State, the Trial shall be at such Place or Places as the Congress may by Law have directed.

Section 3. Treason against the United States, shall consist only in levying War against them, or in adhering to their Enemies, giving them Aid and Comfort. No Person shall be convicted of Treason unless on the Testimony of two Witnesses to the same overt Act, or on Confession in open Court.

The Congress shall have Power to declare the Punishment of Treason, but no Attainder of Treason shall work Corruption of Blood, or Forfeiture except during the Life of the Person attainted.

ARTICLE IV

Section 1. Full Faith and Credit shall be given in each State to the public Acts, Records, and judicial Proceedings of every other State. And the

Judicial Branch
The Articles of Confederation did not set up a federal court system. One of the first things that the framers of the Constitution agreed upon was to set up a national judiciary. With all the laws that Congress would be enacting, there would be a great need for a branch of government to interpret the laws. In the Judiciary Act of 1789, Congress provided for the establishment of lower courts, such as district courts, circuit courts of appeals, and various other federal courts. The judicial system provides a check on the legislative branch; it can declare a law unconstitutional.

Congress has the power to decide the punishment for treason, but it can punish only the guilty person. "Corruption of Blood" means punishing the family of a person who has committed treason. It is expressly forbidden by the Constitution.

Congress may by general Laws prescribe the Manner in which such Acts, Records and Proceedings shall be proved, and the Effect thereof.

Section 2. The Citizens of each State shall be entitled to all Privileges and Immunities of Citizens in the several States.

A Person charged in any State with Treason, Felony, or other Crime, who shall flee from Justice, and be found in another State, shall on Demand of the executive Authority of the State from which he fled, be delivered up, to be removed to the State having Jurisdiction of the Crime.

No Person held to Service of Labour in one State, under the Laws thereof, escaping into another, shall, in Consequence of any Law or Regulation therein, be discharged from such Service or Labour, but shall be delivered up on Claim of the Party to whom such Service or Labour may be due.

The States
States must honor the laws, records, and court decisions of other states. A person cannot escape a legal obligation by moving from one state to another.

Section 3. New States may be admitted by the Congress into this Union; but no new State shall be formed or erected within the Jurisdiction of any other State; nor any State be formed by the Junction of two or more States, or Parts of States, without the Consent of the Legislatures of the States concerned as well as of the Congress.

The Congress shall have Power to dispose of and make all needful Rules and Regulations respecting the Territory or other Property belonging to the United States; and nothing in this Constitution shall be so construed as to Prejudice any Claims of the United States, or of any particular State.

Section 4. The United States shall guarantee to every State in this Union a Republican Form of Government, and shall protect each of them against Invasion; and on Application of the Legislature, or of the Executive (when the Legislature cannot be convened) against domestic Violence.

Section 3 permits Congress to admit new states to the Union. When a group of people living in an area that is not part of an existing state wishes to form a new state, it asks Congress for permission to do so. The people then write a state constitution and offer it to Congress for approval. The state constitution must set up a representative form of government and must not in any way contradict the federal Constitution. If a majority of Congress approves of the state constitution, the state is admitted as a member of the United States of America.

ARTICLE V

The Congress, whenever two thirds of both Houses shall deem it necessary, shall propose Amendments to this Constitution, or, on the Application of the Legislatures of two thirds of the several States, shall call a Convention for proposing Amendments, which, in either Case, shall be valid to all Intents and Purposes, as Part of this Constitution, when ratified by the Legislatures of three fourths of the several States, or by Conventions in three fourths thereof, as the one or the other Mode of Ratification may be proposed by the Congress; Provided that no Amendment which may be made prior to the Year One thousand eight hundred and eight shall in any Manner affect the first and fourth Clauses in the Ninth Section of the first Article; and that no State, without its Consent, shall be deprived of its equal Suffrage in the Senate.

The Amendment Process
America's founders may not have realized just how enduring the Constitution would be, but they did set up a system for changing or adding to it. They did not want to make it easy to change the Constitution. There are two ways in which changes can be proposed to the states and two ways in which states can approve the changes and make them part of the Constitution.

National Supremacy

One of the biggest problems facing the delegates to the Constitutional Convention was the question of what would happen if a state law and a federal law conflicted. Which law would be followed? Who would decide? The second clause of Article VI answers those questions. When a federal law and a state law disagree, the federal law overrides the state law. The Constitution and other federal laws are the "supreme Law of the Land." This clause is often called the supremacy clause.

Ratification

The Articles of Confederation called for all 13 states to approve any revision to the Articles. The Constitution required that 9 out of the 13 states would be needed to ratify the Constitution. The first state to ratify was Delaware, on December 7, 1787. Almost two and a half years later, on May 29, 1790, Rhode Island became the last state to ratify the Constitution.

ARTICLE VI

All Debts contracted and Engagements entered into, before the Adoption of this Constitution, shall be as valid against the United States under this Constitution, as under the Confederation.

This Constitution, and the Laws of the United States which shall be made in Pursuance thereof; and all Treaties made, or which shall be made, under the Authority of the United States, shall be the supreme Law of the Land; and the Judges in every State shall be bound thereby, any Thing in the Constitution or Laws of any State to the Contrary notwithstanding.

The Senators and Representatives before mentioned, and the Members of the several State Legislatures, and all executive and judicial Officers, both of the United States and of the several States, shall be bound by Oath or Affirmation, to support this Constitution; but no religious Test shall ever be required as a Qualification to any Office or public Trust under the United States.

ARTICLE VII

The Ratification of the Conventions of nine States, shall be sufficient for the Establishment of this Constitution between the States so ratifying the Same.

Done in Convention by the Unanimous Consent of the States present the Seventeenth Day of September in the Year of our Lord one thousand seven hundred and Eighty seven and of the Independence of the United States of America the Twelfth. In witness whereof We have hereunto subscribed our Names,

George Washington—
President and deputy from Virginia

NEW HAMPSHIRE
John Langdon
Nicholas Gilman

DELAWARE
George Read
Gunning Bedford, Jr.
John Dickinson
Richard Bassett
Jacob Broom

MASSACHUSETTS
Nathaniel Gorham
Rufus King

MARYLAND
James McHenry
Daniel of St. Thomas Jenifer
Daniel Carroll

CONNECTICUT
William Samuel Johnson
Roger Sherman

NEW YORK
Alexander Hamilton

VIRGINIA
John Blair
James Madison, Jr.

NEW JERSEY
William Livingston
David Brearley
William Paterson
Jonathan Dayton

NORTH CAROLINA
William Blount
Richard Dobbs Spaight
Hugh Williamson

PENNSYLVANIA
Benjamin Franklin
Thomas Mifflin
Robert Morris
George Clymer

Thomas FitzSimons
Jared Ingersoll
James Wilson
Gouverneur Morris

SOUTH CAROLINA
John Rutledge
Charles Cotesworth
  Pinckney
Charles Pinckney
Pierce Butler

GEORGIA
William Few
Abraham Baldwin

Attest:
William Jackson, Secretary

THE AMENDMENTS

Articles in addition to, and Amendment of the Constitution of the United States of America, proposed by Congress, and ratified by the Legislatures of the several States, pursuant to the fifth Article of the original Constitution.

[The First through Tenth Amendments, now known as the Bill of Rights, were proposed to the states for ratification on September 25, 1789, and declared in force on December 15, 1791.]

First Amendment

Congress shall make no law respecting an establishment of religion, or prohibiting the free exercise thereof; or abridging the freedom of speech, or of the press; or the right of the people peaceably to assemble, and to petition the Government for a redress of grievances.

Second Amendment

A well regulated Militia, being necessary to the security of a free State, the right of the people to keep and bear Arms, shall not be infringed.

Third Amendment

No Soldier shall, in time of peace, be quartered in any house, without the consent of the Owner, nor in time of war, but in a manner to be prescribed by law.

Fourth Amendment

The right of the people to be secure in their persons, houses, papers, and effects, against unreasonable searches and seizures, shall not be violated, and no Warrants shall issue, but upon probable cause, supported by Oath or affirmation, and particularly describing the place to be searched, and the persons or things to be seized.

Fifth Amendment

No person shall be held to answer for a capital, or otherwise infamous crime, unless on a presentment or indictment of a Grand Jury, except in cases arising in the land or naval forces, or in the Militia, when in actual service in time of War or public danger; nor shall any person be subject for the same offence to be twice put in jeopardy of life or limb; nor shall be compelled in any criminal case to be a witness against himself, nor be deprived of life, liberty, or property, without due process of law; nor shall private property be taken for public use, without just compensation.

Sixth Amendment

In all criminal prosecutions, the accused shall enjoy the right to a speedy and public trial, by an impartial jury of the State and district wherein the

Bill of Rights
One of the conditions set by several states for ratifying the Constitution was the inclusion of a bill of rights. Many people feared that a stronger central government might take away basic rights of the people that had been guaranteed in state constitutions. If the three words that begin the preamble—"We the people"—were truly meant, then the rights of the people needed to be protected.

The First Amendment protects—among other freedoms—freedom of speech—and forbids Congress to make any "law respecting an establishment of religion" or restraining the freedom to practice religion as one chooses.

A law enforcement official may enter a person's home with a search warrant, which allows the law official to look for evidence that could convict someone of committing a crime.

The Fifth, Sixth, and Seventh Amendments describe the procedures that courts must follow when trying people accused of crimes. The Fifth Amendment guarantees that no one can be put on trial for a serious crime unless a grand jury agrees that the evidence justifies doing so. It also says that a person cannot be tried twice for the same crime.

The Sixth Amendment makes several guarantees, including a prompt trial and a trial by a jury chosen from the state and district in which the crime was committed. The Sixth Amendment also states that an accused person must be told why he or she is being tried and promises that an accused person has the right to be defended by a lawyer.

The Seventh Amendment guarantees a trial by jury in cases that involve more than $20, but in modern times, usually much more money is at stake before a case is heard in federal court.

The Ninth and Tenth Amendments were added because not every right of the people or of the states could be listed in the Constitution.

crime shall have been committed, which district shall have been previously ascertained by law, and to be informed of the nature and cause of the accusation; to be confronted with the witnesses against him; to have compulsory process for obtaining witnesses in his favor, and to have the Assistance of Counsel for his defence.

Seventh Amendment

In Suits at common law, where the value in controversy shall exceed twenty dollars, the right of trial by jury shall be preserved, and no fact tried by a jury, shall be otherwise re-examined in any Court of the United States, than according to the rules of the common law.

Eighth Amendment

Excessive bail shall not be required, nor excessive fines imposed, nor cruel and unusual punishments inflicted.

Ninth Amendment

The enumeration in the Constitution, of certain rights, shall not be construed to deny or disparage others retained by the people.

Tenth Amendment

The powers not delegated to the United States by the Constitution, nor prohibited by it to the States, are reserved to the States respectively, or to the people.

Eleventh Amendment

[Proposed March 5, 1794; declared ratified January 8, 1798]
The Judicial power of the United States shall not be construed to extend to any suit in law or equity, commenced or prosecuted against one of the United States by Citizens of another State, or by Citizens or Subjects of any Foreign State.

The Twelfth Amendment changed the election procedure for president and vice president. This amendment became necessary because of the growth of political parties. Before this amendment, electors voted without distinguishing between president and vice president. Whoever received the most votes became president, and whoever received the next highest number of votes became vice president.

Twelfth Amendment

[Proposed December 9, 1803; declared ratified September 25, 1804]
The Electors shall meet in their respective states, and vote by ballot for President and Vice-President, one of whom, at least, shall not be an inhabitant of the same state with themselves; they shall name in their ballots the person voted for as President, and in distinct ballots the person voted for as Vice-President, and they shall make distinct lists of all persons voted for as President, and of all persons voted for as Vice-President, and of the number of votes for each, which lists they shall sign and certify, and transmit sealed to the seat of the government of the United States, directed to the President of the Senate;—The President of the Senate shall, in the presence of the Senate and House of Representatives, open all the certificates and the votes

shall then be counted;—The person having the greatest number of votes for President, shall be the President, if such number be a majority of the whole number of Electors appointed; and if no person have such majority, then from the persons having the highest numbers not exceeding three on the list of those voted for as President, the House of Representatives shall choose immediately, by ballot, the President. But in choosing the President, the votes shall be taken by states, the representation from each state having one vote; a quorum for this purpose shall consist of a member or members from two-thirds of the states, and a majority of all the states shall be necessary to a choice. ~~And if the House of Representatives shall not choose a President whenever the right of choice shall devolve upon them, before the fourth day of March next following, then the Vice President shall act as President, as in the case of the death or other constitutional disability of the President.~~ —The person having the greatest number of votes as Vice-President, shall be the Vice-President, if such number be a majority of the whole number of Electors appointed, and if no person have a majority, then from the two highest numbers on the list, the Senate shall Choose the Vice-President; a quorum for the purpose shall consist of two-thirds of the whole number of Senators, and a majority of the whole number shall be necessary to a choice. But no person constitutionally ineligible to the office of President shall be eligible to that of Vice-President of the United States.

Thirteenth Amendment

[Proposed January 31, 1865; declared ratified December 18, 1865]

Section 1. Neither slavery nor involuntary servitude, except as a punishment for crime whereof the party shall have been duly convicted, shall exist within the United States, or any place subject to their jurisdiction.

Section 2. Congress shall have power to enforce this article by appropriate legislation.

Although some slaves had been freed during the Civil War, slavery was not abolished until the Thirteenth Amendment took effect.

Fourteenth Amendment

[Proposed June 16, 1866; declared ratified July 28, 1868]

Section 1. All persons born or naturalized in the United States, and subject to the jurisdiction thereof, are citizens of the United States and of the State wherein they reside. No State shall make or enforce any law which shall abridge the privileges or immunities of citizens of the United States; nor shall any State deprive any person of life, liberty, or property, without due process of law; nor deny to any person within its jurisdiction the equal protection of the laws.

Section 2. Representatives shall be apportioned among the several States according to their respective numbers, counting the whole number of per-

In 1833 the Supreme Court ruled that the Bill of Rights limited the federal government but not the state governments. This ruling was interpreted to mean that states were able to keep African Americans from becoming state citizens: if African Americans were not citizens, they were not protected by the Bill of Rights. The Fourteenth Amendment defines citizenship and prevents states from interfering in the rights of citizens of the United States.

sons in each State, ~~excluding Indians not taxed~~. But when the right to vote at any election for the choice of electors for President and Vice President of the United States, Representatives in Congress, the Executive and Judicial officers of a State, or the members of the Legislature thereof, is denied to any of the ~~male~~ inhabitants of such State, ~~being twenty-one years of age,~~ and citizens of the United States, or in any way abridged, except for participation in rebellion, or other crime, the basis of representation therein shall be reduced in the proportion which the number of such ~~male~~ citizens shall bear to the whole number of ~~male~~ citizens ~~twenty-one years of age~~ in such State.

Section 3. No person shall be a Senator or Representative in Congress, or elector of President and Vice President, or hold any office, civil or military, under the United States, or under any State, who, having previously taken an oath, as a member of Congress, or as an officer of the United States, or as a member of any State legislature, or as an executive or judicial officer of any State, to support the Constitution of the United States, shall have engaged in insurrection or rebellion against the same, or given aid or comfort to the enemies thereof. But Congress may by a vote of two-thirds of each House, remove such disability.

Section 4. The validity of the public debt of the United States, authorized by law, including debts incurred for payment of pensions and bounties for services in suppressing insurrection or rebellion, shall not be questioned. But neither the United States nor any State shall assume or pay any debt or obligation incurred in aid of insurrection or rebellion against the United States, ~~or any claim for the loss of emancipation of any slave~~; but all such debts, obligations and claims shall be held illegal and void.

Section 5. The Congress shall have power to enforce, by appropriate legislation, the provisions of this article.

Fifteenth Amendment
[Proposed February 27, 1869; declared ratified March 30, 1870]

Section 1. The right of citizens of the United States to vote shall not be denied or abridged by the United States or by any State on account of race, color, or previous condition of servitude.

Section 2. The Congress shall have power to enforce this article by appropriate legislation.

Sixteenth Amendment
[Proposed July 12, 1909; declared ratified February 25, 1913]

The Congress shall have power to lay and collect taxes on incomes, from whatever source derived, without apportionment among the several States, and without regard to any census or enumeration.

The Fifteenth Amendment extended the vote to African American men.

Seventeenth Amendment

[Proposed May 13, 1912; declared ratified May 31, 1913]

The Senate of the United States shall be composed of two Senators from each State, elected by the people thereof, for six years; and each Senator shall have one vote. The electors in each State shall have the qualifications requisite for electors of the most numerous branch of the State legislatures.

When vacancies happen in the representation of any State in the Senate, the executive authority of such State shall issue writs of election to fill such vacancies: *Provided*, That the legislature of any State may empower the executive thereof to make temporary appointments until the people fill the vacancies by election as the legislature may direct.

~~This amendment shall not be so construed as to affect the election or term of any Senator chosen before it becomes valid as part of the Constitution.~~

The Seventeenth Amendment requires that senators be elected directly by the people instead of by the state legislature.

Eighteenth Amendment

[Proposed December 18, 1917; declared ratified January 29, 1919; repealed by the Twenty-first Amendment December 5, 1933]

~~Section 1. After one year from the ratification of this article the manufacture, sale, or transportation of intoxicating liquors within, the importation thereof into, or the exportation thereof from the United States and all territory subject to the jurisdiction thereof for beverage purposes is hereby prohibited.~~

~~Section 2. The Congress and the several States shall have concurrent power to enforce this article by appropriate legislation.~~

~~Section 3. This article shall be inoperative unless it shall have been ratified as an amendment to the Constitution by the legislatures of the several States, as provided in the Constitution, within seven years from the date of the submission hereof to the States by the Congress.~~

Although many people felt that the Eighteenth Amendment was good for the health and welfare of the American people, it was repealed 14 years later.

Nineteenth Amendment

[Proposed June 4, 1919; declared ratified August 26, 1920]

The right of citizens of the United States to vote shall not be denied or abridged by the United States or by any State on account of sex.

Congress shall have power to enforce this article by appropriate legislation.

Abigail Adams was disappointed that the Declaration of Independence and the Constitution did not specifically include women. It took almost 150 years and much campaigning by groups for women's suffrage to finally achieve voting privileges.

Twentieth Amendment

[Proposed March 2, 1932; declared ratified February 6, 1933]

Section 1. The terms of the President and Vice-President shall end at noon on the 20th day of January, and the terms of Senators and Representatives

In the original Constitution, a newly elected president and Congress did not take office until March 4, which was four months after the November election. The officials who were leaving office were called lame ducks because they had little influence during those four months. The Twentieth Amendment changed the date that the new president and Congress take office. Members of Congress now take office on January 3, and the president takes office on January 20.

at noon on the 3d day of January, of the years in which such terms would have ended if this article had not been ratified; and the terms of their successors shall then begin.

Section 2. The Congress shall assemble at least once in every year, and such meeting shall begin at noon on the 3d day of January, unless they shall by law appoint a different day.

Section 3. If, at the time fixed for the beginning of the term of the President, the President elect shall have died, the Vice-President elect shall become President. If a President shall not have been chosen before the time fixed for the beginning of his term, or if the President elect shall have failed to qualify, then the Vice-President elect shall act as President until a President shall have qualified; and the Congress may by law provide for the case wherein neither a President elect nor a Vice-President elect shall have qualified, declaring who shall then act as President, or the manner in which one who is to act shall be selected, and such person shall act accordingly until a President or Vice-President shall have qualified.

Section 4. The Congress may by law provide for the case of the death of any of the persons from whom the House of Representatives may choose a President whenever the right of choice shall have devolved upon them, and for the case of the death of any of the persons from whom the Senate may choose a Vice-President whenever the right of choice shall have devolved upon them.

~~**Section 5.** Sections 1 and 2 shall take effect on the 15th day of October following the ratification of this article.~~

~~**Section 6.** This article shall be inoperative unless it shall have been ratified as an amendment to the Constitution by the legislatures of three-fourths of the several States within seven years from the date of its submission.~~

The Twenty-first Amendment is the only amendment that has been ratified by state conventions rather than by state legislatures.

Twenty-first Amendment

[Proposed February 20, 1933; declared ratified December 5, 1933]

Section 1. The eighteenth article of amendment to the Constitution of the United States is hereby repealed.

Section 2. The transportation or importation into any State, Territory, or possession of the United States for delivery or use therein of intoxicating liquors, in violation of the laws thereof, is hereby prohibited.

~~**Section 3.** This article shall be inoperative unless it shall have been ratified as an amendment to the Constitution by conventions in the several States, as provided in the Constitution, within seven years from the date of the submission hereof to the States by the Congress.~~

Twenty-second Amendment

[Proposed March 21, 1947; declared ratified February 26, 1951]

Section 1. No person shall be elected to the office of the President more than twice, and no person who has held the office of President, or acted as President, for more than two years of a term to which some other person was elected President shall be elected to the office of the President more than once. ~~But this Article shall not apply to any person holding the office of President when this Article was proposed by the Congress, and shall not prevent any person who may be holding the office of President, or acting as President, during the term within which this Article becomes operative from holding the office of President or acting as President during the remainder of such term.~~

~~**Section 2.** This article shall be inoperative unless it shall have been ratified as an amendment to the Constitution by the legislatures of three-fourths of the several States within seven years from the date of its submission to the States by the Congress.~~

From the time of President Washington's administration, it was a custom for presidents to serve no more than two terms of office. Franklin D. Roosevelt, however, was elected to four terms. The Twenty-second Amendment made into law the old custom of limiting a president to no more than two terms.

Twenty-third Amendment

[Proposed June 16, 1960; declared ratified March 29, 1961]

Section 1. The District constituting the seat of Government of the United States shall appoint in such manner as the Congress may direct:

A number of electors of President and Vice-President equal to the whole number of Senators and Representatives in Congress to which the District would be entitled if it were a State, but in no event more than the least populous state; they shall be in addition to those appointed by the States, but they shall be considered, for the purposes of the election of President and Vice-President, to be electors appointed by a State; and they shall meet in the District and perform such duties as provided by the twelfth article of amendment.

Section 2. The Congress shall have power to enforce this article by appropriate legislation.

Until the ratification of the Twenty-third Amendment, the people of Washington, D.C., could not vote in presidential elections.

Twenty-fourth Amendment

[Proposed August 27, 1962; declared ratified January 23, 1964]

Section 1. The right of citizens of the United States to vote in any primary or other election for President or Vice-President, for electors for President or Vice-President, or for Senator or Representative in Congress, shall not be denied or abridged by the United States or any State by reason of failure to pay any poll tax or other tax.

Section 2. The Congress shall have power to enforce this article by appropriate legislation.

Twenty-fifth Amendment

[Proposed July 6, 1965; declared ratified February 10, 1967]

The illness of President Eisenhower in the 1950s and the assassination of President Kennedy in 1963 were the events behind the Twenty-fifth Amendment. The Constitution did not provide a clear-cut method for a vice president to take over for a disabled president or upon the death of a president. This amendment provides for filling the office of the vice president if a vacancy occurs, and it provides a way for the vice president—or someone else in the line of succession—to take over if the president is unable to perform the duties of that office.

Section 1. In case of the removal of the President from office or of his death or resignation, the Vice-President shall become President.

Section 2. Whenever there is a vacancy in the office of the Vice-President, the President shall nominate a Vice-President who shall take office upon confirmation by a majority vote of both Houses of Congress.

Section 3. Whenever the President transmits to the President pro tempore of the Senate and the Speaker of the House of Representatives his written declaration that he is unable to discharge the powers and duties of his office, and until he transmits to them a written declaration to the contrary, such powers and duties shall be discharged by the Vice-President as Acting President.

Section 4. Whenever the Vice-President and a majority of either the principal officers of the executive departments or of such other body as Congress may by law provide, transmit to the President pro tempore of the Senate and the Speaker of the House of Representatives their written declaration that the President is unable to discharge the powers and duties of his office, the Vice-President shall immediately assume the powers and duties of the office as Acting President.

Thereafter, when the President transmits to the President pro tempore of the Senate and the Speaker of the House of Representatives his written declaration that no inability exists, he shall resume the powers and duties of his office unless the Vice-President and a majority of either the principal officers of the executive department or of such other body as Congress may by law provide, transmit within four days to the President pro tempore of the Senate and the Speaker of the House of Representatives their written declaration that the President is unable to discharge the powers and duties of his office. Thereupon Congress shall decide the issue, assembling within forty-eight hours for that purpose if not in session. If the Congress, within twenty-one days after receipt of the latter written declaration, or, if Congress is not in session, within twenty-one days after Congress is required to assemble, determines by two-thirds vote of both Houses that the President is unable to discharge the powers and duties of his office, the Vice-President shall continue to discharge the same as Acting President; otherwise, the President shall resume the powers and duties of his office.

Twenty-sixth Amendment

[Proposed March 10, 1971; declared ratified July 5, 1971]

Section 1. The right of citizens of the United States, who are eighteen years of age or older, to vote shall not be denied or abridged by the United States or by any State on account of age.

Section 2. The Congress shall have power to enforce this article by appropriate legislation.

Twenty-seventh Amendment

[Proposed September 25, 1789; declared ratified May 7, 1992]

No law, varying the compensation for the services of the Senators and Representatives, shall take effect, until an election of Representatives shall have intervened.

The Voting Act of 1970 tried to set the voting age at 18. However, the Supreme Court ruled that the act set the voting age for national elections only, not state or local elections. This ruling would make necessary several different ballots at elections. The Twenty-sixth Amendment gave 18-year-old citizens the right to vote in all elections.

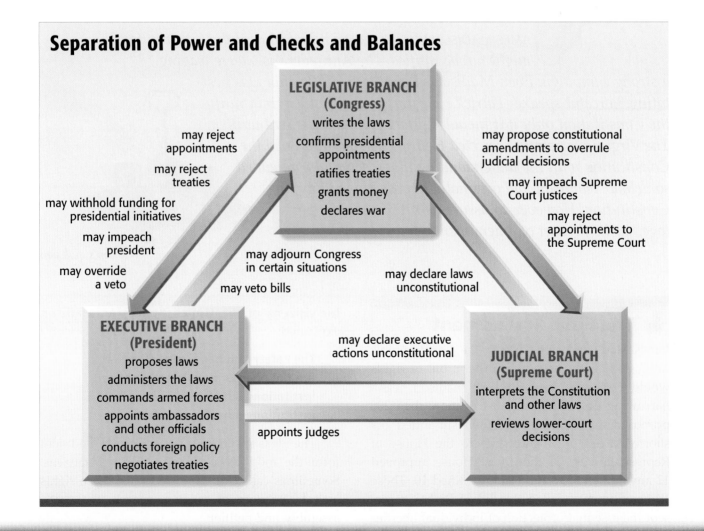

Separation of Power and Checks and Balances

LEGISLATIVE BRANCH (Congress)
- writes the laws
- confirms presidential appointments
- ratifies treaties
- grants money
- declares war

EXECUTIVE BRANCH (President)
- proposes laws
- administers the laws
- commands armed forces
- appoints ambassadors and other officials
- conducts foreign policy
- negotiates treaties

JUDICIAL BRANCH (Supreme Court)
- interprets the Constitution and other laws
- reviews lower-court decisions

may reject appointments
may reject treaties
may withhold funding for presidential initiatives
may impeach president
may override a veto

may adjourn Congress in certain situations
may veto bills

may propose constitutional amendments to overrule judicial decisions
may impeach Supreme Court justices
may reject appointments to the Supreme Court

may declare laws unconstitutional

may declare executive actions unconstitutional

appoints judges

The Bill of Rights

Reading Focus

What are the main freedoms of the First Amendment, and why are they important?

Which constitutional amendments reflect issues with pre-Revolutionary War British officials, and how do the amendments address those concerns?

What rights do the amendments give to people accused of crimes?

Key Terms

petition
search warrant
due process
indict
double jeopardy
eminent domain

AMES MADISON WAS WORRIED. It looked as if the Constitution might not be ratified. The Antifederalists were waging a strong campaign. Even Madison's home state of Virginia was hesitating. Forceful speaker Patrick Henry proposed that Virginia ratify the Constitution only if it included 40 amendments he had written. The Virginia legislature rejected Henry's list, but approved the Constitution with the understanding that it would be amended somehow. Madison had originally opposed amending the Constitution. However, to assure its ratification, he put together its first set of amendments.

Madison's quill pen

 ## The First Amendment

James Madison helped secure the Constitution's ratification with the promise that a bill of rights would be added to it. In 1789 Madison began narrowing down the huge list of more than 200 proposed amendments. He then submitted the shortened list of amendments to the House of Representatives. Of those, the House approved 12 amendments, and the states ratified 10. Those 10 amendments, called the Bill of Rights, represent the essential protection of individual liberties

for citizens of the United States. As Madison explained:

❝ **The safety and happiness of society are the objects at which all political institutions aim and to which all such institutions must be sacrificed.** ❞

The ideas spelled out in the First Amendment form the most basic rights of all U.S. citizens. Sometimes called the five freedoms, these rights include freedom of religion, speech, the press, assembly, and petition.

Freedom of Religion

The First Amendment begins by declaring that "Congress shall make no law respecting an establishment of religion, or prohibiting the free exercise thereof." This means that the government cannot support a religion or interfere with any American's decision to practice a religion or not.

At the time the Constitution was written, most nations had a state religion, a system of religious beliefs supported by the government. For example, the Church of England was the state religion of Great Britain. After the Revolution, some Americans supported the separation of church and state, which would keep the government from establishing an official religion and from favoring any religion over others.

Freedom of Speech and of the Press

The importance of the second and third freedoms in the First Amendment is reflected in an idea expressed by former congresswoman Margaret Chase Smith. "The key to security," she once said, "is public information." Everyone in the United States is guaranteed the freedom of speech. Americans have the right to express their own ideas and opinions and to hear the ideas and opinions of others.

Freedom of speech does not mean that people can say anything they want to, however. The Supreme Court has ruled that speech presenting a serious threat to public safety, such as falsely shouting "Fire!" in a crowded theater, is not protected by the First Amendment. Justice Oliver Wendell Holmes explained:

> **“The question in every case is whether the words used are used in such circumstances and are of such a nature to create a clear and present danger that . . . Congress has a right to prevent.”**

Another kind of unprotected speech is slander, or the intentional telling of lies that damages someone's reputation.

Intentionally writing a lie that harms another person is called libel. In protecting Americans' freedom of the press, the founders recalled the

The Granger Collection, New York

Biography

James Madison

James Madison was born in Virginia in 1751. He attended the College of New Jersey, now Princeton University, before entering Virginia politics. Early in his career Madison became a strong supporter of religious freedom.

Madison served in Congress until 1797. He continued to influence politics from his family plantation, where he remained a slaveholder despite his belief in individual liberty. In 1801 Madison became secretary of state. He served as president from 1809 to 1817 and continued to be active in politics up until his death in 1836. Madison is often called the Father of the Constitution because of his central role in framing the document and adding the Bill of Rights.

case of John Peter Zenger. The publisher of *New York Weekly Journal*, Zenger had gone on trial in 1735 for printing a factual article that criticized New York's royal governor. The jury found Zenger not guilty, establishing that "the truth is a defense against libel."

Freedom of Assembly and Petition

Another freedom Americans have is that of assembly, or of holding meetings. Anyone may gather with anyone else to discuss issues or to conduct

These students express their freedom of speech and of assembly by organizing an Earth Day celebration.

business. As long as those people gather peacefully and are not involved in any illegal activity, the government cannot interfere.

The right to **petition**, or make a request of, the government is another right of the American people. Any American can present a petition, or formal request, to a government official. The right of petition enables Americans to express their dissatisfaction with current laws or to suggest new ones.

★ Protecting Citizens

The Second, Third, and Fourth Amendments all relate to concerns that grew out of the colonists' disputes with British officials before the Revolution. These amendments continue to affect American life today.

Militias

The Second Amendment deals with state militias. As the conflict with Great Britain increased before the Revolution began, colonial militias prepared for war. The "shot heard round the world" that started the Revolutionary War came when British troops tried to seize the weapons of the Massachusetts militia.

The founders believed that the states needed to continue to maintain militias for emergencies. Today the National Guard has replaced state militias. National Guard members

can be called to serve in wars and to help restore order during crises, such as in the event of a natural disaster.

Many people have debated the Second Amendment's intent regarding firearms. Some people argue that gun control laws violate the Second Amendment's declaration that "the right of the people to keep and bear arms shall not be infringed [violated]." In 1939 the Supreme Court approved restrictions for nonmilitary firearms. Years later, a U.S. court of appeals ruled that gun control laws do not violate the Second Amendment. The Supreme Court let that ruling stand in 1983.

Quartering and Search and Seizure

The Third Amendment prohibits the military from forcing citizens to provide housing for soldiers, an idea that may seem odd today. Before the Revolution, however, the British government pressured the colonies to provide food and shelter for British soldiers.

British authorities also issued writs of assistance, which empowered law officials to search colonists' property for illegal goods without first establishing a probable cause of illegal activity. Anger over such actions resulted in the Fourth Amendment's restriction against "unreasonable

These members of the National Guard are helping local citizens prevent a river from flooding.

Judges issue search warrants like this one to allow law enforcement officials to search a suspected criminal's home.

searches and seizures." To conduct a search reasonably, authorities usually must first obtain a **search warrant**. This warrant is a judge's order that authorizes the search because the property in question seems likely to contain evidence relating to a crime.

Authorities do not always need a warrant to conduct a search. Under certain circumstances, such as when a suspect is trying to destroy evidence or conceal a weapon, police can conduct an emergency search. This helps to protect both the officers and any evidence necessary to prove illegal activity.

★ Protection of the Accused

The Fifth, Sixth, Seventh, and Eighth Amendments establish guidelines for trying people accused of a crime. The goal of these amendments is to protect the rights of the accused. No one may be punished for a crime without **due process**, or the fair application, of the law.

Due Process

According to the Fifth Amendment, a court cannot try someone for a serious crime unless a grand jury decides that enough evidence exists to **indict**, or formally accuse, the person. The Fifth Amendment also protects people from being forced to testify in their own trial in a criminal case. To refrain from testifying, the defendant "pleads the Fifth." Anyone found not guilty in a criminal trial cannot face **double jeopardy**, or be tried again for the same crime.

Linking Past to Present

Freedom of Assembly

When Congress first debated what to include in the Bill of Rights, some members thought that guaranteeing citizens' right to meet and speak together was too minor to be a federal issue. Others, however, wanted to make sure that political groups in power did not try to stop rival groups from organizing meetings. Thus, the freedom to assemble became part of the First Amendment.

Over the years Americans have used the right to assemble in many ways, ranging from parades to protests. Citizens have gathered to privately and publicly express their opinions on issues such as civil rights, education, the environment, public policy, and religion. Even in wartime, opponents of U.S. policy have marched to the Capitol and peacefully protested government actions.

Americans do not have unlimited right of assembly, however. Citizens have the right to gather on any public property under guidelines that protect public safety. Parades, for example, usually require a local permit so that traffic flow can be managed during the parade time. Such restrictions are not supposed to be used to prevent people or groups with unpopular beliefs from publicly expressing their opinions.

Understanding What You Read

1. What types of activities might students participate in that are guaranteed under the freedom of assembly?

2. Explain why all groups—even ones with controversial ideas—should have the freedom of assembly.

Amending the U.S. Constitution

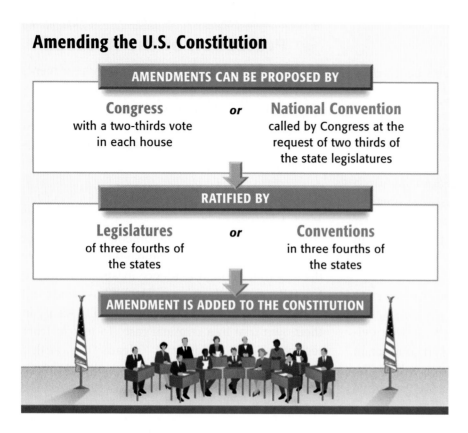

AMENDMENTS CAN BE PROPOSED BY

Congress
with a two-thirds vote
in each house

or

National Convention
called by Congress at the
request of two thirds of
the state legislatures

RATIFIED BY

Legislatures
of three fourths of
the states

or

Conventions
in three fourths of
the states

AMENDMENT IS ADDED TO THE CONSTITUTION

The final clause of the Fifth Amendment states that no one will be deprived of property "without due process of law." The one exception involves the government's power of **eminent domain**, or the right to take personal property to further the public's interest. This would include, for example, the seizing of private lands to build a public road. However, the government must pay the owners a fair amount of money for the property unless the citizens obtained it through illegal activities, such as selling illegal drugs.

Trials

The Sixth Amendment states that someone who is indicted for a crime must have a prompt, public trial by a jury. The accused has the right to know what crime he or she is charged with and to hear and to question the prosecution witnesses. The accused also has the right to an attorney. Today the government pays for the attorney if the person cannot afford legal services.

The accused has the right to refuse any of his or her Sixth Amendment rights. For example, some defendants refuse the services of an attorney, while others choose to have a trial in front of a judge alone instead of before a jury. In many cases, defendants can bypass the trial by agreeing to a plea bargain—pleading guilty to a lesser charge rather than risk being convicted of a crime that may carry a greater sentence.

The Seventh Amendment establishes that juries can decide civil cases. These cases usually involve disputes over money or property. If a person harms another person without breaking the law—for example, by refusing to pay back a debt—the injured party may sue in civil court.

Bail and Punishment

The Eighth Amendment establishes that people accused of a crime have a method of getting out of jail until their trial is over. Defendants gain their release in exchange for bail, money paid to the court to guarantee that they will show up for trial. Whoever pays the bail gets his or her money back at the end of the trial only if the defendant has attended court. If the defendant does not show up for trial, the court keeps all the bail money and issues a warrant for the immediate arrest of the defendant.

The Eighth Amendment prevents courts from setting bail amounts that are too high. How much bail is "too high" depends on the crime, the accused person's financial resources, and the probability that the person will show up. For some people accused of extremely serious crimes, the judge may refuse to grant bail.

The Eighth Amendment also prohibits inflicting "cruel and unusual punishments" against a person convicted of a crime. For many years, Americans have debated the meaning of "cruel and unusual punishments." In 1972 the Supreme Court ruled that the death penalty, as it was carried out by most states at the time, was cruel and unusual. The Court also found that the processes by which many states sentenced people to death were unfair. However, the Court did not rule that all executions are cruel and unusual. All states that use the death penalty must follow guidelines spelled out by the Supreme Court.

⭐ Other Rights of the People

The final two amendments in the Bill of Rights provide a general protection for other individual rights and reserve some governmental powers for the states and for the people. The Ninth Amendment states that listing specific rights in the Constitution does not mean that citizens do not have additional rights. This amendment gives the courts and Congress the ability to determine other fundamental rights of citizens.

Education is one right that was not included in the Constitution but which most Americans consider a fundamental right. "Education is not just another consumer item. It is the bedrock [foundation] of our democracy," explained educational leader Mary Hatwood Futrell. Today state governments provide free education—from elementary to high school—to all citizens.

The Tenth Amendment grants to the states and the people any powers that the Constitution does not specifically give to Congress or prohibit from

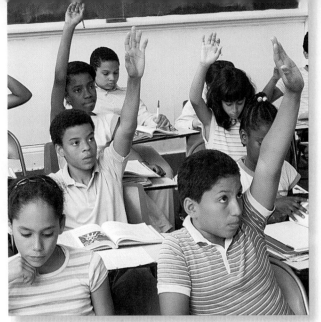
These students benefit from free public education, which many people now consider a right of citizenship.

the states. Recently a group of governors used this amendment to challenge a federal law that required states to pay for and carry out a federal information program. The courts agreed, stating that this requirement interfered with the states' rights, implied under the Tenth Amendment, to determine their own budget priorities. Thus, the last amendment in the Bill of Rights continues to protect the rights of citizens and to balance power between the federal and state governments.

SECTION 2 REVIEW

Identify and explain the significance of the following:
- **James Madison**
- **petition**
- **search warrant**
- **due process**
- **indict**
- **double jeopardy**
- **eminent domain**

Reading for Content Understanding

1 Main Idea What are the five main freedoms guaranteed to U.S. citizens under the First Amendment, and why are they important?

2 Main Idea How do the Second, Third, and Fourth Amendments address concerns from the Revolutionary period?

3 Citizenship and Democracy How does the Ninth Amendment protect people's rights and individual freedoms?

4 Writing *Expressing* What rights of the accused are protected by the Constitution? Do you agree or disagree with protecting these rights? Explain your answer in one or two paragraphs.

5 Critical Thinking *Evaluating* What do you think are the three most important ways that the Bill of Rights influences our lives today? Explain your answers.

Rights and Responsibilities of Citizenship

<table>
<tr><td>

Reading Focus

How can a person become a U.S. citizen?

What are some of the most important responsibilities of citizenship?

Why is it important for citizens to be involved with their community and government?

</td><td>

Key Terms

naturalization
deport
draft
political action committees

</td></tr>
</table>

$\mathbb{P}$ATRICK HENRY ARGUED *that the United States should be open for all people who wanted to become citizens.* "Let . . . Liberty stretch forth her fair hand toward the people of the old world," *he said* "—tell them to come, and bid them welcome." *Many people desiring liberty have become U.S. citizens. Jozef Patyna immigrated to the United States in the early 1980s to flee an unjust government in Poland. "The idea of freedom and democracy is what the people have an instinctive need for," explained Patyna.*

The Statue of Liberty

Becoming a Citizen

The Constitution protects the rights of all U.S. citizens. People can become U.S. citizens in many ways. Anyone born in the United States or a territory it controls is a citizen. People born in Puerto Rico, for example, are citizens because that island is a commonwealth that remains a U.S. territory.

People born in a foreign country can become U.S. citizens if one of their parents is a citizen. People born in a foreign country whose parents are not U.S. citizens can become citizens only if they move to the United States and undergo a long process in gaining citizenship called **naturalization**. The U.S. Immigration and Naturalization Service (INS) oversees this process.

Foreign-born people who permanently move to a new country are called immigrants. In the United States, legal immigrants have many of the same rights and responsibilities as citizens. They cannot vote or hold public office, however. In some states they cannot hold some government jobs either. The U.S. government also has the right to **deport**, or send back to the country of origin, any immigrant who breaks the law or who is in the country illegally.

Only legal immigrants can begin the process of naturalization. All legal immigrants have to be able to support themselves financially or have someone sponsor them and assume that financial responsibility. After living in the United States for five years, legal immigrants over the age of 18 may petition for naturalization. At that point the INS sets a hearing to test the immigrants' qualifications. The immigrants must prove that they are law-abiding and that they support the U.S. Constitution. They must also take a series of tests to prove that they can read, write, and speak English, and that they have a basic understanding of U.S. history and government.

This Asian immigrant is taking the oath of allegiance to become a U.S. citizen.

After the immigrants pass this hearing, the INS conducts a background check on them to make sure they have not hidden any information about themselves. Finally, they go before a naturalization court, where they take an oath of allegiance to the United States and then receive their certificate of naturalization. At that point all young children of the newly naturalized citizens also become citizens.

Becoming a naturalized citizen takes dedication and effort. An elderly Japanese immigrant wrote a poem to celebrate her naturalization:

 **Going steadily to study English,
Even through the rain at night,
I thus attain [acquire],
Late in life,
American citizenship.** "

Naturalized citizens and resident immigrants contribute a great deal to the United States. Many famous Americans, such as scientist Albert Einstein and Secretary of State Madeleine Albright, have been naturalized citizens. The only distinctions between naturalized and native-born citizens are that naturalized citizens can lose their citizenship and they cannot become president or vice president.

⭐ Duties of Citizens

In addition to having certain rights, American citizens have responsibilities to themselves, their government, and other citizens. For the system of representative democracy to work, Americans need to fulfill their civic responsibilities. "The stakes . . . are too high for government to be a spectator sport," explained former Texas congresswoman Barbara Jordan.

Obeying Authority

Citizens elect officials to make laws for them. In turn, citizens must obey the laws passed by those officials. If citizens disagree with a law, they can try to get it changed in a variety of ways, such as by speaking with their local representative, challenging the law in court, petitioning, or voting for elected officials who oppose the law.

Obeying the law includes knowing what the laws are. Thus, citizens need to stay informed of and be aware of changes to laws that affect them. Ignorance of a particular law will not prevent a person from being punished for breaking it.

Citizens also have an obligation to respect the rights of others and to respect people in authority. These people, including parents, teachers, and police officers, have been entrusted with looking out for the welfare of others. Parents, for example, have a responsibility to provide for their children's basic needs, including food, clothing, shelter, and education. In return, children have a responsibility

Consumers like this teenager pay sales tax when they buy goods.

sometimes the state, government. The amount of income tax that a person has to pay depends on the level of his or her income.

Income taxes and property taxes are progressive—they collect a higher percentage of money from those with higher incomes and greater wealth. Regressive taxes, such as sales taxes, are taxes that apply equally to all Americans. If a person buys a product, he or she pays the same amount of sales tax on the item regardless of his or her individual income.

to obey their parents. Government authorities may step in to protect any children whose parents do not take proper care of them.

Paying Taxes

Benjamin Franklin once claimed, "In this world, nothing is certain but death and taxes." Paying taxes is a necessary part of being a good citizen. The government relies on taxes to pay for the many services it provides. If Americans did not pay taxes, the government might be unable to provide public roads, police and fire departments, or even public schools.

People pay many kinds of taxes, such as sales taxes, excise taxes, and tariffs. For example, consumers often pay sales taxes when buying items at a store. Sales tax rates vary from place to place because most sales taxes are set and collected by state and local governments.

Property taxes are taxes people pay based on the value of the property they own. The tax amount owed is a certain percentage of the value of the property. Most school funding comes from property taxes.

April 15 of every year is income tax day. By that day all Americans who earned money the year before must give a certain percentage of their income from that year to the federal, and

Serving in the Military

Citizens also have the duty to protect and defend the nation from harm. This means that if a war breaks out, citizens should try to help in the war effort. U.S. citizens have had to go to war a number of times in the nation's history. In some war situations the federal government has issued a **draft**, or requirement of military service, to raise the needed number of soldiers.

The United States has maintained all-volunteer armed forces since 1973. However, young men are required

Upon turning 18, every male U.S. citizen must fill out a card like this one to register for a potential draft.

to register with the government when they turn 18. This registration provides the government with a record of potential draftees in case a war breaks out. Women are not required to register for the draft, although many women serve in the armed forces.

Serving on Juries

All citizens can be called for jury duty, which involves listening to a court case and reaching a verdict on it. It is important for citizens to serve when called for jury duty, otherwise fulfilling each person's Sixth Amendment right to a trial by jury would be difficult.

Americans also have a duty to testify in court if needed. If a person were to witness a crime, for example, he or she should be willing to testify about the event. Judges may issue subpoenas, or orders to appear in court, to force people to testify.

★ Citizens and Elections

Elections form the basis of representative democracy in the United States. Voting in elections is crucial to maintaining the country's democratic system. Through free elections, U.S. citizens choose who will lead the government. Not all countries allow their citizens to participate in elections.

An active voter should be an informed voter. Citizens should try to find out as much as they can about the issues and candidates before voting. Much of this information is available through newspapers, television, and other forms of media. However, informed voters should watch out for propaganda, or material that is slanted deliberately to support or harm a cause.

Voting is not the only way that Americans participate in elections. Many become involved by campaigning for a particular candidate or issue. Anyone can help campaign, even if he or she is not eligible to vote. Citizens can also contribute money to a candidate directly or through **political action committees** (PACs), organizations that collect money to distribute to candidates who support the same issues as the contributors.

Voters in the United States must be at least 18 years old. Many people younger than 18 can help campaigns by handing out pamphlets, making signs, or otherwise encouraging citizens to vote. Some schools have clubs, such as the Teen-Age Republicans and the Young Democrats, that allow teenagers to get involved in party politics.

High school student Janet Benson's active participation in the Teen-Age Republicans shaped her career goals. "Some people want a career in science or sports," she noted. "For me, it's politics. I love it." Many active members of political clubs get to know political leaders well. Some continue to be active in politics as adults.

★ Citizens and Government

Being involved in elections is just one of the many ways in which citizens can participate in their government. Even after an election, people can influence officials by letting them know what the citizens want done.

Some citizens join interest groups, organizations designed to lobby politicians on behalf of particular issues. People form many kinds of interest groups, and most groups represent the views of a particular segment of society. The American Farm Bureau Federation, for example, is an interest group made up of farmers. It lobbies to get aid for farms—for example, financial assistance to help when a natural disaster destroys crops or to maintain prices of farm products.

Other groups, called public interest groups, lobby for issues that affect all Americans. Mothers Against Drunk Driving (MADD) and Students Against Drunk Driving (SADD) are two public interest groups that work to end drunk driving, which kills thousands of Americans each year. MADD began in 1980 after a drunk driver killed 13-year-old Cari Lightner.

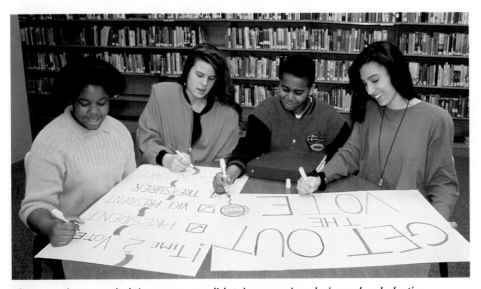

These students are helping run a candidate's campaign during a local election.

These members of Students Against Drunk Driving visited Washington, D.C., to speak out against drinking and driving.

Her mother, Candy Lightner, found out that under her state's law, drunk driving was not a serious crime and that the driver would probably not spend any time in prison. Lightner founded MADD to change that policy. In explaining her motivation, she said:

> **❝ I believe that for every problem there is a solution. . . . I believe in the rights of victims. And I do feel that if you believe in something badly enough, you can make a difference. ❞**

MADD began to lobby for tougher laws against drunk drivers. As a result, every state strengthened its laws against drunk driving. MADD and SADD also work to educate people about the dangers of drunk driving. "We are changing the way people think about drinking and driving," said Lightner. "But more than that, we have caused people to change their behavior, and that is saving lives."

Citizens do not have to join a group to influence political leaders. Individuals can and should let officials know how they feel about certain issues by writing letters and by going to public meetings. Attending city council meetings is a good way to learn about and influence local issues.

If public officials do not know how citizens feel about an issue, they cannot represent them effectively.

★ Citizens and Their Communities

Being part of a representative democracy does not mean that citizens hand over all the responsibility for society to their elected leaders and government. Indeed, a successful democratic society requires the involvement of all citizens in improving the communities in which they live.

Just as there are many interest groups that help U.S. citizens lobby for new legislation, there are numerous groups that organize citizens for community service. Some small communities whose local governments have limited budgets rely on volunteers to provide many public services, such as fire protection. Other volunteer groups assist

These volunteers are helping their neighbor by repainting a fence.

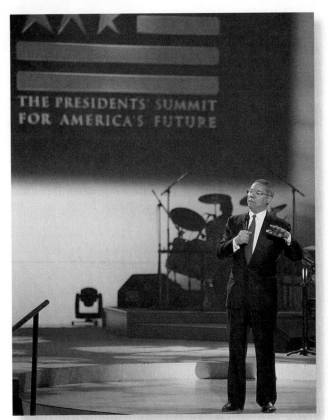
Colin Powell launches an effort to increase volunteerism throughout the country.

citizen patrols usually have lower crime rates than those that do not.

Other groups help do jobs in place of the government. The American Red Cross helps citizens in times of natural disasters or other emergencies. Habitat for Humanity helps to build houses for lower-income families. The Boy Scouts and Girl Scouts organize numerous projects to improve the environment, such as planting trees.

The country's leaders expect all citizens to try to do something to serve others in their communities. Service projects do not have to be big to have an effect. They can include simple acts to improve the appearance of a community, such as picking up trash or painting over graffiti. They may also help individuals—perhaps by volunteering to serve food in a homeless shelter or by visiting an elderly person in a retirement home.

Every day many people in the community need assistance. The nation is strengthened when all citizens do their part to help the country and their fellow citizens. As retired general Colin Powell declared when he launched a campaign to promote volunteerism in 1997:

government-sponsored agencies, including police departments. For example, Citizens on Patrol and the Neighborhood Watch organize volunteers to walk their neighborhoods and inform police of any possible criminal activity they observe in the area. Neighborhoods with

66 **This is the time for each and every one of us . . . to look into our own community, to find someone who is in need . . . to lift up a fellow American and put him on the road to success in this wonderful country of ours.** 99

SECTION 3 REVIEW

Identify and explain the significance of the following:
- **naturalization**
- **deport**
- **draft**
- **political action committees**

Reading for Content Understanding

1 **Main Idea** How can someone become a U.S. citizen?

2 **Main Idea** What responsibilities do citizens have to their country?

3 **Cultural Diversity** What rights do citizens have that immigrants do not?

4 **Writing** *Creating* Write a short poem that might be used to encourage people to volunteer in their communities or to become involved in the government.

5 **Critical Thinking** *Identifying Cause and Effect* Write about a problem within your community—its causes and effects—and give examples of possible ways to get people more involved in correcting the problem.

CHAPTER 2 REVIEW

Chapter Summary

To ensure a system of checks and balances, the framers of the Constitution divided the government into three branches—legislative, executive, and judicial. Leaders later added the Bill of Rights to protect individual liberties. Citizens have certain rights and responsibilities that must be carried out for representative democracy to work. ▪

On a separate sheet of paper, complete the following activities.

Identifying People and Ideas

Describe the significance of the following:

1. representative democracy
2. impeach
3. Sandra Day O'Connor
4. James Madison
5. search warrant
6. due process
7. double jeopardy
8. naturalization
9. draft
10. political action committees

Internet Activity

go.hrw.com
SB1 Supreme Court

Search the Internet through the HRW Web site for more information on Supreme Court justices. Choose one justice who served on the Court during the 1800s. Write a detailed biography of his life, including a summary of the major court cases he helped to decide.

Understanding Main Ideas

1. What are the three branches of the federal government, and what are their primary responsibilities?
2. What are delegated powers, reserved powers, and concurrent powers?
3. Why did the founders add the Bill of Rights to the Constitution?
4. Which amendments focus on the rights of people accused of crimes? What rights do these amendments guarantee?
5. What are the only differences between the rights of naturalized citizens and the rights of native-born citizens?
6. What are the duties and responsibilities of citizenship?

Using the Time Line

Number your paper from 1 to 7. Match the letters on the time line below with the following events.

1. Delegates from 12 of the 13 states meet to create a new system of government.
2. Geraldine Ferraro becomes the first woman to run for vice president on a major-party ticket.
3. Richard Nixon becomes the first president to resign rather than risk impeachment.
4. President Ronald Reagan appoints Sandra Day O'Connor as the first female justice on the Supreme Court.
5. Thurgood Marshall becomes the first African American justice appointed to serve on the Supreme Court.
6. The Supreme Court rules that the death penalty is not cruel and unusual.
7. John F. Kennedy becomes the first Catholic U.S. president.

Reviewing Themes

1. **Citizenship and Democracy** Why is voting an important responsibility in a representative democracy?

2. **Constitutional Heritage** How does the Constitution prevent any one branch of the federal government from becoming too powerful?

3. **Cultural Diversity** Why might it be said that the United States is a nation of immigrants?

Thinking Critically

1. **Determining the Strength of an Argument** Recall the qualifications for becoming president. Why do you think the framers of the Constitution put these in place?

2. **Synthesizing Information** How were some amendments to the Bill of Rights influenced by Americans' experiences before and during the Revolution?

Building Your Portfolio

Complete the following activities individually or in groups.

1. **Freedom of Petition** Think about something in your community that is important to you, such as the existence of crosswalks, parks, or holiday parades. Write a letter to a local official about this element of your community. Make sure the letter explains to the official why you are writing and what you want to be done. Then organize a campaign to get others to sign your letter. Support your campaign by creating signs, letters, flyers, and other items.

2. **The Supreme Court** Use your library or other resources to find out information about the nine Supreme Court justices sitting on the bench today. Then create a detailed time line showing the names of each justice, what year he or she was confirmed, and which president nominated him or her. In addition, include some brief biographical information on each justice.

3. **Identifying Cause and Effect** Serving on juries is required by law and is an important responsibility of citizenship. What problems might arise if people were unwilling to fulfill this responsibility?

Writing About History

1. **Expressing** Imagine that you have immigrated to the United States. Write a letter to a friend back home explaining why you have done so.

2. **Informing** Write a two-paragraph essay explaining how the Constitution guarantees that the federal government considers minority rights while honoring majority rule.

Linking Geography and History

1. **Movement** How might movements of large numbers of people from one part of the country to another affect states' representation in Congress?

2. **Human-Environment Interaction** What actions can people take to physically improve their communities?

History Skills Workshop

Using Primary Sources On February 28, 1963, President John F. Kennedy gave a speech to Congress in support of a civil rights bill. He also took the opportunity to discuss the importance of voting rights for African Americans. Read the following excerpt of his speech. Then explain in a paragraph what Kennedy meant by this passage.

> ❝The right to vote in a free American election is the most powerful and precious right in the world—and it must not be denied on the grounds of race or color. It is a potent [powerful] key to achieving other rights of citizenship.❞

The Living Constitution

The present government of the United States began operation in 1789 and is based on a written Constitution that was adopted by the 13 original states. The United States has remained strong through many crises because its Constitution established a government in which the people choose their leaders to make their laws. The Constitution's principles and methods of governing have been firm enough to enforce its authority, but flexible enough to adapt to great changes over more than 200 years.

Today the original nation of 13 states—which housed fewer than 4 million people—has grown to 50 states and some 270 million people. The United States now stretches across North America, from the Atlantic Ocean to the shores of the Pacific, and includes Alaska in the Northwest and the faraway islands of Hawaii in the Pacific. ■

The Union

The Northwest Ordinance was adopted by Congress in 1787 under the Articles of Confederation, before the Constitution was written. It set out a method for admitting new states to the Union that remains in place today. The last states admitted to the Union were Alaska and Hawaii in 1959.

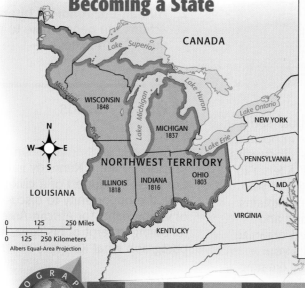

The Northwest Ordinance: Becoming a State

STEPS TO STATEHOOD

Congress specifies that three to five territories will be carved out of the Northwest Territory.

For each territory, Congress appoints a governor, a secretary, and three judges.

When a territory's population reaches 5,000 free male inhabitants of voting age, it elects a territorial legislature and sends a nonvoting delegate to Congress.

Once a territory's population increases to 60,000 free inhabitants, it becomes eligible for statehood and can draft a state constitution.

Congress approves the state constitution, and the territory becomes a state.

Sources: *Record of America; The Oxford Companion to American History*

Geography **Skills**
Reading Political Maps

1. How many people have to be living in a territory for it to be eligible for statehood?
2. Who, or what, has to approve a territory's proposed constitution before the territory becomes a state?
3. In what order did the states of the Northwest Territory join the Union?

Joining the Union

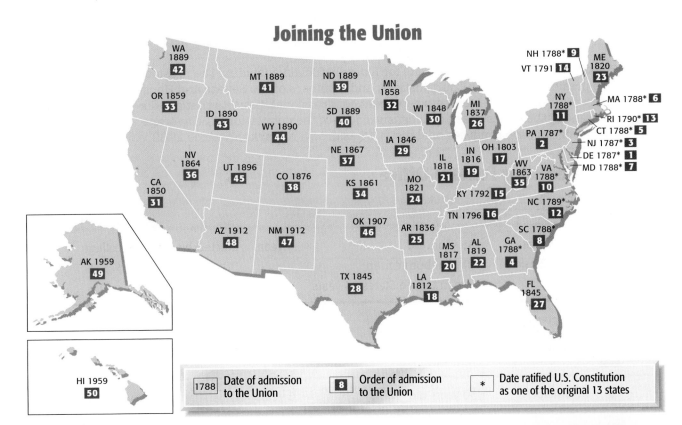

1788	Date of admission to the Union
8	Order of admission to the Union
*	Date ratified U.S. Constitution as one of the original 13 states

Geography Skills
Reading Special-Purpose Maps

1. Which three states ratified the Constitution first?
2. What were the original 13 states?
3. What states were admitted to the Union in the 1900s?

History Note 2

Not all states went through the territory stage before admission to the Union. Texas was an independent country before it became a state. California went directly to statehood because of its rapidly growing population. Kentucky, Maine, Vermont, and West Virginia started out as parts of other states.

History Note 1

Congress established the method for admission of new states to the Union in the Northwest Ordinance of 1787. Before that, however, people in the northeastern portion of present-day Tennessee made the first attempt to create a new state. This proposed state of "Franklin," named after Benjamin Franklin, appealed to Congress for statehood. Franklin's application for statehood came in 1784 after North Carolina turned over the Tennessee territory to the new United States government. Before Congress acted on Franklin's statehood, North Carolina decided to reclaim the region. For a brief time both the state of North Carolina and the proposed state of Franklin tried to enforce laws in the region. Finally, in 1790 North Carolina again turned over control of the region to the national government. Six years later the proposed state of Franklin became part of the new state of Tennessee.

Rocky Mount, capitol for the first territorial government of Tennessee

Representatives and Citizens

The Constitution sets the requirements for federal officials, including the president and vice president, Supreme Court justices, and members of the Senate and House of Representatives. House members represent congressional districts that are distributed among the states based on a census count of the population. The average population size of each congressional district has grown remarkably since 1789.

Requirements for Federal Office

OFFICE	REQUIREMENTS	TERM	SELECTION
President Vice President	• 35 years old • Natural-born citizen • Live in United States 14 years	4 years	Elected by electoral college
Supreme Court Justice	• None	Life	Appointed by president and approved by Senate
Senator	• 30 years old • U.S. citizen 9 years • Live in state where elected	6 years	Originally chosen by state legislature (per Constitution) Currently elected by voters (per Seventeenth Amendment)
Representative	• 25 years old • U.S. citizen 7 years • Live in state where elected	2 years	Elected by voters of district

President Franklin D. Roosevelt gave many radio speeches.

Geography Skills
Reading Charts

1. What are the age requirements for federal officials?

2. Are members of Congress required to live in the states they represent?

History Note 3

Franklin D. Roosevelt, the only president elected to more than two terms, was elected four times. In 1951 the Twenty-second Amendment was ratified, limiting any one president to two terms. In 1995 the U.S. Supreme Court ruled that neither the states nor Congress could pass laws limiting congressmembers' terms. A constitutional amendment that limits the terms of congressmembers has failed to pass Congress.

The Expanding Electorate

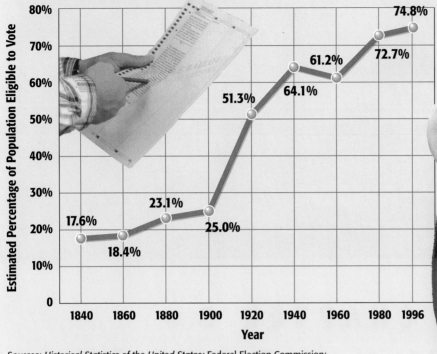

Estimated Percentage of Population Eligible to Vote vs. Year

- 17.6% (1840)
- 18.4% (1860)
- 23.1% (1880)
- 25.0% (1900)
- 51.3% (1920)
- 64.1% (1940)
- 61.2% (1960)
- 72.7% (1980)
- 74.8% (1996)

Sources: *Historical Statistics of the United States;* Federal Election Commission; *Congressional Quarterly's Guide to U.S. Elections; Datapedia of the United States, 1790-2000: America Year by Year*

Geography Skills
Reading Line Graphs

1. What three years show the largest increases in the percentage of the U.S. population eligible to vote?
2. What amendments to the Constitution help explain the changes in 1920 and 1980?

History Note 4

The Constitution generally gives states the right to decide who is eligible to vote in elections. Over the years, however, constitutional amendments have extended the right to vote to more and more people. The Fifteenth Amendment, ratified in 1870, protects the right of people of any race to vote. The Nineteenth Amendment, passed in 1920, gives women the right to vote in all states. The Twenty-sixth Amendment, passed in 1971, lowered the minimum voting age from 21 to 18.

Albert Bierstadt, Emigrants Crossing the Plains, 1867, Oil on Canvas, A011.IT: National Cowboy Hall of Fame, Oklahoma City, OK

▪ CHAPTER 3 ▪
The Nation Expands
(1789–1865)

As the 1800s began, the United States was a young country with limitless opportunities for the future. In his first inaugural address, President Thomas Jefferson described the United States as "a rising nation, spread over a wide and fruitful land, traversing [crossing] all the seas with the rich productions of their industry."

THEMES

Global Relations
Why might nations go to war?

Citizenship and Democracy
How might citizens try to extend equal rights to all people?

Technology and Society
How might changes in technology affect a nation's economy and society?

| 1790 | 1800 | 1810 | 1820 |

1789 George Washington is elected president.

1804 Lewis and Clark set out on their journey west.

1814 Britain and the United States sign the Treaty of Ghent, ending the War of 1812.

Launching the Nation

Reading Focus

What problems did President Washington face at home and abroad?

How did Alexander Hamilton help solve the nation's economic problems?

What challenges did John Adams face during his presidency?

Key Terms

Judiciary Act

strict construction

loose construction

Whiskey Rebellion

political parties

XYZ affair

Alien and Sedition Acts

Twelfth Amendment

ONCE THE STATES HAD *ratified the U.S. Constitution, George Washington looked forward to retiring from public life and living quietly on his Virginia farm. However, his friends soon drew him into politics as a presidential candidate. When Washington hesitated to run, fellow politician Gouverneur Morris told him, "Should the idea prevail [become known] that you would not accept the presidency, it should prove fatal . . . to the new government." Morris concluded confidently, "Of all men, you are the best fitted to fill that office."*

Courtesy of the John Carter Brown Library at Brown University

1788 print of George Washington with state seals

IMAGE ON LEFT PAGE: *Albert Bierstadt's painting* Emigrants Crossing the Plains *shows settlers moving west in the mid-1800s.*

1830

1840

1850

1860

1836 Texas wins its independence from Mexico.

1846 Congress declares war on Mexico.

1865 General Lee surrenders at Appomattox Courthouse, ending the Civil War.

1830 Congress passes the Indian Removal Act.

1857 The Supreme Court issues the *Dred Scott* decision.

Washington Sets Precedents

In February 1789 the electoral college unanimously elected George Washington president, with John Adams as vice president. After taking office, President Washington wrote, "The first of everything in our situation will serve to establish a precedent." A precedent is an action or decision that later serves as an example.

Congress organized the executive branch, creating departments that specialized in different areas of national policy. Washington appointed Alexander Hamilton as secretary of the treasury, Thomas Jefferson as secretary of state, Henry Knox as secretary of war, and Samuel Osgood as postmaster general. Washington began to meet with the department heads as a group, which became known as the cabinet.

In September 1789 Congress passed the **Judiciary Act**, creating the federal court system. Washington appointed John Jay as the first chief justice of the United States and Edmund Randolph as attorney general. Washington wrote to the Supreme Court justices:

> ❝ **The happiness of the people of the United States . . . depend[s] in a considerable degree on the interpretation and execution of its laws.** ❞

President Washington with some of his key advisers (left to right): Washington, Henry Knox, Alexander Hamilton, Thomas Jefferson, and Edmund Randolph

Hamilton and National Finances

As secretary of the treasury, Alexander Hamilton had to deal with the national debt—the amount of money the United States owed to various lenders. The U.S. government had raised some money by selling bonds, or certificates that represent money owed, to citizens. It promised to buy the bonds back later at a higher price. To maintain the trust of lenders, Hamilton proposed that the federal government pay its debt to foreign nations and repay citizens the full value of all bonds. Despite opposition from Thomas Jefferson and Representative James Madison, Congress approved Hamilton's plan.

The U.S. Mint made its first coins in 1792.

Hamilton also wanted the federal government to assume, or pay, most of the debts owed by the states for Revolutionary War expenses. The southern states, which had few war debts, did not want their citizens to be taxed to help pay the debts of other states. However, they did want to move the nation's capital. They believed that having the capital in New York gave the northern states too much influence. As a compromise, Congress approved the debt assumption plan and chose the site of present-day Washington, D.C., as the new national capital.

Hamilton wanted to create a national bank to provide a safe place to deposit government funds and to serve as a source of loans for the government and businesses. Madison and Jefferson opposed the bank because they believed in **strict construction**—that the federal government could do only what the Constitution specifically said it could do. Hamilton argued for **loose construction**, meaning that the federal government could take reasonable actions that the Constitution did not specifically forbid it from taking. In his opinion, the clause in Article I, Section 8, stating that Congress has the right "to make all laws . . . necessary and proper" was "elastic," or intended to be flexible. President Washington and Congress supported Hamilton. In 1791 Congress chartered the Bank of the United States for 20 years.

George Washington

George Washington entered the presidency with a tremendous sense of responsibility to the country. He wanted to be both a proper, dignified leader and a president who listened to the needs of the people.

Washington was sometimes trapped between the importance of his office and his wish to be treated like an ordinary citizen. At his inauguration, for example, Washington told his military guard, "The affection of my fellow citizens is all the guard I want." However, he decided that the escort was necessary to maintain the dignity of the presidency.

The pressure to live up to the country's expectations often made life difficult for Washington. He was very sensitive to attacks made against him in the press, leading Thomas Jefferson to write, "I think he feels those things [criticisms] more than any person I ever met." Washington did not run for re-election in 1796. He had little time to enjoy his retirement from politics, however, because he died in 1799.

New Conflicts

In 1793 France declared war on Britain. On April 22, President Washington issued the Neutrality Proclamation, which stated that the United States would remain neutral toward all nations at war in Europe. However, both Britain and France violated U.S. neutrality. Some French agents tried to recruit American ships to attack the British. Britain seized hundreds of American merchant ships trading with the French West Indies. Rumors spread that the British were also encouraging American Indians to fight against American settlers on the frontier. Washington sent John Jay to London to negotiate a peaceful resolution. The Senate ratified Jay's Treaty in 1795. That same year, diplomat Thomas Pinckney arranged a treaty with Spain, which had closed the port of New Orleans to U.S. trade. In Pinckney's Treaty, Spain agreed to reopen New Orleans to American shipping.

Washington also faced domestic issues. As settlers moved to the Northwest Territory, they forced American Indians off their lands. An Indian confederation led by Chief Little Turtle of the Miami defeated U.S. forces in 1790 and 1791. Then on August 20, 1794, General Anthony Wayne defeated the confederation in the Battle of Fallen Timbers. In 1795 Indian leaders signed the Treaty of Greenville, giving Americans access to Indian lands in most of present-day Ohio.

More conflict broke out after Congress passed a tax on U.S.-made whiskey to help pay off the national debt. Some protesters in rural western Pennsylvania reacted violently. Washington ordered several states to call out their militias and led more than 10,000 soldiers toward the area. Most of the rebels fled as the troops approached, thus ending the **Whiskey Rebellion** in November 1794 without a real battle.

Having faithfully served as president for two terms, Washington decided not to run again. In his Farewell Address, he warned that the greatest threats to America were public debt, foreign alliances, and political divisions at home.

The Granger Collection, New York

Pennsylvanians opposed to the whiskey tax tar and feather a tax collector.

Washington's Farewell Address

On September 19, 1796, President George Washington's Farewell Address first appeared in a Philadelphia newspaper. In the following excerpt he advised the nation on its economy, political parties, and foreign policy.

In contemplating [considering] the causes which may disturb our Union, it occurs as matter of serious concern that any ground should have been furnished for characterizing parties by geographical discriminations: Northern and Southern; Atlantic and Western. . . .

Let me now . . . warn you in the most solemn manner against the baneful [destructive] effects of the spirit of party generally. . . .

Of all the dispositions and habits which lead to political prosperity, religion and morality are indispensable [necessary] supports. . . .

Promote, then, as an object of primary importance, institutions for the general diffusion [spreading] of knowledge. In proportion as the structure of a government gives force to public opinion, it is essential that public opinion should be enlightened.

As a very important source of strength and security, cherish public credit. One method of preserving it is to use it as sparingly as possible, . . . avoiding likewise the accumulation of debt, . . . not ungenerously throwing upon posterity [future generations] the burden which we ourselves ought to bear. . . .

Observe good faith and justice toward all nations. Cultivate [seek] peace and harmony with all. . . .

The great rule of conduct for us, in regard to foreign nations, is in extending our commercial relations to have with them as little political connection as possible. . . .

It is our true policy to steer clear of permanent alliances with any portion of the foreign world.

Understanding Primary Sources

1. What was President Washington's most important advice?

2. Do you think his advice is still important today? Explain your answer.

 President John Adams

Despite George Washington's warning, **political parties**—groups that help elect government officials and influence government policies—played an important role in the 1796 presidential election. Alexander Hamilton helped shape the Federalist Party's policies, which included strengthening the federal government and promoting trade and industry. The Federalists, who were most popular in New England, nominated former vice president John Adams and Thomas Pinckney.

Thomas Jefferson and James Madison started the Democratic-Republican Party, or Republicans, which wanted to limit the power of the federal government. The party was most popular in the South and the West. The Republicans chose Thomas Jefferson and Aaron Burr as their candidates. Adams received 71 electoral votes, and Jefferson came in second with 68. Under the Constitution at that time, the second-place finisher became vice president, even if that person was from a different political party than the president. Thus, Adams and Jefferson served together.

The XYZ Affair

John Adams campaign button

One of Adams's first actions as president was to send a diplomatic team to Paris to improve relations with France. Three French agents informed the U.S. diplomats that negotiations would not begin without a $250,000 bribe. The furious diplomats refused to meet this demand and told Adams that their mission was a failure. On hearing the news of the so-called **XYZ affair**, Federalists called for war with France, crying, "Millions for defense, but not one cent for tribute [forced payment]!" At Adams's urging, Congress strengthened the army and the navy. However, Adams stunned many Federalists by not asking Congress to declare war on France. In 1800 the United States and France signed a treaty that ended the undeclared war that was being fought on the seas.

Republicans criticized Federalist support for war with France. To quiet the criticism, the Federalist-controlled Congress passed the **Alien and Sedition Acts** in 1798. The Alien Act allowed the president to deport, or expel, foreign citizens from the United States on suspicion of antigovernment activities. The Sedition Act made it illegal to "write, print, utter or publish" any false or hostile words against the U.S. government or the administration's policies.

In response, Jefferson and Madison wrote the Virginia and Kentucky Resolutions. They argued that the Alien and Sedition Acts were unconstitutional because they went beyond the powers granted to the federal government and interfered with the powers of the state governments. Future politicians used the resolutions to argue that the states could declare laws or actions of the federal government to be illegal.

The Election of 1800

In the 1800 presidential election, Thomas Jefferson and Aaron Burr defeated John Adams and Charles Pinckney. Jefferson and Burr received 73 electoral votes each. Voters could not vote separately for president and vice president, so the House of Representatives broke the tie, electing Jefferson president. In 1804 the states ratified the **Twelfth Amendment**, which required a separate ballot for president and vice president. The election of 1800 proved that the nation could transfer power peacefully from one party to another. Jefferson later wrote that the election was

❝as real a revolution in the principles of our government as that of 1776 was in its form; . . . [caused] by the rational and peaceable instrument of reform, the suffrage [vote] of the people.❞

SECTION 1 REVIEW

Identify and explain the significance of the following:
- **George Washington**
- **Judiciary Act**
- **strict construction**
- **loose construction**
- **Whiskey Rebellion**
- **political parties**
- **John Adams**
- **XYZ affair**
- **Alien and Sedition Acts**
- **Thomas Jefferson**
- **Twelfth Amendment**

Reading for Content Understanding

1 **Main Idea** What foreign and domestic difficulties did President Washington face?

2 **Main Idea** What issues did John Adams face as president?

3 **Economic Development** What were Alexander Hamilton's plans for improving the U.S. economy?

4 **Writing** *Creating* Write an editorial commenting on the rise of political parties.

5 **Critical Thinking** *Supporting a Point of View* Do you think that the founding of the national bank was constitutional? Explain your answer.

Building a Strong Nation

Reading Focus

What was the significance of the Lewis and Clark expedition?

What led to the War of 1812, and what was the outcome?

How did Andrew Jackson respond to domestic issues during his presidency?

Key Terms

judicial review

Louisiana Purchase

Battle of New Orleans

Treaty of Ghent

Monroe Doctrine

Missouri Compromise

Democratic Party

states' rights

Indian Removal Act

THE DAY WAS MARCH 4, 1801, and Thomas Jefferson was about to be sworn in as president of the United States in the new capital city of Washington. While George Washington and John Adams had worn splendid outfits and ridden in carriages to their inaugurations, Jefferson chose to walk the few blocks from his boardinghouse to the Capitol Building. A reporter observed, "His dress was, as usual, that of a plain citizen, without any distinctive badge of office." Known by some Republicans as "The People's Friend," Jefferson demonstrated his views on government by not wearing fancy clothes to the inauguration.

Coin celebrating Jefferson's inauguration

Jefferson in Office

President Jefferson kept some Federalist policies and institutions, such as the Bank of the United States. However, he decreased military spending and repealed domestic taxes. He also told Secretary of State James Madison to withhold some commissions of judges that President Adams had appointed late in the evening before he left office.

One such "midnight judge," William Marbury, argued that under the Judiciary Act of 1789, the Supreme Court had the authority to force the executive branch to hand over his commission. In *Marbury* v. *Madison* the Court ruled against Marbury, saying that some powers Congress had given the Court in the Judiciary Act were unconstitutional. Chief Justice John Marshall's ruling established the principle of **judicial review**, which means that the Supreme Court has the right to declare an act of Congress to be unconstitutional. The Court gained great power with this ruling. Although the Court's decision supported the actions of Jefferson's administration, the president would face many challenges ahead.

The Louisiana Purchase

President Jefferson was greatly concerned that France once again owned Louisiana:

> 66 **There is on the globe one single spot, the possessor of which is our natural and habitual enemy. It is New Orleans, through which the produce of three-eighths of our territory must pass to market.** 99

In response to a U.S. attempt to buy New Orleans, France offered to sell all of Louisiana for $15 million. On October 20, 1803, the Senate approved the **Louisiana Purchase**, which stretched west from the Mississippi River to the Rocky Mountains.

Jefferson sent a small expedition led by Meriwether Lewis and William Clark to explore the West. In May 1804 the Lewis and Clark expedition began its journey by going up the Missouri River. A Shoshoni woman named Sacagawea (sak-uh-juh-WEE-uh) helped the group cross the Great Plains. Other Shoshoni Indians led Lewis and Clark across the Rocky Mountains. After the difficult journey, the explorers followed the Columbia River to the Pacific Ocean.

Lewis and Clark explored the Pacific Northwest during the winter. In March 1806 the expedition started its long trek home, reaching St. Louis in September. In their reports and journals, Lewis and Clark described the West's lands and people. They also provided scientific information on the region's plants and animals.

An illustrated page from William Clark's journal

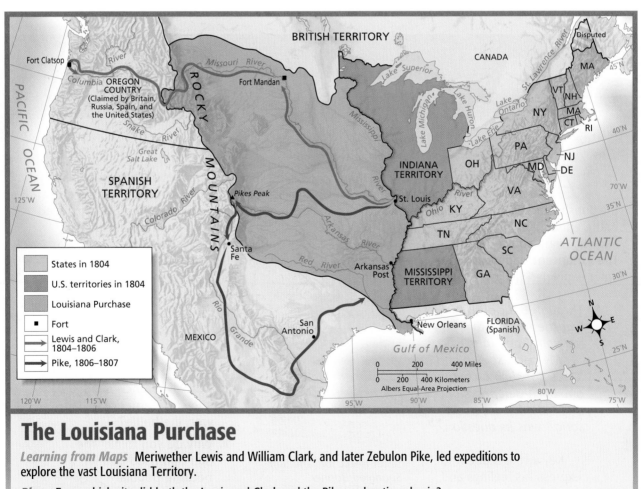

The Louisiana Purchase

Learning from Maps Meriwether Lewis and William Clark, and later Zebulon Pike, led expeditions to explore the vast Louisiana Territory.

Place From which city did both the Lewis and Clark and the Pike explorations begin?

Trouble with Britain

France had agreed to sell Louisiana in part because it was at war with Britain. Neither Britain nor France wanted the United States to supply war materials to its enemy. The British and French navies stopped and searched hundreds of American merchant ships. The British also searched the ships for deserters from the British navy. In a practice called impressment, the British forced these people and others to serve in their navy. British officials even impressed U.S. citizens, despite the protests of the U.S. government.

In 1807 Congress passed the Embargo Act, which in effect prohibited trade with all foreign nations. Northern economies, which relied heavily on trade, suffered, but the act did little to hurt Britain or France. In 1809 Congress repealed the unpopular law and passed the Non-Intercourse Act, which banned trade only with Britain and France. This act went into effect just before James Madison, the newly elected president, took office.

The War of 1812

Britain also angered many Americans by providing military aid to American Indians in the Northwest Territory. Tecumseh, a Shawnee chief, was trying to unite Indian nations into a confederation to oppose settlers. On November 7, 1811, Indiana Territory governor William Henry Harrison fought a group of Indians in the Battle of Tippecanoe. Harrison's soldiers forced the Indians to retreat and destroyed their village near the Tippecanoe River. Tecumseh thus lost the support he needed to create a great Indian confederacy.

Some members of Congress, the War Hawks, wanted to declare war on Britain. Federalists in New England, who preferred to renew friendly business ties with Britain, opposed them. Speaking to Congress on June 1, 1812, President Madison said that Britain was in "a state of war against the United States." In response, Congress declared war. A few months later, Madison was re-elected.

American Arts

The National Anthem

American Francis Scott Key was aboard a British warship when the British attacked Fort McHenry. When the battle ended, Key saw the U.S. flag still flying above the fort. The Americans had won. Key later explained his joy:

66 *Through the clouds of the war the stars of that banner still shone in my view. . . . My heart spoke; and 'Does not such a country and such defenders of their country deserve a song?' was its question.*99

Key wrote a poem to express his feelings and

Sheet music for "The Star-Spangled Banner"

set the verses to the melody of a popular song, which became quite popular. Soon Key's composition was published as "The Star-Spangled Banner." A few months later, Americans played the new piece at the Battle of New Orleans. In 1931 "The Star-Spangled Banner" became the official national anthem of the United States.

Understanding the Arts

1. How did Francis Scott Key know the Americans had won the battle?

2. Why do you think "The Star-Spangled Banner" became popular?

British forces set fire to many government buildings in Washington during the War of 1812.

Early in the war, a U.S. invasion of Canada failed, giving Britain control of the strategic Great Lakes region. On September 10, 1813, U.S. captain Oliver Hazard Perry's fleet won a battle on Lake Erie. Perry sent General William Henry Harrison a message: "We have met the enemy and they are ours." Harrison defeated the British and their American Indian allies in early October near the Thames River in Canada. Tecumseh's death in the battle ended the threat of the British–American Indian alliance in the Great Lakes area.

Farther south, Creek forces led by Red Eagle destroyed Fort Mims in present-day Alabama. Andrew Jackson, a general in the Tennessee militia, led his soldiers in a decisive victory over the Creek at Horseshoe Bend in 1814. Red Eagle surrendered days later, ending the Creek War.

Meanwhile, the British navy was blockading and attacking U.S. seaports. In 1814 the British captured Washington, setting fire to the White House and other buildings. The British then attacked Baltimore, Maryland, which was guarded by Fort McHenry. The Americans refused to surrender, and the British retreated. The British next attacked New Orleans on January 8, 1815. At the **Battle of New Orleans**, General Jackson won a great victory. Meanwhile, a peace treaty ending the war had been signed two weeks earlier.

The peace agreement that Jackson had yet to hear about was the **Treaty of Ghent**, signed on

American flag from 1818

December 24, 1814, in Belgium. Following months of negotiations, the treaty ended the War of 1812 and restored all conquered territory. However, the diplomats found no solutions to the problems of impressment or trade embargoes.

★ Peace and Prosperity

After the War of 1812, the United States entered "the Era of Good Feelings" with the election of James Monroe in 1816. He served two terms. During Monroe's presidency, the Convention of 1818 set the U.S.-Canada border at the 49th parallel and established the joint British and U.S. occupation of Oregon. In the 1819 Adams-Onís Treaty, Spain ceded, or gave up, Florida to the United States. At the time, Spain was involved in struggles with its Latin American colonies. In response, Monroe issued the **Monroe Doctrine** in 1823. The doctrine warned European nations not to colonize or interfere in the Americas.

Monroe faced a domestic crisis in 1819 when Missouri applied for statehood. At that time there were 11 free states and 11 slave states in the Union. Representative Henry Clay of Kentucky proposed the **Missouri Compromise**, which would let Missouri enter the Union as a slave state while Maine joined as a free state. The compromise would also prohibit slavery in any new territories or states formed north of the 36°30' line. Congress approved the compromise in 1820.

To unify the nation economically, Clay proposed the American System, a plan to use protective tariffs to boost domestic industries and to pay for internal improvements. Congress approved a protective tariff, and the first federal road project was the Cumberland, or National, Road. The road eventually ran from Maryland to Illinois. In the Northeast, canals were built because water transportation was usually quicker, easier, and cheaper than overland travel. New Yorkers paid about $7 million to build the Erie Canal, which ran from Buffalo to Albany. When it was completed in 1825, the canal opened up transportation between the Great Lakes region and New York City.

The Monroe Doctrine

1823

On December 2, 1823, President James Monroe issued what became known as the Monroe Doctrine. The following is an excerpt from the doctrine, which has had a significant effect on U.S. foreign policy.

We . . . declare that we should consider any attempt on their [European powers'] part to extend their [political] system to any portion of this hemisphere as dangerous to our peace and safety.

With the existing colonies or dependencies of any European power we have not interfered and shall not interfere. But with the governments who have declared their independence and maintained it, and whose independence we have . . . acknowledged, we could not view any interposition [interference] for the purpose of oppressing [unjustly ruling] them, or controlling in any other manner their destiny, by any European power in any other light than as the manifestation [realization] of an unfriendly disposition toward the United States. . . .

Our policy in regard to Europe . . . remains the same, which is, not to interfere in the internal concerns of any of its powers. . . . But in regard to those continents [the Americas], circumstances are . . . different. It is impossible that the allied powers should extend their political system to any portion of either continent without endangering our peace and happiness. . . .

It is equally impossible, therefore, that we should behold such interposition in any form with indifference.

Understanding Primary Sources

1. What warning did Monroe give to the European powers in the Monroe Doctrine?

2. What do you think is the most important part of this document?

The Age of Jackson

John Quincy Adams won the 1824 presidential election by defeating Andrew Jackson, who had campaigned as a representative of the common people. Jackson's supporters became known as the **Democratic Party**. Many supporters of President Adams began calling themselves National Republicans. Jackson and John C. Calhoun, his running mate, won the 1828 election.

Many white men voted for the first time in 1828. They had gained suffrage when states eliminated property ownership as a voting qualification. Political parties began holding nominating conventions—public meetings to select the party's presidential and vice presidential candidates. This democratic expansion is referred to as Jacksonian Democracy. President Jackson rewarded some of his supporters with government jobs—a practice known as the spoils system.

A national crisis arose before the 1828 election when Congress passed a high protective tariff. Southerners opposed it because the South relied heavily on imported goods. Calhoun, who was from South Carolina, supported **states' rights**, or the belief that state power should be greater than federal power. He wrote that states had the right to nullify, or cancel, federal laws. When Congress passed a new tariff in 1832, Calhoun resigned as vice president. South Carolina's legislature declared the tariffs to be "null, void . . . nor binding upon this State." Jackson threatened to send troops into South Carolina to enforce the law. The nullification crisis ended after Congress agreed to gradually lower the tariffs and South Carolina agreed to enforce the law.

Andrew Jackson

Also in 1832, Jackson vetoed a bill to renew the charter of the Second Bank of the United States. In *McCulloch* v. *Maryland*, the Supreme Court had ruled that the Constitution gave Congress implied powers, such as the right to establish the Bank. However, Jackson disagreed. In spite of his conflicts with Congress and the Court, he remained popular with voters and easily won re-election with Martin Van Buren as his running mate. He then moved most of the Bank's funds to state banks.

Van Buren won the 1836 presidential election. Soon after he took office, a financial crisis, known as the Panic of 1837, struck the nation. The resulting economic depression hurt his re-election campaign in 1840. William Henry Harrison, the hero of the Battle of Tippecanoe, won the election.

 ## Indian Removal

With President Jackson's support, Congress had passed the **Indian Removal Act** in 1830. This act authorized the removal of American Indians living east of the Mississippi River to Indian Territory. This newly created region contained most of present-day Oklahoma. To oversee federal Indian policy, Congress had created the Bureau of Indian Affairs. In the 1840s Indian removal in the former Northwest Territory was completed. In the Southeast, many of the Choctaw, Creek, and Chickasaw were removed in the 1830s.

In Georgia, the Cherokee sued the state, arguing that the tribe was an independent nation. In 1831 the Supreme Court disagreed, saying that tribes were "domestic dependent nations." Later, in *Worcester* v. *Georgia,* the Court ruled that only the federal government had authority over American Indians, but Georgia defied the ruling. The Cherokee were removed to Indian Territory in 1838. Almost one fourth of the 18,000 Cherokee died on this 800-mile walk known as the Trail of Tears.

In present-day Florida, Seminole leader Osceola called for armed resistance to removal:

66 **When the Great Spirit tells me to go with the white man, I go, but he tells me not to go. I have a rifle. . . . I say, we must not leave our homes and lands.** 99

Despite resistance, the U.S. Army removed some 3,000 Seminole and killed many others by 1842.

SECTION 2 REVIEW

Identify and explain the significance of the following:
- **judicial review**
- **Louisiana Purchase**
- **Andrew Jackson**
- **Battle of New Orleans**
- **Treaty of Ghent**
- **Monroe Doctrine**
- **Missouri Compromise**
- **Democratic Party**
- **states' rights**
- **Indian Removal Act**

Reading for Content Understanding

1 **Main Idea** What caused the War of 1812, and how did it end?

2 **Main Idea** How did President Jackson react to domestic crises?

3 **Constitutional Heritage** How did the Cherokee use the courts to resist removal?

4 **Writing** *Expressing* Write a one-paragraph report on the Lewis and Clark expedition explaining why the mission was important.

5 **Critical Thinking** *Evaluating* Why did the nation spend money on internal improvements in the early 1800s?

The North and the South

Reading Focus

How did the Industrial Revolution and the Transportation Revolution change life in the United States?

What effect did the cotton boom have on the South and slavery?

What did some of the major reform movements hope to achieve?

Key Terms

Industrial Revolution

nativists

Transportation Revolution

cotton gin

Nat Turner's Rebellion

abolition

Second Great Awakening

emancipation

Seneca Falls Convention

temperance movement

I N THE 1800S NEW IDEAS *and inventions transformed the way people lived and worked in the northern United States. Massachusetts senator Daniel Webster wrote enthusiastically in 1847 about advances in science and technology, "It is an extraordinary era in which we live. It is altogether new. The world has seen nothing like it before." What most impressed Webster was "the application of this scientific research to the pursuits of life."*

A steam engine design

The Industrial Revolution

In the mid-1700s Britain underwent the **Industrial Revolution**, a period of rapid growth in the use of machines in manufacturing and production. The first factories were textile mills that used water-powered machinery. With the help of Englishman Samuel Slater, American merchants built their first textile mill in Rhode Island in 1793. Most mills were in the Northeast because as one mill owner noted, "Our thousand rivers and streams afford [provide] an inexhaustible supply of . . . power."

Under the Rhode Island system, mill owners hired entire families and divided factory work into simple tasks. In 1813 businessman Francis Cabot

Lowell built his first textile mill in Waltham, Massachusetts. His idea of combining spinning and weaving cloth in one mill and employing single women to work in his factories became known as the Lowell system. When he needed more waterpower to expand, he built more mills in a town later named Lowell. The female workers, mostly from local farms, were known as Lowell girls. Visitors were dazzled by the machinery, clean factories, and workers' boardinghouses.

Changes in Working Life

As factory machines increased in size and speed, employees had to work faster to keep up with the equipment. Mill machinery was also dangerous, with many moving parts. A reporter described the working conditions at Lowell in 1846:

 Each girl usually attends three looms. Doing so requires constant attention. . . . The room is full of cotton filaments [fibers] and dust, which we were told are very harmful to the lungs.

As conditions worsened, immigrants replaced the Lowell girls. Between 1840 and 1860, more than 4 million immigrants, mostly from Ireland and Germany, came to the United States. These immigrants filled the need for cheap labor in the Industrial Revolution. However, many native-born citizens felt threatened by the immigrants' different backgrounds and the economic competition they presented. Americans who opposed immigration were called **nativists**. In 1850 a group of nativists founded what became known as the Know-Nothing Party, whose candidates won several state elections.

Low wages, long hours, and the fear of losing their jobs led many workers to form trade unions—organizations created to improve working conditions. Unions sometimes staged strikes, in which members refused to work in an attempt to force employers to meet union demands. Most early strikes failed because courts and police usually supported companies. To get laws changed, many unions became politically active.

In 1840 President Martin Van Buren granted federal employees a 10-hour workday. Union leaders wanted to extend this protection to employees of private businesses, who often put in 12 hours a day, six days a week. Although some states passed 10-hour-day laws, many companies avoided such laws by requiring workers to sign special contracts. Despite such setbacks, unions continued to fight for workplace reforms.

Changing Factories

As the Industrial Revolution progressed, more factory owners turned to steam instead of water-power to run their machinery. The use of steam engines allowed factories to be built in places that did not have suitable waterpower. Building factories closer to cities and transportation centers lowered the price of labor and shipping costs.

Some businesses also relied on mass production, or the efficient production of large numbers of identical goods. In the 1790s inventor Eli Whitney had tried to mass-produce rifles using a concept called interchangeable parts. This meant that each vital part that went into making a product would be made exactly the same. By the 1840s interchangeable parts allowed some factories to mass-produce goods.

★ The Transportation Revolution

The Industrial Revolution was fueled by the **Transportation Revolution**—a rapid growth in the speed and convenience of transportation. One new transportation method was the steamboat. The first successful commercial steamboat was Robert Fulton's *Clermont*, which sailed up the Hudson River on August 9, 1807. Steamboats were well suited to river travel because they could move quickly against the current and did not rely on uncertain winds. Steamboats shaved months off the travel time from New Orleans to Pittsburgh and lowered shipping prices more than 75 percent. These savings created a boom in trade and encouraged more settlers to move to the Midwest.

What the steamboat did for water travel, the train did for land travel. First developed in Britain,

This scene from an early New England textile mill shows the growing use of machinery in industry.

Science and Technology

The Age of Steam

Before the Industrial Revolution, people relied on natural sources of energy to do work. They used muscle power from animals or humans, waterpower from rivers, and wind power. This limited suitable factory locations and the speed of transportation.

The development of steam power introduced a new source of energy. The first steam engines were built in the early 1700s in Europe. Engineers such as Englishman James Watt greatly improved these early designs, making them more practical. The early steam engines were large and heavy with three main parts: the boiler, the cylinder, and the condenser. In the boiler a fuel such as wood or coal burned to heat water and produce steam. The steam then entered the cylinder, where it built up enough pressure to push a piston back and forth. The condenser increased the engine's power by pulling steam out of the cylinder, thus speeding up the piston.

Other machinery converted the piston's powerful back-and-forth motion into energy that could turn the paddlewheel of a steamboat, the wheels of a train, or the belts on a machine. These early "low-pressure" steam engines produced steady, reliable power.

American Oliver Evans helped develop a more powerful steam engine. Evans designed a smaller engine, without a condenser, that used steam at much higher pressure. Although it required more fuel to operate, Evans's high-pressure steam engine was simple to maintain. Such engines were ideal for steamboats running on the Mississippi or trains racing across the American countryside.

Steam power was often dangerous. As engineers on steamboats or steam trains tried to get the most power out of their engines, the high-pressure boilers often exploded, injuring or killing people. Engineers continued to use and improve steam engines. Eventually, factories began to use steam power, allowing them to be built in areas that did not have access to waterpower.

Understanding What You Read

1. How did early steam engines work?
2. How do you think steam engines changed the way people lived and worked?

Throttle lever · Steam dome · Steam room · Water · Firebox · Steam flow · Steam control valve · Piston steam-powered trains became popular in the United States in the 1830s. By 1860 there were about 30,000 miles of railroad track linking almost every major city in the eastern United States. Senator Daniel Webster declared in 1847 that the railroad "towers above all other inventions of this or the preceding [previous] age."

Around the same time, Samuel Morse invented the telegraph. Telegraph companies strung telegraph lines on poles alongside railroads and opened telegraph offices in many train stations. By 1854 more than 15,000 miles of telegraph cable connected cities throughout the United States.

Slaves made crafts, such as this quilt, that reflected their culture.

★ The South and Slavery

The textile boom increased the demand for cotton. At the same time, the South's major cash crops—tobacco, rice, and indigo—were greatly decreasing in price. Growing cotton became more profitable in the 1790s when inventor Eli Whitney developed the **cotton gin**. This machine removed the seeds from cotton much faster than workers could by hand. By 1860 cotton accounted for more than half of all U.S. exports. Most of the South—from South Carolina to east Texas—formed what is known as the Cotton Kingdom, or cotton belt. This region grew most of the country's cotton crop.

Growing and harvesting cotton required many field hands, as did other southern crops such as rice and Louisiana sugarcane. Rather than hiring workers through a wage-labor system, the South relied heavily on slaves. In the first half of the 1800s, about one third of white southern families owned slaves. A smaller percentage were planters, large-scale farmers who owned more than 20 slaves. Despite their small numbers, planters held a lot of political power. To a smaller degree, slavery was also practiced in the North, but it had much less economic importance than in the South.

By 1860 more than half of all free African Americans lived in the South. To many white southerners, free African Americans threatened the institution of slavery because they proved that

African Americans could live outside the slave system. Many cities and states passed laws limiting the rights of free African Americans, such as the right to vote, travel freely, or hold certain jobs.

Most southern communities also passed strict slave codes prohibiting slaves from traveling or learning to read or write. Slaveholders often relied on harsh punishments and threats to ensure slaves' obedience. On large plantations, the majority of slaves were assigned specific jobs. They usually worked in the fields from sunrise to sunset.

Despite the harsh realities of daily life, many slaves found comfort in their community and culture. The most important unit of slave communities was the family. Slaves feared being sold to another plantation and separated from their families. To

U.S. Cotton Production, 1790–1860

3,841,000 bales 1860

Invention of cotton gin 1793

Cotton (in 100,000 bales)

Year

Source: *Historical Statistics of the United States*

King Cotton The cotton gin led to dramatic increases in southern cotton production, which exceeded 1 million bales by 1835. During what decades did cotton production nearly double?

Slave auctions like this one often resulted in the breakup of slave families.

make sure that the children never forgot their heritage, enslaved parents told them stories passed down from earlier generations. Slaves also told folktales that taught lessons about how to survive under slavery.

Another important aspect of slave culture was religion. Some slaves expressed their religious beliefs through spirituals. These emotional Christian songs blended African and European traditions. Many spirituals, such as "The Heavenly Road," reflected slaves' belief in their equality before God:

❝ Come, my brother, if you never did pray,
   I hope you may pray tonight;
   For I really believe I'm a child of God
   As I walk in the heavenly road. ❞

In small ways, slaves tried to gain a measure of control over their lives. Some slaves ran away. Others worked slowly to protest work conditions. While violent slave revolts were rare, planters lived in fear that such revolts would occur. Nat Turner led the most violent slave revolt in the United States. A well-educated slave from Virginia, Turner believed that God had called on him to overthrow slavery. Almost 60 white people were killed during **Nat Turner's Rebellion** in August 1831. More than 100 slaves were killed in putting down the rebellion, and Turner was tried and executed. As a result of the rebellion, many states strengthened their slave codes.

Frederick Douglass

⭐ The Abolition Movement

During the 1830s Americans organized a movement to support **abolition**, or a complete end to slavery, in the United States. The **Second Great Awakening**, a period of evangelism that began in the 1790s and had become widespread by the 1830s, helped further the abolition movement. Many ministers, in particular Charles Grandison Finney, believed that slavery was morally wrong. These ministers inspired followers to become abolitionists. The ideal of the Declaration of Independence, that all men are created equal, inspired other abolitionists.

Abolitionists furthered their cause with speaking tours, newspapers, and pamphlets. Leading abolitionist William Lloyd Garrison published the *Liberator,* an antislavery newspaper. He also helped found the American Anti-Slavery Society in 1833. This group wanted immediate **emancipation**, or freedom from slavery, as well as equality for African Americans. Two white southerners, sisters Angelina and Sarah Grimké, also became well-known antislavery activists. Angelina Grimké asked southern women to "persuade your husband, father, brothers and sons that slavery is a crime *against God and man.*"

Many former slaves were active in the antislavery movement. Some, like Frederick Douglass, shared powerful stories of their lives in captivity through written slave narratives and speeches. Douglass published a newspaper called the *North Star* and became one of the most important African American leaders of the 1800s. Former slaves Henry Highland Garnet and Sojourner Truth also fought for the abolitionist cause.

By the 1830s a loosely organized group of abolitionists had begun helping slaves escape to the North and to Canada. They created the Underground Railroad, a network of people who arranged transportation and hiding places for fugitives, or escaped slaves. Escaped slave Harriet

Tubman returned to the South and led hundreds of slaves to freedom during her lifetime.

Reforming Society

Women who had to defend their role in the anti-slavery movement, such as Sojourner Truth and the Grimké sisters, also began to fight for women's rights. Elizabeth Cady Stanton and Lucretia Mott organized the **Seneca Falls Convention**, held in Seneca Falls, New York, in July 1848. At the convention, 100 people signed the Declaration of Sentiments, which listed the injustices that women suffered in society.

The convention launched the organized women's rights movement in the United States. Susan B. Anthony, Elizabeth Cady Stanton, and Lucy Stone emerged as its major leaders. Thousands of women participated in the struggle. They demanded equal pay for equal work, equal educational opportunities, property rights for married women, and the right to vote. These women had some success, such as gaining property rights for married women, but did not gain other major reforms, such as the right to vote, for many years.

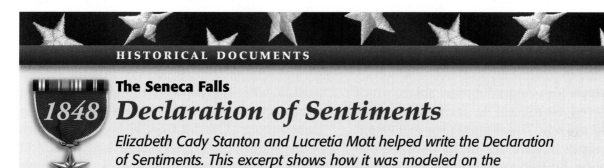

HISTORICAL DOCUMENTS

The Seneca Falls

1848 *Declaration of Sentiments*

Elizabeth Cady Stanton and Lucretia Mott helped write the Declaration of Sentiments. This excerpt shows how it was modeled on the Declaration of Independence.

We hold these truths to be self-evident: that all men and women are created equal; that they are endowed [provided] by their Creator with certain inalienable [permanent] rights; that among these are life, liberty, and the pursuit of happiness....

The history of mankind is a history of repeated injuries and usurpations [seizures] on the part of man toward woman, having in direct object the establishment of an absolute tyranny [unjust rule] over her. To prove this, let facts be submitted to a candid [fair] world.

He has never permitted her to exercise her inalienable right to [vote]....

He has taken from her all right in property, even to the wages she earns....

He has monopolized nearly all the profitable employments, and from those she is permitted to follow, she receives but a scanty remuneration [payment]. He closes against her all the avenues to wealth and distinction which he considers most honorable to himself....

He has denied her the facilities for obtaining a thorough education, all colleges being closed against her....

He has endeavored [tried], in every way that he could, to destroy her confidence in her own powers, to lessen her self-respect, and to make her willing to lead a dependent and abject [hopeless] life....

Resolved, That woman is man's equal—was intended to be so by the Creator, and the highest good of the race demands that she should be recognized as such.

Understanding Primary Sources

1. What are some of the injustices that the declaration describes?

2. How is the Declaration of Sentiments modeled after the Declaration of Independence?

Reformers also tried to improve social conditions in the United States. Cities faced many challenges as a result of the rapid growth that occurred when immigrants and rural inhabitants moved to urban areas in search of jobs. Many urban residents, particularly immigrants, lived in overcrowded and poorly built apartments. Epidemics were fairly common because cities lacked clean water, public health regulations, or sanitary ways to dispose of garbage and human waste. Reformers hoped to improve these urban living conditions.

Reformers also targeted alcohol abuse, which they believed contributed to crime, family violence, and poverty. This **temperance movement** urged people to give up or to limit alcohol consumption. By 1855 thirteen states had banned or restricted alcohol sales.

Dorothea Dix helped reform prisons after finding terrible conditions and poor treatment of people with mental illnesses in Massachusetts jails. Her efforts also led to the establishment of state hospitals where people with mental illnesses could receive professional treatment.

A temperance poster

One of the most important reform efforts was the movement to improve children's education. As the immigrant population grew, reformers argued that the nation needed a better education system to help people acquire the skills needed to become responsible citizens. The common-school movement argued that all children, regardless of their economic background, should be educated in a common place. Reformer Horace Mann led this movement during the mid-1800s.

Educational opportunities improved for women when Emma Willard opened the first college-level institution for female students in the United States. Oberlin College became the first coeducational college, admitting both men and women, and the first college to accept African Americans. Educational opportunities expanded for African Americans when black colleges were founded. Efforts to improve education also extended to people with special needs, such as those with hearing or visual impairments. Thus, the efforts of school reformers reached many parts of American society.

SECTION 3 REVIEW

Identify and explain the significance of the following:

- **Industrial Revolution**
- **nativists**
- **Transportation Revolution**
- **cotton gin**
- **Nat Turner's Rebellion**
- **abolition**
- **Second Great Awakening**
- **emancipation**
- **Seneca Falls Convention**
- **temperance movement**

Reading for Content Understanding

1 **Main Idea** How did the cotton boom affect the South and slavery?

2 **Main Idea** What were the main goals of the women's rights movement?

3 **Economic Development** How did the Industrial Revolution and the Transportation Revolution affect Americans?

4 **Writing** *Creating* Imagine that you are a member of a society for reform, such as abolition or education. Create a poster outlining the goals of your movement.

5 **Critical Thinking** *Making Comparisons* How do you think some of the reform movements of the mid-1800s are similar to or different from reform efforts today?

Expanding West

Reading Focus

What events led Texas to win its independence from Mexico?

What challenges did travelers face on the journey west?

What events led to the Mexican War, and what was its outcome?

Key Terms

Republic of Texas

Oregon Trail

manifest destiny

Treaty of Guadalupe Hidalgo

Mexican Cession

Gadsden Purchase

forty-niners

California Gold Rush

*I*N THE EARLY 1800S *American settlers and traders continued to push west. Pioneer Moses Austin recalled a typical conversation with hopeful early settlers: "Have you any [land]? No, but I expect I can get it. . . . Did you ever see the country? No, but everybody says it is good land." The settlers' quest for land brought them into contact with American Indians and Mexican citizens already living in the West.*

Alamo defender Davy Crockett's rifle

Alamo Collection, photograph courtesy the Daughters of the Republic of Texas Library

 ## American Settlers in Texas

In 1810 Father Miguel Hidalgo y Costilla led Mexicans in a rebellion against Spain. This revolt failed, but in 1821 Mexico became an independent nation. The Mexican government soon changed old Spanish policies. In California, it ended the mission system. In Texas, officials recruited settlers to increase its small population.

In 1821 Stephen F. Austin, the son of Moses Austin, brought 300 American families to Texas. These settlers agreed to become Mexican citizens, obey Mexican laws, and be loyal to the Catholic Church. By 1834 more than 20,000 Americans had moved to Texas. They greatly outnumbered

Tejanos, settlers of Spanish descent living in Texas. After American settlers ignored Mexico's laws, the government restricted U.S. immigration and enforced an existing ban on slavery. People who had brought slaves to Texas were upset. Other Texans believed that Texas was not fairly represented in the Mexican government.

These tensions led some Texans to revolt. The first battle of the Texas Revolution took place near the town of Gonzales in October 1835. In San Antonio, Texans led by William Travis and Jim Bowie occupied the Alamo, an old mission. Some Tennessee volunteers, including frontiersman Davy Crockett, joined them. As Mexican general Antonio López de Santa Anna marched his army toward San Antonio, Travis ignored orders to retreat. When Santa Anna arrived with about 3,000 soldiers, some 150 Texan soldiers were at the Alamo.

Santa Anna's army surrounded the Alamo for 13 days. Travis sent officer Juan Seguín and others to get reinforcements. About 30 arrived before the Mexican army attacked on March 6, 1836. The Mexicans suffered heavy losses, but soon overwhelmed the Texans and killed all the defenders. After the battle, Mexican forces attacked Texas troops near Goliad. Severely outnumbered, the Texans surrendered. Santa Anna charged them with treason and had them executed.

These losses failed to break the spirit of the Texas rebels. Sam Houston, the commander in chief of the new Texas army, decided to make a stand at San Jacinto, near present-day Houston. On April 21, 1836, the Texans attacked, yelling, "Remember the Alamo! Remember Goliad!" Caught by surprise, the Mexican army was destroyed. The Texans captured Santa Anna and forced him to recognize Texas independence. Voters elected Sam Houston as president of the **Republic of Texas**, which had become an independent nation.

★ The Journey West

As some Americans moved to Texas, others headed farther west. Mountain men went to the Rocky Mountains and beyond, trapping animals

Santa Anna surrenders to the wounded Sam Houston after the Battle of San Jacinto.

A mountain man

and selling their furs. The era of fur trading lasted only a few decades. By the 1840s settlers had begun to follow the mountain men to the West. Many Americans traveled to the Pacific Northwest. First missionaries such as Marcus and Narcissa Whitman and then settlers followed the **Oregon Trail**. This route stretched some 2,000 miles across the northern Great Plains and the Rocky Mountains. Most pioneers traveled in wagon trains. Their journey usually began in late spring and lasted about six months. The pioneers kept up a tiring pace from dawn until dusk. American Indians often helped them on their journey.

The Oregon Trail split into two branches. Most settlers followed the trail north to Oregon Country, which had fertile valleys for farming. Others took the southern route, the California Trail. These travelers were interested in trade, not settlement. In 1839 Swiss immigrant John Sutter built a colony known as Sutter's Fort, near the Sacramento River. It became a popular destination for traders. American merchants also traveled on the Santa Fe Trail, which ran from Independence, Missouri, to Santa Fe, New Mexico. The long trip across the desert and mountains was dangerous, but the lure of high profits drew the traders.

Some pioneers who headed west were Mormons, or members of the Church of Jesus Christ of Latter-Day Saints, founded in New York by Joseph Smith in 1830. Mormons were often persecuted for their beliefs and practices. In 1844 an anti-Mormon mob murdered Smith. The Mormons then decided to move west to present-day Utah. Brigham Young, the new head of the Mormon Church, organized the trek along the Mormon Trail. Upon seeing the Great Salt Lake in 1847, Young said, "This is the place whereon we will plant our feet." By 1860 about 40,000 Mormons lived in Utah.

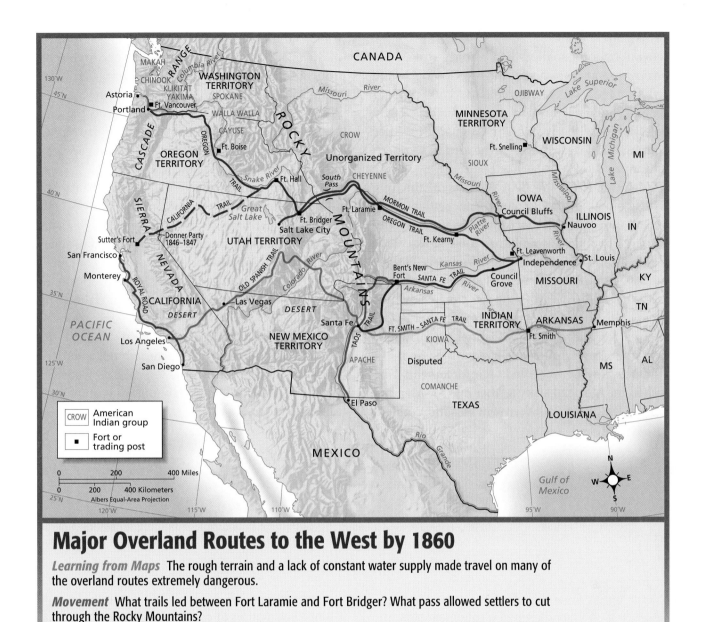

Major Overland Routes to the West by 1860

Learning from Maps The rough terrain and a lack of constant water supply made travel on many of the overland routes extremely dangerous.

Movement What trails led between Fort Laramie and Fort Bridger? What pass allowed settlers to cut through the Rocky Mountains?

★ Manifest Destiny

By the 1840s many Americans believed in **manifest destiny**, the idea that the United States was meant to expand across the continent to the Pacific Ocean. Democrat James K. Polk won the 1844 presidential election on a platform supporting westward expansion. In 1846 Britain agreed to give the United States all Oregon Country land south of the 49th parallel. This treaty established the final portion of the present-day U.S.-Canada border. Oregon became a U.S. territory in 1848.

After Congress voted to annex Texas in March 1845, Mexico cut off diplomatic relations with the United States. In addition, Mexico rejected the U.S. claim that the Rio Grande marked the southern border of Texas. President Polk ordered General Zachary Taylor to take about 3,500 soldiers into the disputed border region. After Polk learned that Mexican troops had crossed the river and attacked U.S. soldiers, he gave this message to Congress:

> **"Mexico has passed the boundary of the United States, has invaded our territory, and shed American blood upon the American soil. . . . The two nations are now at war."**

Two days later, on May 13, 1846, Congress declared war on Mexico.

The Mexican War

General Taylor's soldiers had already driven the Mexican troops back across the Rio Grande. While Taylor waited for reinforcements, Polk ordered General Stephen Kearny to attack Santa Fe. Kearny took the city without a fight in August 1846. After securing New Mexico, Kearny headed to southern California.

Meanwhile, in the Bear Flag Revolt in June 1846 a small group of American settlers near Sutter's Fort declared that California was an independent republic. Commodore John Drake Sloat seized California's capital at Monterey. Farther south, Commodore Robert Stockton planned a naval invasion. With support from Kearny's forces, Stockton captured Mexican-held Los Angeles, San Diego, and San Gabriel. By early 1847 Mexican forces in California had surrendered.

Once Taylor received reinforcements, he pushed the Mexican army farther into the Mexican interior. President Polk then sent General Winfield Scott to the port of Veracruz, the strongest fortress in Mexico. Scott's naval forces laid siege to the city until it fell on March 29. Scott next pushed more than 250 miles inland toward Mexico City. By August, U.S. troops were at the edge of the city. Mexican soldiers and civilians fought fierce battles on the outskirts of the capital. U.S. troops captured Mexico City on September 14, 1847.

Signed in February 1848, the **Treaty of Guadalupe Hidalgo** ceded much of Mexico's northern territory to the United States. This **Mexican Cession** included the present-day states of California, Nevada, and Utah. It also contained most of Arizona and New Mexico, parts of Colorado and Wyoming, and the area claimed by Texas north of the Rio Grande. Five years later, the United States acquired additional land in the **Gadsden Purchase** that included the southern parts of Arizona and New Mexico. The Gadsden Purchase fixed the southern boundaries of the continental United States.

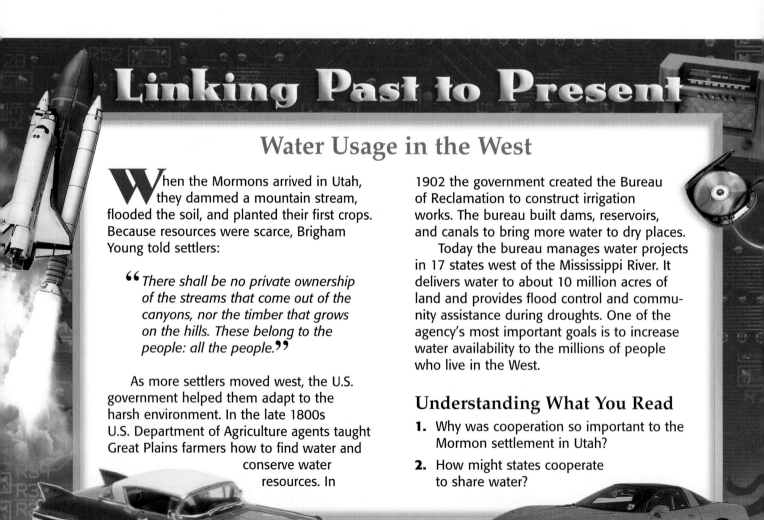

Linking Past to Present

Water Usage in the West

When the Mormons arrived in Utah, they dammed a mountain stream, flooded the soil, and planted their first crops. Because resources were scarce, Brigham Young told settlers:

“ *There shall be no private ownership of the streams that come out of the canyons, nor the timber that grows on the hills. These belong to the people: all the people.*”

As more settlers moved west, the U.S. government helped them adapt to the harsh environment. In the late 1800s U.S. Department of Agriculture agents taught Great Plains farmers how to find water and conserve water resources. In 1902 the government created the Bureau of Reclamation to construct irrigation works. The bureau built dams, reservoirs, and canals to bring more water to dry places.

Today the bureau manages water projects in 17 states west of the Mississippi River. It delivers water to about 10 million acres of land and provides flood control and community assistance during droughts. One of the agency's most important goals is to increase water availability to the millions of people who live in the West.

Understanding What You Read

1. Why was cooperation so important to the Mormon settlement in Utah?

2. How might states cooperate to share water?

The California Gold Rush

On January 24, 1848, James Marshall was building a sawmill near Sutter's Fort when he glanced down:

Gold-mining tools

❝ **My eye was caught with the glimpse of something shining in the bottom of the ditch. . . . I reached my hand down and picked it up; it made my heart thump, for I was certain it was gold.** ❞

In 1849 nearly 100,000 gold-seekers, known as **forty-niners**, traveled to California hoping to become rich. This event became known as the **California Gold Rush**. Some forty-niners took wagon trains across the country, while others traveled by sea. Most of these trips lasted three months or longer.

Few of the forty-niners had any previous gold-mining experience. The forty-niners would prospect, or search for gold, along the banks of streams or in shallow surface mines. The first prospector to arrive at a site would "stake a claim." Arguments and violent disputes often broke out over claims. There were few authorities to provide law and order in the mining communities. Mining camps and boom towns grew quickly when claims opened up and then disappeared just as quickly when claims died out.

In 1853 California's gold production peaked at more than $60 million. Few gold-rush miners became rich, however. Many settlers found that they could make a good living supplying miners with food, equipment, and services. Miners paid high prices for basic necessities because the large amounts of gold in circulation caused severe inflation in California.

The lure of gold in California attracted miners from around the world. Some 24,000 young Chinese men immigrated to California between 1849 and 1853. Prospectors also came from Mexico, South America, and Europe. More than 10,000 immigrants arrived in 1849 alone. Most forty-niners came to San Francisco.

California's economy was transformed by gold mining, trade, and business growth. Without the gold rush, California's population probably would have continued to grow slowly instead of increasing rapidly. The territory became eligible for statehood only two years after it was acquired by the United States.

SECTION 4 REVIEW

Identify and explain the significance of the following:
- **Republic of Texas**
- **Oregon Trail**
- **manifest destiny**
- **Treaty of Guadalupe Hidalgo**
- **Mexican Cession**
- **Gadsden Purchase**
- **forty-niners**
- **California Gold Rush**

Locate and explain the importance of the following:
- **Santa Fe**
- **San Francisco**

Reading for Content Understanding

1 **Main Idea** What difficulties did settlers have as they traveled west?

2 **Main Idea** What events caused the Mexican War, and what was the result?

3 **Geographic Diversity** *Movement* What effect did the gold rush have on California?

4 **Writing** *Informing* Write an article for a newspaper in Texas or Mexico explaining how Texas won its independence from Mexico. Include in your article an account of the fighting at the Alamo and the Battles of Goliad and San Jacinto.

5 **Critical Thinking** *Evaluating* Do you think the United States was justified in declaring war against Mexico? Explain your answer.

The Civil War

Reading Focus

What events demonstrated the growing sectional conflict over slavery?

What events led to the Civil War?

What battles occurred in the eastern and western theaters of war?

Key Terms

Compromise of 1850

Republican Party

Kansas-Nebraska Act

Dred Scott decision

Confederate States of America

Battle of Antietam

Emancipation Proclamation

Battle of Gettysburg

Gettysburg Address

Appomattox Courthouse

IN 1858 ABRAHAM LINCOLN *said, "'A house divided against itself cannot stand.'... I believe this government cannot endure, permanently half* slave *and half* free." *Lincoln stated that he did not expect the house to fall—nor did he think the Union would be dissolved. "But I* do *expect it will cease to be divided," he said. "It will become* all *one thing, or* all *the other." For many Americans in the mid-1800s, the issue of slavery was threatening national unity.*

The Granger Collection, New York

Abraham Lincoln

 ## Conflict over Slavery

California's application for statehood in 1850 threatened the balance between free and slave states that had been maintained since the Missouri Compromise. Senator Henry Clay proposed the **Compromise of 1850**, which let California enter the Union as a free state. The rest of the Mexican Cession was divided into two territories—Utah and New Mexico. Local voters would decide the issue of slavery in these territories. The voters would elect representatives to their legislatures, which would pass laws on slavery. The compromise also abolished the slave trade in the nation's capital and included the Fugitive Slave Act. This act made it a crime to assist runaway slaves and allowed them to be arrested even in areas where slavery was illegal. It increased support for the abolition movement.

Harriet Beecher Stowe's *Uncle Tom's Cabin*, published in 1852, also increased antislavery sentiment. Within a decade, the novel sold more than 2 million copies in the United States. In 1854 the **Republican Party** was formed mainly to prevent the spread of slavery to the West. That same year the **Kansas-Nebraska Act** was passed. It created two new territories, Kansas and Nebraska, where voters would decide the slavery issue. The act also ended the Missouri Compromise's restriction on slavery north of the 36°30' line.

Violence Breaks Out

Antislavery and pro-slavery groups rushed people to Kansas to vote in the election that would determine the issue of slavery there. When the results produced a pro-slavery territorial legislature, antislavery Kansans created their own legislature. Pro-slavery forces destroyed property and killed one man in the town of Lawrence in 1856. Abolitionist John Brown led a group to avenge the attack and killed five pro-slavery men. About 200 people died in the continuing violence, which newspapers called Bleeding Kansas.

In 1857 the U.S. Supreme Court dealt abolitionists a blow with the *Dred Scott* **decision**. Scott was a slave who sued for his freedom, saying that he had become free by living in free territory. The Court ruled that African Americans were not citizens under the Constitution. Therefore, they did not have the right to file suit in federal court. The Court also ruled that the Missouri Compromise's restriction on slavery was unconstitutional. This ruling meant that Congress had no right to ban slavery in any federal territory.

Sectional tensions increased in 1859 when John Brown seized the federal arsenal in Harpers Ferry, Virginia. U.S. Marines soon defeated Brown and his men, ending John Brown's raid. Brown was hanged for his acts on December 2, 1859. Southerners, however, were angered that many abolitionists called John Brown a hero.

Secession

Many southerners associated the Republican Party with abolitionists and John Brown. They were also concerned about the South's loss of power in Congress. They warned that a Republican victory in the 1860 presidential election would mean disunion. Republican Abraham Lincoln won the election. Four days later, South Carolina's legislature called a convention to consider secession, or withdrawing from the Union. On

Jefferson Davis

The Granger Collection, New York

Representatives in the House

YEAR	SLAVE STATES	FREE STATES
1840	88	135
1860	85	155

December 20, 1860, the delegates unanimously voted for secession. Mississippi, Florida, Alabama, Georgia, Louisiana, and Texas soon followed.

On February 4, delegates from the seceding states met in Montgomery, Alabama. They formed a new nation—the **Confederate States of America**, or the Confederacy. The delegates wrote a constitution and elected Jefferson Davis of Mississippi president of the Confederacy. Alexander Stephens of Georgia became vice president.

★ The Civil War Begins

Hoping to prevent more southern states from seceding, President Lincoln pledged in his inaugural address that he would not try to abolish slavery in the South. He promised the South that the federal "government will not assail [attack] you. You can have no conflict without being yourselves the aggressors." However, Lincoln also stated his intention to preserve the Union:

> ❝No State, upon its own mere motion, can lawfully get out of the Union. . . . Acts of violence, within any State or States, against the authority of the United States, are revolutionary.❞

The Confederacy was already seizing federal property and military bases in the South. On April 12, 1861, Confederate soldiers opened fire on Fort Sumter, which controlled the entrance to Charleston Harbor in South Carolina. After more than 30 hours of bombardment, Major Robert Anderson surrendered the fort. Lincoln declared that a state of rebellion existed in the South and called on the states to provide a total of 75,000 militiamen to put down the rebellion. Thousands of volunteers responded to Lincoln's call.

Virginia, North Carolina, Tennessee, and Arkansas joined the Confederacy shortly after Lincoln's request for troops. The largely pro-Union population of western Virginia broke away from the Confederacy. This led to the creation of West Virginia, which joined the Union in 1863. Four slave states—Delaware, Kentucky, Maryland, and Missouri— bordered the North. These border states remained in the Union.

Union army drum

The North had several key advantages over the South. With a much larger population, the North could recruit more soldiers. Most of the nation's factories— particularly those that could produce military supplies—were in the North. The region's network of railways allowed for more efficient movement of troops and supplies to the war front. The Union was also able to raise more money to spend on the war effort.

Union general Winfield Scott developed a two-part military strategy to defeat the South. He wanted to use a naval blockade to cut off southern seaports and strangle the South's economy. Scott also emphasized the need to gain control of the Mississippi River, which would separate Arkansas, Louisiana, and Texas from the Confederacy. Other northern leaders called for an attack on Richmond, Virginia, the Confederate capital.

The Confederacy's strategy was to defend itself against northern attacks and wear down the Union's will to fight. The South also hoped that Britain would support the Confederacy because of southern cotton's importance to Britain's textile industry. However, the South failed to gain any official foreign allies.

⭐ The War in the East

President Lincoln soon ordered General Irvin McDowell to push toward Richmond. In July 1861, Union soldiers met the Confederates about 25 miles southwest of Washington, along a creek called Bull Run. The Union troops drove the Confederate line back. Then a southern officer cried out, "Look! There is [Confederate general] Jackson standing like a stone wall! Rally behind the Virginians!" The Confederates responded and rallied behind "Stonewall" Jackson. When southern reinforcements arrived, the Union army retreated to Washington. As a result of this First Battle of Bull Run, the Union lost its hopes of quickly winning the war.

In the spring of 1862 Lincoln sent Union forces under the command of General George B. McClellan back into Virginia. By April 1862 McClellan had 100,000 troops near Richmond. He faced General Robert E. Lee. In 1861 Lee had refused Lincoln's request to take command of Union forces. After Virginia seceded, Lee resigned from the U.S. Army and joined the Confederates.

On June 26, 1862, Lee attacked McClellan in what became known as the Seven Days Battles. The Confederates suffered more than 20,000 casualties but inflicted nearly 16,000 on the Union and forced McClellan to retreat. Lincoln then ordered General John Pope to advance on Richmond from Washington. Caught off guard by Lee, Pope's army fell apart at the Second Battle of Bull Run. By the end of August 1862, Lee had pushed most of the Union forces out of Virginia.

Confederate leaders hoped that a major victory on Union soil would break northern morale and secure European aid. On September 17, 1862, the Union army met the Confederates along Antietam Creek in Maryland. The **Battle of Antietam** was the bloodiest single-day battle of the war—and in U.S. history. The Confederacy suffered more than 13,700 casualties and the Union

General Robert E. Lee was widely respected in the North and the South for his leadership.

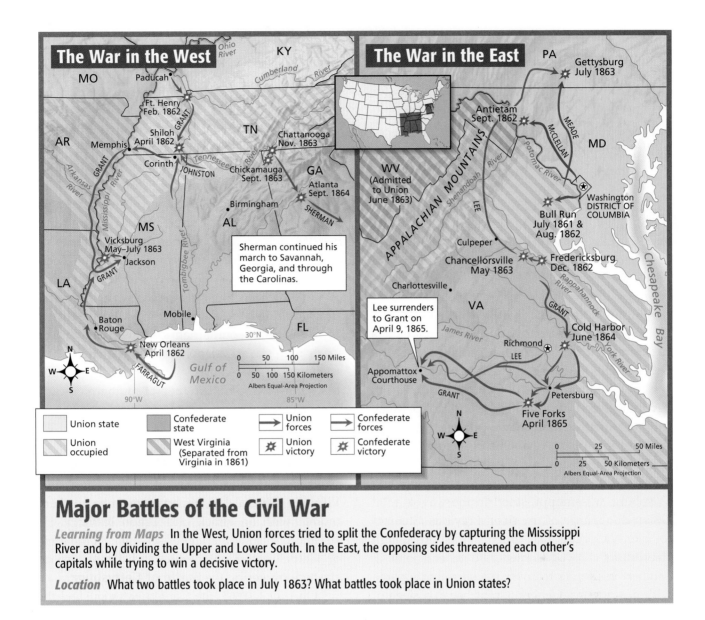

The War in the West

The War in the East

Sherman continued his march to Savannah, Georgia, and through the Carolinas.

Lee surrenders to Grant on April 9, 1865.

| Union state | Confederate state | → Union forces | → Confederate forces |
| Union occupied | West Virginia (Separated from Virginia in 1861) | Union victory | Confederate victory |

Major Battles of the Civil War

Learning from Maps In the West, Union forces tried to split the Confederacy by capturing the Mississippi River and by dividing the Upper and Lower South. In the East, the opposing sides threatened each other's capitals while trying to win a decisive victory.

Location What two battles took place in July 1863? What battles took place in Union states?

about 12,500. The battle was an important victory for the Union. Lee lost nearly a third of his troops, and his advance was stopped. However, McClellan refused to pursue Lee's retreating troops. This led Lincoln to later relieve McClellan of his command.

On September 22, 1862, after the victory at Antietam, Lincoln issued the **Emancipation Proclamation**. This proclamation called for all slaves in nonoccupied areas rebelling against the Union to be freed. It went into effect on January 1, 1863. Abolitionist Frederick Douglass wrote, "We shout for joy that we live to record this righteous decree [order]." Congress then authorized African Americans to enlist in the army. During the war, about 180,000 African Americans served with the Union Army.

 The War in the West

Union strategy in the West focused on controlling the Mississippi River. The most important figure in the western theater of war was General Ulysses S. Grant. When the Civil War broke out, Grant volunteered for service with the Union army. His aggressiveness in battle set him apart from Union leaders such as General McClellan.

In early 1862 Grant led Union troops into Tennessee. With help from Union navy gunboats, Grant took Fort Henry and Fort Donelson. He continued his advance south. On April 6 the Confederates caught Grant by surprise and pushed the Union army back at the Battle of Shiloh. Grant ordered his troops to hold their

Confederate general George Pickett led thousands of troops in a costly charge against Union forces at the Battle of Gettysburg.

ground, whatever the cost. During the night, Union reinforcements arrived. Grant mounted a counterattack the next day and forced the Confederates to retreat.

The Union army next focused on capturing key southern positions along the Mississippi River. In late April, Union naval officer David G. Farragut captured New Orleans. He then proceeded up the Mississippi, taking Baton Rouge, Louisiana, as well as Natchez, Mississippi. Only Vicksburg, Mississippi, stood in the way of total Union dominance of the river. Previous attempts to take Vicksburg had failed. Vicksburg's high river bluffs allowed Confederate general John C. Pemberton's forces to cover the surrounding area with heavy guns. General Grant began a siege of Vicksburg in mid-May. As supplies ran out, the city's residents resorted to eating horses, dogs, and rats. Pemberton surrendered on July 4, 1863. Grant later said, "The fate of the Confederacy was sealed when Vicksburg fell."

 ## Life During Wartime

The war effort affected the lives of most Americans. Women replaced farmers and industrial workers who had left for war. Led by Dorothea Dix, more than 3,000 women served as paid nurses in the Union army. Clara Barton provided medical aid to Union troops and later founded the American Red Cross. Despite such efforts, about twice as many soldiers died of disease than died in combat.

In the North, Peace Democrats, or Copperheads, opposed the war. To silence such critics, President Lincoln suspended *habeas corpus*—the constitutional protection against unlawful imprisonment. Many antiwar activists were arrested. In 1863 antidraft riots occurred after Congress passed a law that allowed the draft of men into the army. Many southerners resented the Confederate draft, passed in 1862. This draft excluded those who owned a large number of slaves. Some southerners said the conflict was a "rich man's war, [a] poor man's fight." In 1863 food shortages—caused in part by the Union blockade—led to riots in several southern cities.

 ## The Battle of Gettysburg

After winning a battle at Chancellorsville, Virginia, General Lee hoped to destroy northern morale with an attack into Union territory. He advanced into southern Pennsylvania. At the town of Gettysburg, Confederate and Union troops clashed, triggering the **Battle of Gettysburg**.

On July 1, 1863, the Confederates pushed the Union line back to Cemetery Ridge. The next day, the Union turned back a major Confederate assault. As General George Meade reinforced the Union line, Lee ordered General George Pickett to attack on July 3. Most of the nearly 15,000 men who took part in Pickett's Charge up Cemetery Ridge were killed or captured. One Union lieutenant wrote, "The battle was now over, but nobody knew it." The Confederacy's casualties were more than 28,000, and the Union's were more than 23,000.

Gettysburg was a turning point in the war. The Union victory there and Grant's capture of Vicksburg on the same day renewed northern support for the war effort. President Lincoln dedicated the Union to winning the war in the **Gettysburg Address**. His speech became one of the most famous in U.S. history.

⭐ The War's End

Impressed with General Grant's successes, President Lincoln made him supreme commander of the Union armies. In early 1864 Grant advanced into eastern Virginia. There he engaged General Lee in battles that stretched Confederate soldiers and supplies to their limits. Although Union forces suffered massive casualties, Grant pressed forward. In June 1864 he reached Petersburg, just south of Richmond, and laid siege to the city.

Meanwhile, General William Tecumseh Sherman marched south from Tennessee with 100,000 troops. On September 2, 1864, he captured Atlanta, Georgia, a vital railroad junction. The capture of Atlanta showed that progress was being made toward victory and helped Lincoln win a landslide re-election in 1864. Shortly after the election, Sherman marched toward Savannah, Georgia. On Sherman's march, he engaged in total war—targeting military and civilian resources to destroy an opponent's ability to fight. Hoping to speed the war's end, he ordered his troops to destroy bridges, railways, crops, and livestock. When Sherman finally reached Savannah on December 10, 1864, his army had left a path of destruction 60 miles wide and almost 300 miles long. Sherman then marched toward the Carolinas.

In April 1865 Grant broke through Lee's defenses at Petersburg. Lee realized the situation

Lee surrenders to Grant at Appomattox Courthouse on April 9, 1865.

was hopeless. He noted, "There is nothing left for me to do but go and see General Grant, and I would rather die a thousand deaths."

The two generals met in the town of **Appomattox Courthouse** on April 9, 1865. Lee signed the surrender documents ending the war. Grant later wrote:

> **❝ I felt . . . sad and depressed at the downfall of a foe who had fought so long and valiantly [bravely], . . . for a cause, though that cause was, I believe, one of the worst for which a people ever fought. ❞**

Some 620,000 Americans had lost their lives in the four years of bloody fighting, making the Civil War the most deadly conflict in U.S. history.

SECTION 5 REVIEW

Identify and explain the significance of the following:

- **Compromise of 1850**
- **Republican Party**
- **Kansas-Nebraska Act**
- *Dred Scott* **decision**
- **Abraham Lincoln**
- **Confederate States of America**
- **Jefferson Davis**
- **Robert E. Lee**
- **Battle of Antietam**
- **Emancipation Proclamation**
- **Ulysses S. Grant**
- **Battle of Gettysburg**
- **Gettysburg Address**
- **Appomattox Courthouse**

Reading for Content Understanding

1 **Main Idea** What events showed the regional tensions over slavery?

2 **Main Idea** Make a time line listing some of the major battles of the Civil War. Be sure to include which side won each battle.

3 **Geographic Diversity** *Region* What was the Union's strategy for winning the war?

4 **Writing** *Informing* Imagine that you are a foreign journalist touring the United States in early 1861. Write an article on the events that were the immediate cause of the Civil War.

5 **Critical Thinking** *Determining the Strength of an Argument* Do you think that President Lincoln was justified in suspending *habeas corpus*? Explain your answer.

The Emancipation Proclamation

When the Union army won the Battle of Antietam, President Lincoln felt that the timing was right for a bold move. In late September 1862 he issued a preliminary Emancipation Proclamation. On January 1, 1863, the following official Proclamation went into effect.

A Proclamation by the President of the United States of America

Whereas on the twenty-second day of September, A.D. 1862, a proclamation was issued by the President of the United States, containing, among other things, the following, to wit [namely]:

"That on the first day of January, A.D. 1863, all persons held as slaves within any state or designated part of a state, the people whereof shall then be in rebellion against the United States, shall be then, thenceforward [afterward], and forever free; and the executive government of the United States, including the military and naval authority thereof, will recognize and maintain the freedom of such persons and will do no act or acts to repress [keep down] such persons or any of them, in any efforts they may make for their actual freedom.

"That the Executive will on the first day of January aforesaid, by proclamation, designate the states and parts of states, if any, in which the people thereof, . . . shall then be in rebellion against the United States; and the fact that any state or the people thereof shall on that day be in good faith represented in the Congress of the United States by members chosen thereto at elections wherein a majority of the qualified voters of such states shall have participated shall, in the absence of strong countervailing [opposing] testimony, be deemed [declared] conclusive evidence that such state and the people thereof are not then in rebellion against the United States."

Now, therefore, I, Abraham Lincoln, President of the United States, by virtue of the power in me vested [empowered] as Commander-in-Chief of the Army and Navy of the United States in time of actual armed rebellion against the authority and government of the United States, and as a fit and necessary war measure for suppressing said rebellion, do, on this first day of January, A.D. 1863, and in accordance with my purpose so to do, publicly proclaimed for the full period of one hundred days from the first day above mentioned, order and designate as the states and parts of states wherein the people thereof, . . . are in this day in rebellion against the United States the following, to wit:

Arkansas, Texas, Louisiana (except the parishes of St. Bernard, Plaquemines, Jefferson, St. John, St. Charles, St. James, Ascension, Assumption, Terrebonne, Lafourche, St. Mary, St. Martin, and Orleans, including the city of New Orleans), Mississippi, Alabama, Florida, Georgia, South Carolina, North Carolina, and Virginia (except the forty-eight counties designated as West Virginia, and also the counties of Berkeley, Accomac, Northampton, Elizabeth City, York, Princess Anne, and Norfolk, including the cities of Norfolk and Portsmouth), and which excepted parts are for the present left precisely as if this proclamation were not issued.

And by virtue of the power and for the purpose aforesaid, I do order and declare that all persons held as slaves within said designated states and parts of states are, and henceforward shall be, free; and that the executive government of the United States, including the military and naval authorities thereof, will recognize and maintain the freedom of said persons.

And I hereby enjoin upon [order] the people so declared to be free to abstain [hold back] from all violence, unless in necessary self-defense; and I recommend to them that, in all cases when allowed, they labor faithfully for reasonable wages.

And I further declare and make known that such persons of suitable condition will be received into the armed service of the United States to garrison [defend] forts, positions, stations, and other places, and to man vessels of all sorts in said service.

And upon this act, sincerely believed to be an act of justice, warranted by the Constitution upon military necessity, I invoke [call upon] the considerate judgment of mankind and the gracious favor of Almighty God.

Understanding Primary Sources

1. What authority did Lincoln claim allowed him to issue the Emancipation Proclamation?

2. In what places does Lincoln free slaves?

3. Why do you think Lincoln did not free all slaves?

Abraham Lincoln's

Gettysburg Address

1863

On November 19, 1863, Abraham Lincoln addressed a crowd gathered to dedicate a cemetery at the Gettysburg battlefield. His short speech reminded Americans of the ideals on which the republic was founded.

Four score and seven years ago our fathers brought forth on this continent, a new nation, conceived [created] in Liberty, and dedicated to the proposition that all men are created equal.

Now we are engaged in a great civil war, testing whether that nation, or any nation so conceived and so dedicated, can long endure. We are met on a great battlefield of that war. We have come to dedicate a portion of that field, as a final resting place for those who here gave their lives that that nation might live. It is altogether fitting and proper that we should do this.

But, in a larger sense, we can not dedicate—we can not consecrate [make holy]—we cannot hallow—this ground. The brave men, living and dead, who struggled here, have consecrated it, far above our poor power to add or detract. The world will little note nor long remember what we say here, but it can never forget what they did here. It is for us the living, rather, to be dedicated here to the unfinished work which they who fought here have thus far so nobly advanced. It is rather for us to be here dedicated to the great task remaining before us—that from these honored dead we take increased devotion to that cause for which they gave the last full measure of devotion—that we here highly resolve that these dead shall not have died in vain—that this nation, under God, shall have a new birth of freedom—and that government of the people, by the people, for the people, shall not perish from the earth.

Understanding Primary Sources

1. Why does Lincoln say that he and the other members of the crowd cannot consecrate the battlefield?

2. For what cause does Lincoln say the soldiers at Gettysburg died? Why—at this particular point in the war—do you think that Lincoln decided to remind Americans of this cause and its importance?

CHAPTER 3 REVIEW

Chapter Summary

The United States expanded its borders with the Louisiana Purchase and fought the War of 1812. Conflict with American Indians broke out as more settlers moved west. The Industrial and Transportation Revolutions changed American life. The South's economy depended on cotton and slavery. The U.S. victory in the Mexican War greatly increased the nation's size. Rising tensions over the issue of slavery led to the Civil War. ▪

On a separate sheet of paper, complete the following activities.

Identifying People and Ideas

Describe the historical significance of the following:

1. Abraham Lincoln
2. Louisiana Purchase
3. John Adams
4. Emancipation Proclamation
5. Industrial Revolution
6. cotton gin
7. Monroe Doctrine
8. Republic of Texas
9. Thomas Jefferson
10. manifest destiny

Internet Activity

go.hrw.com
SB1 Cabinet

Search the Internet through the HRW Web site for information about the president's cabinet, including what departments there are and who heads each one. Then compare the number of cabinet positions today with the number in the first cabinet. Write two short paragraphs discussing what the cabinet reflects about our government today and how that contrasts with government during George Washington's presidency.

Understanding Main Ideas

1. What foreign policy challenges did the young nation face, and how did these tensions lead to the War of 1812?
2. How did western settlement affect American Indians in the early and mid-1800s?
3. Why was the United States divided over slavery, and what compromises were reached on slavery?
4. What were some of the results of increased immigration in the mid-1800s?
5. What reform movements did Americans participate in during the mid-1800s?
6. What was life like for slaves in the South in the 1800s?
7. What were the results of increased American migration to Texas?
8. How did the gold rush affect California?

Using the Time Line

Number your paper from 1 to 5. Match the letters on the time line below with the following events.

1. The Indian Removal Act is passed.
2. Lewis and Clark begin their journey west.
3. General Lee surrenders, ending the Civil War.
4. George Washington is elected the first president of the United States.
5. The United States and Mexico go to war.

| 1790 | 1800 | 1810 | 1820 | 1830 | 1840 | 1850 | 1860 |
| a | b | | | c | d | | e |

Reviewing Themes

1. **Global Relations**   What events led to the Mexican War, and what were the consequences of this war?

2. **Citizenship and Democracy**   How did women try to achieve greater rights?

3. **Technology and Society**   In what ways did the Industrial and Transportation Revolutions change American society?

Thinking Critically

1. **Evaluating**   Do you think Thomas Jefferson's actions as president benefitted the nation? Explain your answer.

2. **Identifying Cause and Effect**   What effect did Abraham Lincoln's election as president have on the country?

3. **Drawing Conclusions**   Why might reformers think it important that all members of society receive an education?

Building Your Portfolio

Complete the following activities individually or in groups.

1. **Regional Differences**   Select a region of the country (either the South, the Northeast, or the West). Then create a brochure that might be used to attract settlers or immigrants to that region in the 1850s. Your brochure should focus on the region's economy, culture, and historical points of interest.

2. **Abolitionist Literature**   Imagine that you have been hired to promote one of the abolitionist newspapers published in the 1800s in the northern United States. Create a poster to advertise one of these works, either William Lloyd Garrison's the *Liberator*, or Frederick Douglass's *North Star*. Be sure that your poster clearly states what these newspapers are about. Your poster should give a brief biography of either publisher and should also discuss the history of the abolition movement.

Writing About History

1. **Expressing**   Write a note to George Washington thanking him for his years of service to the United States. Include Washington's accomplishments in the Revolutionary War and his later political life.

2. **Informing**   Write a newspaper article explaining the resources and strategies of the North and the South during the Civil War. Include information about the final outcome of the war.

Linking Geography and History

1. **Region**   Why did protective tariffs hurt southerners more than northerners?

2. **Movement**   What trails did Americans take to reach California and the Southwest?

History Skills Workshop

Reading Maps   Study the map below. Then answer the following questions: (a) How many slave states were there in 1860? (b) How many free states were there in 1860? (c) What was the total number of senators for the free and slave states in 1860?

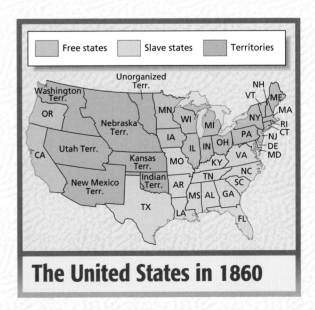

The United States in 1860

History Skills

WORKSHOP

Reading Maps

Maps provide a wealth of historical and geographical information. To read maps, you must understand their terms and symbols.

Types of Maps Types of maps include *physical maps, political maps,* and *special-purpose maps.* Physical maps show the landforms that mark Earth's surface. Political maps illustrate political units such as states and nations. Special-purpose maps present specific information, such as the routes of explorers or the outcome of an election.

Map Features A map's legend, or key, explains any special symbols, colors, or shading used on the map. Labels designate political and geographic place-names as well as physical features.

Most maps in this textbook have a *compass rose,* or directional indicator. The compass rose indicates the four cardinal points: north, south, east, and west. Many maps also include a scale, showing both miles and kilometers, to help you find the distance between two points on the map.

The *absolute location* of any place on Earth is given in terms of latitude and longitude. Latitude is the number of degrees north or south of the equator, an imaginary line that runs around Earth halfway between the North and South Poles. Longitude is the number of degrees east or west of the prime meridian, an imaginary line that runs from the North Pole to the South Pole through western Europe and Africa.

How to Read A Map

1. **Study the title and the legend** Read the map's title and legend to determine the map's subject and the geographic area it covers. Familiarize yourself with any symbols, lines, colors, and shading used.

2. **Study the map** Study the map's basic features and details. If it is a special-purpose map, study the specific information given.

3. **Check directions and distances** Use the compass rose and scale to determine direction, location, and distance.

Practicing the Skill

Study the map below. Then answer the following questions.

1. Near what type of geographic feature are most of the cities located?

2. What type of map is shown here?

The Thirteen Colonies

History in Action

UNIT 1 PORTFOLIO

The United States: The Diorama

Complete the following activity in small, cooperative groups.

Your group will create a diorama showing the history of the United States from the first people to arrive in North America to the Civil War. This three-dimensional exhibit will include a backdrop map of the United States with historical figures in front of it. Each group member will make one figure. Each figure will be from a different time period. Use symbols, colors, or shading on the map to relate to each historical figure. Pay close attention to the clothing your figure wears and the objects he or she carries.

Materials To complete this activity, you will need large sheets of paper for creating the background and cardboard or sticks for making your people stand up. You will also need various art supplies, such as cloth, construction paper, glue, markers, paints, and paper.

Parts of the Project To make your diorama, complete the following tasks:

1. **Overview** You and the members of your group will create figures for your diorama. The group as a whole will decide on the time periods to represent. You should have as many time periods as group members. The time span is from the beginning of North American settlement to the Civil War.

2. **Roles** Here are the different roles that each group member will

need to perform in order to make your project a success:

- **Researchers:** All group members will gather information and images for the time periods and the map. Each group member will also research his or her specific time period to decide on the figure to create and how to relate that figure to the background map.

- **Artists:** The group as a whole will create the map. Each group member will create his or her figure and provide its clothing and objects.

- **Writers:** Each group member will write a paragraph explaining the significance of his or her historical figure. All paragraphs should be written from the figure's point of view. Be sure to include information on what daily life would have been like for your figure. Gather the narratives together as a brochure to accompany the diorama.

3. **Presentation** Once you have completed your diorama, present it to the class. Each group member will read the narrative for his or her figure.

Once all groups have made their presentations, the class as a whole will compare the different time periods represented. The class will then come up with one time line that best identifies the unit.

Teenagers prepare an exhibit.

Industrial America

(1850–1900)

American Teens
IN HISTORY
Young Immigrants

During the 1880s and 1890s about 9 million immigrants poured into the United States. Most were farmers from Austria-Hungary, Italy, Poland, and Russia who brought their families with them. Immigrant children and teenagers found life in the United States both difficult and exciting. Many immigrant teens worked outside the home. Some immigrants came from communities that had a tradition of family labor. For example, many Italian immigrant families operated according to the expression, the "door [of a house] is open to he who contributes—otherwise you stay outside." Italian boys were thus more likely to work than attend school. Other immigrant groups, such as Jews from eastern Europe, tried to keep their children out of the full-time labor force and in school during their teen years.

The rapid increase in the number of immigrant children often led to overcrowded schools. Some schools had students attend in two shifts. Each group received instruction for only half of the school day. Some students also had to share resources. One student remembered sharing a desk with another girl and having to "put an arm around her waist so I shouldn't fall off."

School administrators placed immigrant children in classrooms according to their ability to speak, read, or write English. Many immigrants were put in classrooms with students three to four years younger than they were. One goal of public school instruction was to "Americanize" immigrant students. One student from Serbia recalled that "at school I went as Tomas . . . because the teacher would not pronounce or spell my own [name]." However, many immigrant youths found teachers that provided wonderful instruction. A student named Dora said that her teacher "changed the course of my life. . . . Because of her I was introduced to everything that was good in the United States."

In this unit you will learn more about the immigrants who came to the United States in the late 1800s. You will also learn about Reconstruction and the West, as well as an industrializing America.

The Granger Collection, New York

In the late 1800s and early 1900s most European immigrants arrived at Ellis Island, New York.

LEFT PAGE: *In the late 1800s Pittsburgh, Pennsylvania, became a leading iron and steel producer.*

The Granger Collection, New York

Industrial America

A Pony Express rider

Thomas Watson, Alexander Graham Bell's assistant, holds the first telephone.

UNITED STATES

1860
The Pony Express begins delivering mail in the West.

1865
John Wilkes Booth assassinates President Abraham Lincoln while the president attends a play at Ford's Theater.

1866
Cowboys drive cattle north from Texas on the Chisholm Trail for the first time.

1872
P. T. Barnum opens the "Greatest Show on Earth," his circus in Brooklyn, New York.

1876
Alexander Graham Bell develops the first telephone.

| 1850 | 1854 | 1858 | 1862 | 1866 | 1870 | 1874 |

WORLD

In one of her adventures in "Wonderland," Alice grew tall.

1865
Lewis Carroll publishes *Alice's Adventures in Wonderland.*

1869
The Suez Canal in Egypt opens. It connects the Mediterranean and Red Seas.

1874
Painters stage the first impressionist art exhibition in Paris, France.

Claude Monet's *Impression: Sunrise*

Clipper ships like *Royal Charter* traveled through the Suez Canal.

The opening day for the Brooklyn Bridge

A costume brought by an immigrant from Moravia

1894
Pullman Palace Car Company workers go on strike.

An interior view of a Pullman Palace Car

1883
The Brooklyn Bridge opens to pedestrian traffic. It is the longest suspension bridge in the world.

1886
Geronimo and some of his followers surrender, ending Apache resistance to the U.S. government.

1900
Increased immigration pushes the U.S. population to 76 million.

1878	1882	1886	1890	1894	1898	1900

The Eiffel Tower

1883
The island of Krakatoa in the Pacific Ocean erupts in the greatest volcanic disaster since c. 1470 B.C. More than 36,000 people die.

1889
The Eiffel Tower, designed by Alexandre-Gustave Eiffel, is built in Paris. The steel structure is 984 feet tall.

Medals in honor of the 1896 Olympics

1896
The first modern Olympic Games are held in Athens, Greece.

1899
War breaks out in South Africa between two Boer republics and Great Britain.

A British souvenir cup marking the war in South Africa

USING THE TIME LINE

1. Which entries on the time line refer to new technology?
2. Make a list of the major construction projects mentioned on the time line. How do these projects represent industrialization?
3. Which time line entries refer to "firsts": actions, events, or things?

Activity Create an annotated map of the world using the world events on this time line. Use your library or the world atlas in your textbook to determine the location of the events. Then write the events on your map with brief explanations of what happened. You may also wish to illustrate your map.

◼ CHAPTER 4 ◼

Reconstruction

(1865–1877)

The Civil War was over, but two major issues remained unresolved. First, the federal government had to decide the conditions by which the South could rejoin the Union. Second, the government had to define the rights of the 4 million African Americans freed by the Emancipation Proclamation. As abolitionist Frederick Douglass explained, "The work does not end with the abolition of slavery, but only begins."

THEMES

Constitutional Heritage
How might a nation attempt to rebuild itself following a civil war?

Citizenship and Democracy
Why might a nation's definition of a democratic society change over time?

Cultural Diversity
How might the experiences of a newly freed group affect a nation?

1865

1867

1869

JAN. 1865
Congress proposes the Thirteenth Amendment.

JULY 1866
Race riots erupt in New Orleans.

MAR. 1867
Congress passes the first federal Reconstruction Act.

NOV. 1868
Ulysses S. Grant is elected president.

FEB. 1869
Congress proposes the Fifteenth Amendment.

FEB. 1870
Hiram Revels is elected to the U.S. Senate.

Rebuilding the South

Reading Focus

What effect did the end of the Civil War have on southern life?

How did Lincoln, Congress, and Johnson differ in their views on Reconstruction?

In what ways did the Freedmen's Bureau aid newly freed slaves?

Key Terms

Reconstruction
amnesty
Thirteenth Amendment
Freedmen's Bureau

A SOUTHERNER WHO KEPT A *diary while traveling through Georgia after the Civil War recorded* the destruction he saw: *"Every village and station we stopped at presented an array [group] of ruined walls and chimneys standing useless."* When he reached the once prosperous city of Columbia, South Carolina, burnt and empty buildings greeted him. *The war had dramatically changed the land-scape of the South and the lives of southerners.*

A Georgia newspaper with news of Robert E. Lee's surrender

The Museum of the Confederacy, Richmond, Virginia, Katherine Wetzel, Photographer

IMAGE ON LEFT PAGE: *A school for freedpeople in Vicksburg, Mississippi*

1871	1873	1875	1877

MAY 1872 Fisk Jubilee Singers introduce much of the country to African American spirituals.

NOV. 1874 Republicans lose control of the House of Representatives.

MAR. 1875 Congress passes the Civil Rights Act of 1875.

MAR. 1877 The Compromise of 1877 ends Reconstruction.

The South After the Civil War

After the South's surrender, weary southern soldiers—many permanently disabled—returned home to find their farms destroyed and their cities in ruins. However, the damage went beyond crops and buildings. Former Confederate Josiah Reams reached his home in Tennessee to find:

❝My father and stepmother . . . [had] died. My only brother was killed . . . and a half-brother on the Union side . . . died. So our home was broken up and I was penniless.❞

Many southerners faced the threat of starvation. The Shenandoah Valley in Virginia, once full of rich farmland, was now battle-scarred and barren. Across the South, harvests of cotton, rice, corn, and other crops were well below normal. Many farm animals had been killed or had run away. Food prices, already high because of wartime shortages, remained high.

When food was available, distributing it was difficult. The widespread destruction of railroads by Union troops had disabled transportation and communications throughout the South. Living in Richmond, Virginia, Mary Chesnut wrote in her diary about the isolation: "We are shut in here. . . . All RR's [railroads] destroyed—bridges gone. We are cut off from the world."

Much of Richmond, Virginia, burned in the last days of the war.

In addition, financial institutions, which had begun to collapse during the war, continued to struggle. Banks failed and merchants went bankrupt because few southerners could repay their debts. The Confederate currency they held was now worthless. Former Confederate general Braxton Bragg found that "*all, all* was lost, except my debts."

The Meaning of Freedom

Despite having to suffer through the postwar difficulties, freedpeople, or newly freed slaves, had reason to celebrate as word of emancipation spread slowly through the South. Freedom meant important changes for families. Numerous couples held ceremonies to legalize marriages that had not been recognized under slavery. Many freedpeople searched for relatives who had been sold away from their families years earlier. One man walked 600 miles through Georgia and North Carolina looking for his wife and children. Other freedpeople placed newspaper ads seeking information about their children. Many women began to work at home rather than in the fields.

Now that they could travel without a pass, many freedpeople moved from mostly white counties to places with more African Americans. Some freedpeople in the Upper South tried to find work in Lower South states such as Texas, Florida, and Mississippi, where expanding farms needed new workers. Other freedpeople traveled simply to test their new freedom of movement. A South Carolina woman explained, "I must go, if I stay here I'll never know I'm free."

For most former slaves, freedom to travel was just the first step on a long road toward equal rights and a new way of life. Adults took new last names and began to insist on being called Mr. or Mrs., rather than by their first name or by nicknames. Most freedpeople, such as Henry Adams, wanted the same rights as whites. Adams said, "If I cannot do like a white man I am not free."

Many African Americans left white-controlled churches and created their own congregations. These new churches became the first large

After the Civil War, African Americans bought and filled out family records such as this one.

organizations run by African Americans. Church members established voluntary associations and mutual aid societies to help those in need.

Many freedpeople wanted their own land to farm. At the end of the Civil War, General William Tecumseh Sherman had issued an order to break up plantations in coastal South Carolina and Georgia. He wanted to divide the land into 40-acre plots and give them to freedpeople as compensation for their forced labor during slavery. Many white planters, however, refused to surrender their land. Some freedpeople pointed out that it was only fair that they receive some of this land, because the labor they had performed as slaves had made the plantations prosper. At this time, many freedpeople were unsure about where they would live, what kind of work they would do, and what rights they had.

⭐ Planning Reconstruction

The U.S. government soon stepped in to help freedpeople in the South. The government also faced the task of bringing the defeated southern states back into the Union. **Reconstruction**—the process of reuniting the nation and rebuilding the southern states in the absence of slavery—lasted from 1865 to 1877.

Lincoln's Plan

President Lincoln wanted to reunite the nation as quickly and painlessly as possible. Before the war ended, he proposed a plan for readmitting the southern states. He wanted to offer southerners

amnesty, or an official pardon, for all illegal acts supporting the rebellion. Those southerners who pledged an oath of loyalty to the United States and accepted a ban on slavery would receive amnesty. Any southern state with at least 10 percent of its voters making this pledge could establish a new state government and be readmitted to the Union. Louisiana and other southern states that had been occupied by Union troops before the war's end quickly elected new state legislatures under this Ten-Percent Plan.

The Wade-Davis Bill

Some politicians believed that Congress had the constitutional authority to admit new states. Thus,

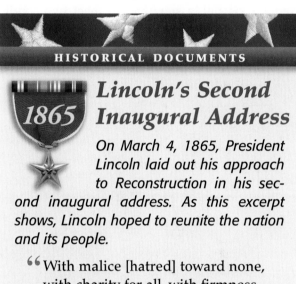

HISTORICAL DOCUMENTS

Lincoln's Second Inaugural Address

1865

On March 4, 1865, President Lincoln laid out his approach to Reconstruction in his second inaugural address. As this excerpt shows, Lincoln hoped to reunite the nation and its people.

❝ With malice [hatred] toward none, with charity for all, with firmness in the right, as God gives us to see the right, let us strive on to finish the work we are in, to bind up the nation's wounds, to care for him who shall have borne the battle, and for his widow, and his orphan—to do all which may achieve and cherish a just, and a lasting peace. ❞

Understanding Primary Sources

1. What is Lincoln asking of the nation?
2. What issues might have prevented Lincoln's request from being fulfilled?

they argued, Congress should handle the southern states' return to the Union. Many Republican members of Congress simply disagreed with Lincoln's plan for Reconstruction. They shared the views of one senator who said,

❝ **The people of the North are not such fools as to . . . turn around and say to the traitors, 'all you have to do [to return] is . . . take an oath that henceforth you will be true to the Government.'** ❞

Two Republicans—Senator Benjamin Wade and Representative Henry Davis—proposed a stricter alternative to Lincoln's plan. Under the Wade-Davis Bill, a state had to meet two conditions before it could rejoin the Union. First, it had to ban slavery. Second, a majority of adult males in the state had to take the loyalty oath. Furthermore, only southerners who swore that they had never supported the Confederacy would be allowed to vote or to hold office. President Lincoln refused to sign this bill into law, because few southerners could fulfill its requirements.

The Thirteenth Amendment

One thing Republicans agreed on was abolishing slavery. The Emancipation Proclamation had freed slaves only in the Confederate states that had been unoccupied by Union forces. The proclamation allowed slavery to continue in the border states. In addition, many people feared that the federal courts might someday declare the Emancipation Proclamation unconstitutional. On January 31, 1865, at Lincoln's urging, Congress proposed the **Thirteenth Amendment** to the Constitution, which made slavery illegal throughout the United States. The amendment then went into effect on December 18, 1865. Abolitionist William Lloyd Garrison declared that his work was now finished and called for the American Anti-Slavery Society to disband. Frederick Douglass, however, insisted that "Slavery is not abolished until the black man has the ballot [vote]."

★ The Freedmen's Bureau

In addition, in 1865 Congress established the **Freedmen's Bureau** to provide relief for all poor people—black and white—in the South. The bureau had a difficult job. At its high point about 900 agents served the entire South. Bureau commissioner

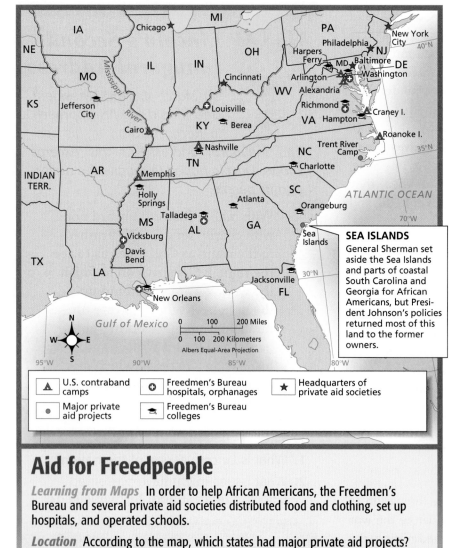

SEA ISLANDS
General Sherman set aside the Sea Islands and parts of coastal South Carolina and Georgia for African Americans, but President Johnson's policies returned most of this land to the former owners.

⚠ U.S. contraband camps	⊕ Freedmen's Bureau hospitals, orphanages	★ Headquarters of private aid societies
• Major private aid projects	🎓 Freedmen's Bureau colleges	

Aid for Freedpeople

Learning from Maps In order to help African Americans, the Freedmen's Bureau and several private aid societies distributed food and clothing, set up hospitals, and operated schools.

Location According to the map, which states had major private aid projects?

Linking Past to Present

Historically Black Colleges and Universities

The Freedmen's Bureau, private donors, and religious organizations helped establish colleges for African Americans in the South. In addition to traditional education, many of these schools—now known as historically black colleges and universities—offered training and teaching degrees.

A half century ago, African Americans had few choices when selecting a college because laws in many states prohibited them from attending white schools. Today, however, African American students can choose which schools to attend. Many continue to choose historically black colleges and universities because of their emphasis on African American identity and history.

According to United Negro College Fund president William H. Gray III, students have support from the faculty, administration, and fellow students in such schools. One Howard graduate noted, "From the minute you walk on campus during freshman orientation, you feel like you finally got to the right place."

Almost 150 years after the founding of the first black college, African American enrollment

African American students study art at Virginia Union University in Richmond, Virginia.

continues to rise at these schools. Many African Americans share the view of one Hampton graduate who said, "I'll always see a need for black colleges. . . . It made me who I am and what I'm going to be."

Understanding What You Read

1. What groups helped establish colleges for African Americans in the South?

2. Why do many African American students choose to attend historically black colleges and universities?

Oliver O. Howard eventually decided to use the bureau's limited budget to distribute food to the poor and to provide education and legal help for freedpeople. The bureau also assisted African American war veterans.

The Freedmen's Bureau played an important role in establishing more schools in the South. Laws against educating slaves meant that most freedpeople had never learned to read or write. Before the war ended, however, northern groups

such as the American Missionary Society began providing books and teachers. The teachers were mostly women who were committed to helping freedpeople. One teacher said of her students:

" I never before saw children so eager to learn. . . . It is wonderful how [they] . . . can have so great a desire for knowledge, and such a capacity for attaining [reaching] it. "

Andrew Johnson

Andrew Johnson had a long political career before becoming president. Born to a poor family in North Carolina, Johnson became a tailor's apprentice. Unhappy with this arrangement, Johnson ran away to Tennessee, where he started his own tailoring business. Eventually, he became a prosperous landowner and entered politics, but he never forgot his humble beginnings. He often criticized wealthy southern planters, calling them a "pampered, bloated, corrupted aristocracy."

Johnson served as governor of Tennessee before becoming a U.S. senator. During the Civil War, he was the only senator from a Confederate state who remained loyal to the Union. Hoping that he would appeal to voters in the border states, Republicans selected Johnson as Lincoln's running mate in the presidential campaign of 1864. He had been vice president for less than six weeks when Lincoln's death elevated Johnson to the presidency.

After the war, some freedpeople organized their own education efforts. For example, Freedmen's Bureau agents found that some African Americans had opened schools in abandoned buildings. Many white southerners continued to believe that African Americans should not be educated. Some whites burned down schools and attacked teachers and students. Despite such opposition, by 1869 more than 150,000 students attended the more than 3,000 schools that had been established. The Freedmen's Bureau also helped establish several colleges for African Americans, including Howard and Fisk.

Students quickly filled the new classrooms. Working adults attended classes in the evening. African Americans made these sacrifices for many reasons, including their desire to learn to read the Bible. They also hoped that education would help them to understand and protect their rights and to enable them to find better jobs. Both black and white southerners benefited from the effort to provide greater access to education in the South.

★ A New President

While the Freedmen's Bureau was helping African Americans in the South, the issue of how the southern states would rejoin the Union remained unresolved. Soon, however, a tragic event ended Lincoln's dream of reuniting the country.

Lincoln's Assassination

On the evening of April 14, 1865, a little more than a month after his second inauguration, President Lincoln and his wife attended the play *Our American Cousin* at Ford's Theater in Washington. During the play, John Wilkes Booth—a southerner hostile to Lincoln's policies—sneaked into the president's theater box and shot him.

Lincoln was rushed to a boardinghouse across the street, where he died at about 7:30 the next morning. Secretary of the Navy Gideon Welles was by the president's side. He later wrote that "strong and brave men wept when I met them" with the news of Lincoln's death.

Vice President Andrew Johnson was sworn into office that morning. Reconstruction was now his responsibility. Republicans approved of President Johnson because he seemed to favor a tougher approach to Reconstruction than Lincoln had. Senator Wade spoke for many Republicans when he told the new president, "Johnson, we have faith in you."

Johnson's Reconstruction Plan

Despite his tough talk, Johnson's plan for the re-entry of the southern states into the Union was similar to Lincoln's Ten-Percent Plan. Johnson gave amnesty to all southerners who pledged an oath of loyalty and who promised to support the abolition of slavery. He also returned all property except slaves to southerners who received amnesty. Johnson did add some special restrictions to his plan. Wealthy southerners and former Confederate officials could not receive amnesty without a presidential pardon. In the end, however, this was not as restrictive as it might seem. Johnson shocked Republicans by eventually pardoning almost 7,000 people.

Johnson established a system for setting up new southern state governments. First, he appointed a temporary governor for each state. Then in each state, southerners who had taken the loyalty oath elected delegates to a convention that would revise their state constitution. Voters then elected state officials and representatives to the U.S. Congress. Once a state government was in place, it had to declare that secession was illegal and refuse to pay Confederate debts before the state could be readmitted to the Union. Virginia and three states that had already set up governments using Lincoln's Ten-Percent Plan—Arkansas, Louisiana, and Tennessee—were allowed to keep their governments in place.

By the end of 1865 all the southern states except Texas had created new governments. Johnson approved all these governments and declared that the United States was restored. When the new representatives from each state came to the capital, he asked Congress to allow them to take their seats in the House and Senate.

Lincoln's funeral procession passes through Springfield, Illinois, in April 1865. A month later, Andrew Johnson issued his plan of Reconstruction.

However, Republicans did not approve of the new representatives, many of whom had been military officers and political leaders in the Confederacy. For example, Alexander Stephens, the former vice president of the Confederacy, was elected a U.S. senator from Georgia. Most Republicans did not believe that people like Stephens were loyal to the United States.

Congress therefore refused either to seat the new representatives or to readmit the southern states into the Union. Clearly, the nation was still divided over who should control Reconstruction and what direction it should take.

SECTION 1 REVIEW

Identify and explain the significance of the following:
- **Reconstruction**
- **amnesty**
- **Thirteenth Amendment**
- **Freedmen's Bureau**
- **John Wilkes Booth**
- **Andrew Johnson**

Reading for Content Understanding

1 Main Idea How did life in the South change after the Civil War?

2 Main Idea What were the various Reconstruction plans, and how did they differ?

3 Citizenship and Democracy How did freedpeople express their new freedom?

4 Writing *Persuading* Write a one-paragraph editorial that explains the importance of the Freedmen's Bureau for both black and white southerners.

5 Critical Thinking *Evaluating* Why might owning farmland have been important for freedpeople?

The Fight over Reconstruction

Reading Focus

How did Black Codes restrict African Americans' freedoms?

Why did Radical Republicans try to impeach President Johnson?

How did Republicans try to protect the civil rights of African Americans?

Key Terms

Black Codes
Radical Republicans
Civil Rights Act of 1866
Fourteenth Amendment
Reconstruction Acts
Fifteenth Amendment

TO TEST HIS NEWFOUND FREEDOM, *in 1865 Henry Adams left the plantation where he had been enslaved. A group of white men stopped Adams on the road and asked who owned him. When Adams replied that he was free, the men beat him. Such incidents of violence were not unusual in the post–Civil War South. Many white southerners opposed African Americans' freedom and feared the consequences of that freedom. This resentment and fear also affected local authorities and state governments.*

A federal soldier protects an African American man from violence.

 ## The Black Codes

While Congress debated the rules for restoring the Union, in 1866 the new state legislatures approved by President Johnson began passing laws to deny African Americans' civil rights. "This is a white man's government, and intended for white men only," declared Governor Benjamin F. Perry of South Carolina. Soon every southern state passed **Black Codes**—laws that greatly limited the freedom of African Americans.

Each state had a set of Black Codes, which were usually designed to help white southerners economically. Black Codes forced African Americans to work on farms or as servants and required them to sign labor contracts that re-created conditions similar to those under slavery. One of South Carolina's Black Codes, for example, stated:

“ **All persons of color who make contracts for service or labor, shall be known as servants, and those with whom they contract shall be known as masters.** ”

In most southern states, any African American who could not prove he or she was employed

Under the Black Codes, white southerners could arrest unemployed African Americans and auction off their labor to the highest bidder.

could be arrested and punished with one year of work without pay. Other Black Codes prevented African Americans from owning guns, holding public meetings, or renting property in cities.

African Americans were alarmed by the Black Codes. As one Civil War veteran declared, "If you call this Freedom, what do you call Slavery?" African Americans organized and took action to oppose the codes. One group sent a petition to officials in South Carolina, which had one of the strictest Black Codes:

66 **We simply ask . . . that the same laws which govern *white men* shall govern *black men*; that we have the right of trial by a jury of our peers; that schools be established for the education of *colored children* as well as white . . . that, in short, we be dealt with as others are—in equity [equality] and justice.** 99

Such calls for equality had little effect on the new state governments, however.

★ The Radical Republicans

The Black Codes angered many Republicans who felt the South was returning to its old ways. Most Republicans were moderates who wanted the South to have loyal state governments but also believed that African Americans should receive their rights as citizens. Most moderates hoped that

the South would not have to be forced to follow the laws passed by the U.S. government.

Another group in Congress, called the **Radical Republicans**, wanted the South to change much more than it had before it could return to the Union. Like the moderates, they considered the Black Codes to be undemocratic and cruel. The Radical Republicans, however, wanted the federal government to be much more involved in Reconstruction, fearing that too many southern leaders remained loyal to the former Confederacy. Thaddeus Stevens of Pennsylvania and Charles Sumner of Massachusetts led the Radical Republicans.

A harsh critic of President Johnson, Stevens was known for his honesty, his sharp tongue, and his interest in economic justice for both African Americans and poor white southerners. Sumner had been a strong opponent of slavery before the Civil War and continued to argue tirelessly for African Americans' civil rights. These included the right to vote and the right to fair laws. Stevens and Sumner both felt that President

Thaddeus Stevens

Johnson's Reconstruction plan was a failure. Although the Radical Republicans did not control Congress, they began to gain support among moderates when President Johnson ignored criticism of the Black Codes. "The same national authority that destroyed slavery must see that this other pretension [the Black Codes] is not permitted to survive," said Sumner.

★ Johnson Versus Congress

In early 1866 Congress proposed a bill to increase the powers of the Freedmen's Bureau by allowing it to use military courts to try individuals accused of violating African Americans' rights. Supporters of the bill hoped that these courts would be more fair than local courts in the South. To the surprise of many members of Congress, Johnson vetoed the bill and insisted that Congress could not pass any new laws until the southern states again were represented in Congress. He also argued that the Freedmen's Bureau was unnecessary because he believed that African Americans did not need any special assistance.

Republicans responded with the **Civil Rights Act of 1866**. This act provided African Americans with the same legal rights as white Americans. Republicans believed that without rights for African Americans, the South would never have a strong economy or democracy.

President Johnson once again used his veto, arguing that the act gave too much power to the federal government. He also rejected the principle of equal rights for African Americans, insisting that they did not understand "the nature and character of our institutions." The Republicans overrode Johnson's veto.

★ The Fourteenth Amendment

Many Republicans were concerned that the Civil Rights Act might be overturned by Congress once the southern states were readmitted. To protect the new civil rights laws from hostile presidents or legislators, Republicans proposed an amendment to the Constitution in the summer of 1866.

President Johnson traveled to cities such as Philadelphia, Cleveland, and St. Louis when he campaigned for Democratic candidates in 1866.

Equal Protection

The **Fourteenth Amendment** guaranteed citizenship and equal protection under the law to all people born or naturalized within the United States with the exception of American Indians. It said that state governments could not "deprive any person of life, liberty, or property, without due process of law."

The amendment also banned many former Confederate officials from holding state or federal offices. In addition, the amendment made state laws subject to federal court review. The final section of the amendment gave Congress the power to pass any laws needed to enforce any part of the amendment. The editors of one black newspaper wrote, "We are entering upon the greatest political contest that has ever agitated [upset] the people of the country."

The 1866 Elections

President Johnson and most Democrats opposed the Fourteenth Amendment. As a result, civil rights for African Americans became a key issue in the 1866 congressional elections. Republican candidates asked Americans to support civil rights by voting for the Republican Party. To help the Democrats, Johnson traveled around the country defending his Reconstruction plan.

Johnson's speaking tour was a disaster and did little to help win votes for the Democratic Party. He got into arguments with spectators and often seemed to wander from the subject. When a spectator at one of his speeches cried out, "Hang Jeff Davis!" Johnson replied angrily, "Why don't you hang Thad Stevens? . . . I can tell you, my countrymen, I have been fighting traitors in the south, and . . . I am prepared to fight traitors at the north, . . . with your help." Such outbursts did not impress many voters.

The Granger Collection, New York

Southern whites fire on African American demonstrators during the New Orleans riot of 1866.

Violence in the South

Two major riots in the South also hurt Johnson's campaign. On May 1, 1866, a dispute in Memphis, Tennessee, between local police and black Union soldiers turned into a three-day wave of violence against African Americans. To make things worse, police officers joined in the attacks on freedpeople. By the time federal troops restored peace, 46 African Americans were dead.

Three months later, another riot took place in New Orleans when African Americans attempted to hold a peaceful political demonstration. This time 34 African Americans and 3 white Radical Republicans were killed. Again, the local police participated in the violence, and federal troops had to restore order. These widely publicized events convinced many voters that Johnson's Reconstruction plan was failing.

 ## Congress Takes Charge

The 1866 elections gave the Republican Party a commanding two-thirds majority in both the House and the Senate. This gave the Republicans

the power to override any presidential veto. In addition, the Republicans became united as the moderates joined with the Radicals. Together they called for a new form of Reconstruction.

The Reconstruction Acts

In March 1867 Congress passed the first of several **Reconstruction Acts**. These acts divided the South into five districts that were controlled by military commanders. The acts also required all southern states to create new state constitutions supporting the Fourteenth Amendment before they could be readmitted to the Union. In addition, the states would be required to give African American men the right to vote.

Thaddeus Stevens was one of the new Reconstruction Acts' most enthusiastic supporters. Defending them before Congress, he argued:

> **" Have not loyal blacks quite as good a right to choose rulers and make laws as rebel whites? Every man, no matter what his race or color . . . has an equal right to justice, honesty, and fair play with every other man; and the law should secure him those rights. "**

President Johnson disagreed strongly with Stevens, arguing that African Americans did not deserve the same treatment as white people. He also insisted that the Reconstruction Acts used "powers not granted to the federal government or any one of its branches."

Impeachment

Congress knew that Johnson did not support its Reconstruction policies. To limit his power, Congress passed an act preventing the president from removing cabinet officials without the approval of the U.S. Senate. Johnson defied the new law soon after by firing Secretary of War Edwin Stanton.

A ticket to President Andrew Johnson's 1868 trial in the Senate

The Granger Collection, New York

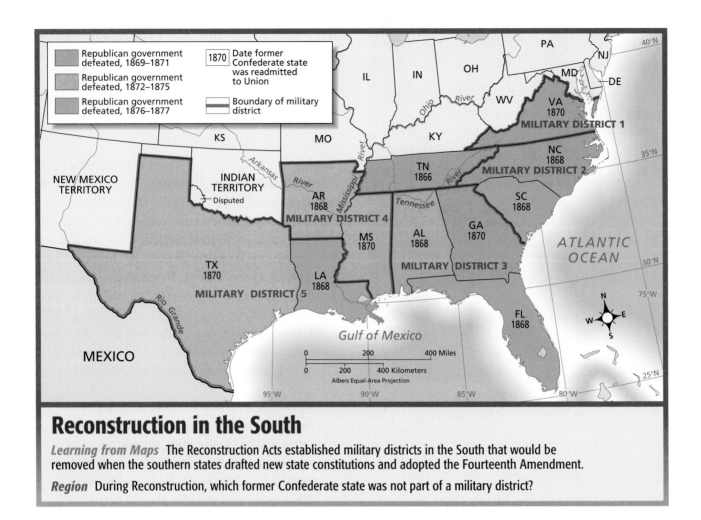

Reconstruction in the South

Learning from Maps The Reconstruction Acts established military districts in the South that would be removed when the southern states drafted new state constitutions and adopted the Fourteenth Amendment.

Region During Reconstruction, which former Confederate state was not part of a military district?

The House of Representatives responded by voting for presidential impeachment for the first time in U.S. history. Impeachment is the process of bringing charges of wrongdoing against a public official. The next step, under Article I of the Constitution, was a trial in the Senate. A two-thirds majority was required to find Johnson guilty and remove him from office.

Although Johnson was unpopular with Republicans, some of them believed he was being judged unfairly. Others did not want to disrupt the balance of powers by interfering with presidential authority over the cabinet. By a single vote, Senate Republicans failed to convict Johnson. Even so, the trial broke his power as president.

★ The Election of 1868

The Democratic Party chose former New York governor Horatio Seymour as its 1868 presidential candidate. The Republican Party chose Ulysses S.

Grant. As a war hero, Grant appealed to many northern voters. He had no political experience but supported the congressional Reconstruction plan. He ran under the slogan "Let Us Have Peace."

Shortly after Grant was nominated, Congress readmitted seven southern states: Alabama, Arkansas, Florida, Georgia, Louisiana, North Carolina, and South Carolina. (Tennessee already had been readmitted in 1866.)

Under the terms of readmission, these seven states approved the Fourteenth Amendment and agreed to let African American men have the vote. During the election, however, white southerners used violence to keep African Americans from the polls in many states.

Ulysses S. Grant

Despite such tactics, thousands of African Americans voted for Grant and the "party of Lincoln." One black newspaper reported that many freedpeople "see clearly enough that the Republican party [is] their political life boat." African American votes helped Grant win a narrow victory.

This poster—which includes images of African American preachers, soldiers, and students—celebrated the passage of the Fifteenth Amendment.

 ## The Fifteenth Amendment

Congressional Republicans wanted to protect their Reconstruction plan, which they believed most African American voters would support. Some Radical Republicans argued that it was not fair that only eight northern states allowed African Americans to vote while all southern states were required to grant suffrage to African American men.

In 1869 Congress proposed the **Fifteenth Amendment**, which gave African American men throughout the United States the right to vote. Abolitionist William Lloyd Garrison praised "this wonderful, quiet, sudden transformation of four millions of human beings from . . . the auction block to the ballot-box." The amendment, which went into effect in 1870, was one of the last important pieces of Reconstruction legislation passed at the federal level.

The Fifteenth Amendment did not please every reformer, however. Women's rights activists were angry because the amendment did not also grant women the right to vote.

SECTION 2 REVIEW

Identify and explain the significance of the following:
- **Black Codes**
- **Radical Republicans**
- **Thaddeus Stevens**
- **Civil Rights Act of 1866**
- **Fourteenth Amendment**
- **Reconstruction Acts**
- **Fifteenth Amendment**

Reading for Content Understanding

1 **Main Idea** What was the purpose of the Black Codes?

2 **Main Idea** Why did Radical Republicans want to remove President Johnson from office?

3 **Constitutional Heritage** What did Congress do to guarantee the civil rights of African Americans?

4 **Writing** *Creating* Write a slogan that might have been used by the Republican or the Democratic Party to appeal to voters in either the 1866 congressional election or the 1868 presidential election.

5 **Critical Thinking** *Making Comparisons* How might a conservative white southerner have viewed the Fourteenth and the Fifteenth Amendments? How might a Radical Republican or an African American have viewed these amendments?

Reconstruction in the South

Reading Focus

What roles did African Americans, northerners, and southern white Republicans play in rebuilding the South?

How did the Ku Klux Klan try to stop Reconstruction?

What factors led to the end of Reconstruction?

Key Terms

carpetbaggers
scalawags
Ku Klux Klan
Panic of 1873
Civil Rights Act of 1875
General Amnesty Act of 1872
Compromise of 1877
Redeemers
poll tax
segregation
Jim Crow laws
Plessy v. *Ferguson*

GOVERNMENTS ELECTED *with the support of African American votes took control of most southern states. This led planter William Henry Ravenel to express concerns about the future in his daily journal: "The experiment [Reconstruction] is now to be tried. . . . It produces a financial, political, and social revolution [in] the South." Ravenel feared how the actions of the new governments would affect southern society, but he still hoped that God would "bless the effort and make it successful."*

William Henry Ravenel

 ## Reconstruction Governments

The Republican Party controlled most southern governments partly because the Fourteenth Amendment banned a large number of former Confederates from holding office. Most of these Republican officeholders were unpopular with the majority of white southerners.

Carpetbaggers and Scalawags

Many white southerners called northern-born Republicans **carpetbaggers**. Most of these northerners had come South after the war, carrying all their possessions in a bag made from carpeting. Many southerners resented "carpetbaggers," believing that they had moved south to profit from Reconstruction. Southern Democrats were no more fond of white southern Republicans. They referred to them as **scalawags**, which means liars and cheats. Democrats believed that "scalawags" had betrayed the South by voting for the Republican Party.

Despite southern resentment, northerners and white southern Republicans had many reasons for taking part in Reconstruction. Some northerners shared the view of one reformer who strongly believed he "had a Mission with a large M" to help

In this cartoon, the South bears the heavy burden imposed by President Grant, federal troops, and carpetbaggers during Reconstruction.

freedpeople. Others hoped to make money while rebuilding the southern economy. An Illinois man who had moved to Texas explained, "I am going to introduce new ideas here in the farming line." Many southern Republicans were small farmers who had supported the Union during the war. Others, like Mississippi governor James Alcorn, were former members of the Whig Party who preferred to become Republicans rather than join the Democrats. By 1872, about 25 percent of southern whites were Republicans.

African Americans in Politics

African Americans seeking equality overwhelmingly supported Reconstruction and were the largest group of southern Republican voters. During Reconstruction, voters elected more than 600 African American representatives to state legislatures and sent 16 to Congress. Other African Americans held important state offices such as lieutenant governor, treasurer, and secretary of state. Many more held local offices in counties throughout the South. Apart from their regular duties, these politicians helped enforce civil rights laws that white officials often ignored. In Georgia, for example, Justice of the Peace Tunis Campbell arrested some white overseers who

mistreated black workers. One African American called Campbell "the champion of their rights and the bearer of their burden."

African American politicians came from many different backgrounds. Hiram Revels was born a free man in North Carolina. He went to college in Illinois and became a Methodist minister. During the Civil War, he served as a chaplain in the Union army. In 1870 Revels became the first African American in the U.S. Senate when he took over the seat previously held by Jefferson Davis. Blanche K. Bruce was another important African American leader. Bruce grew up in slavery in Virginia and later became a prominent Republican politician in Mississippi. He served one term as a U.S. senator and was active in politics for many years.

Reconstruction Reforms

The Reconstruction governments provided money for many new programs and organizations. These governments helped to establish the first state-funded public school systems in the South and built new hospitals, prisons, and orphanages. Republican governments also passed laws prohibiting discrimination against African Americans.

During this period, southern states spent large amounts of money building or repairing railroads, bridges, and public buildings—improvements intended to help the southern economy recover

The first African American members of Congress: (left to right) Hiram Revels, Benjamin Turner, Robert DeLarge, Josiah Wells, Jefferson Long, Joseph Rainey, and Robert Elliott

from the war. To get the money for these projects, the Reconstruction governments raised taxes and issued bonds.

★ Opposition to Reconstruction

Despite all of these efforts to rebuild the South, the majority of white southerners opposed Reconstruction. Democrats claimed that the Reconstruction governments were unjust and illegal. They also disliked having the federal soldiers stationed in their states. Many white southerners disapproved of African American officeholders. One Democrat noted, "'A white man's government' [is] the most popular rallying cry we have."

In 1866 a group of white southerners in Tennessee created the **Ku Klux Klan**. This secret society opposed African Americans obtaining civil rights, particularly suffrage, and used violence

and terror to frighten and discourage them. The Klan's membership grew rapidly as it spread throughout the South. Klan members wore robes and hoods to hide their identities as they attacked—and even murdered—African Americans, white Republican voters, and public officials, usually at night. Charlotte Fowler described her husband's murder by the Klan:

> **"We still had a little grandchild living with me. . . . I heard somebody by the door. . . . The little child followed its grandfather to the door. . . and just then I heard the report [shot] of a pistol, and they shot him down. And this little child ran back to me before I could get out and says, 'Oh grandma, they have killed my poor grandpappy.'"**

Local governments did little to stop the violence because many officials feared the Klan or

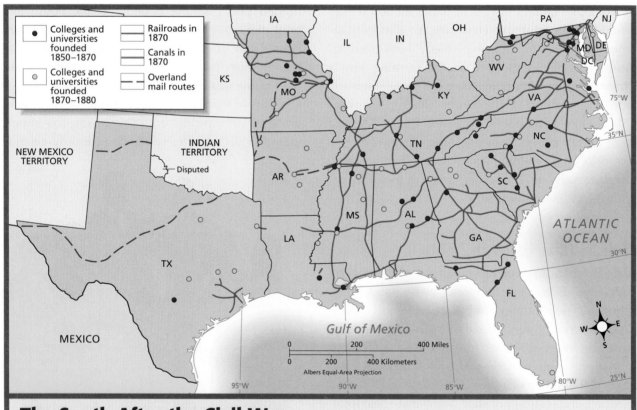

The South After the Civil War

Learning from Maps After the Civil War many Reconstruction programs contributed to the rapid growth in transportation and education in the South.

Place How many colleges and universities were founded in Alabama from 1850 to 1870?

were sympathetic to its activities. In Kentucky a committee of African Americans presented a list of at least 70 murder victims and a formal complaint to the state legislature about the lack of action against the Klu Klux Klan. "We regard them [the Klan] as now being licensed to continue their dark and bloody deeds under cover of the dark night," they wrote.

In 1870 and 1871 the federal government passed a series of laws that made it a federal crime to interfere with elections or deny citizens equal protection under the law. Thus, by the mid-1870s the Klan was no longer an organized threat, although it would re-emerge later. Even with the decline of the Klan, white mobs continued to assault African Americans and Republicans throughout the 1870s. Such actions made federal action and protection necessary for Reconstruction's success.

African American men—one of them a soldier—voting in the South

The Election of 1876

The violence that took place throughout the South was not the only challenge to Reconstruction. Northerners also grew more critical of the Reconstruction policies during the early 1870s.

Republican Support Fades

Although President Grant was re-elected in 1872, his administration suffered many scandals that upset voters. The financial **Panic of 1873**, which helped cause a severe economic downturn, also hurt the Republican Party. In 1874 the Republicans lost control of the House of Representatives to the Democrats. Nevertheless, Republicans managed to pass one last act—the **Civil Rights Act of 1875**, which allowed African Americans to sue private businesses for discrimination.

Southern and national politics had also changed with the passage of the **General Amnesty Act of 1872**. This act repealed Section III of the Fourteenth Amendment and allowed former Confederates, with the exception of those of high rank, to hold public office. Many of these former Confederates were Democrats. As a result, southern state governments gradually became controlled by the Democratic Party.

Republicans could tell that support for Reconstruction was also fading in the North, where people were growing concerned about economic problems and government corruption. Thus, the Republicans selected for their 1876 presidential candidate Ohio governor Rutherford B. Hayes, who believed the time had come to end federal support of the Reconstruction governments. The Democrats nominated New York governor Samuel J. Tilden.

The Compromise of 1877

During the election, Democrats in the South again used violence at the polls. Senator Blanche K. Bruce of Mississippi described the problem:

❝In many parts of the State corrupt and violent influences were brought to bear [used] . . . changing the number of votes cast; . . . threats and violence were practiced directly upon the masses of voters . . . to deter [prevent] them from [voting].❞

The election between Hayes and Tilden was very close. When the votes from the electoral college came in, Tilden appeared to have won, but Republicans questioned the election returns in three southern states.

Reconstruction **139**

The Election Commission hears testimony on disputed returns from the presidential election of 1876.

A special commission of 10 members of Congress and five Supreme Court justices settled the issue. The commission narrowly decided to give all the disputed votes to Hayes. Hayes thus won the election by one electoral vote. In the **Compromise of 1877**, the Democrats agreed to accept Hayes's victory if all remaining federal troops were removed from the South. They also asked for funding for internal improvements in the South and the appointment of a southern Democrat to the president's cabinet. Shortly after he took office in 1877, President Hayes removed the last of the federal troops from the South.

 ## Turning Back the Clock

Reconstruction ended at different times in southern states, depending on when the Democrats regained control of a particular state government. In general, their first order of business was to eliminate the Reconstruction reforms.

The Redeemers

The individuals behind the Democratic Party's return to power in the South were known as the **Redeemers**. The Redeemers included people from many different backgrounds, such as U.S. senator John T. Morgan of Alabama—a former general in the Confederate army—and newspaper editor Henry Grady of Georgia, who was interested in promoting southern industry. "Never was nobler

duty confided [given] to human hands than the uplifting and upbuilding of the… South," said Grady. The Redeemers wanted to reduce the size of state government and limit the rights of African Americans. They lowered state budgets and got rid of social programs. They cut property taxes and reduced public funding for schools. The Redeemers also succeeded in limiting African Americans' civil rights.

In an effort to deny the vote to African Americans, the Redeemers set up the **poll tax**, which required individuals to pay a special tax before they could vote. The poll tax, however, often stopped not only African American men but also some white men from voting. To bypass this result, some states more carefully targeted African American voters by requiring them to pass literacy tests. A "grandfather clause" was usually written into law as well, allowing any man whose father or grandfather could vote before 1867 to avoid poll taxes and literacy tests. This meant that almost every white man could benefit from the clause, but few black men could.

Segregation and Jim Crow

Another change made by the Democratic governments was the introduction of legal **segregation**—the forced separation of whites and African Americans in public places. **Jim Crow laws**—laws that enforced segregation—began appearing in southern states in 1881. African Americans had to stay in different hotels than whites, sit in separate theater sections, and ride in separate railcars. One white southerner described segregated areas as "in every instance . . . the most uncomfortable, uncleanest, and unsafest place[s]."

African Americans challenged these laws in

An African American man is ordered to leave a "whites only" railroad car.

court. In 1883, however, the U.S. Supreme Court ruled that the Civil Rights Act of 1875 was unconstitutional. The Court also ruled that the Fourteenth Amendment applied only to the actions of state governments. This allowed private individuals and businesses to practice segregation.

 ## Plessy v. Ferguson

In 1896 the U.S. Supreme Court returned to the issue of segregation in the case **Plessy v. Ferguson**. Homer Plessy was an African American who had purchased a first-class ticket on a Louisiana train. When he tried to sit in the first-class car, he was arrested because Louisiana's Jim Crow laws did not allow African Americans to ride in first class with whites. Plessy and his lawyers argued that this violated the Fourteenth Amendment's guarantee of equal legal treatment.

The Court ruled against Plessy, arguing that it was legal to force African Americans and whites to use separate facilities as long as the facilities were of equal quality. According to the Court, this was fair so long as "separate-but-equal" facilities were provided for African Americans.

The only justice who disagreed with the Court's decision was John Marshall Harlan. Justice Harlan explained his concerns in a dissenting, or disagreeing, opinion:

> " **In the eye of the law, there is in this country no superior, dominant [controlling], ruling class of citizens. . . . Our Constitution is color-blind, and neither knows nor tolerates classes among citizens. In respect of civil rights, all citizens are equal before the law.** "

Few white Americans agreed with Justice Harlan in 1896, however. Segregation continued to be widespread both in the South and in the North. In addition, the public schools, libraries, parks, and other areas open to African Americans were usually inferior in quality to those created for whites. Thus, in practice, the "separate-but-equal" facilities usually were "separate-and-unequal."

A judge's gavel

SECTION 3 REVIEW

Identify and explain the significance of the following:

- carpetbaggers
- scalawags
- Hiram Revels
- Blanche K. Bruce
- Ku Klux Klan
- Panic of 1873
- Civil Rights Act of 1875
- General Amnesty Act of 1872
- Rutherford B. Hayes
- Compromise of 1877
- Redeemers
- poll tax
- segregation
- Jim Crow laws
- *Plessy v. Ferguson*
- John Marshall Harlan

Reading for Content Understanding

1 **Main Idea** What contributions did African Americans, northern whites, and white southern Republicans make to the Reconstruction process?

2 **Main Idea** Why did some white southerners oppose Reconstruction? Why did some of them form the Ku Klux Klan?

3 **Citizenship and Democracy** What was the Compromise of 1877, and how did it lead to the end of Reconstruction?

4 **Writing** *Persuading* Imagine that you are a newspaper editor who opposes the *Plessy v. Ferguson* ruling. Write an editorial to convince your readers that the ruling is wrong.

5 **Critical Thinking** *Evaluating* Do you think the civil rights aspects of Reconstruction were a short-term failure but a long-term success? Explain your answer.

The New South

*A*FTER RENTING LAND FOR YEARS, *Charley White and his wife, Lucille, saved enough money to buy their own farm in Texas. Reflecting back on the purchase, Charley White said, "The house wasn't much more than a shack." The fact that it belonged to them made all the difference. "It just set us on fire. We didn't seem to get half as tired, or if we did we didn't notice it." Lucille White told her husband that "even the rocks look pretty." Many other African American farmers, however, were not fortunate enough to share the Whites' accomplishment.*

Farmers used harrows such as this one to smooth their soil.

★ Farming in the South

Throughout most of the South, few African Americans could afford to buy or even rent their own farms and the necessary farm supplies. Moving west also was costly. Thus, many African Americans remained on plantations, while others tried to make a living in the cities.

The Growth of Sharecropping

Those African Americans who stayed on plantations often became part of a system known as **sharecropping**, or sharing the crop. Landowners provided the land, tools, and supplies, and sharecroppers provided the labor. At harvest time, the sharecropper gave most of the crop to the owner. Whatever remained belonged to the sharecropper.

The sharecropping system allowed poor African Americans and poor whites to farm land that they could not afford to rent or buy. The system also enabled small farmers to hire people to work on their land. Many sharecroppers hoped to save enough money from selling their share of the crops to buy a farm. Only a few were able to achieve this dream, however.

A Cycle of Debt

When sharecropping families needed food, clothing, or supplies, they went to the general store. Most families bought goods on credit because they had little money. When the harvest came, sharecroppers hoped to sell their crops and pay off their debt to the store. However, bad weather or low crop prices often prevented them from making as much money as they had hoped.

Many merchants cheated sharecroppers by charging them for items they did not purchase. Some landowners also cheated sharecroppers by taking more than their fair share of the crop. Abolitionist Frederick Douglass complained about the treatment of sharecroppers:

> **The merchant puts him [the sharecropper] off with his poorest commodities [goods] at highest prices, and can say to him take these or nothing. . . . By this means the laborer is brought into debt, and hence is kept always in the power of the land-owner. . . . On such a system of fraud and wrong one might well invoke [request] a bolt from heaven.**

As a result of such practices, most sharecroppers found themselves deeper in debt at the end of the harvest than they had been when they planted their crops.

Too Much Cotton

Many farmers saw planting cotton as a sure way to make money. Cotton was one of the South's most important cash crops—crops that farmers grow to sell to others rather than to use themselves. Cotton had a worldwide market and could be sold or stored easily. As a result, numerous landowners and sharecroppers grew cotton, hoping to pay their debts or save money. When too many farmers

Children in the South often had to help their parents pick cotton at harvest time.

African American Property Owners in the South, 1860 and 1870

Total number of African American property owners (in thousands)

Year	Number
1860	9
1870	139

Figures are for owners in former Confederate states.
Source: *The Facts of Reconstruction*

Owning Property   The number of African American property owners in the South dramatically increased in the years following the Civil War. How much did this number increase from 1860 to 1870?

planted cotton, however, the supply became too great and the price per bale dropped. One man wrote his father about a drop in the price of cotton: "It nearly ruined us. . . . The farmers are very blue here. But getting ready to plant cotton again."

Even though many farmers understood the drawbacks of planting cotton, they felt too much pressure from banks or landlords to change their ways. "Cotton raising has grown to be a necessity more than a choice," a farmer in Alabama said. Another southern man explained,

> **Cotton is the thing to get credit on in this country. . . . You can always sell cotton. You leave home with a wagon load of cotton and you will go home that night with money in your pocket; you load up your wagon with wheat or corn . . . and I doubt some days whether you could sell it.**

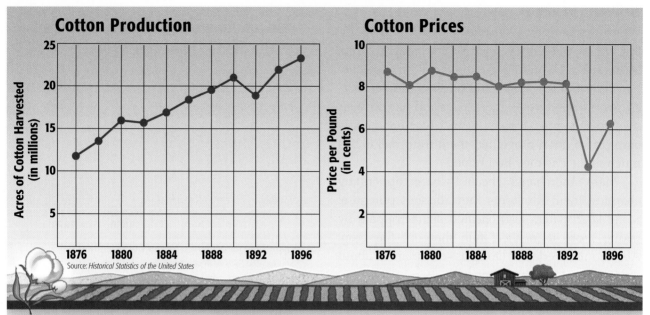

Cotton Production

Acres of Cotton Harvested (in millions)

Source: *Historical Statistics of the United States*

Cotton Prices

Price per Pound (in cents)

King Cotton During the late 1800s cotton remained a primary crop for many farmers. According to the graphs, what generally happened as cotton production increased?

★ The "New South" Movement

The southern economy, like the southern farmer, relied on cash crops such as cotton. This created cycles of good and bad years as prices went up or down. Tired of watching the southern economy suffer, some business leaders wanted to create a "New South" that had an industrial base in addition to its agricultural one. They hoped industry would strengthen the southern economy.

Southern Industry

Henry Grady, a newspaper editor in Atlanta, was one of the leaders of the New South movement. "The new South presents a perfect democracy," he wrote, "and a diversified [varied] industry that meets the complex needs of this complex age." Grady and his supporters wanted to take advantage of the South's resources—such as its cotton production and cheap and abundant labor—to build textile mills and other factories.

Grant Hamilton's From Darkness to Light *(1895) shows the New South rising from the destruction of the Civil War.*

They hoped their plans for development would interest investors.

New industries developed in the South, though not as quickly or in as many areas as Grady hoped. One of the great changes after the Civil War was the repair of the old railroads and the growth of new lines as workers laid thousands of miles of railroad track throughout the South. The new railroads allowed companies to ship goods faster and farther than ever before. The telegraph lines that accompanied the railroads also helped bring news to small southern towns.

The most successful industrial development in the South involved textile production. Businesspeople built textile mills that produced cotton fabric in many small towns, drawing hundreds of people from the countryside to work in the mills. While this industry pumped new life into the southern economy, the New South was far from the "perfect democracy" that Grady had claimed. The most important example of this lack of democracy was the cotton mills' refusal to hire African Americans.

Southern Mill Life

Work in the cotton mills appealed to farm families that had trouble making ends meet. As one mill worker explained, "It was a necessity to move and get a job, rather than depend on the farm." Recruiters sent out by the mills promised good wages and steady work.

Entire families often worked in the same mill. One company in South Carolina asked for "whole families with at least three workers for the mill in each family." Mills employed large numbers of women and children. Many children started working around the age of 12; some started earlier than that. Women did most of the spinning and were valued workers, although few women had the opportunity to advance within the company.

Many mill workers were proud of the skills they used, but they did not enjoy their work. One unhappy worker described it as "the same thing over and over again. . . . The more you do, the more they want done." Workers often labored six days a week, 12 hours a day. Cotton dust and lint filled the air, causing asthma and an illness known as brown-lung disease. Fast-moving machinery caused many injuries and some deaths. Despite the long hours and dangerous working conditions, wages were low. However, mill work did offer an alternative to farming.

Southern Literature

While the New South movement sought to modernize the South, many southerners looked to the arts to reinforce their traditions. Southern literature, an important element of southern culture, gained national popularity in the late 1800s. The most famous writer about the South at the end of Reconstruction was probably Mark Twain. Twain, whose real name was Samuel Clemens, wrote *The Adventures of Tom Sawyer* in 1876. Although Twain wrote about many subjects, his novels and stories about the South were among his most admired.

Part of the reason that southern literature gained national attention was that many of these stories involved people and places in the South that seemed exotic to northerners. The popular writer Mary Noailles Murfree, for example, wrote short stories and novels about the people who lived in the mountains of eastern Tennessee. Another writer, George Washington Cable, wrote novels about the African American community in New Orleans. Cable used his writing as an opportunity to protest racial prejudice in the South.

Mary Noailles Murfree began her writing career by producing short stories, which she read to her family.

Joel Chandler Harris was one of the most popular southern writers. He wrote short stories about a fictional plantation slave named Uncle Remus, a wise old storyteller who taught lessons by reciting folktales. Another author, William J. Faulkner, brought together many more African American folktales in his book *The Days When the Animals Talked*. Both Harris and Faulkner based their work on stories they were first told by enslaved African Americans and later by freedpeople.

Many white southern writers set their stories in a pre–Civil War South full of beautiful plantations and happy slaves. Unlike these authors who presented romantic images of life on southern plantations, African American writer Charles W. Chesnutt wrote plantation stories that showed the greed and cruelty of the slavery system. Chesnutt was born in Ohio but raised in North Carolina. Many of his short stories are in a book called *The Conjure Woman*.

A southern dancing party

American Literature

"The Wife of His Youth"
Charles W. Chesnutt

African American Charles W. Chesnutt wrote about slavery and racial prejudice. In "The Wife of His Youth," the main character, Mr. Ryder, is courting a young widow, Mrs. Dixon. Ryder has been apart from his wife for 25 years. He must choose between his first wife, a woman he married when he was a slave, and the widow. In the following excerpt, Mr. Ryder tells his friends about his wife.

"Suppose that this husband, soon after his escape, had learned that his wife had been sold away, and that such inquiries [investigations] as he could make brought no information of her whereabouts. . . . Suppose, too, that he made his way to the North . . . and there, where he had larger opportunities, had improved [himself]. . . . And then suppose that accident should bring to his knowledge the fact that the wife of his youth, . . . was alive and seeking him, but that he was absolutely safe from recognition or discovery, unless he chose to reveal himself. My friends, what would the man do? . . ."

Charles W. Chesnutt
The Granger Collection, New York

There was something in Mr. Ryder's voice that stirred the hearts of those who sat around him. . . . It was observed, too, that his look rested more especially upon Mrs. Dixon. . . .

She was the first to speak: "He should have acknowledged her." "Yes," they all echoed, "he should have acknowledged her."

"My friends and companions," responded Mr. Ryder, "I thank you, one and all. It is the answer I expected, for I knew your hearts."

He turned and walked toward the closed door of an adjoining room. . . . He came back in a momemt, leading by the hand his visitor of the afternoon. . . .

"Ladies and gentlemen," he said, "this is the woman, and I am the man, whose story I have told you. Permit me to introduce to you the wife of my youth."**

Understanding Literature

1. How does Mr. Ryder become separated from his wife?

2. Why do you think Mr. Ryder chooses to tell his friends about his wife?

Southern Music

Southern music also grew in popularity after the Civil War. Popular musical instruments in the South included the violin, the banjo, and the guitar. Fiddle players provided the music for square dancing, a popular pastime. Mary Noailles Murfree described a country dance in "The Dancin' Party at Harrison's Cove":

"Now and then a guffaw [laugh] mingled with the violin's resonant [loud] strains and the dancers' well-marked pace; the women talked to each other with somewhat more animation [cheerfulness] than was their wont [typical practice], under the stress of the unusual excitement of a dancing party."

One of the most important musical styles of the period was the spiritual. These songs were based on Christian hymns and African music sung in the days of slavery. In these songs the lead singer often called out a verse that the rest of the singers would repeat. Although the lead singer might change the words slightly to reflect current events, the lyrics usually described the sorrows of slavery and the hope for freedom. One of the best-known spirituals, "Swing Low Sweet Chariot," expressed African Americans' longing for "the promised land," where they would be free from slavery:

Many of the original Fisk Jubilee Singers were recently emancipated slaves.

❝ Swing low sweet chariot,
Comin' for to carry me home,
Swing low sweet chariot,
Comin' for to carry me home,
I look'd over Jordan, an' what did I see,
Comin' for to carry me home,
A band of angels comin' after me,
Comin' for to carry me home,
If you get-a there befo' I do,
Tell all of my friends I'm comin' too. ❞

During Reconstruction, the Fisk Jubilee Singers—a group of students from Fisk University in Nashville, Tennessee—traveled widely to earn money for their school. They brought African American music to a national audience. This singing group entertained people with spirituals, touring the United States in 1871 and 1872 and performing in Europe in 1873. Their tours made Fisk University famous and also raised enough money to save the college from financial ruin and build a new campus. Other African American colleges, such as Hampton University in Virginia, formed similar singing groups, which increased the popularity of spirituals.

SECTION 4 REVIEW

Identify and explain the significance of the following:

- sharecropping
- Henry Grady
- Mark Twain
- Mary Noailles Murfree
- Joel Chandler Harris
- Charles W. Chesnutt

Reading for Content Understanding

1 **Main Idea** What were some of the drawbacks of being a sharecropper in the years after the Civil War?

2 **Main Idea** Why did some business leaders want to develop southern industry?

3 **Cultural Diversity** What types of southern culture were popular throughout the United States?

4 **Writing** *Describing* Write a paragraph describing what life might have been like in a southern mill.

5 **Critical Thinking** *Making Comparisons* How were the lives of black and white sharecroppers similar? How were they different?

CHAPTER 4 REVIEW

Chapter Summary

After the Civil War, the United States struggled with restoring the southern states to the Union and dealing with the rights of former slaves. Americans differed in their approach to Reconstruction. At the end of Reconstruction, the Union was restored, but African Americans continued to be denied their full citizenship rights. ■

On a separate sheet of paper, complete the following activities.

Identifying People and Ideas

Describe the historical significance of the following:

1. Thirteenth Amendment
2. Freedmen's Bureau
3. Black Codes
4. Andrew Johnson
5. Hiram Revels
6. Fourteenth Amendment
7. Ulysses S. Grant
8. Ku Klux Klan
9. *Plessy v. Ferguson*
10. sharecropping

Internet Activity

go.hrw.com
SB1 Colleges

Search the Internet through the HRW Web site to find information on one of the historically black colleges or universities that was founded during Reconstruction. Then use the information to create a one-page brochure about that school.

Understanding Main Ideas

1. How did the Reconstruction plans of Lincoln, the Radical Republicans, and Johnson differ?
2. What was the Civil Rights Act of 1866? Why did President Johnson veto it, and how did Congress react to his veto?
3. How did the Reconstruction Acts of 1867 protect the rights of African Americans in the South?
4. What roles did African Americans, northerners, and white southern Democrats play in Reconstruction?
5. Why were most white southerners loyal to the Democratic Party?
6. What crisis was resolved by the Compromise of 1877? What were the elements of this compromise?
7. What musical styles were popular in the South after the Civil War?

Using the Time Line

Number your paper from 1 to 5. Match the letters on the time line below with the following events.

1. Congress proposes the Fifteenth Amendment, giving African American men the right to vote.
2. Democrats take control of the House of Representatives.
3. Hiram Revels becomes the first African American senator.
4. Congress proposes an amendment to make slavery illegal throughout the United States.
5. Americans elect Ulysses S. Grant, a Civil War hero, president.

1865   a   1868   b   c   d   1871   1874   e   1877

Reviewing Themes

1. **Constitutional Heritage**   Which three amendments to the Constitution attempted to protect the rights of African Americans? How did these amendments protect those rights?
2. **Citizenship and Democracy**   How did democracy expand during Reconstruction?
3. **Cultural Diversity**   What contributions did African Americans make to southern society, government, and culture?

Thinking Critically

1. **Drawing Conclusions**   Why might southern culture have increased in popularity during the late 1800s?
2. **Synthesizing Information**   If you were a freedperson living in the South in 1870, how would your life have changed after emancipation?
3. **Evaluating**   How might the Redeemers' efforts to limit the rights of African Americans affect poor whites?

Writing About History

1. **Informing**   Imagine that you are a foreign newspaper reporter in Washington. Write a one-paragraph news article on either the assassination of President Lincoln or President Johnson's impeachment trial.

Building Your Portfolio

Complete the following activities individually or in groups.

1. **Travel Journal**   Imagine that you are traveling through the South during Reconstruction. Create a journal describing what you see. You may wish to include maps of the places you have visited and descriptions of the people you have met.
2. **Freedom**   Write a poem or song about an African American who was set free at the end of the Civil War. If you create a poem, find an image to illustrate it. If you write a song, select a musical style in which it would be performed.

2. **Describing**   Imagine that you are a teacher from the North who moved to the South to teach African Americans after the Civil War. Write a letter to your family telling them about your experiences.

Linking Geography and History

1. **Movement**   Why did many freedpeople leave their homes and towns?
2. **Place**   Explain why the Civil War left the South a poor region.

History Skills Workshop

Reading Maps   Study the map below, which shows historically black colleges and universities, and answer the following questions:
(a) According to the map, which state had the most African American colleges and universities?
(b) Which states located outside the former Confederacy had African American colleges and universities? (c) Why might most African American colleges and universities have been located in the South?

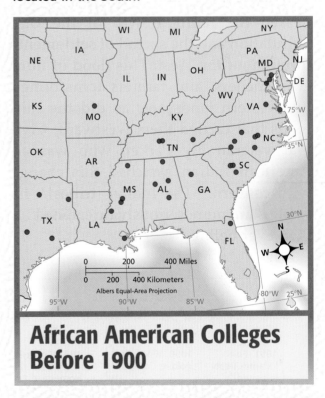

African American Colleges Before 1900

▪ CHAPTER 5 ▪
The West
(1850–1890)

After the Civil War, Americans witnessed the rapid growth of the U.S. population and the spread of settlements throughout the West. This flood of miners, ranchers, and farmers transformed the western landscape, as did the railroads that carried them westward. Civil War veteran Ely Parker, who was an American Indian, watched this change with concern. "The Indian [tribes]," he wrote, "are more seriously threatened . . . than ever before."

THEMES

Economic Development
In what ways might a government promote economic development in a new region?

Cultural Diversity
How might the actions of one group affect the culture of another?

Geographic Diversity
How might people adjust to living in a different environment?

1850	1855	1860	1865	1870

1851 Fort Laramie Treaty is signed.

1858 Miners find gold in Colorado.

1862 Congress passes the Homestead Act.

1869 The first transcontinental railroad is completed.

1874 Gold is discovered in the Black Hills.

1864 The Sand Creek Massacre occurs.

The Wars for the West

Reading Focus

What was life like for American Indians on the Great Plains?

What were the causes and results of conflict between American Indians and U.S. settlers in the West?

How did the reservation system and the Dawes Act affect American Indians?

Key Terms

Fort Laramie Treaty

reservations

Sand Creek Massacre

Bozeman Trail

Treaty of Medicine Lodge

Battle of the Little Bighorn

Long Walk

Ghost Dance

Massacre at Wounded Knee

Dawes General Allotment Act

The Granger Collection, New York

LIKE MANY SIOUX BEFORE HIM, *Standing Bear was eager for his first buffalo hunt. "Watch the buffalo closely. . . . They are very quick and powerful," warned his father. "They can get their horns under your horse and toss him high in the air." When he got close to the buffalo herd, Standing Bear recalled, "I realized how small I was." He brought down a buffalo and rode proudly back to camp to give his mother the buffalo skin. Buffalo hunts were important to American Indians' way of life on the Great Plains.*

Cheyenne warrior's shield

IMAGE ON LEFT PAGE: *Plains Indians observe the westward movement of settlers and the railroad in the late 1800s.*

1875

1876 The Sioux defeat the U.S. Army in the Battle of the Little Bighorn.

1880

1881 Helen Hunt Jackson's *A Century of Dishonor* is published.

1885

1887 Congress approves the Dawes General Allotment Act.

1890

1890 The Massacre at Wounded Knee ends the war between the U.S. Army and Plains Indians.

⭐ The Great Plains

The Great Plains lie between the Mississippi River and the Rocky Mountains, stretching north into Canada and south into Texas. Early explorers such as Stephen Long thought that the Great Plains, which were dry and barren except for grasslands, were no better than a desert.

Despite their harshness, the Great Plains were home to the Plains Indians. Groups such as the Apache and the Comanche lived on the southern Plains around Texas and present-day Oklahoma. The Cheyenne and Arapaho roamed across the central Plains. The Pawnee occupied parts of Nebraska, while the Sioux spread north across Minnesota to Montana. Plains Indians spoke many languages and used a common sign language to communicate with each other.

Sioux moccasins

For survival, Plains Indians depended on two animals—the horse and the buffalo. After the Spanish brought horses to America in the 1500s, Plains Indians traveled on horseback and became highly mobile. Indian hunters were able to move onto the Plains year-round, following the herds of buffalo that roamed the land.

Most hunters used a short bow and arrows to shoot the buffalo at close range from horseback. Plains Indians used the buffalo for food, shelter, and tools. Women dried buffalo meat to make jerky. They also made clothing and tepees from buffalo hides and cups and tools from buffalo horns. As one Sioux explained, "When our people killed a buffalo, all of the animal was utilized [used] in some manner; nothing was wasted." With the buffalo providing many of their needs, the Plains Indians prospered. By 1850 some 75,000 American Indians lived on the Plains.

⭐ Negotiations and Conflicts

When miners and settlers began crossing the Great Plains in the mid-1800s, U.S. officials sent agents to negotiate treaties with the Plains Indians. The first major agreement was the **Fort Laramie Treaty**, signed with northern Plains tribes in Wyoming in

1851. Two years later, several southern Plains tribes signed a treaty at Fort Atkinson in Kansas.

These treaties accepted Indian claims to most of the Great Plains and allowed the United States to build forts and roads and to travel across Indian homelands. The U.S. government promised to pay for any damages to Indian land. The treaties, however, did not keep the peace for long. After the discovery of gold in present-day Colorado in 1858, thousands of miners came into conflict with the Cheyenne and Arapaho.

In 1861 the U.S. government negotiated new treaties that created **reservations**, areas of federal land set aside for Indians. The Bureau of Indian Affairs operated the reservations. The government expected Indians to stay on the reservations, which made hunting buffalo almost impossible. Many Indians refused to live on reservations. Some continued to fight, while others shared the view of Cheyenne chief Black Kettle. "It is not my intention or wish to fight the whites," he declared. "I want to be friendly and peaceable and keep my tribe so."

He did not get his wish. In November 1864 U.S. Army colonel John M. Chivington led a surprise attack on Black Kettle's camp on Sand Creek

Several African American cavalry regiments served in the western U.S. Army. American Indians nicknamed these African American troops "buffalo soldiers."

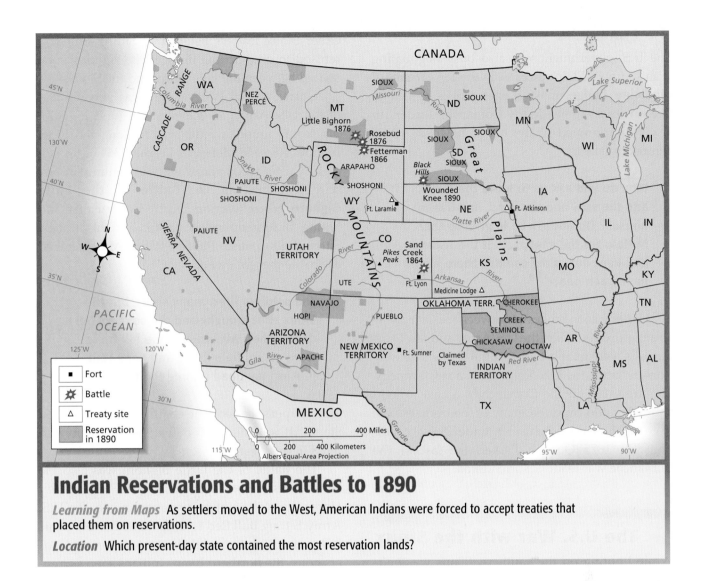

Indian Reservations and Battles to 1890

Learning from Maps As settlers moved to the West, American Indians were forced to accept treaties that placed them on reservations.

Location Which present-day state contained the most reservation lands?

in southeastern Colorado. The Cheyenne raised a white flag and a U.S. flag to show that they were peaceful. Chivington ignored the flags. "Kill and scalp all, big and little," he ordered. The soldiers killed around 200 men, women, and children. Black Kettle was among the Cheyenne who escaped the **Sand Creek Massacre**.

 ## Fighting on the Plains

News of the Sand Creek Massacre spread across the Great Plains. Along with the news came more pioneers, miners, and conflicts.

The Bozeman Trail

Many miners used the **Bozeman Trail**, a route named after pioneer John M. Bozeman that ran from Wyoming to Montana. To protect the miners, the U.S. Army built forts along the trail, which went through Sioux hunting grounds. Sioux chief Red Cloud responded to the army's actions with war. In late 1866 warrior Crazy Horse and a group of Sioux lured 82 cavalry troops to their deaths in an ambush.

William Tecumseh Sherman, the famous Civil War general, had been placed in charge of the western armies. He threatened the "extermination [of the Sioux], men, women, and children." The U.S. Army had little success in this effort, however, and asked Red Cloud to negotiate. He replied, "When we see the soldiers moving away and the forts abandoned, then I will come down and talk." In 1868 the U.S. Army closed the Bozeman Trail and abandoned the forts along it. Many Sioux then moved to the Black Hills Reservation in Dakota Territory.

The Comanche

The U.S. government was also busy negotiating with southern Plains Indians. In the 1867 **Treaty of Medicine Lodge**, most of these tribes agreed to live on reservations. Many Comanche leaders in Texas disapproved of the treaty, however. Chief Ten Bears asked:

❝ Why do you ask us to leave the rivers, and the sun, and the wind, and live in houses? Do not ask us to give up the buffalo for the sheep. . . . If the Texans had kept out of my country, there might have been peace. ❞

Fighting soon broke out between the Comanche and the Texans. When the U.S. Army and the Texas Rangers were unable to defeat the Comanche warriors in battle, the U.S. forces tried a new strategy. The army cut off the Comanche's access to food and water and captured many of their horses. The Comanche could not survive under these conditions. In 1875 Quanah Parker, the last of the Comanche war leaders, surrendered.

★ The U.S. War with the Sioux

While fighting on the southern Plains was ending, new trouble was starting to the north. In 1874 Lieutenant Colonel George Armstrong Custer's soldiers discovered gold in the Black Hills. The U.S. government responded by insisting that the Sioux who lived in the area sell their reservation land in the Black Hills. Sitting Bull, a Sioux shaman, or spiritual leader, protested these new demands:

❝ What treaty that the whites have kept has the red man broken? Not one. What treaty that the white man ever made with us have they kept? Not one. ❞

Other Sioux leaders listened to Sitting Bull and refused to give up the Black Hills. Fighting soon started between the U.S. Army and the Sioux.

Custer, a Civil War veteran, was in command of the U.S. Army 7th Cavalry. On June 25, 1876, his scouts found a Sioux camp along the Little Bighorn River in Montana. Leading 264 of his soldiers, Custer raced ahead without waiting for any reinforcements. In the **Battle of the Little Bighorn**, Sioux warriors led by Crazy Horse and Sitting Bull surrounded Custer and his troops. Sitting Bull's cousin Pte-San-Waste-Win described the battle that followed:

❝ The soldiers fired many shots, but the Sioux shot straight and the soldiers fell dead. When we came to the hill there were no soldiers living and Long Hair [Custer] lay dead among the rest. ❞

Newspapers called the battle "Custer's Last Stand." It was the worst defeat the U.S. Army suffered in the West.

The Battle of the Little Bighorn was also the Sioux's last major victory. In late 1877 Crazy Horse was killed after surrendering to the U.S. Army. Sitting Bull fled to Canada with a few of his followers. With two of their most important leaders gone, the northern Plains Indians soon surrendered to the U.S. Army.

At the Battle of the Little Bighorn, a troop of the 7th Cavalry suffered a devastating defeat at the hands of Sioux warriors. None of the cavalry troops survived the battle.

The Granger Collection, New York

Indians in the Southwest and Far West

Far from the Great Plains, other American Indians fought against their relocation to reservations. Their struggles were rarely successful.

The Long Walk

In 1863 the U.S. government ordered the Navajo of present-day Arizona and New Mexico to settle on a reservation. The Navajo refused. Kit Carson, a former scout, led U.S. troops in raids on the Navajo's fields, homes, and livestock. Then he lay siege to the Navajo warriors, who were in a well-defended canyon in northeastern Arizona.

When the Navajo ran out of food and shelter, they started surrendering to the U.S. Army. In 1864 the army led Navajo captives on the **Long Walk**, a 300-mile march across the desert to a reservation at Bosque Redondo, New Mexico. Along the way, hundreds of Navajo died. At Bosque Redondo the Navajo suffered harsh conditions until 1868, when they negotiated for a new reservation located in Arizona and New Mexico.

The Nez Percé

While the Navajo were moving to their new reservation, the U.S. government was promising to let the peaceful Nez Percé keep their homelands in northeastern Oregon. Within a few years, however, settlers persuaded the government to move the Nez Percé to a reservation in present-day Idaho.

Nez Percé leader Chief Joseph reluctantly agreed to move. Before leaving, a few angry Nez Percé killed some settlers. Fearing revenge, the Nez Percé fled. The U.S. Army chased this band of around 700 Indians across Idaho, Wyoming, and Montana. Although outnumbered, the band defeated or avoided the army for weeks before trying to escape to Canada. Less than 40 miles

American Literature

"I Will Fight No More Forever"
Chief Joseph

Chief Joseph led the Nez Percé from 1871 to 1877. He gave the following speech to the U.S. Army officers who took him prisoner on October 5, 1877.

Chief Joseph

Tell General Howard I know his heart. What he told me before, I have in my heart. I am tired of fighting. Our chiefs are killed. . . . The old men are all dead. It is the young men who say yes and no. He who led on the young men [Joseph's brother, Alokut] is dead. It is cold and we have no blankets. The little children are freezing to death. My people, some of them, have run away to the hills, and have no blankets, no food; no one knows where they are perhaps freezing to death. I want to have time to look for my children and see how many I can find. Maybe I shall find them among the dead. Hear me, my chiefs. I am tired; my heart is sick and sad. From where the sun now stands I will fight no more forever.

Understanding Literature

1. How does Chief Joseph express his grief for the condition of his people?

2. Why does Chief Joseph want to "fight no more forever"?

Biography

Geronimo

Many Apache found it difficult to get along with Geronimo—he had grown bitter after Mexican soldiers killed his wife and children. Despite this bitterness, other Apache admired Geronimo for his intelligence and resourcefulness. "In times of danger he was a man to be relied upon," recalled his cousin.

As a young warrior, Geronimo fought alongside the great Apache leader Cochise. Eventually, Geronimo led his own band of warriors. He was captured several times, but usually managed to escape. Geronimo surrendered to U.S. troops in 1886 and remained a prisoner of war until he died in 1909. His courage and determination to remain free made Geronimo a legend.

from the border, U.S. troops overtook and surrounded the Nez Percé. Chief Joseph surrendered on October 5, 1877, and the U.S. government sent the Nez Percé to a reservation in present-day Oklahoma.

The End of Armed Resistance

By the 1880s most American Indians had stopped fighting. The Apache of the Southwest, however, continued to battle the U.S. Army. The Apache were fierce raiders, known for their ability to survive in the desert. Settlers living illegally on Apache lands feared them. In the 1870s the U.S. Army gathered some Apache on a reservation in San Carlos, Arizona. One Apache called the reservation "nothing but cactus, rattlesnakes, heat, rocks, and insects."

A Chiricahua Apache named Geronimo and his small band of warriors left the reservation and resisted capture until 1884. The next year Geronimo escaped again. When the U.S. Army caught him, he broke free once more on the way to the reservation. "I feared treachery [dishonesty]," he said. This time the army sent 5,000 soldiers to capture Geronimo and 24 of his followers. Finally, in September 1886, he surrendered, ending the Apache armed resistance. The U.S. government sent Geronimo and all Chiricahua Apache to Florida as prisoners of war.

The Ghost Dance and Wounded Knee

Meanwhile, in 1881 Sitting Bull and his Sioux followers returned from Canada after running out of food during the hard winter. "I wish it to be remembered," Sitting Bull said, "that I was the last man of my tribe to surrender my rifle." He joined most of the Sioux on Standing Rock Reservation in Dakota Territory. Black Elk, a Sioux shaman, described the difficulties of reservation life: "All our people now were settling down in square gray houses . . . around them the [whites] had drawn a line to keep them in. . . . The people were in despair."

At this time a religious movement known as the **Ghost Dance** began. Wovoka, a Paiute Indian, predicted the arrival of a paradise in which Indians would live freely and at peace. The buffalo herds would return and the settlers would disappear. This paradise was for those Indians who performed the sacred Ghost Dance.

When the Ghost Dance spread across the Plains, U.S. officials did not understand its meaning. They did, however, fear that it would inspire the Sioux to rebel. While following orders to arrest Sioux leaders, reservation police killed Sitting Bull in 1890. In response, many Sioux left the reservations. Later that year, the U.S. Army found a camp of Sioux near Wounded Knee Creek in South Dakota. When the two groups faced one another, a shot rang out. The U.S. troops began firing and killed at least 150 Indians. This **Massacre at Wounded Knee** marked the end of more than 25 years of war on the Great Plains.

⭐ Policy and Protest

By the 1870s many American Indian tribes were living on reservations. Indian leaders spoke out against the reservation system, complaining that Bureau agents stole government food and money meant for Indians. In addition, reservation land was usually not suitable for farming or buffalo hunting. As a result, many Indians were starving.

In the late 1870s a Paiute Indian named Sarah Winnemucca became one of the first Indians to call for reform. "Day after day my people were begging me to go east to talk for them," she explained. She eventually pleaded her case in Washington. She also gave lectures on the need to reform the reservation system. After listening to her, "many people were moved to tears," according to one spectator.

Another person pushing for reservation reform was writer Helen Hunt Jackson. In 1881 she published *A Century of Dishonor*, which criticized the federal government's treatment of Indians. She wrote that "it makes little difference where one opens the record of the history of the Indians;

every page and every year has its dark stain." The popularity of Jackson's writings helped spread the reform message.

Once the major wars for the West had ended, many reformers believed that Indians would be better off if they adopted the ways of white people. Congress passed the **Dawes General Allotment Act** in 1887 to lessen the tribal influence on Indian society by making land ownership private rather than shared. The Dawes Act split up reservation lands and divided them among individual Indians. Families were supposed to receive 160 acres, single adults 80 acres. The act also promised U.S. citizenship to American Indians.

After it split up the reservations, the government sold the land that remained unassigned. As a result, Indians lost much of the land that they occupied before the Dawes Act. Despite the hopes of reformers, the Dawes Act claimed more land from American Indians than all the wars combined, did not grant them citizenship as promised, and failed to improve their lives.

The Granger Collection, New York

Sarah Winnemucca

Miners and Railroads

Reading Focus

What were some of the challenges of mining in the West?

What obstacles did the builders of the transcontinental railroad face?

How did the transcontinental railroad affect the settlement and development of the West?

Key Terms

Comstock Lode
bonanza
boom towns
Pony Express
transcontinental railroad
Pacific Railway Acts

I N 1859 GREAT EXCITEMENT *swept the United States when news reached the East of a Colorado* gold strike in 1858. Traveling west to examine this find, New York Tribune *editor Horace Greeley announced that the "discovery is . . . the richest and greatest [gold mine] in America." Thousands of prospectors in wagons labeled "Pikes Peak or Bust" raced west to the mining region around Pikes Peak. Most of these "fifty-niners," as they were called, traveled hundreds of miles only to find that the early prospectors had started the rush by filling part of their mine with extra gold.*

Gold ore

 ## The Mining Booms

Many fifty-niners, still full of excitement created by the California Gold Rush, continued to search for strikes. Some miners found gold in other parts of Colorado. Gold rushes also occurred in Idaho in 1862 and two years later in Montana.

The Comstock Lode

The same year that miners rushed to Pikes Peak, prospectors Peter O'Riley and Patrick McLaughlin struck gold and silver in western Nevada. Their good fortune attracted the attention of miner Henry Comstock, who convinced the partners that he owned the water source they were using at the mine. O'Riley and McLaughlin gave Comstock a share in their find to avoid legal trouble. Comstock bragged that he had found the mine, and the discovery became known as the **Comstock Lode**.

Within a year, thousands of California miners arrived, and Virginia City sprang up almost overnight. The Comstock Lode was a **bonanza**—a large deposit of precious ore. In the next 20 years, the Lode produced nearly $400 million worth of gold and silver.

These miners are bringing ore out of a mine shaft along the Comstock Lode in the 1860s.

Mining Companies

Comstock sold his share of the mine to a big corporation for $11,000. Large companies had the funds needed to remove the silver and gold trapped within the quartz rock. To get this quartz, miners dug and blasted tunnels hundreds of feet long into the mountain. Then they loaded the ore onto mining carts and brought it to the surface. The ore was usually shipped by train to a refining center, where powerful stamping mills crushed the ore, and large machines called smelters melted the pieces so that the metal could be separated. Mining became a big business as large companies bought up mining claims from miners who could not afford such expensive equipment.

A Miner's Life

As companies dug bigger and deeper mines in the West, the work became more dangerous. Miners risked their lives every day that they went underground.

Working in the Mines

To ride down into the mines, miners squeezed together on elevator platforms just a few feet wide. These "cages" had no walls, and a careless move or an accident could pin a miner between the wall and the moving cage with deadly results. Down in the poorly lit tunnels, miners used picks, drills, and explosives to get to the gold- and silver-rich rock. In the 1860s miners began using power drills, which produced dust that caused serious lung problems. Unexpected explosions killed or injured many miners. In addition, dynamite explosions sometimes created poisonous gases.

In the deeper tunnels, temperatures often rose above 130°F. An Idaho miner recalled that in the cold winters, "I came off work soaked to the skin, and before reaching home all my clothes were frozen fast on me and I couldn't take them off myself." The hot, stuffy air was often filled with toxic gases. Some tunnels had so little oxygen that candles would not burn. Cave-ins and floods from underground springs sometimes killed miners or trapped them below ground. The threat of fire in the mines was also a great concern. With all these hazards, mining was one of the most dangerous jobs in the country. In the West, concerns about safety and wages led to the creation of several miners' unions in the 1860s.

The Miners

In addition to the dangerous work, miners faced other difficulties. Many Mexican immigrants and Mexican Americans were experienced miners, skilled in assaying, or testing, the contents of valuable ore. Despite their skill, they were often denied the better-paying mining jobs. Chinese immigrants faced similar job discrimination.

People from all over the world worked in the western mines. Some miners came from the eastern United States, while others immigrated from Europe, Central and South America, Asia, and Australia. Some miners hoped to get rich and return to their native countries, but most hoped to stay in the United States.

Mining Towns

Mining booms also produced **boom towns**, communities that grew suddenly when a mine opened and disappeared just as quickly when the mine closed down. Most boom towns had general stores, saloons, and boardinghouses. Business owners charged high prices for goods and services. This was partly to make a big profit and partly because most merchandise had to be shipped west and then transported to the remote mining communities. "The sociable [friendly] man is lost in the money making," admitted one store

Families faced many hardships in the early mining camps.

owner. In his autobiographical work *Roughing It*, Mark Twain described Virginia City during its boom years:

> 66 [It] had grown to be the 'livest' town . . . that America had ever produced. The sidewalks swarmed with people. . . . The streets themselves were just as crowded. . . . Money-getting schemes . . . were . . . in every brain. 99

Boom towns were dangerous places that lacked basic law and order. "To be raised in a mining camp," as one man put it, "means an experience as full of thrills and wounds and scars as going to the war." There were few women or families in most boom towns. In 1860, for example, there were more than 75 men for every woman in Virginia City. Most women who lived in mining towns faced a life of hard work and few friends. "I was never so lonely and homesick in all my life," wrote one young woman.

Women contributed to the local economy by washing, cooking, making clothes, chopping wood, and growing food for the miners. Women also helped turn some mining camps into successful permanent communities by raising families, teaching in schools, and writing for local papers. Such efforts drew more Americans to the West.

★ Crossing the Continent

More Americans began moving west, increasing the need to send goods and information between the East and West. The **Pony Express**, established in 1860, used a system of messengers on horseback to carry mail from one relay station to another along a 2,000-mile route. Telegraph lines, which sent messages faster, quickly put the Pony Express out of business.

Some Americans hoped to improve communication and travel across the country by building a **transcontinental railroad** to connect the East to the West. Many business-people and politicians were confident that such a railroad could be built despite the many geographic obstacles and the expensive labor and resources needed.

Poster advertising the Pony Express

To help railroad companies overcome these difficulties, the federal government passed the **Pacific Railway Acts** in 1862 and in 1864. These acts gave railroad companies loans and large land grants, which could be sold to pay for construction costs. By 1872 Congress had granted more than 125 million acres of public land to railroad companies. In exchange, the government required the railroads to carry U.S. mail and troops at reduced rates. These acts inspired many companies to begin laying tracks.

★ The Great Race

Two companies, the Central Pacific and the Union Pacific, took the lead in the great race to complete the transcontinental railroad. In February 1863 the Central Pacific began building east from Sacramento, California. At the end of the year, the Union Pacific started in Omaha, Nebraska, and headed west.

Working on the Railroad

To build its railroad, the Union Pacific hired thousands of workers, particularly Irish immigrants.

Global Connections

The Railroads of India

While workers were completing the world's first transcontinental railroad in Promontory, Utah, other nations were building their own massive rail systems. Great Britain was developing one of the world's largest railroad networks in India, which was then part of the vast British Empire.

In the early 1800s Britain wanted to increase trade with India by selling British-made manufactured goods there and by getting raw materials from remote Indian regions. A railroad would make such trade easier. In addition, a rail system would allow the British to strengthen their military control over India and to improve communications.

The British pushed to construct the railroad quickly. Between 1859 and 1869, Indian laborers laid more than 5,000 miles of track. As in the United States, laying track in India posed many challenges to workers and engineers. Large rivers and mountains made the work difficult and dangerous. Two sections of land in the Western Ghats Mountains were so rugged and steep that workers had to build 81 bridges and 38 tunnels for the railroad to get through the mountain range. Despite such obstacles, by 1900 some 25,000 miles of railway stretched across India,

Engineers overcame many geographic obstacles to build India's railroads.

making the Indian rail network larger than any other in Asia.

The railroad carried mail, freight, and passengers. Most of the railroad's business came from transporting passengers. In 1855 the newspaper *Friend of India* noted, "The fondness for traveling by rail has become almost a national passion . . . and it is producing a social change in the habits of general society."

Understanding What You Read

1. Why did the British want to build a rail network in India?
2. What benefits did the railroad system in India have in common with the transcontinental railroad in the United States?

Some laborers were Civil War veterans. Under former brigadier general Jack Casement, "the Casement Army" worked long, hard days laying rails across the Great Plains.

Chinese immigrants made up some 85 percent of the Central Pacific workforce. The railroad's part-owner Leland Stanford praised these Chinese workers as "quiet, peaceful, [and] industrious" but paid them less than white laborers. Chinese crews were also given the most dangerous jobs and were

required to work longer hours than other railroad laborers. Nonetheless, Chinese workers took on the job because the $30 a month that the Central Pacific paid was in some cases 10 times as high as wages in China.

Geographic Obstacles

The Central Pacific workers struggled to cross the Sierra Nevada range in California. Breaking apart

The success of the transcontinental railroad led to the creation of other railroad lines linking the East and the West. Here workers on the Northern Pacific pose for an 1886 photograph.

its rock formations required large amounts of blasting powder and the explosive nitroglycerin. In the winter of 1866, many workers were trapped and killed in snow drifts over 60 feet high. "Many of them we did not find until . . . the snow melted," reported a company official.

Meanwhile, the Union Pacific workers faced harsh weather on the Great Plains. In addition, the company pressured them to work at a rapid pace—at times laying 250 miles of track in six months. Faced with greater geographic obstacles, the Central Pacific took four years to lay the first 115 miles of track. For both lines, providing food and supplies for their workers became more difficult as they pushed into remote areas. The railroad companies often relied on local resources. Professional hunters such as "Buffalo Bill" Cody shot thousands of buffalo to feed workers on the Union Pacific as it crossed the Plains.

The Golden Spike

When the two railroads neared completion, Congress required them to connect at Promontory, Utah. On May 10, 1869, workers and reporters watched the two lines meet for the first time. In a dramatic ceremony, a golden spike was used to

Workers from the Central Pacific and the Union Pacific celebrate the completion of the transcontinental railroad at Promontory, Utah.

connect the railroad tie joining the two tracks. Alexander Toponce witnessed the event:

❝ **Governor Stanford, president of the Central Pacific, took the sledge [hammer], and the first time he struck he missed the spike and hit the rail. What a howl went up! Irish, Chinese, Mexicans, and everybody yelled with delight. 'He missed it.' . . . Then Stanford tried it again and tapped the spike. . . . The tap was reported in all the offices east and west.** ❞

The transcontinental railroad had finally united the East and the West. Following its completion, companies continued building railroads until the West was crisscrossed with shining rails.

⭐ The Impact of the Railroads

The transcontinental railroad increased both economic growth and the population in the West. The railroad companies encouraged settlement by providing better transportation for people and goods and by selling land to settlers.

Time and Cargo

Another benefit of railroads was that they saved time. The Union Pacific advertised that a trip from Omaha, Nebraska, to San Francisco, California,

Advertisement for the Union Pacific Railroad

would take four days—instead of a month by wagon. The Union Pacific also promised greater safety: "Travelers for pleasure, health or business will find a trip over the Rocky Mountains healthy and pleasant."

The new railroads also helped businesses. In time, telegraph lines ran alongside railroads, opening up the West to faster and more convenient communication. Western timber companies, miners, cattle ranchers, and farmers used railroads to ship items to the East. Wood, metals, beef, and grain traveled east in exchange for manufactured products that were shipped west.

Railroad Booms and Busts

Railroad companies encouraged people to invest money in the railroads, sometimes unwisely. Railroad speculation and the collapse of railroad owner Jay Cooke's banking firm helped start the

Population of Omaha

102,555

1,833

1860   1900

Sources: Bureau of the Census; U.S. Department of Commerce

City on the Rise   In 1865 the Union Pacific Railroad laid its tracks through the city of Omaha, Nebraska, causing the population to soar. How much did Omaha's population increase between 1860 and 1900?

Panic of 1873 and the depression that followed. By the 1880s many of the smaller western railroads were deep in debt.

Despite such setbacks, Americans remained interested in railroad investments. By 1890 there were around 199,000 miles of railroad track in operation compared to only about 35,000 miles in 1865. Almost 750,000 Americans worked for railroad companies. Railroads had become one of the biggest industries in the United States and one of the most important in the West.

SECTION 2 REVIEW

Identify and explain the significance of the following:
- **Comstock Lode**
- **bonanza**
- **boom towns**
- **Pony Express**
- **transcontinental railroad**
- **Pacific Railway Acts**
- **Leland Stanford**

Reading for Content Understanding

1 **Main Idea** Why was mining one of the most dangerous jobs in the West?

2 **Main Idea** What were some of the difficulties in building a transcontinental railroad?

3 **Cultural Diversity** Why do you think so few women lived in mining towns?

4 **Writing** *Creating* Write a short song that might have been sung at the celebration of the connection of the Union Pacific and Central Pacific Railroads. Your song should focus on how the railroad will change life in the West or improve communication between family members.

5 **Critical Thinking** *Drawing Conclusions* Why do you think the railroad is still one of the most effective ways of transporting goods across the country, even though faster forms of transportation have been developed?

The Cattle Kingdom

Reading Focus

What factors led to a cattle boom in the 1870s?

What was life like for cowboys?

What caused the decline of the Cattle Kingdom?

Key Terms

Texas longhorn   cattle drive

Cattle Kingdom   Chisholm Trail

open range   range wars

range rights

vaqueros

roundup

IN THE MID-1800s *Texas ranchers began gathering up huge herds of wild cattle. Describing these herds, one rancher wrote, "Cattle are permitted to range . . . over a large surface of country, thirty, forty, and even fifty miles in extent [size]." Keeping track of these roaming cattle required great skill. Although the ranch hands who did this work faced many hardships, a rancher wrote that "the young men that follow this 'Cow-Boy' life . . . generally become attached to it." These cowboys and ranchers helped start the cattle-ranching industry in the West.*

A wealthy rancher bought this golden bull clock.

The Roots of Ranching

Spanish settlers brought their cattle to California and Texas in the 1700s. These cattle later mixed with English breeds to create the **Texas longhorn**, which spread rapidly throughout western Texas. Longhorn cattle were lean and tough, with horns up to five feet across. Many butchers said the longhorn had too little meat, calling it "8 pounds of hamburger on 800 pounds of bone and horn." Nonetheless, settlers preferred to raise longhorns because the animals needed very little water and could survive harsh weather.

The new breed was also resistant to a terrible disease commonly called Texas fever. This sickness, which was transmitted by ticks that infested the cattle, was usually deadly. Unfortunately, healthy longhorns were often carriers, which meant they could endanger other cattle breeds and oxen by giving them the ticks.

In the 1850s ranchers rounded up Texas longhorns and sold them to miners, U.S. soldiers, railroad workers, and American Indians living on reservations. During the Civil War, the cattle herds grew because Texas was isolated from its markets and unable to sell cattle for much of the war.

Ranchers brought their cattle to railroad towns to sell them to buyers, who then shipped the cattle to meatpacking plants farther east.

many of their cattle north to Colorado, Wyoming, Nebraska, and Montana. In 1871 more than 600,000 cattle had been moved from Texas onto the Plains. The many ranches in the land stretching from Texas north to Canada formed the **Cattle Kingdom**. Many ranchers grazed their huge herds on the **open range**, or public land. The U.S. government did not charge ranchers for using this public land that was once occupied by Plains Indians and buffalo herds.

 ## Open-Range Ranching

Following the Civil War, the demand for beef in the East increased as the economy and the population expanded. A cow worth $3 to $6 in Texas could be sold for $38 in Kansas or $80 in New York. Nobody drove the longhorns to eastern markets, however, because of the distance and the danger of transmitting Texas fever to other farm animals.

The Cattle Boom

In 1867 businessman Joseph McCoy had the idea "to establish a market whereat the southern . . . [rancher] and the northern buyer would meet." The creation of new western railroads made this possible. McCoy built pens for cattle in the small town of Abilene, Kansas, which was located on the Kansas Pacific Railroad line. Cattle could be shipped by rail from Abilene straight to processing plants in St. Louis, Missouri. The idea was a great success. When rancher J. F. Ellison sold his cattle in Abilene, his son recalled, "This trip proved to be a profitable one. . . . Father had $9,000 cash, which was a lot of money in those days." Soon many Texas ranchers were making the trip north to sell their herds of cattle.

Around the same time, cattle ranching began to expand onto the Great Plains. Ranchers found that the tough longhorns did well on the Plains and were free of disease. In 1890 it was discovered that the cold winters killed the ticks that carried the Texas fever. Ranchers began taking

The Ranches

One of the people who saw the profits of ranching was Elizabeth Collins. When she and her husband had trouble mining gold, Collins decided "to discontinue the business of mining and engage in that of cattle raising." She moved to the Teton Valley in Montana and started ranching. She was so successful she earned the name "Cattle Queen of Montana."

Collins was just one of many ranchers who became prosperous during the cattle boom. Charles Goodnight started the first ranch in the Texas Panhandle, more than 250 miles from any town or railroad. Speculators in the East and in Europe invested money in ranches the same way that they did in railroads. Some of the resulting ranches were huge, such as the XIT Ranch, which covered more than 3 million acres.

Elizabeth Collins

Most ranchers did not own this much land. Instead, they concentrated on buying the **range rights**, or water rights, to ponds and rivers. This gave them access to scarce water as well as ownership of the land around it. With range rights, ranchers could eliminate competition by stopping farmers and other ranchers from using the water.

The West **165**

Cowboys borrowed many of their methods and equipment from the vaqueros who worked on ranches in California and the Southwest.

The remote locations of many ranches meant that some ranchers were the local authority. Joseph McCoy noted that the cattle rancher considered himself "an independent sovereign [ruler] . . . capable of conducting his affairs in his own way." Isolated ranchers needed to be self-reliant and capable of solving their own problems. Mary Jaques, who lived on a Texas ranch for two years, explained:

❝ The ideal ranchman must be butcher, baker, carpenter, . . . blacksmith, plain cook, milker. . . . It is a fact that each of these trades will have to be practiced to some extent sooner or later. ❞

★ The Cowboys

The workers who took care of a rancher's cattle were known as cowhands or cowboys. They became symbols of the American West for many people around the world. Cowboys borrowed many of their techniques from the Mexican **vaqueros** (vah-KER-ohs), ranch hands who tended cattle and horses. From the vaqueros came the western saddle, the lariat—a rope used for lassoing cattle—and the leather chaps that cowboys wore over their pants for protection against the thorny brush. The cowboys borrowed the vaqueros'

broad felt hat and changed it into the familiar high-peaked cowboy hat. Cowboys also adopted the bandanna, a cloth that covered the face to protect it from dust and served as a handkerchief or bandage.

Many cowboys were Mexican Americans or African Americans. African American cowboy Nat Love wrote an autobiography in which he described daily ranch life:

❝ When we were not on the trail taking large herds of cattle or horses to market to be delivered to other ranches, we were engaged in range riding, moving large numbers of cattle from one grazing range to another, keeping them together, and hunting up strays. ❞

Although most cowhands were men, some women worked alongside cowboys. One female rancher explained, "I love to work with my cattle, and have spent a good deal of my time on the range."

Gathering the cattle together was known as the **roundup**. At the spring roundups, cowboys branded young calves and horses. Branding involved burning a ranch's unique mark onto an animal to prevent thieves from stealing horses and cattle and selling them as their own.

Riding the range involved a great deal of hard work as well as danger from cattle thieves, bad weather, and unpredictable livestock. The words to one western song warned potential cowboys,

❝ Some boys go up the trail for pleasure, But that's where you get it most
awfully wrong.
For you haven't any idea of the trouble
they [the cattle] give us
While we go driving them along. ❞

Cowboys worked for low wages, and few were able to make enough money to start their own ranches. Despite these factors, many agreed with Love, who said he enjoyed his days as a cowboy because he had "a genuine love of the free and wild life of the range."

Cowboy Nat Love

Cattle Drives and Cattle Towns

One of the most important and dangerous duties of the cowboy was the **cattle drive**. On these long journeys, cowboys herded cattle to the market or to the northern Plains for grazing. These trips usually lasted several months and covered hundreds of miles.

Riding the Trail

The **Chisholm Trail** was one of the earliest and most popular routes for cattle drives. Blazed by Texas cowboy Jesse Chisholm in 1867, this trail ran from San Antonio, Texas, to the cattle town of Abilene, Kansas. Charles Goodnight blazed a trail leading from Texas to New Mexico Territory that became known as the Goodnight-Loving Trail. The most heavily used route, the Western Trail, headed north from San Antonio, Texas, to Dodge City, Kansas.

Cattle drives usually started in the spring. Some cowboys specialized in cattle drives and took other ranchers' cattle to market for them. These cowboys made several of the long, difficult trips in one year. Cattle driving was rugged and dangerous work. Cowboy James H. Cook described life on the trail:

❞ **There was plenty of rough country, with creeks and steep-banked rivers to be crossed. We had no tents or shelter of any sort other than our blankets.** ❞

The cattle were as difficult to deal with as the geographical challenges. During storms they would stampede. Then cowboys would have to track down the strays and round them up again. At night, cowboys had to stand watch over the cattle herds. Cowboy "Teddy Blue" Abbott complained, "There was never enough sleep. . . . I have often sat in my saddle sound asleep." Most cowboys were happy to reach the end of the cattle drive.

Cowboy's spur

The Cattle Towns

A large cattle town such as Dodge City or Abilene was usually at the end of the trail. Small businesses sprang up as more cowboys passed through town. Many of these businesses were owned or operated by women such as Malinda Jenkins, who ran a boardinghouse in Fort Worth, Texas. To get her business started, she traded her sewing machine for the first month's rent and bought a cookstove on credit. Eventually, she paid off her debts and had a successful business.

Boardinghouses, hotels, saloons, and restaurants in cattle towns counted on tired cowboys spending money during the few days they were in town. Most ranchers paid the cowboys in cash when the drive ended. Cowboys spent their money on food, hot baths, and comfortable beds after long weeks on the trail. John Baumann described his cowboy friends in Dodge City:

❞ **The boys have received their wages; $200 or $300 perhaps, in a lump, and are turning themselves loose. . . . Clean-shaven and [wearing] new store clothes from head to foot, we scarcely recognize each other.** ❞

During the cattle drive season the large number of rowdy cowboys could make life in cattle towns rough and violent. While there were rarely shoot-outs in the streets, there were

Colt revolver

often fights and disorderly behavior. Law officials such as Wyatt Earp made their reputations while keeping the peace in cattle towns.

The End of the Open Range

In the early 1880s cattle ranching became increasingly profitable. In 1882 Gustavus Swift used the newly invented refrigerator railroad car to carry beef from packing plants to the big eastern cities. This increased the national demand for beef and made cities such as Chicago, Illinois, famous for their meatpacking factories.

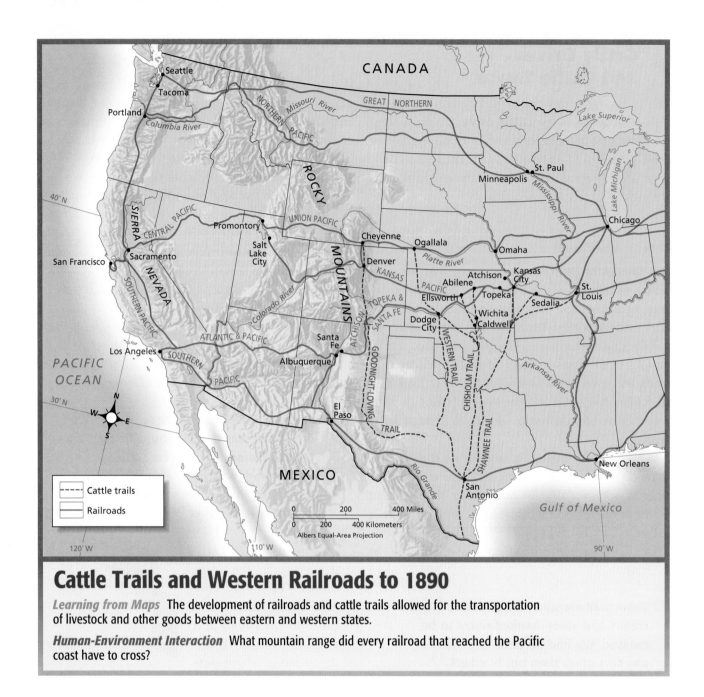

Cattle Trails and Western Railroads to 1890

Learning from Maps The development of railroads and cattle trails allowed for the transportation of livestock and other goods between eastern and western states.

Human-Environment Interaction What mountain range did every railroad that reached the Pacific coast have to cross?

Range Wars

While the cattle business boomed, ranchers faced increased competition for use of the open range. As more settlers came to the Great Plains, farmers began to buy range land where cattle had once grazed. Smaller ranchers also began competing with the large ranches for land. Then in 1873 Joseph Glidden invented barbed wire, which allowed westerners to fence off large amounts of land at a low cost. Westerners had been unable to do this because traditional fencing material, such as stones and lumber, was scarce on the Great Plains.

Large ranchers moved quickly to fence in the open range to keep out farmers and smaller ranchers. Some farmers and small ranchers responded by cutting fences and moving onto the land or stealing cattle. This competition led to **range wars** between large ranchers, small ranchers, and farmers. Although the large ranchers often won these battles, few ranchers could continue to count on letting their cattle roam free on public land.

Cattle ranchers also fought with sheep owners. As the number of sheep increased in the 1880s, so did the competition for grasslands. Sheep chewed the grass down so far that there was nothing left for the cattle. Despite threats and violence against them, sheep ranchers continued to prosper in the West.

The Decline of the Cattle Kingdom

By the 1880s an estimated 7 million cattle roamed the Great Plains. These large numbers drove down cattle prices. To improve prices, ranchers began introducing eastern cattle to the western range. These cattle produced larger amounts of tastier beef than the Texas longhorns but were not well adapted to the conditions on the Plains.

In 1885 and 1886 disaster struck the Cattle Kingdom. The huge cattle herds on the Plains had eaten much of the prairie grass that ranchers depended on for feed. Unusually severe winters in both years made the ranching situation even worse. Thousands of cattle died, particularly the new eastern breeds. Most ranches lost 30 percent of their herd, and some ranchers lost as many as 9 out of 10 cattle. "The prairies were seen thickly dotted with the dead bodies of famished [starved] and frozen animals," according to Elizabeth Collins. Rancher Granville Stuart saw the damage to his herd and vowed,

The Granger Collection, New York

Joseph Glidden's barbed wire made it easier and more affordable to build fences around western ranches and farms, helping lead to the end of the open range.

"I never wanted to own again an animal that I could not feed and shelter."

Many ranchers were ruined financially. To pay their debts, ranchers rushed to sell their cattle, even though the prices were low. Cattle towns were also hard hit. While cattle ranching continued, it became more costly. Ranchers were forced to buy winter feed for their cattle and to raise smaller herds. Low prices, harsh weather, and greater competition for grazing land brought an end to the reign of the Cattle Kingdom.

SECTION 3 REVIEW

Identify and explain the significance of the following:
- **Texas longhorn**
- **Joseph McCoy**
- **Cattle Kingdom**
- **open range**
- **Elizabeth Collins**
- **range rights**
- **vaqueros**
- **Nat Love**
- **roundup**
- **cattle drive**
- **Chisholm Trail**
- **range wars**

Reading for Content Understanding

1 **Main Idea** Why did cattle ranching become profitable in the 1870s?

2 **Main Idea** What factors led to the end of the Cattle Kingdom?

3 **Economic Development** How did ranching and cattle trails help western economic development?

4 **Writing** *Describing* Imagine that you are a cowboy during the late 1800s. Write a paragraph explaining what your daily life is like. Include some of the problems or mishaps you might face.

5 **Critical Thinking** *Drawing Conclusions* Why might American Indians have become cowboys?

Farming the Great Plains

Reading Focus

Why did settlers move to the Great Plains?

What challenges did farming families face on the Plains?

What was daily life like on the Plains?

Key Terms

Homestead Act

Morrill Act

Exodusters

sodbusters

dry farming

IN 1879 SCOTTISH WRITER *Robert Louis Stevenson took the transcontinental railroad across the United States. Most of the other passengers were settlers moving to the West. When a passenger began to play the song "Home Sweet Home," all conversation stopped, "and the faces began to lengthen," noted Stevenson. Then "an elderly, hard-looking man . . . [asked] the performer [to] stop. 'I've heard about enough of that,' he [said]. 'Give us something about the good country we're going to.'" The passengers cheered, and the performer began to play music for dancing. Despite being homesick, most settlers hoped to build a better life in the West.*

Pioneer rail ticket

 ## Settling the Plains

In 1862 Congress passed two important land grant acts that helped open the West to settlers. The **Homestead Act** gave government-owned land to small farmers. Any adult who was a U.S. citizen or planned to become one could receive 160 acres of land in exchange for a small registration fee and a promise to live on the land for five years. The **Morrill Act** granted more than 17 million acres of federal land to the states. The act required each state to sell this land and use the money to build colleges to teach agriculture and engineering.

The federal government also offered land in the present-day state of Oklahoma that had formerly belonged to Creek and Seminole Indians. In March 1889 officials announced that homesteaders could file claims on these lands starting at noon on April 22. Within a month of the announcement, some 50,000 people had rushed to Oklahoma to stake their claim. In all, the settlers claimed more than 11 million acres of former Indian land in the Oklahoma land rush.

Federal land grants encouraged settlers to move west. At first, settlers made this journey in wagons as earlier pioneers had done on the

Before the completion of the transcontinental railroad, pioneers moving west had to travel alone or as part of massive wagon trains that rolled across the Plains.

Oregon Trail. These trips were filled with hard work, boredom, and danger. "I am getting impatient for our journey to come to an end," wrote one pioneer woman. There were dangerous obstacles such as rivers, valleys, and mountains to cross. Rough weather and sickness could also make the trip risky.

The trip west on the railroads was safer and faster. As railroads stretched across the Great Plains, many settlers chose to travel by train. The railroad companies encouraged people to move west by printing posters and pamphlets advertising fertile and inexpensive land. The Union Pacific even promised free houses to settlers on its land in Nebraska. Many railroads also offered lower fares to pioneers.

The Homesteaders

The great stretches of land drew pioneers to the Great Plains. The Plains offered pioneers the chance to make a fresh start.

Moving West

People from all over the country chose to move west. One train traveler noted that "they came from almost every quarter. From Virginia, from Pennsylvania, from New York, from far western Iowa and Kansas." People who had already moved to the Great Plains often chose to move again after a few years. All of these settlers hoped

to find prosperity on the Plains, usually by starting their own farms. Many farming families moved from areas where farmland was becoming scarce or expensive, such as New England. Others were the descendants of earlier pioneers to the Midwest. Many single women moved west because the Homestead Act granted land to unmarried women, which was unusual for the time.

The promise of land also drew a large group of African Americans west. In 1879 Benjamin Singleton led 20,000 to 40,000 southern African Americans to Kansas. These settlers became known as **Exodusters** because of their exodus, or mass departure, from the South. Many of these Exodusters were sharecroppers such as John Solomon Lewis, who explained his reasons for moving his family:

> **❝ I one day said to the man I rented [land] from: 'It's no use, I works hard and raises big crops and you sells it and keeps the money, and brings me more and more in debt, so I will go somewhere else.' ❞**

Soon black communities, such as Nicodemus, Kansas, developed, having drawn many African Americans west with land advertisements. Other Exodusters moved west, seeking not only more economic opportunity but also equal rights, which they were denied in the South after Reconstruction.

Many African American families, such as the Shores, moved to the Great Plains.

The West **171**

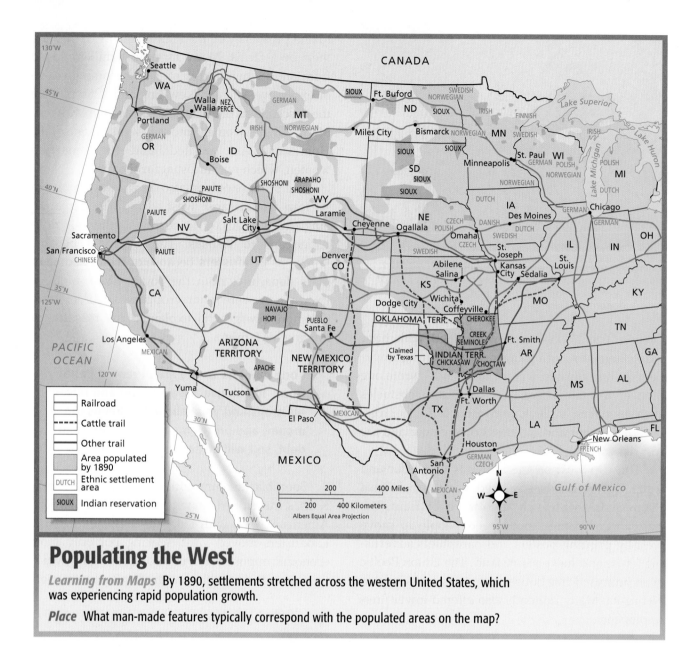

Populating the West

Learning from Maps By 1890, settlements stretched across the western United States, which was experiencing rapid population growth.

Place What man-made features typically correspond with the populated areas on the map?

Immigrants

Western homesteads also appealed to immigrants, who could receive land grants under the Homestead Act if they promised to stay in the United States. Norwegian, Swedish, Danish, German, and Czech immigrants created many small communities on the Great Plains. These groups were looking for economic opportunity. Usually, a relative made the journey to America first and then wrote letters home encouraging family members to come. One immigrant described his good economic prospects to his family, writing "that a farm had been given to him by the government. It was 60 acres of land, [with] good soil."

In addition, thousands of Mennonites, a religious group from Russia, came to the Great Plains. They were some of the first to begin large-scale farming and introduced American farmers to a type of red wheat that grew very well on the Plains.

Farming on the Plains

Although the inexpensive land and rich soil appealed to settlers, the Great Plains presented unique challenges to farmers. "Whatever I had learned of farming in the East, had to be . . . learned over again here," wrote one pioneer.

The Environment

When settlers came to the Plains, they found a mostly flat landscape covered with grass. On the eastern half of the Great Plains, the prairie grass grew up to eight feet tall. In contrast, the grass in the western part of the Plains was just a few inches tall.

Settlers found that the seasons were extreme on the Plains. In the winter, temperatures on the northern Plains could fall to 40° below zero Fahrenheit, while the scorching summer temperatures could reach 110°. Farmers could not raise the same crops that they had grown in the East because the climate of the Plains was much drier. Settlers also faced the threat of blizzards and tornadoes. The dangerous and unpredictable weather made life difficult for the pioneers.

A Storm of Grasshoppers

In the summer of 1874, many farmers in Kansas and nearby states were expecting a very good harvest. Then one day they saw something startling on the horizon—millions of grasshoppers were swarming toward the fields. Settler Mary Lyon described the strange scene: "They began, toward night, dropping to earth, and it seemed as if we were in a big snowstorm where the air was filled with enormous-size flakes." Mary Roberts, another pioneer woman, said "When they came down, they struck the ground so hard it sounded almost like hail."

The grasshoppers covered the fields in a carpet up to four inches thick. They ate settlers' crops from the fields, the food in their houses, and even their clothing. Lyon recalled that by the time the grasshoppers left, "They [had] devoured every green thing but the prairie grass." The huge swarms returned each year, then suddenly stopped. Swarms occasionally returned in later years but never as dramatically as in the 1870s.

★ New Ways of Farming

Farmers learned to cope with the challenges of the Great Plains by developing new farming equipment and methods. The root-filled sod beneath the

Mechanical farming equipment such as the reaper made it easier for western farmers to harvest huge fields of wheat.

grass was very tough and could actually break the plows that many farmers had brought with them to the Plains. Inventor John Deere's deep steel plow made it possible to break through the sod, allowing the farmers to plant crops in the tough soil. The farmers on the Plains, along with the plows they used, were nicknamed **sodbusters** for the hard work they had in breaking up the sod.

In the 1890s a farmer named Hardy Campbell began to teach farmers on the western Plains a new method called **dry farming**. This method shifted the focus from water-dependent crops such as corn to more hardy crops like red wheat. In addition, farmers left part of their fields unplanted each year so that the soil preserved water. Even on the eastern Plains, which received more rain, farmers discovered that the soil required special care. As one observer noted, they "learned that their lands needed feeding as well as their cattle and hogs." Although imperfect, these dry-farming methods helped farmers make it through drought years.

By the 1880s mechanical farming was becoming increasingly common. Cyrus McCormick made his fortune designing, building, and selling farm equipment to thousands of eager customers. Horse-drawn machines such as McCormick reapers collected wheat stalks, and threshing machines separated the grain from the husk. By using machinery, farmers could work much more quickly on large fields with fewer workers.

Corporate farmers who could afford to invest in the needed land and machinery created huge bonanza farms where they grew thousands of bushels of wheat. Farmer Oliver Dalrymple used "eighty horses, twenty-six breaking plows, forty

Causes and Effects of Increased Western Settlement

Long-Term Causes
Desire for new farm and ranch land
Search for natural resources
Growth of national and foreign markets

Immediate Causes
Belief in manifest destiny
Homestead Act, 1862
Completion of the transcontinental railroad in 1869 and the building of other western railroads

Increased Western Settlement Mid-1800s to 1900

Effects
Increased conflict with American Indian cultures in the West
Immigrants and migrants come to the West in search of a new life
Great expansion of the western economy
Creation of new states

cross plows, twenty-one seeders, [and] sixty harrows [spiked farming tools]" to plant crops on 7,000 acres of a North Dakota farm.

Once they harvested their crops, farmers shipped their harvest east by train. From there, crops were shipped overseas. As farming technology improved, the Great Plains became known as the breadbasket of the world because of all of the grains that the region's farmers produced.

★ Daily Life on the Plains

Settler Gro Svendsen described the challenges of Plains life, "When one begins to farm, it takes a great deal to get started—especially when one must begin with nothing." Building a house was one of the first challenges that settlers faced. With very little wood available, many families built houses from bricks of sod cut out of the ground. Although cheap to build, these sod homes were typically very small and uncomfortable. Pioneer May Avery explained a few of the common problems. "The roof leaked something awful [and inside] we killed a snake or two . . . and several centipedes." For all their faults, however, the small homes did provide necessary shelter.

Once a home was built, daily chores kept pioneer families busy. For example, settlers had to make and mend their own clothes. Without machines to do the work, washing clothes was a tremendous chore that usually took an entire day to complete. Pioneers usually made their wash soap from lye and animal fat. One pioneer woman's list of 11 washday chores started with "build fire in back yard to heat kettle of rain water," and ended with "brew cup of tea, set and rest and rock a spell and count blessings." Women also prepared meals and often grew vegetables, raised chickens, or made butter to earn money for the family.

Farming families raised livestock and worked hard in the fields, plowing and planting. Harvesting a crop such as wheat required reaping, binding, and stacking. In addition, pioneers often had to build or repair most of their farm buildings and machinery.

Children helped with many chores around the farm. Farm families were often large, and everyone had a task. Author Laura Ingalls Wilder was one of four children in a pioneer family that plowed its own fields, built its own homes, and made many of its own clothes. In *The Long Winter*, Wilder described harvesting hay:

❝ **While Pa tossed the hay from the wagon she [Laura] spread it as well as she**

Windmills were used to pump water in the West.

could, walking around and around on the stack to pack it tightly. . . . Laura was proud. Her arms ached and her back ached and her legs ached . . . but she did not tell anyone. **"**

Wilder's books about settlers' lives on the prairie gained a large readership and are still popular today.

This group of students in Hecla, Montana, posed with their teacher in October 1893.

Building Communities

Communities were an important part of life on the Plains. Many early settlers found life on their remote farms to be extremely difficult. About her mother's life as a pioneer, Esther Clark explained: "It took [courage] to live twenty-four hours at a time, month in and out, on the lonely and lovely prairie." Farmers developed communities so that they could assist one another in times of need.

One of the first things that many pioneer communities did was establish a local church and a school. Churches served as gathering places for pioneer families. Even small communities made an effort to get schools started. Many communities raised money and ran the schools themselves. One woman recalled proudly, "They [the school board]

and the pupils and I built that school house with our own hands."

Pioneer schools were usually small one-room buildings where children of all ages learned together in one class. Few children had schoolbooks, and many children went to school only part of the year because they had to help with farmwork. Most teachers in these pioneer schools were young women who made little money.

Frontier families worked very hard to provide a community for themselves and for their children. Through these efforts, more people found the West an appealing place to live and raise a family.

SECTION 4 REVIEW

Identify and explain the significance of the following:

- **Homestead Act**
- **Morrill Act**
- **Exodusters**
- **sodbusters**
- **dry farming**
- **Cyrus McCormick**

Reading for Content Understanding

1 **Main Idea** What motivated settlers to move west?

2 **Main Idea** Why was farming on the Plains difficult, and how did that affect pioneers' lives?

3 **Economic Development** What technology helped Plains farmers, and how did it affect the region's economic development?

4 **Writing** *Expressing* Imagine that you are a student on the Plains in the late 1800s. Write a letter to a friend discussing a typical day at your school and on the farm.

5 **Critical Thinking** *Making Comparisons* Do you think it would be easier to be a teenager today or in the West in the 1890s? Explain your answer in a paragraph, using information from the chapter and your personal experiences.

CHAPTER 5 REVIEW

Chapter Summary

When settlers and miners moved west in the mid-1800s, conflicts arose with American Indians. The U.S. government sent Indians to reservations. The discovery of gold, the transcontinental railroad, and offers of free land encouraged more western settlement. The 1870s saw the rise of the Cattle Kingdom. With new farming techniques and inventions, the Great Plains became the breadbasket of the world. ■

On a separate sheet of paper, complete the following activities.

Identifying People and Ideas

Describe the historical significance of the following:

1. reservations
2. Elizabeth Collins
3. Sitting Bull
4. Comstock Lode
5. Pacific Railway Acts
6. Nat Love
7. Chisholm Trail
8. Exodusters
9. Joseph McCoy
10. Homestead Act

go.hrw.com
SB1 Western Paintings

Internet Activity

Imagine that you are putting together a documentary guide to western artists. Search the Internet through the HRW Web site to find at least three paintings about the West. For each image, write a few sentences explaining how the image does, or does not, accurately show life in the West in the late 1800s.

Understanding Main Ideas

1. What was life like for the Plains Indians?
2. How did the wars for the West affect American Indians?
3. What factors made mining in the West such a dangerous job?
4. What dangers did cowboys face?
5. Why was there a cattle boom in the 1870s?
6. What effect did the transcontinental railroad have on western settlement?
7. Why did many immigrants move to the West?

Reviewing Themes

1. **Economic Development**   What factors led to the expansion of the economy in the West in the late 1800s?
2. **Cultural Diversity**   What effect did the movement of American Indians to reservations have on their social and economic life?

Using the Time Line

Number your paper from 1 to 5. Match the letters on the time line below with the following events.

1. A golden spike connects the last railroad tie of the transcontinental railroad.
2. The northern Plains Indians sign the Fort Laramie Treaty.
3. The Homestead Act grants 160-acre plots of land to people who can pay a small fee and will live on the land for five years.
4. Congress passes the Dawes General Allotment Act, which splits up reservation lands.
5. Helen Hunt Jackson publishes *A Century of Dishonor*, criticizing the treatment of American Indians.

1850   1860   1870   1880   1890

a   b   c   d   e

3. **Geographic Diversity** In what ways did the environment affect the crops that farmers planted and the farming methods they used?

Thinking Critically

1. **Identifying Cause and Effect** What effect do you think the invention of cars, trucks, and airplanes has had on the railroad industry?

2. **Evaluating** List two positive and two negative consequences of economic development in the West.

3. **Making Comparisons** What similarities and differences were there among mining towns, cattle towns, and farming communities?

Writing About History

1. **Describing** Imagine that you are in one of the mining boom towns of the late 1860s. Write a two-paragraph letter home to your family back East telling about your life in the West. Describe your work as a miner or a boardinghouse keeper.

Building Your Portfolio

Complete the following activities individually or in groups.

1. **Battle of the Little Bighorn** Imagine that you are a newspaper reporter from the East who has been assigned to cover the Battle of the Little Bighorn. To help your readers understand more about the event, either write a biographical sketch of two key figures in the battle, prepare a relief map of the battle site, or create an illustration of the battle.

2. **Heading West** Imagine that your family has decided to move west in 1870. You are in charge of making sure you are prepared for the challenges that lie ahead. Make a list of 10 things you will take with you. Then imagine that you have arrived in your new home. Write a journal entry about how each item on your list has helped you on the frontier. Note if there are items you wish you had chosen to bring, and explain why.

2. **Creating** Write a four-line stanza for a cowboy song that might have been sung on one of the long cattle drives to the North.

Linking Geography and History

1. **Movement** Most of the Exodusters came from Kentucky, Tennessee, and Mississippi. Why do you think they moved to Kansas and other parts of the West instead of to the North or the Northeast?

2. **Place** Describe the physical environment of the Great Plains.

History Skills Workshop

Reading Graphs Study the graph below and then answer the following questions. (a) How many buffalo (bison) were there in the United States in 1800? (b) How many buffalo were there in the United States in 1889? (c) What was the estimated buffalo population in 1994? (d) What factors led to the decline of the buffalo population?

Estimated Bison Population

In millions
30
25
20
15
10
5

In thousands
200
150
100
50
0

1800   1870 1889   1950   1994

Source: *National Geographic*, November 1994

The Economy of the West

In the last half of the 1800s, great numbers of settlers followed the trails of earlier pioneers westward across North America. People moved west for new economic opportunities in farming, mining, and ranching. Prospectors and miners staked claims throughout the West, hoping to strike it rich. Ranchers bought cattle from Texas to the northern Great Plains. Farmers planted vast wheat fields where once only buffalo had roamed.

Networks of railroads brought more settlers west and connected the West with eastern markets. By 1890 settlement was so extensive throughout the West that the U.S. Census Bureau reported the official end of the frontier. ■

Western Mining and Farming

A mining boom in the late 1800s brought thousands of prospectors to the West. Successful strikes in western mines contributed to a huge increase in the amount of gold and silver produced in the United States. Farmers also moved west in increasing numbers during the late 1800s, looking for fertile land to settle.

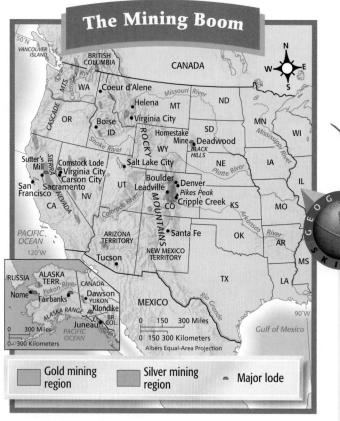

The Mining Boom

Gold mining region
Silver mining region
▲ Major lode

Mining equipment

Geography Skills

Reading Special-Purpose Maps

1. What U.S. cities were located near silver mining regions in the West?
2. What U.S. cities developed near gold mining regions?
3. In what kind of terrain were most of the gold and silver strikes made?

U.S. Land in Farms

States east of the Mississippi River

States west of the Mississippi River

1870:
407,735,000 total acres

24.8%

75.2%

1900:
841,202,000 total acres

56.3%

43.7%

1995:
972,000,000 total acres

21.4%

78.6%

Sources: *Historical Statistics of the United States; 1997 World Almanac and Book of Facts*

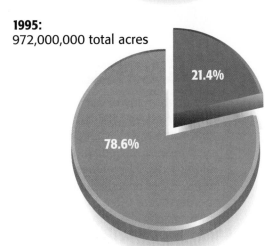

Barns and grain silo

Geography **Skills**
Reading Pie Graphs

1. What percentage of total U.S. farmland was located west of the Mississippi in 1870? in 1995?
2. How has the geographical distribution of total farmland in the United States changed between 1870 and 1995?
3. How many acres of farmland were in the United States in 1995?

The Changing West

In the 1860s the U.S. government passed the Homestead Act, which sold government-owned western lands at a very low cost. The federal government also passed the Pacific Railway Acts, giving railroad companies land for every mile of track they laid. By 1900 a network of railroad lines crisscrossed the mountains and farm-lands of the increasingly populated West.

The West Around 1870

Legend:
- Cattle trails
- Sheep trails (1870–1900)
- Railroads
- Original range of western cattle
- Farming
- Cattle ranching
- Present-day boundaries

Geography Skills
Reading Special-Purpose Maps

1. What towns and cities were served by the Union Pacific and Central Pacific railroad lines by 1870?
2. Where did the cattle trails that ran north to the railroads begin?
3. Why do you think cattle trails ended at towns along railroad lines?

History Note 3

Although many of our images of the West are of cowboys and cattle drives, sheepherders also moved millions of sheep along a network of western trails. Experienced sheep-herders were often immigrants from places like France, Mexico, and Spain. They helped move large western herds with as many as 7,000 sheep. One of the first great sheep drives in the United States provided food for hungry miners during the California Gold Rush.

The West Around 1900

Cattle grazing

Sheep grazing

Railroads to the
Pacific Ocean

Farming

Grazing

Woodlands

Geography Skills
Reading Special-Purpose Maps

1. By 1900 what West Coast cities were linked by railroads to the eastern United States?
2. Where was sheep grazing most common?
3. Compare the map above to the one on page 180. Into what regions of the West had farming expanded between 1870 and 1890?

History Note 4

The construction of railroads in the West contributed much to the settlement of the region and to the industrialization of the U.S. economy. Railroads gave farmers and ranchers a way to get their goods to markets in the East, and at the same time opened new markets for eastern industrial goods in the West.

■ CHAPTER 6 ■
An Industrial Nation
(1876–1900)

To celebrate the nation's 100th birthday, the Centennial Exposition opened in Philadelphia on May 10, 1876. The Chicago *Tribune* urged Americans to come even "if you have to live six months on bread and water to make up for the expense." During the next six months some 10 million visitors viewed "the results . . . of the best brains of all lands." The new technology on exhibit was bringing U.S. agriculture and industry into a new era.

THEMES

Technology and Society
How might new sources of energy and advances in manufacturing transform a country's economy?

Economic Development
How might a government respond to economic and industrial expansion?

Citizenship and Democracy
What political action might citizens take in response to economic changes?

1876   **1878**   **1880**   **1882**   **1884**   **1886**

MAR. 1876 Alexander Graham Bell patents the telephone.

FEB. 1878 Congress passes the Bland-Allison Act.

SEPT. 1882 Thomas Alva Edison begins supplying electricity to buildings in New York City.

MAY 1886 More than 100 people are wounded during the Haymarket Riot.

FEB. 1887 Congress creates the Interstate Commerce Commission.

The Second Industrial Revolution

Reading Focus

How did the Second Industrial Revolution affect the U.S. economy?

What were the key inventions of the Second Industrial Revolution?

How did the inventions of the late 1800s change people's lives?

Key Terms

Second Industrial Revolution
Bessemer process
patent

THE MOST POPULAR EXHIBIT *at the 1876 Centennial Exposition in Philadelphia was the massive Corliss steam engine. Weighing 700 tons and standing 40 feet tall, the engine drew large crowds of spectators as it powered the equipment in the exhibition's Machinery Hall. One exhibition guidebook declared, "The first thing to do is to see the tremendous iron heart."* **Atlantic Monthly** *editor William Dean Howells wrote that machinery such as the Corliss engine demonstrated "the national genius" of the United States. For Howells and many others at the fair, the exhibits in Machinery Hall represented "the glorious triumphs of skill and invention."*

The Corliss Engine ran all the equipment in the exhibition's Machinery Hall.

IMAGE ON LEFT PAGE: *Centennial Exposition in Philadelphia, 1876*

1888   1890   1892   1894   1896   1898

JULY 1890 Congress passes the Sherman Antitrust Act.

JUNE 1892 The Homestead Strike begins.

MAY 1894 The Pullman Strike begins, eventually halting midwestern railroad traffic.

An Industrial Nation **183**

Railroads and Steel

Technological advances such as those displayed at the 1876 Centennial Exposition were vital to the **Second Industrial Revolution**. It was a period of explosive growth in U.S. manufacturing in the late 1800s. By the mid-1890s, the United States had become the world's industrial leader.

An Age of Steel

Some of the most significant advances in technology occurred in the steel industry. Steel is iron that has been strengthened considerably by heating it and combining it with other metals. Skilled workers originally produced steel in small batches, but it was difficult and expensive to make. In the 1850s British inventor Henry Bessemer discovered an easier and less expensive way to make steel. Bessemer found that by blasting hot air through melted iron he could remove the iron's impurities quickly. The **Bessemer process** allowed several tons of iron to be made into steel in only 10 or 20 minutes instead of taking a day or more.

The Bessemer process helped U.S. steel production skyrocket from 77,000 tons in 1870 to more than 1 million tons in 1879. At first the demand for

Steel Production, 1865–1895

Source: *Historical Statistics of the United States*

Built of Steel Steel had many uses, which caused its production to skyrocket in the late 1800s. About how much steel was produced in 1890?

steel rails for railroads fed this growth, but soon steel mills were also making girders for tall buildings and cable for suspension bridges. As production climbed, steel prices dropped from more than $100 per ton in 1873 to $17 per ton by 1900. This made it affordable to use steel for items such as nails, wire, and pipes.

A Railroad Boom

As steel dropped in price, so did the cost of constructing railroads. Companies built thousands of miles of new steel track. Railroad mileage grew from some 30,000 miles in 1860 to 199,000 miles by 1900. These stronger, longer-lasting rails could carry heavier loads. A network of railroad lines soon carried heavy freight traffic across the nation.

New technology also made railroad travel both faster and safer. Steel locomotive boilers could withstand greater steam pressure, making trains more powerful. Improved air brakes designed by George Westinghouse and Granville T. Woods made travel on these new trains safer than on earlier models. In addition, elegant passenger and sleeping cars designed by George Pullman made long-distance travel more comfortable. One group of businessmen heading west called their Pullman car a "beautiful . . . moving hotel."

Other developments also improved railroad service. Cornelius Vanderbilt and other powerful railroad owners began consolidating, or buying smaller companies to form one large company. Consolidation of the many smaller rail lines into a few large networks improved efficiency and decreased travel time. In 1860 it had taken two days and 17 line changes to travel from New York City to Chicago. By 1870 passengers could make the trip in 24 hours without changing trains or railroad lines. Vanderbilt also improved the efficiency of railroad services in urban areas. One newspaper called Vanderbilt "the great railway king of the country."

The railroads had a huge impact on the economy and development of the United States. Manufacturers and farmers could get their products to market more rapidly than ever by rail. Cities such as Chicago and Kansas City grew rapidly where major rail lines crossed. Railroads also promoted western development by offering

The Illinois Central Railroad connected many towns across the Midwest.

free tickets to settlers. Rail travel made the journey west faster and safer for settlers. As rail travel and shipping increased, railroads and their related industries became some of the largest employers in the United States.

Striking Oil

Another important technological breakthrough in the late 1800s was the development of petroleum, or oil, as a power source. People had known about oil for many years but had few ways to use it. This changed in the 1850s, when Dr. Benjamin Silliman Jr. discovered how to refine crude oil into a fuel called kerosene. Kerosene could be used for cooking and heating, but one of its most popular uses was for home lighting. The development of kerosene and other refined fuels greatly increased the demand for oil.

As the demand for oil increased, people began searching for a reliable petroleum source. In 1859 retired railroad conductor Edwin L. Drake proved that it was possible to pump crude oil from the ground. People mockingly referred to his oil well as "Drake's Folly," but they stopped laughing when the well began producing 20 barrels per day. Wildcatters, or oil prospectors, drilled for oil in Ohio, Pennsylvania, and West Virginia. Oil became a big business as these states began producing millions of barrels annually. Companies also built oil refineries to turn the crude oil into finished products, such as kerosene. One superintendent in the industry referred to oil workers as "men who are supplying light for the world."

★ Electric Light and Power

Electricity emerged as another source of light and power during the Second Industrial Revolution. The invention of the electric generator in the mid-1880s allowed electricity to be used in greater quantities and more reliably than ever before.

The possible uses of electricity drew the interest of inventors like Thomas Alva Edison, who began his career as a telegraph operator. He soon started designing improvements to the telegraph equipment, receiving his first **patent** at age 22. A patent is an exclusive right to manufacture or sell an invention. Edison's inventions soon earned him enough money to start his own research laboratory in 1876 in Menlo Park, New Jersey.

Researchers at Menlo Park wanted to create practical items that they could patent. As Edison explained:

> **"I do not regard myself as a pure scientist. . . . I am only a professional inventor . . . with the object of inventing that which will have commercial utility."**

Edison's name eventually appeared on more than 1,000 patents.

In 1878 Edison viewed an experimental light display powered by electricity. He recalled that "this electric light idea took possession of me." Edison announced in the national press that he would soon invent a practical electric light, even though he had not yet started any experiments. Working feverishly, by the end of 1879 Edison and his team of inventors had succeeded in creating the lightbulb.

Although the electric lightbulb received great publicity, Edison was faced with a problem— very few homes or businesses had access to electricity. To address this problem, Edison built a power plant that began

Inventor Thomas Edison and his original electric lightbulb

The Wizard of Menlo Park

Before he turned 30, Thomas Alva Edison was already a talented inventor. In 1876 he used funding from his inventions to build a new laboratory in Menlo Park, New Jersey. There he was given the nickname "The Wizard of Menlo Park."

Edison designed Menlo Park as an "invention factory." He had a team of skilled specialists to help him. Edison also employed young people who wanted to learn about technology firsthand. Many of them began by working for free. In fewer than six years at Menlo Park, Edison patented more than 400 devices or ideas created by his team. Three of their most important inventions were the carbon telephone transmitter, the phonograph, and the electric lightbulb.

The telephone transmitter came first. Edison improved Alexander Graham Bell's original design in several ways that made it possible to send stronger telephone signals. This greatly improved the sound quality of telephone messages. Today many telephones are still based on Edison's ideas.

His success with the telephone encouraged Edison's team to try recording the human voice. Their experiments resulted in the first phonograph. A person operated this device by speaking into a tube and turning a crank. The vibrations caused by the voice moved a small needle up and down on a tin cylinder. This created a pattern of tiny indentations that formed a groove around the cylinder. The pattern was a record of the person's voice. To play the phonograph, a person touched another needle to the groove and turned the crank again. The indentations caused the needle to vibrate and re-created the sound of the voice through a small speaker.

This invention thrilled Americans. Edison even demonstrated the device to President

The Granger Collection, New York

Thomas Edison's team of inventors at Menlo Park work on creating a lightbulb.

Rutherford B. Hayes and his wife, Lucy. Eventually, other inventors improved the phonograph and used it to play music.

One of Edison's greatest achievements at Menlo Park was the creation of the electric lightbulb. After many failures, Edison's team succeeded in using electricity to heat a filament placed inside a glass bulb with no air in it. The material would glow brightly and provide a steady source of light.

In the 1880s few buildings had electricity, so Edison tackled the problem of providing it. In 1882 he left Menlo Park and started an electric power plant in New York City that provided electric lighting for more than 80 buildings. Edison eventually formed an electric power company and built a new, larger laboratory in West Orange, New Jersey. In 1929 a full-scale re-creation of Menlo Park was built in Greenfield Village, Michigan. It remains a popular tourist attraction.

Understanding What You Read

1. What were some of the inventions created at Menlo Park?

2. How did these inventions change people's lives?

supplying electricity to dozens of buildings in New York City in September 1882. The *New York Times* reported that with electric lighting in the newspaper offices, "it seemed almost like writing by daylight."

The typewriter was also invented in the late 1800s.

Edison's power company used direct current (DC) to transmit electricity to the homes and offices of consumers. While safe and relatively powerful, DC is difficult to transmit over long distances. This led Edison's power company to concentrate on providing electricity in heavily populated cities, where there were many customers nearby.

In the late 1880s George Westinghouse bought a patent for an alternating current (AC) generator designed by Serbian immigrant Nikola Tesla. Unlike DC, AC could be transmitted easily over long distances. Tesla's generator design allowed Westinghouse to build an AC-based electrical network that competed with Edison Electric. Electric use spread rapidly, and electric utilities became a growing business. Electricity was used to light urban homes and businesses and to power factories. Electricity also powered hundreds of streetcars in cities across the nation, allowing urban residents to travel quickly and cheaply.

Advances in Communications

There were also great advances in communication technology in the late 1800s. Thomas Edison and other inventors continued to improve the telegraph. By 1861 telegraph wires connected the East and West coasts. Five years later, a cable on the Atlantic Ocean's floor successfully connected the United States and Britain.

The telegraph had some disadvantages. It carried only written messages and was difficult for untrained people to use. These problems were solved in March 1876 when inventor Alexander Graham Bell patented the telephone, or "talking telegraph." A Scottish-born speech teacher who also worked with hearing-impaired people, Bell studied the science of sound. His telephone made long-distance communication

easier than ever before. Bell soon demonstrated the telephone at the Centennial Exposition, where judges called it a "marvel."

Like electric lighting, the telephone depended on a large network of wires. Telephone companies raced to lay thousands of miles of phone lines. By 1884 Boston and New York City were linked by phone. The number of telephones in American homes and businesses increased rapidly, from around 55,000 in 1880 to almost 1.5 million by 1900. Bell became very wealthy as a result of his company's success. He founded a scientific journal and continued to invent a wide range of devices. Eventually, his Bell Telephone Company became American Telephone and Telegraph, one of the nation's largest and longest lasting monopolies.

Automobiles and Planes

The Second Industrial Revolution produced breakthroughs in transportation as well as communications. In 1876 German engineer Nikolaus A. Otto invented an engine powered by gasoline, another fuel produced from oil. Gasoline motors typically were much lighter than steam engines and more efficient than electric motors, which relied on heavy batteries that ran down quickly. Gasoline

Switchboard operators run one of the many telephone systems created after Alexander Graham Bell (right) invented the telephone.

soon competed with steam and electricity as a power source for a new type of transportation, the automobile.

In 1893 Charles and James Duryea used a gasoline engine to build the first practical motorcar in the United States. By the early 1900s thousands of cars were being built in the United States by many different manufacturers. Most of these early cars were too expensive for anyone but the wealthy to afford. As automobiles became more common, states began improving roads, passing traffic laws, and requiring car owners to take driving tests.

New engine technology also helped make another transportation breakthrough possible. Orville and Wilbur Wright were bicycle makers who began experimenting with airplane designs in the 1890s. Fascinated by flight, the brothers used the Smithsonian Institution to research previous flying attempts. They applied this research and their own theories to create a lightweight airplane with a small gas-powered engine.

In Kitty Hawk, North Carolina, Orville Wright made the first piloted flight in a powered plane on December 17, 1903. He later wrote:

> "I got on the machine [airplane] at 10:35 for the first trial. . . . The machine lifted from the truck. . . . [It] would rise

The Wright brothers' first airplane had to be steered while lying down. The plane was so light that a strong gust of wind could knock it over.

> suddenly . . . and then as suddenly, on turning the rudder, dart for the ground. A sudden dart when out about 100 feet from the end of the tracks ended the flight. Time about 12 seconds."

Those few seconds led to fame for the Wright brothers, who eventually achieved a flight of about 24 miles. They patented their airplane in 1906. Few planes were built in the United States before 1914, in part because early planes had limited range and cargo capacity.

Inventions such as the motorcar and the airplane resulted in great public excitement. However, they were not widely used at first, partly because of their cost. They eventually joined many other inventions of the late 1800s in changing the way that Americans worked, traveled, and lived.

SECTION 1 REVIEW

Identify and explain the significance of the following:
- **Second Industrial Revolution**
- **Bessemer process**
- **Thomas Alva Edison**
- **patent**
- **Alexander Graham Bell**
- **Orville and Wilbur Wright**

Reading for Content Understanding

1. **Main Idea** Create a graphic organizer listing at least five important inventions of the Second Industrial Revolution, their inventors, and the years that they were invented.

2. **Main Idea** How did inventions affect people's lives in the late 1800s?

3. **Technology and Society** How did the Second Industrial Revolution transform the U.S. economy?

4. **Writing** *Informing* Imagine that you are an editor of a magazine in the 1880s. Write a short editorial about what you think the most important invention of the period is and why.

5. **Critical Thinking** *Drawing Conclusions* What advantages do inventors gain from patenting an invention? Do you think this encourages inventors to develop new technologies? Explain your answer.

Big Business

Reading Focus

What changes occurred in the way that businesses were organized in the late 1800s?

How did some business leaders explain the reasons for their success?

Why did some Americans oppose monopolies, and what action was taken?

Key Terms

free enterprise
entrepreneurs
corporations
vertical integration
horizontal integration
trust
Sherman Antitrust Act

 N HIS LECTURE TITLED "Acres of Diamonds," minister Russell H. Conwell declared, "I say that you ought to get rich. . . . It is all wrong to be poor." Conwell traveled the United States giving his speech throughout the late 1800s, presenting it some 6,000 times to an estimated 13 million people. He stressed the same theme repeatedly, "that in this country of ours every man has the opportunity to make more of himself." Conwell's audiences shared the fascination of many Americans for the wealth and power generated by big business.

A flyer announcing a Russell H. Conwell speech

⭐ The Growth of Big Business

In the late 1800s the U.S. government generally promoted **free enterprise**—business that is free from government involvement. In 1883 Yale professor William Graham Sumner described free enterprise, also known as laissez-faire:

❝ **Let us translate it into blunt English, and it will read, Mind your own business. It is nothing but the doctrine [idea] of liberty. Let every man be happy in his own way.** ❞

The government did, however, promote the interests of business by giving such aid as protective tariffs for manufacturers and land grants to railroad companies. This assistance and the government's laissez-faire policies benefited **entrepreneurs**—people who start new businesses.

In the late 1800s, many entrepreneurs organized their businesses as **corporations**—companies that sell shares of ownership called stocks. Corporations must be approved and chartered by state governments. Stockholders in a corporation typically receive a dividend, or a percentage of company profits, that is based on how much stock

An Industrial Nation **189**

they own. Although the stockholders actually own the corporation, they do not run its day-to-day affairs. Instead, they elect a board of directors. The board in turn appoints the main officials of the corporation, such as the president and vice president.

Stock certificate

Corporations provided several important advantages over previous methods of organizing companies. Unlike business partners or members of joint-stock companies, the stockholders in a corporation are not personally responsible for the debts of the business. This means that if a corporation fails, the stockholders lose only the money that they invested. Stockholders are also usually free to sell their shares to whomever they want whenever they want. These factors made investing less risky than it had been previously and thus encouraged more investment in businesses. By 1900 more than 100 million shares a year were being traded on the New York Stock Exchange.

For entrepreneurs, stock sales provided a way to raise large amounts of money to pay for modern factories and to expand businesses. One corporate leader explained that shares of stock represented "nothing more than good will and prospective [expected] profits." These profits did not always appear, however.

Throughout the late 1800s, the economy followed a cycle of boom and bust, with businesses succeeding during the boom periods and failing during the busts. During the Panic of 1873, the New York Stock Exchange shut down for 10 days. The depression in 1893 had an even greater effect on the economy, causing unemployment and business failures across the nation. One businessman described his life in such bust times as being "work by day and worry by night, week in and week out, month after month." Despite these bust periods, American businesses continued to grow.

Vertical and Horizontal Integration

Vertical Integration
Companies owned by U.S. Steel

- Steel Mills
- Railroads and Ships
- Coal Mines
- Iron Mines

Horizontal Integration
Competitors bought by Standard Oil Company

Standard Oil Company

Oil-Refining Companies

Big Business Corporations in the late 1800s used methods such as horizontal and vertical integration to increase tremendously in size. U.S. Steel owned companies associated with each step in the steel-making process. Standard Oil bought out most of its competitors. Why would horizontal or vertical integration help a company?

Business Leaders

Entrepreneurs and business leaders were some of the most widely respected members of American society in the late 1800s. Political leaders praised successful businesspeople as fine examples of American individuality and talent.

Carnegie and Steel

Andrew Carnegie was one of the most admired business leaders of the late 1800s. While working as an executive for the Pennsylvania Railroad, Carnegie used personal connections to borrow money that he then invested in iron mills and bridge-building businesses. These investments were so successful that in 1865 Carnegie left the railroad company. "I was no longer merely an official working for others . . . ," he wrote, "but a full-fledged business man."

Inspired by the Bessemer process, in 1873 Carnegie focused his efforts on steelmaking. He expanded by buying out his competitors when steel prices were low. Although he never held a monopoly on steel production in the United States, by 1900 Carnegie's mills were producing more steel than all of Britain's steel mills combined. Carnegie's businesses succeeded in part through his use of **vertical integration**—owning businesses involved in each step of a manufacturing process. To lower his cost of production, Carnegie purchased the iron ore mines, coal fields, and railroads needed to supply and support his steel mills.

Rockefeller and Oil

John D. Rockefeller was also extremely successful in business consolidation. He began his rise to wealth and power as a bookkeeper. By age 21 he was a partner in a wholesale business and soon decided to start an oil-refining company. By 1870 Rockefeller's Standard Oil Company, which started in Cleveland, Ohio, was the nation's largest oil refiner. Like Carnegie, Rockefeller used vertical integration. Standard Oil made its own barrels and cans and controlled most of the pipelines, tank cars, and storage facilities it used. Many railroads that wanted Standard Oil's valuable shipping business offered Rockefeller lower rates and

Biography

Andrew Carnegie

Andrew Carnegie was born in Scotland in 1835 and immigrated to Pennsylvania at age 13. As a teenager, Carnegie worked at a textile mill, then as a machine cleaner in a factory. His big break came when he got a job as a railroad messenger, which led to his becoming a telegraph operator and then an assistant to a railroad manager.

Carnegie constantly impressed his employers with his hard work and ability to learn quickly. One employer, Thomas Scott, loaned Carnegie $600 to make his first investment in a company. Carnegie soon became wealthy by making wise investment choices. Unlike many other successful businesspeople of his era, Carnegie continued to live very simply, warning that "the amassing of wealth is one of the worst species of idolatry [worship of false images]."

rebates—partial returns of payment. At times he even got railroads to agree not to provide service to his competitors.

Rockefeller's company was also organized through **horizontal integration**—owning all the businesses in a particular field. By 1879 his companies controlled more than 90 percent of the U.S. oil-refining business, making them a monopoly. Rockefeller used consolidation as a means of cutting costs. He also formed a **trust**—a legal arrangement grouping together a number of companies under a single board of directors. To earn higher profits, trusts often tried to eliminate competition and to regulate production, raising prices for consumers in the process. Rockefeller stated, "The day of combination [trusts] is here to stay. Individualism has gone, never to return."

★ Social Darwinism and Philanthropy

Many individuals who supported laissez-faire capitalism also believed in social Darwinism. This was a view of society based loosely on scientist Charles Darwin's theory of natural selection.

Darwin argued that over long periods of time species evolved by adapting to their environments. Social Darwinists argued that a similar process took place in human societies, and that

John D. Rockefeller founded several philanthropic organizations.

"survival of the fittest" determined who would succeed. Important social Darwinists such as sociologist Herbert Spencer also claimed that government regulation of businesses harmed the "natural" economic order.

Business leaders such as Andrew Carnegie and John D. Rockefeller supported Spencer's theories. Rockefeller once told a Sunday school class that

> " the growth of large business is merely a survival of the fittest. . . . This is not an evil tendency in business. It is merely the working-out of a law of nature and a law of God. "

Some business leaders used social Darwinism to justify their accumulation of great wealth while their companies supported child labor, low wages, and unsafe working conditions. If poor people wanted to improve their situation, these leaders argued, it was their own responsibility to work hard and rise above the rest of society. Other business leaders claimed that the wealthy had a duty to aid the poor because nature predetermined who was poor and who was rich. These leaders tried to help the poor through philanthropy, or giving money to charities.

Such beliefs led Carnegie to give away most of his fortune. During his lifetime he donated more than $350 million to charity. About $60 million of this money went to found public libraries, in order to expand access to books. Other business leaders, including Rockefeller, also gave large amounts of money to various causes. By the late 1800s, charities had received millions of dollars from philanthropists.

HISTORICAL DOCUMENTS

Andrew Carnegie's
1889 *The Gospel of Wealth*

The following excerpt is from an article written by Andrew Carnegie in 1889. Later called "The Gospel of Wealth," it explains his views on capitalism.

" Individualism, private property, the law of accumulation of wealth, and the law of competition . . . these are the highest results of human experience, the soil in which society so far has produced the best fruit. Unequally or unjustly, perhaps, as these laws sometimes operate, and imperfect as they appear to the idealist, they are, nevertheless, . . . the best and most valuable of all that humanity has yet accomplished. "

Understanding Primary Sources
1. What laws does Andrew Carnegie believe are humanity's highest accomplishments?
2. What flaws does Carnegie note in these laws?

The House of Mirth
Edith Wharton

The House of Mirth was written by Edith Wharton in 1905. It established her as a popular and critically successful author. The novel is the story of Lily Bart, a young woman trying first to advance and then to preserve her place in New York City high society. The novel describes the resentment faced by newly rich families attempting to join this restricted social circle. It also explores the power of money and the changing world of the city. In the following excerpt, the season of dinner parties, entertaining, and theater-going has begun under the watchful eye of the wealthy Mrs. Peniston.

The Granger Collection, New York

Edith Wharton won a Pulitzer Prize in 1920 for her novel The Age of Innocence.

Fifth Avenue had become a nightly torrent [flood] of carriages surging upward to the fashionable quarters about the [Central] Park, where illuminated windows and outspread awnings betokened [showed] the usual routine of hospitality. . . .

This particular season Mrs. Peniston would have characterized as that in which everybody "felt poor" except the Welly Brys and Mr. Simon Rosedale. It had been a bad autumn in Wall Street. . . . Even fortunes supposed to be independent of the market either betrayed a secret dependence on it, or suffered from a sympathetic affection [connection]: fashion sulked in its countryhouses, or came to town incognito [disguised], general entertainments were discountenanced [disapproved], and informality and short dinners became the fashion. . . .

The mere fact of growing richer at a time when most people's investments are shrinking, is calculated to attract envious attention; and according to Wall Street rumours, Welly Bry and Rosedale had found the secret of performing this miracle.

Rosedale, in particular, was said to have doubled his fortune, and there was talk of his buying the newly-finished house of one of the victims of the crash, who, in the space of twelve short months, had made the same number of millions, built a house on Fifth Avenue, filled a picture-gallery with old masters [valuable paintings], entertained all New York in it, and [then] been smuggled out of the country between a trained nurse and a doctor, while his creditors mounted guard over the old masters, and his guests explained to each other that they had dined with him only because they wanted to see the pictures. Mr. Rosedale meant to have a less meteoric [fast-rising and fast-falling] career.

Understanding Literature

1. What has caused many members of New York's upper class to "feel poor"?

2. How does Simon Rosedale attract the attention of high society?

3. What does the story of the "victim of the crash" suggest about the attitudes of some members of New York's upper class?

The Antitrust Movement

Critics of big business argued that many entrepreneurs earned their fortunes not through natural selection but by using unfair business practices. These criticisms grew stronger in the 1880s as corporations became more powerful. Large corporations often used their size and power to drive smaller competitors out of business. Andrew Carnegie and John D. Rockefeller pressured railroads to charge their companies lower shipping rates. Powerful trusts also arranged to sell goods and services at prices below market value. After smaller competitors went bankrupt trying to match these prices, the trusts would raise them again.

Opponents became concerned when trusts gained a monopoly on a product such as oil or a service such as telephone communication. Critics argued that such monopolies reduced the competition that was needed to keep prices low and the quality of goods and services high. Members of monopolistic trusts regularly agreed to match each other's prices to avoid the risks of competition. Other companies merged with their rivals to dominate an industry or a service. Powerful businessman

Monopolies and trusts pick Uncle Sam's pockets in this cartoon.

and banker J. P. Morgan once said, "I like a little competition, but I like combination better." Some Americans were also concerned about the political influence of wealthy trusts. Union leader John W. Hayes called trusts "the common enemy of society."

Many citizens and small businesses demanded government action to help control monopolies and trusts. Supporters of trusts responded that they were more efficient and gave the consumer a reliable product. One newspaper editor declared that "the right to cooperate is as unquestionable as the right to compete."

Although many in Congress were supportive of big business, they could not ignore the concerns of voters. As Senator John Sherman explained, "You must heed their appeal. . . . Society is now disturbed by forces never felt before." In July 1890 Congress passed the **Sherman Antitrust Act**, which stated that any "attempt to monopolize . . . any part of the trade or commerce among the several States" was a crime. However, the act did not clearly define just what a trust was in legal terms. The antitrust laws were thus difficult to enforce, and corporations and trusts continued to grow in size and power.

SECTION 2 REVIEW

Identify and explain the significance of the following:
- free enterprise
- entrepreneurs
- corporations
- Andrew Carnegie
- vertical integration
- John D. Rockefeller
- horizontal integration
- trust
- Sherman Antitrust Act

Reading for Content Understanding

1 **Main Idea** What did social Darwinists argue about society?

2 **Main Idea** How and why did some people try to protect business competition?

3 **Economic Development** What new forms of business ownership and organization developed in the late 1800s?

4 **Writing** *Persuading* Imagine that you are a member of Congress debating antitrust legislation. Write a short speech arguing why trusts and monopolies should or should not be controlled by law.

5 **Critical Thinking** *Supporting a Point of View* Do you agree with the ideas expressed by business leaders such as Andrew Carnegie about the importance of competition, individualism, and philanthropy? Explain your answer.

Industrial Workers

Reading Focus

How did the Second Industrial Revolution affect U.S. workers?

Why did workers form labor unions, and how were they organized?

How did major labor strikes affect workers?

Key Terms

collective bargaining
Knights of Labor
Haymarket Riot
American Federation of Labor
Homestead Strike
Pullman Strike

AT THE BEGINNING OF *the Second Industrial Revolution, skilled workers called puddlers turned hot, liquid iron into steel. One puddler said he felt "like some frantic baker in the inferno kneading a batch of iron bread." Puddlers' skills made them valuable to employers and difficult to replace. However, over time, factory owners began replacing puddlers with machines. Like many other skilled workers, puddlers began losing their jobs as well as their bargaining power with employers.*

Labor union announcement

 ## The New Workplace

During the Second Industrial Revolution, machines run by unskilled workers replaced many skilled craftspeople. Because these low-paid workers required little training, they usually could be replaced easily. Therefore, they feared that complaining about wages or working conditions would cause them to lose their jobs.

As machines became more widely used in industries, factories focused on specialization—having workers repeatedly perform a single step in the production process. Specialization lowered costs and increased production. This focus on reducing costs caused managers to value efficiency.

In the early 1880s Frederick W. Taylor, an efficiency engineer with the Midvale Steel Company, performed time-and-motion studies to standardize worker activity. Taylor examined the steps that workers performed to do their jobs and measured the time each step took. He then found ways to do these tasks more efficiently, in order to lower labor costs and make them a measurable, predictable part of production. Taylor explained that "in the past the man has been first; in the future the system must be first."

Scientific management encouraged the creation of factories like this one, where each worker performed a few specific tasks.

Taylor's ideas became so popular that he left Midvale and became a well-known and successful consultant to many businesses. In 1911 he published *The Principles of Scientific Management* and established efficiency studies as a standard part of U.S. industry.

By focusing on how to reduce the cost of labor, scientific management encouraged managers to see workers as parts of the production process, not as individuals. In factories, managers increasingly ignored working conditions. Managers strictly regulated workers' activities, such as taking a break to get a drink of water. Injuries increased as workers used more machines and were pushed to work at a rapid pace. Companies rarely took responsibility for work-related injuries. As conditions grew worse, workers sought ways to bring about change.

⭐ Labor Unions

To improve working conditions, workers formed labor unions, usually in spite of their employers' objections. Unions increased workers' power because an entire workforce of a business was not as easily replaced as one individual worker. When all workers acted collectively, or together, they had a much greater chance of success. Unions tried to use **collective bargaining**—in which union leaders negotiated for better wages and working conditions on behalf of all workers in a particular factory or industry. Most employers opposed collective

bargaining, sharing the feelings of one company president who said, "I shall never give in. I would rather go out of business."

The Knights of Labor

Founded by Uriah Stephens, the **Knights of Labor** was a union originally organized like a secret society. During a depression in the 1870s, the union built a network of local assemblies. It sought to, as Stephens said, "include men and women of every creed and color." In 1879 Terence V. Powderly became the leader of the Knights. He eliminated the secrecy surrounding the organization and turned it into the first truly national labor union in the United States. Under Powderly's leadership, the Knights worked for goals such as an eight-hour workday, equal pay for equal work, regulation of trusts, and an end to child labor. Unlike most unions at the time, the Knights welcomed both skilled and unskilled workers as members.

Women not only joined the union but also took an active role in it. Union organizer Mary Harris Jones was called Mother Jones by the workers whose rights she fought to protect. Jones organized

The Knights of Labor was one of the few unions to accept African Americans like Frank J. Farrell (left), shown here introducing Terence V. Powderly (center).

196 Chapter 6

many strikes among workers, such as a group of poorly paid Virginia miners whose lives were very difficult. She described their condition:

Mary Harris "Mother" Jones

❝In some of these [company] camps the miners are forced to pay as much as $9 a barrel for sugar, 18 cents a pound for fat pork, and $8 to $10 a month rent for a company shack, the roof of which is so poor that when it rains the bed is moved from place to place in the attempt to find a dry spot. Many a miner works his whole life and never handles a cent of money.❞

Even though workers faced such problems, Powderly was reluctant to support strikes. Local Knights of Labor chapters, however, supported the great railroad strike of 1877 that affected the nation from coast to coast. Such strikes led the Knights to their greatest strength in the mid-1880s. By 1886 the Knights' membership had increased to 700,000.

The Haymarket Riot

By 1886 other unions were gaining strength. In May thousands of union members in Chicago, Illinois, went on strike to support an eight-hour workday. Two strikers were killed in a clash with police. The next night, workers met at Haymarket Square to protest the killings. When police arrived to break up the crowd, someone threw a bomb that wounded more than 60 officers and killed 8 of them. The police responded by firing into the crowd, killing several people and wounding 100 others. The Chicago *Herald* described the event that became known as the **Haymarket Riot** as "wild carnage [slaughter]."

Eight anarchists—people who oppose all forms of government—were arrested and convicted of conspiracy, although there was no hard evidence directly linking them to the bombing. One of the anarchists predicted more violence among union members. "When you shall have hanged us, then—mark my words—they will do the bombthrowing!" he warned.

Although Powderly and the other Knights' leaders never supported the strike or the Haymarket demonstration, several local chapters of the Knights did. One of the convicted anarchists, Albert Parsons, held a Knights of Labor membership card. Public opinion linked the Knights to the Haymarket Riot and its violence. As a result, membership in the Knights declined rapidly.

The AFL

Another union, the **American Federation of Labor** (AFL), fared better than the Knights. Unlike the Knights, the AFL organized individual national unions, such as the mineworkers and the steelworkers unions, into a loose association. Led by Samuel Gompers, the AFL limited its membership to skilled workers, which gave the union great bargaining power but excluded the majority of workers.

Gompers said that the AFL tried to "accomplish the best results in improving the conditions of the working people . . . today and tomorrow" by negotiating for better wages, hours, and working conditions. By 1890 the AFL's membership was larger than that of the Knights and by 1904 it had more than 1.5 million members.

The bombing at Haymarket Square resulted in the deaths of several police officers and a decline in union support.

Strikes Against the Entrepreneurs

Unions continued to use strikes to improve conditions. Sometimes workers went on strike for the right to create a union or establish a chapter of a national union. Sometimes business owners pushed unions into striking in hopes of gaining government support in breaking the union. One such conflict occurred in 1892 at one of Andrew Carnegie's steel plants.

The Homestead Strike

Previously, workers had gotten along well with managers at the Carnegie Steel Company in the mill town of Homestead, Pennsylvania. This changed in 1889 when Henry Frick became chairman of the company. In 1892, union members protested Frick's plan to introduce new machinery to the plant. New machines would reduce the number of workers. When an agreement with the union could not be reached, Frick set out to break the union and cut costs. He announced that the company would negotiate only with individual workers, not the union.

On June 29 the **Homestead Strike** began while Carnegie was out of the country. Frick locked workers out of the plant. He refused to negotiate with the union or allow union members back to work. The workers responded by seizing control of the town of Homestead. Frick then hired private detectives from the Pinkerton agency to break the power of the union by force.

The striking workers were prepared, however. Gunfire erupted on July 6, when the Pinkerton detectives tried to enter the steelworks from barges on the Monongahela River. Nine workers and seven Pinkertons were killed in the battle that followed. After a long standoff, the outnumbered and trapped Pinkertons surrendered. They were then marched through the streets and insulted by crowds. Pennsylvania's governor called out the state militia to restore order. Although the strike continued for four more months, the union was eventually defeated. Frick sent a message to

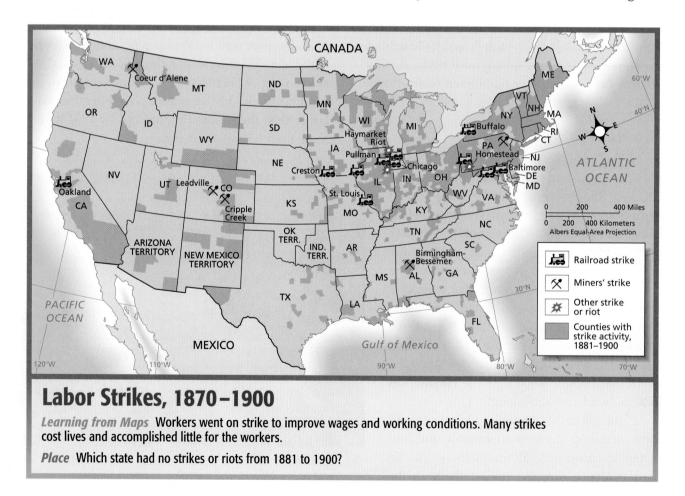

Labor Strikes, 1870–1900

Learning from Maps Workers went on strike to improve wages and working conditions. Many strikes cost lives and accomplished little for the workers.

Place Which state had no strikes or riots from 1881 to 1900?

Carnegie, "Our victory is now complete."

The Pullman Strike

Another major strike occurred among the workers at George Pullman's company. The Pullman Palace Car Company had established the company town of Pullman, Illinois, where most of its workers lived. Workers had to pay higher rents and utility costs than in nearby towns.

During a depression that began in 1893, Pullman laid off nearly half of the company's workers and cut the wages of those who remained by 25–40 percent without lowering rents. On May 11, 1894, workers protesting the wage cuts began the **Pullman Strike**. Support for the strike quickly spread throughout the railroad industry. The American Railway Union, headed by Eugene V. Debs, supported the strikers by refusing to work on trains carrying Pullman cars. By July, traffic on most midwestern rail lines was halted because almost all trains carried Pullman cars. The railroad officials then ordered the Pullman cars to be attached to U.S. mail cars, so that workers who stopped Pullman cars could be charged with the

Pinkertons confront workers during the Homestead Strike.

federal offense of interfering with the U.S. mail.

The federal government backed the railroad companies. Despite the protest of the Illinois governor, President Grover Cleveland sent federal troops to Chicago, the heart of the strike. Cleveland vowed:

66 **If it takes every dollar in the Treasury and every soldier in the United States to deliver a postal card in Chicago, that postal card should be delivered.** 99

The U.S. attorney general broke the strike by securing a court order demanding that the workers stop their strike because they were acting in restraint of trade. He used the Sherman Antitrust Act—originally intended to curb big business, not labor—to get the court order and keep the trains rolling. Debs was arrested and later sentenced to six months in jail for violating the court order. Strikes continued, but defeats like the Pullman Strike and the government's continued support of big business over the unions set the industrial labor movement back for several decades to come.

SECTION 3 REVIEW

Identify and explain the significance of the following:

- **Frederick W. Taylor**
- **collective bargaining**
- **Knights of Labor**
- **Terence V. Powderly**
- **Mary Harris Jones**
- **Haymarket Riot**
- **American Federation of Labor**
- **Samuel Gompers**
- **Henry Frick**
- **Homestead Strike**
- **Pullman Strike**

Reading for Content Understanding

1 **Main Idea** Why were the Knights of Labor and the American Federation of Labor formed, and how were they organized?

2 **Main Idea** How did the major strikes of the late 1800s affect American workers?

3 **Technology and Society** What impact did changes in industry and new technology have on the workplace?

4 **Writing** *Describing* Imagine that you are a newspaper journalist during the Haymarket Riot. Write a short article describing the events and outcome of the riot.

5 **Critical Thinking** *Making Comparisons* Compare the Knights of Labor with the American Federation of Labor. How were the unions similar? How were they different?

Populism

Reading Focus

What effects did industrialization have on farmers, and what actions did farmers take to fight for change?

How did farmers want to change the money supply?

What issues did the Populist Party support?

Key Terms

National Grange

Interstate Commerce Act

Interstate Commerce Commission

free coinage

gold standard

Sherman Silver Purchase Act

Farmers' Alliances

Populist Party

IN THE LATE 1800S *many western farmers blamed their economic hardships on the railroads. Frank Norris's 1901 novel,* The Octopus, *shows the farmers' point of view. The octopus in the story is the railroads, which threaten farmers' livelihoods by charging high rates. When farmer Dyke asks a railroad official on what basis the company raised shipping rates, the response is: "All— the—traffic—will—bear." However, the rate increase will leave Dyke with no profit from his harvest. Unless Dyke pays back the money he borrowed to raise his crops, the bank will foreclose on his home. Dyke realizes that "not only would the Railroad devour every morsel of his profits, but also it would take from him his home."*

Farm family

⭐ Rural Unrest

From 1860 to 1900, the U.S. population more than doubled, from 31.5 million to 76 million. To feed the growing population, the number of farms tripled, from 2 million to 6 million. Many farmers borrowed money to buy land and machinery, as farming became more mechanized. With modern machines, farmers in 1900 could produce a bushel of wheat almost 20 times faster than in 1830. However, the combination of more farms and greater productivity led to overproduction and lower prices for crops. Many farmers responded to lower prices by increasing crop production, which eventually pushed prices even lower.

As their income decreased, many farmers found it more difficult to pay their bills. Those who could not make their mortgage payments lost their farms and homes. Many became tenant farmers. By 1880 one fourth of all farms were rented by tenants, and the number kept growing. Many Americans could not even afford to rent land and thus became farm laborers. By 1900 there were 4.5 million farm laborers in the United States.

Many farmers blamed businesspeople—wholesalers, brokers, grain buyers, grain elevator operators, and particularly railroad owners—for profiting at their expense. Leonidas Polk, an editor of a North Carolina farm journal, expressed this view when he wrote,

> " There is something radically wrong. . . . The railroads have never been so prosperous. . . . The banks have never done a better . . . business. . . . Manufacturing enterprises have never made more money. . . . Towns and cities flourish and 'boom,' . . . and yet agriculture languishes [declines]. "

As economic conditions grew worse for farmers, they began to organize associations—like workers had done—to further their interests.

★ The National Grange

In 1866 clerical worker Oliver Kelley toured the South for the U.S. Department of Agriculture. Kelley saw firsthand how the nation's farmers suffered. After that tour, Kelley and several government clerks founded the National Grange of the Patrons of Husbandry in 1867. The **National Grange** was a social and educational organization for farmers. The Grange wanted to ease the isolation of farm life and improve farmers' living standards. Local granges, or chapters, were quickly established, and membership grew rapidly, to more than 1.5 million by 1874.

Granges formed organizations called cooperatives to buy goods in bulk at lower prices, increasing farmers' buying power. Farmers also formed cooperative societies to sell their crops, hoping that by joining together they could demand higher prices. Unfortunately for farmers, these cooperatives were often run by people who were inexperienced in business. In addition, banks, merchants, and railroads usually organized to oppose these cooperatives. As a result, most of the cooperatives fared poorly.

The Grange then shifted its focus to politics. It campaigned for political candidates who supported farmers' goals and demanded legislation to

This Granger poster shows the group's ideal image of farm life.

regulate rates for the use of railroads and grain elevators. In a few states, the Grange managed to enact laws regulating railroads, which farmers relied on to ship their crops.

The issue of railroad regulation came before the U.S. Supreme Court in 1877 in the case of *Munn* v. *Illinois*. The Court ruled that the government did have the right to regulate the railroads and other businesses that affected the public interest. In the 1886 case of *Wabash* v. *Illinois*, the Court clarified that the federal government could only regulate companies that did business across state lines. Regulation of rates for railroad lines within states fell to the state governments.

Congress also tried to exert its authority. In February 1887 it passed the **Interstate Commerce Act** to provide some uniform national regulations over trade between the states. This act created the **Interstate Commerce Commission** (ICC) to ensure that railroads charged fair rates and did not discriminate in favor of big shippers. However, the commission lacked any real power to enforce its regulations, and the courts gave the agency little help when it appealed to them.

An Industrial Nation **201**

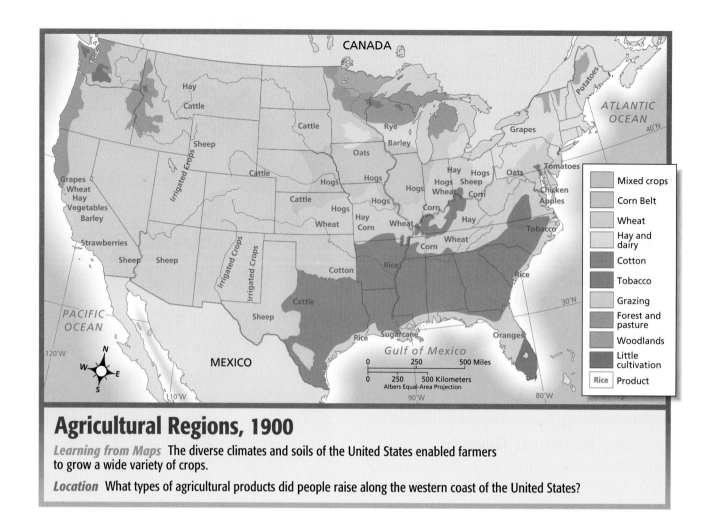

Agricultural Regions, 1900

Learning from Maps The diverse climates and soils of the United States enabled farmers to grow a wide variety of crops.

Location What types of agricultural products did people raise along the western coast of the United States?

⭐ Money Issues

Railroad rates were not the only concern facing farmers. Farmers' problems most often involved money issues, such as debt, credit, and low crop prices. Many farmers thought that assistance would come only from national legislation that affected the money supply.

Farmers for Silver

Since 1792, the United States had allowed free and unlimited coinage. **Free coinage** meant that gold and silver were coined and that paper money was worth a specific amount of gold or silver. The Coinage Act of 1873 placed the United States strictly on a **gold standard**—meaning that only gold could back U.S. currency.

1863 silver half dollar

Tied to the gold standard, the money supply tended to grow more slowly than the nation's population. This meant that there were fewer dollars in circulation for each citizen, which resulted in deflation—a shrinking of the money supply and a general lowering of prices. Farmers supported coining silver to create inflation—an increase in the money supply and a rise in prices. With inflation, farmers hoped that prices for farm products would rise, thus increasing their income and allowing them to pay their debts more easily.

Silver Politics

During the late 1870s there was considerable support for free coinage of silver. Many farmers began backing political candidates who supported free silver coinage. One such politician was William Jennings Bryan of Nebraska, who claimed that with

Grover Cleveland

The Granger Collection, New York

the free coinage of silver all "necessary reforms will be possible." In February 1878 Congress passed the Bland-Allison Act, allowing limited silver coinage, over President Hayes's veto.

A new political party, the Greenback Party, favored inflating the money supply with paper dollars not backed by gold or silver. In the presidential election of 1880 the Greenback Party nominated Iowa congressman James B. Weaver as its candidate. The two major parties, however, largely ignored the money issue.

The Republicans finally made continued coinage of silver an issue in the presidential election of 1888. President Cleveland, a Democrat, lost the election to Republican Benjamin Harrison, grandson of former president William Henry Harrison. After the election, the Republican Congress passed the **Sherman Silver Purchase Act** to increase the amount of silver purchased for coinage. However, this act did not help farmers economically as much as they had hoped.

Farmers' Alliances

Many farmers formed their own political organizations to increase their power. First locally, then regionally, they organized to elect candidates and to achieve policies favorable to them. These political organizations became known as the **Farmers' Alliances**.

The Texas alliance started as a frontier farmers' association in 1877 and quickly grew to become the Grand State Alliance in 1879. Other alliances joined, and membership soared, topping 1.5 million in 1890. The Colored Farmers' Alliance had more than 1 million members of its own.

The Farmers' Alliances were more politically active than the Grange had been. Their goals and proposals put more emphasis on government legislation to help farmers. The Alliances called for increased railroad regulation and lower interest rates.

In the 1890 elections the Alliances ran candidates who emerged as a serious political force, particularly in the West and in the South. These candidates won the governorships of Texas and Georgia and gained control of both houses of the Georgia legislature. Alliance supporters also won more than 35 seats in the U.S. Congress.

★ The Populist Party

Following their state and local successes, farmers raised their political sights and hopes. At a conference in Cincinnati, Ohio, in 1891, Alliance leaders met with representatives from labor and reform organizations. They agreed to organize a new national political party, the People's Party. This organization, better known as the **Populist Party**, represented the high point of farmers' political activity.

The Election of 1892

In 1892 the Populist Party held its first national convention in Omaha, Nebraska, where the group decided on a platform of far-reaching reforms. The Populists' goal was to remove the influence of big

The Colored Farmers' Alliance fought for the rights of African American farmers like this family from Virginia.

business on government and to provide all Americans with greater democracy and voice in the government. Populist Mary Lease expressed their sentiments:

> " Wall Street owns the country. It is no longer a government of the people, by the people, and for the people, but a government of Wall Street, by Wall Street, and for Wall Street. "

To restore the political power of the common people, the Populist platform called for government ownership of railroads and the telephone and telegraph systems, and it supported the "free and unlimited coinage of silver and gold." To attract votes from industrial workers, the Populists supported the eight-hour workday and immigration restrictions.

In the 1892 presidential election the Democrats nominated Grover Cleveland, and the Republicans nominated Benjamin Harrison. The significant issue of the campaign was the Republicans' support for high tariffs. This time Cleveland won. James B. Weaver, the Populist candidate, won an impressive 1 million votes, about 8.5 percent of the total popular vote.

The Panic of 1893

Shortly after Grover Cleveland took office, the Philadelphia and Reading Railroad failed, causing a stock market panic. This triggered the worst economic downturn that Americans had yet experienced. By 1894 millions of Americans

The Granger Collection, New York

In 1895 Mary Lease published her views on populism in a well-known book.

Linking Past to Present

Third Political Parties

Ever since the presidential election of 1796, the United States has had a two-party system. However, at times some Americans have felt that the two major parties did not adequately represent their views. Thus, many Americans formed or joined third political parties, such as the Populist Party.

Dissatisfied with the Democratic and Republican presidential candidates for the 1992 and 1996 elections, Americans supported several new political parties. Ross Perot ran as an independent candidate in 1992. Perot then founded the Reform Party and ran as its candidate in 1996. Each time he campaigned on a platform of government reform. Ralph Nader ran in 1996 for the Green Party, which was formed in 1984. This party had an environmental platform. In 1996 Perot was on the ballot in all 50 states, and Nader was on the ballot in 18 states.

While running as an independent candidate in the 1992 presidential campaign, Perot joined the Republican and Democratic candidates in televised debates. Perot received almost 20 million votes in the election, about 19 percent of the total. Although a third-party candidate has yet to win a presidential election, third parties remain an important part of the democratic process.

Understanding What You Read

1. Why have Americans formed political parties in the past?

2. What role do you think third parties play in the democratic process?

were unemployed and some 690,000 workers went on strike to protest reduced wages.

The depression had multiple causes, but some Americans blamed the money system. Many investors reacted to the downturn by selling their investments in exchange for gold, causing a gold drain. Bank depositors feared a further downturn and exchanged their paper money and silver coins for gold at federal banks. The result was a serious shortage of U.S. gold reserves, which forced the government to sell bonds to increase the gold supply.

Democrat William Jennings Bryan supported many Populist ideas.

The Election of 1896

With the economic panic, many voters began to agree with the Populists' call for reform. In 1896 the Republicans nominated William McKinley for president, and he came out firmly against free coinage of silver. Many Democrats saw this platform as a chance to win Populist and some Republican votes.

At the Democrats' nominating convention their nominee, William Jennings Bryan, swept the crowd with an emotional speech. In support of free coinage of silver he said, "You shall not press down upon the brow of labor this crown of thorns. You will not crucify mankind upon a cross of gold!"

The Democrats had put the Populists in a difficult position by adopting their strongest issue. The Populists had to decide between running their own candidate, and thus splitting the silver vote, or supporting Bryan and possibly being absorbed by the Democrats. The Populists decided to nominate Bryan but chose their own vice president.

The Democrats carried the South and the West. However the Republicans won the election with the strong support of the more heavily populated Midwest and Northeast. The well-financed Republican campaign had convinced many industrial workers in large urban areas that free silver coinage would create high unemployment. McKinley's victory in the election of 1896 marked the end of both the Populist Party and the organized farmers' parties.

SECTION 4 REVIEW

Identify and explain the significance of the following:

- Oliver Kelley
- National Grange
- Interstate Commerce Act
- Interstate Commerce Commission
- free coinage
- gold standard
- Benjamin Harrison
- Sherman Silver Purchase Act
- Farmers' Alliances
- Populist Party
- James B. Weaver
- William Jennings Bryan

Reading for Content Understanding

1 **Main Idea** What problems did farmers face during the late 1800s, and how did they respond?

2 **Main Idea** What issues did farmers support in the National Grange and the Populist Party?

3 **Economic Development** Why did many farmers support the free coinage of silver?

4 **Writing** *Informing* Write a paragraph explaining the goals of the Populist Party and why it did not win the 1896 presidential election.

5 **Critical Thinking** *Making Comparisons* In what ways was the Populist Party different from the Democratic and Republican Parties?

CHAPTER 6 REVIEW

Chapter Summary

The Second Industrial Revolution resulted in the growth of new industries such as steel and new inventions such as the lightbulb. This revolution also changed the way that businesses were organized and how people worked. Industrial workers created unions to gain better working conditions. Farmers formed the National Grange and the Populist Party in an effort to reverse their hard times and increase their political influence. ▪

On a separate sheet of paper, complete the following activities.

Identifying People and Ideas

Describe the historical significance of the following:

1. Bessemer process
2. Thomas Alva Edison
3. free enterprise
4. Andrew Carnegie
5. horizontal integration
6. Pullman Strike
7. Terence V. Powderly
8. American Federation of Labor
9. Mary Harris Jones
10. gold standard

Internet Activity
go.hrw.com
SB1 Inventions

Search the Internet through the HRW Web site to find information about the inventions of the late 1800s. Create a chart showing some of the inventions that are still used today. Include when they were invented, who invented them, and a caption explaining their importance both at the time they were invented and today. You may include drawings of the inventions as well.

Understanding Main Ideas

1. How did technological breakthroughs help bring about the Second Industrial Revolution?
2. What changes took place in the way that American businesses were organized?
3. How did Andrew Carnegie use the method of vertical integration to gain control of the steel industry?
4. What were the causes and outcome of the strike at Carnegie's Homestead plant?
5. Why were the years 1860 to 1900 difficult for American farmers?
6. Why did Congress pass the Sherman Silver Purchase Act?

Reviewing Themes

1. **Technology and Society** What effect did the Second Industrial Revolution have on the U.S. economy?

Using the Time Line

Number your paper from 1 to 6. Match the letters on the time line below with the following events.

1. More than 100 people are wounded in the Haymarket Riot in Chicago.
2. Congress creates the Interstate Commerce Commission to regulate trusts.
3. Thomas Edison begins supplying New York City buildings with electrical power.
4. Congress passes the Sherman Antitrust Act to stop the growing power of the trusts.
5. The Pullman Strike shuts down railroad traffic across the Midwest.
6. Congress passes the Bland-Allison Act, allowing some silver coinage.

1876   1880   1884   1888   1892   1896

a   b   c   d   e   f

2. **Economic Development**   What actions did government take to help big business? What steps did government take to control big business?
3. **Citizenship and Democracy**   How did many industrial workers and farmers react to the economic changes of the Second Industrial Revolution?

Thinking Critically

1. **Supporting a Point of View**   Many business leaders opposed attempts by politicians, unions, and competitors to regulate businesses. Do you agree or disagree with these business leaders? Explain your answer.
2. **Drawing Conclusions**   Why do you think the Knights of Labor sought such a wide range of members, including African Americans, unskilled workers, and women?
3. **Evaluating**   Although the Populist Party lost the presidential election of 1892, several reforms in the party's platform were later put into effect. Which reform do you think was the most important? Explain your answer.

Building Your Portfolio

Complete the following activities individually or in groups.

1. **Oral History**   Create an oral history that might have been told about the Homestead Strike. First, research the events that took place during the strike. Then choose a perspective based on the views of a group of participants in the strike, such as the strikers or the mill management. When you have finished your oral history, relate your account to the rest of the class.
2. **Presidential Elections**   Research and create a campaign poster for a candidate in either the 1892 or the 1896 presidential election. (Remember that in 1892, the third-party candidate made a strong showing.) Make sure that your poster includes the important issues of that election and states the candidate's position on those issues.

Writing About History

1. **Classifying**   Which new invention of the Second Industrial Revolution do you think most changed Americans' lives? What is a modern invention that has had a similar impact on your life? Explain your answers in a paragraph.
2. **Persuading**   Write a newspaper editorial supporting one of the candidates in the 1896 presidential election. Be sure to identify the main issue or issues supported by this candidate.

Linking Geography and History

1. **Location**   Why do you think that most factories were built along major railroads or waterways?
2. **Region**   Why do you think the Populist Party was more popular in the South than it was in the North?

History Skills Workshop

Using Visual Resources   Study the image below, which is an artist's sketch of federal troops firing on Pullman Company workers. Write one paragraph describing this scene from the point of view of the troops and another paragraph from the point of view of the Pullman Company strikers.

The Granger Collection, New York

▪ CHAPTER 7 ▪
Immigrants and Cities
(1870–1900)

In 1870 landscape architect Frederick Law Olmsted spoke to a Boston crowd about the rapid growth of U.S. cities. "There will," he predicted, "soon be larger towns than any the world has yet known." Urban areas were being filled both with immigrants and with migrants from rural areas. These new city residents struggled to adjust to factory work and different lifestyles. They also helped create a distinctive urban culture.

THEMES

Cultural Diversity
In what ways might increased immigration affect a nation?

Technology and Society
How might technology affect people's daily lives?

Geographic Diversity
What effect might the growth of large urban areas have on a nation?

1870 | **1873** | **1876** | **1879** | **1882**

1870 Fourteen U.S. cities have a population of more than 100,000.

1876 The first successful professional baseball league is formed.

1882 Congress passes the Chinese Exclusion Act.

1881 Marshall Fields department store opens in Chicago.

A New Wave of Immigration

Reading Focus

Why did immigrants come to the United States, and where did they emigrate from during the late 1800s?

What was life in the United States like for immigrants in the late 1800s?

How did some Americans try to limit immigration?

Key Terms

old immigrants
new immigrants
steerage
tenements
benevolent societies
Chinese Exclusion Act
Immigration Restriction League

LEE CHEW LIVED IN CHINA *as a poor peasant working on his father's farm. He had little hope of ever owning his own land. When Chew saw a man from his village who had "returned with unlimited wealth, which he had obtained in the country of the American wizards," Chew decided to leave China. Like millions of other immigrants to the United States, he left behind everything and everyone he knew and traveled to a strange land carrying little but the hope of opportunity.*

The Granger Collection, New York

Asian immigrants in the 1800s

IMAGE ON LEFT PAGE: *City streets grew more crowded in the late 1800s as urban populations increased.*

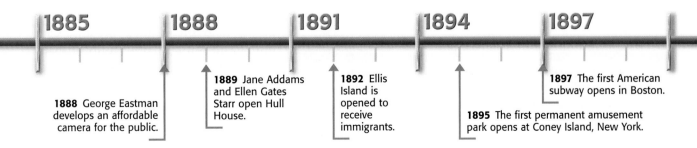

1885   **1888**   **1891**   **1894**   **1897**

1888 George Eastman develops an affordable camera for the public.

1889 Jane Addams and Ellen Gates Starr open Hull House.

1892 Ellis Island is opened to receive immigrants.

1895 The first permanent amusement park opens at Coney Island, New York.

1897 The first American subway opens in Boston.

New Immigrants

Many immigrants shared Lee Chew's vision of America as a land of opportunity and wealth. While immigrants continued to come to the United States by the millions, immigration patterns began to change in the late 1800s. Immigrants who had come to the United States before the 1880s were often called **old immigrants**. They were mostly from Britain, Germany, Ireland, and Scandinavia. Many were skilled workers who spoke English. Most of the old immigrants were also Protestants, except for the Irish and some Germans.

After 1880 many more immigrants came to the United States, often from different countries than previous immigrants. As many immigrants arrived during the 1880s as had come between 1800 and 1860. By 1910 more than 70 percent of these immigrants to the United States were so-called **new immigrants** from southern and eastern Europe. Thousands of Czechs, Greeks, Hungarians, Italians, Poles, Russians, and Slovaks came to the United States looking for a better life. For example, immigrant Miriam Zunser hoped "for all manner of miracles [in] a strange, wonderful land!"

Many of these new immigrants sought economic opportunities while others, including Armenians and Jews, were escaping political and religious persecution. The immigrants who arrived in the late 1800s brought many new cultural practices with them. They also held a variety of religious beliefs, including Eastern Orthodoxy, Roman Catholicism, and Judaism.

Coming to America

The industrial boom of the late 1800s created job opportunities that attracted many immigrants. Immigrants often wrote to family members and friends back home, urging them to come to America. They also sent money for the journey. To attract immigrants, railroad and steamship companies hired business agents. These agents tended to paint unrealistic pictures of easy success in the United States.

Shoes worn by an Ellis Island immigrant

Immigrants usually had to endure a difficult journey. Most immigrants bought the cheapest fares and traveled in **steerage**, an area on a ship's lower levels near where the steering mechanisms were located. In cramped conditions with poor ventilation and no privacy, passengers experienced seasickness, and some died from disease. A journalist emigrating from Naples, Italy, wondered,

❝ **How can a steerage passenger remember that he is a human being when he must first pick the worms from his food . . . and eat in his stuffy, stinking bunk, or in the hot and fetid [foul] atmosphere where 150 men sleep, or . . . [next] to a seasick man?** ❞

Despite the hardships, some immigrants held on to their dreams. One immigrant wrote that a group of them "peered through the portholes into the blackness at night . . . and forgot our seasickness in anticipation of the wonders we were to behold."

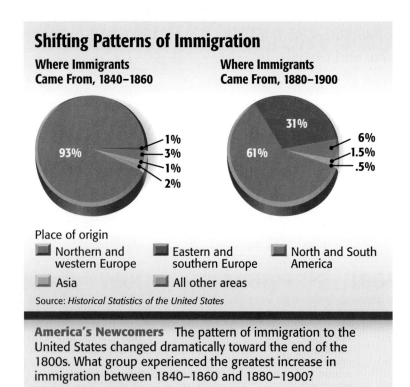

Shifting Patterns of Immigration

Where Immigrants Came From, 1840–1860

93%, 1%, 3%, 1%, 2%

Where Immigrants Came From, 1880–1900

61%, 31%, 6%, 1.5%, .5%

Place of origin
- Northern and western Europe
- Eastern and southern Europe
- North and South America
- Asia
- All other areas

Source: *Historical Statistics of the United States*

America's Newcomers The pattern of immigration to the United States changed dramatically toward the end of the 1800s. What group experienced the greatest increase in immigration between 1840–1860 and 1880–1900?

Ellis Island

Once immigrants reached the United States, they went first to immigration processing centers. For many years, these centers were poorly run by state and local governments. In 1890 the federal government began assuming control of the immigration centers. Two years later the U.S. government opened a new receiving office on Ellis Island in New York Harbor. Millions of immigrants came through Ellis Island over the next 40 years. Italian immigrant Edward Corsi described the approach to Ellis Island:

Ellis Island became so well known that songs were written about it.

❝ **The Statue of Liberty . . . looming shadowy through the mist . . . brought silence. . . . This symbol of America . . . inspired awe in the hopeful immigrants.** ❞

Most Asian immigrants entered the country through West Coast stations such as Angel Island in San Francisco Bay. In the processing centers, officials interviewed immigrants to decide whether to let them enter the country. Officials also conducted physical examinations, deporting any person who carried an infectious disease such as tuberculosis. The majority of immigrants were admitted, however. After admission, they entered the United States in search of work and a new life.

 ## Immigrant Life

Once they arrived in the United States, the majority of new immigrants settled in large cities, where they hoped to find work and other people from their homeland. Because life in their new country was often very different from what they were used to, many immigrants lived in neighborhoods with others who shared their nationality.

In these neighborhoods, immigrants could hear their own language, eat familiar foods, and preserve their customs. Many immigrant groups published newspapers in their own languages and founded schools, churches, synagogues, and other organizations to preserve their beliefs and customs.

In New York City, for example, Jewish immigrants founded a thriving theater that gave performances in the Yiddish language.

Immigrants often opened local shops and small neighborhood banks. Business owners helped new arrivals by extending store credit for food purchases and by giving small loans. Such financial aid was important for newcomers because there were few commercial banks in most immigrant neighborhoods. In 1904 Italian immigrant Amadeo Pietro Giannini started the Bank of Italy in San Francisco, which later became the Bank of America.

Even with neighborhood support, immigrants often found urban life difficult. Many of them lived in **tenements**—poorly built, overcrowded apartments—and worked under exhausting conditions. One girl described the difference between her hopes and reality:

❝ **[I dreamed] of the golden stairs leading to the top of the American palace where father was supposed to live. [I] went 'home' to . . . an ugly old tenement in the heart of the Lower East Side. There were stairs to climb but they were not golden.** ❞

New immigrants often shopped at stores that carried foods from their homeland, like this Italian grocery in New York City.

Immigrant parents emphasized education as a key to their children's success. Students here participate in a physical fitness program.

Some immigrant communities formed **benevolent societies**—aid organizations founded to provide help in cases of sickness, unemployment, and death. At that time, there were few national government agencies to provide such aid.

Despite the challenges, immigrants often found opportunities in the United States that they would not have had at home. Many immigrants tried to adjust to their new country by eagerly embracing American culture. New immigrants encouraged their children to learn English and to become familiar with American customs. Some parents stressed education to their children as a way of improving their future chances for success. Russian immigrant Mashke Antin recalled that free public schools were her father's "chief hope for us children, the essence of American opportunity." Many immigrants successfully met the challenges of living in a new country and were able to build a future for their families in the United States.

★ Immigrant Workers

Although many of the new immigrants had been agricultural workers in their homelands, few could afford to buy land in the United States. Instead, they found work in the cities, where about 90 percent of all manufacturing in the United States took place by 1900.

Global Connections

Coming to America

For many immigrants, the decision to leave their homes was difficult. However, poverty and persecution helped convince millions of Europeans from countries such as Greece, Italy, and Poland to immigrate to the United States in search of a better life.

Many of these immigrants hoped to return home wealthy after earning money overseas. Other immigrants, such as Jews and Armenians, saw the United States as a place to settle to escape religious and ethnic persecution. In Russia, many Jewish mothers sang a lullaby to their children:

66 *America is for everyone*
They say, it's the greatest piece
of luck
For Jews, it's a garden of Eden
A rare and precious place. 99

The political freedom found in the United States also appealed to many immigrants.

These various factors helped attract large numbers of immigrants in the late 1800s and early 1900s. In spite of the cultural and language differences between the United States and their homelands, millions of eastern and southern Europeans came to the United States during this period. Others immigrated to Canada or South American nations such as Argentina and Brazil.

Understanding What You Read

1. What factors encouraged people to emigrate from their homelands in Europe?

2. Why do you think so many European immigrants chose to settle in the Americas?

Because the majority of immigrants came from rural areas, few had any skills in manufacturing or industrial work. With little money and limited knowledge of English, most of these immigrants were forced to take low-paying, unskilled industrial jobs. Many of these jobs were in the construction, garment, or steel industries. "Wherever the heat is most . . . scorching, the smoke and soot most choking," wrote one Hungarian immigrant, "there we are certain to find compatriots [people from the same homeland] bent . . . with toil."

The typical workweek for industrial laborers in the late 1800s consisted of six 10-hour days, but longer hours were also common. Employers offered immigrants relatively low wages, which were nevertheless often higher than they could have earned in their home countries. Women and children earned even less, and many families depended on their wages for survival.

Not all industrial labor took place in large factories. Some immigrants worked long hours for little pay in small shops or factories located in or near working-class neighborhoods. Usually associated with the garment industry, these workplaces were called sweatshops because of the workers' long hours and often unhealthy working conditions. In small rooms, workers crowded around tables and sewing machines. Writer Joseph Kirkland described a sweatshop in New York:

> 66 In one such place there were fifteen men and women in one room, which contained also a pile of mattresses on which some of the men sleep at night. 99

A large number of garment workers were paid by the week, but some earned wages based on the number of garment pieces they completed. These so-called piece workers had to work quickly.

Immigrant women also commonly worked as maids and cooks for middle- or upper-class families. Other women ran boardinghouses in their homes. They cooked for their boarders and laundered their clothes. Women in these occupations worked long hours from dawn until dusk.

Immigrants with the appropriate skills sometimes found work in a wide range of occupations.

The Granger Collection, New York

Immigrant families like this one often worked together in sweatshops making garments.

Some worked as bakers, carpenters, masons, metalworkers, or skilled machinists. Other immigrants saved, shared resources, or borrowed money to open small businesses, such as barbershops, candy stores, laundries, restaurants, or street vending carts. New immigrants tended to open the same types of businesses in which earlier immigrants from the same country were already successful.

Many immigrants traveled back and forth between Europe and the United States before returning permanently to Europe. For example, it was common for Italian male immigrants to eventually return to Italy. The immigrants who stayed in the United States often paved the way for the success of future generations.

★ Opposition to Immigration

The rise in immigration in the late 1800s increased anti-immigrant feeling among some Americans. Nativists argued that U.S. immigration policies allowed in too many new immigrants. Nativists also claimed that the new immigrants' poverty and lack of education would harm American society. Many nativists also held racial and ethnic prejudices against immigrants from Asia, southern Europe, and eastern Europe. Nativists argued that the different languages and cultural backgrounds of these immigrants would prevent them from becoming good U.S. citizens.

Labor unions, particularly in the West, also opposed immigration. They feared that immigrants willing to work for low wages would take jobs away from union members. Some politicians agreed. Senator Henry Cabot Lodge of Massachusetts declared, "If we have any regard for the welfare, the wages, or the standard of life of American workingmen, we should take immediate steps to restrict foreign immigration." Some business leaders, however, favored immigration. They wanted a large supply of workers to keep labor costs down. One businessman said, "Their home countries have borne [paid] the expense of rearing them . . . and then America . . . reaps whatever profits there are" from their work.

In some places, nativists committed violence against immigrants. Other nativists worked to stop or limit immigration by lobbying for anti-immigration legislation. For example, about 105,000 people of Chinese descent lived in the United States in 1880. Two years later, Congress passed the **Chinese Exclusion Act**, which prohibited Chinese people from immigrating to the United States for 10 years. This act marked the first time a nationality was prohibited from entering the country. As a result, the Chinese American

The Granger Collection, New York

This cartoon shows the attitude of nativists who looked down on many new immigrants during the late 1800s.

population suffered a steady decline in the late 1800s. Congress extended the ban into the early 1900s.

To further reduce the number of immigrants, nativists founded the **Immigration Restriction League** in 1894. The league demanded that all immigrants prove that they could read and write before being allowed into the country. Supporters of the league argued that this measure would reduce immigration from eastern and southern Europe while preserving immigration from western and northern Europe. Congress passed a law requiring a literacy test for immigrants in 1897, but President Cleveland vetoed it, saying that the bill was "narrow, and un-American."

Despite the opposition from nativists, immigrants continued to arrive in large numbers and played an essential role in industrial growth in the late 1800s. Immigrants constructed many of the nation's buildings, roads, and railroads. They also performed much of the low-wage factory work that drove the rapid economic growth of the United States.

SECTION 1 REVIEW

Identify and explain the significance of the following:
- old immigrants
- new immigrants
- steerage
- tenements
- benevolent societies
- Henry Cabot Lodge
- Chinese Exclusion Act
- Immigration Restriction League

Reading for Content Understanding

1 **Main Idea** What were living conditions like for many immigrants?

2 **Main Idea** What steps did some Americans take to change U.S. immigration policies?

3 **Geographic Diversity** *Movement* Why did immigrants come to the United States, and what countries did they emigrate from in the late 1800s?

4 **Writing** *Persuading* Imagine that you are an immigrant to the United States in 1885. Write a letter to your family back home, telling them about your good and bad experiences, and try to persuade them to join you.

5 **Critical Thinking** *Identifying Generalizations and Stereotypes* Why did some Americans oppose immigration in the late 1800s?

City Life

Reading Focus

Why did so many people move to cities, and what problems resulted from the rapid urban growth?

What technological developments made larger cities possible?

How did city residents organize to deal with the challenges of urban life?

Key Terms

mass transit
suburbs
department stores
settlement houses
Hull House

*I*N THE 1880S, *Kate Richards O'Hare and her family lived on a Kansas ranch. "Those were wonderful days," she recalled. An economic depression brought hard times to her family, however. O'Hare wrote sadly, "The [live]stock was sold, the home dismantled. . . . Then came the day when we left the ranch and went to the city." There the young girl was shocked by the masses of people and the fierce struggle to find work. The O'Hare family was one of thousands of migrant and immigrant families that moved to U.S. cities in the late 1800s, where they faced new challenges as city-dwellers and industrial workers.*

Train schedules for Boston and Chicago

 ## The Growth of Cities

During the late 1800s immigrants and native-born Americans moved to cities in record numbers, causing rapid urban growth. In 1850 there were only six cities in the United States with a population greater than 100,000. By 1870 this number had grown to 14, and by 1900 there were more than 35 such cities. In particular, the urban population of midwestern cities grew dramatically during those years. Chicago's population rose from 30,000 in 1850 to 1.7 million in 1900.

Although some city residents were business-people and skilled workers, many more were poor laborers. Agricultural hardships drove large numbers of rural residents to the cities. One writer described Chicago's new residents as having "come for the common avowed object [declared goal] of making money." Hoping to escape discrimination and find better economic opportunities, African Americans from the rural South began moving to northern cities in the 1890s. These native-born Americans joined thousands of immigrants also seeking jobs.

People from the country were often amazed by the noise and the crowds in the city. One woman who arrived in New York City in 1901 noted:

❝I never saw so many people on the streets, shouting, going in all directions. Having come from a little bit of a village with a few houses, it was to say the least disturbing.❞

By the turn of the century about 40 percent of Americans lived in urban areas, and the percentage kept climbing in the early 1900s.

 ## The Changing Look of the City

Increased size was not the only change affecting cities in the late 1800s. New technology made living in a large city more convenient, thus encouraging continued urban expansion.

Skyscrapers

In the mid-1800s typical downtown city buildings were five stories tall. Architects were limited to designing buildings of this size for reasons of safety and practicality. Construction materials at that time, such as brick, stone, and wood, were either too weak or too heavy to be used in very tall buildings. Taller buildings also required residents to walk up many flights of stairs. Another inconvenience was that water could not reliably be pumped higher than the fifth floor.

The rapid growth of cities placed a great strain on the available downtown space. Architects, particularly Louis Sullivan of Chicago, and engineers responded by designing skyscrapers—multistory buildings with metal frames. The availability of stronger and lower-cost steel helped make the skyscraper possible. The steam-powered safety elevator, patented by Elisha Otis in 1861, solved the problem of carrying people up and down these towering buildings. Other breakthroughs, such as improved plumbing and ventilation, helped architects create even taller buildings. By 1900 the tallest building in the United States was the 435-foot-tall Park Row Building in New York City—some four times taller than the early skyscrapers.

Public Transportation

Skyscrapers allowed developers to use limited city space more efficiently. As more tall buildings were constructed, city centers became more densely

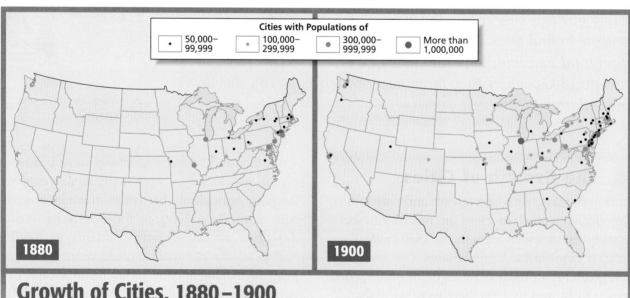

Cities with Populations of

- 50,000–99,999
- 100,000–299,999
- 300,000–999,999
- More than 1,000,000

1880

1900

Growth of Cities, 1880–1900

Learning from Maps The introduction of mass transit systems and continued increases in manufacturing helped many cities grow between 1880 and 1900.

Region Which region had the most large cities in both 1880 and 1900?

Chicago city streets crowded with people, buildings, and public transportation

The Granger Collection, New York

populated. Pedestrians and horse-drawn carts crowded city streets that were often poorly paved or not paved at all.

City planners tried to ease the congestion by creating several forms of **mass transit**, or public transportation. By the 1890s cities like New York and Chicago had elevated railroads that ran on tracks above the streets. A more complicated and expensive option was to build underground railroads known as subways. The first American subway opened in Boston in 1897, followed in 1904 by the much larger New York City subway. Cable cars, first used in the 1860s, were also common. Electric trolleys became popular in the 1890s. These streetcars carried people to and from work cheaply and quickly.

If they could afford it, many middle-class Americans chose to live outside the city, in quieter areas where they could buy their own homes. They moved to **suburbs**—residential neighborhoods outside of downtown areas. The new mass transit networks of trolleys, subways, and commuter trains made it possible for people to live in the suburbs and work in the cities.

★ New Places for the Public

In addition to places for people to live and work, urban leaders in the late 1800s wanted to create public places to enhance a city's image and improve the quality of city life. Not all city residents could afford to move to the suburbs in search of quiet. As cities grew larger, public areas began to disappear. Although town commons and greens had existed in the United States since the 1600s, the public park—a space specially designed for recreation—was unknown until the mid-1800s. About that time New York City began setting aside land for public use to provide residents with quiet, green spaces. The city hired landscape architect Frederick Law Olmsted to design Central Park. The idea of preserving green areas in cities for recreation caught on, and many cities began building parks.

In the 1870s a group of Chicago leaders founded a public library, declaring that "every person in the community, however humble, . . . has a right to be supplied with books." During the late 1800s cities and towns across the country established public libraries to educate and serve their residents. Many communities benefited from the philanthropy of Andrew Carnegie, who donated millions of dollars for library construction.

Philanthropists in several large U.S. cities also began creating museums where the public could see displays of art, natural history, and science. These museums, such as the Metropolitan Museum of Art in New York and the Art Institute of Chicago, were intended to educate the public and to create beautiful city centers. The founders of the Boston Museum of Fine Arts stated that the museum "ought to be a popular institution, in the widest sense of the term."

Giant retail shops known as **department stores** also appeared in some city centers in the late 1800s. These stores provided a great variety of

Streetcars transported people from suburbs to their jobs in the city.

Immigrants and Cities **217**

American Arts

Frederick Law Olmsted

Frederick Law Olmsted, who was one of the first designers to call himself a landscape architect, is best known as the chief architect of New York City's Central Park. In addition to designing Central Park, Olmsted planned Prospect Park in Brooklyn; South Park in Chicago; the Stanford University grounds in California; the grounds of the U.S. Capitol in Washington, D.C.; and the Boston park system.

In 1857 Olmsted was appointed superintendent of Central Park, the first major public park in the United States. He created new plans for the park with designer Calvert Vaux. Olmsted planned Central Park to serve as a rural retreat for city-dwellers. He hoped that it would be a place where they could relax while they explored the park's natural landscape. For this reason, he carefully planned every square foot of the park's surface, including every tree and bush, as well as every arch. Olmsted also hoped that the park would offer a place for people to exercise. He wanted to create a setting where people of all social classes might gather outdoors.

Olmsted's designs for Central Park called for three main bodies of water—the Lake, the Meer, and the Pond. To make the Pond area more attractive to visitors, Olmsted planted trees along its edge and lined its path with benches. He purposely placed the Pond near busy streets, hoping that it would attract walkers, if only for a brief period of rest.

South of the Lake is the Children's District. It was designed as a place where parents could bring their children during the hot summer months. Because infant and child deaths in the city sharply increased during hot weather, staying cool was important. "For them," Olmsted said, "the best that can be done is to spend an occasional day or part of a day in the Park."

The Granger Collection, New York

This 1870 image shows Frederick Law Olmsted's plan for Central Park.

In additon, Central Park offered other leisure activities, such as horseback riding, ice skating, boating, and baseball. Central Park proved extremely popular, attracting an average of 30,000 visitors a day for a total of 10 million in 1871. It remains a popular destination today for New York City's residents as well as its tourists.

Understanding the Arts

1. What did Frederick Law Olmsted hope to achieve with the Pond area of Central Park?

2. What is the Children's District?

3. Why do you think Central Park became such a popular attraction?

goods all in one location. New department stores included Jordan Marsh in Boston and Marshall Fields, which opened in 1881 in Chicago. These grew increasingly popular, relying on low prices, high sales volumes, and newspaper advertising to attract customers. In 1896 one writer described the great success of a department store owned by John Wanamaker:

A Marshall Fields advertising brochure

❝In Philadelphia everybody goes to Wanamaker's. . . . He tells you each morning in the newspapers what he has got today, and if you want it you had better go and get it: the chances are it will be gone tomorrow.❞

Although department stores were designed to sell goods, they were also elaborate buildings designed to awe and impress the public. Many had vaulted ceilings, elegant displays, huge plate glass windows, and bright lighting. As one New Yorker noted in 1899, window-shopping along the street in front of the "gleaming store-windows" provided many people with "a cheap form of social entertainment." Department stores and skyscrapers helped create new "downtown" business sections in the centers of many U.S. cities.

★ Urban Problems

Despite the new public parks, skyscrapers, and streetcars, U.S. cities in the late 1800s suffered from a wide range of problems. Many urban areas were unprepared for the tremendous population growth that they experienced. City leaders worked to meet the many challenges that arose during this time. However, they often lacked the laws, organizations, and resources necessary to protect citizens' health and well-being.

Housing Problems

Cities' rapid population growth often resulted in shortages of affordable housing. Consequently, many families found themselves packed into tiny apartments in overcrowded tenement buildings. Journalist and photographer Jacob Riis described the conditions faced by poor urban residents in his book *How the Other Half Lives:*

❝Nine lived in two rooms, one about ten feet square that served as parlor, bedroom, and eating room, the other a small hall room made into a kitchen. The rent was . . . more than a week's wages for the husband.❞

Overcrowding and lack of sanitation frequently led to disease and health problems. The poor suffered the most. Many tenement buildings were packed together in areas close to city factories. Rooms in these buildings were often dark, with few windows to let in light or to allow air to circulate. Families in many buildings had to walk down to the streets to draw their water from public sidewalk pumps. In most cities, landlords were not required by law to repair their buildings or to maintain safety standards.

Fire and crime were also common problems in urban neighborhoods. By the late 1800s this had

In the late 1880s Jacob Riis photographed crowded living conditions like this room in New York City.

Jane Addams was born into a prosperous midwestern family in 1860. She graduated from college at the head of her class, but illness and injury prevented her from becoming a doctor as she had originally planned. After visiting the Toynbee Hall community center in London, Addams was inspired to found Hull House in Chicago.

Addams was a compassionate and practical leader who responded to the needs of her community. When Chicago failed to clear trash off of the neighborhood streets, Addams became a city garbage inspector and forced the garbage collectors to do their jobs. As a reformer, lecturer, and writer, she reached beyond Chicago to touch many lives for many years. She was a co-winner of the Nobel Peace Prize in 1931 for her work with the Woman's International League for Peace and Freedom. Addams once wrote that democracy must be "a rule of living as well as a test of faith."

led many major cities to hire full-time firefighters and establish permanent police forces. Police officers also provided public services, such as helping lost children and enforcing health and traffic codes. In spite of these improvements, the reform efforts of most city governments were limited by internal corruption or a lack of funds.

Urban Organizations

City residents often established their own organizations to make life easier. Many immigrant communities created benevolent societies. Workers from a variety of backgrounds established associations that assisted injured or unemployed members and provided places to meet socially. Others formed lodges for recreation or political clubs to discuss local and national issues.

In the late 1800s African American religious groups emerged as a powerful force to organize and aid their urban communities. African American ministers often served as political as well as spiritual leaders in black neighborhoods. One report from a Baptist organization described black ministers as "a class of men who . . . have won the confidence, love, and respect of their people."

African American women, who made up the majority of church members and volunteer leaders, often helped these ministers with their work. Through the churches, black women held power and influence in their communities. One woman noted that the typical man in her community believed that men should be the leaders in society. She said, "But whenever it comes to church affairs, he quietly puts his hands in his pockets and steps aside leaving it for the women to do."

African Americans used their own churches in the late 1800s to help address urban problems.

The Granger Collection, New York

★ The Settlement Houses

Many private aid organizations offered assistance to poor people in the late 1800s. In addition to benevolent societies, there were **settlement houses**—neighborhood centers in poor areas, staffed by professionals and volunteers, that offered education, recreation, and social activities.

Settlement houses began in Britain but also became common in the United States. Janie Porter Barrett established an African American settlement house in Norfolk, Virginia. The most famous settlement house was **Hull House**, founded by Jane Addams and Ellen Gates Starr in 1889. Addams and Starr were among the many upper-class women of their era who received a college education but found few job opportunities open to them. Addams wanted to do work that would help the poor. "I was quite settled in my mind that I should study medicine and 'live with the poor,'" she once recalled. Addams and Starr moved into a run-down building in a poor neighborhood in Chicago and turned it into Hull House. The work at Hull House focused most on the needs of immigrant families.

Addams brought in many other women like herself who sought a career that they felt was useful. These female social workers lived at the settlement house. Addams believed that it was best for the workers to live among the people they hoped to help. As she later explained:

Reformer Florence Kelley began her career at Hull House.

❝ **I gradually became convinced that it would be a good thing to rent a house in a part of the city where many . . . needs are found, in which young women who have been given over too exclusively to study might . . . learn of life from life itself; where they might try out some of the things they have been taught.** ❞

Addams and her staff participated in a variety of activities. They established a kindergarten and a public playground. They taught classes in English and U.S. government to help immigrants become citizens. The staff also worked for reforms such as child labor laws and the eight-hour workday for women. Hull House served as a model for other settlement houses. By 1900 there were more than 100 settlement houses in the United States. Many of the women involved in running Hull House later became active in a variety of national reform movements.

SECTION 2 REVIEW

Identify and explain the significance of the following:
- **mass transit**
- **suburbs**
- **Frederick Law Olmsted**
- **department stores**
- **settlement houses**
- **Hull House**
- **Jane Addams**

Reading for Content Understanding

1. **Main Idea** Make a chart listing technological developments in the 1800s and how they helped cities deal with rapid growth.

2. **Main Idea** What organizations did citizens form to help solve some of the urban problems?

3. **Geographic Diversity** Why did so many Americans choose to move from the country to the cities?

4. **Writing** *Describing* Imagine that you are a journalist in New York City in 1900. Write a newspaper article about the positive and negative changes that have taken place in the city over the last few decades.

5. **Critical Thinking** *Drawing Conclusions* What steps do you think a city government could have taken to solve some of the urban problems that developed in the late 1800s?

Society and Culture

IN FEBRUARY 1872 *the partners of "P. T. Barnum's Museum, Menagerie and Circus" held an emergency meeting. The other partners told Barnum that the circus had become too big and expensive and that they needed to cut costs. Barnum replied that he was going to make the circus even bigger and travel from town to town by train instead of by wagons, "so as to hit good-sized towns every day in the season." His gamble paid off, and that year Barnum's circus, billed as the "Greatest Show on Earth," earned record profits as it toured the country.*

Poster for P. T. Barnum's popular circus

★ Mass Culture

P. T. Barnum's success reflected changes in American society in the late 1800s. Increased population, improved transportation, growing cities, and a boom in publishing all contributed to the rise of **mass culture**—leisure and cultural activities shared by large numbers of people.

Early examples of mass culture included world's fairs—international expositions featuring exhibits and participants from all over the world. These fairs grew more popular in the United States after the great success of the Philadelphia Centennial Exposition in 1876. The exposition combined displays of the latest technological inventions with exhibits of world cultures. Fair organizers hoped to attract and educate huge crowds by appealing to people's curiosity.

Millions of visitors came to the world's fairs to see the amazing exhibits. Others saw the fairs as a chance to relax and enjoy themselves during their time off. Beginning with the Chicago Exposition in 1893, fair organizers tried to fill this need for relaxation by providing places for pure entertainment.

Thousands of visitors relaxed and enjoyed themselves at Luna Park on Coney Island.

Shoot-the-Chutes, the Barrel of Fun, and the Ferris wheel offered visitors thrills and new experiences. The parks also gave visitors a chance to relax in an informal setting with people from different backgrounds. "It was a world removed," noted one journalist, "shut away from the . . . clatter and turmoil of the streets." Inexpensive train fares from New York City and affordable admission tickets attracted many low-wage workers to the amusement parks. People from all walks of life made trips to Coney Island each year, enjoying the sights and sounds.

For example, outside of the main exhibit area known as the White City, the Chicago fair featured an attraction called the Midway. This was a mile-long strip of displays, restaurants, shops, and theaters. Rides such as the Ferris wheel were also located in the Midway, which proved to be the most popular site at the exposition.

The demand for public entertainment soon led to the creation of amusement parks, most notably on New York City's Coney Island. The first permanent amusement park, Sea Lion Park, was built in 1895 on the island. Other parks soon followed, and by 1905 thousands of people visited Coney Island to enjoy rides and displays at places such as Luna Park and Dreamland. In 1904 the *New York Times* reported on the opening day of the summer season at Coney Island:

❝ **They took the lid off Coney Island last night, and a quarter of a million men and women got a glimpse of a swaying, rocking, glittering magic city by the sea.** ❞

Part of the appeal of amusement parks was the technology used in them. Mechanical rides such as

⭐ The Rise of Sports

Athletic events also began drawing large crowds of spectators. In 1896 the first modern Olympics—held in Athens, Greece—led to an increased worldwide interest in track and field events.

Spectator Sports

In addition to track and field, other popular spectator sports included baseball and football. Baseball began as an amateur sport that grew in popularity after the Civil War. Early baseball players did not wear gloves, and pitchers tossed the ball underhand toward the batter. Gradually, padded gloves, catcher's masks, and new pitching styles were introduced, making the game safer for players and more exciting for fans. Players were organized into a national professional league in 1876. The professional baseball teams—such as the Philadelphia Athletics, New York Mutuals, and Chicago White Stockings—were located in large cities where they could draw crowds of a few thousand people per game.

An early baseball and glove, now preserved in the Baseball Hall of Fame

Football became an increasingly popular amateur sport on college campuses. Crowds gathered to watch teams such as Harvard and Yale. These early games were very rough, and few players wore helmets. Yale football player and future coach Alonzo Stagg explained that "injuries were disregarded. . . . Two or three dependable substitutes were all that a team thought of needing."

For many people, spectator sports became a way to forget the concerns of their daily lives while watching their local team play. Fans from a wide variety of cultural, social, and economic backgrounds could unite in supporting a team. African Americans, however, were excluded from playing in early professional sports leagues. This led to the creation of independent African American sports leagues in the 1900s.

Exercise and Health

In addition to enjoying organized sports, many Americans became interested in outdoor exercise for fun and health. Popular activities included boating, hiking, and swimming. More Americans also began playing golf and tennis.

In the late 1800s the first modern bicycle was developed. It had two equal-sized wheels and air-filled rubber tires. These safer, more comfortable vehicles led to a boom in bike sales, what New York writer Henry Brown called "the great bicycle craze of the Nineties." Brown wrote, "It was . . . the Bicycle that created the present enormous vogue for [popularity of] athletics amongst women."

Early bicycles had one large wheel and one smaller one. In the 1890s people found bicycles much easier to ride when both wheels were made the same size.

Many young women defied tradition when they wore short pants called bloomers—named after women's rights activist Amelia Bloomer—while riding bicycles. Women also began to participate in increasing numbers in college sports such as field hockey or games such as lawn tennis.

⭐ The Growth of Publishing

To meet the growing interest in athletics, newspapers began running sports sections to report the latest game scores and team news. People interested in reading about sports or other events found more newspapers to read in the late 1800s. The invention in 1884 of the linotype, an automatic typesetting machine, greatly reduced the time and cost of printing. As printed material became less expensive to produce, more newspapers and magazines were published. In 1850 there were fewer than 300 daily newspapers in the United States. By 1900 there were more than 2,000.

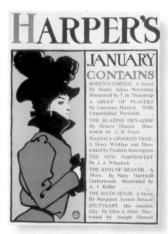

Advertisement for the January 1898 issue of Harper's *magazine*

Big cities often produced many newspapers, some printed in foreign languages for immigrant readers. Newspaper advertisers began running pictures and full-page ads for the first time. Many of these advertisements were for department stores. An editor for the New York *Herald* boasted in 1872, "What a picture of the metropolis [city] one day's advertisements in the *Herald* presents to mankind!"

Competition for readers pushed newspapers into making other changes. In the late 1890s newspaper publishers Joseph Pulitzer and William Randolph Hearst began using color printing for the first time. They also began featuring Sunday comic strips, such as the Yellow Kid and the Katzenjammer Kids.

Magazines also flourished during the late 1800s. They tended to be more focused on specific subjects than newspapers. Popular magazines included the *Delineator* and *Ladies' Home Journal* for women's issues, the political magazine *The Nation*, and literary magazines such as *Scribner's Magazine*. Reduced prices, better printing quality, and improved writing helped such magazines expand their readership.

By 1900 the daily newspaper had become a powerful cultural force in people's everyday lives. It provided news of local, national, and world events, advertisements for the latest products, and information on sports and entertainment. Weekly and monthly magazines carried articles, essays, and short stories on a wide range of topics. Together, magazines and newspapers played an important role in informing Americans and shaping their views of the world.

Popular American Literature

The printing revolution also made books more affordable. Authors experimented with new story locations and writing styles to interest an expanding audience. Some of the best-known authors in the late 1800s used a style known as local color in their writing. Their stories focused on common local scenes and described the landscape and customs of regional America. For example, Samuel Clemens, who wrote under the name Mark Twain, set many of his stories in the Mississippi River region and the Far West. Twain often used exaggerated characters for comic effect.

George Washington Cable was one of several authors who became well known for writing novels and short stories set in the South before the Civil War. The Northeast was represented by the work of writers such as Sarah Orne Jewett. She believed that her writing should inform readers about rural New Englanders and their way of life. "I wanted the world to know their grand, simple lives," Jewett explained.

Dime novels like this one were popular in the late 1800s.

Many authors of the late 1800s wrote novels that offered advice to young people on how to prepare for the future. These stories often reinforced society's ideas about success for men and women. Horatio Alger Jr. wrote a popular series of "rags-to-riches" novels about fictional young men who rose from humble beginnings to achieve great wealth. Alger wrote more than 100 such books, including *Work and Win* and *Risen from the Ranks.* For many people, Alger's books told the story of the American dream—that all Americans could achieve financial success by being honest and hardworking.

Louisa May Alcott's stories about young women and domestic life were very popular even though her characters sometimes challenged the traditional roles of women. *Little Women*, published in 1868, is still widely read today.

The Trend Toward Realism

In the late 1800s some writers turned away from the romantic style of earlier authors such as Nathaniel Hawthorne and James Fenimore Cooper and began writing more realistic stories. Known as **realism**, this writing style concentrated on presenting accurate images of American society. Realist authors often wrote stories with characters who were neither completely good nor completely bad and used plots that explored the lives of everyday people. One of the early realists, *Atlantic Monthly* editor William Dean Howells, described the new style as "nothing more and nothing less than the truthful treatment of material."

Like the realists, naturalists dealt with a variety of topics, particularly the challenges of life during the Second Industrial Revolution. In *The Octopus*, Frank Norris describes the fights over land between farmers and railroad companies. Stephen Crane wrote about people's struggles to survive in stories like "The Open Boat." In 1900 Theodore Dreiser wrote *Sister Carrie*, a novel that describes the experiences of a young woman who moves to Chicago from the country and experiences life in the big city. In one passage

Dreiser describes Carrie's thoughts after she passes by fancy stores for the rich while searching for a job to pay her rent:

" As for Carrie, her understanding of the moral significance of money was the popular understanding, nothing more. The old definition: 'Money: something everybody else has and I must get,' would have expressed her understanding of it thoroughly. "

Other authors of the time, such as Edith Wharton, showed the behavior and attitudes of the American upper class. Henry James wrote several such manners novels, including *Portrait of a Lady*. Both James and Wharton spent many years traveling and living in Europe, as many wealthy Americans did. James preferred to live quietly in England, writing about American life from a distance.

 ## American Painters

In the mid-1800s members of the Hudson River school, also called the American Romantics, had helped create a distinctly American style of painting that celebrated westward expansion. Some artists, such as Albert Bierstadt and George Inness,

James McNeill Whistler used his mother as his model in this painting.

were strongly influenced by the American Romantic painters. "A work of art does not appeal to the intellect," Inness once stated. "Its aim is . . . to awaken an emotion." His bold landscapes were widely admired in Europe.

Other American painters turned away from romantic art. Winslow Homer developed a distinctive style of watercolor painting as he created seascapes and scenes of New England rural life. His images were unsentimental, showing people struggling against the power of nature. In the 1880s he moved to the coast of Maine and painted landscapes and seascapes there until his death.

Describing his isolation, he once wrote, "I am four miles from telegram & P.O. [post office] & under a snow bank most of the time." Homer liked living in the country, telling his brother, "The life I have chosen gives me full hours of enjoyment."

Some other respected American painters worked mainly in Europe, where there were better art schools and many wealthy supporters of the arts. John Singer Sargent became particularly admired for his detailed and realistic portraits. He was hired to paint many of the notable figures in European society. Mary Cassatt was the first American to join the impressionist movement in France. The impressionists painted scenes of everyday life, concentrating on representing light and color accurately. Cassatt usually painted women, particularly

Artist Winslow Homer became famous for his watercolor paintings like The Blue Boat.

mothers with their children. Another artist fascinated by color was James McNeill Whistler. He painted many scenes in watercolor while living in Russia, France, and Britain. To create a certain mood, Whistler often emphasized color in his paintings rather than details of his subjects. "As music is the poetry of sound, so painting is the poetry of sight," Whistler wrote.

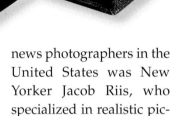

Kodak's first camera could take 100 images. For $10 customers could return the camera and film to Kodak for development.

For Christmas Morning

A KODAK

And throughout the day, the taking of pictures of all that goes to make that day a merry one.

EASTMAN KODAK COMPANY,
ROCHESTER, N. Y., *The Kodak City.*

The Granger Collection, New York

⭐ A New Art Form

Photography offered another way of creating realistic images of the world. In 1880 the wet-plates used by early photographers were replaced by a more convenient type of camera film. George Eastman made further improvements, leading to cheaper cameras and the box camera in 1888. His company, Kodak, sold cameras that people simply mailed back to Kodak when they wanted the pictures developed. Kodak's slogan was "You Press the Button—We Do the Rest."

Advances in photography and printing enabled newspapers to use black and white photos more widely in the 1890s. One of the best-known news photographers in the United States was New Yorker Jacob Riis, who specialized in realistic pictures of urban life and the city's slums.

Art photographers also emerged in the 1890s. Led by Alfred Stieglitz, these photographers used the camera in much the same way as a painter used a brush and canvas. Many people admired the photographs taken by Stieglitz and others. However, many art critics insisted that photography was not a true art form because it relied on machines. Despite these criticisms, photography continued to grow in popularity. In the process, photographers captured many images of work, play, and daily life in the rapidly changing United States.

SECTION 3 REVIEW

Identify and explain the significance of the following:
- mass culture
- Louisa May Alcott
- realism
- William Dean Howells
- Henry James
- Winslow Homer
- Mary Cassatt
- George Eastman

Reading for Content Understanding

1 Main Idea What activities did many Americans enjoy in the late 1800s?

2 Main Idea What changes occurred in American literature and publishing during the late 1800s?

3 Cultural Diversity What new styles of art and photography tried to capture American life?

4 Writing *Informing* Imagine that you are a city resident writing to a friend in the country about the many kinds of public activities that you have in the city. Explain what your favorite activities are and why.

5 Critical Thinking *Synthesizing Information* Why do you think that realist authors chose the story topics that they did? How did these topics reflect society in the late 1800s?

CHAPTER 7 REVIEW

Chapter Summary

Immigration from eastern and southern European countries increased after the Civil War. Many of these immigrants moved to cities, where they joined large numbers of migrants from rural America. Rapidly growing cities faced a variety of problems such as overcrowding and poverty. A new mass culture developed, and Americans began exploring new styles in literature, painting, and photography.

On a separate sheet of paper, complete the following activities.

Identifying People and Ideas

Describe the historical significance of the following:

1. new immigrants
2. benevolent societies
3. Immigration Restriction League
4. suburbs
5. Jane Addams
6. settlement houses
7. realism
8. Louisa May Alcott
9. Winslow Homer
10. mass culture

Internet Activity

go.hrw.com
SB1 Ellis Island

Search the Internet through the HRW Web site to find information about Ellis Island in the late 1800s and early 1900s. Use this information to create a two-page journal describing an immigrant's trip to and arrival in the United States. You may include pictures with your journal.

Understanding Main Ideas

1. How were new immigrants different from old immigrants?
2. What were daily life and work like for immigrants in the late 1800s?
3. Why did cities grow so rapidly?
4. What problems resulted from urban growth?
5. How did popular entertainment begin to change in the late 1800s?
6. What changes took place in American literature in the late 1800s?

Reviewing Themes

1. **Cultural Diversity** What effect did increased immigration have on the United States?
2. **Technology and Society** How did the technological changes of the late 1800s affect Americans?
3. **Geographic Diversity** How did the growth of large cities affect American society?

Using the Time Line

Number your paper from 1 to 5. Match the letters on the time line below with the following events.

1. The first permanent amusement park opens for business in New York.
2. Ellis Island begins receiving immigrants.
3. Jane Addams and Ellen Gates Starr found Hull House, a settlement house to help immigrants and the poor.
4. Congress bans Chinese immigrants from entering the United States for 10 years.
5. Boston opens the first subway in the United States.

1870	1873	1876	1879	1882	1885	1888	1891	1894	1897
				a		b	c	d	e

228 Chapter 7

Thinking Critically

1. **Identifying Generalizations and Stereotypes**   Why did some people oppose the arrival of new immigrants to the United States?

2. **Identifying Cause and Effect**   What factors do you think contributed to the development of mass culture?

3. **Evaluating**   Why do you think city officials felt that libraries, museums, and parks would improve a city's image?

Writing About History

1. **Informing**   Imagine that you are a museum official in the 1890s preparing an exhibit of American art. Write a brief essay discussing the major painters of the period and their artistic styles.

2. **Creating**   Write a short poem or song that expresses the feelings of an immigrant seeing a U.S. city for the first time.

Linking Geography and History

1. **Movement**   Why did many immigrants come to the United States?

2. **Human-Environment Interaction**   How was technology used to help manage the increasing size of cities?

Building Your Portfolio

Complete the following activities individually or in groups.

1. **Immigrant Communities**   Many immigrant communities established during the 1800s, such as Boston's North End and Chinatown in San Francisco and New York, are still thriving parts of U.S. cities today. Research a modern immigrant community and create a tourist brochure to attract visitors to that community. Your brochure should include some historical information about the community as well as descriptions and images of current attractions.

2. **Authors of the Second Industrial Revolution**   Select an American author who began his or her work in the late 1800s or the early 1900s. Authors may include, but are not limited to, the following: Mark Twain, William Dean Howells, Stephen Crane, Frank Norris, Theodore Dreiser, Henry James, Edith Wharton, and Horatio Alger Jr. Use the library or other resources to research your author. Create a script with questions and answers for an interview with the author on his or her life. Include information on one of the author's stories explaining how the story reflects life during the late 1800s. Perform the interview for the class.

History Skills Workshop

Reading Charts   Study the chart below, which shows the number of immigrants arriving in the United States from 1860 to 1900, and answer the following questions: (a) During what period was the growth in immigration the greatest? (b) During what two decades was immigration the highest? (c) Why do you think this was the case?

Total Immigration to the United States, 1860–1900

Source: *Historical Statistics of the United States*

History Skills

WORKSHOP

Reading Charts and Graphs

Charts and graphs categorize and display data in a variety of ways. The type of chart or graph depends on the subject matter and the information being represented.

Charts There are many different kinds of charts. *Flowcharts* show a sequence of events or the steps involved in a process. They are useful in showing cause-and-effect relationships. *Organizational charts* show the structure of an organization. They generally identify the rank and function of an organization's parts and the relationships among them. *Tables* are charts that present categories of data in columns.

How to Read a Chart

1. **Read the title** Read the title to identify the chart's purpose.
2. **Study the chart's parts** Read the chart's heading, subheadings, and labels to identify the categories used.
3. **Analyze the data** When reading quantities, note increases or decreases in amounts presented in the chart. When reading dates, note intervals of time. With flowcharts and organizational charts, follow directional arrows or lines.

Graphs There are several different types of graphs. A *line graph* often plots changes in quantities over time. A line graph has a horizontal axis and a vertical axis. A *bar graph* displays changes in quantities over time or compares quantities within categories. A *pie graph*, or *circle graph*, displays proportions by showing sections of a whole as if they were slices of a pie.

All sections of the circular image add up to an entire pie, or 100 percent.

How to Read a Graph

1. **Read the title** Read the title to identify the subject and purpose of the graph.
2. **Study the labels** Read the labels that define each section of the graph's axes, bars, or sections.
3. **Analyze the data** Note increases or decreases in quantities. Look for trends, relationships, and changes in the data.

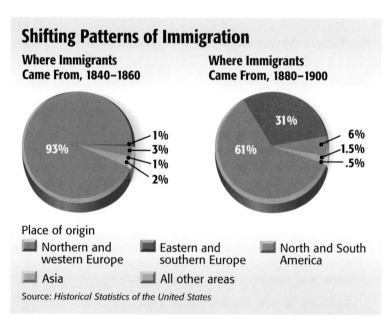

Shifting Patterns of Immigration

Where Immigrants Came From, 1840–1860
93% / 1% / 3% / 1% / 2%

Where Immigrants Came From, 1880–1900
31% / 61% / 6% / 1.5% / .5%

Place of origin
- Northern and western Europe
- Eastern and southern Europe
- North and South America
- Asia
- All other areas

Source: *Historical Statistics of the United States*

Practicing the Skill

Study the graphs above. Then answer the following questions.

1. Which group experienced the greatest percent decrease in immigration between 1840–1860 and 1880–1900?

2. What do these graphs tell you about the actual number of immigrants arriving?

3. What generalizations or conclusions about immigration can you draw based on the information in these graphs?

History in Action

UNIT 2 PORTFOLIO

Journey Across the World: The Travel Agency

Complete the following activity in small, cooperative groups.

Imagine that your class has been transported back in time to the second half of the 1800s. Your group operates a travel agency and is in charge of the travel plans for four groups of people: old immigrants coming to the United States, new immigrants arriving in the United States, cowboys on a cattle drive, and pioneers heading to the West. Your group's job is to provide a complete itinerary, or travel plan, for your customers. A number of travel agencies are competing for the business. You want the travelers to select your company as their travel agency.

Materials To complete this activity, you will need some U.S. and world maps and some blank outline maps to chart the journey for your customers. You will also need some art supplies such as construction paper, markers, pens, and glue to create your brochure.

Parts of the Project To create your itinerary and brochure, complete the following tasks:

1. **Research** Use the library and your textbook to research the journey of each customer group. Your itinerary needs to include point of origin, means of travel, length of travel, arrival time, and cost. You will also need to research the travelers' destinations. Find information on what your customers need to bring with them and what housing and job opportunities they can expect once they reach their destination.

2. **Creating the Itinerary** Graph the course your customers will take on one of the blank maps. Also, provide a detailed travel schedule in the form of a chart or a graph. Include as much information as possible on travel time, meals, weather conditions, and places to stay during the journey.

3. **Writing the Brochure** Organize the information you have gathered into a brochure. The brochure should welcome your travelers to their new home and include information on housing, jobs, schools, and potential difficulties and opportunities. You may want to illustrate your brochure with images or photographs.

4. **Presentation** Present your itinerary and brochure to your customers (the class). This is your last chance to present any information that might influence your customers to select your travel agency.

Continue this activity by having your customers select the travel agency they want to use for their journey. Customers should evaluate your agency's itinerary in terms of detail, historical accuracy, and overall appeal of the brochure.

Students locating places on a map

UNIT 3

A Growing America

(1865–1920)

American Teens
IN HISTORY
Young Workers

During the late 1800s the United States became a leading industrial nation. Many people left their farms and moved to the cities. With the increased number of factories, teenagers' employment opportunities began to change. Cotton textile mills in the Northeast and the South became some of the largest industrial employers of children and teenagers.

In 1850 some 9,000 children who were 14 years old or younger worked in southern cotton mills. By 1900 that number had increased to 25,000. Almost half of these children were younger than 12 years old. For southern girls younger than 14 years old, no job paid better than mill work.

Mill owners tried to attract entire families to work in the mills. One-parent families, usually headed by women, found mill work particularly attractive. Because mill owners usually paid adult men low wages, the entire family was often forced to work to meet expenses. Young mill worker Marie Proulx remembered:

Winslow Homer's painting Cotton Pickers *shows African American girls working in cotton fields in the late 1800s.*

❝ *My father was never able to support a family of eight children on $1.10 per day. . . . Oh, were we miserable! . . . So I had to go work somewhere, and all there was were the mills.* ❞

Teenagers working full-time in the mills often labored 12 hours a day, six days a week.

Coal mines in western Pennsylvania also hired many child laborers. Almost always boys, these workers were sent underground into the mines at the age of 12 or 13. By the age of 17 or 18, these boys had become miners' helpers. Boys were also more likely than girls to sell newspapers on city streets. These positions became more important with the growth of publishing and big cities. Standing wherever people commuted, newsboys could earn more money selling newspapers than any other product.

In this unit you will learn more about the reform movements to limit child labor. You will also learn more about the Progressive Era and the United States as an international power.

LEFT PAGE: *A Currier and Ives print of Broadway in New York City in the late 1800s*

UNIT 3

Time Line: 1865–1920

A Growing America

The Statue of Liberty

"The Republican Vote" is written on the elephant's side.

A Waterman fountain pen

UNITED STATES

1874
Thomas Nast's cartoon in *Harper's Weekly* establishes the elephant as a symbol of the Republican Party.

1884
New York insurance agent Lewis Edson Waterman invents the first practical fountain pen.

1886
The Statue of Liberty, formally known as Liberty Enlightening the World, is dedicated in New York Harbor.

1865	1870	1875	1880	1885	1890

WORLD

1868
French archaeologist Edouard Lartet discovers the remains of Cro-Magnon man. This prehistoric human is believed to be between 10,000 and 35,000 years old.

1874
Alfonso XII is proclaimed king of Spain. Nearly 400 years earlier, King Alfonso's ancestors had helped form modern Spain when they captured Granada from the Moors.

1877
The ballet *Swan Lake,* composed by Russian Pyotr Tchaikovsky, is performed for the first time.

Swan Lake costume

1894
China and Japan fight over control of Korea. Japan forces Korea to open itself to foreign trade.

The Alhambra Palace in Granada displays the style of its original builders, the Moors.

1898
The Spanish-American War is fought.

1900
George Eastman introduces the Kodak Brownie camera.

A Brownie camera box

Row houses in San Francisco after the earthquake

1906
On April 18 a powerful earthquake strikes San Francisco. It lasts less than a minute but destroys property valued at more than $400 million.

1913
The Armory Show in New York City introduces Americans to a new style of art known as cubism. French painter Marcel Duchamp is one of the participants.

Young suffrage supporters

1920
The Nineteenth Amendment, which grants women the right to vote, is ratified.

| 1895 | 1900 | 1905 | 1910 | 1915 | 1920 |

1901
Queen Victoria dies after nearly 64 years as ruler of the British Empire. During her reign, the colonial empire becomes the world's largest.

Queen Victoria

Albert Einstein immigrated to the United States in 1932.

1919
In the Indian city of Amritsar, British troops kill more than 370 unarmed supporters of Indian self-rule.

1905
German Albert Einstein presents his special theory of relativity, $E = mc^2$.

1912
The British luxury passenger liner *Titanic* sinks after hitting an iceberg during its first voyage.

About 1,500 people died when the *Titanic* sank.

USING THE TIME LINE

1. Which entries represent change in American society?

2. Compare the entries on this time line to those on the Unit 2 Time Line. Which entries are from the same time period? Use this information to create a new time line combining the Unit 2 and Unit 3 Time Lines.

Activity Use the information on this time line to create a chart that classifies these entries according to their subject. Your chart should have the dates on one side and the subject headings on the other. Subject headings for the chart might include culture, environment, politics, and science and technology.

■ CHAPTER 8 ■
The Spirit of Reform
(1868–1920)

New York politician George W. Plunkitt described the questionable practices that led to his success. "I've made a big fortune out of the game, and I'm gettin' richer every day . . . ," he boasted. "I seen my opportunities and I took 'em." A growing number of people in the late 1800s were becoming angry with the actions of politicians such as Plunkitt. They soon called for economic, political, and social reform across the nation.

THEMES

Constitutional Heritage
What effect might a Supreme Court ruling have on workers' rights?

Citizenship and Democracy
How might reformers try to address political inequalities in a democracy?

Cultural Diversity
How might a group fight for equal rights?

1870	1875	1880	1885	1890

1868 Ulysses S. Grant is elected president.

1873 The first public kindergarten opens in St. Louis, Missouri.

1880 James Garfield is elected president.

1883 Congress passes the Pendleton Civil Service Act.

1888 Benjamin Harrison is elected president.

The Gilded Age

Reading Focus

In what ways did bosses control city politics?

What were some of the problems in federal government during the Gilded Age?

How did the appointment of federal officials change during the late 1800s?

Key Terms

bosses

political machines

mugwumps

Pendleton Civil Service Act

WHEN MAGAZINE EDITOR *Lincoln Steffens visited St. Louis, Missouri, he noted the citizens' pride in their city. "The visitor is told of the wealth of the residents, of the financial strength of the banks, and of the growing importance of the industries," Steffens wrote. However, Steffens also witnessed a different aspect of the city. It had poorly paved streets littered with garbage. The crumbling City Hospital was crowded with the sick. Even in the hotel, muddy water ran out of the taps of his bath. Steffens's experience highlighted the contrasts that caused people to refer to the late 1800s as the Gilded Age.*

The novel The Gilded Age

IMAGE ON LEFT PAGE: *A suffrage parade in 1912 in New York City*

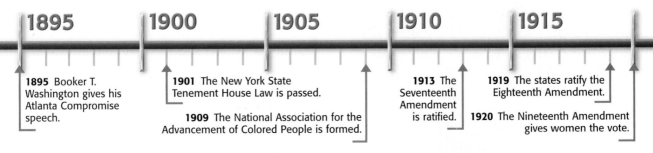

1895	1900	1905	1910	1915

1895 Booker T. Washington gives his Atlanta Compromise speech.

1901 The New York State Tenement House Law is passed.

1909 The National Association for the Advancement of Colored People is formed.

1913 The Seventeenth Amendment is ratified.

1919 The states ratify the Eighteenth Amendment.

1920 The Nineteenth Amendment gives women the vote.

★ Corruption in Politics

In 1873 Mark Twain and Charles Dudley Warner published the best-selling novel *The Gilded Age.* Twain believed that American society looked golden from a distance but was merely gilded, or coated with cheap gold paint, on the outside. This meant that society, despite its positive appearance, was ugly and corrupt on the inside. Twain argued that the country lived by the motto "Get rich; dishonestly if we can, honestly if we must."

Machine Politics

State and local politics suffered from corruption during the Gilded Age. Powerful organizations used illegal methods to control government and grow rich from it. The rapid growth of cities in the late 1800s made possible the rise of **bosses**, political leaders who controlled elections through bribery and payoffs. For example, in return for votes and money, a boss might provide jobs, order neighborhood improvements, or allow an illegal business to stay in operation. Author James Bryce explained that the boss

> ❝rewards the loyal, punishes the mutinous [disloyal], . . . negotiates treaties. He generally avoids publicity . . . and is all the more dangerous because he sits, like a spider, hidden in the midst of his web.❞

The bosses drew much of their support from immigrants. "There's got to be . . . somebody that any bloke [man] can come to—no matter what he's done—and get help," explained one Boston politician. The boss system offered immigrants both jobs and social mobility—opportunities often denied to them in the larger society.

City bosses developed **political machines**—organizations that guaranteed votes at election time through both legal and illegal methods. Political machines usually printed election ballots listing only their party's candidates. These were often printed on colored paper, so the bosses would know how individuals voted. Party organizers also paid citizens for their votes and hired the people who counted the votes. New York City boss William Marcy Tweed declared, "The ballots made no result; the counters made the result." Through their political machines, bosses protected their political positions and controlled the spending of public money. Thus, bosses personally profited from their own dishonesty.

Tammany Hall

New York City's political machine, Tammany Hall, became widely known throughout the country. Through corrupt practices, Boss Tweed may have succeeded in stealing nearly $200 million from the city treasury. He was eventually convicted of another crime, however, and died in jail.

Some politicians thought that the political machines were a fair exchange of money, influence, and jobs for working-class votes. For example, after winning city elections in 1888, Tammany Hall members provided some 12,000 jobs to supporters, particularly Irish immigrants.

National Scandals

In the late 1800s political scandals were also common on the national level. The administration of Republican Ulysses S. Grant—who was elected in 1868 and re-elected in 1872—was widely regarded as corrupt. During his second term, for example, government revenue officials were jailed for their part in the Whiskey Ring. They took bribes from whiskey distillers seeking to avoid paying taxes.

Members of Congress also participated in corrupt activities. In 1872 the *New York Sun* broke the story of a new scandal. The major owners of the

Members of Tammany Hall blame each other for stealing public money.

Union Pacific Railroad had created a construction company called Crédit Mobilier of America. The owners gave or sold shares in this company to the members of Congress responsible for awarding federal land grants to the railroads. The congressmen then gave large federal land grants to Crédit Mobilier. These grants increased the value of the company's stock. The congressmen who received shares and the railroad owners profited at the public's expense.

The Crédit Mobilier scandal damaged the careers of several Gilded Age politicians, including Schuyler Colfax, Grant's vice president. This political corruption led many Americans to angrily question the honesty of those running the federal government.

In this cartoon corrupt officials weigh down the Grant administration.

★ Gilded Age Presidents

During the 1876 presidential campaign, Democrats called for government reform. The Democratic candidate, Samuel J. Tilden, had already attacked corruption in his own party. He promised to establish an honest administration in Washington, D.C. The Republicans nominated Rutherford B. Hayes, a moderate reformer who promised "thorough, radical, and complete" changes in government. He was a war hero who had a reputation for honesty. The House of Representatives declared him the winner by a slim margin over Tilden in a disputed election.

Republicans won another close victory in 1880 with the election of reformer James Garfield and his vice president, Chester Arthur. On July 2, 1881, frustrated federal job-seeker Charles Guiteau confronted President Garfield at a Washington railroad station. He shouted "Arthur [is] President now," and shot Garfield twice. The president died from his wounds in September, and Vice President Arthur became president.

In the 1884 election, Republicans chose James G. Blaine as their nominee rather than another reform candidate. Blaine's record of association with corruption upset many Republican reformers, who came to be known as **mugwumps** (the Algonquian Indian word for big chiefs). Dissatisfied mugwumps left the Republican Party and threw their support behind the Democratic nominee, Grover Cleveland, who had a reputation for political honesty. In a campaign full of personal attacks, American voters chose Cleveland over Blaine as president. Cleveland involved himself in all the day-to-day details of the presidency. He worked hard to hire and fire government employees based on their merit rather than their party loyalty.

Four years later in 1888, Cleveland again won the popular vote. This time, however, he lost the electoral vote and thus the presidential election, to Republican Benjamin Harrison. Harrison controlled inflation and helped pass the Sherman Antitrust Act, which regulated monopolies. Nevertheless, Cleveland remained popular, and in 1892, crowds sang:

❝ **Grover, Grover, four more years of Grover—**
Out they go and in we come and we'll be in the clover. ❞

In 1881 Charles Guiteau shot President James Garfield at a railroad station.

Winning both the popular and electoral vote in 1892, Cleveland defeated Harrison and returned to the White House. During Cleveland's second term the country faced a recession. Cleveland angered many fellow Democrats with his economic policies. In 1896 the Democrats nominated William Jennings Bryan. He lost to Republican William McKinley. The practical, friendly McKinley worked well with Congress and was re-elected in 1900. During his two terms, he helped restore public confidence in the presidency by avoiding the corruption and scandals that had plagued the federal government in the Gilded Age.

 ## Civil Service Reform

Many Americans reacted to the widespread corruption of the Gilded Age by demanding changes in the civil service, or government jobs. The party in control of the government had long taken advantage of the spoils system to award jobs to loyal members, whether they were qualified or not. Every time a new party took power, many current government employees were replaced. This resulted in ruined careers and inefficient administrations. Henry Adams, author and grandson of former president John Quincy Adams, commented on this practice in 1870. He said that "all my friends have been or are on the point of being driven out of the government."

Reformers wanted a system that used competitive exams to award civil service jobs based on merit. They argued that this system would keep out incompetent and corrupt workers. President Hayes had promoted some reform efforts during his administration in the 1870s. Some Americans also believed that the spoils system had been responsible for President Garfield's assassination.

A fellow official congratulates Senator George Pendleton on his plan for civil service reform.

The Nation, a weekly newspaper, noted that "the crime seems to have acted on public opinion . . . like a spark on a powder-magazine [gunpowder storage]." This reaction led to a movement to pass stronger civil service reform legislation.

President Chester Arthur responded to the public's demands by supporting the **Pendleton Civil Service Act**. This act established a merit system controlled by the Civil Service Commission. Passed in January 1883, the act initially only affected about 14,000 out of 130,000 federal jobs. President Cleveland doubled the number of positions covered by the legislation. The act has since been expanded so that it now affects almost 90 percent of government jobs.

SECTION 1 REVIEW

Identify and explain the significance of the following:
- bosses
- political machines
- William Marcy Tweed
- Rutherford B. Hayes
- James Garfield
- Chester Arthur
- mugwumps
- Grover Cleveland
- Benjamin Harrison
- Pendleton Civil Service Act

Reading for Content Understanding

1 **Main Idea** How did scandals affect national politics in the Gilded Age?

2 **Main Idea** How did civil service reform affect the appointment of federal officials?

3 **Citizenship and Democracy** How did bosses and political machines control city governments?

4 **Writing** *Classifying* Make a chart that shows the presidents during the Gilded Age, their political party, and the year they were elected or became president.

5 **Critical Thinking** *Evaluating* Do you agree that civil service jobs should be merit based? Explain your answer.

SECTION 2

Progressive Ideals

Reading Focus

What role did middle-class reformers and muckrakers play in the progressive movement?

How did progressives change government?

How did progressives address the nation's social problems?

Key Terms

progressives

muckrakers

direct primary

Seventeenth Amendment

recall

initiative

referendum

Wisconsin Idea

NE COLD, SNOWY MORNING *in late December 1891, Florence Kelley and her three children arrived on the front steps of Hull House in Chicago. When she knocked on the door, Jane Addams answered. "We were welcomed as though we had been invited," Kelley later wrote. "We stayed." At Hull House, Kelley not only found refuge but also joined the increasingly popular movement for reform. She went on to become one of the nation's leading social reformers.*

Hull House in Chicago

★ The Progressive Movement

In the late 1800s a group of reformers who became known as the **progressives** began working to improve American society. Progressives wanted to address the social and political problems caused by rapid industrial expansion and urban growth. Progressives believed that by studying these issues, they could develop plans that would correct the root causes of the problems. For example, many progressives sought to change the environments that contributed to crime, disease, and poverty.

A large number of progressives were members of the growing middle class. The industrial and urban growth that caused many problems in the late 1800s also contributed to an increase in the number of professionals and small-business owners. These individuals formed an educated group that wanted to improve the quality of life throughout society. They often had leisure time and training, both of which were helpful in organizing reform movements. Although many people in the progressive movement came from middle-class backgrounds, some working-class and wealthy Americans also sought reforms.

The Spirit of Reform **241**

Causes and Effects of the Progressive Movement

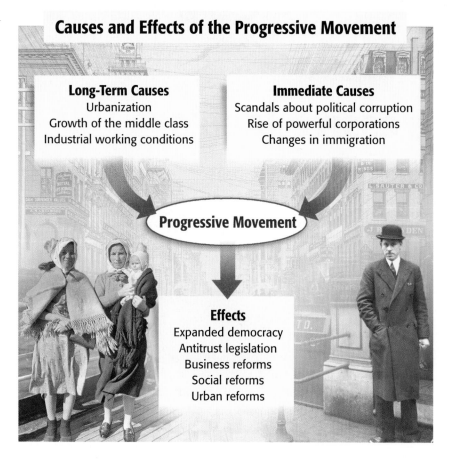

Long-Term Causes
Urbanization
Growth of the middle class
Industrial working conditions

Immediate Causes
Scandals about political corruption
Rise of powerful corporations
Changes in immigration

Progressive Movement

Effects
Expanded democracy
Antitrust legislation
Business reforms
Social reforms
Urban reforms

Progressive leaders did not always agree on which social problems were the most important or how these problems should be solved. As a result, the progressives focused their efforts in a variety of areas. These actions included promoting health and education in poor neighborhoods, reforming government, and improving working conditions. Many progressives believed that to achieve all of these goals, the federal government needed to step in and regulate business, health, and safety issues. Progressives wanted greater cooperation between the government and the public to solve social problems.

★ Muckrakers

Journalists also became involved in the progressive movement. Reporters began writing about corruption in business and politics. They hoped that their articles would lead to greater public awareness of problems and eventually to reform measures. These journalists were soon nicknamed "**muckrakers**" because they "raked up" and exposed the muck, or filth, of society.

Some muckrakers such as Ida Tarbell became well known for articles attacking unfair business practices. Tarbell wrote a series of articles criticizing John D. Rockefeller's Standard Oil Company:

❝ **Very often people who admit the facts, who are willing to see that Mr. Rockefeller has employed force and fraud to secure his ends, justify him by declaring, 'It's business.' That is, 'it's business' has come to be a legitimate [acceptable] excuse for hard dealing, sly tricks, [and] special privileges.** ❞

Tarbell argued that companies had to follow fair business practices to protect competition.

Reporter Lincoln Steffens exposed scandals in city politics in some of the first muckraking articles. They were published in 1902 in *McClure's Magazine*. These articles were later collected in a book called *The Shame of the Cities*. Although the urban corruption that he exposed shocked some readers, Steffens later claimed that "every one of those articles was an understatement."

Ida Tarbell wrote many muckraking articles for McClure's Magazine.

Muckrakers often focused on the plight of poor people, such as this Jewish immigrant, who lived in a coal cellar.

Muckrakers also investigated issues such as slum housing, the use of child labor, and racial discrimination. Their articles angered many city politicians and business leaders. They also helped unite the progressive movement by influencing voters to challenge corrupt practices and by encouraging some politicians to call for reforms.

Expanding Democracy

Concern about political corruption convinced some progressives to reform state and local governments. They helped pass reform measures that gave voters more power in selecting political candidates and in getting laws passed.

Election Reforms

Progressives passed a number of election reforms that reduced political machines' ability to influence the voting process. Reformers in many cities and states introduced ballots that listed all candidates, regardless of their party. Many states also adopted a secret ballot to ensure that a person's vote was confidential. Progressives patterned these ballot changes on methods used in Australia.

Reformers also broadened political participation by introducing the **direct primary**. This allowed voters to choose candidates for public office directly rather than relying on party leaders to select the candidates. In addition, the ratification of the **Seventeenth Amendment** in 1913 allowed Americans to vote directly for U.S. senators. They had previously been elected by state legislatures.

Petitioning for Change

Other reform measures allowed voters to petition for action on political issues even if there was no regular election or vote scheduled. For example, some states like Oregon, as well as cities like Los Angeles, passed a measure known as the **recall**. Voters who are dissatisfied with an elected official can sign a petition asking for a special vote to recall, or remove, that official before the end of his or her term. If enough voters sign the petition, the vote takes place and the official must abide by its results.

Reformers in Oregon and the Midwest also pushed for two reforms that gave voters the power to affect new legislation directly. The **initiative** gives voters the ability to propose a new law by collecting signatures on a petition supporting that law. If enough signatures are collected, the proposed law is placed on the ballot for the public to vote on at the next election. A similar measure, the **referendum**, allows voters to approve or disapprove legislation that has already been proposed or passed by a state or local government. This gives voters the opportunity to overrule laws with which they disagree.

Reforming City and State Governments

In addition to broadening political participation, progressives worked to change the structure of city government and state politics. Many Americans were upset by the corruption and waste in public services that resulted from political machines like the one run by New York's Boss Tweed. Samuel M. "Golden Rule" Jones, a business leader who became mayor of Toledo, Ohio, argued that government should not be used "for the purpose of plundering [stealing from] the poor."

Businesspeople and other professionals often led the effort to make local government more efficient and more responsive to citizens' needs.

Some reformers wanted to replace elected officials with professionals who would run city government more like a business. Several cities changed to a council-manager government, which put power in the hands of professional administrators. Under this system, voters elect a city council that appoints a professional manager to run the city. The system is modeled on a corporation, where a board of directors chooses a chief executive to run the business. By 1914 there was a professional City Managers' Association.

Many other cities took a similar business-influenced approach, called the commission government. This form of city government is headed by a group of elected officials. Each official manages a major city agency, such as housing, sanitation, or transportation.

These new forms of city administration became popular during the Progressive Era. However, many urban residents found that these systems created a city government that was less responsive to their needs. The council-manager and commission forms of government were most popular in small to medium-sized cities, which dealt with fewer problems than large cities.

State governments faced some of the same problems as cities. Corrupt urban officials such as city bosses were often part of a statewide political machine that influenced all party decisions. Some reformers challenged these political machines. In Wisconsin, Republican Robert La Follette opposed the power of the party bosses, arguing that government should be directly responsive to the people. La Follette supported the direct primary, tax reform, new state commissions, and the use of professionals to manage social problems.

Robert La Follette created a popular model for reforming government.

The commission form of city government was first introduced in 1900 in Galveston, Texas, after a severe hurricane destroyed much of the city. The commission made rebuilding efforts more efficient.

As one political writer described La Follette's appeal to voters, "He is eager to be the people's champion; his mind is aglow with visions of great enactments [laws] for the public welfare."

La Follette failed to win his party's nomination for governor in 1896 and in 1898. He finally won the governor's seat in 1900. As governor, La Follette developed the **Wisconsin Idea**—a program of reforms to reduce the influence of political machines and to professionalize state government. This idea became a model for progressive reformers in other states. La Follette later served in the U.S. Senate until he died in 1925.

★ City Planning

Political corruption was just one of many problems faced by growing U.S. cities. Progressive minister Josiah Strong declared that

❝ the city is the nerve center of our civilization. It is also the storm center. . . . The city has become a serious menace [threat] to our civilization.❞

As many native-born Americans and immigrants moved to U.S. cities looking for work, city officials found themselves unable to keep up with demands for housing and social services. The results were unsanitary and unsafe conditions for thousands of families living in poverty. Many people crowded into tenements, whose owners failed to make needed improvements in living conditions. Progressive Lawrence Veiller described the effects of tenement living on children and society:

The Granger Collection, New York

An artist's version of an ideal progressive city—attractive, clean, and safe

 A child living its early years in dark rooms, without sunlight or fresh air, does not grow up to be a normal, healthy person. . . . It is not of such material that strong nations are made. ""

Progressives addressed these problems in a variety of ways. Veiller successfully campaigned for the 1901 New York State Tenement House Law, which made the construction of dark and airless tenements illegal. The law required new buildings to have better ventilation, toilets, and running water. New York's law became a model for other states' housing reform. Many progressives also established settlement houses patterned after Jane Addams's Hull House in Chicago. These organizations worked in immigrant and poverty-stricken communities to improve education, sanitation, and housing conditions.

Urban reforms led to the creation of new professions such as city planning and civil engineering. City planners worked with local officials to control and regulate city growth by establishing zoning laws, creating safer building codes, and developing public park lands. Civil engineers improved city transportation by paving streets and building bridges. Sanitation engineers tried to solve the problems of water supply, waste disposal, and pollution. Cities that addressed these problems experienced a dramatic drop in death rates by the end of the century. The many improvements carried out during the Progressive Era gave urban Americans some of the highest standards of public services in the world.

★ Social Reforms

Progressive leaders were interested in using scientific principles and new organizations to deal with political problems. Progressive leaders also applied this approach to reforming public and professional education.

Public Education

Many progressives believed that by improving public education, they could cure social ills and fulfill the demand from business and industry for better-educated managers. To meet the changing needs of students, high school courses were broadened to include areas such as health, citizenship, and job training. School enrollment increased greatly in the late 1800s. This was largely because the reformers' push for education had led to the creation of new public high schools and to the introduction of public kindergartens. In addition, many states passed laws requiring children to attend school.

Many progressives started kindergarten programs to serve the needs of poor city residents, particularly immigrants. Kindergartens taught basic social skills to children between the ages of three and seven. In 1873 reformer Susan Blow opened the first American public kindergarten in

High school students study science in 1900.

St. Louis, Missouri. By 1898 more than 4,000 kindergartens had opened in the United States.

One supporter of early childhood education, John Dewey, was an important philosopher and educator. As the director of the University of Chicago's Laboratory School, Dewey tried to develop teaching methods suited to the interests and needs of students. Two teachers at the school described the classes as based on "the idea of the school-house as a home." The goal was to nurture children and to give them critical-thinking skills to help them in everyday life. For example, Dewey wanted to teach children problem-solving skills rather than have them simply memorize their lessons. Dewey's teaching methods became the model for progressive education throughout the country.

Progressivism in Medicine

Progressives also tried to improve the education of medical professionals. In the late 1800s the United States suffered from a lack of well-trained and professionally organized doctors. For example, researchers had identified the causes of infectious diseases such as malaria, pneumonia, tuberculosis, and yellow fever. However, there were few medical organizations to help spread this knowledge.

Under the leadership of Joseph McCormack, the American Medical Association (AMA), which brought together local medical organizations, was reorganized in 1901. The AMA supported laws protecting public health. Its reform efforts reflected the progressives' ability to unite professionals to better help society.

Doctors struggled to control contagious diseases.

SECTION 2 REVIEW

Identify and explain the significance of the following:
- progressives
- muckrakers
- Lincoln Steffens
- Ida Tarbell
- direct primary
- Seventeenth Amendment
- recall
- initiative
- referendum
- Robert La Follette
- Wisconsin Idea
- John Dewey
- Joseph McCormack

Reading for Content Understanding

1 **Main Idea** What contributions did middle-class reformers and muckrakers make to the progressive movement?

2 **Main Idea** What social reforms did progressives try to make?

3 **Citizenship and Democracy** How did progressives work to fight corruption in local and state governments?

4 **Writing** *Informing* Imagine that you are a muckraker journalist for *McClure's Magazine*. Write a short article explaining how progressives have addressed problems in U.S. cities in the early 1900s.

5 **Critical Thinking** *Drawing Conclusions* Describe John Dewey's teaching methods. What do you think are the advantages of Dewey's approach?

Reforming the Workplace

Reading Focus

How did progressives attempt to change labor laws?

How did the courts react to labor legislation?

How did labor organize to improve working conditions?

Key Terms

Triangle Shirtwaist Factory Fire
capitalism
socialism
Industrial Workers of the World

*E*VERY DAY AT 7:00 A.M. *15-year-old Sadie Frowne sat down at her machine in a garment factory in Brooklyn, New York. "The machines go like mad all day, because the faster you work the more money you get," she wrote. "Sometimes in my haste I get my finger caught and the needle goes right through it." When her workday ended at 6:00 P.M., she felt exhausted. One of the progressives' main goals was to establish better working conditions for children like Frowne.*

Labor union booklet

⭐ Child Labor Reform

Low wages for unskilled workers in the late 1800s meant that many more children had to work to help support their families. Girls often cooked and cleaned for boarders, and boys sold newspapers or shined shoes on the streets. Girls also worked with their mothers at home, sewing garments or making artificial flowers and costume jewelry.

Many children also worked in industrial areas. In 1900 more than 1.75 million children aged 15 and under worked in mines, mills, and factories. The terrible situation of these children moved many progressives to action. One wealthy reformer, Marie Van Vorst, posed as a poor woman to investigate conditions in a South Carolina textile mill. She saw children as young as five years old working in the mills. She described one young girl:

66 **Through the looms I catch sight of . . . my landlord's little child. She is seven; so small that they have a box for her to stand on. . . . I can see only her fingers as they clutch at the flying spools; her head is not high enough, even with the box, to be visible.** 99

The Spirit of Reform **247**

"Tired?" Van Vorst asked the child, who nodded without stopping. The girl received 40 cents a day for her work, providing cheap labor for the manufacturer, and $2.40 a week for her parents.

Florence Kelley, who had raised her three children at Chicago's Hull House, led the progressive crusade against child labor. Her strategy was to "investigate, educate, legislate, and enforce." Beginning her career as a social reformer at Hull House, Kelley traveled throughout the United States lobbying for labor laws to protect women and children. As a boardmember of the National Consumers' League—the major lobbying group for women's and children's labor issues—Kelley established about 60 local consumer leagues throughout the United States.

The National Child Labor Committee worked with labor committees to pass laws restricting

Progressives wanted to keep companies from using the labor of children, like this young coal miner.

child labor in many states. Although Congress passed federal child labor laws in 1916 and 1919, the Supreme Court declared them unconstitutional. A later attempt to pass a constitutional amendment restricting child labor failed to be ratified.

★ Safety in the Workplace

Child labor reform was only part of the progressive effort to help American workers. Some progressives cooperated with labor unions to get legislation passed that addressed the low wages, long hours, and unsafe working conditions faced by millions of adult workers. Many progressives supported the eight-hour workday. The National Consumers' League led efforts to establish laws to guarantee a minimum wage and limit working hours. As a result, many states passed minimum-wage laws and maximum-hour laws for women.

Tragic accidents also led reformers to call for safety regulations in the workplace. In 1900 some 35,000 people were killed by industrial accidents, and about 500,000 suffered injuries. In 1911 the Triangle Shirtwaist Company in New York City was the site of a shocking accident. As some 500 immigrant women prepared to leave the clothing factory one day, a fire broke out in the 10-story building. The women tried to escape through exit doors but found that the managers had locked them. Other workers crammed into elevators or leaped into the elevator shafts as the fire and smoke spread around them. Some women jumped hand-in-hand from the top of the burning building, falling to their deaths. By the time firefighters finally brought the **Triangle Shirtwaist Factory Fire** under control, 146 workers had died.

The factory owners, insurance company, city building inspectors, and fire departments were all blamed in the investigation. No one was convicted on criminal charges, however. At a memorial service for the victims of the fire, union organizer

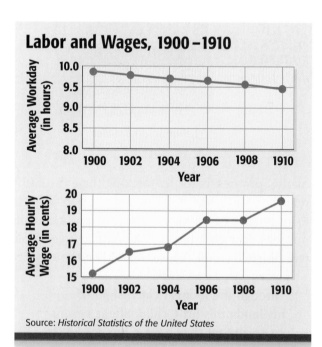

Labor and Wages, 1900–1910

Source: *Historical Statistics of the United States*

Earning a Living In the early 1900s employees worked fewer hours than before but earned a higher hourly wage. What was the average hourly wage in 1902?

Rose Schneiderman appealed to other workers for action:

> " This is not the first time girls have been burned alive in the city. Each week I must learn of the untimely death of one of my sister workers. . . . The life of men and women is so cheap and property is so sacred. . . . It is up to the working people to save themselves. "

Accidents such as the Triangle Shirtwaist Factory Fire encouraged legislation that increased factory safety standards and improved working conditions. State legislatures passed some mine and factory safety laws and new inspection regulations.

Labor leaders and progressive reformers also fought for workers' compensation laws, which would provide money to individuals who were injured on the job. Previously, employers had held workers responsible for any injuries received on the job. In 1902 Maryland became the first of many states to adopt a workers' compensation law. However, the workplace laws were not always strictly enforced, so working conditions remained difficult in many places.

★ The Courts and Labor

Some business leaders opposed workforce regulations and believed that the economy should operate without government interference. State and federal courts often upheld these views. The courts argued that the Fourteenth Amendment protected businesses against regulations that deprived them of property without due process of law.

Lochner v. *New York*

In an 1898 decision the Supreme Court ruled that states could limit the hours worked by people in particularly dangerous jobs such as mining. Under the same principle, the state of New York later passed a law that limited bakers to a 10-hour workday because of the unhealthy working conditions in bakeries. A bakery owner named Joseph Lochner challenged the 10-hour law, claiming that

The loss of life in the Triangle Shirtwaist Factory Fire shocked the country.

it interfered with his right to run his business. The case eventually went to the U.S. Supreme Court.

In *Lochner* v. *New York* the Court ruled that states could not restrict ordinary workers' hours and that the New York law was unconstitutional. Justice Rufus Peckham's opinion stated:

> " The freedom of master and employee to contract with each other . . . cannot be prohibited or interfered with without violating the Fourteenth Amendment's guarantee of liberty. "

Muller v. *Oregon*

The Supreme Court did uphold some laws that limited the hours that women and children worked. In the 1908 case *Muller* v. *Oregon,* the Court upheld laws limiting women's hours. Defense attorney Louis Brandeis enlisted the help of progressive reformers Florence Kelley and Josephine Goldmark. Together they collected medical and labor study data to support their legal argument. After hearing this evidence, the Court ruled that pregnancy and other health factors distinguished female workers from male workers. The justices wrote that a woman's health is a matter of public concern and that this public interest allowed the government to regulate women's working hours.

For the progressives, this was an important decision because *Muller* v. *Oregon* was the first case successfully argued from economic, scientific, and social evidence rather than prior legal principle. Progressives and union leaders continued using such evidence in their efforts to win similar legal protection for male workers.

Josephine Goldmark fought to protect the rights of female workers.

 ## Labor Organizations

While progressives used the nation's courts and legislatures to try to change labor laws, unions continued to negotiate with employers for improved working conditions. A major union goal was gaining higher wages. In 1910 millions of working men and women lived in poverty. Union membership increased from more than 800,000 in 1900 to about 5 million in 1920. Most unions discouraged women from joining, so some female workers organized their own unions. For example, reformers started the national Women's Trade Union League (WTUL) in 1903.

The American Federation of Labor (AFL) continued to be one of the most powerful labor unions, with some 4 million members by 1920. The AFL concentrated on organizing workers in skilled trades. Its goals were higher wages, better working conditions, and union recognition. These goals followed AFL president Samuel Gompers's idea of "pure and simple unionism."

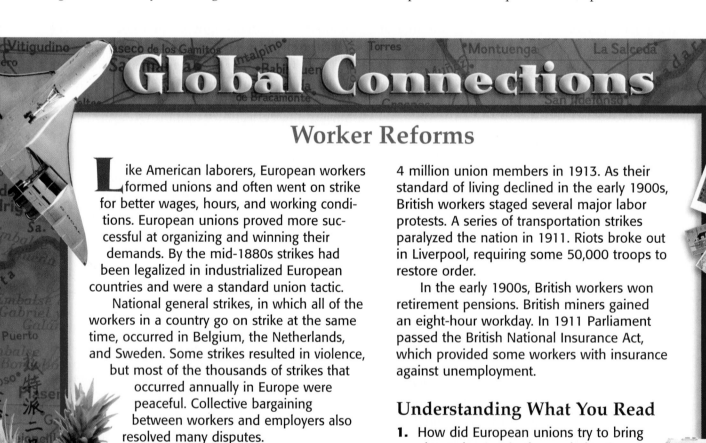

Global Connections

Worker Reforms

Like American laborers, European workers formed unions and often went on strike for better wages, hours, and working conditions. European unions proved more successful at organizing and winning their demands. By the mid-1880s strikes had been legalized in industrialized European countries and were a standard union tactic.

National general strikes, in which all of the workers in a country go on strike at the same time, occurred in Belgium, the Netherlands, and Sweden. Some strikes resulted in violence, but most of the thousands of strikes that occurred annually in Europe were peaceful. Collective bargaining between workers and employers also resolved many disputes.

The labor movement was strongest in Britain, where there were about 4 million union members in 1913. As their standard of living declined in the early 1900s, British workers staged several major labor protests. A series of transportation strikes paralyzed the nation in 1911. Riots broke out in Liverpool, requiring some 50,000 troops to restore order.

In the early 1900s, British workers won retirement pensions. British miners gained an eight-hour workday. In 1911 Parliament passed the British National Insurance Act, which provided some workers with insurance against unemployment.

Understanding What You Read

1. How did European unions try to bring about changes in the workplace?

2. What gains did British workers make?

Gompers and others like him supported the system called **capitalism**, in which private businesses run most industries, and competition determines how much goods cost and how much workers are paid.

Some union members embraced more radical ideas than those supported by the AFL. These workers claimed that capitalism was unfair. Instead, they supported **socialism**, a system in which the government or the workers own and operate a nation's means of production. Socialists hoped that if the government ran industries and manufacturing, it would be more sympathetic to workers' concerns.

Some socialists and union leaders founded the **Industrial Workers of the World** (IWW) in 1905. Led by William D. "Big Bill" Haywood, the IWW worked to bring all laborers together into one large industrial union that would try to overthrow capitalism. The IWW unionized many workers who were unwelcome in the AFL, including unskilled laborers, immigrants, women, African Americans, and migrant workers.

Haywood said that workers and capitalists were engaged in a bitter "class struggle." As part of this struggle, the IWW organized many strikes across the country. The IWW gained supporters in 1912 after its successful textile mill strike in Lawrence, Massachusetts. The next year, however, the union lost a major silkworkers' strike in Paterson, New Jersey.

Labor Union Membership, 1900–1920

Source: *Historical Statistics of the United States*

The Growing Unions The nation's industrial growth and the efforts of progressive reformers helped labor unions' membership grow. During which five-year period was union membership the highest?

The beliefs and actions of the IWW frightened many Americans, particularly wealthy and powerful leaders of big business. Political opposition, arrests of union leaders, and government investigations weakened the IWW. By 1920 the union had practically disappeared.

SECTION 3 REVIEW

Identify and explain the significance of the following:
- **Florence Kelley**
- **Triangle Shirtwaist Factory Fire**
- **capitalism**
- **socialism**
- **Industrial Workers of the World**
- **William D. Haywood**

Reading for Content Understanding

1 **Main Idea** How did many progressives try to reform labor practices?

2 **Main Idea** How did labor unions try to address workplace issues?

3 **Constitutional Heritage** What did the Supreme Court decide in *Muller* v. *Oregon* and *Lochner* v. *New York*? What reasons did the Court give in its rulings?

4 **Writing** *Describing* Write a half-page news article about the Triangle Shirtwaist Factory Fire in 1911.

5 **Critical Thinking** *Determining the Strength of an Argument* Do you think that the courts should or should not have attempted to regulate the workplace? Explain your answer.

SECTION 4

Women's Suffrage and Temperance

Reading Focus

How did higher education and women's social clubs lead to reform efforts in the late 1800s and early 1900s?

How did women participate in the temperance movement?

What methods did women's rights activists use to gain the vote?

Key Terms

Woman's Christian Temperance Union

Anti-Saloon League

Eighteenth Amendment

National American Woman Suffrage Association

National Woman's Party

Nineteenth Amendment

DURING THE SUMMER OF 1910, *a campaign tour for women's right to vote stopped in Warren, Illinois. The local crowd greeted the female activists with colorful banners and enthusiasm. The activists told Warren's residents that their state representative had opposed the Woman Suffrage bill. The crowd brought the representative forward and demanded to know if he would change his vote and support the bill the next time. "It looks as if I would have to," he responded. To the delight of the crowd, he shouted, "I can't fight against a woman's campaign. I'm for you."*

Suffrage supporter

⭐ Progressive Women

In the years following the Seneca Falls Convention of 1848, women's rights activists had achieved some important breakthroughs. These included property rights for married women and increased access to higher education.

In the late 1800s women began attending college in record numbers. Several women's colleges had been founded in the mid-1800s, including Vassar, Smith, and Wellesley. Women's colleges were designed "to develop as fully as may be the powers of womanhood," said Sophia Smith, founder of Smith College. In addition, many of the new state universities admitted both men and women. Some educators opposed women's higher education, however. For example, in 1874 a professor at Harvard Medical School argued that the physical and mental strain of too much thinking would harm a woman's health.

American Arts

Mary Cassatt

Mary Cassatt was born into a wealthy Pennsylvania family in 1844. From an early age she was interested in the arts, but she found the American art school she attended dull. She moved to Europe, where she studied painting for years, developing her own vivid, colorful style. Her successful career showed the increased opportunities available to women in the late 1800s.

French painter Edgar Degas saw one of Cassatt's paintings in the 1870s. He remarked, "There is a person who feels as I do." Degas invited Cassatt to become the only American to exhibit with the impressionists, a school of painters who created richly colored scenes of everyday life. Cassatt later became the first impressionist to exhibit in the United States.

While many impressionists painted public scenes, Cassatt often chose mothers and young children as her subjects, creating sensitive portraits. Her work helped to increase American interest in impressionist painting. In the early 1890s she painted a large mural, titled *Modern Woman,* for the Women's Building at the World's Columbian Exposition in Chicago. The mural was lost after the exposition ended.

Cassatt was also influenced by Japanese prints displayed in Paris, France. Inspired by the exhibition, Cassatt created some prints in her own style. She was uninterested, however, in most of the styles of modern art that were introduced during the early 1900s.

Cassatt was a precise and outspoken person who painted only who and what she wanted. She never taught any students because she believed that each artist had to develop his or her own personal

Mary Cassatt's paintings, such as Young Mother Sewing, *often showed mothers and daughters sharing daily activities.*

style. When Cassatt died in 1926, she was regarded as one of the finest American artists of her time.

Understanding the Arts

1. Why did Mary Cassatt go to Europe to study art?

2. How was Cassatt's work similar to and different from that of the other impressionists? Why do you think this was the case?

3. What do you think Cassatt is trying to show in the above painting?

Frances Willard

Frances Willard was born in Churchville, New York, in 1839. She attended North Western Female College in Illinois and graduated in 1859. After graduating, she supported herself as an educator and travel writer.

Willard later became involved in the Woman's Christian Temperance Union (WCTU). Her fiery speeches and effective organizing skills led to her election as WCTU president in 1879, a position she held for the next 20 years.

Willard was interested in a wide range of women's rights issues. She expanded the work of the WCTU beyond temperance drives. She supported the ballot for women as a "weapon for the protection of the home." In addition, she helped the WCTU create departments dealing with issues such as public health, education, and prison reform. When Willard died in 1898, the WCTU had expanded its membership worldwide.

Despite such views, many women seized the opportunity to expand their education. More than 20 percent of college students were women in 1870. That number rose to about 40 percent in 1910. After graduation, however, most of these women found that there were few jobs available for them. Jane Addams explained the frustration this caused her and other women. She stated that she could "not understand this apparent waste of herself, this elaborate [complex] preparation, if no work is provided for her." Many female graduates entered fields such as teaching, social work, and library management. However, they found it harder to join male-dominated professions such as law and medicine.

Women who were denied access to such careers often played a central role in progressive reform movements. Many middle-class women became active as members of local women's social clubs. The General Federation of Women's Clubs (GFWC) was founded in 1890 with more than 200 member organizations. It grew steadily throughout the Progressive Era and had almost 1 million members by 1910. Middle-class African American women formed their own clubs when they were denied membership in most clubs established by white women. One African American women's club adopted the motto "Lifting As We Climb."

In addition to providing places for women to meet and discuss social and political issues, these clubs often supported community improvements. Locally, club members raised money and provided volunteers for projects such as improved libraries, better schools, and scholarship fund-raising. National clubs helped organize local club efforts and schedule lecturers to speak to club members on a wide range of topics. Charlotte Perkins Gilman, a writer and women's rights activist, praised the positive influence of clubs on women's participation in reform movements:

“**The woman's clubs reached almost everyone and brought her out of the sacred selfishness of the home and into the broader contact and relationship so essential to social progress. . . . The clubs are united and federating [organizing] by towns, states, nations.**”

⭐ The Temperance Movement

Another area in which female progressives were vital participants was the temperance movement. Temperance reformers had been arguing since the 1840s that alcohol was to blame for many of society's problems. They claimed that alcohol abuse disrupted the family and led to crime and poverty. In the 1870s many reformers renewed the fight against alcohol.

One of the first temperance crusades of this period began in Hillsboro, Ohio. Women demanded that liquor dealers give up their trade

❝in the name of our . . . ruined lives . . . for the good of the town, in the name of God who will judge you and us, [and] for the sake of our souls.❞

During the 1870s the movement spread to hundreds of small towns as reformers shut down more than 1,000 saloons. A few women even followed the example of temperance leader Carry Nation, who stormed into saloons with a hatchet, chopping bars and smashing liquor bottles and glasses.

In 1874, reformers created the **Woman's Christian Temperance Union** (WCTU). This organization united women from many different backgrounds in the fight against alcohol abuse. Frances Willard served as president of the WCTU from 1879 to 1898. She created a highly effective organization with 10,000 local branches that represented every state, territory, and major city in the nation. Under Willard's leadership, the WCTU began addressing issues beyond temperance, including the fight for women's suffrage.

The size and success of the WCTU inspired other temperance organizations. The **Anti-Saloon League** was founded in 1893 and became particularly active in the early 1900s. As a result of such widespread

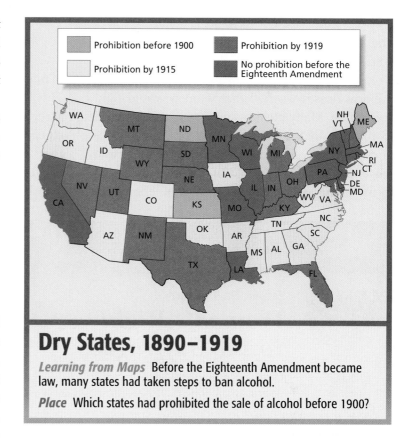

| Prohibition before 1900 | Prohibition by 1919 |
| Prohibition by 1915 | No prohibition before the Eighteenth Amendment |

Dry States, 1890–1919

Learning from Maps Before the Eighteenth Amendment became law, many states had taken steps to ban alcohol.

Place Which states had prohibited the sale of alcohol before 1900?

temperance efforts, by 1916 the sale of alcohol was illegal in 23 states, primarily in the rural West and South. In 1919, temperance efforts eventually led to the passage of the **Eighteenth Amendment**, which outlawed the "manufacture, sale, or transportation" of alcoholic beverages in the United States.

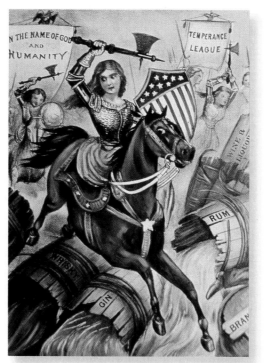

Cartoons often showed temperance leader Carry Nation as a warrior attacking alcohol.

★ Women's Suffrage

In addition to focusing on reform projects such as the temperance movement and settlement houses, women during the Progressive Era also organized in a renewed effort to gain suffrage. Although progressives supported other women's reform efforts, some progressive leaders still considered the suffrage issue controversial. Many Americans shared their opinion.

The Spirit of Reform **255**

Resistance to Suffrage

The suffrage movement had many opponents. Some people feared that the vote would give women too much political power. For example, political bosses worried that women would fight corruption. Many businessmen were also opposed to reforms that a large number of women supported, such as child labor laws and the minimum wage. Other people argued that women belonged in the home as homemakers and mothers, rather than in the world of politics. This argument was also accepted by many women's club members, who believed that women should lead efforts for social change but avoid politics.

Suffragists strongly challenged such claims. One suffragist leader responded to her opponents by arguing that women

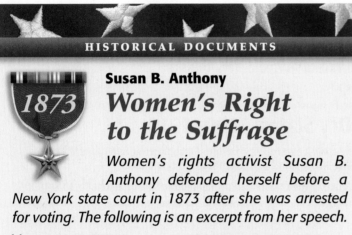

> **HISTORICAL DOCUMENTS**

Susan B. Anthony
1873

Women's Right to the Suffrage

Women's rights activist Susan B. Anthony defended herself before a New York state court in 1873 after she was arrested for voting. The following is an excerpt from her speech.

" Friends and fellow citizens: I stand before you to-night under indictment for the alleged crime [accusation] of having voted at the last presidential election, without having a lawful right to vote. It shall be my work this evening to prove to you that in thus voting, I not only committed no crime, but, instead, simply exercised my citizen's rights, guaranteed to me and all United States citizens by the National Constitution. . . . It was we, the people, not we, the white male citizens; nor yet we, the male citizens; but we, the whole people, who formed the Union. And we formed it, not to give the blessings of liberty, but to secure them; not to the half of ourselves and the half of our posterity, but to the whole people—women as well as men. "

Understanding Primary Sources

1. What crime was Susan B. Anthony accused of committing?

2. Why does Anthony believe that women should have the vote?

Carrie Chapman Catt waves to supporters.

" **must go beyond the house. No longer is home compassed [contained] by four walls. Many of its most important duties lie now involved in the bigger family of the city and state.** "

Suffrage Organizations

In 1890 Elizabeth Cady Stanton and Susan B. Anthony began the **National American Woman Suffrage Association** (NAWSA) to focus on getting the vote for women. That same year, women gained full suffrage in the state of Wyoming. Colorado, Idaho, and Utah followed in the 1890s. Despite these early successes, the NAWSA faced great challenges as it tried to lobby for suffrage across the nation.

Carrie Chapman Catt, who had fought successfully for women's suffrage in the West, became the president of the NAWSA in 1900. Catt mobilized more than 1 million volunteers for the movement. She promoted the NAWSA's goals through campaigns and speeches. Catt argued that female voters were needed to help bring about progressive reforms. She also pointed out that women deserved to have a voice in creating the laws that affected them.

Some women believed that the efforts of the NAWSA did not go far enough. In 1913 former NAWSA member Alice Paul founded what would become the **National Woman's Party** (NWP). The NWP used methods such as parades and public demonstrations to draw attention to its cause, as well as more controversial activities such as pickets, hunger strikes, and civil disobedience. Paul and other NWP leaders were jailed on several occasions for such actions.

The NWP and the NAWSA campaigned for a constitutional amendment to grant women the vote. The success of other progressive reforms encouraged these groups. In 1916 both the Democratic and Republican Parties supported women's suffrage. In 1920 the combined efforts of the NAWSA and the NWP resulted in the passage of the **Nineteenth Amendment**. This amendment gave women in the United States the vote.

The NWP continued to push for women's rights by supporting an equal rights amendment. The NAWSA helped create the League of Women Voters, an organization that encouraged women to educate themselves on public issues, to vote regularly, and to support additional social reform measures.

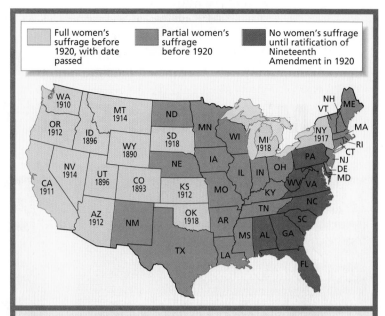

| Full women's suffrage before 1920, with date passed | Partial women's suffrage before 1920 | No women's suffrage until ratification of Nineteenth Amendment in 1920 |

Women and Suffrage, 1890–1920

Learning from Maps The National American Woman Suffrage Association and the National Woman's Party successfully led the fight for women's suffrage.

Place Which states had no women's suffrage before the ratification of the Nineteenth Amendment?

SECTION 4 REVIEW

Identify and explain the significance of the following:
- **Woman's Christian Temperance Union**
- **Frances Willard**
- **Anti-Saloon League**
- **Eighteenth Amendment**
- **Susan B. Anthony**
- **National American Woman Suffrage Association**
- **Carrie Chapman Catt**
- **Alice Paul**
- **National Woman's Party**
- **Nineteenth Amendment**

Reading for Content Understanding

1 **Main Idea** What role did higher education and women's social clubs play in reform efforts during the late 1800s and early 1900s?

2 **Main Idea** In what ways did women contribute to the temperance movement?

3 **Constitutional Heritage** How did some women fight for suffrage? What legislation was passed as a result of their efforts?

4 **Writing** *Creating* Imagine that you have just joined the NAWSA. Write a brief paragraph and a slogan for a poster supporting the women's suffrage movement.

5 **Critical Thinking** *Evaluating* What do you think were the most important contributions made by women to the progressive movement? Explain your answer.

Minorities Fight for Change

Reading Focus

What reforms did African Americans seek during the Progressive Era?

What difficulties did American Indians face during the Progressive Era?

What major changes occurred for Chinese Americans and Mexican Americans during the Progressive Era?

Key Terms

Atlanta Compromise

Niagara Movement

National Association for the Advancement of Colored People

National Association of Colored Women

Society of American Indians

ON JULY 25, 1900, *African American professor and writer W. E. B. Du Bois stepped up to a podium in London's Westminster Town Hall. Before him sat reporters and delegates from around the world, gathered for the first Pan-African Conference. In solemn tones, Du Bois asked his audience to consider the key question facing the world. That problem, he declared, was how and why racial differences were used as "the basis of denying to over half the world the right of sharing . . . the opportunities and privileges of modern civilization."*

W. E. B. Du Bois

 African Americans Fight for Change

White reformers in the progressive movement often ignored issues such as racial discrimination. While other areas of life were improving during the late 1800s, discrimination and segregation increased throughout the nation.

Booker T. Washington

Some African American leaders, particularly Booker T. Washington, promoted efforts to improve the economic conditions of African Americans. Born a slave in 1856, Washington became a respected educator while in his twenties. In 1881 he founded the Tuskegee Institute in Alabama to educate and train black schoolteachers. Washington explained the practical goals of Tuskegee in his autobiography *Up from Slavery.* "The student shall be so educated that he shall be enabled to meet conditions as they exist *now.*" Tuskegee also drew African American teachers such as scientist George Washington Carver. Carver's agricultural research addressed many farming problems in the South.

In addition to his administrative duties at Tuskegee, Washington was an influential writer and public speaker. He argued that African Americans should not spend their time fighting discrimination and segregation but instead should focus on improving their own educational and economic well-being. Washington explained his philosophy in 1895 before a group at the Cotton States Expo in Atlanta, Georgia. In his **Atlanta Compromise** speech he noted:

> 66 **In all things that are purely social we [whites and African Americans] can be as separate as the fingers, yet one as the hand in all things essential to mutual [shared] progress.** 99

Other African American leaders believed that economic progress alone was not enough.

Ida B. Wells-Barnett

One such leader was journalist Ida B. Wells-Barnett. She was a suffragist and an outspoken opponent of violence against African Americans. After three of her friends were lynched, or killed by a mob, Wells-Barnett began writing antilynching editorials in her Memphis newspaper, *Free Speech.* These courageous articles drew national attention to the lynching of black men in the South. She also helped organize an international crusade against lynching.

In 1895 Wells-Barnett published the book *Red Record,* which reported lynching statistics for a three-year period. Although repeated death threats forced Wells-Barnett to move to the North, she continued her antilynching campaign.

Ida B. Wells-Barnett was orphaned as a teenager and raised her five brothers and sisters.

W. E. B. Du Bois

The approach of W. E. B. Du Bois also contrasted with that of Booker T. Washington. Born in Massachusetts in 1868, Du Bois went to Fisk University and later earned a doctoral degree from Harvard. He criticized Washington for holding African Americans responsible for correcting racial injustice. Du Bois also disagreed with Washington's emphasis on job training rather than liberal arts education.

Du Bois challenged Washington's arguments in a collection of essays published in 1903 called *The Souls of Black Folk.* "The problem of the twentieth century," wrote Du Bois, "is the problem of the color-line." Du Bois explained that his goal was "to make it possible for a man to be both a Negro and an American . . . without having the doors of Opportunity closed roughly in his face." Du Bois brought attention to cases of racial prejudice and wrote dozens of articles, speeches, and influential books on African American history.

★ African American Organizations

In 1905 W. E. B. Du Bois and other African Americans who shared his views met at Niagara Falls, Canada. Calling themselves the **Niagara Movement**, they demanded economic and educational equality, as well as an end to segregation and discrimination. Their platform insisted that "to ignore, overlook, or apologize for these wrongs is to prove ourselves unworthy of freedom."

To help further the goals of the Niagara Movement, Du Bois joined with reformers such as Mary White Ovington to found the **National Association for the Advancement of Colored People** (NAACP) in 1909. The new organization included many well-known leaders in the progressive movement, such as Jane Addams and John Dewey. These progressives were appalled by the lynchings and recent tide of race riots against African Americans in northern and southern cities. Du Bois acted as director of publicity and research and also as the editor of the NAACP journal, *The Crisis.*

The NAACP worked to bring racial inequality to the attention of white Americans and attacked racial discrimination through the court system. In *Guinn* v. *United States* in 1915, the NAACP won the first of several important Supreme Court decisions. This ruling outlawed the grandfather clause, which had been widely used in southern states to prevent African Americans from voting.

The National Urban League was an influential black organization founded in 1911. This group helped many African Americans—particularly those moving from the South to northern cities—find jobs and housing and adjust to a new life in an urban environment. The **National Association of Colored Women** (NACW), led by antilynching activist Mary Church Terrell, supported political reforms for African Americans. These reforms included women's suffrage and protecting the voting rights of black men in the South.

Gertrude S. Bonin helped found the Society of American Indians.

★ American Indians

Progressive reforms did not address the many problems—such as widespread poverty and a shrinking population—that the majority of American Indians faced. Most Indians lived on reservations, where living conditions were often hard, housing was poor, and medical care was limited. Many Indian children were sent away from the reservations to boarding schools that taught little or nothing about traditional Indian culture. These schools provided basic or vocational education, but students found few jobs available when they returned home.

Several American Indians founded the **Society of American Indians** in 1911 to assist those living on the reservations. Members believed that the Dawes Act, which authorized the breakup of the reservation system, was the best solution to Indians' poverty and unemployment. The group also argued that Indians should adopt the beliefs and practices of the larger American society in an effort to gain U.S. citizenship.

Most of the Society's members, however, did not understand the views of Indians who lived on the reservations and who wanted to preserve traditional Indian culture. A large number of Indians saw the breakup of reservations under the Dawes Act not as a benefit but as the end of the traditional Indian way of life. The importance of traditional beliefs was stressed in advice given by Sioux chief Sitting Bull: "Take the best of the old Indian ways—always keep them. They have been proven for thousands of years. Do not let them die."

Some American Indians protested the policies of the Dawes Act by refusing their government land allotments. Other Indians wanted to slow down the allotment process and allow people to remain on reservations. These efforts met strong resistance from the federal government.

★ Chinese Americans

Asian immigrants also faced barriers. Many Chinese immigrants who came to the United States were men who mined gold and built railroads. Although most had planned to return home, many later decided to stay.

The Chinese American population grew slowly as a result of laws passed in the 1880s that severely restricted Chinese immigration. In 1900 the Chinese American population was less than 90,000. Chinese Americans also faced other forms of discrimination. Ing Weh-teh wrote his friend in China that in America he had "to labor, to suffer, floating from one place to another, persecuted by the whites, for more than twenty years."

Chinese Americans often formed their own neighborhoods in cities such as San Francisco.

The first Chinese telegraph operator in San Francisco

One man recalled how he and his friends tried to preserve a sense of community by gathering at neighborhood shops:

> ❝They all just like to get together. . . . Sometimes they even get some idea [news] from China. . . . We communicate, see, otherwise you're alone. You know nothing.❞

Even with such efforts to maintain their cultural ties, life was often difficult for many Chinese Americans.

Many Mexican immigrants were agricultural workers, like these laborers knocking walnuts out of trees in an orchard.

Mexican Americans

While Chinese immigration declined during the early 1900s, immigration from Mexico increased greatly. Between 1900 and 1930 nearly 1 million Mexicans crossed the border into the United States. Immigrants could move freely across the U.S. borders with Mexico and Canada during this time. The lyrics to one Mexican song from the period tells of the sadness many immigrants felt and explains why many made the journey:

> ❝For I am not to blame
> That I leave my country thus;
> The fault lies in the poverty,
> Which keeps us all in want.❞

Most Mexican immigrants moved into areas that had previously been part of Mexico, such as Texas or California. Cities with existing Hispanic communities—such as San Antonio and El Paso, Texas, and Los Angeles, California—grew in size as a result. The majority of Mexican immigrants took agricultural jobs, although large numbers also worked in factories or meatpacking plants.

Although Mexican immigrants and Mexican Americans played an important role in the economy of the Southwest, many faced discrimination and harsh labor conditions. Despite these challenges, immigrants often returned to Mexico to encourage other family members and friends to move to the United States.

SECTION 5 REVIEW

Identify and explain the significance of the following:
- Booker T. Washington
- Atlanta Compromise
- Ida B. Wells-Barnett
- W. E. B. Du Bois
- Niagara Movement
- National Association for the Advancement of Colored People
- National Association of Colored Women
- Society of American Indians

Reading for Content Understanding

1 **Main Idea** How did the Society of American Indians try to overcome the hardships faced by American Indians?

2 **Main Idea** What changes in immigration took place for Chinese Americans and Mexican Americans in the late 1800s and early 1900s?

3 **Cultural Diversity** How did some African Americans work to end racial injustice?

4 **Writing** *Informing* Write a short essay explaining the challenges faced by minority groups in the Progressive Era.

5 **Critical Thinking** *Making Comparisons* Compare and contrast the approaches of Booker T. Washington and W. E. B. Du Bois to improving life for African Americans.

CHAPTER 8 REVIEW

Chapter Summary

The Progressive Era was a time when many concerned Americans attempted to reform society. They worked to reform such areas as politics, government, the workplace, public schools, and cities. Other Americans tried to improve the lives of women, African Americans, American Indians, immigrants, and other groups. ■

On a separate sheet of paper, complete the following activities.

Identifying People and Ideas

Describe the historical significance of the following:

1. political machines
2. John Dewey
3. capitalism
4. Industrial Workers of the World
5. Frances Willard
6. Carrie Chapman Catt
7. Nineteenth Amendment
8. Atlanta Compromise
9. Booker T. Washington
10. W. E. B. Du Bois

 go.hrw.com
SB1 Suffrage Movement

Internet Activity

Search the Internet through the HRW Web site to find information about the women's suffrage movement. Create a time line of at least 10 important events in the women's suffrage movement, ending with the Nineteenth Amendment. Briefly explain in a caption why each event was important.

Understanding Main Ideas

1. How did bosses use political machines to control local and city governments?
2. How did reforms give voters more choice in selecting their candidates for public office?
3. What was the Wisconsin Idea?
4. What were working conditions like for child laborers and other factory workers in the late 1800s?
5. Why did some women form the Woman's Christian Temperance Union?
6. How did Booker T. Washington and W. E. B. Du Bois differ in their approaches to fighting for equal rights?

Reviewing Themes

1. **Constitutional Heritage** What was the significance of the ruling in *Lochner* v. *New York*? How did the Supreme Court's decision in

Using the Time Line

Number your paper from 1 to 6. Match the letters on the time line below with the following events.

1. Grover Cleveland loses the presidency to Benjamin Harrison.
2. The first public kindergarten opens in St. Louis, Missouri.
3. Leaders of the progressive movement form the National Association for the Advancement of Colored People.
4. The New York State Tenement Law outlaws the construction of dark and airless tenements.
5. The Pendleton Civil Service Act establishes a merit system for federal jobs.
6. The Nineteenth Amendment is passed.

1870   1880   1890   1900   1910

a   b   c   d   e   f

Muller v. *Oregon* partially reverse its earlier ruling?

2. **Citizenship and Democracy**   Why did women form the National American Woman Suffrage Association?

3. **Cultural Diversity**   How did African American leaders try to gain equal rights during the late 1800s and early 1900s?

Thinking Critically

1. **Identifying Cause and Effect**   What events led the public to call for civil service reform during the Gilded Age? What was the result of this public outcry?

2. **Making Comparisons**   How were progressives similar to and different from previous reformers?

3. **Evaluating**   Which of the progressive reform efforts do you think was the most significant? Explain your answer.

Writing About History

1. **Informing**   Imagine that you are writing a section of a history book that explores women's participation in various reform efforts during the Progressive Era. Write a half-page feature on this topic.

2. **Expressing**   Write a letter to Booker T. Washington telling him whether you agree with his Atlanta Compromise speech. Include reasons to support your position.

Linking Geography and History

1. **Region**   What problems did residents of urban areas in the United States face that rural residents did not?

2. **Human-Environment Interaction**   Why did many American Indians object to the breakup of reservation lands and tribal society?

Building Your Portfolio

American History

Complete the following activities individually or in groups.

1. **Muckrakers**   If muckrakers were investigating problems in American society today, what do you think would be the top five problems they would address? Find newspaper and magazine articles and images on these topics. Use this information to create a bulletin-board display titled Reforming Society Today.

2. **The Supreme Court**   Use your textbook or the library to find information about an important Supreme Court reform case of the late 1800s. Create arguments for the defending and prosecuting attorneys, as well as for the justices' ruling. Present your case to the class. Include whether you think the decision supported progressive reform.

History Skills Workshop

Using Primary Sources   In his book *How the Other Half Lives,* reformer Jacob Riis described the living conditions of many poor urban people. Read the excerpt to the right, which is Riis's description of a New York City tenement house, and answer the following questions: (a) What connection is Riis making between tenement houses and the child's illness? (b) Why do you think Riis chose this example to illustrate poor people's living conditions? (c) How do you think readers might have responded to these descriptions?

66 Suppose we look into [a tenement] on Cherry Street. . . . Here is a door. Listen! that short hacking cough, that tiny helpless cry—what do they mean? . . . The child is dying of measles. With half a chance it might have lived. But it had none. That dark bedroom killed it. 99

The Granger Collection, New York

■ CHAPTER 9 ■
The Progressive Presidents
(1900–1920)

Activist Jane Addams joined other reformers in 1912 at the Progressive Party's national convention in Chicago. She described the mix of social workers, religious leaders, scholars, and politicians: "Suddenly, as if by magic, the city of Chicago became filled with men and women from every state in the Union who [had] . . . like [similar] hopes." These people hoped to create democratic reforms on the national level.

THEMES

Economic Development
In what ways might a government try to reform business?

Geographic Diversity
How might a nation try to protect the natural environment?

Citizenship and Democracy
How might political parties and political leaders respond to voters' concerns?

1900　　**1902**　　**1904**　　**1906**　　**1908**

SEPT. 1901 Vice President Theodore Roosevelt is sworn in as president after William McKinley's assassination.

NOV. 1904 Roosevelt is elected to a second term as president.

JUNE 1906 Congress passes the Pure Food and Drug Act.

NOV. 1908 William Howard Taft is elected president.

Roosevelt Becomes President

Reading Focus

How did President Roosevelt try to balance the needs of both business and labor?

What did Roosevelt do to regulate businesses and railroads?

Why did Roosevelt and others promote the conservation movement?

Key Terms

arbitration
Square Deal
Pure Food and Drug Act
conservation
National Park Service

HE SUMMER TOUR *following President William McKinley's second inauguration in 1901 was filled with friendly crowds eager to shake the president's hand. In September McKinley greeted a group of well-wishers in Buffalo, New York. The event turned to tragedy, however, when anarchist Leon Czolgosz (CHAWL-gawsh) pulled out a pistol and shot the president at point-blank range. As he lay fatally wounded, the president whispered, "My wife, be careful how you tell her—oh be careful!" A little more than a week later, McKinley was dead.*

President McKinley is assassinated in 1901.

IMAGE ON LEFT PAGE: *Theodore Roosevelt campaigning for the Progressive Party in 1912*

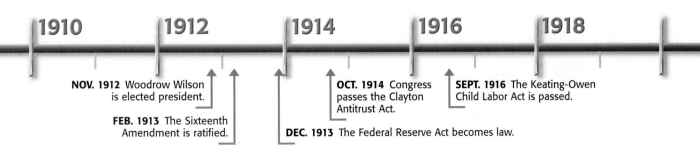

1910 1912 1914 1916 1918

NOV. 1912 Woodrow Wilson is elected president.

FEB. 1913 The Sixteenth Amendment is ratified.

OCT. 1914 Congress passes the Clayton Antitrust Act.

DEC. 1913 The Federal Reserve Act becomes law.

SEPT. 1916 The Keating-Owen Child Labor Act is passed.

★ Roosevelt's Path to the Presidency

After President McKinley's assassination in early September 1901, Vice President Theodore Roosevelt took the oath of office. At age 42 he was the youngest man ever to become president.

Roosevelt was greatly influenced by his father, who taught him to be hardworking and fair-minded. Although Roosevelt came from a wealthy family, he was sympathetic to the problems of the less fortunate. After graduating from Harvard University, Roosevelt became a politician, serving in the New York state legislature. He earned a reputation for being a moderate reformer with a stubborn streak. During an early dispute with other members of the Republican Party, Roosevelt once declared:

> ❝ **I would rather go out of politics having the feeling that I had done what was right than stay in . . . knowing in my heart that I had acted as I ought not to.** ❞

Roosevelt's early political career was successful, but the death of his first wife, Alice Lee, in 1884 was a great blow to him. "The light has gone out of my life," he wrote. Leaving politics, he moved west to the Dakotas, where he ran a ranch for several years. While there, he transformed himself into a rugged outdoorsman. Roosevelt then returned to politics, eventually serving as governor of New York. He was chosen to run as McKinley's vice presidential candidate in 1900. He also remarried, this time to childhood friend Edith Carow.

Theodore Roosevelt served as assistant secretary of the navy in 1897 and 1898.

The Granger Collection, New York

Although he promised Republican leaders that he would "continue, absolutely unbroken, the policy of President McKinley," Roosevelt quickly made his own mark on the nation. Unlike most of the Gilded Age presidents, who had seen themselves more as administrators, Roosevelt believed the president should be an active leader. He pushed for his legislation to be passed and aggressively used his executive powers. He also tried to be responsive to public opinion.

A 1902 cartoon that showed Roosevelt saving a bear cub inspired the first Teddy Bear.

★ Labor and Business

President Roosevelt believed that the interests of business, labor, and consumers should be balanced in order to protect the public good. In his opinion, if any one group gained too much power, it might take unfair advantage of the others.

Coal Miners Strike

President Roosevelt demonstrated his beliefs in his response to a Pennsylvania coal miners' strike in 1902. Coal mine operators had refused to meet the demands of the United Mine Workers for better pay, an eight-hour workday, and acceptance of their union. In May more than 150,000 miners went on strike in protest throughout Pennsylvania's vast coalfields.

The strike lasted several months, leading to coal shortages and rising prices. Roosevelt declared that the strike had "become a matter of vital concern to the whole nation" because it threatened to leave the country without heating fuel in the coming winter. He argued that as president it was his responsibility to become involved in the dispute.

Many of the mine owners believed that Roosevelt would send the U.S. Army into Pennsylvania to force the strikers back to work. Instead, Roosevelt brought the strikers and managers together for **arbitration**, a formal meeting to discuss and settle disagreements.

To get both sides to agree to arbitration, Roosevelt threatened to have the federal government take over the mines if the two groups did not cooperate. As a result of the negotiations, the strike was settled and the crisis ended in time to supply coal to the nation for the winter.

The Square Deal

President Roosevelt's actions broke with the traditional presidential approach to labor disputes. In the past, presidents had either refused to become involved or had sided against labor. Roosevelt's actions helped the efforts of labor unions to bargain with management. In 1903 Roosevelt described his approach during the strike as part of a program to treat every citizen fairly, a plan he called the **Square Deal**. He promised:

> ❝The labor unions shall have a square deal, and the corporations shall have a square deal, and in addition all private citizens shall have a square deal.❞

When some critics questioned whether Roosevelt's Square Deal was going to interfere with competition, he explained, "I do not mean . . . it is possible to give every man the best hand. . . . All I mean is that there shall not be any crookedness in the dealing." The Square Deal soon became a key part of Roosevelt's political program.

★ Roosevelt Takes on the Trusts

President Roosevelt made regulating trusts one of the most important goals of his administration. He later recalled, "The absolutely vital question was whether the government had power to control them at all." He believed that it did.

Roosevelt accepted that the economic changes that occurred during the Second Industrial Revolution had encouraged the growth of large corporations and trusts. While many progressives believed that all trusts were threats to fair competition, Roosevelt argued instead that there were "good" trusts and "bad" trusts. According to Roosevelt, a good trust was efficient and provided

Theodore Roosevelt

Theodore Roosevelt was born into a wealthy family in New York City in 1858. Despite his privileged upbringing, Roosevelt believed that his success came as a result of his hard work. As a boy, he suffered from severe asthma and poor eyesight. "I was nervous and timid," Roosevelt remembered.

At the age of 11, however, he began improving his health through exercise and outdoor activities. His asthma got better and he became a strong and confident young man. Roosevelt was very energetic and always seemed to be rushing from one task to the next. He was impatient with anyone who could not keep up with his rapid pace. Reporter Lincoln Steffens once wrote about Roosevelt, "He took joy in everything he did, in hunting, camping, in ranching, in politics, in reforming the police or the civil service."

At the age of 55 Roosevelt still had an adventurous spirit. As he explained about a trip to the jungles of Brazil, "I had just one more chance to be a boy, and I took it!"

consumers with needed products and services at reasonable prices. A bad trust, however, restricted trade unfairly and used its influence to charge high prices. Roosevelt's goal was to shut down the bad trusts but to allow the good ones to stay in business.

The first bad trust that Roosevelt tackled was the Northern Securities Company, an enormous corporation that had a monopoly on the major railroad lines in the Northwest. In 1902 he ordered the Justice Department to prosecute this powerful trust under the Sherman Antitrust Act. The influential businessman J. P. Morgan, an executive of

THE LION-TAMER

President Roosevelt, the trustbuster, taming powerful businesses

Northern Securities, was shocked at Roosevelt's action. He visited the White House and told the president, "If we have done anything wrong, send your man to my man and they can fix it up."

Roosevelt refused Morgan's offer, insisting that every citizen, rich or poor, had to obey the law. In 1904 the U.S. Supreme Court narrowly upheld the Sherman Antitrust Act and then dissolved Northern Securities. The Court's decision sent a warning to large corporations. Roosevelt followed this victory by supporting legislation that regulated the railroads and their shipping rates. Such actions gained Roosevelt a reputation as a trust-buster, even though his administration did not actually attack a large number of trusts.

 The 1904 Election

Roosevelt faced the 1904 presidential election with some concern. Although he had strong public support, his antitrust efforts had angered powerful business leaders. Some Americans also feared his expansion of the federal government's powers and disapproved of government interference in the economic system. The Democrats chose former New York judge Alton Parker to run against Roosevelt. Parker accused Roosevelt of being a radical. Former president Grover Cleveland declared that the Democrats were filled with "hope and confidence" at their chances of winning the election.

The Republicans began a well-organized campaign to promote their candidate across the country. Roosevelt was already an expert at dealing with the press because he had met regularly with reporters throughout his first term. His witty and direct manner of speaking charmed the public and helped him become a widely recognized figure. By contrast, Parker was neither well known nor a gifted speaker. The result was a huge victory in November 1904 for Roosevelt and his Square Deal platform of equal opportunity and reform.

 Roosevelt and the Muckrakers

In some cases, public pressure forced President Roosevelt to seek reform. Newspaper and magazine articles by muckraking journalists helped raise public awareness of problems within the food and drug industries. The American Medical Association also called for better food standards and proper labeling. Nevertheless, Congress resisted the pressure to pass reforms.

The turning point came in 1906 when muckraker Upton Sinclair published *The Jungle*, a novel that exposed the practices of the meatpacking industry. The book's vivid descriptions of spoiled meat being packed and sold to consumers shocked readers, including Roosevelt.

He responded to the public outcry by launching a federal investigation. His report concluded that

❝ the stockyards and packing houses are not kept even reasonably clean, and . . . the method of handling and preparing food products is uncleanly and dangerous to health. ❞

Although he did not get the strict regulation that he wanted, Roosevelt persuaded Congress to pass the **Pure Food and Drug Act** in June 1906.

American Literature

The Jungle
Upton Sinclair

Upton Sinclair wrote The Jungle *to create sympathy for the conditions under which immigrants lived and worked. Readers were shocked by his descriptions of the unsanitary practices in the meatpacking industry. Sinclair later said about Americans' reaction, "I aimed at the public's heart, and by accident I hit it in the stomach." In the following excerpt from* The Jungle, *the Rudkus family describes conditions at a Chicago meat plant.*

Meat sales dropped after The Jungle *was published.*

The family had a first-hand knowledge of the great majority of Packingtown swindles. For it was the custom, as they found, whenever meat was so spoiled that it could not be used for anything else, either to can it or else to chop it up into sausage. . . .

Jonas had told them how the meat that was taken out of pickle [vinegar solution] would often be found sour, and how they would rub it up with soda to take away the smell, and sell it to be eaten on free-lunch counters; also of all the miracles of chemistry which they performed, giving to any sort of meat, fresh or salted, whole or chopped, any color and any flavor and any odor they chose. . . .

It was only when the whole ham was spoiled that it came into the department of Elzbieta. . . . Mixed with half a ton of other meat, no odor that ever was in a ham could make any difference. There was never the least attention paid to what was cut up for sausage; there would come all the way back from Europe old sausage that had been rejected. . . . There would be meat that had tumbled out on the floor, in the dirt and sawdust, where the workers had tramped and spit uncounted billions of . . . germs. There would be meat stored in great piles in rooms; and the water from leaky roofs would drip over it, and thousands of rats would race about on it. This is no fairy story.

Understanding Literature

1. What happened to spoiled meat?
2. Why do you think *The Jungle* led to new health laws?

This act prohibited the manufacture, sale, or transportation of mislabeled or contaminated food and drugs sold in interstate commerce. Congress also passed the Meat Inspection Act, which required inspections of meat plants.

Roosevelt was not always in favor of the muckrakers' work. "Men with the muck rake are often indispensable [vital] to the well-being of society, but only if they know when to stop raking the muck," he once commented. Nonetheless, the articles written by muckrakers helped generate public support for Roosevelt's expansion of the federal government's regulatory powers. His activism set a standard for later progressive presidents. At the same time, though, Roosevelt's reform efforts increased the tension within the Republican Party between progressive and traditional Republicans.

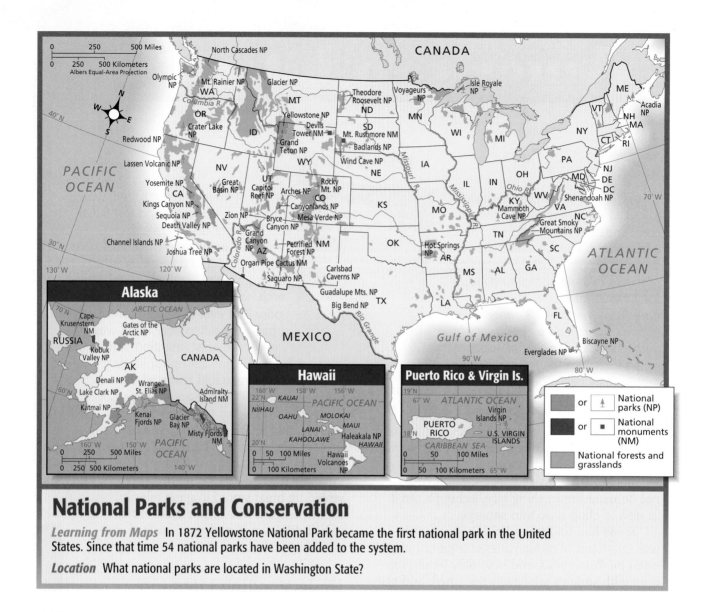

National Parks and Conservation

Learning from Maps In 1872 Yellowstone National Park became the first national park in the United States. Since that time 54 national parks have been added to the system.

Location What national parks are located in Washington State?

⭐ Conservation

One reform effort of great personal importance to President Roosevelt was the **conservation** movement, or the effort to protect nature and its resources. Roosevelt had been interested in nature for many years. As a boy he read many books on birds and wildlife and often spent hours in the American Museum of Natural History, which his father had helped found. Later in life he became an eager hunter and birdwatcher. Roosevelt's love of the outdoors made him the first president to consider conservation an important issue.

There were two different points of view among the members of the conservation movement. Those calling themselves preservationists believed that nature should be preserved because of its beauty. Many preservationists, such as John Muir and Charles Sargent, argued that the remaining ancient forests of the West should be completely protected from logging and enjoyed as an unspoiled part of nature. Muir wrote:

❝**Thousands of tired, nerve-shaken, over-civilized people are beginning to find out that going to the mountains is going home; that wildness is a necessity; and that mountain parks and reservations are useful not only as fountains of timber and irrigating rivers, but as fountains of life.**❞

Muir became a widely respected forest expert and a leader of the conservation movement.

Other members of the conservation movement were more concerned with conserving the natural resources of the United States. Known as conservationists, this group wanted to manage the use of these natural resources more efficiently. "Forestry is the art of using a forest without destroying it," Chief of Forestry Gifford Pinchot (PIN-shoh) declared. He argued that forests should not be preserved simply "because they are beautiful," but more importantly because they produced the materials necessary to build "prosperous homes."

Despite their different opinions on how people should interact with nature, preservationists and conservationists fought together to establish national and state parks on public lands. They also pushed for the foundation of wildlife refuges to protect endangered animals. Roosevelt supported these measures, stating, "We are not building this country of ours for a day." He hoped that parks could provide "rest, health, and recreation" for the American people for many years to come.

By 1870 millions of acres of federal lands had already been sold or given to private mining, logging, and railroad companies. These companies

President Roosevelt meets with preservationist John Muir at Yosemite Valley, California, site of the first national park.

opposed the efforts made during the Progressive Era to conserve federal land. When Roosevelt took office, only 46 million acres of land had been set aside as national reserves.

Roosevelt took advantage of a federal law that allowed the president to set aside forest land. During his administration nearly 150 million acres of public land moved under the control of the Forest Service. These lands were equal in size to Great Britain and France combined. Roosevelt also doubled the number of national parks, created 16 national monuments, and established 51 wildlife refuges. This newly protected territory included the Grand Canyon and the Petrified Forest in Arizona and Zion in Utah. To help supervise the growing number of parks and monuments, the **National Park Service** was created in 1916. The National Park system has continued to expand with the addition of new land and services, as well as the establishment of urban parks.

SECTION 1 REVIEW

Identify and explain the significance of the following:
- **Theodore Roosevelt**
- **arbitration**
- **Square Deal**
- **Pure Food and Drug Act**
- **conservation**
- **National Park Service**

Locate and explain the importance of the following:
- **Grand Canyon**
- **Zion**

Reading for Content Understanding

1. **Main Idea** How did President Theodore Roosevelt try to help business and labor?

2. **Main Idea** What actions did Roosevelt take against corporations and railroads?

3. **Geographic Diversity** *Human-Environment Interaction* Why did supporters of the conservation movement want to protect America's natural resources?

4. **Writing** *Persuading* Imagine that you are a Republican Party leader. Write a brief essay arguing for or against Roosevelt's reform efforts. Give examples to support your argument.

5. **Critical Thinking** *Evaluating* Why might people have called Theodore Roosevelt an "activist president"?

The Taft Administration

Reading Focus

How was William Howard Taft's administration similar to and different from Roosevelt's administration?

Why did progressives turn against President Taft?

What events took place during the election of 1912?

Key Terms

Payne-Aldrich Tariff

New Nationalism

Bull Moose Party

New Freedom

THEODORE ROOSEVELT DECLARED *in 1904 that he would not run for a third term in 1908. Many people doubted him, however, and Roosevelt grew upset with the rumors that he would run again for president. In early 1908 he told his press secretary that a new candidate needed to be chosen, saying, "We had better turn to Taft." William Howard Taft was secretary of war and a good friend of Roosevelt. When the press secretary brought him the news, Taft said in surprise, "I must go over and thank Theodore." When Taft arrived, Roosevelt encouraged him, saying, "Yes, Will, it's the thing to do."*

The Granger Collection, New York

President William Howard Taft

★ William Howard Taft

President Roosevelt was confident that Taft was a responsible leader and the best choice to continue the Square Deal. "There will be no backward step under Taft," he assured one supporter during the 1908 election.

The Reluctant President

Taft was born in Ohio in 1857. His family was moderately wealthy and his parents pushed him

to pursue a legal career. After graduating second in his class at Yale, Taft completed law school and went on to hold a variety of appointed government offices. He spent eight years serving as a U.S. Circuit Court judge and found the judiciary to be his true calling. "I love judges, and I love courts," he said on one occasion. His greatest ambition was not to become president but to be appointed to the U.S. Supreme Court and serve as chief justice.

Taft disliked political campaigns, and only Roosevelt's encouragement persuaded him to run for president. "A national campaign for the presidency is to me a nightmare," he once admitted. With Roosevelt's support and advice, however, Taft overcame his lack of campaign experience. He then easily defeated progressive Democrat William Jennings Bryan in the November 1908 election. Many pro-business Republicans were pleased with the election results because they believed Taft would be easier to work with than Roosevelt.

Taft and Roosevelt

Despite their friendship, Taft and Roosevelt had different personalities and different ideas about the role of the president. While Roosevelt was a skilled public speaker who enjoyed public attention, Taft often gave his speeches without enthusiasm. Unlike Roosevelt, Taft avoided the press and did not like to be interviewed by reporters. Although he was a friendly and polite man, Taft often seemed stiff and awkward in public.

Politically, Taft supported the regulation of big business and promised to continue Roosevelt's reform policies. Whereas Roosevelt had often acted swiftly in response to public concerns, however, Taft was more cautious. Most importantly, Taft thought that Roosevelt had claimed too much presidential power and had too often gone beyond the letter of the law. Taft felt strongly that the law, not personal beliefs or public opinion,

William Howard Taft and his wife, Helen, traveling to his inauguration

should control the actions of the government and the president. For these reasons he was opposed to progressive reforms such as the recall, which he felt gave the voters too much power. Taft also believed that the government should not interfere too much in society. He explained his views:

 There is a line beyond which government cannot go with any good practical results in seeking to make men and society better. "

★ Taft Angers the Progressives

Supporters hoped that Taft's honesty and sense of duty would overcome his lack of experience in holding an elected office. Just before Taft took office, Roosevelt told one reporter, "He's [Taft is] all right, he means well, and he'll do his best." Even so, President Taft soon disappointed the progressive Republicans who had been so loyal to Roosevelt.

Reforms Under Taft

Taft replaced many of the members of Roosevelt's cabinet with corporate lawyers. Progressives claimed that these new cabinet members would be too pro-business to support reform. Taft argued that he needed their business experience and legal advice.

Taft started 90 antitrust lawsuits—more than double the number initiated by Roosevelt. These included lawsuits against the corporate giants U.S. Steel and International Harvester. Such court battles were lengthy and there was no guarantee that the government would win its cases against the trusts. One of the biggest antitrust victories for the Taft administration was the case against Standard Oil, which had begun during Roosevelt's administration.

Despite this victory, many progressives wanted bolder action from Taft. Some progressives, such as William Jennings Bryan and Robert La Follette, wanted new laws that would eliminate the trusts entirely.

Senator Nelson Aldrich and his tariff are defeated by public opinion as President Taft watches in concern.

reduction. The **Payne-Aldrich Tariff**, passed in 1909, reduced many tariffs but raised others. It was criticized by progressive Republicans and by Democrats.

In a speech Taft responded to his critics by insisting that the Payne-Aldrich Tariff was "the best tariff bill that the Republican Party ever passed." This claim quickly drew an angry reaction from many people in the Midwest. The new tariff had hurt local industries there while providing little relief on the price of goods.

Taft's inability to push such laws through Congress disappointed them. Business leaders, who had been some of Taft's strongest supporters, were also angry at the administration's prosecution of their companies. Taft believed that he was doing his duty by following the existing antitrust laws. He therefore ignored complaints from both sides on the issue.

Roosevelt watched Taft's actions with concern. He claimed that Taft was failing to distinguish between good and bad trusts and was hurting the U.S. economy in the process. Roosevelt wanted a special commission created to help regulate big business without filing so many lawsuits.

The Tariff

Another major issue that separated Taft from the progressives was the tariff. Many Republicans favored the existing high tariff rates. These made imported goods more expensive and thus helped protect American industries from foreign competition. Progressives and many Democrats believed that the high tariff made the cost of living too expensive for most Americans. Some people also argued that the tariff hurt the ability of American businesses to sell goods overseas. Roosevelt had avoided dealing with the tariff question during his terms in office because it was so complicated. Taft, however, had promised during his campaign that he would lead a fight to lower the tariff rates.

Taft's inexperience in dealing with Congress hurt his efforts to push for any significant tariff

★ A Conservation Controversy

President Taft often felt misunderstood by the public. Perhaps the greatest public relations disaster of Taft's administration occurred in his battle with Roosevelt's close friend and ally, Chief of Forestry Gifford Pinchot. In 1909 Pinchot accused Secretary of the Interior Richard Ballinger of hurting conservation efforts by siding with the interests of big business and by leasing public lands. Taft tried without success to get the two officials to settle their differences quietly. Pinchot continued to attack Ballinger, and the issue began to attract national attention.

The Ballinger-Pinchot controversy soon turned into a public debate over whether Taft truly supported conservation as strongly as Roosevelt had. Taft was embarrassed by the situation and convinced that the charges made against Ballinger were unfounded. Taft finally decided to fire Pinchot. This act outraged conservationists and many other progressives, including Roosevelt. Taft defended himself, saying:

Gifford Pinchot

❝ If I were to turn Ballinger out, in view of his innocence and in view of the conspiracy against him, I should be a white-livered skunk. ❞

President Taft balances awkwardly as he tries to satisfy both sides during the Ballinger-Pinchot affair.

Congress launched an investigation of Ballinger that resulted in no official charges but which made Taft's administration look worse to many conservationists. Taft was unable to win back progressive support, even though he expanded many of Roosevelt's conservation policies. He also transferred almost as much land into government reserves as Roosevelt had.

★ Roosevelt and the Progressive Party

As the election of 1912 neared, President Taft seemed to be losing much public support. The Republicans had already lost control of the House of Representatives in 1910, which shocked many party leaders.

The New Nationalism

Roosevelt had remained politically active and continued to develop his political philosophy. He expressed his views in a plan for government called the **New Nationalism**. This program called for a strong executive, more active business regulation, and the passage of additional social welfare

measures. In 1910 Roosevelt described his new plan for government:

> ❝ The New Nationalism puts the national need before sectional or personal advantage. This New Nationalism regards the executive power [the president] as the steward of the public welfare. It demands of the judiciary that it shall be interested primarily in human welfare rather than property, just as it demands that the representative body [Congress] shall represent all the people rather than any one class of or section of the people. ❞

Taft was greatly angered by Roosevelt's speech, which he felt insulted the judiciary system and Taft's own antitrust efforts. He began working to reduce Roosevelt's influence in the Republican Party by seeking support from traditional Republicans. Many of these Republicans agreed that Roosevelt had gone too far with his support of government involvement in business and society.

The division between Taft and Roosevelt grew wider. Roosevelt told his oldest son that Taft "has not the slightest idea of what is necessary if this country is to make social and industrial progress." Many progressives agreed with Roosevelt. In 1912, nine Republican governors sent him a letter asking him to run for an unprecedented third term. Roosevelt knew that if he ran again he would be criticized but he agreed anyway. A reporter asked Roosevelt if the rumors about his candidacy were true. "My hat is in the ring!" Roosevelt replied. "The fight is on."

The Bull Moose Party

Roosevelt and his supporters rapidly put together a campaign

A button and bull moose pendant from the presidential campaign

staff. The former president began traveling around the country to challenge Taft for the Republican nomination. In states with direct primaries, Roosevelt was the clear winner, receiving almost twice as many popular votes and many more delegates than Taft. Roosevelt lost the Republican nomination to Taft, however, in a party convention controlled by Taft's supporters.

In response, Roosevelt and his followers formed the Progressive Party. It was nicknamed the **Bull Moose Party** after Roosevelt told a crowd that he was "as strong as a bull moose." The party built its platform around Roosevelt's New Nationalism, promising to give more political power to the American people. Roosevelt declared, "We must drive the special interests out of politics. . . . For every special interest is entitled to justice, but not one is entitled to a vote in Congress."

A cartoon showing Socialist candidate Eugene V. Debs as the king of the labor unions

⭐ The Election of 1912

Three major political opponents ran for the presidency in 1912: Theodore Roosevelt, William Howard Taft, and Democratic Party candidate Woodrow Wilson. In addition, Socialist Party candidate Eugene V. Debs ran for the fourth time.

The Republicans Split

The Progressive Party faced a great challenge, for it had to organize itself quickly to get on the ballot in every state in time for the November election. The young party also had to compete with the powerful Democratic and Republican political machines. Roosevelt's party did receive support from many progressive leaders. For example, Hull House founder Jane Addams stated that "the Progressive Platform contains all I have been fighting for for a decade."

Roosevelt threw himself into the campaign. During one frightening moment in Milwaukee, Wisconsin, Roosevelt was shot by a would-be assassin just before a scheduled speech. Bleeding from the wound,

Roosevelt insisted on giving the speech anyway. Roosevelt told the stunned crowd, "I have just been shot, but it takes more than that to kill a Bull Moose." Despite Roosevelt's energetic campaign efforts, Taft trusted that voters would respect his record and reject Roosevelt's calls for reform.

Woodrow Wilson

The Democratic Party decided to challenge Taft by running pro-reform candidate Woodrow Wilson. Born in Virginia, Wilson earned a doctoral degree in history from the Johns Hopkins University and became a professor in 1890. Beginning in 1902 he served as president of Princeton University until he accepted the Democratic nomination to run for governor of New Jersey in 1910. Wilson's reforms while governor received national attention.

Wilson based his presidential campaign on a program called the **New Freedom**. This program called for government action against monopolies to ensure free competition. In his speeches, Wilson challenged the influence of

The speech and eyeglass case that Theodore Roosevelt was carrying when he was shot on October 14, 1912

big business, encouraged small businesses, and supported reducing the tariff rate.

Wilson began his campaign without much political experience and without support from the Democratic Party. After struggling to gain the Democratic nomination, he won approval as he toured the nation. Wilson impressed voters with his intelligence, bold ideas, and independence from traditional machine politics.

Although Wilson did not receive a majority of the popular vote, he won a majority of electoral votes and thus the presidency. The November 1912 election results showed how damaging the split between Taft and Roosevelt had been for the Republican Party. Together their votes might have been enough to win the election. The number of votes won by Debs, Roosevelt, and Wilson—all reform candidates—also demonstrated the degree to which Americans favored progressive efforts to change society.

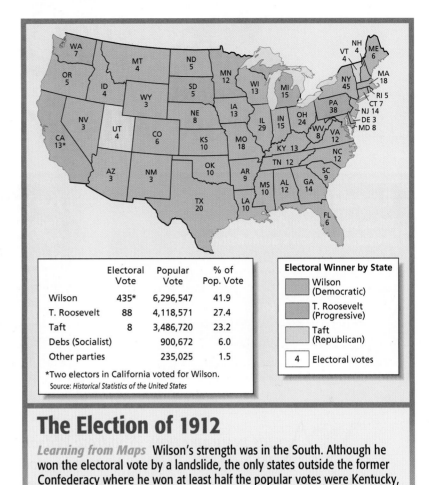

	Electoral Vote	Popular Vote	% of Pop. Vote
Wilson	435*	6,296,547	41.9
T. Roosevelt	88	4,118,571	27.4
Taft	8	3,486,720	23.2
Debs (Socialist)		900,672	6.0
Other parties		235,025	1.5

*Two electors in California voted for Wilson.
Source: Historical Statistics of the United States

Electoral Winner by State
- Wilson (Democratic)
- T. Roosevelt (Progressive)
- Taft (Republican)
- 4 Electoral votes

The Election of 1912

Learning from Maps Wilson's strength was in the South. Although he won the electoral vote by a landslide, the only states outside the former Confederacy where he won at least half the popular votes were Kentucky, Maryland, and Oklahoma.

Location Which state split its electoral vote?

SECTION 2 REVIEW

Identify and explain the significance of the following:
- **William Howard Taft**
- **Payne-Aldrich Tariff**
- **Gifford Pinchot**
- **Richard Ballinger**
- **New Nationalism**
- **Bull Moose Party**
- **Woodrow Wilson**
- **New Freedom**

Reading for Content Understanding

1 **Main Idea** What were the similarities and the differences between Taft's and Roosevelt's views of the presidency?

2 **Main Idea** Why did President Taft's policies upset many progressives?

3 **Citizenship and Democracy** Why and by whom was the Progressive Party created in 1912? What effect did the Progressive Party have on the outcome of the 1912 presidential election?

4 **Writing** *Classifying* Write one or two paragraphs comparing the goals of Roosevelt's New Nationalism program with the goals of Wilson's New Freedom program.

5 **Critical Thinking** *Supporting a Point of View* Do you think that third political parties, such as the Progressive Party, help or hurt the democratic process? Explain your answer.

Woodrow Wilson's Reforms

Reading Focus

What were some characteristics of President Wilson's administration?

What economic reforms did Wilson pursue?

How did Wilson try to regulate corporations?

Key Terms

Underwood Tariff Act

Sixteenth Amendment

Federal Reserve Act

Clayton Antitrust Act

Federal Trade Commission

Keating-Owen Child Labor Act

Adamson Act

Federal Farm Loan Act

AT HIS INAUGURATION, *Woodrow Wilson looked formal and serious as he stood next to a smiling William Howard Taft. While Taft seemed relieved to be leaving office, Wilson concentrated on the responsibility now facing him. In his brief inaugural address, Wilson emphasized the challenges that faced the United States. "This is not a day of triumph, it is a day of dedication," he declared in a calm voice. Wilson asked the crowd before him to look beyond their party loyalties and to consider the work that needed to be done to improve the nation.*

Woodrow Wilson and his family

Wilson in Office

Unlike Taft, who had served in the shadow of Theodore Roosevelt, President Wilson established himself as the clear leader of his administration. As one journalist observed, "[T]his administration is Woodrow Wilson's, and none other's. He is the top, the middle, and the bottom of it."

Many people were puzzled by Woodrow Wilson. He was a capable manager and a good public speaker, but he sometimes seemed cold and proud. While he had strong moral beliefs, he was also willing to be practical about political issues. Wilson was also very private about his ideas. He wrote many official papers on his own, typing them himself late at night. He established regular press meetings at the White House, but he very rarely answered questions directly and refused to be directly quoted in the newspapers.

Wilson was the first Democrat to be elected president in 20 years. In addition, the Democratic Party controlled both houses of Congress. Wilson also appointed many Democrats to government positions. He filled his cabinet with influential

278 Chapter 9

Woodrow Wilson entered the presidency with many new ideas and goals for reform.

party leaders such as William Jennings Bryan, who became secretary of state. Wilson also brought many southern politicians into his administration.

Democrats were eager to prove that they were ready to take charge of the country after so many years of Republican control. They united behind Wilson and his new policies. Wilson convinced congressional leaders to pass his reform measures. In addition, he became the first president since Thomas Jefferson to promote legislation in person before Congress.

 ## Economic Reforms

During his presidential campaign, Wilson had supported two key economic reform measures: tariff reduction and banking reform. Once in office he moved quickly to push these reforms into law.

A New Tariff

President Wilson made tariff reduction the first part of his economic reform plan because he believed that lower tariff rates would help consumers. He therefore threw his support behind the **Underwood Tariff Act** of 1913, overcoming initial resistance from industries that had lobbied to keep rates high. The passage of the Underwood Tariff Act resulted in the lowest tariff rates in many years.

To help make up for the lost tariff revenue, the act also introduced a version of the modern-day income tax on personal earnings. Progressives had fought for years to pass a federal income tax, but the U.S. Supreme Court ruled that such taxes were unconstitutional. The **Sixteenth Amendment**, ratified by the states in February 1913, amended the Constitution and allowed the federal government to pass direct taxes, such as the income tax. Although it was a significant step in government policy, the new tax was quite low and did not affect most Americans.

Reforming the Banking Industry

After the Underwood Tariff Act was passed, Wilson turned his attention to improving the banking system. There were no national regulations governing banks, which resulted in great confusion and an unreliable money supply. Wilson knew banking reform would be much more difficult to pass than the tariff legislation. However, he told his friends confidently, "There is nothing that succeeds in life like boldness, provided you believe you are on the right side."

The Federal Reserve Building in Washington, D.C.

Income Tax

Before the creation of an income tax in 1913, the federal government raised its money primarily from duties and tariffs, which became increasingly unpopular. In the late 1800s, even millionaires such as Andrew Carnegie and John D. Rockefeller paid no tax on their personal earnings.

The IRS Data Processing Center in Austin, Texas

The new income tax was a progressive tax. This meant that it took a larger percentage from someone with a high income than from someone with a low income. The tax was quite small, with a maximum rate of 7 percent. The income tax applied to about 4 percent of wage earners because yearly income below $4,000 was exempt, or free, from taxes. This was at a time when the average annual income was about $900.

Despite these modest beginnings, the income tax quickly became an important way for the federal government to raise money, particularly during wartime. Just a few years after the tax law was passed, for example, the maximum tax rate was temporarily raised to 77 percent to help fund national defense.

Many states also began collecting personal income tax in the early 1900s to help pay the cost of running state governments and of establishing new urban reforms.

As late as 1939, most Americans still did not have to pay federal taxes. This changed during the 1940s, when the minimum taxable income was lowered. As the federal government has received more tax money, it has greatly increased the number of benefits and services it provides to the public.

Today, the majority of Americans who earn wages must pay federal income taxes. In 1994 the federal government received more than 115 million personal income tax returns and collected almost $600 billion in income tax. The Internal Revenue Service (IRS) employs thousands of people to process these returns, which represent the government's single largest source of revenue.

Understanding What You Read

1. Why do the federal and state governments tax personal income?

2. What might motivate a government to raise or lower taxes?

One obstacle to banking reform was the lack of agreement on this issue among Wilson's fellow Democrats in Congress. Some wanted a central banking system controlled by the government. Others favored a decentralized system run by private bankers. Banking reform also met strong opposition from Republican leaders. Senator Henry Cabot Lodge, for example, called the president's economic reforms "dreadful assaults on business." In spite of these challenges, Wilson stayed firm. He insisted that the banking system had to be changed and that it needed to be run by the government to ensure fairness.

The result was a compromise called the **Federal Reserve Act**. Passed in December 1913, the act created a banking system called the Federal Reserve. This system is made up of 12 regional Federal Reserve banks as well as privately owned banks. The Federal Reserve is overseen by an independent decision-making body that controls banking policy. The passage of the Federal Reserve Act gave stability to the national banking system. Over time, the Federal Reserve has also become responsible for regulating bank deposits and interest rates. This gives the federal government a way to try to minimize sudden changes between boom and bust cycles in the economy.

 ## Regulating Big Business

Having created what he felt was a sound economic foundation for the country, President Wilson pushed for additional legislation regulating big business. Like Taft, Wilson distrusted the power of monopolies and trusts. "If there are men in this country big enough to own the government of the United States, they are going to [try to] own it," he warned. Wilson wanted a more powerful version of the Sherman Antitrust Act that could be used to break up these trusts.

The **Clayton Antitrust Act**, passed in October 1914, strengthened federal laws against business monopolies. The act also specifically stated that labor unions had the right to bargain collectively and go on strike. This prevented the new law from being used against organized labor as the Sherman Antitrust Act had been. Union leaders such as AFL president Samuel Gompers praised the Clayton Antitrust Act as a breakthrough for organized labor. However, state and federal courts often continued to favor business interests when interpreting the new law.

To further regulate corporations, Congress established the **Federal Trade Commission** (FTC) in 1914. The five-person commission was given broad powers to examine company records and investigate business practices. The commission passed along this information to the president and Congress. The FTC was also able to issue restraining orders to stop "unfair trade practices" from continuing. Over time, the FTC's role has expanded. Today, it also enforces business regulations and establishes standards for advertising and product labeling.

Wilson hoped that his antitrust efforts would provide open and fair competition while allowing

President Wilson using antitrust laws to challenge the power of greedy trusts

business to prosper. He predicted that the legislation he helped pass would be "the final step in setting the business of this country free." However, Republicans rejected Wilson's claim that his economic reforms had helped business. One Republican politician declared that business leaders were convinced Wilson had "put through a dangerous and destructive legislative program in which he has ignored every protest made by them."

 ## Changes in Policy

Wilson believed that many social issues, such as women's rights, were best addressed by state governments rather than by the federal government. He also wanted to keep the support of business leaders and of southern Democrats. For these reasons he was at first reluctant to support laws intended to help organized labor or to support women's suffrage.

Wilson was also hesitant to reach out to minority groups. Although he had pledged during his campaign to support greater opportunities for

Progressive Presidential Reforms, 1906–1914

REFORM LAWS	PASSED UNDER PRESIDENT	RESULTS
The **National Monuments Act** (1906) allowed the president to declare certain areas on federal lands to be protected historic or scientific landmarks.	T. Roosevelt	Roosevelt created national monuments that later became national parks, including the Grand Canyon in Arizona and Zion in Utah. Later presidents have added to this list.
The **Pure Food and Drug Act** (1906) prohibited the manufacture, sale, or transportation of mislabeled or contaminated food and drugs sold in interstate commerce.	T. Roosevelt	The law was a breakthrough in public health reform. It also increased Roosevelt's public support.
The **Payne-Aldrich Tariff** (1909) lowered tariffs on raw materials such as coal, iron, and lumber.	Taft	Progressives opposed the law, which left many tariff rates unchanged and raised some others.
The **Underwood Tariff Act** (1913) reduced tariffs on many goods by one third and created the first federal income tax.	Wilson	The public applauded the lower tariff rates, and the income tax became an important source of federal revenue.
The **Federal Reserve Act** (1913) created a special board to regulate the banking industry.	Wilson	The Federal Reserve provided stability to the banking industry and now influences the economy by setting the prime interest rate.
The **Clayton Antitrust Act** (1914) greatly strengthened antimonopoly laws and recognized organized labor's right to collective bargaining and to strike.	Wilson	For many years the law was limited by Supreme Court rulings. It is still in effect today.
The **Federal Trade Commission Act** (1914) created an independent commission to investigate businesses and issue complaints about unfair practices.	Wilson	The Federal Trade Commission still investigates business practices and helps enforce laws such as the Clayton Antitrust Act.

African Americans, he did not keep this promise. In "An Open Letter to Woodrow Wilson," W. E. B. Du Bois wrote:

> **"Not a single act and not a single word of yours since election has given anyone reason to infer [believe] that you have the slightest interest in the colored people or desire to alleviate [make easier] their intolerable position."**

In order to satisfy the demand of southern politicians, Wilson agreed to the racial segregation of federal facilities in Washington, D.C. This action was met by protests from African American leaders and caused Wilson to lose support among some progressives.

As the presidential race of 1916 approached, Wilson increased his support for progressive reforms by focusing on the needs of farmers and wage earners. He appointed Louis Brandeis, a progressive lawyer, to the U.S. Supreme Court. Brandeis was known nationally as "the people's attorney" for taking cases free of charge on behalf of consumers and laborers. The appointment sparked controversy. Nevertheless, after a fierce four-month battle between progressive supporters and conservative opponents, Brandeis was confirmed, becoming the first Jewish American to sit on the U.S. Supreme Court.

W. E. B. Du Bois challenged racism as the editor of the NAACP magazine, The Crisis.

In September 1916 Wilson helped pass the **Keating-Owen Child Labor Act**. This legislation prohibited companies from shipping their products across state lines if they employed children under the age of 14. In 1918, however, the Supreme Court overturned the act by ruling that only the states could regulate child labor.

Other progressive reforms backed by Wilson included a law requiring workers' compensation for federal employees. He also supported the **Adamson Act**, which limited the workday on the nation's railroads to eight hours. Finally, to help farmers, he supported the **Federal Farm Loan Act**. This act made it easier for farmers to obtain credit.

Although Republicans attacked these measures, many progressives and some socialists approved of Wilson's new reform efforts. As a result, they began to rally around the president. At the start of his 1916 presidential campaign, Wilson announced proudly:

❝ **We have in four years come very near to carrying out the platform of the Progressive Party as well as our own; for we are also progressives.** ❞

The Keating-Owen Child Labor Act was an effort to address the situation of children such as these cannery workers.

In the campaign Wilson faced Republican Charles Evans Hughes, a former U.S. Supreme Court justice. Both Wilson and Hughes received support from former members of the Progressive Party. Wilson won a narrow victory, receiving 277 electoral votes to Hughes's 254.

Wilson displayed great skill and determination at guiding his reform programs through Congress. His work helped unite a Democratic Party that included members with very different views. Wilson explained to a friend that he had a talent for putting his mind "at the service of others for the accomplishment of a common purpose." His impressive legislative record reflects the many progressive reforms put into place by 1920.

SECTION 3 REVIEW

Identify and explain the significance of the following:
- **Underwood Tariff Act**
- **Sixteenth Amendment**
- **Federal Reserve Act**
- **Clayton Antitrust Act**
- **Federal Trade Commission**
- **Louis Brandeis**
- **Keating-Owen Child Labor Act**
- **Adamson Act**
- **Federal Farm Loan Act**

Reading for Content Understanding

1 **Main Idea** What was the style of President Wilson's administration?

2 **Main Idea** What steps did Wilson take to regulate big business?

3 **Economic Development** What economic reforms did Wilson achieve in his first term?

4 **Writing** *Informing* Imagine that you are a member of the Democratic Party in 1912. Explain how your party gained influence following the presidential election.

5 **Critical Thinking** *Drawing Conclusions* Why do you think Wilson's reform policies changed during his presidency? Give several reasons to support your answer.

The Progressive Presidents **283**

CHAPTER 9 REVIEW

Chapter Summary

The progressive movement gained supporters in both the Democratic and Republican Parties. In 1912 the Progressive Party was formed. Presidents Theodore Roosevelt, William Howard Taft, and Woodrow Wilson each helped pass a series of progressive reforms. These included efforts to control big business, improve the economy, build relations between labor and management, and conserve the environment. ▪

On a separate sheet of paper, complete the following activities.

Identifying People and Ideas

Describe the historical significance of the following:

1. Theodore Roosevelt
2. arbitration
3. Pure Food and Drug Act
4. conservation
5. William Howard Taft
6. Bull Moose Party
7. Woodrow Wilson
8. Sixteenth Amendment
9. Federal Reserve Act
10. Clayton Antitrust Act

Internet Activity

go.hrw.com
SB1 Federal Reserve

Search the Internet through the HRW Web site to find information about how the Federal Reserve system works today. Use this information to create a graphic organizer that shows how the Federal Reserve's actions affect the economy.

Understanding Main Ideas

1. What was President Roosevelt's Square Deal?
2. How did Roosevelt respond to Upton Sinclair's *The Jungle*?
3. What were President Taft's business and economic reform policies?
4. Why did Taft lose the support of Roosevelt and many other progressives?
5. How did President Wilson help reform the banking industry?
6. What labor reforms were passed during Wilson's presidency?

Reviewing Themes

1. **Economic Development**   What actions did Presidents Roosevelt, Taft, and Wilson take to regulate large corporations?
2. **Geographic Diversity**   What was the conservation movement? Who were some of its leaders?
3. **Citizenship and Democracy**   Why was the Progressive Party created?

Using the Time Line

Number your paper from 1 to 5. Match the letters on the time line below with the following events.

1. **President McKinley is assassinated.**
2. **William Howard Taft is elected president of the United States.**
3. **The Sixteenth Amendment is ratified, allowing a personal income tax.**
4. **Public concern over food safety leads to the passage of the Pure Food and Drug Act.**
5. **The Clayton Antitrust Act is passed.**

| 1900 | 1902 | 1904 | 1906 | 1908 | 1910 | 1912 | 1914 | 1916 | 1918 |

a   b   c   d   e

Thinking Critically

1. **Making Comparisons**   How did Roosevelt's view of the presidency differ from that of previous presidents? Use examples from his administration to explain your answer.

2. **Evaluating**   Which of the progressive presidents do you think was most successful in reforming American society? Explain your answer.

3. **Identifying Cause and Effect**   What effect did the formation of the Progressive Party have on the presidential election of 1912?

Writing About History

1. **Informing**   Write a short newspaper article comparing Roosevelt's New Nationalism program with Wilson's New Freedom platform.

2. **Expressing**   Write a letter to the editor stating your view on whether Roosevelt was right to choose Taft as his successor to the presidency.

Linking Geography and History

1. **Region**   In what region of the country were most of the national parks and natural forests created? Why do you think this was the case?

2. **Human-Environment Interaction**   What issue divided some members of the conservation movement?

Building Your Portfolio

Complete the following activities individually or in groups.

1. **Theodore Roosevelt**   Use your textbook or the library to find information about the life of Theodore Roosevelt. Focus on the following topics: Roosevelt the Conservationist, Roosevelt the Rancher, Roosevelt the Trustbuster, Roosevelt the Family Man, or Roosevelt the President. Use this information to write a biography about several aspects of Roosevelt's life. You should include some quotations by Roosevelt himself, as well as by other people talking about Roosevelt.

2. **National Parks**   Use the library or other resources to find information about the national parks, monuments, wildlife refuges, or forests nearest you. Choose one of these locations and create a small brochure describing the area and explaining when and why it was founded. You should include pictures or a map with the brochure.

History Skills Workshop

Using Visual Resources   Study the image to the right, which is a political cartoon of Theodore Roosevelt during the presidential campaign of 1912. The box behind Roosevelt is labeled *Vox Populi Vox Mei,* which in Latin means "The voice of the public is my voice." (a) Why do you think the artist drew Roosevelt as a king? (b) What message do you think the cartoon is trying to communicate to the public about Roosevelt's campaign? (c) What is the cartoon suggesting about Roosevelt's personality?

■ CHAPTER 10 ■
America As a World Power
(1865–1914)

While campaigning for the Senate in 1898, Albert J. Beveridge declared, "If England can govern foreign lands, so can America." Previously the United States had expanded only across the North American continent. However, as the 1800s came to a close, many Americans began to look overseas for a source of new lands. Beveridge summed up this attitude by saying that "the ocean does not separate us from lands of our duty and desire."

THEMES

Geographic Diversity
Why might a nation attempt to expand its boundaries?

Economic Development
For what reasons might a nation want to increase international trade?

Global Relations
How might a nation's overseas territories bring it into conflict with another nation?

1865	1870	1875	1880	1885

1867 The United States purchases Alaska.

1877 Porfirio Díaz takes power in Mexico.

1881 A French company begins building a canal across the Isthmus of Panama.

1887 Planters force King Kalakaua to grant more power to the Hawaiian parliament, which they control.

The United States Gains Overseas Territories

Reading Focus

Why did some people favor expansion over isolationism?

What events led to the U.S. annexation of Hawaii?

What was the goal of U.S. foreign policy in Japan and China?

Key Terms

imperialism
isolationism
McKinley Tariff
subsidy
spheres of influence
Open Door Policy
Boxer Rebellion

O N THE MORNING OF MARCH 16, 1889, *the crews of one British, three German, and three U.S. war-ships prepared for a possible battle. At any moment the peace of Apia Harbor—a port in the Pacific island-nation of Samoa—might erupt with blasts of heavy guns. The United States, Germany, and Britain had each sent their ships to gain control of the Samoa Islands. Before the warships could do battle, however, a sudden typhoon swept into the harbor, destroying all the ships except the British vessel. Although the typhoon had prevented hostilities that day, it did not end Western nations' competition for territories around the world.*

Cartoon showing the United States and European nations struggling for power over the Samoans

IMAGE ON LEFT PAGE: *Battle of Manila Bay during the Spanish-American War*

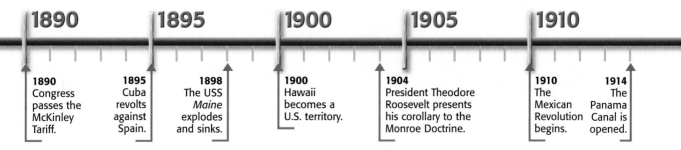

1890

1895

1900

1905

1910

1890
Congress passes the McKinley Tariff.

1895
Cuba revolts against Spain.

1898
The USS *Maine* explodes and sinks.

1900
Hawaii becomes a U.S. territory.

1904
President Theodore Roosevelt presents his corollary to the Monroe Doctrine.

1910
The Mexican Revolution begins.

1914
The Panama Canal is opened.

★ Imperialism and Isolationism

Powerful Western nations were willing to risk war in such far-off places as Samoa to establish a naval base and to protect shipping routes in the Pacific. By the late 1800s the nations of Europe had become engaged in **imperialism**—the practice of extending a nation's power by gaining territories for a colonial empire. Between 1870 and 1914, Europeans built vast colonial empires, seizing control of most of Africa and much of Southeast Asia.

Several forces drove this wave of imperialism. Nations wanted new and plentiful sources of raw materials, such as copper, tin, and rubber, to maintain their industrial growth. At the same time, businesspeople needed new markets in which to sell their goods. Many people also saw colonies as a source of power and national pride.

The United States, however, had not built an overseas colonial empire like many European nations had. Americans were pursuing a limited policy of **isolationism**—avoiding involvement in the affairs of other nations. In his Farewell Address, President George Washington had advised the United States "to steer clear of permanent alliances" with other nations, particularly in Europe. U.S. leaders had tried to follow this advice by avoiding involvement in conflicts overseas.

Washington's advice had been fairly easy to follow partly because the United States enjoyed the security of a wide ocean separating it from Europe. Good relations with Britain meant that the powerful British navy stood between the United States and possible European enemies. Despite their support of isolationism, many Americans favored expanding the U.S. economy through foreign trade and building a strong military to protect U.S. interests.

★ Expansion

Many Americans thought that the United States needed to expand its lands to maintain its economic strength. One well-known supporter of expansion was Alfred T. Mahan. In his book *The Influence of Sea Power upon History*, Mahan argued that the United States needed a strong navy to protect its economic interests. Mahan also explained that a strong navy required overseas bases and coaling stations—places where steamships could take on coal for fuel. Senator Henry Cabot Lodge echoed the call for economic expansion through naval power. "Commerce follows the flag," Lodge declared, "and we should build up a navy strong enough to give protection to Americans in every quarter of the globe."

In 1867 the United States greatly expanded its territory when Secretary of State William Seward arranged the purchase of Alaska from Russia for $7.2 million, less than two cents per acre. People laughed at the purchase, calling it "Seward's Folly" and the "Alaskan Icebox." Despite such criticism, Alaska added some 600,000 square miles to the United States—an area more than twice the size of Texas. Alaska contained natural resources such as furs, timber, and mineral wealth. The 1896 Klondike Gold Rush in Canada's Yukon Territory brought many miners to the region. Around 1900, miners found gold in Alaska, bringing more settlers to the region.

Seward believed that the United States "must continue to move on westward," and in 1867 the nation annexed the Midway Islands. The islands' location, about halfway between the U.S. West

Uncle Sam begins to reap the harvest of imperialism.

The Granger Collection, New York

Alaska's beautiful scenery and natural resources made it a valuable addition to the United States in the long run.

Coast and Japan, made Midway an excellent base and coaling station for the U.S. Navy. The United States also wanted the island group of Samoa for similar reasons, and in 1899 Germany and the United States agreed to divide the Samoa Islands. Britain, interested in territories elsewhere, had given up its part of Samoa to Germany.

Hawaii

Even more appealing than Samoa were the Hawaiian Islands. The Hawaiian people had first come in contact with Europeans in 1778, when British explorer Captain James Cook arrived in the islands.

Economic Interests

Soon after Cook's arrival, Pacific trading and whaling ships from the United States and other countries began stopping in Hawaii for supplies. After the sailors' arrival, American missionaries came to convert the Hawaiians to Christianity. Many of these missionaries remained in the islands, establishing businesses and raising crops such as sugarcane. Some missionary families eventually became wealthy sugar planters.

In 1795 Chief Kamehameha (kuh-may-uh-MAY-huh) had created a monarchy that united Hawaii's eight major islands. In 1839 Hawaii adopted written laws and a constitution based on U.S. and British models.

By the 1840s some 80 percent of the ships arriving in Hawaii were American owned, as were most shops, warehouses, and shipyards. By this time, sugar had become a leading export of the Hawaiian economy. Thousands of workers, particularly Chinese and Japanese, arrived to work on the sugar plantations. An 1875 treaty allowed Hawaiian sugar to be shipped duty-free to the United States. In exchange, Hawaii agreed not to grant territory or special privileges to any nation other than the United States. Hawaiian sugar production boomed, and the planters' influence grew. In 1887 they forced King Kalakaua (kah-LAH-KAH-ooh-ah) to sign a new constitution granting more power to the Hawaiian parliament, which the planters controlled. Many Hawaiians worried that foreigners were becoming too powerful.

Political Control

Sugar planters in Hawaii suffered a severe economic setback when Congress passed the **McKinley Tariff** in 1890. This law allowed all countries to ship sugar duty-free to the United

Pineapple plantations like this one were among the most profitable businesses on the Hawaiian Islands.

Queen Liliuokalani

Liliuokalani was born in Honolulu in 1838 and was educated by American missionaries. In 1887 she traveled across the United States and visited with President Grover Cleveland in Washington.

Liliuokalani became queen in 1891. After the revolt that ended her short reign, Liliuokalani continued to work to reclaim her throne. In her autobiography, *Hawaii's Story*, she wrote that "the United States could become a successful rival of the European nations in the race for conquest, and could create a vast military and naval power." She asked, "But is such an ambition laudable [admirable]?" Until her death in 1917 Liliuokalani served as a symbol of Hawaiian pride and a link to the islands' history.

States but gave U.S. sugar producers a **subsidy**, or bonus payment, of two cents per pound. Prices for Hawaiian sugar dropped, and the islands' economy collapsed.

In 1893 Queen Liliuokalani (li-lee-uh-woh-kuh-LAHN-ee), who had taken the throne in 1891, announced a new constitution that returned power to the monarchy. The planters revolted. John L. Stevens, U.S. ambassador to Hawaii, called 150 marines ashore to support the revolt. The revolt succeeded without any shots being fired. The planters established a new government with lawyer Sanford B. Dole as president. Acting without authority from the state department, Stevens recognized the new government and declared Hawaii to be under U.S. control on February 1, 1893. He wrote to the U.S. State Department that "the Hawaiian pear is now fully ripe, and this is the golden hour for the United States to pluck it." On a U.S. speaking tour at the time, Liliuokalani's 17-year-old niece, Princess Kaiulani, asked Americans to oppose annexation:

> ❝ I am strong . . . in the strength of seventy million people who in this free land will hear my cry, and will refuse to let their flag . . . dishonor . . . mine. ❞

President Grover Cleveland disapproved of the revolt and refused to annex Hawaii. However, he took little effective action to help restore the monarchy. The islands remained an independent republic until July 7, 1898, when Congress annexed them. Hawaii became a U.S. territory in 1900 and the 50th state in 1959.

★ The Opening of Japan

By the mid-1800s some European powers had established strong trade ties to much of East Asia—with the notable exception of Japan. The island-nation of Japan had isolated itself from the rest of the world for centuries. In the 1500s Japan was ruled by several competing family groups, some led by warrior-lords called shoguns. After an extended period of civil war, the leader of the Tokugawa family unified the country.

Suspicious of outsiders, the Tokugawa shoguns had expelled all westerners in the early 1600s. Only the Dutch East India Company was allowed to trade, and only at one port. The Tokugawa had also forbidden travel abroad.

Perry in Japan

The United States looked upon Japan as a trade market it could open before Europeans got there. The *Democratic Review* expressed the feelings of many Americans when it wrote that "the opening of commerce with Japan is demanded by reason, civilization, progress and religion." Eager to overcome Japan's isolationism, President Millard Fillmore sent Commodore Matthew Perry to secure "friendship, commerce, a supply of coal and provisions."

On July 8, 1853, an astonished Japanese crowd watched a fleet of four U.S. warships move into Edo (now called Tokyo) Harbor. Perry delivered a letter from President Fillmore suggesting a peaceful trade relationship. Perry's fleet then sailed off, and he returned in February 1854 with seven warships. To show some of the technological gains that trade with the United States would offer, Perry presented Japanese leaders with gifts of a telegraph transmitter and a model train. However, it was mostly the U.S. show of force that persuaded Japanese leaders to sign a treaty opening trade with the United States. Many Japanese leaders also pushed for trade because they believed that their country needed to industrialize.

In 1856 Townsend Harris arrived in Japan as the first U.S. consul general, or chief diplomat. His instructions were to secure a treaty that would open Japan to further trade. This was difficult because, as Harris wrote, "the absence of a man-of-war [warship] . . . tends to weaken my influence with the Japanese." He eventually overcame Japanese opposition and in 1858 negotiated a commercial treaty.

Japan Expands

In 1868, supporters of industrialization came to power in Japan and began a period of modernization known as the Meiji [MAY-jee] Restoration. Over the next 40 years, Japanese leaders invested heavily in industry and in strengthening the nation's military. The government sent Japanese students to Western schools to learn about modern science and technology and Western government. One such student, Yukichi Fukuzawa, realized

❝ **what policy Japan must take to preserve herself among the powers of the**

Global Connections

Japanese Immigrants in Hawaii

Japanese immigrants began arriving in Hawaii in the 1860s but did not immigrate in large numbers until later in the 1800s. By 1923 they made up almost 43 percent of the population. Many Japanese were recruited and signed labor contracts to work on the islands' many sugar plantations. They came in search of more opportunities.

Japanese fieldworkers in Hawaii

Life on the plantations was difficult. The workday began at sunrise and ended at sundown. The working conditions were harsh, as workers planted, weeded, fertilized, watered, harvested, and hauled the sugarcane.

Many Japanese immigrants remained in Hawaii once their contracts expired because they could not afford to return to Japan. Some, believing there was a potential market for Japanese products, started their own businesses, such as importing food, clothing, and hardware.

Today people of Japanese descent make up about one fourth of Hawaii's population. They live on all the major islands and work in all occupations, including government, law, and education.

Understanding What You Read

1. Describe the working conditions on Hawaii's sugar plantations.

2. How have Japanese immigrants contributed to Hawaiian society?

world. . . . The final purpose of all my work was to create in Japan a civilized nation as well equipped in the arts of war and peace as those of the Western world."

By the end of the century, Japan was emerging as a major imperial power. Japan's invasion and defeat of China in 1894-95 gave the Japanese the same trade privileges in China as European nations had.

Japan dealt a similar blow to Russia. In 1904 the Japanese attacked Russian forces stationed in China. The Japanese won early victories over the Russians in the Russo-Japanese War. Japan sank an entire Russian fleet in a single battle. In 1905 U.S. president Theodore Roosevelt helped negotiate a peace treaty to end the war. Japan had won the respect it desired and had gained Korea, as well as a lease on Port Arthur in China, and other rights. In less than 50 years Japan had gone from an isolated nonindustrial country to a major world power. Hilary Herbert, U.S. secretary of the navy, said that "Japan has leaped, almost at one bound, to a place among the great nations of the earth."

Asian goods like this fan were popular trade items.

Peabody Essex Museum, Salem, Massachusetts

★ Foreign Powers in China

Economic interests drew the United States not only to Hawaii and Japan but also to China. There the United States and many European nations engaged in a profitable trade.

Spheres of Influence

Japan's 1894 invasion of China with a modern, well-equipped army had resulted in a swift and surprisingly easy victory. In its defeat, China granted Japan trade privileges and formally accepted Japan's control of Korea. China surrendered Taiwan and other territories to Japan.

Other nations quickly took advantage of China's weakness to seize **spheres of influence**—areas where foreign nations control trade and natural resources. Many nations joined in what was called "the carving up of the Chinese melon." Germany took control of a harbor in Shandong Province in November 1897. Other nations followed suit—Russia in the north, Great Britain on the coast opposite Hong Kong Island, and France and Japan in the southern provinces.

The Open Door

The United States feared that it would be closed out of Chinese markets. Some of President William McKinley's advisers called for a U.S.

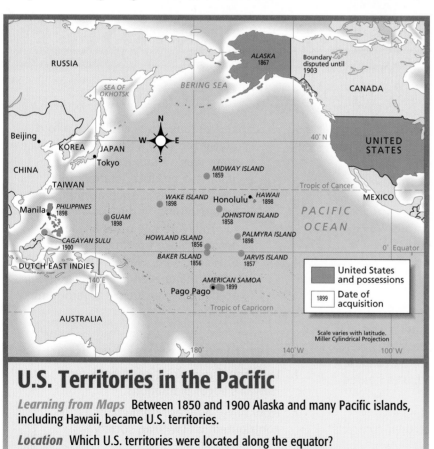

U.S. Territories in the Pacific

Learning from Maps Between 1850 and 1900 Alaska and many Pacific islands, including Hawaii, became U.S. territories.

Location Which U.S. territories were located along the equator?

sphere of influence, but the nation lacked the naval power to accomplish this. Instead, the United States turned to diplomacy.

In 1899 Secretary of State John Hay sent a series of notes to Japan and most European nations outlining what became known as the **Open Door Policy**—that all nations should have equal access to trade with China. The goal of this policy was to protect U.S. trade interests. Japan and the European powers neither accepted nor rejected the Open Door Policy. Hay took advantage of this situation to announce that the policy had been accepted.

Participants in the Boxer Rebellion

The Boxer Rebellion

Within China, there was strong resentment of the power and control held by foreign nations. In 1900 this antiforeign hostility boiled over, producing the **Boxer Rebellion**. The Boxers were Chinese nationalists who were members of the "Fists of Righteous Harmony." The Boxers were angered by foreign involvement in Chinese affairs, mismanagement by the Chinese government, and the hunger and homelessness caused by a series of natural disasters.

In June 1900 the Boxers took to the streets of Beijing, China's capital, and murdered two foreign diplomats. They then laid siege to the walled settlement in which foreigners lived, killing more than 200 people. Knowing the attack was doomed, the Chinese government did not support the Boxers.

The siege continued for two months until military forces including U.S. Marines fought their way from the port of Tianjin to Beijing. The Boxers were soon defeated. Afterward, China was forced to accept a harsh settlement that included a $333 million cash payment, $25 million of which went to the United States. Secretary of State Hay then sent another Open Door note to Japan and the European nations, restating the U.S. position that all nations should have equal access to Chinese markets. Hay wanted to prevent any European colonization of China that would limit U.S. influence there. The Open Door Policy remained in effect long after the Boxer Rebellion.

SECTION 1 REVIEW

Identify and explain the significance of the following:
- **imperialism**
- **isolationism**
- **William Seward**
- **McKinley Tariff**
- **subsidy**
- **Liliuokalani**
- **Matthew Perry**
- **spheres of influence**
- **Open Door Policy**
- **Boxer Rebellion**

Reading for Content Understanding

1 **Main Idea** What arguments did people make for isolationism and for expansion in the 1800s?

2 **Main Idea** How did Hawaii become a part of the United States?

3 **Global Relations** What did U.S. leaders hope to accomplish in relations with Japan and China?

4 **Writing** *Persuading* Imagine that you are a member of Congress at the time William Seward proposes the purchase of Alaska from Russia. Write a short speech you might give to Congress, explaining why you are voting for or against the proposed purchase.

5 **Critical Thinking** *Making Comparisons* How were China's and Japan's reactions to foreign trade similar? How were they different?

SECTION 2

The Spanish-American War

Reading Focus

How did the press affect U.S. involvement in the conflict in Cuba?

What enabled the United States to win the war with Spain?

How did the Spanish-American War affect the Philippines, Cuba, and Puerto Rico?

Key Terms

yellow journalism

Teller Amendment

Anti-Imperialist League

Platt Amendment

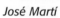

JOSÉ MARTÍ WAS BORN in Havana, Cuba, on January 28, 1853. At the age of 15, Martí joined in a revolt against Cuba's Spanish rulers. For his actions, Martí was banished to Spain, where he earned a university degree. He later worked in Mexico as a journalist and in Guatemala as a teacher. Martí returned to Cuba in 1878 but was banished again for his actions. This time, he moved to New York City, where he continued to work tirelessly for Cuban independence. While anxiously watching events in his homeland, Martí waited for the day when he could return to fight the Spanish once again.

José Martí

 ## Revolts Against Spain

In the late 1800s only Cuba and Puerto Rico remained of Spain's once-great American empire. In 1868, Cubans revolted, beginning a decade-long struggle for freedom. Spain eventually regained control and forced many members of the Cuban independence movement, like José Martí, to leave the country.

After the revolt, U.S. trade with Cuba grew, and the United States invested some $50 million in Cuba, mostly in sugar and mining. However, in 1894 the Wilson-Gorman Tariff removed Cuban

sugar from the list of duty-free products. This made Cuban sugar more expensive in the United States and harmed the Cuban economy.

In 1895 Cuba again erupted in revolt, further damaging its trade with the United States. Martí returned to Cuba to fight the Spanish but was killed soon after. He quickly became a Cuban hero. Spain decided to crack down harshly on Cuba, and sent General Valeriano Weyler to crush the rebellion. Because so many civilians supported the rebels, Weyler gathered several hundred thousand Cubans into barbed-wire camps, called *reconcentrados*, or reconcentration camps. He

294 Chapter 10

reasoned that anyone not in the camps was a rebel. More than 100,000 Cubans died in the camps because of bad and inadequate food and lack of sanitation. Weyler's harsh measures led many Americans to support the rebels.

The Road to War

Many Americans sympathized with the rebels, believing that the Cubans' struggle for liberation was similar to that of the United States in 1776. The conflict was widely reported, even exaggerated, in the American press, further increasing support for the Cubans.

The Press

Two newspapers—Joseph Pulitzer's New York *World* and William Randolph Hearst's *New York* *Journal*—were particularly critical of the Spanish. Their harsh words and stories were part of a competition between Pulitzer and Hearst to sell the most newspapers. This use of sensational, often exaggerated stories to attract readers is known as **yellow journalism**.

Pulitzer was the first to engage in yellow journalism, but Hearst soon outdid Pulitzer at his own game. Describing General Weyler as "pitiless, cold, an exterminator of men," the *New York Journal* went so far as to create the stories that Hearst wanted. To increase support for U.S. action in Cuba and to sell papers, Hearst hired artist and illustrator Frederic Remington to provide pictures of the conditions on the island. Remington supposedly telegraphed Hearst from Cuba, saying, "Everything is quiet. There is no trouble here. There will be no war." Hearst is said to have replied, "You furnish the pictures and I'll furnish the war."

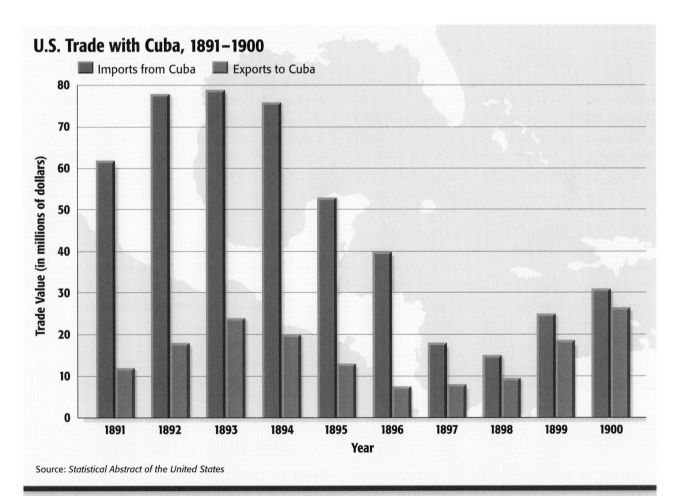

U.S. Trade with Cuba, 1891–1900

Source: *Statistical Abstract of the United States*

The Value of Trade The valuable trade with Cuba was a factor in the U.S. decision to go to war with Spain. What was the value of imports from Cuba in 1896?

Political Pressure

Despite growing support for military action, President Cleveland remained strongly opposed to involvement in Cuba. In 1896, however, William McKinley, who supported Cuban independence, was elected president.

Growing international protest over the treatment of Cubans led the Spanish government to recall General Weyler in October 1897. Attempting to end the rebellion, Spain offered to grant Cubans autonomy—self-government without independence. However, Cuban rebels were committed to independence and refused the offer.

"Remember the *Maine*"

Several events led to war in Cuba. On February 9, 1898, Hearst published a letter that Dupuy de Lôme, the Spanish minister to the United States, had written to a friend. In it, de Lôme called President McKinley "weak and a bidder for the admiration of the crowd." The Spanish government was embarrassed by the letter, but many Americans were outraged.

On January 25, before Hearst published de Lôme's letter, the U.S. battleship *Maine* arrived in Havana Harbor to protect U.S. citizens and economic interests. Senator Mark Hanna compared this action to "waving a match in an oil well for fun." On February 15 the *Maine* exploded and sank with a loss of 260 men. Although the cause of the explosion was unclear, many Americans immediately blamed Spain. "Remember the *Maine!*" quickly became a rallying cry for angry Americans.

Congress approved $50 million that McKinley requested to prepare for war. Spain offered to negotiate but would not consider Cuban

independence. Even though Cuba was not a U.S. territory, on April 20 Congress issued a resolution that declared Cuba independent. That same resolution also gave Spain three days to leave the island. Attached to the resolution was the **Teller Amendment**, which declared that the United States had no intention of taking over Cuba. In response to the U.S. resolution, Spain declared war on April 24. The next day, Congress passed and McKinley signed a declaration of war.

President William McKinley

⭐ Fighting in the Pacific

While attention was focused on Cuba, the U.S. Navy won a quick and spectacular victory nearly halfway around the world in the Pacific Ocean. Commodore George Dewey, commander of the American Asiatic squadron at Hong Kong, had orders to be prepared to attack the Spanish Philippines in the event of war. On April 30 Dewey arrived at the Philippines with four large warships and two smaller gunboats. The next day, ignoring reports that mines barred his way, he boldly sailed into Manila Bay and destroyed Spain's Pacific fleet there. Dewey's forces sank or captured 10 ships. While the Spanish lost 381 lives, none of Dewey's men were killed.

Dewey's victory put him in an awkward position—he had defeated the Spanish but did not have the troops necessary to occupy the islands. He decided to wait for reinforcements. Troops eventually arrived and on August 13, one day after the war had ended, U.S. troops and Filipino rebels led by Emilio Aguinaldo (ahg-ee-NAHL-doh) took control of the Philippine capital, Manila.

⭐ The War in the Caribbean

Many people expected victory in Cuba to come as quickly as it had in the Philippines. However, training and supplying thousands of volunteer troops took longer than getting the navy under way.

The New York Journal *announces the explosion aboard the* Maine.

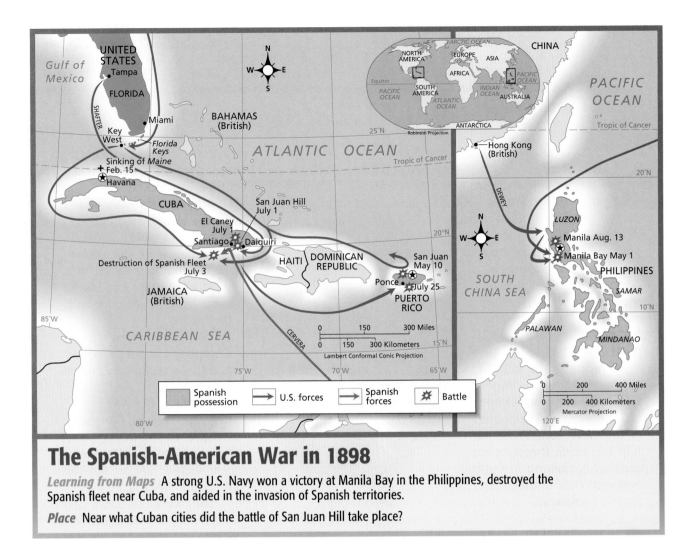

The Spanish-American War in 1898

Learning from Maps A strong U.S. Navy won a victory at Manila Bay in the Philippines, destroyed the Spanish fleet near Cuba, and aided in the invasion of Spanish territories.

Place Near what Cuban cities did the battle of San Juan Hill take place?

The Soldiers

At the start of the war, only about 28,000 soldiers were serving in the regular U.S. Army. The army was unprepared to train and supply the more than 280,000 soldiers who would see active duty. There were shortages of bullets and rifles, and soldiers received warm woolen uniforms to wear in the tropical heat. Once in Cuba, many soldiers were struck by deadly diseases such as yellow fever. For food the army purchased canned meat that one general called "embalmed beef." Of the few thousand U.S. forces who died during the war, only a small percentage died in battle. The rest died from food poisoning, disease, and other causes.

The most colorful group of soldiers in the war were the Rough Riders, the First Volunteer Cavalry commanded by General Leonard Wood. Second in command was Lieutenant Colonel Theodore Roosevelt. Anxious to join the fighting, Roosevelt organized a group of volunteers to fight in Cuba. The Rough Riders came from many walks of life. They included college athletes, miners, American Indians, ranchers, and cowboys.

Newspaper accounts of Roosevelt's charm and the Rough Riders' heroic achievements in battle earned the group the admiration of the American public. Many other U.S. soldiers also served bravely. Four privates of the African American 10th Cavalry rowed through heavy gunfire to rescue 15 members of a U.S. landing party. All four received the Congressional Medal of Honor for their actions.

The Battles

On June 1, 1898, U.S. ships caught the Spanish Caribbean fleet in the harbor of Santiago de Cuba. The more numerous and powerful U.S. Navy blockaded the harbor and made it safe for U.S. troops to land nearby. Set ashore on June 22 and

The War Dispatches of Stephen Crane

Although more readers know of Stephen Crane for his novel The Red Badge of Courage, *he also worked as a journalist during the Spanish-American War. He published many gripping war reports. While in his twenties, Crane was already such a popular reporter that his editors made a point of putting his name in their front-page headlines to attract more readers. The following war dispatch, "Night Attacks on the Marines and a Brave Rescue," appeared in the New York* World *on July 16, 1898. It reports an account of fighting in Cuba between U.S. Marines and Spanish soldiers.*

Stephen Crane
The Granger Collection, New York

GUANTANAMO, July 4.—
Once upon a time there was a great deal of fighting between the marines and the guerrillas [Spanish soldiers] here, and during that space things occurred.

The night attacks were heart-breaking affairs, from which the men emerged in the morning exhausted to a final degree, like people who had been swimming for miles. From colonel to smallest trumpeter went a great thrill when the dawn broke slowly in the eastern sky, and the weary band quite cheerfully ate breakfast. . . . Afterward the men slept, sunk upon the ground in an abandon [physical exhaustion] that was almost a stupor [daze].

Lieut. Neville, with his picket [forward group] of about twenty men, was entirely cut off from camp one night, and another night Neville's picket and the picket of Lieut. Shaw were cut off, fighting hard in the thickets [forests] for their lives. At the break of day the beleaguered [surrounded] camp could hear still the rifles of their lost pickets.

The problem of rescue added anxiety to the already tremendous anxiety of the fine old colonel. . . . The guerrillas were still lurking [sneaking] in the near woods, and it was unsafe enough in camp without venturing into the bush.

Volunteers from Company C were called for, and these seventeen privates volunteered:

Boniface, Conway, Fitzgerald, Heilner, Harmson, Hemerle, Lewin, Mann, Mills, Monahan, Nolan, O'Donnell, Ryan, Riddle, Sinclair, Sullivan, W. A., and Smith, J. H.

They went out under Lieut. Lucas. They arrived in Neville's vicinity just as he and his men, together with Shaw and his men, were being finally surrounded at close range. Lucas and his seventeen men broke through the guerrillas and saved the pickets, and the whole body then fell back to Crest Hill. That is all there is to it.

Understanding Literature

1. How did the soldiers feel after the night attacks?

2. How did Lieutenant Lucas and his men save the pickets?

3. Why do you think the U.S. soldiers from Company C volunteered to help in the rescue of the pickets that were cut off from camp?

4. What effect do you think this war dispatch had on readers in the United States?

aided by Cuban rebels, the U.S. troops moved to capture the hills around the main Spanish forces at Santiago. At the village of El Caney on July 1, some 7,000 U.S. soldiers overwhelmed about 600 Spanish defenders. The main U.S. force under General Hamilton Hawkins then attacked and captured San Juan Hill. A smaller force, including the Rough Riders and the African American 9th and 10th Cavalries, captured nearby Kettle Hill. A journalist on the scene described their charge:

The Rough Riders and the 9th and 10th Cavalries fight to help secure Santiago.

> **❝It was a miracle of self-sacrifice, a triumph of bulldog courage. . . . The fire of the Spanish riflemen . . . doubled and trebled [tripled] in fierceness, the crests of the hills crackled and burst in amazed roars and rippled with waves of tiny flame. But the blue line [of U.S. soldiers] crept steadily up and on.❞**

On July 3 the U.S. artillery was within range of the Spanish fleet, so the Spanish commander decided to try breaking through the U.S. blockade. Every Spanish ship was destroyed in the battle, with 474 Spaniards killed and 1,750 others captured. American forces suffered only two casualties. Santiago surrendered on July 17. A few days later, U.S. troops commanded by Nelson Miles invaded Puerto Rico, where they met little resistance. Puerto Rico soon surrendered. Spain asked for peace and signed a cease-fire on August 12, 1898.

The Peace Treaty

The peace treaty between Spain and the United States placed Puerto Rico, Guam, Cuba, and the Philippines under U.S. control. Groups like the **Anti-Imperialist League**, made up of Americans who opposed the treaty, accused the United States of building a colonial empire. Despite such protests, the treaty was ratified by a vote of 57 to 27, one vote more than the two-thirds majority needed.

The Philippines

Spain had surrendered the Philippines in return for a $20 million payment from the United States. Many Americans wondered why their nation wanted the islands. Some believed that it would be wrong to annex the islands without the consent of the Filipinos. Other people agreed with President McKinley, who said that the United States would benefit from the islands' naval and commercial value, and that annexing the islands would keep Europeans from seizing them.

Filipino rebels, however, had helped U.S. forces capture Manila, and expected to gain their independence after the war. When the United States decided to keep the islands, the rebels began a guerrilla war against the U.S. forces. Some 70,000 U.S. soldiers fought in the Philippines, and hundreds of thousands of Filipinos died, before the war ended more than three years later in 1902.

On July 1, 1902, the U.S. Congress passed the Philippine Government Act. This act provided that the Philippines would be ruled by an appointed governor and a two-house legislature, the lower house of which was elected. In 1946 the United States granted full independence to the Philippines.

Cuba

Although the Teller Amendment had stated that the United States would not annex Cuba, President McKinley established a military government there. McKinley wanted to create stability and increase U.S. trade and influence in the region. He appointed General Leonard Wood as governor, and Wood quickly began building schools and a sanitation system. To combat disease, Dr. Walter

Reed, head of the Army Yellow Fever Commission, was sent to Cuba in 1900. He and his volunteers proved that yellow fever was transmitted by mosquitoes. Getting rid of standing water reduced the mosquito population, which in turn helped health officials to effectively control the disease.

Wood also oversaw the drafting of a Cuban constitution, which also included the **Platt Amendment**. The amendment limited Cuba's right to make treaties, required Cuba to sell or lease land to the United States for naval stations, and authorized the United States to intervene in Cuban affairs. Cuban leaders compared this to

> ❝ **handing over the keys to our house so that they [the Americans] can enter it at any time, whenever the desire seizes them, day or night, whether with good or evil design [intentions].** ❞

The Cubans reluctantly accepted the Platt Amendment, and U.S. troops withdrew. The amendment remained in force until 1934.

Puerto Rico

Like Cuba, Puerto Rico had hoped for independence after the war. Instead, the U.S. government made the island a territory like the Philippines. On April 12, 1900, the Foraker Act established a civil

After the United States acquired Puerto Rico, the government built many new schools.

government that was headed by a governor and included a two-house legislature.

A debate soon arose over the citizenship status of the people of the new territories. Residents of Puerto Rico were considered citizens of the island but not of the United States. In 1917 the Jones Act granted Puerto Ricans U.S. citizenship and made both houses of the legislature elective. However, another 30 years passed before Puerto Ricans could elect their own governor. In 1952 Puerto Rico became a commonwealth. This unique status means that the island has its own constitution and elected officials. As with the 50 states, Puerto Rico can change its constitution as long as it does not conflict with that of the United States.

SECTION 2 REVIEW

Identify and explain the significance of the following:
- José Martí
- Joseph Pulitzer
- William Randolph Hearst
- yellow journalism
- Teller Amendment
- Emilio Aguinaldo
- Theodore Roosevelt
- Anti-Imperialist League
- Platt Amendment

Reading for Content Understanding

1 **Main Idea** How did the American press influence relations between the United States and Spain?

2 **Main Idea** What led to U.S. victory in the Spanish-American War?

3 **Global Relations** How did the war affect the Philippines, Cuba, and Puerto Rico?

4 **Writing** *Expressing* Imagine that you are a soldier during the Spanish-American War. Write a journal entry describing the war and the dangers you face.

5 **Critical Thinking** *Supporting a Point of View* If you had been a U.S. diplomat in Cuba in the 1890s, would you have supported going to war? Explain your answer.

The United States and Latin America

Reading Focus

What steps did the United States take to build a canal across Panama?

How did U.S. involvement in Latin America change under President Theodore Roosevelt?

How did Presidents Taft and Wilson enforce the Monroe Doctrine?

Key Terms

Hay-Herrán Treaty
Hay–Bunau-Varilla Treaty
Panama Canal
Roosevelt Corollary
dollar diplomacy

The USS Oregon

W HEN THE SPANISH-AMERICAN WAR *began in 1898, the U.S. battleship* Oregon *was stationed at Puget Sound in Washington State. After receiving its orders, the* Oregon *set out at top speed on a 12,000-mile voyage. It traveled around the southern tip of South America to join the fighting in Cuba. Newspapers charted the* Oregon's *daily progress while the American public "breathlessly pushed her along." The trip lasted from March 19 to May 24, 1898—67 days!*

 ## The Panama Canal

Despite the best efforts of the *Oregon*'s crew, the ship barely arrived in time to take part in the major battle around Cuba. The delay concerned many people. The United States needed to be able to quickly transfer key naval forces between the Caribbean and the Pacific. However, travel around the southern tip of South America took weeks.

Spanish explorer Vasco Núñez de Balboa had crossed the narrow Isthmus of Panama in Central America in the early 1500s. Since then, many people had dreamed of building a canal there to link the Pacific and Atlantic Oceans. In the late 1800s some U.S. leaders began to explore ways to dig a canal across the narrow neck of Central America. Such a canal would cut 8,000 miles off the voyage and join the Atlantic and Pacific naval fleets.

Negotiations

In 1850 the United States and Great Britain had signed the Clayton-Bulwer Treaty, which called for them to jointly build and maintain a canal. Despite the treaty, the countries never built a canal. In 1881 a French company headed by Ferdinand de Lesseps, who had engineered the Suez Canal in Egypt, began work. After spending nearly $300 million and losing some 20,000 lives, the company went bankrupt in 1887. At that time, less than one third of the planned 51-mile canal had been dug.

No one was a stronger supporter of a Central American canal than Theodore Roosevelt, who had become president in 1901 after the assassination of William McKinley. Influenced by the ideas of Alfred Mahan, Roosevelt believed that naval power was essential to U.S. strength and security. Earlier, Roosevelt had written to Mahan, "I believe we should build the [Central American] canal at once, and, in the meantime, . . . we should build a dozen new battleships." In 1901 Secretary of State John Hay completed negotiations with the British for the Hay-Pauncefote Treaty. Britain surrendered its interest in building and operating a Central American canal in exchange for a U.S. agreement to keep the canal open to all vessels at all times.

With this agreement settled, Secretary Hay began negotiating with Colombia, because the Isthmus of Panama was part of that country. Hay and the Colombian minister Thomas Herrán soon reached an agreement. The United States would pay $10 million plus $250,000 a year for a 99-year lease on a five-mile wide strip of land across the isthmus.

The U.S. Senate ratified the **Hay-Herrán Treaty** in March 1903, but the Colombian senate rejected it in hopes of better terms. President Roosevelt refused to pay more money to Colombia. He considered other ways of gaining the Isthmus of Panama, such as seizing it by force.

A New Nation

Philippe Bunau-Varilla, chief engineer with the French Canal Company, offered an alternative plan. In a meeting with Hay and Roosevelt, Bunau-Varilla informed them about the possibility of a revolt in the Colombian province of Panama. Bunau-Varilla knew about the effort, as he himself was organizing the plot. Bunau-Varilla came away from the gathering with the assumption that the United States would support—or at least not strongly discourage—the Panamanian revolt.

On November 2, 1903, a U.S. warship arrived in Colón, Panama. The next day the revolution broke out. Although Colombian forces tried to stop the rebellion, dense jungles blocked the land routes and the U.S. warship blocked the sea lanes to Panama. On November 4 Panama declared itself an independent nation. The United States recognized, or formally acknowledged, the new nation almost immediately. On November 13, Bunau-Varilla arrived in Washington, D.C., as the Panamanian minister to the United States. He met with the Roosevelt administration and five days later signed the **Hay–Bunau-Varilla Treaty**. The terms of this treaty were identical to the Hay-Herrán Treaty, except that the canal zone was widened to 10 miles. The United States was ready to build the canal.

This cartoon shows President Roosevelt digging the Panama Canal and throwing the dirt on Colombia, which had rejected an earlier canal plan.

★ Building the Canal

Building the canal proved to be very difficult. The first obstacle to overcome was tropical disease, particularly yellow fever, which had been a serious problem for the earlier French effort. The canal route ran about 51 miles through jungles and

The Panama Canal

Gaillard Cut

Gatún Locks

Culebra

Canal

Gatún

To Pacific

To Atlantic

Locks

Sea level

Locks

Once the U.S. Congress approved construction of a canal across the Isthmus of Panama, the massive undertaking began. The project faced many obstacles, including disease, floods, mountains, and swamps.

A big hurdle in the project was completing the Gaillard Cut through a mountain range. Even with dozens of huge shovels, removing all the rock and mud took workers years. Engineers built a large railroad to carry away the debris. It took workers 10 years to dig a path eight miles long and about 40 feet deep. Then engineers built a dam to control flooding from the nearby Chagres River. This dam created the great Gatún Lake.

Engineers then designed and built six enormous locks. A lock is a section of a canal with large gates at either end. Each of the six locks is eight stories tall and longer than three football fields. When a ship enters a lock, operators close the gates and raise or lower the water level inside the lock. When water is at the desired height, the gates are opened and the ship continues on its way.

To travel from the Atlantic to the Pacific Ocean, a ship enters the Panama Canal near the town of Colón. The ship travels through the Gatún Locks, where the water level and therefore the ship is raised 85 feet. Then the ship travels down a long channel in Gatún Lake until it passes through the Gaillard Cut in the mountains. There the vessel is lowered 31 feet. The ship is eventually lowered to sea level by another series of locks, after which it follows another channel out to the ocean. The entire Panama Canal is about 51 miles long. A typical trip takes about nine hours. The canal reduces the distance a ship has to travel from one coast of the United States to another by about 8,000 miles. Completed in 1914, the Panama Canal remains one of the greatest engineering feats of the 1900s.

Understanding What You Read

1. What were some construction challenges in building the Panama Canal?

2. How do ships travel through the Panama Canal?

Some 43,000 workers dug through jungles and mountains to complete the Panama Canal.

Roosevelt and Latin America

With the construction of the Panama Canal, the United States had increased its involvement in Latin America. In 1823 President James Monroe had announced U.S. interest in Latin America when he warned European nations not to interfere in either Central or South America. In what became known as the Monroe Doctrine, he declared that "the American continents . . . are henceforth not to be considered as subjects for future colonization by any European powers." The United States would view any such actions as a threat to its safety.

swamps filled with mosquitoes, many of which carried malaria and yellow fever. Having helped Dr. Walter Reed combat disease in Cuba, Dr. William C. Gorgas organized a vast effort to rid the canal route of disease-carrying mosquitoes. Without his success in slowing the spread of deadly diseases, the canal's construction would have taken much longer. It also would have cost much more, in terms of lives and money.

Even with the reduced risk of disease, the work was very dangerous. Much of the canal had to be blasted out of solid rock. On one occasion, a bolt of lightning struck a 12-ton explosive charge, setting it off prematurely and killing seven workers. In several other incidents, workers died when their shovels struck the cap of an unexploded charge. One West Indian worker recalled, "The flesh of men flew in the air like birds many days."

The high mountain range of central Panama also stood as a challenge to the canal-building effort. To overcome this obstacle, chief engineers John Stevens and George W. Goethals directed workers to cut a narrow, eight-mile-long channel through solid rock using dozens of steam shovels.

Some 6,000 lives were lost building the **Panama Canal**, which finally opened to traffic on August 15, 1914. The cost was $367 million on top of the nearly $300 million spent in the failed French effort. In the end, however, the world had its "highway between the oceans."

The Monroe Doctrine had become a defining principle of U.S. foreign policy. At the time that Monroe announced it, however, the United States lacked the military power to enforce the policy. Fortunately, no situation required direct U.S. involvement. President Monroe's administration relied on Britain's large navy as well as British interest in keeping the area free of other European powers to enforce the Monroe Doctrine. This situation changed as the United States grew stronger and expanded its influence, particularly after the Spanish-American War.

George W. Goethals (center) directed the building of the Panama Canal. Dr. William C. Gorgas is second from the right.

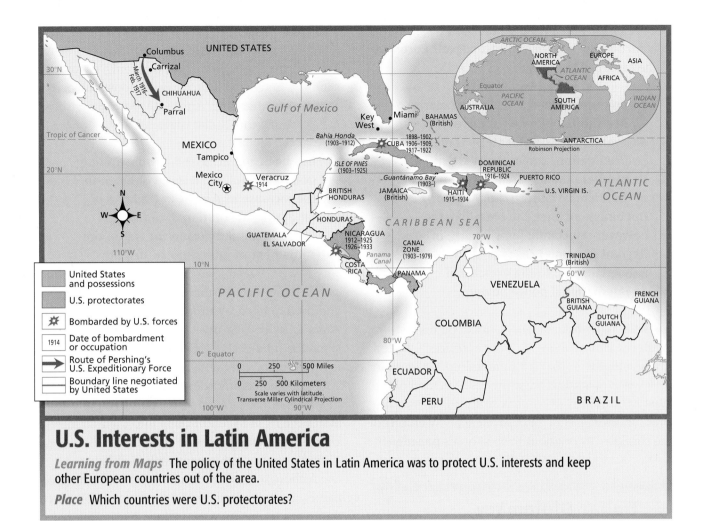

Map labels:

UNITED STATES

Columbus
Carrizal
March 1916 / Feb. 1917
CHIHUAHUA
Parral

Gulf of Mexico

30°N
Tropic of Cancer
20°N

MEXICO
Tampico
Mexico City ★
Veracruz 1914

Key West
Miami
BAHAMAS (British)

Bahía Honda (1903–1912)
CUBA 1898–1902, 1906–1909, 1917–1922
ISLE OF PINES (1903–1925)
Guantánamo Bay (1903–)
JAMAICA (British)
HAITI 1915–1934
DOMINICAN REPUBLIC 1916–1924
PUERTO RICO
U.S. VIRGIN IS.

ATLANTIC OCEAN

BRITISH HONDURAS

CARIBBEAN SEA

HONDURAS
GUATEMALA
EL SALVADOR
NICARAGUA 1912–1925 1926–1933
COSTA RICA
PANAMA
Panama Canal
CANAL ZONE (1903–1979)
70°W
60°W
TRINIDAD (British)

N W E S

110°W
10°N
0° Equator
100°W
90°W
80°W

PACIFIC OCEAN

VENEZUELA
COLOMBIA
BRITISH GUIANA
DUTCH GUIANA
FRENCH GUIANA

ECUADOR
PERU
BRAZIL

Inset globe: ARCTIC OCEAN, NORTH AMERICA, EUROPE, ASIA, ATLANTIC OCEAN, AFRICA, PACIFIC OCEAN, Equator, AUSTRALIA, SOUTH AMERICA, INDIAN OCEAN, ANTARCTICA, Robinson Projection

Legend:
- United States and possessions
- U.S. protectorates
- ✴ Bombarded by U.S. forces
- 1914 Date of bombardment or occupation
- → Route of Pershing's U.S. Expeditionary Force
- Boundary line negotiated by United States

0   250   500 Miles
0   250   500 Kilometers
Scale varies with latitude.
Transverse Miller Cylindrical Projection

U.S. Interests in Latin America

Learning from Maps The policy of the United States in Latin America was to protect U.S. interests and keep other European countries out of the area.

Place Which countries were U.S. protectorates?

A Larger Role

During the late 1800s many European banks had invested in, and made loans to, a number of Latin American countries. When some of these nations had difficulty repaying their loans, European nations used force to collect their debts. Venezuela, under the rule of dictator Cipriano Castro, fell deeply in debt to British and German investors. In 1902 the Venezuelan government refused to repay these debts or to have the claims settled by a neutral third party.

European leaders wanted to act but were concerned about the Monroe Doctrine. In 1901, however, President Roosevelt had declared that the United States did "not guarantee any State against punishment if it misconducts itself." The only condition Roosevelt set was "that punishment does not take the form of acquisition [taking] of territory by any non-American power." The European nations interpreted this to mean that they could collect their debts—by force if necessary. Britain

and Germany sent ships to blockade Venezuela. The Venezuelan dictator then asked Roosevelt to propose having the matter settled by a third party, which the Europeans accepted.

A similar situation developed in the Caribbean nation of the Dominican Republic in 1904. Again, European nations considered using force to collect their debts. This time Roosevelt worried that the foreign forces might not leave afterward. The presence of European forces in the Caribbean would not only have violated the Monroe Doctrine but also could have threatened U.S. power in the region and control of the Panama Canal.

The Roosevelt Corollary

President Roosevelt realized that if the United States prevented European creditors from collecting what was owed them, U.S. officials would need to intervene. The United States would have to force the debtor nations to repay their loans. In

December 1904 the president outlined his thinking in what became known as the **Roosevelt Corollary** to the Monroe Doctrine:

> 66 **Chronic wrongdoing . . . may in America, as elsewhere, ultimately require intervention [involvement] by some civilized nation, and in the Western Hemisphere the adherence [observance] of the United States to the Monroe Doctrine may force the United States, however reluctantly [unwillingly], in flagrant [extreme] cases of such wrongdoing . . . to the exercise of an international police power.** 99

This new role of the United States as the Western Hemisphere's "police officer" suited Roosevelt's style. He had summed up his ideas in 1900 when he said, "I have always been fond of the West African proverb: 'Speak softly and carry a big stick, you will go far.'" Roosevelt actively enforced the corollary throughout the rest of his presidency.

★ Dollar Diplomacy

When William Howard Taft became president in 1909, he also acted to protect U.S. interests in Latin America. Instead of Roosevelt's "big-stick" approach of using military force, Taft used a policy known as **dollar diplomacy**, which emphasized

Many Americans thought that President Taft struggled with issues that Theodore Roosevelt had handled with ease.

using U.S. economic power and business investment to influence Latin American governments. Taft believed he could influence events, encourage stability, and keep European nations out of the region by expanding American businesses there. He explained that dollar diplomacy

> 66 **has been characterized as substituting dollars for bullets. It is . . . directed to the increase of American trade . . . [and] the substitution of arbitration [discussion] and reason for war in the settlement of international disputes.** 99

Taft supported American businesses overseas and tried to replace European investments in Latin America with U.S. investments. In an agreement signed in June 1911, the United States declared that it would help Nicaragua secure private loans from American banks in order to pay its national debt. In exchange, Nicaraguan officials gave the United States the right to send troops into their country if U.S. leaders felt it necessary. The United States also signed a similar agreement with Honduras.

Although the U.S. Senate rejected both agreements, the Taft administration informally observed the treaty terms anyway. In July, Nicaragua failed to repay a large loan from British investors. Secretary of State Chase Knox helped secure a $1.5 billion loan for Nicaragua from American bankers. In exchange, the bankers received control of the National Bank of Nicaragua and the government-owned railway. Local dissatisfaction over this agreement soon led to a revolt in Nicaragua. Taft sent in U.S. Marines to protect American interests. The marines remained until 1925, returned the next year, and finally left in 1933.

★ Wilson's Foreign Policies

President Woodrow Wilson, who took office in 1913, rejected the dollar diplomacy of the Taft administration. Wilson disapproved of the role of big business in foreign affairs and said he would not act to support any "special group or interests." Instead, he believed the United States had a moral obligation to

The Granger Collection, New York

promote democracy in Latin America. He sought to protect U.S. interests in the region by encouraging the growth of state government. One newspaper responded to Wilson's policy by writing, "There is . . . not a word [here] to stir the greed of a dictator."

Wilson tended to oppose imperialist ideas. Nevertheless, he eventually sent more troops into Latin America than any previous president in an attempt to bring democracy to the region. For example, the Caribbean nation of Haiti had long been in financial disorder. The country also suffered a series of political revolutions that threatened people's lives and safety. In 1915 Haitian president Guillaume Sam ordered 167 political prisoners executed. As a result, he was overthrown and assassinated in another revolt. Previously, Germany and France had temporarily sent troops to Haiti to protect their interests. Wilson feared that those countries might try to seize control of Haiti during the violence. To prevent this, U.S. Marines landed in Haiti on July 29, 1915, and quickly restored peace. The United States took control of collecting customs taxes to pay Haiti's debts and installed a new government there.

Similar events occurred in the Dominican Republic. The customs arrangements established by President Roosevelt in 1905 had brought a

These U.S. Marines were among the many that President Wilson sent to restore order in Haiti.

stable government to this nation. In 1911, however, the Dominican president was assassinated and instability returned. By threatening to withhold customs revenue, Secretary of State Knox forced the Dominicans to accept a U.S.-supported government.

In 1913 William Jennings Bryan, the new secretary of state, began to oversee the Dominican Republic's finances. After Bryan resigned in 1916, however, the Dominican president opposed the appointment of a new financial adviser. Fearing more political unrest, Wilson declared martial law on the island and established a government run by the U.S. Navy. Wilson, like Roosevelt and Taft before him, refused to let internal political unrest in Latin America threaten U.S. interests there.

SECTION 3 REVIEW

Identify and explain the significance of the following:

- **Hay-Herrán Treaty**
- **Philippe Bunau-Varilla**
- **Hay–Bunau-Varilla Treaty**
- **William C. Gorgas**
- **Panama Canal**
- **Roosevelt Corollary**
- **dollar diplomacy**

Reading for Content Understanding

1 **Main Idea** What was President Theodore Roosevelt's foreign policy in Latin America?

2 **Main Idea** In what ways did Presidents Taft and Wilson differ from Roosevelt in enforcing the Monroe Doctrine?

3 **Technology and Society** Describe the steps that led to the completion of the Panama Canal.

4 **Writing** *Describing* Imagine that you are a worker helping to build the Panama Canal. Write a letter home to your family, describing the difficulties you have encountered during your time in Panama.

5 **Critical Thinking** *Determining the Strength of an Argument* President Roosevelt believed that the United States needed to serve as the international police officer of the Western Hemisphere. Do you agree? Explain your answer.

The United States and Mexico

Reading Focus

Why did the Mexican people revolt against their government in 1911?

Why did President Woodrow Wilson intervene in the Mexican Revolution?

Why did Mexican immigration to the United States increase in the early 1900s?

Key Terms

Mexican Revolution
ABC Powers

IN 1910 MEXICO CELEBRATED *the 100th anniversary of Father Miguel Hidalgo's call for revolution,* known as the Grito de Dolores. *Mexican president Porfirio Díaz treated guests from around the world to entertainment and fine food and toasted Mexico's successful revolt against Spain. Francisco Madero, another Mexican leader, celebrated the* Grito *in a different way. He published a pamphlet demanding that Díaz resign and calling for free elections. When Díaz refused, Madero began another revolution.*

The Granger Collection, New York

Porfirio Díaz

★ The Mexican Revolution

For 34 years, from 1877 to 1911, Porfirio Díaz ruled Mexico and eagerly welcomed foreign investment. The United States became the biggest investor in Mexico, and by 1913 had invested more than $1 billion in Mexican land, mining, oil, railways, and manufacturing. More than 500,000 U.S. citizens lived and worked in Mexico. To open Mexico to foreign investors, Díaz had ruled the Mexican people harshly. He imprisoned his opponents and rewarded his supporters. Most of Mexico's 15 million people were landless and poor.

Many Mexicans found a new leader in democratic reformer Francisco Madero, who began the **Mexican Revolution** in 1910. After capturing Ciudad Juárez and gaining support throughout the country, Madero forced Díaz to resign in May. Madero was elected president. The Taft administration wanted a stable government in Mexico and quickly recognized Madero as president.

Despite Madero's victory, a struggle for power continued in Mexico. In February 1913 General Victoriano Huerta seized power and had Madero killed. The violence angered Woodrow Wilson, who was about to take office as U.S. president.

These women were among the many people who fought in the Mexican Revolution.

Wilson refused to recognize the new Mexican government, saying:

> **We hold, as I am sure all thoughtful leaders of republican government everywhere hold, that just government rests upon the consent of the governed.** "

When a revolt led by Venustiano Carranza began gathering force, Wilson proposed that the two sides cease fighting and agree to a free election. If they agreed, Wilson said he would help the new elected Mexican government secure loans from U.S. banks. However, Wilson insisted that Huerta could not be a candidate in the election because he had seized power by force. Not surprisingly, Huerta refused.

Wilson then lifted the U.S. restrictions against selling arms in Mexico so that weapons could be supplied to the forces opposing Huerta. Wilson also stationed U.S. warships near Veracruz, Mexico, to block any foreign aid to Huerta. In addition to Carranza, two other major revolutionaries—Francisco "Pancho" Villa in the north and Emiliano Zapata in the south—led movements to overthrow Huerta. Like Carranza, both Villa and Zapata had supported Madero against Díaz. Both were heroes to Mexico's poor.

Although Carranza, Villa, and Zapata had a common goal in hoping to overthrow Huerta, they were not close allies. Their relationship was best described by the saying, "The enemy of my enemy is my friend." Each wanted to replace Huerta as Mexico's leader, leading to a strong rivalry among them.

★ The United States Reacts

The fighting in Mexico weakened its economy, leading a number of American business leaders to fear that they would lose their investments there. They wanted Huerta out of office, by force, if necessary. President Wilson, however, refused their demands.

The public pressure to intervene continued to grow. Many members of Congress demanded military action. The press at home and abroad also criticized Wilson's policy, but he refused to be swayed by such attacks. Wilson explained to his secretary, "I have to pause and remind myself that I am President of the United States and not of a small group of Americans with vested interests [investments] in Mexico."

President Wilson adopted a policy of "watchful waiting" toward the unrest in Mexico. At the same time, he looked for an opportunity to act against Huerta.

Tampico

In 1914 an incident finally gave Wilson the opportunity to act. The U.S. ship *Dolphin* was patrolling

Pancho Villa (left) and Emiliano Zapata (right) led revolutionaries against Victoriano Huerta's government.

America As a World Power **309**

in Mexican waters. A group of its sailors went ashore at Tampico, Mexico, which was under military rule. When these soldiers accidentally entered a restricted area, Huerta's troops arrested them.

The sailors were soon released, and the local commander in Tampico apologized to Admiral Mayo, who was commanding the U.S. fleet. Mayo, however, was not satisfied with the apology. Even though he lacked the proper authorization, he wrote to the Mexican general in charge of Tampico:

❝ I must require that you send me . . . [an] apology for the act, together with your assurance that the officer responsible for it will receive severe punishment. Also that you publicly hoist the American flag in a prominent [important] position on shore and salute it with twenty-one guns. ❞

Wilson supported Mayo's demands. The Mexican general delivered the written apology, and Huerta expressed regret over the incident. The salute, however, was not delivered. On April 20, 1914, Wilson asked Congress for approval to use the armed forces "to obtain from General Huerta . . . the fullest recognition of the rights and dignity of the United States."

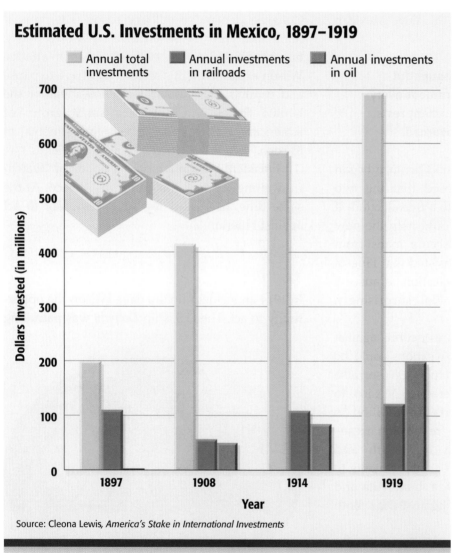

Estimated U.S. Investments in Mexico, 1897–1919

Annual total investments · Annual investments in railroads · Annual investments in oil

Dollars Invested (in millions) / Year

Source: Cleona Lewis, *America's Stake in International Investments*

Investment Concerns The disorder of the Mexican Revolution gave many Americans concern about money they had invested in Mexico's economy. In which category—railroads or oil—had U.S. investment increased the most by 1919?

Veracruz

Before the Tampico crisis could be resolved, Wilson learned that a German ship carrying a large supply of arms was cruising toward the port city of Veracruz, Mexico. Wilson did not want Huerta to receive these weapons, so the president ordered U.S. Marines to seize Veracruz. In late April 1914, U.S. forces captured the city. This action took the lives of 19 Americans and wounded 47 others. Some 200 Mexicans were killed and 300 more were wounded in the fighting.

The quick assault on Veracruz united Mexicans against the United States. Huerta broke off diplomatic relations, and the two nations stood on the brink of war. Then the **ABC Powers**—Argentina, Brazil, and Chile—offered to negotiate the dispute. Wilson accepted but Huerta rejected the proposed settlement. However, Huerta was soon forced to leave office. In

August, Carranza and his forces occupied Mexico City and established a new government. The United States and several Latin American nations recognized Carranza as president of Mexico, and the U.S. troops withdrew from Veracruz.

Pursuing Pancho Villa

Despite Huerta's overthrow, Pancho Villa and Emiliano Zapata continued their revolts. Villa hoped to destroy the Carranza government and win the support of the Mexican people by attacking the United States. In January, Villa and his troops stopped a train at Santa Ysabel, Mexico, and killed 18 American mining engineers on board.

On March 9, 1916, Villa and his troops attacked Columbus, New Mexico, burning the town and killing 17 U.S. citizens. In response, President Wilson sent General John J. Pershing and 15,000 soldiers into Mexico. Pershing's forces chased Villa more than 300 miles but failed to capture him. Mexicans greatly resented having U.S. troops in their country. Wilson eventually agreed to Carranza's demands for withdrawal and recalled the troops.

In 1917 Carranza approved a liberal constitution to bring orderly rule to Mexico. However, in 1920 the forces of Álvaro Obregón revolted and killed Carranza. After 1920, peace gradually returned to Mexico.

General John J. "Black Jack" Pershing led the failed effort to capture Pancho Villa.

The Mexican Revolution resulted in a large-scale Mexican migration to the United States. Many Mexicans fled the destruction of the war. Others fled to escape political persecution. These immigrants included upper- and middle-class refugees, as well as farmers and urban poor. Many hoped to find industrial jobs in the United States.

Between 1905 and 1909 more than 28,000 Mexicans immigrated to the United States. By 1915 about three times that number had arrived. Since then, economic and political factors have continued to draw many Mexican immigrants to the United States.

SECTION 4 REVIEW

Identify and explain the significance of the following:
- Porfirio Díaz
- Francisco Madero
- Mexican Revolution
- Victoriano Huerta
- Venustiano Carranza
- Francisco "Pancho" Villa
- Emiliano Zapata
- ABC Powers
- John J. Pershing

Reading for Content Understanding

1 **Main Idea** Why did Francisco Madero begin the Mexican Revolution?

2 **Main Idea** Why did the United States become involved in the Mexican Revolution?

3 **Cultural Diversity** Why did Mexican immigration to the United States increase during and after the Mexican Revolution?

4 **Writing** *Informing* Write an article that might have appeared in a Mexican newspaper in 1920 about the role Pancho Villa played in the Mexican Revolution.

5 **Critical Thinking** *Identifying Cause and Effect* Why did the revolution in Mexico make U.S. businesspeople uneasy?

CHAPTER
10 REVIEW

Chapter Summary

As the U.S. economy grew, so did the desire to secure new foreign markets for American products. In the mid- and late 1800s the United States purchased Alaska from Russia, annexed the islands of Hawaii, and tried to open markets in Asia. Victory in the Spanish-American War gave the United States additional territories. Afterward, the United States became more involved in events in Latin America, including a revolution in Mexico. ◼

On a separate sheet of paper, complete the following activities.

Identifying People and Ideas

Describe the historical significance of the following:

1. imperialism
2. Liliuokalani
3. Boxer Rebellion
4. José Martí
5. Teller Amendment
6. Platt Amendment
7. Roosevelt Corollary
8. Francisco Madero
9. ABC Powers
10. John J. Pershing

Internet Activity

go.hrw.com
SB1 Panama Canal

Search the Internet through the HRW Web site to find information about the operation of the Panama Canal. Use the information to create a drawing that shows how ships pass through the canal. Be sure to provide a caption for your drawing.

Understanding Main Ideas

1. What was the Open Door Policy?
2. How did the press help spark U.S. involvement in the conflict in Cuba?
3. How did the outcome of the Spanish-American War affect the United States, Spain, and Cuba?
4. Explain the steps that the United States took to build and control the Panama Canal.
5. Why did President Wilson refuse to recognize General Huerta's government in Mexico?
6. Why did President Wilson order U.S. troops into Mexico?

Reviewing Themes

1. **Geographic Diversity** Why did the United States want control of certain Pacific islands?
2. **Economic Development** What steps did the United States take to expand trade with China and Japan?

Using the Time Line

Number your paper from 1 to 5. Match the letters on the time line below with the following events.

1. Secretary of State William Seward negotiates the purchase of Alaska from Russia.
2. Revolution breaks out in Mexico.
3. Congress passes the McKinley Tariff, allowing all countries to ship sugar duty-free to the United States.
4. The USS *Maine* explodes and sinks, killing 260 people.
5. Despite most Hawaiians' opposition, Hawaii becomes a U.S. territory.

| 1865 | 1870 | 1875 | 1880 | 1885 | 1890 | 1895 | 1900 | 1905 | 1910 |

a   b   c d   e

3. **Global Relations** Why did the United States defend Cuba against Spain?

Thinking Critically

1. **Supporting a Point of View** Do you think the United States had good reasons for purchasing Alaska? Explain your answer.
2. **Synthesizing Information** Why did many Americans want to gain more overseas territory?
3. **Identifying Cause and Effect** What effect did the Mexican Revolution have on the people of Mexico?

Writing About History

1. **Creating** Imagine that you are a member of the Anti-Imperialist League. Create a pamphlet explaining your group's position and encouraging people to join your organization.
2. **Informing** Imagine that you are a journalist covering the Mexican Revolution. Write a half-page news story explaining the events leading to the revolution, as well as describing the involvement of the United States and the revolution's outcome.

Linking Geography and History

1. **Human-Environment Interaction** What physical obstacles stood in the way of building a canal across Panama?
2. **Location** Why did the United States want to acquire the Philippines?

History Skills Workshop

Using Visual Resources Study the image to the right, which is a 1904 cartoon by Joseph Keppler. In this cartoon an eagle symbolizing America stretches all the way from the United States to the Philippines. Then answer the following questions: (a) What message do you think Keppler was trying to get across to the viewer? (b) Do you agree with his message? Explain your answer.

Building Your Portfolio

Complete the following activities individually or in groups.

1. **Latin America** Choose one of the following Latin American nations: Argentina, Cuba, the Dominican Republic, Haiti, Mexico, Nicaragua, Panama, or Venezuela. Present a short report in class on the country's historical and present-day relationship with the United States. Your report should include appropriate images and a map of the country.

2. **Yellow Journalism** Select an event you have studied recently in class or one that is in the news. Then write two half-page newspaper articles, with headlines, on that topic. One article should report the facts as accurately as possible, and the other should be written in the style of yellow journalism. Finally, share your news articles with the class. Have the class vote for which articles they think best represent each style of journalism.

The Granger Collection, New York

Geography & History

The United States in the Modern Age

During the late 1800s many powerful nations, particularly European powers, tried to create global empires through conquest and political influence. The United States began acquiring overseas territories in the 1890s. Despite this expansion, the scope of U.S. possessions around the world remained much smaller than that of nations such as France, Germany, and Great Britain.

The expansion of U.S. power overseas helped develop U.S. foreign trade. American merchants exported increasing amounts of goods to consumers in global markets. American consumers were also able to buy more imported goods. ∎

Latin America and the Pacific

As a result of the Spanish-American War, the United States took control of Spanish colonies in the Pacific and the Caribbean. These new possessions helped the United States protect its growing trade with those regions.

U.S. Overseas Expansion, 1898–1899

COLONY/COUNTRY	U.S. INVOLVEMENT	CURRENT STATUS
Cuba	Occupied by U.S. forces during Spanish-American War in 1898	Independent nation; the United States gave up right to intervene in Cuban affairs in 1934
Hawaii	Annexed by the United States in 1898	Became 50th U.S. state in 1959
Philippines	Ceded by Spain to the United States in 1898	Independent nation since 1946
Puerto Rico	Ceded by Spain to the United States in 1898	U.S. commonwealth since 1952
Samoa	Agreement in 1899 divided islands between the United States and Germany	Western Samoa independent since 1962; American Samoa still under U.S. control

Pineapples and sugarcane were some of the Pacific crops prized by Americans.

Geography Skills
Reading Charts

1. What Spanish colonies did the United States gain as a result of the Spanish-American War?
2. What other territories came under U.S. control by the end of the 1800s?
3. When did the United States annex Hawaii?

The flag of the common-wealth of Puerto Rico (top), the national flag of the Philippines (center), and the state flag of Hawaii (bottom)

U.S. Exports and Imports, 1865–1915

- ●━ Exports to Latin America (including the Caribbean)
- ●━ Imports from Latin America (including the Caribbean)
- ●━ Exports to Asia and the Pacific
- ●━ Imports from Asia and the Pacific

Source: *Historical Statistics of the United States*

History Note 1

Taking possession of Hawaii, the Philippines, and Puerto Rico helped the United States expand trade in the Pacific, Asia, and Latin America. "We want new markets," President William McKinley declared in 1898, "and as trade follows the flag, it looks very much as if we are going to have new markets."

Geography **Skills**
Reading Line Graphs

1. During which five-year period did the value of U.S. exports to Latin America grow the most?
2. By which year had the value of exports to Asia and the Pacific grown to more than $100 million?
3. During which five-year periods did imports from Latin America decline?

History Note 2

By the late 1800s the United States exported more goods to Europe than it imported from European nations. U.S. exports to Europe soared even higher after World War I began in 1914. American businesses provided money and supplies needed by the huge European armies. The war also caused a decline in exports from Europe. Americans responded by purchasing more goods from Asia and Latin America.

Global Expansion

Nations such as France, Germany, Great Britain, and Japan competed fiercely to establish overseas colonies and control foreign markets. This competition left regions such as Africa and southern Asia with only a few independent nations.

History Note 3

European powers controlled large areas of the world by 1900. However, they had few possessions in Latin America, where many former European colonies had won their independence in the early 1800s. The announcement of the Monroe Doctrine by the United States in 1823 helped keep European powers out of Latin America.

Global Possessions in 1914

Countries and Possessions in 1914

Great Britain	Germany
Denmark	France
Netherlands	Spain
Belgium	Portugal
Italy	United States
Ottoman Empire	Independent/ No foreign possessions
Russia	
Japan	→ Trade routes

Major Resources

Co Cocoa	Di Diamond	I Iron	R Rubber	T Tobacco
Cf Coffee	F Fish	Me Meat	S Silk	W Wool
Cp Copper	Fr Fruit	O Oil	Sp Spices	
C Cotton	G Gold	P Palm products	Su Sugar	
D Dairy products	Gr Grain	Ri Rice	Te Tea	

History Note 4

During the late 1800s and early 1900s, several nations tried to gain control of China's huge economic market. Although China kept its own government, countries such as Britain, Germany, Japan, and the United States gained great influence over Chinese affairs. Japan in particular concentrated on expanding its power in Asia. By 1905 Japan had established control over Korea and Formosa (modern-day Taiwan) and was threatening to expand into northern China.

Geography Skills

Reading Special-Purpose Maps

1. What were Australia's major resources?
2. What nations had colonies in South America?
3. What Asian country had foreign colonies in 1914?

History Skills

Identifying Cause and Effect

Identifying and understanding cause-and-effect relationships is crucial to the study of history. To investigate why an event took place and what happened as a result of that event, historians ask questions. These questions include: What were the immediate actions that triggered the event? What was the background of the event? Who was involved?

How to Identify Cause and Effect

1. **Look for clues** Certain words and phrases are clues to the existence of a cause-and-effect relationship. Note the following examples.

Clue Words and Phrases

Cause	Effect
because	aftermath
brought about	as a consequence
gave rise to	as a result of
inspired	depended on
led to	originating from
produced	outcome
provoked	outgrowth
spurred	proceeded from
the reason	resulting in

2. **Identify the relationship** Read carefully to identify how historical events may be related. Writers do not always state clearly the link between cause and effect. Sometimes a reader of history has to infer, or draw a conclusion about, the cause or the effect of a particular event or action.

3. **Check for complex connections** Beyond the immediate cause and effect, check for other, more complex connections. Note, for example, whether (1) there were additional causes of a given effect, (2) a cause had multiple effects, and (3) these effects themselves caused further events.

Example The following diagram presents important cause-and-effect relationships on the events leading up to the Spanish-American War. In the late 1800s some Cubans rebelled against Spanish rule. They wanted independence. To protect American interests in Cuba, the United States sent the battleship *Maine* to Havana Harbor. The *Maine* exploded, killing 260 people. Many Americans thought that Spain was responsible for the explosion. Responding to President William McKinley's request, Congress declared war on Spain in 1898.

> **Cause**
> Some Cubans wanted independence and rebelled against Spanish rule.
>
> **Effect/Cause**
> The U.S. government sent the battleship *Maine* to Cuba to protect American interests there. The *Maine* exploded, killing 260 people. Many Americans suspected that Spain was responsible.
>
> **Effect**
> Congress declared war on Spain in 1898.

Practicing the Skill

Reread Chapter 10, Section 4, in your textbook, which discusses the causes of the Mexican Revolution. Draw a diagram like the one above, showing the relationships between the actions and the outcomes of important events leading up to the Mexican Revolution.

318 History Skills Workshop

History in Action

UNIT 3 PORTFOLIO

American History

Muckraker Magazine

Complete the following activity in small, cooperative groups.

Imagine that you are a journalist working for the fictitious news publication *Muckraker Magazine* during the early 1900s. Your editor has asked you to prepare a special issue examining the causes, effects, problems, and reforms of the Progressive Era. Five teams of reporters will work to put this special issue together. Each team will create one section of the magazine that focuses on a specific topic.

Materials To complete this activity, you will need posterboard, construction paper, or typing paper. You may wish to write your article on a computer. In addition, you will need markers, pens, pencils, and glue, tape, or rubber cement.

Parts of the Project To create your magazine, complete the following tasks:

1. **Planning and Writing** You will work on one of the following topics: urban living conditions; working conditions; politics and government; monopolies, trusts and big business; or social reform. As a group decide on the articles to include in your section of the magazine. Then decide who will research and write each article. Remember to identify the causes and effects of Progressive Era problems and reforms.

Students prepare their school newspaper.

2. **Editing** When you have completed your article(s), pair off with another member of your group and exchange articles. Edit your partner's article(s) and offer constructive comments. Revise your own article(s) and prepare a final typed draft.

3. **Designing** Meet in your group to plan the design and layout for your magazine section. Decide how to organize the articles, and discuss images, charts, and maps that you might use to improve the layout.

4. **Laying out the Magazine** Next, decide who will be news editors and who will be photographers. News editors will begin laying out the magazine and writing headlines. The photographers will be selecting or creating images and writing captions. When these tasks have been completed, paste your section together. Combine it with other groups to make a complete issue of *Muckraker Magazine*.

Elect someone in the class to design the cover and table of contents for the magazine. Display the finished magazine in your classroom or in another area of your school.

UNIT 4

The Changing Nation

(1914–1929)

American Teens
IN HISTORY
Young War Supporters

Young people across the United States supported the nation's fight in World War I. These teenagers performed essential services and helped the Allies win.

Boy Scouts and Girl Scouts, who took an oath to serve their country when they joined their troops, fulfilled their duty with enthusiasm during the war. Under the slogan "Every Scout to Save a Soldier," Scouts sold almost half a billion dollars in Liberty Bonds and War Savings Stamps.

Some young people donated their own money to the war effort. Sunday school pupils in Cleveland, Ohio, each gave a dime toward the cost of a new warship. Victory Boys and Girls also pledged money, up to $10 a child, toward the war effort. They worked at odd jobs to earn money. These jobs included raising and selling guinea pigs, gathering nuts, and polishing shoes.

Other young people volunteered their labor. Girls joined knitting parties to make scarves and gloves for soldiers. Boys on vacation from school signed up with the U.S. Boy's Working Reserve "agricultural army" to help farmers grow food for soldiers overseas. One writer credited the Reserve workers "with saving the sugar-beet crop in Michigan, the apple crop in Georgia, [and] the berry crop in Oregon."

Some young people even left school to help boost agricultural production. The New York legislature, for example, proposed laws to allow 12-year-olds to stay out of school seven months out of the year to work on farms. After the war, however, the government urged these young people to return to school. One poster read:

> **Boys and Girls**
> *The School Is Your Training Camp*
> *Uncle Sam Says*
> *ENLIST TODAY.*

The U.S. government created posters to encourage young people to join in the war effort.

Young war supporters often found that their work offered unexpected benefits. One teen who served as a machine operator earned $3.50 a day—several times what he could have earned before the war. Other young adults got the chance to travel. All had the satisfaction of serving their country.

In this unit you will learn about how Americans responded to World War I. You will also learn about American life during the 1920s—the exciting Jazz Age.

LEFT PAGE: *U.S. soldiers prepare to "ship out" for service in World War I.*

UNIT 4

The Changing Nation

A World War I recruiting poster

UNITED STATES

A radio with speaker from the 1920s

1917
The U.S. Congress declares war on Germany after the German navy resumes unrestricted submarine warfare.

1918
President Woodrow Wilson proposes his Fourteen Points for a lasting peace after World War I.

1920
WWJ in Detroit becomes the first radio station to air regular commercial broadcasts.

1921
Langston Hughes's poem "The Negro Speaks of Rivers" appears in *The Crisis* magazine.

1914	1915	1916	1917	1918	1919	1920	1921

WORLD

1914
World War I begins after Austria-Hungary declares war on Serbia.

1915
A German submarine sinks the *Lusitania,* a British passenger liner. About 1,200 people, including 128 Americans, die.

1916
Determined Turkish resistance fighters battle the Allies in Gallipoli.

1917
The Bolshevik Revolution sweeps Russia and ends the rule of the czars.

1919
Leaders of the nations involved in World War I sign the Treaty of Versailles.

1921
Leading naval powers meet at the Washington Conference and agree to limit the size of their navies.

An early newspaper headline reports inaccurate information.

St. Basil Cathedral in Moscow

Little Orphan Annie
and her dog, Sandy

1922
To protest
cuts in their
wages, some
400,000
railroad
workers
go on strike.

1924
*Little Orphan
Annie* first
appears in
the New
York *Daily
News.*

Charles
Lindbergh

1927
Charles
Lindbergh
becomes the
first person
to fly solo
across the
Atlantic
Ocean.

1929
American
automakers
sell more
than 4.8
million cars
in one year.

"Fronty Ford"
Speedster

| 1922 | 1923 | 1924 | 1925 | 1926 | 1927 | 1928 | 1929 |

1922
The tomb of
Tutankhamen
is uncovered
by British
archaeolo-
gists near
Luxor, Egypt.

1923
Adolf Hitler
leads an
attempt to
overthrow
the Weimar
Republic in
Germany.

1926
Hirohito
ascends the
Japanese
throne after
the death
of his
father,
Emperor
Yoshihito.

1928
Ras Tafari
assumes
power in
Ethiopia. He
will later
serve as
Emperor
Haile Selassie.

1929
The first
exhibition
by Spanish
painter
Salvador Dali
opens
in Paris.

The burial mask of
Tutankhamen

Emperor Hirohito
and his wife,
Nagako Kuni

Detail from Salvador Dali's
The Persistence of Memory

USING THE TIME LINE

1. Which entries shown on the time line relate to World War I?
2. In what order did the major international agreements occur?

Activity Choose one of the entries shown on the time line. Use your library or your textbook to find some additional information and events related to this entry. Be sure to note when these events occurred and their significance. Create a new time line focusing on this entry. (Your new time line might only include the months of one year.) Place the events and information for this entry in correct chronological order. You may also wish to illustrate your time line.

▪ CHAPTER 11 ▪
World War I
(1914–1919)

On the afternoon of June 28, 1914, Gavrilo Princip walked the streets of Sarajevo (sahr-uh-YAY-voh), the capital of Bosnia. That morning, his accomplices had failed to complete their deadly mission—to kill Archduke Franz Ferdinand, the heir to the throne of Austria-Hungary. Suddenly, the archduke's car appeared. Stepping forward, Princip fired two shots, killing the archduke and his wife. With them died years of peace in Europe.

THEMES

Citizenship and Democracy
How might a government encourage citizens to support a war effort?

Global Relations
How might a local conflict expand into a world war?

Technology and Society
How might new forms of technology change warfare?

1914　　　　**1915**　　　　**1916**

JUNE 1914 A Serb nationalist assassinates Archduke Franz Ferdinand and his wife.

JULY 1914 Austria-Hungary declares war on Serbia, beginning World War I.

SEPT. 1914 The First Battle of the Marne occurs.

MAY 1915 A German U-boat sinks the *Lusitania*.

NOV. 1916 Woodrow Wilson is re-elected president.

The Road to War

Reading Focus

What were the main causes of World War I?

How did most of Europe become involved in the war?

Where was the early fighting in the war, and what were the results?

Key Terms

nationalism
militarism
balance of power
Triple Alliance
Triple Entente

mobilize
Central Powers
Allied Powers
First Battle of the Marne

IN THE EARLY 1900S *Europe seemed to be at peace. There had not been a major war in the region since 1871. Political tensions were building, however, and most nations had continued to strengthen their armed forces. In 1888 German chancellor Otto von Bismarck had introduced a bill to the German parliament that added 750,000 soldiers to the German army. In his address he exclaimed, "We no longer ask for love, either from France or Russia. We run after nobody. We Germans fear God and nothing else on earth!" Before long the political tensions would explode into war on the European continent.*

German citizens listen to an official announce the beginning of World War I.

IMAGE ON LEFT PAGE: *During World War I, millions of soldiers fought and died in trenches like this one.*

1917

APR. 1917 The United States declares war on Germany.

MAR. 1917 U.S. newspapers publish the Zimmerman Note.

1918

JAN. 1918 President Wilson announces the Fourteen Points.

NOV. 1918 Germany agrees to an armistice, ending World War I.

1919

NOV. 1919 The U.S. Senate refuses to approve the Treaty of Versailles.

★ Causes of War

Despite the peace in Europe, relationships among nations were filled with fear and distrust. In this unstable political environment, even a minor incident could destroy the calm.

Nationalism

During the 1800s **nationalism**—the feeling that a specific nation, language, or culture is superior to all others—had become a force for unification. In 1871 Kaiser Wilhelm I unified a number of German states into the German Empire. Later the Pan-German movement sought to unite most of the other German-speaking people in Europe under Germany.

Although nationalism helped to create and enlarge Germany, it threatened the stability of some nations. Austria-Hungary included people of many nationalities and languages. One of these groups, the Slavs, wanted to create a nation of their own. Serbia was already an independent Slavic country on the Balkan Peninsula. The Serbs encouraged Slavs within Austria-Hungary to break free and join them in creating an independent, united Slavic empire in the Balkans. Russia, itself largely Slavic, supported Serbia's goal.

Austro-Hungarian leaders saw this movement as a threat to their authority. One Austrian official predicted that Slavic nationalism was "one of the powerful national movements which can neither be ignored nor kept down." The hostilities in the Balkan region became so intense that many people referred to the Balkans as a "powder keg." The Balkan region seemed a likely place to ignite a major European war.

THE BOILING POINT

In this 1912 British cartoon, European leaders try to keep trouble in the Balkans from boiling over.

Imperialism

Tensions also grew as many European nations competed to gain territories and build overseas empires. By the late 1800s Britain was the world's largest imperial power. France, Germany, Italy, and Russia wanted to create similar empires. These countries also struggled over territory in Europe. France, for example, wanted to recover Alsace-Lorraine (al-sas law-rayn), an area it had lost in a war with Germany in 1871.

As relationships grew more strained, some nations turned to **militarism**, a policy of aggressive military preparedness. European nations built larger militaries than ever before. Germany created the most powerful army in Europe. In 1912 and 1913 alone, Germany increased the size of its army by more than 20 percent. Germany also built a navy to rival Britain's, the world's most powerful.

New Alliances

In the late 1800s European nations began to form alliances to try to create a **balance of power**—a situation in which the strength of rival alliances is nearly equal. European leaders thought that no country would start a war without a real advantage in military strength. In 1879 Germany allied with Austria-Hungary. Three years later Italy joined the union, making it the **Triple Alliance**. Austria-Hungary, Germany, and Italy pledged to support each other in case of attack.

Concerned by Germany's growing power, France formed a military alliance with Russia in 1893. Britain feared Germany's growing naval force and signed an entente, or understanding, with France. In 1907 Russia and Britain reached a similar agreement. The **Triple Entente** alliance united Britain, France, and Russia.

The Triple Alliance and the Triple Entente created a balance of power in Europe that was complicated and fragile. Many people, like Helmuth von Moltke, a German general, felt that "a European war is bound to come sooner or later."

The Spark

In 1878 the Balkan province of Bosnia and Herzegovina had gained independence from Turkish rule. In 1908 Austria-Hungary annexed the province. This annexation angered many

Felix Schwarmstadt's painting captures the 1914 assassination of Archduke Franz Ferdinand and his wife, Sophie.

The Granger Collection, New York

Slavic nationalists who wanted the region allied with Serbia. Many of these nationalists belonged to a secret group known as the Black Hand, which used violence to achieve its goals.

On June 28, 1914, Archduke Franz Ferdinand, the heir to the throne of Austria-Hungary, visited Sarajevo with his wife, Sophie. As the visitors rode through the streets, Gavrilo Princip, a 19-year-old Serb nationalist and member of the Black Hand, stepped out from the crowd and shot them to death.

The archduke's assassination lit the fuse on the "powder keg" of Europe. The president of France advised an Austro-Hungarian official:

66 With a little good will, this Serbian business is easy to settle. But it can just as easily become acute [severe]. Serbia has some very warm friends in the Russian people. And Russia has an ally, France. 99

Austro-Hungarian leaders disregarded his advice. They wanted an excuse to crush Serbia and the Serbian-led Slavic nationalist movements. On July 28, 1914, Austria-Hungary declared war on Serbia.

Europe Goes to War

The next day Austria-Hungary began shelling the Serbian city of Belgrade. An earlier promise of support required Russia to defend Serbia. Initially, however, Russian czar Nicholas II hesitated to **mobilize**, or prepare his military for war. According to his foreign minister:

66 The Tsar was silent. Then he said to me, in a voice full of deep feeling: 'This would mean sending hundreds of thousands of Russian people to their death. How can one help hesitating to take such a step?' 99

The czar decided to keep his earlier promise of support, however. Russia's mobilization led other countries to fulfill their own alliance obligations. In support of Austria-Hungary, Germany declared war on Russia on August 1, and on France, Russia's ally, two days later.

German troops invaded Belgium on August 3 to begin their march toward France. Britain, which had pledged to defend Belgian neutrality, then declared war on Germany. On August 5 Austria-Hungary declared war on Russia. The Great War—which later generations would know as World War I—had begun.

The alliance of Austria-Hungary and Germany became known as the **Central Powers**. Bulgaria and the Ottoman Empire would later join the

Russia mobilized its enormous army in response to Austria-Hungary's attack on Serbia.

Resistance by Belgian soldiers, such as these defending Antwerp, slowed the German army and prevented a quick victory over France.

Central Powers. Britain, France, and Russia fought together as the **Allied Powers**, or the Allies. Despite its alliance with Austria-Hungary and Germany, Italy joined the Allies in 1915. Eventually, 30 nations would fight in World War I.

Many Europeans expected the war to last no more than six months. Kaiser Wilhelm II told departing German troops, "You will be home before the leaves have fallen from the trees." Wilhelm's confidence came from the Schlieffen Plan, the military strategy by which Germany hoped to quickly defeat France before Russia had a chance to fully mobilize its army. The Schlieffen Plan called for a rapid two-pronged attack on France—one in the north through Belgium and one in the south—and a later attack on Russia.

The Belgians fiercely resisted the German army, upsetting the timetable of the Schlieffen Plan. The Belgian effort gave France and Britain valuable time to mobilize their troops.

★ The Battle of the Marne

Belgian resistance slowed German troops but did not stop them. By early September 1914 the Germans were 25 miles from Paris, the capital of France. The military governor warned, "I have received the order to defend Paris against the invader. This order I shall fulfill to the end." In the **First Battle of the Marne**, French troops launched a daring counterattack against the Germans. The French rushed to stop them along the Marne River east of Paris. After a few days of fighting, the Germans retreated. By mid-September the armies faced each other across the western front, a battle line extending from Switzerland to the North Sea.

Meanwhile, the Russians attacked the Central Powers in mid-August on the eastern front, which extended from the Black Sea to the Baltic Sea. The Russians quickly advanced into East Prussia, but Germany counterattacked and crushed the Russian forces. By late September 1914 the Central and Allied Powers both realized that the war would not be a short one.

SECTION 1 REVIEW

Identify and explain the significance of the following:

- nationalism
- militarism
- balance of power
- Triple Alliance
- Triple Entente
- Franz Ferdinand
- Nicholas II
- mobilize

- Central Powers
- Allied Powers
- Wilhelm II
- First Battle of the Marne

Reading for Content Understanding

1. **Main Idea** How did nationalism, imperialism, and militarism help cause World War I?

2. **Main Idea** Describe the early fighting in the war.

3. **Global Relations** Explain how Britain, France, Germany, and Russia became involved in the war.

4. **Writing** *Informing* Imagine that you are a German army officer in September 1914. Write a memo to the kaiser explaining the outcome of the Schlieffen Plan. Describe the plan in your memo.

5. **Critical Thinking** *Supporting a Point of View* Do you think that other European nations should have entered a war that originally started between Austria-Hungary and Serbia? Support your answer.

SECTION 2

Wilson and Neutrality

Reading Focus

What was trench warfare like?

How did new weapons affect the fighting in World War I?

How did the United States try to remain neutral in the war, and what events forced the United States to enter the war?

Key Terms

trench warfare

no-man's-land

stalemate

U-boats

Lusitania

Sussex pledge

Zimmerman Note

THE DAY'S FIGHTING *seemed over. Two Allied officers sat on a hill in southwestern Belgium. As they looked out over fields and villages, a dog barked at some sheep, and a girl sang as she walked. Soldiers laughed as they cooked their evening meal. Darkness fell. Then, as one officer remembered, "without a moment's warning, . . . we saw the whole horizon burst into flame." The Germans had begun to bombard the area. Stunned, the officers soon concluded that World War I had "a merciless, ruthless aspect [part] that we had not realized till then."*

Soldiers from the 8th Battalion eating lunch

 ### The War in Europe

Soon after World War I began, military leaders began to revise old battle plans. The new war strategies—along with new weapons—made the Great War a conflict unlike any other.

Trench Warfare

After French troops stopped the enemy advance in the First Battle of the Marne, the Germans dug in and prepared to hold their ground. Both armies soon turned to **trench warfare**—the strategy of defending a position by fighting from the protection of deep ditches. Two massive systems of opposing trenches stretched for 400 miles across the western front. Trenches ranged from simple holes to complex networks that were six to eight feet deep with rooms for sleeping and eating.

The trenches were typically cold, wet, and dirty. A reporter described one very uncomfortable aspect of trench warfare:

❝ **Men standing in slime for days and nights in field boots . . . lost all sense of feeling in their feet. These feet of theirs,** so cold and wet, began to swell, and then go 'dead' and then suddenly to burn as though touched by red hot pokers. "

Trench warfare brought many health problems. In the trench environment, disease spread rapidly.

The area between opposing trenches, called **no-man's-land**, varied in width from about 200 to 1,000 yards. Much of the fighting took place in no-man's-land, which, according to a British soldier, was "littered with the bodies of men."

New Technology

New weapons made the war even more dangerous. In the trenches, soldiers set up groups of machine guns that fired 400 to 600 rounds of ammunition per minute. In addition, huge guns launched artillery shells, which exploded into deadly metal fragments over enemy positions.

Exposure to the elements, disease, and unsanitary conditions made trenches nearly as dangerous to soldiers as enemy fire.

Some shells contained poison gases, such as chlorine gas and mustard gas. These gases destroyed soldiers' lungs, killing the men slowly. Gas masks were effective, but soldiers had to either wear them all the time or be ready to slip them on in seconds.

The armies also used tanks and airplanes in the war. British and French forces developed tanks to support infantry attacks on trenches. Tanks were hard to destroy and could cause very heavy damage. Pilots used airplanes to gather information, shoot down enemy planes, and fire on trenches.

⭐ The Battle for Verdun

By late 1914 the war had become a **stalemate**—a situation in which neither side can win a decisive victory. In December 1915 German general Erich von Falkenhayn decided to capture the fortified French city of Verdun, located near the southern end of the trench line. The French, however, had

other plans. When the Germans attacked in February 1916, French general Philippe Pétain (PAY-tan) vowed: "They shall not pass." The German advance stalled outside the city, but the battle for Verdun raged for months.

To relieve the pressure on Verdun, in July Allied forces launched an offensive along the Somme River, in northeastern France. Almost 20,000 Allied troops were killed the first day of fighting. When the battle ended in November, the Allies had forced the Germans to retreat only a few miles. However, the attack did succeed in drawing some German forces away from Verdun.

The fighting at Verdun dragged on for 10 months, making it the longest battle of the war. Although France held the city, both armies suffered great losses. The death total at the Somme and Verdun reached almost 1 million. On average, more than 138 soldiers died every single hour.

⭐ The War in the Atlantic

The stalemate on land made the battle in the North Sea and the Atlantic Ocean even more important. Britain used its large navy to cut off German supplies by blockading ports and placing mines in the North Sea. The British searched neutral ships for war materials before guiding them through the minefields.

German **U-boats**, or submarines, attacked British shipping to prevent supplies from reaching

Months of fierce fighting and intense bombing reduced Verdun and many other European cities to rubble.

The Airplane in World War I

On December 17, 1903, brothers Orville and Wilbur Wright made history at Kitty Hawk, North Carolina. Orville made the first piloted flight in a powered airplane. Wilbur made the longest flight that day, remaining aloft for 59 seconds.

The Wrights wanted to sell flying machines to the U.S. government, but officials were not interested. The Wrights then took their invention to Europe. After countries there showed interest, the U.S. Army finally tested the airplane. In 1909 the army began supporting the Wrights' efforts to manufacture their machines.

Early airplanes were fragile. Most were biplanes, which meant that they had two wings, one above the other. Biplanes were made mostly of wood and fabric, light materials that sometimes broke apart if the planes climbed or dove too quickly. Most planes had a single propeller, usually in the front, and could not fly very fast.

At first, the Allies and the Central Powers used airplanes only for scouting. While pilots flew high over the battlefield, observers onboard took pictures of enemy troops and equipment.

The pictures provided valuable information for military commanders. These scout planes did not carry weapons. Opposing pilots sometimes waved when flying by each other.

This friendliness changed, however. To prevent spying, both sides' armies installed machine guns on fighter planes and shot down enemy scouts. Engineers improved fighter planes' speed and maneuverability. Both the Allies and the Central Powers also built large bombers and developed planes that could take off from ships. Thousands of planes were built during the war.

Improvements in airplane design led to new uses after the war. Airmail service began in the United States in 1918, with World War I veterans serving as pilots. Regular airline travel began on a limited basis in the 1920s. The Wright brothers' dream of flying had become part of everyday life.

Understanding What You Read

1. How were airplanes used in World War I?

2. How were airplanes used in civilian life after the war?

Machine guns

Rudder

Ailerons

Struts

No F1283

Engine

Elevator

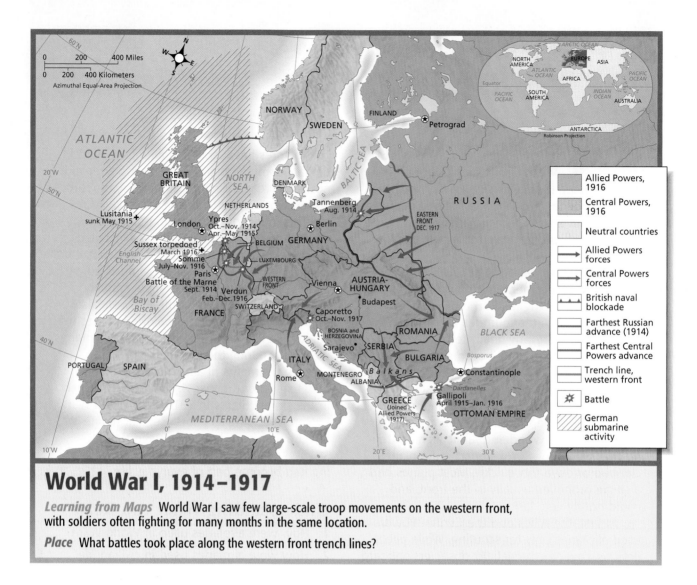

World War I, 1914–1917

Learning from Maps World War I saw few large-scale troop movements on the western front, with soldiers often fighting for many months in the same location.

Place What battles took place along the western front trench lines?

Britain and the Allies. Germany also began targeting neutral merchant ships suspected of carrying war supplies. Germany's submarine fleet, the world's largest and most advanced, caused heavy losses to Allied shipping.

 ## Wilson Pursues Neutrality

Shortly after the war began in Europe, President Woodrow Wilson announced that the United States would remain neutral. Wilson's declaration of neutrality reflected the nation's policy of isolationism, or noninvolvement in foreign affairs.

American Opinion

Most Americans viewed the war as a European conflict. A popular American song title—"I Didn't Raise My Boy to Be a Soldier"—reflected this view. When forced to take a side, most Americans supported the Allies because of long-standing ties with Britain and France. However, millions of Americans had immigrated from and sympathized with the nations of the Central Powers.

Britain, France, and Germany used propaganda to influence public opinion in the United States. British propaganda represented Germany as cruel and inhumane. German propaganda pictured President Wilson as falsely claiming neutrality while actively favoring the Allies.

U.S. neutrality did not prevent American merchants from trading with the warring European nations. U.S. ships carried most of the supplies, including war materials, to the Allies. American banks invested $2 billion in European war bonds, though only $20 million of that was invested in German bonds.

Woodrow Wilson

To many people, President Woodrow Wilson seemed cold and distant. In private, however, Wilson could be warm and lively. He credited his wife, Ellen Axson Wilson, with freeing his true personality. In August 1914, after 29 years of marriage, Ellen died. Wilson threw himself into his work to cope with his grief.

Seven months later, while still mourning his wife's death, Wilson met Edith Bolling Galt. He took her horseback riding and sailing. Wilson discussed affairs of state with her and even had a private telephone line installed between the White House and Edith's home.

Wilson and Galt married in December 1915. Wilson adored his new wife, and often sang her the popular hit "Oh, You Beautiful Doll!" With the entry of the United States into the war, however, the president's attention turned to more serious matters.

Americans Under Fire

The United States moved closer to entering the war on the Allies' side when Germany violated the rules of neutrality in the Atlantic. The rules required German submarines to stop and search merchant ships. The Germans often simply attacked without warning, however, knowing that their submarines were defenseless above water.

In May 1915 a U-boat sank the British passenger liner **Lusitania** off the coast of Ireland, killing nearly 1,200 people, including 128 Americans. The *Lusitania* attack infuriated the American public. President Wilson condemned the attack as "a violation not only of international law but of the fundamental decencies of civilization." The German government argued that the *Lusitania* had been carrying war materials and that Americans had been warned against traveling through the war zone.

Even after the *Lusitania* incident, Wilson tried to keep the nation out of the war. When a U-boat torpedoed the French passenger ship *Sussex* on March 24, 1916, however, he threatened to end diplomatic relations with Germany. Germany then issued the **Sussex pledge**, which included a promise not to sink merchant vessels "without warning and without saving human lives."

★ Campaigning for Peace

As President Wilson campaigned for re-election during the fall of 1916, he pledged to keep the country neutral and to work for peace. Wilson's opponent was Republican Charles Evans Hughes, a Supreme Court justice and former governor of New York. Hughes attacked Wilson for not strongly defending American rights in Europe.

The race was surprisingly close. Many Americans opposed Wilson's foreign policy. Other voters were less certain that Wilson could maintain his

In the Lusitania's *1915 voyage announcement the German Embassy warned Americans about the danger of traveling across the Atlantic.*

This 1917 U.S. Army Air Service recruiting poster asks Americans to join the fight in World War I.

campaign promise to keep the United States out of the war. In the end, however, Wilson won a narrow victory in November 1916 with 277 electoral votes to Hughes's 254.

Once re-elected, Wilson began work on a settlement to end the war. In a speech to the Senate on January 22, 1917, Wilson proposed "peace without victory," in which the Allies and the Central Powers would both declare peace, with neither side the winner. Wilson's speech angered the Allies, particularly Britain. The Allies blamed the Central Powers for the war and wanted them to pay for wartime destruction. The Allies wanted territory, money, or at the very least, a German admission of guilt.

 Congress Declares War

All hopes for a peaceful settlement ended when the Germans violated the *Sussex* pledge and resumed unrestricted submarine warfare on February 1, 1917. President Wilson soon broke off diplomatic relations with Germany and ordered U.S. merchant ships to be fitted with guns. Tensions increased when American newspapers published a decoded German telegram in March. In the note, dated January 19, German foreign minister Arthur Zimmermann proposed an alliance between Germany and Mexico against the United States. He told the German minister in Mexico that for its part, Mexico would "reconquer the lost territory in New Mexico, Texas, and Arizona." The telegram, known as the **Zimmerman Note**, outraged the American public.

In early April President Wilson responded to the new threats by asking Congress to declare war on Germany. Saying that "the world must be made safe for democracy," Wilson called on Americans to

❝ **fight for the things which we have always carried nearest our hearts, for democracy . . . [and to] bring peace and safety to all nations and make the world itself at last free.** ❞

Congress approved Wilson's request, and on April 6, 1917, the United States declared war on Germany.

SECTION 2 REVIEW

Identify and explain the significance of the following:
- **trench warfare**
- **no-man's-land**
- **stalemate**
- **U-boats**
- ***Lusitania***
- ***Sussex* pledge**
- **Charles Evans Hughes**
- **Arthur Zimmermann**
- **Zimmerman Note**

Locate and explain the importance of the following:
- **Verdun**
- **North Sea**

Reading for Content Understanding

1 **Main Idea** What was World War I like for soldiers fighting in the trenches?

2 **Main Idea** What did President Wilson do to enforce neutrality? Why did the United States finally decide to declare war against Germany in 1917?

3 **Technology and Society** What effect did machine guns, poison gas, tanks, and airplanes have on the fighting in World War I?

4 **Writing** *Describing* Imagine that you are a member of a German U-boat crew, or a passenger aboard the *Lusitania*. Write a short diary entry describing the *Lusitania* incident. You might analyze how the Germans' submarine warfare contributed to the U.S. entry into World War I.

5 **Critical Thinking** *Determining the Strength of an Argument* Do you think Wilson had good reasons to ask Congress to declare war? Explain your answer.

Americans Prepare for War

Reading Focus

How did the U.S. government prepare the military for war?

What contributions did women and African Americans make to the war effort?

How did the war affect industry and labor?

Key Terms

Committee on Public Information

Selective Service Act

Liberty bonds

War Industries Board

Food Administration

National War Labor Board

S HORTLY AFTER CONGRESS *declared war, Major Palmer E. Pierce, an aide to the secretary of war, appeared before the Senate Finance Committee. Pierce was there to answer questions about how the War Department planned to spend the $3 billion it had requested. He explained that the money would go for "clothing, cots, camps, food, pay. . . . And we may have to have an army in France." The chairman of the Senate Finance Committee exclaimed, "Good Lord! You're not going to send soldiers over there, are you?" Even though most people supported the declaration of war, few were ready to risk American lives.*

Blindfolded, the U.S. secretary of war drew the first numbers for the military draft on June 5, 1917.

 Rallying the Public

Two weeks after Congress declared war on Germany, President Wilson created a new agency, the **Committee on Public Information** (CPI), to increase public support for the war effort. George Creel, the head of the CPI, launched a nationwide publicity campaign. Creel used rallies, parades, posters, and pamphlets to persuade Americans to support the war. The committee recruited movie stars to entertain troops. Hollywood produced movies like *The Kaiser: The Beast of Berlin* that

showed enemy leaders as evil people, even monsters. Some 75,000 "four-minute men" explained the importance of American involvement in the Great War. These speakers gave short patriotic speeches in movie theaters, churches, and schools.

The government also restricted some freedoms. The Espionage Act of 1917 and the Sedition Act of 1918 provided severe penalties for aiding the enemy, refusing military duty, or speaking disloyally about the U.S. government, Constitution, or flag. Some 900 opponents of the war—including some labor leaders and socialists such as

Eugene Debs and Bill Haywood—were jailed as a result of the laws.

Some Americans criticized religious groups that were committed to nonviolence, characterizing them as traitors. German Americans faced harassment and charges of disloyalty because of strong anti-German feelings. In order to show their dislike for German things, people renamed familiar items: hamburgers became liberty sandwiches, and dachshunds became liberty pups.

U.S. troops prepare at a New Jersey training camp to fight in the war.

Mobilizing for War

Encouraged by the CPI's publicity, some 73,000 men enlisted in the army in the six weeks following the declaration of war. However, these new recruits and the 98,000 men already in the armed forces were not enough to fight a modern war.

Drafting Soldiers

On May 18, 1917, Congress passed the **Selective Service Act**, which required men between the ages of 21 and 30 to register to be drafted into the armed forces. Almost 3 million men who served during the war were draftees. Some Americans saw the draft as a violation of their civil liberties. Others, such as Quakers, refused to fight because of their religious beliefs. Many of these men served in noncombat roles.

To organize and train the soldiers, the army built dozens of training camps. Most were located in the South, where mild winters allowed year-round training. Soldiers learned to dig trenches, survive poison-gas attacks, string barbed wire, fire rifles and machine guns, and throw hand grenades.

African American Soldiers

After the U.S. declaration of war, the government trained African American soldiers to fill noncombat roles. Pressure from the National Association for the Advancement of Colored People (NAACP) led the military to create some combat units and one officer-training camp for African Americans.

The majority of the 400,000 African Americans who served in the armed forces, however, did so in segregated units commanded by white officers. Once in Europe, most African American troops fought with divisions of the French army. U.S. officials worried that conflict might erupt within their army if white and black soldiers fought together.

While black soldiers fought "to make the world safe for democracy," African Americans at home protested ongoing discrimination and racially motivated violence. On July 28, 1917, some 15,000 African Americans marched in silence down New York City's Fifth Avenue. They carried signs and passed out leaflets declaring their message. Their *Why We March* leaflet stated:

> **We march because we are thoroughly opposed to Jim Crow cars, segregation, discrimination, and disfranchisement [denial of voting rights], lynching, and the host of evils that are forced on us. We march because we want our children to live in a better land and enjoy fairer conditions than have fallen to our lot.** "

Organizing for War

In addition to raising troops, the government needed to raise money and supplies. To do so, it expanded its involvement in the economy.

Supplying the Armies

Congress increased income taxes, imposed a tax on business profits, and, most importantly, authorized the issue of war bonds. Money from the sale of **Liberty bonds** provided loans to the Allies to allow them to purchase food and war supplies. Liberty bonds raised more than $20 billion.

To oversee the production and distribution of goods manufactured by the nation's war industries, President Wilson created the **War Industries Board** (WIB). According to Bernard Baruch, head of the WIB, "No steel, copper, cement, rubber, or other basic materials could be used without our [WIB] approval." Most producers eagerly cooperated with the WIB. The automobile and steel industries, however, hesitated to yield to government control. The automakers gave in only after Baruch threatened to stop railroad service into and out of their plants. Steel producers also agreed to cooperate when Baruch threatened to take over their factories.

Feeding the Troops

With the passage of the Lever Food and Fuel Control Act of 1917, the federal government gained even greater control over the war effort. The act gave Wilson the right to establish price and production controls over food and fuel. Herbert Hoover took control of the **Food Administration**, an agency created to increase food supplies for the troops by expanding agricultural production and decreasing domestic consumption.

Hoover motivated farmers to produce at high levels by guaranteeing them high prices for their food crops. Production, as well as prices, increased greatly. Announcing that "food will win the war," Hoover promoted "meatless Mondays" and "wheatless Wednesdays" and encouraged people to plant vegetables at home in "victory gardens."

★ Women's War Efforts

American women contributed to the war effort in many ways. Some 25,000 female volunteers served in France. They worked as nurses, signalers, typists, and interpreters. The "Hello Girls" of the U.S. Army Signal Corps handled military telephone service, including translating calls and sending battle orders. None of the women in the military received any pension for their service.

Although officially not allowed in combat, many female nurses and ambulance drivers worked at the front lines. One female driver remembered the dangers:

66 We had our first air-raid work last night. I was the night-driver on duty. . . . Some bombs fell very near just as I got to the [evacuation hospital]. . . . I had just stopped . . . when shrapnel [metal fragments] whizzed past my head and there was a tremendous crash close beside. . . . Then an ambulance call came and I tore off. 99

Many other women volunteered for the Red Cross and served at home and abroad. First Lady Edith Wilson regularly served coffee and

The U.S. government used posters like these to inspire patriotism and encourage support for the war effort.

CAN
Vegetables
Fruit AND
the Kaiser too

Tomatoes   Peas

Kaiser Brand
Unsweetened

Write for Free Book to
NATIONAL WAR GARDEN COMMISSION
WASHINGTON, D.C.

Charles Lathrop Pack, President   P. S. Ridsdale, Secretary

OVER THE TOP
FOR YOU

Buy U.S. Gov't Bonds
THIRD LIBERTY LOAN

Women joined the war effort by serving as ambulance drivers, often transporting wounded soldiers directly from the front lines to hospitals.

sandwiches to soldiers in Washington, D.C. On the home front, women filled important industrial jobs. More than 1.5 million women worked in factory positions left vacant by departing soldiers.

Some women, including social reformer Jane Addams, opposed U.S. entry into the war and worked for peace. Jeannette Rankin of Montana, the first woman elected to the U.S. Congress, cast one of the few votes against President Wilson's war resolution. She stated, "I want to stand by my country but I cannot vote for war."

 ## Labor and the War

The effort to supply the troops overseas benefited all workers. Three conditions combined to produce high wages and a favorable environment for labor.

First, American products were essential to Allied troops fighting in Europe, so it was important to maintain full production. Second, the war created a serious labor shortage as production increased and workers left to join the armed forces. The new female workers could not fill all the empty positions. Third, immigration to the United States nearly stopped during the war.

The new and remaining workers took advantage of the labor shortage to press for higher wages and better working conditions. They formed and joined unions and sometimes went on strike. During the course of the war more than 4 million workers went on strike—the highest proportion of the workforce to do so before or since the war. Unable to replace striking workers and faced with steady production orders, most companies gave in to worker demands and agreed to pay higher wages.

In April 1918 President Wilson created the **National War Labor Board** to settle disputes between workers and management and prevent strikes. The board was sympathetic to workers and supported their right to collective bargaining. It also outlined minimum-wage and maximum-hour standards in the workplace, and required fair pay for female workers.

SECTION 3 REVIEW

Identify and explain the significance of the following:
- **Committee on Public Information**
- **George Creel**
- **Selective Service Act**
- **Liberty bonds**
- **War Industries Board**
- **Bernard Baruch**
- **Food Administration**
- **Jeannette Rankin**
- **National War Labor Board**

Reading for Content Understanding

1 **Main Idea** What changes did U.S. government officials make to organize an army to fight in Europe during World War I?

2 **Main Idea** How did the war affect industry and labor? How did this situation benefit each?

3 **Cultural Diversity** How did women and African Americans serve in the war effort?

4 **Writing** *Creating* Create a poster to encourage Americans to support the war effort. You might advise Americans why it is important to buy Liberty bonds or to join the Red Cross.

5 **Critical Thinking** *Determining the Strength of an Argument* Do you agree with the government's action in punishing some people who opposed the war? Explain your answer.

Americans "Over There"

Reading Focus

What were the experiences of U.S. soldiers in World War I?

How did the final battles of the war progress?

Why did Germany finally agree to an armistice?

Key Terms

American Expeditionary Force
Communists
Treaty of Brest-Litovsk
Second Battle of the Marne
armistice

I N JUNE 1917 *the first U.S. forces arrived in France. In Paris the French Republican Guard band greeted the soldiers with "The Star-Spangled Banner," followed by the French national anthem, "La Marseillaise" (mahr-suh-layz). The sidewalks overflowed with people welcoming the troops. An American journalist traveling with the soldiers reported, "From the crowded balconies and windows overlooking the route, women and children tossed down showers of flowers and bits of colored paper. . . . There came from the crowds a good old genuine American whoop-em-up yell."*

Sheet music cover of George M. Cohan's World War I song

★ The Americans Arrive

By the time the first U.S. troops arrived, the Allies were in bad shape. German troops were occupying Belgium and part of France. The German navy was destroying Allied ships at an alarming rate. Russia was barely able to hold the Germans back.

Joining the Fight

The French and British armies wanted U.S. troops on the front lines immediately. However, General John J. "Black Jack" Pershing refused to send soldiers to join French and British units. He wanted U.S. troops, known as the **American Expeditionary Force** (AEF), to serve as individual units. He wanted the AEF to be a "distinct and separate component of the combined forces, the identity of which will be preserved." The AEF included the regular army, the National Guard, and the new larger force of volunteers and draftees.

Starting in the fall of 1917, Pershing hurried his troops through a three-month training program. The U.S. soldiers, called doughboys, trained in

World War I soldiers carried all their necessary equipment on their backs. A condiment can (top right) had compartments for coffee, sugar, and salt. A bacon tin (bottom right) stored meat.

Germany launched a series of major attacks to break the the stalemate on the western front.

During these weeks, the first U.S. troops experienced the grim realities of war. Unlike the practice trenches, the trenches at the front were filled with trash, lice, and rats, and sometimes the remains of long-dead soldiers. The troops' diet consisted of hard biscuits, bacon, dried beef, and canned emergency rations. Once in battle, however, these hardships seemed unimportant. One U.S. Marine remembered, "I had been so horrified at the death, destruction, and danger on all sides that I had forgotten about my stomach."

On March 21 the Germans attacked along the Somme River near St. Quentin in northern France. The battle began with a five-hour bombardment by more than 6,000 heavy guns. Two days later, German artillery bombarded Paris from 75 miles away. After pushing some 40 miles into Allied lines, the German advance stalled as troops advanced farther and faster than their supplies. The attack cost the German army 250,000 casualties. Combined British and French losses were 133,000.

In April the German army launched its second offensive against the British line in northwestern France, near Belgium. British field marshal Douglas Haig told his troops:

> 66 **There is no other course open to us but to fight it out! Every position must be held to the last man. . . . With our backs to the wall, and believing in the justice of our cause, each one of us must fight on to the end.** 99

They did just that and the Germans failed to reach their target—a major railway junction. In 20 days of combat, both sides suffered about 110,000 casualties.

Farther south, the Germans forced French troops across the Aisne River and back toward the Marne River. German forces reached the Marne River and were threatening to break through the thin French line toward Paris. Ferdinand Foch, French commander of the Allied forces, declared, "Lose not another meter of ground!" At this point,

specially dug trenches and practiced with real shells and rifles. Pershing's plan was to train these troops for victory. The Allies, however, grew impatient for the soldiers to enter the war.

Russia Leaves the War

The Allies feared defeat as their situation worsened. In November 1917, the Bolsheviks seized control of the Russian government. The Bolsheviks were **Communists**, or people who favor the equal distribution of wealth and the end of all forms of private property. The new government, led by Vladimir Lenin, faced famine and civil war. Russia withdrew from the fighting in December. In March 1918 the Central Powers and Russia signed the **Treaty of Brest-Litovsk**, a peace agreement removing Russia from the war.

 ## The Final Battles

With Russia out of the war and most U.S. troops not yet ready to fight, Germany saw its last chance to win the war and seized it. In the spring of 1918

These German sharpshooters are moving into position near the front lines during fighting near the Aisne River in France.

two divisions of the American Expeditionary Force joined French forces to strike back.

U.S. troops stopped the German advance at the town of Château-Thierry (sha-toh-te-ree), fewer than 50 miles from Paris. French and U.S. troops then attacked the Germans at Belleau Wood. The battle started poorly for the Allies. When an observer asked a U.S. officer about

withdrawing, however, he responded: "Retreat[?] . . . We just got here." The Allies then gradually drove back this second German offensive.

By the beginning of July 1918, 1 million U.S. troops and military personnel were stationed in France. At midnight on July 14, the Germans launched their last, desperate offensive at the **Second Battle of the Marne**. During the fighting, the U.S. 3rd Division blew up every bridge that the Germans had built across the Marne River. Both sides suffered heavy casualties, but the German losses crippled their ability to launch another offensive. The turning point of the war had finally come.

★ Driving The Germans Back

With the last German offensive beaten, the Allies attacked. In September—in the first distinctly American assault—U.S. forces defeated German troops at Saint-Mihiel near Alsace-Lorraine, on the border of France and Germany. One wounded but

American Arts

John Philip Sousa

John Philip Sousa was born in 1854 in Washington, D.C. He earned a place in the world of music by writing more marches than anyone else in history. In all, Sousa wrote some 140 military marches, including "Semper Fidelis" and "The Stars and Stripes Forever." His marches were hugely popular and still inspire strong feelings of patriotism.

During World War I, Sousa joined the U.S. Naval Reserve at the age of 62 to organize its band units. He toured with a navy band of more than 300 sailors. In addition to entertaining the troops, Sousa's band also assisted in the Liberty Loan and Red Cross drives. He wrote his "Liberty Loan" march at the request of Secretary of the Treasury William McAdoo.

John Philip Sousa

Sousa wrote many marches during the war, including "The Chantyman's March" and "Sabre and Spurs." In 1918, when anti-German feelings were running high, the American Relief Legion asked Sousa to write a wedding march to replace the often-used music of German composers. Sousa's "Wedding March" was performed at many wedding ceremonies held during World War I.

Understanding the Arts

1. How did John Philip Sousa serve in World War I?

2. Why do you think Sousa's music was so popular?

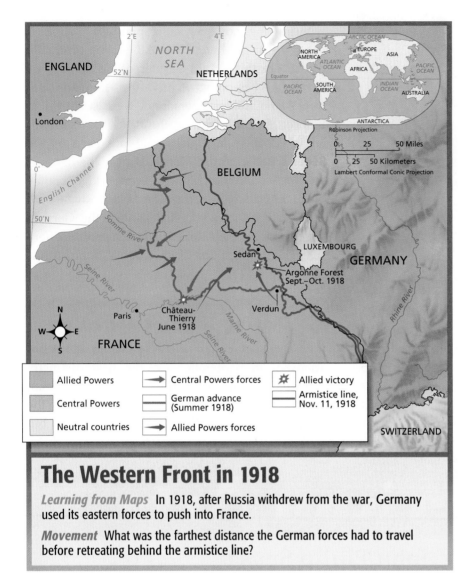

The Western Front in 1918

Learning from Maps In 1918, after Russia withdrew from the war, Germany used its eastern forces to push into France.

Movement What was the farthest distance the German forces had to travel before retreating behind the armistice line?

and fields were strewn [covered] with dead Germans, horses, . . . helmets, [and] guns."

The Allies continued to advance toward the railway at Sedan on the Belgian border, which was the main supply line for German forces. Other Allied forces advanced all along the front. The German soldiers were so exhausted that a U.S. soldier with an empty pistol captured 300 of them simply by asking them to surrender.

★ Armistice

By the fall of 1918 the German people were as tired of the war as their soldiers. In October 1918, a German newspaper even dared to ask, "Do the people wish to continue war?" Many German civilians were without food or supplies. By 1918 an average of 800 Germans were dying daily from starvation, up from 240 per day in 1915. Food riots and strikes occurred in Germany and the other Central Powers nations.

German soldiers also rebelled. In October, when senior German naval officers planned a final suicide attack to break the British blockade, German sailors mutinied. They refused to sail on the mission and seized control of the naval station at Kiel, Germany. The Germans did not have enough soldiers to continue fighting. In the three months since the last Allied offensive began in August, the Allies had captured one quarter of all German soldiers in the field and one half of all German guns. By early November the commandant of Berlin sent a telegram that read, "All troops deserted."

Germany's allies in the Central Powers also began leaving the war. Bulgaria signed a truce on September 30, and a month later the Ottoman

proud soldier informed his parents, "Folks, we have them on the run." The Americans then joined the other Allies under the leadership of Ferdinand Foch to attack along the Meuse River and in the Argonne Forest.

Every available U.S. unit joined the fighting, including the African American soldiers of the 369th U.S. Infantry—the so-called Harlem Hell Fighters. The 369th spent more time in combat than any other U.S. unit and was the first Allied regiment to reach the Rhine River on the German border. The members of the 369th were awarded France's highest military honor—the Croix de Guerre (krwah-di-ger)—for their bravery.

By November 1918 General Pershing was able to report, "For the first time the enemy lines were completely broken through." One U.S. private recalled the scene after the fighting: "The roads

These African American soldiers received the Croix de Guerre (right) from France for their bravery during the war.

Empire also quit the war. On November 4, 1918, the Allies reached a peace agreement with Austria-Hungary. Just four days later, German representatives traveled to the Allied headquarters at Compiègne (kohm-pyayn), France, to receive the terms of a cease-fire. As part of the agreement, Kaiser Wilhelm II abandoned the German throne and fled to the Netherlands. Germany became a republic.

The Allies demanded that Germany evacuate all occupied territory. German aircraft, tanks, and heavy artillery were to be destroyed, and Germany had to surrender its U-boats. Germany was also required to accept the possible occupation of German territory by Allied troops. The Germans had no choice but to agree to the Allies' terms. On the 11th hour of the 11th day of the 11th month, the **armistice**, or truce, went into effect. The Great War had ended. An Allied soldier described the troops' reaction to the news:

66 **There came a second of expectant silence, and then a curious rippling sound. . . . It was the sound of men cheering from the Vosges [a mountain range located in northeastern France] to the sea.** 99

In a different location, U.S. pilots yelled, "I've lived through the war!" and "We won't be shot at any more." However, the tragedy of the war took away from some of the celebration. When asked what the armistice meant, one British soldier replied, "Time to bury the dead."

SECTION 4 REVIEW

Identify and explain the significance of the following:
- **John J. Pershing**
- **American Expeditionary Force**
- **Communists**
- **Treaty of Brest-Litovsk**
- **Ferdinand Foch**
- **Second Battle of the Marne**
- **armistice**

Locate and explain the importance of the following:
- **Château-Thierry**
- **Argonne Forest**

Reading for Content Understanding

1 **Main Idea** What was World War I like for U.S. soldiers?

2 **Main Idea** Why, after so many early victories, did Germany finally surrender in World War I?

3 **Global Relations** What did the Allies demand of Germany following the armistice?

4 **Writing** *Informing* Imagine that you are a reporter for an American newspaper who has been assigned to cover the western front in 1918. In a one- or two-paragraph story, explain the condition of the German and Allied troops in the final battles, and describe the war's end.

5 **Critical Thinking** *Synthesizing Information* Do you think that the Allies could have won the war without the help of U.S. troops? Use information from the text to explain your answer.

Establishing Peace

Reading Focus

What were the human and economic costs of the war?

What were the terms of the Treaty of Versailles?

How did Americans respond to the Treaty of Versailles?

Key Terms

Fourteen Points
self-determination
League of Nations
Big Four
reparations
Treaty of Versailles

O N NOVEMBER 7, 1918, *an American reporter saw German officials arrive in France and mistakenly wired New York that the war was over. Celebrations erupted in hundreds of towns and cities. In New York City, thousands of men and women poured into the streets in a "wild, whooping dance of celebration." Famed Italian opera singer Enrico Caruso appeared at the window of his hotel and sang "The Star-Spangled Banner" to a joyous crowd below. Later, on November 11, when the armistice was actually signed, Americans celebrated all over again.*

Two women sweep this marine off his feet after the armistice.

 Europe After The War

World War I carried a heavy human cost. The Allies lost more than 5 million soldiers as a result of the war. Some 116,000 U.S. troops died. More than half of them died of influenza, a viral infection. The Central Powers lost about 3.4 million soldiers. More than 20 million soldiers on both sides had been wounded. Thousands of civilians were also killed during the four years of fighting.

The economies of the nations involved in the war were ruined. The war also destroyed the land itself. A British visitor described the French countryside after the war:

66 **The horror . . . of war was made visible . . . on an extraordinary scale. . . . The completeness of the destruction was evident. For mile after mile nothing was left. No building was habitable [livable] and no field fit for the plow.** 99

The cost of the war has been estimated at more than $145 billion for the Allies and $63 billion for the Central Powers. In addition, more than $30 billion in property had been destroyed and over $1 billion was spent on aid efforts. Industry and agriculture had nearly been wiped out in Belgium, France, and other parts of Europe.

France and Britain owed American banks billions of dollars for money borrowed during the war. Germany also faced debt and severe food shortages. Many people feared that these economic troubles would allow the communist revolution in Russia to expand to other nations.

⭐ Wilson's Fourteen Points

While Americans welcomed the armistice, President Wilson focused on making an enduring peace. Even before the United States entered the war, Wilson had been preparing for its end.

On January 8, 1918, Wilson outlined a vision for postwar Europe and a system to avoid future wars. This plan was called the **Fourteen Points**, because it contained 14 basic principles. (See pages 350–51.) The president believed that the peace terms must not be so hard on the Central Powers that the settlement would lead to another war.

Many of the Fourteen Points concerned the future of specific nations and regions. Some points called for freedom of ships on the seas, smaller armies and navies, and lower trade tariffs. Other points related to fair settlement of colonial claims

These members of the Disarmament Conference of the League of Nations are struggling with the problems of enforcing the peace.

of independence and an end to secret agreements between nations. Wilson also emphasized the right of people to decide their own political status—the right of **self-determination**. The last point called for the creation of the **League of Nations**—a congress of nations designed to settle international disputes and protect democracy.

Other Allied leaders, however, wanted a different kind of peace. An American journalist reported that Allied leaders wanted "a new world domination with themselves and ourselves dominating; what they decidedly do not want is a democratic peace." France and Britain also wanted to punish Germany for its role in the war and to ensure that Germany would never again be a world power. As one reporter wrote, Britain and France wanted Germany to "pay, pay, pay."

Many Americans agreed with these Europeans. A Montana rancher who had three sons fighting in France, however, wanted the government to do more than just punish Germany. The rancher knew that one or two of his sons could die in battle, and he accepted that possibility. As he explained in a letter to a member of Wilson's cabinet, the rancher wanted something in return:

❝ **What I ask is that they do not give themselves in vain [for nothing]. . . . Take steps to see that there shall never be another tragedy like this. See that they do not die for anything less worthwhile. Fix the matter so that neither Germany nor any other nation can ruin the world.** ❞

⭐ The Paris Peace Conference

President Wilson arrived in Europe on December 13, 1918, ready to persuade the Allies to propose peace based on his Fourteen Points. He ignored his advisers, who feared that if he attended the peace conference, Allied leaders would force him to compromise. Wilson went because he felt "it is now my duty to play my full part in making good what [our soldiers] offered their lives to obtain."

Deciding Europe's Future

Leaders of the Allied nations attended the peace conference at the palace of Versailles (ver-sy), outside of Paris. The new leaders of Russia refused to attend, and no representatives of the Central Powers were invited. The **Big Four**—President Woodrow Wilson of the United States, British prime minister David Lloyd George, French premier Georges Clemenceau (kle-mahn-soh), and Italian prime minister Vittorio Orlando—dominated the conference.

National leaders from around the world gathered in the Hall of Mirrors at Versailles on June 28, 1919, to sign the peace treaty.

The peace conference was a clash between Wilson's ideals of peace and democracy and the European leaders' desire to reward their allies and punish their enemies. Lloyd George was most interested in keeping the British Empire together and protecting its long-term interests. Clemenceau wanted to punish Germany so severely that it could never again threaten France. Orlando was most concerned with ensuring that Italy received the territory that it had been promised when it entered the war on the Allies side.

Wilson was unable to persuade the other members of the Big Four to accept his goal of "peace without victory." The other leaders insisted that Germany accept the blame and pay the Allied Powers for the entire cost of the war. Forced to compromise, Wilson agreed that Germany would have to pay **reparations**—payments for damages

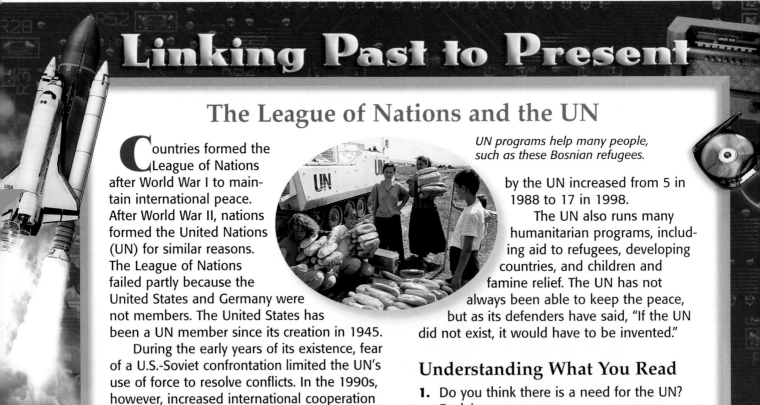

Linking Past to Present

The League of Nations and the UN

UN programs help many people, such as these Bosnian refugees.

Countries formed the League of Nations after World War I to maintain international peace. After World War II, nations formed the United Nations (UN) for similar reasons. The League of Nations failed partly because the United States and Germany were not members. The United States has been a UN member since its creation in 1945.

During the early years of its existence, fear of a U.S.-Soviet confrontation limited the UN's use of force to resolve conflicts. In the 1990s, however, increased international cooperation has strengthened the UN. The number of ongoing peacekeeping missions conducted by the UN increased from 5 in 1988 to 17 in 1998.

The UN also runs many humanitarian programs, including aid to refugees, developing countries, and children and famine relief. The UN has not always been able to keep the peace, but as its defenders have said, "If the UN did not exist, it would have to be invented."

Understanding What You Read

1. Do you think there is a need for the UN? Explain your answer.

2. What does the United Nations do today?

and expenses brought on by war. The amount was eventually set at $33 billion. To provide France the defensive security that it desired, the president also agreed that Germany must return the border region of Alsace-Lorraine. Also, the Allies would gain control of the Rhineland and Saar Valley region in western Germany.

Wilson's Victories

The final peace settlement of World War I, the **Treaty of Versailles**, included a number of the Fourteen Points. The treaty partially incorporated the right of national self-determination. The people of some nations won the right to decide their own political situation, rather than have an outside empire decide it. Some new nations were formed and old ones were restored. Czechoslovakia and Yugoslavia were created and Poland was restored. Estonia, Finland, Latvia, and Lithuania became free nations. The Central Powers were also forced to surrender control of their colonies to the Allies.

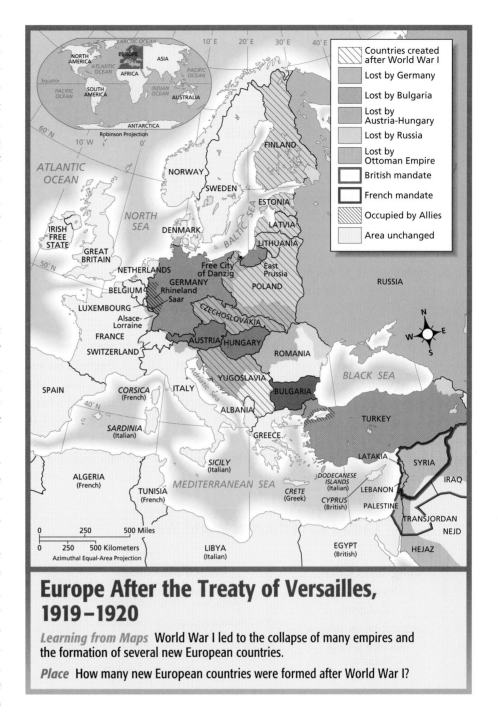

Europe After the Treaty of Versailles, 1919–1920

Learning from Maps World War I led to the collapse of many empires and the formation of several new European countries.

Place How many new European countries were formed after World War I?

However, the victorious Allies would not keep the Central Powers' colonies as their own. A system of mandate, or authority, gave the League of Nations control over these areas. The League assigned nations, such as France and Britain, to administer these areas until they were ready for independence.

Although the treaty was not everything that Wilson wanted, he felt that the League of Nations could resolve any problems that the treaty created or failed to solve. Wilson addressed the peace conference in February 1919. He said that although the war had caused many terrible things,

❝some very beautiful things have come out of it. Wrong has been defeated, but the rest of the world has been more conscious than it was before of the majesty of right. People that were suspicious of one another can now live as friends . . . in a single family.❞

All that remained was to persuade the U.S. Senate to ratify the treaty. Wilson was not prepared for the opposition he met there.

★ The League of Nations

For President Wilson, the most important part of the treaty was the creation of the League of Nations, which he believed would be "a definite guarantee of peace." In Wilson's plan, the League of Nations would include representatives from democratic nations. It would consist of a council, an assembly, and a permanent administrative staff. The League would promote peace by working cooperatively to settle disputes and to reduce armaments.

Each member nation would be represented in the assembly and would have one vote. The council would have four rotating members elected by the assembly, and five permanent members—Britain, France, Italy, Japan, and the United States. Eventually, all independent nations would be allowed to join, but the former Central Powers nations could not be members at first.

Member nations would present disagreements to the Permanent Court of International Justice, or World Court. If a member nation did not obey the court's judgment, the League could impose penalties. They might include a ban on trade or even the use of military force.

★ Peace Without a Treaty

When President Wilson returned to the United States in July 1919, he found that Congress did not share his enthusiasm for the Treaty of Versailles or the League of Nations. Republican senator Henry Cabot Lodge, chairman of the Foreign Relations Committee, said:

> ❝ No peace that satisfied Germany in any degree can ever satisfy us. It can not be a negotiated peace. It must be a dictated peace, and we and our allies must dictate it. ❞

To secure the two-thirds majority needed to ratify the treaty, Wilson needed the support of the Republicans in Congress. They had won control of the House and the Senate in 1918. Wilson had offended some Republicans by not including them in the U.S. delegation to the peace conference. Although most Democratic senators supported the treaty, many Republican senators disagreed with certain parts of it and demanded changes. Wilson, expecting the treaty to pass without change, refused to negotiate.

A group of 14 Republican senators, called the irreconcilables, rejected the peace treaty outright. The remaining Republican senators were divided between mild reservationists, who wanted small changes, and strong reservationists, who demanded drastic revisions.

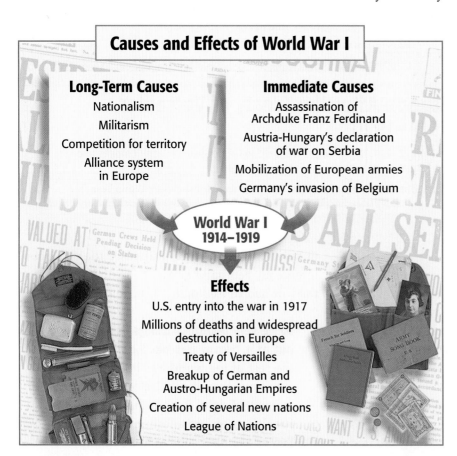

Causes and Effects of World War I

Long-Term Causes
Nationalism
Militarism
Competition for territory
Alliance system in Europe

Immediate Causes
Assassination of Archduke Franz Ferdinand
Austria-Hungary's declaration of war on Serbia
Mobilization of European armies
Germany's invasion of Belgium

World War I 1914–1919

Effects
U.S. entry into the war in 1917
Millions of deaths and widespread destruction in Europe
Treaty of Versailles
Breakup of German and Austro-Hungarian Empires
Creation of several new nations
League of Nations

The Foreign Relations Committee, led by Senator Henry Cabot Lodge, demanded changes to the Treaty of Versailles.

Most of the Republicans' concerns focused on the extreme instances when the League of Nations could use military force to carry out its decisions. The Republicans were suspicious of European countries' motives. Many of them believed that membership in the League conflicted with Congress's constitutional power to declare war. Senator Lodge led the strong reservationists. In an attempt to force Wilson to compromise, Lodge delayed the treaty vote.

Wilson took his cause to the American public. He went on an extended speaking tour to defend the treaty and to get the public to pressure Republicans to pass it. As he traveled across the country, Wilson spoke to enthusiastic crowds. After a speech in Pueblo, Colorado, in September Wilson

collapsed. He was rushed back to Washington, D.C., where he suffered a stroke in early October. Although he survived, Wilson never fully recovered. His wife, Edith Galt Wilson, took care of him and tried to persuade him to compromise on the treaty.

In November, Lodge presented the treaty for ratification with his list of reservations. He wanted to limit U.S. military involvement in the League, but otherwise his reservations did not change the treaty significantly. Wilson still refused any compromise on the League and ordered Democrats to vote against Lodge's version of the treaty.

In November 1919, the Senate defeated both versions—with and without reservations—of the Treaty of Versailles. Neither the Democrats nor the Republicans would vote for the other's version, but neither side had enough votes for the two-thirds majority. After further debate, the Senate again defeated the treaty in March 1920.

Congressional opposition and President Wilson's refusal to negotiate doomed the Treaty of Versailles to defeat in the Senate. Wilson's continued refusal to compromise cost him his goal of U.S. membership in the League of Nations. In the end, the United States negotiated separate peace treaties with Austria, Germany, and Hungary. The United States never joined the League of Nations, and the League's future as a world peace organization seemed uncertain.

SECTION 5 REVIEW

Identify and explain the significance of the following:
- **Fourteen Points**
- **self-determination**
- **League of Nations**
- **Big Four**
- **reparations**
- **Treaty of Versailles**
- **Henry Cabot Lodge**

Reading for Content Understanding

1 Main Idea How did the war affect the people and the economies of the nations involved?

2 Main Idea What were the conditions and requirements of the Treaty of Versailles?

3 Geographic Diversity *Human-Environment Interaction* How did World War I affect the European landscape?

4 Writing *Describing* Imagine that you are a visitor to the Capitol on the day that Senator Lodge presents his reservations about the Treaty of Versailles. In a letter to a friend, describe the different opinions expressed about the treaty.

5 Critical Thinking *Evaluating* If you had been a member of the Senate in 1919, what would your approach to a postwar peace have been?

Woodrow Wilson's
The Fourteen Points

President Wilson announced his specific proposals for a postwar peace—the Fourteen Points—in an address to Congress on January 8, 1918. An excerpt of the Fourteen Points appears below.

Gentlemen of the Congress:

It will be our wish and purpose that the processes of peace, when they are begun, shall be absolutely open and that they shall involve and permit henceforth no secret understandings of any kind. . . . The program of the world's peace, therefore, is our program; and that program, the only possible program, as we see it, is this:

I. Open covenants [agreements] of peace, openly arrived at, after which there shall be no private international understandings of any kind but diplomacy [negotiations] shall proceed always frankly and in the public view.

II. Absolute freedom of navigation upon the seas, outside territorial waters, alike in peace and in war, except as the seas may be closed in whole or in part by international action for the enforcement of international covenants.

III. The removal, so far as possible, of all economic barriers and the establishment of an equality of trade conditions among all the nations consenting to the peace and associating themselves for its maintenance.

IV. Adequate guarantees given and taken that national armaments [military equipment] will be reduced to the lowest point consistent [in agreement] with domestic safety.

V. A free, open-minded, and absolutely impartial [fair] adjustment of all colonial claims, based upon a strict observance of the principle that in determining all such questions of sovereignty [who should rule] the interests of the populations concerned must have equal weight with the equitable [just] claims of the government whose title is to be determined.

VI. The evacuation of all Russian territory and such a settlement of all questions affecting Russia as will secure the best and freest cooperation of the other nations of the world in obtaining for her an . . . opportunity for the independent determination of her own political development and national policy and assure her of a sincere welcome into the society of free nations under institutions of her own choosing; and more than a welcome, assistance also of every kind that she may need and may herself desire.

VII. Belgium, the whole world will agree, must be evacuated and restored, without any attempt to limit the sovereignty [self-rule] which she enjoys in common with all other free nations. No other single act will serve as this will serve to restore confidence among nations in the laws which they have themselves set and determined for the government of their relations with one another. Without this healing act the whole structure and validity [authority] of international law is forever impaired [damaged].

VIII. All French territory should be freed and the invaded portions restored, and the wrong done to France by Prussia in 1871 in the matter of Alsace-Lorraine, which has unsettled the peace of the world for nearly fifty years, should be righted, in order that peace may once more be made secure in the interest of all.

IX. A readjustment of the frontiers of Italy should be effected along clearly recognizable lines of nationality.

X. The peoples of Austria-Hungary, whose place among the nations we wish to see safeguarded and assured, should be accorded [given] the freest opportunity of autonomous [independent] development.

XI. Rumania, Serbia, and Montenegro should be evacuated; occupied territories restored; Serbia accorded free and secure access to the sea; and the relations of the several Balkan states to one another determined by friendly counsel [agreement] along historically established lines of allegiance and nationality; and international guarantees of the political and economic independence and territorial integrity [completeness] of the several Balkan states should be entered into.

XII. The Turkish portions of the present Ottoman Empire should be assured a secure sovereignty, but the other nationalities which are now under Turkish rule should be assured an undoubted [beyond dispute] security of life and an absolutely unmolested [unquestioned] opportunity of autonomous development, and the Dardanelles should be permanently opened as a free passage to the ships and commerce of all nations under international guarantees.

XIII. An independent Polish state should be erected which should include the territories inhabited by indisputably Polish populations, which should be assured a free and secure access to the sea, and whose political and economic independence and territorial integrity should be guaranteed by international covenant.

XIV. A general association of nations must be formed under specific covenants for the purpose of affording mutual guarantees of political independence and territorial integrity to great and small states alike.

Understanding Primary Sources

1. What freedoms does President Wilson want to guarantee?

2. What countries does Wilson want created or restored?

3. Do you think the Fourteen Points were fair to all the countries involved? Explain your answer.

The Granger Collection, New York

The Big Four; seated from left to right, Italian prime minister Vittorio Orlando, British prime minister David Lloyd George, French premier Georges Clemenceau, and U.S. president Woodrow Wilson

CHAPTER
11 REVIEW

Chapter Summary

Long-simmering tensions in Europe caused World War I to break out in 1914. The United States initially pursued a policy of neutrality. Then German U-boats killed Americans on neutral ships and newspapers published the Zimmerman Note. The United States entered the war in 1917 and helped the Allies win the conflict. Despite President Wilson's quest for "peace without victory," the Allies forced harsh postwar conditions on Germany. ▪

On a separate sheet of paper, complete the following activities.

Identifying People and Ideas

Describe the historical significance of the following:

1. Franz Ferdinand
2. mobilize
3. stalemate
4. *Sussex* pledge
5. George Creel
6. National War Labor Board
7. American Expeditionary Force
8. John J. Pershing
9. reparations
10. Henry Cabot Lodge

Internet Activity go.hrw.com
SB1 Soldiers

Search the Internet through the HRW Web site to find information on U.S. soldiers who served in World War I. Create a profile of the regiments that fought together in a particular battle.

Understanding Main Ideas

1. What events led to U.S. entry into World War I?
2. What was war like in the trenches?
3. How did the war affect African Americans and women?
4. How did Americans at home contribute to the war effort?
5. Why was the Second Battle of the Marne the turning point of the war?
6. Why was the League of Nations part of the Treaty of Versailles?
7. How and why did American opinions differ on the League of Nations?

Reviewing Themes

1. **Citizenship and Democracy** How did the United States attempt to increase support for World War I at home?
2. **Global Relations** How did the assassination of Archduke Franz Ferdinand and his wife trigger a world conflict?
3. **Technology and Society** Explain how the machine gun and the airplane changed fighting in World War I.

Using the Time Line

Number your paper from 1 to 5. Match the letters on the time line below with the following events.

1. President Wilson announces the Fourteen Points.
2. Woodrow Wilson is re-elected president.
3. Gavrilo Princip assassinates Archduke Franz Ferdinand and his wife, Sophie.
4. The U.S. Senate rejects the Treaty of Versailles.
5. A German U-boat attacks and sinks the *Lusitania*.

1914   1915   1916   1917   1918   1919

a   b   c   d   e

Thinking Critically

1. **Evaluating**   President Wilson thought that the last of his Fourteen Points was the most important. Of the points described in the chapter, which do you think is the most important? Explain your answer.

2. **Supporting a Point of View**   Do you think that Germany should have been held totally responsible for the cost of World War I? Explain your answer.

3. **Identifying Cause and Effect**   How did nationalism and imperialism contribute to tensions in Europe before World War I?

Writing About History

1. **Persuading**   Imagine that you are preparing to vote in the 1916 presidential election. Make a campaign poster for the candidate of your choice. Be sure that your poster includes a slogan and the candidate's campaign pledges.

2. **Expressing**   Imagine that you are a French soldier fighting with a unit of American soldiers. Write a letter home describing how they fought. Include your feelings on the benefits of having U.S. troops on your side.

Building Your Portfolio

Complete the following activities individually or in groups.

1. **The War on the Home Front**   Create three posters to promote the war effort on the home front. You might develop posters for recruiting, for the war effort in the United States, or for the Food Administration. Write a paragraph that explains each poster. Then explain how each poster would have helped the war effort.

2. **Cataloging World War I**   Imagine that you and your classmates are reporters. Each of you will write a story on one of the following: an airplane fight, trench warfare, the spotting of a U-boat, or the sinking of the *Lusitania.* Then combine this information with images and maps to create a booklet titled "Fighting in World War I."

Linking Geography and History

1. **Place**   How did the borders of European nations change as a result of World War I? What nations lost territory and what new nations were formed?

2. **Human-Environment Interaction**   How did trenches help soldiers survive the fighting in World War I? How did they expose soldiers to new dangers?

History Skills Workshop

Reading Maps   Study the map below of the American advances during the fall of 1918. Then answer the following questions: (a) Which American advance covered more territory? (b) How did these advances relate to the armistice line?

American Advances During World War I, Sept.–Nov. 1918

▫ CHAPTER 12 ▫
The 1920s:
An Unsettled Decade
(1919–1929)

Florence Harriman was working for the Red Cross in Paris when World War I ended. She spent a joyous day wandering the streets with the crowds. To Harriman it seemed that "everything in the world were possible, and everything was new, and that peace was going to be what we had dreamed about." Peace, however, brought its own challenges, as Americans turned away from foreign affairs and concentrated on domestic concerns.

THEMES

Citizenship and Democracy
How might fear of radical politics affect citizens?

Economic Development
In what ways might the end of a war affect economic growth?

Technology and Society
How might advances in manufacturing technology affect people's work environment?

1919	1920	1921	1922	1923

JAN. 1920 The strike against U.S. Steel ends.

JULY 1919 A deadly race riot breaks out in Chicago, Illinois.

NOV. 1921 The Washington Conference begins.

JULY 1922 Some 400,000 railroad workers go on strike to oppose wage cuts.

AUG. 1923 President Harding dies unexpectedly.

Returning to "Normalcy"

Reading Focus

What difficulties did the United States face in making the transition from war to peacetime?

What were some of the causes of the strikes and riots of 1919?

How did the Red Scare affect American society?

Key Terms

demobilization
Red Scare
anarchists
Palmer raids
xenophobia
American Civil Liberties Union

*O*NE AFTERNOON IN FEBRUARY 1919, *teenager Bernard Katz headed up New York City's Fifth Avenue with a group of friends. Suddenly they saw a parade for the returning 369th U.S. Infantry, a heavily decorated African American unit. Caught up in the joy of the moment, Katz and his friends "stepped out into the middle of the street . . . and swung up Fifth Avenue behind the 369th and the fantastic sixty-piece band." When the parade ended, the participants, like the rest of the nation, had to face the challenges that accompanied the end of the war.*

The U.S. government encouraged different groups, such as industrial workers and soldiers, to work together after World War I.

IMAGE ON LEFT PAGE: *Howard Thain's painting* The Great White Way

1924	1925	1926	1927	1928

NOV. 1924 Calvin Coolidge is elected president.

AUG. 1927 Nicola Sacco and Bartolomeo Vanzetti are executed.

AUG. 1928 The United States, France, and 13 other nations sign the Kellogg-Briand Pact.

The Transition to Peace

Following World War I, the United States struggled through **demobilization**—the process of returning to a peacetime economy. Several challenges awaited the some 4.5 million soldiers who returned home after the war. Many soldiers found that the jobs they had left behind had been filled by others. Women had entered the industrial workforce in record numbers during wartime. When the war ended, government officials and union leaders asked women to give up these jobs. One American Federation of Labor (AFL) union insisted that women should quit work to make room for returning veterans:

> 66 **The same patriotism which induced [convinced] women to enter industry during the war should induce them to vacate their positions after the war.** 99

Many female workers disagreed with this point of view. "We stand now by your side. . . . We're equal, free at last," declared a group of female machinists. Despite their protests, many women were forced out of factory jobs. Some women found lower-paying work. However, by 1920 the percentage of women working outside the home had dropped below wartime levels.

While working women were being displaced and soldiers were returning to the job market, businesses began laying off employees. Billion-dollar military contracts had enabled many industries to expand during the war. During demobilization the government canceled these contracts. These cutbacks forced companies to slow production and reduce their workforce. As a result, unemployment soared from less than 2 percent in 1919 to almost 12 percent in 1921. The nation suffered a severe recession.

The recession hit American workers hard. Many people had been hoping for a bright economic future. During the war, wages had risen steadily, and unemployment had been extremely low. Some labor unions had enjoyed large increases in membership. However, prices had also risen during the war. The cost of living—the price of basic necessities such as food, shelter, and clothing—doubled between 1915 and 1920.

Immediately after the war, high inflation caused the cost of living to continue rising. Wages, however, remained about the same or declined. Unemployed Americans were particularly hard hit by rising prices. The weak economy created a tension between business and labor that worried many Americans.

Industrial Workers Strike

As economic conditions grew worse around the nation, thousands of industrial workers went on strike for better pay. In 1919 alone there were more than 3,600 strikes involving more than 4 million workers.

The Seattle General Strike

One of the strongest union towns in the United States in 1919 was Seattle, Washington. The wartime prosperity of the Seattle shipyards had encouraged workers in some 110 AFL-affiliated unions to organize a Central Labor Council. After the war, shipyard companies rejected union demands for

During World War I, large numbers of women took industrial jobs such as welding bomb casings.

The Granger Collection, New York

The Influenza Epidemic of 1918–1919

One of the most frightening events of World War I was a global epidemic of influenza, or flu. The epidemic had three major waves, the first beginning in Camp Funston, Kansas, in 1918. Soldiers from Camp Funston and other army bases are believed to have carried the epidemic to Europe as they went to fight in the war. Transmitted through the air, the flu spread rapidly among soldiers in the trenches, leading to an even deadlier second outbreak. Soldiers returning to the United States brought the flu to major cities. Other travelers soon spread the sickness around the world.

The flu epidemic was different from most diseases because it struck otherwise healthy adults in large numbers. As quickly as an hour after exposure, victims developed raging fevers and severe headaches. Those with the worst cases literally suffocated as their lungs filled with fluid. A young woman at Camp Funston recalled the shock caused by the outbreak. "We'd be working with someone one day, and they'd go home because they didn't feel good, and the next day they were gone [dead]."

The Granger Collection, New York

Red Cross nurses make gauze masks to help prevent the spread of the flu.

The epidemic killed more than half a million people in the United States, about 10 times the number of Americans killed in battle during World War I. Worldwide some 30 million people died from the flu. The epidemic of 1918–19 was one of the deadliest outbreaks of disease in recorded history.

Understanding What You Read

1. What were the symptoms of the flu, and whom did it affect?

2. Why did the flu spread so quickly?

---

higher wages. In response, the Metal Workers Union went on strike in January 1919.

The Metal Workers Union was one of the largest on the council. The metalworkers also had the sympathy of many other Seattle laborers. As a member of a local barbers' union explained, "We felt in duty bound to support those who support us." A plasterers' union member put the issue more bluntly: "We knew that if the metal trades were forced to their knees our turn would come next." In February the Central Labor Council called for a work stoppage in support of the metalworkers' strike. Some 60,000 union members went on a general strike—a strike involving all the union members in a community. "The eyes of the nation are fixed on Seattle," announced the council's secretary.

Business leaders and city officials viewed the strike as a dangerous challenge to their authority. Hoping to turn public opinion against the strikers,

During the Seattle general strike, unions provided groceries to striking members.

However, thousands of steelworkers were unhappy with their long hours and low pay. Steelworker Frank Smith was one of many who wondered "how a man is going to make a living for himself and his wife and . . . children" on such low wages. To improve their situation, steelworkers formed a union. They demanded eight-hour workdays, six-day workweeks, and wage increases to make up for the rising cost of living.

The leaders of the steel industry refused to recognize the union or meet with its representatives. On September 22, 1919, some 250,000 steelworkers walked off the job in Pittsburgh, Pennsylvania. They represented more than half of the industry's workforce. By week's end more than 350,000 workers were on strike. The steel industry was in danger of shutting down.

As in Seattle, the press accused the strike leaders, such as union organizer and communist William Z. Foster, of being revolutionaries. Company officials accused strikers of being anti-American radicals. Steel-mill owners hired armed guards. They also brought in so-called scabs—nonunion replacement workers—to run the mills. In addition, mill owners tried to divide strikers along ethnic lines. For example, owners in Chicago told Serb strikers that Italian strikers were going back to work to take the Serbs' jobs. By early January 1920, 20 strikers had been killed in violent confrontations. Some 100,000 union workers were

many officials claimed that foreign radicals had started the strike. The press called the strikers "riffraff from Europe intent on terrorizing the community." Mayor Ole Hanson labeled the general strike "an attempted revolution." Hanson deputized 2,500 additional police. He also called in the state militia to patrol the streets. "Shoot on sight anyone causing disorder," he instructed.

Union leaders set up community kitchens and milk stations to feed the strikers and their families. Veterans among the strikers helped patrol the streets to keep order. Although the city remained peaceful, the majority of the public opposed the strike. After five days the strikers returned to work. None of their demands had been met.

The Steel Strike

The tension that led to the Seattle general strike was also present in the nation's largest industry—steel. The largest steel corporation, U.S. Steel, employed several hundred thousand workers. Such companies had great influence over their employees' lives. Steelworkers and their families typically lived in company-owned housing and shopped at company stores. In 1919 U.S. Steel chairman Elbert H. Gary said that this control benefited workers. He declared that his company wanted to "make the Steel Corporation a good place for the [workers] to work and live."

Heavily armed police officers patrolled the streets during a 1919 labor strike in New Jersey.

still off the job and $112 million in wages had been lost. The unsuccessful struggle had broken the power of the union. Union bosses called off the strike. Labor leaders would wait years before trying to organize workers in heavy industries again.

The Boston Police Strike

In September 1919 a different type of strike drew national attention. Like the members of many other police departments, the Boston police were poorly paid. They wanted to form a union to negotiate for better wages and working conditions. Police Commissioner Edwin Curtis refused to allow police officers to unionize. After Curtis dismissed 19 police officers for trying to create a union, the police went on strike.

The actions of the police officers raised the question of whether government employees had the right to strike. Massachusetts governor Calvin Coolidge insisted that "the action of the police in leaving their posts is not a strike, it is desertion." President Wilson even declared the strike a "crime against civilization." With the police on strike, violence and looting broke out across the city. After two nights of disorder, two people were dead and nine others wounded. Coolidge called in the state militia to restore order.

The strike was broken, but Curtis refused to allow the officers to return to work. Coolidge backed Curtis, saying, "there is no right to strike against the public safety by anybody, anywhere, at any time." The entire police force was dismissed and replaced with a new one made up of unemployed veterans. These replacements received the higher wages and improved working conditions demanded by the strikers.

The Red Scare

The strikes and riots of 1919 led some Americans to worry that a communist revolution like the one in Russia might occur in the United States. In 1919 and 1920 these concerns led to a **Red Scare**. This was a widespread fear of Communists—also called Reds—and other radicals in the United States.

This Red Scare cartoon appeared in the Philadelphia Inquirer in 1919.

Political Threats

Some political groups wanted to bring enormous change to American society. They challenged democracy and the capitalist system. U.S. leaders feared the political goals of Communists, who wanted to share all property and wealth equally. Officials were also concerned about **anarchists**, who wanted to abolish all forms of government. Some Communists and anarchists were willing to use violence to accomplish their goals. Socialists made up a third political group that challenged the social structure of the United States. Some socialists supported revolution, but the majority wanted peaceful change through elections.

The most active Communists and anarchists were often recent immigrants from Europe. This led many Americans to stereotype most European immigrants as dangerous revolutionaries. In addition, major newspapers often reported labor strikes as the work of communist agents. However, in 1919 the communist parties in the United States had fewer than 40,000 members. Despite this fact, many Americans suspected that Reds were everywhere.

The Palmer Raids

Public concern increased following a series of bombings in 1919 aimed at business leaders and government officials. In June a bomb attack by an anarchist damaged the house of Attorney General A. Mitchell Palmer. He responded by ordering raids on suspected radical organizations, beginning in November 1919. The largest raids took place in January 1920. Federal agents in more than 30 cities arrested some 6,000 suspected radicals. These so-called **Palmer raids** often took place without warrants. In addition, there was little evidence against many of those arrested. Hundreds of immigrants were eventually deported as a result of the raids. Some were never officially charged with a crime.

Gradually, these violations of civil rights began to upset the public. When the New York state legislature expelled five representatives because they belonged to the Socialist Party, many people protested. Palmer then warned that radicals were planning a revolution on May 1, 1920, or May Day, an international labor holiday. When the revolution failed to take place, the public lost confidence in Palmer.

Sacco and Vanzetti

The Red Scare contributed to an atmosphere of **xenophobia**—fear and hatred of foreigners—that lingered long after the Palmer raids had ended. This xenophobia greatly influenced the trial of Italian immigrants Nicola Sacco and Bartolomeo Vanzetti. In May 1920 the two men were arrested and charged with robbing a Massachusetts shoe factory and murdering the paymaster and guard.

Sacco and Vanzetti were anarchists. They had lied to authorities about their political activities, fearing that they would be deported. This helped persuade some officials of their guilt. However, much of the evidence that the police had against the two anarchists was inconclusive. Sacco even had witnesses who said he was in another town on the day of the murders. Both men insisted that they were innocent and were being unjustly targeted because of their political beliefs.

Following a trial that many observers considered unfair, the two men were found guilty and sentenced to death in

Poet Edna St. Vincent Millay was one of many Americans who protested the trial of Sacco and Vanzetti.

the electric chair. After the sentence was read, Vanzetti stood and gave a final statement:

> 66 **This is what I say: I would not wish to a dog or to a snake, to the most low and misfortunate creature of the earth—I would not wish to any of them what I have had to suffer for things that I am not guilty of. . . . I am suffering because I am a radical.** 99

Thousands of people protested the verdict. Leading the protests was the new **American Civil Liberties Union** (ACLU), an organization formed to protect people's constitutional rights. However, an official commission reviewed the case and found no grounds for retrial. Massachusetts governor Alvan T. Fuller refused to change the sentence. On August 23, 1927, Sacco and Vanzetti were executed. In 1977 Governor Michael Dukakis of Massachusetts issued a proclamation stating that Sacco and Vanzetti had been unjustly treated.

Ben Shahn, Bartolomeo Vanzetti and Nicola Sacco (1931–1932)

Immigrant artist Ben Shahn created this painting in the 1930s as part of a series showing the events of the Sacco and Vanzetti trial.

★ Racial Violence

Foreigners and radicals were not the only targets of violence following World War I. The economic difficulties caused by demobilization also increased existing racial tensions, particularly in urban areas. Hundreds of thousands of African Americans had moved to northern cities during the war, often filling new factory jobs. African American communities grew in northern cities in formerly white neighborhoods. Many white northerners feared competition from the African American residents for housing and jobs. In the summer of 1919, called "Red Summer," these tensions exploded into urban race riots.

Many African Americans had to seek safe areas during the Chicago race riots of 1919.

The worst riot took place in Chicago, Illinois. After several violent race-related confrontations, antilynching activist Ida B. Wells-Barnett asked, "Will the legal, moral and civic forces of this town stand idly by?" Officials did nothing. Another incident soon occurred. In July 1919 a young African American named Eugene Williams went to a Lake Michigan beach near Chicago. Williams crossed into a whites-only area, where people began throwing rocks at him. He drowned. Fighting then broke out between white and African American bathers on the beach. The violence spread to the city. A week of rioting followed in which nearly 40 people were killed and more than 530 were injured.

Similar riots occurred in other cities, including Washington, D.C., and Tulsa, Oklahoma. By late 1919 there had been more than 25 race riots across the nation. Lynchings of African American men also took place, particularly in the South. The National Association for the Advancement of Colored People (NAACP) tried to stop these attacks. Despite such efforts, more than 70 African Americans were lynched in 1919.

SECTION 1 REVIEW

Identify and explain the significance of the following:
- demobilization
- Red Scare
- anarchists
- A. Mitchell Palmer
- Palmer raids
- xenophobia
- Nicola Sacco and Bartolomeo Vanzetti
- American Civil Liberties Union

Reading for Content Understanding

1 **Main Idea** Why did workers across the country go on strike in 1919?

2 **Main Idea** What began the Red Scare, and how did it affect Americans?

3 **Economic Development** What economic problems arose during demobilization, and why did these problems occur?

4 **Writing** *Creating* Make a pamphlet protesting either the guilty verdict in the Sacco and Vanzetti case or the race riots in Chicago in 1919. Be sure to include arguments to persuade others to join your protest.

5 **Critical Thinking** *Synthesizing Information* How might the economic troubles experienced during demobilization have affected race relations in northern cities?

Republicans in Power

Reading Focus

How did the Harding and Coolidge administrations address economic issues?

What scandals plagued President Harding and the Republicans?

What was U.S. foreign policy during the 1920s?

Key Terms

Ohio Gang
Teapot Dome scandal
disarmament
Washington Conference
Five-Power Naval Treaty
Kellogg-Briand Pact

*F*OR THE PRESIDENTIAL ELECTION OF 1920, *Republican candidate Warren G. Harding chose to campaign from his home in Marion, Ohio. In May, however, Harding traveled to Boston and gave a speech before a large crowd of supporters. He declared that "America's present need is not heroics but healing; not nostrums [fake remedies] but normalcy." When reporters asked him what he meant by normalcy, Harding replied, "I mean normal procedures, the natural way, without excess." Many Americans were troubled by the postwar problems. Harding's simple words promised a return to better times.*

Harding campaign button

★ The Election of 1920

The Republicans were confident that they could win the presidency in 1920. Some Americans were angry with Democratic leaders for bringing the United States into World War I. Many people also blamed the Democratic Party for the economic troubles that followed the war. Republican leaders tried to appeal to voters by running a simple campaign that promised a return to prosperity.

The Republican Party nominated Ohio senator Warren G. Harding for president and Massachusetts governor Calvin Coolidge for vice president. Harding was chosen more for his charming and friendly nature than for his political talents. Coolidge had impressed voters by ending the Boston police strike. Together they campaigned on a pro-business platform. Harding also supported immigration restrictions and aid to farmers.

Republican leaders were careful to keep Harding, who was often not well informed on issues, from making many public appearances. One politician told campaign organizers:

❝ **Keep Warren at home. Don't let him make any speeches. If he goes out on a tour somebody's sure to ask him questions, and Warren's just the sort of . . . fool that will try to answer them.**❞

While Harding remained at his Ohio home during most of the campaign, his Democratic challengers traveled across the country. The Democrats chose Ohio governor James M. Cox to run for president and Assistant Secretary of the Navy Franklin D. Roosevelt to run for vice president. Both candidates tried to avoid domestic issues and emphasize foreign policy. They also supported the League of Nations.

Unfortunately for the Democrats, Americans cared little about the League. Most people wanted to avoid further involvement in European affairs. On election day, Harding took about 60 percent of the popular vote. A Democratic adviser declared, "It wasn't a landslide; it was an earthquake." A sizable number of voters were dissatisfied with both major parties, however. Socialist Party candidate Eugene V. Debs received some 900,000 votes despite still being in prison for his opposition to World War I.

 Harding's Administration

Although he was popular with voters, President Harding was not a particularly gifted leader. He once told a journalist that he was often overwhelmed by the responsibilities of the presidency. Harding's main strengths were his party loyalty and ability to make political allies. Harding quickly assembled a talented cabinet. He appointed Charles Evans Hughes as secretary of state and Herbert Hoover as secretary of commerce. Hughes was a former governor of New York and associate justice of the Supreme Court. Hoover, a wealthy mining engineer, had been very successful in organizing wartime relief for millions of Belgians.

From the start, the Harding administration focused on strengthening the U.S. economy.

President Harding included several important business leaders in his cabinet.

Harding believed that government should promote the growth of business but otherwise leave the economy alone. He soon faced a tough decision over whether to raise or lower taxes. He admitted, "I can't make a . . . thing out of this tax problem. I listen to one side and they seem right, and then . . . I talk to the other side, and they seem just as right." To solve the dilemma, Harding turned to Secretary of the Treasury Andrew Mellon, a successful banker and business investor. He was also one of America's richest men.

Mellon declared, "The government is just a business and can and should be run on business principles." He proposed numerous tax cuts, many of which benefited businesses and wealthy Americans. Congress passed several of these tax cuts.

Mellon's critics questioned whether his tax cuts truly benefited most citizens. However, the public was generally pleased as business boomed and the post–World War I recession ended. The United States soon entered a period of rapid economic growth. Both unemployment and prices declined.

 Political Scandals

Not all of President Harding's appointments were wise, however. He made a habit of choosing old friends to fill government posts, regardless of their qualifications. One group of officials in Harding's administration was known as the **Ohio Gang** because they had all been acquaintances of Harding in Ohio. Even Harding eventually recognized that

The 1920s: An Unsettled Decade **363**

The Teapot Dome scandal was a major threat to Harding's presidency.

most of these individuals were poorly qualified for their positions. He once declared to a reporter:

> " I have no trouble with my enemies. I can take care of my enemies all right. But my . . . friends . . . [are] the ones that keep me walking the floor nights. "

Harding had reason to worry. For example, an investigation into the management of the Veterans Bureau discovered that its chief, Charles Forbes, had taken bribes. Forbes was fined $10,000 and sentenced to two years in prison.

The biggest scandal of the Harding administration involved Secretary of the Interior Albert Fall. Fall's heavy personal spending triggered a Senate investigation. This investigation revealed that Fall had transferred control of two naval oil reserves to his department. One of the reserves was at Teapot Dome, Wyoming. He then illegally leased the reserves to two oil companies. In return, he received cash and thousands of dollars in gifts and personal "loans." When caught, Fall claimed that he was acting in the nation's best interest. However, the **Teapot Dome scandal** led to his conviction for taking bribes. He was sentenced to a year in jail and fined $100,000.

Eventually, six members of Harding's administration resigned as a result of corruption charges. Harding never had to face these scandals publicly.

On August 2, 1923, he died suddenly while on a western speaking tour. The scandals came to light shortly after his death. He was not directly involved in any of the corrupt activities. However, the trouble that his "friends" caused greatly damaged Harding's reputation.

★ Coolidge in Office

The scandals also hurt the reputation of the Republican Party. Vice President Calvin Coolidge, however, was not involved in the corruption. After he was sworn in as president, Coolidge fired those who were involved.

Coolidge was born on a Vermont farm and attended a one-room schoolhouse. To many people he symbolized old-fashioned values. Coolidge was a quiet man who once told a colleague, "If you don't say anything, you won't be called on to repeat it." His no-nonsense attitude comforted many Americans. His reputation for honesty helped the Republicans recover from the scandals.

Coolidge easily won the Republican presidential nomination in 1924. He ran on an even stronger pro-business platform than Harding had, stating that "the man who builds a factory builds a temple." Coolidge's conservative policies upset some progressive Republicans. They broke away to nominate Senator Robert La Follette of Wisconsin as the Progressive Party candidate. The Democrats were deeply divided between urban and rural interests. They finally nominated little-known lawyer John W. Davis.

Coolidge won a landslide victory in November 1924, receiving nearly 16 million votes. Davis received more than 8 million, while La Follette finished with nearly 5 million votes. The key to Coolidge's victory was his promise of continued economic prosperity. He retained several key members of Harding's cabinet to help plan his economic policies, which favored low taxes, low interest rates

Calvin Coolidge was often called Silent Cal by reporters.

on loans, and little economic regulation. He further reduced government spending and gave Treasury Secretary Mellon the freedom to propose more tax cuts. Tariffs were raised to increase the price of foreign goods and prevent them from competing with domestic goods.

Although these measures tended to benefit primarily those with higher incomes, the national economy steadily improved during Coolidge's administration. Coolidge firmly believed that the best government was one that rarely interfered in daily life. He once advised, "Never go out to meet trouble." For four years he kept government activity to a minimum. With a booming economy, he received few complaints from the public.

Coolidge was a pro-business presidential candidate.

★ Foreign Policy

During the 1920s the Republicans faced a difficult challenge in foreign policy. As a leading world power, the United States needed to protect its foreign interests. Many Americans, however, supported isolationism—the policy of avoiding involvement in other nations' affairs.

The Washington Conference

Republican leaders compromised by concentrating on foreign-policy issues that promoted economic growth and peace. Even most isolationists could accept these goals. Diplomats hoped that new treaties would prevent another world war and would strengthen the global economy. A healthy world economy would help the United States. During World War I, European allies had borrowed billions of dollars from the United States. To repay their loans, these countries needed peaceful conditions that would allow their economies to recover.

Many world leaders believed that the key to peace was **disarmament**—limiting or reducing military weapons. In November 1921 the United States invited other major nations to the **Washington Conference** to discuss naval disarmament and Asian affairs. During his opening speech, Secretary of State Charles Evans Hughes

surprised the assembled foreign delegates. He challenged them to join the United States in destroying a total of 2 million tons of naval ships. Hughes also called for limits on the total naval strength of the major world powers. A journalist reported that the delegates reacted with a "mad chorus of approval."

The Washington Conference led to the **Five-Power Naval Treaty**. In addition to calling for reductions in naval strength, this treaty limited the maximum size of each nation's navy. The treaty allowed the United States and Great Britain to have the two largest navies, each of equal size and strength. Japan was allowed a navy three fifths that size. France and Italy were assigned navies roughly half the size of Japan's.

The conference also produced two treaties addressing Asian affairs. In the Four-Power Treaty, France, Great Britain, Japan, and the United States agreed to respect each other's rights in the Pacific. The Nine-Power Treaty pledged support for the Open Door policy. It also promised to respect "the independence, and the territorial and administrative integrity [organization] of China."

The Granger Collection, New York

AFTER THE NAPOLEONIC WARS

AFTER OUR OWN CIVIL WAR

AFTER THE WORLD WAR

After World War I some Americans called for an end to war and the destruction it caused.

The Kellogg-Briand Pact

Diplomats took additional steps toward achieving world peace. France's foreign minister, Aristide Briand, and U.S. Secretary of State Frank Kellogg led efforts to create an agreement to end war. In August 1928 the United States and 14 other nations signed the **Kellogg-Briand Pact**. This pact tried to outlaw warfare. Eventually, most of the countries of the world signed the agreement.

There was no agreement on how to enforce the treaty, however. One U.S. senator remarked that the pact would be "as effective to keep down war as a carpet would be to smother an earthquake." Like the treaties signed at the Washington Conference, the Kellogg-Briand Pact was well intentioned but could not guarantee an end to military aggression. For American isolationists, this was a risk they were willing to take to avoid involvement in future foreign conflicts.

Herbert Hoover used new technologies such as radio and film in his presidential campaign. This truck showed a Hoover campaign film to voters.

★ The Election of 1928

Foreign policy played only a small role in the 1928 presidential election. Each candidate concentrated on domestic issues, which interested the public more than international issues did. The Democratic candidate was Alfred E. Smith, the governor of New York. Smith represented urban interests. This concerned many rural Americans who distrusted big-city politicians. A large number of Protestants also opposed Smith because he was Catholic.

Calvin Coolidge decided not to run for re-election in 1928. Republicans nominated Secretary of Commerce Herbert Hoover. In contrast to Smith, Hoover seemed to represent traditional values. Hoover and the Republicans also benefited from the nation's economic prosperity.

Hoover's campaign platform consisted largely of promises of continued economic good times. His slogan "A Chicken for Every Pot and a Car in Every Garage" helped carry him to an easy victory. Hoover received more than 21 million votes to Smith's 15 million. Voters in the nation's 12 largest cities, however, supported Smith. The election results demonstrated the growing political differences between urban and rural America.

SECTION 2 REVIEW

Identify and explain the significance of the following:
- **Warren G. Harding**
- **Ohio Gang**
- **Charles Forbes**
- **Albert Fall**
- **Teapot Dome scandal**
- **Calvin Coolidge**
- **disarmament**
- **Washington Conference**
- **Five-Power Naval Treaty**
- **Kellogg-Briand Pact**
- **Herbert Hoover**

Reading for Content Understanding

1 **Main Idea** How did Presidents Harding and Coolidge attempt to strengthen the U.S. economy?

2 **Main Idea** What foreign policy did the leaders of the United States pursue during the 1920s?

3 **Citizenship and Democracy** Why did the Republicans have the advantage in the 1920 and 1928 elections?

4 **Writing** *Describing* Write a brief magazine article that details the scandals of the Harding administration.

5 **Critical Thinking** *Drawing Conclusions* Why do you think the international treaties of the 1920s were difficult to enforce?

"The Business of America Is Business"

Reading Focus

How did the assembly line affect manufacturing?

What effect did the automobile have on the economy and people's everyday lives?

How did advertising and the installment plan change people's buying habits?

Key Terms

Model T
assembly line
installment plan

THE MANUFACTURER'S CHALLENGE CUP, one of the first major automobile races, was held on October 25, 1902. One entry—Henry Ford's car—stood out from the rest. An observer said the car was "low, rakish [streamlined], and makes more noise than a freight train." Ford's 70-horsepower 999 was so fast that he feared for his driver's safety. However, the car turned out to be both fast and safe. The 999 led the race from the start and won by a large margin, covering five miles in five minutes and 20 seconds. The victory brought fame to Ford, who continued to experiment with car design.

Ford's 999 race car

⭐ The Model T

Henry Ford founded the Ford Motor Company in 1903. He wanted to create a vehicle "so low in price that no man making a good salary will be unable to buy one." Ford explained the basic principles of the car he wanted to build:

❝ **It will be large enough for the family but small enough for the individual to run and care for. It will be constructed** of the best materials, by the best men to be hired, after the simplest design that modern engineering can devise. ❞

After eight different models, Ford achieved his goal in 1908 with the **Model T**. Affectionately nicknamed the Tin Lizzie by the public, the Model T was easy to repair and maintain. It was not fancy or flashy. Ford had decided to produce the car only in black. It was, however, durable and reliable. It could be driven on any surface. This ability was

Henry Ford

Henry Ford was born in 1863 on a farm near Dearborn, Michigan. From an early age he loved working with machines. "My toys were all tools," he later recalled, adding, "they still are." When he was a teenager, Ford left the family farm for Detroit and worked in a machine shop. He eventually became an engineer for the Edison Illuminating Company. In his free time he worked on designing and building a gasoline-powered automobile.

From the Collections of The Henry Ford Museum and Greenfield Village

Ford's success with the Model T made him wealthy and powerful. He even ran for the U.S. Senate in 1918, losing in a close race. Ford remained old-fashioned. In later years he often complained that the country was losing its traditional values. To encourage Americans to respect their past, he built Greenfield Village in Dearborn, Michigan. This historical town contains the original homes of famous Americans such as Orville and Wilbur Wright.

important because most roads in the 1920s were unpaved and filled with potholes and ruts.

Perhaps most importantly, the Model T was fairly inexpensive compared to previous automobiles. The low cost allowed many Americans to buy the Model T as their first car. As Ford and his engineers improved their manufacturing methods, prices dropped even lower. The cost of a Model T dropped from around $950 in 1909 to about $350 in 1920. By 1921 Ford controlled some 55 percent of the U.S. automobile market. He was selling more than 1 million cars annually.

The Model T, also called the Tin Lizzie

The Granger Collection, New York

Ford's Methods

To manufacture so many cars so cheaply, Henry Ford and his engineers developed a new assembly process. In the past, teams of workers built each car one at a time from start to finish. Ford's factories used a new, faster method.

The Assembly Line

This method was the moving **assembly line**. This system of chains, slides, and conveyor belts moved parts from one worker to another. Each car began on the assembly line as a simple chassis, or frame, with no parts attached. As it moved down the line, the chassis stopped at stations. At each stop one type of part, such as doors or seats, was quickly installed. When it reached the end of the line, the car was complete.

The assembly line controlled the pace of all the work in the factory. The key to the assembly line was that each worker performed only one simple task over and over again. Ford's engineers also introduced special machines to help workers perform their tasks more efficiently. In this way they divided the manufacturing process into many small steps. This approach was influenced by the theories of researcher Frederick W. Taylor. Taylor had described his ideas in the book *The Principles of Scientific Management.*

The benefits to production were tremendous. After the assembly line was introduced, the time needed to build a Model T fell from more than 12 hours to less than 2 hours. The assembly line also lowered manufacturing costs. In Michigan, Ford built several huge assembly lines at the River Rouge complex, the largest factory in America. This plant mass-produced hundreds of thousands of cars a year.

Assembly-line work was dull and tiring. Workers had to keep up with the line's speed at all times. The wife of one worker wrote to Ford, "The chain system [assembly line] you have is a *slave driver!*" Another worker explained why assembly-line work could be so tiring:

> **❝The weight of a tack . . . is insignificant, but if you have to drive eight tacks in every Ford cushion that goes by your station within a certain time, and you know that if you fail to do it you are going to tie up the entire platform, and you continue to do this for four years, you are going to break under the strain.❞**

This stress caused assembly-line workers to quit on a regular basis.

Fordism

Constantly replacing these workers and training the new employees cost Ford's company a great deal of money. Unhappy autoworkers were also easy for unions to recruit. This troubled Ford, who was strongly antiunion.

To keep his workers from quitting their jobs or joining unions, Ford tried to create a better working environment. He offered an eight-hour workday and wages of up to $5 per day, a high amount for the time. Workers were encouraged to suggest ways to improve productivity. Ford also employed African Americans at a time when most auto plants hired only white workers. In addition, the company employed more than 9,000 people with disabilities. Visually impaired workers, for example, sorted parts.

Along with higher wages and other benefits, however, Ford placed strict requirements on his employees. Workers who drank alcohol, smoked tobacco, or joined unions could be fired. Ford also required immigrant employees to attend "Americanization" classes. Such classes taught civics and English to immigrant workers. These programs had been common in the early 1900s, and Ford continued them at his plants.

In the 1920s many people used the term "Fordism" to describe the assembly-line mass production of goods. Although not all owners agreed with Ford's higher salaries or his work policies, many companies began to imitate Fordism.

Mexican artist Diego Rivera painted this mural of a Ford assembly line in the 1930s.

The Car Craze

Mass production transformed the U.S. auto industry. Instead of producing a few expensive luxury vehicles for the rich, mass production supplied inexpensive transportation to the public.

In 1929 nearly 5 million automobiles were manufactured in the United States. Automakers employed some 375,000 workers. Millions more workers held jobs that supported automobile manufacturing. For example, the automobile industry used large quantities of glass, paints, rubber, and steel. Oil and gas consumption in the United States also doubled from 1920 to 1929.

Cars changed the landscape of America. New communites sprang up along country roads. Auto-industry towns boomed. For example, the population of Detroit, Michigan, jumped from around 285,000 in 1900 to about 1.5 million in 1930. The widespread use of trucks to ship goods was also important. Factories moved to the outskirts of cities, where real estate was cheaper. Most factories had previously been located in downtown areas that had access to central water and rail connections. The convenience of owning a car also allowed more people to move from city centers to suburbs. For the first time, millions of people commuted to work by car. As more people moved to the suburbs, construction companies built new communities.

Although there were many cars, there were few good roads. Soon federal and state governments were pouring millions of dollars into the construction of bridges, tunnels, and highways. By 1925 more than $200 million a year was being spent on roads. As traffic problems increased, automobile accidents multiplied. Some mechanics started body shops to repair the damage. As the number of accidents increased, drivers also needed insurance. The insurance industry expanded to meet this need.

Families began taking driving vacations. Responding to a survey, one woman

An advertisement for a driving vacation

declared, "I never feel as close to my family as when we are all together in the car." "Motor hotels," also known as motels, appeared throughout the country. Americans created auto clubs and magazines to encourage leisure travel. *Motor Car* magazine explained the joys of a driving vacation:

 You are your master, the road is ahead; you eat as you please . . . , sleeping when you will . . . , waking with the dawn. . . . Time and space at your beck and call; your freedom is complete. "

The increase in traffic led to the development of new roadside businesses. Service stations provided fuel for the millions of cars on the roads. Roadside restaurants fed hungry drivers and passengers. To catch the eyes of passing motorists, advertisers constructed billboards along highways across the nation. The automobile had transformed the economy and society of the United States.

★ Business Booms

Many other industries also experienced economic growth in the 1920s. Electric utilities brightened

Electricity and new appliances made cooking and cleaning easier in the most modern homes of the 1920s.

homes and streets. Telephone companies made instant communication possible. By the 1920s most homes in cities and suburbs had electricity. This led to the growing use of electrical household conveniences. People used small electrical appliances to iron their clothes, make their morning toast, or play their musical recordings.

Electricity also powered growing factories. The quantity of goods manufactured nearly doubled between 1921 and 1929. This growth was largely because of an increased production of durable consumer goods. These are large, long-lasting home appliances such as washing machines and refrigerators.

Food-processing plants produced large quantities of canned goods and packaged food products. Such foods were more convenient to prepare. Many goods were now sold on a national basis instead of only in smaller local markets. Trucks shipped these goods affordably across the country.

Chains of grocery and retail stores opened or expanded in the 1920s. They brought wider varieties of products to small towns at lower prices. Grocery stores such as A&P and Piggly Wiggly sold food at cheaper prices than many local stores. They did this by stocking and selling items in large quantities. Catalog retailers such as Sears, Roebuck, & Co. and F. W. Woolworth also began opening department stores across the country. These chains offered consumers a wide range of goods such as appliances, clothing, and home furnishings.

This growth in products and stores contributed to the rise of a consumer society. In a consumer society, people are continually encouraged to buy products to improve their lives and help the economy.

To make it easier to purchase goods, more companies offered the **installment plan**. This program allowed customers to buy goods by making a small initial down payment followed by additional monthly payments with interest. This increased the total cost of the item purchased, but the plan was convenient and popular. In the past many people delayed purchases until they had enough cash. These people were able to buy goods more quickly using the installment plan. During the 1920s, some 60 percent of all cars and furniture were purchased on credit.

A Consumer Culture

Households with Electricity

Automobile Sales

Source: *Historical Statistics of the United States*   The Granger Collection, New York

A Better Life During the 1920s the number of households with electricity increased, as did automobile sales. During what year were automobile sales the highest?

⭐ Selling to the People

The existence of new products led to a boom in advertising as businesses tried to sell their goods. Large manufacturers were now producing for a national market. Advertisers helped create brand names that were recognizable across the country, such as Coca-Cola and Campbell's Soup. Billboards, magazines, and newspapers carried ads encouraging Americans to buy. Radios also broadcast a steady stream of commercials. Advertising executive Bruce Barton explained the purpose of advertising:

❝The American conception [idea] of advertising is to arouse desires and stimulate wants, to make people dissatisfied with the old and out-of-date . . . to send them out to work harder to get the latest model—whether that model be an icebox or a rug, or a new home.❞

Advertising was particularly important to the automobile industry. Americans were earning more money. As a result, people began considering comfort and style more strongly when buying a car. Automobile companies such as General Motors recognized this trend. They began to gain

Advertisements often emphasized a product's advanced technology.

rapidly on Ford Motor Company in the 1920s by advertising the variety of body styles and colors they offered. Most ads for home appliances were targeted at women. Many ads promised that new gadgets would allow consumers to enjoy more leisure time.

Some people accused advertisers of misleading consumers about products. Critics also claimed that advertisers urged consumers to spend more than they could afford. Home appliance ads tried to pressure wives into believing that they needed all the latest products to keep themselves and their families happy. "Why drown your soul in a greasy dishpan?" asked a dishwasher ad. Car ads suggested to men that they needed new, stylish cars to gain respect.

Ad writer Helen Woodward admitted that her job required "a passion for converting the other fellow, even if it is to something you don't believe in yourself." Advertising executives defended their agencies, however. They argued that by encouraging people to consume new products, advertisements stimulated the economy.

SECTION 3 REVIEW

Identify and explain the significance of the following:
- **Henry Ford**
- **Model T**
- **assembly line**
- **installment plan**

Reading for Content Understanding

1 Main Idea How did manufacturing change with the introduction of the assembly line?

2 Main Idea How did many Americans' lives change with the new prosperity of the 1920s? What role did advertising

and installment plans play in these changes?

3 Technology and Society What effect did the Model T and other cars have on the economy and society of the United States?

4 Writing *Describing* Imagine that you work on the assembly line at Ford's River Rouge plant. Describe the benefits and drawbacks of your job.

5 Critical Thinking *Identifying Cause and Effect* How did automobiles affect other industries in the 1920s?

The U.S. Economy

Reading Focus

What caused the stock market boom in the 1920s?

Why did organized labor's influence decline during the 1920s?

What difficulties did farmers experience during the 1920s?

Key Terms

synthetic
American Plan
Fordney-McCumber Tariff Act

ONE DAY IN WASHINGTON, D.C., *Supreme Court Justice Louis Brandeis was going down the street when he saw an advertisement for tires that read, "Ride Now, Pay Later." The judge was outraged over the growth of consumerism in the nation. "I can't understand where all this . . . money comes from," he later told his brother. "We are certainly not earning it as a nation." Brandeis doubted that the U.S. economy was as strong as businesspeople believed it to be. However, he was one of a minority of Americans who openly questioned the prosperity of the 1920s.*

Catalogs displayed hundreds of goods for consumers.

★ Prosperity and Growth

The U.S. economy grew rapidly for much of the 1920s. This prosperity led many Americans to dream of achieving great wealth. Some Americans thought that buying stocks was the easiest way to fulfill these dreams. The federal government's pro-business policies and the production boom of the 1920s led to increased profits for many companies. For example, in 1929 manufacturing profits tripled those made in 1920. As company profits rose, so did stock values and the dividends returned to the stockholders.

Thousands of Americans invested in the stock market. From 1923 to 1928, the amount of stock sold on the New York Stock Exchange on Wall Street increased by more than 400 percent. As author Frederick Lewis Allen observed:

66 **All sorts of people to whom the stock ticker had been a[n] . . . alien mystery were carrying [owned] a hundred shares of Studebaker . . . and whipping open the early editions of afternoon papers to catch the 1:30 quotations [on stock prices] from Wall Street.** 99

The 1920s: An Unsettled Decade **373**

Allen reported stories of men and women who had made thousands of dollars by investing in companies about which they knew very little.

Many of these individuals borrowed money to invest in the stock market. They were confident that stock values would continue rising. Experts such as professor Irving Fischer of Yale University supported this view. Fischer predicted that the stock market growth would continue to be strong. He encouraged people to buy stocks.

This 1920s bracelet shows the New York City skyline.

Some financial experts, however, were more cautious. They reminded Americans of the old proverb "What goes up must come down."

Despite the hopes of many investors, only a few Americans became extremely wealthy during the 1920s. Some earned their fortune outside the stock market by inventing new machines or creating successful businesses. Henry Ford, for example, went from tinkering in his garage to earning millions. J. C. Penney started as a general store clerk and went on to found a successful chain of department stores. He offered stock options to his managers so they could share in company profits. This profit sharing encouraged hard work. By 1929 the J. C. Penney Company had nearly 1,400 stores nationwide.

One of the most successful female entrepreneurs of the early 1900s was Madame C. J. Walker. Her "Walker System" of hair and skin care products for African Americans became the foundation for a thriving national business. Walker never forgot how she achieved her success. She often said, "I got my start by giving myself a start." She became a philanthropist and was also active in the NAACP. Although Walker died in 1919, her company continued to prosper. In the 1920s her daughter maintained the family tradition of supporting important African American causes.

Madame C. J. Walker became a successful entrepreneur.

The Limits of Prosperity

Certain "sick," or economically depressed, industries did not share in the nation's prosperity. Despite the economic boom, organized labor also suffered setbacks during the 1920s.

Sick Industries

Struggling industries included coal, textiles, and lumber. The coal industry suffered because coal was being replaced by oil, natural gas, and hydroelectric power as a source of energy. The introduction of **synthetic**, or artificial, fabrics such as rayon hurt the cotton textile industry. So did overproduction of cotton. The lumber industry faced a similar challenge as materials such as concrete replaced wood in many buildings. These industries were slow to adapt to changing technology and consumer demands. As a result, they did not share in the prosperity of the 1920s.

Many workers also faced financial difficulties. Skilled workers at large corporations generally received good pay and benefits. However, workers at smaller companies in service industries such as the retail or grocery trades were often less fortunate. In addition, unskilled factory and industrial workers usually received poor pay and few benefits. Several million unskilled workers were employed in these troubled industries.

During the 1920s the prices of many cotton fabrics dropped because of overproduction and competition with synthetic fibers.

374 Chapter 12

The Great Gatsby
F. Scott Fitzgerald

In 1925 F. Scott Fitzgerald published The Great Gatsby, *which many consider the novel that most represents the 1920s. The* Great Gatsby *is the story of the newly rich Jay Gatsby of Long Island, New York, and his tragic love for the beautiful Daisy Buchanan. Fitzgerald's novel describes an obsession with wealth and spending money that was true of some Americans in the 1920s. In the following excerpt, Nick Carraway—the novel's narrator and Gatsby's neighbor—describes the typical atmosphere of one of Gatsby's parties.*

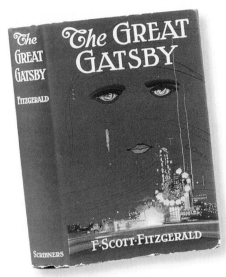

The Great Gatsby *was F. Scott Fitzgerald's most popular novel.*

There was music from my neighbor's house through the summer nights. . . . At high tide in the afternoon I watched his guests diving from the tower of his raft or taking the sun on the hot sand of his beach while his two motor boats slit the waters of the Sound. . . . On week-ends his Rolls-Royce became an omnibus [bus], bearing parties to and from the city, past nine in the morning and long after midnight, while his station wagon scampered like a brisk yellow bug to meet all trains. And on Mondays eight servants including an extra gardener toiled all day with mops and scrubbing-brushes and hammers and garden shears, repairing the ravages [damages] of the night before. . . .

At least once a fortnight [every two weeks] a corps [army] of caterers came down with several hundred feet of canvas and enough colored lights to make a Christmas tree of Gatsby's enormous garden. . . .

By seven o'clock the orchestra has arrived—no thin five piece affair but a whole pit full of oboes and trombones and saxophones . . . and cornets and piccolos and . . . drums. The last swimmers have come in from the beach now and are dressing upstairs; the cars from New York are parked five deep in the drive. . . . I believe that on the first night I went to Gatsby's house I was one of the few guests who had actually been invited. People were not invited—they went there. They got into automobiles which bore [transported] them out to Long Island and somehow they ended up at Gatsby's door. Once there they were introduced by somebody who knew Gatsby and after that they conducted themselves according to the rules of behavior associated with amusement parks. Sometimes they came and went without having met Gatsby at all.

Understanding Literature

1. What jobs were performed to prepare for the party and to entertain the guests once they had arrived?

2. Why do you think Gatsby spent so much money entertaining strangers?

3. How does F. Scott Fitzgerald's description of Gatsby's parties reflect the prosperity of the 1920s?

Labor in the 1920s

Organized labor also struggled to share in the decade's boom times. During World War I the federal government had feared work stoppages in war industries and thus supported union demands for higher wages. This led to increases in union membership. After the war ended, the government no longer supported labor. In addition, the labor supply increased. These changes allowed many businesses to avoid hiring union workers.

The violent strikes of 1919 had inspired strong antiunion feelings across the United States. Many Americans believed that unions were radical political organizations run by individuals who wanted to weaken American society. During the 1920s union membership declined sharply. It fell from a high of more than 5 million in 1920 to around 3.6 million just three years later.

At the same time, the courts often struck down pro-worker legislation and upheld companies' attempts to ban unions. Labor unions had worked to make industries into "closed shops" where only union members could be employed. The closed shop increased the power of unions. Union leaders could usually rely on the support of all the workers in a closed-shop industry. Business leaders responded by launching an open-shop campaign called the **American Plan**. In an open shop, union membership was not required and was sometimes even forbidden. Republicans openly supported the drive against unions. Attorney General Harry Daugherty said:

> 66 **So long and to the extent that I can speak for the government of the United States, I will use the power of the government to prevent the labor unions of the country from destroying the open shop.** 99

Unions fought the American Plan but with little success. One of the worst defeats suffered by labor occurred in July 1922. Some 400,000 railroad workers went on strike to oppose wage cuts. Daugherty secured a federal restraining order against the strikers in September. The strike collapsed. As union membership declined in the 1920s, business leaders no longer pushed for open shops.

★ Hard Times for Farmers

The postwar years were also difficult for farmers. Demobilization ended the prosperity that World War I had brought to American agriculture. Keeping the Allies supplied during the war had created high demand and high prices for agricultural products. In response, American farmers had increased their production. They often bought land and equipment on credit. When the war ended, so did the huge Allied demand for U.S. farm products.

Many farmers found themselves producing much more than they could sell. Food prices dropped dramatically. Nebraska corn, which had sold for $1.22 a bushel in 1919, sold for only 41 cents in 1920. When farm earnings dropped drastically, many farmers found it impossible to pay their debts. Nearly half a million farmers lost their land. To drive prices up, farmers needed to produce less. However, many farmers planted more in an attempt to recover their losses. Additional crops only made the problem worse by driving prices even lower.

To try to solve their problems, farmers in the Midwest elected a group of pro-agriculture

The drop in farm prices following World War I meant hard times for many farm families.

congressmen known as the Farm Bloc. The Farm Bloc helped pass legislation intended to ease the farm crisis. The **Fordney-McCumber Tariff Act** was designed to raise the demand and price for domestic crops by placing high taxes on imported farm products. The high tariff prevented many foreign farm goods from being sold in the United States. However, it also raised the cost of many consumer goods—which hurt everyone, including farmers.

Other suggestions included a government subsidy, or aid. One plan proposed that the government buy basic goods such as cattle, corn, cotton, and wheat. American farmers would receive more than market-value prices for these goods. The government would then sell the crops overseas at the lower world-market rates. Critics attacked this plan as unworkable. President Coolidge vetoed it.

Farmers kept pressing the federal government for assistance. Republican leaders, however, did not want to interfere with the free-enterprise system by regulating prices. Only large farms and ones with expensive, modern machinery prospered in the 1920s. Some of the biggest farms were run by agricultural corporations. These

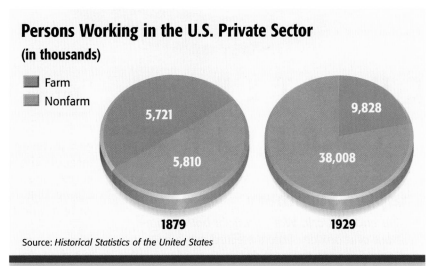

Persons Working in the U.S. Private Sector
(in thousands)

■ Farm
■ Nonfarm

5,721
5,810
1879

9,828
38,008
1929

Source: *Historical Statistics of the United States*

Leaving the Farm Between 1880 and 1930, the increased use of farm machinery and the growth of industry contributed to a decrease in the number of farm jobs. How many more people worked in nonfarm jobs in 1929 than in 1879?

farms benefited from increased efficiency and large-scale operations.

Most farmers, however, were not so fortunate. In 1929 the average annual income of farmers was about a third of that of nonfarmers. Farm laborers, particularly migrant workers, fared even worse. They often received poor pay and worked under difficult conditions. A minister reported that in a settlement in California, "shelters were made of almost every conceivable [imaginable] thing—burlap, canvas, palm branches." The booming economy of the 1920s brought prosperity for many Americans, but did not bring good times for large numbers of farmers and union workers.

SECTION 4 REVIEW

Identify and explain the significance of the following:

• J. C. Penney
• Madame C. J. Walker
• synthetic
• American Plan
• Fordney-McCumber Tariff Act

Reading for Content Understanding

1. **Main Idea** What factors contributed to the stock market boom in the 1920s?

2. **Main Idea** What difficulties did unions face in the 1920s?

3. **Economic Development** How did the end of World War I affect farmers?

4. **Writing** *Informing* In a paragraph, explain why some industries struggled to compete during the 1920s.

5. **Critical Thinking** *Drawing Conclusions* What steps might farmers or the government have taken to ease the farm crisis?

CHAPTER 12 REVIEW

Chapter Summary

The end of World War I brought both excitement and anxiety. Voters elected pro-business Republicans to the presidency. Fear of communism led to a Red Scare that swept the nation. Race riots also broke out in many U.S. cities. The automobile industry and the stock market boomed as Americans bought more goods. Although many Americans enjoyed prosperity, some groups—such as union members and farmers—faced hard times. ■

On a separate sheet of paper, complete the following activities.

Identifying People and Ideas

Describe the historical significance of the following:

1. demobilization
2. Red Scare
3. xenophobia
4. Warren G. Harding
5. Teapot Dome scandal
6. Calvin Coolidge
7. Henry Ford
8. assembly line
9. installment plan
10. Madame C. J. Walker

go.hrw.com
Internet Activity **SB1 The Twenties Abroad**

Choose a country other than the United States that was involved in World War I. Search the Internet through the HRW Web site to find information about what happened in that country's economy during the 1920s. Then use this information to write a report.

Understanding Main Ideas

1. What was the overall outcome of the major labor strikes that took place in the United States following World War I?
2. What was the Republican Party's economic policy during the 1920s?
3. What were the goals of the Five-Power Naval Treaty, the Nine-Power Treaty, and the Kellogg-Briand Pact?
4. How did the automobile spark tremendous growth in the U.S. economy?
5. How did advertising and the installment plan contribute to the creation of a consumer society in the 1920s?
6. Why did the stock market expand greatly during the 1920s?
7. Which groups benefited the most and the least from the general economic prosperity of the 1920s?

Using the Time Line

Number your paper from 1 to 5. Match the letters on the time line below with the following events.

1. **President Harding dies suddenly while on a speaking tour.**
2. **Union leaders call off the unsuccessful strike against U.S. Steel.**
3. **Race riots break out in Chicago, Illinois, leaving nearly 40 people dead and more than 530 injured.**
4. **The United States and 14 other nations sign the Kellogg-Briand Pact, outlawing war.**
5. **Calvin Coolidge defeats Democrat John W. Davis and Progressive Party candidate Robert La Follette in the presidential election.**

1919   1921   1923   1925   1927

a   b   c   d   e

Reviewing Themes

1. **Citizenship and Democracy** In what ways did the Red Scare affect the civil rights of many Americans?
2. **Economic Development** What effects did demobilization have on the U.S. economy?
3. **Technology and Society** How did the development of the assembly line and mass production change Americans' working lives?

Thinking Critically

1. **Evaluating** Do you think advertising had a positive or negative effect on American society in the 1920s? Explain your answer.
2. **Identifying Generalizations and Stereotypes** What factors do you think contributed to the rise in lynchings and race riots following World War I?
3. **Identifying Cause and Effect** How did events in 1919 influence the outcome of the presidential election of 1920?

Writing About History

1. **Expressing** Imagine that you are a resident of Seattle, Washington, during the general strike of 1919. Write a brief diary entry on how the strike has affected you, your family, and your community.
2. **Informing** Imagine that you are a reporter for a local radio station in the Midwest during the 1920s. Write a news story on the economic situation facing midwestern farmers.

Linking Geography and History

1. **Movement** How did the automobile affect Americans' travel habits?
2. **Human-Environment Interaction** How did the widespread use of the automobile change the American landscape?

History Skills Workshop

Reading Charts Radios were initially a luxury item. Their use increased dramatically during the 1920s as costs declined and people began to make purchases using the installment plan. Study the chart below. Then answer the following questions: (a) About how many households had radios in 1923? (b) Between what two years did the number of households with radios increase the most? (c) From 1925 to 1930, how many additional households bought radios?

Building Your Portfolio

Complete the following activities individually or in groups.

1. **Advertising** Imagine that you are an advertising executive in the early 1920s and are in charge of a new ad campaign for Ford's Model T. Create two advertisements, one that might have appeared in a magazine and one that might have been broadcast on the radio.

2. **Campaigning for President** Create a campaign poster that might have appeared for a Democratic, Republican, or third-party candidate in the 1920, 1924, or 1928 presidential election. Make sure that your campaign poster contains a slogan and at least one of the party's platform issues.

Households with Radios, 1922–1930

Y-axis: U.S. Households (in millions), marked 0, 2, 4, 6, 8, 10, 12, 14

X-axis: Year — 1922 1923 1924 1925 1926 1927 1928 1929 1930

Source: *Historical Statistics of the United States*

The Granger Collection, New York

CHAPTER 13
The Roaring Twenties
(1920–1929)

On July 2, 1921, the Radio Corporation of America (RCA) broadcast the Jack Dempsey–Georges Carpentier boxing match. Few Americans owned radios, so thousands gathered in clubs and theaters to hear the fight. Some 100,000 people in Manhattan stood outside the New York Times Building listening to loudspeakers. Radio broadcasting was one of the many developments that transformed American culture in the 1920s.

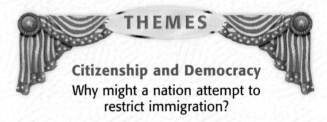

THEMES

Citizenship and Democracy
Why might a nation attempt to restrict immigration?

Technology and Society
How might advances in communication technology affect people's lives?

Cultural Diversity
How might the experiences of a particular group affect the culture of an entire country?

1920 **1921** **1922** **1923** **1924**

JAN. 1920 The Eighteenth Amendment goes into effect.

NOV. 1920 KDKA in Pittsburgh airs the presidential election results.

MAY 1921 President Harding signs the Emergency Quota Act.

DEC. 1923 The National Woman's Party proposes an Equal Rights Amendment.

JUNE 1924 Congress passes the Indian Citizenship Act.

Prohibition America

Reading Focus

What social changes took place among American teenagers after World War I?

How did prohibition affect the United States in the 1920s?

How did Fundamentalism develop, and what role did it play in the Scopes trial?

Key Terms

flappers

prohibition

Volstead Act

bootleggers

speakeasies

Twenty-first Amendment

Fundamentalism

Scopes trial

IN A 1924 INTERVIEW, *an Indiana woman explained how her family and others had spent their leisure time in the past. "We were all much more together. People brought chairs and cushions out of the house and sat on the lawn. . . . We'd sit out so all evening." She went on to describe how neighbors would stop by, and how the young and the old would play games or music together. After World War I, however, this woman's family and many other American families began spending less of their leisure time together. This change was partly the result of young Americans, particularly teenagers, spending more of their free time with friends their own age.*

Many Americans spent their leisure time listening to records played on phonographs.

IMAGE ON LEFT PAGE: *Magazine covers showing the changing fashions and music of the 1920s*

1925 **1926** **1927** **1928** **1929**

JULY 1925
The Scopes trial takes place in Dayton, Tennessee.

MAY 1927
Charles Lindbergh completes the first solo flight across the Atlantic Ocean.

OCT. 1927 Warner Brothers releases the first talkie film, *The Jazz Singer*.

FEB. 1929
The St. Valentine's Day massacre occurs in Chicago.

★ A Changing Nation

After World War I, popular support for public education grew. The improved economy also enabled more children to attend school rather than having to work to help support their families. As a result, from 1915 to 1930, high school enrollment more than tripled.

American Youth

Changes in public education transformed the social lives of many young Americans. High schools began offering a wider range of classes, including job-training courses. Schools also offered extracurricular activities, which had been rare during the late 1800s. Organized sports and social clubs became widespread and popular. School-related activities such as sports events and dances took up an increasing amount of students' time each week.

Technology also changed the lives of young Americans. Radio broadcasts spread popular songs across the nation. The growing use of automobiles gave teenagers greater freedom, which worried some parents. Many teens preferred to go out with their friends rather than spend time with their families. "The two older children never go out when the family motors [drives]. They always have something else on," complained one mother.

A high school boys' basketball team

Straight dresses and short haircuts were popular among flappers.

Critics who did not approve of these changes in social activity accused American youth of being irresponsible. Journalist John Carter challenged these claims in a 1920 article in *Atlantic Monthly*:

> ❝I would like to say a few things about my generation. . . . A keen interest in political and social problems, and a determination to face the facts of life, ugly or beautiful, characterizes us.❞

Young Americans like Carter saw themselves as a new generation that was preparing for the challenges of a modern age.

Throughout the 1920s, many young Americans sought to break away from traditional standards of dress and behavior. For example, some young women stopped wearing long hair and uncomfortable clothing such as heavy corsets. Instead, they wore looser clothes, used cosmetics, and cut their hair short in a style called a bob. The *Ladies' Home Journal* called these women **flappers** because their style of loose clothing and unbuckled coats flapped when they walked. Being a flapper was not just about new fashions, however. As one observer noted, flappers pursued a wide variety of interests, "whether it were a marathon dancing contest, . . . a political campaign, or a social-service settlement."

Rural and Urban America

To many rural Americans, flappers and other new social trends reflected the growing division between the cultures of the city and country. During the 1920s the United States became an increasingly industrial and urban society. For the first time, more than half of the nation's population lived in cities or towns.

As cities grew, so did the number of industrial workers and the power of political machines. Big cities also often had large immigrant populations.

These trends concerned many rural inhabitants. They felt that city life threatened traditional values.

At the same time, some popular urban writers criticized small-town America. These critics claimed that rural residents were ignorant of new technologies and unprepared to live in modern times.

 ## The Prohibition Debate

One of the key disagreements between urban and rural Americans involved **prohibition**—the banning of the manufacture, sale, and transportation of alcohol. The debate over alcohol use had gained national attention in the 1840s. At that time temperance reformers argued that Americans should limit their alcohol consumption. Later temperance supporters included political progressives, conservative Protestant Christian groups, and women's organizations such as the Woman's Christian Temperance Union. These groups believed that alcohol contributed to crime, poverty, and the breakup of families.

In the 1890s the temperance movement had gained new momentum with the founding of the national Anti-Saloon League. The league encouraged its members to vote only for pro-temperance candidates. By 1917 such political efforts had led 19 states to become "dry"—that is, places where liquor sales were banned.

Many prohibition supporters lived in rural areas. Prohibition opponents were concentrated in cities. They included large numbers of immigrants and industrial workers. Opponents of prohibition argued that it would give the government too much power over people's lives. Many Americans feared the law would make criminals out of ordinary people who drank moderately.

The outbreak of World War I tipped popular support in favor of prohibition. Public opinion turned against brewery owners partly because many brewers were of German descent and the United States was at war with Germany. Other Americans argued that all grain should be used for food in the war effort, not wasted in making alcohol. Congress responded by passing a prohibition amendment in December 1917. The states finally ratified the Eighteenth Amendment in 1919, and it went into effect in January 1920.

The Eighteenth Amendment did not actually specify how prohibition would be enforced. Congress passed the **Volstead Act** in October 1919. This act established federal penalties for the manufacture and sale of alcohol. It also made the Bureau of Internal Revenue responsible for enforcing prohibition.

 ## A Dry Nation

Supporters of prohibition expected little opposition once it was signed into law. John F. Kramer, the first prohibition commissioner, declared that liquor would not be "sold, nor given away, nor hauled in anything on the surface of the earth or under the earth or in the air." In areas that had already been dry before prohibition, Kramer was often able to fulfill this pledge.

Enforcing the Law

Police officers and prohibition agents arrested more than 500,000 people for violating prohibition. However, large quantities of illegal liquor remained readily available in cities and towns across the nation. Illegal alcohol came from a variety of sources. Some people stole industrial alcohol

Supporters of prohibition celebrated the ratification of the Eighteenth Amendment in 1919.

intended for legal products such as perfume and antifreeze. Other Americans produced their own alcohol at home. If improperly made, such alcohol could be deadly. Smugglers also brought liquor in from other nations, particularly Canada and Mexico. People involved in the illegal liquor traffic were called **bootleggers**. This name came from an older term that described how smugglers used to hide bottles of alcohol in their boots.

Some speakeasies advertised on cards.

In addition to stopping bootleggers, prohibition agents attempted to locate and close down **speakeasies**. These were secret, illegal clubs that served alcohol. The name speakeasy came from the need for customers to keep quiet about the location of the clubs. Speakeasies were common in most major U.S. cities.

To shut down speakeasies, agents had to be determined and resourceful. None were more so than Isadore "Izzy" Einstein and Moe Smith. The pair made more than 4,000 arrests in five years, often using outrageous disguises to gain entrance to the clubs. On one occasion, Einstein stood outside a speakeasy in light clothing in the bitter cold. Smith knocked on the door and shouted, "Give this man a drink! He's been frostbitten." The startled owner looked at the blue and shivering Einstein and quickly brought him a drink. The agents made their arrest.

Organized Crime

In major cities such as Chicago and New York, criminals organized powerful gangs to control the illegal liquor trade. Chicago was home to one of the nation's most famous and financially successful gangsters, Al "Scarface" Capone.

By 1927 Capone was making about $60 million a year. He dominated the bootlegging business through blackmail, bribery, and murder. Capone defended his actions by saying:

66 **I make my money by supplying a public demand. If I break the law, my customers, who number hundreds of the best people in Chicago, are as guilty as I am. Everybody calls me a racketeer. I call myself a businessman.** 99

Capone's business, however, was deadly. There were several hundred gang-related murders in Chicago alone during the 1920s. During a gang war in September 1926, eight carloads of gangsters sprayed Capone's headquarters with machine-gun fire in broad daylight. On February 14, 1929, Capone had his own gangsters—some disguised

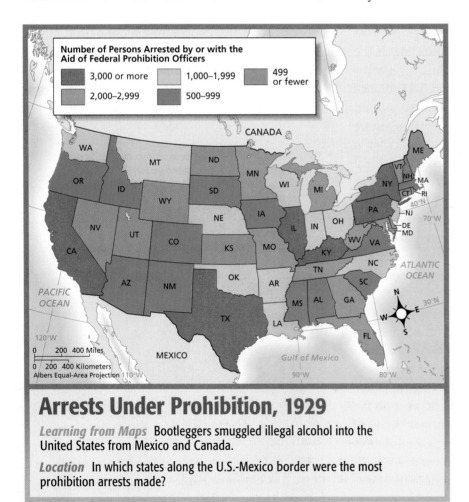

Number of Persons Arrested by or with the Aid of Federal Prohibition Officers

- 3,000 or more
- 2,000–2,999
- 1,000–1,999
- 500–999
- 499 or fewer

Arrests Under Prohibition, 1929

Learning from Maps Bootleggers smuggled illegal alcohol into the United States from Mexico and Canada.

Location In which states along the U.S.-Mexico border were the most prohibition arrests made?

Police take Al Capone's brother, Matthew Capone, into custody.

as police officers—kill seven members of the rival gang. The attack was known as the St. Valentine's Day Massacre. Capone's career finally ended in 1931, when he was convicted for income tax evasion. He was ill when released from prison in 1939 and died eight years later.

The growth of organized crime greatly concerned many Americans. Alcohol consumption decreased during prohibition. However, it soon became clear that the law was very difficult to enforce nationwide. As a result, a movement to repeal prohibition began slowly gaining strength. On December 5, 1933, the **Twenty-first Amendment** ended national prohibition.

⭐ Fundamentalism

Many Protestant groups were united by their support for prohibition but found themselves divided by other issues. One of the central debates involved how to interpret the Bible. Many Christians, often referred to as "modernists," believed that the Bible was divinely inspired but not literally true. An increasing number of Christians, however, joined a movement called **Fundamentalism**. Fundamentalists believe that the Bible is literally true and that it can be relied on as an unquestioned authority.

The movement's name came from a series of booklets, *The Fundamentals,* published between 1910 and 1915. These volumes set forth a series of conservative Protestant beliefs. Fundamentalism appealed to many people who were suspicious of modern industry and science. One Fundamentalist wondered what the value of scientific advances was. "While they are contributing to our material prosperity, they are more rapidly still undermining [destroying] our morals."

Fundamentalist churches were strongest in rural areas and small towns. They were also found in large cities where rural residents had moved to find work. Fundamentalist preacher Billy Sunday drew huge crowds to revival meetings in Chicago. Sunday, a former professional baseball player, was a fiery speaker. He traveled the country holding religious services. Sunday challenged the opponents of prohibition. "I will fight them till hell freezes over, then I'll buy a pair of skates and fight 'em on the ice."

A Canadian-born preacher named Aimee Semple McPherson used a different approach to spread Fundamentalism. McPherson emphasized the blessings and personal joy brought by faith. She preached in the immense Angelus Temple in Los Angeles. Built by her followers, the temple could hold some 5,000 people. In her religious services she used an orchestra, a chorus, and elaborate backgrounds that resembled movie sets. An observer described McPherson as "a superb actress. . . . She sweeps her audience as easily as the harpist beside her sweeps the wires."

Aimee Semple McPherson was a preacher for nearly 20 years.

McPherson broadcast her sermons over the radio with a transmitter so powerful that it frequently interfered with other stations. Using such new methods in addition to traditional revival meetings, Fundamentalist preachers like McPherson and Sunday carried their religious messages to millions of Americans.

⭐ The Scopes Trial

Many Fundamentalists strongly opposed Charles Darwin's theory of evolution because it contradicted the biblical account of creation. Darwin had argued that humans had evolved from simpler forms of life over millions of years. In 1925 the Tennessee legislature passed a law making it illegal to teach any theory contrary to the biblical account of creation. The American Civil Liberties Union (ACLU) argued that the law was unconstitutional and offered to defend anyone who challenged it. The ACLU's chance came when high school science teacher John T. Scopes volunteered to teach Darwin's theory. Scopes was arrested in Dayton, Tennessee, for breaking the law. He was brought to trial in July 1925.

Many Americans saw the **Scopes trial** as a symbol of how American society was struggling to cope with changing times. Some people supported Scopes, while others sided with the Fundamentalists. Clarence Darrow, a famous criminal attorney, led the defense. Three-time presidential candidate William Jennings Bryan led the prosecution. The quiet town of Dayton was transformed by the trial. More than 100 newspaper, magazine, and radio reporters from across the United States and abroad covered the event. Preachers held meetings in tents on the edge of

"*When Shall We Three Meet Again?*"

The monkey standing between William Jennings Bryan (left) and Clarence Darrow (right) represents Darwin's theory of evolution.

town. Vendors sold soda, hot dogs, fans, and Bibles to the many visitors.

The judge in the case refused to allow scientific experts to testify about the theory of evolution. Darrow therefore tried to find some inconsistency in the prosecution's argument. The prosecution argued that the biblical theory of creation was the literal truth. Bryan agreed to testify as an expert on the Bible. When he took the stand, the crowd was so large that the trial was moved outdoors. Darrow questioned Bryan at length. During his testimony, Bryan seemed to accept that some parts of the Bible might be open to interpretation.

Nevertheless, Scopes was convicted and fined $100. The Tennessee Supreme Court overturned Scopes's conviction in 1927 on a technicality but upheld the law against teaching evolution. The controversy over evolution did not end. Religious beliefs continued to influence debates in American politics and culture.

SECTION 1 REVIEW

Identify and explain the significance of the following:

- flappers
- prohibition
- Volstead Act
- bootleggers
- speakeasies
- Al Capone
- Twenty-first Amendment
- Fundamentalism
- Billy Sunday

- Aimee Semple McPherson
- John T. Scopes
- Scopes trial
- Clarence Darrow
- William Jennings Bryan

Reading for Content Understanding

1 **Main Idea** What was the effect of prohibition on the United States in the 1920s?

2 **Main Idea** How did Fundamentalism grow in the 1920s?

3 **Cultural Diversity** In what ways were the experiences of young Americans in the 1920s different from those of previous generations?

4 **Writing** *Describing* Imagine that you are a newspaper reporter covering the Scopes trial. Write a brief article describing the trial. Include the views of both Scopes's supporters and his Fundamentalist opponents.

5 **Critical Thinking** *Synthesizing Information* What were some of the key differences between rural and urban Americans in the 1920s?

SECTION 2

A Changing Population

<table>
<tr>
<td>

Reading Focus

How did nativism affect immigration after World War I?

What challenges did minority groups in the United States face during the 1920s, and what progress did they make?

How did women's political and economic opportunities change during the 1920s?

</td>
<td>

Key Terms

Emergency Quota Act

National Origins Act

Great Migration

Universal Negro Improvement Association

Indian Citizenship Act

</td>
</tr>
</table>

N JULY 1923 Henry Curran became commissioner of the immigration station on Ellis Island. In his first week of work Curran witnessed a scene that he later recorded in his memoirs. From his office window he watched hundreds of immigrants being forced to return home because of new laws restricting immigration. "They trooped aboard the big barges . . . some carrying little American flags, most of them quietly weeping." Such scenes, which Curran said "twisted something in my heart that hurts to this day," became increasingly common in the 1920s as Congress passed stricter immigration laws.

A coversheet for a 1923 song protesting immigration

 ## Opposing Immigration

Immediately after World War I, the U.S. economy suffered a brief recession. Rapid demobilization led to layoffs and labor strikes. Many Americans blamed the hard times on the millions of immigrants living in the United States.

Nativism

A wave of nativism, or strong anti-immigrant feeling, swept the nation. Opponents of immigration claimed that immigrants took jobs away from U.S.

citizens. Some Americans were also influenced by the Red Scare. They believed that immigrants introduced politically radical ideas—such as communism and anarchism—that were dangerous to American democracy. Alabama senator James Heflin claimed that:

❝[immigrants] fill places that belong to the loyal wage-earning citizens of America. They preach a doctrine [belief] that is dangerous and deadly to our institutions. . . . They constitute a menace and danger to us every day.❞

Nativists focused their criticism on immigrants from southern and eastern Europe. The languages, customs, and religious beliefs of these individuals were often different from those of earlier immigrants from northern and western Europe. Nativists considered these differences a threat to American culture. Arriving into this atmosphere of suspicion and hostility, one immigrant asked:

❝ **Isn't it strange that here we are coming to a country where there is complete equality, but not quite so for the newly arrived immigrants?** ❞

Restricting Immigration

Even after the postwar recession ended, nativists were concerned by increasing immigration to the United States. More than 800,000 immigrants arrived in 1921 alone. In May 1921 President Harding signed the **Emergency Quota Act**. This law limited total immigration to the United States to 357,000 a year. It also restricted the number of immigrants from any European nation to only 3 percent of each nationality's U.S. population according to the 1910 U.S census.

Some pamphlets tried to help immigrants become U.S. citizens.

This law excluded many eastern and southern European immigrants because there were relatively small numbers of them living in the United States in 1910. The act set no limits, however, on immigration from nations in the Western Hemisphere. American farmers and business owners benefited from this policy because they hired many Canadian and Mexican immigrants.

Congress passed the **National Origins Act** in May 1924, further reducing total immigration. For example, this act completely banned Japanese immigration to the United States. In addition, the new law based the limits on European immigration on the 1890 U.S. census. As a result, the law gave even greater preference to immigrants from northern and western Europe. The act also made it much easier for the government to deport immigrants already living in the United States.

This 1920s cartoon argues that many new immigrants did not mix well into American society.

The Granger Collection, New York

⭐ The Ku Klux Klan

The growing hostility toward immigrants also contributed to the rebirth of the Ku Klux Klan. Re-formed in 1915 by minister William J. Simmons in Stone Mountain, Georgia, the Klan grew slowly during World War I. Until 1920 the Klan had only a few thousand members. Its scope was confined to Alabama and Georgia. After 1920, however, the Klan began using recruiters and modern advertising to promote itself as a defender of "Americanism."

Klan leaders pledged to protect the nation's white, Protestant society from threats of radical change and from people of different cultures and color. Members of the Klan not only were hostile toward African Americans but also targeted Catholics, Jews, and foreigners. The Klan used cross-burnings, beatings, kidnappings, and murders to terrorize its victims. Recruiters downplayed the Klan's racism and use of violence. Instead, they compared the Klan to the business and social clubs popular at the time. As a result, the Klan grew at an amazing rate. At its peak in the mid-1920s, the Ku Klux

An anti-immigration Ku Klux Klan poster

Klan claimed about 4 million members, including thousands of women and children.

Soon the Klan became a strong force in local politics and influenced elections in states from Maine to Oregon. In Indiana, Klan leader David Stephenson virtually controlled local and state politics. He boasted, "I am the law." In 1925 Stephenson's career ended when he was convicted of second-degree murder. When his political allies abandoned him, he exposed widespread corruption within the Klan.

The news that Klan leaders, promoters, and recruiters were getting rich on membership dues greatly decreased the Klan's influence. The scandals and congressional investigations that followed further reduced the Klan's power nationwide.

☆ Challenging Discrimination

Even before the expansion of the Klan, racism and poverty motivated many African Americans to leave the South. During the labor shortage of World War I, some 500,000 African Americans moved to midwestern and northern cities. They hoped to find better jobs and greater social opportunities. This mass movement was known as the **Great Migration**.

The NAACP and the UNIA

Even after they moved to northern communities, African Americans faced job discrimination and the threat of violence. Black leaders responded to these challenges in different ways. The National Association for the Advancement of Colored People (NAACP) fought segregation and racial inequality. It used the courts as well as writings to call attention to discrimination. W. E. B. Du Bois, a founding member of the NAACP, wrote that he expected change to come "through reason, human sympathy, and the education of children."

Marcus Garvey clashed with Du Bois and other NAACP leaders over integration. Garvey stated that he would not "waste time . . . waiting for white people to recognize me." He was born in Jamaica, where he first organized the **Universal Negro Improvement Association** (UNIA) in 1914. The UNIA's goals were to end imperialism in Africa and discrimination in the United States. In 1916 Garvey moved to the neighborhood of Harlem in New York City and founded a UNIA chapter. A powerful speaker, Garvey attracted an estimated 1 million members worldwide to the UNIA by 1921.

Garvey's Program

Garvey supported a movement called black nationalism, which encouraged African Americans to be economically independent and to take pride in their African heritage. As part of this effort he supported a "back to Africa" movement. This effort was intended to help African Americans resettle in Africa and rebuild its economy. Garvey also urged African Americans to start their own businesses in the United States. He personally

Marcus Garvey organized several international conventions of the UNIA.

Mexican immigrants Lupe and Juan Salvador Villaseñor were married in 1929. In a traditional ceremony these coins, called *arras*, are given by the groom to the bride to show that he will always provide for her.

In addition to this Mexican American migration north, between 500,000 and 1 million Mexicans immigrated to the United States during the 1920s. Some immigrants were searching for new economic opportunities. Others were escaping the problems caused by the Mexican Revolution. Most families of Mexican descent settled in the West and Southwest, particularly in California and Texas. There they worked mainly as agricultural laborers.

Life in their new country could be difficult for Mexican immigrants. They were usually poorly paid. The struggle to make ends meet often meant that young women had to work outside the home, which was a change from their traditional role. Immigrants often lived in temporary camps filled with shacks constructed of scrap wood. In some communities, Spanish-speaking residents formed barrios, or neighborhoods, where they shared a common culture. In the barrio, author and educator Ernesto Galarza recalled, "we heard Spanish on the streets and in the alleys." In contrast, when Galarza and his family left the barrio to go downtown they felt "like aliens in a foreign land."

established several companies. In 1919 he founded the Black Star steamship line to provide trade and transportation between Africa and the Americas. In addition, the UNIA funded the *Negro World*. This publication quickly became the most widely read black newspaper in America.

In 1922, however, Black Star suspended operations. After the federal government investigated Black Star's finances, Garvey was convicted of mail fraud, fined $1,000, and sentenced to five years in jail. He served two years before being released in 1927 and deported to Jamaica. Despite his legal problems, the *Amsterdam News* described Garvey as having "made black people proud of their race. In a world where black is despised he taught them black is beautiful."

★ American Indians

The thousands of American Indians living on reservations also faced hardships. Officials of the

A delegation of Pueblo Indians arrived in Washington, D.C., in 1923 to protest the mistreatment of tribal members and threats to tribal lands.

★ Mexican Americans

Like African Americans, many Mexican Americans had moved north to fill jobs during World War I. This migration continued during the 1920s as restrictions on European immigration and the expanding U.S. economy created a labor shortage. Thousands of Mexican American workers went to manufacturing centers such as Chicago, Detroit, and Pittsburgh.

federal Bureau of Indian Affairs had hoped to address the problems of poverty and poor housing with the Dawes Act, passed in 1887. This act took reservation land away from American Indian tribes and allotted sections of it to individual Indians. Reservation land that was left over after this distribution was usually sold to non-Indians.

The breaking up of the reservations was intended to help establish independent Indian ranches and farms. Instead, the Dawes Act greatly disrupted tribal culture and removed millions of acres of land from Indian control. By 1934, American Indians owned only about a third of the land they had owned in 1887.

American Indians also faced political restrictions. Many Indians living within the United States were not recognized as U.S. citizens. Despite this restriction, during World War I around 10,000 American Indians served in the U.S. military. At home, American Indians purchased an estimated $25 million in war bonds. Indian leaders pointed to these patriotic acts and demanded U.S. citizenship. "Many of our young men . . . gave their lives for you," argued Deskaheh, a Cayuga chief. In response to these demands, Congress passed the **Indian Citizenship Act** in June 1924. This legislation granted all American Indians the legal protections and voting privileges of U.S. citizenship.

Indian leaders won another political victory in 1922 when the Pueblo tribes united to fight the Bursum Bill. This legislation would have taken away thousands of acres of Pueblo land. Receiving national support from groups such as the General Federation of Women's Clubs, the Pueblo successfully defended their ownership of tribal lands. Such political accomplishments gave some Indian leaders hope for future reforms. Many Indians, however, continued to suffer economic hardship and social discrimination during the 1920s.

★ Women in the 1920s

American women also made political gains during the decade. In 1920 they gained the vote with the ratification of the Nineteenth Amendment. Voting gave women the ability to influence national politics directly. It also increased women's opportunities to become political leaders.

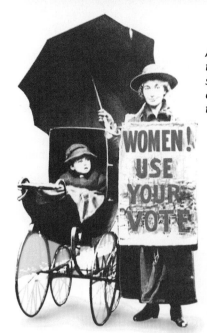

After women gained the vote in 1920, suffragists encouraged them to go to the polls.

Women in Politics

In 1924 Nellie Tayloe Ross of Wyoming and Miriam "Ma" Wallace Ferguson of Texas became the first two female governors in the United States. By 1928, 145 women held seats in state legislatures, and 2 women had been elected to the U.S. House of Representatives.

The National Woman's Party (NWP), led by Alice Paul, sought broader social gains. The NWP called for the abolition of laws that regulated the type of work women could do, the pay they could receive, and the loans they could get. In December 1923 the NWP proposed an Equal Rights Amendment (ERA) to the U.S. Constitution.

Disagreements over the ERA divided the women's movement. The Women's Trade Union League had fought for labor legislation to protect women. It was concerned that the ERA would remove these legal safeguards. The League of Women Voters argued that the ERA was too broad and would interfere with women's roles in society. Paul disagreed with such arguments:

66 **If we get freedom for women, then they are probably going to do a lot of things that I wish they wouldn't do. But it seems to me that isn't our business to say what they should do with it. It is our business to see that they get it.** 99

The ERA failed to pass despite the efforts of the NWP and other supporters.

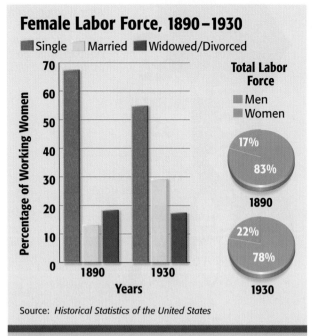

Female Labor Force, 1890–1930

■ Single ■ Married ■ Widowed/Divorced

Percentage of Working Women

Total Labor Force
■ Men
■ Women

17%
83%
1890

22%
78%
1930

Source: *Historical Statistics of the United States*

Women at Work By 1930 both the size and the distribution of the female labor force had changed significantly. What percentage of working women were married in 1890? in 1930?

Women at Work

Even without the passage of an Equal Rights Amendment, women's roles in the workplace were changing during the 1920s. World War I had provided thousands of women with the opportunity to enter industrial jobs traditionally held by men. As suffrage leader Harriot Stanton Blatch explained, "When men go a-warring, women go to work." After the war, business and union leaders asked women to give up these industrial jobs so that returning war veterans could go back to work.

Thousands of women sought other work because they were unwilling to surrender their economic and social independence. By the end of the 1920s the number of women working outside the home had risen by 2 million. Many of these women worked in offices as secretaries, telephone operators, or typists. The number of women in professional fields such as nursing and teaching also increased. Some professional women gained national recognition. For example, Dr. Florence R. Sabin became the first female member of the National Academy of Sciences.

In spite of these gains, women continued to face obstacles in the workforce. Most clerical, nursing, and teaching jobs paid relatively little for the skills required. In addition, employers often refused to hire minority women for such jobs. As a result, many African American and Hispanic women took lower-paying domestic or factory work. Women's rights activists continued to struggle throughout the 1920s to achieve greater social and economic equality.

SECTION 2 REVIEW

Identify and explain the significance of the following:

- **Emergency Quota Act**
- **National Origins Act**
- **Great Migration**
- **Marcus Garvey**
- **Universal Negro Improvement Association**
- **Indian Citizenship Act**
- **Alice Paul**

Reading for Content Understanding

1 Main Idea How did Congress respond to nativist concerns over immigration?

2 Main Idea What problems did African Americans face during the 1920s, and what solutions did black leaders seek?

3 Citizenship and Democracy What political and economic gains did women achieve during the 1920s?

4 Writing *Describing* Imagine that you are a journalist interviewing a Mexican immigrant family in the United States during the 1920s. Write a short article describing the family's experiences, including where its members live, their work, and any difficulties that they have encountered.

5 Critical Thinking *Identifying Cause and Effect* Why do you think that the participation of American Indians in World War I helped convince Congress to grant them U.S. citizenship?

Americans at Play

Reading Focus

What led to the rise of fads in the 1920s?

How did radio and movies affect American culture?

What did Americans think of movie actors and professional athletes during the 1920s?

Key Terms

fads

nickelodeons

talkies

*O*NE DAY IN 1927 *Alvin "Shipwreck" Kelly climbed onto a flagpole and did not come down. Day after day, he perched on top of the pole. When he was hungry or thirsty, Kelly hauled food and drink up in a bucket. At night he slept only briefly, fearing he would fall to his death. He never slept for more than 20 minutes at a time. After 23 days and seven hours on his flagpole, Kelly finally climbed down, having achieved his goal. Shipwreck Kelly was the new world-record holder in flagpole sitting. Some hotels actually hired him to attract business by sitting on flagpoles. Kelly sat on flagpoles for 145 days in 1929, earning $29,000.*

Alvin "Shipwreck" Kelly sits on top of a flagpole in New York City.

⭐ Fads and Fun

Shipwreck Kelly's stunts were part of an adventurous spirit that led some Americans to nickname the decade the Roaring Twenties. The national economy enjoyed spectacular growth. Americans were encouraged to buy new consumer products and experiment with new leisure activities.

The 1920s were also a time of **fads**—interests followed with great enthusiasm by many people for a short time. Fads owed much of their existence to the increased influence of mass media in the 1920s. Across the nation people could watch the same movies and listen to the same radio broadcasts. They could also read the same articles and view the same advertisements. This ability allowed people throughout the country to share cultural activities such as fads.

Fads varied widely. In 1923 a Chinese game known as mah jongg

Mah jongg sets contain either 136 or 144 tiles.

was particularly popular. Another widespread fad was the self-improvement program taught by Emile Coué, a French hypnotist. In 1923 millions of Americans were repeating Coué's simple self-help formula, "Every day, in every way, I'm growing better and better." Other popular new pastimes included crossword puzzles and miniature golf.

 ## Radio

Listening to the radio was much more than a fad. Radio's popularity continued well beyond the 1920s. In 1920 WWJ in Detroit became the first radio station to air regular broadcasts. On November 2, 1920, KDKA in Pittsburgh reported the results of that year's presidential election.

Consumers had to buy magazines and newspapers to read the articles. Radio broadcasts, however, were free to anyone who had access to a radio. To make a profit, radio stations turned to advertising. The first radio advertisements were aired in 1922. Businesspeople loved radio advertising. Business sponsors brought in money that funded more powerful broadcasting equipment and additional radio programming.

Radio broadcasts fascinated many Americans and brought the larger world into individual homes. "We could pull unseen voices out of the air and into the living room from all over the world," remembered one man. Most radio airtime was devoted to live music. Major elections and special events also received live radio news coverage. WGN in Chicago, for example, captured its listeners' attention with live broadcasts of the Scopes trial. Broadcasts of sporting events also helped radio grow in popularity. Radio listeners cheered on their favorite teams during the 1921 World Series.

In 1926 the National Broadcasting Company (NBC) was created, followed the next year by the Columbia Broadcasting System (CBS). By gathering together many radio stations to broadcast their shows, NBC and CBS could reach large numbers of listeners. Soon the networks were broadcasting shows coast-to-coast. A woman working at home in rural Idaho, for example, could hear the daily news from New York City.

By 1929 some 10 million Americans owned radios. Families and friends often gathered to listen to their favorite shows. One woman remembered how her neighbor invited his friends

to come listen to the 'Grand Old Opera' on [each] Saturday night. . . . We were thrilled and looked forward to this each week."

Radio exposed people all around the country to the same programs, news stories, and advertisements. Live events in politics, sports, and entertainment could be shared by thousands. This common experience bridged cultural differences and helped to link American society.

America Goes to the Movies

Movies were another form of entertainment that brought Americans together. Thomas Edison and others had invented moving pictures, also called movies, in the late 1800s.

The Film Industry

Early films were often short, silent scenes of trains or waterfalls. Many early theaters, which were

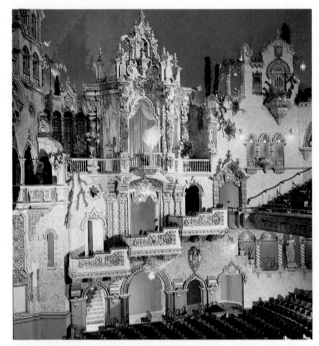

The Majestic Theater in San Antonio, Texas, was one of many grand movie theaters built in the 1920s.

Movie Special Effects

On April 14, 1894, the Holland brothers' amusement arcade opened in New York City. Inside the converted shoe store were 10 cabinets containing Thomas Edison's latest invention—the kinetoscope. For five cents these machines would display a 20-second film of moving images.

In 1896 special-effects pioneer Georges Méliès, a French magician, developed the technique of stop-action to film his magic tricks. Méliès discovered that by stopping and starting the camera, he could make objects seemingly appear, disappear, or change into other objects. His special effects in the 1902 film, *A Trip to the Moon,* influenced filmmakers everywhere.

The next year Edwin S. Porter thrilled audiences with *The Great Train Robbery.* Running about 10 minutes, the drama told the story of four bandits who robbed a train. By editing the film, Porter was able to cut backward in time and back and forth across space. These cuts allowed the audience to understand the entire story even though events were happening in different places at the same time.

In more recent years, technological breakthroughs have included color films, wide screens, and stereo. Other inventions were less successful. These included gimmicks such as three-dimensional movies, which required viewers to wear special paper eyeglasses. Smell-O-Vision, which tried to add smells to the movie experience, also flopped.

Movie special effects have come a long way. Today, moviemakers are using digital sound and computer-generated special effects in their films. In his

Animators used computers to create the advanced three-dimensional insects in the film A Bug's Life.

1990s films *Jurassic Park* and *The Lost World,* director Steven Spielberg used computer animation to draw the dinosaurs. He also used computers to make the dinosaurs' muscles appear to move naturally when they ran. Other new film technologies include interactive movies that allow the audience members to determine the outcome. There is even an updated version of three-dimensional movies without the glasses.

Movie theaters themselves are being redesigned to improve the moviegoing experience. Some of these new design features include gigantic screens and seats that move to allow audiences to feel the action taking place on screen.

Understanding What You Read

1. What special effect did Georges Méliès develop?

2. How did Edwin S. Porter influence the way that movies were directed?

3. Why do you think that many moviemakers use special effects in their films?

Mary Pickford

Born in 1893, Mary Pickford made her first stage appearance at the age of five. When she was a teenager she began making movies with director D. W. Griffith. She soon rose to stardom. By the end of World War I, Pickford was making $10,000 a week. Movies such as *Cinderella* and *Rebecca of Sunnybrook Farm* established the little-girl image that earned her the title of "America's Sweetheart."

Pickford tried to play different parts, but fans wanted her to play more familiar roles in films such as *Pollyanna*. Determined to find new challenges, she joined Griffith, Charlie Chaplin, and Douglas Fairbanks to found the independent film distributor United Artists in 1919. Pickford retired after acting in more than 200 films. She was one of Hollywood's greatest legends when she died in 1979.

called **nickelodeons** because admission was usually five cents, were stuffy, converted stores. After World War I, luxurious new theaters with balconies and enormous screens replaced the nickelodeons. Some of these "movie palaces" included orchestras to accompany the silent films. A New York woman described entering one of these theaters as "stepping into another world of fantasy."

By 1928 there were some 20,000 movie theaters in the United States. Millions of Americans went to the movies each year. Even people who lived in small towns made going to the movies a regular event. For example, on Saturdays one young girl's family would walk three miles from their farm in Massachusetts to the nearest town. "How we loved the serials [multipart movies] . . . and how we hoped never to miss a part," she remembered fondly.

In 1927 the first **talkies**—movies with sound or dialogue—thrilled American moviegoers. The first full-length feature talkie was Warner Brothers' *The Jazz Singer*, released in October 1927. Starring Al Jolson, it was an enormous box-office success. One theater owner described the film as "just about the most wonderful thing I had ever seen in my life." Other movie studios quickly adopted the new sound technology. In 1928 Walt Disney's talkie cartoon *Steamboat Willie* introduced audiences to Mickey Mouse.

The American film industry began its existence in New York and New Jersey. By the 1920s the industry was centered in Hollywood, California.

Mickey Mouse became one of the country's most popular cartoon characters in the 1920s and 1930s.

Film companies began moving to Hollywood in 1911. They were attracted by sunny weather, cheap real estate, and beautiful natural scenery. Many studio founders were immigrants from eastern Europe. Their achievements were impressive during a time when nativism was strong. Samuel Goldwyn and the Warner Brothers—Harry, Sam, and Albert—emigrated from Poland. Louis B. Mayer arrived from Russia, and William Fox came from Hungary.

Movie Stars

American audiences were less interested in moviemakers than in movie stars. In the early 1920s, 40 million Americans went to the movies every week. By 1929 the number had increased to 80 million. These huge audiences turned their favorite actors and actresses into celebrities almost overnight. One teenager recalled how at the movies he and his friends would "stamp, whistle, holler, cheer, clap, and do everything possible to urge on our hero or heroine." Films also influenced national fashion and culture. Young Americans copied their idols' clothes, hairstyles, and ways of walking and talking.

Charlie Chaplin's lovable but pathetic character, the Tramp, may have been the best-known figure in America. Female movie-goers across the country packed theaters to watch heartthrob Rudolph Valentino ride across the desert in *The Sheik*. When Valentino died in 1926, tens of thousands of people, mostly women, lined up for blocks outside the funeral home. Other movie stars included Greta Garbo, Douglas Fairbanks, Clara Bow, and Mary Pickford. Many wealthy movie stars began to draw attention as much for their expensive lifestyles as for their film appearances.

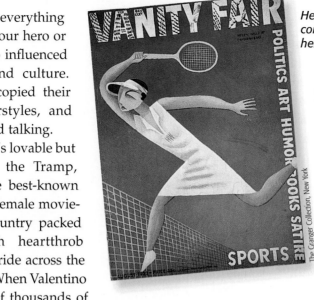

The Granger Collection, New York

Helen Wills was noted for her concentration on the court and her powerful serves.

Sports Stars

As organized sports became increasingly popular, Americans also made celebrities out of star athletes. Perhaps the greatest athlete of the 1920s was Jim Thorpe, an American Indian of Sauk and Fox descent. Thorpe won gold medals at the 1912 Olympics in Stockholm, Sweden, in the pentathlon and decathlon. He later played professional baseball and football. In 1920 he became president of the newly formed National Football League. Thorpe played for and coached a number of teams before retiring in 1928.

Other outstanding athletes of the 1920s, such as swimmer Gertrude Ederle and tennis player Helen Wills, also became celebrities. At the 1924 Olympics, Ederle won a gold medal and two bronze medals. Two years later, she swam the English Channel in 14 hours and 31 minutes— nearly two hours faster than the men's record. Wills won four consecutive Wimbledon singles titles from 1927 to 1930. She won more than 30 Grand Slam events during her career.

Team sports were also popular. Thousands of fans packed college football stadiums to see powerful teams from such schools as Notre Dame and the University of Michigan. One of the greatest football players of the 1920s was Harold "Red" Grange, the "Galloping Ghost." He played halfback for the University of Illinois. After his spectacular senior year in 1925 Grange became the first athlete to appear on the cover of *Time* magazine.

As the 1920s began, professional baseball was stunned by a scandal. Players for the Chicago White Sox had accepted money to lose the 1919 World Series. Baseball recovered from the scandal with the help of an exciting young star named George "Babe" Ruth. He became one of baseball's greatest home-run hitters while playing for the New York Yankees. In 1920 he hit more home runs in one season than any previous player. The Yankees became the first team to draw more than 1 million fans in a season. Yankee Stadium was later called The House That Ruth Built. Ruth led the Yankees to four world championships and hit 714 home runs during his career, a record that stood for nearly 40 years.

African Americans were excluded from playing in the major leagues. In response, some black baseball players formed the Negro National League. Stars of these new teams included pitcher Satchel Paige, catcher and home-run hitter Josh Gibson, and outfielder "Cool Papa" Bell. These players were eventually included in baseball's Hall of Fame in Cooperstown, New York.

Home-run hitter Babe Ruth

★ Daring Aviators

Pilot Charles Lindbergh was one of the biggest celebrities of the 1920s. Lindbergh took off from Long Island, New York, on the morning of May 20, 1927. His goal was to become the first person to fly solo across the Atlantic Ocean. Six expert pilots had already died while attempting this feat. By comparison, Lindbergh was a little known pilot without much financial backing. Few people thought that he could succeed where others had failed so tragically.

Lindbergh, who was called the Lone Eagle as well as Lucky Lindy, beat the odds. About 33 and a half hours after taking off, he landed his plane, the *Spirit of St. Louis,* in Paris. News of his arrival on the night of May 21 drew more than 100,000 French people to the airport to meet the daring pilot. Lindbergh later recalled:

The Granger Collection, New York

Charles Lindbergh posing just before his historic flight across the Atlantic Ocean

❝My name was called out over and over again. . . . I opened the door, and started to put my foot down onto ground. But dozens of hands took hold of me—my legs, my arms, my body. . . . I found myself lying . . . up on top of the crowd, in the center of an ocean of heads that extended as far out into the darkness as I could see.❞

Back in the United States, Lindbergh's achievement captured the imagination of the American public. He was honored with parades, given multiple medals, and featured on a new postage stamp. Lindbergh's flight even helped boost investment in the aviation industry.

Lindbergh inspired other daring aviators. In 1928 Amelia Earhart became the first woman to fly across the Atlantic. Earhart continued to thrill Americans with her long-distance journeys until she disappeared in 1937 while trying to fly around the world. In a time when many Americans felt that the frontier had disappeared, pilots such as Lindbergh and Earhart seemed to represent the return of the nation's old pioneering spirit.

SECTION 3 REVIEW

Identify and explain the significance of the following:

- **fads**
- **nickelodeons**
- **talkies**
- **Charlie Chaplin**
- **Mary Pickford**
- **Jim Thorpe**
- **George "Babe" Ruth**
- **Charles Lindbergh**
- **Amelia Earhart**

Reading for Content Understanding

1 **Main Idea** Why were fads so common during the 1920s?

2 **Main Idea** How did Americans treat movie and sports stars in the 1920s?

3 **Technology and Society** How did developments such as radio and movies affect American culture in the 1920s?

4 **Writing** *Expressing* Imagine that you have just heard a radio broadcast for the first time. Write a short letter about the experience of listening to the broadcast to a friend who has never heard a radio.

5 **Critical Thinking** *Drawing Conclusions* Why do you think many Americans considered individuals like Charles Lindbergh to be national heroes? Who do you consider to be a modern-day hero, and why?

SECTION 4

The Arts

Reading Focus

How did the blues and jazz affect American culture?

Why were the Harlem Renaissance and the Lost Generation significant?

What were some of the other major developments in American arts in the 1920s?

Key Terms

Jazz Age
Harlem Renaissance
Lost Generation
expatriates
Armory Show

*I*N 1926, *African American writer Langston Hughes published an influential essay in the magazine* The Nation. *In it he declared that a new era of African American literature and art was beginning. "We young Negro artists who create now intend to express our individual dark-skinned selves without fear or shame," he announced. "We know we are beautiful." African American arts flourished during the 1920s and helped shape the cultural development of the decade.*

Poet Langston Hughes

 ### The Jazz Age

One of the arts in which African Americans had the greatest influence during the 1920s was music. Two of the most popular musical styles were the blues and jazz. Both styles had deep roots in African American culture.

The Blues

The blues emerged from the countryside and small towns of the rural Mississippi Delta region in the South. The blues evolved from the spirituals and work chants that had been sung by enslaved African Americans. By the 1890s the blues had become a distinct musical style. Blues musicians often used instruments to imitate the singing voice. The most popular blues instruments were the guitar, harmonica, and piano. Blues performers sang lyrics dealing with a wide range of topics, including daily struggles, racism, and lost love.

Born in Alabama, musician W. C. Handy helped popularize the blues in the North. Known as the Father of the Blues, Handy wrote songs such as "St. Louis Blues." This hit song described life in a St. Louis neighborhood of the 1890s. The most

The Roaring Twenties **399**

Bessie Smith was known as the Empress of the Blues, while Louis Armstrong's fans nicknamed him "Satchmo."

Ellington began appearing at jazz clubs in New York City. Ellington composed jazz classics such as "Black and Tan Fantasy." He used a large band and skillfully blended its many instruments. Ellington continued to compose and perform songs into his seventies. In addition to big-band hits, he wrote scores for movies, Broadway shows, and operas.

Other bandleaders such as Benny Goodman and Paul Whiteman helped popularize jazz and bring it to an even wider audience. Whiteman paid composer George Gershwin to write a jazz symphony, "Rhapsody in Blue," that mixed elements of popular and classical music. People worldwide were soon enjoying this uniquely American style of music. Jazz became so popular in the 1920s that the decade is often called the **Jazz Age**.

successful blues recording artist of the 1920s was Bessie Smith. Jazz singer and trumpeter Louis (LOO-ee) Armstrong said that Smith had a "certain something in her voice no other blues singer could get. She had music in her soul." Other notable blues singers of the 1920s included Mamie Smith and Gertrude "Ma" Rainey.

Jazz

Like the blues, jazz music originated in the South, in cities such as New Orleans, Louisiana. Jazz was influenced by the blues as well as another African American music style—ragtime. Musician Scott Joplin helped create this lively piano music that was popular in the early 1900s. Other influences on jazz included West African folk music.

Important early jazz musicians included cornet player Joseph "King" Oliver, pianist Ferdinand "Jelly Roll" Morton, and Louis Armstrong. Armstrong was known for his deep singing voice as well as his trumpet-playing. He played with Oliver before forming the Louis Armstrong Hot Five. Armstrong developed performance techniques, such as stepping out from the group to play a solo, that are still popular with audiences today.

During the 1920s many musicians traveled from the South to northern cities like Chicago, bringing jazz music to urban African American audiences. In 1927 Edward "Duke"

★ The Harlem Renaissance

Jazz was one of many art forms that flourished in the New York City neighborhood of Harlem. As a result of the Great Migration, Harlem's population boomed, making the neighborhood the nation's largest African American community. Many African Americans involved in the arts—actors, musicians, painters, and writers—moved to Harlem. As a result, Harlem became a major center of African American cultural activity during the 1920s. As artist and writer Elton Fax said:

> **Harlem epitomized [symbolized] a kind of freedom that we did not know: 'Once I get to Harlem, I won't need to worry about anything. Nobody's gonna bother me in Harlem.'**

The **Harlem Renaissance**—a remarkable period of African American artistic achievement in the 1920s—took its name from the neighborhood. However, many artists who were identified with the Harlem Renaissance did not live in Harlem. Through their work, Harlem Renaissance artists expressed frustration and anger with racial inequality. They also showed

Brass horns such as the trumpet were popular with many jazz musicians.

their pride and hope for the future. This future was represented for many people by the ideal of the "New Negro". The New Negro was an independent African American proud of his or her artistic and intellectual achievements.

Literature

As editor of the magazine *The Crisis,* W. E. B. Du Bois published the works of many young African American writers. Scholar Alain Locke and NAACP leader and author James Weldon Johnson also published the works of other writers as well as their own material.

Much of the literature of the Harlem Renaissance showed the struggles of African American life. Poets Countee Cullen, Claude McKay, and Langston Hughes were each respected. McKay expressed his anger and resentment in poems such as "The Lynching" and "If We Must Die." Hughes was possibly the most famous of the Harlem Renaissance poets. He used his writing to explore the African heritage of black Americans. The poem "I, Too" expressed both his pride in being an African American and his optimism for the future:

" I, too, sing America.
I am the darker brother.
They send me to eat in the kitchen
When company comes,
But I laugh,
And eat well,
And grow strong.

Tomorrow,
I'll be at the table
When company comes.
Nobody'll dare
Say to me,

'Eat in the kitchen,'
Then.

Besides,
They'll see how beautiful I am
And be ashamed—

I, too, am America. "

Harlem Renaissance, 1920s and 1930s

Learning from Maps The New York City neighborhood known as Harlem became an important center for African American art, literature, and music during the 1920s.

Movement What happened to the African American neighborhood in Harlem between 1920 and 1930?

Theater

The theater also thrived during the Harlem Renaissance. Leading roles in the theater had previously been off-limits to African Americans. In 1921, however, the black musical comedy *Shuffle Along* appeared on Broadway. Its success paved the way for other popular African American musicals. These shows introduced performers such as singer and dancer Josephine Baker, who became an international star.

Paul Robeson was one of the best-known African American actors and singers. Robeson was an all-American football player and class valedictorian at Rutgers University. He attended Columbia University Law School before deciding to become an actor. His dynamic but disciplined acting style and powerful singing voice received praise from critics. Robeson starred in a wide range of productions, from the musical *Show Boat* to Shakespearean plays. He went on to make successful records and appeared in a variety of films. Performers such as Robeson, Charles Gilpin, and Rose McClendon helped open doors for other black actors.

Paul Robeson gained rave reviews for his performance in the title role of Shakespeare's *Othello*.

The Lost Generation

Harlem Renaissance writers were not alone in examining American society. Many writers of the 1920s were disgusted by the death and destruction of World War I. Author Ernest Hemingway had served as an ambulance driver during the war. He wrote that it was "the most colossal, murderous, mismanaged butchery that has ever taken place on earth. Any writer who said otherwise lied."

Some authors believed that the democratic ideals for which the war was fought had been abandoned when it ended. These writers also thought that American culture was too devoted to greed and money. Author Gertrude Stein called the writers who criticized postwar American society the **Lost Generation**.

After World War I many American writers moved to Europe to live as **expatriates**—people who leave their native country to live elsewhere. Other writers, including playwright Eugene O'Neill and poet Edna St. Vincent Millay, remained in the United States. Some expatriates who returned settled in New York City's Greenwich Village, which became a cultural center similar to Harlem.

Author Sinclair Lewis was a particularly harsh critic of big business and small-town America. One of Lewis's most popular novels, *Babbitt,* attacked businesspeople as narrow-minded. Lewis later became the first American to win a Nobel Prize in literature.

Some of the most influential members of the Lost Generation began writing in their early twenties. These authors included Ernest Hemingway, John Dos Passos, and F. Scott Fitzgerald. Many young Americans were drawn to their works. Hemingway developed a direct and simple writing style that inspired later authors. His novel *A Farewell to Arms* was a romantic tragedy based on his own experiences in World War I. The main character expressed a common attitude of the Lost Generation when he said, "I was always embarrassed by the words sacred, glorious, and sacrifice. . . . I had seen nothing sacred, and the things that were glorious had no glory."

Author F. Scott Fitzgerald also served in the armed forces during World War I. Fitzgerald's works, such as *This Side of Paradise* and *The Great Gatsby,* captured the spirit of the Jazz Age. He and his wife, Zelda, demonstrated the spirit of the Roaring Twenties. They were known for dancing until dawn and even jumping into a fountain at the end of a party. Fitzgerald struggled, however, to make enough money to maintain his lifestyle and still produce quality writing. In some ways, he and other members of the Lost Generation were like the main characters of *The Great Gatsby*. These characters seem to be successful but are unable to find happiness and satisfaction.

Edward Hopper's 1928 painting Manhattan Bridge Loop

New Directions in Art

The visual arts thrived in the 1920s. Leading artists broke away from traditional styles and explored new techniques and subjects.

The Armory Show

In the early 1900s Spanish artist Pablo Picasso helped create a new style of art, called cubism. This style combined images of a subject from multiple points of view into a single painting. Americans were introduced to cubism and other new painting styles at the **Armory Show**, an art exhibition held in New York City in 1913. The Armory Show inspired artists like Aaron Douglas to experiment with new cubist methods. Like other artists of the Harlem Renaissance, Douglas drew from the culture and history of African Americans in his work.

Other American painters were inspired by the Armory Show to paint nontraditional subjects. For example, artist Edward Hopper painted the urban landscape. Artist Georgia O'Keeffe probably best described the attitude of leading American artists in the 1920s. Explaining why she developed her own painting style, O'Keeffe said:

> **I thought someone could tell me how to paint a landscape, but I never found that person. . . . They could tell you how they painted their landscape, but they couldn't tell me how to paint mine.**

Photography

By the 1920s photography had gained new popularity as an art form, due largely to the efforts of Alfred Stieglitz, the founder of modern art photography. Stieglitz promoted exhibitions and displayed modern art in his New York City gallery. He explained that the goal of his work was to use simple photography techniques "to hold a moment, to record something . . . completely." James Van Der Zee was another notable photographer of the 1920s who, like Stieglitz, was interested in recording scenes of daily life. Van Der Zee took hundreds of photographs of life in Harlem.

Although many artists of the 1920s focused on urban life, photographer Ansel Adams turned his camera to the drama of the wilderness. Adams became well known for his sharply

Photographer Ansel Adams took this picture of Vernal Fall in Yosemite National Park, California, in 1920.

American Arts

Georgia O'Keeffe

Georgia O'Keeffe was born in Wisconsin in 1887. She saw the world from an artist's perspective at a very young age. "My first memory," she once recalled, "is of the brightness of light . . . light all around."

O'Keeffe studied art in Chicago and New York City and later taught in Amarillo, Texas. In Texas she often hiked into nearby Palo Duro Canyon, where the rock walls rose up to 1,000 feet and seemed to take on different colors in the light. There she first began to sketch the western landscapes that later became so important in her art. In 1916 a friend took a few of O'Keeffe's sketches to photographer Alfred Stieglitz in New York City. He loved her work and agreed to show it in his art gallery. It was the start of a brilliant career.

O'Keeffe moved to New York City and married Stieglitz. She began painting skyscrapers and other city buildings. She is best known, however, for her paintings of two other subjects—flowers and desert scenes. O'Keeffe painted single flowers at close range, showing tiny details. "Most people in the city rush around so, they have no time to look at a flower," she said. "I want them to see it whether they want to or not." O'Keeffe's flower paintings became very popular during the 1920s, often selling for more than $25,000 each.

After becoming a successful artist, O'Keeffe started to spend time in New Mexico, an area she called "the faraway" because of its lonely landscape. She began painting desert scenes—bleached bones, old churches, storms sweeping in over the mountains. O'Keeffe's work used rich color and complicated shapes. "I found that I could say things with color and shapes that I couldn't say in any other way—

Georgia O'Keeffe's painting Cow's Skull: Red, White, and Blue

things that I had no words for," she explained.

Toward the end of her life, O'Keeffe remembered that "the men like to put me down as one of the best women painters. I think I'm one of the best painters." Many critics have agreed with her.

Understanding the Arts

1. What attracted Georgia O'Keeffe to both flowers and the desert as subjects for her paintings?

2. Why do you think O'Keeffe used red, white, and blue in this painting? How do these colors add different meaning to the skull?

focused photographs of mountains in the Yosemite Valley. Adams tried to create images that communicated the emotions he felt as he saw the landscape. He believed that "to photograph truthfully and effectively is to see beneath the surfaces and record the qualities of nature and humanity which live . . . in all things."

 ## Architecture

Some of the most dramatic landscapes of the 1920s were built in big cities such as New York and Chicago. These cities were home to towering skyscrapers, which used the most advanced building materials. In the late 1800s technological advances had been combined with new artistic designs to create the first skyscrapers. In the 1890s architect Louis H. Sullivan had helped to make the design of tall buildings an art as well as a science. Sullivan's idea that "form follows function" greatly influenced the design of skyscrapers in the 1920s.

During the 1920s many American architects adopted what was known as the International style. They designed tall towers using modern materials such as reinforced concrete, glass, and steel. Architect Frank Lloyd Wright, a student of Sullivan's, had helped pioneer the use of these mass-produced materials in his designs during the early 1900s.

As a result of new building methods and great public interest, the construction of skyscrapers boomed. By 1929, skyscrapers had transformed the skylines of cities across the country. The Manhattan borough of New York City was well known for its skyline. Architects competed to build the tallest skyscraper. This competition led to the construction of the 102-story Empire State Building in Manhattan. Completed in 1931, it was the tallest building in the world at that time. To many Americans, the size and majesty of skyscrapers represented the limitless creative power of the 1920s.

The Chrysler Building was one of the best-known skyscrapers built in the 1920s.

SECTION 4 REVIEW

Identify and explain the significance of the following:
- **Bessie Smith**
- **Louis Armstrong**
- **Edward "Duke" Ellington**
- **Jazz Age**
- **Harlem Renaissance**
- **Langston Hughes**
- **Ernest Hemingway**
- **Lost Generation**
- **expatriates**
- **F. Scott Fitzgerald**
- **Armory Show**
- **Georgia O'Keeffe**
- **Ansel Adams**

Locate and identify the importance of the following:
- **Harlem**
- **Manhattan**

Reading for Content Understanding

1 **Main Idea** What were some of the accomplishments of the Harlem Renaissance?

2 **Main Idea** Make a chart listing some of the most significant American architects, painters, and photographers of the 1920s. Include a brief explanation of their major achievements.

3 **Cultural Diversity** In what ways did the blues and jazz influence American culture?

4 **Writing** *Informing* Imagine that you are writing a magazine review of the authors of the Lost Generation. Briefly describe their work and how it commented on life in the 1920s.

5 **Critical Thinking** *Making Comparisons* How were the writers of the Harlem Renaissance and the Lost Generation similar in their views of American society in the 1920s?

CHAPTER 13 REVIEW

Chapter Summary

The 1920s were a time of great social change and economic prosperity in the United States. Social movements such as Fundamentalism, nativism, and prohibition sparked heated debates about education, immigration, and alcohol consumption. New forms of mass media and mass entertainment—including movies and radio—also strongly influenced American culture. In addition, actors, musicians, painters, and writers made many contributions to the arts in America. ■

On a separate sheet of paper, complete the following activities.

Identifying People and Ideas

Describe the historical significance of the following:

1. prohibition
2. Fundamentalism
3. John T. Scopes
4. National Origins Act
5. Marcus Garvey
6. talkies
7. Charles Lindbergh
8. Harlem Renaissance
9. Bessie Smith
10. Ernest Hemingway

go.hrw.com
SB1 Silent Movies

Internet Activity

Search the Internet through the HRW Web site to find information about movies and movie stars of the silent screen. Use the information to create a movie poster advertising a popular 1920s film. Include the names of the film's stars.

Understanding Main Ideas

1. Why was prohibition difficult to enforce?
2. What were some reasons why Fundamentalism spread in the 1920s?
3. How did Marcus Garvey promote black nationalism?
4. What political and economic advances did women achieve during the 1920s?
5. What forms of mass entertainment developed during the 1920s?
6. What were the major literary movements of the 1920s?

Reviewing Themes

1. **Citizenship and Democracy** Why did U.S. immigration policy change during the 1920s?
2. **Technology and Society** How did the development of radio and movies affect the lives of Americans?
3. **Cultural Diversity** How did African Americans contribute to the cultural changes in the United States during the 1920s?

Using the Time Line

Number your paper from 1 to 6. Match the letters on the time line below with the following events.

1. The teaching of the theory of evolution is challenged in court.
2. The United States passes an emergency quota on immigration.
3. The first American radio station broadcasts the results of the 1920 presidential election.
4. Prohibition goes into effect.
5. American Indians gain citizenship.
6. The first motion picture with sound is made.

1920	1921	1922	1923	1924	1925	1926	1927	1928
a	b c			d	e		f	

Thinking Critically

1. **Making Comparisons** How did the NAACP and the UNIA differ?
2. **Evaluating** Why do you think fads became common during the 1920s?
3. **Identifying Cause and Effect** How did prohibition contribute to a rise in organized crime?

Writing About History

1. **Expressing** Imagine that you are a supporter or opponent of national prohibition. Write a letter to the editor explaining your position.
2. **Describing** Imagine that you are the parent of a high school student during the 1920s. Describe how school life and social activities have changed since you went to school in the 1890s.

Linking Geography and History

1. **Movement** How did the Great Migration affect the spread of jazz music in the United States?
2. **Region** What social divisions developed between urban and rural communities during the 1920s?

Building Your Portfolio

Complete the following activities individually or in groups.

1. **Coming to America** Imagine that you are a European visitor to the United States during the 1920s. Choose one or several areas of the country to visit. Create a journal describing your travels to share with your friends back home. Along with your journal entry, you may wish to include maps of your travels, illustrations of the things you saw, and descriptions of the people you met and their activities.
2. **Radio Program** Imagine that you are the writer of a radio show about the rise of celebrities during the 1920s. Select one or more famous people from the decade to discuss on your show and write a script for your radio program. You may wish to interview someone, describe his or her accomplishments, or broadcast one of the person's games or performances. You may also discuss what makes someone a celebrity in the United States during the 1920s. When you have finished, present your radio show for the class.

History Skills Workshop

Using Visual Resources Study the image to the right, which is a painting by Jacob Lawrence. Then answer the following questions: (a) Where do you think the people in the painting are going? (b) What ideas or emotions do you think the artist is trying to communicate in the painting? (c) Draw a picture or write a description about what these people encountered upon reaching their destinations.

The Phillips Collection, Washington, D.C.

American Migrations, 1865–1930

 The United States became increasingly industrialized from 1865 to 1930. Some of today's major U.S. cities, such as Chicago, Detroit, and St. Louis, grew rapidly as people moved there in search of better economic opportunities. Many Americans left rural areas, hoping to find industrial jobs in large towns and cities. For example, many African Americans relocated, first to southern mill towns, and later to northern cities.

Immigration also increased the urban population. Millions of immigrants came from all across Europe. Large numbers of immigrants also arrived from Mexico. Many European immigrants moved to cities in the Northeast and Midwest. Most Mexican immigrants settled in rural areas in the Southwest. Eventually, many Mexican Americans moved to cities, particularly in Texas and California. Gradually, all these different migrations reshaped U.S. cities. ■

Farms to Cities

Between 1880 and 1930, the United States shifted from being a largely rural nation to a mostly urban one. Many people moved to cities to find work.

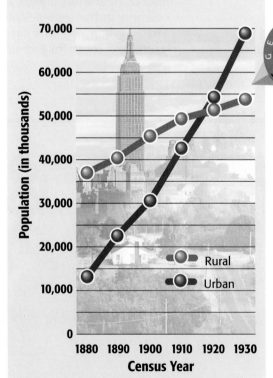

Population Shift: Rural to Urban, 1880–1930

Population (in thousands)

70,000
60,000
50,000
40,000
30,000
20,000
10,000
0

1880 1890 1900 1910 1920 1930
Census Year

Rural
Urban

Source: *Historical Statistics of the United States*

Geography **Skills**
Reading Line Graphs

1. In what census year did the urban population of the United States become larger than the rural population?
2. In what decade did rural population experience the least growth?
3. In what decade did urban population experience the most growth?
4. What do you think the graph would show if it continued on to the present?

Mexican American Population in 1930

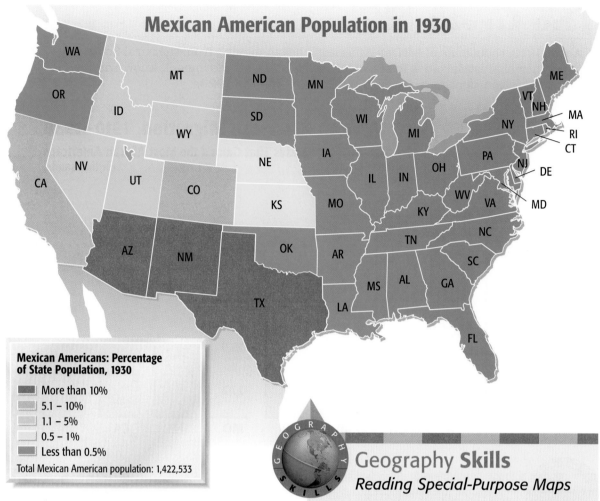

Mexican Americans: Percentage of State Population, 1930

- More than 10%
- 5.1 – 10%
- 1.1 – 5%
- 0.5 – 1%
- Less than 0.5%

Total Mexican American population: 1,422,533

Geography **Skills**
Reading Special-Purpose Maps

1. How many states in 1930 had a Mexican American population that was 1.1 percent or more of the state's total population?
2. In which states did the highest percentage of Mexican Americans live?

History Note 1

In the early 1900s large numbers of Mexican immigrants began arriving in the United States. Between 1920 and 1930, nearly 500,000 Mexican immigrants settled in the United States, mostly in the West and the Southwest. In the first years after these new immigrants arrived, most lived in rural areas. By the 1930s, however, many Mexican Americans had migrated to large cities—such as Chicago, Los Angeles, and San Antonio—in search of higher-paying industrial jobs.

In 1937 this family of Mexican American migrant workers from Texas picked sugar beets in Minnesota.

The Great Migration

About 1910, thousands of African Americans began moving from the rural South to northern industrial cities in search of better jobs. This movement, known as the Great Migration, continued through World War I and the 1920s.

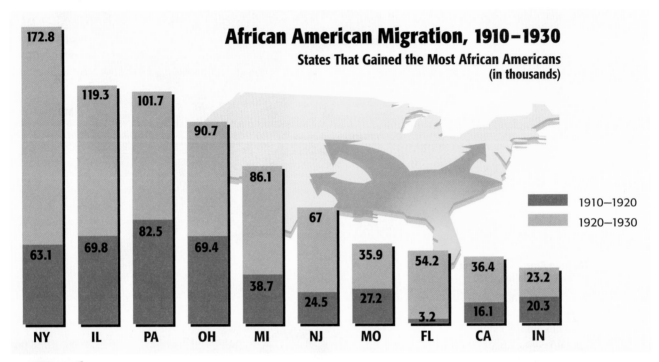

African American Migration, 1910–1930

States That Gained the Most African Americans
(in thousands)

Legend:
- 1910–1920
- 1920–1930

State	1910–1920	1920–1930	Total
NY	63.1	(172.8 top)	172.8
IL	69.8	119.3	
PA	82.5	101.7	
OH	69.4	90.7	
MI	38.7	86.1	
NJ	24.5	67	
MO	27.2	35.9	
FL	3.2	54.2	
CA	16.1	36.4	
IN	20.3	23.2	

Geography Skills
Reading Bar Graphs

1. Which states' African American population increased by more than 200,000 between 1910 and 1930? by more than 100,000?

2. In which states was the gain in African American population between 1920 and 1930 more than double the gain between 1910 and 1920?

History Note 3

Even though racial discrimination was common in the South before 1900, few African Americans left the region in the late 1800s. As late as 1910, more than 80 percent of African Americans still lived in the South. Beginning in 1910, however, many African Americans began moving to northern and western cities. They were hoping to improve their lives with better jobs and opportunities.

History Note 2

In 1930, three northern cities—Chicago, Detroit, and New York—had an African American population three times greater than it had been in 1910. The impact of this movement of African Americans, known as the Great Migration, can be seen in current population statistics. Today, around half of all African Americans in the United States live outside the South.

In 1912 this African American family moved to Chicago from the rural South.

Discrimination Against African Americans in 1930

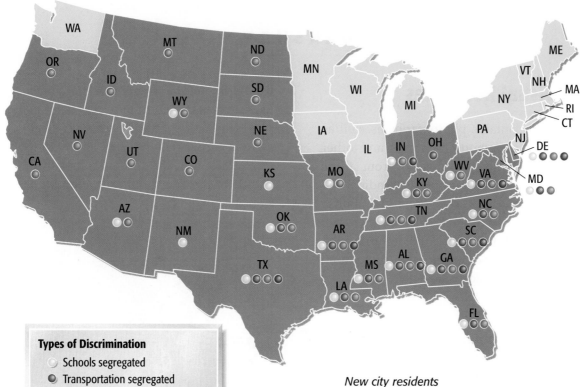

Types of Discrimination
- ◯ Schools segregated
- ◓ Transportation segregated
- ◑ Interracial marriage outlawed
- ⬤ Voting restricted
- ▢ No state laws enforcing discrimination

New city residents

Geography **Skills**
Reading Special-Purpose Maps

1. Which geographic region of the United States had the fewest discriminatory laws?
2. Which geographic region had the most discriminatory laws?
3. In which states did African Americans face the most discriminatory legislation? the least?

History Note 4

During the 1930s many African Americans moved north hoping to escape the economic hardships of the Great Depression. However, northern cities were experiencing high unemployment and poverty. During these hard times the National Association for the Advancement of Colored People fought to ensure equal treatment for African Americans.

NEW YORK

History Skills

WORKSHOP

Using Visual Resources

This textbook contains photographs as well as reproductions of famous paintings and other artwork. Gathering information from these sources is a key strategy to understanding history. Visual resources can provide a better understanding of how people in the past behaved, dressed, thought, and communicated with one another. Images can also provide an accurate record of historical events.

Gathering Information from Art

To effectively gather information from artwork, follow these steps.

1. **Determine the subject of the work** Study the people, objects, and actions in the artwork. Check the title or caption. In cartoons, artists often use familiar images to represent complex ideas.

2. **Examine the details** Study the background of the painting or drawing. Remember that *all* the visual evidence is important to understanding the historical event or period.

3. **Note the artist's point of view** If possible, determine whether the events are shown favorably or unfavorably. Ask yourself how the artwork might affect others.

4. **Use the information carefully** Remember that a work of art may be an artist's *interpretation* of an event. Try to determine how accurately the art shows the event before deciding how to use the information.

Using Cartoons as Primary Sources

Follow these steps to use cartoons as primary sources.

1. **Study the subject** Identify the people, events, or locations in the cartoon.

2. **Check for details** Note the expression, action, or setting. Look closely at the style of clothing and other details.

3. **Do not be misled** Remember that an artist uses images in a cartoon to represent people, ideas, and events. Because political cartoons are usually created shortly after an event occurs, the artist assumes that people have some familiarity with the subject.

The Granger Collection, New York

Practicing the Skill

Study the image above, which is a political cartoon from 1921 entitl~d *Spoiling the Broth*. The cartoon shows some Americans' fears about the number of immigrants arriving in the United States. Then answer the following questions.

1. How does the artist represent immigrants, the U.S. government, and the United States?

2. What does the melting pot represent? Why do you think the artist used this image?

3. What is the artist's opinion about immigration? How can you tell?

4. Write a three-sentence caption that might accompany the cartoon.

History in Action

American History

Life in the Twenties: The Play

Complete the following activity in small, cooperative groups.

You and the members of your group are the writers, producers, directors, and actors of a play called *Life in the Twenties.* The play will include short segments on different aspects of society during the 1920s. You want to focus mainly on the arts and culture of the time, such as radio, movies, music, sports, and literature. You and your group need to decide what specific topics you will include.

Materials To complete this activity, you will need art supplies, costumes, and perhaps a cassette or compact disc player for the musical accompaniment.

Parts of the Project To create your play, complete the following tasks:

1. **Research** Use the library and your textbook to gather information. You will focus on the arts and culture of the 1920s, such as radio, movies, music, sports, and literature. Be sure to include information on some visual artists such as photographers and painters. As much as possible, you want to use the words of the people in the 1920s in your play. For example, find something Charles Lindbergh wrote about his trip across the Atlantic Ocean. Have someone play the role of Lindbergh and speak his words.

Students present a play to their class.

2. **Writing** Once you have gathered enough information, write your play. You might want to include some songs as well as spoken passages in your script. Your play will contain brief segments on different topics. Because your play does not have a plot, you will need to write some transitions between the different people or topics. Add stage directions to show how the characters will sing, speak, and move. You might want some characters to perform the different dances that were popular in the 1920s. In addition, you might want to play music from the 1920s.

3. **Rehearsal and Production** Once the play is written, decide who will direct it and who will play each of the characters. Prepare the necessary props and costumes. Finally, rehearse your play several times.

Perform your play after you have finished rehearsals. Provide the audience with an illustrated program, which includes some visual resources representing the subjects.

UNIT 5 A World in Crisis

(1929–1945)

American Teens
IN HISTORY
Young Relief Workers

When the Great Depression hit, it placed a significant burden on young Americans. Economic hardship forced many young people to drop out of school or college to look for work. However, jobs were scarce. By May 1935 more than 1 million Americans between the ages of 16 and 24 were unemployed.

In June 1935 President Franklin D. Roosevelt created the National Youth Administration (NYA), a special division of the Works Progress Administration. The NYA was one of many relief programs designed to help young people. It offered part-time jobs for young Americans still in school. For those no longer in school, the NYA provided jobs and work training.

High school students in campus work programs received jobs in or around their schools. They earned only about $6 a month, but the pay made a huge difference to the 1.5 million students enrolled in the program. The money allowed students to stay in school. These teenagers used the money to pay for their own schoolbooks, supplies, and bus fare. Other young people took part in out-of-school programs. Boys on the Onondaga Indian reservation in New York built a summer camp for children. Other young workers painted buildings, maintained city parks, performed carpentry tasks, and much more.

The NYA provided new opportunities for all its participants. Rural teenagers, for example, learned industrial skills. The NYA also attempted to integrate teenagers of different races. One boy recalled the program's meaning in his life:

The Granger Collection, New York

The Civilian Conservation Corps was one of many relief programs. It provided jobs for young men 17 to 24 years old.

> ❝ Maybe you don't know what it's like to come home and have everyone looking at you, and you know they're thinking, . . . 'He didn't find a job.' It gets terrible. You just don't want to come home. . . . I tell you, the first time I walked in the front door with my paycheck, I was somebody! ❞

In this unit you will learn about the Great Depression and government efforts to help Americans. You will also learn about how World War II transformed the United States and the world.

LEFT PAGE: *Missouri residents wait for food at a Salvation Army center.*

UNIT 5

A World in Crisis

FDR as "Man of the Year"

Fallingwater

A Texas Ranger badge

UNITED STATES

1929
The stock market crash sends the United States into an economic depression.

1932
Franklin D. Roosevelt is elected to his first term as president.

1934
The Texas Rangers end the crime spree of Bonnie Parker and Clyde Barrow.

1936
Architect Frank Lloyd Wright begins work on Fallingwater. The stone and concrete house sits on top of a waterfall in Bear Run, Pennsylvania.

1929   **1931**   **1933**   **1935**

WORLD

1930
Mohandas Gandhi leads Indians on the Salt March, an act of civil disobedience protesting a tax on salt imposed by the British.

1932
British scientist John Cockcroft and Irish physicist Ernest Walton split an atom for the first time in history. The men will receive the Nobel Prize for Physics in 1951 for their work.

Mao Zedong marching with Chinese revolutionaries

Indian leader Mohandas Gandhi

1934
Mao Zedong leads Chinese Communists on a Long March into northern China.

1936
Germans begin building the *Bismarck,* which will later be called the most powerful warship in the world. In May 1941, British naval forces sink the battleship.

A model of the *Bismarck*

An ad for "holeproof" hosiery

Letters written by a U.S. soldier in World War II

1940
The first nylon stockings go on sale in the United States. Earlier stockings were made of wool or silk.

1941
Japanese warplanes bomb a U.S. naval base at Pearl Harbor, Hawaii. As a result, the United States enters World War II.

1945
After a difficult battle on the island of Iwo Jima, U.S. soldiers defeat Japanese troops and raise the American flag.

Iwo Jima memorial

| 1937 | 1939 | 1941 | 1943 | 1945 |

1939
Nazi leader Adolf Hitler orders an invasion of Poland, which leads to World War II.

An ENIGMA code machine used by the Germans during World War II

The Little Prince

1943
French author and pilot Antoine de Saint-Exupéry writes *The Little Prince,* a fable. As a volunteer pilot for the U.S. Air Force, he is shot down over North Africa in 1944.

1945
After the United States drops two atomic bombs on Japan, the country surrenders, ending World War II.

Peace Memorial Park in Hiroshima, Japan

USING THE TIME LINE

1. Which entries on the time line are related to World War II?
2. Using only the time line, determine some of the countries that fought in World War II.

Activity Use the information on this time line and in your textbook to create a time line for World War II.

Your time line should match the design of this time line, with U.S. events on the top and world events on the bottom. You will need to select the beginning and ending dates for your time line and divide the time line into intervals. You might want to include some images to illustrate your time line.

▪ CHAPTER 14 ▪

The Great Depression

(1929–1939)

In May 1934, E. W. Bakke began another day of searching for work. He applied at many places, including a clock shop, an auto equipment factory, a rubber plant, and a candy factory. He received the same answer everywhere: "No help wanted." At one office a woman cut him off before he could begin, "No use—sorry." For millions of Americans like Bakke, the Great Depression brought unemployment, hard times, and worries about survival.

THEMES

Economic Development
What factors might cause a nation to experience an economic depression?

Constitutional Heritage
What role might the Supreme Court play during times of economic crisis?

Citizenship and Democracy
How might the government respond to an economic depression?

1929   **1930**   **1931**   **1932**   **1933**   **1934**

OCT. 1929 The stock market crashes.

JUNE 1930 The Smoot-Hawley Tariff goes into effect.

MAY 1932 The Bonus Army arrives in Washington, D.C.

NOV. 1932 Franklin D. Roosevelt is elected president.

MAR. 1933 The Hundred Days begins when Roosevelt's administration creates many new relief agencies.

The End of Prosperity

Reading Focus

Why did many Americans invest in the stock market in the 1920s?

What took place during the stock market crash, and how did it affect the nation?

What economic factors contributed to the Great Depression?

Key Terms

bull market

buying on margin

speculation

bear market

Black Tuesday

Panic of 1929

Great Depression

business cycle

Smoot-Hawley Tariff

OR MANY AMERICANS, *the 1920s were a time of economic prosperity. That was the message of Republican presidential candidate Herbert Hoover in 1928. Hoover expressed his confidence in the economy in a speech at Stanford University. "We in America today," he stated proudly, "are nearer to the final triumph over poverty than ever before in the history of any land." Hoover promised that if elected president he would continue with the approach of Calvin Coolidge's administration. He would "go forward with the policies of the last eight years." Hoover and many others believed that there was no need for change.*

Republicans Herbert Hoover and Charles Curtis ran for president and vice president in the 1928 election.

IMAGE ON LEFT PAGE: *The good times of the 1920s came to a screeching halt when the stock market crashed in October 1929.*

1935   **1936**   **1937**   **1938**   **1939**

JAN. 1935 The Second New Deal begins.

AUG. 1935 Congress passes the Social Security Act.

NOV. 1936 President Roosevelt defeats Alfred Landon to win re-election.

FEB. 1937 Roosevelt presents his plan to change the Supreme Court.

MAR. 1938 The unemployment rate jumps as the U.S. economy continues to decline.

★ The Stock Market Soars

American businesses boomed during the 1920s. Production and employment were high and on the rise. In 1921 about 1.5 million cars were sold. By 1929 that number reached some 4.5 million. More Americans than ever before owned houses,

and about 80 million Americans per week were going to the movies.

Further evidence of the decade's prosperity was the increase in stock prices in the late 1920s. For example, RCA stock jumped from $85 a share to $420 during 1928. Many Americans, from homemakers to business executives, bought and sold stocks. The number of major investors totaled about half a million, but it seemed as though everyone were interested in the stock market. The increased demand for stocks led to higher share prices and more possibility of investment profits.

A March 1929 Life *magazine cover highlighting the interest in the stock market*

Many experts saw no end to this **bull market**, or continuing rise in stock market prices. Business leaders such as General Motors executive John J. Raskob encouraged the public to participate in the stock market boom. In a magazine article titled "Everyone Ought to Be Rich," Raskob stated that if a person invested $15 a week in stocks, "at the end of twenty years he will have at least $80,000. . . . He will be rich."

Many people who invested in the stock market were **buying on margin**—purchasing stocks on credit with a loan from a broker. Brokers borrowed this money from banks. This activity was **speculation**—the investing of money in a high-risk venture in hopes of making a profit. It was based on the belief that no matter how much a person paid for the stock, someone else would pay more. Few people predicted that a **bear market**, or a continuing drop

in stock prices, would occur. At his inauguration in March 1929, President Herbert Hoover told Americans, "I have no fears for the future of our country. It is bright with hope."

★ The Great Crash

On September 3, 1929, stock prices hit an all-time high. Shortly thereafter, prices began to slide downward. On Thursday morning, October 24, large-scale investors sold huge blocks of shares, causing prices to fall even more. However, the stock market rallied by the close of the business day.

President Hoover tried to reassure the American public, saying that "the fundamental business of the country . . . is on a sound and prosperous basis." Investors remained uneasy, however. *New York Times* reporter Elliott Bell recalled that around the New York Stock Exchange (NYSE) people were asking, "Who was in trouble? Who had gone under last? Where was it going to end?"

The stock market collapsed on October 29, 1929, which became known as **Black Tuesday**. As prices began to drop drastically, panicked investors began frantically selling their stocks. People who had bought on margin were forced to sell their stocks to try to raise money to pay their

The newspaper headline explains the panic outside the New York Stock Exchange (below).

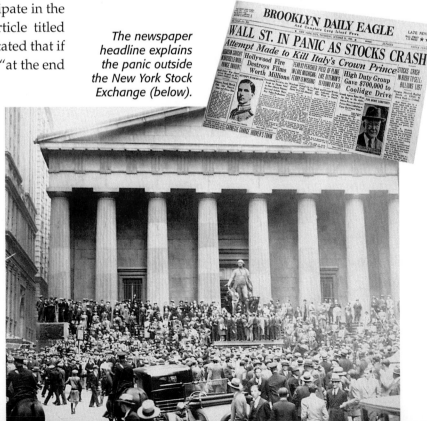

loans. Other investors hoped to sell their stocks before the shares lost all value.

Fearful and confused investors mobbed Wall Street, where the NYSE is located. Telephone lines were jammed. Brokerages were filled with people trying to sell stock. Traders fought with each other on the floor of the exchange. Many people could not find any buyers for their stocks, causing the price of shares to continue falling. When no buyers could be found for the stock of the White Sewing Machine Company, a young messenger bid $1 per share and became a major stockholder in the company.

By the end of Black Tuesday more than 16 million shares had been traded, and some $15 billion in stock value had been lost. An investment banker recalled the mood on Wall Street. "It was like a thunderclap. Everybody was stunned. Nobody knew what it was all about." A journalist wrote, "When the closing bell rang, the great bull market was dead and buried."

The drop in stock prices continued, and the one-day stock market crash turned into the **Panic of 1929**. U.S. Steel stock fell from $261 to $150 a share, while General Electric stock dropped from $396 to $168 a share. By the end of November, losses had climbed to $50 billion. Many speculators who had bought on margin lost everything. They were forced to pay their brokers with savings or by pawning jewelry, china, and clothing to get cash. Even Americans who never invested in the market soon felt the lasting effects of the Great Crash. Author Frederick Lewis Allen wrote about how the crash affected people:

> 66 **Prosperity is more than an economic condition; it is a state of mind. . . . There was hardly a man or woman in the country whose attitude toward life had not been affected by it [the crash] in some degree and was not now affected by the sudden and brutal shattering of hope.** 99

★ The Economy Collapses

In the first months following the Panic of 1929, the nation's leaders played down its importance. Treasury Secretary Andrew Mellon even

Just three weeks before the Great Crash, cartoonist Rollin Kirby warned investors that a bear market could quickly wipe out their profits.

suggested to President Hoover that "a panic was not altogether a bad thing" because Americans had been living beyond their means in the 1920s.

Businesses Go Under

Mellon and many other leaders were slow to realize how serious a blow the stock market crash was to the economy. After the crash many businesses slowed production and laid off workers. As a result, these individuals found it difficult to buy new products or continue making payments on their installment plans. Frederick Lewis Allen noted, "Men and women were wondering how they could meet the next payment on the car or the radio or the furniture."

With fewer people buying goods, factories slowed their production even more and began laying off additional workers. This created a vicious cycle in which layoffs led to decreased consumer spending, which in turn led to more layoffs. These circumstances began affecting even prosperous companies. In Detroit in 1931, for example, the Ford Motor Company stopped producing its once successful Model A because demand slowed.

The nation became locked in a downward economic spiral known as the **Great Depression**. The gross national product (GNP), the total value of all

The illustration Sold Out *expresses the feelings of many Americans in the Panic of 1929.*

The Granger Collection, New York

goods and services produced in a given year, fell by almost 30 percent between 1929 and 1931. While the GNP fell, unemployment jumped. In 1932 the unemployment rate rose to more than 20 percent. Many people began to believe that the hard times were not going to end quickly.

The Banking Crisis

The Great Depression also affected the banking industry. Many banks were hard hit when customers were unable to repay their bank loans. These bankrupt customers included investors who had lost everything in the stock market crash and farmers who were suffering from a drastic drop in agricultural prices. Unable to collect the money they were owed, many local banks could not repay the money they had borrowed from larger banks. As a result, many of these smaller banks failed.

News of these bank failures triggered a panic among depositors because bank deposits were not insured. If a bank failed, depositors lost their entire savings. Fearing more bank failures, people across the country rushed to their banks to withdraw their money. However, banks usually kept on hand only a fraction of the total amount of money that people had deposited. The rest of the money was invested or loaned out to individuals and businesses. Therefore, few banks were able to pay all the depositors who tried to withdraw their money. These runs, or sudden demands, on banks had a devastating effect on the banking industry. Businesses that relied on bank loans to operate or expand could not function.

Unpaid loans, bad debts, and mass withdrawals by depositors led more than 9,700 American banks to fail between 1929 and 1933. These bank failures wiped out the savings that many people had counted on for their survival during hard times.

⭐ What Happened?

The Panic of 1929 did not cause the Great Depression. However, it revealed weaknesses in the economy that contributed to the depression.

The Business Cycle

Many economists argued that a recession in 1930 was a natural part of the **business cycle**—the pattern of alternating prosperity and recession in a free-enterprise economy. According to this cycle, people buy more goods during times of prosperity.

New York City bank customers stood in long lines to try to withdraw their money.

To meet this greater demand, businesses increase production and hire extra workers. Eventually, more goods are produced than sold, creating a surplus. To reduce the surplus, companies lower prices and therefore profits. Industries cut back production and lay off workers, which causes a recession. If a recession continues for an extended period of time, it becomes a depression. As factory output decreases, surpluses are gradually used up. Industries then increase production and rehire workers. These workers spend money, and the economy enters the recovery stage. Eventually, recovery leads to prosperity and the cycle repeats itself.

The Typical Business Cycle

Economic Trends At first, most Americans thought the stock market crash had caused only a temporary recession. What do you think a graph of the business cycle during the Great Depression would look like?

Predictions

Many economists in the late 1920s believed that a brief recession was bound to follow the prosperity. In 1928 housing construction slowed, consumer spending declined, and inventories began piling up. Before the Great Crash, some industries had reduced production and laid off workers. The decline in workers' incomes combined with the drop in bank deposits limited the money supply—the amount of money available for spending or investment.

Even as the economy worsened, leaders such as Treasury Secretary Mellon believed that the nation's economic problems were not serious. Mellon declared that prosperity would soon return. "People will work harder [and] . . . enterprising people will pick up the wrecks from less competent people," he said confidently. Instead, the recession turned into the most severe depression in U.S. history.

Industry and Agriculture

Overproduction, bank failures, and the stock market crash contributed to the Great Depression. Other causes included struggling industries, an unequal distribution of wealth, and unwise trade policies. Industries such as lumber, mining, and textiles had expanded during World War I. During peacetime these industries could not maintain this growth and became "sick."

Agriculture never recovered fully from the recession of 1920–21. Farmers had to pay high prices for farm equipment, labor, land, and transportation. At the same time, overproduction caused crop prices to fall. As a result, many farmers could not repay their bank loans. Farmers had to declare bankruptcy and lost their property through foreclosure. Lenders foreclose on, or take possession of, mortgages when borrowers can no longer make their loan payments. Lenders often sell the mortgaged properties to pay off the loan.

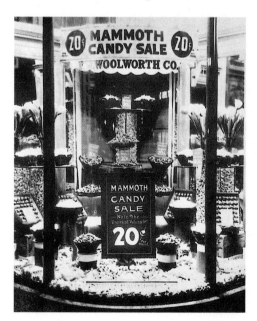

In the 1930s candy remained an affordable item. For 20 cents customers could buy one pound of candy.

Wealth and Trade

Another economic weakness was the unequal distribution of wealth in the United States. In 1929 a mere 1 percent of the U.S. population held about one third of all personal wealth. At the same time, an estimated 60 percent of all American families earned less than the $2,000 a year needed to buy basic necessities. The result was that most people could not afford to buy the goods produced. In addition, many Americans had bought goods on credit. After the crash, they were not able to pay for these products.

A 1932 article in *Current History* described the frustration shared by many Americans:

In the 1930s the Ford Motor Company had to stop production of many of its cars, like the Model A Deluxe Phaeton.

❝**There is too much bread, too much wheat and corn, meat and oil. . . . We are not able to purchase the abundance that modern methods of agriculture, mining and manufacture make available. . . . Why is mankind being asked to go hungry and cold and poverty stricken in the midst of plenty?**❞

In order to reverse the economic decline, people needed to be able to buy the surplus of available goods. During the early 1930s, most Americans had little money to spend. Wealthy Americans could not invest enough or buy enough items, like automobiles, to make up for the decline in purchases. As a result, the recovery did not occur.

President Hoover blamed world economic problems for the depression. In the late 1920s some European countries still struggled to make war reparations, while others tried to repay loans from World War I. Certain U.S. trade policies made matters worse. The June 1930 **Smoot-Hawley Tariff** raised U.S. duties on imports to all-time highs. Foreign governments responded by imposing their own trade restrictions. Higher foreign tariffs limited the markets in which American goods could be sold and made the worldwide depression worse. As the depression deepened, many Americans began to worry that a return to prosperity was unlikely anytime soon.

SECTION 1 REVIEW

Identify and explain the significance of the following:
- bull market
- buying on margin
- speculation
- bear market
- Black Tuesday
- Panic of 1929
- Andrew Mellon
- Great Depression
- business cycle
- Smoot-Hawley Tariff

Reading for Content Understanding

1 **Main Idea** Why did some people see the stock market as a way to get rich quickly?

2 **Main Idea** What were some of the causes of the Great Depression?

3 **Economic Development** What took place during the stock market crash, and what effect did it have on Wall Street and the U.S. economy?

4 **Writing** *Describing* Imagine that you are a business leader giving a magazine interview after October 29, 1929. Explain the business cycle and whether you think the events following the stock market crash support this pattern.

5 **Critical Thinking** *Drawing Conclusions* Do you think President Hoover could have taken any actions to prevent the Great Depression? Explain your answer.

Hoover and the Depression

Reading Focus

In what ways did the Great Depression affect the everyday lives of Americans?

What actions did President Hoover take to help Americans during the depression?

How did Hoover respond to the Bonus Army's demands?

Key Terms

Hoovervilles
relief
Reconstruction Finance Corporation
public works
Agricultural Marketing Act
Federal Home Loan Bank Act
Bonus Army

IN LATE OCTOBER 1929, *teenager Gordon Parks read a newspaper article describing the stock market crash. "I couldn't imagine financial disaster touching my small world; it surely concerned only the rich," he recalled. Parks was working part time, but soon felt the effect of the crash when his employer laid him off the next week. "Along with millions of others across the nation, I was without a job," he wrote. Unable to find a job that paid as well as his part-time job, Parks quit school to look for full-time work. He became one of the many Americans whose lives were suddenly changed by the Great Depression.*

Unemployed workers gather in front of the White House to demand help.

 ## The Depression Hits Home

Following the stock market crash in October 1929, production and investment slowed dramatically. Most construction ground to a halt. Across the nation, millions of Americans struggled to protect themselves and their families from economic ruin.

Out of a Job

In 1932 the U.S. unemployment rate was at more than 20 percent. In New Orleans, several hundred people answered an advertisement for a single position. In cities like New York, jobless people sold apples and pencils on the street. Several hundred thousand people, most of them men, left their homes in search of work. They traveled across the country on foot, by car, or by rail. One reporter called them "the nomads of the depression."

Although the depression affected all segments of society, African Americans, Mexican Americans, and recent immigrants were particularly hard hit. Members of minority groups were usually the first to be laid off from factory jobs so that white employees could keep their jobs. One African American steelworker whose factory laid him off

Unemployment During the Depression

Source: *Historical Statistics of the United States*

Work Wanted At the depth of the depression, about 25 percent of employable Americans did not have jobs. During what year was unemployment the highest?

had been set outside the back door of a restaurant. American citizens fighting for scraps of food like animals!**"**

Farm families were somewhat better equipped to provide themselves with basic necessities. However, poverty and drought made daily life a struggle for many rural residents. In one rural school in the Appalachian Mountains, a teacher told a sick-looking girl to go home and get something to eat. "I can't," the child replied. "It's my sister's turn to eat."

The depression also reached into the suburbs of the once prosperous middle class. The greatest fear among the middle class was the possibility of losing their homes.

Some people who lost their homes built clusters of shacks from cardboard boxes or old boards. They named these camps **Hoovervilles** because they blamed President Hoover for their situation. People in Hoovervilles typically camped outside of major cities. They used old newspapers, which they called "Hoover blankets," to keep warm. At times, desperate Americans begged for money or stole food. Some people eventually starved to death.

was told "he needn't trouble looking for a job as long as there is so many white men out of work."

Women found it somewhat easier to get jobs during the depression. They found work primarily as clerks, maids, or waitresses—positions that survived the hard times better than factory jobs. However, these positions usually paid very low wages. Women who found jobs in other professions were generally paid less than men.

Hard Times All Over

The Great Depression affected Americans in every part of the country. Wages were so low that men and women who did have jobs often did not earn enough to support their families without making great sacrifices. Living conditions in urban areas became particularly difficult. Thousands of unemployed people competed for scarce jobs, food, and shelter. Louise Armstrong, author of *We, Too, Are the People*, wrote of a shocking scene in a large city:

"We saw a crowd of some fifty men fighting over a barrel of garbage which

During the depression, some Americans slept where they found space to put down a mattress.

American Literature

Their Eyes Were Watching God
Zora Neale Hurston

Zora Neale Hurston's novel Their Eyes Were Watching God *was published in 1937. The novel centers around Janie Crawford's life story and her search for true love.* Their Eyes Were Watching God *also gives some insight into the lives of African Americans during the Great Depression. In order to find work, many African Americans traveled throughout the South. The following excerpt describes the arrival of migrant farmhands to a bean farm.*

Cover from Hurston's 1937 book, Their Eyes Were Watching God

Day by day now, the hordes [crowds] of workers poured in. Some came limping in with their shoes and sore feet from walking. It's hard trying to follow your shoe instead of your shoe following you. They came in wagons from way up in Georgia and they came in truck loads from east, west, north and south. Permanent transients [drifters] with no attachments and tired looking men with their families and dogs. . . . All night, all day, hurrying in to pick beans. Skillets, beds, patched up spare inner tubes all hanging and dangling from the ancient cars on the outside. . . .

People ugly from ignorance and broken from being poor. . . .

Finally no more sleeping places. Men made big fires and fifty or sixty men slept around each fire. But they had to pay the man whose land they slept on. He ran the fire just like his boarding place—for pay. But nobody cared. They made good money, even to the children. So they spent good money. Next month and next year were other times. No need to mix them up with the present.

Understanding Literature

1. Describe how the workers looked and felt as they came to work in the bean fields.

2. Why do you think they are only looking to the present?

Trying to Cope

The poverty caused by the Great Depression was a blow to the pride of many Americans. They resisted asking for assistance as long as they could. As the depression worsened, however, many people turned to traditional community support networks to help them. These networks included relatives, neighbors, and churches.

As the pressure on community networks increased, private organizations began providing direct **relief**—food, clothing, shelter, and money—to the needy. Organizations such as the Red Cross and the Salvation Army set up soup kitchens and breadlines. Hungry people could get free food there. People would often line up around the block for a piece of bread and a small cup of thin soup. Peggy Terry, who was a young girl during the depression, recalled going to the soup kitchen after school. "If you happened to be one of the first ones in line, you didn't get anything but water that was on top." The Red Cross and the Salvation Army also operated lodging houses where homeless men could spend the night.

As the depression worsened some desperate Americans took aggressive actions. In 1930 more than 1,000 New Yorkers standing in a Salvation Army breadline robbed two bakery trucks that were making a delivery at a nearby hotel. In Arkansas, hungry residents used guns to force Red Cross workers to give out food.

Few private relief organizations were prepared to cope with the severity of the depression. In Philadelphia, wealthy residents who contributed millions of dollars to local relief were stunned when the money ran out within months. Some business leaders were unsympathetic to the hardships faced by the unemployed. They were therefore reluctant to donate money to relief organizations. John Edgerton, president of the National Association of Manufacturers, accused the jobless of failing to save money or spend wisely. "[How] is our economic system, or government, or industry to blame?" he asked.

Many suffering Americans wondered when the government was going to get involved in fighting the depression. Some citizens wrote letters to the government in anger or desperation. They tried to convince leaders to change their hands-off policies. One New Jersey resident wrote to President Hoover in 1930:

"Our children have Schoolless days and Shoeless days and the land full of plenty and Banks bursting with money. Why does Every Thing have Exceptional Value. Except the Human being—why are we reduced to poverty and starving and anxiety and Sorrow. . . . Why not End the Depression have you not a Heart[?]"

★ Hoover's Philosophy

Those looking for government assistance found little support from President Hoover or his advisers. For months Hoover insisted that the economic downturn was temporary. In 1930 he told a group of businesspeople, "The Depression is over."

In spite of what many Americans thought, Hoover was sympathetic to the troubles of the poor. For example, during World War I he had led efforts to help starving refugees in war-torn Europe. However, Hoover firmly opposed federal programs such as unemployment relief because he worried about destroying Americans' self-reliance. He was convinced that private charity, not federal aid, was the "American way." Hoover hoped that Americans would rise to the challenges posed by the Great Depression. He once wrote:

"The spread of government destroys initiative [independent action] and thus destroys character. Character is made in the community as well as in the individual by assuming responsibilities, not by escaping them."

Hoover also believed that businesses should operate without interference from or involvement by the federal government. He asked business leaders to voluntarily maintain wage rates, keep up production, and cooperate with the government to build confidence in the economy. "We have passed the worst," he claimed in March 1930.

Hungry men hoped to find a good meal at a New York City soup kitchen in 1931.

The Granger Collection, New York

⭐ Hoover's Aid Policies

When economic conditions did not improve, President Hoover was forced to act. He decided to try a program to stimulate the economy. However, he also wanted to preserve what he called "the principles of individual and local responsibility."

Fixing the Economy

Hoover believed that providing money to American businesses was the best solution. In 1932 he established the **Reconstruction Finance Corporation** (RFC), which loaned money to businesses and banks to help keep them operating. The RFC saved many corporations, but the economy continued to decline. Hoover cut federal taxes and encouraged the federal government to spend about $150 million on **public works**. These building projects—such as hospitals, roads, and schools—would benefit the public. One public-works project was the construction of Boulder Dam along the Colorado River. The dam was later renamed Hoover Dam. The president hoped that programs like these would create jobs and thus help relieve the suffering of the poor and unemployed.

Helping Farmers

The agricultural industry also needed help. It had been depressed since the early 1920s. Most farmers reacted angrily to new hardships in the 1930s. Some people tried to stop bank agents and government officers from foreclosing on farms and evicting farmers from their homes. Other farmers protested the low prices paid for their products by publicly destroying crops.

Hoover was willing to assist farmers in obtaining loans to buy animal feed or farm equipment. However, he opposed giving farmers direct federal aid to pay for food, clothing, or shelter for their families. In 1929 Congress had passed the **Agricultural Marketing Act**. This act ended some

As this 1931 cartoon shows, many Americans blamed President Hoover for the depression.

farm subsidies and established the Federal Farm Board. As crop prices fell, Hoover instructed the board to help buy surplus wheat, cotton, and other farm products. By buying these commodities and taking them off the market, Hoover hoped to reduce the supply and generally boost prices. The federal government planned to store these crops and sell them later, when prices were higher.

This plan failed, however. The government did not purchase enough crops to make up for the huge supply. Farmers had also reacted to low market prices by growing more crops. The more they produced, the more prices fell, and the less money they made. Overall, the Federal Farm Board spent more than $180 million before it went out of existence in 1933.

Helping Homeowners

Hoover also tried to give indirect aid to homeowners. He supported the 1932 **Federal Home Loan Bank Act**. This act provided money to banks, financial institutions, and insurance companies so they could offer low-interest mortgages. Hoover believed that the act would reduce the number of foreclosures on homes. He also hoped that the act would encourage home construction, thus boosting employment and increasing the amount of money in the economy.

Despite such efforts, Hoover had little success in ending the depression. Many Americans believed that he had done too little, too late. One woman told her young nephew in 1932, "People were starving because of Herbert Hoover. My mother was out of work because of Herbert Hoover."

⭐ The Bonus Army

Veterans of World War I also suffered during the Great Depression. In 1924 Congress had passed the so-called bonus bill. This legislation

The Great Depression **429**

Police clash with World War I veterans while trying to drive them from their camps in Washington, D.C.

authorized the payment of a bonus to all World War I veterans. The money would be put in a fund until 1945, when each veteran would receive an average of $1,000. Because the depression had left many veterans hungry and penniless, they wanted their money right away. In 1931 Congress passed a bill, over Hoover's veto, to loan veterans up to 50 percent of the bonus. Later that year Democrats in Congress proposed to pay the entire bonus in cash.

A group of veterans left Portland, Oregon, in the spring of 1932. They were headed to Washington, D.C., to pressure Congress to pay the bonus in cash. These veterans urged others to join them. They called themselves the Bonus Expeditionary Force but later became known as the **Bonus Army**. They arrived in May. By June about 15,000 other veterans had joined them in Washington. Some veterans carried signs that read, "Heroes in 1917—Bums in 1932." Their protest

convinced the House of Representatives to pass a bill to immediately pay the bonus, but the Senate blocked the bill.

Most of the veterans went home, but some 2,000 marchers refused to obey a police order to leave. A small riot began. Two police officers and two veterans were killed. President Hoover ordered General Douglas MacArthur to restore order. MacArthur led a group of army troops against the veterans and their families. The troops threw tear gas, set the campgrounds on fire, and used bayonets to remove people from the area. A baby died from the tear gas. Reporter Thomas L. Stokes remembered walking through the demolished camp after the attack: "Some of the occupants watched their shacks burn quietly, standing beside piles of their few belongings. Then, one after another, they . . . wandered away."

Hoover and MacArthur defended their actions as necessary to protect the public. Photographs and news accounts of these unarmed and unemployed veterans of World War I being driven off by tear gas and bayonets outraged the public. One newspaper editor wrote, "If the Army must be called out to make war on unarmed citizens, this is no longer America." The public's reaction to the Bonus Army was another serious blow to Hoover's popularity. As the nation prepared for the 1932 presidential election, one observer declared, "If you put a rose in Hoover's hand it would wilt."

SECTION 2 REVIEW

Identify and explain the significance of the following:
- **Hoovervilles**
- **relief**
- **Reconstruction Finance Corporation**
- **public works**
- **Agricultural Marketing Act**
- **Federal Home Loan Bank Act**
- **Bonus Army**

Reading for Content Understanding

1 **Main Idea** How did the Great Depression affect most Americans?

2 **Main Idea** What was President Hoover's response to the Bonus Army?

3 **Citizenship and Democracy** In what ways did Hoover try to help businesses, workers, and farmers during the Great Depression?

4 **Writing** *Informing* Imagine that you are a political reporter. Write a short column on how you think Hoover's handling of the Bonus Army will affect the upcoming presidential election.

5 **Critical Thinking** *Evaluating* How does Hoover's quotation on page 428 reveal his philosophy about the role of government?

SECTION 3

Roosevelt and the New Deal

Reading Focus

What steps did President Roosevelt take to fight the depression immediately after taking office?

How did New Deal programs address the problem of unemployment?

What programs addressed the needs of industry and agriculture?

Key Terms

New Deal

Brain Trust

Hundred Days

fireside chats

Federal Deposit Insurance Corporation

Federal Emergency Relief Administration

National Industrial Recovery Act

Tennessee Valley Authority

A$T THE DEMOCRATIC NATIONAL CONVENTION *in Chicago, many party members believed they could defeat President Hoover in the 1932 election. The Democrats were less confident that anyone would be able to lead the nation out of the Great Depression. When Democrat Franklin D. Roosevelt found out that he had been nominated for the presidency, he hurried to Chicago to address the convention. He wanted to rally his supporters. "I pledge you, I pledge myself to a new deal for the American people . . . ," he declared. "This is more than a political campaign; it is a call to arms. Give me your help . . . to restore America to its own greatness."*

The Granger Collection, New York

A 1932 campaign bumper plate

★ The Election of 1932

As the Great Depression worsened, it became clear that no Republican candidate was likely to win the presidency in 1932. Many voters had given Republicans credit for the prosperity of the 1920s. These voters now blamed Republicans for the economic collapse. President Hoover had little popular support. The Republicans lacked a better candidate, however, and decided to nominate him again.

Democrats nominated Franklin D. Roosevelt. He had served as assistant secretary of the navy in

the Wilson administration and had run for vice president in 1920. Roosevelt won the New York governorship in 1928. While many viewed Hoover as a cold and uncaring man, Roosevelt appeared more concerned about people.

As the campaign progressed, Hoover continued to oppose any government takeover of relief efforts from communities and private charities. In contrast, Roosevelt promised that if elected, he would provide a **New Deal** to help the American people. He thought it was "common sense to take a method and try it. If it fails, . . . try another. But

The Great Depression **431**

above all, try something." Americans responded positively to Roosevelt's message. He won the November election in a landslide, receiving 472 electoral votes to Hoover's 59. Democrats also gained 90 seats in the House and 12 in the Senate, giving them large majorities in Congress.

A 1933 magazine cover showing the differing personalities of Hoover and Roosevelt

The Brain Trust

Between Franklin Roosevelt's election as president and his inauguration in March 1933, the U.S. economy worsened. Industrial production dropped to its lowest point. As more banks failed, some states restricted banking operations. During these months, Roosevelt gathered together a group of experts for advice on policies and programs. Most members of this so-called **Brain Trust** were college professors, lawyers, labor leaders, and social workers. Key members included professors Rexford Tugwell and Raymond Moley.

Roosevelt also included some experienced reformers in his cabinet. The president appointed labor reformer Frances Perkins as secretary of labor, making her the nation's first female cabinet member. For secretary of the interior, Roosevelt chose Harold Ickes, a longtime leader of the urban reform movement in Chicago. Roosevelt also appointed many African Americans to government positions.

First Lady Eleanor Roosevelt also played an important role in the administration. Already an active member of several women's reform movements, as first lady she continued to fight for the underprivileged. During her husband's first term, she traveled some 50,000 miles to meet with political allies and reform leaders.

Roosevelt's advisers disagreed on precisely how to fight the Great Depression. However, they agreed that ending the depression would require a new level of government involvement.

The Hundred Days

On March 4, 1933, millions of Americans crowded around their radios to hear President Roosevelt's inaugural address. Trying to lift people's spirits, he declared, "The people of the United States have not failed." Humorist Will Rogers wrote that the address inspired confidence in the new president:

66 **America hasn't been as happy in three years as they are today. No money, no banks, no work, no nothing, but they know they got a man in there who is wise to Congress, wise to our so-called big men. The whole country is with him.** 99

Instead of attending the Inaugural Ball, Roosevelt and his advisers met through the night. The next day Roosevelt called for a special session of Congress. This legislative session, which lasted from March 9 until mid-June, came to be called the **Hundred Days**. The bulk of the early New Deal programs was passed during this time.

Bank Reform

Roosevelt's first step was to save the nation's banks. On March 5, he announced that a four-day "bank holiday" would begin the next day. Every bank not already closed would be

First Lady Roosevelt established a precedent when she was regularly photographed with African Americans.

closed by federal order. On March 9, Congress passed the Emergency Banking Act. This act authorized the actions Roosevelt had already taken and allowed the government to examine bank records. Only stable banks were allowed to reopen.

On Sunday evening, March 12, some 60 million Americans sat around their radios. They heard the first of many **fireside chats**—radio broadcasts that Roosevelt made from the White House. The president assured Americans that it was safe to return their money to the banks. Most of the nation's banks reopened for business. Congress also created the **Federal Deposit Insurance Corporation** (FDIC) to protect bank accounts. During the depression the FDIC insured deposits up to $5,000 per account.

To protect investors and guard against stock fraud, Congress passed the Federal Securities Act and created the Securities and Exchange Commission (SEC). The SEC regulates companies that sell stocks or bonds.

Loan Assistance and Relief

Roosevelt's administration also moved quickly to help people who could not pay their mortgages. Some 250,000 families lost their homes in 1932 because they were unable to make loan payments. Congress created the Home Owners Loan Corporation (HOLC). The HOLC provided low-interest, long-term mortgage loans to many families. One woman who kept her home with the help of the HOLC wrote the president, "You have saved my life."

Roosevelt also reorganized all farm credit agencies into the Farm Credit Administration (FCA). Each day FCA loans typically saved 300 farms from foreclosure. In addition, the FCA refinanced about one fifth of all farm mortgages and kept thousands of rural banks from closing.

In May 1933 Congress authorized $500 million for the **Federal Emergency Relief Administration** (FERA). The president chose Harry L. Hopkins, a former relief supervisor in New York, as the FERA administrator. At least half of the FERA's relief money went to the states for direct distribution

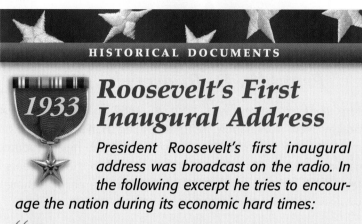

HISTORICAL DOCUMENTS

1933 Roosevelt's First Inaugural Address

President Roosevelt's first inaugural address was broadcast on the radio. In the following excerpt he tries to encourage the nation during its economic hard times:

"This great nation will endure as it has endured, will revive and will prosper. So, first of all, let me assert [state] my firm belief that the only thing we have to fear is fear itself. . . .

Our greatest primary task is to put people to work. This is no unsolvable problem if we face it wisely and courageously. It can be accomplished in part by direct recruiting by the government itself, treating the task as we would treat the emergency of a war, but, at the same time, through this employment, accomplishing greatly needed projects to stimulate and reorganize the use of our natural resources. . . .

I shall ask the Congress for the one remaining instrument to meet the crisis—broad executive power to wage a war against the emergency, as great as the power that would be given to me if we were in fact invaded by a foreign foe. For the trust reposed in [given to] me I will return the courage and the devotion that befit the time. I can do no less."

Understanding Primary Sources

1. What does President Roosevelt mean by "the only thing we have to fear is fear itself"?

2. Why do you think Roosevelt asks for broad executive power?

Franklin D. Roosevelt

Franklin D. Roosevelt was born in 1882 into a wealthy New York family. After attending Harvard University and Columbia University Law School, he practiced law. In 1911 Roosevelt won a seat in the New York legislature. He modeled his political career on that of his distant cousin Theodore Roosevelt, whose niece Eleanor he married in 1905. Although he was popular and intelligent, Franklin Roosevelt was not then considered a strong leader.

His life changed dramatically in 1921 when he suffered an attack of polio. The disease left him paralyzed in both legs. After extensive physical therapy, Roosevelt learned to move again with the help of leg braces.

He re-entered politics and enjoyed great success. Roosevelt's private battle with polio made him more compassionate and gave him the strength to lead the nation during great crisis. He once explained the source of his determination: "If you had spent two years in bed trying to wiggle your toe, after that anything would seem easy."

to families. By 1935 the FERA had spent some $3 billion helping Americans. However, many people disliked this kind of aid. They wanted jobs, not handouts. One aid recipient in Michigan told a FERA official: "It's very hard for me to ask for help. I don't want charity. I want work—any kind of work. I'll do road work, or anything."

The Civilian Conservation Corps (CCC) addressed this issue. The CCC provided government jobs for unmarried 17- to 24-year-old men. These men lived in U.S. Army camps while they planted trees, fought forest fires, and restored national historic sites and parks. During its lifetime, the CCC put nearly 3 million men to work. The Civil Works Administration (CWA) was a temporary work relief program in the winter of 1933. The CWA provided jobs for more than 4 million Americans in less than a year. "When I got that [CWA] card it was the biggest day in my whole life," a former insurance salesman in Alabama said. "At last I could say, 'I've got a job.'"

★ Reviving Business and Industry

President Roosevelt saw relief programs as a short-term solution. Economic recovery was his long-term goal. A key part of this plan was the **National Industrial Recovery Act** (NIRA), passed in 1933. The NIRA was an attempt to suspend antitrust laws, eliminate unfair competition, and prevent business failures. In a fireside chat Roosevelt explained the idea behind the NIRA:

> **If all employers in each competitive group agree to pay their workers the same wages—reasonable wages—and require the same hours—reasonable hours—then higher wages and shorter hours will hurt no employer.**

The Civilian Conservation Corps hired single young men to conserve and develop natural resources.

The NIRA created the Public Works Administration (PWA), a program to distribute government funds to help stimulate the economy. Headed by Secretary of the Interior Harold Ickes, the PWA provided some $3.3 billion for public works. Eventually, this figure rose to more than $6 billion.

Not all businesses that displayed the blue eagle followed the NRA's codes.

Although some people criticized Ickes for being slow to spend money, the PWA completed more than 34,000 projects. PWA workers completed work on Boulder Dam, built a new courthouse for Kalamazoo, Michigan, and created the Triborough Bridge in New York City. Between 1933 and 1939, the PWA helped build most of the country's new schools and many new courthouses, city halls, and sewage plants. The PWA also built thousands of miles of streets and highways.

The NIRA also addressed labor's concerns, guaranteeing workers the right to organize and bargain collectively. The NIRA created the National Recovery Administration (NRA) to develop codes that established prices, wages, and work hours for each industry. The NRA outlawed such practices as child labor and sweatshops. Merchants and manufacturers who supported NRA standards displayed a blue eagle with the slogan "We Do Our Part."

Although the NRA helped many people, it also had its problems. Some labor leaders referred to the NRA as the "National Run Around." Businesses that had agreed to NRA codes often found ways to avoid labor reforms and wage increases. When Secretary of Labor Frances Perkins was on a tour of major steel towns, local leaders in Homestead, Pennsylvania, tried to prevent her from meeting with unhappy workers. The workers wanted to discuss wages and working conditions. Perkins responded by holding a meeting at the local post office, which was federal property.

The limited achievements of the National Industrial Recovery Act did not last long. In May 1935 the Supreme Court unanimously declared the NIRA to be unconstitutional. The Court ruled that the federal government had no authority in peacetime to regulate interstate commerce so closely. The Court also ruled that the NIRA gave the president too much power.

Helping Rural America

In addition to helping workers and trying to revitalize business, the Roosevelt administration wanted to improve living conditions in rural America. A first step was to help farmers.

The AAA

New Deal officials encouraged farmers to grow fewer crops. The officials wanted this reduction to increase demand, raise prices, and increase farmers' earnings. Under the Agricultural Adjustment Act (AAA) of 1933, farmers received subsidies, or government payments, for not planting corn, cotton, rice, tobacco, and wheat. They were also paid not to raise hogs or produce dairy products. To raise money for the subsidies, the government taxed businesses that processed foods, such as wheat mills and meatpacking plants.

In 1933, for example, the government paid farmers to plow under 10 million acres of already planted cotton. Many farmers, and even some government officials, found these measures hard to accept. "To have to destroy a growing crop is a shocking commentary on our civilization," said Agriculture Secretary Henry Wallace.

The AAA helped stabilize farm prices, but critics complained that too many benefits were paid to large-scale farms. The AAA also often hurt the poorest farmers. Some landowners cut

Dairy farmers dump milk from their trucks to protest low prices.

The Tennessee Valley Authority, 1933–1945

Learning from Maps The Tennessee Valley Authority provided electricity to a wide area, built dams to control flooding, and created jobs to lessen poverty.

Place In which state did the TVA build the most dams?

used to pay the subsidies was unconstitutional.

The TVA

In May 1933 Congress created the **Tennessee Valley Authority** (TVA). The TVA was a rural reform effort targeting the Tennessee Valley region. TVA workers constructed a series of dams in seven states along the Tennessee River basin. The dams controlled flooding, reduced soil erosion, and generated inexpensive hydroelectric power. Soon, thousands of rural families had electricity in their homes for the first time.

The TVA was perhaps the most ambitious and successful New Deal program. The TVA's long-term goal was to attract industry to the region and provide rural Americans with more dependable employment than farming. President Roosevelt hoped that the TVA and the many other pieces of legislation passed during the Hundred Days would put the nation on the road to recovery.

production by forcing renters and sharecroppers off their land. Because subsidies were based on the size of the farms, they were often not enough to help small-scale farmers.

In early 1936 the Supreme Court struck down the AAA. The Court ruled that the tax

SECTION 3 REVIEW

Identify and explain the significance of the following:
- Franklin D. Roosevelt
- New Deal
- Brain Trust
- Eleanor Roosevelt
- Hundred Days
- fireside chats
- Federal Deposit Insurance Corporation
- Federal Emergency Relief Administration
- Harry L. Hopkins
- National Industrial Recovery Act
- Tennessee Valley Authority

Reading for Content Understanding

1 **Main Idea** What actions did President Roosevelt take after his inauguration?

2 **Main Idea** How did Roosevelt try to solve the unemployment problem during the Hundred Days?

3 **Constitutional Heritage** What New Deal legislation did the Supreme Court declare unconstitutional, and why?

4 **Writing** *Classifying* Identify the programs created to help businesses and rural residents. Briefly explain what each program did and whether it was successful.

5 **Critical Thinking** *Making Comparisons* Compare and contrast Herbert Hoover's and Franklin D. Roosevelt's solutions to the Great Depression.

The Second New Deal

Reading Focus

Why were some people critical of the New Deal?

What programs were passed during the Second New Deal?

How did President Roosevelt try to prevent the Supreme Court from overturning his New Deal programs?

Key Terms

American Liberty League

Share-Our-Wealth

Second New Deal

Social Security Act

Rural Electrification Administration

Emergency Relief Appropriation Act

Works Progress Administration

welfare state

deficit spending

A cartoon showing the Supreme Court rejecting the AAA

*A*FTER THE SUPREME COURT *struck down the NIRA in May 1935, Justice Louis Brandeis walked back to his cloakroom. There he met with Thomas Corcoran, a young lawyer helping plan President Roosevelt's New Deal. Brandeis gave Corcoran a stern message. "I want you to go back and tell the President that we're not going to let this government centralize [take control of] everything. It's come to an end." Corcoran and the others who favored the New Deal chose to ignore this warning, but it revealed the strength of the opposition to the New Deal.*

 New Deal Critics

Some opponents of the New Deal claimed that it discouraged free enterprise and was the beginning of socialism in the United States. These critics included leaders of powerful corporations such as Du Pont and General Motors. In 1934 a group of business leaders opposed to the New Deal created the **American Liberty League**.

Other critics argued that the New Deal had not done enough for the public. To help older Americans, Dr. Francis Townsend of California

proposed the Old Age Revolving Pension (OARP). The plan would give citizens over 60 years old $200 a month and require them to spend the money within 30 days. Townsend hoped that the OARP would assist the elderly while putting more money into the economy. Thousands of Americans, particularly in the West, supported Townsend's plan.

Father Charles Coughlin, a Catholic priest in a Detroit suburb, was another critic of the New Deal. His radio show, *The Golden Hour of the Little Flower,* had millions of listeners nationwide. He often

The Great Depression　437

discussed political and social issues on his program. At first, Coughlin supported President Roosevelt. Then Coughlin became impatient with the slow progress of the New Deal. He organized the National Union for Social Justice and the Union Party, as a challenge to the Democratic Party. The Union Party called for stronger government control over banking, business, and the money supply.

Huey Long was another critic who had supported Roosevelt's early New Deal programs. Known as the Kingfish, Long called himself a defender of the common people. As governor of Louisiana, Long had attacked corporations and built bridges and roads in the poorest sections of the state. He also gave free schoolbooks to children. His critics accused him of stealing state funds and ruthlessly using his political machine to crush all opponents.

As a U.S. senator in 1934, Long organized the **Share-Our-Wealth** plan. It had the slogan "Every Man a King." Long's plan seemed simple. He wanted the federal government to limit the size of all personal fortunes so that every family would be guaranteed a minimum income of $2,500 a year. Long declared that this would "break up the swollen fortunes of America and . . . spread the wealth among all our people." Many economists dismissed Long's program as far too expensive to work. Although New Deal critics like Long gained some popularity, Americans showed their support for Roosevelt in the 1934 congressional elections. Voters increased the Democrats' majorities in both houses of Congress.

New Reform Efforts

In response to New Deal critics and to the 1934 congressional elections, the Roosevelt administration proposed a new program of reforms in January 1935. Historians refer to this program as the **Second New Deal**.

Social Security

Congress passed the **Social Security Act** in August 1935. This act created Social Security, a pension plan for retired workers over age 65. The federal government would administer the plan. Its funds would come from a payroll tax on businesses and a tax on workers' wages. The Social Security Act also established unemployment insurance for workers. In addition, it provided financial aid for older Americans, people with disabilities, and families of deceased male workers.

The original law did not cover farmworkers or domestic workers. It also did not help people who lost their jobs because of illness. Nevertheless, the Social Security Act became one of the most far-reaching and long-lasting pieces of legislation from the Second New Deal. Over the years Social Security has been expanded to cover people who were previously excluded.

Other Reforms

Perhaps in response to Senator Long's Share-Our-Wealth campaign, Roosevelt supported the Revenue Act of 1935, better known as the Wealth Tax Act. This act raised taxes on the nation's wealthiest people and levied an "excess profits" tax on wealthy corporations. Congress wanted

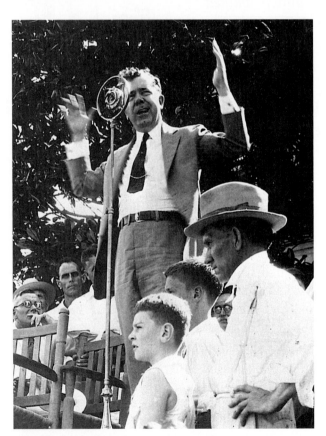

Senator Huey Long was an exciting speaker and drew large crowds wherever he spoke.

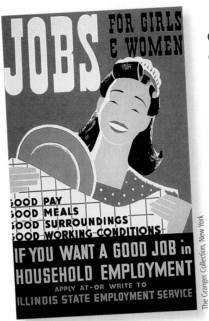

Most women employed by relief programs were given jobs such as cleaning or sewing.

to use the tax money to boost the U.S. economy. However, corporate leaders complained that the taxes actually discouraged business expansion by taking away funds that could be invested.

The government also improved utility services provided to rural areas. The **Rural Electrification Administration** (REA) soon extended electrical power lines into isolated rural areas. When the REA was established, only about 12 percent of American farms had electricity. By 1941 about 40 percent of the nation's farms did.

Congress passed a law allowing a federal commission to regulate the interstate transmission and sale of electricity. Roosevelt also tried to lower the prices public utility companies charged for electricity and gas.

☆ The WPA

Unemployment remained one of the biggest problems facing the Roosevelt administration. Even though the jobless rate had fallen, some 10 million Americans were still out of work. In April 1935 Congress passed one of the most important measures of the Second New Deal, the **Emergency Relief Appropriation Act**. This act provided close to $4.9 billion to help the unemployed. It also established a new federal public-works agency, the **Works Progress Administration** (WPA).

Linking Past to Present

Social Security

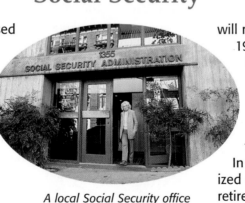

A local Social Security office

When Congress passed the Social Security Act in 1935, critics complained that it ignored large segments of the population who needed assistance. Since that time, lawmakers have created numerous amendments to expand the act. By the late 1990s, Social Security programs covered 95 percent of the nation's workers.

The Social Security old-age pension program has proved expensive. By 1989 it accounted for one fourth of the federal budget. As the nation's population ages, many Americans worry that Social Security funds will run out. In the 1980s and 1990s, Congress began taking steps to protect Social Security funds. Congress increased the number of workers paying Social Security taxes and the amount of those taxes. In addition, Congress authorized a gradual increase in the retirement age from 65 to 67.

Understanding What You Read

1. How has the Social Security program expanded since 1935?

2. What have lawmakers done to ensure that there is enough money to fund Social Security?

Headed by Harry L. Hopkins, the WPA employed more than 8.5 million Americans between 1935 and 1943. At the program's peak, more than 3 million people received a monthly WPA check. WPA workers built or repaired thousands of bridges, parks, public buildings, and roads. The WPA also had a special women's division. It provided work in fields such as bookbinding, home care for the elderly, nursing, sewing, and teaching.

The WPA Handicraft Project provided jobs for older Americans and people with disabilities.

Recognizing that creative artists also needed work, Hopkins launched Federal Project One. This program employed about 40,000 actors, artists, musicians, and writers in a variety of projects. The Federal Writers' Project paid writers to produce state and regional guidebooks and to record volumes of oral histories, including the narratives of former slaves. The Federal Theater Project produced plays such as *The Living Newspaper*. A popular all–African American version of William Shakespeare's *Macbeth* was set in Haiti instead of Scotland. The Federal Arts Project sponsored folk art, murals, and paintings. The Federal Music Project helped create new symphony orchestras and supported public performances. When asked why he was spending government money to support artists, Hopkins replied, "They've got to eat just like other people."

WPA artists painted this mural inside Coit Tower in San Francisco to celebrate California agriculture.

Some WPA relief money went to the newly formed National Youth Administration (NYA). The NYA gave part-time employment to more than 4.5 million high school and college-age students.

★ The Election of 1936

As the presidential election of 1936 drew near, Americans had to decide whether to vote for President Roosevelt and his New Deal programs. Despite the efforts of the Roosevelt administration, millions of Americans remained unemployed. Hundreds of factories were still closed.

The Republican Party chose Kansas governor Alfred M. Landon to run against Roosevelt. Landon had the support of many business interests, most major newspapers, and wealthier Americans. During the campaign, Landon criticized the inefficiency and expense of the New Deal. He called the Social Security Act "unjust, unworkable, stupidly drafted and wastefully financed." However, Republicans realized that many New Deal programs were popular. Therefore, Landon promised to continue helping the elderly and unemployed and to protect workers' rights.

Many Democrats were concerned that a third-party candidate would take votes away from Roosevelt and allow the Republicans to win the election. Huey Long had announced his entry into the presidential race, but the son-in-law of one of his political opponents assassinated the senator in September 1935.

The Democrats officially nominated Roosevelt for re-election in 1936. During the campaign, the president defended his New Deal programs. He told a crowd, "When Americans suffered, we refused to pass by on the other side. Humanity came first." A majority of Americans believed that Roosevelt had saved them from economic disaster. Several million people were working again. Some large companies, such as General Motors, were also recovering.

Roosevelt won re-election in November 1936 with one of the largest majorities in U.S. history. He carried every state except Maine and Vermont. Roosevelt received more than 60 percent of the popular vote, and Landon just over 36 percent. Coughlin's Union Party received about 2 percent. The London magazine *The Economist* suggested that "on the whole, the poor won the election from the well-to-do."

The 1936 election marked the first time that one party had received a majority of votes from organized labor, farmers, and African Americans. Previously most African Americans had voted for the Republican Party because it had ended slavery under President Abraham Lincoln. In 1936, African Americans supported the Democratic Party because some New Deal programs had provided them with work and relief opportunities.

 ## The Supreme Court

President Roosevelt saw his landslide victory as approval for his New Deal programs. In his second inaugural address, Roosevelt described his goals for the term. He wanted to help the millions of Americans who

> " at this very moment are denied the greater part of what the very lowest standards of today call the necessities of life. . . . I see one-third of a nation ill-housed, ill-clad [ill-clothed], ill-nourished. "

Roosevelt saw only one major roadblock standing in the way of greater reform—the Supreme Court. The Court had already struck down the NIRA and the AAA. With the constitutionality of the TVA and Social Security Act to be decided in upcoming Supreme Court cases, the whole future of the

Select New Deal Programs

FIRST NEW DEAL, 1933–1934	PROVISIONS
Emergency Banking Act	Gave the executive branch the right to regulate banks
Farm Credit Administration (FCA)	Refinanced loans to keep farmers from losing their land
Civilian Conservation Corps (CCC)	Employed young men on public-works projects
Federal Emergency Relief Administration (FERA)	Provided relief to the needy
Agricultural Adjustment Act (AAA) of 1933	Paid farmers to grow fewer crops; later declared unconstitutional
Tennessee Valley Authority (TVA)	Built dams and power plants in the Tennessee Valley region
Home Owners Loan Corporation (HOLC)	Lent money to homeowners to refinance their mortgages
Federal Deposit Insurance Corporation (FDIC)	Insured deposits in individual bank accounts
National Recovery Administration (NRA)	Regulated industry and raised wages and prices
Public Works Administration (PWA)	Set up public-works projects to increase employment
Civil Works Administration (CWA)	Provided federal jobs to the unemployed
Securities and Exchange Commission (SEC)	Regulated the securities market
Federal Housing Administration (FHA)	Insured bank loans for building and repairing homes
SECOND NEW DEAL, 1935–1938	PROVISIONS
Works Progress Administration (WPA)	Created jobs in public works, research, and the arts
Rural Electrification Administration (REA)	Provided electricity to rural areas lacking public utilities
National Youth Administration (NYA)	Provided job training and part-time jobs to students
National Labor Relations Act (NLRA)	Recognized labor's right to bargain collectively
Social Security Act	Provided unemployment benefits and retirement pensions
Farm Security Administration (FSA)	Provided loans to help tenant farmers buy land
Agricultural Adjustment Act (AAA) of 1938	Paid farmers to voluntarily limit crop production
Fair Labor Standards Act	Established a minimum wage and a 40-hour workweek

OF COURSE WE MAY HAVE TO CHANGE REMEDIES IF WE DON'T GET RESULTS

F.D.R.

NEW DEAL REMEDIES

CONGRESS

NRA

President Roosevelt was willing to try a variety of remedies to help the ailing U.S. economy.

Democrats' New Deal legislation appeared to be in jeopardy.

In February 1937, two weeks after his second inauguration, Roosevelt stunned Congress and the nation. He submitted a bill to change the structure of the Supreme Court. He proposed to increase the maximum number of justices from 9 to 15. Because Roosevelt would appoint the additional judges, this plan would allow the president to establish a majority of justices that would be friendly to his reform programs.

Roosevelt's opponents quickly accused him of "court packing"—trying to pack, or fill, the Court with his own judges. The *Chicago Tribune* urged Congress to vote against the bill, declaring that "if Congress answers yes, the principle of an impartial and independent judiciary will be lost." Even some of Roosevelt's allies were uncomfortable with his plan. They believed it would upset the checks and balances of the federal government.

As the court-packing debate continued, the Supreme Court surprised observers by upholding several key pieces of New Deal legislation, including the Social Security Act. Many Americans wondered if Roosevelt's plan had influenced how the justices voted. One journalist noted that a "switch

in time saved nine," meaning that the change in the justices' ruling kept their number at nine. Although Congress soon defeated the court-packing plan, Roosevelt filled seven Court vacancies, caused by death or retirement, within the following four years. Thus, Roosevelt got what he wanted. He appointed new justices and ensured that the Supreme Court contained a majority that supported his New Deal policies. However, the battle over Roosevelt's court-packing proposal had divided the Democratic Party. It also ended up costing Roosevelt valuable support within his party.

★ The End of the New Deal

During 1936 and early 1937 the economy seemed to be improving. To cut federal spending, President Roosevelt reduced the total number of people employed by WPA and other New Deal projects from more than 3 million to just under 2 million.

Recession

Unfortunately, private industries were not able to employ all of these workers. In August 1937 the economy began to decline again, and unemployment rose rapidly. The president's critics called this situation the "Roosevelt recession." In October the stock market dropped again. Unemployment greatly increased in March 1938. President Roosevelt and Congress responded by approving more than $3 billion to expand the WPA, restart the PWA, and fund other agencies.

The increase in federal spending reduced some unemployment and prevented the new recession from becoming much worse. The strain of the lengthy economic problem was beginning to show, however. During the congressional elections of 1938, the Democratic Party was divided between supporters of Roosevelt and those opposed to the New Deal. Republicans took advantage of this division and picked up 7 seats in the Senate and 75 in the House, as well as many governorships.

Evaluating the New Deal

By 1938 the New Deal was reaching the limits of what it could do for the economy. The federal budget had grown by several billion dollars. However, this spending increase was not enough to make up for lost private investment. Critics charged that the New Deal created a **welfare state**. This system of government institutions provides for basic needs of citizens. These needs might include health care and unemployment benefits. Critics also argued that the New Deal promoted **deficit spending**—having the government spend more money than it receives in revenue—for the first time during a period of peace.

Supporters of the New Deal argued that the federal government took on a necessary role. New Deal programs helped many people. Home loans, farm subsidies, bank deposit insurance, relief payments and jobs, pension programs, and unemployment insurance helped Americans survive the Great Depression. The New Deal also established minimum standards for working conditions and the protection of workers' rights. Many Americans believed that Roosevelt and the federal government were concerned with their well-being. One man recalled:

❝ My mother looks upon the President as someone so immediately concerned with

President Roosevelt's fireside chats gave many people the feeling that the president cared for them personally.

her problems and difficulties that she would not be greatly surprised were he to come to her house some evening and stay to dinner. ❞

The New Deal's effectiveness in fighting the depression remains a topic of much historical debate. Nonetheless, it has had lasting results, creating programs and agencies that still exist today. In addition, Roosevelt's leadership and popularity helped shift the balance of power in the federal government from the legislative branch to the executive branch.

SECTION 4 REVIEW

Identify and explain the significance of the following:

- **American Liberty League**
- **Francis Townsend**
- **Charles Coughlin**
- **Huey Long**
- **Share-Our-Wealth**
- **Second New Deal**
- **Social Security Act**
- **Rural Electrification Administration**
- **Emergency Relief Appropriation Act**
- **Works Progress Administration**
- **welfare state**
- **deficit spending**

Reading for Content Understanding

1 **Main Idea** Why did some Americans criticize President Roosevelt's New Deal policies?

2 **Main Idea** Make a graphic organizer that describes five important programs created during the Second New Deal.

3 **Constitutional Heritage** How did Roosevelt try to influence the Supreme Court's rulings on New Deal programs?

4 **Writing** *Informing* Write a paragraph on how New Deal programs might affect Americans today.

5 **Critical Thinking** *Synthesizing Information* Do you think the New Deal was successful in helping Americans and in ending the depression? Explain your answer.

CHAPTER 14 REVIEW

Chapter Summary

The stock market crash on October 29, 1929, marked the beginning of the Great Depression. The depression left millions of Americans unemployed. They became dissatisfied with President Hoover's efforts to help them. President Roosevelt introduced a wide range of New Deal programs to help businesses and individuals recover from the devastating effects of the depression.

On a separate sheet of paper, complete the following activities.

Identifying People and Ideas

Describe the historical significance of the following:

1. speculation
2. Black Tuesday
3. Franklin D. Roosevelt
4. New Deal
5. Eleanor Roosevelt
6. fireside chats
7. National Industrial Recovery Act
8. Tennessee Valley Authority
9. Social Security Act
10. relief

Internet Activity go.hrw.com
SB1 New Deal

Search the Internet through the HRW Web site for information about life histories that were collected as part of the Works Progress Administration. Then use this information to write a short biographical sketch of one of the people interviewed.

Understanding Main Ideas

1. What happened during the 1929 stock market crash?
2. How did President Hoover and many business leaders respond to the crash?
3. How did the Great Depression affect Americans' daily lives?
4. How did President Roosevelt try to revive banking and industry during the Hundred Days?
5. How did the New Deal try to help farmers and rural residents?
6. What alternatives to the New Deal did Francis Townsend, Charles Coughlin, and Huey Long propose?
7. Why did Roosevelt try to pass his court-packing plan, and what were the results?

Reviewing Themes

1. **Economic Development** What economic factors contributed to the Great Depression?

Using the Time Line

Number your paper from 1 to 5. Match the letters on the time line below with the following events.

1. Roosevelt wins re-election by a record-breaking margin.
2. Angry veterans known as the Bonus Army arrive in Washington, D.C.
3. The Social Security Act is passed to provide security for older Americans and the unemployed.
4. The passage of the Smoot-Hawley Tariff raises tariffs on foreign goods and contributes to the global depression.
5. The stock market crashes on what becomes known as Black Tuesday.

1929   1931   1933   1935   1937   1939

a   b   c   d   e

2. **Constitutional Heritage**   What role did the Supreme Court play in the New Deal?

3. **Citizenship and Democracy**   How were some New Deal programs targeted to directly help the unemployed?

Thinking Critically

1. **Identifying Cause and Effect**   Explain the cause of the banking crisis and its effect on the economy.

2. **Making Comparisons**   Compare and contrast the programs that Hoover passed to help farmers during the depression with Roosevelt's New Deal programs.

3. **Evaluating**   Do you think the New Deal was successful in fighting the effects of the Great Depression? Explain your answer.

Building Your Portfolio

Complete the following activities individually or in groups.

1. **Oral History Project**   Interview at least three people in your community who were alive during the Great Depression. You may wish to ask them about how their family survived the depression, what they thought of Presidents Hoover and Roosevelt, or how the New Deal programs affected them. Combine your interviews into a brochure, audiotape, or videotape that you can present to your class.

2. **The Stock Market**   Imagine that you are an investor in the stock market. Get a current copy of the financial section of the newspaper and select a company that you think will be successful in the future. Now imagine that you have 100 shares in this company and note the value of these shares. For the next month, keep track of how your stock is doing. At the end of the month, note the final value of your 100 shares. Then write a short report that details how your stock did and whether you made or lost money. Include a line graph that shows the gains and losses of your stock.

Writing About History

1. **Describing**   Imagine that you are a teenager working for the CCC. Write a letter home describing the work you are doing and why it is important to other Americans.

2. **Creating**   Imagine that you are an artist on Federal Project One. Create a flyer or song lyrics describing the effect of the WPA on life in your community.

Linking Geography and History

1. **Region**   How did the TVA improve the lives of rural people in the Tennessee Valley?

2. **Human-Environment Interaction**   How did agencies such as the CCC and PWA change the landscape of the United States?

History Skills Workshop

Reading Charts   Study the chart below, which shows the collapse of share prices during the 1929 stock market crash. Then answer the following questions: (a) Which stock shown lost the most points between September 3 and November 13, 1929? (b) Which stock was worth the most on November 13, 1929? (c) Which stock lost the greatest percentage of its starting value?

The Crash

Company	High Price Sept. 3, 1929	Low Price Nov. 13, 1929
American Telephone and Telegraph	304	197 1/4
General Electric	396 1/4	168 1/8
General Motors	72 3/4	36
Montgomery Ward	137 7/8	49 1/4
U.S. Steel	261 3/4	150
Woolworth	100 3/8	52 1/4

Source: Frederick Lewis Allen, *Only Yesterday*

Alexandre Hogue, *Drouth Stricken Area*, 1936, Oil on canvas, Dallas Museum of Art, Dallas Art Association Purchase, 1945.6

■ CHAPTER 15 ■
The Depression at Home and Abroad
(1929–1939)

One day during the Great Depression young Clara Hancox found her piggy bank empty. Her mother told her that her father had taken the money. He needed it to look for work, and Clara was the only one in the family with any money. To Clara, it was not the missing money that was painful. Rather, "it was to see this happen to the man who in my eyes could do no wrong." In the 1930s, many people shared similar experiences.

THEMES

Economic Development
In what ways might the government help citizens economically?

Cultural Diversity
How might different groups be affected by an economic downturn?

Global Relations
How might a nation's government change in response to economic difficulties?

| 1929 | 1930 | 1931 | 1932 | 1933 | 1934 |

SEPT. 1931
Japan invades Manchuria.

FEB. 1932
Duke Ellington records his hit song "It Don't Mean a Thing (If It Ain't Got That Swing)."

JUNE 1934
The Indian Reorganization Act is passed.

Workers and Farmers in the New Deal

Reading Focus

How did New Deal legislation help organized labor?

What new labor unions were formed, and what new strategies did the unions use during the Great Depression?

What happened to farmers and farmworkers during the Great Depression?

Key Terms

National Labor Relations Act

Fair Labor Standards Act

Congress of Industrial Organizations

sit-down strike

Southern Tenant Farmers' Union

Dust Bowl

Farm Security Administration

A child during the 1930s

I N THE WINTER OF 1931–32, *newspaper editor Oscar Ameringer traveled the Midwest recording the stories of desperate and starving Americans. He offered a ride to one Arkansas family. The woman was hugging a dead chicken under her ragged coat. When asked where she had found the chicken, she said she had found it dead in the road. Then—referring to Herbert Hoover's 1928 campaign slogan—she added with grim humor, "They promised me a chicken in the pot, and now I got mine."*

IMAGE ON LEFT PAGE: *Alexandre Hogue's 1934 painting of the drought-stricken United States*

1935 · 1936 · 1937 · 1938 · 1939

JULY 1935 The National Labor Relations Act is passed.

OCT. 1935 Italy invades Ethiopia.

JULY 1936 The Spanish Civil War begins.

DEC. 1936 A sit-down strike begins at General Motors.

JULY 1937 The Farm Security Administration is created.

NOV. 1938 Nazis attack Jews on *Kristallnacht.*

DEC. 1939 The movie *Gone With the Wind* is released.

★ New Deal Labor Programs

In the mid-1930s the Roosevelt administration revised some of its New Deal labor programs, particularly after the Supreme Court struck down the National Industrial Recovery Act. In 1935 Senator Robert Wagner of New York sponsored legislation to strengthen and restore workers' rights. In July, Congress passed the **National Labor Relations Act** (NLRA), or Wagner-Connery Act. The NLRA gave workers the right to select their own unions by majority vote. Workers also gained the right to strike, boycott, and picket. The NLRA required employers to negotiate wages, hours, and working conditions with the workers' unions.

United Auto Workers buttons from the late 1930s

To enforce these rights, the NLRA created the National Labor Relations Board (NLRB). This board supervised secret-ballot elections among employees to determine if they wanted union representation. The NLRB also investigated charges of unfair labor practices and antiunion activities.

In 1938 Congress passed legislation on employee hours and wages. The **Fair Labor Standards Act** established a minimum wage of 40 cents an hour by 1940. The act also set a maximum standard workweek of 40 hours. In addition, the act banned the employment of children under 16 years of age.

★ Industrial Unions

With the passage of pro-labor laws, union membership increased. During the 1920s most workers had belonged to craft unions associated with the American Federation of Labor (AFL). Skilled workers who performed the same craft, or trade, belonged to these unions. Because industrial production required workers with many different skills, there were sometimes several different craft unions in one industry.

After the NLRA passed, some workers tried to organize industrial unions. These unions represent all skilled and unskilled workers in an industry.

John L. Lewis, president of the United Mine Workers (UMW), and some other union leaders argued that industrial unions would give unions more power. Lewis failed to persuade the AFL leadership to abandon craft unions. He did, however, form the Committee for Industrial Organization. It brought together workers in the automobile, rubber, steel, and textile industries. In 1936 this group was organizing workers in mass-production industries. The committee became the **Congress of Industrial Organizations** (CIO) in 1938. The CIO joined together industrial unions. Lewis wanted the CIO to "organize the unorganized." The congress welcomed unions that had African Americans, immigrants, unskilled workers, and women as members. Industrial unions in the CIO included the International Ladies' Garment Workers Union, the United Auto Workers, and the United Mine Workers.

Union membership totals jumped from roughly 3 million in 1932 to more than 8 million in 1938. Unions used their influence to help elect pro-labor candidates and to lobby Congress.

With greater union strength came an increasing number of strikes. In early 1936, workers went on strike at the Goodyear Tire Factory in Akron, Ohio. Instead of leaving the factory to form a picket line, the striking workers sat on the production floor. They refused to leave until management met their demands. This was the first major **sit-down strike**, one in which workers remain in

Sit-down strikers at a General Motors plant established committees to provide for meals, education, and entertainment.

the factories but refuse to work. With workers occupying the plants, employers could not replace them. The sit-down strike forced factories to halt production until the conflict was resolved. The Akron workers won their demands and inspired others to stage similar strikes.

In late December 1936, autoworkers at a General Motors (GM) factory in Flint, Michigan, staged a sit-down strike. It soon spread to other company plants. Inside the Flint factory, striking workers prepared for a long strike. Outside, the wives of striking workers marched on picket lines, raised money, and mobilized support.

The autoworkers had no formal means to express their grievances to management. Their complaints ranged from the fast-paced speed of the work to frequent and lengthy layoffs. One woman said that the long, hard hours had turned her husband into

"a young man grown old from the speed-up. He has come home at night . . . so tired he couldn't eat. He was wakened the next morning with his hands so swollen he couldn't hold a fork."

The strike lasted six weeks. It virtually halted GM's car production until the workers' demands were met. One autoworker recalled that "the inhuman high speed [was] *no more*." Within eight months of the strike, the membership of the United Auto Workers had increased to about 400,000—up from 30,000 one year earlier. Soon workers in other industries staged sit-down strikes. In 1937 more than 470 sit-down strikes occured. There had been less than 50 in 1936.

 ## Farmers in the Depression

Organized labor gained strength with the New Deal, but farmers did not fare so well. During the 1920s, farmers had struggled with crop surpluses, low prices, and high costs. The stock market crash worsened their crisis. Many farmers found themselves unable to repay their loans. Banks took over ownership of many indebted farms. Between 1930 and 1935 as many as 750,000 farms were lost through bankruptcy or foreclosure.

The Southern Tenant Farmers' Union fought to protect the rights of sharecroppers and tenant farmers.

Farmers Take Action

Frustrated farmers often fought against foreclosures. When banks held auctions to sell animals, equipment, and farms, many people refused to bid market prices. They offered a few dollars for a barnyard of animals or for an entire farm. With no other offers, the banks accepted these low bids. The purchasers usually returned the items to their neighbors.

The Agricultural Adjustment Act (AAA) helped some farmers pay their mortgages. It hurt other farm families, however. Poor families, tenants, and sharecroppers often lost their jobs when farmers reduced production as the AAA required. In response, tenants, sharecroppers, and farm laborers joined forces in Arkansas. They organized the **Southern Tenant Farmers' Union** (STFU) in July 1934. STFU president J. R. Butler urged black and white farmworkers to join together. "The landlord is always betwixt us, beatin' us and starvin' us and makin' us fight each other," explained one farmer. The STFU had limited success, but it did bring attention to the problems that sharecroppers and tenant farmers faced.

The Dust Bowl

An environmental disaster also hurt farmers. In order to grow more crops, many Great Plains farmers had plowed up grazing land and the grasses that protected the topsoil. A severe drought and heat wave struck the Great Plains in the early 1930s. The land dried out. Soon heavy winds swept away the dried-out topsoil. These dust storms turned parts of the Great Plains into the so-called **Dust Bowl**. One woman from Kansas remembered dust storms

66 **covering everything—including ourselves—in a thick, brownish gray blanket. . . . The door and windows were all shut tightly, yet those tiny particles seemed to seep through the very walls. It got into cupboards and clothes closets; our faces were as dirty as if we had rolled in the dirt; our hair was gray and stiff and we ground dirt between our teeth.** 99

YEARS OF DUST

RESETTLEMENT ADMINISTRATION
Rescues Victims
Restores Land to Proper Use

Many Americans were forced to leave their farms as drought turned their farmland to dust.

The dust came in all colors—brown, black, yellow, gray, and even red—depending on its source. A single dust storm could rage from one hour to three and a half days, often reducing visibility to zero.

The dust storms destroyed farm life in the area. Many farm families, often called "Okies"

because they came from Oklahoma, abandoned their farms. They headed west to California looking for work. A documentary film created in the 1930s described these migrants:

66 **Nothing to stay for . . . nothing to hope for . . . homeless, penniless, and bewildered they joined the great army of the highways.** 99

Migrant Workers

When Dust Bowl refugees arrived in California, they competed for jobs with migrant workers already there. By 1933 more than twice as many people were looking for work on California farms as there were jobs.

Many of these migrant workers were Mexican citizens. Because they were not U.S. citizens, some state and local governments did not allow them to participate in public-works projects. Other Mexican citizens were forced to leave the United States. Nearly 400,000 Mexican nationals were deported during the 1930s. Their American-born children, who were U.S. citizens, were also sent to Mexico.

Some Mexican migrant workers who remained in the United States organized for better working conditions. In 1933, for example, some 12,000 laborers in the San Joaquin Valley went on strike for higher wages for picking cotton. Migrant worker Lydia Ramos joined the strikers, explaining, "*We* were not going to break a strike." The strikers won a wage-rate increase. However, many migrant workers continued to experience hardship during the depression.

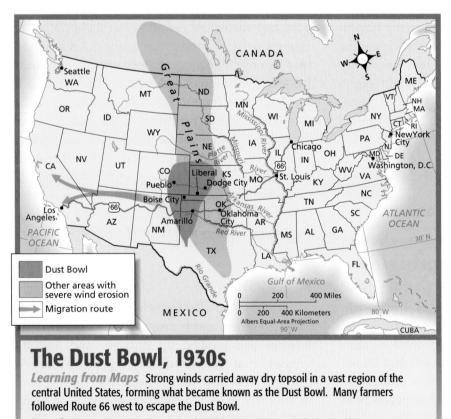

The Dust Bowl, 1930s

Learning from Maps Strong winds carried away dry topsoil in a vast region of the central United States, forming what became known as the Dust Bowl. Many farmers followed Route 66 west to escape the Dust Bowl.

Location From New Mexico, through which states did the typical migration route pass?

American Literature

The Grapes of Wrath
John Steinbeck

John Steinbeck's The Grapes of Wrath *was published in 1939. The novel describes the Joad family's struggle during the Great Depression. After losing their farm in Oklahoma, the Joads travel to California. They find hard, miserable work as migrant farm laborers. In the following excerpt, the Joads prepare to leave their farm.*

For The Grapes of Wrath, *John Steinbeck won a Pulitzer Prize. The novel describes the hardships and suffering many Americans experienced during the 1930s.*

Now they were ready. Granma . . . saying, "What's all this? What you doin' now, so early?" But she was dressed and agreeable. And Ruthie and Winfield were awake, but quiet with the pressure of tiredness and still half dreaming. . . . And the movement of the family stopped. They stood about, reluctant [not wanting] to make the first active move to go. They were afraid, now that the time had come—afraid in the same way Grampa was afraid. . . .

And Tom shook himself free of the numbness. . . . "We got to get goin'." And the others came out of their numbness and moved toward the truck.

"Come on," Tom said. "Let's get Grampa on." Pa and Uncle John and Tom and Al went into the kitchen where Grampa slept. . . . They took him under the elbows and lifted him to his feet, and he grumbled and cursed thickly. . . . Out the door they boosted him, and when they came to the truck Tom and Al climbed up, . . . hooked their hands under his arms and lifted him gently up, and laid him on top of the load. . . .

They got into the cab, and then the rest swarmed up on top of the load. Connie and Rose of Sharon, Pa and Uncle John, Ruthie and Winfield, Tom and the preacher. Noah stood on the ground, looking up at the great load of them sitting on top of the truck. . . . Noah said, "How about the dogs, Pa?"

"I forgot the dogs," Pa said. He whistled shrilly, and one bouncing dog ran in, but only one. Noah caught him and threw him up on the top, where he sat rigid and shivering at the height. "Got to leave the other two," Pa called. "Muley, will you look after 'em some? See they don't starve?"

"Yeah," said Muley. "I'll like to have a couple dogs. Yeah! I'll take 'em."

"Take them chickens, too," Pa said.

Al got into the driver's seat. The starter whirred and caught. . . . And then the loose roar of the six cylinders and a blue smoke behind. "So long, Muley," Al called.

And the family called, "Good-by, Muley."

Understanding Literature

1. How do the Joads feel about leaving their farm?

2. How does John Steinbeck's *The Grapes of Wrath* reflect many people's everyday experiences during the Great Depression?

The Agricultural New Deal

In 1935 the federal government addressed some of the problems that migrant workers and tenant farmers faced. The Resettlement Administration (RA) helped farm laborers to resettle in areas with better land. In July 1937 the RA became part of the **Farm Security Administration** (FSA). The FSA was created to increase farm ownership. It issued long-term loans at low interest rates so tenants and sharecroppers could buy farms. The FSA also set up camps to provide shelter and medical care for migrant workers.

In addition, the FSA hired photographers and filmmakers to create a record of rural life. FSA photographer Dorothea Lange wanted to use her camera "to register the things about these people that were more important than how poor they were—their pride, their strength, their spirit." Lange's photograph *Migrant Mother* is one of the most famous images of the Great Depression.

Dorothea Lange's Migrant Mother *captures this woman's determination to survive the depression.*

Other FSA photographers included Margaret Bourke-White and Gordon Parks. Pare Lorentz produced two documentary films, *The Plow That Broke the Plains* and *The River,* that showed the need for New Deal agricultural programs.

Other New Deal agricultural reforms focused more on the land than the people who worked it. The Soil Conservation Act of 1935 encouraged farmers to use new grasses and crops. It also established rain-conservation programs to protect the soil. A second Agricultural Adjustment Act (AAA) was passed in 1938. It allowed for payments to farmers who voluntarily restricted the number of acres in use. The AAA also placed limits on the amount of certain goods that could be marketed. It provided for storage of surpluses and for loans to farmers based on the value of stored crops. By the late 1930s, the aims of the first and second AAA and other New Deal agricultural programs had been partly met.

SECTION 1 REVIEW

Identify and explain the significance of the following:
- **National Labor Relations Act**
- **Fair Labor Standards Act**
- **John L. Lewis**
- **Congress of Industrial Organizations**
- **sit-down strike**
- **Southern Tenant Farmers' Union**
- **Dust Bowl**
- **Farm Security Administration**
- **Dorothea Lange**

Locate and explain the importance of the following:
- **Great Plains**
- **Oklahoma**

Reading for Content Understanding

1 **Main Idea** How did the NLRA help unions?

2 **Main Idea** What new unions and labor strategies were developed in the 1930s?

3 **Geographic Diversity** *Human-Environment Interaction* How did farmers' practices contribute to the Dust Bowl?

4 **Writing** *Classifying* Imagine that you are a federal official sent to investigate the problems of farmers and farmworkers during the Great Depression. Describe the different situations of each group.

5 **Critical Thinking** *Evaluating* Look at the photograph *Migrant Mother.* Do you think this image helped the FSA achieve its goal of gaining sympathy for farmers' difficulties? Explain your answer.

Americans Face Hard Times

Reading Focus

How did the Great Depression affect families and women?

How did the New Deal affect American Indians?

What were the New Deal's efforts to help African Americans during the depression?

Key Terms

Indian Reorganization Act
Black Cabinet

*I*N THE DIFFICULT DAYS *of the fall of 1931, Freda Stallings gave birth to her third child, a boy. Unfortunately, her husband, Odie, had lost his job. Freda and Odie Stallings did everything they could to take care of their two older children and their new baby. Odie Stallings walked miles looking for work. He insulated their shack with newspapers. Freda and Odie often slept with their baby in between them to keep him warm. After one cold night they woke to find their infant son dead. With no money for a coffin, they buried him in a cardboard box.*

During the depression, homeless Americans took shelter wherever they could.

★ Family Life

During the Great Depression many Americans could not afford even the basic necessities of life—food, clothing, and shelter. For help, people often turned to their families. One person recalled that "the safety net was the big families. Even though you were unemployed, there was always somebody working, and the families somehow managed to hold together." Women tried to keep their households together with little income, often relying on the proverb "Use it up, wear it out, make it do, or do without."

Some men left their families and crisscrossed the country in search of jobs. Some never returned. Selma Hannish remembered that her father left home because he "didn't make seven dollars a month to pay the rent." Men who stayed with their families often found that their traditional role as the head of the household had changed. Some women replaced their husbands as their family's main economic support because they found it a little easier to get work. Many jobs traditionally held by women, such as clerical or service positions, were not as affected by the economic downturn as industrial jobs.

The Depression at Home and Abroad **453**

Frances Perkins

Born in 1882 in Boston, Massachusetts, Frances Perkins grew up in a middle-class family. She earned a degree from Mount Holyoke College in chemistry and physics. In her senior year, she heard Florence Kelley of the National Consumers' League speak. Perkins later said that Kelley "first opened my mind to the necessity for and the possibility of work which became my vocation."

As a social worker, Perkins held a variety of positions, including one with the National Consumers' League and one as New York's industrial commissioner. When President Roosevelt offered to appoint her as his secretary of labor, she hesitated. Then she remembered her grandmother's advice: "If anybody opens a door, one should always go through." During her 12 years as secretary of labor, Perkins gained the respect of labor leaders.

★ Women in the Depression

Many married working women faced public hostility. One magazine editor's solution to end the depression was: "Simply fire the women, who shouldn't be working anyway, and hire the men. Presto! No unemployment. . . . No depression." In some cases, the government discriminated against women. For example, 26 states introduced legislation to prohibit married women from working. The U.S. government decided that only one member of a family could work in the federal civil service. As a result, thousands of women resigned from the civil service because they generally earned less than their husbands.

Many relief programs covered only men or families, so the depression hit single women particularly hard. For example, in 1934 there were some 75,000 homeless, single women in New York City. With no shelters available to them, these women often rode the subways all night.

African American and Hispanic women also faced hardships. Many who held domestic service jobs lost them to white women who were now looking for work. The percentage of African American women with jobs fell more than 12 percent during the 1930s.

Some New Deal programs offered relief to women. The Works Progress Administration (WPA) employed large numbers of women. Two WPA teachers in San Antonio, Texas, wrote First Lady Eleanor Roosevelt:

 Just when all seemed lost . . . this Adult Educational Program came, providing us with a means of livelihood, a ladder up which we could climb again to patriotism and self-respect. "

In addition to helping women through New Deal programs, President Roosevelt appointed many women to important positions at the federal level. He appointed Frances Perkins secretary of labor and made Florence Allen the first female federal court judge. In 1933 Ruth Bryan Owen became the first American woman appointed to an important diplomatic position. Mary Dewson, head of the Women's Division of the Democratic National Committee, used her position to encourage more federal appointments for women.

★ New Programs for American Indians

For American Indians, the New Deal brought programs designed to improve tribal life. Indians suffered from the deepest and most widespread poverty of any group in the United States in the early 1930s. They had a short life expectancy and a death rate about twice that of the white population. Social worker and educator John Collier hoped to change these disturbing statistics.

Collier was appointed commissioner of the Bureau of Indian Affairs in 1933. He planned to reverse the Dawes Act and end what he called "a huge white land grab, . . . a blow, meant to be fatal, at Indian tribal existence." The **Indian Reorganization Act** (IRA) was passed in June 1934. It ended land allotment to individual Indians and allowed some lands to be returned to tribal ownership. The IRA also organized reservation tribes into self-governing bodies. The tribes had to write constitutions for their new governments and submit them to the federal government for approval.

Unlike previous treaties, the IRA required that Indian tribes vote to accept the act before it would go into effect. Many tribes rejected the legislation. The Navajo expressed a common sentiment: "We Indians don't think it is right for Collier to tell us we should govern ourselves, and then tell us how to do it." Other tribes felt differently:

❝We have been led by the white people for 122 years since the white people came into this country. . . . We have no voice in anything. . . . Let us try a new deal. It can not be any worse than what it has been.❞

More than 70 percent of the tribes voted to accept the IRA. This act restored some land to Indian tribes and generally improved the federal government's treatment of American Indians.

The signing of the Indian Reorganization Act

African Americans in the Depression

The Great Depression increased the economic problems of black workers. They typically had received lower wages than white workers. Poet Langston Hughes observed that "the depression brought everybody down a peg or two. And the Negroes had but a few pegs to fall."

New Deal Programs

Like women, African Americans were often the last ones hired and the first to be fired. African Americans worked in fields particularly hard hit by the depression. These industries included construction, lumber, unskilled manufacturing, and mining. Elmer Thomas, a black stockyard worker, argued that more African Americans lost their jobs because white laborers needed jobs. Thomas said, "They were hiring young, white boys, sixteen and eighteen years old, raw kids, didn't know a thing."

Hundreds of thousands of African Americans received relief and work from New Deal programs. In particular, the Federal Emergency Relief Administration and the Works Progress Administration offered aid. The Farm Security Administration began to employ some African Americans in supervisory positions. The aid many African Americans received from New Deal programs was more assistance than they had ever received from the federal government. Even the minimum WPA wages were much more than what many African Americans had been earning.

However, some African Americans said that the New Deal programs were discriminatory. Professor Ralph Bunche noted that for African Americans the New Deal meant "the same thing, but more of it." For example, black men in the Civilian Conservation Corps worked in units segregated from white men. The National Industrial Recovery Act (NIRA) established industrial codes that allowed employers to pay African Americans lower wages. In May 1935 President Roosevelt issued an executive order banning discrimination on WPA projects.

Roosevelt's Record

Roosevelt sought the advice of African American leaders on matters ranging from economics to education. He appointed so many African Americans to significant government positions that they made up an unofficial **Black Cabinet**. Members of the Black Cabinet such as Mary McLeod Bethune and Robert Weaver met informally to discuss how the government could help African Americans. At the group's first meeting, Bethune urged all present to "think in terms as a 'whole' for the greatest service of our people." Many members also advised the Democratic Party on issues important to African Americans.

Despite his efforts to include African Americans in New Deal programs, Roosevelt did not support a federal antilynching law introduced in 1935. The president feared political backlash from white southern Democrats. Roosevelt needed their support in order to get his New Deal legislation passed. As he explained privately to NAACP supporters of the bill:

" **I've got to get legislation passed by Congress to save America. . . . If I come out for the anti-lynching bill now, they [southern congressional leaders] will block every bill I ask Congress to pass to**

Mary McLeod Bethune urged the federal government to do more for African Americans during the depression.

keep America from collapsing. I just can't take that risk. "

Congress never passed the antilynching law. Nevertheless, Roosevelt received more than 75 percent of the African American vote in the 1936 presidential election. As one person explained, "It was not civil rights, it was jobs" that persuaded many African Americans to support Roosevelt.

First Lady Eleanor Roosevelt publicly supported minority rights. She and Bethune met regularly to discuss civil rights issues to bring to the president's attention. In 1939, members of the patriotic organization Daughters of the American Revolution (DAR) refused to allow Marian Anderson, a world-famous African American singer, to use their hall for a concert. The first lady resigned from the DAR in protest. With her support, Anderson performed at the Lincoln Memorial in March 1939 in front of 75,000 people. The concert was also broadcast nationwide. For many Americans, the event signified a bright spot. Bethune called it "a story of hope for tomorrow—a story of triumph—a story of pulling together—[a] story of splendor and real democracy."

SECTION 2 REVIEW

Identify and explain the significance of the following:
- **Mary Dewson**
- **Indian Reorganization Act**
- **Black Cabinet**
- **Mary McLeod Bethune**
- **Robert Weaver**
- **Marian Anderson**

Reading for Content Understanding

1 **Main Idea** What were the effects of the Great Depression on families and women?

2 **Main Idea** How did the Indian Reorganization Act change American Indian life?

3 **Cultural Diversity** How were African Americans affected by the New Deal?

4 **Writing** *Informing* Imagine that you are a reporter during the depression. Write an article noting how the depression and the New Deal changed living situations for a white farm family, an African American family, and an American Indian family.

5 **Critical Thinking** *Drawing Conclusions* Do you think President Roosevelt's appointment of women and African Americans to government positions helped them fight discrimination in society? Explain your answer.

SECTION 3

Arts and Entertainment

Reading Focus

How did the arts reflect Americans' experiences in the depression?

How did government programs help support the arts during the Great Depression?

How did Americans entertain themselves during the depression?

Key Terms

regionalists

swing

N 1931 PRESIDENT HERBERT HOOVER *was hoping to lift the spirits of Americans suffering through the Great Depression. "What the country needs is a good big laugh. There seems to be a condition of hysteria. If someone could get off a good joke every ten days I think our troubles would be over." Americans often turned to laughter during the depression to lighten their lives.*

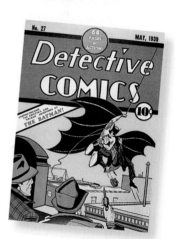

A May 1939 comic book featuring Batman

⭐ The Arts

Depression-era readers turned to detective stories and newly printed comic books to escape their woes. Superman, the Lone Ranger, Batman, and Wonder Woman all made their appearances in the 1930s. Popular magazines included *Family Circle, Life,* and *Time.*

Literature

Paperback books, designed to appeal to readers with limited budgets, were published in large quantities. The first ones cost 25 cents. One of the most popular books was Margaret Mitchell's novel *Gone With the Wind.* Many Americans left their own troubles behind and followed those of Scarlett O'Hara, the main character. In the best-seller, O'Hara, a once wealthy woman raised on a southern plantation, struggles to rebuild her family's fortune after the Civil War. Many readers identified with O'Hara's determination to triumph over hard times.

The pre–Civil War South was a popular setting for many other novels. William Faulkner created a mythical Mississippi county, Yoknapatawpha, to use as a setting for 14 novels and many short stories. From 1929 to 1942 Faulkner published

The Depression at Home and Abroad **457**

William Faulkner

eight novels, including *The Sound and the Fury* and *Absalom, Absalom!* His characters confront issues of plantation life, slavery, and the Civil War. One character asks a southerner to "tell about the South. What's it like there. What do they do there. Why do they live there." In 1950 Faulkner received a Nobel Prize in literature.

Poet Robert Frost wrote about rural New England. He received the Pulitzer Prize four times for his poetry. Laura Ingalls Wilder also wrote about regional issues. Between 1932 and 1942 Wilder published a series of books about her childhood, including *Little House in the Big Woods* and *Little House on the Prairie.* Readers enjoyed her tales of surviving blizzards, grasshopper plagues, illness, and debt.

Other authors, such as James T. Farrell and John Dos Passos, wrote about the economic and social troubles of the Great Depression. Writer James Agee and Farm Security Administration photographer Walker Evans lived with sharecroppers in Alabama for about six weeks in 1936. From their experiences, they produced a nonfiction account of the lives of three families in *Let Us Now Praise Famous Men.* These books helped Americans realize that others shared in their economic difficulties.

Depression-Era Painting

Some visual artists helped Americans become more aware of the beauty of their nation. Painters who sought inspiration from regional customs and folk themes became known as the **regionalists**. They included Thomas Hart Benton, John Steuart Curry, and Grant Wood. Benton explained that art for the regionalists meant "American life as known and felt by ordinary Americans." Benton and Wood painted scenes of rural people at work. Curry's subjects were often American folk legends and history.

Other well-known artists of the 1930s included Edward Hopper, who painted realistic scenes of urban life. Anna "Grandma" Moses, in her seventies during the 1930s, became famous for painting images of what she called "old-timey" farm life.

Helping Artists

Unemployment hit actors, dancers, and other artists particularly hard. Critic Malcolm Cowley commented, "If we want to have poets in this country, we will have to keep them alive." One artist sent a plea to the government: "Kind of work: will accept any position. Salary: Enough to make a living on. At Present: Broke." The Roosevelt administration created several programs to help artists.

Federal arts projects, like the Works Progress Administration's Federal Project One, allowed many artists to continue practicing their craft. As writer Ralph Ellison noted, "Actually to be *paid* for writing . . . why that was a wonderful thing!" John Steinbeck wrote *The Grapes of Wrath* based on his Federal Writers' Project experiences. Richard Wright published an essay in a WPA collection of writings that provided the basis for his autobiographical work *Black Boy.* Painters, including Jacob Lawrence, used WPA-sponsored workshops and training to learn and improve their art. Lawrence later produced paintings of famous African Americans. The WPA's success guaranteed future generations of artists.

Grant Wood's painting American Gothic *reflects the hardworking spirit of many farm families.*

★ Moving Music

When many Americans wanted to be entertained, they listened to music. Jazz remained popular during the Great Depression. Count Basie, Duke Ellington, Benny Goodman, and other big-band leaders helped develop a new style of jazz called **swing**. Fletcher Henderson was an important composer and arranger of swing music. Swing musicians played in groups larger than most jazz groups in the 1920s. Swing also involved more written music than spontaneous compositions.

Bandleader Duke Ellington (front left) successfully blended the sounds and talents of his musicians.

The term *swing* became commonly used after Ellington's hit "It Don't Mean a Thing (If It Ain't Got That Swing)" was recorded in February 1932. Millions of Americans forgot their troubles, at least briefly, while dancing to the fast-paced rhythms of swing music. Swing dancers became known as jitterbugs. Goodman, who was called the King of Swing, described the dancers as

 bugs, literally glued to the music, [who] would shake. . . . Their eyes popped, their heads pecked, their feet tapped out the time, arms jerked to the rhythm. 〞

At the height of the swing craze, many people seemed to be trying to dance their cares away.

Americans also drew inspiration and comfort from gospel, a traditional church-based form of African American music. Gospel developed from spirituals, jazz, and blues music. Singers Mahalia Jackson and Sister Rosetta Tharpe were among the best-known gospel artists of the time. They helped the music gain a wider group of listeners.

Folk music, particularly the work of singer and songwriter Woody Guthrie, was also very popular. Born in Oklahoma, Guthrie traveled and performed throughout the country during the depression. He often sang in migrant-worker camps in California. His songs were tales of loss and struggle. One song contained the line, "All along your green valley I'll work till I die"—a sad reality for some Americans.

★ Movies and Radio

Many Americans also watched movies and listened to radio programs to escape the Great Depression. Despite the economic hard times, growing numbers of Americans found the money to buy movie tickets and radios. One theater owner explained that audiences wanted "the type of picture that lifts people into a happy world." They did not want "serious and sad pictures— they have too much of that at home!"

Movies

Moviegoers watched cartoons, comedies, gangster films, and westerns. The Marx Brothers' comedies made Americans laugh. Many others were amazed by Walt Disney's first full-length animated feature, *Snow White and the Seven Dwarfs*. Musicals also became popular as producers mastered the talkie. Dancers Fred Astaire and Ginger Rogers began their long-time association in the film *Flying Down to Rio*. Other popular movie stars included James Cagney, Marlene Dietrich, Greta Garbo, James Stewart, and John Wayne.

Fred Astaire and Ginger Rogers danced together in many movies.

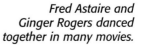
The Granger Collection, New York

The Depression at Home and Abroad **459**

Many Americans bought Shirley Temple dolls like this one made in the 1930s.

Katharine Hepburn also made her first movie appearance in the 1930s. She won an Academy Award for Best Actress in 1934 for her role in *Morning Glory*. She became one of the nation's greatest actors. She received a fourth Academy Award in 1982 at the age of 75.

Child actor Shirley Temple was the top box-office draw in Hollywood from 1935 to 1938. Most of her movies earned more than $5 million each. In 1934 she appeared in her first starring role, *Stand Up and Cheer*. She was only five years old. Temple danced and sang in many more movies.

Dorothy's ruby-red slippers

One of the most popular movies of all time, the screen version of *Gone With the Wind*, was released in December 1939. Depression-weary crowds wanted to believe Scarlett O'Hara as she vowed, "I'm going to live through this and when it's all over, I'll never be hungry again!" The *Wizard of Oz* was another popular movie released that year. It told the story of Dorothy, a young girl swept away by a tornado from her home in Kansas. She ended up in the magical land of Oz, where she met many interesting characters.

Despite the great economic difficulties of the 1930s, each week an estimated 90 million Americans scraped together the 25 to 35 cents needed for a ticket to the movies. By September 1939 there were some 17,000 movie theaters in more than 9,000 towns. That meant there

Gone With the Wind made Clark Gable and Vivien Leigh international movie stars.

was one cinema seat on average for every 12 Americans.

Radio

Even more Americans listened to radio programs. As many as 97 million Americans, out of a population of almost 129 million, listened to a family-owned radio in 1938. By the 1930s there were many popular radio series, including comedies such as *The Jack Benny Show,* mysteries like *The Shadow,* and soap operas like *The Guiding Light.* Soap operas got their name from the fact that so many of the original advertising sponsors were soap companies.

Listeners also tuned in regularly to shows such as *Little Orphan Annie* and *The Lone Ranger.* Will Rogers hosted a popular radio show during the early days of the depression. On one program he joked about one cause of the depression—installment buying: "We'll show the world we are prosperous, even if we have to go broke to do it."

On the night of October 30, 1938, many radio listeners heard their program cut off by a special "news" bulletin. The "correspondent" sobbed,

> " Ladies and gentleman, this is the most terrifying thing I have ever witnessed. . . . There, I can see the thing's body. It's large as a bear and it glistens like wet leather. . . . The eyes are black and gleam like a serpent. "

Listeners heard that strange vehicles were landing in New Jersey and that martians were coming out of them. CBS had said at the beginning of the program that the show was fictional. However, many listeners tuned in late and panicked. One man recalled, "I don't know what I did exactly, but I know I prayed harder and more earnest than ever before." The panic created by Orson Welles's *War of the Worlds* radio production was one demonstration of the influence of radio.

Spectator Sports

The popularity of radio helped some spectator sports survive during the Great Depression. In the early 1930s attendance at sporting events fell. However, fans kept up with their favorite teams by listening to their games on the radio. When the economy improved, fans went back to the ball parks. Minor league and Negro League baseball attracted more people to their games by offering something new. They began to play games at night, when more people could attend.

Baseball stars of the 1930s included Dizzy Dean, Lou Gehrig, and Satchel Paige. Gehrig, known as the Iron Horse, played in 2,130 consecutive games. His streak, which started in 1925, ended 14 years later. Two months after his retirement, the New York Yankees honored Gehrig. He was dying from a rare muscle disease. He told the crowd:

"Fans, for the past two weeks you have been reading about a bad break I got.

New York Yankee manager Joe McCarthy (right) presents Lou Gehrig (left) with a trophy on "Lou Gehrig Day."

Yet today I consider myself the luckiest man on the face of the earth."

Many other athletes made their mark in the 1930s. Helen Wills continued to dominate women's tennis. Mildred "Babe" Didrikson Zaharias conquered almost all other women's sports. She played basketball and won Olympic medals in the javelin and hurdle events. Zaharias then turned to playing golf, where she was also successful. She said her childhood ambition "was to be the greatest athlete who ever lived."

African American track star Jesse Owens challenged Didrikson for that title. Owens was a sprinter and long jumper. On a single day in 1935, he broke five world records and tied one. The next year at the 1936 Olympic Games in Berlin, Germany, Owens won four gold medals. For many Americans, watching these athletes was a wonderful escape from their problems during the depression.

SECTION 3 REVIEW

Identify and explain the significance of the following:

- **Margaret Mitchell**
- **William Faulkner**
- **regionalists**
- **Thomas Hart Benton**
- **Duke Ellington**
- **Benny Goodman**
- **swing**
- **Woody Guthrie**
- **Shirley Temple**
- **Lou Gehrig**
- **Mildred Didrikson Zaharias**
- **Jesse Owens**

Reading for Content Understanding

1 **Main Idea** In what ways did artists focus on American life during the Great Depression?

2 **Main Idea** What forms of entertainment did Americans turn to in the 1930s?

3 **Economic Development** How did government programs support artists during the depression?

4 **Writing** *Expressing* Imagine that you are a folk singer like Woody Guthrie. Write the lyrics for a song that expresses how the depression has affected you.

5 **Critical Thinking** *Evaluating* What role do you think art and entertainment should play during a national economic crisis? Explain your answer in a brief paragraph.

SECTION 4

The Depression Abroad

Reading Focus

How did the Good Neighbor policy differ from previous U.S. foreign policies toward Latin America?

Why did dictators rise to power in certain European nations?

How did the United States respond to events in Europe and Asia in the 1930s?

Key Terms

Good Neighbor policy

totalitarianism

Blackshirts

fascism

Nazis

Axis Powers

Kristallnacht

Neutrality Acts

I N 1930 MANY COFFEE FARMERS *in the tiny Central American country of El Salvador decided not to pick their crop. According to one observer, "The country became permeated [filled] with the sick-sweet smell of rotting coffee fruits." There was nothing wrong with the crop. In fact, coffee was one of the country's main crops and sources of income. The berries were left to rot because the price of coffee was so low that harvesting the crop was not worth the farmers' time or money.*

Coffee beans

⭐ The Depression in Latin America

The Great Depression took a heavy toll on the people and governments of Latin America. The situation in El Salvador was typical of many Latin American countries. As a U.S. diplomat explained:

❝ **Roughly 90 percent of the wealth of the country is held by about one-half of one percent of the population. . . . The [rest of the] population has practically nothing.** ❞

President Roosevelt's Latin American policy was to make the United States a "good neighbor— the neighbor who . . . respects the rights of others—the neighbor who respects his obligations and . . . his agreements." As part of his **Good Neighbor policy**, Roosevelt recognized that the United States "cannot merely take, but must also give." The Good Neighbor policy included a plan to increase economic aid to the nations of Latin America. The U.S. government also negotiated new trade agreements with many Latin American countries. For many of these countries, the United States was their most important trading partner.

For Roosevelt, the Good Neighbor policy also meant respecting the borders of Latin American nations and following a course of nonintervention. In 1934 the Roosevelt administration nullified the Platt Amendment. The United States had used this law to intervene in Cuban affairs. Roosevelt also withdrew U.S. Marines who had been stationed in Haiti.

In 1938 Mexican president Lázaro Cárdenas put Mexico's oil industry under national control. The Roosevelt administration refused to intervene on behalf of U.S. companies. Roosevelt recognized that Mexico had the right to control its own resources. After negotiations, Mexico agreed to pay the oil companies for their property. Roosevelt's nonintervention policy, along with increased trade and cultural exchanges, improved U.S. relations with Latin America.

Soviet posters supporting Stalin and his policies

★ Dictators in Europe

Overseas, Europeans faced the enormous task of rebuilding their shattered nations. Debts from World War I still burdened European economies when the Great Depression struck. Nations took a variety of approaches to handling the economic disaster. For example, Great Britain raised tariffs and focused on increasing domestic production. Its government remained relatively stable. However, other nations experienced political turmoil. Several countries moved toward **totalitarianism**. In this political system, the government controls every aspect of citizens' lives.

The Soviet Union

The Soviet Union had experienced economic and political troubles for years. In the late 1920s, Soviet leader Joseph Stalin introduced a Five-Year Plan. It called for the rapid industrialization of the economy, particularly in heavy industries such as iron and steel and in machinery.

Stalin also forced farmers and peasants to give up their land to work on collectives—large government-owned farms. At the time, some 80 percent of the nation's people worked on farms. If farmers refused to give up their land, Soviet officials had them killed or deported to Siberia. Several million Soviets died as a result of the Soviet policy of forced collectivization. By 1935 more than 90 percent of the country's land was organized into collectives.

Stalin's totalitarian government increasingly controlled every aspect of people's lives. According to one young Communist, "All you heard about day and night was Stalin." Stalin closed churches and had his political opponents killed. Few people knew details of what Stalin and his supporters were doing. As a result, many foreigners were impressed by Stalin's economic plan. The Soviet Union industrialized while much of the rest of the Western world suffered from the depression. The U.S. government, which had withheld official recognition since 1917, formally recognized the Soviet Union in November 1933.

Italy

Elsewhere in Europe, many Italians were bitter that their country had not received new territory in return for its efforts during World War I. Suffering from economic difficulties after the war, many Italians began to look for strong leadership. They found it in former journalist and soldier Benito Mussolini.

During the 1920s Benito Mussolini and his supporters used force to gain power in Italy.

In 1922 Mussolini and his followers threatened to march on Rome. His supporters were known as **Blackshirts** after the color of their uniforms. Soon after, the Italian king gave Mussolini temporary dictatorial powers, which ended up lasting more than two decades. Mussolini's government was based on the political theory of **fascism**. This theory calls for a strong government headed by one individual. In fascist systems, the state—or government—is seen as more important than individuals. In accordance with this belief, the state has the duty to limit or destroy all opposition.

In October 1935 Mussolini expanded Italy's territory by invading the African nation of Ethiopia. Under Emperor Haile Selassie (HY-lee suh-LAS-ee), the Ethiopian forces fought bravely. However, they could not defend themselves against the modern weaponry of the Italian army. Italy quickly conquered Ethiopia and made it a colony. The League of Nations responded with penalties but lacked the authority to enforce them. The United States remained neutral during the conflict.

 ## Germany

Many Germans felt particularly bitter about the outcome of World War I. The Treaty of Versailles required Germany to pay war reparations, which crippled its economy. The Great Depression brought about its near collapse. Amid this suffering, war veteran and politician Adolf Hitler rose to power.

Hitler offered Germans a scapegoat, or someone to blame for problems. He had outlined his theories in *Mein Kampf (My Struggle)*. He wrote this book while in prison for attempting to overthrow the German government. In *Mein Kampf*, Hitler blamed intellectuals, Communists, and particularly Jews for Germany's defeat in World War I and its postwar problems. *Mein Kampf* also presented Hitler's plan for Germany's rise to regional and global power.

Hitler quickly gained a large following. In 1932 his National Socialist Party, or **Nazis**, won around 37 percent of the vote in national elections. The next year, Hitler became the chancellor of Germany. He soon seized absolute power and became a fascist dictator. He also established the Third Reich, an aggressive new German empire.

The Nazis used large, showy parades to encourage feelings of national pride and gain support.

Hitler reduced Germany's unemployment and became more popular. Between March 1933 and March 1934, unemployment fell by more than 2 million. State spending helped many groups recover from the depression. German farmers, for example, received guaranteed prices for their produce. The government also funded housing and highway construction projects. One German woman who was a teenager during Hitler's rise to power explained his appeal:

“ **He promised us . . . that Germany would once again take its place in the world as a state worthy of respect. . . . So this man was not only admired but welcomed.** ”

Many Germans also found work in weapons factories. Hitler violated the Treaty of Versailles by rebuilding Germany's military and by moving to occupy the Rhineland, a border region in western Germany.

Hitler's plans included a campaign against Jews. The Nazis banned Jews and non-Nazis from government positions, and destroyed or seized their property. In September 1935 the government assigned Jews a lower class of citizenship. Despite these actions, Germany's capital city, Berlin, remained the site of the 1936 Olympic Games. During the Games, the German government tried to hide the evidence of its discrimination against Jews. Germany's economic accomplishments during a depression impressed many of the thousands of people in attendance at the Games.

After the Olympics, the German government returned to its plan for world domination. In October 1936 Germany and Italy formed a military alliance, the **Axis Powers**. In late 1936 Germany entered into a similar agreement with Japan.

The German government also revived many of its anti-Jewish activities, such as expelling Jews from all professions and from studying in universities. Jews faced increasing hardship and isolation, but the majority of them did not want to leave Germany. The Nazis, however, attempted to drive them out. On November 9, 1938, Nazis went on a rampage called **Kristallnacht**, or the "night of broken glass." On *Kristallnacht*, Nazi mobs killed more than 90 Jews and seriously injured hundreds more. As one Jew remembered:

> " **Yesterday the synagogues burned. They burned in Germany. They burned in Austria. They burned in Czechoslovakia. . . . Most Jewish business was demolished. My synagogue was plundered [robbed].** "

The crowds demolished some 7,500 Jewish businesses and burned or destroyed nearly 200 synagogues. Violence against Jews spread throughout Germany and Austria. After *Kristallnacht* the Nazi persecution of Jews increased dramatically.

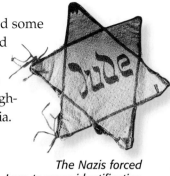

The Nazis forced Jews to wear identification patches on their clothing.

★ Civil War in Spain

As fascism spread through Italy and Germany, fascists also threatened to take over Spain's republican government. In July 1936 General Francisco Franco led a revolt that began three years of warfare. Germany and Italy provided Franco and his troops with military assistance. The Republicans received supplies from France, Mexico, and the Soviet Union.

Global Connections

The Spanish Civil War

The brutality of the Spanish Civil War attracted international attention. One particular event became representative of the war's viciousness. On April 26, 1937, a squadron of German aircraft flew over the tiny Spanish town of Guernica. The town hardly seemed an important strategic area. It had only one weapons plant and one bridge that might have been important for troop movement.

Nevertheless, German fighter planes bombed the town for three hours. It was market day in Guernica, so the town's population had swelled to around 10,000. More than 1,600 people were killed, and 800 others were wounded in the attack. About the only parts of the town left untouched by the bombing were the munitions plant and the bridge.

The horror of this event stunned people worldwide. The story of the town's slaughter became the focus of Spanish painter Pablo Picasso's *Guernica.* One of the most famous modern paintings, *Guernica* was displayed at the 1937 Paris World Exhibition. The painting hung in New York City's Museum of Modern Art until 1981. At Picasso's request, the museum returned the painting to Spain once democracy had been restored there.

Understanding What You Read

1. Why were so many people horrified by the events in Guernica?

2. Why do you think Pablo Picasso wanted his painting returned to Spain after democracy was restored?

Many people saw the Spanish Civil War as part of a struggle to contain fascism. About 40,000 foreigners, including some 2,800 Americans, volunteered to fight with the Republicans against Franco. Novelist Ernest Hemingway drew on his experience there as a war correspondent to write *For Whom the Bell Tolls,* published in 1940. In this novel, an American character explained the importance of fighting in the war: "You believe in Life, Liberty, and the Pursuit of Happiness. . . . If this war is lost all of those things are lost."

In the spring of 1939, Republican forces disbanded. Franco's troops entered Madrid, Spain's capital, and Franco became dictator. An estimated 500,000 soldiers and civilians had died during the war.

 ## Japan's Military Expansion

On the other side of the world, Japan also used military force to solve its economic problems. Japan's military leaders wanted to seize new territories to take control of their natural resources. They hoped to reduce Japan's reliance on foreign imports. In September 1931 Japan invaded Manchuria, in northern China. The League of Nations and the United States condemned the invasion, but neither wanted to fight a war to oppose it. By 1937 Japan occupied much of northern China.

Japan also began a massive naval buildup, which violated its pledge given at the Washington Conference in the early 1920s. The buildup upset the balance of power in the Pacific.

Japanese Expansion, 1931–1938

Learning from Maps Japan's military leaders believed that conquering neighboring lands would solve their country's economic problems.

Place What important Chinese cities had Japan captured by 1938?

On December 12, 1937, Japan tested the U.S. commitment to isolationism. Japanese planes destroyed the *Panay*, a U.S. gunboat, killing 2 people and wounding 30 others. President Roosevelt demanded an apology, payment for damages, and a guarantee against future incidents. In a letter dated December 16, Roosevelt wrote about the United States: "this nation wants peace." Japan's government agreed to the terms. The United States had avoided war for the moment.

 ## Roosevelt's Response

President Roosevelt tried to maintain a balance between stopping aggression and keeping the United States out of war. Many Americans favored a policy of isolationism. They wanted the government to focus on domestic economic problems and not on international affairs. In the late 1930s Congress passed four **Neutrality Acts** to keep the nation out of international incidents. The first act, passed in 1935, prohibited the U.S. government from shipping arms to nations at war. Later neutrality acts extended the ban to include groups involved in civil wars.

Some Americans wanted to stop the expansion of Germany, Italy, and Japan. By October 1937,

The Granger Collection, New York

Japan's aggression and refusal to honor its agreements are pictured in this 1931 cartoon.

Roosevelt had begun to believe that the growing aggression of these nations required action. He warned "that the epidemic of world lawlessness is spreading." Roosevelt saw war as a disease that must be contained to prevent further infection. Many Americans, however, still favored isolationism and were upset by Roosevelt's speech. They hoped that an isolationist policy would keep the government's focus on improving the U.S. economy.

SECTION 4 REVIEW

Identify and explain the significance of the following:

- **Good Neighbor policy**
- **totalitarianism**
- **Joseph Stalin**
- **Benito Mussolini**
- **Blackshirts**
- **fascism**
- **Adolf Hitler**
- **Nazis**
- **Axis Powers**
- ***Kristallnacht***
- **Neutrality Acts**

Locate and explain the importance of the following:

- **Japan**
- **Manchuria**

Reading for Content Understanding

1 Main Idea How did President Roosevelt change U.S. policy in Latin America?

2 Main Idea How did the United States respond to the territorial aggressions of Germany, Italy, and Japan?

3 Global Relations What brought dictators to power in Europe during the Great Depression?

4 Writing *Persuading* Imagine that you are an American living during the Great Depression. Write a letter to Congress persuading its members to pass the Neutrality Acts.

5 Critical Thinking *Making Comparisons* Compare the leadership styles and goals of Joseph Stalin, Benito Mussolini, and Adolf Hitler.

CHAPTER 15 REVIEW

Chapter Summary

The Great Depression was a period of tremendous suffering for Americans and others around the world. The New Deal strengthened the position of organized labor. For farmers, African Americans, American Indians, and women, the New Deal had a more mixed record. Americans turned to new and old forms of entertainment during the 1930s. In some foreign nations, the depression led to the rise of dictators. ■

On a separate sheet of paper, complete the following activities.

Identifying People and Ideas

Describe the historical significance of the following:

1. John L. Lewis
2. sit-down strike
3. Dust Bowl
4. Dorothea Lange
5. Indian Reorganization Act
6. regionalists
7. William Faulkner
8. totalitarianism
9. Joseph Stalin
10. Nazis

Internet Activity

go.hrw.com
SB1 Great Depression

Search the Internet through the HRW Web site to find information about the Great Depression. Use the information to create a script for a play showing the difficulties one family might have faced.

Understanding Main Ideas

1. How did the New Deal respond to the needs of African Americans?
2. In what ways did organized labor change during the 1930s?
3. What forms of entertainment did Americans enjoy during the Great Depression?
4. How did families cope with the effects of the depression?
5. How did the lives of some women change during the 1930s?
6. In what ways did the United States respond to international events in the 1930s?

Reviewing Themes

1. **Economic Development** How did the New Deal help farmers and artists?
2. **Cultural Diversity** How did the Great Depression affect American Indians and Mexican migrant workers?
3. **Global Relations** How did the governments of Germany and Italy change in the 1930s?

Using the Time Line

Number your paper from 1 to 5. Match the letters on the time line below with the following events.

1. **Congress passes the Indian Reorganization Act.**
2. **Nazis attack Jews and Jewish properties in Germany on *Kristallnacht*.**
3. **Italian forces attack Ethiopia.**
4. **A sit-down strike begins that will virtually shut down General Motors.**
5. **Japanese troops attack the northern Chinese region of Manchuria.**

1929   1931   1933   1935   1937   1939

a   b   c   d   e

Thinking Critically

1. **Drawing Conclusions** How might poor economic conditions lead to dictatorship?
2. **Evaluating** Why did African Americans support the New Deal, even though some of its programs discriminated against them?
3. **Synthesizing Information** Was the New Deal successful? Explain your answer.

Writing About History

1. **Informing** Imagine that you are a radio announcer in the 1930s. Provide reviews to your listeners of the movies that are playing in theaters.
2. **Creating** Imagine that you are a WPA writer. Create a short story about your experiences during the depression.

Linking Geography and History

1. **Region** What was President Roosevelt's Latin American policy during the depression?
2. **Human-Environment Interaction** How did farmers' practices contribute to soil erosion in the Dust Bowl?

Building Your Portfolio

Complete the following activities individually or in groups.

1. **Feeding the Hungry** Imagine that you are a farmer during the Great Depression. You have crops to sell, but you cannot afford to ship them to market. People in cities need food but cannot afford to buy it. Propose a New Deal program that will get food to the hungry and income to the farmers. Create a proposal for Congress using visuals and an oral or written report.

2. **Movies and the Great Depression** Imagine that you are a movie producer in the 1930s who wants to create a short film that focuses on a well-known person from the era. Your subject can be from any field, such as government, sports, or entertainment. Your movie can be a documentary, a fictional account of his or her life, or a musical. Create a script and visuals for your film. You may want to perform or videotape your movie for the class.

History Skills Workshop

Using Primary Sources Mexican American César Chávez and his family were migrant workers during the Great Depression. Read the excerpt to the right, which is Chávez's recollection of his life during the depression. Then answer the following questions: (a) Why did Chávez sometimes miss school? (b) How did Chávez's family try to stay alive one winter? (c) How do you think their experiences compare to those of other families during the depression?

> ❝We all of us climbed into an old Chevy that my dad had. And then we were in California, and [were] migratory workers. . . . Well, it was a strange life. . . . When we moved to California, we would work after school. Sometimes we wouldn't go [to school]. 'Following the crops,' we missed much school. Trying to get enough money to stay alive the following winter, the whole family picking apricots, walnuts, prunes. We were pretty new, we had never been migratory workers. We were taken advantage of quite a bit by the labor contractor.❞

The Global Depression

Although it began in the United States, the Great Depression soon became a global economic disaster. The economies of many countries were badly shaken. Industrial production fell, millions of people lost their jobs, and many people lost their entire life savings.

As the depression deepened, countries' economies continued to shrink. Unemployment rates skyrocketed, affecting nearly a fourth of the workforce in some industrial nations. *In the United States, more than 20 percent of the labor force was out of work by 1932. The average amount of money people earned was cut nearly in half.*

In the United States and other countries, governments increased spending to help the unemployed and the poor. Nevertheless, the depression did not end until World War II. Wartime production increased employment as people produced military supplies and other goods to support their country's war effort. ■

A World in Crisis

Many countries saw their gross national product (GNP)—the total value of all goods and services produced by a country in one year—fall dramatically during the depression. In addition, unemployment rates soared.

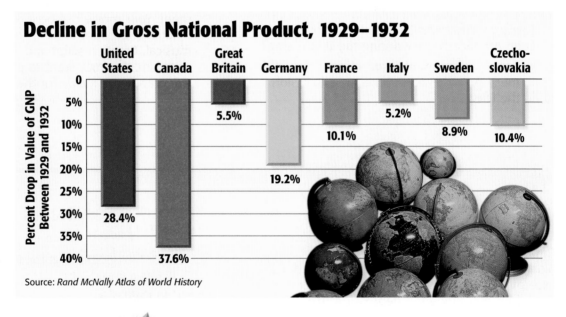

Decline in Gross National Product, 1929–1932

Country	Percent Drop in Value of GNP Between 1929 and 1932
United States	28.4%
Canada	37.6%
Great Britain	5.5%
Germany	19.2%
France	10.1%
Italy	5.2%
Sweden	8.9%
Czechoslovakia	10.4%

Source: *Rand McNally Atlas of World History*

Geography Skills
Reading Bar Graphs

1. Which country's GNP declined the most between 1929 and 1932?
2. Which country's GNP declined the least during that period?
3. How much did the U.S. GNP fall between 1929 and 1932?

Effects of the Depression

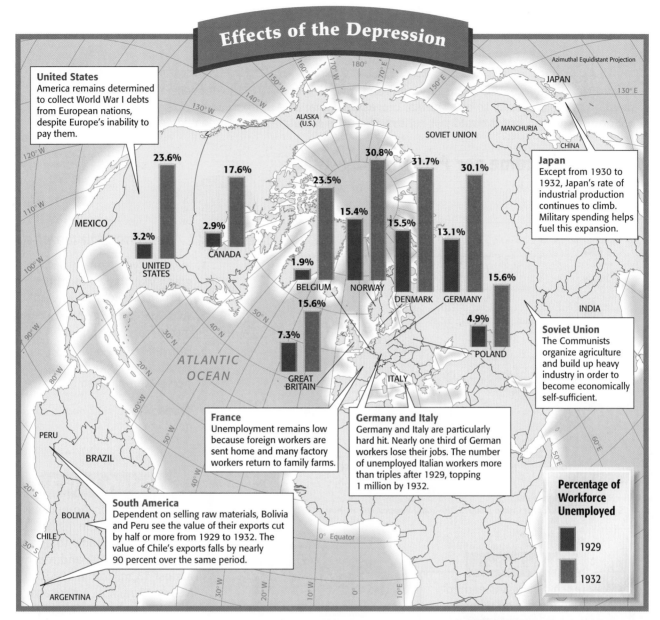

United States
America remains determined to collect World War I debts from European nations, despite Europe's inability to pay them.

Japan
Except from 1930 to 1932, Japan's rate of industrial production continues to climb. Military spending helps fuel this expansion.

Soviet Union
The Communists organize agriculture and build up heavy industry in order to become economically self-sufficient.

France
Unemployment remains low because foreign workers are sent home and many factory workers return to family farms.

Germany and Italy
Germany and Italy are particularly hard hit. Nearly one third of German workers lose their jobs. The number of unemployed Italian workers more than triples after 1929, topping 1 million by 1932.

South America
Dependent on selling raw materials, Bolivia and Peru see the value of their exports cut by half or more from 1929 to 1932. The value of Chile's exports falls by nearly 90 percent over the same period.

Azimuthal Equidistant Projection

- UNITED STATES: 3.2%, 23.6%
- CANADA: 2.9%, 17.6%
- BELGIUM: 1.9%, 23.5%
- NORWAY: 15.4%, 30.8%
- DENMARK: 15.5%, 31.7%
- GERMANY: 13.1%, 30.1%
- POLAND: 4.9%, 15.6%
- GREAT BRITAIN: 7.3%, 15.6%

Percentage of Workforce Unemployed
- 1929
- 1932

Geography **Skills**
Reading Special-Purpose Maps

1. In which three countries was more than 30 percent of the workforce jobless by 1932?

2. How were some South American countries affected by the depression?

3. Which country saw the greatest increase in its percentage of unemployed between 1929 and 1932?

4. How did Japan increase its rate of industrial production during the depression?

While traveling around Britain in search of work, this man lived in this mobile home he built.

The Depression in the United States

In addition to increasing unemployment and lowering the GNP, the depression left people with less money to buy things. Increased government spending helped the economy recover, but it could not relieve all of the country's economic problems.

Average Income per Person, 1929–1940

Dollars / Year

Source: *Datapedia of the United States, 1790–2000: America Year by Year*

Geography Skills
Reading Line Graphs

1. In which year shown on this graph was the average income per person highest? lowest?
2. What happened to the average income per person in 1939?
3. Between 1933 and 1939, in which year was income per person the highest?

History Note 2

About 1.5 million Americans were out of work in 1929. That number grew rapidly to about 12 million in 1932 and reached almost 13 million in 1933. Nearly 10 million Americans were still out of work when World War II broke out in Europe in 1939. During World War II, millions of American civilians found jobs in factories and plants producing war goods.

History Note 1

How much Americans earned largely depended on where they lived. Workers in the Lower South, for example, generally earned far less than the national average in 1929. This remained true a decade later. On average, Mississippians earned about $216 each in 1940—about one third of the national average of $593 a year. The average worker in Alabama, Arkansas, and South Carolina earned about $300 or less in 1940. Those four states also had the lowest average personal income levels in 1929.

Some unemployed workers earned money selling apples on street corners.

Growth in Federal Spending, 1928–1940

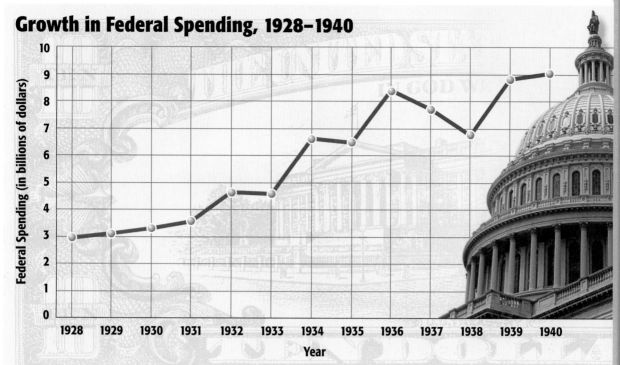

Federal Spending (in billions of dollars)

Year

Source: *Historical Statistics of the United States*

Geography Skills
Reading Line Graphs

1. About how much more did the U.S. government spend in 1940 than it did in 1929?
2. What happened to U.S. government spending in 1937 and 1938? in 1939?

History Note 3

Under President Franklin D. Roosevelt's New Deal programs, the federal government gradually spent more money each year to pull the country out of the depression. The unemployment rate did drop—from about 25 percent in 1933 to some 14 percent in 1937—but not as much as was necessary to pull the nation out of the depression. The economy weakened again in 1937 and 1938, causing unemployment to rise and contributing to still higher federal spending.

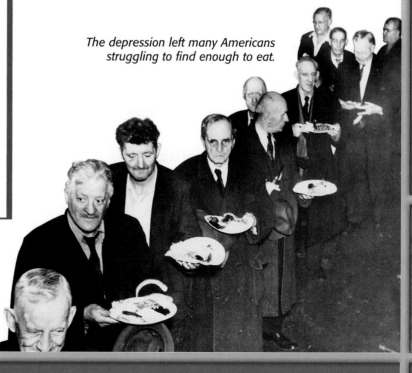

The depression left many Americans struggling to find enough to eat.

NEW YOR

The Granger Collection, New York

◼ CHAPTER 16 ◼
World War II
(1938–1945)

Just past 7:00 A.M. on Sunday, December 7, 1941, two U.S. soldiers were operating a radar station on the Hawaiian island of Oahu. They noticed "something completely out of the ordinary." A large formation of airplanes appeared to be headed their way. Within an hour, almost 200 Japanese warplanes attacked U.S. battleships anchored at Pearl Harbor. More than 2,300 U.S. soldiers and sailors were killed. Soon after, the United States entered World War II.

THEMES

Citizenship and Democracy
How might involvement in a foreign war affect people's rights?

Economic Development
What effect might fighting a war have on a nation's economy?

Global Relations
Why might a nation become involved in a war on another continent?

1938

1939

1940

1941

SEPT. 1938
The Munich Conference takes place.

SEPT. 1939
Germany invades Poland.

MAR. 1941
Congress passes the Lend-Lease Act.

DEC. 1941
Japanese planes attack Pearl Harbor.

World War II Begins

Reading Focus

What parts of Europe did Germany conquer by mid-1940?

How did President Roosevelt aid Britain while preserving U.S. neutrality?

What events led to the conflict between the United States and Japan?

Key Terms

Munich Conference

appeasement

nonaggression pact

Allied Powers

Blitzkrieg

Maginot Line

Battle of Britain

Lend-Lease Act

Battle of the Atlantic

Atlantic Charter

ON THE NIGHT OF AUGUST 31, 1939, *a group of special German troops attacked a radio station in the German town of Gleiwitz (GLY-vits) on the Polish border. Their mission was to stage an "incident" that the German government could use to justify an invasion of Poland. To make the Poles look responsible for the attack, the Germans dressed several convicted criminals in Polish military uniforms, shot them, and left the bodies at the station. Within hours, German forces began streaming across the Polish border in retaliation for the "attack." The incident at Gleiwitz helped trigger a war that would soon spread around the world.*

German soldiers chop down a border gate between Germany and Poland on the first day of the invasion.

IMAGE ON LEFT PAGE: *The USS* Shaw *explodes in Pearl Harbor after being bombed by Japanese planes.*

1942

1943

1944

1945

FEB. 1942 The U.S. government decides to intern Japanese Americans.

JULY 1943 Allied forces invade Sicily.

JUNE 1944 The D-Day invasion takes place.

MAY 1945 Germany surrenders.

AUG. 1945 The United States drops atomic bombs on Japan.

SEPT. 1945 Japan surrenders.

Hitler's War Machine

In 1935, two years after Adolf Hitler became chancellor of Germany, he launched a massive program to rebuild the country's military. Hitler had long dreamed of revenge for Germany's defeat in World War I. He began in 1936 by sending German troops to reoccupy the Rhineland, a demilitarized zone established by the Treaty of Versailles. Two years later, Hitler forced Austria to unite with Germany.

Many nations were still focused on their own economic problems from the Great Depression and ignored these actions. However, in 1938 Hitler drew the world's attention. He demanded that Czechoslovakia turn over the Sudetenland (soo-DAYT-uhn-land)—an area with many ethnic Germans—to Germany. The Czechs refused the demand, and Hitler threatened war. French and British leaders met with Hitler at the **Munich Conference**, held in September 1938. In an act of **appeasement**—giving in to an aggressor to preserve peace—they persuaded the Czechs to surrender the Sudetenland. Hitler promised this was "the last territorial claim I have to make in Europe." Upon hearing of the appeasement, British admiral Winston Churchill said, "The government had to choose between shame and war. They have chosen shame. They will get war."

Hitler seized the rest of Czechoslovakia in March 1939. He then demanded that Poland return the city of Danzig (present-day Gdańsk). It had been part of Germany until World War I.

To hide its military buildup, Germany disguised warplanes like this one as mail planes.

Britain and France—who became known as the **Allied Powers**—declared war against Germany.

German forces attacked Poland in a **Blitzkrieg**, a new kind of fast-moving "lightning war." The Blitzkrieg concentrated airplanes and tanks in strategic areas in order to break through enemy lines. German troops swept across Poland from the west, and soon after the Soviets invaded from the east. By the end of the month, the two armies occupied Poland and sent its government into exile.

Hitler Looks West

When Germany attacked Poland, Britain and France began to mobilize their armed forces. The French massed their troops behind the **Maginot Line**—a fortified wall that France had built along its border with Germany after World War I.

In April 1940, German troops occupied Denmark and invaded Norway. In May, Germany seized the Low Countries of Belgium, Luxembourg, and the Netherlands. In doing so, Germany moved north of the Maginot Line. From there, German troops rushed southward behind the fortified line into France. The Germans trapped Belgian, British, and French soldiers at the French port of Dunkirk. In a daring evacuation, British

The Fighting Begins

Britain and France responded to Hitler's demands by pledging to defend Poland if Germany attacked. To keep the Soviet Union out of the war, Hitler secretly negotiated an agreement with Soviet leader Joseph Stalin in August 1939. In this **nonaggression pact**, Hitler and Stalin agreed not to attack one another and to divide Poland between their countries.

Poland Falls

World War II began on September 1, 1939, when German forces invaded Poland. Two days later,

Allied troops stream toward ships waiting to evacuate them from Dunkirk, France. Hundreds of ships of all sizes, including many privately owned boats, were used in the effort.

Axis Powers

Allied Powers

Neutral countries

Axis advances

Controlled by Axis

Controlled by Allies

Area of the
Battle of Britain

Farthest Soviet
advance, 1940

Maginot Line

World War II in Europe, 1939–1941

Learning from Maps Within two years of unleashing its Blitzkrieg, or "lightning war," in 1939, Germany controlled most of Europe and North Africa.

Place What European countries remained free from Axis control?

ships carried hundreds of thousands of soldiers across the English Channel to safety between May 26 and June 3, 1940.

As Hitler's forces advanced on the French capital of Paris in June 1940, Italy joined Germany and declared war on the Allied Powers. Together, Italy and Germany were known as the Axis Powers. On June 22 France surrendered to Germany, which then took control of northern France. In central France a German-controlled French government was established in the city of Vichy. Many French soldiers who had escaped at Dunkirk continued to participate in the fight against Germany. Based in London, French general Charles de Gaulle (gohl) organized a "Free French" army to serve with other Allied troops.

Britain Stands Alone

With France defeated, Hitler prepared to invade Britain. To launch a successful invasion across the English Channel, Germany would first need to defeat the British Royal Airforce (RAF). In July 1940 the *Luftwaffe*—the German air force— began to attack RAF airfields and aircraft. For months the two sides fought for air supremacy in what is known as the **Battle of Britain**.

In late August, Hitler ordered the *Luftwaffe* to bomb civilian targets in hopes of destroying British morale. A new invention called radar helped the RAF detect incoming German aircraft. Without control of the skies, Hitler canceled his plans for a ground invasion of Britain in mid-September. Winston Churchill, now British prime minister, expressed his nation's gratitude to the RAF pilots: "Never in the field of human conflict was so much owed by so many to so few."

 ## U.S. Neutrality

The United States remained neutral in the early stages of the war. Although most Americans opposed Hitler, they did not want to fight in a European war. Many well-known Americans, such as pilot Charles Lindbergh, supported isolationism.

U.S. neutrality laws prevented President Franklin D. Roosevelt from providing war supplies to the Allies. In 1939 he asked Congress to adjust these laws. Congress later approved the "cash-and-carry" system. The Allies could purchase U.S. weapons, but they had to pay for the arms in cash and carry them back to Europe on their own ships. In another effort to supply the Allies, Roosevelt swapped 50 U.S. destroyers for 99-year leases on several of Britain's naval bases in the Caribbean. After France fell in 1940, Congress greatly increased the U.S. defense budget.

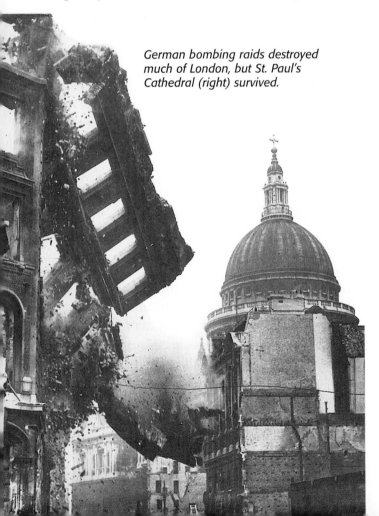

German bombing raids destroyed much of London, but St. Paul's Cathedral (right) survived.

With the war in Europe, Roosevelt broke with tradition in 1940 and ran for a third term as president. The Republicans chose lawyer Wendell Willkie as his opponent. Most Americans decided to stick with a leader they knew, and Roosevelt won an easy victory. During the election, Roosevelt had reassured Americans that "your boys are not going to be sent into any foreign wars." Even so, he was convinced that the United States would eventually have to enter the war. Roosevelt again asked Congress to expand U.S. aid to the Allies. He argued that if all of Europe fell to Hitler,

> **"it is no exaggeration to say that all of us in the Americas would be living at the point of a gun. . . . We must be the great arsenal [arms supplier] of democracy."**

Congress passed the **Lend-Lease Act** in March 1941. This act offered to loan $7 billion worth of weapons and other war supplies to cash-poor Britain. After Hitler broke the nonaggression pact and invaded the Soviet Union in June 1941, Roosevelt extended Lend-Lease to the Soviets.

The Battle of the Atlantic

As U.S. aid to Britain increased, Germany focused its submarine forces on stopping the transportation of weapons. The result was a long fight, called the **Battle of the Atlantic**, to control the ocean trade routes. German U-boats sank many Allied cargo ships and tried to cut Britain off from the United States, its main source of supplies. To reduce their losses, the Allies organized their cargo ships into protective groups called convoys. The U.S. Navy began escorting the convoys across the Atlantic as far as Iceland. The navy also tracked U-boats and notified the British of the submarines' locations.

In August 1941 President Roosevelt and Prime Minister Winston Churchill signed a document of cooperation known as the **Atlantic Charter**. In it they pledged not to acquire new territory as a result of war and to work for peace after the current conflict. Just a month after the signing, a German U-boat fired on a U.S. destroyer. When Roosevelt ordered U.S. forces to "shoot on sight," war between the United States and Germany seemed certain.

★ Conflict with Japan

Like Germany and Italy, Japan had aggressively sought new territory. After conquering much of China during the 1930s, Japan set its sights on Southeast Asia and its valuable natural resources. Japan also allied itself with Germany and Italy in the late 1930s and became part of the Axis Powers in 1940. In July 1941 Japanese forces seized French Indochina. In response, President Roosevelt froze Japanese funds in the United States and blocked the sale of products critical to Japanese industry. Both actions deeply angered Japanese leaders. U.S. officials also demanded that Japan leave China and French Indochina.

Meanwhile, the Japanese military developed a plan to attack Hawaii. In late November 1941, aircraft carriers left Japan. Led by Admiral Isoroku Yamamoto, the Japanese fleet planned to destroy U.S. forces at Pearl Harbor and then complete the conquest of Southeast Asia.

On December 7, 1941, Japanese warplanes swept down out of the sky and attacked the base. One sailor aboard the USS *Oklahoma* remembered:

“ **Suddenly the ship lurched! . . . As she rolled over, I was . . . buffeted [knocked]**

Naval destroyers protected ship convoys like this one.

and tossed about. Then the dark waters closed over me as the ship came to rest upside down on the bottom of the harbor. ”

The attack sank or damaged U.S. battleships in Pearl Harbor. That same day, Japanese forces attacked U.S. military bases in the Philippines and on Guam, Midway, and Wake Island.

The surprise attack on U.S. soil shocked many Americans. The next day Roosevelt asked Congress to declare war on Japan, calling December 7 “a date which will live in infamy [disgrace].” Germany then declared war on the United States. Less than 25 years after its entry into World War I, the United States joined the Allies in another global conflict.

SECTION 1 REVIEW

Identify and explain the significance of the following:
- **Munich Conference**
- **appeasement**
- **nonaggression pact**
- **Allied Powers**
- **Blitzkrieg**
- **Maginot Line**
- **Battle of Britain**
- **Winston Churchill**
- **Wendell Willkie**
- **Lend-Lease Act**
- **Battle of the Atlantic**
- **Atlantic Charter**

Locate and explain the importance of the following:
- **Munich**
- **Poland**
- **Danzig**
- **Belgium**
- **Dunkirk**
- **Vichy**

Reading for Content Understanding

1 **Main Idea** How did the United States aid the Allies while remaining neutral?

2 **Main Idea** Why did Japan attack Pearl Harbor?

3 **Geographic Diversity** *Movement* Make a graphic organizer describing and explaining Germany's early conquests in Europe.

4 **Writing** *Expressing* Imagine that it is June 1940 and France has just fallen to Germany. Create a script for a radio editorial expressing your support for or opposition to U.S. involvement in World War II.

5 **Critical Thinking** *Determining the Strength of an Argument* Some historians have suggested that World War II might have been prevented if the Allies had refused Hitler's demands at the Munich Conference. Do you agree? Explain your answer.

Mobilizing for War

Reading Focus

How did the United States mobilize for World War II?

What effects did World War II have on civilian women and minorities?

Why did the U.S. government intern Japanese Americans during the war?

Key Terms

War Production Board
Selective Training and Service Act
Fair Employment Practices Committee
braceros
zoot-suit riots
internment

*A*FTER THE UNITED STATES *entered World War II, the government called upon all U.S. citizens to join the war effort. Officials asked civilians to limit their use of canned foods, gasoline, tires, and other items needed to supply the troops. Most of Mary Speir's neighbors in Westminster, Maryland, flew American flags outside their homes, but she did not. She understood the great sacrifices that Americans would have to make to win the war. One day a man said to her, "You're not very patriotic, are you?" Speir—whose 20-year-old son had died in battle—answered, "It takes more than waving a flag to win a war."*

The U.S. government used ration stamps to control the supply of materials important to the war effort.

★ Working for the War Effort

Still suffering from the Great Depression, the United States took on a huge and costly task when it entered World War II. However, the economy began to recover as the country mobilized to meet the demands of war.

Industry Gears Up for War

Production boomed as American factories turned out enormous quantities of tanks, jeeps, guns, and ammunition. Perhaps the most remarkable example of wartime production was the construction of Liberty ships—transport vessels designed to carry troops and supplies. Workers could build one of these ships in a matter of days, leading observers to joke that they were "built by the mile and chopped off by the yard."

Most workers were employed and earnings rose. Many Americans, including some rural residents, relocated to take high-paying factory jobs in the North and Midwest or shipyard jobs along the West Coast. Even so, U.S. agricultural production remained high. Farmers managed to feed Americans as well as the European Allies.

To prepare the nation for war, the government expanded its role and increased its regulation of the economy. The **War Production Board** (WPB) oversaw the conversion of factories to war production. In 1942, for example, the WPB banned the production of cars so that automotive plants could focus on producing military equipment. The WPB was later replaced by the Office of War Mobilization (OWM).

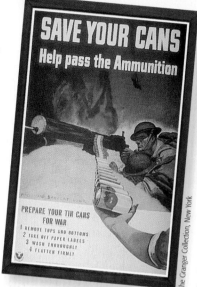

SAVE YOUR CANS
Help pass the Ammunition

PREPARE YOUR TIN CANS
FOR WAR
1 REMOVE TOPS AND BOTTOMS
2 TAKE OFF PAPER LABELS
3 WASH THOROUGHLY
4 FLATTEN FIRMLY

The Granger Collection, New York

A poster urging Americans to recycle

of the war expenses, however. The government borrowed the difference, mostly by selling war bonds to the public.

★ Opportunities and Obstacles

The mobilization for war brought new opportunities to women and minorities. However, as they entered the workplace these groups still sometimes encountered unfair treatment.

The Troops

In addition to reorganizing the economy, the U.S. government had to recruit and train millions of soldiers. Congress had prepared for this in 1940 when it passed the **Selective Training and Service Act**, the first peacetime draft in U.S. history. At first, the law required all men between the ages of 21 and 35 to register, but it later included men aged 18 to 38. Local draft boards granted deferments, or postponements of service, for medical or religious reasons. People who held jobs that were vital to the war effort were also excused from the draft.

More than 16 million Americans, including 1 million African Americans and some 300,000 Mexican Americans, served in the military. African American troops faced discrimination in the armed forces and generally served in segregated units. As the war went on, however, African Americans gradually won increased opportunities to serve in infantry, tank, and air force units and to train as officers.

Support and Sacrifice

After the attack on Pearl Harbor, the American people rallied together to support the war effort. The government worked hard to keep morale high, knowing that people had to endure shortages, hardships, and worse—the loss of loved ones.

To pay for the war effort, the government drastically increased taxes. For the first time, middle- and lower-income Americans had to pay income taxes. These tax increases paid only 40 percent

Women

With the U.S. entry into the war, there were many new jobs and not enough workers. The government urged women to fill these new positions. As men left for war, women replaced them in factories and business offices. One female worker recalled her job at Rohr Aircraft:

> ❝[I] learned how to use an electric drill, . . . how to rivet. . . . I was an eager learner, and I soon became an outstanding riveter. At Rohr I worked riveting the boom doors on P-38s [fighter planes]. . . . The war really created opportunities for women. It was the first time we got a chance to show that we could do a lot of things that only men had done before.❞

These men are signing up to join the 99th Pursuit Squadron—the first U.S. Army Air Corps unit to allow African Americans to enlist.

Although they did the same work as men, women often faced discrimination and received less pay.

Some 300,000 women worked in the armed forces. They joined organizations such as the Women's Auxiliary Army Corps (WAAC) and the Women's Airforce Service Pilots (WASP). Women performed a variety of military jobs. Some helped operate military communications systems. Others flew planes from factories to military units. Army and navy nurses served in combat areas.

African Americans

As during World War I, many African American civilians migrated from the South to cities in the North to join the industrial labor force. Despite their important contributions, African Americans often received less pay than white workers in similar jobs.

To protest this discrimination, African American labor leader A. Philip Randolph organized a march on Washington, D.C. Randolph agreed to cancel the march when President Roosevelt issued an executive order banning racial discrimination in defense industries. Roosevelt also created the **Fair Employment Practices Committee** (FEPC) to prevent discrimination in war industries and government jobs. African Americans gained new opportunities in some defense companies, earning better pay than before.

Mexican Americans

Many Mexican American civilians moved to the West Coast and the Midwest to take advantage of wartime job opportunities. In 1942, to meet a labor shortage in the Southwest, the U.S. government authorized Mexican workers called **braceros** to enter the United States. Some 200,000 braceros became a critical part of the agricultural economy in the West and the Southwest.

Mexican Americans faced discrimination during World War II despite supporting the war effort. Many young Mexican American men of the time

American Arts

Oklahoma!

In 1943 writer Richard Rodgers and composer Oscar Hammerstein II created *Oklahoma!*, one of the most popular musicals of all time. *Oklahoma!* is a simple, down-home story—the tale of two cowboys wooing two farm girls.

Oklahoma! opened on Broadway at the St. James Theatre on March 31, 1943. The musical was so popular that the theater often displayed the sign "We have no tickets for *Oklahoma!*" in the lobby. One night, a young couple showed up at the St. James box office hoping to get tickets, but the show was sold out. When the man mentioned that he was heading to Europe the next day to fight in the

The upbeat musical Oklahoma! lifted the spirits of many Americans during the war years.

war, the ticket seller silently pushed over a pair of tickets. It might have been the man's last chance to see the show.

Oklahoma! was so popular that it was used to promote the war effort. Some *Oklahoma!* sheet-music covers contained a note in the left-hand corner urging people to buy U.S. War Savings Bonds. The musical ended its long run at the St. James in May 1949.

Understanding the Arts

1. Why did *Oklahoma!* appeal to wartime audiences?

2. Why do you think *Oklahoma!* was chosen to promote the war effort?

wore zoot suits—outfits with oversized jackets, wide-brimmed hats, and baggy pants that fit tightly at the ankles. In Los Angeles in June 1943, groups of sailors attacked Mexican Americans wearing these outfits in the so-called **zoot-suit riots**. For 10 days, mobs roamed the city, assaulting Mexican Americans. Riots against Mexican Americans broke out in seven other cities. Nevertheless, many Mexican Americans made patriotic contributions.

These Japanese American women are standing outside the barber shop at the internment center in Malheur County, Oregon.

Japanese American Internment

Wartime anger after the Pearl Harbor attack led to widespread discrimination against Japanese Americans. In 1941 more than 125,000 people of Japanese descent lived in the United States, mostly on the West Coast. Some were issei, Japanese immigrants, but more were nisei, U.S. citizens born to Japanese immigrants.

After Pearl Harbor, many Americans questioned the loyalty of issei and nisei. Fearing the possibility of spying or sabotage, in February 1942 the U.S. government began a process of **internment**, or forced relocation and imprisonment. As part of this policy, the government moved most Japanese Americans to remote camps, which were largely located in the western United States. One woman remembered

> **that sad morning when we realized suddenly that we wouldn't be free. . . . Suddenly you realized that human beings were being put behind fences just like on the farm where we had horses and pigs in corrals.**

Despite the internment policy, many Japanese Americans volunteered for military service. Many nisei served in the 442nd Regimental Combat Team, a highly distinguished unit that fought in Europe. Other Japanese Americans played a vital role in the Pacific campaign as interpreters and translators with military intelligence units.

SECTION 2 REVIEW

Identify and explain the significance of the following:

- **War Production Board**
- **Selective Training and Service Act**
- **A. Philip Randolph**
- **Fair Employment Practices Committee**
- **braceros**
- **zoot-suit riots**
- **internment**

Reading for Content Understanding

1 **Main Idea** What did the United States do to prepare for its entry into World War II?

2 **Main Idea** How did the war affect women, African Americans, and Mexican Americans?

3 **Citizenship and Democracy** Why did the U.S. government move Japanese Americans into internment camps during the war? How did some Japanese Americans show their patriotism despite this internment?

4 **Writing** *Describing* Imagine that you are a female defense worker during the war. Write several diary entries describing your new job.

5 **Critical Thinking** *Drawing Conclusions* Why do you think the U.S. government needed to regulate the economy during the war?

SECTION 3

The War in North Africa and Europe

Reading Focus

Why was the Allies' North Africa campaign so important?

What were the major turning points of the war in Europe?

How did the Allies drive the Germans out of France?

Key Terms

Battle of El Alamein
Battle of Stalingrad
D-Day
Battle of the Bulge

AFTER THE DUNKIRK EVACUATION in May and June 1940, British prime minister Winston Churchill declared, "We shall defend our Island, whatever the cost may be." His words inspired the nation. During the Battle of Britain, the RAF prevented a German invasion. However, the Luftwaffe continued to bomb London through the spring of 1941. Churchill had said, "We shall fight on the beaches. We shall fight in the fields and in the streets, . . . we shall never surrender." Despite widespread damage to their nation, the British people lived up to his words.

Some of the Dunkirk evacuation boats

⭐ A Desperate Situation

In the fall of 1941, the Axis Powers pressed the Allies nearly to the breaking point. German submarine attacks were severely straining Britain's North Atlantic supply lines. Axis forces had occupied Greece and Yugoslavia and were steadily advancing in North Africa and the Soviet Union.

Two weeks after the attack on Pearl Harbor, President Roosevelt and Prime Minister Churchill met in Washington, D.C. They agreed to focus on defeating Germany first, rather than launching a full attack on Japan. The two leaders also discussed a possible attack on Axis positions in North Africa. In January 1942, China and the Soviet Union agreed to these war aims and pledged their resources to defeating the Axis Powers. They also agreed not to make a separate peace with any Axis nation.

In 1942 the war in the Atlantic looked more hopeful after the Allies introduced new sonar technology, which helped locate and track German submarines. New long-range patrol bombers also offered some protection to ships far out at sea.

While Allied naval forces fought for command of the Atlantic, Allied air forces tried to destroy Germany's economic resources. Flying out of Britain, Allied bombers primarily targeted factories, railroads, and military centers, but they also hit many German cities. To improve the accuracy and effectiveness of their raids, U.S. bombers flew their missions in daylight. As a result, bomber crews suffered very high casualties but made large contributions to winning the war.

★ North Africa and Italy

In September 1940, Italian forces in Libya had attacked Egypt. They had hoped to capture the Suez Canal, a vital Allied supply route. The British counterattacked, however, and drove back the Italians. Adolf Hitler then sent the German *Afrika Korps*, commanded by General Erwin Rommel, to the region. For the next two years a back-and-forth battle raged over some 1,500 miles.

A master of warfare and surprise attacks, Rommel soon became known as the Desert Fox. By the summer of 1942, Rommel seemed ready to take Egypt, but a shortage of troops and supplies slowed his offensive. In November, British forces under General Bernard Montgomery stopped Rommel's advance in the **Battle of El Alamein**. About the same time, a combined British-American force under U.S. general Dwight D. Eisenhower landed west of Egypt in French North Africa. Eisenhower was an expert at organization and planning and soon had U.S. troops pushing back the German forces. Montgomery's and Eisenhower's troops trapped Rommel's retreating *Afrika Korps* between them. After a series of hard-fought battles in early 1943, the *Afrika Korps* surrendered.

Having driven the Axis troops from North Africa, the Allies decided to invade Italy, the place that Winston Churchill

German sharpshooters search for enemy troops in North Africa. Wide-open spaces, dust, sand, heat, and disease all made desert fighting very difficult.

Biography

Daniel Inouye

Daniel Inouye was born in Hawaii in 1924. After Japan attacked Pearl Harbor in 1941, he volunteered for military service and served in the famous 442nd Regimental Combat Team.

While in Italy, the 442nd captured Mount Folgorito, a heroic and spectacular accomplishment. Inouye recalled that while his unit was climbing the cliffs "some men had slipped and bounced as much as 100 feet down the steep slopes . . . but not one of them cried out and the soundless advance went on." They took the Germans by surprise and captured the mountain. In a later battle with the Germans, Inouye was wounded and lost his right arm.

After the war Inouye studied law and entered politics. He eventually became a U.S. representative and later a senator.

called the enemy's "soft underbelly." In July 1943, Allied forces landed on the island of Sicily. After winning control of the island, they began landing troops on the Italian mainland in September.

As the Allies advanced, the Italian government overthrew dictator Benito Mussolini in order to make peace. Hitler, however, was determined to stop the Allies in Italy. He stepped in to save Mussolini. German troops then took control of Italy and slowed the Allied advance with fierce fighting. In January 1944 the Allies tried to take the Germans by surprise by landing a force behind

German lines at the seaport of Anzio. The landing force failed to break through the German lines and remained trapped at Anzio for four months. Allied forces fighting their way up the Italian Peninsula eventually linked up with the Anzio force. Together they captured Rome, Italy's capital, in June. In late April 1945 the Allies drove the Germans out of Italy. That same month, Mussolini tried to flee the country but was instead captured and executed.

U.S. Rangers charged across the beach under heavy fire from German forces and then climbed these steep cliffs during the D-Day invasion.

Turning Points

In early 1943 the Allies had begun the final push to defeat the Axis Powers, and victories during the winter of 1942–43 brought the Allies closer to their goal. As British and U.S. troops advanced in North Africa and Italy, Soviet forces began driving the Axis Powers out of the Soviet Union. The turning point in the war between Germany and the Soviet Union came in the city of Stalingrad.

Stalingrad

After their initial invasion in June 1941, Axis forces had advanced deep into the Soviet Union. In mid-1942 a German army tried to capture the city of Stalingrad.

The **Battle of Stalingrad** was a fierce struggle. Soldiers fought hand-to-hand combat for each city block. As the harsh winter weather set in, Soviet reinforcements arrived and surrounded the German army. One German soldier described the scene:

> 66 The men in field grey just slouched on, . . . filthy and . . . louse-ridden, their weary shoulders sagging. . . . Skin now loose-stretched over bone, so utter [complete] was the exhaustion, so utter the starvation. . . . And whenever any individual could do no more, when even the . . . fear of death ceased to have meaning, . . . the debilitated [weakened] body . . . came to a standstill. Soon . . . snow covered the object and only the toe of a jackboot or an arm frozen to stone could remind you that what was now an elongated [long] white hummock [small hill] had quite recently been a human being. 99

Finally, in late January 1943, with supplies running desperately low, the remaining German troops in Stalingrad surrendered. The Axis Powers had lost some 200,000 soldiers in the fighting.

Six months after the Battle of Stalingrad, the Soviets dealt another great blow to the Germans in a huge tank battle near the Soviet city of Kursk.

Soviet soldiers scramble across a ditch that used to be a street in the city of Stalingrad. Most of the city was destroyed during the six months of fighting.

The combined Soviet victories at Stalingrad and Kursk marked a turning point in the war. Hitler's attempt to conquer the Soviet Union was crushed. Axis troops retreated west toward Germany.

D-Day

President Roosevelt's top military adviser, General George C. Marshall, had long supported an Allied invasion of German-occupied France. General Eisenhower was put in charge of planning the invasion, called Operation Overlord. The plan called for a massive landing on the beaches of Normandy, in northern France. To mislead the Germans about the exact location of the attack, the Allies staged several decoy landings in other places.

On the morning of June 6, 1944—a date recorded in history as **D-Day**—some 150,000 Allied soldiers swarmed ashore in Normandy. Hundreds

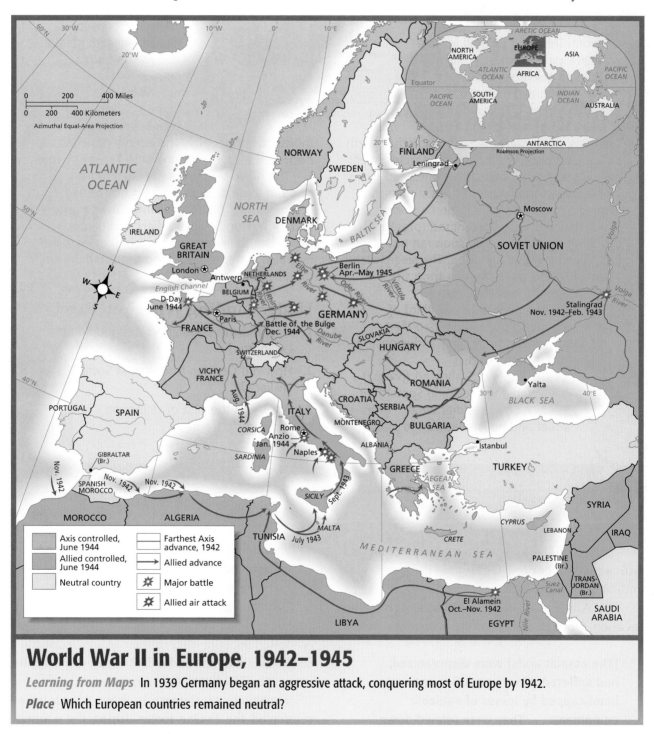

World War II in Europe, 1942–1945

Learning from Maps In 1939 Germany began an aggressive attack, conquering most of Europe by 1942.

Place Which European countries remained neutral?

The Eastern Front

While the Allies fought the Axis Powers in western Europe, a fierce battle raged in the east. Millions of German and Soviet soldiers fought along the 4,000-mile eastern front. This front opened in June 1941, when some 13 million German soldiers invaded the Soviet Union. As the Germans swept eastward, they killed many civilians. Desperate to stop the Germans, the Soviets followed a scorched-earth policy, destroying anything the Germans might have found useful, such as factories and dams.

As part of their eastern-front strategy, the Germans tried to capture important Soviet cities. They blockaded Leningrad (present-day St. Petersburg), which soon ran out of fuel, running water, and food. The siege lasted around 900 days. By the time the Germans retreated, about 1 million people, or one third of Leningrad's population, had died. Many died from hunger and exposure to the extreme cold.

The Battle of Stalingrad (present-day Volgograd) began in September 1942. A Soviet soldier wrote, "Every street and house has turned into a

This poster encouraged Soviet citizens to help rebuild their country.

battlefield." In January 1943, exhausted by both the fighting and the harsh winter weather, many of the German troops in Stalingrad surrendered.

As the German armies retreated westward, they burned hundreds of villages and killed thousands of people. "The enemy has destroyed everything," one Soviet soldier wrote.

The Allied victory on the eastern front came at a great price. German troops had pushed some 1,200 miles into Soviet territory, and 14 million Soviet soldiers had died defending their country. At least 6 million civilians also lost their lives, and thousands of children became orphans.

Understanding What You Read

1. How did the siege affect the people of Leningrad?

2. How did German troops treat Soviet civilians?

3. What was the cost of victory on the eastern front?

---

of warships off the coast attempted to protect them with a cover of gunfire. D-Day was the largest sea-and-land invasion in history.

The Allies faced fierce resistance during the invasion. One U.S. officer on the scene reported:

" [The assault units] were disorganized, had suffered heavy casualties and were handicapped by losses of valuable equipment. . . . They were pinned down by intense enemy fire. . . . Personnel and equipment were being piled up ashore . . . where congested [crowded] groups afforded good targets for the enemy."

Nonetheless, the determined Allies continued their assault. By the end of D-Day, they had landed more than 155,000 troops in France.

Hundreds of thousands more Allied troops reinforced the D-Day forces during the summer.

Victorious Allied troops move under Paris's Arc de Triomphe, *the largest triumphal arch in the world, and receive a warm welcome.*

The Battle of the Bulge

After liberating Paris, the Allies began to push through Belgium and France toward Germany itself. Although defeat seemed certain, Hitler refused to surrender.

In December 1944 Hitler made a desperate attempt to split the advancing Allied armies by trying to recapture Antwerp, Belgium, the Allies' major supply port. The Germans' target was the Ardennes (ahr-den), a densely forested region defended by a few U.S. divisions. On December 16, some 25 divisions of the German army attacked in the heavy snow and almost broke the Allied lines. Surprised, outnumbered, and without air support, the Americans fought bravely in the **Battle of the Bulge**. U.S. losses were heavy—some 77,000 casualties—but the American resistance had slowed the German counterattack.

As Allied reinforcements arrived, the German offensive stalled, then turned into a general retreat. The Battle of the Bulge ended Germany's ability to wage an offensive war. As 1945 began, the Soviets pushed toward Berlin, Germany's capital. U.S. and British troops prepared to cross the Rhine River into Germany from the west.

With increased forces, U.S. general Omar Bradley led the breakout from the beaches and the Allied advance into France. Tank forces under General George Patton then broke through the German lines in July. Meanwhile, new Allied forces landed in southern France and began to advance northward. The liberation of France was at last in sight.

In August, fighting broke out in Paris as French citizens rose up against the German occupation forces. On August 24 a small unit of Free French troops entered the city. The next morning, Bradley arrived with his 12th Army Group. As one person described, "All Paris surged out to meet the Allied columns and welcome their liberators."

SECTION 3 REVIEW

Identify and explain the significance of the following:
- Erwin Rommel
- Bernard Montgomery
- Battle of El Alamein
- Dwight D. Eisenhower
- Battle of Stalingrad
- George C. Marshall
- D-Day
- Omar Bradley
- George Patton
- Battle of the Bulge

Reading for Content Understanding

1 **Main Idea** What military goals did the Allied forces achieve in their North Africa campaign?

2 **Main Idea** What battles were turning points for the war in Europe?

3 **Geographic Diversity** *Movement* Create a flow chart describing how the Allies pushed the Germans out of France.

4 **Writing** *Informing* Imagine that you are an American reporter during World War II. Write a brief article informing your readers about the Battle of the Bulge.

5 **Critical Thinking** *Synthesizing Information* How was cooperation among Allied nations important to the D-Day invasion?

War in the Pacific

Reading Focus

Where did Japan attack after its bombing of Pearl Harbor?

What three battles were the major turning points of the war in the Pacific?

How did the Allies advance toward Japan?

Key Terms

Bataan Death March
Battle of the Coral Sea
Battle of Midway
island-hopping
Battle of Leyte Gulf
kamikaze

ON NOVEMBER 20, 1943, *U.S. Marines swarmed into the lagoon of Tarawa, one of the Gilbert Islands in the Pacific Ocean. Many flat-bottomed boats became stuck on reefs. As the marines waded ashore in chest-deep water, they came under a hail of Japanese machine-gun fire. "The water seemed never clear of . . . men," one witness recalled. "They kept falling, falling, falling . . . singly, in groups, and in rows." Yet the marines pressed on. Three days and 3,000 casualties later, they had overrun the island. Tarawa was just one of many difficult Allied landings in the Pacific.*

U.S. Marines charge onto Tarawa and into Japanese machine-gun fire.

Japan Advances Across the Pacific

In 1931, years before the battle at Tarawa, Japan had begun its wars of expansion in Asia by conquering Manchuria in China. Under General Hideki (hee-dek-ee) Tojo, Japan continued to expand across East Asia and the Pacific Ocean. Immediately after bombing Pearl Harbor, Japanese forces struck quickly to grab U.S. holdings in the Pacific and British and Dutch possessions in Southeast Asia.

By early 1942 Japan had seized the British colonies of Hong Kong and Singapore. Advancing through the independent country of Thailand, Japanese forces invaded Burma, a British colony. They then took control of the oil-rich Netherlands East Indies (present-day Indonesia) from the Dutch.

The Japanese also raced to strengthen their position against an expected U.S. counterattack in the Pacific. In December 1941 Japan had attacked and captured Guam and Wake Island, both U.S. territories. Farther north, Japanese forces landed on the U.S.-owned Aleutian islands of Kiska and

These U.S. soldiers were among the thousands of prisoners who suffered brutal treatment on the Bataan Death March.

The Battle of the Coral Sea

To stop Japan's advance, the Allies had to defeat the Japanese navy. The U.S. Navy, commanded in the Pacific by Admiral Chester Nimitz, had a critical, top-secret advantage. Navy experts had cracked the Japanese communication code and could read secret Japanese messages. As a result, Nimitz learned that the Japanese planned to capture Port Moresby, in New Guinea.

To cut them off, Nimitz sent an Allied fleet to attack the Japanese invasion force in the Coral Sea northeast of Australia. In early May 1942, U.S. planes sank one Japanese carrier and damaged another in the **Battle of the Coral Sea**. The United States suffered losses as well. Japanese planes sank the U.S. carrier *Lexington* and damaged the *Yorktown*, but the Allies had stopped the Japanese advance for the first time.

Attu, near Alaska. Japan also invaded the Philippines, another U.S. possession.

Under the direction of General Douglas MacArthur, U.S. and Filipino forces made a determined stand against the Japanese invasion. The capital of Manila fell quickly, however, and the islands' defenders retreated across Manila Bay to the Bataan Peninsula. Short of food, they held out on the fortified island of Corregidor as long as possible. In March 1942 President Roosevelt ordered MacArthur to go to Australia. "I shall return," he vowed before making his escape.

Weak and hungry, U.S. and Filipino units on the Bataan Peninsula and Corregidor surrendered soon afterward. The Japanese then made the more than 70,000 American and Filipino prisoners—many of whom were sick and wounded—march 65 miles up the peninsula to prison camps. In what became known as the **Bataan Death March**, the Japanese treated the prisoners harshly, killing many. More than 600 Americans and 10,000 Filipinos died on the Bataan Death March.

The Battle of Midway

The secret work of the navy's code breakers contributed to a second important victory just weeks after the Battle of the Coral Sea. From intercepted messages, Nimitz learned that the Japanese planned to seize Midway, two islands located northwest of Hawaii. Nimitz ordered U.S. carriers to catch the Japanese by surprise.

The **Battle of Midway**, which took place between June 3 and 6, was a battle of carrier-based airplanes. Japanese and U.S. warplanes fought in

The Navajo Code Talkers used a special code in the Navajo language that the Japanese were never able to crack.

★ Halting Japan's Advance

In early 1942 Japan seemed unstoppable and ready to strike at India, Australia, Hawaii, and even the West Coast of the United States. Over the course of the year, however, Allied forces began to turn the tide of the war against Japan.

the air trying to sink each others' aircraft carriers. When the battle was over, the United States had crippled the Japanese navy by sinking four of its carriers, while losing only one of its own. An officer on the Japanese carrier *Akagi* described his ship's fate:

> "Within five minutes all her planes would be launched. Five minutes! Who would have dreamed that the tide of battle would shift completely in that brief interval of time? . . . The first Zero fighter [Japanese warplane] gathered speed and whizzed off the deck. At that instant a lookout screamed, 'Hell-divers!' I looked up to see three black enemy planes plummeting [diving] toward our ship. . . . Bombs! Down they came straight toward me! "

After its defeat at Midway, the Japanese navy was on the defensive for the remainder of the war.

Guadalcanal

The Allies pressed the Japanese war effort even further on the island of Guadalcanal, one of the Solomon Islands in the Southwest Pacific. From Guadalcanal the Japanese air force could threaten the vital sea link between Australia and the United States. In August 1942 the United States began landing marines on the island to prevent Japanese troops from completing an airstrip there. The fighting on Guadalcanal was ferocious, but by early 1943 the Allies had won control of the island.

★ Taking the Offensive

In early 1943, despite their loss at Guadalcanal, the Japanese forces continued to advance through Burma toward India. They also were in firm control of China.

Yet with the victories in the Coral Sea, at Midway, and on Guadalcanal, the Allies finally had the chance to take the offensive in the Pacific. By 1943, U.S. submarines were attacking Japanese transport ships and cutting off the flow of raw materials to Japan. Allied commanders prepared to advance toward Japan itself.

Island-Hopping

The Allies planned to conquer one Pacific island after another, gradually moving closer to Japan. Allied forces would land only on the most important islands, thus isolating Japanese troops on bypassed islands. The Allies planned this strategy of **island-hopping** to gain bases from which they could bomb and later invade Japan. U.S. leaders used the strategy quite effectively.

The island-hopping began in late 1943. As forces under General MacArthur battled the Japanese on New Guinea in November, other troops attacked the Gilbert Islands. In the Gilberts the Japanese had heavily fortified the island of Tarawa. U.S. troops suffered a high casualty rate landing there, but the survivors fought hard and captured the island. Tarawa was just the beginning, and attacks followed on the Marshall, Mariana, Volcano, and Bonin Islands. With the capture of the islands of Saipan and Tinian in the Marianas, U.S. planes began bombing the main islands of Japan.

Massive landing craft, like these in the waters of the Philippines, delivered U.S. troops to enemy-held beaches. These vessels were crucial to the U.S. strategy of island-hopping in the Pacific.

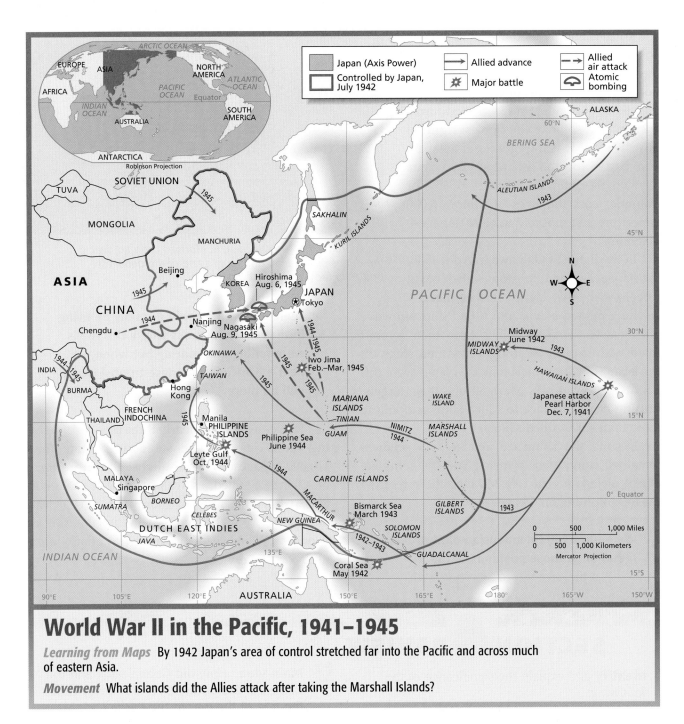

World War II in the Pacific, 1941–1945

Learning from Maps By 1942 Japan's area of control stretched far into the Pacific and across much of eastern Asia.

Movement What islands did the Allies attack after taking the Marshall Islands?

Liberating the Philippines

Having secured New Guinea, General MacArthur turned to the liberation of the Philippines in October 1944. The Japanese navy gathered to block the Allied invasion force and was decisively defeated in the **Battle of Leyte Gulf**—the largest naval engagement in history.

Shortly after the battle, MacArthur waded ashore on Leyte, keeping his promise to return to the Philippines. Aided by Filipino guerrillas, Allied forces began the advance toward Manila. In

January 1945, Allied troops landed on the main island of Luzon. On March 3 they captured Manila. Fighting against fierce Japanese resistance, it was summer before all the main towns, roads, and airfields of the country were in Allied hands.

★ Final Battles

By spring 1945 the war against Japan had entered its final phase. U.S. bombers hit targets in Japan and caused enormous damage. A raid on Tokyo in March 1945 destroyed much of the Japanese capital. Despite the devastation and the heavy loss of life, the Japanese refused to surrender. In fact, Allied forces encountered some of the fiercest fighting of World War II as they got closer to Japan. The battle for the island of Iwo Jima (EE-woh JEE-mah) in February 1945, for example, cost the lives of almost 6,000 Americans and most of the 22,000 Japanese defenders.

In the Battle of Okinawa in April 1945, the Japanese tried to stop Allied naval forces with the tactic of **kamikaze**— crashing piloted planes into Allied ships. In wave after wave, kamikaze pilots flew their aircraft filled with explosives straight at Allied ships off the island of Okinawa. Kamikaze planes were difficult to shoot down. Many struck their targets, causing heavy damage to Allied ships and killing more than 4,000 Allied sailors.

Despite the kamikaze attacks, U.S. soldiers remained committed to their goal—the complete defeat of Japan. One U.S. Marine officer recalled the hard fighting on Okinawa:

66 **We poured a tremendous amount of metal in on those positions. . . . It**

On February 19, 1945, these U.S. Marines charged over the dunes of Iwo Jima and fought one of the deadliest battles in the war against Japan.

seemed nothing could possibly be living in that churning mass where the shells were falling and roaring but when we next advanced, [Japanese troops] would still be there.99

The losses during nearly three months of fighting on Okinawa were staggering. More than 110,000 Japanese troops—almost the entire force on Okinawa—died, as well as some 80,000 civilians. The Allies suffered more than 11,000 dead and some 33,000 wounded. With the fall of Okinawa, Allied leaders planned to attack Japan itself for a final victory.

SECTION 4 REVIEW

Identify and explain the significance of the following:
- **Hideki Tojo**
- **Douglas MacArthur**
- **Bataan Death March**
- **Chester Nimitz**
- **Battle of the Coral Sea**
- **Battle of Midway**
- **island-hopping**
- **Battle of Leyte Gulf**
- **kamikaze**

Reading for Content Understanding

1 **Main Idea** What areas did Japan conquer after bombing Pearl Harbor? Why did Japan want to control these areas?

2 **Main Idea** How did Guadalcanal and the Battles of the Coral Sea and Midway turn the tide of the war in the Pacific?

3 **Geographic Diversity** *Region* What role did geography play in the U.S. strategy to advance toward Japan itself?

4 **Writing** *Describing* Imagine that you are a sailor on a U.S. warship in the Pacific during World War II. Write a letter home describing a kamikaze attack.

5 **Critical Thinking** *Identifying Cause and Effect* Why did the destruction of its aircraft carriers at Midway destroy Japan's ability to wage an offensive war?

SECTION 5

Final Victory and Consequences

Reading Focus

How did the Allies force Germany and Japan to surrender?

What were the human and economic costs of World War II?

What events led to the Holocaust?

Key Terms

atomic bomb
Manhattan Project
Holocaust
genocide

TOWARD THE END *of the war, the Allies mounted heavy bombing raids against the Axis Powers. In long flights over the Pacific Ocean, U.S. bombers battled Japanese fighter planes to drop tons of explosives on fortified enemy positions. One crew member described an attack on a Japanese airstrip in which "black puffs of ack-ack [antiaircraft fire] surround us, and some of the stuff hits. . . . The plane lurches and reels." The bomber survived, but that one mission to New Guinea lasted nine hours and covered more than 1,500 miles. The Allies would fight many more such battles before final victory.*

Victory medal from World War II

★ Victory in Europe

As they did against Japan, the Allies bombed Germany heavily during the final months of World War II. The German cities of Berlin, Hamburg, and Leipzig sustained massive damage. In January 1945, Allied bombers destroyed the historic German city of Dresden. One U.S. soldier remembered, "Dresden was an inferno. . . . I have nightmares, even today, about the charred bodies." Bombing raids meant to destroy an enemy's ability to manufacture weapons killed many civilians, Allied and Axis alike.

During the early months of 1945, the Allies pushed the Germans back. British and U.S. forces raced toward the Rhine River to enter Germany from the west. These troops moved fast to capture bridges across the Rhine before the Germans destroyed them. Some Allied leaders—particularly Winston Churchill—thought it was important for the noncommunist Allies to occupy as much of Germany as possible to keep it out of Soviet hands.

Allied tanks roll through Berlin at the end of the war.

not only disintegrated the steel tower that held the bomb but also melted the desert sand into glass for 800 yards in all directions. President Truman called it "the most terrible thing ever discovered" and struggled with the decision to use such a deadly weapon. When Japan refused the Allies' demand for an unconditional surrender, Truman gave the order to use the bomb.

On August 6, 1945, the B-29 bomber *Enola Gay* dropped an atomic bomb on the Japanese city of Hiroshima. One survivor recalled:

> **When I saw a very strong light, a flash, I put my arms over my face unconsciously. Almost instantly I felt my face was inflating. . . . I saw people looking for water and they died soon after they drank it. . . . The whole city was destroyed and burning. There was no place to go.**

In almost an instant, the atomic blast killed between 70,000 and 80,000 people. Thousands more died later from serious burns and radiation poisoning.

Despite the destruction, Japan refused to surrender. On August 9, U.S. forces dropped a second atomic bomb, this time on the city of Nagasaki. On September 2, 1945, Japan formally surrendered.

By mid-March 1945, British and U.S. forces had crossed the Rhine and were advancing east toward Berlin. Meanwhile, the Soviets pushed westward toward the city. With his enemies closing in, Hitler retreated to his underground bunker, or shelter, in the heart of the city. On April 30, as the Soviets advanced, Hitler committed suicide. Days later, on May 7, German officers surrendered unconditionally to the Allies. The next day—May 8, 1945—was declared V-E (Victory in Europe) Day. It marked the official end of World War II in Europe. For Americans, the joy was mixed with sorrow because only weeks before, on April 12, President Roosevelt had died of a stroke. Vice President Harry S Truman became president.

★ Victory in the Pacific

As Germany surrendered, the Allies were also near victory in the Pacific. Yet Allied leaders feared that a final invasion of Japan would result in enormous Allied loss of life.

The **atomic bomb**, a weapon that produced tremendous power by splitting atoms, offered an alternative to invasion. Since 1942, Allied scientists had been working on a secret program known as the **Manhattan Project** to develop an atomic bomb. In July 1945, they exploded the world's first atomic bomb in the desert near Alamogordo, New Mexico.

The bomb's destructive power was beyond all expectations. The explosion

The atomic bomb dropped on Hiroshima destroyed everything within 1.5 miles of the spot where it exploded. This watch, found in the ruins, had stopped at the exact moment of the explosion—8:15 A.M.

Science and Technology

Antibiotics

During World War I, wound infections killed some 15 percent of all soldiers who died. Infections were fast-moving and deadly—a scratch from barbed wire could kill a soldier in days if it became infected. By the end of World War II, such deaths were rare among Allied troops, thanks to a new drug called penicillin.

Sir Alexander Fleming discovered the lifesaving antibiotic penicillin.

British scientist Alexander Fleming discovered penicillin by accident in 1928. He noticed that a small dish of bacteria was covered with mold, which seemed to be killing the bacteria. This mold was penicillin, the first antibiotic ever discovered. Antibiotics prevent bacteria from growing, and in some cases, kill them. This allows the body's immune system to fight against disease and infection caused by bacteria.

It took years of work by researchers to refine the mold into a useful drug. By 1942, scientists were making small amounts of pure penicillin. The British could not produce enough penicillin to supply the military doctors. So in 1943 the U.S. government made penicillin production a top research priority, second only to the atomic bomb program. Scientists developed a method of growing a new type of mold in huge vats instead of small dishes or bottles. Scientists also used X rays to alter this penicillin mold so that it would produce even more penicillin.

By 1944 there was enough of the precious drug to treat thousands of wounded soldiers. After World War II, doctors began using penicillin to treat many different kinds of diseases and infections. Today, penicillin and other antibiotics are widely available and commonly prescribed by doctors. The drug that was such a lifesaver during the war is still saving lives.

Understanding What You Read

1. What is penicillin, and what does it do?
2. Why was penicillin important during World War II?
3. How might life be different today without antibiotics?

★ The Costs of the War

With Japan's surrender, World War II finally ended after six devastating years. Approximately 50 million people died—more than half of them civilians. Millions more were injured or left suffering from disease or malnutrition. China, Poland, and the Soviet Union were particularly hard hit. Both Germany and Japan lost many people as well.

In Europe, as in Asia, the war devastated national economies. Food production, industry, and transportation networks were destroyed in many areas. Millions of people found themselves homeless, lacking even the most basic necessities of food, fuel, water, and shelter. From London to Warsaw to Leningrad, large urban areas lay in ruins. Much of the world's great art and architecture was lost forever.

The United States escaped almost all of the physical destruction that Europe and Asia suffered. In addition, U.S. government spending on war efforts finally lifted the nation out of the Great Depression. The U.S. economy emerged from the war more powerful than ever.

Prisoners were separated upon arrival at Auschwitz concentration camp. One survivor recalled that an SS officer sent prisoners to a line "on his right or his left, and this is the life or death of each of us."

 ## The Holocaust

One of the most horrifying aspects of World War II was the **Holocaust**—Hitler and the Nazis' systematic attempt to kill the Jews of Europe. Soon after taking power in 1933, the Nazis wrote laws that stripped German Jews of their civil rights, jobs, and property. The Nazis tried to force German Jews to emigrate. The Nazis imprisoned those who remained in concentration camps, such as Dachau (DAH-kow) near Munich.

Early Measures

German expansion in Europe brought many more Jews under Hitler's control. Thousands of Jews lived in France, the Low Countries, and eastern Europe. Millions more lived in Poland and the Soviet Union. Hitler and other high-ranking Nazis found it impossible to force all these Jews to emigrate or to put them in concentration camps. Therefore, the Nazis took other steps.

In Poland, the Germans uprooted Jews from their homes in the countryside and forced them into isolated urban areas known as ghettos. Between April 1942 and April 1943, a ghetto in the Polish capital of Warsaw became the site of a brave but unsuccessful uprising against the Nazis.

The Germans also used special killing squads that were known as the *Einsatzgruppen* (YN-sahts-groo-puhn) to round up and shoot Jews. For three days in 1941, the *Einsatzgruppen* machine-gunned some 33,000 Jewish men, women, and children at Babi Yar near the Soviet city of Kiev. By the end of 1941, the *Einsatzgruppen* troops had killed around 600,000 Jews.

The Final Solution

In January 1942, senior Nazi officials met in a suburb of Berlin called Wannsee. At the Wannsee Conference these leaders agreed on a "final solution to the Jewish question." For the Nazis this "final solution"

Causes and Effects of World War II

Long-Term Causes
- Treaty of Versailles
- Debts from World War I
- Global and local economic problems
- Totalitarian governments
- Repeated acts of aggression

Immediate Causes
- Germany's invasion of Poland
- Japanese aggression in Asia
- Japanese attack on Pearl Harbor

World War II

Effects
- Millions of deaths and widespread destruction in Europe and Asia
- The Holocaust
- The emergence of the United States as a superpower

was **genocide**—the deliberate murder of an entire people.

The Nazis planned to eliminate the Jews in specially built death camps. These camps were equipped with gas chambers to kill great numbers of people. The camps also had large furnaces to cremate the remains of the murdered people. By mid-1942 the Nazis had begun to ship Jews from throughout German-occupied Europe to the camps. People were packed shoulder-to-shoulder in railroad boxcars. Nazi officers sorted the Jews by age, sex, and health, often ripping families apart. Camp officers forced physically fit Jews to work in camp factories. The Nazis sent many other prisoners—mostly women and children, the elderly, the weak, and the sick—directly to the gas chambers for immediate execution.

Moritz Vegh, age 13, was sent from his home in the former Czechoslovakia to Auschwitz—the most notorious of the death camps. He recalled his terrifying arrival:

66 **When we got off the cattle truck, they ordered, 'Men, right; women, left.' . . . I went with my father. My little sister, Esther, she went with my mother. Esther was only eleven. She was holding my mother's hand. When they made a selection of the women, Esther clung to my mother. My mother wouldn't give her up. . . . They went straight to the gas chamber.** 99

The Nazis sent Moritz to work at Auschwitz for the rest of the war. As the Allies began to liberate the concentration camps in early 1945, many of the survivors were too weak or ill to move.

The Allied liberation revealed the horrifying magnitude of the Holocaust. Some 6 million Jews—about two thirds of all Jews living in Europe before the war—had perished in the Holocaust. The Nazis also sent thousands of other people—including gypsies, Slavs, political and religious radicals, and others—to be killed in the camps. Perhaps more than any other event, the Holocaust serves as a chilling reminder of the brutal, inhumane nature of Nazi thought and of the terrible cost of Nazi aggression.

Prisoners at this concentration camp in Evensee, Austria, were liberated by U.S. troops in 1945.

SECTION 5 REVIEW

Identify and explain the significance of the following:
- **Harry S Truman**
- **atomic bomb**
- **Manhattan Project**
- **Holocaust**
- **genocide**

Reading for Content Understanding

1 **Main Idea** What were the consequences of World War II in both human and economic terms?

2 **Main Idea** Create a time line of the events that led to the Holocaust.

3 **Global Relations** How did the Allies eventually force both Germany and Japan to surrender?

4 **Writing** *Expressing* Imagine that you are one of the Allied soldiers who helped defeat Germany. Write a letter to your hometown newspaper expressing your feelings on V-E Day.

5 **Critical Thinking** *Supporting a Point of View* Do you agree or disagree with the decision to drop atomic bombs on Japan? Explain your answer.

CHAPTER 16 REVIEW

Chapter Summary

In 1939 Germany's invasion of Poland began World War II. The United States aided Britain against Germany but remained neutral until Japan attacked Pearl Harbor in 1941. From 1941 to 1945, the United States and the other Allies waged war against the Axis Powers. After Germany surrendered, the horror of the Holocaust was revealed to the world. The war finally came to an end in September 1945 with the surrender of Japan. ■

On a separate sheet of paper, complete the following activities.

Identifying People and Ideas

Describe the historical significance of the following:

1. appeasement
2. Winston Churchill
3. internment
4. Omar Bradley
5. Dwight D. Eisenhower
6. Battle of the Bulge
7. Bataan Death March
8. Battle of Midway
9. Manhattan Project
10. Holocaust

Internet Activity

go.hrw.com
SB1 Veterans

Search the Internet through the HRW Web site to find more information about American veterans of World War II. Use the information to design a memorial to the veterans.

Understanding Main Ideas

1. How did the United States remain neutral during the early part of World War II while still helping the Allies?
2. How did World War II affect American women?
3. How did the war create new opportunities for African American civilians?
4. What were the turning points in the war in Europe and in the Pacific?
5. Why did the United States decide to drop atomic bombs on Japan?

Reviewing Themes

1. **Citizenship and Democracy**   How did the war affect the rights of nisei?
2. **Economic Development**   How did mobilizing for war change the U.S. economy?
3. **Global Relations**   Why did President Franklin D. Roosevelt feel that the United States needed to serve as "the arsenal of democracy" for the world and become involved in World War II?

Using the Time Line

Number your paper from 1 to 6. Match the letters on the time line below with the following events.

1. **After Adolf Hitler commits suicide, German authorities surrender to the Allies.**
2. **The atomic bomb is dropped on Hiroshima.**
3. **The invasion of Poland begins.**
4. **Allied troops invade Normandy, France.**
5. **Pearl Harbor is bombed.**
6. **The Allies invade the Italian island of Sicily.**

1938   1939   1940   1941   1942   1943   1944   1945

a   b   c   d   e f

Thinking Critically

1. **Making Comparisons** How did Allied strategy differ in Germany and Japan?
2. **Evaluating** What were Adolf Hitler's reasons for starting World War II?
3. **Synthesizing Information** Why might fighting a war on multiple fronts be difficult?

Writing About History

1. **Informing** Imagine that you are a war correspondent covering D-Day. Write a newspaper article informing your readers about the event and the soldiers' reactions.
2. **Describing** Write a paragraph describing what might have happened if Britain had fallen to the Germans. Use examples from the chapter in your description.

Linking Geography and History

1. **Location** Look at the map of Europe on page xxviii and select several alternative locations to Normandy for the D-Day invasion. Why do you think Eisenhower selected Normandy?
2. **Movement** How was fighting in western Europe different from fighting along the western front during World War I?

Building Your Portfolio

Complete the following activities individually or in groups.

1. **Supporting the War Effort** Imagine that you work in the government's public relations office during World War II. Create an advertisement that would encourage people to make sacrifices for the war. Your advertisement might target a particular group—teenagers, for example—or appeal to all Americans. Then present the advertisement to your supervisor along with a short report explaining why the advertisement would be effective.

2. **Under Fire** Imagine that you were a soldier during World War II. You want to record your experiences before your memories fade with time. Choose either the war in Europe or in the Pacific and create a scrapbook of your experiences. Include descriptions of battles and sketches of some of the places you saw. Begin with the U.S. entry into the war and end with the final victory.

History Skills Workshop

Reading Maps In April 1942 the Allied forces in the Philippines surrendered to the Japanese. Some 70,000 Americans and Filipinos—both soldiers and civilians—were taken prisoner. The Japanese forced these starving survivors to march from Mariveles to San Fernando. The prisoners were loaded onto cargo trains at San Fernando and transported to prison camps farther north. Some 10,000 prisoners died during the Bataan Death March alone. Study the map of the Bataan Death March at the right. Then answer the following questions: (a) How far did the prisoners march before they were put on trains? (b) Where did their journey finally end?

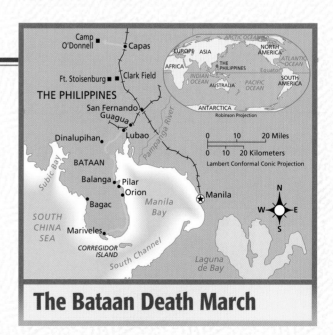

The Bataan Death March

History Skills
WORKSHOP

Distinguishing Fact from Opinion and Identifying Bias

Historical sources may contain both facts and opinions. Sources such as diaries, letters, and speeches usually express personal views. The ability to distinguish fact from opinion is essential to judging the soundness of an argument or the reliability of a historical account.

When reading historical sources, try to identify a writer's *bias*—prejudices or strong feelings—that he or she might have about the subject. Many famous historical people had strong opinions that appear in their writings and speeches. Remember that just because a person is famous does not mean that you must agree with his or her opinions.

How to Distinguish Fact from Opinion

1. **Identify the facts** Ask yourself: Can the statement be proven? Determine whether the idea can be checked for accuracy in a source such as an almanac or encyclopedia. If so, it is probably factual. If not, it probably contains an opinion.
2. **Identify the opinions** Look for clues that signal a statement of opinion: phrases such

as *I think* and *I believe,* comparative words like *greatest* and *more important,* and value-filled words like *extremely* and *ridiculous* imply a judgment, and thus an opinion.

How to Identify Bias

1. **Evaluate the information presented** What are the sources of information? How reliable are they? Why might a historical figure support one view over another? Be sure to distinguish between provable facts and someone's preferences or opinions.
2. **Make your own judgment** Remember that many of the historical documents you read are created by people who have their own opinions and points of view. It is up to you to read each document critically and to draw your own conclusions.

Practicing the Skill

Read the excerpt below, in which Father Charles Coughlin tells voters why they should not re-elect Franklin D. Roosevelt in 1936. Coughlin is running against the president. Then answer the questions that follow.

66 The hand of Moscow backs communist leaders in America . . . [and] aims to support FDR. . . . I ask you to purge [get rid of] the man who claims to be a Democrat from the Democratic Party, and I mean Franklin Double-Crossing Roosevelt. 99

1. Is this excerpt an example of a fact or an opinion? Which words let you know?
2. What bias, if any, does the author express about President Roosevelt? Why might Charles Coughlin be expressing bias?

History in Action

American History

The New Deal Game Show

Complete the following activity in small, cooperative groups.

You will be creating a game show called "The New Deal." The goal of the game is to help your classmates identify New Deal agencies and programs. Your group will come up with the specific format of the game. You will design all components of this new game.

Materials To complete this activity, you will need index cards, posterboard, scissors, pens, pencils, markers, and your textbook.

Parts of the Project To create your game, complete the following tasks:

1. **Question Cards** Choose eight New Deal programs or agencies discussed in Unit 5. Write the acronym, or abbreviation made by initials, of each program on an index card. For each program, create four additional cards. On one side of these cards, write one of the following categories: full name, date, description, or "Fact or Opinion." On the opposite side of the card include the information for that category. "Fact or Opinion" might include information such as who headed the organization or opinions about how helpful the program was. For this category, game players will identify the New Deal agency and identify whether the information is fact or opinion. You should be able to find most of this information in your textbook. You may also need to consult an encyclopedia or other library resources.

2. **Game Show Format** Once you have made the game cards, you will decide how to use them in your game show format. You will need to decide how players will win the game. You should also consider whether you want to have a game show host or allow the players to lead the show. You might also want to assign different point values to the categories based on their difficulty. Depending on the format you select, you might need to design some sort of signaling device for players.

3. **Rule Book** Write a set of rules for your game. The rules should be clear, easy to follow, and thorough.

When you have finished creating your game show, exchange it with another group. Have class members play the game. Select the best game show.

Students use index cards to record information.

UNIT 6 Postwar America
(1945–1960)

CHAPTER 17 **The Cold War Begins** (1945–1955)

CHAPTER 18 **Peace and Prosperity** (1945–1960)

American Teens

IN HISTORY

Young Musicians

When he was just 14 years old, Buddy Holly saw what his future held. A friend played a Fats Domino record for him, and suddenly Holly knew he wanted to be a rock 'n' roll star. However, he had doubts about whether he could succeed. In 1953, after just a few years of practice, Holly and a friend won regular spots on a weekly radio show in their hometown of Lubbock, Texas. "You're destined to be a star," a manager at the radio station told Holly.

The manager's prediction came true. In 1957 Buddy Holly and the Crickets topped the charts with the hit single "That'll Be the Day." Later that year, after Holly performed on *The Ed Sullivan Show,* the host asked him about his rapid rise to stardom. Holly admitted, "Well, we've had a few rough times, I guess you'd say, but we've been real lucky, getting it this quick."

Holly was just one of many young musicians who became famous in the late 1950s. Following the great success of Elvis Presley—a huge star by the age of 19—many young people took up instruments and started bands. Excited teenagers crowded concert halls to listen to these new singing sensations.

The Everly Brothers perform with Sam Cooke (center) on Shindig, *a popular television show.*

One popular concert tour was called "America's Greatest Teenage Performing Stars." That show included the Everly Brothers—Don and Phil. This duo started in show business at a young age. They made radio appearances on the *Everly Family Show* when they were just eight and six. In 1955 the teenage brothers headed to Nashville to write songs for a country music publisher. Two years later they recorded their first #1 hit with "Bye Bye Love."

Some other young stars of the 1950s included Richie Valens and Frankie Lymon and the Teenagers. Valens died at age 17 in a plane crash that also killed Buddy Holly. Young musicians such as "Little" Stevie Wonder and the Jackson Five continued to top the charts throughout the 1960s and 1970s.

In this unit you will learn more about the cultural and social changes that swept the United States after World War II. You will also learn about the political challenges that faced the country, both at home and abroad.

LEFT PAGE: *Teenagers at a dance*

Postwar America

A DNA model

Coin-operated music box from the 1940s

Seal of the OAS

1951
American scientist James D. Watson meets British scientist Francis Crick. Their work will lead to the discovery of the double helix structure of DNA in 1953.

1946
ENIAC is one of the first automatic electronic digital computers.

1947
Big-band jazz is popular but Charlie Parker's be-bop form of jazz is gaining listeners.

1948
The United States and many countries in the Western Hemisphere join together in the Organization of American States (OAS).

1949
President Harry S Truman announces his Fair Deal program.

1950
As part of a UN force, the United States joins with South Korea in a war against North Korea.

UNITED STATES

1945	1946	1947	1948	1949	1950	1951	1952

WORLD

1947
The Diary of Anne Frank, a Jewish girl's account of hiding out during World War II, is published.

1948
Following the UN's division of Palestine, the Jewish state of Israel is founded.

1949
Communists assume power in China. The People's Republic of China is established.

1951
After leading Great Britain during World War II, Winston Churchill is again elected as prime minister.

1952
Eva Perón dies. She had served her husband, Argentine president Juan Perón, as an unofficial adviser.

Anne Frank and a page from her diary

The Great Wall of China

1954
The Supreme Court rules in *Brown v. Board of Education* that separate educational facilities for black and white children are unconstitutional.

The Supreme Court Building in Washington, D.C.

Elvis "The King" Presley

1956
Singer Elvis Presley performs live on *The Ed Sullivan Show.*

1958
Two major credit cards, American Express and BankAmericard (later VISA), are introduced. They will change the spending habits of Americans.

1959
The United States and other countries sign an agreement to preserve Antarctica for scientific interests.

King penguins in Antarctica

1953	1954	1955	1956	1957	1958	1959	1960

1953
New Zealand explorer Edmund Hillary and Nepalese mountaineer Tenzing Norgay reach the summit of Mount Everest, the highest mountain in the world.

Hillary (left) and Norgay

1956
Soviet troops crush anti-communist rebellions in Poland and Hungary.

1958
A seventeen-year-old player known as Pelé leads Brazil's soccer team to victory in the World Cup.

The Jules Rimet World Cup trophy

1959
The Dalai Lama, the spiritual leader of Tibetan Buddhists, is forced to flee China.

Buddhist Wheel of Life

USING THE TIME LINE

1. On what significant topic did the Supreme Court rule in the 1950s, and how did this decision reverse earlier practices?

2. What did James D. Watson and Francis Crick discover?

3. When did Communists assume power in China and establish the People's Republic?

Activity Use information from Unit 5 and Unit 6 Time Lines to identify a possible link between the world time line entry in 1947 and the world time line entry in 1948. Explain why Anne Frank was in hiding during World War II. Write a diary entry for her. Identify events that might have helped lead to the creation of the Jewish state of Israel.

■ CHAPTER 17 ■
The Cold War Begins
(1945–1955)

Cooperation during World War II had encouraged many Americans to trust the Soviet Union. President Franklin D. Roosevelt had even said, "I think the Russians are perfectly friendly; they aren't trying to gobble up all the rest of Europe or the world." Soon after the war ended, however, this view changed. The United States and the Soviet Union became locked in a struggle for world power.

THEMES

Economic Development
Why might one country give economic aid to another?

Global Relations
How might political differences cause conflict and competition between two nations?

Citizenship and Democracy
How might global conflicts affect civil rights at home?

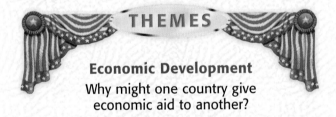

| 1945 | 1946 | 1947 | 1948 | 1949 |

NOV. 1945 War crimes trials begin in Nuremberg, Germany.

MAR. 1947 President Truman announces the Truman Doctrine.

MAY 1948 The nation of Israel is founded.

APR. 1949 NATO is created.

JUNE 1948 The Soviet Union blockades the city of Berlin.

The World After War

What agreements did the Allies reach at the Yalta and Potsdam Conferences?

What measures did the Allies take to prevent another world war?

What postwar events led to increased tensions between the Western Allies and the Soviet Union?

Key Terms

Yalta Conference
Potsdam Conference
United Nations
Nuremberg Trials

AT 5:47 P.M. ON APRIL 12, 1945, *news announcers interrupted every radio and television program in the United States. They reported that President Roosevelt had died. Americans were shocked. The man who had led the United States through the Great Depression and most of World War II was gone. Harry S Truman became the new president. He told reporters, "When they told me yesterday what had happened, I felt like the moon, the stars, and all the planets had fallen on me." After just 82 days as vice president, Truman had to fill the great man's shoes.*

Roosevelt's death stunned many Americans.

IMAGE ON LEFT PAGE: *Winston Churchill, Franklin D. Roosevelt, and Joseph Stalin (seated left to right) at Yalta*

| 1950 | 1951 | 1952 | 1953 | 1954 |

JUNE 1950 The Korean War begins.

FEB. 1950 Senator Joseph McCarthy claims that Communists are working in the U.S. State Department.

JUNE 1953 Julius and Ethel Rosenberg are executed for spying.

JULY 1953 A cease-fire ends the Korean War.

The Cold War Begins **509**

⭐ Yalta and Potsdam

In February 1945 the Allies were close to victory in Europe. In the Soviet town of Yalta, a meeting took place between the "Big Three." These leaders were Franklin D. Roosevelt of the United States, Winston Churchill of Great Britain, and Joseph Stalin of the Soviet Union. At the **Yalta Conference**, they made plans for the postwar world. The resulting agreement would shape international affairs for years to come.

Clement Attlee, Harry S Truman, and Joseph Stalin (seated left to right) at the Potsdam Conference

The Yalta agreement called for the creation of a world peacekeeping organization. It also supported free elections and democratic governments in the nations being freed from Axis control. In addition, Stalin agreed to join the war against Japan after Germany surrendered. The agreement seemed to solve many problems. One of President Roosevelt's close advisers recalled, "We really believed in our hearts that this was the dawn of the new day we had all been praying for and talking about for so many years."

Stalin did not honor all of the agreements he had made at Yalta. For example, he did not want a democratic government established in Poland. Stalin saw Poland as a crucial buffer between Germany and his own country. After the Soviets liberated Poland from German control, they installed a pro-communist government in June 1945. This government later refused to allow free elections in Poland.

After Roosevelt's death in April, Harry S Truman had become president. Germany surrendered the following month. Soviet armies occupied most of Eastern Europe. In July, Truman traveled to Potsdam, Germany, to meet with Churchill and Stalin. At the **Potsdam Conference**, the three leaders divided Germany into four zones of occupation. Britain, France, the Soviet Union, and the United States would each control one zone. The former German capital of Berlin, located within the Soviet zone, was also divided into four sections.

Meanwhile, in the Pacific the Allies continued to fight Japan. The Allies demanded unconditional surrender from the Japanese government. Shortly before his arrival at Potsdam, Truman had learned of the successful atomic bomb test at Trinity Site, New Mexico. He decided to tell Churchill about the test, but not Stalin. Truman later approved the use of this new weapon against Japan. After the atomic bombing of Hiroshima and Nagasaki, Japan surrendered in September 1945.

⭐ Political Changes

While in Germany, President Truman visited Berlin. Shocked by the wartime devastation of the city, he and other political leaders looked for ways to prevent future wars.

The United Nations

The solution seemed to be an international organization that could resolve conflicts peacefully. In 1944, British, Chinese, Soviet, and U.S. representatives had met in Washington, D.C. They drafted a plan for a new organization to promote world peace—the **United Nations** (UN). The following year, representatives from 50 nations came together in San Francisco, California, to write the UN charter. The charter was unanimously approved and signed in June 1945. The first official UN session took place in January 1946.

The flags of member nations fly at the UN Building in New York City.

The UN charter created two major bodies, the Security Council and the General Assembly. Fifteen member nations belong to the Security Council. Five nations—China, France, Great Britain, present-day Russia, and the United States—have permanent seats on the council. The other 10 nations are elected to the council for two-year terms. The Security Council authorizes diplomatic, economic, and military actions to settle disputes. The General Assembly is made up of all UN member nations. It meets annually to debate policy, vote on membership, and approve the budget. The UN charter also created the International Court of Justice, based in The Hague, Netherlands.

These Nazi officials were the first of many charged with war crimes. Seated on the far left is Hermann Göring, head of Hitler's secret police.

The War Crimes Trials

To discourage future acts of aggression, the Allies also held war crimes trials. These are trials of individuals accused of crimes against humanity and the international laws of warfare. Beginning in November 1945, the International Military Tribunal tried high-ranking Nazi officers. The trials were held in Nuremberg, Germany—the former site of huge Nazi rallies. The chief American attorney highlighted the importance of these **Nuremberg Trials**.

" **The wrongs which we seek to condemn and punish have been so calculated, so malignant [harmful] and devastating, that civilization cannot tolerate their being ignored because it cannot survive their being repeated.** "

The tribunal at Nuremberg found 21 Nazi leaders guilty of crimes against humanity and sentenced 12 of them to death. The tribunal also tried and convicted thousands of lesser officials. Many of the ex-Nazis were convicted for helping to run concentration camps during the Holocaust.

The International Military Tribunal for the Far East conducted similar war crimes trials in Japan. The tribunal convicted and executed former prime minister Hideki Tojo and six other Japanese leaders. It also convicted some 4,000 lesser Japanese war criminals.

During the trials soldiers could not use the defense that they had simply been following

orders. The war crimes trials established that there is no defense for committing crimes against humanity. The trials also showed that nations could cooperate to prosecute war criminals.

The Birth of Israel

The Nuremberg Trials further exposed the horrors of the Holocaust. International support increased for the creation of a Jewish homeland. In 1947 the UN General Assembly divided Palestine, which Britain had occupied since World War I. Two states were to be formed—one Arab, one Jewish. In May 1948 the independent Jewish nation of Israel was established.

The United States immediately recognized Israel's independence. Just as swiftly, the armies of neighboring Arab states attacked the new nation. Israeli forces drove back the attackers and advanced to occupy

Israel's national flag

Arab territory. After a bitter fight, the two sides signed an armistice in the spring of 1949. The Jews had a homeland. However, the war had created about 1 million Palestinian Arab refugees. Israel joined the United Nations in 1949.

★ A Divided Europe

Despite the efforts of Allied leaders to establish world peace after World War II, tensions in Europe remained high. Western diplomats were becoming very concerned about the plans of Stalin and the Soviet Union.

The United States and the Soviet Union disagreed strongly about the political future of Central and Eastern Europe. The status of Germany was a major issue. The United States wanted an independent and united Germany. The Soviets feared that if Germany united, it might once again invade their country—as it had in both world wars.

The Soviet armies of occupation remained in Eastern Europe. They helped establish communist "satellite states" loyal to the Soviet Union. The Soviets argued that they were simply protecting their borders. Western diplomats viewed these actions differently. British prime minister Winston Churchill warned Americans about the threat posed by Soviet expansion in Europe:

66 **An Iron Curtain has descended across the [European] Continent. Behind that**

The Iron Curtain cut nations such as Czechoslovakia off from Western Europe.

Editorial cartoon by Tom Little, 1948; courtesy of the *Nashville Tennessean*.

line lie all the capitals of the ancient states of Central and Eastern Europe. . . . All these famous cities and the populations around them lie in the Soviet sphere and all are subject . . . to a very high and increasing measure of control from Moscow. 99

British and U.S. leaders feared that the Soviet Union's influence would continue to expand. This growth would threaten the democracies of Western Europe. Many observers were also troubled by stories of Stalin's use of terror and violence against Soviet citizens. These brutal acts suggested that Stalin would stop at nothing to protect and increase his power.

Some U.S. politicians were even concerned that Communists at home were cooperating with Soviet spies. Senator Arthur Vandenberg asked other members of Congress, "What is Russia up to? . . . We ask it in eastern Europe. . . . We ask it sometimes even in connection with events in our United States."

SECTION 1 REVIEW

Identify and explain the significance of the following:
- Yalta Conference
- Harry S Truman
- Potsdam Conference
- United Nations
- Nuremberg Trials

Reading for Content Understanding

1 **Main Idea** What plans did the Allies discuss at the Yalta and Potsdam Conferences?

2 **Main Idea** What created postwar tensions between the Soviet Union and the Western Allies?

3 **Global Relations** How did the Allies try to preserve world peace after World War II?

4 **Writing** *Expressing* Imagine that you are a Jew who lived through the Holocaust. Write a short article for an Israeli newspaper expressing your reaction to the Nuremberg Trials.

5 **Critical Thinking** *Drawing Conclusions* Why do you think the United States was willing to join the United Nations when it had not been willing to join the League of Nations after World War I?

SECTION 2

The Roots of the Cold War

Reading Focus

What were the major U.S. foreign-policy strategies after World War II?

What was the purpose and the result of the Marshall Plan?

What were the major events in the Cold War between the United States and the Soviet Union from 1946 to 1950?

Key Terms

Cold War
Truman Doctrine
Marshall Plan
containment
Berlin Airlift
North Atlantic Treaty Organization

O ne day in the spring of 1945, *U.S. and Soviet troops met each other at the Elbe River in Germany. The Soviets waited on the eastern shore of the river. Private Joseph Polowsky and a few other U.S. soldiers approached the Soviets cautiously. Through translators the two sides spoke to each other. "There were tears in the eyes of most of us . . . ," recalled Polowsky. They then pointed to the ruins around them, he remembered. "We embraced. We swore never to forget." Despite their shared relief at the end of the war, Polowsky felt "a sense of foreboding [uneasiness] that things might not be as perfect in the future as we anticipated."*

A stamp showing the meeting at the Elbe River

★ Allies Become Enemies

The Soviet Union and the United States had allied against Germany in World War II. After the war they were the two most powerful nations in the world. Their alliance quickly turned into a bitter competition.

The so-called superpowers had little in common economically or politically. The United States was based on free enterprise and democracy. The Soviet Union was a communist country. Both governments wanted to spread their influence around the world. As a result, both countries became increasingly involved in the affairs of other nations. For example, the Soviet Union supported pro-communist independence movements in many colonized regions. The United States often opposed these efforts, fearing the spread of communism.

U.S. presidential adviser Bernard Baruch described U.S.-Soviet relations by saying, "Let us not be deceived—we are today in the midst of a cold war." Many people began using the term **Cold War** to describe the struggle between the

The Cold War Begins **513**

United States and the Soviet Union for global power.

One of the first trouble spots was Greece. In August 1946, communist guerrillas revolted against the corrupt monarchy of Greece. The rebels were supported by the independent communist government of Yugoslavia. President Truman, however, believed the Soviets were behind the revolt. He decided to stop further Soviet expansion in Europe.

In March 1947 Truman announced that the United States would provide economic aid to help foreign countries fight communism. This policy became known as the **Truman Doctrine**. Congress approved $400 million in aid for Greece and its neighbor Turkey. This aid helped the Greek army defeat the rebels. The Truman Doctrine was successful in protecting the anti-communist governments of Greece and Turkey. However, it greatly angered Soviet leaders.

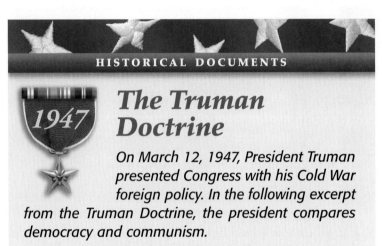

The Truman Doctrine

1947

On March 12, 1947, President Truman presented Congress with his Cold War foreign policy. In the following excerpt from the Truman Doctrine, the president compares democracy and communism.

"At the present moment in world history nearly every nation must choose between alternative ways of life. . . . One way of life is based upon the will of the majority, and is distinguished by free institutions, representative government, free elections, and . . . freedom from political oppression. The second way of life is based upon the will of a minority forcibly imposed upon the majority. It relies upon terror and oppression . . . and the suppression of personal freedoms. I believe it must be the policy of the United States to support free peoples. . . .

The free peoples of the world look to us for support in maintaining their freedoms. If we falter in our leadership, we may endanger the peace of the world—and we shall surely endanger the welfare of our own nation."

Understanding Primary Sources

1. What distinguishes democracy from communism according to President Truman?

2. Who does Truman say the United States should support, and why?

★ The Marshall Plan

Some Europeans thought that communism would solve their economic troubles. The European economy had been severely damaged by World War II. Millions of people were unemployed and major industries were in ruin. Many people were homeless. Countless others were in danger of starvation.

General George C. Marshall had helped plan the D-Day invasion in World War II. He became U.S. secretary of state in 1947. Marshall argued that Europe's economic recovery was necessary to protect world peace. European recovery would also benefit the U.S. economy, which relied on trade with Europe. Marshall said:

"It is logical that the United States should do whatever it is able to do to assist in the return of normal economic health in the world, without which there can be no political stability and no assured peace."

In what became known as the **Marshall Plan**, the United States offered "friendly aid" to help the nations of Europe rebuild. Some members of Congress thought the Marshall Plan would be too expensive. Others argued

Tons of goods helped Europeans recover after the war.

that Communists might gain control of Western European nations if their economies did not recover.

This argument persuaded many officials. Congress eventually approved $6 billion for Marshall Plan aid. Congress later increased funding for the plan after it went into effect.

The United States offered to assist the Soviet Union under the Marshall Plan, but the Soviets refused the offer. The Soviet foreign minister called the plan a plot to enslave Europe by making it dependent on U.S. aid. Marshall insisted that his plan was not directed "against any country or doctrine but against hunger, poverty, desperation, and chaos." Soviet leaders ignored such statements. They prevented their Eastern European satellites from participating in the Marshall Plan and accepting U.S. aid.

The Marshall Plan helped Western Europe recover from the war. "We grabbed the lifeline with both hands," remembered a British minister. The plan also created a market for American exports. However, the Marshall Plan widened the division between the Soviet Union and the United States.

★ Containment

As the Cold War continued, the United States adopted a new foreign policy. This foreign policy, called **containment**, sought to contain the spread of communism by reacting quickly to any Soviet-backed aggression. U.S. officials saw containment as a defensive strategy. Soviet leaders , however, regarded the policy as an offensive strategy.

The Berlin Airlift

In the late 1940s a crisis in occupied Germany tested the containment policy. England, France, and the United States wanted an independent German nation. In June 1948 they proposed merging their areas of control to create the country of West Germany. The divided city of Berlin, however, would still be located in Soviet-controlled eastern Germany. Angered by this proposal, the Soviets blocked off all highway and rail traffic between West Berlin and Western Europe.

West Berlin could not survive without food and other necessities from the West. To solve the crisis without a direct military confrontation, U.S. officials decided to fly supplies into the city. In June 1948, U.S. and British planes began the **Berlin Airlift**. They brought food and supplies to the more than 2 million people in West Berlin. The effort was massive. Planes landed in Berlin every minute for weeks.

The Marshall Plan, 1948–1951

Learning from Maps The Marshall Plan lasted from 1948 until 1951, during which time the United States sent about $13 billion in aid to European countries recovering from World War II.

Location Which country in Western Europe did not receive aid under the Marshall Plan?

Linking Past to Present

American Military Bases Abroad

The United States has maintained overseas military bases since the mid-1800s. In the 1860s and 1870s, the U.S. Navy gained the use of Pacific islands as refueling stations. Victory in the Spanish-American War brought bases in Cuba and the Philippines under U.S. control.

After World War II, U.S. presidents believed that Soviet aggression required a near-global U.S. military presence. As a result, the United States built many more bases in foreign countries. With Soviet-dominated East Germany as a neighbor, West Germany was particularly vulnerable. Therefore, the United States built multiple army command headquarters, airfields, and smaller bases there. The United States also built bases in other Western European nations, as well as in Japan, South Korea, and the Philippines. To protect its interests in the Persian Gulf, the United States built bases in Bahrain and Saudi Arabia.

Thousands of U.S. military personnel and their families have lived on these overseas bases. Their experiences have been both rewarding

Camp Foster on the Japanese island of Okinawa

and challenging. One air force colonel's son fondly remembers the years he lived in Italy. "We went to festivals where there were big floats and people threw confetti." Others, however, did not experience the local culture. An army sergeant's daughter recalls, "We were pretty much isolated. We lived in this compound, and for all we figured, that was the way everybody lived."

In the post–Cold War era, the Department of Defense re-examined strategic needs and foreign-policy goals. It concluded that there was less need for overseas bases. The United States has thus closed or reduced the size of many overseas bases, mostly in Europe.

Understanding What You Read

1. Why and when were most U.S. overseas military bases established?
2. Why were so many U.S. military bases located in West Germany?

In September 1948 Ernst Reuter, the mayor of West Berlin, declared:

" **We cannot be bartered [traded], we cannot be negotiated, we cannot be sold. . . . Whoever would surrender the people of Berlin, would surrender a world. . . . People of the world, look upon this city! You cannot, you must not, forsake us!** "

The so-called Operation Vittles lasted 321 days. During this time, planes brought more than 2 million tons of food and supplies into West Berlin. The Soviets did not want to risk a war by stopping the airlift. On May 12, 1949, the Soviet Union lifted its blockade. That same year, Germany became two nations—the Federal Republic of Germany (West Germany) and the German Democratic Republic (East Germany).

Defensive Moves

Concern over the growing military strength of the Soviet Union led the United States, Canada, Iceland, and nine Western European nations to form a military alliance in April 1949. Each member of this **North Atlantic Treaty Organization** (NATO) pledged to defend the others. The treaty then went to the U.S. Senate to be ratified. Some senators worried that NATO might require the United States to go to war without congressional approval. Similar concerns had stopped the United States from joining the League of Nations after World War I. Yet the threat of Soviet expansion convinced the Senate to approve NATO. In 1955 the Soviet Union created its own military alliance, the Warsaw Pact, with the Eastern European nations it controlled.

Another concern for U.S. leaders was the rise of a Soviet nuclear threat. In August 1949 the Soviets shocked U.S. military experts by detonating their own atomic bomb. The Cold War grew more intense. In 1950 the U.S. National Security Council issued NSC-68, a foreign-policy paper. This

This NATO badge bears the Latin inscription "Vigilance is the price of liberty."

paper argued that the Soviet Union sought to control not just Europe but the entire world. According to NSC-68, U.S. leaders had to be prepared to oppose Soviet-backed Communists worldwide. The United States might have to use force in small or remote countries to protect its interests.

Not all Americans agreed with this viewpoint. Some critics argued that the resources of the United States would be stretched too thin if it tried to fight communism everywhere. They also worried that the United States would be tempted to support even undemocratic governments that were anticommunist. Despite such criticisms, global containment had strong support among many American politicians and military leaders.

To support containment, the United States strengthened its international alliances. It also quadrupled defense spending. President Truman authorized the development of even more powerful nuclear weapons for national defense. Just a few years after the end of World War II, the Cold War between the United States and the Soviet Union was spreading around the world.

SECTION 2 REVIEW

Identify and explain the significance of the following:

- **Cold War**
- **Truman Doctrine**
- **George C. Marshall**
- **Marshall Plan**
- **containment**
- **Berlin Airlift**
- **North Atlantic Treaty Organization**

Locate and explain the importance of the following:

- **Berlin**
- **East Germany**
- **West Germany**

Reading for Content Understanding

1 Main Idea What major foreign policies did the United States develop at the start of the Cold War?

2 Main Idea Create a graphic organizer listing the major events of the Cold War between 1946 and 1950. Include the year that each event occurred and its outcome.

3 Economic Development Why did the United States create the Marshall Plan, and what were its results?

4 Writing *Persuading* Imagine that you are a member of Congress in 1949. Write a short speech persuading other members to support or oppose the North Atlantic Treaty Organization.

5 Critical Thinking *Drawing Conclusions* Why do you think the Western Allies put so much effort and money into keeping the Soviets from controlling West Berlin?

The Truman Era

Reading Focus

How did the U.S. government try to ease the transition to peacetime?

What were the major issues and the outcome of the 1948 presidential election?

What did President Truman hope to accomplish with his Fair Deal?

Key Terms

GI Bill of Rights
United Mine Workers
Taft-Hartley Act
Dixiecrats
Fair Deal

*A*S A YOUNG MAN, *Chesterfield Smith just wanted to have a good time. He entered the University of Florida in 1935. By 1940 he had completed only three and a half years of school. "I'd go to school a semester and then drop out a semester," Smith explained. "I chose the easy life in college." Then World War II came, and Smith served in France. In 1946 he returned to college and quickly finished the classes he needed to graduate. Smith's wife explained: "Something happened to Chesterfield's attitude in the war, I don't know just what, but he was a serious man when he returned." Smith was one of many Americans who became serious about the future after the war.*

Like many Americans, these people were overjoyed by the victory in World War II.

 ## Returning to Peace

After World War II, President Truman wanted the United States to return to a peacetime economy. He considered loosening wartime price controls and canceling defense contracts. Yet he worried that too much spending by consumers would cause inflation. Truman also feared that canceling defense contracts might cause a recession. This had taken place following World War I. Truman believed that the United States needed a strong economy to compete in the Cold War.

Postwar Jobs

More than 16 million men and women had served in the armed forces. Most of them needed jobs when they returned to civilian life. To provide more positions for these veterans, the government encouraged the millions of women who had gone to work during wartime to give up their jobs.

Many women resented the loss of the income and independence that their jobs had provided. "They say a woman doesn't belong behind a factory machine or in any business organization," one female worker remarked. "But . . . who will give

Harry S Truman

Harry S Truman was born in May 1884 in Lamar, Missouri. From an early age he was a good student. "I don't know anybody in the world ever read as much or as constantly as he did," a friend remem-

bered. Truman also studied human nature, a skill that helped him in his political career. "When I was growing up," Truman said, "it occurred to me to watch the people around me to find out what they thought and what pleased them the most."

After the United States entered World War I, Truman felt a deep obligation to serve his country. A number of personal factors—his age and poor eyesight, for example—would have allowed him to avoid military service. He enlisted nonetheless, saying it was "a job somebody had to do." After serving in a command position, Truman returned to Missouri and soon began his political career. He became a U.S. senator in 1934. Ten years later he was elected vice president.

my family the help they have been getting from me? No one has thought to ask me whether or not I need my job."

New laws provided veterans with benefits that eased the transition to civilian life. Government officials had feared that 8 million people would be unemployed by the spring of 1946. The figure never rose above 2.7 million.

The GI Bill

The Servicemen's Readjustment Act, also called the **GI Bill of Rights**, helped keep unemployment

These veterans are entering Austin College in Sherman, Texas.

low. Congress passed the GI Bill in 1944. It offered veterans educational benefits to attend colleges and technical schools. The bill also provided veterans with affordable home and business loans.

Guy Owen was a veteran from North Carolina who became a novelist and a professor. He explained how the GI Bill changed his life:

 The GI Bill, I can't emphasize enough, really saved me. [Without it] I don't think I would have been able to go on for the doctorate [graduate degree]. . . . The GI Bill took me . . . to places . . . where I had different experiences from what I would have ever seen in Carolina. "

Nearly 9 million veterans took advantage of the GI Bill's educational benefits.

★ Labor Unrest

Despite President Truman's efforts, there were some postwar economic troubles. When Truman ended rationing and price controls on goods, consumers rushed to buy products. As a result, prices skyrocketed. Food prices rose by more than 25 percent between 1945 and 1947. The inflation rate for 1946 rose to just over 18 percent.

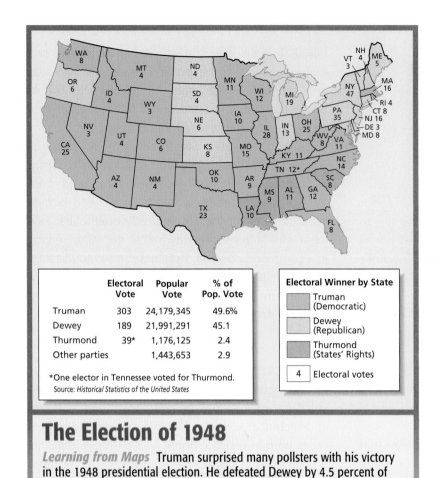

	Electoral Vote	Popular Vote	% of Pop. Vote
Truman	303	24,179,345	49.6%
Dewey	189	21,991,291	45.1
Thurmond	39*	1,176,125	2.4
Other parties		1,443,653	2.9

*One elector in Tennessee voted for Thurmond.
Source: Historical Statistics of the United States

Electoral Winner by State
- Truman (Democratic)
- Dewey (Republican)
- Thurmond (States' Rights)
- 4 Electoral votes

The Election of 1948

Learning from Maps Truman surprised many pollsters with his victory in the 1948 presidential election. He defeated Dewey by 4.5 percent of the popular vote.

Region What parts of the country voted primarily for Dewey in 1948?

As inflation soared, unions went on strike to demand higher wages. In 1946 alone, some 4.5 million workers took part in nearly 5,000 strikes across the country. In April of that year some 400,000 members of the **United Mine Workers** (UMW) went on strike. When President Truman could not negotiate a settlement, he placed the mines under government control.

In November, UMW president John Lewis called a second strike even though the mines were still under federal control. This time, Truman said, it would be a "fight to the finish." He ordered U.S. troops to take control of the mines. The government ordered Lewis to stand trial for contempt, or disobeying an official order. "You can't dig coal with bayonets," replied Lewis. He refused to send the miners back to work. After a federal court fined the UMW $3.5 million, however, he finally halted the strike.

Republicans in Congress wanted to weaken labor unions. They were particularly concerned with the closed shop. A closed shop is a workplace in which job applicants have to join a union before they can be hired. In 1947 Senator Robert Taft of Ohio led the drive to pass the **Taft-Hartley Act**. This act outlawed closed shops. It also required union leaders to take an oath saying that they were not Communists. The act gave the president the authority to obtain court orders forcing striking unions to call off their strikes for an 80-day "cooling off" period. Despite his conflicts with the UMW, Truman thought that the Taft-Hartley Act placed too many restrictions on unions. He vetoed it, but Congress overrode his veto.

★ The 1948 Election

The labor unrest caused many Americans to question Truman's presidential skills. The Republicans had gained control of Congress in 1946. They believed they could win the White House in 1948. Republicans nominated New York governor Thomas Dewey for president and California governor Earl Warren for vice president.

Even leaders of the Democratic Party did not think that Truman could win re-election in 1948. Many wanted to dump him in favor of another candidate. At the 1948 national convention, the Democrats were sharply divided. Nonetheless, Truman managed to win the nomination.

Stunning the experts and forcing newspapers to rewrite headlines, President Truman won the 1948 election.

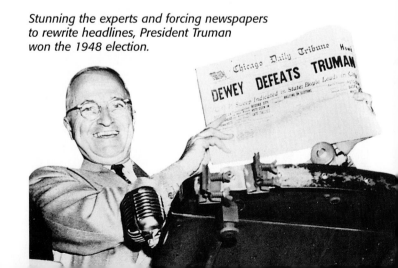

Some southern Democrats were upset with Truman's actions on civil rights issues. They walked out of the convention. Many of them joined the newly formed States' Rights Party, known as the **Dixiecrats**. The Dixiecrats favored racial segregation and wanted to restrict African American voting rights. The party nominated South Carolina governor Strom Thurmond for president. A second group of Democrats disliked the way Truman had dealt with the labor strikes. These politicians formed a new Progressive Party. They nominated Henry Wallace for president. Wallace had previously served as vice president in Franklin D. Roosevelt's third administration.

Truman campaigned with tremendous energy. He traveled more than 30,000 miles by train and delivered hundreds of speeches. He attacked Congress as the "do-nothing, good-for-nothing, worst Congress." Nonetheless, public opinion polls predicted a landslide victory for Dewey, right up to election night.

When the results were in, Truman had won a surprising victory. He later declared:

A donkey made for President Truman by a supporter

❝ **It seemed to have been a terrific political upset. It was not—it was merely a continuation of the policies . . . that the people wanted.** ❞

Truman's success was based on several factors. His veto of the Taft-Hartley Act had won back union support. He also gained a large number of African American votes. In addition, many Wallace supporters switched to Truman when it looked as if Dewey would win.

The recovering economy was another reason for Truman's victory. By 1948 American industries had successfully shifted back to peacetime production. Personal income began to increase. Cold War spending also created new jobs. As one Truman supporter explained, "I own a nice house, I have a new car. . . . Why change?"

Truman was confident that the American public supported his policies. He proposed a series of reform programs that became known as the **Fair Deal**. The Fair Deal was intended to provide full employment, a higher minimum wage, and a national health insurance plan. Truman also called for more affordable housing, expanded Social Security benefits, and aid for farmers.

Congress approved a few key Fair Deal reforms. It extended Social Security and raised the minimum wage. Congress rejected some civil rights legislation, federal aid to education, and national health insurance. The government also spent billions on domestic improvements and the GI Bill. This government spending helped to sustain the postwar boom.

SECTION 3 REVIEW

Identify and explain the significance of the following:
- **GI Bill of Rights**
- **United Mine Workers**
- **John Lewis**
- **Taft-Hartley Act**
- **Dixiecrats**
- **Fair Deal**

Reading for Content Understanding

1 **Main Idea** What public concerns affected the outcome of the 1948 presidential election?

2 **Main Idea** What were the main goals of the Fair Deal?

3 **Economic Development** What steps did the U.S. government take to avoid a recession after World War II?

4 **Writing** *Describing* Imagine that you are a reporter observing the labor unrest of 1946. Write an article describing President Truman's efforts to end the labor strikes.

5 **Critical Thinking** *Identifying Cause and Effect* How did the GI Bill help promote long-term economic growth?

The Korean War

Reading Focus

What events led China to become a communist nation?

Why was the United States involved in Korea and how did the Korean War end?

How did the Korean War affect the 1952 presidential election?

Key Terms

Long March
38th parallel

IN 1911 A GROUP OF YOUNG *Chinese army officers revolted against the 2,000-year-old Chinese empire.*
Early the next year, China's 400 million people learned that China had become a republic. The emperor, Pu Yi, was only six years old when he received the news that he would no longer rule the nation. Pu Yi was confined in the Imperial Palace with his servants. "It was in this tiny world that I was to spend the most absurd childhood possible . . . ," he later wrote. "When China was called a republic . . . I was still living the life of an emperor, breathing the dust of the nineteenth century."

The Imperial Palace in Beijing

★ Communist China

When China's monarchy fell in 1912, it caused great political unrest. During the 1920s the Chinese Nationalist Party and the Chinese Communists struggled for power. This struggle turned into a bitter civil war. In 1934 about 100,000 Communists had to flee from a Nationalist army attack. Led by Mao Zedong (MOW DZUH-DOOHNG), the Communists began a 6,000-mile, 12-month retreat to northwestern China. This escape became known as the **Long March**.

During the mid-1930s the Nationalists joined with the Communists to fight against the invading Japanese. After World War II, however, the civil war resumed. Suspicious of any communist government, the United States backed the Nationalists led by Chiang Kaishek (chang-ky-SHEK). However, his government lacked popular support. U.S. Army general Joseph Stilwell wrote that he saw "corruption, neglect, chaos" in the Nationalist government and military.

Nevertheless, the United States gave millions of dollars in aid to the Nationalists to fight the

Communists. This U.S. support was not enough to defeat the Communists. In 1949 they drove the Nationalists off the Chinese mainland to the island of Taiwan. Mao then founded the communist People's Republic of China.

Relations between the United States and China were poor. The United States refused to formally recognize Mao's new government. Instead, the United States continued diplomatic relations with Taiwan. Many Americans were concerned that the People's Republic of China would join forces with the Soviet Union. Such an alliance would threaten U.S. security.

U.S. secretary of state Dean Acheson wrote that the takeover of China by the Communist Party "was beyond the control of the government of the United States." Despite such claims, many U.S. leaders thought that the United States had "lost" China to the Communists because of foreign-policy mistakes. Some U.S. politicians vowed never to lose another nation in Asia to communism.

The Chinese government made posters celebrating the Communists' victory in 1949.

the United States and the Soviet Union each established a government in its area of occupation.

The Soviets backed the communist Democratic People's Republic of Korea in the northern half of the peninsula. The United States supported the Republic of Korea in the southern half. U.S. officials realized that this compromise was awkward. They hoped that the division would keep the peace and prevent further communist expansion in Asia.

The U.S. and Soviet troops finally pulled out in 1949. Both the North and South Korean governments then claimed the entire country. The Soviets had left behind a well-equipped and well-trained North Korean army. On June 25, 1950, North Korean forces crossed the **38th parallel**, the line of latitude dividing the two countries. The South Korean army was no match for the invaders. North Korean forces quickly advanced. The UN Security Council immediately called for a cease-fire. The North Koreans, however, continued their attack. Top U.S. advisers were determined not to allow another Asian nation such as South Korea to become communist.

 ## The Cold War in Asia

The postwar period also brought new governments to other Asian nations. After World War II, U.S. forces occupied Japan and began rebuilding Japan's devastated economy. Military leaders such as General Douglas MacArthur also helped create a U.S.-style constitution. The new government placed more power in the hands of the Japanese people. It also granted women the right to vote. In addition, the Japanese constitution prohibited Japan from waging war.

Japan had controlled Korea from 1910 until the end of World War II. In 1945 the Allies divided Korea. U.S. forces occupied the southern half of the Korean Peninsula. Soviet troops occupied the north. The United States then asked the United Nations to allow national elections in Korea to reunite the country. The Soviet Union vetoed this proposal in the UN Security Council. As a result,

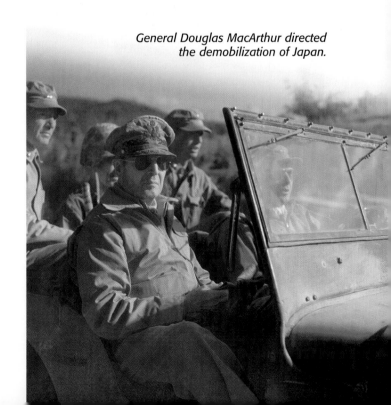

General Douglas MacArthur directed the demobilization of Japan.

War in Korea

On June 27, 1950, the UN Security Council called on UN members to support South Korea. The Soviet ambassador was not present to veto this proposal. That same day President Truman announced to Americans, "I have ordered United States air and sea forces to give the Korean government troops cover and support."

General Douglas MacArthur flew to Korea to review the situation. He reported that South Korea needed ground troops immediately. In response, the United States and 15 other nations offered troops to the UN effort. It was the first time that UN forces had fought in a major conflict. In July, MacArthur was named commander of the UN forces. These troops consisted largely of U.S. and South Korean soldiers.

Changes of Fortune

By late July the North Korean army had driven UN forces to the southeastern tip of the peninsula, into a small area near the port city of Pusan. General Walton "Bulldog" Walker told his men, "There will be no more retreating. . . . We must fight to the end. We must fight as a team. If some of us die, we will die fighting together."

For six weeks, fierce fighting raged along the Pusan front. The situation seemed desperate at times. MacArthur and other military leaders developed a daring plan to turn the tide of the war—a surprise attack behind enemy lines. On September 15, UN forces landed near the port city of Inchon. There they attacked the North Korean troops from behind. The UN forces quickly drove the invading army out of South Korea.

MacArthur's forces pursued. Just over a month later, they captured Pyongyang (pyuhng-YANG), North Korea's capital. Eventually, they reached the Yalu River, the border between China and North Korea. U.S. soldiers looked forward to a quick end of the war. MacArthur boasted that he would "have the boys [the soldiers] home by Christmas."

China Enters the War

During the fighting, it had become clear that some Chinese troops were fighting alongside the North Koreans. Hundreds of thousands more Chinese troops joined the North Koreans in launching a counteroffensive. They drove the UN forces back below the 38th parallel in brutal fighting. One platoon leader in the U.S. 24th Infantry described a battle that took place in a rice paddy:

> "The medics could scarcely keep up with the men who had been hit. . . . How we managed to survive I don't know, but when we reached the top of the hill, the enemy had cut and run, and we collapsed on the ground, not bothering to dig in."

The Korean War, 1950–1953

Learning from Maps After three years of fighting, the boundary between North and South Korea remained roughly the same.

Movement Which country increased in size after the armistice line of 1953 was established?

Boundary set by Allies after World War II.

Armistice line, July 1953

Farthest advance of communist forces, Sept. 1950

Farthest advance of UN forces, Nov. 1950

Farthest advance of Chinese/North Korean forces, Jan. 1951

Fighting during the Korean winters was uncomfortable and difficult.

General MacArthur knew President Truman did not want the war to expand beyond Korea. Nonetheless, MacArthur publicly called for air strikes on Chinese cities and a ground attack on the Chinese coast. Truman refused. MacArthur then criticized the president openly. He wrote that "there is no substitute for victory." In response, Truman relieved MacArthur of his command in April 1951. Truman's decision was not a popular one. MacArthur returned home to parades and celebrations in his honor.

In early 1951 a UN offensive pushed the Chinese and North Koreans back across the 38th parallel. The fighting then settled into a standstill. Groups of diplomats from both sides attempted unsuccessfully to hammer out a peace treaty.

 The Election of 1952

By the spring of 1951 it had become clear that neither side in Korea was going to defeat the other on the battlefield. As one British soldier stated, "Everybody could see that we had reached stalemate, unless someone started chucking atom bombs." Peace negotiations began in July but saw little progress. As the negotiations and the war dragged on, the American public grew increasingly frustrated.

The Korean War became the major issue in the presidential election of 1952. Knowing that many voters blamed him for the war, President Truman chose not to seek re-election. The Democrats nominated Adlai Stevenson, the governor of Illinois, for president. Stevenson was intelligent and quick-witted. However, his speaking style made him seem out of touch with the "real world" to many voters.

Hoping to win the White House for the first time since the election of 1928, the Republicans nominated General Dwight D. Eisenhower. Ike, as he was often called, was a respected war hero. He was also charming and popular with the American public. For vice president, the Republicans nominated Senator Richard Nixon of California. Nixon was a strong anticommunist.

The Eisenhower-Nixon campaign faced a potential problem. Nixon was accused of receiving illegal gifts and money from a number of wealthy donors. Eisenhower considered replacing Nixon with a new candidate. Nixon then went on television to offer an explanation to the American people. He said that one of the gifts was a small puppy named Checkers. Nixon declared that he could not return it because his children loved the dog. The Checkers speech, as it became known, saved Nixon's place on the ticket.

A 1952 Eisenhower campaign sign

Already leading the polls, Eisenhower probably secured the election when he said in October:

> ❝ **The first task of a new administration will be to . . . bring the Korean War to an early and honorable end. That is my pledge to the American people. For this task a wholly new administration is necessary. The reason for this is simple. The old administration cannot be expected to repair what it failed to prevent. . . . That job requires a personal trip to Korea. . . . I shall go to Korea.** ❞

Eisenhower easily won, gaining 442 electoral votes to Stevenson's 89 electoral votes.

On his trip to Korea, Eisenhower joined his old army unit for a meal.

The End of the War

President-elect Eisenhower made good on his promise to go to Korea. He flew to Korea and met with U.S. commanders in early December 1952. Despite his visit, the peace negotiations remained stalled. Eisenhower was desperate for a solution. He let the Chinese and North Koreans know that the United States might use atomic weapons if the conflict continued.

After the death of Soviet leader Joseph Stalin on March 5, 1953, the new Soviet leadership also pushed both sides to end the war. As the peace talks slowly progressed, fighting flared up again. Thousands more soldiers were killed or wounded.

The war remained at a stalemate while the negotiations continued. On July 27, 1953, the two sides signed a cease-fire that effectively ended the Korean War. After three years of fighting that devastated both sides, the two countries were once again divided roughly along the 38th parallel. The U.S. forces suffered more than 155,000 casualties. The South Korean army suffered about 845,000 casualties. North Korean and Chinese military casualties totaled more than 1.5 million. Some 3 million North and South Korean civilians had also died. Many thousands more Koreans were left homeless as a result of the war.

The Korean War was over so far as the United Nations and the United States were concerned. However, North and South Korea had signed a truce rather than a peace treaty. Tensions remained high between both governments. A narrow demilitarized zone (DMZ) was established between the two nations along the 38th parallel. On each side, thousands of soldiers continue to face each other across a no-man's-land. Thousands of U.S. troops are still stationed along the DMZ to help defend South Korea against an invasion from the North.

SECTION 4 REVIEW

Identify and explain the significance of the following:
- **Mao Zedong**
- **Long March**
- **Chiang Kaishek**
- **Douglas MacArthur**
- **38th parallel**
- **Adlai Stevenson**
- **Dwight D. Eisenhower**

Locate and explain the importance of the following:
- **North Korea**
- **South Korea**
- **Inchon**

Reading for Content Understanding

1 **Main Idea** Create a graphic organizer to show the events that resulted in China becoming a communist nation.

2 **Main Idea** How were the results of the 1952 presidential election influenced by the Korean War?

3 **Global Relations** Why did the United States become involved in the Korean War?

4 **Writing** *Describing* Imagine that you are a U.S. soldier who has been stationed in South Korea since the start of the war. In a series of short journal entries, describe the main events of the conflict, including its conclusion.

5 **Critical Thinking** *Supporting a Point of View* Do you agree with President Truman's decision to remove General MacArthur? Explain your answer.

Cold War Fears

Reading Focus

What caused the new Red Scare?

What role did Senator Joseph McCarthy play in the new Red Scare?

How did popular culture after World War II reflect Cold War fears?

Key Terms

House Un-American Activities Committee
blacklisting
Internal Security Act
McCarthyism
Army-McCarthy hearings

T O ATTORNEY GENERAL *J. Howard McGrath and many other Americans, the signs were everywhere. The Soviet Union controlled Eastern Europe. Communists governed in China as well, and they had fought fiercely in Korea. Were there Communists in the United States, too? McGrath answered the question by saying, "There are today many Communists in America. They are everywhere—in factories, offices, butcher shops, on street corners." He warned that every Communist "carries . . . the germs of death for society." Soon some Americans were caught up in a hunt for Communists.*

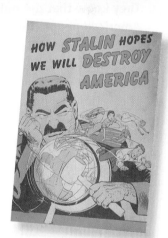

Anticommunist images were common during the Cold War.

★ A New Red Scare

The Cold War shaped American life at home, where intense fears of Communists and communism led to a new Red Scare. The first Red Scare had begun just after World War I, following the communist revolution in Russia. It took place amid postwar social unrest in the United States.

The new Red Scare started in the late 1930s. The scare reached its full strength during the late 1940s and early 1950s. Several factors help explain this new scare. The growth of domestic communism during the 1930s worried many Americans. The growth of the U.S. Communist Party was a particular concern. Fears intensified after World War II, when the Soviet Union expanded its influence across Eastern Europe. The Communists' takeover of China and communist aggression in Korea further increased anticommunist feelings in the United States.

In May 1938 Congress had established the **House Un-American Activities Committee** (HUAC) to investigate disloyalty and harmful foreign influences in the United States. In 1947 the

HUAC launched a series of widely publicized hearings. Their purpose was to prove the presence of Communists both in the Hollywood movie industry and in the U.S. State Department.

The committee often disregarded citizens' rights in its rush to expose Communists. In the tense climate of the late 1940s, being questioned by the HUAC could ruin people's lives. Having a past association with a communist organization was often seen as proof of disloyalty. One writer called before the committee charged that the HUAC "has conducted an illegal and indecent trial of American citizens." He added:

> **❝ I . . . appear here as a representative of 130 million Americans because the illegal conduct of this committee has linked me with every citizen. If I can be destroyed, no American is safe. . . . Forces are trying to introduce fascism in this country. They know that the only way to trick the American people into abandoning their rights and liberties is to manufacture an imaginary danger. ❞**

The HUAC investigations revealed that some people in the motion picture industry had communist sympathies. They did not, however, uncover widespread communist activity. Nonetheless, executives in film, radio, television, and theater began **blacklisting**, or refusing to hire, suspected Communists. The most famous blacklisted individuals were called the Hollywood Ten. This group of writers refused to cooperate with the HUAC.

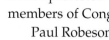

Some magazines claimed that Communists controlled the media.

In response to HUAC investigations, actor Lauren Bacall helped create and lead the Committee for the Fifth Amendment. The committee protested the anticommunist tactics of some members of Congress.

Paul Robeson, an African American singer and actor, was also affected by the new Red Scare. After the HUAC accused Robeson of being a

Actors Lauren Bacall and Humphrey Bogart lead members of the Committee for the Fifth Amendment on their way to Congress.

Communist, promoters canceled many of his shows. Mob attacks disrupted his two remaining concerts. Concerned by Robeson's support of a close U.S.-Soviet friendship, the State Department took away his passport in 1950. An interviewer later asked Robeson why he did not move to the Soviet Union. "My father was a slave, and my people died to build this country," Robeson said. "No . . . people will drive me from it."

★ Spies in Government

After World War II, many Republicans accused President Truman of having let Communists sneak into the government. In response, Truman created the Loyalty Review Board in March 1947. Its purpose was to investigate the background of some 16,000 federal workers. The board's reviews failed to discover any Communists. However, about 100 people lost their jobs because of "reasonable grounds" to suspect their loyalty. Many other organizations soon began requiring loyalty oaths. These groups included the FBI, the Justice Department, state and local governments, and schools and universities. Thousands more people lost their jobs because of suspected communist ties.

In 1950 Congress passed the **Internal Security Act**. The act required suspected communist organizations to register with the government. The law also gave the government the right during times of national emergency to arrest people suspected of treasonous activities.

In the late 1940s, explosive spy cases deepened Cold War fears. In 1948 journalist Whittaker Chambers confessed that he had spied for the Soviet Union. Testifying before the HUAC, Chambers claimed that Alger Hiss, a former State Department officer, was also a communist spy. Hiss denied the charges. Chambers later produced secret government papers that he claimed Hiss had passed to the Soviets. Although Hiss maintained his innocence, he was tried and found guilty of perjury. He was sentenced to five years in prison.

The Rosenberg case shocked the nation.

The spy cases continued into the 1950s. In 1951 Julius and Ethel Rosenberg were convicted of passing secret atomic weapons information to the Soviet Union. The case divided Americans. Many people claimed that the Rosenbergs were innocent victims of the Red Scare. Others argued that the Rosenbergs were part of a communist spy ring that threatened national security. Despite protests from their supporters, the Rosenbergs were executed in June 1953 for spying.

★ McCarthyism

More than anyone else, Senator Joseph McCarthy helped stir up Cold War fears. In 1950 McCarthy, a Republican from Wisconsin, began a campaign to expose Communists in the U.S. government.

McCarthy's Rise to Power

In February 1950 McCarthy told a West Virginia audience, "This is the time for the show-down between the democratic . . . world and the Communist." McCarthy blamed the spread of communism on

66 **the traitorous actions of those . . . individuals who have been helping to shape our foreign policy.**

> . . . The State Department . . . is thoroughly infested with Communists. I have in my hand fifty-seven cases of individuals who would appear to be either card-carrying members or certainly loyal to the Communist Party, but who nevertheless are still helping to shape our foreign policy. 99

McCarthy's charges stunned many people. Members of Congress challenged him to reveal the names on his list. McCarthy refused. When an early investigation labeled McCarthy's claims a fraud, however, he responded by making new charges. He even accused the head of the investigation of being pro-communist. His practice of making serious accusations without providing proof became known as **McCarthyism**.

Few Americans challenged McCarthy. Some accepted his charges because they were not used to questioning their public officials. Others were afraid of being labeled "soft on communism." In addition, many Americans wanted an explanation for the spread of communism in Eastern Europe and Asia. McCarthy gave them one.

The Truth Revealed

A few people attempted to stop Senator McCarthy. Journalist Edward R. Murrow tried to expose McCarthy's unfair methods on the television show *See It Now.* Murrow was not congratulated for his courage. Instead, he received bundles of hate mail from McCarthy supporters.

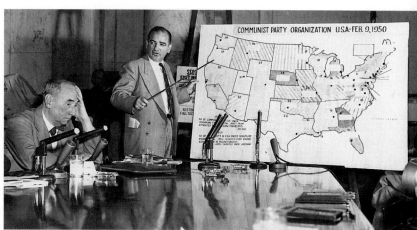

Senator McCarthy charged that there were Communists plotting to overthrow the U.S. government.

The Crucible
Arthur Miller

In his 1953 play, The Crucible, *author Arthur Miller compared McCarthyism to the Salem witch trials of 1692. Miller suggested that in both cases individuals were accused without evidence of wrongdoing. He wrote that this treatment violated their civil liberties. In the excerpt that follows, John Proctor has confessed to witchcraft in an effort to save himself from being hanged. Deputy Governor Danforth wants Proctor to identify other witches—just as the HUAC asked its witnesses to identify other Communists.*

A film version of Arthur Miller's play The Crucible

[DEPUTY GOVERNOR] DANFORTH: Mr. Proctor. When the Devil came to you did you see Rebecca Nurse in his company? *Proctor is silent.* Come, man, take courage—did you ever see her with the Devil?

[JOHN] PROCTOR, *almost inaudibly:* No. *Danforth, now sensing trouble, glances at John and goes to the table, and picks up a sheet—the list of condemned.*

DANFORTH: Did you ever see her sister, Mary Easty, with the Devil?

PROCTOR: No, I did not.

DANFORTH, *his eyes narrow on Proctor:* Did you ever see Martha Corey with the Devil?

PROCTOR: I did not.

DANFORTH, *realizing, slowly putting the sheet down:* Did you ever see anyone with the Devil?

PROCTOR: I did not.

DANFORTH: Proctor, you mistake me. I am not empowered [allowed] to trade your life for a lie. You have most certainly seen some person with the Devil. *Proctor is silent.* Mr. Proctor, a score of people have already testified they saw this woman with the Devil.

PROCTOR: Then it is proved. Why must I say it?

DANFORTH: Why "must" you say it! Why, you should rejoice to say it if your soul is truly purged of any love for Hell!

PROCTOR: They [the accused] think to go [be executed] like saints. I like not to spoil their names [reputation].

DANFORTH, *inquiring, incredulous:* Mr. Proctor, do you think they go like saints?

PROCTOR, *evading:* This woman never thought she done the Devil's work.

DANFORTH: Look you, sir. I think you mistake your duty here. It matters nothing what she thought—she is convicted. . . . Your soul alone is the issue here, Mister, and you will prove its whiteness or you cannot live in a Christian country. Will you tell me now what persons conspired with you in the Devil's company? *Proctor is silent.* To your knowledge was Rebecca Nurse ever—

PROCTOR: I speak my own sins; I cannot judge another. *Crying out, with hatred:* I have no tongue for it.

Understanding Literature

1. Why does John Proctor refuse to accuse others of witchcraft?

2. Why do you think that the court insists that Proctor testify against others?

In late 1953, however, the senator went too far. McCarthy charged that there were Communists in the military. He wanted to pressure the army to go easy on an assistant of his who had been drafted. A group of senators decided to hold televised hearings to investigate his charges. These **Army-McCarthy hearings** proved to be McCarthy's downfall.

During the hearings, Joseph Welch, the army's attorney, won the support of viewers with his charm and humor. At one point the desperate McCarthy revealed that Welch's law firm employed a former member of a pro-communist legal group. Welch was stunned by this statement, which had nothing to do with the hearings. He replied, "I think I never really gauged [understood] your cruelty. . . . Have you left no sense of decency, sir, at long last?" At this remark, the people watching burst into applause.

Viewers across the nation finally saw McCarthy for what he was—a bully. One commentator wrote that McCarthy "lied vividly and with bold imagination." In 1954 the Senate voted 67 to 22 to condemn McCarthy. For the people whose careers and lives had been destroyed by McCarthy's lies, however, it was a classic case of too little, too late.

Science fiction movies like Forbidden Planet *reflected Americans' concerns about Cold War technology.*

★ Fears at Home

During the Red Scare popular culture reflected many Americans' fear of communism. Magazines published articles like "How Communists Get That Way" and "Communists Are After Your Child." Between 1948 and 1954, Hollywood produced more than 40 anticommunist films. News-oriented trailers offered frightening details about international communist expansion.

Science fiction movies such as *Invasion of the Body Snatchers* and *Forbidden Planet* also revealed Americans' Cold War fears. Such movies were so popular that the 1950s became known as the Golden Age of Science Fiction. Science fiction films often combined anxiety over new forms of technology with the fear of communism. In the 1954 film *Gog*, for example, a Russian spy takes control of an important U.S. computer. Despite the postwar power of the United States, Americans were worried about the potential threat presented by the Soviet Union and other communist nations.

SECTION 5 REVIEW

Identify and explain the significance of the following:

- **House Un-American Activities Committee**
- **blacklisting**
- **Internal Security Act**
- **Alger Hiss**
- **Julius and Ethel Rosenberg**
- **Joseph McCarthy**
- **McCarthyism**
- **Army-McCarthy hearings**

Reading for Content Understanding

1 **Main Idea** What factors led to a Red Scare in the late 1940s and 1950s?

2 **Main Idea** How did the Cold War influence American popular culture?

3 **Citizenship and Democracy** In what ways did Cold War anxieties and fear of communism affect Americans' rights and freedoms?

4 **Writing** *Informing* Imagine that you are a radio broadcaster who has observed Joseph McCarthy's rise to power. Write the script to a radio editorial explaining McCarthy's role in the new Red Scare.

5 **Critical Thinking** *Evaluating* Review the material on the HUAC investigations and the Loyalty Review Board. Do you think the government has the right to investigate citizens' political beliefs? Explain your answer.

CHAPTER 17 REVIEW

Chapter Summary

The postwar world was marked by the spread of communism and the creation of the United Nations. The U.S.-funded Marshall Plan helped European countries rebuild their economies. The United States issued the Truman Doctrine and fought the Korean War to prevent the spread of communism. At home, a postwar recession was followed by a new Red Scare. The Cold War between the United States and the Soviet Union deepened. ◻

On a separate sheet of paper, complete the following activities.

Identifying People and Ideas

Describe the historical significance of the following:

1. Yalta Conference
2. Nuremberg Trials
3. George C. Marshall
4. GI Bill of Rights
5. Fair Deal
6. Harry S Truman
7. 38th parallel
8. Dwight D. Eisenhower
9. blacklisting
10. McCarthyism

Internet Activity

go.hrw.com
SB1 Cold War

Search the Internet through the HRW Web site to find information about Cold War–era science fiction films. Use the information to outline a scene from a movie that reveals Cold War fears.

Understanding Main Ideas

1. What was the goal of containment?
2. What steps did the Allies take to prevent another world war?
3. What was the Fair Deal?
4. Why was President Truman's victory in the 1948 election a surprise?
5. What were the causes and the outcome of the Korean War?
6. What led to a new Red Scare in the United States?

Reviewing Themes

1. **Economic Development** Why did Secretary of State George C. Marshall think that aiding European economies would help prevent the spread of communism?
2. **Global Relations** What events led to the Cold War between the United States and the Soviet Union?
3. **Citizenship and Democracy** How did the Cold War affect Americans' freedoms?

Using the Time Line

Number your paper from 1 to 5. Match the letters on the time line below with the following events.

1. The Soviets blockade West Berlin.
2. North Korea invades South Korea.
3. The Nuremberg Trials begin to try high-ranking Nazi officials.
4. Israel declares its independence.
5. The Rosenbergs are executed for passing secret atomic weapons information to the Soviets.

1945 1946 1947 1948 1949 1950 1951 1952 1953 1954

a   b c   d   e

Thinking Critically

1. **Drawing Conclusions**   Why do you think the United States offered economic aid to the Soviet Union? Why do you think the Soviet Union refused?

2. **Identifying Cause and Effect**   How did Americans' fear of communism during the Cold War affect U.S. foreign policy?

3. **Making Comparisons**   How did Americans' view of foreign involvement after World War II differ from their view following World War I?

Writing About History

1. **Persuading**   Imagine that you are a Harry S Truman supporter in 1948. Write a letter to your friends persuading them to vote for Truman instead of Thomas Dewey.

2. **Creating**   Imagine that you are a member of the Hollywood Ten. Write the opening two paragraphs to an autobiography describing your life after the blacklists.

Linking Geography and History

1. **Region**   Why did the United States consider Greece and Korea strategically important in the fight against communism?

2. **Location**   How did West Berlin's location make it difficult for the Western Allies to aid the city?

Building Your Portfolio

Complete the following activities individually or in groups.

1. **The Cold War**   Imagine that you are a U.S. government official assigned to evaluate the threat posed by Communists during the Cold War. Create a map of the world in the 1950s. Identify countries that are of strategic importance to the United States. When deciding what is strategically important, be sure to consider criteria such as a nation's location and its resources. You might consider dividing the countries you choose into the most and the least strategically vital. Include a brief caption for each strategic country explaining why it is important to the United States. Present your map to the class.

2. **Honoring the Veterans**   The Korean War is often called the "Forgotten War." Imagine that you have been chosen to design a memorial to the soldiers of the Korean War. Consider the causes, major battles, and results of the war and decide what your memorial should look like. Create a sketch of the memorial and write a paragraph explaining what the memorial represents. Hold a ceremony to present the memorial to your class.

History Skills Workshop

Using Primary Sources   Even before World War II ended, the Women's Advisory Committee (WAC) was concerned that returning veterans would displace female workers. WAC issued the following report urging government officials to protect women's jobs. After reading the excerpt to the right, answer the following questions: (a) What did WAC ask for in this excerpt? (b) Who did WAC appeal to for support? (c) Why do you think WAC referred to "democratic ideals"?

66 Prospects for job security and other new job opportunities after the war are as important to women as to men. The American people therefore must demand consideration of the status of women in all postwar plans. . . . No society can boast of democratic ideals if it utilizes womanpower in a crisis and neglects it in peace. 99

The Cold War

The end of World War II left much of Europe and parts of Asia in ruins. Great Britain and France, two traditional world powers, were greatly weakened. Much of Germany and Japan had been destroyed.

After the war only two great powers remained—the capitalist and democratic United States and the communist Soviet Union. For some 45 years, the two superpowers were locked in an ongoing struggle that became known as the Cold War.

The United States and the Soviet Union competed to establish alliances and spread their influence. The two superpowers never openly went to war with each other, but they supported opposing sides in many small wars and conflicts.

The superpower rivalry also created a new kind of arms race, as the United States and the Soviet Union competed to build huge arsenals of nuclear weapons. This nuclear arms race was one of the most frightening aspects of the Cold War. ■

A World Divided

By the end of the 1950s, much of the world was divided into two camps. Many countries were allied with either the United States or the Soviet Union. In Europe, the U.S.-backed North Atlantic Treaty Organization (NATO) faced the Soviet-backed Warsaw Pact.

The Height of the Cold War, 1960

ARCTIC OCEAN

CANADA

UNITED STATES

PACIFIC OCEAN

ATLANTIC OCEAN

MEXICO

CUBA

PUERTO RICO (U.S.)

United States and allies
Soviet Union and allies
▲ NATO member
■ Warsaw Pact member
○ Received aid under Marshall Plan

History Note 1

When the United States offered the Marshall Plan to aid countries weakened by World War II, the Soviet Union refused to participate. Instead the Soviets set up a similar plan for their own allies, the so-called Molotov Plan, named after Soviet foreign minister Vyacheslav Molotov.

The Marshall Plan created new opportunities through economic aid.

Geography **Skills**

Reading Special-Purpose Maps

1. Which countries in 1960 were members of NATO? Which were members of the Warsaw Pact?
2. Which non-NATO nations in Europe received aid under the Marshall Plan?
3. Which East Asian and Pacific countries were allies of the United States in 1960?

A U.S. Air Force B-52 bomber

Defending America

U.S. military spending fell dramatically in the years just after World War II. However, after communist North Korea invaded South Korea in 1950, the United States increased its military spending in an attempt to contain communist expansion around the world. Over the next 40 years, the United States spent more than a trillion dollars on defense.

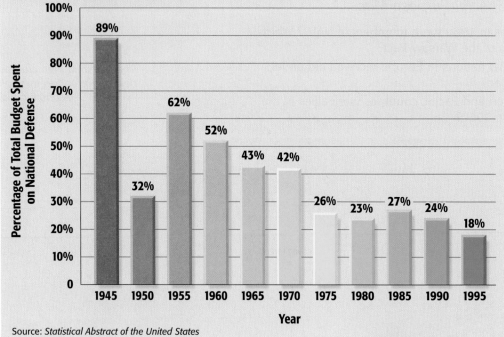

Defense Spending As Part of Total U.S. Budget, 1945–1995

Percentage of Total Budget Spent on National Defense

- 1945: 89%
- 1950: 32%
- 1955: 62%
- 1960: 52%
- 1965: 43%
- 1970: 42%
- 1975: 26%
- 1980: 23%
- 1985: 27%
- 1990: 24%
- 1995: 18%

Year

Source: *Statistical Abstract of the United States*

History Note 2

As part of its Cold War defense program, the United States put great effort into building a vast nuclear stockpile. At first the United States and the Soviet Union relied mainly on intercontinental bombers to carry nuclear weapons, but these were largely replaced by nuclear missiles by 1970. Most estimates made during the Cold War showed that the United States had more nuclear warheads than the Soviet Union until the late 1970s or early 1980s.

Geography Skills
Reading Bar Graphs

1. In which year did the United States spend the highest percentage of its national budget on defense? What was the next highest year?

2. By how many percentage points did defense spending increase from 1950 to 1955?

3. By how many percentage points did defense spending decrease between 1990 and 1995?

Cold War Defenses

Political status as of 1960.

Legend:
- United States and allies
- Soviet Union and allies
- ⊙ Major U.S. base
- North American Defense System (NORAD) Warning line or system
- ✷ Point of conflict

0 1,000 2,000 Miles
0 1,000 2,000 Kilometers
Azimuthal Equidistant Projection

*Map labels:*
MALAYSIA, CAMBODIA, SOUTH VIETNAM, THAILAND, NORTH VIETNAM, LAOS, BURMA, EAST PAKISTAN, INDIA, INDIAN OCEAN, WEST PAKISTAN, Peshawar, Dhahran, IRAN 1953, SAUDI ARABIA, Subic Bay, Clark, PHILIPPINES, TAIWAN, CHINA, EGYPT, Suez Canal 1956, Incirlik, TURKEY, Ankara, LIBYA, OKINAWA, SOUTH KOREA, Kimpo, MONGOLIA, GREECE, YUGOSLAVIA, Wheelus, Sasebo, Korean War 1950–1953, U-2 Incident 1960, SOVIET UNION, HUNGARY 1956, Naples, ITALY, Yokosuka, NORTH KOREA, JAPAN, Berlin 1958–1959, WEST GERMANY, Wiesbaden, ALGERIA (French), FINLAND, SWEDEN, NORWAY, NATO HQ, FRANCE, Zaragoza, SPAIN, 150° E, ARCTIC OCEAN, North Pole, Holy Loch, UNITED KINGDOM, MOROCCO, Adak, Ballistic Missile Early Warning System, GREENLAND (Danish), Thule, ICELAND, Keflavik, PORTUGAL, 180°, Midway, AZORES (Portuguese), Lajes, Unalaska, ALASKA, Sondrestrøm, ATLANTIC OCEAN, 30° W, Distant Early Warning Line, Goose, CANADA, Pearl Harbor, HAWAII, PACIFIC OCEAN, Mid-Canada Line, 150° W, Pinetree Line, 60° W, 30° N, Minot, Grand Forks, K.I. Sawyer, Grissom, BERMUDA (British), NORAD HQ, SAC HQ, UNITED STATES, U.S. Naval Space Surveillance System, Roosevelt Roads, PUERTO RICO (U.S.), MEXICO, CUBA, Guantánamo Bay, GUATEMALA 1954, Howard, PANAMA, CANAL ZONE

Missiles were a major part of Cold War defenses.

Geography **Skills**
Reading Special-Purpose Maps

1. Where did conflicts occur in 1956?

2. How many major military bases did the United States have in Western Europe?

3. What system did the United States put into place to provide the first warning of a Soviet attack?

NEW YOR

▪ CHAPTER 18 ▪
Peace and Prosperity
(1945–1960)

While on a family trip to Washington, D.C., Kemmons Wilson saw a special opportunity. Many of the nation's motels were dirty. Some charged extra for children to stay in the rooms. Wilson thought he could do better. He decided to go into the hotel business. His Holiday Inns proved very popular as people traveled the nation's new highways in their cars.

THEMES

Technology and Society
In what ways might the existence of weapons of mass destruction affect a society?

Economic Development
How might economic prosperity affect people's daily lives?

Constitutional Heritage
Why might minority groups use the courts to fight for increased rights?

1945

1947

1949

1951

DEC. 1946 President Harry Truman appoints the Committee on Civil Rights.

JULY 1948 President Truman issues an executive order banning segregation in the military.

JAN. 1950 The United States begins to develop the hydrogen bomb.

OCT. 1951 The *I Love Lucy* show premieres.

Eisenhower's Foreign Policy

Reading Focus

How did the existence of nuclear weapons influence President Eisenhower's foreign policy?

What methods did the United States use to fight communism abroad?

What Cold War crises occurred during Eisenhower's presidency?

Key Terms

hydrogen bomb

Sputnik

National Aeronautics and Space Administration

massive retaliation

brinkmanship

covert operations

Central Intelligence Agency

Suez Canal crisis

Eisenhower Doctrine

U-2 incident

HERMAN ADAMS, *the governor of New Hampshire, had a problem. He wanted to enter Dwight D. Eisenhower in the state's Republican presidential primary. However, he did not know for certain if the quiet World War II general was a Republican. Adams contacted the county clerk in Abilene, Kansas—Eisenhower's boyhood town—for more information. The letter Adams received in reply stated, "I don't think [Eisenhower] has any politics." Eisenhower, who was often called Ike, campaigned on his personal popularity with the American people. His approach was successful, and he won the 1952 presidential election.*

General Dwight D. Eisenhower was a decorated war hero.

IMAGE ON LEFT PAGE: *A suburban family takes to the open road in the 1950s.*

1953	1955	1957	1959

MAY 1954 The *Brown* v. *Board of Education* ruling declares segregation in public schools illegal.

DEC. 1955 Rosa Parks is arrested in Montgomery, Alabama.

NOV. 1956 The Soviet Union invades Hungary.

SEPT. 1957 Federal troops arrive in Little Rock, Arkansas, to enforce the desegregation of Central High School.

MAY 1960 The U-2 incident increases Cold War tensions.

The Nuclear Age

Shortly after Eisenhower was elected president, the U.S. military tested the first **hydrogen bomb**. The United States had begun developing this nuclear weapon in January 1950. It was far more powerful than the atomic bombs dropped on Japan in World War II. An observer recalled the test of the bomb, which was exploded on an island in the South Pacific:

> **The fireball expanded to three miles in diameter. Observers, all evacuated to 40 miles or more away, saw . . . that the island . . . had vanished, vaporized also. In its place a crater 1/2 mile deep and two miles wide had been born.**

Less than a year later, the Soviet Union tested its own hydrogen bomb. "The United States no longer has a monopoly," one Soviet official bragged. Both the United States and the Soviet Union were afraid to let the other side gain nuclear superiority. As a result, each nation built more nuclear bombs.

The nuclear arms race frightened many Americans. Some families created underground bomb shelters to protect themselves in case of attack. Children practiced emergency "duck-and-cover" drills at school. They would duck under their desks and cover their heads in case of emergency. A few Americans formed antinuclear groups, such as the Committee for a Sane Nuclear Policy, to protest the arms race. They argued that nuclear weapons tests released radioactive particles that caused birth defects and disease.

Despite such protests, the arms race continued. In October 1957 the Soviet Union launched *Sputnik*, the first artificial satellite, into orbit. Many Americans worried that the advanced technology used in *Sputnik* gave the Soviets a military advantage. One reporter asked President Eisenhower, "What are we going to do about it?"

In January 1958 the United States launched its first satellite. Later that same year, Congress established the **National Aeronautics and Space Administration** (NASA) to conduct space research. Congress also cre-

The launch of Sputnik started a space race between the United States and the Soviet Union.

ated programs to improve math, science, and foreign language education in public schools. Officials hoped that better-educated students would help the nation win the arms and space races.

During the Truman years, the United States had tried to contain the spread of communism around the world. President Eisenhower and Secretary of State John Foster Dulles established a "New Look" in U.S. foreign policy. Eisenhower wanted the United States to actually "roll back" communism from certain regions.

The New Look relied on a strategy known as **massive retaliation**, or the threat to use nuclear weapons to halt communist aggression. Few diplomats supported the use of nuclear weapons. However, most accepted that the nation might have to go to the brink of war to oppose communism. This approach was known as **brinkmanship**. Dulles explained the strategy by saying, "The ability to get to the verge [brink, or edge] without getting into war is the necessary art." Brinkmanship was a difficult policy to pursue, however. In 1953 the Soviets crushed anticommunist protests in three East German cities. U.S. leaders sympathized with the protesters but were unwilling to become involved and risk a nuclear war.

The first test of the hydrogen bomb

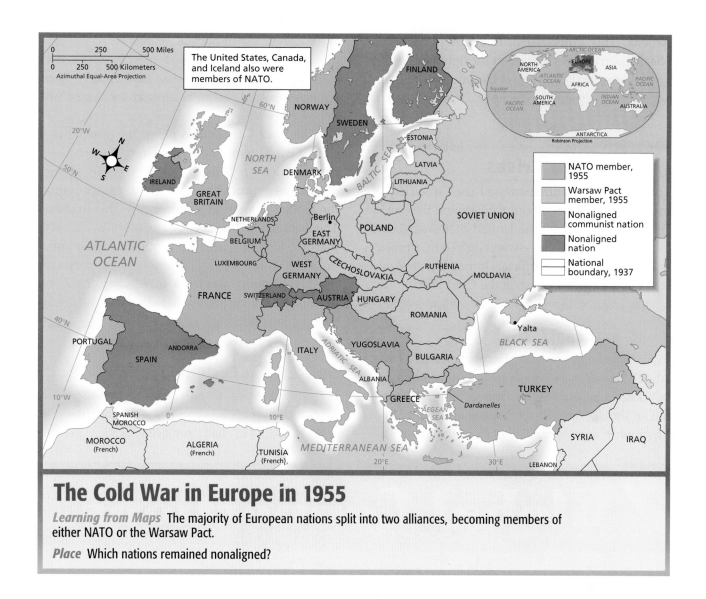

The Cold War in Europe in 1955

Learning from Maps The majority of European nations split into two alliances, becoming members of either NATO or the Warsaw Pact.

Place Which nations remained nonaligned?

Map legend:
- NATO member, 1955
- Warsaw Pact member, 1955
- Nonaligned communist nation
- Nonaligned nation
- National boundary, 1937

The United States, Canada, and Iceland also were members of NATO.

★ Covert Operations

Some Americans criticized brinkmanship. They argued that not every Cold War conflict required the threat of nuclear weapons. A single nuclear attack might lead to a nuclear war that could destroy the world. President Eisenhower sometimes used **covert operations**, or secret missions, to expand his foreign-policy options. The **Central Intelligence Agency** (CIA), a secretive intelligence organization established by the National Security Act in 1947, conducted these covert operations. During Eisenhower's presidency, the CIA's size and influence increased greatly.

The CIA's first major covert operation took place in the Middle Eastern nation of Iran. In 1951 Mohammad Mosaddeq (MAWS-ad-dek) became Iran's premier. He grew more powerful than the shah, Iran's ruler and a U.S. ally. Mosaddeq nationalized, or placed under government control, Iran's oil industry. His actions made U.S. diplomats fear that he was a Communist. In 1953 British and U.S. leaders organized "Operation Ajax." This mission overthrew Mosaddeq and returned sole power to the shah.

The CIA also became involved in the Central American nation of Guatemala. In 1951 Colonel Jacobo Arbenz Guzmán became president of Guatemala and began land and labor reforms. He nationalized the local fields and processing plants of the American-owned United Fruit Company.

After the takeover, Secretary of State Dulles went to the UN World Court to protest Arbenz's actions. He argued that Guatemala had turned to "international communism." In 1954 the CIA hired an army to invade Guatemala and overthrow

Arbenz. This army failed, but CIA pilots using Nicaraguan aircraft continued the fight. These CIA actions resulted in an anticommunist military government replacing Arbenz.

★ Cold War Crises

The Eisenhower administration used a variety of methods to oppose communism around the world. For example, in 1955 the United States agreed to help Egypt pay for the Aswan High Dam, a project on the Nile River. U.S. officials hoped Egypt would support the United States in the Cold War.

The Suez Canal Crisis

Just a year later, however, Egyptian leader Gamal Abdel Nasser was cooperating with communist nations. In response, the United States dropped out of the Aswan project. Nasser announced that Egypt would pay for the dam by nationalizing the Suez Canal, an important waterway connecting the Mediterranean and Red Seas. Nasser's decision upset Britain, France, and Israel. These nations invaded the areas around the Suez Canal in November 1956.

The **Suez Canal crisis** raised the possibility of a third world war. The Soviet Union threatened to fire missiles on Britain and France. To prevent a broader conflict, the United States joined the Soviet Union in condemning the invasion. The Suez Canal crisis ended peacefully. To show that the United States still opposed communism in the Middle East, Eisenhower announced the **Eisenhower Doctrine** in January 1957. He promised U.S. aid to any Middle Eastern country facing communist aggression.

Uprisings in Eastern Europe

Before the Suez Canal crisis erupted, Nikita Khrushchev (KROOSH-chawf) shocked the communist world. He had replaced Soviet premier

Global Connections

The Eisenhower Doctrine

After the Suez Canal crisis, President Eisenhower reconsidered his Middle Eastern policy. In 1957 he announced the Eisenhower Doctrine, in which he asked Congress for money to help Middle Eastern nations fight communism.

Many in Congress disliked Eisenhower's plan. One senator asked, "Why is it necessary to make this commitment here in such broad terms of permanent military and economic aid to these countries? It leaves us open now to be blackmailed." Secretary of State Dulles argued that if the United States did not aid the free nations of the Middle East, "then

President Eisenhower and Secretary of State John Foster Dulles

that critical area will almost certainly be taken over by Soviet communism."

After a long debate, Congress adopted a revised version of the Eisenhower Doctrine. It stated that the United States would use armed force to help countries in the Middle East resist aggression.

Understanding What You Read

1. Why did Secretary of State Dulles support the Eisenhower Doctrine?

2. How might the geographic location of the Middle East encourage Soviet aggression?

Joseph Stalin after his death in 1953. Khrushchev announced that Stalin had committed criminal acts, including mass murder, against the Soviet people. He argued that Stalin's policies should no longer be followed. Khrushchev also said that capitalism and communism could peacefully coexist in the world.

Stalin's death and Khrushchev's speech were followed by unrest in communist Eastern Europe. In Hungary, for example, new leaders argued for democratic reforms. The Soviet army invaded Hungary in November 1956 to stop this uprising. Hungarians fought back against the tanks with stones, rifles, and homemade bombs. The United States refused to intervene, and the Soviets easily crushed the revolt.

The U-2 Incident

In 1959 it appeared that the Cold War might be thawing. Vice President Richard Nixon visited the Soviet Union. Nikita Khrushchev then visited the United States. However, a new crisis erupted. On May 5, 1960, Khrushchev announced that the Soviets had shot down a U.S. spy plane. At first U.S. officials denied the charge. Khrushchev then

The U-2 was an advanced spy plane that flew at very high altitudes.

revealed that the pilot, Francis Gary Powers, had survived. Powers admitted that he had been on a secret mission in a U-2 spy plane. The event was called the **U-2 incident**.

Eisenhower admitted that he had approved the U-2 flight. In a speech he explained:

" **Our safety, and that of the free world, demand, of course, effective systems for gathering information about the military capabilities of other powerful nations . . . to guard ourselves and our allies against surprise attack.** "

Despite the U-2 incident Eisenhower and Khrushchev attended a summit in Paris, France. The meeting was a disaster. The summit talks collapsed. The thaw in the Cold War was over.

SECTION 1 REVIEW

Identify and explain the significance of the following:

- **Dwight D. Eisenhower**
- **hydrogen bomb**
- *Sputnik*
- **National Aeronautics and Space Administration**
- **John Foster Dulles**
- **massive retaliation**
- **brinkmanship**
- **covert operations**
- **Central Intelligence Agency**
- **Suez Canal crisis**
- **Eisenhower Doctrine**
- **Nikita Khrushchev**
- **U-2 incident**

Locate and explain the importance of the following:

- **Soviet Union**
- **Hungary**

Reading for Content Understanding

1 **Main Idea** How did the United States attempt to fight communism abroad?

2 **Main Idea** Make a graphic organizer showing major Cold War events that took place in East Germany, Egypt, Guatemala, Hungary, and Iran in the 1950s. Include the dates and outcomes of the events.

3 **Technology and Society** What role did nuclear weapons play in President Eisenhower's foreign policy?

4 **Writing** *Informing* Imagine that you are a member of the State Department under John Foster Dulles. Write a memo explaining the U.S. reaction to the Suez Canal crisis and the uprisings in Eastern Europe.

5 **Critical Thinking** *Making Comparisons* How are the policies of brinkmanship and covert operations similar? How are they different?

A Prosperous Nation

Reading Focus

How did economic prosperity increase under President Eisenhower?

In what ways did inventions help change American industry and society in the 1950s?

What was life like in the suburbs?

Key Terms

Sun Belt

automation

Highway Act

Levittown

baby boom

urban renewal

IN THE 1950S REVEREND *Norman Vincent Peale was one of the best-selling authors in the United States. In* The Power of Positive Thinking, *his most popular book, Peale told Americans that "happiness is achievable and the process for obtaining it is not complicated. Anyone who desires it, who wills it, and who learns and applies the right formula may become a happy person." Peale's books were very influential in the 1950s, a time when many Americans were confident that they could achieve wealth and happiness.*

The 1952 edition of Peale's book

 ## America Under Eisenhower

The economy boomed during the 1950s. Undamaged by World War II, American industries were the strongest in the world. The federal government spent millions of dollars on Cold War defense, creating new jobs. President Dwight D. Eisenhower took a middle-of-the-road approach to managing the growing economy. He wanted to reduce the size of the federal government and give states and private companies control over some federal projects. However, during his presidency Congress increased the minimum wage and expanded Social Security.

During Eisenhower's administration, personal income soared for most Americans. By the mid-1950s nearly 60 percent of the population qualified as middle class, with annual incomes between $3,000 and $10,000. As a result, more Americans were able to buy luxuries such as large home appliances and TV sets. One woman proudly noted:

❝When we were married my husband earned $30 a week. . . . Now we have . . . an income of over $25,000 a year. We own our own eight-room house—also a nice house on a lake. . . . Our oldest child goes to a prep school.❞

Science and Technology

Television

Television, or TV, developed from radio broadcasting technology. In the late 1920s, researchers discovered how to add a video signal to radio broadcasts. The video signal carries information about the shape, brightness, and color of the images being filmed. This video signal is transmitted to the television set.

When a television receives this transmission, it turns the signal into beams of electrons. These electron beams scan rapidly back and forth in alternating lines across the TV screen. When the electron beams hit the screen, they activate tiny strips of material called phosphors. The phosphors then light up in the appropriate colors. Together all the phosphors on a screen create a picture.

TV sets typically show about 30 still images every second—a rate so fast that the viewer's eyes cannot see individual pictures. The eyes are also tricked into seeing a moving picture instead of a series of many still images.

Early televisions showed only black-and-white pictures on small screens about a foot wide. Much like early radio programs, the first TV shows were live broadcasts. Broadcasters also televised political speeches and debates.

TV changed how people saw the world. Televised congressional hearings were widely watched in the 1950s. Dwight D. Eisenhower's presidential campaign in 1952 was the first to rely heavily on TV ads. Eventually, the nightly news broadcast pictures from around the globe.

Television technology continued to change. In 1968 color TV sets outsold black-and-white TVs for the first time. Today cable and satellite television provide many channels for a fee. A new technology known as high-definition television (HDTV) offers a sharper TV image.

Understanding What You Read

1. How do televisions work?
2. In what ways has TV changed daily life?

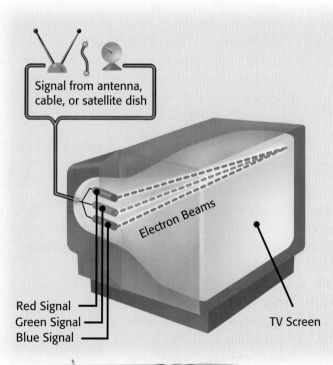

Signal from antenna, cable, or satellite dish

Electron Beams

Red Signal
Green Signal
Blue Signal

TV Screen

Beams scan at high speed across the screen to create images.

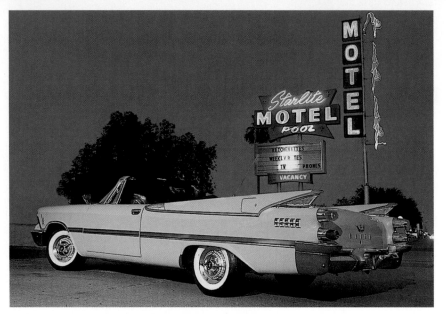

Large cars such as this Dodge convertible were popular in the 1950s.

New technology also caused changes in the workforce. Many factories increased **automation**, or the use of machines in production. This change affected labor unions. Automation took jobs away from industrial workers, who often were strong union supporters. At the same time, few new managers, clerical workers, or sales staff joined unions.

In an effort to remain powerful, the nation's two largest unions—the American Federation of Labor (AFL) and the Congress of Industrial Organizations (CIO)—merged in 1955. They formed the AFL–CIO. Led by George Meany, the new union represented both skilled and unskilled workers. Despite such efforts, unions faced tough challenges. In the 1950s the Senate investigated the illegal use of union funds. Reports also surfaced that unions were pro-socialist or even Communist. As a result of such developments, the power of unions declined.

The healthy economy helped Eisenhower easily win re-election in 1956.

The new prosperity brought many changes. Millions of Americans moved to the **Sun Belt** states of the South and Southwest. They were attracted to the region by the warm winters, low taxes, and job opportunities. As a result, the population of the Sun Belt rose much faster than the national average. Families were on the move in other ways as well. They bought houses in the suburbs, took vacations, and sent their children to college. However, not everyone shared in the prosperity of the 1950s. In 1960 more than 20 percent of all families earned less than $3,000 a year.

A Changing Workforce

Many changes also occurred in the workforce in the 1950s. New corporate structures greatly increased the number of middle managers. The growth of the service sector created a greater need for clerical and sales workers. Women filled many of these typically low-paying positions. Such jobs offered little chance for advancement. Women who pursued careers often faced harsh criticism. One woman recalled:

66 **The only person who approved of me in those days was my father. He had encouraged me to be an accountant and whatever I did was all right with him.** 99

Technological Advances

Factories were not alone in being changed by technology in the 1950s. Advances in medical technology helped millions of Americans. Some devices, such as hearing aids and better contact lenses, improved the quality of life. Other advances were lifesaving breakthroughs, such as Dr. Jonas Salk's polio vaccine. Polio was a serious disease that had affected many Americans, including former president Franklin D. Roosevelt. The disease often caused paralysis or death.

During the late 1940s and early 1950s a polio epidemic swept across the United States, infecting thousands of children. In 1952 Dr. Salk developed a vaccine that

Dr. Jonas Salk on the cover of Time magazine.

ended the epidemic and helped eliminate polio around the world. One reporter called this vaccine "one of the greatest triumphs in the history of medicine."

Many new technologies developed out of military research begun during World War II and the Cold War. The government spent millions of dollars on research projects for national defense. For example, researchers improved computer technology, which was first developed during World War II. Computers remained bulky and expensive. However, they were very useful for sorting large amounts of data.

Other advances included jet planes. In the 1950s Boeing introduced the first successful commercial jetliner, the 707. These large jet planes made long-distance travel cheaper because they could carry more passengers.

Some technologies affected home life. Engineers put nuclear technology to civilian use by building the first nuclear power plant. Nuclear power provided electricity to homes and businesses. The introduction of affordable home air conditioners helped residents of the Sun Belt endure hot summers.

★ Suburban America

Federal government programs also altered the countryside of the United States. In June 1956 Congress passed the **Highway Act**. This act funded

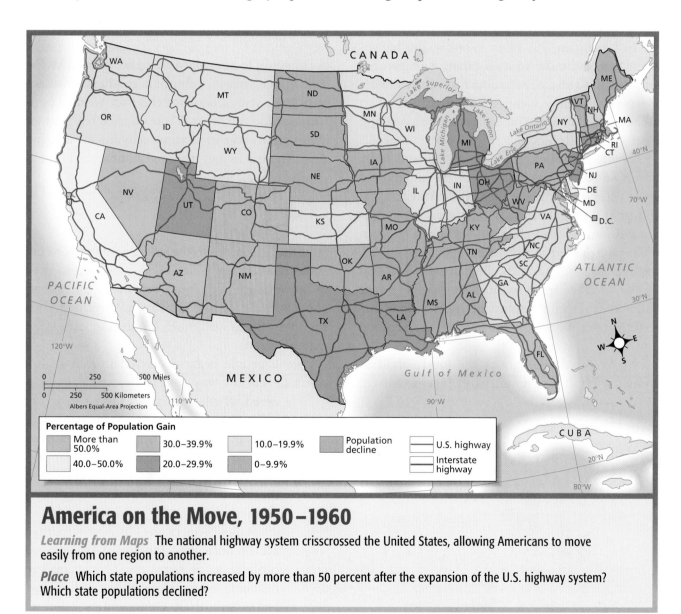

America on the Move, 1950–1960

Learning from Maps The national highway system crisscrossed the United States, allowing Americans to move easily from one region to another.

Place Which state populations increased by more than 50 percent after the expansion of the U.S. highway system? Which state populations declined?

a new national system of interstate highways. This system greatly increased business and personal travel throughout the nation. The number of cars sold between 1946 and 1960 tripled. In addition, the highway system made it easier for many middle-class Americans to move to suburbs and commute to work. By 1960 more than one fifth of the entire U.S. population lived in suburbs.

Life in the Suburbs

As more Americans moved out of the cities, developers built new suburban neighborhoods. These sprawling subdivisions soon included their own parks, schools, and public services. William Levitt created **Levittown** on Long Island, New York. Levittown was an early example of a preplanned and mass-produced housing development.

In Levittown and other suburbs, the houses often looked similar to each other, with garages and large yards. Most suburban homes were inexpensive. Many were equipped with modern kitchens and labor-saving devices such as washing machines and dryers.

Americans welcomed these comforts. A **baby boom**—a significant increase in the number of babies born—took place after World War II. Most suburban neighborhoods centered activities around families and children. Suburban children often participated in organized activities, including music lessons, sports, Boy Scouts, and Girl Scouts. Mothers spent so much time driving their children from one activity to another that one commentator referred to the task as "motherhood on wheels."

Many people thought of the ideal suburban woman as a full-time mother who devoted most of

"I'm Mrs. Edward M. Barnes. Where do I live?"

Some people made fun of the similar appearance of houses in the suburbs.

her energies to her children and her home. Despite this image, many suburban mothers, particularly those with school-age children, worked part-time outside the home. Their wages often paid for after-school and summertime activities for the children. These activities included summer camps and dance or music lessons.

Suburban Culture

Suburban culture placed a strong emphasis on consumer goods. Many neighbors quietly competed to see which family could buy the latest clothes, gadgets, and cars. The growing advertising industry often encouraged much of this competition for material goods.

Some people began to complain that such a consumer culture was wasteful. Social critics wondered whether people really needed new cars every two years, or new kitchen appliances every three years. Others wondered whether material things could make people happy. One woman called suburban life "quite stale," despite her family's many possessions.

A few Americans disliked suburban life because they thought it encouraged conformity, or sameness. Most suburban residents were white and middle class. Some suburban communities tried to

Magazines promoted an idealized image of suburban life.

prevent people who did not fit their mold—whether because of race, ethnicity, or religion—from moving into their neighborhoods. Despite critics' complaints about the suburbs, residents often praised their communities. Many residents appreciated the strong social networks provided by suburban life.

★ Life in the City

As more white, middle-class Americans moved to the suburbs from the cities, they left behind many poor and nonwhite residents. Fewer tax dollars remained in the cities, leading to a decline in urban conditions and services.

As urban decay set in, the federal government launched an **urban renewal** program to improve life in the cities. The project began with a plan to improve public services and housing in the cities. The program called for replacing buildings in poor, run-down neighborhoods with large housing projects. Additional legislation in the 1950s provided further funds and a wide-ranging urban renewal plan.

Some city residents, however, felt that the plain-looking, multilevel housing projects destroyed the unique culture of older neighborhoods. Responding to these concerns, officials gradually altered the program to focus on restoring old buildings rather than demolishing them and building new ones. Despite the various efforts to improve living conditions, many city residents struggled to match the prosperity of the suburbs.

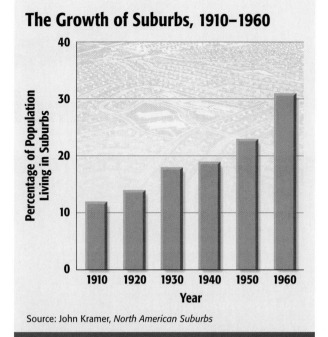

The Growth of Suburbs, 1910–1960

Percentage of Population Living in Suburbs / Year

Source: John Kramer, *North American Suburbs*

Suburban Life With improved roads, people increasingly moved to the suburbs and commuted to nearby cities for work. By about how much did the percentage of Americans living in suburbs increase between 1950 and 1960?

SECTION 2 REVIEW

Identify and explain the significance of the following:
- **Sun Belt**
- **automation**
- **Jonas Salk**
- **Highway Act**
- **William Levitt**
- **Levittown**
- **baby boom**
- **urban renewal**

Reading for Content Understanding

1 **Main Idea** How did inventions bring change to American life during the 1950s?

2 **Main Idea** What aspects of suburban life appealed to Americans in the 1950s? What aspects were criticized?

3 **Economic Development** In what ways did national prosperity increase during President Eisenhower's terms in office?

4 **Writing** *Describing* Imagine that you are a reporter living in a Sun Belt state after World War II. Write an article describing how the population has changed and explaining some of the reasons why this has happened.

5 **Critical Thinking** *Identifying Cause and Effect* What factors contributed to the economic prosperity of the 1950s? Consider the contributions of businesses and government programs in your answer.

Peace and Prosperity **549**

A Changing Culture

Reading Focus

How did television affect American culture?

What comments did some writers make about American society?

Why did certain films and music appeal to teenagers during the 1950s?

Key Terms

beats
silent generation
rock 'n' roll

*S*OON AFTER ITS DEBUT *in 1951,* I Love Lucy *became the most popular program on television. Millions of Americans tuned in to the 1953 episode in which actor Lucille Ball's character gave birth. In fact, more people watched that episode than tuned in the next day to see Dwight D. Eisenhower's inauguration. "It looks like Lucy is more popular than Ike," declared her co-star and husband, Desi Arnaz. "I wonder if we could run her for President in fifty-six?"*

Lucille Ball doll

Hake's Americana, York, PA

 The Golden Age of Television

The 1950s have been called television's golden years. In 1946 there were fewer than 10,000 television sets in the United States. Ten years later there were almost 35 million households with a TV set. Much like radio, television allowed many Americans to share the same experiences. Millions of viewers could watch a single program, whether a sports event or a news broadcast.

Milton Berle was one of television's earliest stars. As a boy he appeared in vaudeville shows—stage productions that combined singing, dancing, and comedy routines. When vaudeville became less popular Berle turned to television. He headlined *Texaco Star Theatre,* a popular variety show. He eventually appeared in so many TV shows that many people called him "Mr. Television."

Lucille Ball was another TV star of the 1950s. Her weekly series *I Love Lucy* started in October 1951. It co-starred her real-life husband, Cuban American bandleader Desi Arnaz. Week after week the couple found themselves in unusual situations. Ball's character was constantly trying to get herself into show business, while Arnaz always acted bewildered by her wild ideas. The result was a huge comedy hit. A TV producer later explained how Ball had appealed to her as a young girl:

Frozen TV dinners became popular in the 1950s.

 The main thing that Lucy did for me was that she acted. She was an active person who was having a grand adventure. . . . And I felt [when] watching Lucy that she wasn't afraid of anything.

In addition to comedy shows, popular types of programs included dramas, game shows, soap operas, and westerns. Usually a TV show was sponsored by only one company. During the show the stars took short breaks to encourage viewers to buy the sponsor's product. Companies hoped that TV advertising would be even more successful than radio advertising. The success of this strategy led to the creation of more commercials and more elaborate advertising approaches. By 1955, advertisers were spending more than $1 billion a year on TV commercials. Television encouraged millions of American families to buy the latest products and participate in the expanding consumer culture.

★ Writers and Artists

For many Americans, the prosperity of the 1950s was an enjoyable relief from the strains of wartime. However, some writers criticized American society as being too focused on conformity. For example, in *The Lonely Crowd* writer David Riesman argued that social pressure to fit in discouraged people from being creative.

African American authors also served as powerful social critics during the 1950s. In his 1952 novel, *Invisible Man*, Ralph Ellison explores a young African American man's search for identity in the postwar world. James Baldwin also wrote about racism in his novel *Notes of a Native Son*. Baldwin viewed his work as an act of patriotism:

 I love America more than any other country in the world, and, exactly for this reason, I insist on the right to criticize her.

A young group of writers called beatniks, or **beats**, used their unusual writing styles and rebellious behavior to criticize American life. In *On the Road*, beat author Jack Kerouac urged people to reject traditional society and choose their own path.

Some American artists also challenged traditional styles. Painter Jackson Pollock developed a bold new method called action painting. David Smith sculpted steel into unusual geometric shapes. Critics of such experimental writing and art claimed that the new styles did not have any real meaning. They accused the beats and other artists of being self-absorbed and immature.

Some people called teenagers and college students of the time the **silent generation** because young people appeared to conform to social expectations without protest. However, some teenagers rebelled by reading materials such as *Mad* magazine, which made fun of 1950s society.

★ Movies

Many young people also identified with and tried to imitate the young rebels that they saw in popular movies of the era. Actor James Dean was particularly popular. Dean starred in only three films

James Dean and Natalie Wood were the young stars of Rebel Without a Cause.

Jackson Pollock

Paul Jackson Pollock was born in Cody, Wyoming, in 1912. He grew up in California and Arizona. When he was still a teenager, he began studying art with regionalist painter Thomas Hart Benton. During the Great Depression, Pollock worked on the Federal Arts Project.

At first, Pollock experimented with different styles and subjects. Around 1947, he began the work that would make his reputation—the so-called drip and splash paintings.

Pollock's method was bold and original. He spread a huge piece of canvas across the floor and then stood over it, dripping different types and colors of paint onto the canvas. Pollock argued that his new method helped his painting. "On the floor I am more at ease, I feel nearer, more a part of the painting, since this way I can walk around it, work from the four sides and internally be in the painting," he said.

Pollock's drip and splash paintings stunned the art world and the larger public. Unlike traditional paintings, Pollock's pieces did not feature identifiable subjects in standard places on the canvas. His paintings were wild combinations of color, shape, and texture. "The painting has a life of its own," Pollock commented. "I try to let it come through."

Jackson Pollock titled this 1948 drip and splash painting Silver over Black, White, Yellow, and Red.

Pollock's creations were leading examples of a new movement in art called action painting. During the 1950s, the action painters looked for freedom—the freedom to paint abstract images in a new style.

Understanding the Arts

1. Why did Jackson Pollock prefer to paint with his canvas on the floor?

2. How did Pollock use colors and shapes in new ways?

3. What 1950s art movement did Pollock represent?

before dying in a car wreck at the age of 24. In *Rebel Without a Cause*, Dean plays a troubled middle-class teen. His character feels like an outcast and a failure because he cannot live up to other people's expectations of him.

Actor Marlon Brando also appealed to young audiences. In *The Wild One,* Brando plays a wild biker who challenges the rules of adult society—settle down, work hard, get ahead. When one character in the film asks, "What are you rebelling against?" Brando replies, "Whadda ya got?"

 Music

Young people also rebelled by listening to new kinds of music. During the 1950s two important new styles of music became popular.

Bebop

Bebop, or bop, got its start in the 1940s, when African American jazz musicians Charlie Parker and Dizzy Gillespie paired up. This complex type of jazz music, often played at a rapid pace, thrilled listeners. "It was new, and it was fresh, . . . it was so inventive," recalled bebop bandleader Lionel Hampton.

Rock 'n' Roll

Even more popular than bebop was the loud and enthusiastic sound of **rock 'n' roll**. This new musical style drew heavily from African American rhythm and blues. Rock 'n' roll musicians used new instruments such as electric guitars to create a fast-paced sound. Rock 'n' roll attracted many teenagers who wanted to challenge social restrictions.

The biggest rock star of the 1950s was Elvis Presley. Born in Tupelo, Mississippi, Presley was influenced by the blues and by country and western music. His silky voice, good looks, and energetic stage performances made him hugely popular with audiences, particularly teenage

Elvis Presley

girls. During his career he sold millions of records. He also starred in more than 30 movies, mainly musicals.

Other rock 'n' roll stars included Chuck Berry, Fats Domino, Buddy Holly, Jerry Lee Lewis, and Little Richard. Berry and Holly were noted for their guitar playing, while Domino, Lewis, and Little Richard were piano players.

Critics argued that rock 'n' roll contributed to youth crime. Other adults simply thought it was bad music—too loud and filled with lyrics, such as "do-wop, do-wop," that meant nothing. Still others worried that rock 'n' roll cut across racial lines. Many teenagers were fans of white rock 'n' roll artists such as Presley, Lewis, and Holly as well as black artists such as Berry, Domino, and Little Richard. In spite of its critics, rock 'n' roll continued to grow in popularity. The new sound even attracted large audiences in other countries, particularly in Europe. Eventually, rock 'n' roll was seen by many people as a uniquely American contribution to music, similar to jazz or the blues.

SECTION 3 REVIEW

Identify and explain the significance of the following:
- **Lucille Ball**
- **Ralph Ellison**
- **James Baldwin**
- **beats**
- **Jack Kerouac**
- **Jackson Pollock**
- **silent generation**
- **rock 'n' roll**
- **Elvis Presley**

Reading for Content Understanding

1 Main Idea How did television change American culture in the 1950s?

2 Main Idea What attracted teenagers to rock 'n' roll and to movies such as *Rebel Without a Cause*?

3 Cultural Diversity What did authors such as James Baldwin, Ralph Ellison, David Riesman, and Jack Kerouac write about American life in the 1950s?

4 Writing *Persuading* Imagine that you are a student in the 1950s writing an article about bebop or rock 'n' roll for your school newspaper. Try to persuade your readers that these new forms of music are or are not exciting and worthwhile.

5 Critical Thinking *Evaluating* Did American teenagers in the 1950s deserve the label of "silent generation"? Explain your answer.

The Early Civil Rights Movement

Reading Focus

How did African American World War II veterans influence the early civil rights movement?

What were some of the main events in the struggle for school desegregation?

Why did the Montgomery bus boycott succeed?

Key Terms

Committee on Civil Rights

Brown v. *Board of Education*

Little Rock Nine

Montgomery bus boycott

Montgomery Improvement Association

Southern Christian Leadership Conference

MANY AFRICAN AMERICAN VETERANS *came home from service in World War II filled with anger. Civil rights lawyer Constance Baker Motley explained their feelings. "Black servicemen were overseas dying for this country," she said, "and . . . they would be coming home to a situation that said, in effect, You're a second-class citizen. . . . You can't stay in a hotel or eat in a restaurant because you're black." James Hicks, an African American veteran, described the response of many fellow ex-soldiers: "I paid my dues over there and I'm not going to take this anymore over here." Black veterans prepared to take up another fight—this one against discrimination in the United States.*

Civil rights picketer outside the 1948 Democratic National Convention

Segregation After World War II

Many returning African American veterans focused their efforts on voting discrimination. Fees, literacy tests, and threats of violence in some states—particularly those in the South—prevented African Americans from voting or even registering to vote. Some white politicians encouraged such discrimination when they ran for office.

The drive for African American voting rights brought intense conflict. As the violence grew, many black leaders asked President Truman for help. In the summer of 1946, a group of civil rights activists protested outside the White House. They held signs that read "SPEAK, SPEAK, MR. PRESIDENT." That same summer nearly 15,000 protesters marched to the Lincoln Memorial to demand an end to the threats and violence carried out by the Ku Klux Klan.

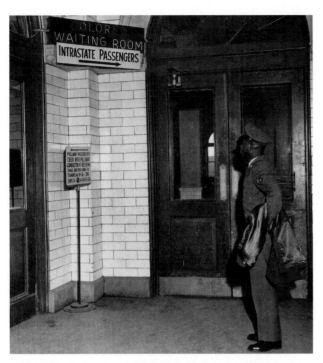

Even though the U.S. military had been desegregated, this airman still faced segregation at the Atlanta Terminal Station in 1956. Such segregation inspired many African Americans to work for civil rights.

President Truman responded to these requests in December 1946. He appointed the **Committee on Civil Rights** to investigate racial discrimination and suggest federal solutions to the problem. The committee's report, *To Secure These Rights*, noted the existence of racial discrimination throughout the country. The report also recommended a number of federal actions to help African Americans. The recommended actions included passing new laws to better protect all voters, desegregating the armed forces, and establishing a permanent Fair Employment Practices Commission. Truman pledged to support the committee's recommendations.

President Truman's verbal support for civil rights pleased African American leaders. They began, however, to express frustration as months dragged on with little real action by the president or Congress. Finally, African American labor leader A. Philip Randolph threatened to organize a massive protest if Truman did not at least desegregate the armed forces. In July 1948 Truman issued an executive order banning segregation in the military. That same year he also announced an executive order banning racial discrimination in the hiring of federal employees.

Brown v. Board of Education

Early civil rights leaders, particularly members of the National Association for the Advancement of Colored People (NAACP), had one main goal. They wanted to end the segregation of black and white Americans. They were particularly concerned with school segregation.

A Long Struggle

Many states, in both the North and the South, maintained separate schools for black and white students. Most officials argued that these institutions were "separate but equal." However, African American schools typically received far less money and supplies than did white schools.

The NAACP legal defense team won a series of court cases that challenged the practice of maintaining separate-but-equal educational facilities. In 1938 the U.S. Supreme Court had issued a ruling declaring that every state had to offer equal educational opportunities within its borders. In other words, a state that offered a law school or a medical school for white students had to provide a school for black students as well. Some states already had such separate facilities, and a few others established them after the ruling.

The NAACP then tried to show that separate schools did not provide equal educational opportunities for black students. In 1946 an African American named Heman Sweatt applied to the law school at the University of Texas. The law school did not accept black students, and school officials refused to admit Sweatt. Instead, they created a separate black law school. In 1950 the Supreme Court ruled in *Sweatt* v. *Painter* that the new school did not provide African Americans with access to equal academic prestige, facilities, or instructors. The Court ordered the university to admit Sweatt into its law school.

A Crucial Case

Starting around 1950, the NAACP focused on abolishing segregation in public schools in the United States. Thurgood Marshall, the NAACP attorney who had argued the *Sweatt* case, led the courtroom battles. A number of school segregation cases came together under the title of **Brown v. Board of Education**. The title case involved Linda Brown, a seven-year-old girl from Topeka, Kansas. Even though she lived very close to a school for white children, she had to travel across town to attend an all-black school. Her father sued to allow Linda to attend the nearby white school.

The NAACP team used studies by African American psychologist Kenneth Clark to oppose segregation. Clark argued that segregation led many black children to feel that they were less important than white children. "Segregation was, is, the way in which a society tells a group of human beings that they are inferior to other groups of human beings in the society," he explained.

The Court Ruling

In May 1954 the U.S. Supreme Court decided *Brown* v. *Board of Education*. The Court ruled that segregation in public schools is illegal. The majority opinion said:

> ❝To separate [black students] from others of similar age and qualifications solely because of their race generates a feeling of inferiority as to their status in the community that may affect their hearts and minds in a way very unlikely ever to be undone. . . . In the field of

Many schools segregated students on the basis of race. Nearly 90 African American children crowd into this kindergarten class.

public education the doctrine [belief] of 'separate but equal' has no place. Separate educational facilities are inherently [by their very nature] unequal.❞

The Court's decision effectively overturned the 1896 *Plessy* v. *Ferguson* ruling that had established the "separate-but-equal" doctrine. In 1955 the Court strengthened its ruling by ordering public schools to desegregate "with all deliberate speed."

Public reaction to the *Sweatt* and *Brown* decisions was mixed. Some white leaders promised to follow the law. Others such as South Carolina governor James F. Byrnes predicted the very collapse of American culture. Byrnes argued that desegregation "would mark the beginning of the end of civilization in the South as we have known it." Some white citizens pledged to close their local public schools and open private, all-white academies.

Most African Americans were pleased with the Court decisions but wondered whether white leaders would really support desegregation. As one black lawyer explained years before the *Brown* v. *Board of Education* ruling, African Americans knew from experience that there was a "difference between the law in books and the law in action."

★ The Little Rock Nine

Despite the Court's "all deliberate speed" order, desegregation proceeded slowly in most places. Only three school districts in the entire South began desegregating in 1954. Most other school districts adopted gradual desegregation plans. The school board in Little Rock, Arkansas, decided to integrate one high school first, then slowly work down to the elementary level. The school board selected nine outstanding black students, nicknamed the **Little Rock Nine**, to attend Central High School in 1957.

At first, most African American leaders expected the Little Rock integration plan to go smoothly. Although Little Rock was highly segregated, it had a reputation for being moderate. As the start of the 1957 school year got closer, however, many white residents tried to stop the

556 Chapter 18

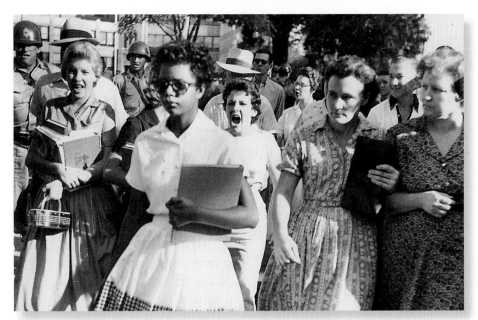

Elizabeth Eckford tries to make her way into Little Rock's Central High School.

a feeling of pride and hope that yes, this is the United States; yes, there is a reason I salute the flag; and it's going to be okay.**"**

integration plan. Arkansas governor Orval Faubus arranged for a group to appeal to a judge to halt integration. When the effort failed, he went on television the day before school started and declared that state National Guard units would prevent the Little Rock Nine from starting school. Faubus claimed that the reason for his action was to prevent violence over integration.

Daisy Bates, the president of the Arkansas NAACP, told the students to meet her on the morning of September 4 to get rides to school. Bates forgot to notify Elizabeth Eckford, a member of the Little Rock Nine. When Eckford went to school by herself, a mob greeted her at Central High. With the screaming crowd behind her, the National Guard soldiers refused her entrance to the school. She was alone and without protection, facing a large mob of enraged protesters. About that time, Eckford recalled, "Somebody started yelling, *'Lynch her! Lynch her!'*" Eckford ran to a nearby bus stop to escape, but the crowd followed. Finally, a white man and woman guided her to safety.

The tense situation continued for several weeks. President Eisenhower tried to persuade Faubus to follow the law, but he refused. In late September, Eisenhower sent federal troops to enforce desegregation at Central High. One of the Little Rock Nine, Melba Pattillo Beals, remembered the soldiers' presence at the school:

❝ I went in not through the side doors, but up the front stairs, and there was

Problems resumed after the federal troops left, and Eisenhower asked that Arkansas National Guard units protect the students.

Despite these efforts, the Little Rock Nine continued to suffer insults and abuse from white students. Even so, eight of the nine remained. In May 1958 Ernest Green became the first African American student to graduate from Central High School. "When they called my name . . . there was eerie silence. Nobody clapped," Green remembered. "But I figured they didn't have to . . . because after I got that diploma, that was it. I had accomplished what I had come there for."

Governor Faubus continued to fight integration. He even closed the Little Rock public schools during the 1958–59 school year. The schools finally reopened under a court order in 1959 and began a process of slow integration.

The Montgomery Bus Boycott

Even before the Arkansas NAACP helped integrate Central High, the Alabama NAACP worked to desegregate public transportation in Montgomery, Alabama. In most southern cities all public facilities, including buses, were segregated. In Montgomery, white passengers rode in the front of the buses and black passengers rode in the back section. If the front section filled up, black passengers had to give up their back seats to white passengers. The Montgomery system also required that African American passengers enter through the front door to pay their fare, then get off the bus, walk to the back door, and board.

Rosa Parks

Rosa Parks spent most of her early life in Montgomery, Alabama, and attended a high school run by Alabama State College. She worked as a seamstress after graduation.

Parks became involved with the local NAACP and served as the secretary of the Montgomery branch as well as its youth council adviser. In the summer of 1955, she attended a workshop on race relations at the Highlander Folk School in Tennessee. This integrated school taught people how to organize movements for social reform. As Parks recalled years later, "At Highlander I found out for the first time in my adult life that this could be a unified society." This lesson inspired her later actions and beliefs.

Parks lost her seamstress job after her arrest for refusing to give up her seat on the Montgomery bus. She and her husband later moved to Detroit, Michigan, where she continued to work for civil rights.

The Rosa Parks Case

In the mid-1950s the NAACP was prepared to challenge Montgomery's segregated bus system. On December 1, 1955, African American seamstress Rosa Parks refused to give up her bus seat to a white passenger, as required by law. She was quickly arrested.

Parks later explained that years of ill treatment had led to her bold act:

66 Having to take a certain section [on a bus] because of your race was humiliating, but having to stand up because a particular driver wanted to keep a white person from having to stand was, to my mind, most inhumane. 99

After Parks's arrest, former NAACP leader E. D. Nixon organized an effort to use her case to challenge Montgomery's bus segregation law. Jo Ann Robinson, a local professor, organized a campaign to get African Americans to boycott the city bus system. This effort became known as the **Montgomery bus boycott**.

To help strengthen the boycott and coordinate their efforts, local African American leaders formed an organization that they called the **Montgomery Improvement Association**. They chose 26-year-old Baptist minister Martin Luther King Jr. to lead the association. King had a reputation as an inspiring speaker who could motivate listeners. In addition, he was new to town. The other members of the association thought that he might have less to lose from his participation in the protest.

Martin Luther King Jr., his wife, Coretta, and their children

A Community Effort

The majority of the city's African Americans supported the Montgomery bus boycott. They refused to ride the buses, depriving the system of about 70 percent of its regular passengers. Some sympathetic white citizens also supported the boycott. City buses were practically empty.

African American leaders established a carpool system to replace the buses. The community pitched in to help with the cost of gas and other items. Jo Ann Robinson explained why so many people supported the boycott: "I think people were fed up, they had reached the point that they knew there was no return."

The city of Montgomery refused to integrate its public transit system. Some white residents resorted to violence in their attempt to break the boycott. The homes of King and Nixon were bombed by people who wanted to maintain segregation. The boycott continued, however. It inspired similar protests in cities such as Birmingham, Alabama, and Tallahassee, Florida.

In November 1956 the U.S. Supreme Court ruled that Montgomery's segregated bus system

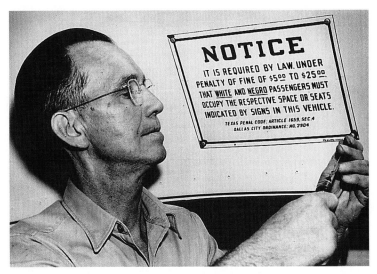

After a 1956 Supreme Court ruling, companies began removing separate seating signs on buses.

was illegal. The victory brought Martin Luther King Jr. to the forefront of the civil rights movement. In 1957 King helped found the **Southern Christian Leadership Conference**, a group of ministers that helped lead the struggle for civil rights. The boycott victory also energized the black community. "We had won self-respect," Robinson remembered. "It . . . makes you feel that America is a great country and we're going to do more to make it greater."

SECTION 4 REVIEW

Identify and explain the significance of the following:

- **Committee on Civil Rights**
- **Thurgood Marshall**
- ***Brown* v. *Board of Education***
- **Little Rock Nine**
- **Rosa Parks**
- **Montgomery bus boycott**
- **Montgomery Improvement Association**
- **Martin Luther King Jr.**
- **Southern Christian Leadership Conference**

Reading for Content Understanding

1 **Main Idea** What effect did African American war veterans have on the early civil rights movement?

2 **Main Idea** What events led to school desegregation?

3 **Constitutional Heritage** How did African Americans use the court system to try to gain equal rights?

4 **Writing** *Informing* Imagine that you have played an important role in the Montgomery bus boycott. Civil rights supporters in another state have asked you to give a speech explaining why the Montgomery protest worked. Write a detailed outline of your speech.

5 **Critical Thinking** *Drawing Conclusions* How do you think the example of the Little Rock Nine affected other African Americans?

CHAPTER 18 REVIEW

Chapter Summary

The 1950s were a decade full of contrasts. Americans enjoyed peace, while the shadow of the Cold War hung over the United States. Many Americans moved to new suburbs and enjoyed prosperity. Some people objected to the emphasis on material success in American society. African Americans battled discrimination in courtrooms and communities with some success. ■

On a separate sheet of paper, complete the following activities.

Identifying People and Ideas

Describe the historical significance of the following:

1. Dwight D. Eisenhower
2. John Foster Dulles
3. brinkmanship
4. *Sputnik*
5. Levittown
6. baby boom
7. Lucille Ball
8. Little Rock Nine
9. Rosa Parks
10. Montgomery bus boycott

Internet Activity

go.hrw.com
SB1 Suez Canal

Search the Internet through the HRW Web site to find information about the Suez Canal today. Use the information to create a "then and now" chart with information on the canal and the region in both 1956 and the present.

Understanding Main Ideas

1. What were President Eisenhower's main domestic policies?
2. How did the United States attempt to fight communism overseas?
3. What business trends affected workers during the 1950s?
4. How did some writers criticize American society during the 1950s?
5. What areas did African American civil rights leaders focus their reform efforts on in the 1950s?
6. What happened as a result of the Montgomery bus boycott?

Reviewing Themes

1. **Technology and Society** How did nuclear weapons affect U.S. foreign policy and American society during the Cold War?
2. **Economic Development** How did post-war prosperity affect the daily lives of many middle-class Americans?

Using the Time Line

Number your paper from 1 to 5. Match the letters on the time line below with the following events.

1. **Rosa Parks's arrest leads to the Montgomery bus boycott.**
2. **Federal troops enforce school desegregation in Little Rock, Arkansas.**
3. **The Soviet Union shoots down a U.S. U-2 spy plane.**
4. ***I Love Lucy* first appears on television.**
5. **An executive order integrates the U.S. military.**

1945   1950   1955   1960

a   b   c   d   e

3. **Constitutional Heritage** How did important court decisions affect African Americans' civil rights?

Thinking Critically

1. **Evaluating** What economic factors helped make the Montgomery bus boycott a success?

2. **Making Comparisons** How were the beats similar to and different from other writers who criticized society during the 1950s?

3. **Drawing Conclusions** Were U.S. efforts to halt the spread of communism in the 1950s successful? Explain your answer.

Writing About History

1. **Describing** Imagine that you are a newspaper reporter sent to Little Rock, Arkansas, in the fall of 1957. Write a feature story describing the events at Central High.

2. **Creating** Imagine that you work as a television editor in Hollywood during the late 1950s. Create a proposal for a comedy program set in a suburb.

Building Your Portfolio

Complete the following activities individually or in groups.

1. **Designing the Perfect Suburb** Imagine that you are an architect in a large downtown firm. Draw a plan or build a model for a new suburb just outside the city. Your plan should include designs for houses, streets, and community buildings. Include a brief paragraph explaining why people would want to live in your suburb.

2. **Fighting for Civil Rights** Imagine that you are the grandchild of a black World War II veteran who played an important role in the early civil rights movement. Create a scrapbook of the period to present to your grandparent at his or her birthday party. Your scrapbook might include photographs and captions, drawings, time lines, articles, interviews, and more.

Linking Geography and History

1. **Region** Why did many Americans move to the Sun Belt states?

2. **Human-Environment Interaction** How did the 1956 Highway Act change Americans' ability to travel?

History Skills Workshop

Reading Maps After petitioning for statehood for many years, the territories of Alaska and Hawaii became U.S. states in the late 1950s. Study the maps of Alaska and Hawaii below. Then answer the following questions: (a) On which dates did Alaska and Hawaii gain statehood? (b) Why was Alaska strategically important during the Cold War? (c) Approximately how far is Hawaii from the West Coast of the United States?

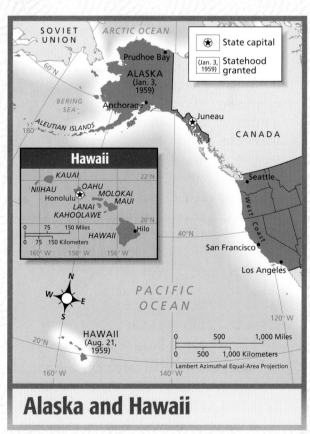

Alaska and Hawaii

History Skills

WORKSHOP

Using Primary and Secondary Sources

There are many sources of firsthand historical information, including diaries, letters, editorials, and legal documents such as wills and titles. All of these are *primary sources.* Newspaper reports are also considered primary sources, even though they are generally written after an event has taken place. The same is true for personal memoirs and autobiographies, which are usually written late in a person's life. Paintings, photographs, and editorial cartoons that make up history's visual record are also primary sources. Because they provide an opportunity to learn how people felt and what they believed, primary sources are valuable historical tools.

    Secondary sources are descriptions or interpretations of events written after the events have occurred, by persons who did not participate in or witness the events. History books, biographies, encyclopedias, and other reference works are examples of secondary sources. Writers of secondary sources have the advantage of knowing an event's long-term consequences. This knowledge helps shape writers' analyses.

How to Study Primary and Secondary Sources

1. **Study the material carefully** Consider the type of material. Is it verbal or visual? Is it based on firsthand information or on the accounts of others? Note the major ideas and supporting details.

2. **Consider the audience** Ask yourself: For whom was this message meant originally? Whether material was intended, for example, for the general public or for a specific, private audience may have influenced its style or content.

3. **Check for bias** Watch for words or phrases that signal a one-sided view of a person or event.

4. **When possible, compare sources** Study more than one source on a topic if you can. Comparing sources gives you a more complete, balanced account.

Practicing the Skill

1. How can you use paintings and photographs as primary sources?

2. What kinds of sources are available on the Internet? How can you distinguish between primary and secondary sources on Web sites?

3. Select a topic from Unit 6. Write a brief report using at least two primary sources and two secondary sources. Create a bibliography and explain why each source is considered a primary or a secondary source.

History in Action

UNIT 6 PORTFOLIO

A Cold War Scrapbook

Complete the following activity in small, cooperative groups.

You and the members of your group will be researching and creating items to be included in a Cold War Scrapbook. Each group member will be responsible for five scrapbook items. All of these items must be primary sources. Each group member will then write a paragraph using the information from the primary sources. This paragraph must be an unbiased account of the Cold War events discussed in the primary source documents. As a group, you will need to decide on which aspects of the Cold War each group member should focus.

Materials To complete this activity, you will need butcher paper, posterboard, construction paper, and various art materials, such as pens, pencils, paper, twine, glue, paints, or cloth for creating scrapbook items.

Parts of the Project To create your scrapbook, complete the following tasks:

1. **Research** Conduct research to locate primary sources relating to the Cold War. These sources might include diaries, letters, newspaper articles, photographs, quotes, or speeches. Use your textbook and library resources to find your sources. Be sure to include sources from a variety of media.

2. **Writing** When you have finished with your research, each group member should use information from the sources to write a one-paragraph account of the events represented. However, your account must be factually accurate and unbiased. You may need to use your textbook for additional information and to help you identify bias. You also need to write captions for your scrapbook items. In addition, one or two members of the group will be responsible for writing (and typing, if possible) a table of contents and an introduction for the scrapbook.

3. **Presentation** One or two group members will be responsible for putting the scrapbook together. For the layout, students should consider the visual impact. Use a variety of shapes and colors on each page. The other group members will make a cover for the scrapbook.

Display your group's finished scrapbook for the class. Have one member of your group read his or her paragraph aloud. Ask the class to identify some differences in opinion and bias between the paragraph and the primary sources.

Students use a variety of materials and sources to create a scrapbook.

UNIT 7 Searching for Solutions

(1945–1978)

American Teens

IN HISTORY

Young Politicians

During the 1960s many American teenagers became interested in political issues. Some participated in civil rights protests and free-speech movements. Other teenagers became involved in the U.S. political process.

Some teenagers received experience as politicians at special programs in Washington, D.C. For example, the American Legion sponsored programs for teen leaders from each state. Participants visited sites in the nation's capital. Delegates met with U.S. senators and in some cases the president.

In the late 1960s high school student Susan Collins participated in the William Randolph Hearst Foundation's Senate Youth Program. She visited the office of Margaret Chase Smith, a Republican senator from Maine. According to Collins,

Bill Clinton, a Boys Nation delegate from Arkansas, shakes hands with President John F. Kennedy in July 1963.

> **"**I remember leaving her office thinking that women can do anything, and that women can get to the highest level of government and make a real difference.**"**

Their experience in Washington inspired many teenagers to seek political office in later years. Teenagers participated in other educational programs designed to introduce them to politics and leadership roles.

Other teenagers became involved in local politics. Some participated on junior city councils. In the mid-1960s Bob Torricelli became the youngest person ever elected as junior mayor of Franklin Lakes, New Jersey. He was 14 years old. In 1996 Torricelli was elected a U.S. senator.

Many teenagers campaigned for local and national candidates even though they were too young to vote. High school student Hillary Rodham was a "Goldwater Girl." She campaigned for Senator Barry Goldwater, the Republican presidential candidate in 1964.

For many teenagers in the 1960s these activities represented just one of the many ways they became active in politics. In this unit you will learn more about how young Americans helped bring about great changes in society. You will also learn about U.S. involvement in Vietnam and the role of young people in the war.

LEFT PAGE: *U.S. astronaut Edwin "Buzz" Aldrin on the moon in July 1969*

Searching for Solutions

Peace Corps logo

1947
Jackie Robinson becomes the first African American to play in major league baseball.

Jackie Robinson

UNITED STATES

George Nelson's marshmallow sofa

1955
Americans Charles Eames, Florence Knoll, and George Nelson are among the pioneers of furniture design.

1958
Americans buy more than 25 million hula hoops, but the fad ends quickly.

1961
President John F. Kennedy establishes the Peace Corps. Many Americans will volunteer to assist other countries in development projects.

1945	1948	1951	1954	1957	1960

WORLD

1948
The National Party gains control in South Africa and introduces its policy of apartheid.

Godzilla

1954
The Japanese movie *Gojira* (or *Godzilla* in the United States) features a dinosaur-like monster, created as a result of nuclear weapons testing.

1945
George Orwell's novel *Animal Farm,* a political fable based on the story of the Russian Revolution, is published.

1960
The capital of Brazil is moved from Rio de Janeiro to the planned city of Brasília. Architects designed the shape of the city to resemble an airplane or a bird.

Cathedral of Brasília

1963
In Washington, D.C., some 200,000 people march for civil rights to the Lincoln Memorial.

The Lincoln Memorial

Ms. magazine covers

A bicentennial pitcher

1969
Astronaut Neil Armstrong becomes the first person to walk on the moon.

1972
Feminist Gloria Steinem begins publishing *Ms.* magazine, which presents women's issues.

1976
The United States celebrates 200 years of independence.

1963	1966	1969	1972	1975	1978

1964
Beatlemania continues to sweep the world as the Beatles release a movie, *A Hard Day's Night.*

1970
The Concorde, an airplane developed by Great Britain and France, travels at twice the speed of sound.

1973
Egyptian troops launch an attack on Israel across the Suez Canal on Yom Kippur, a Jewish holy day.

1975
The war in Vietnam ends. Saigon, the capital of South Vietnam, falls to the communist forces of North Vietnam. Saigon is renamed Ho Chi Minh City.

South Vietnamese medal

Beatles' harmonica box

USING THE TIME LINE

1. Which entries on the time line represent cultural or artistic events?

2. Which entries on the time line are related to civil rights?

Activity Using the entries listed on Unit 7 Time Line, create a new time line. Illustrate the time line with new images. These images should represent the entries without images on the Unit 7 Time Line. Use images from newspapers, magazines, or books or create drawings. Write captions for the new images, questions for the new time line and a new time-line activity.

CHAPTER 19

The Sixties

(1960–1969)

For many people, Bob Dylan's song "The Times They Are A-Changin'" captured the spirit of the 1960s:

> "Come mothers and fathers
> Throughout the land
> And don't criticize
> What you can't understand
> Your sons and your daughters
> Are beyond your command
> Your old road is
> Rapidly agin'.
> Please get out of the new one
> If you can't lend your hand
> For the times they are a-changin'."

THEMES

Global Relations
What events might bring countries close to waging a nuclear war?

Economic Development
How might a government increase citizens' economic opportunities?

Citizenship and Democracy
In what ways might a group work to change society?

1960	1961	1962	1963	1964

NOV. 1960 John F. Kennedy is elected president.

AUG. 1961 The Berlin Wall is erected.

OCT. 1962 The Cuban missile crisis occurs.

NOV. 1963 President Kennedy is assassinated.

OCT. 1964 The free-speech movement is launched at the University of California at Berkeley.

Kennedy and the Nation

What were some of the important elements in the 1960 presidential campaign?

How did John F. Kennedy's presidency inspire young Americans?

What advances and setbacks did Kennedy's domestic programs face?

Key Terms

mandate

New Frontier

ON THE EVENING OF SEPTEMBER 26, 1960, *American viewers watched the first-ever televised debate between presidential candidates. Looking at their television screens, most Americans saw John F. Kennedy as calm and confident. He seemed comfortable in front of the cameras. Richard Nixon appeared tense and sweaty, with a tight smile. "As the moderator signed off," one Kennedy adviser remembered, "our small band erupted in cheers. . . . It was over! We had won! Not just the debate. We had won the election!" Even Kennedy admitted, "We wouldn't have had a prayer without that gadget [television]." The prediction proved true in November, when Americans turned to Kennedy to lead the nation in the 1960s.*

Campaign pins from the 1960 presidential election

IMAGE ON LEFT PAGE: *John F. Kennedy arrives in Los Angeles for the Democratic National Convention.*

1965	1966	1967	1968	1969

JULY 1965 President Johnson signs Medicare into law.

SEPT. 1966 The National Traffic and Motor Vehicle Safety Act is signed into law.

JULY 1969 U.S. astronauts walk on the moon.

AUG. 1969 More than 400,000 people attend the Woodstock Music and Art Fair.

★ The Election of 1960

Many Americans considered the presidential election of 1960 to be an opportunity for change. The Republican Party nominated Richard Nixon. During his service as vice president in the 1950s, Nixon made his reputation as a conservative anticommunist. In 1960 he declared himself to be a "new Nixon." He promised to focus on domestic and economic reforms if elected president. Nixon chose United Nations ambassador and former senator Henry Cabot Lodge of Massachusetts as his running mate.

The Democratic Party nominated Massachusetts senator John F. Kennedy, a moderate on most issues. He chose Texan Lyndon B. Johnson, the Senate majority leader, as his running mate. During the campaign, Kennedy argued

This carriage was part of a parade in Cookeville, Tennessee, in support of Kennedy's campaign.

that the economy had stalled. He promised to make changes and to "get the country moving again."

Kennedy and Nixon differed little on issues. However, Kennedy had the advantage of style, as demonstrated by his success in the televised debates. Kennedy was only four years younger than Nixon, but he appeared youthful and energetic on camera. In contrast, Nixon seemed tired and unsure of himself. Referring to Kennedy, one young voter said: "The idea that this guy, who looked like your cool older brother might be President . . . was . . . really exciting."

Early in the campaign, some people raised questions about Kennedy's religion. These critics argued that as a Catholic, Kennedy might allow the pope to influence his political decisions. Kennedy answered these charges in a speech:

> ❝I am a Catholic, but . . . does that mean that I can't be president of the United States? I'm able to serve in Congress and my brother was able to give his life [in World War II], but we can't be president? . . . I will not allow any pope or church to dictate to the president of the United States.❞

Kennedy's speech quieted many people's doubts about the role his religion would play in his presidency.

Another boost to Kennedy's campaign came from one short telephone call. Civil rights leader Martin Luther King Jr. was in a

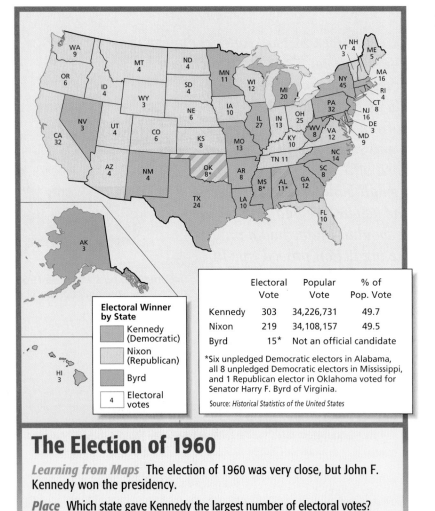

	Electoral Vote	Popular Vote	% of Pop. Vote
Kennedy	303	34,226,731	49.7
Nixon	219	34,108,157	49.5
Byrd	15*	Not an official candidate	

*Six unpledged Democratic electors in Alabama, all 8 unpledged Democratic electors in Mississippi, and 1 Republican elector in Oklahoma voted for Senator Harry F. Byrd of Virginia.

Source: *Historical Statistics of the United States*

Electoral Winner by State
- Kennedy (Democratic)
- Nixon (Republican)
- Byrd
- 4 Electoral votes

The Election of 1960

Learning from Maps The election of 1960 was very close, but John F. Kennedy won the presidency.

Place Which state gave Kennedy the largest number of electoral votes?

Georgia jail for participating in a protest. Kennedy, who had not met King or his wife, Coretta Scott King, called Mrs. King to offer support. King was released but never publicly endorsed Kennedy. One of his aides, however, told a crowd celebrating King's release to "take off your Nixon buttons." Kennedy won about 70 percent of the African American vote.

This support proved important in one of the closest elections of the 1900s. On election day in November 1960, Kennedy won the popular vote by less than 120,000 votes out of more than 68 million cast. This narrow victory did not give Kennedy a clear **mandate**, or public support, for his plans.

President Kennedy saw his inauguration as "a celebration of freedom."

The Kennedy Era

At age 43, John F. Kennedy was the youngest person ever elected president. His youthful image helped to define a new era. The media focused attention on Kennedy's family, particularly his elegant wife, Jacqueline, and their two young children.

The Kennedys brought a sense of style and glamour to the White House. They invited many famous artists, musicians, and writers there. The first lady was an enthusiastic supporter of the arts. She believed, "Whoever lives in the White House must preserve its traditions, enhance it, and leave something of herself there." As a result of her efforts, Congress passed new legislation declaring the mansion's furnishings to be property of the White House. Presidents could no longer give away china, furniture, or other property as gifts.

First Lady Jacqueline Kennedy shows television viewers the White House. She called it "a showcase of American art and history."

Scenes of President Kennedy playing sports contributed to his image of youth and strength. In reality, he suffered from many health problems. "At least one half of the days he spent on this earth were days of intense physical pain," his brother Robert recalled. In addition to serious back problems, Kennedy suffered from Addison's disease, an often fatal ailment. Few Americans knew of Kennedy's illnesses.

Kennedy's New Frontier

President Kennedy assembled a group of highly educated advisers who were active in a variety of causes. The press nicknamed this group "the best and the brightest." Many of Kennedy's advisers were admirers of the New Deal. They believed in using government to bring about positive reform.

In his inaugural address, Kennedy announced a set of domestic- and foreign-policy proposals he called the **New Frontier**. He asked Americans to work for freedom and justice throughout the world:

   " And so, my fellow Americans—ask not what your country can do for you—ask what you can do for your country. My fellow citizens of the world—ask not what America will do for you but what together we can do for freedom of man. "

Kennedy's call inspired many young people to become involved in reform movements and to enter public service.

Conflict with the Steel Industry

One goal of the New Frontier was to improve the economy. A slight economic decline in the late 1950s caused many Americans to worry that the prosperity of the postwar era was over. In 1961 the economy improved slightly—largely because of increased defense spending. However, the next year unemployment rose again, reaching about 7 percent. Kennedy took steps to lower inflation and reduce unemployment. He proposed a series of voluntary wage and price controls for businesses.

Initially, he focused his efforts on the steel industry, whose workers were preparing for new contract negotiations. Kennedy appealed to union members to accept smaller wage increases. He also asked business owners not to raise prices. Steelworkers agreed to smaller raises, which owners could pay without increasing prices.

However, U.S. Steel raised its prices significantly. Kennedy's secretary of labor called the act a "double cross." Several other steel companies joined in this price increase. Kennedy ordered the Federal Trade Commission to investigate whether the steel industry had violated antitrust laws when it raised prices. U.S. Steel soon backed down and lowered its prices. It took longer for Kennedy to repair his relationship with business leaders, who had objected to his involvement in the steel crisis.

Conflicts with Congress

President Kennedy looked for other ways to boost the economy. In August 1962 he proposed a major tax cut to stimulate investment and consumer spending. As part of his New Frontier policies, Kennedy had also proposed new programs to help the poor and expand the military and the space program. Worried about the cost of these programs, Republicans and conservative southern Democrats blocked much of the legislation.

Kennedy did help to pass laws that increased the minimum wage and funded improvements in urban areas and education. He also advanced the cause of mental health. In 1963 Congress approved new funding for local mental-health centers. The purpose of these centers was to reduce the number of people in psychiatric institutions.

Kennedy's proposal to expand health insurance for the elderly did not pass. In general, Kennedy focused his efforts more on foreign policy than on domestic issues. He once remarked to Nixon, "Foreign affairs is the only important issue for a President to handle, isn't it?"

The Defense Department was one of the leading buyers of steel.

SECTION 1 REVIEW

Identify and explain the significance of the following:
- **John F. Kennedy**
- **Jacqueline Kennedy**
- **mandate**
- **New Frontier**

Reading for Content Understanding

1 **Main Idea** What were some of the factors that influenced voters in the 1960 presidential campaign?

2 **Main Idea** What were some of President Kennedy's successes and failures with his domestic programs?

3 **Citizenship and Democracy** Why did many young people become interested in government during Kennedy's presidency?

4 **Writing** *Informing* Imagine that you are a political commentator. Write a newspaper column on the roles that television and style played in the 1960 presidential campaign.

5 **Critical Thinking** *Drawing Conclusions* Why do you think Kennedy's 1961 inaugural address inspired the nation? How do you think you would have responded?

SECTION 2

Kennedy's Foreign Policy

Reading Focus

Why did President Kennedy develop a new Cold War strategy?

How did the Bay of Pigs invasion and the Berlin Wall reflect on Kennedy's administration?

What caused the Cuban missile crisis?

Key Terms

flexible response
Alliance for Progress
Peace Corps
Bay of Pigs
Berlin Wall
Cuban missile crisis
Limited Nuclear Test Ban Treaty

ON JANUARY 23, 1961—*just days after President Kennedy's inauguration*—Newsweek *magazine published a special section on the foreign-policy issues facing the new president. The article began, "Around the restive [uneasy] globe from Berlin to Laos, the Communist threat seethed [raged], and nowhere more . . . than in Cuba." The special section concluded with a warning, "The greatest single problem that faces John Kennedy—and the key to most of his other problems—is how to meet the aggressive power of the Communist bloc."*

Newsweek *magazine published a special section on President Kennedy's New Frontier.*

Flexible Response

In foreign policy, President Kennedy continued the policies of Eisenhower's administration. Kennedy maintained a strong military and increased the nation's supply of nuclear weapons. However, he thought that Eisenhower had relied too heavily on the threat of nuclear weapons. Such weapons were not practical for use in regional conflicts.

Kennedy wanted to increase the number of military forces and conventional, or non-nuclear, weapons such as tanks. He hoped that this increase would give the United States more military options, an approach he called **flexible response**. Kennedy explained the policy in July 1961: "We intend to have a wider choice than humiliation or all-out war." Part of Kennedy's new flexible-response policy involved the use of "counter-insurgency" forces. These troops would lead secret operations to weaken communist movements in other countries.

Kennedy also pursued a nonmilitary approach to foreign policy. Under his leadership, the United States attempted to fight communism in Africa, Asia, and Latin America with economic assistance rather than military force.

The Sixties **573**

The Kennedy administration developed the **Alliance for Progress**. This aid program sought to encourage economic development and promote democracy in Latin America. The United States pledged $20 billion in aid. The assistance did little to improve conditions in Latin America or U.S. relations with the region, however. The Alliance, one scholar later wrote, "attempted to accomplish in a decade what could only be attained [reached] in several generations."

As part of his New Frontier, Kennedy created the **Peace Corps**. This program sends American volunteers to developing countries to work on a wide variety of improvement projects. Thousands of young people responded to Kennedy's call to "make a difference." In 1961 the Peace Corps began sending volunteers overseas. One early volunteer explained her decision to apply:

❝ **The idea was to go there and help people to help themselves. . . . I felt that this was a way that I could give something back. I don't think any of us who joined the Peace Corps had an international view of the world. We just thought that . . . the Peace Corps was a way in which we could bring the best of our nation to these . . . countries.** ❞

★ The Bay of Pigs

President Kennedy was particularly interested in helping Latin America because of a new political situation in Cuba. In 1959 Fidel Castro had led a rebellion that overthrew an unpopular dictator. Castro organized a social and economic revolution, promising all Cubans "neither bread without liberty nor liberty without bread." However, by 1960 he had established a communist dictatorship in Cuba and formed an alliance with the Soviet Union. Cuba is located less than 90 miles from

Linking Past to Present

The Changing Peace Corps

In March 1961 President Kennedy established the Peace Corps to "promote world peace and friendship." Since then, more than 125,000 Americans have served in more than 100 countries.

In the early 1960s, Peace Corps volunteers were primarily young college graduates who served in Africa, Asia, and Latin America. They worked on agriculture, education, engineering, and health projects.

Today, however, the Peace Corps actively recruits retired people because of their broad experience and knowledge. In recent years, many countries have requested help in new areas, particularly economic development.

A Peace Corps volunteer in Honduras

The Peace Corps has expanded its program to include places such as Eastern Europe and the former Soviet Union.

Many Peace Corps veterans say that they learned a lot from their experiences. One volunteer explained: "I have come to appreciate not only the luxuries, but also the freedoms we, as Americans, take for granted."

Understanding What You Read

1. How has the Peace Corps helped both volunteers and those they serve?

2. Why do you think the Peace Corps did not send early volunteers to the Soviet Union?

Florida. Many Americans were worried about having a communist nation so close. They feared that the Soviet Union might use Cuba as a base from which to attack the United States or spread communism in Latin America.

Before he left office, President Eisenhower approved a secret plan for the Central Intelligence Agency to train Cuban exiles and help them invade the island. When Kennedy took office, he approved the final plan. In April 1961 some 1,500 exiles waded ashore at the **Bay of Pigs** on the southwest coast of Cuba. Castro's forces quickly attacked them, and the invasion turned into a disaster. Kennedy decided not to send in U.S. military air support. After three days of fighting, about 300 of the invaders had been killed and the rest captured. Castro remained firmly in power.

At a news conference, Kennedy admitted that the U.S. government had sponsored the invasion. He accepted blame for its failure, saying, "I am the responsible officer of the government." The failed invasion reflected poorly on the administration.

Communist leaders Fidel Castro of Cuba and Nikita Khrushchev of the Soviet Union

The Berlin Wall

Soviet leader Nikita Khrushchev viewed the Bay of Pigs disaster as a sign of American weakness. He decided to test the determination of the U.S. government to continue the Cold War. He chose Berlin as the testing ground.

After World War II, the Soviet Union and the Western Allies had divided the city of Berlin. The western sections became West Berlin, while the Soviet section became East Berlin. For many people in East Berlin, West Berlin stood as a model of prosperity and freedom. Gradually, East Berliners began crossing into West Berlin. Their numbers soon increased. In the summer of 1961, more than 1,000 people a day were fleeing East Berlin.

On the morning of August 13, 1961, Berliners woke to find East German workers building the **Berlin Wall**. This wall between East and West Berlin was a 28-mile barrier of barbed wire and cement. The Berlin Wall was a desperate attempt to stop the border crossings. President Kennedy protested the "brutal border closing." He also sent 1,500 U.S. troops to West Berlin as a show of support for the city's residents. However, neither Kennedy nor Congress wanted to go to war with the Soviet Union.

On June 26, 1963, Kennedy restated his public support for West Berlin in a speech at the Berlin Wall. He assured thousands of West Berliners that the United States was prepared to "risk its cities to defend yours because we need your freedom to protect ours." Kennedy's symbolic support reassured Americans that he would not back down from communism. However, he had no intention of involving the United States in a military operation. The Berlin Wall would stand for decades as a symbol of the Cold War.

The Cuban Missile Crisis

After the Berlin Wall went up, Soviet premier Khrushchev continued to challenge President Kennedy. The most serious Cold War crisis occurred in Cuba in the fall of 1962.

Built in August 1961, the Berlin Wall became a visible symbol of the Cold War and of the Iron Curtain that separated Western and Eastern Europe.

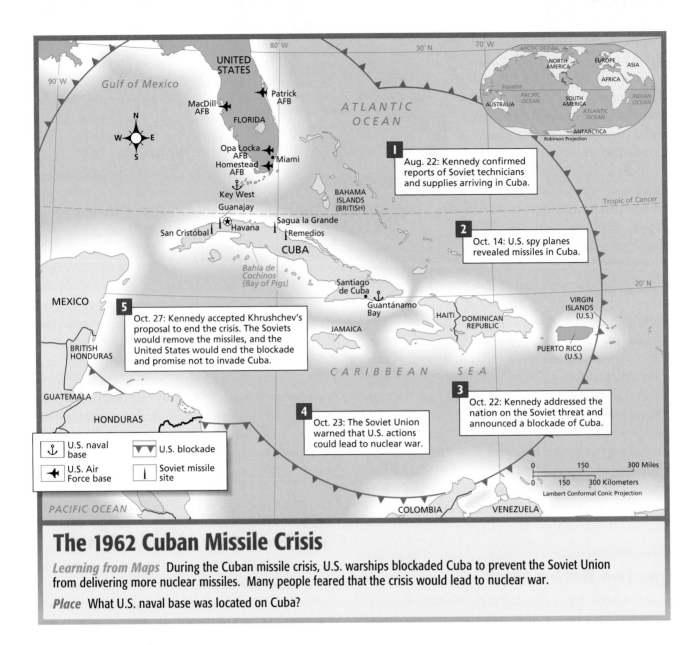

The 1962 Cuban Missile Crisis

Learning from Maps During the Cuban missile crisis, U.S. warships blockaded Cuba to prevent the Soviet Union from delivering more nuclear missiles. Many people feared that the crisis would lead to nuclear war.

Place What U.S. naval base was located on Cuba?

Map labels:
- **1** Aug. 22: Kennedy confirmed reports of Soviet technicians and supplies arriving in Cuba.
- **2** Oct. 14: U.S. spy planes revealed missiles in Cuba.
- **3** Oct. 22: Kennedy addressed the nation on the Soviet threat and announced a blockade of Cuba.
- **4** Oct. 23: The Soviet Union warned that U.S. actions could lead to nuclear war.
- **5** Oct. 27: Kennedy accepted Khrushchev's proposal to end the crisis. The Soviets would remove the missiles, and the United States would end the blockade and promise not to invade Cuba.

Legend:
- U.S. naval base
- U.S. Air Force base
- U.S. blockade
- Soviet missile site

Missiles in Cuba

Beginning in 1961 the Soviet Union sent increasing numbers of military personnel to Cuba. The Soviets started arming Cuba with missiles during the summer of 1962. Cuban and Soviet officials claimed that these weapons were only to protect the country against another invasion like the Bay of Pigs. "We can now repel an American invasion," said Raul Castro, Fidel Castro's brother.

In September, Kennedy warned Soviet leader Khrushchev against putting on Cuban soil missiles that could attack U.S. targets. Khrushchev denied he was doing so. In mid-October, however, photographs from U.S. spy planes provided evidence that the Soviets were installing nuclear missiles. These missiles had enough range to hit major U.S. population centers, such as Miami, Florida, and Atlanta, Georgia. Over the next several days, while the Soviets prepared the missiles for operation, Kennedy met with his advisers to plan his response.

During a televised address on October 22, Kennedy demanded that Khrushchev withdraw the missiles. He also pledged that the United States would attack the Soviet Union if the Soviets fired any missile in the Western Hemisphere. Kennedy warned that he had ordered the U.S. Navy to surround Cuba and prevent Soviet ships from bringing in more missiles.

Kennedy's speech alarmed people worldwide. Many feared that the crisis would lead to nuclear war and global destruction. One American newspaper reported that local high school students were breaking down in class and sobbing, "I don't want to die."

A Soviet nuclear missile on parade in Moscow

A Tense Standoff

Soviet ships loaded with missile parts continued toward Cuba. The world waited anxiously to see what would happen that October in the **Cuban missile crisis**. Attorney General Robert Kennedy later recalled the president's reaction as the superpowers came closer to a confrontation.

" **I think those few minutes were the time of gravest concern for the President. Was the world on the brink [edge] of a holocaust [destruction]? Was it our error? . . . His face seemed drawn, his eyes pained. . . . He would have to wait.** "

Soon word came that at the last moment the Soviet ships had turned back. One Kennedy adviser described the moment, "We're eyeball to eyeball, and the other fellow just blinked." Later, Kennedy and Khrushchev agreed to a compromise. "We and you ought not to pull on the ends of the rope in which you have tied the knot of war," the Soviet leader wrote him. "Let us take measures to untie that knot." The Soviets removed their

missiles from Cuba in return for a U.S. promise not to invade the island. Kennedy also agreed to remove some U.S. missiles from Italy and Turkey. In 1963 Kennedy and Khrushchev established a teletype "hot line." The leaders of the two superpowers could use the hotline to communicate with each other at a moment's notice.

The two leaders also signed the **Limited Nuclear Test Ban Treaty** in August 1963. This treaty banned the testing of new nuclear weapons aboveground. More than 90 nations eventually signed the treaty.

The outcome of the Cuban missile crisis restored public confidence in Kennedy's foreign policy. Unlike his actions during the Bay of Pigs crisis, Kennedy had relied less heavily on his advisers and more on his instincts. He believed that the compromise agreement and the easing of tensions after the crisis showed the effectiveness of flexible response. "It was a combination of toughness and restraint [holding back], of will, nerve, and wisdom," observed Kennedy adviser Arthur Schlesinger Jr. "It dazzled the world." Although the Cold War continued, the United States and the Soviet Union made efforts to prevent future conflicts.

SECTION 2 REVIEW

Identify and explain the significance of the following:
- flexible response
- Alliance for Progress
- Peace Corps
- Fidel Castro
- Bay of Pigs
- Berlin Wall
- Cuban missile crisis
- Limited Nuclear Test Ban Treaty

Locate and explain the importance of the following:
- Cuba
- Miami

Reading for Content Understanding

1 **Main Idea** Why did President Kennedy develop the strategy of flexible response?

2 **Main Idea** How did the Bay of Pigs and the Berlin Wall affect Kennedy's presidency?

3 **Global Relations** Why did the United States and the Soviet Union come so close to nuclear war over the placing of offensive missiles in Cuba?

4 **Writing** *Classifying* Create a chart listing the foreign-policy crises during the Kennedy administration. Classify their outcomes as positive or negative.

5 **Critical Thinking** *Identifying Cause and Effect* How did the Bay of Pigs invasion contribute to the Cuban missile crisis?

The Johnson Administration

Reading Focus

How did people react to President Kennedy's assassination?

How did President Johnson's domestic programs help many Americans?

What was Johnson's approach to foreign policy?

Key Terms

Warren Commission
War on Poverty
Great Society
Medicare
Medicaid
Immigration and Nationality Act

 IN NOVEMBER 1963 *President Kennedy began a quick tour of Texas cities. On the morning of November 22, he polished a speech he planned to deliver that day in Dallas. "We ask therefore that we may be worthy of our power and responsibility," he planned to say, "and that we may achieve in our time and for all time the ancient vision of 'peace on earth, good will toward men.'" Kennedy never delivered that speech. By that afternoon, he had died from an assassin's bullet. That same day, Vice President Lyndon B. Johnson assumed the presidency.*

The Dallas Citizens Council
The Dallas Assembly
The Science Research Center
request the pleasure of
the company of
Mr. Carlos Hedstrom Jr.

at a luncheon in honor of
The President and Mrs. Kennedy
The Vice-President and Mrs. Johnson
The Governor and Mrs. Connally
Friday, the twenty-second of November
at twelve noon
The Trade Mart

An invitation to a luncheon in Dallas for Kennedy

⭐ The Kennedy Assassination

On November 22, 1963, as President Kennedy's car traveled through Dallas, shots rang out. Kennedy slumped forward, severely wounded. He died soon afterward. Vice President Lyndon B. Johnson, traveling in another car, was unharmed. Just hours after the assassination, *Air Force One,* the presidential airplane, carried Kennedy's body back to Washington, D.C. Standing next to First Lady Jacqueline Kennedy, Johnson took the presidential oath of office.

The assassination shocked Americans. One Kennedy administration official remembered his reaction on hearing of the president's death:

❝ I was crying. It was unbelievable, stunning. An awful feeling of helplessness—nothing could be done, no recall. It—he—was over, done, finished. . . . John Kennedy was not the sixties. But he fueled the smoldering embers [fire], and, for a brief while, was the exemplar [prime example] who led

Lyndon B. Johnson

Lyndon B. Johnson was born in 1908 in central Texas. His father was a local politician, and Johnson grew up with politics in his blood.

Johnson became known as the wonder kid of Texas politics for his early accomplishments. In 1935 President Franklin D. Roosevelt appointed Johnson director of the Texas National Youth Administration (NYA), a New Deal program. He was the youngest state NYA director. Under his leadership the NYA constructed highways, parks, and playgrounds throughout Texas. Johnson won election to the House of Representatives in 1937 at age 29.

Johnson continued his rise into the Senate, on to the vice presidency, and then the presidency. A former colleague described Johnson's ambitious pace: "Lyndon behaves as if there were no tomorrow coming and he had to do everything today."

---

others to discover their own strength and resurgent [renewed] energy. ”

People around the world also mourned Kennedy's death. More than 90 percent of American homes and millions of people worldwide watched Kennedy's funeral on television.

Within hours of the assassination, police arrested Soviet sympathizer and former U.S. Marine Lee Harvey Oswald. Two days later, officials prepared to transfer Oswald to another jail. Nightclub owner Jack Ruby pushed his way through a crowd and killed Oswald.

Oswald's death left many unanswered questions. To try to clear up the mystery surrounding Kennedy's assassination, President Johnson appointed a special commission headed by Chief Justice Earl Warren. The **Warren Commission** spent months studying the evidence. It concluded that Oswald was the assassin and that he had acted alone. Not everyone agreed with that conclusion, however. The controversy surrounding the Kennedy assassination continues to this day.

After Kennedy's death, the media created an idealized image of him. Jacqueline Kennedy also popularized this view of her late husband. Days after his funeral, she told a journalist of Kennedy's love of Camelot. This legendary court of King

Arthur was featured in a popular Broadway musical in the early 1960s. The first lady referred to the Kennedy administration as

" a magic moment in American history, when gallant men danced with beautiful women, when great deeds were done, when artists, writers, and poets met at the White House. . . . There'll never be another Camelot again. ”

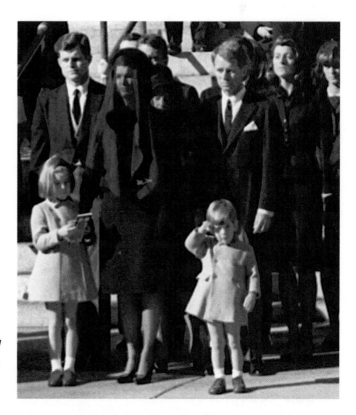

On his third birthday, John F. Kennedy Jr. saluted his father's coffin in the funeral procession.

★ President Johnson

The new president tried to comfort the nation in its grief. Five days after the assassination, President Johnson addressed Congress and the American public: "All I have I would gladly have given not to be standing here today." He promised to push for New Frontier reforms.

The Johnson Style

President Johnson differed from Kennedy in his personal background and leadership style. Johnson grew up in the rural Hill Country of central Texas. He worked his way through a local teacher's college. Kennedy had appeared athletic and poised, while Johnson was known for his physical clumsiness and use of crude language.

Johnson, however, had much more political experience than Kennedy. Johnson served in the House of Representatives for 12 years before moving to the Senate. After his first term as senator, he became majority leader. Johnson worked hard to get to know his fellow senators and to learn what it took to win their votes. He was extremely skilled in the art of compromise, even if his methods were sometimes sharp. One member of Congress recalled Johnson's forceful manner: "Lyndon got me by the lapels [collar] and put his face on top of mine and he talked and talked."

The Kennedy Legacy

As president, Johnson was determined to win the civil rights and education legislation that he had favored as a senator and that Kennedy had supported. Johnson also wanted to help poor Americans. In the 1962 book *The Other America,* journalist Michael Harrington had reported that about 50 million Americans were living in poverty. They earned less than $3,500 per year for a family of four. The news disturbed many people and created some support for government action.

Harrington explained that many Americans enjoyed one of the highest standards of living in the world. At the same time, however, many poor

The Head Start program helped many underprivileged children.

people in the United States were becoming poorer. "If the nation does not measure up to the challenge . . . ," he warned, "poverty in the 1960s might be on the increase." Groups that had limited political power and influence were more likely to be poor. About 50 percent of African Americans and female-headed households were living in poverty. An estimated one third of people over 65 years of age also lived at the poverty level.

To help poor Americans, Johnson launched what he called the **War on Poverty**. He created a new agency, the Office of Economic Opportunity (OEO), to develop programs to help poor people earn money. The OEO started a new Job Corps to teach young adults basic job skills. The agency funded Head Start, an educational program to prepare poor children for school. The OEO also created a domestic version of the Peace Corps—the Volunteers in Service to America (VISTA).

The 1964 Election

Johnson's popularity soared because of his success in establishing such programs. The Democrats nominated him as their candidate for president in 1964. Johnson's choice for vice president was Minnesota senator Hubert Humphrey. After Kennedy's assassination, Johnson had served without a vice president.

Barry Goldwater ran as the Republican presidential candidate. A conservative senator from Arizona, Goldwater wanted to reduce federal social programs and expand the U.S. military. The Democrats accused him of being an extreme anticommunist who might lead the nation into war. Many voters seemed to agree. Johnson won with more than 60 percent of the popular vote and with 486 electoral votes to Goldwater's 52.

A campaign pin for Lyndon B. Johnson, also known as LBJ

⭐ The Great Society

President Johnson saw his election victory as a mandate for his policies. He set out to expand his domestic reforms. Johnson called his new program for reform and aid for Americans living in poverty the **Great Society**. In a speech before the 1964 election, Johnson had described his vision:

❝ **The Great Society rests on abundance and liberty for all. It demands an end to poverty and racial injustice. . . . The Great Society is a place where every child can find knowledge to enrich his mind and to enlarge his talents. . . . It is a place where the city . . . serves not only the needs of the body and the demands of commerce but the desire for beauty and the hunger for community.** ❞

President Johnson was a teacher before he turned to politics.

New Reforms

Johnson considered his Great Society to be an expansion of Roosevelt's New Deal of the 1930s. During Johnson's first 100 days in office in 1965, he introduced and won passage of his Great Society legislation. Some Great Society reforms focused on improving health care and education. These programs continue today. **Medicare** helps people over age 65 meet medical expenses by including them in a government health care plan. **Medicaid** provides health insurance for people with low incomes. President Harry S Truman had first proposed these reforms in 1945. Johnson signed the bill for Medicare in July 1965.

The Elementary and Secondary School Education Act supplied more than $1 billion in aid to assist students with special needs. To help improve housing for low-income families, Congress created the Department of Housing and Urban Development (HUD). Johnson appointed former New Deal reformer Robert Weaver as HUD's secretary. Weaver was the first African American appointed to a presidential cabinet.

Immigration Policy

Johnson's Great Society plan also included a revision of national immigration policy. In October 1965 Congress passed the **Immigration and Nationality Act**. The legislation set the quota for all immigrants from countries in the Western Hemisphere at 120,000. For other immigrants, the annual limit was 170,000, with no more than 20,000 from any one country. Close relatives of individuals already in the United States, however, would be admitted regardless of the quota. As a

President Johnson signed the Medicare bill in former president Truman's hometown.

result, many more newcomers immigrated than legislators had planned. In particular, the number of immigrants from Asia and Latin America rose.

Partly because of Johnson's Great Society, poverty in the United States declined. Overall unemployment levels stayed low in the second half of the 1960s. The percentage of Americans living below the poverty level dropped to about 12 percent by 1969. Americans' income levels rose more during the 1960s than during the prosperous years of the 1950s.

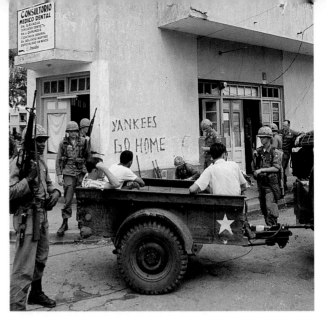

Some Dominican citizens resented the arrival of U.S troops in 1965.

Johnson and Foreign Policy

President Johnson devoted most of his attention to his Great Society programs. Unlike Kennedy, Johnson had little interest in international affairs. However, like former presidents Eisenhower and Kennedy, Johnson regarded communism as a major threat to democracy and world peace.

Johnson relied heavily on Kennedy's foreign-policy advisers as he tried to maintain a strong Cold War policy. During his presidency, Johnson increased the U.S. military presence in South Vietnam to help defend it from communist North Vietnam. (See Chapter 21 for more information.)

In April 1965 Johnson sent U.S. Marines to stop rioting in the Dominican Republic. He feared that Communists allied with Cuban leader Fidel Castro

wanted to take over the nation's unstable government. Overall, Johnson sent some 22,000 soldiers and marines to the small country. Latin American and Caribbean leaders were angered by this use of U.S. force. They viewed U.S. involvement as an extreme reaction to an internal conflict. Eventually, a group of these leaders met with U.S. and Dominican officials. They created a plan for restoring local control to the country.

Most of Johnson's foreign-policy decisions were a response to his fear of communist aggression. However, some Americans wondered if military intervention was the best course to take.

SECTION 3 REVIEW

Identify and explain the significance of the following:
- **Lyndon B. Johnson**
- **Warren Commission**
- **Michael Harrington**
- **War on Poverty**
- **Barry Goldwater**
- **Great Society**
- **Medicare**
- **Medicaid**
- **Robert Weaver**
- **Immigration and Nationality Act**

Reading for Content Understanding

1 **Main Idea** How did Americans respond to the assassination of President Kennedy?

2 **Main Idea** What was President Johnson's foreign policy?

3 **Economic Development** Make a graphic organizer listing Johnson's domestic programs. Include the goals and results of these efforts.

4 **Writing** *Informing* Imagine that you are a TV newscaster in 1963. Write a script informing your audience of Kennedy's assassination and what his death might mean for the nation.

5 **Critical Thinking** *Identifying Generalizations and Stereotypes* How might Michael Harrington's *The Other America* have changed or reinforced people's ideas about poverty in the United States?

New Movements in America

Reading Focus

What did students protest in the 1960s?

What were some aspects of the counterculture?

How were cultural changes reflected in art and music?

Key Terms

Students for a Democratic Society
generation gap
counterculture
hippies
pop art
Motown Records
Woodstock

*I*N THE FALL OF 1964, *school administrators at the University of California at Berkeley took steps that stunned students. The administrators announced that students could no longer conduct political activity on campus. They could not even hand out pamphlets outside the main gate of the campus. The school's decision angered many students. They objected to their loss of the right to free speech as guaranteed in the First Amendment. They soon took action that captured the attention of the nation.*

Student protests occurred on many college campuses.

Student Protests

Mario Savio led some 2,000 other Berkeley students in a free-speech movement in October 1964. Savio had gained much experience from his earlier work with the civil rights movement. He issued a document criticizing university officials.

When there was no response, the students began a strike. They also took over an administration building in an effort to shut down the university. Savio explained:

❝There is a time when the operation of the machine [the university] becomes so odious [hated], . . . that . . . you've got to put your bodies upon the gears and upon the wheels, upon the levers, upon all the apparatus [parts] and you've got to make it stop. And you've got to indicate to the people who run it . . . that unless you're free, the machine will be prevented from running at all.❞

Police arrested more than 770 protesters, but other students continued the strike. Eventually, university officials agreed to some reforms.

Student protests occurred across the nation. The civil rights movement greatly inspired some

Mario Savio addresses students at the University of California at Berkeley.

In the early 1960s much of society and culture looked a lot like it had in the 1950s. The media celebrated white, middle-class suburban values and institutions. The optimism of the time could perhaps be summed up in the words one high school principal had written in a graduating senior's yearbook:

" **As you in the class of 1959 go on to higher education, you are in full accord [agreement] with the times. . . . The signposts everywhere read, 'Opportunity Unlimited!'** "

students in the **Students for a Democratic Society** (SDS). This organization saw nuclear arms and racial discrimination as two great threats to American society. SDS activist Tom Hayden helped explain these issues of concern in the Port Huron Statement. SDS and other students launched protests against racial discrimination, rigid college rules, and the growing U.S. military presence in Vietnam. (See Chapters 20 and 21 for more information.)

 The Youth Revolt

The student protests shocked many older Americans. For them, the protests showed a lack of respect for authority.

The Generation Gap

During the 1960s some children of the post–World War II baby boom were beginning to enter young adulthood. The number of people aged 15 through 24 increased almost 50 percent from 1960 to 1970. In 1964 the first wave of the baby-boom generation entered college. Columbia University president Grayson Kirk declared, "I know of no other time in our history when the gap between the generations has been wider or more potentially dangerous." This **generation gap**, or division between older and younger people, grew as more young people rejected their parents' values and beliefs.

The Counterculture

Some young people rejected traditional society and chose instead to "drop out." They created a **counterculture**—an alternative culture with values that ran counter to, or against, those of the main society. The counterculture emphasized individual freedom, nonviolence, and communal sharing. Members of the counterculture, who called themselves **hippies**, experimented with different lifestyles. They often wore their hair long and dressed in unconventional clothing. African, American Indian, and Indian clothing were popular with hippies. Many hippies dyed their own clothes in a process known as tie-dying. Some hippies experimented with drugs.

Some young leaders tried to bring together members of the student movement and the counterculture. In 1967, protesters in San Francisco organized the Human Be-In. This event attracted some 20,000 young people from both movements.

Hippies explored new styles of clothing and behavior.

American Arts

Andy Warhol

Andy Warhol was born in Pittsburgh, Pennsylvania. His parents were immigrants from Czechoslovakia. After graduating from the Carnegie Institute of Technology in 1949, he worked as a commercial artist in New York City. Many of his commercial drawings were used in advertisements and greeting cards. In the late 1950s Warhol began to paint and create his own art.

In the 1960s Warhol exhibited his prints of Campbell's soup cans, a turning point in his career. His work was known as pop art—art that uses popular or common objects as subjects. Warhol often reproduced brightly colored copies of familiar everyday objects and celebrities. These images of mass culture were intended to question American materialism in the 1960s and the seriousness of traditional art. As one critic stated, Warhol turned products into art.

Warhol's prints of Marilyn Monroe and other celebrities became symbols

Andy Warhol, Campbell's Soup. © 1965. The Andy Warhol Foundation for the Visual Arts, Inc./ Artists Rights Society (ARS), New York.

Andy Warhol turned soup cans into art and showed that art could be found in anything.

of the 1960s. Warhol used a process known as silk-screen printing to mass-produce his art. With silk-screen printing, a person rubs or forces color through a patterned screen made of silk. The pattern will create the image on the material to be printed. This process allows many copies of one image to be made quickly and easily.

As the 1960s progressed, Warhol became more involved with filmmaking, producing, and writing. He established a studio in New York City called the Factory, which attracted well-known artists and celebrities. In 1968 Warhol made his often quoted prediction about the age of mass media: "In the future everyone will have 15 minutes of fame."

Understanding the Arts

1. What is pop art?
2. Why do you think pop art was so popular in the 1960s?

Many student leaders believed, however, that the aims of the counterculture were too different from their goals. Student activists wanted to challenge society in order to improve it. Hippies rejected society and tried to create an alternative culture. Many students believed the counterculture abandoned its responsibility to society by encouraging unhealthy behavior, such as drug abuse.

The counterculture and the student rights movement challenged the way many Americans viewed their world. The movements encouraged a greater tolerance for differences in dress, music, and personal relationships.

★ A Different Perspective

Changes in the art world reflected this new point of view. The **pop art** movement took its name from the popular, commonplace images and objects shown in its works. Pop art challenged the values of traditional art and criticized it for a lack of humor and humanity.

Robert Rauschenberg was one of the first artists to use mass media images in his artwork. In the early 1960s he began to fill large canvases with images from the news and anonymous photographs of city scenes.

Andy Warhol was pop art's most famous artist. His best-known paintings are of brightly colored Campbell's soup cans and of 1950s movie star Marilyn Monroe's face. Art critics debated whether Warhol was criticizing consumer culture or celebrating it. Although some critics saw little merit in pop art, it forced people to discuss the question "What is Art?"

 ## A Musical Revolution

Popular music also underwent many changes during the 1960s. Musical styles and song lyrics reflected the frequent experimentation and social changes of the era.

The "British Invasion"

The popularity of British performers increased in the United States during the mid-1960s. This "British Invasion" began with the Beatles, a foursome from Liverpool, England. Their early songs were upbeat, romantic tunes such as "I Want to Hold Your Hand" and "She Loves You."

The Beatles' 1964 American tour sparked a tremendous wave of excitement among their fans. Reporters labeled the reaction "Beatlemania." One journalist was puzzled by the screaming adoration of excited teenage girls. He concluded, "The Beatles themselves don't know how they do it."

The Beatles' popularity in the United States created opportunities for other British bands. The Rolling Stones, The Who, the Moody Blues, and many other British bands toured the United States and sold millions of records. The success of the Beatles and other rock 'n' roll bands made the growing

Beatles fans react to the arrival of the "Fab Four."

generation gap in the United States more obvious. Most older Americans could not understand why young women screamed excitedly for the Beatles, or why young men copied their shaggy hairstyles.

Motown

Changes in the music business resulted in increased opportunities for African Americans. In 1959 businessman Berry Gordy founded **Motown Records** in Detroit, Michigan. The name Motown is a contraction of "Motortown" and refers to Detroit's main industry, automobile manufacturing. Motown Records was the first major record label owned by an African American. In 1960 the company produced the first of many gold records—records selling 500,000 or more copies.

The "Motown sound" was a form of soul music, the most popular black music in the 1960s.

Album covers from 1960s artists Jimi Hendrix, Aretha Franklin, and Bob Dylan

Soul music combined the strong beat of traditional rhythm and blues with smoother sounds and melodies. Some of the most successful soul artists included Aretha Franklin, Marvin Gaye, the Jackson Five, Diana Ross and the Supremes, and Stevie Wonder. Diana Ross gave Motown Records credit for the success of the Supremes: "Had it not been for Berry Gordy searching for talent in our black community we wouldn't have been discovered." Many Motown performers were popular with white listeners as well as black fans.

Folk Music

During the 1960s folk music also became popular. Musician Odetta Gordon performed a wide range of blues, folk, and gospel songs. Folk musicians such as Joan Baez performed songs that addressed political and social issues of the times. Inspired by 1930s folk singer Woody Guthrie, Bob Dylan wrote songs about the struggles of poor and powerless people to rise above their troubles. Although one critic complained that Dylan's voice sounded like "a dog with his leg caught in barbed wire," few critics denied that his lyrics reflected the spirit of the times.

A ticket for Woodstock

Rock Music

In the 1960s rock 'n' roll became the most popular American music. Electrically amplified instruments, particularly the electric guitar, became the driving sound. Jimi Hendrix incorporated electronic distortions, called feedback, into his guitar playing. In his version of "The Star-Spangled Banner," Hendrix used his guitar to produce the screaming sound of the "rockets' red glare."

Blues singer Janis Joplin's instrument was her voice. With her loud vocals and enthusiastic performances, Joplin was a symbol of 1960s rebellious youth. A fan once asked Joplin if she worried that she might ruin her voice. She replied, "Why should I hold back now and sound mediocre [average] just so I can sound mediocre twenty years from now?" Joplin died in 1970 at the age of 27.

In August 1969 more than 400,000 people gathered in upstate New York for the Woodstock Music and Art Fair. In spite of rain, overcrowding, and food shortages, many fans considered it the cultural high point of the 1960s. **Woodstock** soon became a symbol of the counterculture's idealistic spirit. "I call it a cosmic event myself," said folk singer Richie Havens, who performed at Woodstock. "I felt . . . the vibration which was freedom."

SECTION 4 REVIEW

Identify and explain the significance of the following:
- **Mario Savio**
- **Students for a Democratic Society**
- **Tom Hayden**
- **generation gap**
- **counterculture**
- **hippies**
- **pop art**
- **Andy Warhol**
- **Beatles**
- **Berry Gordy**
- **Motown Records**
- **Bob Dylan**
- **Janis Joplin**
- **Woodstock**

Reading for Content Understanding

1 **Main Idea** What were some of the characteristics of the counterculture?

2 **Main Idea** How did art and music reflect social and cultural changes in the 1960s?

3 **Citizenship and Democracy** What issues motivated students to stage protests during the 1960s?

4 **Writing** *Describing* Imagine that you are a reporter. Write an article describing the differences between the student movement and the counterculture.

5 **Critical Thinking** *Making Comparisons* Compare the various musical styles of the 1960s. How do these styles reflect experimentation and social change?

SECTION 5

Science in the 1960s

Reading Focus

What goal did President Kennedy set for the U.S. space program?

What applications did space technology have in daily life?

How did scientific advances raise environmental concerns?

Key Terms

Apollo program

National Traffic and Motor Vehicle Safety Act

I N MARCH 1961 *"Ivan Ivanovich" was launched into space aboard the Soviet spacecraft* Vostok. *He orbited for a while, then re-entered Earth's atmosphere and was ejected from the spacecraft. He parachuted into the snowy Ural Mountains. Since then he has remained in his spacesuit. Ivanovich appeared so lifelike that "model" was written on his forehead so that anyone who found him would not be confused. Model astronaut Ivan Ivanovich now hangs in the Smithsonian National Air and Space Museum in Washington, D.C.*

"Ivan Ivanovich" is the Russian-language equivalent of "John Doe."

★ The Space Race

On April 12, 1961, the Soviets launched a real person into space. Soviet cosmonaut Yuri Gagarin became the first human space traveler. He orbited Earth once, a trip that took less than 90 minutes. With Gagarin's successful orbit, the Soviet Union had beaten the United States into space again. NASA, established after the Soviets launched *Sputnik,* was still trying to catch up. Project Mercury was NASA's attempt to put the first American in space.

The Astronauts

In early 1959 NASA had begun its selection process for the project, choosing from a group of military test pilots. NASA required that the astronaut "not be taller than five feet eleven inches, he must weigh less than one hundred eighty pounds, and must be under forty years of age." The 32 pilots who volunteered underwent a series of medical examinations, psychiatric interviews, and physical endurance tests. For example, doctors measured the pilots' ability to withstand extreme cold and heat.

588 Chapter 19

Photographers and camera crews pressed around the seven test pilots selected to be Project Mercury astronauts.

On April 9, 1959, NASA formally introduced the seven selected astronauts to the public. The media attention on the astronauts and their families was enormous.

Into Space

Despite the excitement of the astronaut selection, the successful Soviet spaceflight disappointed many Americans. Astronaut John Glenn told the press:

 [The Soviets] just beat the pants off us, that's all. There's no use kidding ourselves about that. But now that the space age has begun, there's going to be plenty of work for everybody. "

On May 5, 1961—23 days after Gagarin's flight—Alan Shepard Jr. became the first American to enter space. His *Mercury* space capsule reached a maximum altitude of 116 miles above Earth's surface but did not orbit Earth. Later that month, President Kennedy committed the nation to "landing a man on the moon and returning him safely to the earth" before the end of the decade. Kennedy wanted the United States to win the space race because he believed it would be an important symbol of national strength during the Cold War.

In February 1962 John Glenn became the first American to orbit Earth. As the space program advanced, NASA launched the **Apollo program** to prepare for a moon landing. NASA soon pushed far ahead of the Soviets. On July 20, 1969—beating Kennedy's target date by nearly six months—U.S. astronauts reached the moon. As their *Apollo 11* spacecraft settled into lunar orbit, Neil Armstrong and Edwin "Buzz" Aldrin launched themselves in a lunar lander toward the moon's surface. Some 500 million people around the world watched on television as Armstrong took the first steps on the moon.

Most viewers were amazed to see a human on the moon. However, some critics complained that the space program cost a great deal while contributing little to daily life. The Apollo program cost between $25 and $35 billion. Each moon trip cost about half a billion dollars. Nevertheless, the majority of Americans saw the moon landing as a human triumph. *New York Times* reporter James Reston wrote:

" The great achievement of the men on the moon is not only that they made history, but that they expanded man's vision of what history might be. "

★ Technology in Daily Life

The live television broadcast of Armstrong's historic moon walk was an example of a practical application of space research. In the late 1950s the U.S. government began developing satellites to gather scientific data and to send and receive messages. NASA launched its first communications satellite, *Echo I*, in 1960. Once in place, radio waves could be bounced off *Echo I* and redirected to another location.

Private companies began using the technology to improve communications. American Telephone and Telegraph (AT&T), the country's largest communications company, sponsored the building of a satellite. In 1962 *Telstar* was launched. *Telstar* was the first satellite to transmit live television signals and telephone conversations across the Atlantic.

The United States joined with several countries to develop Intelsat, a worldwide commercial

The Apollo Program

On July 20, 1969, two *Apollo 11* astronauts landed on the moon. As Mission Commander Neil Armstrong first touched the surface of the moon, he said, "That's one small step for [a] man, one giant leap for mankind." The people who made this leap possible were the astronauts, engineers, and scientists of the Apollo program.

The Apollo program was created to fulfill the long-range goal of landing an American on the moon. By the time of the first Apollo flight, NASA engineers had built all the equipment as light and small as possible to save fuel for the long trip. Even with careful planning, the Apollo astronauts faced great danger. Three astronauts had died in a fire during a prelaunch test for *Apollo 1,* the first planned flight. Later, on *Apollo 13,* a malfunction left the crew dangerously low on oxygen while in space. Quick thinking and technical skill brought the astronauts safely back to Earth.

Despite its difficulties, the Apollo program was very successful. Altogether, there were eight missions to the moon, six of which landed on the surface. The final Apollo moon mission took place in 1972.

Along with increasing our scientific knowledge of the moon and space, the Apollo program contributed to the development of new technologies. These "spin-offs" included improved computers, satellites, medical equipment, and high-tech construction materials.

After the Apollo program ended, space exploration changed. Today, astronauts work mainly in space stations that orbit Earth or on new types of spacecraft, such as the space shuttle. NASA uses robots, not humans, to explore space. For now, at least, history remembers the 12 Apollo astronauts who landed on the moon as the only human beings to set foot on another world.

Understanding What You Read

1. Who was the first person on the moon? What year did he land?

2. What were some of the benefits of the Apollo program?

Astronauts

Main rocket engine

Fuel tanks

Guidance rocket

satellite system. Intelsat provided the global television coverage of the *Apollo* moon landing. Satellites soon became the most common way of transmitting telephone messages and TV images.

The U.S. military also launched spy satellites, which could provide detailed pictures of the Soviet Union. Perhaps the most useful technology to come out of the space program was the development of weather satellites. During the 1960s the United States launched many weather satellites. The information they relayed allowed for the early detection of hurricanes. Warnings could then be delivered to areas in danger.

Biologist and author Rachel Carson in the woods near her home

used insect poison, or pesticide—had caused the bird deaths. The birds were poisoned by bugs that had eaten leaves on trees sprayed with DDT. Carson feared that DDT would harm humans. Additional studies confirmed her findings. In 1972 the United States restricted the use of DDT.

In the mid-1960s lawyer Ralph Nader raised concerns about other dangers to consumers. In his 1965 book, *Unsafe at Any Speed*, he criticized the auto industry for unsafe car designs. According to Nader, car bumpers could not withstand an impact of three miles per hour. Head-on collisions, even at 25 miles per hour, were often fatal. Nader's efforts led to the passage of the **National Traffic and Motor Vehicle Safety Act** in September 1966. This law required the federal government to enact safety standards for all cars sold in the United States.

Nader then turned his attention to other consumer issues. He called for new government regulation to protect citizens. His associates, known as Nader's Raiders, investigated baby food, gas pipelines, land use, and the meat industry. For many Americans, Nader's efforts were an example of the reform spirit of the 1960s.

Science and the Environment

While NASA pioneered space exploration, scientists discovered new dangers on Earth. Some problems were created by scientific advances. Biologist Rachel Carson, for example, studied an outbreak of bird deaths in Massachusetts. In her 1962 book, *Silent Spring*, she examines why "the voices of spring in countless towns in America" have been silenced. Carson concluded that DDT—a widely

SECTION 5 REVIEW

Identify and explain the significance of the following:
- **Alan Shepard Jr.**
- **John Glenn**
- **Apollo program**
- **Neil Armstrong**
- **Edwin "Buzz" Aldrin**
- **Rachel Carson**
- **Ralph Nader**
- **National Traffic and Motor Vehicle Safety Act**

Reading for Content Understanding

1 **Main Idea** What was the goal of the U.S. space program in the 1960s?

2 **Main Idea** How did space technology improve daily life?

3 **Geographic Diversity** *Human-Environment Interaction* Why did scientific advances increase environmental awareness?

4 **Writing** *Describing* Imagine that you are one of Nader's Raiders in the 1960s. Write a press statement about a consumer issue you are investigating.

5 **Critical Thinking** *Synthesizing Information* Why do you think sending an American to the moon was such an important symbolic goal during the Cold War?

CHAPTER 19 REVIEW

Chapter Summary

In 1961 President John F. Kennedy brought a sense of energy and hope to the White House. He successfully guided the United States through the Cuban missile crisis. After Kennedy's assassination, President Lyndon B. Johnson tried to create a Great Society with many social reform programs. At the same time, many American youths rebelled against society and began a student movement. The moon landing of U.S. astronauts inspired great national pride. ■

On a separate sheet of paper, complete the following activities.

Identifying People and Ideas

Describe the historical significance of the following:

1. John F. Kennedy
2. Lyndon B. Johnson
3. Cuban missile crisis
4. Bay of Pigs
5. Great Society
6. Mario Savio
7. hippies
8. Apollo program
9. Neil Armstrong
10. Rachel Carson

Internet Activity go.hrw.com SB1 Apollo Program

Search the Internet through the HRW Web site to find information about the Apollo program. Use the information to create a multimedia display of the astronauts' experience during the Apollo missions.

Understanding Main Ideas

1. What major Cold War crises took place during President Kennedy's administration?
2. What major legislation was passed while President Johnson was in office?
3. What made the student movement of the 1960s new and different?
4. What were some of the characteristics of the counterculture?
5. How was the space race related to the Cold War?
6. What contributions did space technology make to everyday life?

Reviewing Themes

1. **Global Relations**   Why did the United States and the Soviet Union almost fight a nuclear war in the 1960s?
2. **Economic Development**   How did President Johnson's War on Poverty and Great Society programs improve many citizens' economic situations?

Using the Time Line

Number your paper from 1 to 6. Match the letters on the time line below with the following events.

1. The Woodstock Music and Art Fair attracts thousands of people.
2. U.S. astronauts make the first moon landing.
3. People fear the Cuban missile crisis may lead to nuclear war.
4. Medicare legislation is signed into law.
5. John F. Kennedy is assassinated.
6. The free-speech movement begins.

1960 | 1961 | 1962 | 1963 | 1964 | 1965 | 1966 | 1967 | 1968 | 1969

a   b   c   d   e f

3. **Citizenship and Democracy** How did hippies and student groups attempt to change society?

Thinking Critically

1. **Identifying Cause and Effect** How did the Bay of Pigs invasion contribute to increased Cold War tensions in the 1960s?

2. **Making Comparisons** How did the interests and leadership styles of Presidents Kennedy and Johnson contribute to their administrations?

3. **Drawing Conclusions** Why do you think the civil rights movement was important to Students for a Democratic Society and the free-speech movement?

Writing About History

1. **Persuading** Write a television commercial persuading people to vote for either John F. Kennedy or Richard Nixon for president.

2. **Expressing** Imagine that it is 1969 and the Soviet Union has made the first moon landing instead of the United States. Write a science-fiction short story expressing the consequences.

Linking Geography and History

1. **Location** Why did the Kennedy administration view the Soviet missiles in Cuba as a serious threat?

2. **Movement** Why did the Communists build a wall in Berlin?

History Skills Workshop

Using Visual Resources Study the image below, which is Robert Rauschenberg's 1963 painting *Estate.* Then answer the following questions: (a) What media does Rauschenberg appear to use? (b) How does this picture represent the pop art movement? (c) What can you learn about 1960s culture from this painting? Explain your answer.

Building Your Portfolio

Complete the following activities individually or in groups.

1. **Peace Corps Recruitment** Imagine that you are a Peace Corps volunteer who is recruiting Americans to work on a specific project in a foreign country. Design a recruitment program that offers information about what the project is, where it is, what it will accomplish, and what kinds of skills volunteers will need. Create a poster and a recruiting brochure to advertise your program.

2. **Community Activist** Pick an issue in your community that is important to you and that you think needs attention. Start a campaign to get your local government to take action. Your campaign should include a petition for signatures and a speech to present your position at the next city government meeting.

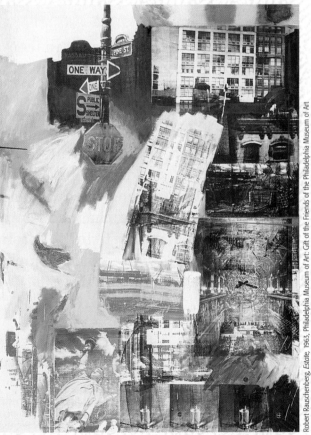

Robert Rauschenberg, *Estate,* 1963, Philadelphia Museum of Art: Gift of the Friends of the Philadelphia Museum of Art

■ CHAPTER 20 ■
The Search for Equal Rights
(1960–1978)

During the 1960s many American teenagers participated in movements to extend equal rights to all citizens. "Young people [today] should realize that it was people just like them, their age, that formulated goals and strategies," recalled activist Diane Nash. "When they look around now, and see things that need to be changed, they should say: 'What can I do?'" Nash and many others answered that question in their search for equal rights.

THEMES

Citizenship and Democracy
How might groups work to change a society?

Constitutional Heritage
In what ways might a government help its citizens gain civil rights?

Geographic Diversity
How might civil rights efforts vary in different regions?

1960	1962	1964	1966	1968

FEB. 1960 Sit-ins begin in Greensboro, North Carolina.

MAY 1961 Freedom Riders leave for the South.

JULY 1964 President Johnson signs the Civil Rights Act of 1964.

AUG. 1966 César Chávez forms a union for farmworkers.

OCT. 1966 Betty Friedan and other feminists found the National Organization for Women.

The Civil Rights Movement

Reading Focus

What events led to new civil rights laws?

Why were Freedom Summer and the marches in Selma successful in bringing about the Voting Rights Act of 1965?

How did the civil rights movement change in the late 1960s and 1970s?

Key Terms

sit-in

Student Nonviolent Coordinating Committee

Freedom Rides

Civil Rights Act of 1964

Freedom Summer

Voting Rights Act of 1965

Black Power

affirmative action

University of California v. *Bakke*

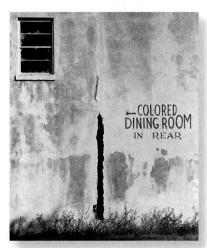

Restaurants throughout the South segregated white and black customers.

ON FEBRUARY 1, 1960, *Joseph McNeil bought a tube of toothpaste at a Woolworth's department store in Greensboro, North Carolina. His friend Franklin McCain bought some school supplies. Then the two black college students sat down together at the lunch counter and ordered coffee. The waitress refused to serve them. McCain asked her, "Why is it that you serve me at one counter and deny me at another?" The two shoppers were joined by two other African American students. They sat at the counter without being served until the store closed for the day. They returned the next morning with about 20 more students. Soon other African American students throughout the South were staging similar protests that captured the nation's attention.*

IMAGE ON LEFT PAGE: *More than 200,000 Americans participated in the March on Washington.*

| 1970 | 1972 | 1974 | 1976 | 1978 |

JAN. 1970 La Raza Unida Party is formed.

FEB. 1973 Members of the American Indian Movement stage a protest at Wounded Knee.

NOV. 1975 The Education for All Handicapped Children Act is passed.

The Sit-Ins

The four young men who started the Greensboro protest—McCain, McNeil, Ezell Blair, and David Richmond—had become friends at college. They had spent hours discussing race relations in the United States. They hungered for action. However, as McCain recalled, "There were many words and few deeds." During one conversation, McNeil declared, "It's time that we take some action." The four students decided to start by protesting racial segregation in local businesses.

They targeted Woolworth's, a popular variety store with a racially segregated lunch counter. On February 1, 1960, the four students sat down at the "whites only" section of the local Woolworth's lunch counter. They were staging a **sit-in**— a demonstration in which protesters sit down in a location and refuse to leave. Newspapers throughout the country reported their protest. Their sit-in inspired other African American students to protest segregation.

To achieve their goals, the sit-in protesters practiced nonviolent resistance. This strategy of peaceful protest rejected the use of violence, even for self-defense. Remaining nonviolent was not always easy. Crowds of angry white citizens often shouted insults at the protesters, threw food on them, and even assaulted them. An African American named Anne Moody described her appearance after a sit-in that turned violent:

 [My hair] was stiff with dried mustard, ketchup and sugar. . . . I didn't have on any shoes because I had lost them when I was dragged across the floor at Woolworth's. My stockings were sticking to my legs from the mustard that had dried on them.

Over time, Woolworth's began to integrate its lunch counters. Some other businesses in the South also integrated. This success encouraged African American student leaders to organize. Civil rights activist Ella Baker gathered student leaders together in the spring of 1960. They formed the **Student Nonviolent Coordinating Committee** (SNCC) to coordinate civil rights demonstrations and provide training for protesters.

☆ Freedom Rides

Despite the move toward integration in some businesses, bus stations all over the South still required travelers to use segregated facilities. In December 1960 the Supreme Court had ruled this practice illegal, but it continued nonetheless. The Congress of Racial Equality (CORE), a civil rights organization, decided to pressure the federal government to enforce the Court ruling. CORE organized **Freedom Rides** to protest segregation. On these rides, black and white riders traveled in buses throughout the South. Black riders would use "whites only" facilities. White riders would use facilities reserved for African Americans.

The Freedom Rides started in May 1961, when 13 riders began a bus trip from Washington, D.C., to New Orleans, Louisiana. By the time the bus reached Anniston, Alabama, a white mob had gathered. The mob pounded the riders with clubs and threw a firebomb through the bus's back window. The riders narrowly escaped with their lives.

Another mob attacked a second bus with CORE riders in Birmingham, Alabama. CORE leaders called off the bus protests because of the threats to the riders' lives. In spite of the enormous danger, SNCC leaders stepped in and decided to

Anne Moody (seated, far right) wrote about her experiences in the civil rights movement in Coming of Age in Mississippi.

continue the Freedom Rides. Nashville student leader Diane Nash said:

"These people faced the probability of their own deaths before they ever left Nashville. Several made out wills. A few more gave me sealed letters to be mailed if they were killed. Some told me frankly that they were afraid, but they knew this was something that they must do because freedom was worth it."

In late May, SNCC riders arrived in Montgomery, Alabama. A mob immediately attacked them. The Kennedy administration feared more violence and wanted the Freedom Rides to end. Attorney General Robert Kennedy advised the riders to observe a "cooling-off period." Ride organizer James Farmer responded, "Please tell the attorney general that we have been cooling off for three hundred and fifty years."

The attorney general provided a police escort, and the rides continued. Many Freedom Riders were jailed in Jackson, Mississippi. Despite the arrests, new people volunteered to participate.

The Freedom Rides ended only after the Interstate Commerce Commission banned bus and railroad companies from using segregated facilities. The ban went into effect on November 1. One SNCC member recalled, "From that moment on, segregation was dead." Although segregation did not die then, the Freedom Riders had struck an important blow.

★ Working for Freedom

In the fall of 1962 the fight for civil rights continued. Some 20,000 federal troops protected black student James Meredith as he registered at the all-white University of Mississippi. A few months later, Alabama governor George Wallace declared that he would fight for "segregation now, segregation tomorrow, segregation forever."

The 1961 Freedom Rides

Learning from Maps Civil rights workers staged Freedom Rides throughout the South to protest the region's segregated bus stations.

Location In which states did the Freedom Riders meet with violence?

Demonstrations in Birmingham

Following these incidents, Martin Luther King Jr. decided to force the end of Jim Crow laws that segregated the South. In 1963 the Southern Christian Leadership Conference (SCLC) chose Birmingham as the site for a campaign of boycotts, sit-ins, and demonstrations. Reverend Fred Shuttlesworth, a Birmingham civil rights leader, hoped to break down the city's segregation policies.

In April, King was arrested during one of the protests. While in custody, King wrote his now famous *Letter from Birmingham Jail*. This letter confirmed his commitment to nonviolence. Responding to a plea for patience made by white clergymen, King wrote:

"When you have to concoct [make up] an answer for a five-year-old son asking . . . 'Daddy, why do white people treat colored people so mean?' . . . then you will understand why we find it difficult to wait."

The Search for Equal Rights **597**

Martin Luther King Jr.

Martin Luther King Jr. was born in Atlanta, Georgia, in 1929. His family included many preachers and reformers who taught him the importance of fighting for justice. King entered college at age 15. After graduating, he studied at a seminary to become a minister. This seminary was the first integrated school King had attended. His experiences there greatly shaped his personal philosophies. King also studied the writings of Mohandas Gandhi, an Indian leader who used nonviolent resistance to help end British rule over India. These ideas helped shape King's later tactics in the civil rights movement.

While doing graduate work at Boston University, King met and married Coretta Scott. She would become one of his most important allies in his civil rights work. In 1954 the Kings moved to Montgomery, Alabama, where King became a minister at Dexter Avenue Baptist Church. He joined the local NAACP and began his lifelong participation in the civil rights movement.

The demonstrations continued after King's release from jail. In early May some 2,500 marchers walked through downtown Birmingham streets. Police Commissioner Eugene "Bull" Connor ordered the fire department to turn high-pressure hoses on the demonstrators. Connor then ordered his officers to release their attack dogs. TV camera crews captured the violence in shocking detail. The televised events gave many Americans their first real understanding that the civil rights movement in the South was a life-and-death struggle.

March on Washington

With public pressure mounting, President Kennedy announced his support for a new civil rights bill to end racial discrimination. African American leaders were hopeful but cautious. They decided to hold a nationwide demonstration—known as the March on Washington—to encourage support for the bill. A. Philip Randolph presided over the march, which was originally planned only for African Americans.

On August 28 more than 200,000 people—both black and white—filled the area around the Washington Monument. They marched to the Lincoln Memorial, where they listened to speakers. In his "I Have a Dream" speech, Martin Luther King Jr. filled the crowd with hope. According to one marcher, King's speech "just seemed to move you almost off the platform, off the earth."

Two weeks after the march, however, the hopeful mood crumbled in a wave of violence. A bomb exploded at an African American church in Birmingham and killed four young girls. A near riot followed. Two months later, President Kennedy was assassinated. After Kennedy's death, President Johnson took up the challenge of civil rights legislation. Johnson signed the **Civil Rights Act of 1964** in July 1964. The law banned segregation in public places, such as restaurants and transportation facilities. The law also prohibited employers, unions, or universities with federal government contracts from discriminating on the basis of color, sex, religion, and national origin.

Some participants in the March on Washington stood in front of the Lincoln Memorial as they listened to the speeches.

Voting Rights

That same summer, SNCC leader Robert Moses organized hundreds of volunteers. Most of them were white students from northern colleges. They volunteered for **Freedom Summer**, a campaign in Mississippi to register African Americans to vote. In Mississippi and some other southern states, threats of job loss, unfair election rules, and violence kept most African Americans from voting.

MISSING CALL FBI

THE FBI IS SEEKING INFORMATION CONCERNING THE DISAPPEARANCE AT PHILADELPHIA, MISSISSIPPI, OF THESE THREE INDIVIDUALS ON JUNE 21, 1964. EXTENSIVE INVESTIGATION IS BEING CONDUCTED TO LOCATE GOODMAN, CHANEY, AND SCHWERNER, WHO ARE DESCRIBED AS FOLLOWS:

ANDREW GOODMAN   JAMES EARL CHANEY   MICHAEL HENRY SCHWERNER

SHOULD YOU HAVE OR IN THE FUTURE RECEIVE ANY INFORMATION CONCERNING THE WHEREABOUTS OF THESE INDIVIDUALS, YOU ARE REQUESTED TO NOTIFY ME OR THE NEAREST OFFICE OF THE FBI. TELEPHONE NUMBER IS LISTED BELOW.

President Johnson ordered the Federal Bureau of Investigation to help locate the missing civil rights workers.

Murder in Mississippi

On June 21, 1964, three Freedom Summer volunteers disappeared. Andrew Goodman and Michael Schwerner, white activists from the North, and James Chaney, a black activist from Mississippi, remained missing for weeks. The search for them focused national attention on civil rights. Rita Schwerner, the wife of Michael Schwerner, noted:

> ❝ I personally suspect that if Mr. Chaney . . . had been alone at the time of the disappearance, that this case, like so many others, . . . would have gone completely unnoticed. ❞

Searchers found the men in early August. All three had been shot to death. Violence against other volunteers continued throughout the summer.

Selma

The brutal murders made voter registration a national issue. The Johnson administration prepared a new bill to protect black voters. To dramatize the need for the law, the SCLC organized a series of marches in Selma, Alabama. Martin Luther King Jr. chose Selma because, as in much of the state, only about 2 percent of African Americans of voting age were registered.

SCLC leaders had planned to march from Selma to Montgomery, the state capital, on March 7. Alabama state troopers ordered the civil rights marchers to stop. Then, as one marcher recalled, "they came upon us and started beating us with their nightsticks." More than 70 marchers were injured. The day became known as Bloody Sunday. Televised images of the violence shocked millions of Americans.

One week later President Johnson appealed to the nation to support a voting rights bill. On March 21, some 4,000 people completed a march from Selma to Montgomery. In August, Johnson signed the **Voting Rights Act of 1965**. The act gave the federal government the power to inspect voter registration procedures and to protect all citizens' right to vote. Within three years, more than half of all black voters in the South had registered to vote.

 ## Black Leaders

While Martin Luther King Jr. had become the best-known civil rights leader, other African Americans also inspired action. Many young black activists, particularly in northern cities, supported Malcolm X, a leader of the Nation of Islam. The religious group, also known as Black Muslims, supported black separatism. They encouraged black people to form their own, all-black communities.

In the early 1960s Malcolm X argued that the African American community should work for social and economic independence rather than integration. Unlike Martin Luther King Jr., Malcolm X insisted that African Americans had the right to protect themselves from violence:

> ❝ You're getting a new generation . . . and they're beginning to think with their own minds and see that you can't negotiate up on freedom nowadays. If something is yours by right, then fight for it or shut up. If you can't fight for it, then forget it. ❞

Malcolm X posed for this picture while visiting Egypt in 1964.

In the spring of 1964 Malcolm X split with the Nation of Islam and formed the Organization of Afro-American Unity. He then traveled to the Islamic holy city of Mecca in Saudi Arabia. There he met Muslims of many races and began to reconsider his antiwhite views. However, Malcolm X still remained committed to African Americans relying mainly on themselves. He still believed that the use of violence was sometimes justifiable. "There can be no revolution without bloodshed," he proclaimed. In February 1965, three members of the Nation of Islam assassinated Malcolm X in New York City.

Shortly after Malcolm X was killed, the civil rights movement reached a crossroads. King continued to support moderation and interracial participation. However, many young SNCC reformers became frustrated by the slow rate of change. They believed that the federal government had not done enough to stop violence against African Americans. Other critics believed that the movement should focus on improving the economic situation of African Americans.

In June 1966 SNCC leader Stokely Carmichael called for "black power." The **Black Power** movement wanted African Americans to have greater economic and political power. Carmichael explained its goals: "We determined to win political power, with the idea of moving on from there into activity that would have economic effects."

That same year Black Power supporters Huey Newton and Bobby Seale organized the Black Panther Party. Seale described the group's goals: "We want power to determine our own destiny in our own black community." The Panthers called for

WE WANT BLACK POWER

IF YOU ARE NOT PART OF THE SOLUTION YOU are part OF THE PROBLEM

Civil rights leaders Stokely Carmichael and Eldridge Cleaver helped spark the Black Power movement.

full employment and provided some community services. To reduce harassment against African Americans, the Panthers formed disciplined patrols to "police the police."

The Panthers' willingness to use violence to achieve their goals frightened many Americans. The Panthers engaged in gun fights with police, federal officers, and other black leaders. At least 19 Panthers were killed and many others jailed as a result of these various incidents. By 1969 the Black Panthers had virtually broken up.

★ Racial Riots

In the mid- to late 1960s racial riots occurred in many urban areas. The first major riot took place in the Watts section of Los Angeles in August 1965. The immediate cause of the riot was the arrest of a black motorist. However, frustrations over discrimination and economic hardships kept many African Americans rioting for several days. Some 30,000 people rioted, looted, and set fires for five days. The riot ended only after some 14,000 National Guard troops came in to restore order. After the riot, more than 20 people lay dead.

Over the next three years, hundreds more riots broke out. President Johnson appointed the Kerner Commission to investigate the violence. In its 1968 report, the commission identified racial issues as a leading cause of the riots. The report also warned that "the nation is rapidly moving toward two increasingly separate Americas"—one white and wealthy, the other black and poor.

In early 1968 Martin Luther King Jr. announced plans for a march to begin the "Poor People's Campaign." He wanted poor people of all races to unite to address economic problems such as poverty and unemployment. Before the march began, King traveled to Memphis, Tennessee, to support striking garbage workers. On April 4, 1968, as he stood talking with supporters, a hidden gunman fired at him. King was hit and died instantly. Some two months later, ex-convict James Earl Ray was arrested for the murder.

King's assassination horrified many people worldwide. Riots erupted in more than 100 U.S. cities. The violence ended with nearly 50 people dead. The nonviolent part of the civil rights movement seemed in danger of dying with King. However, other leaders vowed to pursue his goal.

Educational opportunities for African Americans increased in the 1970s.

★ Reaction and Successes

In the 1970s, civil rights leaders focused on school desegregation. The Supreme Court had declared racial segregation in public schools illegal in 1954. Yet school segregation continued, particularly in the North. Most students went to local schools in their neighborhoods. However, most neighborhoods were segregated. To desegregate schools, some judges ordered forced busing. As a result, students were taken to schools outside their neighborhoods.

Many parents, particularly white parents, objected to forced busing. One mother said it violated "the basic right for a parent to choose how . . . and where the child should be educated." Extreme antibusing protests took place in Boston in 1974. A federal judge had ordered the busing of nearly half of all Boston students to schools outside their neighborhoods.

Some people also opposed **affirmative action**, the practice by some businesses and government agencies of giving special consideration to nonwhites or women to make up for past discrimination. Some critics argued that any race- or gender-based preference was unfair. In June 1978 in ***University of California* v. *Bakke***, the Supreme Court ruled that white applicant Allan Bakke had been unfairly denied admission to medical school. The university had set a quota, or a specific number of spaces, for African Americans. The Court ruled that race could be a factor in admissions, but that setting quotas was illegal. Despite this ruling, affirmative action programs continued to offer new opportunities to many African Americans.

African Americans made gains in other areas. The number of African Americans enrolled in college in the 1970s increased significantly. More African Americans became involved in politics. Between 1966 and 1973, the number of African Americans serving in Congress more than doubled. The percentage of African American elected officials was still low, but African Americans hoped that progress would continue.

SECTION 1 REVIEW

Identify and explain the significance of the following:
- sit-in
- Ella Baker
- Student Nonviolent Coordinating Committee
- Freedom Rides
- Martin Luther King Jr.
- Civil Rights Act of 1964
- Freedom Summer
- Voting Rights Act of 1965
- Malcolm X
- Black Power
- affirmative action
- *University of California* v. *Bakke*

Reading for Content Understanding

1 **Main Idea** What led to the passage of the Civil Rights Act of 1964?

2 **Main Idea** What changes occurred in the civil rights movement in the late 1960s and early 1970s?

3 **Geographic Diversity** Why did civil rights activists stage campaigns for voting rights in Mississippi and Alabama? Why was this strategy successful?

4 **Writing** *Expressing* Imagine that you are a participant in a civil rights sit-in. Write a poem expressing your reaction to the protest.

5 **Critical Thinking** *Making Comparisons* Compare and contrast the goals, strategies, and achievements of Malcolm X and Martin Luther King Jr.

1963

Martin Luther King Jr.'s

I Have a Dream

On August 28, 1963, more than 200,000 people participated in the March on Washington in support of civil rights. The demonstrators marched from the Washington Monument to the Lincoln Memorial, where Martin Luther King Jr. delivered his "I Have a Dream" speech. His address is remembered as one of the most powerful and effective speeches of modern times. An excerpt appears here.

Five score [100] years ago, a great American, in whose symbolic shadow we stand, signed the Emancipation Proclamation. This momentous decree [important order] came as a great beacon [light of hope] to millions of Negro slaves who had been seared [burned] in the flames of withering injustice. It came as a joyous daybreak to end the long night of captivity.

But one hundred years later, we must face the tragic fact that the Negro is still not free. One hundred years later, the life of the Negro is still sadly crippled by the manacles [handcuffs] of segregation and the chains of discrimination. . . .

In a sense we have come to our nation's Capital to cash a check. When the architects of our republic wrote the magnificent words of the Constitution and the Declaration of Independence, they were signing a promissory note [note promising payment] to which every American was to fall heir [inherit]. This note was a promise that all men would be guaranteed the unalienable [permanent] rights of life, liberty, and the pursuit of happiness.

It is obvious today that America has defaulted [failed to pay] on this promissory note insofar as her citizens of color are concerned. Instead of honoring this sacred obligation, America has given the Negro people a bad check; a check which has come back marked "insufficient funds." But we refuse to believe that the bank of justice is bankrupt. . . .

But there is something that I must say to my people who stand on the warm threshold [entrance] which leads into the palace of justice. In the process of gaining our rightful place we must not be guilty of wrongful deeds. Let us not seek to satisfy our thirst for freedom by drinking from the cup of bitterness and hatred. We must forever conduct our struggle on the high plane of dignity and discipline. We must not allow our creative protest to degenerate [fall] into physical violence. Again and again we must rise to the majestic heights of meeting physical force with soul force. . . .

I say to you today, my friends, that in spite of the difficulties and frustrations of the moment I still have a dream. It is a dream deeply rooted in the American dream.

I have a dream that one day this nation will rise up and live out the true meaning of its creed [formal statement]: "We hold these truths to be self-evident; that all men are created equal."

I have a dream that one day on the red hills of Georgia the sons of former slaves and the sons of former slaveowners will be able to sit down together at the table of brotherhood.

I have a dream that one day even the state of Mississippi, a desert state sweltering with the heat of injustice and oppression [persecution], will be transformed into an oasis of freedom and justice.

I have a dream that my four little children will one day live in a nation where they will not be judged by the color of their skin but by the content of their character.

I have a dream today.

I have a dream that one day the state of Alabama, whose governor's lips are presently dripping with the words of interposition [interference] and nullification [refusal], will be transformed into a situation where little black boys and black girls will be able to join hands with little white boys and white girls and walk together as sisters and brothers.

I have a dream today.

I have a dream that one day every valley shall be exalted [glorified], every hill and mountain shall be made low, the rough places will be made plain, and the crooked places will be made straight, and the glory of the Lord shall be revealed, and all flesh shall see it together.

This is our hope. This is the faith with which I return to the South. With this faith we will be able to hew [carve] out of the mountain of despair a stone of hope. With this faith we will be able to transform the jangling discords [disagreements] of our nation into a beautiful symphony of brotherhood. . . .

This will be the day when all of God's children will be able to sing with new meaning, "My country 'tis of thee, sweet land of liberty, of thee I sing. Land where my fathers died, land of the Pilgrims' pride, from every mountainside, let freedom ring."

And if America is to be a great nation, this must become true. So let freedom ring from the prodigious [vast] hilltops of New Hampshire. Let freedom ring from the mighty mountains of New York. Let freedom ring from the heightening Alleghenies of Pennsylvania!

Let freedom ring from the snowcapped Rockies of Colorado! Let freedom ring from the curvaceous peaks of California! But not only that; let freedom ring from Stone Mountain of Georgia! Let freedom ring from Lookout Mountain of Tennessee!

Let freedom ring from every hill and molehill of Mississippi. From every mountainside, let freedom ring.

When we let freedom ring, when we let it ring from every village and every hamlet [community], from every state and every city, we will be able to speed up that day when all of God's children, black men and white men, Jews and Gentiles [non-Jews], Protestants and Catholics, will be able to join hands and sing in the words of the old Negro spiritual, "Free at last! Free at last! Thank God Almighty, we are free at last!"

Understanding Primary Sources

1. What did Martin Luther King Jr. mean when he said that the United States had given African Americans a "bad check"?

2. What did King caution African Americans against in their fight for freedom?

Originally intended to be a protest over African American unemployment, the March on Washington became a wider civil rights demonstration. Here Martin Luther King Jr. waves to the crowd.

Rights for Hispanics

<table>
</table>

Reading Focus

How did César Chávez and the United Farm Workers help migrant workers?

In what ways did other Mexican Americans fight for civil rights?

What were some goals of the Chicano movement?

Key Terms

League of United Latin American Citizens
United Farm Workers
Chicano movement
Mexican American Youth Organization
La Raza Unida Party
Voting Rights Act of 1975

LIKE MANY OTHER AMERICANS, *Félix Longoria* answered the call to serve his country in World War II. After he was killed in action, his body was returned to his hometown in Texas for burial. The local funeral home director refused to hold services in the chapel for him because he was a Mexican American. Lyndon B. Johnson, a U.S. senator from Texas, stepped in to settle the dispute. He arranged for Longoria to be buried with full honors alongside other veterans at Arlington National Cemetery in Virginia.

World War II veteran Félix Longoria

Political Activism

Hispanics in the United States had faced discrimination for years. The mistreatment of World War II veterans pushed many Hispanics into action. "We have proven ourselves true and loyal Americans by every test that has confronted us," declared a Hispanic newspaper. The newspaper demanded "social, political and economic equality and the opportunity to practice that equality." The Longoria case inspired Héctor P. García, a highly decorated U.S. Army surgeon. He formed the American GI Forum to defend the rights of Mexican Americans.

One of the oldest Hispanic civil rights organizations also responded with greater action. In 1929, Mexican Americans had joined together to form the **League of United Latin American Citizens** (LULAC). LULAC's mission was to "make living conditions better for future generations of Mexican Americans." LULAC concentrated its efforts on civil rights, education, and employment.

In the 1940s LULAC won two important school desegregation cases—*Méndez* v. *Westminster School District* (1945) and *Delgado* v. *The Bastrop Independent School District* (1948). In these cases the federal courts established that segregating Mexican American children in public schools was illegal. The courts ordered the school districts to stop this practice, but discrimination continued.

 ## The United Farm Workers

In the 1960s the Hispanic population in the United States continued to grow. Encouraged by the success of the African American civil rights movement, Hispanics launched a fight for their own rights. Some Hispanic rights activists focused on improving economic opportunities.

Migrant Workers

Mexican Americans and Mexicans formed the largest ethnic group of migrant workers. Most of these farm laborers earned low wages and worked in unhealthy conditions. Their employers frequently took advantage of them. One California farmer admitted that

66 **farmworkers . . . were considered just another item in producing . . . like fertilizers. . . . Most growers didn't treat their workers with any degree of respect or dignity.** 99

Mexican American César Chávez had worked in farm fields since childhood. In the early 1960s he began organizing other migrant farmworkers. Chávez shared Martin Luther King Jr.'s belief in nonviolent protest. Chávez explained:

66 **Naturally, nonviolence takes time. But poverty has been with us since the beginning of time. We just have to work for improvement. I despise exploitation [unfair gain] and I want change, but I'm willing to pay the price in terms of time. There's a Mexican saying, 'Hay más tiempo que vida'—there's more time than life. We've got all the time in the world.** 99

Migrant workers picked grapes for long hours for little pay.

Biography

César Chávez

César Chávez was born in Arizona in 1927. He lived in dozens of towns as his family moved in search of farmwork. His early experience led him to help form unions for migrant workers. Chávez viewed union work as a part of a larger fight for human rights—a goal he called *La Causa*, or "The Cause."

Frail and soft-spoken, Chávez seemed to be an unlikely protest movement leader. However, his patience and dedication to the cause of human rights inspired many people and won many supporters. He helped make migrant farmworkers' rights a national issue. Some of his followers called him a "twentieth-century saint." Before his death in 1993, Chávez insisted, "It's not me who counts, it's the Movement."

In 1962 Chávez and Mexican American political lobbyist Dolores Huerta organized the National Farm Workers Association (NFWA). In September 1965 Chávez decided that the NFWA should help Mexican American and Filipino grape workers. They were on strike for higher wages in Delano, California. According to Chávez, the grower kept saying, "I can't pay. I just haven't got the money." Nonetheless, Chávez noted, the grower managed to meet the strikers' demands: "He must have found the money somewhere, because we were asking for $1.40 and we got it."

The Search for Equal Rights **605**

Later that year, Chávez led a larger strike of table-grape workers in California's San Joaquin Valley. Growers brought in other workers to pick the grapes before they rotted. In early 1966 Chávez organized a 250-mile march from Delano to Sacramento, the state capital. He used the march to connect farmworker issues with those of the African American civil rights movement. Some 10,000 workers and supporters participated in the march. In August 1966 Chávez brought together NFWA members and Filipino workers to create what would become the **United Farm Workers** (UFW). Huerta served as its first vice president.

Striking for Rights

Chávez also called for a consumer boycott of table grapes. By 1968 neither the boycott nor the continuing strike was succeeding. Chávez used an unusual tactic to encourage strikers. In March 1968 he began a hunger strike. Presidential candidate Robert F. Kennedy met with Chávez on the 24th day of his fast. Kennedy promised to commit

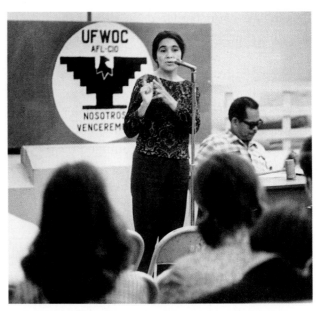

Dolores Huerta reports on union activities during a meeting in Delano, California.

himself to the farmworkers' cause. Televised images of a thin and weak Chávez revived the consumer boycott of grapes. At the peak of the boycott some 17 million Americans stopped buying grapes. The boycott cost growers millions of dollars. The strike was finally settled in 1970. Huerta led the negotiations. The union won a series of favorable three-year contracts with most table-grape growers.

Chávez and the UFW continued to fight for the rights of migrant workers. In 1975 California governor Jerry Brown introduced the Agricultural Labor Relations Act. This act officially provided migrant farmworkers the right to strike and to bargain collectively. Chávez's success in California inspired many farmworkers in Arizona, Florida, Texas, and the Midwest to organize.

A poster announcing a concert by the musical group Peter, Paul and Mary to benefit la huelga, *or the UFW strike*

★ Hispanic Civil Rights Leaders

During the 1960s the activities of Reies López Tijerina also gained public attention. Tijerina founded La Alianza Federal de Mercedes, or the Federal Alliance of Land Grants. He hoped to regain land for Mexican Americans in New Mexico.

According to Tijerina, Mexican Americans had been losing their land since the 1848 Treaty of Guadalupe Hidalgo. The treaty had guaranteed that Mexicans living in the Mexican Cession would still own their lands even after the area became U.S. territory. Tijerina charged that over time, state and local governments had been taking some of the Mexican Americans' land grants. Tijerina explained why he became involved in the issue:

> " Our land was stolen, we wanted it back. Our towns were alive and now they're dead, they're frozen, and the common lands that belonged to the towns were taken away. "

After legal appeals failed, Tijerina turned to direct action. In October 1966 some Alianza members briefly occupied part of the Kit Carson National Forest. Tijerina claimed that the area was part of a disputed land grant. The following June, Tijerina and Alianza members raided a county courthouse. The incident ended in a shoot-out between Alianza members and local officials. A massive search for the raiders followed. Officials used helicopters, planes, and tanks. Tijerina was captured, arrested, and charged with numerous offenses. Before he was convicted, Tijerina led a group of Hispanics in the 1968 Poor People's March on Washington, D.C.

Rodolfo "Corky" Gonzales, a young Hispanic activist, participated in this march. In 1966 Gonzales had begun protesting city government policies toward Mexican Americans in Denver, Colorado. Gonzales declared that "a new crusade for justice had been born." His Crusade for Justice emphasized cultural nationalism, or Mexican American ethnic pride. Gonzales also encouraged greater Hispanic economic and political independence. He issued *Demandas de la Raza,"* which called for reform in education, employment, housing, and land. Gonzales also helped organize a Crusade community center. It included classrooms, a library, a gymnasium, a meeting hall, and a social center.

American Literature

Poetry of Angela de Hoyos

Angela de Hoyos is a poet and graphic artist. Born in Mexico, de Hoyos was raised in San Antonio, Texas. Her first book of poetry was ARISE, CHICANO! and Other Poems.

Angela de Hoyos

BRINDIS*: FOR THE BARRIO
"Brothers, today we drink
the fresh milk of dawn
—for once, not tasting
of sourness.

For once,
the table is set
with plates full of hope,
and in our illiterate hands
some kind fate has placed
a promise of gold for tomorrow.

Not that the hollows
in your sad face of death
will ever be filled
—or the seedy, stale figure
of the poor
feel at ease in fine clothes—

but today we eat
to soothe a pain
—a pain of alien-hungers
Vallejo** never knew."

Understanding Literature

1. How does the poem express issues in the Mexican American community? Use specific words from the poem.

2. What do you think the phrase *a promise of gold for tomorrow* means?

*a toast **Mariano G. Vallejo (1808–90); California leader born in Mexico

The Chicano movement sought to end discrimination and increase Mexican American pride.

Gonzales influenced many young Hispanics with his poem *"Yo Soy Joaquín"* (I am Joaquín):

" **I am Joaquín,**
 lost in a world of confusion,
 caught up in the whirl of a
 gringo [white] society,
 . . .
 My fathers
 have lost the economic battle
 and won
 the struggle of cultural survival. "

★ The Chicano Movement

Gonzales inspired many younger Hispanic activists to join the struggle to end discrimination and increase Hispanic cultural pride. Their efforts became known as the **Chicano movement**, or *el movimiento*. Young Mexican Americans turned the word "Chicano" into a term of pride.

Student Protests

During the 1960s the number of Hispanics attending high school and college increased. Many of these students began to demand bilingual education, or instruction in two languages. They also

wanted more Hispanic teachers. Some Mexican American students staged walkouts in protest. They remained out of school until administrators met some of their demands.

In March 1968 teacher Sal Castro led a student walkout in East Los Angeles. More than 15,000 students walked out as the protest spread to five Los Angeles area high schools. The sight of the students on picket lines prompted one reporter to call the walkouts "the Birth of Brown Power." School authorities called in the police. Officers broke up meetings and made mass arrests. Similar walkouts occurred throughout the Southwest the following school year.

In the Crystal City, Texas, school system, about 85 percent of the student body was Hispanic. However, most of the administrators and teachers were not. Severita Lara recalled life at school:

" **In all of our activities, like for example, cheerleaders . . . there's always three Anglos and one mexicana. . . . We started questioning. Why should it be like that? . . . [We] started looking at other things.** "

In the fall of 1969, students staged a massive walkout to end discrimination. The **Mexican American Youth Organization** (MAYO), formed in 1967 by José Angel Gutiérrez, supported the walkout. The students stayed out of school until January 1970, when the Crystal City school board agreed to a series of reforms.

La Raza Unida

Following the events in Texas, Gutiérrez and some 300 other Hispanic activists organized to increase Hispanic political power. They founded **La Raza Unida Party** (LRUP), or the "United People's Party," in January 1970. In elections that spring, Gutiérrez and two other LRUP members won seats on the school board in Crystal City.

Two Mexican Americans were also elected to the city council.

One Hispanic reported, "Chicanos were in a state of jubilation [happiness]." Hispanic women played an important role in the elections. Party leader Marta Cotera recalled that women "were very much in evidence as . . . candidates, [and] as organizers in leadership positions." Organizers performed the crucial task of getting supporters registered to vote and attracting new members to the party.

Some Hispanics set up alternative schools when students boycotted the public schools.

 New Laws

As a result of the Hispanic civil rights movement, new legislation was enacted. Congress passed the 1968 Elementary and Secondary Education Act. It required that children whose first language is not English be instructed in two languages until they mastered English. The Bilingual Education Act of 1974 provided further federal funding for such programs. From 1969 to 1978 federal funding of bilingual education increased from $7.5 million to $135 million.

Hispanic leaders also hoped to increase the turnout of voters who had limited understanding of English. The **Voting Rights Act of 1975** required areas with large immigrant populations to provide ballots in the voters' preferred language.

By 1970 the Hispanic population in the United States had increased to more than 10 million. People of Mexican descent made up the largest number. However, many people from Puerto Rico, Cuba, other Caribbean islands, and Latin America also moved to the United States. In 1992 one activist declared, "We are still building. . . . There are a lot of fights [left]."

SECTION 2 REVIEW

Identify and explain the significance of the following:

- **Héctor P. García**
- **League of United Latin American Citizens**
- **César Chávez**
- **Dolores Huerta**
- **United Farm Workers**
- **Reies López Tijerina**
- **Rodolfo "Corky" Gonzales**
- **Chicano movement**
- **Mexican American Youth Organization**
- **La Raza Unida Party**
- **Voting Rights Act of 1975**

Reading for Content Understanding

1 **Main Idea** How did César Chávez and the UFW expand the rights of migrant workers?

2 **Main Idea** What actions did other Mexican American civil rights leaders take to gain their rights?

3 **Cultural Diversity** What changes did the Chicano movement achieve?

4 **Writing** *Informing* Imagine that you are the historian for La Raza Unida Party. Write a paragraph informing party members of the role that women played in helping Hispanic Americans gain equal rights.

5 **Critical Thinking** *Identifying Cause and Effect* How did the treatment of Hispanic war veterans help inspire the movement for Hispanic rights?

SECTION 3

The Women's Rights Movement

Reading Focus

Why was the year 1963 significant to the women's rights movement?

What were the goals and tactics of younger feminists?

What were the successes and failures of the women's rights movement?

Key Terms

Commission on the Status of Women
Equal Pay Act
The Feminine Mystique
feminism
National Organization for Women
Equal Rights Amendment

ONE NIGHT IN FEBRUARY 1960, Jerrie Cobb checked into a motel in New Mexico. She was about to begin a week of astronaut qualification tests. A veteran pilot, Cobb had set three speed and altitude records. She had more flying hours than some of the men then training to be astronauts. Despite her qualifications and her exceptional performance on the tests, Cobb never flew into space. At that time women were banned from spaceflight. Cobb brought her case to Congress, where several people opposed having women in the space program. "The men go off and fight the wars and fly the airplanes.... The fact that women are not in this field is a fact of our social order," one astronaut testified. "It may be undesirable."

Jerrie Cobb in front of her jet plane in 1961

⭐ New Frontiers for Women

In the 1960s some women began to challenge this social order. By 1960 nearly 40 percent of women over the age of 16 held jobs. Those workers included almost 40 percent of women with school-age children. An increasing number of working women were college educated. Yet most women were wage laborers or in low-paying, traditionally female professions such as teaching and nursing. Women earned on average only 60 percent of what men with the same experience, responsibility, and

skills earned. Women were paid less than men even when they performed the same job. They also had fewer opportunities for advancement. This situation led one magazine to wonder in 1960, "Wives with Brains: Babies, Yes—But What Else?"

In 1961 President Kennedy appointed Esther Peterson to lead the Women's Bureau in the Department of Labor. She persuaded the president to establish a **Commission on the Status of Women** to study workplace inequality. Former first lady Eleanor Roosevelt and Peterson headed the commission.

610 Chapter 20

Its report, released in 1963, offered contradictory messages. The report declared that motherhood was the major role of American women. It also supported special training to prepare young women for marriage. However, the commission also brought attention to women's lower wages and fewer job opportunities. The commission declared, "Equality of rights under the law for all persons . . . must be reflected in the fundamental law of the land." The report recommended paid maternity leave and the expansion of public child-care facilities to help female workers.

In 1963 Kennedy issued an executive order banning gender discrimination in civil service jobs. That same year, Congress passed the **Equal Pay Act**. This act required employers to pay men and women the same wages for the same job. In the next 10 years, more than 170,000 female employees received about $84 million in back pay under the act.

Despite such legislation, the Kennedy administration had a mixed record on women in the workplace. Kennedy appointed fewer women to high-level federal posts than other presidents. He was the only president since Herbert Hoover not to have a female cabinet member.

★ The Movement Begins

For many women, the commission's report led to a re-evaluation of their roles in American society. In 1957 part-time journalist and full-time mother Betty Friedan attended a Smith College reunion. Like Friedan, some classmates had become dissatisfied with their lives after giving up their careers to become homemakers.

Friedan studied this situation further. She reported her findings in **The Feminine Mystique**, published in 1963. Friedan challenged what she defined as the "feminine mystique." This myth said that all a woman needed to be happy and fulfilled was a husband and family. Friedan described the frustrations of some homemakers:

❝ **As she made the beds, shopped for groceries, matched slipcover material,**

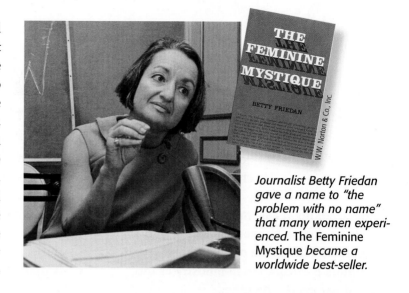

Journalist Betty Friedan gave a name to "the problem with no name" that many women experienced. The Feminine Mystique *became a worldwide best-seller.*

ate peanut butter sandwiches with her children, chauffeured Cub Scouts and Brownies, lay beside her husband at night—she was afraid to ask even of herself the silent question—'Is this all?' ❞

Many white, college-educated women agreed with Friedan's argument.

NOW

The modern women's rights movement began when more Americans began to question the traditional role of women in society. The movement was based on **feminism**. This theory states that women are entitled to economic, political, and social equality with men. The Civil Rights Act of 1964 provided a legal basis for women's call for equal rights. It prohibited employers from discriminating on the basis of sex, among other categories. The act also established the Equal Employment Opportunity Commission (EEOC) to investigate and evaluate discrimination complaints.

In the mid-1960s many people began to think that the government was not doing enough to protect women's rights. In October 1966 Betty Friedan and other feminist leaders founded the **National Organization for Women** (NOW). NOW lobbied for political issues that affected women. "Now that we've organized," declared one supporter, "it must be apparent that feminism is no passing fad but indeed a profound, universal . . . revolution." NOW focused on an "equal partnership of the sexes" in education, government, household

NOW was both the name of the organization and when women wanted their rights.

responsibilities, and job opportunities. The leaders of NOW sought to challenge

> **the traditional assumption that a woman has to choose between marriage and motherhood on the one hand and serious participation in industry or the professions on the other.**

NOW leaders launched a massive attack on gender discrimination. NOW filed lawsuits against newspapers that printed employment advertisements specifying "male only" or "female only" applicants. Other women's rights groups, such as the Women's Equity Action League (WEAL), joined NOW's fight. WEAL filed suit against more than 300 colleges and universities for paying female professors less than their male professors. WEAL ultimately won millions of dollars in salary raises for female faculty members. NOW and WEAL also achieved important legal and political changes for women.

Critics

As the women's rights movement grew, so did its critics. Some African American and Hispanic women criticized organizations like NOW for not addressing the needs of nonwhite women. Most feminists were middle-class, college-educated white women. As a result, some African American women viewed the women's movement as "basically a family quarrel between White women and White men."

Other African Americans argued that the movement needed to do more to help working-class women. They wanted higher wages and more benefits. White women wanted to receive wages equal to white men's wages. Black women wanted their wages to be at least the same as white women's. Hispanic and Asian women were more likely to participate in organizations such as the United Farm Workers. These organizations addressed concerns in their communities.

★ Younger Feminists

In the late 1960s a new group of feminists emerged. These women called for more radical change. Many of these women belonged to a "second wave" of younger activists. They had first worked in the student or civil rights movements. For some women, their experiences with these movements changed their outlook. SNCC activist Mary King noted:

> **If you are spending your time [doing] community organization, . . . opening people's awareness to their own power in themselves, it inevitably strengthens your own conceptions, your own ability.**

Many women were angry that male leaders in activist organizations did not treat them with respect. According to one male member of Students for a Democratic Society, women in SDS "made peanut butter, waited on tables, cleaned up. . . . That was their role." Feminist Shulasmith Firestone broke with a student protest movement after the men on an equal-rights panel refused to allow her to discuss women's rights. "Move on little girl," one man told her. "We have more important issues to talk about here than women's liberation."

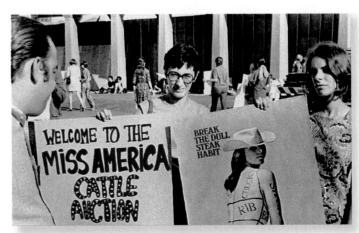

Many feminists believed that beauty pageants presented women as objects, not as human beings.

Linking Past to Present

Women in the Workplace Today

As a result of the women's rights movement, many women gained greater employment opportunities. Today, women make up almost half of the workforce in the United States. Gail Shaffer, executive director of an association of professional women, views the women's movement as a success. "One of the most significant developments of our century," according to Shaffer, is "the progress of women into nontraditional roles and their emergence as a major economic and political force."

Women today hold more professional positions and political offices than in 1970. By 1997 more than 44 percent of executives and managers were women. Women have made progress in nearly all employment and educational areas. Women have served as U.S. Supreme Court justices, secretary of state, and astronauts. These changes led one mother to write in 1998:

In 1997 Madeleine Albright became the first female secretary of state and the highest-ranking woman in the U.S. government.

> **"** *I know we feminists have made progress, because my 12-year-old daughter believes she can do, say and be anything, and go anywhere her male friends can. She not only believes it—she expects it to be that way.* **"**

That same year, however, 30 percent of people who responded to a survey said that inequality in the workplace was still a problem. In fact, workplace inequality was the main problem that women, but not men, faced. Almost 40 years after Congress passed the Equal Pay Act, most women still earn less money than men. This inequality exists even when men and women have comparable positions. For example, in 1997 women in professional and managerial positions earned about 70 percent of men's salaries for similar positions.

Women in the United States are also more likely than men to be poor. About 45 percent of women earn too little money to support a family of three. One explanation for some women's low wages is their employment in traditionally female occupations. These jobs include sales clerks, cashiers, child care workers, home health care workers, cooks, and office cleaners. More than half of all American women are employed in these positions, which are poorly paid. The women's rights movement has made women's presence in the workplace standard. However, complete equality in the workplace has not yet been achieved.

Understanding What You Read

1. Compare and contrast jobs held by women today and in the 1960s.

2. Do you think that the women's movement has succeeded? Explain your answer.

In response, many young female activists focused more of their energies on women's rights. Firestone and other feminists began organizing "consciousness-raising" groups to increase awareness of discrimination that women faced. These female activists called not only for equal rights but also for "women's liberation." Rejecting NOW's politically oriented methods, these women launched dramatic protests. They pushed their way into all-male clubs and restaurants. They also held sit-ins at magazine offices to protest the media's portrayal of women.

The leaders of the National Women's Political Caucus in 1971 (from left to right): Gloria Steinem, Bella Abzug, Shirley Chisholm, and Betty Friedan

⭐ The ERA

Despite differences among feminists, the movement gained strength in the early 1970s. NOW called for a Women's Strike for Equality. In response, thousands of women marched in cities across the country on August 26, 1970. In 1971 Betty Friedan, political leaders Bella Abzug and Shirley Chisholm, and writer Gloria Steinem helped found the National Women's Political Caucus. The organization wanted to increase women's political participation.

According to Abzug, 1972 was "a watershed year." It was a turning point for women's rights. Congress approved the **Equal Rights Amendment** (ERA) and submitted it to the states for ratification. The amendment stated, "Equality of rights under the law shall not be denied or abridged [reduced] by the United States or by any State on account of sex." Many women's groups supported the constitutional amendment. By mid-1973, 28 of the necessary 34 states had ratified the ERA.

Many men and women began organizing to defeat the amendment. Opponents believed that feminism destroyed women's true nature. Connie Marshner, a leading antifeminist, wrote:

❝ The less time women spend thinking about themselves, the happier they are. . . . Women are ordained [appointed] by nature to spend themselves in meeting the needs of others. ❞

Political lobbyist Phyllis Schlafly was the most outspoken ERA critic. She founded STOP–ERA (Stop Taking Our Privileges) to block ratification. She also presented her objections to the ERA in the *Phyllis Schlafly Report.* Schlafly warned that if the ERA passed, women would be drafted into the military. She stated that husbands would no longer be required to provide for their wives. Schlafly also warned that separate rest rooms for men and women would become illegal.

Women in the Labor Force

Percentage of Women in the Labor Force

60
50
40
30
20
10
0

1950 1955 1960 1965 1970 1975 1980 1985
Year

Source: *Statistical Abstract of the United States*

A Widening Workforce Increasing numbers of women joined the workforce after 1950. By about how much did the percentage of women in the workforce increase between 1950 and 1980?

People on both sides of the ERA issue showed their position by wearing pins.

Anti-ERA groups strongly objected to the amendment because they believed that it would hurt the family. Gradually, such arguments weakened support for the amendment. The ERA never became law because it fell three states short of ratification by its June 30, 1982, deadline.

Achievements for Women

Despite the ERA's failure, other reform projects that started in 1972 met with greater success. Journalist Gloria Steinem began publishing *Ms.*, a magazine committed to covering the women's movement. New legislation included Title IX of the Education Amendments Act of 1972. This law prohibited any college or university that received federal aid from discriminating against women. Male-only schools began admitting women. With more education, women's career opportunities improved. More women entered traditionally male professions, such as business, law, and medicine.

Some women turned to politics. Between 1968 and 1972 the percentage of female delegates to the Democratic National Convention jumped from 13 to 40 percent. The percentage of women at the Republican National Convention rose from 17 to 30 percent. In addition, more women began to seek and win political office. In 1968 Shirley Chisholm became the first African American woman elected to Congress. She ran for the Democratic presidential nomination in 1972. Despite such political gains, only 14 of 435 U.S. Representatives in 1973 were women. No women served in the U.S. Senate between 1973 and 1978.

Many women in the 1970s continued to face economic challenges. Women's wages remained less than two thirds of the wages of men. The number of female-headed households rose. The number of those households living in poverty also increased.

The women's rights movement did change the roles and status of women in society. "The point of feminism . . . ," an activist once said, "is to win women a wider range of experience." The movement succeeded with that goal.

SECTION 3 REVIEW

Identify and explain the significance of the following:

- **Commission on the Status of Women**
- **Equal Pay Act**
- **Betty Friedan**
- *The Feminine Mystique*
- **feminism**
- **National Organization for Women**
- **Bella Abzug**
- **Shirley Chisholm**
- **Gloria Steinem**
- **Equal Rights Amendment**
- **Phyllis Schlafly**

Reading for Content Understanding

1 Main Idea What did the "second wave" of feminists want, and what methods did they use to reach these goals?

2 Main Idea Create a graphic organizer that lists the successes and failures of the women's rights movement. Include the year that each event occurred.

3 Constitutional Heritage What was the debate over the Equal Rights Amendment?

4 Writing *Describing* Write a short newspaper editorial on the significant events in the women's rights movement that took place in 1963.

5 Critical Thinking *Determining the Strength of an Argument* Do you agree or disagree with Phyllis Schlafly's opposition to the Equal Rights Amendment? Explain your answer.

Rights for All

Reading Focus

How did American Indians protest their treatment by the federal government?

What were the goals of the disability rights movement?

How were older Americans and young Americans affected by the civil rights movement?

Key Terms

American Indian Movement
Disabled in Action
Education for All Handicapped Children Act
Children's Defense Fund
Gray Panthers
ageism

IN 1947 AN ALASKAN TLINGIT *woman wrote a letter to Ruth Muskrat Bronson. Bronson had played an important role in achieving New Deal legislation for American Indians. The Tlingit woman complained that the U.S. government was trying to take away Indian lands. Noting that the government protected endangered animals, the woman wrote, "Perhaps if we were wolves or bears we could have . . . protection. But we are only human beings."*

An Alaskan Tlingit headdress

★ American Indian Rights

In the 1950s the U.S. government reversed some of its policies protecting American Indian tribes. The Termination Resolution began a plan to end federal control over tribes and reservations. From 1954 to 1960, federal support to more than 60 tribes was ended. Some tribes sank deeper into poverty without the assistance of federally supported educational, health, and social services. Other Indian tribes lost land to private groups seeking control of natural resources such as oil and timber. Within a few years some tribes ceased to exist as organized groups.

In 1961 some 420 American Indians from 67 tribes gathered in Chicago to find solutions to these problems. They wanted Indians from all tribes to unite. The conference's declaration of purpose called for changes in how the federal government treated the tribes. The statement began, "We, the Indian People, must be governed . . . in a democratic manner, with a right to choose our own way of life." Some reformers worked with the National Congress of American Indians (NCAI) to win passage of the Indian Civil Rights Act in 1964. This law protected the constitutional rights of American Indians. It also affirmed their right to self-government on reservations.

Red Power

Some Indians rejected the NCAI's efforts as too slow and started the "Red Power" movement. In 1968, Indian activists formed the **American Indian Movement** (AIM). This group fought for the rights and properties that had been guaranteed in earlier treaties. AIM leader Russell Means expressed the group's goal: "We don't want civil rights in the white man's society—we want our own sovereign [self-governing] rights." AIM inspired cultural and racial pride among Indians.

AIM organized a number of protests to bring attention to its cause. In 1969 some members seized the deserted federal prison on Alcatraz Island in San Francisco Bay. They stayed there for 19 months. In 1972, AIM organized thousands of Indians in the "Trail of Broken Treaties." This group traveled to Washington, D.C., to demand the return of 110 million acres of land. The group ended its protest by temporarily occupying some federal offices.

AIM members made their most dramatic protest in February 1973. They seized a trading post and church at Wounded Knee, South Dakota. In 1890 the U.S. Army had massacred many Sioux at that location. After a 71-day standoff, a gun battle broke out. Two protesters died. One federal marshal suffered serious injuries. AIM's protests increased awareness of American Indian issues. However, AIM's tactics frightened many non-Indian supporters. The organization achieved few of its long-term goals.

Fights in the Courts

Some Indians fought more successfully through the legal system. In 1971 many Alaskan Indian tribes settled their land claims with the federal government. They received more than $962 million and some 44 million acres of land. Other American Indian tribes won more than $800 million in damages.

The Indian movement achieved more success when the federal government

American Indian Movement leader Russell Means

officially replaced its termination policy with a policy of Indian self-determination. This approach gave the Indians the right to govern themselves on reservations.

★ The Disability Rights Movement

In the 1960s, Americans with disabilities also began fighting for their rights. In particular, they wanted better educational and job opportunities and better access to buildings. Ed Roberts, a quadriplegic paralyzed by polio, was denied admission to the University of California at Berkeley. The university refused to admit students with disabilities because its facilities could not accommodate wheelchairs. After Roberts challenged this policy, the school admitted him in 1962.

By 1967 Roberts was working on a graduate degree. Eleven other students with serious disabilities had joined him on campus. They called themselves the "Rolling Quads." These students protested university efforts to restrict their use of student facilities. They demanded that public areas be made wheelchair accessible.

In the fall of 1970 the Rolling Quads received federal funds for the Physically Disabled Students'

Ed Roberts became director of the California Department of Rehabilitation in 1975.

Program. Two years later, Roberts set up the Center for Independent Living. People with disabilities ran both organizations. Program counselors helped people find accessible apartments and set up workshops to fix broken wheelchairs. The goal was to help people with disabilities function in the community.

Leaders of the disability rights movement also insisted on equal job opportunities. In 1970 the New York City Board of Education refused to give Judy Heumann a teaching certificate because she was a quadriplegic. Heumann, who had studied for the certificate for years, sued for discrimination. She took her campaign to the newspapers. One headline read, "You Can Be President, Not Teacher, with Polio." The newspaper was referring to former president Franklin D. Roosevelt.

Heumann's campaign introduced her to other people facing similar discrimination. In 1970 she founded the group **Disabled in Action** (DIA) to coordinate reform efforts. DIA brought together people with many different disabilities. One member said, "We all felt powerful. . . . Everybody who came out felt, We are beautiful, we are powerful, we are strong, we are important."

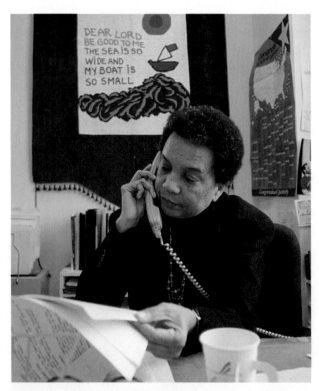

Attorney Marian Wright Edelman worked for the civil rights movement in Mississippi before founding the Children's Defense Fund.

Protests by DIA achieved some legislative successes. The Rehabilitation Act of 1973 made it illegal for any federal agency to discriminate against persons with disabilities. Passed in November 1975, the **Education for All Handicapped Children Act** required public schools to provide a quality education for children with disabilities.

 Rights of Young and Old Americans

Attorney Marian Wright Edelman had provided some of the information that helped lead to the passage of the 1975 education act. In 1973 she had learned that about 750,000 American children between the ages of 7 and 13 did not attend school. Edelman founded the **Children's Defense Fund** (CDF) in part to discover why. She learned that the majority of children not enrolled in school were children with disabilities.

Through the CDF, Edelman expanded her focus to include issues affecting all children. She found that politicians were not doing enough to help children. Edelman observed:

66 **Everybody loves children. Everybody is for them in general. Everybody kisses them in elections. . . . But when they get into the budget rooms, or behind closed doors—to really decide how they're going to carve up money—children get lost in the process because they are not powerful.** 99

The CDF wanted to expand the Head Start program, reform the system of foster parent care, and improve children's health care.

Older Americans also struggled to protect their rights. In 1970 Margaret Kuhn was forced to retire at age 65. In response, she and other retired Americans founded the **Gray Panthers** to defend the interests of the elderly. The Gray Panthers fought **ageism**, discrimination against an age group, particularly the elderly. The Panthers opposed forced retirement. They also fought to improve health care treatment in nursing homes. Believing that older Americans were often being ignored, Kuhn reminded anyone younger than she that "every one of us is growing old."

⭐ The Warren Court

During the 1960s Chief Justice Earl Warren led the U.S. Supreme Court in many rulings that affected equal rights. In a series of cases about state legislative districts, the Court ruled that the number of districts must be based on the state's population. In some states the legislative districts had not changed with the state's population. For example, in Alabama, one state senator represented more than 600,000 people. Another senator had only about 15,000 voters in his district. As a result, political power was not evenly distributed. In *Reynolds* v. *Sims* (1964), the Court required states to create districts of nearly equal population.

Warren also led the Court in rulings that expanded the legal rights of Americans accused of crimes. In 1963 in *Gideon* v. *Wainwright,* a poor Florida man accused of burglary appealed to the U.S. Supreme Court. In a petition he wrote himself, Clarence Earl Gideon argued that the trial judge's refusal to provide him with a lawyer was unconstitutional. The Court agreed and ruled that people accused of a crime had a constitutional right to free legal counsel. The ruling required states to provide an attorney for people unable to afford one.

DEFENDANT | LOCATION
SPECIFIC WARNING REGARDING INTERROGATIONS
1. You have the right to remain silent.
2. Anything you say can and will be used against you in a court of law.
3. You have the right to talk to a lawyer and have him present with you while you are being questioned.
4. If you cannot afford to hire a lawyer one will be appointed to represent you before any questioning, if you wish one.
SIGNATURE OF DEFENDANT | DATE
WITNESS | TIME
REFUSED SIGNATURE   SAN FRANCISCO POLICE DEPARTMENT   PR.9.1.4

After the Miranda *ruling, police officers began asking suspects to sign a form acknowledging their rights.*

In *Escobedo* v. *Illinois* (1964) and *Miranda* v. *Arizona* (1966), the Court expanded the protections for the accused. *Escobedo* established that suspects have a right to have their attorney present during police questioning. *Miranda* ordered police to notify suspects of their rights prior to any questioning. Justice Warren wrote that an accused

> ❝ **person must be warned that he has a right to remain silent, that any statement he does make may be used in evidence against him, and that he has a right to the presence of an attorney, either retained [hired] or appointed.** ❞

The *Miranda* decision was controversial. Some critics complained that the *Escobedo* and *Miranda* rulings hurt the police's ability to investigate crimes.

Throughout the 1960s and the early 1970s, many Americans became more aware of inequalities in society. As a result, many different groups worked to gain their equal civil and political rights during these years.

SECTION 4 REVIEW

Identify and explain the significance of the following:
- **American Indian Movement**
- **Russell Means**
- **Ed Roberts**
- **Disabled in Action**
- **Education for All Handicapped Children Act**
- **Marian Wright Edelman**
- **Children's Defense Fund**
- **Gray Panthers**
- **ageism**

Reading for Content Understanding

1 **Main Idea** What did American Indians do to protest government policies?

2 **Main Idea** What did the disability rights movement want to achieve?

3 **Citizenship and Democracy** How did the civil rights movement affect the rights of young and old Americans?

4 **Writing** *Informing* Write a short paragraph that provides information about some of the rulings of the Supreme Court during the 1960s.

5 **Critical Thinking** *Drawing Conclusions* Do you think the protests by American Indians in the late 1960s and early 1970s were effective? Explain your answer.

CHAPTER 20 REVIEW

Chapter Summary

The 1960s was an era of change. African Americans struggled to gain civil rights. In turn, the civil rights movement inspired other groups, including Mexican Americans, women, and American Indians, to fight for their rights. These groups used sit-ins, boycotts, marches, and other efforts to demand equal rights. By the 1970s these movements had affected the lives of nearly all Americans. ■

On a separate sheet of paper, complete the following activities.

Identifying People and Ideas

Describe the historical significance of the following:

1. sit-in
2. Martin Luther King Jr.
3. Civil Rights Act of 1964
4. César Chávez
5. United Farm Workers
6. Betty Friedan
7. National Organization for Women
8. Russell Means
9. American Indian Movement
10. Malcolm X

Internet Activity

go.hrw.com
SB1 Civil Rights

Search the Internet through the HRW Web site to find quotations and images for an exhibit on the 1960s civil rights movement. Use this information to make a collage reflecting the goals and important figures of the movement.

Understanding Main Ideas

1. How did the sit-ins, the Freedom Rides, and the March on Washington help bring about new civil rights laws?
2. What events helped lead to the passage of the Voting Rights Act of 1965?
3. What role did César Chávez play in helping Mexican Americans gain equal opportunities?
4. What were the goals of the women's rights movement?
5. What were the economic and political conditions that led to protests by some American Indian groups?
6. List some of the groups that became involved in civil rights efforts in the 1960s and early 1970s. Explain their roles.

Reviewing Themes

1. **Citizenship and Democracy** List four tactics used by different groups in the United States to gain equal rights. Give a specific example of each tactic and a group that used it.

Using the Time Line

Number your paper from 1 to 5. Match the letters on the time line below with the following events.

1. **Congress passes the Education for All Handicapped Children Act.**
2. **Hispanics form La Raza Unida Party.**
3. **The National Organization for Women is founded.**
4. **Members of the American Indian Movement seize federal property at Wounded Knee.**
5. **Four African American students stage a sit-in in North Carolina.**

1960	1962	1964	1966	1968	1970	1972	1974	1976
a			b		c	d		e

2. **Constitutional Heritage** What legislation did the U.S. government pass to help American Indians gain their constitutional rights?

3. **Geographic Diversity** Why did leaders of the civil rights movement focus most of their efforts in the South?

Thinking Critically

1. **Evaluating** Do you think requiring workers to retire at a certain age is good or bad for society? Explain your answer.

2. **Synthesizing Information** How did women respond to the feminist movement?

3. **Identifying Cause and Effect** Why do you think that the African American civil rights movement inspired other groups to fight for their civil rights?

Writing About History

1. **Creating** Imagine that you are a migrant worker striking against grape growers. Create a brochure to hand out in support of the strike.

Building Your Portfolio

Complete the following activities individually or in groups.

1. **Then and Now** Prepare a list of questions to ask of someone who is at least 50 years old. At least five questions should ask the person about his or her life today and at least five questions should be about when he or she was a teenager. Interview this person and write a short report of how that person's life has changed with age.

2. **Civil Rights Movements** Imagine that you are the author of a children's book titled *The 1960s Civil Rights Movements.* Write a chapter on one of the following groups: African Americans, Mexican Americans, American Indians, women, or people with disabilities. Use images and maps to illustrate your chapter.

2. **Expressing** Imagine that you have just heard Martin Luther King Jr.'s "I Have A Dream" speech. Write a journal entry expressing what the speech and the march mean to American society.

Linking Geography and History

1. **Region** What was the importance of the particular route the Freedom Riders selected for their demonstration?

2. **Location** Why do you think that the American Indian Movement chose Wounded Knee, South Dakota, as the site for a dramatic protest?

History Skills Workshop

Reading Maps Study the map below, which shows African American voter registration after the passage of the Voting Rights Act of 1965. Then answer the following questions: (a) Which states show the smallest increase in African American voter registration? (b) Which states show the greatest increase in voter registration? (c) What reasons can you give for the different levels of increase in voter registration?

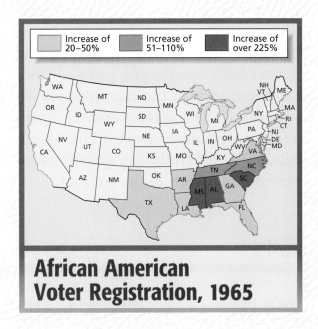

African American Voter Registration, 1965

■ CHAPTER 21 ■
War in Vietnam
(1945–1975)

In Vietnam, U.S. soldiers faced uncertainty with every step. As they marched through rice paddies and dense jungles, they tried to avoid land mines and other hidden traps. According to one GI, soldiers asked themselves: "Should you put your foot to that flat rock or the clump of weeds to its rear?" The wrong answer could have deadly consequences. The war in Vietnam raised troubling questions for everyone involved in the conflict.

THEMES

Global Relations
Why might a nation become involved in a war in a distant place?

Geographic Diversity
How might geography affect the outcome of a war?

Citizenship and Democracy
How might legislation change the roles of the different branches of a government?

1945

1955

1960

1945 Ho Chi Minh declares Vietnam an independent nation.

1954 Vietnam is divided into North Vietnam and South Vietnam.

1956 President Ngo Dinh Diem of South Vietnam refuses to let his nation participate in elections to reunify Vietnam.

1961 President Kennedy sends more U.S. military advisers to Vietnam.

Early Conflicts in Vietnam

Reading Focus

How did French colonization affect Vietnam?

Why was Vietnam divided into two countries in 1954?

Why did many South Vietnamese oppose their government, and how did they express their disapproval?

Key Terms

Vietminh
domino theory
Geneva Accords
National Liberation Front
Vietcong

IN 1873 FRENCH EXPLORER *Francis Garnier pub-lished* Voyages of Exploration, *a description of his expedition to Southeast Asia. Garnier encouraged the French to colonize this area for trade and to bring Western culture to its people. However, one of Garnier's associates believed that it was a mistake for France to impose its culture on the peoples of the region. "The extraordinary resistance, sometimes violent, sometimes passive [inactive] in nature, day by day more hateful . . . by all classes of the people, is stronger now than at any time since the conquest," he warned. "We must open our eyes."*

A villager pulls a French colonist in Vietnam.

IMAGE ON LEFT PAGE: *The Vietnam Veterans Memorial in Washington, D.C., honors the dead and missing in action from the Vietnam War.*

1965

1970

1975

1964 Congress passes the Tonkin Gulf Resolution.

1965 The first U.S. combat troops arrive in Vietnam.

1968 Communist forces attack throughout South Vietnam in the Tet Offensive.

1970 U.S. troops invade Cambodia.

1973 The Paris Peace Accords are signed.

1975 Saigon falls to North Vietnamese forces.

War in Vietnam **623**

★ French Vietnam

Vietnam is a small country in Southeast Asia. It has endured many foreign invasions and occupations. The Vietnamese fiercely opposed the invading powers. In the late 1700s the French became interested in Vietnam after Catholic missionaries journeyed there. By 1883, French forces had conquered Vietnam. France soon combined it with neighboring Laos and Cambodia to create a new colony called French Indochina. The French imposed harsh taxes and limited political freedoms. Many of the people in Indochina, particularly the Vietnamese, fought French colonization for years.

Starting about 1900, Vietnamese nationalists began to renew the fight for independence. The most successful nationalist was born as Nguyen That Thanh (NY-en TAHT TAHN) in central Vietnam in 1890. Later he adopted the name Ho Chi Minh (HOH CHEE MIN), meaning "He who enlightens." Ho spent years studying in France. Over time, he came to believe that the best way to fight colonial imperialism was through a communist revolution.

During World War II Japanese troops and local nationalists drove French soldiers out of Indochina. Ho then refused to accept Japanese rule. To fight the Japanese, Ho organized the League for the Independence of Vietnam, also called the **Vietminh** (vee-ET-MIN). After Japan surrendered to the Allies, he declared the independence of the Democratic Republic of Vietnam in a great celebration in Hanoi on September 2, 1945.

Ho Chi Minh led his people through wars with Japan, France, South Vietnam, and the United States.

French Indochina

Learning from Maps French Indochina consisted of Vietnam, Laos, and Cambodia. At the end of World War II, Vietnam sought independence from French control.

Place What were the capitals of the three countries that made up French Indochina?

★ War Breaks Out

Vietnam was not yet free, however. The French insisted that Vietnam was still part of Indochina. Ho tried to make peace with the French, but he warned:

66 **If they [the French] force us into war, we will fight. The struggle will be atrocious [extremely bad], but the Vietnamese people will suffer anything rather than renounce [give up] their freedom.** 99

The French refused Ho's offers and moved to retake Vietnam. President Eisenhower's administration funded and supplied the French fight based on the belief in the **domino theory**. Like others, the president argued that if Vietnam fell to the Communists—as

China and North Korea had done—all of Southeast Asia would fall as well, like dominoes in a row.

The Vietminh slowly weakened the better-equipped French forces with hit-and-run guerrilla attacks and ambushes. In 1954 the Vietminh trapped and surrounded 12,000 French troops at the village of Dien Bien Phu (DYEN BYEN FOO). The fighting was fierce, and the French suffered more than 7,000 casualties in the battle. Finally, on May 7, the French surrendered.

Just weeks before the French defeat, representatives from the major world powers and delegates from Southeast Asia had met in Geneva, Switzerland. The day after the battle in Dien Bien Phu, the leaders discussed the future of Indochina. In July the parties worked out a compromise known as the **Geneva Accords**. This agreement temporarily divided Vietnam into two separate nations—North Vietnam and South Vietnam. North Vietnam was a communist state led by Ho Chi Minh and the Vietminh. South Vietnam was a Western-style government led by Ngo Dinh Diem (en-GOHDIN de-EM), a committed anticommunist. The Geneva Accords also called for free elections in July 1956 to reunite North and South Vietnam under one government.

★ A Divided Country

U.S. officials fully supported Diem and South Vietnam. They hoped the anticommunists

U.S. troops trained South Vietnamese soldiers and supplied them with the latest weapons.

President Diem, on the left, ruled South Vietnam with the help of his family. Together, they worked to reduce opposition to his government.

would win control of the entire country in the 1956 elections.

Rival Governments

The new government in South Vietnam was dishonest and brutal. President Diem put family members in top positions and used a secret police force to silence his enemies. His methods raised some concerns, but the Eisenhower administration saw his government as the only alternative to a communist state. The United States began sending supplies and providing military training to Diem's forces.

Many North Vietnamese favored the widespread social reforms and land redistribution policies carried out by Ho Chi Minh's communist government. One North Vietnamese man recalled:

❝The living conditions of the people were getting better and better every day. The people were well off. They had enough to eat. . . . They had land to work and buffaloes to help them plow the land.❞

Not everyone benefited in Ho's new nation, however. Ho blamed landlords for North Vietnam's poverty. Communist government officials searched out landowners, imprisoning and killing thousands of them.

The Vietcong

As the planned 1956 reunification elections approached, Diem refused to allow South Vietnam to participate. He feared that the northern communist government would win. U.S. officials backed his decision. To stamp out growing support for Ho and the Vietminh in South Vietnam, Diem began arresting thousands of citizens.

As discontent mounted in South Vietnam, many nationalists there joined the **National Liberation Front** (NLF), an organization dedicated to fighting Diem's government. The NLF largely relied on the **Vietcong**, communist guerrilla forces, as its army. North Vietnam supplied and funded the Vietcong as its soldiers began a civil war against Diem's government in the late 1950s.

Diem's forces arrest Buddhist monks after an antigovernment protest.

 The Division Grows

As fighting between the Vietcong and Diem's Army of the Republic of Vietnam (ARVN) increased, President Eisenhower sent more aid and advisers to South Vietnam. By the end of 1960, about 800 U.S. military advisers were stationed in Vietnam.

As senator, John F. Kennedy had called Vietnam a "test of American responsibility and determination in Asia." As president, he sent more military advisers and 400 special forces soldiers there in May 1961. By 1963 some 16,000 U.S. military personnel were serving in Vietnam.

Despite U.S. support, Diem's government steadily lost power. Diem became more unpopular when his troops fired on Buddhist demonstrators. Some Buddhist monks set themselves on fire in protest. Media images of these protests helped turn U.S. public opinion against Diem.

Over time, some of Diem's military leaders had come to believe that his unpopularity hurt the war effort. In November 1963 a group of South Vietnamese generals took over the government and killed Diem and his brother. After the takeover, the political situation in South Vietnam grew worse.

SECTION 1 REVIEW

Identify and explain the significance of the following:

- **Ho Chi Minh**
- **Vietminh**
- **domino theory**
- **Geneva Accords**
- **Ngo Dinh Diem**
- **National Liberation Front**
- **Vietcong**

Locate and explain the importance of the following:

- **Vietnam**
- **Laos**
- **Cambodia**
- **Dien Bien Phu**

Reading for Content Understanding

1 **Main Idea** What were the long-term effects of French colonization in Vietnam?

2 **Main Idea** What were the terms of the Geneva Accords? Why do you think all sides agreed to the compromise?

3 **Global Relations** Why was the United States involved in Vietnamese affairs?

4 **Writing** *Informing* Imagine that you are a State Department officer. Write a report explaining why many South Vietnamese oppose Diem's government. Explain how they are expressing their disapproval.

5 **Critical Thinking** *Determining the Strength of an Argument* Do you think Americans had good reason to believe in the domino theory during the 1950s? Explain your answer.

The Escalation of the War

Reading Focus

Why did President Johnson continue supporting the war in Vietnam?

What tactics did the U.S. military use to fight the Communists in Vietnam?

How did the Vietnam War affect U.S. soldiers?

Key Terms

Tonkin Gulf Resolution
Operation Rolling Thunder
Ho Chi Minh Trail
escalation
search-and-destroy missions
pacification

TWO DAYS AFTER President Kennedy's assassination on November 22, 1963, President Lyndon B. Johnson met with his foreign-policy advisers to decide how to proceed in Vietnam. One aide recalled Johnson's worry that the Communists would think that the new president was weak—that "with Kennedy dead [the Americans] have lost heart." Johnson decided to increase U.S. military support for the new government in South Vietnam. The message went out to South Vietnamese officials "that Lyndon Johnson intends to stand by [the United States's] word."

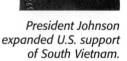
President Johnson expanded U.S. support of South Vietnam.

 ## Johnson's Vietnam Policy

The new president, Lyndon B. Johnson, faced a complicated situation in Vietnam. Some of the new South Vietnamese leaders wanted to negotiate with the Communists. Johnson and his advisers, however, refused to accept the possibility of a communist South Vietnam.

The Tonkin Gulf Resolution

In the summer of 1964, a naval incident between U.S. and North Vietnamese ships led to a further increase in U.S. involvement in Vietnam. On August 2, a navy vessel exchanged gunfire with North Vietnamese vessels in the Gulf of Tonkin, a body of water off the North Vietnamese coast. Two days later, during bad weather, U.S. ships reported that their radar showed torpedo attacks. Although the ships were not damaged, Johnson branded the reported attack an act of war. He ordered air strikes against bases in the North.

On August 7, Congress passed the **Tonkin Gulf Resolution**. It gave President Johnson the authority "to take all necessary measures to repel any armed attack against the forces of the United

States." The resolution shifted the power to determine the course of the Vietnam War from Congress to the president. Johnson would use his increased powers to expand U.S. involvement in the conflict.

Operation Rolling Thunder

With the authority given to him by the Tonkin Gulf Resolution, Johnson dramatically increased U.S. military involvement in Vietnam. In March 1965 the first U.S. combat troops arrived in South Vietnam. At the same time, Johnson ordered **Operation Rolling Thunder**, a series of air strikes to destroy war industries in North Vietnam. Johnson also saw the operation as a way to destroy the **Ho Chi Minh Trail**. This network of paths, small roads, and tunnels led from North Vietnam through neighboring Laos and Cambodia and into South Vietnam. The Vietcong used the Ho Chi Minh Trail as their major supply route. Johnson and his advisers believed that if they destroyed North Vietnam's ability to supply the Vietcong, the United States could end the war.

Dense jungle covered much of the trail and hid the movement of the supplies. To burn off the forests, U.S. airplanes dropped napalm, or jellied gasoline. The planes also released chemical poisons, such as Agent Orange, that killed vegetation and tree leaves. These chemicals were later blamed for environmental damage in the area and serious health problems among Vietnamese civilians and U.S. veterans alike.

The bombing raids lasted until late 1968. During the operation, U.S. planes dropped more than a million tons of explosives, much of it on South Vietnam. Operation Rolling Thunder killed many Vietnamese soldiers and civilians, but the effort did not stop the Communists' ability to wage war.

Legend:
- Major U.S. air strikes
- Major U.S. bases
- Areas under attack in Tet Offensive, 1968
- Base areas/war zone
- Areas of prolonged fighting

North Vietnam bombed 1965–1968 (Operation Rolling Thunder), 1972 (Linebacker I and II)

Gulf of Tonkin incident, 1964

Laos invaded, 1971

Cambodia bombed, 1969–1973; invaded, 1970

Surrender of South Vietnam, 1975

The Vietnam War

Learning from Maps North Vietnam used the Ho Chi Minh Trail to supply communist forces in the South.

Movement Through which countries did the Ho Chi Minh Trail pass?

★ The Ground War

In the mid-1960s, President Johnson authorized an increase in the use of ground forces. The number of U.S. soldiers grew rapidly from 1965 to 1967 as Johnson pursued a policy of **escalation**, or increased U.S. involvement in the war. North Vietnam also escalated its involvement, sending more of its regular army units, the North Vietnamese Army (NVA), to fight alongside the Vietcong.

General William Westmoreland, who commanded the U.S. ground forces

The Vietcong placed sharpened bamboo sticks, called punji stakes, *in covered holes to injure enemy soldiers.*

in Vietnam, developed a new fighting strategy. With his **search-and-destroy missions**, U.S. patrols searched for enemy camps and supplies hidden in the jungle, then destroyed them with massive firepower and air raids. Officials expected the missions, backed as they were by superior U.S. military technology, to quickly defeat the Vietcong and the NVA. One U.S. general said, "The solution in Vietnam is more bombs, more shells, more napalm." However, U.S. generals underestimated the North Vietnamese, who proved difficult to defeat.

The Vietcong and the NVA offset their inferior firepower with effective guerrilla tactics and a better knowledge of the local geography. Moving secretly, they set traps and land mines to kill and injure Americans. When the Vietcong and the NVA attacked, they usually did so in quick surprise assaults. U.S. Marine Philip Caputo recalled the effects of this kind of fighting:

> **"The discovery that the men we had scorned [disregarded] as peasant guerrillas were, in fact, a lethal [deadly], determined enemy . . . broke our early confidence."**

South Vietnamese villagers were caught in the middle of the fighting with no safe place to go. U.S. and South Vietnamese officials tried to win the support of villagers through a policy of **pacification**. Under this program, they created civilian areas guarded by government troops.

Linking Past to Present

The United States and Vietnam Today

After the war, hostility between the United States and Vietnam continued. Recently, however, the countries have established closer ties. The United States lifted its trade embargo against Vietnam in 1994. In May 1997 a new U.S. embassy opened there.

The U.S. ambassador to Vietnam, Douglas "Pete" Peterson, symbolized the new relationship. A pilot during the war, Peterson was shot down and spent nearly seven years in a North Vietnamese prison. Yet he returned to Vietnam with an eager, forgiving spirit.

Sign in Vietnam for an American corporation

Like Peterson, Vietnam seems focused on the future. Leaders have encouraged American businesses to open operations in Vietnam. Today, signs for well-known American products can be seen all over the streets of Hanoi and Ho Chi Minh City, formerly Saigon.

Understanding What You Read

1. Give examples of the new relationship between Vietnam and the United States.
2. How did Ambassador Peterson symbolize the new relationship?

Even in areas protected by soldiers, however, the Vietcong attacked. At night, while the government forces remained in their camps, the Vietcong came out of hiding. They assaulted or killed the people they believed had cooperated with the South Vietnamese government.

South Vietnamese civilians also suffered at the hands of their own government and U.S. forces. Sometimes U.S. troops destroyed the villages and crops of innocent civilians in the mistaken belief that they belonged to Vietcong. Soldier Kenneth Campbell recalled how an officer justified the destruction of two seemingly peaceful farming villages: "He said they were probably feeding the NVA with rice anyway, so therefore they are the enemy." Such reasoning contributed to high civilian casualty rates and lessened any chance the Americans had of winning local support or loyalty.

U.S. troops grew weary from the fighting and from trying to avoid traps and ambushes.

 ## The Soldiers' Stories

The war in Vietnam greatly affected the more than 2 million U.S. soldiers who served in it. Many soldiers were very young. Their average age was 19, about six years younger than in previous wars. Most of the soldiers had been drafted into service. They tended to be from minority groups and poor families. College students—most of whom were white and from the middle and upper classes—could earn draft releases called deferments.

Many young men who served in Vietnam supported the war in the beginning. However, as the war dragged on, support among soldiers declined as casualty rates increased. By mid-1967 more than 300 U.S. soldiers a week were dying in combat.

More than 7,500 women also served in the military during the war. One nurse recalled watching a soldier die:

66 **When you are sitting there working on . . . a 19-year-old kid who's 10,000 miles from home, and you know that he's going to die before dawn . . . and you're the only one that he's got . . . well it [gets] into your soul.** 99

Like the nurse, many of those who served in Vietnam found that the experience "got into their souls" and left them forever changed.

SECTION 2 REVIEW

Identify and explain the significance of the following:
- **Tonkin Gulf Resolution**
- **Operation Rolling Thunder**
- **Ho Chi Minh Trail**
- **escalation**
- **William Westmoreland**
- **search-and-destroy missions**
- **pacification**

Reading for Content Understanding

1 **Main Idea** Why did President Johnson think it was important to fight the Communists in South Vietnam?

2 **Main Idea** How did U.S. troops try to defeat the Communists in Vietnam, and what were the results?

3 **Geographic Diversity** *Place* How did Vietnam's landscape affect the war?

4 **Writing** *Describing* Imagine that you are a U.S. soldier stationed in Vietnam. In a letter home, describe how the war has affected you. You might also describe the difficulties of fighting in Vietnam.

5 **Critical Thinking** *Identifying Cause and Effect* How did the Vietnam War affect South Vietnamese civilians?

SECTION 3

A Divided Nation

Reading Focus

How did the Tet Offensive change public opinion on the Vietnam War?

How did the Vietnam War affect the Democratic Party?

What factors led to Richard Nixon's victory in the 1968 presidential election?

Key Terms

doves
hawks
Tet Offensive

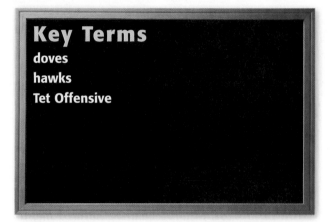

THE WOMEN GATHERED ABOUT 6:00 A.M. outside the military office. Soon the new recruits would arrive, ready to go to boot camp—and then to Vietnam. The women shouldered signs reading "I Support Draft Refusal" and began to walk up and down the sidewalk. Some of the women sat down in the street, preventing the recruits' buses from moving. When the police arrived, an officer told an older woman, "Missus, you don't want to get arrested." She said, "I have to, my grandson's in Vietnam." As more U.S. soldiers went off to fight—and to die—in Vietnam, the antiwar movement gained strength.

Peace button

⭐ Divided Opinions

Journalists, particularly television reporters, played an important role in shaping public opinion about the war. Through television, civilians saw real images of the war's brutality right in their own homes. As journalists continued to cover stories about the war, some began to report their growing suspicions that the fighting was not going as well as the military claimed. Gradually, some people who had originally supported the Vietnam War began to call for U.S. withdrawal from the conflict. They were called **doves**—named after the birds that symbolize peace.

Arkansas senator J. William Fulbright became a leading dove. As the chairman of the Senate Foreign Relations Committee, Fulbright had strongly supported the Tonkin Gulf Resolution. Later, Fulbright came to believe that the Johnson administration had exaggerated the communist threat and that it was unwilling to allow a peaceful settlement in the region. He accused a group of Johnson's advisers with the words: "You don't want to negotiate. . . . You're bombing that little . . .

Television reporters, like Morley Safer, brought the horror of the war into Americans' homes. Vietnam was the first "televised" war.

country up there, and you think you can blow them up."

Other doves, such as Martin Luther King Jr., warned that the war effort was preventing the growth of important social programs. President Johnson, with congressional approval, tried to provide funding for both his Great Society programs and the Vietnam War. However, he believed that communism in Southeast Asia posed a more serious threat because it affected world peace.

A majority in Congress agreed with Johnson. They believed that winning the Cold War against communism in Vietnam took priority over domestic reform. Called **hawks** for their warlike opinions, these leaders pushed for increased military spending in order to send more forces to Vietnam.

★ Protest Groups

Many citizens opposed the hawks' point of view. They organized protests to pressure the government to change its war policy. College students—many of whom had already been activists in the student rights and civil rights movements—often led the protests against the Vietnam War. The Students for a Democratic Society (SDS) became one of the most active antiwar groups. SDS protested the draft system and the companies that manufactured weapons used in the war. In 1965, SDS led a 20,000-person protest march to Washington, D.C.

As the war continued, the student movement grew more aggressive and sometimes even violent. These violent demonstrations were very different from earlier civil rights protests, which were almost entirely nonviolent. At Columbia University in New York City, students took over several campus buildings in March 1968 to protest the school's research ties to the defense industry. Violent clashes erupted between the protesters and police. A strike by students shut down the campus. School administrators eventually yielded to the students' demands. The Columbia strike inspired other student actions. By the end of 1968, students had protested the war on almost 75 percent of the country's college campuses.

Students were not the only protesters. Many other Americans voiced their concerns as well. Charlotte Keyes helped organize a group called Women Strike for Peace. She described the different types of people in the antiwar movement:

 The peaceniks [war protesters] these days are legion [many]—they are ninety years old and fifteen, heads of families and housewives with babies, students, (and) young people. 〞

★ The Tet Offensive

Despite the growth of the antiwar movement, a majority of Americans continued to support the Vietnam War until early 1968. On January 30, during Tet—the Vietnamese New Year—enemy forces

SDS organized this early antiwar march in 1965. As the war escalated, marches grew larger and were sometimes violent.

launched the **Tet Offensive**. In previous years, a cease-fire had halted all fighting during Tet, so the attack came as a complete surprise. North Vietnamese and Vietcong soldiers attacked U.S. forces throughout the South and even invaded the U.S. Embassy in the heart of Saigon. In most places, the U.S. and South Vietnamese troops overcame the communist forces quickly.

Nonetheless, the extent of the Tet Offensive shocked Americans and changed many people's opinions about the war. A short time earlier, General Westmoreland had said that the war would soon be over. There is "a light at the end of the tunnel," he promised. The Tet Offensive showed the opposite—that the enemy forces still had the strength and the will to fight.

The Tet Offensive convinced many Americans that officials could not be trusted to tell the truth about the war. Several well-known journalists, including television news anchor Walter Cronkite, expressed doubts about claims of success. "To say that we are closer to victory today is to believe, in the face of the evidence, the optimists [people who hope for the best] who have been wrong in the past," Cronkite declared in late February 1968. That same month, Westmoreland requested 206,000 more troops for service in Vietnam. With about 510,000 U.S. troops already there, many people questioned whether such an increase was necessary if the United States was really winning the war. President Johnson denied Westmoreland's request.

⭐ The Democrats in 1968

The Tet Offensive weakened public confidence in the government's conduct of the war. One poll showed that after the offensive, only 33 percent of Americans believed that the United States was winning the Vietnam War. About 49 percent said that the United States should never have gotten involved in the conflict. During this time of increasing doubts, the 1968 presidential primary elections began.

The Primaries

Initially, President Johnson's main opponent in the Democratic primaries was Eugene McCarthy, a senator from Minnesota. McCarthy was a major antiwar critic who ran largely on this issue. "The

U.S. Troops in Vietnam, 1964–1972

Number of Troops in Vietnam

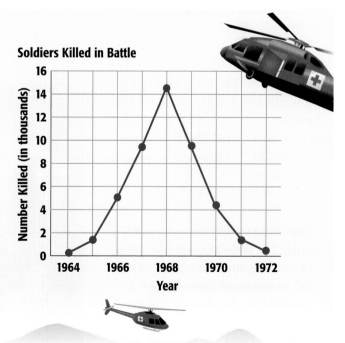

Soldiers Killed in Battle

Source: National Archives and Records Administration

A Costly War The number of U.S. troops sent to Vietnam escalated as the United States became more involved in the conflict. In what year did the number of U.S. troops in Vietnam peak?

President Johnson was troubled by the course of the war but felt obligated to support South Vietnam.

because we want them to but because that is the only way in which this struggle can be settled."

Democratic Party in 1964 promised 'no wider war,'" he reminded voters. "Yet the war is getting wider every month."

Johnson, who had won the presidency by a landslide in 1964, was expected to win the 1968 Democratic primaries easily. However, the Tet Offensive and the war situation in general had produced a massive shift in voter sympathies. In the New Hampshire primary, Johnson narrowly beat McCarthy—48 percent to 42 percent. His slim victory in this first primary of the year showed how unpopular Johnson's Vietnam policies were and how much his political support had declined. On March 31 Johnson withdrew from the election entirely, promising to spend the last months of his presidency trying to end the war.

After McCarthy's strong showing in New Hampshire, Senator Robert F. Kennedy of New York, the former attorney general, entered the race for the Democratic nomination. He believed that the United States should do everything it could to negotiate a peaceful end to the war as soon as possible. During the Tet Offensive, he said:

"Unable to defeat our enemy or break his will—at least without a huge, long, and ever more costly effort—we must actively seek a peaceful settlement. . . . We must be willing to foresee a settlement which will give the Vietcong and the National Liberation Front a chance to participate in the political life of the country. Not

Like his brother, the late president John F. Kennedy, Robert Kennedy believed in civil rights reform and assistance to the poor. These beliefs, along with his position on the war, drew many idealists and reformers to his campaign.

Johnson threw his support for the Democratic nomination behind yet another candidate—his vice president, Hubert Humphrey. Voters tended to dislike Humphrey for his long-standing support of the war. Kennedy soon began to gain ground on Humphrey. On June 5, 1968, Kennedy won the California primary, a major step before the upcoming Democratic National Convention in Chicago. That night, Kennedy declared to his supporters, "On to Chicago and let's win there." Moments later, as he departed, a gunman named Sirhan Sirhan assassinated him.

The Convention

Robert Kennedy's death almost guaranteed that Humphrey would win the nomination. However, the party was still bitterly divided. Many delegates wanted a candidate who was not associated with Johnson and the war. Angry debates soon flared inside the convention hall.

Robert Kennedy won the California Democratic primary on a platform opposing the Vietnam War. Yet some doves criticized him for not entering the presidential race earlier.

Some distance outside the convention hall, hundreds of antiwar protesters joined together. They marched in the city streets, shouting, "Peace now! Peace now!" Under orders from Chicago mayor Richard J. Daley, police officers moved in to stop the demonstration.

A riot broke out. TV cameras broadcasted live images of the event. "Instead of nice young people ringing doorbells," one protester said, "the public saw the image of mobs shouting obscenities and disrupting the city." To the millions of Americans watching, the events in Chicago illustrated the loss of law and order in society and politics. Many voters blamed the Democrats.

More people, including returned veterans, protested the war as it escalated.

★ A Republican Victory

Although divisions marked the convention, Humphrey won the Democratic nomination for president. Humphrey was a long-time supporter of civil rights. He chose Maine senator Edmund Muskie as his running mate.

The conservative governor of Alabama, George Wallace, entered the race as the candidate of the American Independent Party. He wanted to overturn civil rights legislation and most federal social programs. Wallace also criticized what he called the "over-educated, ivory-tower folks with pointed heads" who advised President Johnson.

The Republican candidate, former vice president Richard Nixon, claimed that he could restore order to American society. He also hinted that he had a "secret plan" for ending the Vietnam War.

The election of 1968 was quite close. Nixon received only 43.4 percent of the popular vote, but won the presidency with 302 electoral votes. Humphrey received 191 electoral votes. Wallace won 45 votes, all from southern states. As President-elect Nixon prepared to take office, Americans watched developments in Vietnam closely.

SECTION 3 REVIEW

Identify and explain the significance of the following:

- **doves**
- **hawks**
- **Tet Offensive**
- **Eugene McCarthy**
- **Robert F. Kennedy**
- **Hubert Humphrey**
- **George Wallace**
- **Richard Nixon**

Reading for Content Understanding

1 Main Idea What effect did the Tet Offensive have on Americans' attitudes?

2 Main Idea How did disagreements about the Vietnam War affect the Democratic Party?

3 Citizenship and Democracy Why did Richard Nixon win the presidency in 1968? What might the Democrats have done differently to try to beat him?

4 Writing *Persuading* Imagine that you are either a hawk or a dove during the Vietnam War. Write a letter to the editor trying to persuade others to agree with your position toward the war, whether for or against it.

5 Critical Thinking *Evaluating* Can people disagree with the policies and actions of their government and still be loyal citizens? Explain your answer.

The War Under Nixon

Reading Focus

What was President Nixon's Vietnam policy?

What was the outcome of the presidential election of 1972?

What were some of the war's lasting effects?

Key Terms

Vietnamization
Khmer Rouge
Twenty-sixth Amendment
Paris Peace Accords
MIAs
War Powers Act
Vietnam Veterans Memorial

ON JANUARY 20, 1969—the day of President Nixon's inauguration—a top aide distributed a detailed questionnaire about Vietnam to high-level military and diplomatic personnel. One question was implied but not directly asked: Could the United States win the war, even at that late date? The responses came back with a concrete answer. "The differences . . . were largely ones of degree," remembered one army general who participated in the study. "Nobody believed the war could be won in the foreseeable future." That left the new president with another pressing issue: How to end the Vietnam War.

U.S. combat troops arriving in Vietnam

 ## Peace with Honor

Although President Nixon said that he wanted to "end the war as quickly as was honorably possible," he also wanted to avoid the appearance of defeat. "I will not be the first President of the United States to lose a war," he told Republican leaders.

Nixon and his national security adviser, Henry Kissinger, created a policy to bring about "peace with honor." They planned to gradually turn over all of the fighting to the South Vietnamese army, a process they called **Vietnamization**. Under the new policy, the United States would continue to provide supplies and training to South Vietnam even as U.S. troops left the country.

Nixon also believed that he could bluff the North Vietnamese into thinking that he would use nuclear weapons as a last resort to end the war. In a private talk with an aide, he said:

" I call it the madman theory. . . . I want the North Vietnamese to believe I've reached the point where I might do

Richard Nixon

Richard Nixon was born in 1913 and grew up in and around Whittier, California. Even as a young man, Nixon demonstrated the opposites in his nature that would drive him throughout his life. Shy and socially awkward, he nevertheless pushed himself to meet people and win their backing and support. Gradually, through his own determination and will to succeed, he became a leader. He was twice elected student-body president, first at Whittier College and later at Duke Law School.

Nixon's desire to win political office continued after he graduated. After practicing law and then serving in World War II, he ran as a Republican for Congress in 1946. He won against the odds, and as writer David Halberstam described it, "Once he started in politics, he could never stop: there would always be one more office to run for."

anything to stop the war. We'll just slip the word to them that, . . . 'Nixon is obsessed [crazed] about Communists. We can't restrain [control] him when he's angry—and he has his hand on the nuclear button,'—and Ho Chi Minh himself will be in Paris in two days begging for peace. "

Yet, like other U.S. officials before them, Nixon and Kissinger underestimated the determination of the North Vietnamese and the Vietcong. Even after Ho Chi Minh died in September 1969, his followers vowed to continue the fight to reunite Vietnam and rid it of foreign troops. To achieve this, the North Vietnamese leaders refused to consider any peace agreement that did not include the immediate withdrawal of all U.S. troops.

★ The Attack on Cambodia

After he took office, President Nixon did begin withdrawing U.S. ground troops from Vietnam. At the same time, however, he secretly expanded the war by increasing air attacks in Laos and Cambodia.

A Wider War

Laos and Cambodia were officially neutral countries in the Vietnam War. Yet the use of the Ho Chi Minh Trail and other Vietcong supply lines drew these countries into the war. Nixon ordered bombing raids on Cambodia in 1969 to cut the supply routes. He did so without the knowledge of the American public or Congress.

In reaction to the bombings, the North Vietnamese increased their support of the **Khmer Rouge** (kuh-MER ROOZH), the Cambodian communist army. The Khmer Rouge increased its attacks in Cambodia, and Nixon sent U.S. troops in May 1970 to protect the country's pro-U.S. government. When he announced the invasion of Cambodia, many Americans were outraged. Instead of working for peace, the United States was expanding the war even further.

U.S. troops hoped that NVA papers captured in Cambodia would reveal military secrets.

The killings of antiwar protesters by National Guardsmen at Kent State in 1970 hardened many people's attitudes against the war.

New Protests

After the announcement, students demonstrated at hundreds of college campuses. When students at Kent State University in Ohio attacked a military training building to protest the war, the governor called in the National Guard to restore order. On May 4, 1970, Kent State students started to demonstrate again. Campus police ordered them to leave, but the students refused. National Guard troops then advanced on the protesters and tried to break up the demonstration with tear gas. As the students threw rocks at the soldiers, some of the guardsmen opened fire. When the smoke cleared, 4 students were dead and 14 others were wounded.

The Kent State killings horrified the public. Outraged antiwar activists increased their protests. Some of these new demonstrations also ended in violence. In one such instance in May, police killed two student protesters at Mississippi's Jackson State University.

A Shift in Policy

As the year progressed, political and public opinion continued to turn against the war. In December 1970 Congress acted by repealing the Tonkin Gulf Resolution.

Public opinion became further divided with the publication in the *New York Times* of secret U.S. government documents known as the Pentagon Papers. Daniel Ellsberg, a former Pentagon official, leaked the papers to the newspaper. The papers revealed that U.S. government officials had been

lying about the progress of the Vietnam War for years. "This is a system . . . that lies automatically from top to bottom," claimed Ellsberg.

After the publication of the Pentagon Papers, some members of Congress threatened to cut off funds for the Vietnam War altogether. As his 1972 re-election campaign approached and as public opinion hardened against the war, President Nixon began to revise his strategy. He ordered an end to the invasion of Cambodia and became more open to compromise. In 1972 Henry Kissinger began secret peace negotiations with North Vietnamese officials.

The Election of 1972

The presidential election of 1972 offered voters a choice of candidates with very different positions on ending the war. The Democratic candidate was South Dakota senator George McGovern, an outspoken and long-standing opponent of the war. McGovern promised that he would immediately withdraw all U.S. troops from Vietnam. "The doors of government will be opened, and that brutal war will be closed," he pledged.

McGovern tried to appeal to young voters. In 1971 the **Twenty-sixth Amendment** had lowered the federal voting age from 21 to 18. Many Americans saw this change as fair, because men from this age group were being drafted to serve in Vietnam. Some politicians expected this amendment to lead to a "youth rebellion" in the election.

Although McGovern won the support of a majority of younger voters, most older voters from both parties supported Nixon. Most Americans were tired of the war, but they feared continued disorder and protests. Nixon also promised to end the war soon if re-elected. "Help him finish the job," his campaign advertisements said. The public re-elected Nixon by a huge margin—520 electoral votes compared to 17 for McGovern.

The End of the War

President Nixon kept his promise to end the war, although the peace process was rocky. Negotiations stalled after the election. The United

States began large-scale bombings of North Vietnam in December 1972—the so-called Christmas bombing. Finally, the peace talks resumed. On January 27, 1973, representatives of the National Liberation Front, North Vietnam, South Vietnam, and the United States signed a cease-fire and a series of peace agreements in Paris.

The agreement, known as the **Paris Peace Accords**, called for the removal of all U.S. troops and the return of all American prisoners of war (POWs). To maintain peace between South and North Vietnamese troops, the Paris Peace Accords established a demilitarized buffer zone in the South to separate the two sides. Under the agreement, the Communists in South Vietnam could take part in politics. Further decisions about unification of the country were put off until later.

Late in 1974, however, fighting broke out again between North and South Vietnam. The United States made it clear that it would not send troops back to South Vietnam. The following year, North Vietnam invaded the South in large numbers. South Vietnamese resistance collapsed rapidly. By the end of April 1975, the North Vietnamese had captured the southern capital of Saigon.

Panic gripped the city in the final days of the war. South Vietnamese citizens who had helped the United States during the war swarmed the U.S. Embassy. They hoped to escape before the communist takeover. They feared imprisonment or death in the unified Vietnam. U.S. helicopters managed to carry many people to safety, but more were left behind. Watching the frightened people, one

Many South Vietnamese tried to flee before the North Vietnamese army arrived in 1975.

U.S. official wondered, "What will happen to them?"

★ The Consequences of War

The Vietnam War left long-lasting problems in both Southeast Asia and the United States. Many have yet to be resolved.

Southeast Asia

In Vietnam, life was extremely difficult after the war. The fighting had killed a huge number of citizens. About 1 million North Vietnamese and Vietcong soldiers, more than 185,000 South Vietnamese soldiers, and some 500,000 civilians had died. Almost 1 million Vietnamese children were orphans. Cities and villages lay in ruins. Forests and farmlands lay bare. One Vietnamese editor noted, "The war lasted thirty years, but it will take another twenty years before we will be

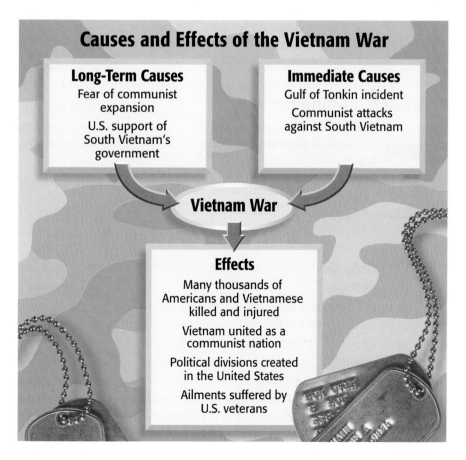

Causes and Effects of the Vietnam War

Long-Term Causes
Fear of communist expansion

U.S. support of South Vietnam's government

Immediate Causes
Gulf of Tonkin incident

Communist attacks against South Vietnam

Vietnam War

Effects
Many thousands of Americans and Vietnamese killed and injured

Vietnam united as a communist nation

Political divisions created in the United States

Ailments suffered by U.S. veterans

American Arts

The Vietnam Veterans Memorial

In November 1982 the Vietnam Veterans Memorial in Washington, D.C., opened as a monument to the Americans who served in the Vietnam War. Designed by Maya Ying Lin, a 21-year-old Yale architecture student, the memorial is a wall of black granite, described by Lin as a "rift [crack] in the earth." The wall rises from the ground on one end and slopes back to the earth on the other end. The names of the more than 58,000 dead or missing Americans are listed according to the date that each died or disappeared. These names are the only words on the wall. They force visitors to confront the human cost of the war.

The wall brings out strong emotions in visitors. Many leave tokens of remembrance. Some people leave military items, such as medals and hats. Others leave personal items such as photos and letters. C. D. Jackson, a Vietnam veteran, left a can of sliced peaches for his friend, James C. Harper. "I brought these 'specially for you," he said, touching Harper's name on the wall. "I know how much you like them."

Many U.S. veterans have found visiting the Vietnam Veterans Memorial to be an emotional experience.

Understanding the Arts

1. Describe the appearance of the Vietnam Veterans Memorial.

2. Why do you think this memorial brings out such strong emotions for the visitors?

able to overcome the legacy [history] of the problems it has left."

Laos and Cambodia also had difficulties after the war. Both countries fell to communist dictatorships in 1975. In Cambodia the Khmer Rouge killed an estimated 2 million people in a massive campaign to destroy supposed enemies of communism. Eventually, the Vietnamese and Cambodian Communists clashed. In 1979 Vietnam invaded Cambodia to drive out the Khmer Rouge.

Since then, Cambodia and its people have experienced ongoing conflict and little peace.

The United States

The war also carried huge costs for the United States. About 58,000 Americans died in the fighting. More than 2,000 remain **MIAs**, which stands for missing in action. The conflict also left the nation deeply divided.

The discoveries of government deception had weakened many Americans' trust in officials, including the president. In 1973 Congress passed the **War Powers Act**. It required the president to get congressional approval before committing U.S. troops to an armed struggle. The act did not apply to Vietnam, but was written to prevent undeclared wars. President Nixon vetoed the measure, but Congress overrode the veto. Passage of the War Powers Act gave Congress increased responsibility for setting U.S. war policy. Since then, presidents have had to exercise more caution in sending troops into war zones and to consult with Congress more fully when they did.

Many Southeast Asians fled their homelands after the war, hoping to escape instability and brutal communist governments. Between 1975 and 1985, more than 1.5 million people left the region. Many of them died while trying to escape. About half of the Southeast Asian refugees immigrated to the United States. Le Ly Hayslip, for example, was a former Vietcong supporter who fled Vietnam and later became a successful businesswoman in California. In her memoirs she addressed the

Air Force captain Ronald Bliss runs to greet his wife after spending seven years as a POW in Vietnam.

U.S. soldiers who had fought in the war, saying:

66 **Most of you did not know, or fully understand, the different wars my people were fighting when you got [to Vietnam]. . . . The least you did—the least any of us did—was our duty. For that we must be proud.** 99

American Veterans

Hayslip's words reflected the difficulties that some American veterans experienced after the war. Instead of a warm welcome, some veterans faced insults from antiwar protesters. Most readjusted well to civilian life, but some veterans suffered from depression and a condition known as post-traumatic stress disorder.

On Veterans Day in 1982, officials dedicated the **Vietnam Veterans Memorial** to honor those who died in the war. Designed by Maya Ying Lin, the memorial is a black granite wall that displays the names of the dead and the missing. Bruce Weigl explained why he and other veterans have visited the wall: "We came to find the names of those we lost in the war, as if by tracing the letters cut into the granite we could find what was left of ourselves."

SECTION 4 REVIEW

Identify and explain the significance of the following:
- **Henry Kissinger**
- **Vietnamization**
- **Khmer Rouge**
- **George McGovern**
- **Twenty-sixth Amendment**
- **Paris Peace Accords**
- **MIAs**
- **War Powers Act**
- **Vietnam Veterans Memorial**

Reading for Content Understanding

1 **Main Idea** What policy did President Nixon pursue in Vietnam?

2 **Main Idea** How did the Twenty-sixth Amendment affect the outcome of the 1972 presidential election? Who won?

3 **Global Relations** Make a graphic organizer listing the consequences of the Vietnam War, both in Southeast Asia and in the United States.

4 **Writing** *Persuading* Imagine that you are a member of Congress in 1973. Respond to a letter that criticizes your support of the War Powers Act. Note the specific events that led you to support the act and why you think it is necessary.

5 **Critical Thinking** *Drawing Conclusions* Why do you think the United States did not send troops back to South Vietnam in 1974 to protect it from invasion by North Vietnam?

CHAPTER 21 REVIEW

Chapter Summary

In the 1950s the United States began sending aid, and in the 1960s troops, to help anti-communist South Vietnam fight against a takeover by communist North Vietnam. Many Americans protested U.S. involvement in the Vietnam War. In 1973 the United States signed a cease-fire agreement and withdrew its troops. The many years of war left deep scars, both in Southeast Asia and the United States. ■

On a separate sheet of paper, complete the following activities.

Identifying People and Ideas

Describe the historical significance of the following:

1. Ho Chi Minh
2. domino theory
3. Vietcong
4. Ngo Dinh Diem
5. escalation
6. hawks
7. Vietnamization
8. Tet Offensive
9. Richard Nixon
10. Paris Peace Accords

go.hrw.com
SB1 South
Vietnam

Internet Activity

Search the Internet through the HRW Web site to find information about the Republic of Vietnam (South Vietnam). Make a graphic organizer showing the leaders of that country from 1954 to 1973, how they came to power, and what difficulties they faced while in office.

Understanding Main Ideas

1. How did French colonization affect Vietnam?
2. What was President Kennedy's policy in South Vietnam, and why did President Johnson continue it?
3. How did U.S. troops fight the Communists in Vietnam, and what were the effects on U.S. soldiers?
4. How did Americans react to the Tet Offensive?
5. How did the Vietnam War affect the presidential election of 1968?
6. How did the war end, and what were its long-term effects?

Reviewing Themes

1. **Global Relations**   Why did the United States fight in Vietnam?
2. **Geographic Diversity**   How did Vietnam's geography make the U.S. military effort there difficult?

Using the Time Line

Number your paper from 1 to 5. Match the letters on the time line below with the following events.

1. The first U.S. combat troops arrive in Vietnam.
2. U.S. ships exchange fire with North Vietnamese forces in the Gulf of Tonkin.
3. By signing the Paris Peace Accords, the United States agrees to withdraw from Vietnam.
4. Ho Chi Minh announces the independent nation of Vietnam.
5. President Nixon sends U.S. troops into Cambodia.

1945   1955   1965

a   b c   d   e

3. **Citizenship and Democracy**   How did the Gulf of Tonkin Resolution and the War Powers Act affect the relationship between the legislative and executive branches of the government?

Thinking Critically

1. **Evaluating**   What could President Diem of South Vietnam have done differently to try to win the support of people in his country?
2. **Drawing Conclusions**   Why did Americans' attitudes toward the war change?
3. **Identifying Cause and Effect**   How did U.S. military strategies affect the outcome of the Vietnam War?

Writing About History

1. **Describing**   Imagine that you are a European reporter visiting the United States in 1970. Write a magazine article describing the different opinions on the Vietnam War.
2. **Classifying**   Imagine that you are a U.S. official just returning from a trip to Vietnam in

1965. Write a memo to President Johnson noting the pros and cons of sending combat troops to South Vietnam.

Linking Geography and History

1. **Location**   How did Cambodia and Laos become part of the war in Vietnam?
2. **Movement**   What different kinds of passages did the Ho Chi Minh Trail allow?

History Skills Workshop

Using Primary Sources   Presidents John F. Kennedy and Lyndon B. Johnson committed U.S. forces to Vietnam without congressional approval. The Tonkin Gulf Resolution gave Johnson some authority to send troops. However, Congress never declared war on Vietnam. In November 1973, Congress passed the War Powers Act over President Nixon's veto. This law outlined the authority of the president and Congress in relation to war. Read the excerpt below and then answer the following questions: (a) How does this act clarify the executive office's military powers? Refer to the Constitution, p. 44. (b) Why do you think that Congress passed this law after U.S. troops pulled out of Vietnam?

Building Your Portfolio

Complete the following activities individually or in groups.

1. **Southeast Asia Map**   Imagine that you work in the map bureau of the State Department. A new U.S. diplomat to Southeast Asia has asked for a historical map of the region spanning the years 1954 to 1975. Create a detailed map for the diplomat. Make sure that your map explains important historical events in the region.
2. **Vietnam War Veteran**   Imagine that you are a Vietnam War veteran who is proud of serving the United States but has mixed emotions about the war. Create a collage for your children and grandchildren to show them what you did and how you feel. Your collage could include artifacts, drawings, news accounts, photographs, and poems. Write a paragraph explaining the parts of your collage.

66 Whenever United States Armed Forces are introduced into hostilities . . . the President shall . . . report to the Congress . . . on the status of such hostilities. . . . Within sixty calendar days after a report is submitted . . . the President shall terminate any use of the United States Armed Forces . . . unless the Congress (1) has declared war . . . (2) has extended by law such sixty-day period, or (3) is physically unable to meet as a result of an armed attack upon the United States. 99

The Struggle for Vietnam

In 1954 a peace agreement divided Vietnam into two countries. North Vietnam had a communist government, while South Vietnam struggled to establish a democracy. Soon the Communists began to support rebels in South Vietnam. U.S. leaders wanted to prevent the spread of communism in Asia. By 1964, the United States and South Vietnam were fighting a war against North Vietnam and the Communist-backed Vietcong rebels.

The inland mountains and dense jungles of Vietnam provided excellent cover for communist guerrilla forces and made it difficult for the U.S. military to wage war. The United States finally withdrew its troops from Vietnam in 1973. ■

A Foreign Battlefield

Most communist troops and their supplies entered South Vietnam along the Ho Chi Minh Trail or the Sihanouk Trail. U.S. bombing was unable to stop the flow of enemy troops and weapons along these jungle and mountain roads.

Geography Skills
Reading Special-Purpose Maps

1. What countries did the Ho Chi Minh Trail pass through?
2. What mountain range did the Ho Chi Minh Trail cross?
3. What South Vietnamese city lay at the end of the Sihanouk Trail?

Vietcong Tunnel Complex

Hidden Entrance

Conference Room

Kitchen

False Tunnel with Trap

Air-Raid Shelter

Sleeping Chamber

To Rest of Tunnel Network

Storage Room

Well

A South Vietnamese soldier explores a Vietcong tunnel complex.

Geography **Skills**
Reading Diagrams

1. Identify the various underground chambers shown in this diagram.
2. Which chambers were nearest the surface?
3. What do you think were some of the advantages the tunnels provided the Vietcong?

History Note 1

Communist forces built tunnels to hide from bombing attacks and to store supplies. Troops often waited until nightfall to emerge from the tunnels.

Americans and the War

The Vietnam War lasted more than eight years, making it the longest continuous conflict in U.S. history. Thousands of Americans died in Vietnam. The economic cost of the war was second only to that of World War II.

U.S. Armed Forces Serving During Wartime

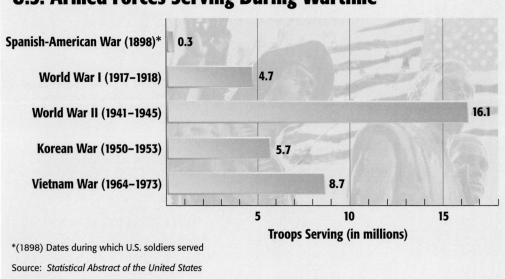

War	Troops Serving (in millions)
Spanish-American War (1898)*	0.3
World War I (1917–1918)	4.7
World War II (1941–1945)	16.1
Korean War (1950–1953)	5.7
Vietnam War (1964–1973)	8.7

Troops Serving (in millions)

5   10   15

*(1898) Dates during which U.S. soldiers served

Source: *Statistical Abstract of the United States*

Geography **Skills**
Reading Bar Graphs

1. How many U.S. military personnel served during the Vietnam War?
2. How many more U.S. military personnel served during the Vietnam War than in World War I?
3. What is one reason suggested by the graph for why more troops served in Vietnam than in Korea, World War I, or the Spanish-American War?

History Note 2

Millions of Americans served in the U.S. armed forces during the Vietnam War. However, not all of these service personnel were stationed in Vietnam during the war. Many served in the United States or in European nations. The majority of those serving during the Vietnam War were not combat personnel. An estimated five noncombat personnel—such as drivers, mechanics, medical staff, and instructors—were required to support each combat soldier.

Helicopters were widely used by the U.S. military for the first time in the Vietnam War.

American Opinions on the Vietnam War, 1965–1971

Percentage of People Who Believed the Vietnam War Was a Mistake

Year

Source: *Trends in Public Opinion: A Compendium of Survey Data*

The Vietnam Service Medal was awarded to members of the U.S. armed forces who served in Vietnam between 1965 and 1973.

Geography **Skills**

Reading Bar Graphs

1. What percentage of respondents opposed the Vietnam War in 1967?

2. Which year's poll had the highest percentage of respondents who opposed the war?

History Note 3

As troop levels and casualties increased, more Americans began to challenge U.S. military involvement in Vietnam. In 1968 the number of U.S. troops serving in Vietnam peaked. That same year more than 14,000 Americans were killed in action—the highest total for any year during the war. By 1969, polls showed that a majority of Americans across the country believed that it was a mistake for the United States to be fighting in Vietnam.

A squad of U.S. soldiers returning to its base from a jungle patrol

History Skills
WORKSHOP

Doing Research and Making an Outline

To complete a paper or a special project, you may need to do some research at a library or on the Internet. An outline will help you organize your research and plan your project.

Gathering Information A catalog, which may be in the form of cards or computer listings, notes the locations of all the library's books. Catalogs list each nonfiction book by title, author's last name, and subject topic—all arranged in alphabetical order.

A library's reference section contains other sources for research, such as encyclopedias, maps, specialized dictionaries, and periodical indexes. Encyclopedias contain information about people, places, events, and general subject topics. Specialized dictionaries, such as geographical dictionaries, contain definitions of terms and important information in a specific subject area.

Making an Outline An outline is a way to organize the information you collected in your research. An outline summarizes your main points. Note only your main ideas in an outline, saving the facts and details for your paper or project. If your outline is thorough and well thought-out, it helps you organize your ideas and makes writing the paper or project much easier.

How to Find Information

1. **Search the library catalog** Use the catalog to find a specific book or author, or find books on certain topics.
2. **Search reference works** Use reference works to find more information. Encyclopedias include information on many topics. In periodical indexes, you can find which magazine and newspaper articles cover your subject.

How to Create an Outline

1. **Order your material** Decide what to emphasize, then organize your material. Decide what information belongs in your paper's introduction, body, and conclusion.
2. **Identify main ideas** Identify the main ideas, then make these your outline's main headings.
3. **List supporting details** List the details that support each main heading as subheadings. Subheadings must come in pairs, at the least: no *A*'s without *B*'s, no *1*'s without *2*'s.

Example:

The Civil Rights Movement
I. The Sit-Ins
   A. Sit-ins in Greensboro
   B. Spread of sit-ins
     1. nonviolent resistance
     2. SNCC formed
II. The Freedom Rides
   A. Supreme Court Decision
   B. CORE Freedom Rides
     1. violence against riders
     2. violence in Anniston
     3. violence in Birmingham
   C. SNCC Freedom Rides
     1. violence in Alabama
     2. arrests in Mississippi

4. **Put your outline to use** Structure your report according to your outline. Each main heading might form the basis for a topic sentence of a paragraph. Subheadings would then make up the content of the paragraph.

Practicing the Skill

1. How are nonfiction library books listed in the catalog?
2. Read the subsection in Chapter 19 titled "A Musical Revolution" (pages 586–87) and create an outline of the material.

History in Action

American History

Vietnam War Documentary

Complete the following activity in small, cooperative groups.

You and the members of your group are trying to create a documentary on the Vietnam War. Your first step is to present your idea to ATW video production company. If ATW likes your idea, they will make your documentary. Your presentation will consist of a series of storyboards—images that show what each scene in the video will look like. To go along with the images, each storyboard should also have a written text that a narrator will read during each scene.

Materials To complete this activity, you will need a tape recorder, posterboard, glue, and various art supplies.

Parts of the Project To create your storyboards, complete the following tasks:

1. **Planning** Meet as a group and assign one of the following topics to each group member: The history of Vietnam, the major battles of the war, U.S. soldiers, the antiwar movement, news coverage of the war, and the effects of the war on U.S. politics. Create an outline for your documentary. In it, note the order in which these topics will be covered and the kinds of images to use for each topic.

2. **Research** Each group member will conduct research to find news articles, quotations, maps, images, and any other information available about their topic.

3. **Creating the Storyboards** Using several pieces of posterboard, draw or paste together the images you want to use for each scene in your portion of the documentary. Under each image, write a short description of the scene.

4. **Writing the Narration** Organize the information you gathered into an outline. Use the outline to write the narrator's script. The script should tell the story in words that the images tell visually. While the text should relate to the images, it does not have to describe them exactly. For example, you could show a picture of an antiwar demonstration in Chicago while the narrator describes the whole antiwar movement.

5. **Editing and Recording** Meet as a group and organize your storyboards in the order they will be presented. Choose one group member to be the narrator. Record the narrator reading the script. You may also want to include sound effects, news reports, or music from the Vietnam War era.

6. **Presentation** Meet with the executives at ATW (the class) and make your presentation. Display the storyboards one at a time while playing the tape of the narrator.

You may want to continue this project by creating your proposed documentary.

Students use computers and a video camera to complete an assignment.

Modern America

(1968–Present)

American Teens
IN HISTORY
Young Volunteers

"I think everybody should volunteer," says high school student Beth Kungel. "You don't need to get paid to help somebody else. It's fun, and it makes you feel good." Many children and teenagers from across the nation share Kungel's feelings. Through their volunteer work, these active young people have improved the world around them. They have saved animals, protected the environment, tutored classmates, fed the homeless, and built homes—among many other projects.

Young people have volunteered to protect the environment in different ways. Some young volunteers raise money to buy and preserve acres of tropical rain forest. Others focus their efforts closer to home. Some junior high school students from the Chicago area took part in the Spring into Action campaign. The project cleaned up local parks, planted trees, and restored sports fields in the community. In 1998 the Rouge River Rescue Cleanup in Michigan received assistance from MTV. The cable music channel held a cleanup party for volunteers to encourage more young people to join the effort.

Young people at work on a community garden project

Other young people have chosen to help fellow citizens and community members. Many have joined Habitat for Humanity, a nonprofit organization that relies on volunteers to build homes for poor people. When asked why she chose to spend her vacations working for free, teenager Regan Beard answered, "Because it's awesome. It's definitely worth it. . . . We start with a concrete base and end with walls." Some volunteers have even met former president Jimmy Carter, a longtime Habitat worker who makes time to visit with the young volunteers.

Other young volunteers like to help their friends and classmates. Peer-tutoring programs match students who want to teach with students who need extra help. Many schools have also begun "cross-age" tutoring programs in which older students work with younger students.

In this unit you will learn more about recent American history. You will learn about political and economic challenges, advances in science and technology, and the spirit with which Americans start the new century.

LEFT PAGE: *Fireworks brighten the sky over the Statue of Liberty during a bicentennial celebration.*

Time Line: 1968–Present

Modern America

President Reagan

UNITED STATES

1968
Democratic presidential candidate Robert F. Kennedy is assassinated in Los Angeles after winning the California primary.

Microphones used by the Watergate burglars

1972
A burglary at the Watergate building will lead to the resignation of President Richard Nixon.

1976
The Muppet Show begins. The TV show features animal-like puppets.

1979
The worst nuclear accident in U.S. history occurs at the Three Mile Island power plant in Pennsylvania.

Nuclear reactors at Three Mile Island

1981
53 Americans return to the United States after being held hostage in Tehran, Iran, for 444 days.

1984
Republican Ronald Reagan is elected to a second term as president.

1968	1971	1974	1977	1980	1983

WORLD

1969
Golda Meir, a former teacher in the United States, is elected as Israel's first female prime minister.

Golda Meir

1974
Chinese farmers working near the city of Xi'an accidentally discover the tomb of emperor Shi Huangdi. It contains an army of more than 6,000 life-sized terra-cotta soldiers.

1979
Nicaraguan dictator General Anastasio Somoza flees from Sandinista rebels, who take over the government.

1981
Great Britain's Prince Charles weds Lady Diana Spencer. The televised ceremony is watched by an estimated 700 million people worldwide.

The terra-cotta soldiers in military formation

Prince Charles and Princess Diana

1988
American sprinter Florence Griffith Joyner wins three gold medals at the Seoul Olympics.

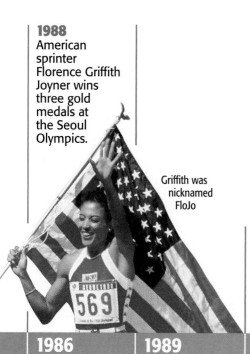

Griffith was nicknamed FloJo

Sojourner vehicle on Mars

1993
Toni Morrison becomes the first African American writer to receive a Nobel Prize.

1997
On July 4 the *Pathfinder,* a three-foot-tall U.S. spacecraft, lands on Mars. It contains a small, remote-controlled vehicle that explores the planet.

1998
In December the House of Representatives impeaches President Bill Clinton. His trial in the Senate begins in January 1999.

Ticket for President Clinton's impeachment trial

| 1986 | 1989 | 1992 | 1995 | 1998 | Present |

A Chinese protestor in Beijing

1994
African National Congress leader Nelson Mandela is elected president of South Africa.

1995
Johan Reinhard leads an expedition up Mount Ampato in Peru. He discovers a 500-year-old Inca maiden buried there.

1999
Yugoslav troops attack Kosovo residents. NATO forces bomb Serbia in response.

1989
Pro-democracy activists lead mass demonstrations in Beijing's Tiananmen Square. The protestors demand freedom of speech and other rights.

Figurine found with the Inca maiden

USING THE TIME LINE

1. What information do the time line entries provide about U.S. presidents from 1968 to the present?

2. What information do the entries provide about world leaders?

Activity Select one of the following topics: culture, economy, politics, social issues, or technology. Using the information on the time line, write a brief history of one of these topics from 1968 to the present. Use the Internet, the library, your textbook, or other sources to find additional information to complete the history.

▫ CHAPTER 22 ▫
A Search for Order
(1968–1980)

In February 1972 President Richard Nixon boarded the presidential airplane for his trip to communist China. In good spirits, he waved and shook hands as thousands cheered him. Speaking to the crowd, Nixon compared his journey to China with a recent moon landing. The U.S. astronauts had left a plaque on the moon that read, "We came in peace for all mankind." Nixon said he was going to China for the same reason.

THEMES

Economic Development
What role might energy resources play in a nation's economy?

Citizenship and Democracy
How might the office of the U.S. presidency be affected by scandals?

Global Relations
How might U.S. foreign policy change depending on the president in office?

| 1968 | 1969 | 1970 | 1971 | 1972 | 1973 | 1974 |

NOV. 1968
Richard Nixon is elected president.

APR. 1970
Millions of Americans celebrate the first Earth Day.

FEB. 1972
President Nixon visits China.

OCT. 1973
Egypt and Syria attack Israel, beginning the Yom Kippur War.

The Nixon Presidency

Reading Focus

How did President Nixon try to address the concerns of the Silent Majority?

What effect did the poor economy and the energy crisis have on Americans?

How did realpolitik affect U.S. relations with other countries?

Key Terms

Silent Majority

southern strategy

stagflation

New Federalism

Organization of Petroleum Exporting Countries

energy crisis

realpolitik

Strategic Arms Limitation Talks

détente

OME 100,000 WORKERS—most of them construction workers—jammed shoulder to shoulder on already crowded New York City streets. "All the way with the U.S.A.," they yelled. They were determined to show their support for President Richard Nixon. Many of these workers considered themselves the backbone of the nation and saw student protesters as dangerous and anti-American. A few days later, one worker presented the president with a hard hat, calling it "a symbol, along with our great flag, for freedom and patriotism to our beloved country."

Demonstrators fill the streets of New York City to show their support for Richard Nixon.

IMAGE ON LEFT PAGE: *President Nixon at the Great Wall of China*

1975	1976	1977	1978	1979	1980

NOV. 1976 Jimmy Carter is elected president.

SEPT. 1978 The Camp David Accords are signed.

MAR. 1979 A nuclear accident occurs at Three Mile Island, Pennsylvania.

AUG. 1974 Nixon resigns the presidency, and Gerald Ford is sworn in as president.

NOV. 1980 Ronald Reagan wins the presidency.

The Silent Majority

A cartoon dollar showing American concerns over inflation

Many Americans voted for Richard Nixon in November 1968 because they disliked the changes taking place in the 1960s. President Nixon called these voters the **Silent Majority**. One Nixon supporter expressed some views of this group:

❝I want my children to live and grow up in an America as I knew it, where we were proud to be citizens of this country. I'm ... sick and tired of listening to all this nonsense about how awful America is.❞

The Silent Majority blamed the federal government for high taxes and social unrest. Nixon promised to restore law and order. He called antiwar protesters criminals and supported policies that increased the power of the police and the courts. He also tried to reduce the size of the government.

In addition, Nixon wanted to limit further civil rights legislation. He said, "The laws have caught up with our consciences." This position was part of the Republicans' so-called **southern strategy**. Nixon hoped this strategy would win the support of white southern Democrats and other opponents of civil rights reforms.

The U.S. Supreme Court blocked some of Nixon's efforts. For example, the Court supported busing programs to desegregate public schools. Nixon opposed such programs. In 1969 he replaced retiring Chief Justice Earl Warren with Warren E. Burger, a more conservative judge. Nixon eventually appointed three additional conservative justices. Following these changes, the Court began to alter some of its earlier civil rights decisions.

The Economy

One critical problem facing President Nixon was the U.S. economy. In the early 1970s the country suffered from **stagflation**, a period of high inflation and high unemployment.

Several factors caused stagflation. The cost of social programs and the Vietnam War had increased the national debt. Paying the interest on this debt cost the federal government billions of dollars a year. These payments contributed to inflation. In addition, American manufacturers faced stronger foreign competition. As a result, some major industries downsized to cut costs. Many Americans lost their jobs. Even those who kept working were hurt by rising prices caused by inflation. From 1967 to 1974, the buying power of the U.S. dollar dropped by 30 percent. "I used to keep a budget," said one San Francisco woman, "but it got so discouraging, I gave it up."

Nixon hoped the economy would correct itself. He believed the federal government should avoid interfering with businesses and state governments. Instead, he proposed a system of revenue sharing called the **New Federalism**. Under this system, the federal government gave grants to the states. Local leaders then decided how to use this money. However, when inflation hit 6 percent in 1971, Nixon placed limits on wage and price increases. These controls temporarily slowed inflation.

The Energy Crisis

Scarce energy resources and rising oil prices also contributed to U.S. economic problems. By 1974

Long lines at the gas pump during the energy crisis

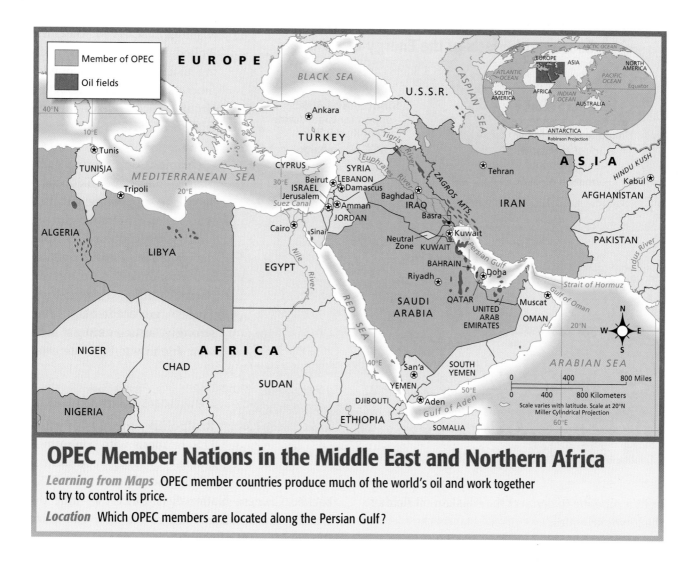

Member of OPEC

Oil fields

EUROPE

BLACK SEA

U.S.S.R.

CASPIAN SEA

ARCTIC OCEAN

EUROPE ASIA NORTH AMERICA

ATLANTIC OCEAN PACIFIC OCEAN

SOUTH AMERICA AFRICA INDIAN OCEAN AUSTRALIA

Equator

ANTARCTICA

Robinson Projection

40°N

10°E

Ankara

TURKEY

Tigris River

Tehran

ASIA

HINDU KUSH

Kabul

Tunis

TUNISIA

MEDITERRANEAN SEA

CYPRUS

30°E

SYRIA

Euphrates River

ZAGROS MTS.

IRAN

AFGHANISTAN

Tripoli

20°E

Beirut LEBANON

ISRAEL Damascus

Baghdad

Jerusalem

Suez Canal

Amman

IRAQ

Basra

PAKISTAN

Indus River

ALGERIA

Cairo

Sinai

JORDAN

Neutral Zone

Kuwait

LIBYA

EGYPT

KUWAIT

Persian Gulf

BAHRAIN

Doha

Strait of Hormuz

Gulf of Oman

N

RED SEA

Riyadh

QATAR

Muscat

W E

NIGER

AFRICA

SAUDI ARABIA

UNITED ARAB EMIRATES

OMAN

20°N

S

CHAD

40°E

San'a

SOUTH YEMEN

ARABIAN SEA

0 400 800 Miles

SUDAN

YEMEN

50°E

0 400 800 Kilometers

NIGERIA

DJIBOUTI

Aden

Gulf of Aden

Scale varies with latitude. Scale at 20°N
Miller Cylindrical Projection

ETHIOPIA

SOMALIA

60°E

OPEC Member Nations in the Middle East and Northern Africa

Learning from Maps OPEC member countries produce much of the world's oil and work together to try to control its price.

Location Which OPEC members are located along the Persian Gulf?

the United States was importing more than a third of its oil. Much of it came from Middle Eastern nations. In 1960, five major oil-producing nations had formed the **Organization of Petroleum Exporting Countries** (OPEC). The membership of OPEC later expanded to include 13 countries. OPEC hoped to maintain a high price for oil by controlling its production and sale.

In the early 1970s OPEC controlled much of the world's oil supply. It used this power to influence international politics. Most OPEC members were Arab countries opposed to Israel, an ally of the United States. In October 1973 Egypt and Syria attacked Israel on Yom Kippur, a Jewish holy day. The United States sent military supplies to Israel during this Yom Kippur War. This act upset Egypt and Syria's OPEC allies.

OPEC declared an embargo, or a ban, on the sale of oil to the United States and some other countries. The oil embargo caused a worldwide

energy crisis that was marked by high fuel prices and fuel shortages. Many gasoline stations remained open only part of the day. Customers waited in long lines to buy gas. The high cost of gasoline hurt sales of American-made cars, most of which got poor gas mileage.

Some schools and businesses had to shut down because they lacked fuel for heat and transportation. One Detroit hospital told its patients to stay in bed to keep warm. A hospital official explained, "We had so little oil left that we just had to cut back the thermostats."

President Nixon encouraged people to use less fuel by lowering their thermostats and limiting air travel. He asked Congress to lower speed limits so that cars would use less gas. Nixon also supported research into nuclear power. In addition, the president announced Project Independence, a plan to end the use of foreign oil by 1980. Under Project Independence, the United States

A Search for Order **657**

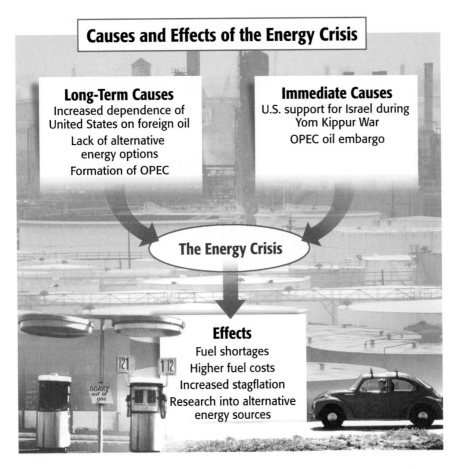

Causes and Effects of the Energy Crisis

Long-Term Causes
Increased dependence of United States on foreign oil
Lack of alternative energy options
Formation of OPEC

Immediate Causes
U.S. support for Israel during Yom Kippur War
OPEC oil embargo

The Energy Crisis

Effects
Fuel shortages
Higher fuel costs
Increased stagflation
Research into alternative energy sources

built a pipeline to connect the Alaskan oil fields to the lower 48 states.

 Foreign Diplomacy

The energy crisis showed how complicated foreign policy had become. President Nixon had already begun developing a new foreign-policy approach to deal with such issues.

Realpolitik

Henry Kissinger served as Nixon's senior foreign-policy adviser. Kissinger was a respected German American professor of political science at Harvard University. He served as national security adviser during Nixon's first term. He became secretary of state during Nixon's second term.

Kissinger based his foreign policy on the idea of **realpolitik**. This German word means "practical politics." Kissinger argued that protecting U.S. interests was more important than defending political or moral ideals overseas. For example,

Kissinger believed that the United States should be willing to cooperate with nondemocratic countries under some circumstances. Nixon agreed with most of Kissinger's policy views.

Some observers complained that realpolitik encouraged U.S. support for dictators who violated human rights. In Latin America, for example, the United States gave military and economic aid to several harsh military dictatorships. These governments were strongly anticommunist and were friendly to U.S. interests.

Relations with China

Realpolitik greatly affected U.S. relations with communist China. In 1949, communist rebels had defeated the U.S.-backed Chinese Nationalists. Since that time the United States had refused to officially recognize the government of communist China.

Many U.S. officials had long assumed that China and the Soviet Union were close allies. In early 1969, however, the two communist nations had argued over their shared border. This dispute almost caused a war. By 1970 China and the Soviet Union had become bitter rivals.

Hoping to widen this split, Nixon administration officials began secret talks with the Chinese. In February 1972 President Nixon and his wife, Pat, visited China. Journalists and television news teams covered the Nixons' trip extensively. Americans saw images of the Great Wall and the Imperial Palace. They also saw pictures of the Nixons at state banquets with Chinese leader Mao Zedong and his wife, Jiang Qing.

Although some people criticized Nixon for establishing closer ties with Communists, many Americans supported him. One observer said:

❝I applaud [Nixon's] timely acceptance of the changing conditions in the world today. . . . **If pragmatism [practicality] is indeed to be the byword [guiding principle] for U.S. policy, then all the better for the American people.** "

Negotiating with the Soviet Union

The Soviets wanted to prevent the United States from allying with China. This concern encouraged them to negotiate with U.S. officials. In May 1972 Nixon became the first U.S. president to visit Moscow. He met with Soviet leader Leonid Brezhnev (BREZH-nef). The two leaders focused their talks on the nuclear arms race. The nuclear buildup was costing both nations billions of dollars. The risk of nuclear war also worried many observers.

To slow the arms buildup, the two leaders signed the **Strategic Arms Limitation Talks** (SALT) treaty. The treaty limited the numbers and types of long-range nuclear missiles each country could have. The SALT treaty began a period of **détente** (day-TAHNT), or an easing of tensions,

Henry Kissinger (center) played a key role in U.S. negotiations with foreign governments.

between the United States and the Soviet Union. U.S. and Soviet officials continued to meet for diplomatic talks.

Détente also improved U.S.-Soviet economic relations. Trade between the United States and the Soviet Union tripled in 1972. The Soviets bought millions of tons of grain from American farmers. Many Americans were pleased that realpolitik had opened up new markets in the Soviet Union. Business leaders hoped this market expansion would improve the U.S. economy.

SECTION 1 REVIEW

Identify and explain the significance of the following:

- Silent Majority
- southern strategy
- stagflation
- New Federalism
- Organization of Petroleum Exporting Countries
- energy crisis
- Henry Kissinger
- realpolitik
- Leonid Brezhnev
- Strategic Arms Limitation Talks
- détente

Locate and explain the importance of the following:

- Egypt
- Syria
- Israel

Reading for Content Understanding

1. **Main Idea** How did President Nixon appeal to the Silent Majority?

2. **Main Idea** How did stagflation and the energy crisis affect Americans?

3. **Global Relations** What effect did realpolitik have on U.S. foreign relations?

4. **Writing** *Informing* Imagine that you work in Nixon's public affairs office. Write a brief brochure on his plans to ease the energy crisis.

5. **Critical Thinking** *Drawing Conclusions* Why do you think some people supported détente with China and the Soviet Union?

Watergate and Beyond

Reading Focus

How did the events of Watergate lead to President Nixon's resignation?

What constitutional issues were addressed during the Watergate scandal?

What challenges did President Ford face while in office?

Key Terms

Watergate
executive privilege
Saturday Night Massacre
trade deficit

ROUND 2:00 A.M. ON JUNE 17, 1972, *a security guard at the Watergate apartment and office complex in Washington, D.C., conducted a routine inspection. At first, everything seemed quiet. Then he discovered that the doors to the Democratic National Committee headquarters were open. He called the police, who soon arrested five men. These were no ordinary burglars—they carried camera equipment, big rolls of cash, and secret electronic recording devices. Bob Woodward, a reporter for the* Washington Post, *was convinced there was more to the story than simple burglary.*

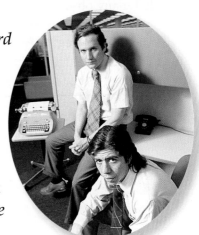

Reporters Bob Woodward (top) and Carl Bernstein (bottom)

 The Beginning of a Scandal

The police discovered that some of the Watergate burglars had ties to President Richard Nixon's administration. One worked for the Committee to Re-elect the President (CRP). Other people associated with the crime had been White House aides. The incident developed into **Watergate**, a political scandal named after the burglarized building.

President Nixon quickly denied that anyone in his administration was involved. The story had little effect on the presidential election of 1972.

Nixon won in a landslide over the Democratic challenger, Senator George McGovern of South Dakota. However, Bob Woodward and Carl Bernstein, two reporters for the *Washington Post,* continued to investigate the break-in.

At first, all the key figures refused to talk. Then a secret White House informant contacted Woodward. This source, whom Woodward called Deep Throat, gave the reporter valuable inside information about Watergate. Like secret agents in a spy movie, the two men met in quiet places such as dark parking garages.

Deep Throat's information led Woodward and Bernstein to a startling discovery. The CRP had used "dirty tricks" to help Nixon and other Republicans win the election. The CRP had hidden illegal campaign contributions and spread false rumors concerning Democratic candidates. The reporters began publishing articles about the CRP's activities in the *Washington Post.*

Nixon adviser John Ehrlichman testifying before the Senate

Evidence also began to build of a Watergate cover-up. Convicted Watergate burglar James McCord spoke out in January 1973. He claimed that he had been pressured to plead guilty and keep silent. In addition, McCord stated that there had been more people involved in the break-in than just the five who had been arrested.

★ The Investigation

Many members of Congress believed James McCord's claim of a Watergate cover-up. Some people even suspected that President Nixon was involved in the Watergate scandal. In the summer of 1973 the Senate launched its own investigation of the Watergate break-in.

The Senate Hearings

Nixon tried to shift blame to others in his administration. He forced H. R. Haldeman, his chief of staff, and John Ehrlichman, a chief adviser, to resign. He also fired White House attorney John Dean. Nixon agreed to Senate demands to appoint an independent special prosecutor to investigate the Watergate scandal. Attorney General Elliot Richardson chose Harvard law professor Archibald Cox. Professor Cox had a reputation for honesty and legal skill. The Senate approved Cox's appointment.

Senator Sam Ervin of North Carolina led the Senate Select Committee that investigated Watergate. Millions of Americans watched the Senate hearings on television. Accusations against the president and his closest advisers soon unfolded. The most damaging witness was former White House attorney John Dean. In his testimony Dean claimed that Nixon was directly involved in the cover-up. Dean also said that he had warned Nixon that the cover-up was "a cancer eating away at his presidency." As the investigations continued, a newspaper columnist wrote that Watergate was "a political bomb that could blow the Nixon administration apart."

Dean had no proof of his claims. However, another witness revealed that Nixon had recorded most of the conversations in his office. When the Senate committee asked Nixon to turn over the tapes, he refused. Nixon based his refusal on **executive privilege**, the president's right to keep information secret to protect national security.

The Battle over the Tapes

The tapes were the key to determining the truth of Dean's claims. Special Prosecutor Cox asked for a court order to get them. President Nixon and his attorneys believed that Cox's demand violated the special rights of the office of the president. Cox responded, "There is no exception for the President. . . . Even the highest executive officials are subject to the rule of law." The federal judge presiding over the case ordered Nixon to hand over the tapes.

The Senate hearings on the Watergate break-in were filled with reporters and cameras.

Nixon asked if he could provide summaries of the tapes rather than the originals. Cox refused. On Saturday evening, October 20, 1973, Nixon instructed Attorney General Richardson to fire the special prosecutor. Nixon claimed that Cox had to be replaced to protect the national interest. Richardson replied, "Mr. President, it would appear that we have a different assessment [view] of the national interest." He resigned rather than fire Cox. So did the next-highest officer in the Justice Department.

Nixon then named Robert H. Bork acting attorney general. Bork fired Cox. One senator called the firing "a reckless act of desperation." The resignations and firing became known as the **Saturday Night Massacre**. Nixon's approval rating dropped to 22 percent in some polls. Many government officials began discussing the possibility of impeaching the president.

Nixon's troubles were made worse by a scandal involving Vice President Spiro Agnew. Agnew faced charges that he had failed to pay his taxes and that he had taken bribes as a public official.

ROTHCO MARGULIES

I KNOW THERE IS A DANGEROUS CONSPIRACY WHICH IS OUT TO GET ME BECAUSE...

AND YOU PUBLISH ALL OF THAT EVIDENCE—

THE PRESS

ALL YOUR INVESTIGATIONS PRODUCE ONLY DAMAGING EVIDENCE—

CONGRESS

AND YOU READ EVERY WORD OF IT !!!

THE PUBLIC

As the Watergate investigations continued, Nixon claimed that his opponents were plotting against him.

He resigned just a few days before the Saturday Night Massacre, receiving a fine and probation. His resignation led *Time* magazine to declare that the White House was filled with "an atmosphere of immorality [corruption]." Nixon selected Michigan representative and House minority leader Gerald Ford as his new vice president.

★ Nixon's Resignation

Following the Saturday Night Massacre, some members of Congress began the formal process of requesting President Nixon's impeachment. The president then handed over a few of the tapes. He provided a heavily edited transcript of the rest. Investigators found that a large portion of one of the tapes had been erased.

The new special prosecutor, Leon Jaworski, demanded the release of all the tapes. In July 1974 the U.S. Supreme Court ordered the president to turn over the complete set. This time Nixon obeyed the court order. Conversations on the tapes proved that Nixon had ordered the Watergate cover-up. The president had also lied to Congress and the American people about his involvement.

The truth shocked many Americans who had until then believed the president. The evidence on the tapes moved Congress to act. The House

The Impeachment Process

Grounds	Officials establish grounds for impeachment, which could include treason, bribery, and other offenses.
Phase 1	The House of Representatives announces articles of impeachment, thus formally accusing an official.
Phase 2	The Senate holds a trial for the accused, with a two-thirds vote needed for a conviction.
Penalty	A convicted official is removed from his or her post and cannot hold any public office in the future.

Judiciary Committee soon made a bipartisan recommendation. It asked the full House of Representatives to vote to impeach the president on three articles. The committee accused Nixon of abusing his authority, obstructing justice, and "violating the constitutional rights of citizens."

Texas congresswoman Barbara Jordan was a committee member. Like others, she believed that Nixon had violated his oath to uphold the nation's laws. She explained why she favored Nixon's impeachment:

> 66 **My faith in the Constitution is whole, it is complete, it is total, and I am not going to sit here and be an idle spectator to the . . . destruction of the Constitution.** 99

After the release of the tapes, there was little support for Nixon in Congress. If the House voted to impeach him, it was very possible that the Senate would then find him guilty. Yet Nixon refused to believe that he would be impeached. It was not until former supporters began asking for his resignation that he realized he was defeated.

In a televised announcement on August 8, 1974, Nixon became the first U.S. president to resign from office. In a shaky voice, he admitted only to "a few mistakes in judgment." The next day, Vice President Gerald Ford was sworn in as president. He was the first person to become president without being elected as either vice president or president.

The Watergate scandal damaged many Americans' faith in the government. "We [now] assume that politicians are without honor," wrote poet and journalist Adrienne Rich. Others, however, disagreed. They viewed the hearings and Nixon's resignation as evidence that the U.S. government had successfully fought against corruption. Senator Sam Ervin later wrote:

> 66 **Watergate . . . proved our Constitution works. That instrument commands the President to 'take care that the laws be faithfully executed.' When President**

After resigning and making a farewell speech, Richard Nixon left the White House.

> **Nixon was untrue to his constitutional obligation, Congress and the federal judiciary remained true to theirs. As a consequence, the United States weathered a great national crisis without turmoil [disturbance] and with all its institutions intact.** 99

The Ford Presidency

President Gerald Ford had established a reputation in Congress for honesty and cooperation. Many Americans hoped that Ford would restore confidence in the government.

The Pardons

Ford referred to Watergate as a "long national nightmare," which he declared was over. He granted a pardon to Richard Nixon soon after taking office. This pardon meant that Nixon would never face trial for any illegal activities committed during his presidency.

Many Americans received the news of the pardon with relief. They believed the pardon was a way to finally move beyond the Watergate scandal. Others, however, questioned why Nixon was allowed to escape punishment. Other Watergate figures had gone to jail. Ford's approval rating dropped from more than 70 to less than 50 percent.

Ford also offered a conditional pardon to young men who had illegally avoided the draft during the Vietnam War. Under Ford's plan, these people could avoid criminal charges by performing community service. Many veterans argued that the plan was too easy on those who had avoided military service. Antiwar activists thought it punished them unfairly for doing what they believed was morally right.

Ford faced another controversy in the mid-1970s. Congressional investigations revealed that both the CIA and the FBI had abused their power. The FBI, for example, had spied on radical groups without proper cause. Ford tried to reorganize and reform the agencies. He hoped these efforts would further restore Americans' faith in government.

The Economy

Within months of taking office, Ford admitted that the nation's economy was nearing the point of recession. Business had slowed because of high oil prices and continuing stagflation. The United States also had a growing **trade deficit**—a trade imbalance that occurs when a nation imports more goods than it exports. Japan and Western European nations were selling large amounts of manufactured products to the United States. These products included automobiles and electronics. For example, many

President Gerald Ford and First Lady Betty Ford

American automakers struggled to compete with popular new import cars such as the Volkswagen Beetle. The trade deficit made inflation and unemployment even worse.

Ford's anti-inflation campaign was unsuccessful.

Ford believed that inflation was "public enemy Number 1." If the United States could control inflation, it could reduce prices for its products. Lower prices would make it easier for American companies to compete against inexpensive foreign imports. Reduced prices would also make American exports more affordable overseas. In addition, American consumers would benefit from lowered prices. Ford hoped that all these factors would combine to improve the economy.

To fight inflation, Ford launched a campaign called Whip Inflation Now (WIN). He asked Americans to save their money and businesses to voluntarily keep wages and prices down to reduce inflation. With no way to enforce these requests, however, the WIN campaign had little effect.

Ford also wanted to reduce government spending to reduce inflation. However, the Democrat-controlled Congress wanted to increase spending to help the poor and unemployed. As a result of this disagreement, little legislation was approved. Ford vetoed more than 30 Democrat-sponsored spending bills during his first year in office. It was not until 1975, when unemployment topped 9 percent, that the president and Congress finally compromised. They agreed to expand unemployment benefits and to cut some taxes. The economy recovered slightly. However, inflation and unemployment remained high, and the national deficit increased.

★ Ford's Foreign Policy

In foreign affairs, President Ford tried to continue Nixon's policy of détente. He achieved some success when he and Soviet leader Brezhnev agreed to limit underground nuclear testing. The two leaders also discussed a second SALT treaty to further limit nuclear arms.

There were also some gestures of friendship between the United States and the Soviet Union. One of the most dramatic events took place in outer space. In July 1975 the U.S. *Apollo 18* spacecraft linked up with the Soviet *Soyuz 19* spacecraft in orbit around Earth. The U.S. astronauts and Soviet cosmonauts then performed a series of joint experiments. The effort showed the benefits of international cooperation.

Despite such events, détente was increasingly unpopular with conservative politicians. Critics of détente had several concerns. They worried that other NATO members might disapprove of U.S. cooperation with the Soviet Union. If NATO nations did not trust the United States as an ally, U.S. foreign policy in Western Europe would be damaged. Some conservatives also believed that the Soviet Union might interpret détente as a sign of American weakness.

President Ford shared these concerns. In the spring of 1975, communist Cambodians captured the American cargo ship *Mayaguez*. Ford was determined to show that the United States would not be bullied. He authorized a military operation to rescue the 40 crew members. The rescue attempt failed, resulting in the deaths of 41 U.S. Marines. It was later discovered that the hostages had already

An artist's drawing of the historic meeting of the U.S. Apollo 18 *(left) and the Soviet* Soyuz 19 *spacecraft (right)*

been released. Some observers charged that Ford had acted too hastily. His supporters, however, called the rescue attempt "a daring show of nerve and steel."

Support for détente decreased even further. Conservatives in Congress took a firm position against communism and opposed future compromises with the Soviet Union. The Soviets also became less cooperative. Further SALT discussions stalled, and Congress blocked several proposed economic agreements. By 1976 little remained of the cooperation between the Soviet Union and the United States.

SECTION 2 REVIEW

Identify and explain the significance of the following:
- **Richard Nixon**
- **Watergate**
- **Bob Woodward and Carl Bernstein**
- **executive privilege**
- **Saturday Night Massacre**
- **Gerald Ford**
- **Barbara Jordan**
- **trade deficit**

Reading for Content Understanding

1 **Main Idea** Create a time line describing the events of Watergate up to President Nixon's resignation.

2 **Main Idea** How did President Ford address domestic and foreign challenges?

3 **Constitutional Heritage** Why did Barbara Jordan and many other Americans believe that President Nixon deserved to be impeached?

4 **Writing** *Expressing* Imagine that it is 1974 and President Ford has just granted Nixon a full pardon. Write a letter to a friend explaining why you do or do not agree with Ford's action.

5 **Critical Thinking** *Supporting a Point of View* Do you agree or disagree with the House Judiciary Committee's conclusion that Nixon's role in Watergate was a serious violation of the Constitution? Explain your answer.

The Carter Administration

Reading Focus

How did President Carter differ from other politicians, and why did he lose public support?

How did Carter handle economic problems during his presidency?

What was Carter's approach to foreign policy?

Key Terms

Panama Canal treaties
Camp David Accords
apartheid
sanctions
Iran hostage crisis

THE MORNING OF JULY 4, 1976, dawned clear and cool over New York Harbor. A steady wind filled the sails of 225 tall ships as they silently made their way past the Statue of Liberty. For a few days most Americans set aside their worries about the economy and foreign policy to celebrate the country's bicentennial, or 200th birthday. Citizens across the country gathered to ring in the event and honor the nation. One person declared that the bicentennial had "become a way of clearing the American soul in a very positive way."

The bicentennial celebration in New York Harbor

 ## The Election of 1976

Democratic Party leaders hoped that the bicentennial would also mark a Democratic presidential victory. Democrats thought they had a good chance to win the White House in 1976. Many Americans associated the Republicans with the Watergate scandal. In addition, a large number of voters were disappointed with President Gerald Ford's handling of economic and diplomatic issues. Other Americans were upset that he had pardoned former president Nixon.

Despite these challenges, Ford won a tough battle for the Republican presidential nomination. He defeated former California governor Ronald Reagan. Ford chose Kansas senator Bob Dole as his running mate. The Democrats wanted a candidate free from political scandals. At first there was no clear front-runner. During the primaries, however, an unexpected candidate emerged. This individual was Jimmy Carter, a little-known former governor of Georgia.

The two most important factors in Carter's life were his family and his religion. These personal

Jimmy Carter

James Earl Carter Jr. was born in Plains, Georgia, in 1924. Carter attended the U.S. Naval Academy. After graduation he served as an engineer in the nuclear submarine program. He planned to make the navy his career. After his father died, however, he returned to Georgia to help his family rebuild their peanut warehouse. He became active in local politics, serving on the local school board and later in the state senate. In 1970 he was elected governor of Georgia.

When he began campaigning in January 1975, few politicians thought that Carter could win the Democratic nomination for the presidency. He stunned political pollsters by winning the New Hampshire primary. By the time of the Democratic National Convention in New York City, he had won 18 state primary elections. Convention delegates nominated him for president.

values strongly shaped Carter's political career. His mother, "Miss Lillian," had taught him the value of community service. She told him that "sharing yourself with others . . . is the most precious gift of all." Carter's religious faith played a key role in his political beliefs. He thought that political decisions should be based on moral ideals such as equality and justice.

Carter's campaign focused more on his personal character than on his political platform. His background and his open, straightforward approach impressed many people. "I will never lie to you," he told voters. He promised a "new era of honest, compassionate, responsive government." His words struck a deep chord with Americans still troubled by the Watergate incident. Carter won a narrow victory over Ford in the November 1976 election. Carter's overwhelming support among African American and Hispanic voters helped secure his victory.

As president, Carter wanted to show a new spirit of openness and modesty in the White House. On Inauguration Day, he and his family walked down Pennsylvania Avenue instead of riding in a limousine. Carter also tried to make the presidency more personal. He had few politicians from Washington in his cabinet. He also reduced the size of the presidential staff. Early in his administration, the public seemed to approve of Carter's approach.

Jimmy Carter chose to walk to his inauguration to show that he would be accessible to the American public.

Domestic Challenges

President Carter faced two major domestic problems—the economy and the energy crisis. The economy was still sluggish. Carter proposed a tax cut and increases in government spending. He also tried to get management and organized labor to cooperate. Carter hoped they would hold down prices and wages. His efforts met with little

Linking Past to Present

The Changing Automobile

The energy crisis of the 1970s led car companies to make smaller, more fuel-efficient cars. Since then, however, the price of oil has generally dropped. Americans have bought record numbers of large vehicles. Big trucks, sport utility vehicles (SUVs), and vans are very popular, but not very fuel-efficient.

Automakers are also developing cars that use less fuel and cause less pollution. Some designs use alternative energy sources. These electric, electric-gas "hybrid," and hydrogen cars create less pollution than autos with conventional engines. However, early models of these new vehicles are also more expensive than traditional cars.

Electric cars run on powerful batteries instead of gasoline. They are quiet and produce no pollution. However, early electric cars could only travel about 100 miles before the batteries had to be recharged. Engineers have tried to increase this driving range. Hybrid cars combine electric batteries with small gasoline engines. This design extends battery life and provides high fuel efficiency. In the late 1990s, engineers developed hybrid cars capable of traveling up

An advanced fuel-efficient concept car

to 70 miles per gallon of gasoline. These early hybrid cars are quite small, however.

Hydrogen-powered cars were still in the early design stages in the 1990s. These cars use devices called fuel cells to turn hydrogen and oxygen into electricity. Fuel cells that use pure hydrogen produce no pollution. The major drawbacks of these cars are that pure hydrogen is highly flammable and there are few places where it can be purchased.

Understanding What You Read

1. How did the energy crisis of the 1970s affect automobile manufacturers?

2. What are some of the new technologies being developed for cars?

---

success, however. Inflation soared again. It reached more than 13 percent in 1980.

The energy crisis continued to hurt the economy. Oil prices remained high, and the United States was still largely dependent on foreign oil. Nuclear energy was not a popular alternative. Many Americans began to fear nuclear power after an accident on Three Mile Island, Pennsylvania. In March 1979 a nuclear power plant's reactor core overheated, almost releasing deadly radiation into

the air. The accident raised new questions about the safety of nuclear power.

Carter created a detailed energy policy and asked Americans to use less fuel. He also supported the development of alternative energy sources such as solar power. However, Carter had difficulty gaining public support for energy conservation.

As an inexperienced political "outsider," Carter also had trouble winning support in

Congress. For example, Carter did not want Congress to make any changes to his complex energy proposal. As a result, only some of the plan was passed. One historian has said that Carter had a tendency

" to equate [make equal] his political goals with the just and the right, and to view his opponents as representative of some selfish or immoral [not moral] interest. "

Carter's inexperience and rigid approach hurt his effectiveness. Although his own party controlled Congress, few of his proposals were passed.

★ Carter's Foreign Policy

President Carter rejected the strategy of realpolitik. Instead, he used his own strict moral standards as guidelines for U.S. foreign policy. Carter declared that "fairness, not force, should lie at the heart of our dealings with the nations of the world." Carter condemned foreign governments that tortured or unlawfully jailed their citizens. He insisted that other governments protect citizens' human rights—the basic rights and freedoms owed to all human beings. Carter reduced U.S. aid to some former allies, such as Argentina and Ethiopia, for violations of these basic rights.

Latin America

President Carter soon applied his new foreign-policy approach to U.S. relations with Latin America. Many Latin Americans resented previous U.S. interference in their countries. In particular, they saw the Panama Canal, built and controlled by the United States, as a major symbol of U.S. influence in Latin America. In 1977 Carter signed the **Panama Canal treaties**, which would transfer control of the canal to Panama by the year 2000.

Many Americans opposed the treaties because of the canal's economic value. However, the Senate ratified them in 1978. Like Carter, the

Senate hoped that the treaties would encourage friendship and cooperation between the United States and Latin America. U.S. leaders also thought that such treaties would reduce communist influence in Latin America. Panamanian leader Omar Torrijos Herrera assured a U.S. senator:

" I believe we have entered on an entirely new era, one in which our two countries are partners, are friends, [and] are going to work together. "

The Middle East

President Carter also became involved in Middle Eastern diplomacy. In September 1978 he brought Egyptian president Anwar Sadat and Israeli prime minister Menachem Begin (BAY-gin) together for peace talks. The leaders met at Camp David, the U.S. presidential retreat.

In two weeks of meetings they crafted a set of peace agreements known as the **Camp David Accords**. The accords marked the first time that an Arab nation had established peaceful relations with Israel. Afterward, Sadat announced: "The barrier of distrust that has been between us [Egypt and Israel] during the last 30 years has been broken down." Many historians consider the Camp David Accords to be President Carter's greatest achievement.

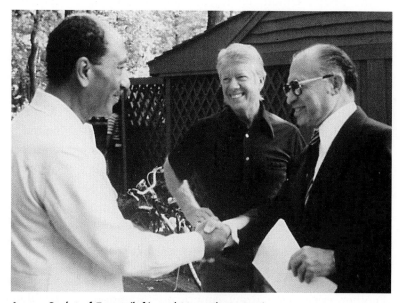

Anwar Sadat of Egypt (left) and Menachem Begin of Israel (right) signed the first peace treaty between Israel and an Arab nation.

South Africa

In Africa, Carter tried to encourage respect for human rights and win allies. He provided economic assistance to developing nations, many of which had new governments. These countries were struggling to establish economic independence after years of colonial rule by European nations. At the same time, Carter tried to preserve U.S. trade interests in the region.

Carter's administration also addressed the issue of **apartheid**, the system of laws requiring racial segregation in South Africa. Andrew Young, the U.S. ambassador to the United Nations, was a strong critic of apartheid. Young supported **sanctions**, or economic penalties, to persuade South Africa to desegregate. The United States began applying sanctions against South Africa in 1985.

Iranian revolutionaries parade some of the U.S. hostages through the streets of Tehran.

The Soviet Union

U.S. relations with the Soviet Union grew worse during Carter's administration. Carter was very critical of the Soviet government's many human rights abuses. This criticism upset Soviet leaders. The situation became even more serious in 1979 when the Soviets invaded the central Asian country of Afghanistan. Carter reacted by postponing talks on SALT II—a new arms-control treaty. He also placed an embargo on U.S. grain shipments to the Soviet Union. Finally, Carter declared a U.S. boycott of the 1980 Summer Olympics in Moscow.

The Olympic boycott and the grain embargo upset many U.S. athletes and farmers. Some Americans believed that beating the Soviets in competition was a better way to show U.S. strength than the boycott. Other Americans were concerned about the economic impact of the grain embargo. "We think of ourselves as patriotic," said one Kansas farmer. "But we shouldn't have to go broke being patriotic."

⭐ The Iran Hostage Crisis

Another crisis soon drew Americans' attention. In the 1950s the United States had helped bring the shah of Iran, Mohammad Reza Pahlavi

(RAY-zah pah-HLAHV-ee), to power. Over the next two decades, the shah had supported U.S. interests in the region. In the late 1970s, however, Islamic fundamentalists began to challenge the shah's power. They called for a strict return to Islamic teachings and an end to cooperation with the United States.

By February 1979, followers of religious leader Ayatollah Khomeini (eye-uh-TOH-luh koh-MAY-nee) had overthrown the shah. In his place they established a fundamentalist dictatorship. This new government was hostile to the United States. In October U.S. officials allowed the shah into the United States for medical treatment. In response, angry Iranian revolutionaries staged massive protests. They also attacked the U.S. Embassy in Tehran, the capital of Iran. On November 4 they seized 54 American hostages, whom they abused and tortured. One hostage was released, but the other 53 were still held captive.

The **Iran hostage crisis** dragged on for months. There was no solution in sight. The crisis horrified Americans. Many saw the hostage situation as evidence of America's declining strength. In April 1980 a rescue attempt by the U.S. military went terribly wrong. Confusion and mechanical problems caused several of the rescue helicopters to crash in the desert. The rescuers never reached Tehran. News of this failure decreased many

Americans' confidence in Carter's ability to end the crisis. One American said bluntly:

66 **America today needs a tough-talking and tough-acting leader. America's strength was built on national pride and morale [positive feeling], and both of these have dropped under the weight of the defeat in Vietnam, the scandal of Watergate, and the catastrophic [disastrous] policies of Jimmy Carter.** 99

As the crisis continued, some of the hostages began to lose hope. One hostage later said, "I think there were times when all of us felt like we'd been left there and forgotten."

⭐ The Election of 1980

While President Carter prepared to run for re-election in 1980, his popularity was falling. Many people blamed him for the hostage crisis and the country's economic problems. He had also lost the support of many Democratic leaders in Congress. One southern Democratic senator said privately, "He hasn't a single friend up here [on Capitol Hill]."

Now it was the Republicans' turn to challenge an unpopular president. They chose Ronald Reagan,

the former governor of California, to run against Carter. In his campaign ads, Reagan claimed that the country needed new leadership:

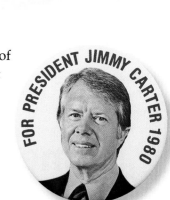

Carter was unable to generate wide-spread support in 1980.

66 **I will not stand by and watch this great country destroy itself under mediocre [average] leadership. . . . This is the greatest country in the world. We have the talent, we have the drive, we have the imagination. Now all we need is the leadership.** 99

When Reagan asked voters, "Are you better off than you were four years ago?" many of them answered "No."

In the November 1980 election Reagan defeated Carter in a landslide, 489 electoral votes to 49. Republicans also gained control of the Senate for the first time in 28 years. On January 20, 1981—the day of Reagan's inauguration—Iran finally released the hostages after 444 days of imprisonment. When they returned home, people all over the nation welcomed them with banners and parades.

SECTION 3 REVIEW

Identify and explain the significance of the following:
- Jimmy Carter
- Panama Canal treaties
- Anwar Sadat
- Menachem Begin
- Camp David Accords
- apartheid
- sanctions
- Ayatollah Khomeini
- Iran hostage crisis

Reading for Content Understanding

1 **Main Idea** What made many Americans see President Carter as a unique leader? Why did he lose public support?

2 **Main Idea** What ideas shaped Carter's foreign policy?

3 **Economic Development** What economic problems faced the nation during Carter's presidency? How did Carter address these problems?

4 **Writing** *Expressing* Imagine that you are an Olympic athlete in 1980. Write a letter to President Carter sharing your opinions on the boycott of the 1980 Summer Games in Moscow.

5 **Critical Thinking** *Evaluating* Do you think Jimmy Carter was a successful president? Use at least two examples from this section to support your answer.

American Society in the 1970s

Reading Focus

How did the U.S. population change during the 1970s?

What environmental concerns drew Americans' attention, and how did they react?

In what ways did health care and popular entertainment change in the 1970s?

Key Terms

Earth Day
Environmental Protection Agency
Endangered Species Act

 ESPITE THE PROBLEMS *the United States faced in the 1970s, it was still a land of opportunity for many immigrants. Many were like Erasmo and Eloina Ortega, who emigrated from the Dominican Republic in the 1970s. Although their family struggled to earn a living in the troubled U.S. economy, they were happy to be in the United States. "The political situation [in the Dominican Republic] was bad," recalled Eloina. "We're very glad that our children have a future that our country could never provide them."*

The flag of the Dominican Republic

★ Population Changes

The Ortegas were part of a changing pattern of immigration in the United States. Until the mid-1960s most people who immigrated to the United States came from Europe. By the 1970s, however, the majority of immigrants were coming from Latin America and Asia.

In Search of Opportunity

These immigrants were often political refugees. For example, thousands of people fled communist Cuba and came to the United States. Many of these Cuban immigrants were educated professionals. They helped create a powerful Cuban American political movement in southern Florida. Some Asian immigrants were also refugees from communist nations, such as Vietnam.

Thousands of other immigrants came to the United States seeking economic opportunities. Mexican immigrants looking for jobs made up the majority of Latin American immigrants during the 1970s. Although the U.S. economy was struggling, for many immigrants it provided better opportunities than the economies of their homelands.

Immigrants also sought educational opportunities. A large number of Asians came to the United States to attend college. After graduating, these students often decided to stay and work in technical industries. Sometimes they brought their families over to join them. Chinese immigrant Subi Lin Felipe recalled how her brother-in-law "brought in a sister and his wife, who brought over one of her brothers and me." Immigrants from many countries shared the outlook of Korean Kim Ta Tai. Kim explained:

Many older Americans enjoyed active lifestyles in the warm climate of the Sun Belt.

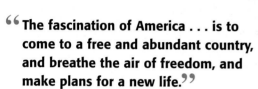
66 **The fascination of America . . . is to come to a free and abundant country, and breathe the air of freedom, and make plans for a new life.** 99

Growth in the Sun Belt

Thousands of immigrants settled in the Sun Belt states of the South and the West. Migrants from the Northeast and the Midwest also moved to the Sun Belt. By 1970 California had become the most populous state in the Union. The populations of other Sun Belt states such as Arizona and Florida also increased dramatically during the 1970s. By comparison, the population of the Midwest and Northeast grew slowly or even shrank.

Many people moved to the Sun Belt states to take new jobs in growing high-tech industries. These industries included aerospace and electronics. A large number of companies got their start in these industries by filling federal defense contracts during the Cold War military buildup. California, Florida, North Carolina, and Texas experienced the most growth in these defense fields.

Many older Americans moved to the Sun Belt for its warm climate. They were part of a major change in the U.S. population. More Americans were living longer because of improvements in health care. At the same time, the birthrate was declining. More adults were waiting longer to have

children and were having smaller families. As a result of these trends, the percentage of the U.S. population aged 65 and older grew rapidly. These senior citizens gained financially from the expansion of Social Security benefits in the 1960s. These improved benefits made retirement easier for many older Americans.

⭐ Environmental Issues

Some Americans worried about the effect of rapid growth on the environment of the Sun Belt and northwestern states. The worldwide energy crisis also led to growing concern about the consumption of natural resources.

American activists tried to raise environmental awareness by sponsoring the first **Earth Day** on April 22, 1970. They declared that:

66 **Earth Day is to remind each person of his [or her] equal responsibility . . . to preserve and improve the Earth and the quality of life thereon.** 99

Many thousands of people have observed Earth Day since the first celebration was held in 1970.

Since then, people around the world have held similar celebrations. Organizations also provide information on practices such as conserving energy, picking up litter, and recycling.

Protecting the Environment

Congress addressed concerns about the environment in the late 1960s and early 1970s. It passed laws to improve air and water quality and to limit pollution. In 1970 Congress established the **Environmental Protection Agency** (EPA) to enforce these laws. The EPA had a challenging task. It had to work with companies that opposed some of the new regulations. Many environmentalists, however, thought the new antipollution laws were not strict enough.

The EPA also inherited problems that had been created before there was great public concern about pollution. Years of unregulated or illegal dumping of industrial waste had created pollution problems across the country. One of the most shocking cases occurred in 1978. Some residents of Niagara Falls, New York, discovered that their homes had been built over an old toxic waste dump.

The dump was known as Love Canal, because it was located in an abandoned canal system. It was leaking dangerous levels of toxic chemicals into the water and soil. Scientists linked this toxic waste to health problems in the community, particularly among young children. "Do I let my three-year-old stay?" asked one concerned resident. Many people chose to move rather than risk exposure to dangerous chemicals.

In 1980 the government established a "Superfund" to pay for cleaning up toxic-waste dump sites such as Love Canal. These clean-up projects can cost millions of dollars and take years to complete.

Endangered Animals

Some environmentalists also asked for better protection of another natural resource—wildlife. As the human population expanded throughout the United States, new housing and suburban development pushed wildlife species into smaller habitats. In 1966 Congress had passed one of the earliest environmental measures, the **Endangered Species Act**. This act protects animals threatened with extinction.

The Department of the Interior maintains a list of species that are in danger. Federal law forbids hunting these species or destroying their natural habitats. The Endangered Species Act directs the government to "halt and reverse the trend toward species extinction, whatever the cost."

Some activists have used the Endangered Species Act to stop building projects. Critics have responded by claiming that the law goes too far. Many critics agree that wildlife should be protected but argue that people need the jobs that new development brings. As the debate continues, some developers search for ways to both protect the environment and make a profit.

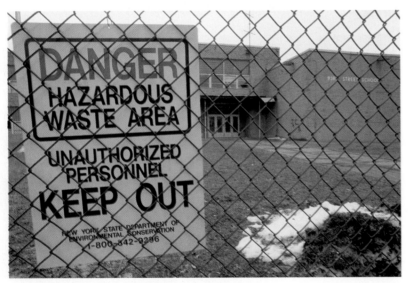

Many places in Love Canal, such as this school, were still considered unsafe in the 1990s.

★ Safety and Health

Environmental concerns played a part in the consumer activist movement of the 1970s. This movement showed that concern for public health could change business practices and safety regulations.

Led by consumer advocate Ralph Nader, activists pushed for improved safety and environmental standards for a wide range of consumer goods. These activities led to stricter rules for product safety and tougher pollution standards for automobiles. In 1977 the federal government also banned the use of chemicals that were believed to weaken Earth's atmospheric ozone layer. The ozone layer helps shield Earth's surface from solar radiation. As a result of new laws, appliance and automobile manufacturers designed products that were safer, more efficient, and produced less air pollution.

Concern for public health also led to many advances in medical technology in the 1970s. The MRI machine was patented in 1972. This machine could detect tumors and other problems with greater accuracy than X-ray machines. The following year, researchers created a system known as the CAT scan, which can detect tumors and brain injuries.

Treatment of illnesses and injuries also improved. In 1977 a German doctor invented angioplasty, a surgical method for clearing

The smiley face became a symbol of positive thinking and mental health in the 1970s.

clogged arteries to prevent heart attacks. In addition, doctors improved the success rate of organ transplants. This breakthrough prolonged the lives of those who received vital organs such as a heart, kidney, or liver.

Possibly the best medical news of the decade was how many Americans were taking responsibility for their own health. Research showed that people could significantly lower their risk of certain diseases by exercising and improving their diets.

These studies encouraged many Americans to adopt a healthier lifestyle during the 1970s. "There is no question that we are in the midst of a fitness explosion," declared one expert in 1977. Jogging, dance, and other aerobic activities became popular. Scientists credited improvements in diet and exercise with a 20 percent decline in the death rate from heart disease between 1969 and 1977.

American Arts

Twyla Tharp

Born in 1941, Twyla Tharp studied every kind of dance available as a child, including ballet, jazz, and tap. After beginning her own dance company in 1965, she described her goal: "I had to become the greatest choreographer of my time. That was my mission." Tharp's 1971 piece, *The Fugue* (FYOOG), named after a type of music composition, was a huge success. Tharp went on to choreograph many theater productions.

Tharp's unique style stretches the boundaries between classical and modern dance. It combines traditional ballet techniques with natural movements like running, walking, and skipping.

Twyla Tharp and dancers

Some of her dance pieces use no music at all. One critic wrote,

"*Whether sashaying [gliding] across the stage to the music of Jelly Roll Morton, Frank Sinatra or the Beach Boys, Twyla Tharp can razzle-dazzle her way into the hearts of the most reluctant modern dance goer.*"

Understanding the Arts

1. What was Twyla Tharp's goal?
2. What is original about Tharp's style of choreography?

Advances in Computers

Computer technology also advanced during the 1970s. Computer designers began making wide use of the microchip, invented in 1958. A microchip is a tiny piece of silicon that contains many miniaturized electronic parts. Placing all of these parts on a single chip allowed computers to become smaller and faster.

As computers became more powerful and less expensive, their use increased. The most powerful machines, known as "supercomputers," were used mainly for advanced scientific research. The military also used computers in many of its new defense and weapons systems. In addition, scientists created the first computer networks for military research. These networks allowed computer users in different locations to share data.

For the first time small personal computers became practical. In 1977 Steven Jobs and Stephen Wozniak founded the Apple computer company. Their first successful home computer had crude graphics and could run only a few programs. Despite these limitations, Apple had sold thousands of computers by 1980.

Although computer designers made many improvements during the 1970s, few Americans owned a computer. For most people, the new machines were still too expensive and not practical enough.

Popular Culture

New technology found its way into the entertainment industry. Technology had a large effect on moviemaking.

Blockbuster Films

Directors such as Francis Ford Coppola and Robert Altman achieved success among adult audiences. The biggest hits of the 1970s, however, were aimed at younger moviegoers. The most successful film of the decade

The Apple II was the first fully assembled home computer.

was George Lucas's 1977 classic, *Star Wars*. The movie tells the story of a battle between good and evil in a distant galaxy. It used familiar themes from traditional action films, such as westerns.

Lucas said that he felt the story appealed to young audiences because it dealt with "universal themes like friendship, loyalty, [and] morality [right and wrong]." The film also used new filmmaking and sound-recording techniques to create amazing special effects that fascinated audiences.

Star Wars earned more than $100 million during its initial release, a record at that time. Its success led to a new era of "blockbuster" films—big-budget, special-effects movies that targeted younger audiences. Director Steven Spielberg, who made hits such as *Close Encounters of the Third Kind*, praised this change:

❝*Star Wars* was a seminal [creative and original] moment when the entire industry instantly changed. For me, personally, it's when the world recognized the value of childhood.❞

Star Wars dazzled audiences with its images of alien worlds.

Movie studios also benefited from making blockbusters because these action movies were popular in foreign countries. As a result, films became an increasingly valuable U.S. export. Audiences all around the world watched American movies and movie stars. The trend toward expensive movies filled with special effects also posed risks for movie studios, however. Big-budget films cost so much to make that if one failed it could ruin a studio. In addition, some viewers began to complain that blockbuster movie plots were too simple and violent.

Flashing lights and mirrored balls were common features of disco clubs.

fast beat with a great melody behind it. When I danced, I wasn't just moving my legs up and down, I was flowing with the music.**"**

The disco craze inspired outrageous fashions, such as glittering sequined outfits that reflected the colorful strobe lights used in dance clubs. Dances like "The Hustle" were popular, and musicians such as the Bee Gees and Donna Summer made best-selling records. In addition to her many hit records, Summer won both a Grammy and an Academy Award for her song "Last Dance" in 1979.

As with big-budget movies, the new music had its critics. Some argued that disco lyrics encouraged irresponsible behavior. Other opponents thought that disco dances and fashions were foolish. Despite such criticisms, disco music remained popular with young fans in the 1970s in much the same way as rock 'n' roll had appealed to youth in the 1950s.

The Disco Craze

Music also changed during the 1970s. Americans began to turn to dance-oriented styles such as disco. Millions of Americans crowded dance clubs called discotheques, or discos. New Yorker Gus Rodriguez described the appeal of disco music:

"Dancing to disco provided me with this incredible release. The music had this

SECTION 4 REVIEW

Identify and explain the significance of the following:
- **Earth Day**
- **Environmental Protection Agency**
- **Endangered Species Act**
- **George Lucas**
- **Donna Summer**

Reading for Content Understanding

1 **Main Idea** What environmental issues concerned Americans in the 1970s? How were these concerns addressed?

2 **Main Idea** How did popular films and music change during the 1970s?

3 **Geography** *Region* How was the population of the United States affected by changes in immigration and migration during the 1970s?

4 **Writing** *Describing* Imagine that you are a doctor attending a medical conference in the late 1970s. Write a short speech describing the latest medical breakthroughs and noting how the health habits of Americans have changed during this decade.

5 **Critical Thinking** *Evaluating* Why might it be important to protect an endangered species from extinction? What steps might help make this possible?

CHAPTER 22 REVIEW

Chapter Summary

Many Americans hoped that the 1970s would be a time of stability and order after the social protests of the 1960s. Instead, the 1970s brought an economic downturn, an energy crisis, and the Watergate scandal. Presidents Ford and Carter struggled with domestic issues during their terms. They also faced new foreign-policy challenges. Americans witnessed technological breakthroughs in computers and medicine. Environmental concerns also increased. ▪

On a separate sheet of paper, complete the following activities.

Identifying People and Ideas

Describe the historical significance of the following:

1. Richard Nixon
2. stagflation
3. Strategic Arms Limitation Talks
4. Watergate
5. Barbara Jordan
6. Jimmy Carter
7. apartheid
8. Iran hostage crisis
9. Earth Day
10. Environmental Protection Agency

Internet Activity

go.hrw.com
SB1 Wildlife Preserves

Search the Internet through the HRW Web site to locate wildlife preserves in the United States. Create a map with shaded areas indicating the different kinds of wildlife preserves.

Understanding Main Ideas

1. How did President Nixon try to address the concerns of the Silent Majority?
2. How was Nixon's role in Watergate gradually revealed?
3. Why did many people consider Jimmy Carter to be an "outsider" to Washington politics?
4. How did President Carter help bring peace to the Middle East?
5. In what ways did popular films and music change during the 1970s?
6. What actions did the federal government take to improve the environment in the 1970s?

Reviewing Themes

1. **Economic Development** How did U.S. dependence on foreign oil affect the economy during the mid-1970s?
2. **Citizenship and Democracy** How did Watergate affect the presidency?
3. **Global Relations** How did President Carter's foreign-policy approach differ from that of President Nixon?

Using the Time Line

Number your paper from 1 to 6. Match the letters on the time line below with the following events.

1. **Begin, Carter, and Sadat sign the Camp David Accords.**
2. **The Yom Kippur War begins.**
3. **An accident takes place at a nuclear power plant on Three Mile Island, Pennsylvania.**
4. **Jimmy Carter wins the presidency.**
5. **President Nixon announces his resignation.**
6. **The first Earth Day is celebrated.**

1968   1970   1972   1974   1976   1978   1980
         a   b   c   d   e f

Thinking Critically

1. **Supporting a Point of View**   Which do you think would have been better for the nation—pardoning President Nixon for Watergate or trying him in a court of law? Explain your answer.

2. **Synthesizing Information**   How did Presidents Nixon, Ford, and Carter try to improve economic conditions during the 1970s?

3. **Identifying Cause and Effect**   How did President Nixon's opening of relations with China affect U.S. relations with the Soviet Union?

Writing About History

1. **Expressing**   Imagine that you are a citizen writing a letter to the editor after Nixon's resignation. Express how the Watergate scandal has affected your view of the federal government and why.

Building Your Portfolio

Complete the following activities individually or in groups.

1. **Recruiting Residents**   Imagine that you are an official of a Sun Belt city hoping to attract new residents. Design a booklet advertising your city and region. Determine what advantages your city offers and include information about subjects such as business and industry, housing costs, taxes, cultural resources, recreation, and the crime rate. As part of your sales pitch, draw a general map of the city, highlighting places you think will be attractive to new residents.

2. **Celebrating Earth Day**   Create a poster and leaflets that might be used for the next Earth Day celebration. On your poster, use art or photographs to show why Earth Day is important. In the leaflets, persuade people to work to preserve the environment and explain how to accomplish that goal.

2. **Persuading**   Imagine that you are a U.S. State Department official. Write a memo to your superior explaining which foreign-policy approach—Nixon's or Carter's—would be the most successful and why.

Linking Geography and History

1. **Human-Environment Interaction**   Why do some environmental activists attempt to stop building projects?

2. **Movement**   What effects did migration to the Sun Belt have on the region and the rest of the United States?

History Skills Workshop

Using Visual Resources   Study the cartoon below, which shows President Ford and a snake. Then answer the following questions: (a) What does the snake represent? (b) What is President Ford doing and why? (c) What do you think the cartoon's message is?

"You've got to admit we're getting Watergate behind us."

THE PARDON · COVER-UP · TRIAL · "TRANSITIONAL" EXPENSES · NIXON SUIT · TAPES

Draper Hill/ © 1974 *The Commercial Appeal, Memphis*

▫ CHAPTER 23 ▫
The Republican Years
(1980–1992)

In 1983 President Ronald Reagan called the Soviet Union the "focus of evil in the modern world." Yet when he met Soviet leader Mikhail Gorbachev (gawr-buh-CHAWF) in 1985, he liked him. Afterward Reagan said, "We've seen what the new Russian looks like. Now maybe we can figure out how to deal with him." At the time neither leader could have guessed that democratic reforms would soon sweep the Soviet Union.

THEMES

Economic Development
How might new U.S. economic policies affect Americans?

Global Relations
How might events in one nation lead to political changes in other nations?

Technology and Society
How might scientific advances lead to changes in daily life?

1980	1981	1982	1983	1984	1985

MAR. 1981
An assassin tries to kill President Reagan.

AUG. 1981 Congress passes the Economic Recovery Tax Act.

JUNE 1983
Sally Ride becomes the first American woman in space.

NOV. 1984
Ronald Reagan is elected to a second term as president.

The Reagan Years

Reading Focus

Why was President Reagan popular with American voters?

How did Reagan hope to balance the budget and improve the nation's economy?

In what ways did Reagan's economic policies affect Americans?

Key Terms

New Right
supply-side economics
Economic Recovery Tax Act
Gramm-Rudman-Hollings Act
Black Monday

DURING RONALD REAGAN'S *first week as president, he was eager to explore his new home, the White House. He flipped light switches, explored closets, and even paid a sudden visit to the kitchen, startling the cooks. One morning, to President Reagan's delight, the Marine Band played "Hail to the Chief" as he ate breakfast. Despite his joy in the moment, he joked with the musicians that he would not expect the performance every day. A Reagan aide explained that although the president was "impressed with the history of it all, . . . he's not overwhelmed." Reagan's obvious ease in his all-important position reassured many Americans.*

Ronald Reagan at his ranch in Santa Barbara, California

IMAGE ON LEFT PAGE: *President Reagan and Soviet leader Gorbachev in Moscow in 1988*

1986	1987	1988	1989	1990	1991	1992

JAN. 1986 The space shuttle *Challenger* explodes.

OCT. 1987 The U.S. stock market crashes.

NOV. 1989 Germans tear down the Berlin Wall.

FEB. 1991 The UN launches a ground attack in the Persian Gulf War.

DEC. 1991 The Commonwealth of Independent States is formed.

⭐ Reagan's Style

At age 69, Ronald Reagan was the oldest person ever elected president. His age and experience seemed to provide comfort for some Americans. One woman described the Reagan effect: "He made people feel good about being American." Reagan reassured Americans that better days were ahead for the United States. He was highly skilled at presenting this simple, yet effective message. After the Watergate scandal and the Iran hostage crisis, many Americans welcomed Reagan's message. His ability to motivate people through his speeches earned Reagan the nickname "The Great Communicator."

First Lady Nancy Reagan also paid attention to the image of the United States. In one of her first efforts, she decided to redecorate the White House. She believed that the residence needed to be updated to better entertain world leaders. She also decided to replace the official White House china set, which had many cracked and missing pieces. The White House "should be something very special," she explained.

Early in his first term Reagan showed how he used humor to put Americans at ease. In March 1981 John Hinckley Jr. tried to assassinate the president as he left a hotel after giving a speech. Hinckley fired several shots and hit Reagan, Press Secretary James Brady, a Secret Service agent, and a local police officer. Brady suffered permanent injury from the shooting. At the hospital, Reagan, although severely injured, reassured people around him with his humor. "Honey, I forgot to duck," he told his wife, Nancy.

Reagan recovered quickly from his injuries, and his popularity soared. One member of Congress remarked, "This [assassination attempt] is a long-term plus for Reagan. He has been through the fire and escaped."

Nancy Reagan selected new White House china in red, her favorite color.

⭐ The Rise of the Republicans

President Reagan received support from a conservative coalition, or alliance, of voters known as the **New Right**. This coalition included traditionally Republican voters, fundamentalist Christians, and so-called Reagan Democrats, who opposed some federal social programs. These conservatives wanted to limit the size of government and create a strong anticommunist foreign policy. Reagan supporters also wanted to decrease government regulation of business. Many members of the New Right opposed the Equal Rights Amendment and busing to achieve school integration. Most of them also supported capital punishment—the death penalty—and mandatory time for prayer in public schools.

Many conservative evangelicals joined the Moral Majority, a group led by minister Jerry Falwell. The Moral Majority wanted to organize people to achieve conservative Christian political goals. In describing the group's purpose, Falwell expressed the beliefs of many conservatives in the New Right:

❝ **Right living must be re-established as an American way of life. We as American citizens must recommit ourselves to the faith of our fathers. . . . We must be willing to live by the moral convictions we claim to believe.** ❞

Critics of the New Right complained that Falwell and his supporters defined "right living" in a narrow way. Throughout much of the 1980s, however, the New Right was an important influence on the Reagan presidency.

Like President Richard Nixon, Reagan wanted to appoint conservatives to the U.S. Supreme Court. In 1981 he appointed Sandra Day O'Connor, a conservative judge, as the first female Supreme Court justice. In the mid-1980s Reagan appointed Antonin Scalia and Anthony M. Kennedy. These appointments shifted the Court toward a more conservative outlook.

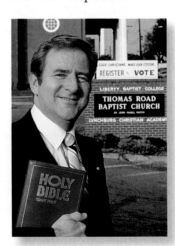

Jerry Falwell led a conservative religious group called the Moral Majority.

Ronald Reagan

Ronald Reagan was born in Tampico, Illinois, in 1911. He took a Hollywood screen test in 1937 and later became a popular actor. Reagan's experience in front of the camera would help him in politics.

Reagan twice served as president of his union, the Screen Actors Guild. At first, he was a Democrat. However, he became convinced that the party placed too much emphasis on social reform. Reagan switched to the Republican Party.

Reagan became involved in national politics in 1964, when he gave campaign speeches for Republican presidential candidate Barry Goldwater. Two years later, Reagan's combination of wit, positive thinking, and conservative politics helped him win election as governor of California. Reagan told voters, "It is time we ended our obsession with what is wrong, and realized how much is right." He carried this message with him to the White House.

Reagan also appointed several women to cabinet-level positions. Elizabeth Dole served as the secretary of transportation and Margaret Heckler served as secretary of health and human services. The decade marked a new trend as increasing numbers of conservative women entered politics.

★ Reagan's First Term

In his 1981 inaugural address President Reagan had expressed his views on the proper role of government:

 Government is not the solution to our problems; government is the problem. . . . It is not my intention to do away with government. It is, rather, to make it work—work with us, not over us. 〞

Reagan's main goals were to balance the federal budget, cut taxes, reduce regulations on business, and expand the military. He also wanted to scale back the size and role of the federal government. According to Republican senator Howard Baker, the Reagan administration had three immediate priorities:

To reduce the deficit, Americans needed to buy goods made in the United States.

"economic recovery, economic recovery, and economic recovery."

Reagan's economic policies, which became known as Reaganomics, rested on an idea called **supply-side economics**. According to this economic theory, the government could eventually balance the budget by cutting taxes. A tax cut would increase personal income and business profits. People would then save or invest this extra income, thus expanding the economy and creating new jobs. Over time this increase in business activity would produce greater tax revenues. With more money coming in to the federal government, Congress would be able to balance the budget.

Tax Cuts and a New Budget

Congress passed the **Economic Recovery Tax Act** (ERTA) in August 1981. The act reduced personal income taxes by 25 percent. The ERTA also cut some other taxes. In total, the tax reduction amounted to some $750 billion. The wealthiest Americans received the greatest tax relief.

To help offset short-term reductions in tax revenues, Congress agreed to cut $500 billion from social programs over a five-year period. These programs included school lunches, unemployment

U.S. Defense Spending, 1945–1995

Source: *Statistical Abstract of the United States*

The Price of the Cold War The United States spent billions of dollars on national defense during the Cold War. During what five-year period did defense spending increase the most?

compensation, low-income housing, and the National Endowments for the Arts and Humanities. Congress did not, however, reduce overall spending on some of the most significant social welfare programs. For example, spending for Social Security rose significantly during Reagan's presidency.

The Reagan administration and Congress also spent more money to increase U.S. military capabilities. From 1981 to 1985, defense spending increased from about $134 billion to some $250 billion. Over time, defense and other federal spending greatly exceeded new tax revenues and budget cuts. As a result, the deficit—the amount by which a government's borrowing and expenditures exceed its revenues—increased dramatically. During Reagan's presidency, the national debt grew from less than $1 trillion to more than $2.6 trillion.

Recession

Early in Reagan's presidency, the nation experienced an economic recession. Heavy industries like steel and automobiles were losing sales to foreign competitors. For example, in 1982, Japanese cars accounted for more than 20 percent of all auto sales in the United States. This figure was 4 percent in 1970. In 1982 the United States imported almost $25 billion more in goods and services than it exported. By 1988 this trade deficit grew to about $150 billion.

As a result, companies began laying off thousands of workers. For example, in 1981 the American automobile industry laid off more than 200,000 workers, about 25 percent of its workforce. In 1982 and 1983, about 10 percent of American workers were out of a job.

The PATCO Strike

Some federal workers took action in response to the bad economic news. Members of the Professional Air Traffic Controllers Organization (PATCO) were dissatisfied with a new contract offer. In August 1981 they went on strike. Union members were violating a ban that prohibited federal employees from striking.

In response, President Reagan fired some 12,000 striking controllers. He told his aides, "The law says they can't strike. By striking they've quit their jobs." He also prohibited the Federal Aviation

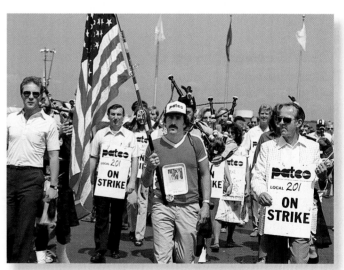

Air traffic controllers at the John F. Kennedy Airport in New York walked the picket line as part of a larger strike of air traffic controllers.

Administration (FAA) from ever rehiring these controllers. The training of new, nonunion controllers ended up costing more money than asked for by PATCO. Nevertheless, the president had won an important symbolic victory.

 ## The 1984 Election

By the time of the 1984 election, the economy had begun to turn around. The gross national product increased by almost 7 percent in 1984—its largest increase since 1951. Unemployment and inflation also dropped significantly. Many Americans gave President Reagan credit for the prosperous economy. The Republican Party nominated him for re-election. His campaign focused on the economic recovery with the slogan "It's Morning Again in America."

The Democratic Party chose Walter Mondale, Jimmy Carter's vice president, as its presidential candidate. Mondale selected Geraldine Ferraro as his running mate. She became the first woman to run for vice president on a major-party ticket. Ferraro told voters:

> " **By choosing an American woman to run for our nation's second-highest office, you send a powerful signal to all Americans. . . . We will place no limits on achievement. If we can do this, we can do *anything*.** "

Mondale's campaign claimed that Reagan's economic policies greatly favored the rich. In one advertisement, Mondale said, "I refuse to let your family pay more while millionaires pay less." In November 1984 Reagan won the election in a landslide, capturing 515 electoral votes to Mondale's 13. He became the first president since Dwight D. Eisenhower to serve two complete terms.

 ## The Financial World

After the election, the federal deficit continued to rise. To control future deficits, Congress passed the **Gramm-Rudman-Hollings Act** in December 1985. The law required the government to cut spending when the deficit grew above a certain level. Yet the nation's total debt continued to grow. A 1986 tax cut contributed to its growth. The tax cut further reduced the tax rate for the wealthiest Americans and lowered corporate taxes.

The tax cut helped some businesspeople make fortunes in the 1980s. Real-estate developer Donald Trump was one of them. Yuppies, or young urban professionals, were also part of this newly rich group. Many became wealthy by buying "junk" bonds, or bonds for companies that were risky investments. Financier Michael Milken pioneered the selling of these bonds. People could receive a large return on their investment if the companies succeeded. However, investors could lose their money if these risky businesses failed.

Milken and his associates raised almost $100 billion selling these bonds. They loaned this capital, or money, to investors who wanted to take over, or buy a controlling interest in, companies. One of the largest corporate transactions in financial history took place in 1988 when an investment firm purchased RJR Nabisco for $25 billion.

Ivan Boesky managed many corporate takeovers. He also summed up the attitude that many people had in the 1980s: "Greed is all right. . . . Everybody should be a little bit greedy." Boesky, however, proved to be a little too greedy. He paid for advance knowledge of mergers and takeovers. He used that information to buy and sell stocks, an illegal practice known as insider trading. Boesky and Milken both ended up in jail, convicted of illegal business activities.

Geraldine Ferraro was a U.S. representative from New York when she ran for vice president in 1984.

In the fall of 1987 even prosperous groups suffered. After reaching an all-time high in August, the stock market dropped more than 20 percent on October 19. The day became known as **Black Monday**. The market continued to drop, eventually losing some 40 percent of its value. Most economists had no clear explanation for the crash. Some blamed the crash on the rising federal deficit. Unlike the Panic of 1929, this stock market crash did not devastate the economy. The Federal Reserve helped stabilize the economy. One Wall Street broker remembered:

> **" It was bad the day the market crashed, but it wasn't as bad as most people think it was. . . . Good news, bad news, as long as there was news, we would make money. "**

On Black Monday, traders on the floor of the New York Stock Exchange tried to sell shares and cut losses.

 Reagan's Critics

Some of President Reagan's critics noted that the prosperity of the mid- to late 1980s did not include everyone. Reagan's budget director, David Stockman, promised that all Americans would eventually benefit from the effects of supply-side economics. However, he also admitted that the plan required "short-run pain in the name of long-run gain."

Farmers suffered both short- and long-term pain. They faced low prices for their products as well as falling land values. Many farmers had borrowed heavily. Some lost their land when they could not pay their debts.

Critics also pointed to the high unemployment rate among African Americans and Hispanics. The working poor—people who work, usually at unskilled positions, but do not earn enough to live above poverty level—also faced difficulties. The reductions in federal social welfare programs deeply affected these citizens. Nonetheless, many Americans believed that they were better off during the 1980s.

SECTION 1 REVIEW

Identify and explain the significance of the following:
- **Ronald Reagan**
- **New Right**
- **Jerry Falwell**
- **supply-side economics**
- **Economic Recovery Tax Act**
- **Walter Mondale**
- **Geraldine Ferraro**
- **Gramm-Rudman-Hollings Act**
- **Black Monday**

Reading for Content Understanding

1 **Main Idea** What qualities made President Reagan popular with many voters?

2 **Main Idea** In what ways did Reagan try to balance the budget and improve the economy?

3 **Economic Development** How were different groups in American society affected by Reagan's economic policies?

4 **Writing** *Describing* Imagine that you are Reagan's budget director. Write a two-paragraph speech describing supply-side economics for the president to present to Congress.

5 **Critical Thinking** *Synthesizing Information* How did political and economic events influence Reagan's election victories?

Reagan's Foreign Policy

Reading Focus

In what ways did the Reagan administration try to stop the spread of communism in Central America?

What actions led to the Iran-contra affair?

How did changes within the Soviet Union affect the Cold War?

Key Terms

Sandinistas

contras

Iran-contra affair

Strategic Defense Initiative

perestroika

glasnost

Intermediate-Range Nuclear Forces Treaty

*O*NE MORNING IN JANUARY 1981, *an Iranian guard told American hostage Barry Rosen, "Pack your bags. You're leaving." After 444 days in captivity, Rosen was blindfolded and marched onto a bus. When the bus stopped, he ripped off his blindfold and ran toward the airplane he saw. The plane carried the hostages home. In the United States, Rosen and the other hostages were greeted as heroes. According to Rosen, "In some ways, I think the people were celebrating what they believed was American power." For many Americans, President Ronald Reagan was the symbol of that power.*

In Washington, D.C., Americans celebrate the release of the hostages in Iran.

 ## Foreign-Policy Challenges

Many Americans believed that the prolonged Iranian hostage crisis had damaged the international reputation of the United States. President Reagan was determined to restore the public's sense of confidence and security. To demonstrate U.S. strength, he supported increased defense spending and military intervention.

Reagan also vigorously opposed communism. He saw the Cold War as a fight of "good versus evil, right versus wrong." The president and his

advisers placed a priority on stopping the spread of communism. Jeane Kirkpatrick, U.S. ambassador to the United Nations (UN), explained Reagan's policy. The Reagan administration refused to support governments it saw as totalitarian, or controlling every aspect of its citizens' lives. However, the administration was willing to support governments with questionable human rights practices if those governments strongly opposed communism.

In October 1983 Reagan sent U.S. troops to overthrow the pro-communist government of

Grenada, a tiny island in the Caribbean Sea. The U.S. mission was short and successful. Reagan hoped that it would encourage Americans to support anticommunist efforts in Central America. The Reagan administration considered stopping the spread of communism in Central America important to U.S. national security.

The U.S. position on El Salvador was particularly complicated. During President Carter's administration, the U.S. government had supported the Salvadoran government in a civil war against communist revolutionaries. The Salvadoran government allowed "death squads" to kill anyone who opposed its cause. In 1980 some 10,000 people were killed. Three American nuns and another American volunteer were among those killed. In response, Carter halted all U.S. aid to El Salvador. In one of his last actions as president, however, Carter renewed aid to El Salvador. He feared that the guerrilla forces would overthrow the government.

Soon after taking office, President Reagan approved $20 million in aid for El Salvador's government. The U.S. government shipped arms and supplies to El Salvador. Some Salvadoran soldiers came to the United States for training. In addition, U.S. military advisers went to El Salvador. During the 1980s the United States provided some $4 billion in aid to El Salvador's government.

★ U.S. Policy in Nicaragua

The United States was also involved in Nicaraguan affairs. In 1979 a revolutionary Nicaraguan political party known as the **Sandinistas** had overthrown its country's pro-American dictator. Sandinista Daniel Ortega became the country's new leader.

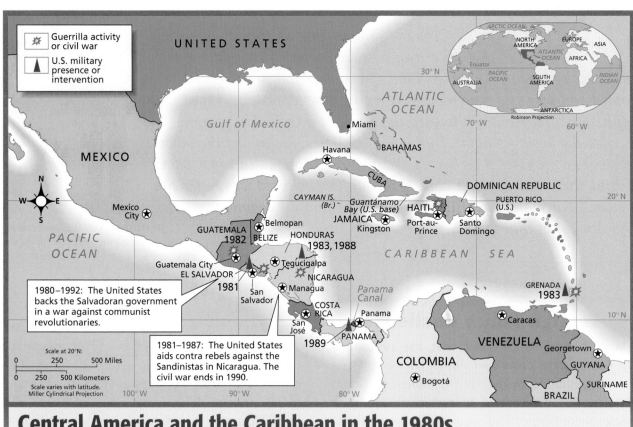

Central America and the Caribbean in the 1980s

Learning from Maps The United States played an active role in the political and military affairs of several countries in Central America and the Caribbean.

Place In which Central American and Caribbean countries did the U.S. military maintain a presence or intervene during the 1980s?

Stopping Communism

The Reagan administration became convinced that the Sandinistas wanted to set up a communist dictatorship. President Reagan worried that if this happened, Central American nations would fall to communism.

In early 1981 the U.S. government demanded that the Nicaraguans stop helping "their revolutionary brothers" in El Salvador. The United States suspended some $15 million in economic aid and millions of dollars of wheat shipments to Nicaragua. Reagan also decided to support anti-Sandinista Nicaraguan rebels known as **contras**. He signed a national security order that provided the Central Intelligence Agency (CIA) with nearly $20 million. The CIA used this money to secretly recruit, train, arm, and pay the contras. By 1985 the contras' fighting force numbered some 20,000.

The CIA provided military aid to the contras.

In 1982 this secret operation against the Sandinista government became public knowledge. Some Americans feared that a war against communism in Nicaragua would turn into a drawn-out conflict like that in Vietnam. In response, Congress passed a series of measures banning U.S. assistance for the overthrow of the Sandinista government. The Boland Amendment of 1984 prohibited any U.S. government agency, including the CIA, from providing military aid to the contras.

The Iran-Contra Affair

In the mid-1980s, issues surrounding contra aid became a wider controversy. Pro-Iranian terrorists in Lebanon had taken some Americans hostage. In secret dealings, the terrorists offered to free the hostages. In return, they demanded that the United States sell arms—including ammunition and missiles—to Iran. A trade of arms for hostages would violate U.S. policy against dealing with terrorists. Therefore, the plan called for Israel to pass the weapons to Iran. The United States would then resupply Israel's weapons.

Oliver North, a U.S. Marine lieutenant colonel who served as a national security aide, arranged

Contra rebels train for their military effort against the Sandinistas.

the secret deal. In 1986 North passed some of the profits from the weapon sales to the contras. His actions violated the Boland Amendment. One man who assisted North explained why he helped:

> **They [the contras] looked to the United States for guidance and for help. We had been supplying them with beans and bullets and blankets and Band-Aids and boots. . . . With the signing of the Boland Amendment, the U.S. Congress was about to walk away. . . . I didn't believe that the United States could just let this happen.**

In the fall of 1986 the **Iran-contra affair**—the name given to the arms deal and resulting scandal—became public. After the story broke, Reagan said:

> **We did not—repeat—did not trade weapons or anything else for hostages nor will we. We . . . have had nothing to do with other countries or their shipment of arms.**

Many Americans doubted his denials. The Senate held hearings to investigate the Iran-contra affair. Members of Reagan's administration initially blamed North. Other people saw North as unfairly taking the blame for the incident.

The Senate hearings turned up no proof of illegal activity by the president. However, North and other White House officials were convicted of crimes associated with the Iran-contra affair. A court later overturned many of the convictions on technical grounds.

U.S. Marines in Lebanon dig through the remains of their barracks after they were bombed by terrorists.

⭐ U.S. Troops in Lebanon

Other foreign-policy actions taken by the Reagan administration included sending U.S. Marines to Lebanon. The U.S. troops were part of a multinational force. They arrived in 1982 to keep the peace between Lebanon and Israel. However, not everyone wanted the troops there. In April 1983, explosions tore apart the U.S. Embassy in Beirut, Lebanon's capital. The explosions killed 63 people, including 17 Americans. In October some Muslim fundamentalists drove a truck loaded with dynamite into the U.S. Marine headquarters compound. The resulting blast killed 241 marines.

In a televised address, President Reagan told the story of a marine wounded in Lebanon. Unable to speak, the soldier wrote the Marine Corps motto, "*Semper fi* [always faithful]," on a piece of paper. Reagan tried to tell the story numerous times before he was able to complete it without becoming too emotional. He used the story to celebrate the courage of the troops.

Yet problems in Lebanon continued. In February 1984 Reagan ordered the U.S. Marines out of Lebanon. Later that year terrorists bombed the newly rebuilt U.S. Embassy in Beirut. The terrorists wanted the United States out of Beirut completely.

⭐ U.S.-Soviet Relations

In addition to these problems in the Middle East, the United States faced continuing Cold War pressures. During his first term, President Reagan saw the Soviet Union as an "evil empire." Therefore, he greatly expanded the U.S. defense budget. In addition, he supported the development of the **Strategic Defense Initiative** (SDI). This defense system was designed to shoot down Soviet missiles in space with laser weapons. Critics referred to the SDI as Star Wars. Congress approved $26 billion to develop the SDI, but scientists never produced a workable version of the system.

Political changes in the Soviet Union eventually softened Reagan's hard-line stand in the Cold War. In the early 1980s, three consecutive Soviet leaders died. When Mikhail Gorbachev became the Soviet leader in 1985, a new era of U.S.-Soviet relations began. Gorbachev realized that the Soviet Union was in desperate economic trouble. The country's economy suffered as it tried to keep up with the United States in the nuclear arms race. Gorbachev said, "We cannot remain a major power

The Strategic Defense Initiative was designed to work as a shield protecting the United States from Soviet missiles.

Many Soviets welcomed Mikhail Gorbachev's reforms.

Soviet writer Chengiz Aitmatov described Gorbachev, the new Soviet hero:

❝ Now comes a man who has stirred up the sleeping kingdom. He . . . arose from within this very system, possibly as our last chance of survival. . . . He dared, it would seem, the impossible—a revolution of minds.❞

in world affairs unless we put our domestic house in order." He began a series of political and economic reforms, known as **perestroika**, to restructure the economy. He also started a policy called **glasnost**, or freedom of expression.

To achieve these goals, Gorbachev needed to stabilize international relations. He also had to reduce defense spending and attract Western investment. He decided to reduce Soviet support for communist nations and to dismantle the Soviet "empire" in Eastern Europe. He also worked to reach new arms agreements with the United States.

For the first time since the earliest days of the Soviet state, the Soviet Union held free elections. These changes excited many Soviet citizens.

In November 1985 Reagan met with Gorbachev. The leaders held four different summit meetings to discuss nuclear arms reductions. In Iceland the men discussed cutting strategic nuclear forces in half.

In December 1987 the two leaders signed the **Intermediate-Range Nuclear Forces (INF) Treaty**. This treaty eliminated all medium-range nuclear weapons from Europe. The INF Treaty was the first to require the destruction of nuclear missiles. Cold War tensions between the United States and the Soviet Union appeared to be lessening. When asked if he still considered the Soviet Union to be an evil empire, Reagan responded, "No, I was talking about another time, another era."

Pershing II missiles were removed from Europe.

SECTION 2 REVIEW

Identify and explain the significance of the following:
- Sandinistas
- contras
- Iran-contra affair
- Strategic Defense Initiative
- Mikhail Gorbachev
- perestroika
- glasnost
- Intermediate-Range Nuclear Forces Treaty

Reading for Content Understanding

1 Main Idea How did the United States attempt to prevent communism from spreading in Central America?

2 Main Idea Make a graphic organizer of the events that led to the Iran-contra affair.

3 Global Relations What political changes took place in the Soviet Union in the 1980s?

4 Writing *Informing* Imagine that you are a U.S. State Department official. Write a memorandum explaining how Mikhail Gorbachev's reforms have led to a decrease in Cold War tensions.

5 Critical Thinking *Determining the Strength of an Argument* Why do you think President Reagan argued that Central America was an important national security concern?

George Bush's Presidency

Reading Focus

What were some of President Bush's major domestic actions?

What events led to the final breakup of the Soviet Union?

What caused the Persian Gulf War, and how did the conflict end?

Key Terms

War on Drugs
Americans with Disabilities Act
Commonwealth of Independent States
Operation Desert Storm

*T*HE BRANDENBURG GATE *was originally built in the late 1700s as an entrance to the city of Berlin. Since 1961 the Berlin Wall had surrounded the gate. Instead of being an opening, the gate helped to close off Soviet-supported East Berlin. Standing at the gate in 1987, President Reagan asked Mikhail Gorbachev to show his commitment to democratizing efforts in Eastern Europe. Reagan shouted, "If you seek liberalization, come here to this gate. Mr. Gorbachev, open this gate! Mr. Gorbachev, tear down this wall!"*

The Brandenburg Gate

★ The Election of 1988

As President Reagan's vice president, George Bush benefited from Reagan's popular tough stance on communism. In 1988 the Republican Party nominated Bush for president. Republicans hoped that he would appeal to Reagan supporters. However, some Americans did not think Bush was as effective a communicator as Reagan.

The Democrats had a difficult time selecting a candidate. Many challengers entered the presidential primaries, including African American civil rights leader Jesse Jackson. No one, though,

clearly led the field. By the end of the primary season, Massachusetts governor Michael Dukakis had won the most presidential delegates. He became the Democratic nominee for president. Dukakis chose Senator Lloyd Bentsen of Texas as his running mate.

Bush selected Dan Quayle, a young, little-known senator from Indiana, as his running mate. During the campaign, Bush vowed to support no new taxes. He told American voters, "Read my lips: no new taxes." He also promised a "kinder, gentler America." The election battle itself, however, was bitter and hard fought. In November,

The Republican team in 1988 (from left to right): Marilyn Quayle, Dan Quayle, George Bush, and Barbara Bush

Bush won the presidency with 426 electoral votes to Dukakis's 111.

The Savings and Loan Crisis

Public awareness of a savings and loan (S&L) crisis was one of the first issues that President Bush faced. Traditionally, S&L financial institutions accepted savings from individuals and invested their deposits in mortgages. During the Reagan years, the government had lifted restrictions on the types of investments S&Ls could make. As a result, some S&Ls rapidly expanded their lending. Many S&L owners invested recklessly in the stock market, commercial real estate, and "junk" bonds.

In some cases, bank officials acted fraudulently. They used their clients' deposits to buy themselves yachts, mansions, and corporate jets. When the stock market crashed in 1987, many S&Ls went bankrupt. Reagan's last economic report to the nation concluded, "The irony is that Federal Government policies have led to this debacle [general collapse]."

Many of these failing S&Ls were in Texas and other Sun Belt states. Texas financial institutions had made bad loans to real estate and oil entrepreneurs. As the price of oil dropped, these people were unable to repay their loans. The S&Ls then did not have the money

The ADA helps many Americans gain greater access to educational facilities.

to pay their depositors. However, the federal government insured depositors' savings in S&Ls up to $100,000 per account.

In August 1989 President Bush authorized $166 billion to close or merge many S&Ls. The S&L crisis, the federal deficit, and the need to balance the federal budget forced Bush to break his campaign pledge. In 1990 he agreed to a significant tax increase.

Bush's Domestic Policies

President Bush also responded to other domestic issues. In 1989 he launched a **War on Drugs**—an organized effort at home and abroad to end the trade and use of illegal drugs. As part of the War on Drugs, the Bush administration supported drug treatment centers and education programs. The effort also used law enforcement to end the drug trade. U.S. officials offered legal assistance and financial aid to help foreign nations arrest major drug smugglers. In December 1989 Bush authorized a military invasion of Panama to capture the country's dictator, Manuel Noriega. He was charged with drug smuggling. In 1992 a U.S. federal court convicted Noriega and sent him to prison.

Other domestic programs included an update of the Clean Air Act. This 1990 law required a reduction in the emission, or release, of ozone-destroying chemicals.

That same year the president approved the **Americans with Disabilities Act** (ADA). The ADA guaranteed people with disabilities equal access to public accommodations, transportation, and employment opportunities. Congress estimated that the act would affect many millions of Americans.

Bush had more difficulty with one of his nominations to the U.S. Supreme Court. In 1990 the Senate

Global Connections

The Fall of the Berlin Wall

Encouraged by new freedoms in the Soviet Union, many East Germans began to demand similar rights for themselves. These demands eventually led to the destruction of the Berlin Wall. East Germans filled the streets of East Berlin in 1989 to protest rules that restricted free movement. Eventually, the East German government withdrew its restrictions on crossing into the West.

Thousands of people gathered for the opening of the gates. At the designated hour of midnight, they streamed into the western side. Celebrators began to dismantle the wall piece by piece. A woman striking blows against the crumbling wall said, "This one's for my mother, [and] this one's for Aunt Frieda." She claimed that the wall had destroyed her family. Other people danced on top of the wall. Some chanted, "The Wall is gone, the Wall is gone." Members of the West German Green Party suggested that the process of breaking down the wall be halted until a waste management program could be administered. Most

Removing the Berlin Wall

Germans, however, felt that the wall had stood too long. They did not wait for a trash system to be designed.

The fall of the Berlin Wall—perhaps the most fearsome symbol of communist rule in Eastern Europe—inspired people in many parts of the world. Hundreds of South Koreans living in West Berlin witnessed the emotional celebration at the wall. The event recalled bittersweet memories of their own still-divided country. One American observer was so moved by the wall's destruction that he declared, "It [removal of the wall] shows the indomitability [strength] of the human spirit."

Understanding What You Read

1. How and why was the Berlin Wall torn down?

2. Do you think that the fall of the Berlin Wall demonstrates "the indomitability of the human spirit"? Explain your answer.

---

easily confirmed David Souter's appointment. The next year Justice Thurgood Marshall, the first African American appointed to the Court, retired. Bush nominated Clarence Thomas, an African American federal judge, to fill Marshall's seat. During the confirmation process, law professor Anita Hill accused Thomas of sexual harassment, or unwanted sexual language or behavior in the workplace. Hill had worked with Thomas at the Equal Employment Opportunity Commission.

Thomas and Hill testified before the Senate in the televised confirmation hearings. The Senate narrowly confirmed Thomas by a vote of 52 to 48. The hearings ignited a national debate. Many women were angry that there were no female senators on the Senate committee. Senate Judiciary Committee chairman Joe Biden summed up the Senate's handling of the hearings, "The judge was wronged, Anita Hill was wronged, the process was wronged."

The End of the Cold War

Meanwhile, dramatic changes continued to sweep the Soviet Union. Soviet leader Mikhail Gorbachev pushed for even greater reforms. President Bush quietly encouraged these changes, and the country moved closer toward democracy.

Independence

Gradually, some Soviet republics—Estonia, Latvia, and Lithuania—declared their independence. In 1989 changes in the countries of Eastern Europe—Bulgaria, Czechoslovakia, East Germany, Hungary, Poland, and Romania—also began to occur more rapidly. Political and civil freedoms increased. East Germans found it easier to leave their country.

By the fall, nearly 250,000 people—almost 300 an hour—had left. Faced with this emigration explosion, East Germany's government officially opened its borders.

In November 1989 pro-democracy activists began tearing down the Berlin Wall. An American student living in West Berlin at the time described the historic moment:

A piece of the Berlin Wall

❝ **For . . . [East Germans] this was a day of newfound freedom. . . . There was also a feeling that the rules had changed—that people did not need police or armies or government, even if just for one day.** ❞

In October 1990 West Germany and East Germany officially reunited. After the Berlin Wall fell, anticommunist revolutions continued throughout Eastern Europe.

The Collapse of the Soviet Union

Demands for democracy also intensified in the Soviet Union. In November 1990 the United States, the Soviet Union, and many European nations signed a treaty of security and cooperation. The Cold War was over.

Many Soviet republics declared independence. As hard-line Communists watched their nation dissolve, one military group made a desperate move to stop the reforms. In August 1991 the group took Gorbachev hostage. Military leaders ordered troops into the streets of Moscow to put down protests. Instead, crowds of people filled the streets. Pro-democracy leader Boris Yeltsin encouraged the people to stand strong and resist. Many soldiers joined the crowd and promised to fight for democracy. The hard-line Communists recognized their defeat and recalled the troops. Soon after, the Soviet Union disbanded. In December 1991 many of the former Soviet republics formed an alliance, the **Commonwealth of Independent States**.

Many people believed that the buildup of the U.S. military under President Reagan had played a decisive role in winning the Cold War. These observers argued that the Soviet Union's

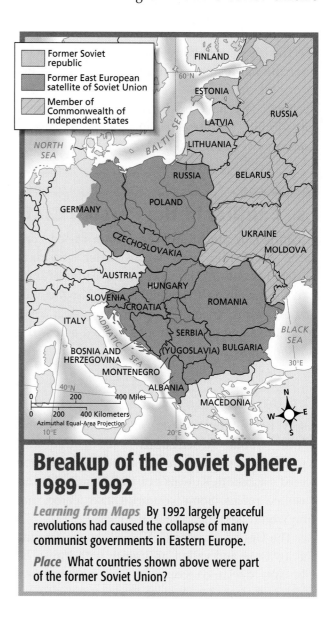

Breakup of the Soviet Sphere, 1989–1992

Learning from Maps By 1992 largely peaceful revolutions had caused the collapse of many communist governments in Eastern Europe.

Place What countries shown above were part of the former Soviet Union?

Standing on top of a tank, Boris Yeltsin (center, with papers) asks the Russian people to resist the military leaders who took Mikhail Gorbachev hostage.

attempt to keep up with increased U.S. defense spending had destroyed the Soviet economy. With the government unable to provide its citizens with jobs and food, the Soviet people had demanded democratic reforms.

The breakup of the Soviet Union transformed international relations. President Bush voiced his hope for newfound peace and stability. He declared, "We have before us the opportunity to forge [build] for ourselves and for future generations a new world order."

★ Conflict in the Persian Gulf

A conflict in the Middle East soon raised concerns about this "new world order." Saddam Hussein (sah-DAHM hoo-SAYN), the leader of Iraq, had long claimed that neighboring Kuwait was actually a province of Iraq. On August 2, 1990, Iraqi tanks and ground troops poured across the border into Kuwait.

The Beginnings of War

Many nations depend on oil from Kuwait and Saudi Arabia, which borders both Iraq and Kuwait. Iraq's invasion threatened to limit the world's access to Kuwait's oil and to raise oil and gasoline prices. Some countries also feared that Iraq would next invade Saudi Arabia.

The United Nations (UN) quickly condemned the invasion and called on Iraq to withdraw. The UN also declared economic sanctions banning trade with Iraq. On August 7, U.S. troops began arriving in Saudi Arabia to protect the country. The next day President Bush explained to the American public why he was involving the United States in a faraway conflict:

❝ **In the life of a nation, we're called upon to define who we are and what we believe. Sometimes these choices are not easy. But today as President, I ask for your support in a decision I've made to stand up for what's right and condemn what's wrong.** ❞

Troops from 27 other nations eventually joined the U.S. forces in a UN military coalition.

While fighting in Kuwait and Saudi Arabia, U.S. and UN troops wore uniforms designed to help them blend in with the desert sand.

The UN gave Iraq until January 15, 1991, to remove its troops from Kuwait. Bush warned Saddam Hussein, "A line has been drawn in the sand. . . . Withdraw from Kuwait unconditionally and immediately, or face the terrible consequences." Many Americans supported this policy. One journalist wrote, "Like all bullies [Saddam Hussein] will in the end be deterred [stopped] only by superior force."

Operation Desert Storm

When the Iraqi forces did not withdraw from Kuwait by the deadline, the UN coalition launched **Operation Desert Storm**. During this offensive, airplanes dropped bombs and missiles on Iraq for six weeks. On February 23, the UN coalition launched a massive ground invasion into Kuwait and Iraq. U.S. Army general Norman Schwarzkopf (SHWAWRTS-kawf) commanded the UN troops. UN forces soon freed Kuwait from Iraqi control. Just four days after the invasion, Bush ordered a cease-fire. The United States had lost some 150 soldiers in battle. An estimated 100,000 Iraqi soldiers and civilians had died.

The Persian Gulf War made heroes out of both Schwarzkopf and Colin Powell, chairman of the Joint Chiefs of Staff of the U.S. armed forces.

1 Jan. 16: Operation Desert Storm began with massive bombing of strategic targets in Iraq and Kuwait.

2 Deployment of U.S. Marines off the coast made the Iraqis expect a landing there.

3 Iraqis set oil fields and storage tanks ablaze and pumped oil into the Persian Gulf in an effort to foul a Saudi water plant.

4 Feb. 23: The four-day ground war began.

5 Feb. 25: Iraqi Scud missile killed 28 U.S. service personnel in their barracks.

6 Feb. 26: Helicopters brought in the 101st Air Assault Division to block the escape of Iraqi forces.

7 Feb. 27: President Bush announced that the allies had liberated Kuwait City and would cease fire.

Legend:
- UN allied forces
- Neutral countries
- U.S. base
- UN bombing
- Scud missile attack
- Iraqi nuclear site
- UN advance
- Iraqi forces
- U.S. naval vessels
- Oil field

The 1991 Persian Gulf War

Learning from Maps After more than a month of bombing, the UN coalition forces ended the Persian Gulf War with a brief ground offensive.

Movement From which country did most of the UN troops advance during the ground war?

General Powell was the highest-ranking African American to have served in the U.S. military. Even before the cease-fire, Powell had confidence in the coalition forces:

❝I had no doubt that we would be successful. We had the troops, the weapons, and the plan. What I did not know was how long it would take, and how many of our troops would not be coming home.❞

The U.S. government prohibited women from taking part in combat as fighter pilots or ground soldiers. However, more than 35,000 American women served in the Gulf War. One female soldier, a medical officer assigned to a combat unit, recalled, "I wasn't afraid that I would panic in combat or fail to do my job; I knew I could do it." After the Persian Gulf War, the debate over whether to expand the role of women in combat intensified. In December 1991 Congress voted to allow women to serve as combat pilots.

For many Americans, the victory in the Persian Gulf War eased some of the painful memories from the Vietnam War. However, the war did not completely resolve the situation in Iraq. Hussein reaffirmed his authority despite heavy economic

In the Persian Gulf War, female soldiers were not allowed in combat positions.

sanctions following Iraq's military defeat. The Iraqi leader also failed to keep some of the cease-fire terms. For example, he prevented the UN from finding and destroying Iraq's remaining weapons of mass destruction. The situation in Iraq remained unstable throughout the 1990s.

SECTION 3 REVIEW

Identify and explain the significance of the following:
- **George Bush**
- **Michael Dukakis**
- **War on Drugs**
- **Americans with Disabilities Act**
- **Commonwealth of Independent States**
- **Saddam Hussein**
- **Operation Desert Storm**
- **Norman Schwarzkopf**
- **Colin Powell**

Reading for Content Understanding

1 **Main Idea** What domestic issues did President Bush tackle?

2 **Main Idea** Create a flowchart that describes the events leading to the collapse of the Soviet Union.

3 **Geographic Diversity** *Region* Which nations border Kuwait, and what important natural resource do they have?

4 **Writing** *Expressing* Imagine that you are a historian who is writing a brief account of the Persian Gulf War. Write two paragraphs on the war's causes and outcomes.

5 **Critical Thinking** *Drawing Conclusions* What do you think might have happened if the United States had not taken a stand against Iraq? Give reasons to support your answer.

Technology and Culture

Reading Focus

What important advances were made in medical research and space exploration in the 1980s?

What new technological advances occurred in the 1980s?

How did music and movies change in the 1980s?

Key Terms

Acquired Immune Deficiency Syndrome
genetic engineering
Challenger
compact discs

I N THE EARLY 1980s *scientists inserted the gene that produces human insulin into E. coli. This bacterial microorganism lives in humans' intestines. The scientists then manipulated the genes of the E. coli. The bacteria became capable of producing human insulin for diabetics. In 1982 scientist Robert Sinsheimer encouraged others to examine the possible effects of this ability to manipulate genes, the basic building blocks of human life. He worried that people were interfering with nature. He asked three crucial questions: "Is it safe? Is it wise? Is it moral?"*

Colored electron micrograph of E. coli

★ Medical Research

In 1981, scientists first reported the disease known as **Acquired Immune Deficiency Syndrome** (AIDS). Caused by the human immunodeficiency virus (HIV), AIDS forces the body's immune system to shut down. The probability increases that victims will contract other illnesses, such as pneumonia, and die.

In the early 1980s, AIDS spread quickly and threatened to become an epidemic. By the end of the decade an estimated 1 to 1.5 million Americans were infected with the virus. By 1997 the number

of deaths from AIDS in the United States had reached more than 385,000. Scientists tried to find a cure or drug therapies to stop the disease.

By the end of the 1980s, medical researchers had also determined the causes of other diseases, including cystic fibrosis, muscular dystrophy, and some cancers. Some scientists thought that **genetic engineering**, the deliberate altering of genes, could prevent many diseases from developing in individuals. The biological office of the U.S. Department of Energy created the Human Genome Project to advance such research. The goal of the project is to "map" the human genome, the complete set of genetic material. The genome is made up of about 60,000 to 100,000 genes. The project has sparked worldwide interest and involves an international network of genetic researchers.

The Space Shuttle

New scientific advances also occurred in space exploration. In 1981 NASA launched the world's first space shuttle, a cost-saving reusable spacecraft. The shuttle is launched as a rocket. While in orbit, it operates like a typical spacecraft. When the shuttle returns to Earth, however, it lands like an airplane on a runway. During the 1980s NASA sent several different space shuttles into orbit.

On a space shuttle mission in June 1983, scientist and astronaut Sally Ride became the first American woman to fly into outer space. After the voyage she noted that what she would "remember most about the flight was that it was fun. In fact, I'm sure it was the most fun that I'll ever have in my life."

In 1984 NASA opened the space program to include selected civilians on its missions. Social studies teacher Christa McAuliffe was the first person chosen for this honor. She explained her interest in the space program:

> " I remember the excitement in my home when the first satellites were launched. . . . I watched the Space Age being born and I would like to participate."

Seconds after the flight carrying McAuliffe lifted off in January 1986, a small cloud of smoke escaped from the space shuttle *Challenger*. A little over a minute into the flight, the shuttle exploded and fell toward Earth. The NASA announcer reported that there was "obviously, a major malfunction." All seven crew members aboard *Challenger* were killed. Millions of people watched the horrifying event on live television. An investigation later concluded that the explosion had begun in the fuel tank. An O-ring, a tiny sealing ring, had failed. NASA worked for more than two years to improve the shuttle. In September 1988 NASA successfully launched the space shuttle *Discovery*.

Technological Developments

Technological advances during the 1980s affected many areas of society. New inventions changed the way people lived, worked, and played.

Personal Computers

In the 1980s the personal computer (PC) became a popular household item. The market for PCs began to grow after IBM produced its first PC in 1981. With aggressive marketing, IBM's PC sales climbed in three years from 25,000 to 3 million. Most of these PCs used a basic operating system called MS-DOS. This software was created

An early computer mouse from the late 1960s

by American programmer Bill Gates. The company Gates founded, Microsoft, was the world's first personal computer software business. It soon became the largest software company in the world.

In 1984 Apple Computer introduced the Macintosh personal computer. These computers had an operating system that allowed people to use icons, or pictures, to perform many computer commands. The Macintosh also popularized the use of the "mouse," a device used to move a cursor across the computer screen. These

American artist George Segal created realistic, life-size sculptures for the cover of Time *magazine.*

American Literature

"Mother Tongue"
Amy Tan

Chinese American author Amy Tan

Amy Tan became famous in 1989 with her best-selling novel The Joy Luck Club. *She often writes about the lives and concerns of Asian American women. In this essay excerpt Tan explores what it meant to grow up hearing different patterns of language.*

I am a writer. And by that definition, I am someone who has always loved language. I am fascinated by language in daily life. . . .

Lately, I've been giving more thought to the kind of English my mother speaks. Like others, I have described it to people as "broken" or "fractured" English. . . .

. . . I was ashamed of her English. I believed that her English reflected the quality of what she had to say.

. . . It wasn't until 1985 that I finally began to write fiction. . . .

I later decided I should envision a reader for the stories I would write. And the reader I decided upon was my mother, because these were stories about mothers. So with this in mind . . .

I began to write stories using all the Englishes I grew up with: the English I spoke to my mother, which for lack of a better term might be described as "simple"; . . . my translation of her Chinese, which could certainly be described as "watered down"; and what I imagined to be her translation of her Chinese if she could speak in perfect English. . . . I wanted to capture . . . her intent, her passion, her imagery, the rhythms of her speech and the nature of her thoughts.

. . . I knew I had succeeded where it counted when my mother finished reading my book and gave me her verdict: "So easy to read."

Understanding Literature

1. What were the different ways that language was used in Amy Tan's household?

2. Do you think that hearing different languages when growing up would be an advantage or a disadvantage? Explain your answer.

"user-friendly" features were soon widely copied by other computer makers.

The potential influence of the personal computer was so great that in 1983 *Time* magazine chose a computer as Machine of the Year instead of the magazine's typical Man of the Year. By 1988 the sales of personal computers had reached 10 million. PCs had become an important part of many people's daily lives.

New Recording Inventions

The 1980s also saw the growth of the videocassette recorder (VCR). These machines allowed owners to program them to record TV shows. Most VCR owners, however, used them to play movie videotapes.

In the mid-1980s **compact discs**, or CDs, offered a new way

An early CD, or compact disc

to record and play music. This new technology created a clearer sound than possible on record albums or cassette tapes.

CDs were also used for storing huge quantities of data, such as the contents of an encyclopedia, on a single disc. These discs were usually "read-only memory," or CD–ROM. Beginning in 1985, CD–ROM drives were built into some personal computers. By the early 1990s the CD had almost made the long-playing record album, or LP, extinct.

Bruce Springsteen's Born in the U.S.A. *tour lasted 18 months. "The Boss" often performed for four hours.*

★ Music and Movies

The invention of compact discs helped rock music to continue its popularity. Bruce Springsteen was among the most popular performers of the 1980s. His 1984 recording *Born in the U.S.A.* sold more than 13 million copies in its first year and a half.

Springsteen also participated in some of the fund-raising musical events that became popular in the 1980s. Numerous musicians performed at Live Aid, a televised show of simultaneous concerts in London and Philadelphia. Live Aid was a fund-raiser for African famine relief. Some 1.5 billion people watched the show and pledged more than $40 million to help with relief efforts. One Live Aid organizer saw its appeal as a way for rock fans to participate in a good cause. The volunteer said, "The point is not problems. The point is, we can become winners."

Other musicians in the United States sponsored similar fund-raising concerts, called Farm Aid, to benefit American farmers. One concert supporter explained: "The main point of Farm Aid is to bring the plight [problems] of the American farmer to the attention of the nation."

Some movies in the mid-1980s also brought attention to the situation affecting farmers. These movies included *Places in the Heart, Country,* and *The River.* One of the most popular movie actors in the 1980s was Meryl Streep. She took on a different look, nationality, or accent in almost every one of her movie roles. Streep played a British woman, a Nazi concentration camp

survivor, and a Danish writer. Responding to a question about her use of accents, Streep responded, "I'm always baffled by this question. How could I play that part and talk like me?" Streep received six Academy Award nominations for Best Actress.

Science fiction, adventure, and fantasy movies also gained popularity. George Lucas and Steven Spielberg, working separately or together, made some of the most popular movies of the 1980s. Following the success of *Star Wars* in 1977, Lucas released two sequels—*The Empire Strikes Back,* in 1980, and *Return of the Jedi,* in 1983. Spielberg's movie *E.T.—The Extraterrestrial* told the story of friendship between a lonely boy on Earth and an alien from space. *E.T.* introduced the phrase "Phone home" to many Americans. Lucas and Spielberg worked together on an action-adventure series of movies with archaeologist Indiana Jones as the hero. These movies contained spectacular special effects made possible by the technical advances of the 1980s.

★ Trends in Television

The television industry was also experiencing change. Cable television first began in the late 1960s, but grew rapidly during the 1980s. With

In the movie E.T., *Elliott helps an alien find his way home, which is 3 million light-years away.*

cable television, television signals are sent to an antenna and then relayed by cable to paying customers. By the end of the 1980s, nearly 60 percent of American homes had cable service. The average number of cable channels had risen to nearly 30. Many channels focused on one type of programming. For example, Cable News Network (CNN), an all-news channel, debuted in 1980. Owner Ted Turner said he created CNN to "offer those who want it a choice." All-sports and all-movie channels also began broadcasting.

In the early 1980s MTV, a rock music cable channel, went on the air. This channel showed music videos, which were first made in the late 1970s to promote bands. MTV videos featured experimental editing styles that became popular in movies and television.

⭐ Sports in the 1980s

Television was also important to one of the biggest sporting events of the decade—the 1984 Summer Olympics held in Los Angeles, California. The American Broadcasting Company (ABC) paid some $225 million to broadcast the Games in

Mary Lou Retton received perfect scores in her last two events to win a gold medal.

the United States. An estimated 2 billion viewers worldwide watched the Games. One writer described the Summer Games as

❝ceremony and celebration, anticipation and achievement. For those who were there as participants and witnesses, the feeling and the images of that summer's fortnight [two weeks] will forever tarry [stay awhile] in memory.❞

One of the most memorable competitors was American sprinter and long jumper Carl Lewis. Lewis won four gold medals, matching Jesse Owens's accomplishments in the 1936 Olympics.

At age 16, U.S. gymnast Mary Lou Retton won five medals, including a gold in individual all-around gymnastics. Speaking of the Olympics, Retton said, "It was just like I dreamt it, the excitement, the tension, the crowd."

The competition, however, did not include all nations. The Soviet Union and some other communist nations boycotted the 1984 Summer Olympics. The 1988 Olympics in Seoul, South Korea, reflected the easing of Cold War tensions. The United States and the Soviet Union both participated for the first time since 1976.

SECTION 4 REVIEW

Identify and explain the significance of the following:

- **Acquired Immune Deficiency Syndrome**
- **genetic engineering**
- **Sally Ride**
- **Christa McAuliffe**
- *Challenger*
- **Bill Gates**
- **compact discs**
- **Meryl Streep**
- **Steven Spielberg**
- **Carl Lewis**

Reading for Content Understanding

1 **Main Idea** What new advances in medical research and space exploration were made in the 1980s?

2 **Main Idea** What were some of the trends in movies and music in the 1980s?

3 **Technology and Society** What new technological inventions became popular in the 1980s? How did they affect Americans?

4 **Writing** *Describing* Imagine that you are preparing a time capsule to be opened in 100 years. Write a description of the new entertainment technologies that were developed in the 1980s.

5 **Critical Thinking** *Drawing Conclusions* Why do you think an event like Live Aid was successful?

CHAPTER 23 REVIEW

Chapter Summary

During the 1980s President Reagan tried to improve the U.S. economy. He also fought against communism in Central America. He increased military spending, which encouraged political changes in the Soviet Union. President Bush presided over the end of the Cold War and the victory in the Persian Gulf War. New scientific and technological advances in the 1980s included the space shuttle, personal computers, and CDs. ■

On a separate sheet of paper, complete the following activities.

Identifying People and Ideas

Describe the historical significance of the following:

1. New Right
2. supply-side economics
3. Iran-contra affair
4. Mikhail Gorbachev
5. War on Drugs
6. Americans with Disabilities Act
7. Colin Powell
8. George Bush
9. *Challenger*
10. genetic engineering

go.hrw.com
SB1 End of the Cold War

Internet Activity

Search the Internet through the HRW Web site to find sites on the fall of the Berlin Wall. Write down five quotations that describe how people on both sides of the wall felt about its destruction. Use the quotations as part of a news broadcast about the event.

Understanding Main Ideas

1. How did Ronald Reagan's presidency represent a new era in the United States?
2. What were some of the business gains and setbacks in the 1980s?
3. Why was Central America an important foreign-policy concern for Reagan?
4. Why did the Cold War end?
5. How did the United States respond to Iraq's invasion of Kuwait? What were the results?
6. What were some of the technological advances of the 1980s?

Reviewing Themes

1. **Economic Development**   How did Reagan's use of supply-side economics affect Americans?
2. **Global Relations**   How did reforms in the Soviet Union lead to changes in Europe?
3. **Technology and Society**   In what ways did the scientific and technological advances of the 1980s change the lives of Americans?

Using the Time Line

Number your paper from 1 to 6. Match the letters on the time line below with the following events.

1. The Economic Recovery Tax Act reduces personal income taxes.
2. The Berlin Wall is torn down.
3. Sally Ride becomes the first American woman to fly on a space shuttle.
4. American voters re-elect Ronald Reagan.
5. UN forces stage a massive ground invasion of Kuwait.
6. The stock market experiences Black Monday.

Thinking Critically

1. **Making Comparisons**   Compare and contrast the foreign-policy actions of Presidents Reagan and Bush.

2. **Identifying Cause and Effect**   How might women's participation in the Persian Gulf War have changed some people's opinions about women's role in the military?

3. **Drawing Conclusions**   Why do you think most Americans supported U.S. involvement in the Persian Gulf War?

Writing About History

1. **Persuading**   Imagine that you are an organizer for Farm Aid. Write a brochure persuading musicians to perform at the event. Be sure to explain how their participation will help American farmers.

2. **Expressing**   Write a letter to the head of NASA expressing your opinion concerning the role the United States should play in space exploration over the next 20 years. Base your opinion on previous space missions. Be sure to explain your point of view.

Linking Geography and History

1. **Location**   Why was Kuwait's fate seen as important to U.S. national interests?

2. **Region**   Why did Reagan see communism in Nicaragua as such a threat?

Building Your Portfolio

Complete the following activities individually or in groups.

1. **Technology in Action**   Design a science museum exhibit to show the medical and technological advances made in the 1980s. Be sure to include as much information as possible on how these different inventions or techniques work. You will need to include diagrams and photographs of the inventions as well as items related to them. Write a paragraph to accompany the images. Explain how each invention or advance was something new in the 1980s. Discuss the role the invention or advance plays in society today.

2. **A Modern Time Capsule**   Imagine that a special government commission has asked you to create a time capsule from the 1980s. Design a storage plan and a box for your time capsule. Then create a "time capsule must have" document that lists the included items and explains their importance. Finally, write a speech to deliver to the American public when you bury your time capsule.

History Skills Workshop

Using Visual Resources   Study the image to the right, which is a political cartoon from the 1980s. Briefly describe what the cartoon means and what the artist probably thinks of President Reagan's Strategic Defense Initiative. Then draw your own political cartoon showing one of the Reagan administration's accomplishments.

CHAPTER 24

The United States Looks to the Future

(1992–Present)

One high school student expressed his view of the twenty-first century:

>"I have a good feeling about the future. The people of my generation are . . . more in tune with what's going on, and I'd like to think that when my generation are in [power], they're gonna be more sensitive and more representative of the people of our country. I think a lot of progress has been made . . . But more . . . needs to be done."

THEMES

Constitutional Heritage
Why might the House of Representatives impeach a president?

Global Relations
How might a nation try to keep world peace and encourage the spread of democracy?

Technology and Society
How might technology improve international communication?

1992

1993

1994

1995

APR. 1992 Riots erupt in Los Angeles, California.

NOV. 1992 Democrat Bill Clinton is elected president.

NOV. 1993 The Senate ratifies the North American Free Trade Agreement.

DEC. 1995 The Dayton peace accords are signed.

The Clinton Administration

Reading Focus

What domestic issues were addressed during President Clinton's administration?

Why were Republicans able to gain majorities in Congress in 1994?

What issue troubled the Clinton presidency in his second term?

Key Terms

Family and Medical Leave Act
North American Free Trade Agreement
Brady Bill
terrorism
independent counsel
Contract with America

IN AN INTERVIEW, *a young man in Dallas, Texas, proudly displayed photos of his military service during Operation Desert Storm. Crowds had cheered as his ship left San Diego, California, for the Middle East. Parades had greeted the soldiers when they returned home. Life got tougher after the young man left the army, though. He answered help-wanted advertisements and made the rounds of employment agencies, but he could not find a job. The recession that had begun in 1990 was in full swing. Many companies were laying off people. Many Americans who had praised President Bush for his leadership in the Persian Gulf War now blamed him for the hard times.*

American workers protest losing jobs to Japan

IMAGE ON LEFT PAGE: *A restaurant at the Los Angeles airport reflects space-age design.*

1996 | 1997 | 1998 | 1999

JULY 1997 The *Pathfinder* spacecraft lands on Mars.

NOV. 1998 John Glenn becomes the oldest space traveler.

MAR. 1999 NATO launches air attacks on Serbia.

DEC. 1998 The House of Representatives impeaches President Clinton.

FEB. 1999 The Senate finds Clinton not guilty.

The Election of 1992

Business had boomed during much of the late 1980s. However, the overall economy had weakened as the federal deficit grew. By 1991 the United States was in a recession. President George Bush downplayed the severity of the recession. He reminded Americans of his leadership during the Persian Gulf War:

❝ **We can bring the same . . . sense of common purpose to the economy that we brought to Desert Storm. And we can defeat hard times together.** ❞

The Republican Party nominated Bush for re-election. Bill Clinton, governor of Arkansas, won the Democratic nomination. He chose Tennessee senator Al Gore as his running mate. Clinton called himself a New Democrat—a Democrat who favors some traditionally Republican policies. These policies included balancing the budget, limiting government spending, and encouraging private enterprise. Clinton also wanted an "end to welfare as we know it." He pledged to introduce an extensive job training program. In addition, he suggested a $200 billion, four-year program of domestic investments. He criticized Bush for raising taxes and failing to end the recession.

Texas billionaire Ross Perot (per-OH) entered the race as an independent candidate. He pledged to balance the budget and run the government like a business. Perot said his lack of experience in government was an asset: "I don't have any experience in running up a $4 trillion debt. I don't have any experience in gridlock [stalled] government."

Perot's campaign as an independent candidate, along with the nation's significant economic problems, contributed to increased voter interest and participation. Some 55 percent of registered voters turned out in November 1992. This turnout was a greater percentage than for any presidential election since 1972. Clinton won the election with 370 electoral votes to Bush's 168. Perot did not win any electoral votes, but he received 19 percent of the popular vote.

Clinton's First Term

At age 46, Bill Clinton was the youngest president elected since John F. Kennedy. Vice President Al Gore was about one year younger. They were the youngest team ever in the White House. After 12 years of Republican leadership, President Clinton promised in his inaugural address to bring an end to gridlock. He announced:

❝ **A new season of American renewal has begun. To renew America, we must be bold. We must do what no generation has had to do before. We must invest more in our own people, in their jobs, in their future, and at the same time cut our massive debt. . . . We must do what America does best: offer more opportunity to all and demand responsibility from all.** ❞

He called for "bold, persistent [continuing] experimentation" to help solve the nation's problems.

Clinton was determined to improve the economy. The budget he submitted to Congress called for a large reduction of the federal deficit and a tax increase. The House of Representatives passed a revised version of the budget by two votes. Vice President Gore cast a tie-breaking vote in the Senate, and the budget was approved.

Health Care

In February 1993 Clinton signed the **Family and Medical Leave Act**.

Born after World War II, the Clintons and the Gores are members of the baby-boom generation.

Bill Clinton

William Jefferson Blythe IV was born in 1946 in Hope, Arkansas. His father had died before he was born. Blythe later changed his last name to that of his stepfather, Roger Clinton. Bill Clinton grew up in Hot Springs, Arkansas. As a young man, he was determined to succeed. He frequently earned academic honors. At age 16, he was selected as a delegate to a high school program in Washington, D.C. On the trip Clinton met President John F. Kennedy. Clinton would later say that the encounter inspired him to enter a life of public service.

After graduating from Georgetown University, Clinton studied at Oxford University as a Rhodes Scholar. In 1973 he received a law degree from Yale University. He then returned to Arkansas to teach law and to prepare himself for a career in politics. In 1978 Clinton was elected governor of Arkansas. He was the nation's youngest governor. Clinton suffered his biggest political loss when he was defeated for re-election in 1980. Clinton revised his political strategy and won the governorship again in 1982. He held that position until he was elected president in 1992.

The law provided many workers with up to 12 weeks of unpaid leave for family or medical purposes. Under this law, employees could take time off to care for themselves or sick family members, or to have or adopt a child. The law guaranteed that these workers would have a job when they returned to work.

In September, Clinton announced a plan to reform the health care system. He had appointed First Lady Hillary Rodham Clinton, a Yale-educated lawyer, to lead the President's Task Force on National Health Care Reform. The task force made several recommendations. Its main priority was to provide universal medical coverage to all Americans. At the time, nearly 40 million Americans lacked health insurance. Many Americans, small business owners, in particular, opposed the plan. The plan failed to pass in Congress and was a major defeat for the Clinton administration.

In 1996 the president achieved some success in health care reform. He signed legislation to allow workers who changed or lost their jobs to pay to keep their health insurance coverage. At the signing ceremony, Clinton called the bill "a long step toward the kind of health-care reform our nation needs."

Trade

Clinton also persuaded the Senate to pass a trade agreement initiated by the Bush administration. In November 1993 the Senate ratified the **North American Free Trade Agreement** (NAFTA). NAFTA eliminated trade barriers between the United States, Canada, and Mexico. Supporters saw NAFTA as a way to increase international trade and business profits. Opponents feared that it would shift production and jobs out of the United States.

Some labor leaders feared that NAFTA would eliminate many jobs in the United States.

Fighting Crime

President Clinton also pushed for new anticrime laws. In November 1993 Congress approved the Handgun Violence Prevention Act, or the **Brady Bill**. This legislation was named after President Reagan's press secretary, James Brady. He had been wounded during an assassination attempt on the president in 1981. The Brady Bill established a five-day waiting period for handgun purchases. In 1998 a computerized system that provides immediate background checks on potential gun buyers replaced the waiting period.

In 1994 Clinton supported a bill to provide funding for 100,000 new police officers and for new prisons and crime-prevention programs. The legislation also prohibited the sale and possession of some assault weapons. Clinton hoped these measures would reduce violent crime. For a variety of reasons, the rate of violent crime fell during the mid-1990s.

Although crime decreased, many Americans were shocked by an increase in **terrorism**. This type of violence is used by individuals or small groups to advance political goals. In February 1993 a bomb exploded in New York City's World Trade Center. The explosion killed 6 people and injured more than 1,000. Several members of an Arab terrorist group were later arrested and sentenced to life imprisonment for the bombing.

In April 1995, terrorists bombed the Alfred P. Murrah Federal Building in Oklahoma City, Oklahoma. The explosion killed 169 people, including many children, and injured many others. One army veteran who was an eyewitness said it was "as bad as anything I'd ever witnessed in Vietnam." The federal government tried and convicted two Americans—Timothy McVeigh and Terry Nichols—for the crime. The government also took measures, such as increasing airport security, to reduce the risk of terrorism at home and abroad.

Sarah Brady lobbied for a gun control law after her husband, James Brady, was wounded.

Republicans Gain Strength

The Clinton administration faced setbacks in 1994. Attorney General Janet Reno appointed Kenneth Starr as **independent counsel**—a special prosecutor to investigate accusations against government officials. After the Watergate scandal, Congress had questioned whether the executive branch could investigate itself adequately. In 1978 Congress established the office of independent counsel to look into charges of wrongdoing by high-ranking government officials. Starr's initial assignment was to investigate the role of the president and the first lady in the so-called Whitewater affair. Whitewater was a failed Arkansas real estate development. The investigation was a significant issue during Clinton's first term.

Contract with America

As the 1994 congressional elections approached, Republican representative Newt Gingrich of Georgia helped create the **Contract with America**. Many Republican candidates signed this campaign pledge. The Contract included promises for smaller government, a balanced budget amendment, tax reforms, and term limits for members of Congress. Republicans proposed to introduce this legislation in 100 days.

Newt Gingrich became Speaker of the House after the Contract with America helped Republicans gain majorities in Congress.

Many voters responded favorably to the Contract. Republicans gained majorities in both houses of Congress for the first time since the 1952 elections. The House passed all items in the Contract, except one to limit the number of terms in office for members of Congress. By the end of 1995, five items in the Contract had become law.

Budget and Welfare Reform

According to Gingrich, the Republicans in Congress "changed the whole debate in American politics. There is now a universal agreement [that] you've got to balance the budget." The Republicans lost some public support, however, when they tried to force the president to accept their proposed budget.

After President Clinton refused to sign the budget, the federal government shut down twice in late 1995 and early 1996. Only necessary federal government agencies were open. Nonessential federal government employees did not work because there was no money to pay them. Federal museums and national parks were closed. After a public outcry, the Republicans and Democrats compromised on a budget. The government began to operate again.

Congress also passed a major revision of the federal welfare system. In 1996 Clinton signed a bill that ended the Aid to Families with Dependent Children (AFDC). This federally funded program had provided cash assistance to poor families. The welfare reform bill replaced AFDC with direct grants to states. Each state became responsible for designing and operating its own welfare program.

★ The 1996 Election

In 1996, Americans turned their attention to the presidential election. Republicans chose Senator Bob Dole of Kansas as their candidate for president. Dole was a World War II veteran and longtime congressional leader. Based on their success in the midterm elections, Republicans thought they might be able to win back the presidency. The Democrats nominated the Clinton-Gore ticket for re-election.

During the campaign, Dole noted that President Clinton seemed to be supporting conservative Republican measures. Dole joked, "If this keeps up, Bill Clinton won't have to make speeches anymore. All he'll have to do is find out my stand on an issue and say 'Me too.'"

Total Federal Debt, 1981–1995

Amount of Debt (in trillions of dollars)

Year

Source: *Statistical Abstract of the United States*

The Growing Debt Despite efforts to reduce the rate of growth of the federal debt, it continued to rise throughout the 1980s and the 1990s. How much was the federal debt in 1992?

Clinton made a campaign pledge to "build a bridge to the twenty-first century." In particular, he wanted to improve public education. Many voters credited Clinton with the booming economy. He won 379 electoral votes to Dole's 159. Republicans maintained majorities in both houses of Congress.

★ Clinton's Second Term

Following the election, the president and Congress worked on the federal budget. In 1997 they reached an agreement to balance the budget by the year 2002. The deal included tax cuts and reductions in domestic spending, including a $75 billion decrease in defense spending. Funding would be increased for education, health insurance, and welfare.

Questions about President Clinton's personal conduct dominated much of his second term. During the mid-1990s, Independent Counsel Kenneth Starr had widened the scope of his investigation. In 1998 he released a lengthy report charging that, among other things, the president had lied under oath before a grand jury. Clinton denied lying under oath, but he did apologize for other actions cited in the report.

> **❝ I let you down. I let my family down. I let this country down. But I'm trying to make it right. I'm determined to never let anything like that happen again. ❞**

Chief Justice William Rehnquist presided over the impeachment trial.

As a result of Starr's report, the House Judiciary Committee began an impeachment inquiry.

Despite the investigation, Democrats gained five new seats in the House in the November 1998 congressional elections. Many people interpreted these results as a sign that the public opposed impeachment. Some people questioned whether the investigation had gone beyond its original assignment.

Nonetheless, the House continued its inquiry. It approved two of four articles of impeachment against the president. In December, Clinton became the second U.S. president to be impeached. According to the articles of impeachment, Clinton

> **❝ has undermined [weakened] the integrity of his office, has brought disrepute [dishonor] on the Presidency, has betrayed his trust as President, and has acted in a manner subversive of [doing harm to] the rule of law and justice, to the . . . injury of the people of the United States. ❞**

On February 12, 1999, the Senate acquitted Clinton of both charges. He therefore remained in office.

SECTION 1 REVIEW

Identify and explain the significance of the following:
- Bill Clinton
- Ross Perot
- Family and Medical Leave Act
- Hillary Rodham Clinton
- North American Free Trade Agreement
- Brady Bill
- terrorism
- independent counsel
- Newt Gingrich
- Contract with America

Reading for Content Understanding

1 **Main Idea** On what domestic issues did President Clinton focus while in office?

2 **Main Idea** Why did the Republicans win majorities in Congress in 1994?

3 **Constitutional Heritage** What was the result of Kenneth Starr's investigation of the president?

4 **Writing** *Persuading* Write a letter to your congressmember to persuade him or her to reach a budget agreement in late 1995. Be sure to include why re-opening the federal government is important.

5 **Critical Thinking** *Making Comparisons* Compare Clinton's domestic policies with those of the Republicans in Congress.

Clinton's Foreign Policy

Reading Focus

What role did the United States play in the post–Cold War era?

How did the United States respond to problems with Iraq after the Persian Gulf War?

How did the United States react to events in the Balkans in the 1990s?

Key Terms

Operation Restore Hope

Operation Desert Fox

Dayton peace accords

URING THE 1992 PRESIDENTIAL CAMPAIGN, Bill Clinton had promised that if elected he would support a more aggressive role for the United States in Bosnia. A bitter civil war had erupted in the Balkan nation. Clinton charged: "The [Bush] administration is turning its back on violations of basic human rights and our own democratic values." During the 1990s, many Americans debated the role the United States should play in helping other nations maintain peace.

UN troops in Bosnia tried to maintain peace.

New Challenges Abroad

The end of the Cold War and the collapse of the Soviet Union changed the goals of U.S. foreign policy. The United States became the world's only superpower. One White House official noted, "No other nation has the muscle . . . or the trust to mediate [settle] disputes . . . or . . . help enforce the terms of an agreement." In the 1990s the United States played a greater role in trying to strengthen democracy, protect human rights, and negotiate peace in different parts of the world.

Haiti

For example, the United States tried to support democracy in Haiti. Haitian military leaders had overthrown the country's democratically elected president, Jean-Bertrand Aristide (ah-ree-steed), in 1991. These military leaders led a campaign of violence against their political opponents. Tens of thousands of Haitians left their country between 1991 and 1994. Most of them headed to the United States.

Concerned about the flood of refugees, the U.S. government pressured the Haitian military

The United States Looks to the Future **713**

government to resign. The Clinton administration also called for the return of Aristide, who was in exile in the United States. In September 1994 President Clinton sent a peace mission to Haiti. Former president Jimmy Carter, former chairman of the Joint Chiefs of Staff Colin Powell, and Senator Sam Nunn negotiated a compromise. Some 20,000 U.S. troops soon arrived in Haiti to help restore order and the Aristide government. The military rulers quickly withdrew. One month later President Aristide returned to Haiti. He urged Haitians to say "no to violence, no to vengeance, yes to reconciliation [coming to peaceful agreement]."

Peace Accords

The United States also supported peace efforts in the Middle East. After years of conflict, Israel and the Palestine Liberation Organization (PLO), an Arab political group, reached a peace agreement. At the White House in 1993 Israeli prime minister Yitzhak Rabin and PLO leader Yasir Arafat signed the historic agreement in which Israel and the PLO officially recognized each other. The agreement also set guidelines for Palestinian self-rule in occupied areas of Israel.

In 1994 Israel and Jordan also agreed to peace. They signed the Washington Declaration at the White House. This peace agreement formally ended the 46-year-long state of war between Israel and Jordan.

Terrorist actions by both Israelis and Palestinians slowed the Israeli-PLO peace process. In 1995 an Israeli opposed to Palestinian self-rule assassinated Rabin. The Palestinians gained self-rule in some occupied areas in 1997. However, no final agreements were reached about the creation of an independent Palestinian state.

American Arts

Worldbeat Music

As barriers between nations were removed in the post–Cold War era, musicians turned to many countries for inspiration. Worldbeat music is one example of this new global music. Unlike traditional Western music, which has its roots in Europe, worldbeat music combines many cultural sounds, including Caribbean, calypso, African, and funk.

Reggae, a type of Jamaican music, combines African and European styles. It comes in different forms including raggamuffin, hip-hop, and dancehall. Musicians such as Bob Marley and Shabba Ranks have popularized reggae.

In Japan, worldbeat music may combine Brazilian and Caribbean beats and West African dance music with rhythms of the island of Okinawa. For example, Japanese musician Kikusuimaru blends story-telling music and reggae sounds. As more people worldwide

The Brazilian percussion group, Olodum

draw inspiration from a variety of cultures, new styles of music are developed.

Understanding the Arts

1. What is worldbeat music?

2. Why do you think worldbeat music is becoming more popular?

Changes in Africa

Meanwhile, significant political changes were also occurring in Africa. The United States played a variety of roles in events in Africa.

Nelson Mandela's release from prison and election as South Africa's president made him a symbol of change.

South Africa

One of the greatest changes occurred in South Africa, which had practiced apartheid and denied black citizens many basic rights. Within South Africa, political groups like the African National Congress (ANC) had fought to end apartheid. In the 1980s many countries had applied political and economic pressure to the South African government to end apartheid. The U.S. Congress approved economic sanctions against South Africa and overrode President Reagan's veto of them. Many American college students encouraged divestment, or removal, of funds invested in South African businesses.

Combined with protest in South Africa, international pressure helped lead to reform. ANC founder Nelson Mandela, who had been held as a political prisoner since 1964, was released in 1990. The next year South Africa's white government repealed the basic apartheid laws. In 1994 the nation held its first elections in which adult South Africans of all races could vote. Mandela became the nation's first black president.

Somalia and Rwanda

In other African countries, the United States took military action and operated as part of a larger United Nations force. In late 1992 President Bush had sent U.S. troops to the African country of Somalia, which was in the midst of a civil war. U.S. soldiers joined **Operation Restore Hope**, a UN relief effort to help Somalia. UN forces opened roads and distributed food to starving Somalis. However, the civil war continued.

In 1993, 18 U.S. soldiers were killed in a gun battle. A number of others were captured. The United States began to re-evaluate its involvement in Somalia. President Clinton removed most of the U.S. troops in 1994. Although problems in Somalia continued, the remaining UN troops left in 1995.

The events in Somalia affected the U.S. response to a bloody ethnic war in the African nation of Rwanda. In 1994 the UN sent a peacekeeping force to Rwanda, but Clinton refused to send U.S. troops. The fighting there was particularly brutal. The UN established a war-crimes tribunal to investigate the murder of some 500,000 Tutsi, a minority ethnic group in Rwanda. The situation in Rwanda demonstrated some of the difficult foreign-policy choices the United States faced in the 1990s.

Tensions in Iraq

As part of a UN delegation, the United States continued to play a role in Iraq. After the Persian Gulf War, Iraq had agreed in the cease-fire agreement to destroy its weapons of mass destruction. UN officials were to inspect Iraq's industrial, chemical, and biological facilities to make sure the weapons were destroyed. However, Iraqi leader Saddam Hussein hindered the efforts of the UN inspectors.

An Iraqi soldier watches as UN inspectors prepare to leave the country.

In 1998 Hussein's actions pushed the UN coalition to act. Secretary of State Madeleine Albright explained the U.S. position:

> ❝ **Our fundamental goal . . . is to contain or end the threat posed by Saddam Hussein to Iraq's neighbors and the world. . . . We retain the authority, the responsibility, the means and the will to use military force if that is required.** ❞

By the fall, all diplomatic efforts to convince Iraq to allow UN inspection teams to do their job had failed. The inspectors left the country. In December 1998 President Clinton launched **Operation Desert Fox**. This military operation included a series of joint U.S. and British air strikes against military and strategic targets in Iraq.

Even after the air strikes, problems with Iraq continued. In 1999 more air attacks were launched on Iraq. The United Nations continued to watch the area for more cease-fire violations.

★ War in the Balkans

The United States also tried to help resolve conflicts in the Balkans, a region in southeastern Europe. Following World War II, the nation of Yugoslavia was created. This communist country was a federation of six republics. Each republic had several ethnic populations. Differences had divided these ethnic groups for centuries. In the early 1990s, four republics—Bosnia and Herzegovina (often referred to as Bosnia), Croatia, Macedonia, and Slovenia— declared their independence. The republics of Serbia and Montenegro remained as the nation of Yugoslavia.

Fighting in Bosnia

Tension among the Balkans' three main ethnic groups— Serbs, Croats, and Muslims— soon led to war. Fighting erupted in the new nations of Croatia and Bosnia. Some of the worst violence was between Serbs and Muslims in Bosnia. Serb president Slobodan Milosevic (sloh-buh-DAHN mi-LOH-suh-vitch) supported Bosnian Serbs who did not want to separate from Yugoslavia.

The Bosnian Serbs practiced ethnic cleansing— the violent removal of ethnic minority groups by a dominant ethnic group. The Serbs used threats, destroyed homes and villages, and killed many Muslims to "cleanse" parts of Bosnia. In November 1994 the International Tribunal for the Prosecution of War Crimes announced that it would prosecute some Serbs for actions related to ethnic cleansing. The trials were the first war crimes trials to be held since World War II.

Fighting in Croatia stopped in 1994. UN efforts to stop the violence in Bosnia were unsuccessful. During President Clinton's first term, U.S. diplomats hosted a peace conference at Wright Patterson Air Force base in Dayton, Ohio. The presidents of Bosnia, Croatia, and Serbia participated in the negotiations. The plan was to reach a permanent peace agreement and a settlement on the boundaries of Bosnia. Richard Holbrooke was

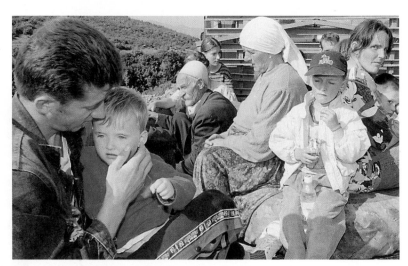

Thousands of Kosovar Albanians fled their homes. Many children ended up in refugee camps separated from their parents.

the chief U.S. negotiator. The warring sides signed the **Dayton peace accords** in December 1995. NATO and Russia sent thousands of peacekeeping troops to the area. Many were from the United States. For a short while the accords were successful, but unrest in Bosnia continued.

Conflict in Kosovo

In early 1998 President Milosevic extended his campaign of ethnic cleansing to the Serbian province of Kosovo. Serbian nationalists regard Kosovo as the birthplace of Serbian culture. The Serbs in Kosovo were the largest of several minorities. However, of the province's approximately 2 million inhabitants, more than 90 percent were of Albanian heritage.

Some of these Kosovars, or residents of Kosovo, began to demand independence. In response, Milosevic's troops killed thousands of Kosovar Albanians and forced thousands more to leave their homes. Serbian military forces increased their attacks on the Kosovars in March 1999. NATO responded by launching air strikes on Serbia.

Retired U.S. diplomat James Hooper, head of the Balkan Action Council, explained the significance of the problem. He wrote,

❝ The Kosovo problem is as much about the resolve of American leadership and

NATO celebrated its 50th anniversary in April 1999.

the credibility of NATO as it is about the complexities of Balkan politics. ❞

Russia also played a role in the peace process. In June 1999 NATO and Yugoslavia reached an agreement that required Serbian troops to leave Kosovo. NATO agreed to send a security force of more than 50,000 to the area.

NATO's actions in the Balkans represented its first effort as an expanded organization. After the breakup of the Soviet Union, several Eastern European nations had established democratic governments. As communist nations, they had belonged to the Warsaw Pact. In the post–Cold War era, some of these countries became members of NATO.

SECTION 2 REVIEW

Identify and explain the significance of the following:
- **Jean-Bertrand Aristide**
- **Nelson Mandela**
- **Operation Restore Hope**
- **Madeleine Albright**
- **Operation Desert Fox**
- **Dayton peace accords**

Reading for Content Understanding

1 **Main Idea** How did U.S. foreign policy change after the end of the Cold War?

2 **Main Idea** What actions did the United States and the United Nations take against Iraq in the 1990s?

3 **Global Relations** Make a graphic organizer showing the actions the United States took in Haiti, Iraq, Bosnia, and Kosovo. Indicate the kind of action and the results.

4 **Writing** *Describing* Write two paragraphs describing the role of NATO in the post–Cold War era.

5 **Critical Thinking** *Determining the Strength of an Argument* Do you believe that as the world's only superpower the United States has a responsibility to promote peace and democracy? Use specific examples to support your argument.

Americans in the 1990s

Reading Focus

What changes did Congress make to immigration laws in the 1980s and 1990s?

How have professional sports changed in recent years?

What effect have computers had on people's access to information?

Key Terms

Immigration Reform and Control Act
Los Angeles riots
Information Revolution
Internet

IN SEPTEMBER 1978 *Juan Chanax set out from the Guatemalan highlands of Totonicapán. The United States was his destination. He left his village because he thought he had no choice. "With little land and little education and little money, I had no chance to sobresalir [excel]." Chanax ended up in Houston, Texas, where he found work in a supermarket. He sent home as much as $100 a week—twice as much money as most people earned in Guatemala. He was the first person from his hometown to immigrate. Within 15 years about half of the village's population had immigrated to the United States.*

A Guatemalan weaving

 ## Immigrants in the 1990s

Juan Chanax and his Guatemalan neighbors were part of an enormous increase in the number of immigrants to the United States in the 1980s and 1990s. This increase in immigration was the largest since the 1910s. The populations of California, Florida, and Texas grew in part as a result of this immigration. Many of these recent immigrants came from Latin America and Asia. Like previous immigrants, they often settled in large cities with other people from their native countries.

In response to this increased immigration, Congress passed the **Immigration Reform and Control Act** in 1986. This act granted legal status to illegal aliens, or noncitizens, who could prove they had lived continuously in the United States since before January 1, 1982. The act also called for employers who knowingly hired illegal aliens to receive large fines. Illegal aliens had until May 1988 to register with the Immigration and Naturalization Service. By the deadline, more than 1 million illegal aliens had sought legal status. More than 70 percent of these aliens were from Mexico.

The Immigration Act of 1990 set a permanent limit of 675,000 immigrants per year after 1994. Of these immigrants, 80,000 were to be aliens with special skills. The law also increased the number of visas for immigrants with families already living in the United States.

★ The Los Angeles Riots

Other changes in the 1990s included increased tensions among some citizens. Many Americans were shocked by a videotape that showed four white police officers beating black motorist Rodney King. In April 1992 a jury found the Los Angeles officers not guilty of assault. The verdict triggered the **Los Angeles riots**. During four days of rioting, more than 50 people died and hundreds of businesses were destroyed. On the second day of rioting, King asked the people of Los Angeles to stop their rampage. At a news conference, he asked, "People, I just want to say, . . . can we all get along? Can we stop making it horrible for the older people and the kids?"

Many illegal aliens had to wait in long lines to submit their request to become legal immigrants.

Most of the riot damage occurred in South Central Los Angeles. Frustration over rising poverty in the area contributed to the violence. In many cases, immigrant businesses were the target of the attacks. The riots were one of the most violent episodes of urban unrest in the United States in the 1900s.

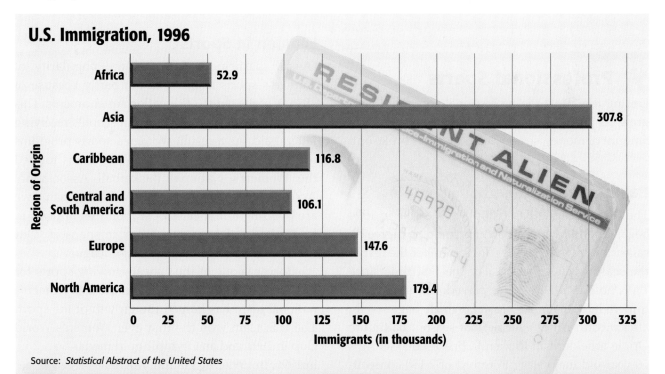

U.S. Immigration, 1996

Region of Origin

Region	Immigrants (in thousands)
Africa	52.9
Asia	307.8
Caribbean	116.8
Central and South America	106.1
Europe	147.6
North America	179.4

Immigrants (in thousands)

Source: *Statistical Abstract of the United States*

Changes in Immigration In the 1990s an increasing number of immigrants came to the United States from Asia and Latin America. More than one third of all immigrants to the United States in 1996 came from five countries: China, India, Mexico, the Philippines, and Vietnam. According to the chart above, how many immigrants came to the United States from other countries in the Americas in 1996?

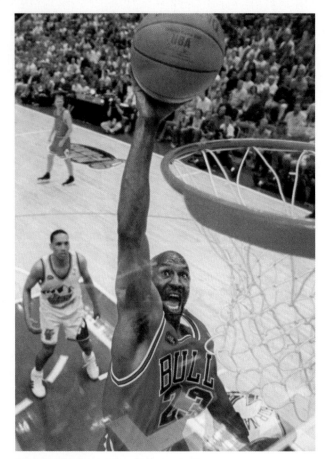

Michael Jordan of the Chicago Bulls

⭐ Professional Sports

During the 1990s the professional sports industry grew. As professional sports involved an increasing amount of money, several labor disputes broke out.

Baseball and Basketball

The Major League Baseball players' strike in 1994 began after players and owners could not agree on salary and revenue issues. In September the rest of the season was canceled. For the first time since 1905, no World Series was played. The strike continued into the next season, which began only after a court order. During that season, Baltimore Oriole infielder Cal Ripken Jr. broke Lou Gehrig's 56-year-old major league record of 2,130 consecutive games played. In September 1998 Ripken sat out one game and ended his streak at 2,632 games.

Angered by the strike, many baseball fans did not return to the games until the summer of 1998. Mark McGwire of the St. Louis Cardinals and

Sammy Sosa of the Chicago Cubs were trying to break Roger Maris's 37-year-old record for the most home runs—61—in a single season. One fan saw the race as "what we need." Referring to the Clinton investigation, the fan noted,

66 **This is what the country needs to help with the healing process and all the trouble that's going on in Washington. This will help cure the ills of the country.** 99

On September 8, 1998, McGwire broke Maris's record. Sosa also broke the record later in the season.

In professional basketball several spectacular players, including Larry Bird, Julius "Dr. J" Erving, Earvin "Magic" Johnson, and Michael Jordan, helped attract fans. During the 1990s, Jordan led the Chicago Bulls to six world championships. He also contributed to the growth of professional basketball as a business. According to what one magazine called the "Jordan Effect," his presence in the NBA added an estimated $10 billion to the economy. This figure included ticket sales, television revenue, and merchandise.

Women in Sports

Overall participation in and the popularity of women's sports also increased, partly because of Title IX of the federal Education Amendments. This act banned sex discrimination in schools receiving federal aid. As a result, women's sports programs received more funding. In 1997, 10 teams formed the Women's National Basketball Association. According to league president Val Ackerman, "we are building a first-class operation that appeals to fans, players, television, corporate sponsors. Our dream is to become the fifth major league."

Soccer is one of the fastest-growing sports for girls and women. The success of the U.S. women's national team has helped the growth of the sport. The U.S. team won the first ever Women's World Cup in 1991 and an Olympic gold medal in 1996. In 1999 Mia Hamm, Michelle Akers, and Brandi Chastain led the U.S team to its second World Cup.

The largest crowd ever for a women's sporting event watched the 1999 cup final.

Computers

In the modern world computers are almost everywhere. Banks, businesses, governments, and schools use computers to keep records, send information, and solve problems. The computer industry earns billions of dollars a year and creates millions of jobs. Yet computers are a fairly recent development.

Scientists built the first computers during World War II. These early models, such as ENIAC, filled entire rooms. They used bulky vacuum tubes for electrical switches. One of the first major improvements in computer design was the transistor. Invented in 1948, the transistor is a tiny electrical switch that works at very high speeds.

In the 1950s, engineers created the integrated circuit, or microchip. A microchip has many transistors on a single silicon chip. Microchip technology was used in the early 1970s to create the microprocessor. An advanced chip, the microprocessor carries out the instructions that allow a computer to operate. By the early 1970s advances in microchip technology allowed a handheld calculator to solve problems faster than the giant ENIAC.

All of these changes improved computer hardware—the physical parts that carry out functions. Other improvements involved computer software, the instructions that tell a computer how to operate. Computers process information using binary code, or a code with two numbers. A program written entirely in binary code is very long and difficult to revise. In the 1950s, researchers developed programming languages. These languages allow people to write complicated instructions that computers then translate into binary code. Researcher Grace Murray Hopper developed COBOL, the first widely used programming language. Modern programming languages such as C++ are even more advanced.

Computers use increasingly powerful hardware and software. For example, by the early 1990s, the microprocessor that runs a computer had more than a million transistors. Computers have also become much less expensive. In addition, new products ranging from cars to washing machines use some form of computer technology. The abilities and uses of computers continue to expand in ways that few people imagined only 50 years ago.

Understanding What You Read

1. What are the basic parts of a computer?

2. Describe some of the most important computer improvements that have been developed since the 1940s.

The mother board (here in green) connects the various parts of a computer.

Computer Technology

Many people worldwide began keeping up with sporting events and other news on their computers. In the 1990s, computers increased and simplified the transfer of information—a development called the **Information Revolution**. Computers became essential to business, education, and every activity that requires the organization and processing of information.

In the 1980s, new technologies linked computers into networks. These networks allowed different computers to communicate and work together. With computers linked to one network, whole systems have been networked to create a worldwide link. This link is the **Internet**—a system of computer networks in which people anywhere in the world can communicate and share information. Some people have referred to the system as the information superhighway.

The Internet had its roots in a 1960s Defense Department project. However, the Internet's growth exploded in the 1990s with the creation of the World Wide Web. By 1998 as many as 60 million Americans, and more than 100 million people globally, were using the World Wide Web.

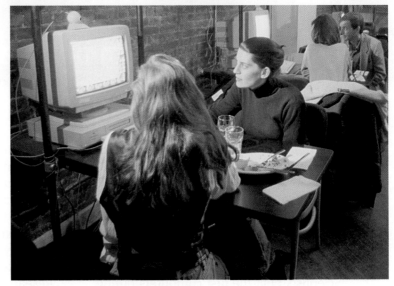

Some cafes and restaurants provide their customers with access to the Internet.

Microsoft chairman Bill Gates saw the growth of the Internet as a major step in the Information Revolution. Gates predicted some of the changes that would result:

66 **The information highway is going to break down boundaries. . . . We are watching something historic happen, and it will affect the world . . . the same way the scientific method, the invention of printing, and the arrival of the Industrial Age did.** 99

SECTION 3 REVIEW

Identify and explain the significance of the following:
• **Immigration Reform and Control Act**
• **Los Angeles riots**
• **Mark McGwire**
• **Michael Jordan**
• **Information Revolution**
• **Internet**

Reading for Content Understanding

1 **Main Idea** How did Congress try to change immigration in the 1980s and 1990s?

2 **Main Idea** In what ways did professional sports change in the 1980s and 1990s?

3 **Technology and Society** How have advances in computer technology changed the way information is shared?

4 **Writing** *Describing* Imagine that you have just immigrated to the United States. Write a brief journal entry describing life in your new country.

5 **Critical Thinking** *Synthesizing Information* Why do you think Bill Gates compared the information highway to the Industrial Revolution?

Preparing for the Twenty-first Century

Reading Focus

What environmental issues gained attention in the 1990s?

What did the space program accomplish in the 1990s?

How has the global economy changed?

Key Terms

global warming
El Niño
European Union

*T*EENAGERS MARIA PEREZ, *Fabiola Tostado, and Nevada Dove spent hours studying test results, chemical analyses, and groundwater-safety studies. Sometimes they read the reports aloud and made note of anything that sounded odd to them. The girls were not preparing for a school test. These environmental activists were preparing for a meeting. They lobbied for the temporary closing of a middle school so that potentially hazardous materials could be cleaned up at the site. Dove explained why the teenagers took action: "We're the new generation. One day you're going to have to stand up on your own two feet for something you believe in. Why not get an early start?"*

The disposal of harmful materials has become a major concern.

 ## The Environment

During the 1980s and 1990s more Americans began to share such concerns about the environment. In 1990 Congress took steps to limit industrial and auto pollution. Congress hoped that reducing pollution would limit urban smog and acid rain. Toxins from air pollution combine with water vapor to form acid rain. This rain can damage forests, lakes, and rivers.

Global Concerns

Increasingly, Americans became aware that environmental problems required worldwide cooperation. Many people were concerned that a thinning of the ozone layer would increase cases of skin cancer. This thin layer of gas in the upper atmosphere prevents harmful solar rays from reaching Earth's surface. To protect the ozone layer, many countries, including the United States, agreed to limit the release of certain chemicals into the air.

Environmental hazards include smog, a type of air pollution (as shown above in Los Angeles), and holes in the ozone layer (shown in the satellite image).

Another issue of concern was **global warming**. Some scientists argue that excessive heat is being trapped in Earth's atmosphere. Thus, temperatures around the globe are rising. Scientists blame this "greenhouse effect" on the buildup of carbon dioxide in the atmosphere. This buildup is caused in part by the burning of fossil fuels and the destruction of forests. Environmentalists warn that this climate change could have dangerous consequences. Other scientists disagree about the extent of the problem, however.

In 1992 the United States participated in the Earth Summit, a large gathering of world leaders, to discuss Earth's environment. Most of the 178 nations represented made a commitment to protect Earth's environment and resources.

Senator Al Gore played an active role in the summit. He had written a book on the environment, *Earth in the Balance*. As vice president, he continued to play an active role in environmental issues. In 1997 Gore spoke about the need to continue research on global warming. He said,

❝ We don't have all the answers today. But we know we must reverse the trend of global warming. We must safeguard our precious natural resources, and put a premium on public health and safety. ❞

Weather Extremes

Some people blamed global warming for a series of weather-related disasters in the 1990s. In 1993 some of the worst flooding in U.S. history occurred in the Midwest. From North Dakota to Missouri, heavy rains forced rivers out of their banks.

During 1996 parts of the Great Plains and the Southwest experienced a drought almost as bad as the Dust Bowl of the 1930s. Parts of Arizona, Colorado, Kansas, New Mexico, Oklahoma, Texas, and Utah suffered extremely dry conditions. According to a New Mexico state official, parts of his state had received "more rain during the Dust Bowl." The drought ruined wheat and corn crops. Having learned from the Dust Bowl problems, many farmers had crop insurance for such natural disasters.

Later that same year scientists noticed the first indications of a particularly strong **El Niño** weather system. El Niño, Spanish for "the boy child," is an irregularly occurring flow of warm surface water along the Pacific coast of South America. It is often accompanied by weather extremes. In 1998 El Niño was blamed for one of the worst heat waves of the century. Record heat and drought occurred throughout the Great Plains and Texas. Scientists also saw El Niño as the cause of severe flooding and tornadoes. In 1999 the mid-Atlantic states were hurt by record heat and drought.

⭐ Space 2000

While some scientists studied conditions on Earth, others were looking into space. In the 1990s the United States entered into many new space ventures. Some of these projects resulted from a new relationship between the United States and the former Soviet Union.

U.S. astronaut Shannon Lucid had to stay longer than expected on Mir, the Russian space station, because of mechanical problems.

The United States and Russia agreed in 1993 to jointly design and build an international space station. Two years later the U.S. space shuttle *Atlantis* linked up in orbit with the Russian space station, *Mir*, for five days. The mission was the first in preparation for the construction of the new space station. In 1996 U.S. astronaut Shannon Lucid spent 188 days stationed aboard *Mir*. Her stay was the longest by any American.

In November 1998, 77-year-old John Glenn, who had been the first American to orbit Earth, became the oldest space traveler. He flew on a shuttle mission and performed medical tests on the effects of weightlessness.

The U.S. space program began a new phase of exploration in the 1990s. This program used smaller spacecraft to explore other planets. NASA launched *Pathfinder*, a three-foot-tall spacecraft, toward Mars. On July 4, 1997, *Pathfinder* landed on Mars. *Sojourner*, a small robotic car known as a rover, emerged from the spacecraft. It traveled over the planet collecting information and sending back images. Rover engineer Henry Moore remarked, "Nobody has ever driven a car on Mars before." The Pathfinder project cost an estimated $250 million.

In 1999 NASA launched another spacecraft headed for Mars. For the first time in NASA's history, three female scientists were in charge of the project. According to manager Sarah Gavit, the age and gender of the team gave it a new outlook:

 [NASA] didn't want people with the old ways of thinking because they knew it was a really challenging mission.

★ A Global Economy

NASA's decision to establish an international space station reflected a trend toward globalization. Increased international trade has made economies of different countries more closely

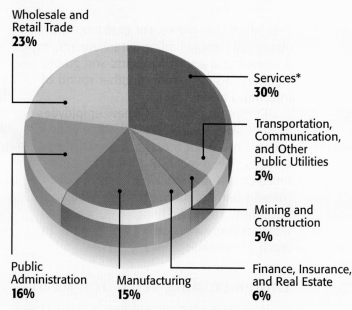

U.S. Employment

Distribution of Employment by Industry, March 1998

Wholesale and Retail Trade **23%**

Services* **30%**

Transportation, Communication, and Other Public Utilities **5%**

Mining and Construction **5%**

Public Administration **16%**

Manufacturing **15%**

Finance, Insurance, and Real Estate **6%**

Predicted Fastest-Growing Jobs, 1996–2006

1. Database administrators and computer specialists
2. Computer engineers
3. Systems analysts
4. Personal and home care aides
5. Physical and corrective therapy assistants and aides
6. Home health aides
7. Medical assistants
8. Desktop-publishing specialists
9. Physical therapists
10. Occupational therapy assistants and aides

*Includes business, computer education, entertainment, health, legal, and repair services, among others.
Sources: Bureau of Labor Statistics; *1998–99 Occupational Outlook Handbook*

Concerns for the Future Due to the widespread use of computers, jobs related to the computer industry are expected to skyrocket in the coming years. According to the list above, what other industry is expected to expand significantly by the year 2006?

Linking Past to Present

Careers in the Twenty-first Century

In the twenty-first century, many careers will require people to have computer or technological knowledge. The job market for college students graduating in the late 1990s was typical of this change. Some of the biggest growth was in computer-related fields. Workers in these areas include computer engineers, computer support specialists, database administrators, and systems analysts. Many of these positions require a good deal of computer knowledge. According to one writer, "If you can work a computer by the time you stroll to the podium [at graduation], you can, it seems, get a great job."

High-tech workers, like this one inspecting a computer microchip, will be in demand in the twenty-first century.

The industries that need more workers than they have been able to hire include high-tech, engineering, accounting, finance, and health care. The growth in health care positions such as home health aides and physical therapists is largely a result of the aging of the U.S. population. High growth is also expected in jobs for cashiers, retail salespersons, receptionists, and information clerks. The increase in these positions reflects the fact that the U.S. economy is becoming more service-oriented. American companies are producing fewer goods or products but are offering more services.

Even though many companies desperately need technical workers, some of these same companies are making their hiring practices more strict. According to one career placement adviser, "Companies are more concerned with organizational fit." To achieve a proper fit between employer and employee, some employers are requiring three to four sets of interviews. For example, one young job seeker had an interview and took a written test analyzing charts and graphs. He then had to perform another round of interviews and tests.

Companies want their new employees to have skills such as team work, organization, time management, and analytical thinking. The director of an employment research institute explained why the fast-paced environment made these skills so important. He said, "Things are moving so fast that companies can't take the time to teach [these skills]."

Understanding What You Read

1. How have employment needs in the United States changed in the 1990s? What may have contributed to these changes?

2. What skills are in demand for careers in the twenty-first century?

connected and dependent on each other. The rise of multinational corporations—corporations that operate in more than one country at a time—has also shaped the global economy.

Some nations have even joined together to increase their global economic power. In 1991, 11 nations of Western Europe joined together to form the **European Union** (EU). The EU wanted to join its members' economies into one single market with a common currency and a common central bank. In 1999 the EU introduced the "euro," its common currency. One European proudly announced, "There are now two economic superpowers [the EU and the United States]."

In 1995, 125 nations joined together in the World Trade Organization (WTO), which supervises international trade. The WTO replaced the General Agreement on Tariffs and Trade (GATT). GATT was a series of trade agreements reached since World War II to reduce quotas and limit tariffs.

As global markets become more integrated, there is more risk that difficult times in one nation will hurt the economies of other countries. In 1994 and 1995, for example, Mexico suffered a serious economic crisis. The value of its currency, the peso, dropped significantly. The crisis threatened the financial situations of international investors. President Clinton and the United Nations' World

The European Union created 11 different versions of the euro. Each version has an image or symbol of the member nation that designed it.

Bank supported a $50 billion package to get Mexico's economy back on track.

The World Bank helps its member nations establish international economic cooperation. The International Monetary Fund (IMF) of the World Bank lends money to countries in need. The number of loans and the amount of money loaned by the IMF has increased as international trade has expanded. After the Cold War ended, the IMF loaned money to Russia and a number of Eastern European nations. Russia has had difficulty making the transition from communism to a free-market economy.

In 1997 the IMF also provided more than $100 billion in financial assistance to several Asian countries experiencing economic crisis. A downturn in their economies threatened to cause currency problems throughout the world. Russia was one of the nations affected. The IMF agreed to loan the country more than $17 billion.

The IMF is just one way that nations can work together to keep the global economy strong. The United States continues to look for new ways to support economic stability with its trading partners throughout the world.

SECTION 4 REVIEW

Identify and explain the significance of the following:
- **global warming**
- **El Niño**
- **Shannon Lucid**
- **European Union**

Reading for Content Understanding

1 **Main Idea** What environmental issues and weather-related events were important in the late 1980s and the 1990s?

2 **Main Idea** What did NASA achieve in its space programs in the 1990s?

3 **Economic Development** How have economic ties among nations changed?

4 **Writing** *Informing* Imagine that you are a scientist who thinks that global warming is a serious problem. Write a paragraph explaining the situation.

5 **Critical Thinking** *Drawing Conclusions* What advantages might European nations gain by forming the European Union?

CHAPTER 24 REVIEW

Chapter Summary

Voters elected Bill Clinton president in 1992 and 1996. The Clinton administration and Congress balanced the federal budget and reformed welfare. However, President Clinton faced many challenges. In the post–Cold War world, the United States tried to help some nations achieve peace. Countries have become more connected through computer technologies and the global economy. ■

On a separate sheet of paper, complete the following activities.

Identifying People and Ideas

Describe the historical significance of the following:

1. Bill Clinton
2. Brady Bill
3. independent counsel
4. Newt Gingrich
5. Contract with America
6. Madeleine Albright
7. Immigration Reform and Control Act
8. Information Revolution
9. global warming
10. Shannon Lucid

Internet Activity

go.hrw.com
SB1 Environment

Search the Internet through the HRW Web site to find sites related to environmental issues in the United States. In particular, find out how students are involved in environmental projects. Use the information to create an action guide listing possible issues and projects in which students might want to participate.

Understanding Main Ideas

1. What health care and welfare reforms did President Clinton support? Which were successful?
2. What did many Republicans running for Congress promise to do after the 1994 elections?
3. How did acts of terrorism affect the United States during the 1990s?
4. Why did President Clinton send U.S. troops to Haiti?
5. What immigration reforms did Congress approve in the 1980s and 1990s?
6. What are some of NASA's recent efforts in space?

Reviewing Themes

1. **Constitutional Heritage**   Why did the House of Representatives impeach President Clinton? What was the outcome?

Using the Time Line

Number your paper from 1 to 5. Match the letters on the time line below with the following events.

1. **President Clinton is impeached.**
2. **The United States and NATO launch air strikes on Serbia.**
3. **The North American Free Trade Agreement is ratified.**
4. **Bill Clinton is the first Democrat elected president since 1976.**
5. **NASA lands the *Pathfinder* spacecraft on Mars.**

1992 1993 1994 1995 1996 1997 1998 1999 2000

a   b   c   d e

2. **Global Relations**   What international role has the United States assumed in the 1990s?

3. **Technology and Society**   How has the Information Revolution changed international communication?

Thinking Critically

1. **Identifying Cause and Effect**   How did the 1994 congressional elections affect Clinton's presidency?

2. **Drawing Conclusions**   What historical reasons might the United States have for being concerned about events in the Balkans?

3. **Evaluating**   How do you think the women's rights movement in the 1960s and 1970s contributed to the growth of women's sports in the 1990s?

Writing About History

1. **Creating**   Imagine that you are a campaign adviser during the 1992 presidential campaign. Select one of the candidates mentioned in the chapter. Create a flyer explaining why U.S. voters should support your candidate.

2. **Persuading**   Write a letter to the head of the World Bank urging the bank to help other countries that are experiencing financial problems. Be sure to include reasons why the World Bank should offer aid to these nations.

Linking Geography and History

1. **Location**   How did the breakup of Yugoslavia lead to conflict in the Balkans?

2. **Movement**   Why did many Haitians leave their country in the early 1990s?

Building Your Portfolio

Complete the following activities individually or in groups.

1. **A Nation of Many**   Create a collage on the theme that the United States is a nation of many people with different cultural and ethnic backgrounds. Use as many newspaper and magazine clippings as you can find, and write captions for them.

2. **Journey into the Future**   Imagine that you have been transported 50 years into the future. You will stay there just long enough to write a guide to life at that time for the next person to be transported into your future. Your guide should explain how people live, what kinds of careers they have, and how technology affects their daily lives. Your guide should also include information about food, clothing, and transportation. Be sure to include illustrations.

History Skills Workshop

Using Primary Sources   Maya Angelou is an African American writer, poet, and civil rights activist. She is best known for her autobiographical novels. Bill Clinton asked her to compose and read a poem for his 1993 inauguration. When she read "On the Pulse of Morning," she became the second poet to read his or her work at a presidential inauguration. Robert Frost had presented a poem at John F. Kennedy's inauguration in 1961. Read the following excerpt from "On the Pulse of Morning." Then answer the following questions: (a) What does Maya Angelou mean by "the pulse of this new day"? (b) What message is Angelou offering? (c) Why do you think Bill Clinton selected Angelou to participate in his inauguration?

> ❝Here on the pulse of this new day
> You may have the grace to look up
>   and out
> And into your sister's eyes, and into
> Your brother's face, your country
> And say simply
> Very simply
> With hope
> Good morning.❞

The World's Energy

The United States is the world's largest consumer of energy, using about one fourth of the world's commercial power. The United States, as well as other nations with industrial economies, consumes much of that energy in running factories and in powering homes, businesses, and public facilities. Less industrialized nations, called developing countries, consume much less energy. Energy sources for heating buildings and cooking food in developing countries often are wood, charcoal, and manure.

Much of the world's energy resources consist of fossil fuels. These fuels include oil, natural gas, and coal. Fossil fuels were formed from the remains of prehistoric plants and animals. These fuels are limited and cannot be replaced, leading some people to fear energy depletion. Leaders from the United States and other nations are working to protect Earth's limited resources. ∎

Energy Resources

Many wealthy countries, such as the United States and Canada, are among the biggest consumers and producers of energy.

Top World Consumers of Energy, 1994

Energy Consumed (in quadrillion Btu*)

Top 10 Consumers	Energy Consumed
United States	85.64
China	33.93
Russia	27.94
Japan	20.7
Germany	13.87
Canada	11.64
India	9.46
United Kingdom	9.27
France	9.24
Italy	7.03

*Btu—British thermal unit

Source: Energy Information Administration, U.S. Department of Energy

Geography **Skills**
Reading Bar Graphs

1. About how much energy did the United States consume compared to the second-largest energy consumer in 1994?

2. Use the world map on page xxvi to check the location of the countries listed in this bar graph. On which continent is each country located?

3. Which continent consumes the most energy?

Leading Energy Producers, 1990–1992

Oil Producers

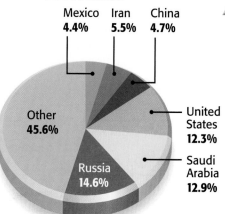

Mexico 4.4%
Iran 5.5%
China 4.7%
Other 45.6%
United States 12.3%
Saudi Arabia 12.9%
Russia 14.6%

Coal Producers

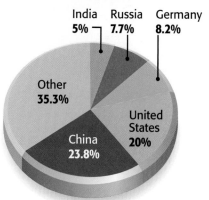

India 5%
Russia 7.7%
Germany 8.2%
Other 35.3%
United States 20%
China 23.8%

Natural Gas Producers

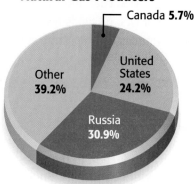

Canada 5.7%
United States 24.2%
Other 39.2%
Russia 30.9%

Source: *Rand McNally Goode's World Atlas*

Geography **Skills**
Reading Pie Graphs

1. What nation ranked in the top three in all areas of energy production?
2. What percentage of the world's coal was produced by China, Russia, and the United States combined?
3. What energy source owes more than half of its production to two nations?

Natural gas, oil, and coal provide most of the world's energy.

History Note 1

These pie graphs show the three major sources of energy in the world today. These fossil fuels—oil, coal, and gas—made up about 90 percent of the world's total commercial energy production at the beginning of the 1990s.

Energy at Home

Most of the United States's energy is produced at home. The United States does buy large amounts of oil, as well as certain other fuels, from other countries. Foreign fuel is important because of high U.S. consumption.

Energy Sources in the United States

Major oil-producing field

Minor oil-producing field

Major natural gas field

Major coal deposit

Minor coal deposit

Uranium deposits

Nuclear power plants

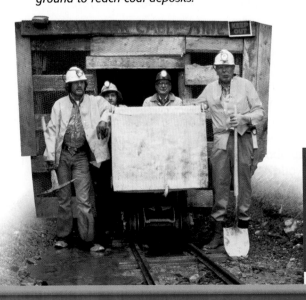

Miners tunnel deep into the ground to reach coal deposits.

Geography Skills
Reading Special-Purpose Maps

1. Where are major U.S. coal deposits located?
2. Where are major U.S. oil fields found?
3. What energy sources can be found off the coast in the Gulf of Mexico?

History Note 2

About 80 percent of U.S. energy production in the mid-1990s came from fossil fuels. Power generated by nuclear plants accounted for another 10 percent of the country's energy production. Coal has been the largest single source of U.S. energy production since the mid-1970s and is the country's largest energy-resource export.

U.S. Energy Use, 1970–1995

■ Consumption ■ Production ■ Imports ■ Exports

Energy Consumed (in quadrillion Btu*)

*Btu–British thermal unit

Source: Energy Information Administration, U.S. Department of Energy

Geography Skills

Reading Line Graphs

1. During what five-year period shown on the graph did U.S. energy consumption decrease?
2. During what five-year period shown on the graph did U.S. energy consumption increase by the greatest amount?
3. In what year shown on the graph did the United States import the most energy? How much energy was imported in that year?
4. How much more energy did the United States import in 1990 than it exported in that year?

History Note 3

Texas and California, the nation's two most populous states, rank first and second among the 50 states in the amount of energy consumed. However, Alaska—where winters are long and extremely cold—consumes more energy per person than any other state. The typical New York resident on average consumes less energy than residents of any other state.

Derricks like this one pump oil from beneath Earth's surface.

History Skills

WORKSHOP

Writing a Paper

When writing a paper, you should keep a particular focus in mind. You may want to analyze some information, inform your audience about a particular topic, or persuade someone on an important issue.

Stages of Writing a Paper When you are writing a paper, divide your work into steps. Focus on completing each before you begin the next.

Writing with a Purpose Always keep your purpose for writing the paper in mind—it will determine the best approach to take. Different types of writing require their own tone and content. For example, you would use a different tone in writing a paper analyzing the causes of the oil embargo than you would in trying to persuade readers to recycle.

Research is an important part of writing a paper.

How to Write a Paper

Regardless of what you are writing, you should follow certain basic steps.

1. **Choose a topic** If possible, choose a topic that interests you. Keep the subject of your topic specific so that your research and writing is focused and clear.

2. **Identify your purpose in writing** Understand the directions for your assignment so that you can plan your paper.

3. **Consider your audience** When writing for a specific audience, choose the tone and style that will best communicate your message.

4. **Collect information** Use your library and/or the Internet and take notes of the information you collect on your subject.

5. **Create an outline** Organize your themes, main ideas, and supporting details into an outline.

6. **Write a first draft and evaluate it** Use your outline as a guide. Each paragraph should express one main idea and contain details to support it. Use transitions—sentences that build connections between paragraphs—to show the relationships between ideas.

7. **Review, revise, and proofread** Read your draft and reorganize it as needed to make your points. Improve sentences by adding appropriate adjectives and adverbs. Make your writing clearer by changing the length or structure of awkward sentences. Check for proper spelling, punctuation, and grammar.

8. **Write your final version** Prepare a neat, clean final version. Appearance is important. It can affect the way people understand your writing.

Practicing the Skill

1. Why is it important to consider the audience for whom you are writing?

2. What steps should you take to edit a first draft?

3. Choose one of the presidents in this unit and write a three-paragraph paper about his administration. Along with the paper's final version, turn in your research notes, outline, first draft, and revisions.

American History

History in Action

UNIT 8 PORTFOLIO

Textbook Final Chapter

Complete the following activity in small, cooperative groups.

History is more than just what happened long ago. Events taking place today are also part of the continuing story of history. Your editor has asked you to add a chapter to this textbook. This chapter will cover the important events in U.S. history that have occurred since the end of Chapter 24. Your class will be divided into four teams and each team will create one section of the chapter.

Materials To complete this activity, you will need posterboard, construction paper, or typing paper. You may wish to use a computer to write your chapter. In addition, you will need markers, pens, pencils, and glue, tape, or rubber cement.

Parts of the Project Complete the following tasks to create your chapter:

1. **Planning and Outlining** Each group will take one of the following topics—American Culture; The Election of 2000; Major World Events; or Science and Technology—as the subject for its section. Meet as a group and create an outline for your section. Review the last few chapters of this book for ideas on how to organize your section. Further divide your section's main topic into smaller, more specific topics. Use these topics to divide your sections into subsections. Assign each person a subsection.

2. **Researching and Writing** Use recent newspapers and magazines, the library, and other sources to gather information on your topic. Compare what you find with what you have already learned and take note of any

These students are selecting photographs for their project.

new developments or changes that have occurred. Also gather any images, maps, or charts you think will be useful. Then, write your subsection.

3. **Editing** When you have finished writing, meet as a group again. Have each group member exchange his or her subsection with another group member. Read and edit the subsection you have received, checking spelling and grammar. Ask questions about anything that seems unclear and offer constructive suggestions to improve the work. Get back your original subsection, revise it, and write a final draft.

4. **Laying out the Chapter** Meet as a group and decide how to arrange the images and text of your section. Paste the subsections with images onto posterboard to create the pages of your section. Combine it with the other groups' sections to create a chapter.

Have the class vote on a title for the chapter. Display the chapter in your classroom or another area of the school and use it to answer questions about recent history.

American flag

Cotton, an important southern product

I LIKE IKE

Dwight Eisenhower campaign item

Space shuttle

Streetcar

Saxophone and jukebox

Iwo Jima memorial

Call to FREEDOM

1865 to the Present

The Statue of Liberty

REFERENCE

Magazines
reflecting
the spirit of
the 1920s

The Granger Collection,
New York

Model T
automobile

The Granger
Collection,
New York

Campaign
pins

Camera
box

Presidents of the United States

The Official Portraits

1 GEORGE WASHINGTON
Born: 1732   Died: 1799
Years in Office: 1789–97
Political Party: None
Home State: Virginia
Vice President: John Adams

2 JOHN ADAMS
Born: 1735   Died: 1826
Years in Office: 1797–1801
Political Party: Federalist
Home State: Massachusetts
Vice President: Thomas Jefferson

3 THOMAS JEFFERSON
Born: 1743   Died: 1826
Years in Office: 1801–09
Political Party: Republican*
Home State: Virginia
Vice Presidents: Aaron Burr,
  George Clinton

4 JAMES MADISON
Born: 1751   Died: 1836
Years in Office: 1809–17
Political Party: Republican
Home State: Virginia
Vice Presidents: George Clinton,
  Elbridge Gerry

5 JAMES MONROE
Born: 1758   Died: 1831
Years in Office: 1817–25
Political Party: Republican
Home State: Virginia
Vice President: Daniel D. Tompkins

6 JOHN QUINCY ADAMS
Born: 1767   Died: 1848
Years in Office: 1825–29
Political Party: Republican
Home State: Massachusetts
Vice President: John C. Calhoun

7 ANDREW JACKSON
Born: 1767   Died: 1845
Years in Office: 1829–37
Political Party: Democratic
Home State: Tennessee
Vice Presidents: John C. Calhoun,
  Martin Van Buren

* The Republican Party of the third through sixth presidents is not the party of Abraham Lincoln, which was founded in 1854.

8 MARTIN VAN BUREN
Born: 1782   **Died:** 1862
Years in Office: 1837–41
Political Party: Democratic
Home State: New York
Vice President: Richard M. Johnson

9 WILLIAM HENRY HARRISON
Born: 1773   **Died:** 1841
Years in Office: 1841
Political Party: Whig
Home State: Ohio
Vice President: John Tyler

10 JOHN TYLER
Born: 1790   **Died:** 1862
Years in Office: 1841–45
Political Party: Whig
Home State: Virginia
Vice President: None

11 JAMES K. POLK
Born: 1795   **Died:** 1849
Years in Office: 1845–49
Political Party: Democratic
Home State: Tennessee
Vice President: George M. Dallas

12 ZACHARY TAYLOR
Born: 1784   **Died:** 1850
Years in Office: 1849–50
Political Party: Whig
Home State: Louisiana
Vice President: Millard Fillmore

13 MILLARD FILLMORE
Born: 1800   **Died:** 1874
Years in Office: 1850–53
Political Party: Whig
Home State: New York
Vice President: None

14 FRANKLIN PIERCE
Born: 1804   **Died:** 1869
Years in Office: 1853–57
Political Party: Democratic
Home State: New Hampshire
Vice President: William R. King

15 JAMES BUCHANAN
Born: 1791   **Died:** 1868
Years in Office: 1857–61
Political Party: Democratic
Home State: Pennsylvania
Vice President: John C. Breckinridge

16 ABRAHAM LINCOLN
Born: 1809   **Died:** 1865
Years in Office: 1861–65
Political Party: Republican
Home State: Illinois
Vice Presidents: Hannibal Hamlin,
Andrew Johnson

17 ANDREW JOHNSON
Born: 1808 **Died:** 1875
Years in Office: 1865–69
Political Party: Republican
Home State: Tennessee
Vice President: None

18 ULYSSES S. GRANT
Born: 1822 **Died:** 1885
Years in Office: 1869–77
Political Party: Republican
Home State: Illinois
Vice Presidents: Schuyler Colfax,
Henry Wilson

19 RUTHERFORD B. HAYES
Born: 1822 **Died:** 1893
Years in Office: 1877–81
Political Party: Republican
Home State: Ohio
Vice President: William A. Wheeler

20 JAMES A. GARFIELD
Born: 1831 **Died:** 1881
Years in Office: 1881
Political Party: Republican
Home State: Ohio
Vice President: Chester A. Arthur

21 CHESTER A. ARTHUR
Born: 1829 **Died:** 1886
Years in Office: 1881–85
Political Party: Republican
Home State: New York
Vice President: None

22 GROVER CLEVELAND
Born: 1837 **Died:** 1908
Years in Office: 1885–89
Political Party: Democratic
Home State: New York
Vice President: Thomas A. Hendricks

23 BENJAMIN HARRISON
Born: 1833 **Died:** 1901
Years in Office: 1889–93
Political Party: Republican
Home State: Indiana
Vice President: Levi P. Morton

24 GROVER CLEVELAND
Born: 1837 **Died:** 1908
Years in Office: 1893–97
Political Party: Democratic
Home State: New York
Vice President: Adlai E. Stevenson

25 WILLIAM MCKINLEY
Born: 1843 **Died:** 1901
Years in Office: 1897–1901
Political Party: Republican
Home State: Ohio
Vice Presidents: Garret A. Hobart,
Theodore Roosevelt

PRESIDENTS OF THE UNITED STATES

26 **THEODORE ROOSEVELT**
Born: 1858   Died: 1919
Years in Office: 1901–09
Political Party: Republican
Home State: New York
Vice President: Charles W. Fairbanks

27 **WILLIAM HOWARD TAFT**
Born: 1857   Died: 1930
Years in Office: 1909–13
Political Party: Republican
Home State: Ohio
Vice President: James S. Sherman

28 **WOODROW WILSON**
Born: 1856   Died: 1924
Years in Office: 1913–21
Political Party: Democratic
Home State: New Jersey
Vice President: Thomas R. Marshall

29 **WARREN G. HARDING**
Born: 1865   Died: 1923
Years in Office: 1921–23
Political Party: Republican
Home State: Ohio
Vice President: Calvin Coolidge

30 **CALVIN COOLIDGE**
Born: 1872   Died: 1933
Years in Office: 1923–29
Political Party: Republican
Home State: Massachusetts
Vice President: Charles G. Dawes

31 **HERBERT HOOVER**
Born: 1874   Died: 1964
Years in Office: 1929–33
Political Party: Republican
Home State: California
Vice President: Charles Curtis

32 **FRANKLIN D. ROOSEVELT**
Born: 1882   Died: 1945
Years in Office: 1933–45
Political Party: Democratic
Home State: New York
Vice Presidents: John Nance Garner,
  Henry Wallace, Harry S Truman

33 **HARRY S TRUMAN**
Born: 1884   Died: 1972
Years in Office: 1945–53
Political Party: Democratic
Home State: Missouri
Vice President: Alben W. Barkley

34 **DWIGHT D. EISENHOWER**
Born: 1890   Died: 1969
Years in Office: 1953–61
Political Party: Republican
Home State: Kansas
Vice President: Richard M. Nixon

35 JOHN F. KENNEDY
Born: 1917   **Died:** 1963
Years in Office: 1961–63
Political Party: Democratic
Home State: Massachusetts
Vice President: Lyndon B. Johnson

36 LYNDON B. JOHNSON
Born: 1908   **Died:** 1973
Years in Office: 1963–69
Political Party: Democratic
Home State: Texas
Vice President: Hubert H. Humphrey

37 RICHARD M. NIXON
Born: 1913   **Died:** 1994
Years in Office: 1969–74
Political Party: Republican
Home State: California
Vice Presidents: Spiro T. Agnew,
 Gerald R. Ford

38 GERALD R. FORD
Born: 1913
Years in Office: 1974–77
Political Party: Republican
Home State: Michigan
Vice President: Nelson A. Rockefeller

39 JIMMY CARTER
Born: 1924
Years in Office: 1977–81
Political Party: Democratic
Home State: Georgia
Vice President: Walter F. Mondale

40 RONALD REAGAN
Born: 1911
Years in Office: 1981–89
Political Party: Republican
Home State: California
Vice President: George Bush

41 GEORGE BUSH
Born: 1924
Years in Office: 1989–93
Political Party: Republican
Home State: Texas
Vice President: J. Danforth Quayle

42 BILL CLINTON
Born: 1946
Years in Office: 1993–
Political Party: Democratic
Home State: Arkansas
Vice President: Albert Gore Jr.

PRESIDENTS OF THE UNITED STATES

Facts About the States

STATE	YEAR OF STATEHOOD	1997 POPULATION	REPS. IN CONGRESS	AREA (SQ. MI.)	POPULATION DENSITY (SQ. MI.)	CAPITAL
Alabama	1819	4,319,154	7	51,705	83.5	Montgomery
Alaska	1959	609,311	1	591,004	1.0	Juneau
Arizona	1912	4,554,966	6	114,000	40.0	Phoenix
Arkansas	1836	2,522,819	4	53,187	47.4	Little Rock
California	1850	32,268,301	52	158,706	203.3	Sacramento
Colorado	1876	3,892,644	6	104,091	37.4	Denver
Connecticut	1788	3,269,858	6	5,018	651.6	Hartford
Delaware	1787	731,581	1	2,045	357.7	Dover
District of Columbia	—	528,964	—	69	7,666.1	—
Florida	1845	14,653,945	23	58,664	249.8	Tallahassee
Georgia	1788	7,486,242	11	58,910	127.1	Atlanta
Hawaii	1959	1,186,602	2	6,471	183.4	Honolulu
Idaho	1890	1,210,232	2	83,564	14.5	Boise
Illinois	1818	11,895,849	20	56,345	211.1	Springfield
Indiana	1816	5,864,108	10	36,185	162.1	Indianapolis
Iowa	1846	2,852,423	5	56,275	50.7	Des Moines
Kansas	1861	2,594,840	4	82,277	31.5	Topeka
Kentucky	1792	3,908,124	6	40,410	96.7	Frankfort
Louisiana	1812	4,351,769	7	42,752	101.8	Baton Rouge
Maine	1820	1,242,051	2	33,265	37.3	Augusta
Maryland	1788	5,094,289	8	10,460	487.0	Annapolis
Massachusetts	1788	6,117,520	10	8,284	738.5	Boston
Michigan	1837	9,773,892	16	58,527	167.0	Lansing
Minnesota	1858	4,685,549	8	84,402	55.5	St. Paul
Mississippi	1817	2,730,501	5	47,689	57.3	Jackson
Missouri	1821	5,402,058	9	69,697	77.5	Jefferson City
Montana	1889	878,810	1	147,046	6.0	Helena
Nebraska	1867	1,656,870	3	77,355	21.4	Lincoln
Nevada	1864	1,676,809	2	110,561	15.2	Carson City
New Hampshire	1788	1,172,709	2	9,279	126.4	Concord
New Jersey	1787	8,052,849	13	7,787	1,034.1	Trenton
New Mexico	1912	1,729,751	3	121,593	14.2	Santa Fe
New York	1788	18,137,226	31	49,108	369.3	Albany
North Carolina	1789	7,425,183	12	52,669	141.0	Raleigh
North Dakota	1889	640,883	1	70,702	9.1	Bismarck
Ohio	1803	11,186,331	19	41,330	270.7	Columbus
Oklahoma	1907	3,317,091	6	69,956	47.4	Oklahoma City
Oregon	1859	3,243,487	5	97,073	33.4	Salem
Pennsylvania	1787	12,019,661	21	45,038	266.9	Harrisburg
Rhode Island	1790	987,429	2	1,212	814.7	Providence
South Carolina	1788	3,760,181	6	31,113	120.9	Columbia
South Dakota	1889	737,973	1	77,116	9.6	Pierre
Tennessee	1796	5,368,198	9	42,144	127.4	Nashville
Texas	1845	19,439,337	30	266,807	72.9	Austin
Utah	1896	2,059,148	3	84,899	24.3	Salt Lake City
Vermont	1791	588,978	1	9,614	61.3	Montpelier
Virginia	1788	6,733,996	11	40,767	165.2	Richmond
Washington	1889	5,610,362	9	68,139	82.3	Olympia
West Virginia	1863	1,815,787	3	24,232	74.9	Charleston
Wisconsin	1848	5,169,677	9	56,153	92.1	Madison
Wyoming	1890	479,743	1	97,809	4.9	Cheyenne

Important Supreme Court Cases

MARBURY v. MADISON, 1 CRANCH (5 U.S.) 137 (1803)

Significance: This ruling established the Supreme Court's power of judicial review, giving the Court the power to decide whether laws passed by Congress are constitutional. This decision greatly increased the prestige of the Court and gave the judiciary branch a powerful check against the legislative and executive branches.

Background: William Marbury and several others were commissioned as judges by Federalist president John Adams during his last days in office. This act angered the new Democratic-Republican president, Thomas Jefferson. Jefferson ordered his secretary of state, James Madison, not to deliver the commissions. Marbury took advantage of a section in the Judiciary Act of 1789 that allowed him to take his case directly to the Supreme Court. He sued Madison, demanding the commission and the judgeship.

Decision: This case was decided on February 24, 1803, by a vote of 5 to 0. Chief Justice John Marshall spoke for the Court, which decided against Marbury. The court ruled that although Marbury's commission had been unfairly withheld, he could not lawfully take his case to the Court without first trying it in a lesser court. Marshall said that the section of the Judiciary Act that Marbury had used was actually unconstitutional, and that the Constitution must take priority over laws passed by Congress.

MCCULLOCH v. MARYLAND, 4 WHEAT. (17 U.S.) 316 (1819)

Significance: This ruling established that Congress had the constitutional right to charter a national bank. The case also established the principle of national supremacy, which stated that the Constitution and other laws of the federal government take priority over state laws. In addition, the ruling reinforced the loose construction interpretation of the Constitution favored by many Federalists.

Background: In 1816 the federal government set up the Second Bank of the United States to stabilize the economy following the War of 1812. Many states were opposed to the competition provided by the new national bank. Some of these states passed heavy taxes on the Bank. The national bank refused to pay the taxes. This led the state of Maryland to sue James McCulloch, the cashier of the Baltimore, Maryland, branch of the national bank.

Decision: This case was decided on March 6, 1819, by a vote of 7 to 0. Chief Justice John Marshall spoke for the unanimous Court, which ruled that the national bank was constitutional because it helped the federal government carry out the other powers granted to it by the Constitution. The Court declared that any attempt by the states to interfere with the duties of the federal government could not be permitted.

GIBBONS v. OGDEN, 9 WHEAT. (22 U.S.) 1 (1824)

Significance: This ruling was the first case to deal with the clause of the Constitution that allows Congress to regulate interstate and foreign commerce. This case was important because it reinforced both the authority of the federal government over the states and the division of powers between the federal government and the state governments.

Background: Steamboat operators who wanted to travel on New York waters had to obtain a state license. Thomas Gibbons had a federal license to travel along the coast, but not a state license for New York. He wanted the freedom to compete with state-licensed Aaron Ogden for steam travel between New Jersey and the New York island of Manhattan.

Decision: This case was decided on March 2, 1824, by a vote of 6 to 0. Chief Justice John Marshall spoke for the Court, which ruled in favor of Gibbons. The Court stated that the congressional statute (Gibbons's federal license) took priority over the state statute (Ogden's state-monopoly license). The ruling also defined commerce as more than simply the exchange of goods, broadening it to include the transportation of people and the use of new inventions (such as the steamboat).

WORCESTER v. GEORGIA, 6 PET. (31 U.S.) 515 (1832)

Significance: This ruling made Georgia's removal of the Cherokee illegal. However, Georgia, with President Andrew Jackson's support, defied the Court's decision. By not enforcing the Court's ruling, Jackson violated his constitutional oath as president. As a result, the Cherokee and other American Indian tribes continued to be forced off of lands protected by treaties.

Background: The state of Georgia wanted to remove Cherokee Indians from lands they held by treaty. Samuel Worcester, a missionary who worked with the Cherokee Nation, was arrested for failing to take an oath of allegiance to the state and to obey a Georgia militia order to leave the Cherokee's lands. Worcester sued, charging that Georgia had no legal authority on Cherokee lands.

Decision: This case was decided on March 3, 1832, by a vote of 5 to 1 in favor of Worcester. Chief Justice John Marshall spoke for the Supreme Court, which ruled that the Cherokee were an independent political community. The Court decided that only the federal government, not the state of Georgia, had authority over legal matters involving the Cherokee people.

SCOTT v. SANDFORD, 19 HOW. (60 U.S.) 393 (1857)

Significance: This ruling denied enslaved African Americans U.S. citizenship and the right to sue in federal court. The decision also contradicted the Missouri Compromise, which had prevented slavery in territories north of the 36° 30' line of latitude. The ruling increased the controversy over the expansion of slavery in new states and territories.

Background: John Emerson, an army doctor, took his slave Dred Scott with him to live in Illinois and then Wisconsin Territory, both of which had banned slavery. In 1842 the two moved to Missouri, a slave state. Four years later, Scott sued for his freedom according to a Missouri legal principle of "once free, always free." The principle meant that a slave was entitled to freedom if he or she had once lived in a free state or territory.

Decision: This case was decided March 6–7, 1857, by a vote of 7 to 2. Chief Justice Roger B. Taney spoke for the Court, which ruled that slaves did not have the right to sue in federal courts because they were considered property, not citizens. In addition, the Court ruled that Congress did not have the power to abolish slavery in territories because that power was not strictly defined in the Constitution. Furthermore, the Court overturned the once-free, always-free principle.

PLESSY v. FERGUSON, 163 U.S. 537 (1896)

Significance: This case upheld the constitutionality of racial segregation by ruling that separate facilities for different races were legal as long as those facilities were equal to one another. This case provided a legal justification for racial segregation for more than 50 years until it was overturned by *Brown* v. *Board of Education* in 1954.

Background: An 1890 Louisiana law required that all railway companies in the state use "separate-but-equal" railcars for white and

African American passengers. A group of citizens in New Orleans banded together to challenge the law and chose Homer Plessy to test the law in 1892. Plessy took a seat in a whites-only coach, and when he refused to move, he was arrested. Plessy eventually sought review by the U.S. Supreme Court, claiming that the Louisiana law violated his Fourteenth Amendment right to equal protection.

Decision: This case was decided on May 18, 1896, by a vote of 7 to 1. Justice Henry Billings Brown spoke for the Court, which upheld the constitutionality of the Louisiana law that segregated railcars. Justice John M. Harlan dissented, arguing that the Constitution should not be interpreted in ways that recognize class or racial distinctions.

LOCHNER v. NEW YORK, 198 U.S. 45 (1905)

Significance: This decision established the Supreme Court's role in overseeing state regulations. For more than 30 years *Lochner* was often used as a precedent in striking down state laws, minimum-wage laws, child labor laws, and regulations placed on the banking and transportation industries.

Background: In 1895 the state of New York passed a labor law limiting bakers to working no more than 10 hours per day or 60 hours per week. The purpose of the law was to protect the health of bakers, who worked in hot and damp conditions and breathed in large quantities of flour dust. In 1902 Joseph Lochner, the owner of a small bakery in New York, claimed that this law violated his Fourteenth Amendment rights by unfairly depriving him of the liberty to make contracts with employees. This case went to the U.S. Supreme Court.

Decision: This case was decided on April 17, 1905, by a vote of 5 to 4 in favor of Lochner. The Supreme Court judged that the Fourteenth Amendment protected the right to sell and buy labor, and that any state law restricting that right was unconstitutional. The Court rejected the argument that the limited workday and workweek were necessary to protect the health of bakery workers.

MULLER v. OREGON, 208 U.S. 412 (1908)

Significance: A landmark for cases involving social reform, this decision established the Court's recognition of social and economic conditions (in this case, women's health) as a factor in making laws.

Background: In 1903 Oregon passed a law limiting workdays to 10 hours for female workers in laundries and factories. In 1905 Curt Muller's Grand Laundry was found guilty of breaking this law. Muller appealed, claiming that the state law violated his freedom of contract (the Supreme Court had upheld a similar claim that year in *Lochner* v. *New York*). When this case came to the Court, the National Consumers' League hired lawyer Louis D. Brandeis to present Oregon's argument. Brandeis argued that the Court had already defended the state's police power to protect its citizens' health, safety, and welfare.

Decision: This case was decided on February 24, 1908, by a vote of 9 to 0 upholding the Oregon law. The Court agreed that women's well-being was in the state's public interest and that the 10-hour law was a valid way to protect their well-being.

BROWN v. BOARD OF EDUCATION, 347 U.S. 483 (1954)

Significance: This ruling reversed the Supreme Court's earlier position on segregation set by *Plessy* v. *Ferguson* (1896). The decision also inspired Congress and the federal courts to help carry out further civil rights reforms for African Americans.

Background: When the Browns, an African American family, moved into an all-white neighborhood in Topeka, Kansas, they were told that their daughter would have to attend a distant all-black school that was supposedly "separate but equal." Oliver Brown sued the school board, saying that school segregation violated the equal protection clause of the Fourteenth Amendment.

Decision: This case was decided on May 17, 1954, by a vote of 9 to 0. Chief Justice Earl Warren spoke for the unanimous Court, which ruled that segregation in public education created inequality. The Court held that racial segregation in public schools was by nature unequal, even if the school facilities were equal. The Court noted that such segregation created feelings of inferiority that could not be undone. Therefore, enforced separation of the races in public education is unconstitutional.

GIDEON v. WAINWRIGHT, 372 U.S. 335 (1963)

Significance: This ruling was one of several key Supreme Court decisions establishing free legal help for those who cannot otherwise afford representation in court.

Background: Clarence Earl Gideon was accused of robbery in Florida. Gideon could not afford a lawyer for the trial, and the judge refused to supply him with one for free. Gideon tried to defend himself and was found guilty. He eventually appealed to the U.S. Supreme Court, claiming that the lower court's denial of a court-appointed lawyer violated his Sixth and Fourteenth Amendment rights.

Decision: This case was decided on March 18, 1963, by a vote of 9 to 0 in favor of Gideon. The Court agreed that the Sixth Amendment (which protects a citizen's right to have a lawyer for his or her defense) applied to the states because it fell under the due process clause of the Fourteenth Amendment. Thus, the states are required to provide legal aid to those defendants in criminal cases who cannot afford to pay for legal aid.

MIRANDA v. ARIZONA, 384 U.S. 436 (1966)

Significance: This decision ruled that an accused person's Fifth Amendment rights begin at the time of arrest. The ruling caused controversy because it made questioning suspects and collecting evidence more difficult for law enforcement officers.

Background: In 1963 Ernesto Miranda was arrested in Arizona for a kidnapping. Miranda signed a confession and was later found guilty of the crime. The arresting police officers, however, admitted that they had not told Miranda of his right to talk with an attorney before his confession. Miranda appealed his conviction on the grounds that by not informing him of his legal rights the police had violated his Fifth Amendment right against self-incrimination.

Decision: This case was decided on June 13, 1966, by a vote of 5 to 4. Chief Justice Earl Warren spoke for the Court, which ruled in Miranda's favor. The Court decided that an accused person must be given four warnings after being taken into police custody: (1) the suspect has the right to remain silent, (2) anything the suspect says can and will be used against him or her, (3) the suspect has the right to consult with an attorney and to have an attorney present during questioning, and (4) if the suspect cannot afford a lawyer, one will be provided before questioning begins.

REED v. REED, 404 U.S. 71 (1971)

Significance: This ruling was the first in a century of Fourteenth Amendment decisions to say that gender discrimination violated the equal protection clause. This case was later used to strike down several other statutes that violated women's rights.

Background: Cecil and Sally Reed were separated. When their son died without a will, the law gave preference to Cecil to be appointed the administrator of the son's estate. Sally sued Cecil for the right to administer the estate, challenging the gender preference in the law.

Decision: This case was decided on November 22, 1971, by a vote of 7 to 0. Chief Justice Warren Burger spoke for the unanimous Supreme Court. Although the Court had upheld laws based on gender preference in the past, in this case it reversed its position. The Court declared that gender discrimination violated the equal protection clause of the Constitution and therefore could not be the basis for a law.

Gazetteer

Abilene   Cattle town in east-central Kansas. (39°N 97°W) **168**

Africa   Second-largest continent. Lies in both the Northern and the Southern Hemispheres. **xxx**

Aisne River   River in northern France. **340**

Akron   City in northeast Ohio. (41°N 81°W) **448**

Alabama (AL)   State in the southern United States. Admitted as a state in 1819. Capital: Montgomery. (33°N 87°W) **xx**

Alamogordo   City in southern New Mexico. (33°N 106°W) **496**

Alaska (AK)   U.S. state in northwestern North America. Admitted as a state in 1959. Capital: Juneau. (64°N 150°W) **xx**

Albany   Capital of New York State. (42°N 74°W) **16**

Alcatraz Island   Island in San Francisco Bay once used as a federal prison. **617**

Aleutian Islands   Chain of islands off the coast of Alaska. (52°N 176°W) **493**

Alsace-Lorraine   Region between Belgium, France, Germany, and Switzerland. Part of the German Empire from 1871 to 1918; returned to France by the Treaty of Versailles in 1919. Held by Germany during World War II from 1940 to 1944. **347**

Anniston   City in northeastern Alabama. (34°N 86°W) **597**

Antietam Creek   Creek in northern Maryland. **109**

Antwerp   City in northern Belgium. (51°N 5°E) **487**

Anzio   Town in central Italy. (41°N 12°E) **487**

Appalachian Mountains   Mountain system in eastern North America that extends from Canada to central Alabama. **xxii**

Appomattox Courthouse   Town in central Virginia. (37°N 79°W) **109**

Arctic Circle   Line of latitude that encircles the northern frigid zone of Earth. **7**

Ardennes   Forest in southern Belgium and northwestern France. **489**

Argentina   Republic located in the south-central and southern part of South America. Capital: Buenos Aires. (34°S 64°W) **xxvii**

Argonne Forest   Wooded plateau in northeastern France. **342**

Arizona (AZ)   State in the southwestern United States. Became a territory in 1863. Admitted as a state in 1912. Capital: Phoenix. (34°N 113°W) **xx**

Arkansas (AR)   State in the south-central United States. Admitted as a state in 1836. Capital: Little Rock. (35°N 93°W) **xx**

Asia   Largest continent. Occupies the same land mass as Europe. **xxix**

Atlanta   Capital of Georgia. (33°N 84°W) **109**

Atlantic Ocean   Vast body of water separating North and South America from Europe and Africa. **xxiv**

Attu   Island located off the coast of southwestern Alaska. (53°N 173°E) **491**

Australia   Island-continent and country located between the Indian and Pacific Oceans. Capital: Canberra. (25°S 135°E) **xxxi**

Austria   Republic in central Europe. Capital: Vienna. (48°N 16°E) **xxviii**

Austria-Hungary   Monarchy in central Europe from 1867 to 1918. Consisted of Austria, Bohemia, Hungary, and parts of Italy, Poland, Romania, and Yugoslavia. **332**

Bahamas   Country in the Atlantic Ocean consisting of a chain of islands. Capital: Nassau. (26°N 76°W) **xxvi**

Bahrain   Nation made up of islands located in the Persian Gulf off the coast of the Arabian Peninsula. Capital: Manama. (26°N 50°E) **xxix**

Balkans   Region that occupies the Balkan Peninsula and includes Albania, Bulgaria, Greece, Romania, Yugoslavia, and northwestern Turkey. **332**

Baltic Sea   Arm of the Atlantic Ocean in northern Europe. **xxviii**

Baltimore   Maryland city northeast of Washington, D.C., on the Chesapeake Bay. (39°N 76°W) **xx**

Bataan Peninsula   Peninsula in the western Philippines. (14°N 120°E) **491**

Baton Rouge   Capital of Louisiana. (30°N 91°W) **109**

Bay of Pigs   Bay on the western coast of Cuba. Also called Bahía de Cochinos. **576**

Beirut   Capital of Lebanon. (34°N 35°E) **xxix**

Belgium   Kingdom in northwestern Europe. Capital: Brussels. (51°N 13°E) **xxviii**

Belgrade   Capital of Yugoslavia and of Serbia. (45°N 20°W) **xxviii**

Belleau Wood   Forest in northern France. **341**

Beringia   Land bridge that once connected present-day Alaska with Siberia. **6**

Berkeley   City on California's San Francisco Bay. (38°N 122°W) **xx**

Berlin   Capital of Germany. Divided into East Berlin and West Berlin in 1945. Reunited in 1990. (52°N 13°E) **477**

Birmingham   City in north-central Alabama. (33°N 86°W) **xx**

Black Hills   Mountains in western South Dakota and northeastern Wyoming. **153**

Black Sea   Sea between Europe and Asia. **xxviii**

Bonin Islands   Group of islands in the western Pacific Ocean. (27°N 142°E) **492**

Bosnia and Herzegovina   Country annexed to Austria-Hungary in 1908; after World War I became part of what would become Yugoslavia; declared independence in 1992. Capital: Sarajevo. (44°N 17°E) **xxviii**

Bosque Redondo   Location of a former Navajo reservation in New Mexico. **155**

Boston   Capital of Massachusetts. (42°N 71°W) **16**

Boston Harbor   Massachusetts port that was the scene of the Boston Tea Party in 1773. **22**

Brandywine Creek Creek in Pennsylvania and Delaware that was the site of the Revolutionary War's Battle of Brandywine Creek in 1777. **24**

Brazil Republic in eastern South America. Largest country on the continent. Ruled by Portugal from 1500 to 1822. Capital: Brasília. (9°S 53°W) **xxvii**

Breed's Hill Hill in Boston, Massachusetts, that was one site of the Revolutionary War's Battle of Bunker Hill in 1775. **23**

Brooklyn Borough that is part of New York City. **218**

Buffalo City in western New York. (43°N 79°W) **xx**

Bulgaria Republic in southeastern Europe. Capital: Sofia. (42°N 23°E) **xxviii**

Bull Run Creek in northeastern Virginia where the Confederates won two major battles during the Civil War. **109**

Bunker Hill Hill in Boston, Massachusetts, that was one site of the Revolutionary War's Battle of Bunker Hill in 1775. **23**

Burma Country in southeast Asia. Now called Myanmar. Capital: Rangoon. (16°N 96°E) **xxix**

California (CA) State in the western United States. Admitted as a state in 1850. Capital: Sacramento. (38°N 121°W) **xx**

Cambodia Republic in southeastern Asia. Capital: Phnom Penh. (11°N 105°E) **xxix**

Canada Country in northern North America. Capital: Ottawa. (50°N 100°W) **xxvi**

Cape of Good Hope Southern tip of Africa. **10**

Caribbean Sea Arm of the Atlantic Ocean bounded by the West Indies, Central America, and South America. **xxvi**

Central America Region of land connecting North and South America. **xxvi**

Chagres River River in Panama that is dammed to form Gatún Lake. **303**

Chancellorsville Town in northeastern Virginia where Confederate forces won a major victory during the Civil War. Now called Chancellor. **109**

Charleston Port city in southeastern South Carolina. (33°N 80°W) **16**

Château-Thierry Town in northern France. (49°N 3°E) **342**

Chesapeake Bay Inlet of the Atlantic Ocean in Virginia and Maryland. **xxii**

Chicago City in northeastern Illinois on Lake Michigan. (41°N 87°W) **xx**

Chile Country in southwestern South America. Capital: Santiago. (35°S 72°W) **xxvii**

China Vast country in Asia. Capital: Beijing. (36°N 93°E) **xxix**

Ciudad Juárez City in the Chihuahua state of northern Mexico. (31°N 106°W) **308**

Colombia Republic in northwestern South America. Capital: Bogotá. (3°N 72°W) **xxvii**

Colón City in north-central Panama. (9°N 80°W) **302**

Colorado (CO) State in the western-central United States. Admitted as a state in 1876. Capital: Denver. (39°N 107°W) **xx**

Colorado River River located in the southwestern United States. **xxii**

Columbia Capital of South Carolina. (34°N 81°W) **123**

Columbia River River that flows from southeastern British Columbia, Canada, through Washington and Oregon, where it empties into the Pacific Ocean. **89**

Columbus Town in southwestern New Mexico. (32°N 107°W) **305**

Compiègne Town in northern France. (49°N 3°E) **343**

Concord Town in northeastern Massachusetts. (42°N 71°W) **22**

Coney Island Section of southern Brooklyn in New York City that has been home to several amusement parks. **223**

Confederacy (Confederate States of America) Nation made up of 11 southern states during their secession from the United States from 1860 to 1865. **107**

Connecticut (CT) State in the northeastern United States. One of the original thirteen colonies. Capital: Hartford. (41°N 73°W) **xx**

Coral Sea Part of the southwestern Pacific Ocean. **xxxi**

Corregidor Island located in Manila Bay off of the Bataan Peninsula. (14°N 120°E) **491**

Croatia Country in southeastern Europe; was part of the republic of Yugoslavia until 1991. Capital: Zagreb. (45°N 15°E) **xxviii**

Crystal City City in southern Texas. (28°N 100°W) **608**

Cuba Nation south of Florida in the Caribbean Sea made up of the large island of Cuba and other surrounding small islands. Capital: Havana. (22°N 79°W) **xxvi**

Cumberland Road First U.S. federal road; began in Cumberland, Maryland, and ended in St. Louis, Missouri. **91**

Czechoslovakia Former republic in central Europe made up of present-day Czech Republic and Slovakia. **xxviii**

Czech Republic Country in central Europe. Capital: Prague. (50°N 14°E) **xxviii**

Dakota Territory Former territory in the northwestern United States made up of much of the region on both sides of the Missouri River and west of the Red River of the North. Admitted to the Union as North Dakota and South Dakota in 1889. **153**

Dallas City in northeastern Texas. (32°N 96°W) **xx**

Danzig Seaport on the Gulf of Gdańsk. Polish name: Gdańsk. (54°N 18°E) **477**

Dayton City in southwestern Ohio. (40°N 84°W) **xx**

Delaware (DE) State in the eastern United States. One of the original thirteen colonies. Capital: Dover. (38°N 75°W) **xx**

Delaware River River that forms the boundary between Pennsylvania and New Jersey. **23**

Denmark Kingdom in northwestern Europe. Capital: Copenhagen. (56°N 10°E) **xxviii**

Denver Capital of Colorado. (39°N 105°W) **xx**

Detroit City in southeastern Michigan. (42°N 83°W) **xx**

Dien Bien Phu Village in northwestern Vietnam. (21°N 102°E) **624**

Dodge City Town in southern Kansas. (38°N 100°W) **168**

Dominican Republic Country in the Caribbean Sea. Located on the eastern part of the island of Hispaniola. Capital: Santo Domingo. (19°N 70°W) **xxvi**

Dresden City in east-central Germany that was destroyed by Allied bombing during World War II. (51°N 13°E) **495**

Dunkirk Seaport in northern France. (51°N 2°E) **477**

East Germany   *See* Germany.

East Prussia   Former province of Prussia located in central Europe. Divided between Poland and the Soviet Union in 1945. **347**

Egypt   Country in northeastern Africa on the Mediterranean Sea. Capital: Cairo. (27°N 27°E) **xxx**

Elbe River   River that flows through Germany and the Czech Republic. **513**

El Caney   Community in eastern Cuba. **297**

Ellis Island   Island in New York Bay where the Statue of Liberty is located. (40°N 74°W) **211**

El Paso   City in western Texas. (32°N 106°W) **261**

El Salvador   Country in Central America. Capital: San Salvador. (14°N 89°W) **xxvi**

England   Region of the United Kingdom that makes up of most of the southern part of the island of Great Britain. Capital: London. (51°N 1°W) **xxviii**

English Channel   Strait between southern England and northern France that connects the Atlantic Ocean with the North Sea. **xxviii**

Erie Canal   Canal that extends from Buffalo, New York, to Albany, New York. **91**

Estonia   Country in northeastern Europe. Annexed to the Soviet Union in 1940. Became an independent republic in 1991. Capital: Tallinn. (55°N 23°E) **xxviii**

Ethiopia   Country in eastern Africa. Capital: Addis Ababa. (7°N 38°E) **xxx**

Europe   Continent occupying the same land mass as Asia. **xxviii**

Finland   Country in northeastern Europe. Capital: Helsinki. (62°N 26°E) **xxviii**

Flint   City in southeast-central Michigan. (43°N 83°W) **449**

Florida (FL)   State in the southeastern United States. Admitted as a state in 1845. Capital: Tallahassee. (30°N 84°W) **xx**

Fort McHenry   U.S. fort that guarded Baltimore, Maryland, during the War of 1812. **91**

Fort Mims   Site in Alabama where Creek Indians massacred settlers in 1813. **91**

Fort Sumter   Fort in Charleston Harbor, South Carolina. Attack by Confederate forces there started the Civil War. **107**

Fort Ticonderoga   Strategic fort in northern New York that Patriots secured from the British in 1775 during the Revolutionary War. **23**

Fort Worth   City in northern Texas. (33°N 97°W) **172**

France   Country in Western Europe. Capital: Paris. (46°N 0°E) **xxviii**

French Indochina   Former colony in southeastern Asia that France held from 1887 to 1940 and from 1946 to 1955. **493**

Gatún Lake   Lake in Panama that forms part of the system of the Panama Canal. **303**

Geneva   City in southwestern Switzerland. (46°N 6°E) **625**

Genoa   Port city in northwestern Italy. (44°N 10°E) **11**

Georgia (GA)   State in the southeastern United States. One of the original thirteen colonies. Capital: Atlanta. (32°N 84°W) **xx**

Germany   Country in central Europe. Divided into German Democratic Republic (East Germany) and Federal Republic of Germany (West Germany) after World War II. Reunified in 1990. Capital: Berlin. (51°N 8°E) **xxviii**

Gettysburg   Town in southern Pennsylvania. (40°N 77°W) **109**

Gilbert Islands   Group of islands in the western Pacific Ocean. (0°S 174°E) **493**

Gleiwitz   City in southwestern Poland. Polish name: Gliwice. (50°N 18°E) **475**

Gonzales   Town in south-central Texas. (30°N 97°W) **101**

Grand Canyon   Gorge in the Colorado River, located in northwestern Arizona, that is now a national park. **270**

Great Basin   Elevated region made up of parts of California, Idaho, Nevada, Oregon, Utah, and Wyoming that was home to many American Indian groups. **7**

Great Britain   Kingdom in Western Europe. Consists of England, Scotland, and Wales. Capital: London. (54°N 4°W) **xxviii**

Great Lakes   Chain of lakes located in central North America and extending across the U.S.-Canada border. Includes Lake Erie, Lake Huron, Lake Michigan, Lake Ontario, and Lake Superior. **xxii**

Great Plains   Region of central North America that lies between the Mississippi River and the Rocky Mountains and stretches north into Canada and south into Texas. **7**

Great Salt Lake   Saltwater lake in northern Utah. **103**

Greece   Southeastern European country on the Balkan Peninsula that includes numerous surrounding islands. Capital: Athens. (39°N 21°E) **xxviii**

Greenland   Island located in northeastern North America. Capital: Godthåb. (71°N 40°W) **xxvi**

Greensboro   City in north-central North Carolina. (36°N 80°W) **597**

Grenada   Country in the Caribbean Sea made up of the island of Grenada and the southern Grenadines. Capital: St. George's. (12°N 61°W) **xxvi**

Guadalcanal   One of the Solomon Islands in the western Pacific Ocean. (9°S 160°E) **493**

Guam   Pacific island that became a U.S. territory after the Spanish-American War. Capital: Agana. (14°N 143°E) **xxxi**

Guatemala   Republic in Central America. Capital: Guatemala City. (15°N 91°W) **xxvi**

Hague, The   City in the southwestern Netherlands that serves as the seat of the Dutch government. (52°N 4°E) **xxviii**

Haiti   Country in the Caribbean Sea located on the western part of the island of Hispaniola. Capital: Port-au-Prince. (19°N 72°W) **xxvi**

Hamburg   City in northern Germany. (53°N 10°E) **xxviii**

Hanoi   Capital of Vietnam. (21°N 106°E) **624**

Harlem   Area of northern Manhattan in New York City. **401**

Harpers Ferry   Town in present-day northeastern West Virginia where John Brown attempted to start a slave revolt in 1859. (39°N 78°W) **107**

Havana   Capital and seaport of Cuba located on the northwest coast. (23°N 82°W) **297**

Hawaii (HI)   State in the central Pacific Ocean that is made up of the Hawaiian Islands. Organized as a U.S. territory in 1900. Admitted as a state in 1959. Capital: Honolulu. (20°N 157°W) **xx**

Hillsboro   City in southern Ohio. (39°N 83°W) **255**

Hiroshima   Japanese city bombed by a U.S. atomic weapon in August 1945. (34°N 132°E) **493**

Ho Chi Minh Trail   Former system of trails running from North Vietnam to South Vietnam. **628**

Hollywood   District in Los Angeles, California, known for its association with the motion picture industry. **396**

Homestead   Town in southwestern Pennsylvania. (40°N 80°W) **198**

Honduras   Republic in Central America. Capital: Tegucigalpa. (15°N 86°W) **xxvi**

Hong Kong   British colony from 1842 to 1997 located off the coast of China. Returned to China in 1997. Capital: Victoria. (21°N 115°E) **xxix**

Honolulu   Capital of Hawaii. **292**

Houston   City located in southeastern Texas. (30°N 95°W) **xx**

Hudson Bay   Inland sea in east-central Canada. **xxvi**

Hudson River   River flowing from northeastern to southern New York. **xxii**

Hungary   Republic in central Europe. Capital: Budapest. (47°N 19°E) **xxviii**

Iceland   Island republic located between the Arctic and North Atlantic Oceans. Capital: Reykjavík. (65°N 18°W) **xxviii**

Idaho (ID)   State in the northwestern United States. Admitted as a state in 1890. Capital: Boise. (44°N 15°W) **xx**

Illinois (IL)   State in the north-central United States. Admitted as a state in 1818. Capital: Springfield. (40°N 90°W) **xx**

Independence   City in western Missouri that was the starting point of the Santa Fe and Oregon Trails. (39°N 94°W) **103**

India   Large republic in southern Asia. Capital: New Delhi. (28°N 77°E) **xxix**

Indiana (IN)   State in the north-central United States. Admitted as a state in 1816. Capital: Indianapolis. (40°N 86°W) **xx**

Indiana Territory   Former territory created from the division of the Northwest Territory in 1800 that included present-day Illinois, Indiana, Wisconsin, much of Michigan, and part of Minnesota. **89**

Indian Ocean   Vast body of water east of Africa, south of Asia, west of Australia, and north of Antarctica. **xxiv**

Indian Territory   Former territory that included most of present-day Oklahoma. **103**

Indonesia   Country in southeastern Asia. Capital: Jakarta. (7°S 106°E) **xxix**

Iowa (IA)   State in the north-central United States. Admitted as a state in 1846. Capital: Des Moines. (42°N 94°W) **xx**

Iran   Country in southwestern Asia. Capital: Tehran. (31°N 53°E) **xxix**

Iraq   Country in southwestern Asia. Capital: Baghdad. (32°N 43°E) **xxix**

Ireland   Island in the British Isles. Divided into Northern Ireland (Capital: Belfast), which is part of the United Kingdom, and the independent republic of Ireland (Capital: Dublin). (54°N 6°W and 54°N 8°W) **xxviii**

Israel   Country in southwestern Asia on the eastern Mediterranean coast. Established by Jews after the United Nations divided Palestine in 1948. Capital: Jerusalem. (32°N 34°E) **511**

Isthmus of Panama   Landmass that links North America to South America and separates the Atlantic and the Pacific Oceans. Forms the Republic of Panama. **305**

Italy   Country in southern Europe. Capital: Rome. (44°N 11°E) **xxviii**

Jackson   Capital of Mississippi. (32°N 90°W) **597**

Jamaica   Island-nation in the Caribbean Sea. Capital: Kingston. (18°N 78°W) **xxvi**

Jamestown   First permanent English colony in America. Established in eastern Virginia in 1607. **16**

Japan   Country made up of a chain of islands in the western Pacific Ocean. Capital: Tokyo. (37°N 134°E) **xxix**

Kansas (KS)   State in the central United States. Admitted as a state in 1861. Capital: Topeka. (38°N 99°W) **xx**

Kentucky (KY)   State in the east-central United States. Admitted as a state in 1792. Capital: Frankfort. (37°N 87°W) **xx**

Kiel   Seaport city in northern Germany. (54°N 10°E) **342**

Kiska   Island located off the coast of southwestern Alaska. (52°N 177°E) **490**

Kitty Hawk   Town in eastern North Carolina. (36°N 76°N) **188**

Korea   Peninsula and former country of eastern Asia located between the Yellow Sea and the Sea of Japan. Officially divided into two independent nations, North Korea (40°N 127°E) and South Korea (36°N 128°E), in 1948. **xxix**

Kosovo   Province in southwestern Serbia, in southern Yugoslavia. (42°N 21°E) **717**

Kuwait   Country on the northeast Arabian Peninsula at the northern end of the Persian Gulf. Capital: Kuwait City. (29°N 48°E) **xxix**

Labrador   Mainland section of the Newfoundland province in eastern Canada. **8**

Lake Erie   One of the Great Lakes, located in the United States and Canada. **89**

Laos Country in southeastern Asia. Capital: Vientiane. (18°N 102°E) **xxix**

Latin America Spanish-speaking countries of North and South America that once belonged to the Spanish empire and Portugal. **xxiv**

Latvia Country in northern Europe on the Baltic Sea. Former republic of the Soviet Union. Capital: Riga. (57°N 24°E) **xxviii**

Lawrence (KS) City in eastern Kansas. (39°N 95°W) **107**

Lawrence (MA) City in northeastern Massachusetts. (42°N 71°W) **251**

Lebanon Country at the eastern end of the Mediterranean Sea. Capital: Beirut. (34°N 36°E) **xxix**

Leipzig City in eastern-central Germany. (51°N 12°E) **495**

Lexington Town in northeastern Massachusetts. (42°N 71°W) **22**

Leyte Gulf Inlet of the Pacific Ocean in the eastern Philippines. **493**

Libya Republic in northern Africa on the Mediterranean Sea. Capital: Tripoli. (27°N 17°E) **xxx**

Lithuania Country in northern Europe on the Baltic Sea. Declared independence from the Soviet Union in 1990. Capital: Vilnius. (59°N 25°E) **xxviii**

Little Bighorn River River in southern Montana. **153**

Little Rock Capital of Arkansas. (34°N 92°W) **xx**

London Capital of the United Kingdom. Located in England. (51°N 0°W) **xxviii**

Long Island Island in southeastern New York that is located between the Atlantic Ocean and Long Island Sound. (41°N 73°W) **398**

Los Angeles Large city in southwestern California. (34°N 118°W) **xx**

Louisiana (LA) State in the southeastern United States carved out of the Louisiana Territory. Admitted as a state in 1812. Capital: Baton Rouge. (31°N 93°W) **xx**

Louisiana Territory Huge region of land stretching from the Mississippi River to the Rocky Mountains and from the Gulf of Mexico to present-day Canada. Acquired by the U.S. government from France through the Louisiana Purchase of 1803. **89**

Low Countries Name given to the region made up of the countries of the Netherlands, Belgium, and Luxembourg. **498**

Lowell Massachusetts city on the Merrimack River northwest of Boston. (42°N 71°W) **94**

Macedonia Republic in southeastern Europe. Declared independence from Yugoslavia in September 1991. Capital: Skopje. (41°N 23°E) **xxviii**

Maine (ME) State in the northeastern United States. Admitted as a state in 1820. Capital: Augusta. (45°N 70°W) **xx**

Manchuria Region in northeastern China. (47°N 125°E) **493**

Manhattan Island Island at north end of New York Bay; one of the five boroughs that make up New York City. **401**

Manila Capital of the Philippines. (15°N 121°E) **297**

Manila Bay Large inlet of the South China Sea located in western Luzon, an island in the Philippines. **297**

Marianas Islands in the western Pacific Ocean. (16°N 145°E) **493**

Marne River River in northeastern France. **342**

Marshall Islands Group of islands in the western Pacific Ocean. Capital: Majuro. (9°S 152°E) **493**

Maryland (MD) State in the east-central United States. One of the original thirteen colonies. Capital: Annapolis. (39°N 76°W) **xx**

Massachusetts (MA) State in the northeastern United States. One of the original thirteen colonies. Capital: Boston. (42°N 72°W) **xx**

Mediterranean Sea Large sea bordered by southern Europe, southwestern Asia, and northern Africa. **xxviii**

Memphis City in southwestern Tennessee. (35°N 90°W) **126**

Menlo Park Community in central New Jersey. (40°N 74°W) **185**

Mesoamerica Extremely fertile region made up of present-day Mexico and parts of Central America that was the home to the first major Native American cultures. Also known as Middle America. **7**

Meuse River River in western Europe that flows from northeastern France to the North Sea. **342**

Mexico Country in southern North America. Capital: Mexico City. (23°N 104°W) **xxvi**

Mexico City Capital of Mexico. (19°N 99°W) **xxvi**

Miami City in southeastern Florida. (26°N 80°W) **xx**

Michigan (MI) State in the north-central United States. Admitted as a state in 1837. Capital: Lansing. (46°N 87°W) **xx**

Middle East Vast region made up of countries in southwestern Asia and northeastern Africa. **657**

Midway Islands Two islands northwest of Hawaii that have been under U.S. administration since 1867. (28°N 177°W) **493**

Milwaukee City in southeastern Wisconsin. (43°N 88°W) **276**

Minnesota (MN) State in the north-central United States. Admitted as a state in 1858. Capital: St. Paul. (46°N 90°W) **xx**

Mississippi (MS) State in the southeastern United States. Admitted as a state in 1817. Capital: Jackson. (32°N 89°W) **xx**

Mississippi River River that flows from Minnesota to the Gulf of Mexico. **xxii**

Mississippi River valley Vast area of land drained by the Mississippi River. **6**

Missouri (MO) State in the central United States. Admitted as a state in 1821. Capital: Jefferson City. (38°N 93°W) **xx**

Missouri River River located in the central and northwest-central United States. **xxii**

Missouri River valley Vast area of land drained by the Missouri River. **6**

Monongahela River River in northern West Virginia and southwestern Pennsylvania that merges with the Allegheny River at Pittsburgh to form the Ohio River. **198**

Montana (MT) State in the northwestern United States. Admitted as a state in 1889. Capital: Helena. (47°N 112°W) **xx**

Monterey City in western California that was the province's capital when the region was held by Mexico. (36°N 122°W) **103**

Montgomery Capital of Alabama. (32°N 86°W) **xx**

Montreal City in southeastern Canada that was founded by the French in 1642. (46°N 74°W) **23**

Moscow Capital of Russia. (61°N 60°E) **xxviii**

Munich City in southern Germany. (48°N 11°E) **xxviii**

Nagasaki Second Japanese city bombed by a U.S. atomic weapon in August 1945. (32°N 130°E) **493**

Nashville Capital of Tennessee. (36°N 87°W) **126**

Natchez City in southwestern Mississippi. (31°N 91°W) **110**

Nebraska (NE) State in the central United States. Admitted as a state in 1867. Capital: Lincoln. (41°N 101°W) **xx**

Netherlands Kingdom located in northwestern Europe. Capital: Amsterdam. (52°N 5°E) **xxviii**

Nevada (NV) State in the western United States. Admitted as a state in 1864. Capital: Carson City. (39°N 117°W) **xx**

New Amsterdam Dutch settlement on Manhattan Island founded c. 1625. **18**

New England Northeastern section of the United States made up of Connecticut, Maine, Massachusetts, New Hampshire, Rhode Island, and Vermont. **16**

Newfoundland Island off the eastern coast of Canada. (48°N 56°W) **xxvi**

New France Former French territory in North America that included eastern Canada and the Mississippi Valley. France lost all North American territory to Britain in 1763. **16**

New Guinea Island in the western Pacific Ocean. Western half is part of Indonesia, and eastern half is part of Papua New Guinea. (5°S 140°E) **xxxi**

New Hampshire (NH) State in the northeastern United States. One of the original thirteen colonies. Capital: Concord. (44°N 71°W) **xx**

New Jersey (NJ) State in the eastern United States. One of the original thirteen colonies. Capital: Trenton. (40°N 75°W) **xx**

New Mexico (NM) State in the southwestern United States. Organized as a U.S. territory that included Arizona and part of Colorado in 1850. Capital: Santa Fe. (34°N 107°W) **xx**

New Netherland Former Dutch colony in North America from c. 1613 to 1664 that included parts of present-day New Jersey and New York. **13**

New Orleans Port city in southeastern Louisiana, located between the Mississippi River and Lake Pontchartrain. (30°N 90°W) **89**

New Sweden Swedish colony that was located in eastern North America on the Delaware River. **13**

New York (NY) State in the northeastern United States. One of the original thirteen colonies. Capital: Albany. (42°N 78°W) **xx**

New York Bay Atlantic Ocean inlet located at the mouth of the Hudson River in southeastern New York State. **24**

New York City Largest city in the United States. First capital of the United States. (41°N 74°W) **xx**

Niagara Falls City in New York State on the Niagara River on the border of the United States and Canada. (43°N 79°W) **259**

Nicaragua Central American country on the Caribbean Sea and the Pacific Ocean. Capital: Managua. (12°N 86°W) **xxvi**

Nicodemus Town in Kansas settled by African Americans in the late 1800s. **171**

Nile River River that flows through east and northeast Africa. **xxx**

Norfolk City in southeast Virginia. (38°N 76°W) **221**

Normandy Historic region in northern France that was the site of the D-Day invasion during World War II. (49°N 0°W) **487**

North America Continent in the northern Western Hemisphere. **xxvi**

North Carolina (NC) State in the southeastern United States. One of the original thirteen colonies. Capital: Raleigh. (35°N 81°W) **xx**

North Dakota (ND) State in the north-central United States. Admitted as a state in 1889. Capital: Bismarck. (47°N 102°W) **xx**

North Sea Arm of the Atlantic Ocean that separates the British Isles from the European continent. **xxviii**

Northwest Territory Region of the north-central United States that extended from the Ohio and Missouri Rivers to the Great Lakes. Awarded to the United States by the Treaty of Paris of 1783 and organized as a U.S. territory in 1787. Later divided into the present-day states of Illinois, Indiana, Michigan, Ohio, Wisconsin, and part of Minnesota. **31**

Norway Kingdom in northwestern Europe. Capital: Oslo. (62°N 10°E) **xxviii**

Nuremberg City in southern Germany where the Nuremberg Trials were held from 1945 to 1946. (49°N 11°E) **511**

Oahu Third-largest Hawaiian island. (21°N 158°W) **xx**

Ohio (OH) State in the north-central United States. Admitted as a state in 1803. Capital: Columbus. (40°N 83°W) **xx**

Ohio River valley Region of land drained by the Ohio River. **6**

Okinawa Japanese island captured by U.S. forces after tremendous resistance during World War II. (26°N 128°E) **493**

Oklahoma (OK) State in the southwest-central United States. Organized as a territory in 1890. Admitted as a state in 1907. Capital: Oklahoma City. (36°N 98°W) **xx**

Oklahoma City Capital of Oklahoma. (36°N 98°W) **xx**

Omaha City in eastern Nebraska. (41°N 96°W) **168**

Oregon (OR) State in the northwestern United States. Admitted as a state in 1859. Capital: Salem. (43°N 122°W) **xx**

Oregon Country Region in western North America that extended from the Pacific coast to the Rocky Mountains and from the northern border of California to Alaska. So called from 1818 until it became Oregon Territory in 1848. **103**

Ottoman Empire Former empire in Europe, Asia, and Africa whose remaining territory was proclaimed Republic of Turkey in 1923. Capital: Constantinople. (42°N 28°E) **332**

Pacific Ocean Body of water extending from the Arctic Circle to Antarctica and from western North America and South America to Australia, the Malay Archipelago, and eastern Asia. **xxiv**

Palestine Historic region in southwestern Asia that is now present-day Israel and part of Jordan. **511**

Panama Country in southern Central America that occupies the Isthmus of Panama. Location of the Panama Canal. Capital: Panama City. (8°N 81°W) **xxvi**

Paris Capital of France. (49°N 2°E) **xxviii**

Paterson City in northern New Jersey. (41°N 74°W) **251**

Pearl Harbor Harbor on the Hawaiian island of Oahu where the Japanese launched a surprise attack against the U.S. Pacific Fleet in 1941. (21°N 158°W) **493**

Pennsylvania (PA) State in the eastern United States. One of the original thirteen colonies. Capital: Harrisburg. (41°N 78°W) **xx**

Persian Gulf Arm of the Arabian Sea between the Arabian Peninsula and southwestern Iran in southwestern Asia. **xxix**

Philadelphia City in southeastern Pennsylvania. Capital of the United States from 1790 to 1800. (40°N 75°W) **xx**

Philippines Archipelago of about 7,100 islands lying approximately 500 miles off the southeast coast of Asia. Gained full independence from the United States in 1946. Capital: Manila. (14°N 125°E) **xxix**

Pikes Peak Mountain in east-central Colorado that was part of an important mining region in the mid- to late 1800s. **153**

Pittsburgh City in southwestern Pennsylvania. (40°N 80°W) **xx**

Plymouth Town in Massachusetts that is the site where the Pilgrims first landed in North America in 1620. (42°N 70°W) **16**

Poland Country in central Europe bordering on the Baltic Sea. Capital: Warsaw. (52°N 17°E) **xxviii**

Portugal Country in southwestern Europe on the western Iberian Peninsula. Includes the island groups of Madeira and the Azores in the Atlantic Ocean. Capital: Lisbon. (38°N 8°W) **xxviii**

Princeton Town in west-central New Jersey. (40°N 75°W) **23**

Promontory Location in northwestern Utah where the Central and Union Pacific Railroads were joined in 1869. **168**

Providence Settlement established by Roger Williams in 1636 that later became Rhode Island. Present-day capital of Rhode Island. (42°N 71°W) **16**

Puerto Rico Island east of Cuba and southeast of Florida that is a U.S. commonwealth. Capital: San Juan. (18°N 67°W) **xxvi**

Puget Sound Arm of the Pacific Ocean located in western Washington State. **301**

Pullman Town established near Chicago, Illinois, in 1880 by the Pullman Palace Car Company for its workers. **198**

P'yŏngyang Capital of North Korea. (39°N 126°E) **524**

Quebec City in eastern Canada on the St. Lawrence River. (47°N 71°W) **xxvi**

Red Sea Inland sea between the Arabian Peninsula and northeastern Africa. **xxix**

Rhine River River in western Europe that flows from Switzerland to the North Sea. **342**

Rhineland Region west of the Rhine River in western Germany. **347**

Rhode Island (RI) State in the northeastern United States. One of the original thirteen colonies. Capital: Providence. (41°N 71°W) **xx**

Richmond Capital of Virginia. (37°N 77°W) **109**

Rio Grande "Great River" that forms the border between Texas and Mexico. **xxii**

Roanoke Island Island off the coast of North Carolina. **13**

Rocky Mountains Mountain range in western North America that extends from Mexico to the Arctic. **xxii**

Romania Republic in southeastern Europe. Capital: Bucharest. (46°N 25°E) **xxviii**

Rome Capital of Italy. (42°N 12°E) **487**

Russia Country in Eastern Europe and northwestern Asia. Formerly part of the Soviet Union. Capital: Moscow. (61°N 60°E) **xxviii**

Rwanda Republic in east-central Africa. Capital: Kigali. (2°S 30°E) **xxx**

Saar Valley Region around the Saar River near the western German border. **347**

Sacramento Capital of California. (38°N 121°W) **168**

Sacramento River River in northwestern California. **102**

Sahara Vast desert in northern Africa. **9**

Saigon City in South Vietnam that is now known as Ho Chi Minh City. (11°N 106°E) **624**

Saint-Mihiel Community in northeastern France. (49°N 5°E) **341**

Saipan One of the Mariana Islands, located in the western Pacific Ocean. (15°N 146°E) **492**

Samoa Group of volcanic islands in the southwestern-central Pacific Ocean. Divided into American Samoa and Western Samoa. (14°S 171°W) **292**

San Antonio City in south-central Texas. (29°N 99°W) **89**

San Carlos Location of an Apache reservation in Arizona. **156**

Sand Creek Site in southeastern Colorado of the Sand Creek Massacre in 1864. **153**

San Diego City in southwestern California on San Diego Bay, an inlet of the Pacific Ocean near the Mexican border. (33°N 117°W) **xx**

San Francisco City in western California on a peninsula between the Pacific Ocean and San Francisco Bay. (37°N 122°W) **168**

San Francisco Bay Inlet of the Pacific Ocean in western-central California. **xx**

San Gabriel City in southwestern California. **104**

San Jacinto River River in southeastern Texas that flows into Galveston Bay. Site of the Mexican surrender to the Texans in 1836 that ended the Texas Revolution. **102**

Santa Fe Capital of New Mexico. (35°N 106°W) **103**

Santiago de Cuba Seaport located on the southern part of Cuba. Captured by U.S. forces during the Spanish-American War. (20°N 76°W) **297**

Sarajevo Capital of Bosnia and Herzegovina. (44°N 17°E) **xxviii**

Saratoga Site in eastern New York of the Revolutionary War's Battle of Saratoga in 1777. **23**

Saudi Arabia Kingdom on the Arabian Peninsula in southwest Asia. Capital: Riyadh. (22°N 46°E) **xxix**

Savannah Port city in southeastern Georgia. (32°N 81°W) **16**

Scandinavia Region of northern Europe that includes Denmark, Norway, and Sweden. **xxviii**

Scotland Northern part of the island of Great Britain. Capital: Edinburgh. (57°N 4°W) **xxviii**

Seattle City in west-central Washington. (47°N 122°W) **xx**

Selma City in southwest-central Alabama. (32°N 87°W) **597**

Seneca Falls Town in west-central New York State. (43°N 77°W) **99**

Seoul Capital of South Korea. (37°N 127°E) **xxix**

Serbia Part of Yugoslavia, located in southeastern Europe. Capital: Belgrade. (45°N 20°E) **xxviii**

Shandong Province Coastal province in northeastern China. **292**

Shenandoah Valley Valley in Virginia that is located between the Allegheny and the Blue Ridge Mountains and is drained by the Shenandoah River. **124**

Sicily Italian island in the Mediterranean Sea. (37°N 14°E) **xxviii**

Sierra Nevada Large mountain range in eastern California. **xxii**

Singapore Southeastern Asian republic made up of Singapore Island and several smaller islands. Capital: Singapore. (1°N 104°E) **xxix**

Slovakia Country in central Europe. Capital: Bratislava. (48°N 17°E) **xxviii**

Slovenia Country in southern Europe. Declared independence from Yugoslavia in June 1991. Capital: Ljubljana. (46°N 15°E) **xxviii**

Solomon Islands Island group in the southwestern Pacific Ocean. (8°S 159°E) **493**

Somalia Country in eastern Africa. Capital: Mogadishu. (3°N 44°E) **xxx**

Somme River River in northern France. **332**

South Africa Country in southern Africa. Pretoria is the administrative capital, Cape Town is the legislative capital, and Bloemfontein is the judicial capital. (30°S 26°E) **xxx**

South America Continent in the southern Western Hemisphere. **xxvii**

South Carolina (SC) State in the southeastern United States. One of the original thirteen colonies. Capital: Columbia. (34°N 81°W) **xx**

South Dakota (SD) State in the north-central United States. Organized as part of the Dakota Territory in 1861. Admitted as a state in 1889. Capital: Pierre. (44°N 102°W) **xx**

South Korea Country in southeastern Asia. Established in 1948. Capital: Seoul. (40°N 127°E) **xxix**

Soviet Union Former communist country in Eastern Europe and Asia. **515**

Spain Kingdom in southwestern Europe occupying the greater part of the Iberian Peninsula and including the Balearic and Canary Islands. Capital: Madrid. (40°N 4°W) **xxviii**

Springfield Capital of Illinois. (40°N 89°W) **129**

Sri Lanka Independent island state in the Indian Ocean. Capital: Colombo. (7°N 81°E) **xxix**

Stalingrad Present-day Volgograd. City in southwestern Russia. (48°N 42°E) **487**

St. Louis City in Missouri on the Mississippi River. (38°N 90°W) **89**

St. Petersburg City in northwestern Russia that was formerly called Leningrad. (60°N 30°E) **487**

Stockholm Capital of Sweden. (59°N 18°E) **397**

Stone Mountain Large rocky mass near Atlanta, Georgia. **388**

Sudan Republic in northeast Africa. Capital: Khartoum. (15°N 30°E) **xxx**

Sudetenland Region in the northwestern Czech Republic along the Polish border. Ceded to Germany in 1938 and restored to Czechoslovakia in 1945. **476**

Suez Canal International waterway in the Middle East that connects the Red Sea and the Mediterranean Sea. **487**

Sumatra Island in the western part of Indonesia. (0°S 102°E) **9**

Sutter's Fort Colony established in 1839 in northern California. **103**

Sweden Kingdom in northwestern Europe. Capital: Stockholm. (62°N 15°E) **xxviii**

Switzerland Federal republic in central Europe. Capital: Bern. (47°N 7°E) **xxviii**

Syria Country in southwestern Asia on the eastern Mediterranean coast. Capital: Damascus. (35°N 37°E) **xxix**

Taiwan Island-nation off the southeastern coast of China. Capital: Taipei. (23°N 121°E) **xxix**

Tallahassee Capital of Florida. (30°N 84°W) **xx**

Tampico Seaport in eastern Mexico. Arrest of U.S. solders there in 1914 led to the sending of troops to Mexico. (22°N 98°W) **305**

Tarawa Pacific island captured by the Allies in 1943. (1°N 173°E) **xxxi**

Tehran Capital of Iran. (31°N 53°E) **xxix**

Tennessee (TN) State in the south-central United States. Admitted as a state in 1796. Capital: Nashville. (36°N 88°W) **xx**

Texas (TX) State in the southwest-central United States. Admitted as a state in 1845. Capital: Austin. (31°N 101°W) **xx**

Thames River River that flows from southeastern Ontario, Canada, and empties into Lake St. Clair. **91**

Three Mile Island Island in the Susquehanna River in Pennsylvania. **668**

Tinian One of the Mariana Islands, located in the western Pacific Ocean. (15°N 145°E) **493**

Tippecanoe River River that flows from northern Indiana to join the Wabash River in west-central Indiana. **90**

Tonkin, Gulf of Arm extending from the South China Sea, east of North Vietnam. **624**

Topeka Capital of Kansas. (39°N 95°W) **xx**

Trenton Capital of New Jersey. (40°N 75°W) **23**

Tulsa City in northeast Oklahoma. (36°N 96°W) **xx**

Turkey Country in southwestern Asia and southeastern Europe between the Mediterranean and the Black Seas. Capital: Ankara. (38°N 32°W) **xxix**

United States of America Federal republic in central North America. Capital: Washington, D.C. (39°N 77°W) **xx**

Utah (UT) State in the western United States. Admitted as a state in 1896. Capital: Salt Lake City. (39°N 112°W) **xx**

Valley Forge Site in southeastern Pennsylvania where General George Washington and his troops spent the harsh winter of 1777–78 during the Revolutionary War. **23**

Venezuela Country in northern South America on the Caribbean Sea. Capital: Caracas. (8°N 65°W) **xxvii**

Venice City and trading center in northeastern Italy that was particularly important during the Renaissance. (45°N 12°E) **10**

Veracruz Seaport in eastern Mexico. (19°N 96°W) **305**

Verdun City in northeastern France. (44°N 1°E) **332**

Vermont (VT) State in the northeastern United States. Capital: Montpelier. (44°N 73°W) **xx**

Vicksburg City in western Mississippi on the bluffs above the Mississippi River. (42°N 85°W) **109**

Vietnam Country in southeastern Asia that was divided into North Vietnam and South Vietnam between 1954 and 1975. Capital: Hanoi. (18°N 107°E) **xxix**

Virginia (VA) State in the eastern United States. One of the original thirteen colonies. Capital: Richmond. (37°N 80°W) **xx**

Virginia City Town in western Nevada that was established in 1859 when people came to mine the Comstock Lode. (39°N 119°W) **158**

Volcano Islands Small group of islands in the western Pacific Ocean. (25°N 141°E) **492**

Wake Island Island in the northern Pacific Ocean. A U.S. territory since the 1890s. (19°N 166°E) **493**

Waltham City in northeastern Massachusetts. (43°N 71°W) **94**

Warsaw Capital of Poland. (52°N 21°E) **xxviii**

Washington (WA) State in northwestern United States, bounded by British Columbia, Canada, to the north and by the Pacific Ocean to the west. Admitted as a state in 1889. Capital: Olympia. (47°N 121°W) **xx**

Washington, D.C. Capital of the United States, located on the Potomac River between Virginia and Maryland. (39°N 77°W) **xx**

Watts Neighborhood in southwestern Los Angeles. (34°N 118°W) **600**

Western Ghats Mountain range in southern India. **161**

West Germany *See* Germany.

West Indies Islands between North and South America enclosing the Caribbean Sea. **xxvi**

West Virginia (WV) State in the east-central United States. Admitted as a state in 1863. Capital: Charleston. (39°N 81°W) **xx**

Wisconsin (WI) State in the north-central United States. Admitted as a state in 1848. Capital: Madison. (44°N 91°W) **xx**

Woodstock Town in southeastern New York. (42°N 74°W) **587**

Wounded Knee Site in southwestern South Dakota of the Massacre at Wounded Knee in 1890. **153**

Wyoming (WY) State in the northwestern United States. Admitted as a state in 1890. Capital: Cheyenne. (43°N 108°W) **xx**

Yalta Town in the Ukraine. (44°N 34°E) **510**

Yalu River River that flows between northeastern China and North Korea. **524**

Yorktown Town in southeastern Virginia. (41°N 74°W) **23**

Yugoslavia Country in southeastern Europe that was formed as the Kingdom of the Serbs, Croats, and Slovenes after the collapse of Austria-Hungary in 1918; renamed Yugoslavia in 1929; Serbia and Montenegro formed new Republic of Yugoslavia in 1992. Capital: Belgrade. **xxviii**

Yukon Territory Territory in northwestern Canada. **288**

Zion Canyon in southwestern Utah that is now a national park. **270**

Glossary

This Glossary contains terms you need to understand as you study American history. After each key term there is a brief definition or explanation of the meaning of the term as it is used in *Call to Freedom.* The page number refers to the page on which the term is introduced in the textbook.

Phonetic Respelling and Pronunciation Guide

Many of the key terms in this textbook have been respelled to help you pronounce them. The letter combinations used in the respelling throughout the narrative are explained in the following phonetic respelling and pronunciation guide. The guide is adapted from *Webster's Tenth New College Dictionary, Merriam-Webster's New Geographical Dictionary,* and *Merriam-Webster's New Biographical Dictionary.*

MARK	AS IN	RESPELLING	EXAMPLE
a	alphabet	a	*AL-fuh-bet
ā	Asia	ay	AY-zhuh
ä	cart, top	ah	KAHRT, TAHP
e	let, ten	e	LET, TEN
ē	even, leaf	ee	EE-vuhn, LEEF
i	it, tip, British	i	IT, TIP, BRIT-ish
ī	site, buy, Ohio	y	SYT, BY, oh-HY-oh
	iris	eye	EYE-ris
k	card	k	KAHRD
ō	over, rainbow	oh	OH-vuhr, RAYN-boh
ù	book, wood	ooh	BOOHK, WOOHD
ò	all, orchid	aw	AWL, AWR-kid
òi	foil, coin	oy	FOYL, KOYN
aù	out	ow	OWT
ə	cup, butter	uh	KUHP, BUHT-uhr
ü	rule, food	oo	ROOL, FOOD
yü	few	yoo	FYOO
zh	vision	zh	VIZH-uhn

*A syllable printed in small capital letters receives heavier emphasis than the other syllable(s) in a word.

ABC Powers Argentina, Brazil, and Chile. 310

abolition An end to slavery. 98

Acquired Immune Deficiency Syndrome (AIDS) Disease caused by the human immunodeficiency virus (HIV) that forces the body's immune system to shut down, making it easier for a person to contract other illnesses. 699

Adamson Act Reform legislation passed during President Woodrow Wilson's administration that limited the workday on the nation's railroads to eight hours. 283

affirmative action Practice by some businesses and government agencies of giving special consideration to nonwhites or women to make up for past discrimination. 601

ageism Discrimination against an age group, particularly the elderly. 618

Agricultural Marketing Act (1929) Legislation that ended some farm subsidies and established the Federal Farm Board. 429

Alien and Sedition Acts (1798) Laws passed by a Federalist-dominated Congress that made it illegal to print or speak words hostile to the government; used against Republicans. 87

Alliance for Progress Aid programs developed by President John F. Kennedy's administration that sought to encourage economic development and promote democracy in Latin America. 574

Allied Powers World War I alliance that included Britain, France, Russia, and later the United States; also the World War II alliance between Britain and France, and later the United States and other countries, that fought against the Axis Powers. 328, 476

amendments Official changes, corrections, or additions to a constitution. 33

American Civil Liberties Union (ACLU) Organization formed in 1920 to protect civil rights. 360

American Expeditionary Force (AEF) U.S. troops that served overseas in World War I. 339

American Federation of Labor (AFL) One of the first large labor unions in the United States; organized in the

1880s by Samuel Gompers as an association of individual skilled craft unions. **197**

American Indian Movement (AIM) Organization formed in 1968 to fight for the rights of American Indians. **617**

American Liberty League Group formed by business leaders to oppose the New Deal. **437**

American Plan Campaign launched by business leaders in the early 1900s to create open shops, or businesses where union membership was not required and was sometimes forbidden. **376**

Americans with Disabilities Act (ADA) (1990) Law that guarantees people with disabilities equal access to public accommodations, transportation, and employment opportunities. **693**

amnesty An official pardon issued by the government for an illegal act. **125**

anarchists People who want to abolish all forms of government. **359**

Anti-Imperialist League Group of Americans who opposed the treaty ending the Spanish-American War because they believed that the sections of the treaty acquiring former Spanish territories was the beginning of a U.S. colonial empire. **299**

Anti-Saloon League Organization founded in 1893 to fight alcohol abuse; particularly active during the early 1900s. **255**

apartheid System of laws in South Africa that required racial segregation. **670**

Apollo program The National Aeronautics and Space Administration's program to land astronauts on the Moon. **589**

appeasement The act of giving in to an aggressor to preserve peace. **476**

Appomattox Courthouse Town in which Union general Ulysses S. Grant accepted the surrender of Confederate general Robert E. Lee, ending the Civil War. **111**

apportionment The use of population to determine how many legislative representatives an area will have. **38**

arbitration Formal meetings to discuss and settle disagreements. **266**

armistice A truce between warring groups or countries. **343**

Armory Show An art exhibition held in New York City in 1913. **403**

Army-McCarthy hearings Televised hearings in the 1950s of the U.S. Senate's investigations into Senator Joseph McCarthy's charges that Communists were in the U.S. military. **531**

Articles of Confederation (1777) Document that created the first permanent national government for the United States; was replaced by the U.S. Constitution in 1789. **30**

artifacts Remains of objects that have been made by humans. **6**

assembly line A system that moves parts and partly assembled products among factory workers to reduce production time. **368**

Atlanta Compromise (1895) Speech given by Booker T. Washington stating that African Americans should focus on improving their education and economic situation instead of fighting discrimination and segregation. **259**

Atlantic Charter (1941) Pledge signed by U.S. president Franklin D. Roosevelt and British prime minister Winston Churchill not to acquire new territory as a result of World War II and to work for peace after the war. **478**

atomic bomb A nuclear weapon that produced an explosion by splitting atoms; the United States dropped two atomic bombs on Japan during World War II. **496**

automation The use of machines in production. **546**

Axis Powers Military alliance formed by Italy and Germany in 1936; later joined by other countries. Fought against the Allied Powers in World War II. **465**

baby boom A significant increase in the number of children being born; one took place in the United States after World War II. **548**

Bacon's Rebellion (1676) Attack led by Nathaniel Bacon against American Indians and the colonial government in Virginia. **15**

balance of power A situation in which the strength of rival nations is nearly equal. **326**

Bataan Death March (1942) Forced march of tens of thousands of American and Filipino prisoners during World War II up the Bataan Peninsula to internment camps. **491**

Battle of Antietam (1862) Union victory in Maryland during the Civil War that marked the bloodiest single-day battle in U.S. military history. **108**

Battle of Britain (1940–41) Series of bombing raids launched against British cities by the German air force. **477**

Battle of Bunker Hill (1775) Revolutionary War battle in Boston that demonstrated that the colonists could fight well against the British army. **23**

Battle of El Alamein (1942) British victory in World War II that stopped Axis forces from advancing in North Africa. **485**

Battle of Gettysburg (1863) Union victory at Gettysburg, Pennsylvania, during the Civil War that turned the tide against the Confederates; resulted in the loss of more than 50,000 soldiers. **110**

Battle of Leyte Gulf (1944) World War II battle in the Philippines that was the largest naval battle in history. **493**

Battle of Midway (1942) World War II battle in which U.S. warplanes crippled Japan's navy. **491**

Battle of New Orleans (1815) Greatest U.S. victory in the War of 1812; actually took place two weeks after the signing of a peace treaty that ended the war. **91**

Battle of Saratoga (1777) Revolutionary War battle in New York that resulted in a major defeat of British troops; marked the Patriots' greatest victory up to that point in the war. **24**

Battle of Stalingrad (1942–43) Allied victory by the Soviet Union in World War II in which the Axis Powers lost many soldiers. **486**

Battle of the Atlantic Long-lasting World War II naval war to control Atlantic Ocean trade routes. **478**

Battle of the Bulge (1944–45) World War II battle in which Allied forces ended Germany's ability to wage an offensive war. **489**

Battle of the Coral Sea (1942) World War II battle in which the Allies stopped the Japanese advance to New Guinea. **491**

Battle of the Little Bighorn (1876) "Custer's Last Stand"; battle between U.S. soldiers led by George Armstrong Custer and Sioux warriors led by Crazy Horse; resulted in the worst defeat of the U.S. Army in the West. **154**

Battle of Yorktown (1781) Last major battle of the Revolutionary War; site of British general Charles Cornwallis's surrender to the Patriots in Virginia. **25**

Bay of Pigs Bay on the coast of Cuba that Cuban exiles, secretly trained by the United States, tried to invade; the exiles were quickly defeated. **575**

bear market A stock market with declining stock prices. **420**

beats Young writers who criticized American life in the 1950s through their writings and behavior; also called beatniks. **551**

benevolent societies Organizations that helped immigrants in cases of sickness, unemployment, and death. **212**

Berlin Airlift (1948) Joint effort by the United States and Britain to fly food and supplies into West Berlin after the Soviets blocked off all ground routes to the city. **515**

Berlin Wall Wall constructed in 1961 between East and West Berlin to prevent East Berliners from crossing into the West. **575**

Bessemer process Less expensive, easier way to make steel; developed by British inventor Henry Bessemer in the 1850s. **184**

bicameral legislature A lawmaking body made up of two houses. **19**

Big Four Collective name given to U.S. president Woodrow Wilson, British prime minister David Lloyd George, French premier Georges Clemenceau, and Italian prime minister Vittorio Orlando during the post–World War I peace conference at Versailles. **346**

Bill of Rights First 10 amendments to the U.S. Constitution; ratified in 1791. **33**

Black Cabinet Group of African Americans who were appointed to significant government positions by President Franklin D. Roosevelt. **456**

Black Codes Laws passed in the southern states during Reconstruction that greatly limited the freedom and rights of African Americans. **130**

blacklisting Refusing to hire a person; common action toward suspected Communists during the 1950s. **528**

Black Monday October 19, 1987; the day the stock market dropped more than 20 percent after reaching an all-time high in August. The market continued to drop following this day, eventually losing some 40 percent of its value. **686**

Black Power Social and political movement in the 1960s that called for greater African American economic and political power. **600**

Blackshirts Group of Italians led by Benito Mussolini that gained power in the early 1920s. **464**

Black Tuesday October 29, 1929; the day the stock market collapsed. Led to the Panic of 1929. **420**

Blitzkrieg "Lightning war"; type of fast-moving warfare used by German forces against Poland in 1939. **476**

bonanza A large find of precious ore. **158**

Bonus Army Group of World War I veterans that marched on Washington, D.C., in 1932 to demand the immediate payment of their government war bonuses in cash. **430**

boom towns Western communities that grew quickly because of mining booms and often disappeared soon after. **159**

bootleggers People who smuggled liquor into the United States from Canada and Mexico during prohibition. **384**

bosses Corrupt political leaders who used bribery and payoffs to win elections. **238**

Boston Massacre (1770) Incident in which British soldiers fired into a group of colonists, killing five people. **22**

Boxer Rebellion (1900) Revolt in which Chinese nationalists known as the Boxers attacked foreigners in order to end outside involvement in China's affairs; put down by U.S. Marines and other forces after two months. **293**

Bozeman Trail Trail used by miners, named after pioneer John M. Bozeman; ran from Wyoming to Montana. **153**

braceros Mexican workers authorized by the U.S. government to enter and work in the United States during World War II. **482**

Brady Bill (1993) Handgun Violence Prevention Act; legislation that established a five-day waiting period for handgun purchases. **710**

Brain Trust Group of expert policy advisers who worked with President Franklin D. Roosevelt in the 1930s to end the Great Depression. **432**

brinkmanship The Eisenhower administration's policy of being willing to go to the very brink of war to oppose communist expansion. **540**

Brown v. Board of Education (1954) Supreme Court ruling that declared that segregation in public schools is illegal; overturned the separate-but-equal doctrine established in 1896 case *Plessy* v. *Ferguson.* **556**

bull market A stock market with rising stock prices. **420**

Bull Moose Party Nickname for the Progressive Party, which was formed by Theodore Roosevelt and his supporters in 1912. **276**

business cycle Economic pattern in which business goes through periods of prosperity and depression. **422**

buying on margin Purchasing stocks on credit. **420**

cabinet Group made up of the heads of the executive departments that advises the U.S. president. **41**

California Gold Rush (1849) Migration of thousands of people to California after gold was first discovered there. **105**

Camp David Accords (1978) Peace agreements between Israel and Egypt, negotiated by President Jimmy Carter. **669**

capitalism Economic system in which private businesses own and operate most industries; competition determines the cost of goods as well as workers' pay. **251**

carpetbaggers Republicans from the North who moved to the South during Reconstruction. **136**

cattle drive Long journeys on which cowboys herded cattle to northern markets or better grazing lands. **167**

Cattle Kingdom Area of the Great Plains, stretching from Texas to Canada, on which many ranchers raised cattle during the late 1800s. **165**

Central Intelligence Agency (CIA) An organization established by the federal government in 1947 to conduct covert operations. **541**

Central Powers World War I alliance led by Austria-Hungary and Germany and later joined by Bulgaria and the Ottoman Empire. **327**

Challenger U.S. space shuttle that exploded in 1986 after takeoff, killing all seven crew members. **700**

charter Official English document that gave a person or group the right to establish a colony. **13**

checks and balances A system established by the Constitution that shares power between branches of government and prevents any one branch from becoming too powerful. **32**

Chicano movement Effort of young Hispanic activists to end discrimination and increase cultural pride. **608**

Children's Defense Fund Program founded in the 1970s by Marian Wright Edelman to protect the rights of children. **618**

Chinese Exclusion Act (1882) Law prohibiting Chinese people from immigrating to the United States for a period of 10 years; was extended into the early 1900s. **214**

Chisholm Trail Trail from San Antonio, Texas, to Abilene, Kansas, established by Jesse Chisholm in 1867 for cattle drives. **167**

Civil Rights Act of 1866 Law that gave African Americans legal rights equal to those of white Americans. **132**

Civil Rights Act of 1875 Law allowing African Americans to sue private businesses for racial discrimination. **139**

Civil Rights Act of 1964 Law banning segregation in public places and prohibiting employers, unions, and universities from discriminating on the basis of color, sex, religion, and national origin. **598**

Clayton Antitrust Act (1914) Act that strengthened federal laws against monopolies. **281**

Cold War Power struggle between the United States and the Soviet Union that lasted from 1945 to 1991. **513**

collective bargaining Process in which union leaders negotiate with factory owners on behalf of workers in a particular business or industry for better wages and working conditions. **196**

Columbian Exchange Transfer of plants, animals, and diseases between the Americas and Africa, Asia, and Europe. **12**

Commercial Revolution Period of economic development that took place in Europe in the 1400s and greatly expanded trade. **10**

Commission on the Status of Women Commission formed by President John F. Kennedy in 1961 to study workplace inequality; headed by Esther Peterson and former first lady Eleanor Roosevelt. **610**

Committee on Civil Rights (1946) Committee appointed by President Harry S Truman to investigate racial discrimination and to suggest federal solutions to the problem. **555**

Committee on Public Information (CPI) Agency created by President Woodrow Wilson in 1917 to increase public support for World War I. **335**

Commonwealth of Independent States (CIS) An alliance formed by many of the former Soviet republics in December 1991. **695**

Communists People who favor the equal distribution of wealth and the end of all forms of private property. **340**

compact discs (CDs) Devices on which to record music or sounds; also capable of storing huge quantities of data. **701**

Compromise of 1850 Agreement proposed by Henry Clay that allowed California to enter the Union as a free state and divided the rest of the Mexican Cession into two territories where slavery would be decided by popular sovereignty; also settled land claims between Texas and New Mexico, abolished the slave trade in Washington, and introduced the Fugitive Slave Act. **106**

Compromise of 1877 Agreement to settle the disputed presidential elections of 1876; Democrats agreed to accept Republican Rutherford B. Hayes as president in return for the removal of federal troops from the South. **140**

Comstock Lode (1859) Nevada gold and silver mine that Henry Comstock claimed to have discovered. **158**

concurrent powers Powers that are shared by the federal and state governments. **38**

Confederate States of America Nation formed by the southern states on February 4, 1861; also known as the Confederacy. **107**

Congress of Industrial Organizations (CIO) Labor group formed in 1938 that joined together industrial unions. **448**

conservation Preservation of nature and its resources. **270**

Constitutional Convention (1787) Meeting in Philadelphia at which delegates from the states wrote the U.S. Constitution. **31**

containment U.S. foreign policy followed during the Cold War that sought to prevent the expansion of Soviet communism. **515**

Contract with America Ten-point Republican reform plan created in the mid-1990s. **710**

contras A group of anti-Sandinista rebels in Nicaragua. **689**

corporations Companies that sell shares of ownership, called stocks, to investors in order to raise money. **189**

cotton gin Device refined by Eli Whitney in the 1790s to separate the seeds from the fibers in cotton plants; revolutionized the cotton industry. **97**

counterculture An alternative culture with values that run counter to, or against, those in the main society. **584**

covert operations Secret missions. **541**

Crusades (1096–1221) Series of five wars launched by European Christians to gain possession of the Holy Land. **9**

Cuban missile crisis (1962) Military crisis that almost led to nuclear war when U.S. naval ships blockaded Cuba until the Soviet Union agreed to remove its nuclear missiles from the island; in return, the United States promised not to invade Cuba and to remove certain missiles from Europe. **577**

culture Common values and traditions of a society, such as language, government, and family relationships. **6**

Dawes General Allotment Act (1887) Legislation passed by Congress that split up Indian reservation lands among individual Indians and promised them citizenship; goal was to lessen tribal influence. **157**

Dayton peace accords (1995) Peace agreements signed in Dayton, Ohio, by the presidents of Bosnia, Croatia, and Serbia; unrest in Bosnia continued in spite of the accords. **717**

D-Day June 6, 1944; date of Allied invasion of France during World War II. **487**

Declaration of Independence (1776) Statement of the Second Continental Congress that defined the colonists' rights and explained their complaints against Britain; declared the colonies independent. **23**

deficit spending Government spending that exceeds the amount received in revenue. **443**

delegated powers Powers that are granted to the federal government. **38**

demobilization The process of returning to a peacetime economy. **356**

Democratic Party Political party formed by supporters of Andrew Jackson after the presidential election of 1824. **92**

department stores Large retail shops that first appeared in cities in the late 1800s. **217**

deport To send an immigrant back to his or her country of origin. **71**

détente Period in the 1970s when relations between the United States and the Soviet Union were less hostile than in the past. **659**

direct primary   Method of allowing voters to choose their own candidates for office. **243**

Disabled in Action (DIA)   Group formed in 1970 to coordinate reform efforts for people with disabilities. **618**

disarmament   The act of limiting military weapons. **365**

Dixiecrats   Members of the States' Rights Party; formed in the 1940s by southern Democrats who were upset with President Harry S Truman's support for civil rights. **521**

dollar diplomacy   President William Howard Taft's policy of influencing Latin American governments through economic, not military, intervention. **306**

Dominion of New England (1686–89) Unpopular union of some northeastern American colonies under one government organized by King James II. **19**

domino theory   Belief common during President Dwight D. Eisenhower's administration and beyond; stated that if one nation in Southeast Asia fell to communism, the rest of Southeast Asia would also fall. **624**

double jeopardy   Act of trying a person twice for the same crime. **67**

doves   Americans who called for U.S. withdrawal from the Vietnam War. **631**

draft   A system of required service in the armed services. **72**

Dred Scott **decision** (1857)   Supreme Court ruling that declared African Americans were not U.S. citizens, that the Missouri Compromise's restriction on slavery was unconstitutional, and that Congress did not have the right to ban slavery in any federal territory. **107**

dry farming   Hardy Campbell's farming method taught to Great Plains farmers in the 1890s; allowed farmers to grow certain crops with less water. **173**

due process   Fair application of the law. **67**

Dust Bowl   Name given to parts of the Great Plains in the 1930s after a severe drought dried out the region. **450**

Earth Day   Day celebrated annually on April 22 to increase environmental awareness; first celebrated in 1970. **673**

Economic Recovery Tax Act (ERTA) (1981)   Federal legislation that reduced personal income taxes by 25 percent and cut some other taxes, amounting to some $750 billion in tax reduction. **683**

Education for All Handicapped Children Act (1975)   Legislation that required public schools to provide a quality education for children with disabilities. **618**

Eighteenth Amendment (1919)   Constitutional amendment that outlawed the production, sale, and transportation of alcoholic beverages in the United States; repealed in 1933. **255**

Eisenhower Doctrine (1957)   President Dwight D. Eisenhower's promise of U.S. aid to any Middle Eastern nation fighting communist aggression. **542**

elastic clause   Article I, Section 8, of the U.S. Constitution that has been interpreted as giving Congress authority to stretch its delegated powers to address issues not otherwise specified in the document. **38**

El Niño   Weather system marked by an irregularly occurring flow of warm surface water along the Pacific coast of South America; often accompanied by weather extremes. **724**

emancipation   Freedom from slavery. **98**

Emancipation Proclamation (1863)   Order announced by President Abraham Lincoln in 1862 that freed the slaves in nonoccupied areas rebelling against the Union; took effect January 1, 1863. **109**

Emergency Quota Act (1921)   Law that limited the number of immigrants to the United States to 357,000 per year. **388**

Emergency Relief Appropriation Act (1935)   Second New Deal legislation that provided close to $4.9 billion to help the unemployed. **439**

eminent domain   The government's right to take personal property to further the public's interest. **68**

Endangered Species Act (1966)   Legislation that protects animals threatened with extinction. **674**

energy crisis   Situation in the 1970s marked by high fuel prices and fuel shortages. **657**

entrepreneurs   People who organize new businesses. **189**

Environmental Protection Agency (EPA)   Agency established by Congress in 1970 to enforce environmental laws. **674**

Equal Pay Act (1963)   Legislation that required employers to pay men and women the same wages for the same job. **611**

Equal Rights Amendment   Proposed constitutional amendment that would guarantee women's rights by prohibiting discrimination based on sex; passed by Congress in 1972 but never ratified by enough states to become a constitutional amendment. **614**

escalation   President Lyndon B. Johnson's policy of increasing U.S. involvement in the Vietnam War. **628**

European Union (EU)   Group of 11 European nations that joined together in 1991 to form a single market with a common currency and a common bank in order to increase their global economic power. **727**

executive branch   Division of the federal government that includes the president and the administrative departments; enforces the nation's laws. **32**

executive orders   Nonlegislative directives issued by the U.S. president in certain circumstances; executive orders have the force of congressional law. **41**

executive privilege   Right of the president to keep information secret to protect national security. **661**

Exodusters   Some 20,000 to 40,000 southern African Americans who settled in western lands in the late 1800s. **171**

expatriates   People who leave their native country to live elsewhere. **402**

exports   Items that a country sells to other countries. **19**

fads   Interests followed for a short time with great enthusiasm. **393**

Fair Deal   Series of reform programs proposed by President Harry S Truman. **521**

Fair Employment Practices Committee (FEPC)   Committee created during World War II to prevent discrimination in war industries and government jobs. **482**

Fair Labor Standards Act (1938)   Legislation that established a minimum wage of 40 cents an hour by 1940. **448**

Family and Medical Leave Act (1993)   Legislation that provides workers with up to 12 weeks of unpaid leave for family or medical purposes. **708**

Farmers' Alliances   Political groups formed by farmers in the late 1800s that worked to elect candidates favorable to farmers. **203**

Farm Security Administration Federal agency created in the 1930s to increase farm ownership by issuing long-term loans at low interest rates. **452**

fascism Political theory that calls for a strong government headed by one individual and in which the state is more important than the individual. **464**

Federal Deposit Insurance Corporation (FDIC) Organization created by Congress during the Hundred Days to protect bank accounts by insuring deposits. **433**

Federal Emergency Relief Administration (FERA) Organization authorized by Congress in 1933 to provide money directly to families in need. **433**

Federal Farm Loan Act Legislation passed during President Woodrow Wilson's administration that made it easier for farmers to obtain credit. **283**

Federal Home Loan Bank Act (1932) Legislation that provided money to banks, financial institutions, and insurance companies so they could offer low-interest mortgages. **429**

federalism U.S. system of government in which power is distributed between a central authority and the individual states. **32**

Federal Reserve Act (1913) Act that created a national banking system to help the government control the economy. **280**

Federal Trade Commission (FTC) (1914) Commission established to investigate corporations to try to keep them from conducting unfair trade practices. **281**

Feminine Mystique, The Book published by Betty Friedan in 1963 that drew national attention to the lives of female homemakers. **611**

feminism Theory that states that women are entitled to economic, political, and social equality with men. **611**

feudalism System of government that arose during the Middle Ages in which people pledge their loyalty to a lord in exchange for protection. **8**

Fifteenth Amendment (1870) Constitutional amendment that gave African American men the right to vote. **135**

fireside chats President Franklin D. Roosevelt's radio addresses to the American people. **433**

First Battle of the Marne (1914) World War I battle in which French forces stopped a German advance near Paris. **328**

Five-Power Naval Treaty Treaty following the Washington Conference that called for reductions in naval strength and imposed a limit on the maximum size of each nation's navy. **365**

flappers Young women in the 1920s who challenged social traditions with their dress and behavior. **382**

flexible response President John F. Kennedy's policy of increasing the number of military forces and conventional weapons, thus providing more military options. **573**

Food Administration Agency created during World War I to increase the food supply for the war by expanding agricultural production and decreasing domestic consumption. **337**

Fordney-McCumber Tariff Act Legislation passed in the 1920s that placed high taxes on imported farm products. **377**

Fort Laramie Treaty (1851) Agreement with the northern Plains Indians that allowed the U.S. government to build forts and roads in Indian homelands while promising to pay for any damage to Indian land. **152**

forty-niners Gold-seekers who traveled to California during the gold rush. **105**

Fourteen Points (1918) President Woodrow Wilson's plan for organizing post–World War I Europe and for avoiding future wars. **345**

Fourteenth Amendment (1868) Constitutional amendment passed by Congress in 1866 giving full rights of citizenship to all people born or naturalized in the United States, except for American Indians. **132**

free coinage Type of monetary system in which both gold and silver were coined; the value of paper money was worth a specific amount of gold or silver. **202**

Freedmen's Bureau Agency established by Congress in 1865 to help poor people in the South. **126**

Freedom Rides (1961) Bus trips by civil rights workers through several southern states in which protesters challenged illegal bus segregation. **596**

Freedom Summer (1964) A campaign in Mississippi to register African Americans to vote. **599**

free enterprise System in which businesses operate free from government involvement. **189**

Fundamentalism Protestant religious movement that teaches that the Bible is literally true. **385**

Gadsden Purchase (1853) United States's purchase of land from Mexico that included the southern parts of present-day New Mexico and Arizona. **104**

General Amnesty Act of 1872 Law that repealed the section of the Fourteenth Amendment that forbade former Confederates from holding public office. **139**

generation gap Division between older and younger people. **584**

genetic engineering The deliberate altering of genes by scientists. **699**

Geneva Accords (1954) Agreement that temporarily divided Vietnam into North and South Vietnam and called for free elections in 1956 to reunite the country. **625**

genocide Deliberate murder of an entire people. **499**

Gettysburg Address (1863) Speech given by Abraham Lincoln in which he praised Union soldiers' bravery and renewed his commitment to winning the Civil War. **110**

Ghost Dance A religious movement among American Indians that spread across the Great Plains in the 1880s. **156**

GI Bill of Rights (1944) Servicemen's Readjustment Act, which offered World War II veterans education benefits and loans for houses, farms, and businesses. **519**

glasnost Soviet policy established in the 1980s that promoted political openness and freedom of expression. **691**

global warming Potential environmental threat caused by the rising temperature on Earth from heat trapped in the planet's atmosphere. **724**

gold standard Type of monetary system in which money is worth a specific amount in gold. **202**

Good Neighbor policy President Franklin D. Roosevelt's foreign policy of promoting better relations with Latin America by using economic influence rather than military force in the region. **462**

Gramm-Rudman-Hollings Act (1985) Law that required the government to cut spending when the deficit grew above a certain level. **685**

Gray Panthers Group formed by Margaret Kuhn to defend the rights of the elderly. **618**

Great Awakening A Christian evangelical movement that became widespread in the American colonies in the 1730s and 1740s. **20**

Great Compromise (1787) Agreement worked out at the Constitutional Convention; established that a state's population would determine representation in the lower house of the legislature, while each state would have equal representation in the upper house of the legislature. **31**

Great Depression Serious, global economic decline that began with the crash of the U.S. stock market in 1929. **421**

Great Migration Mass migration of some 500,000 African Americans to midwestern and northern U.S. cities during and after World War I. **389**

Great Society Legislation introduced by President Lyndon B. Johnson to create government programs to end poverty and racism. **581**

Harlem Renaissance Period of great African American artistic achievement in the 1920s; named for the Harlem neighborhood of New York City. **400**

hawks Americans who pushed for increased military spending and involvement in the Vietnam War. **632**

Hay–Bunau-Varilla Treaty (1903) Agreement between the United States and Panama that gave the United States a 99-year lease to build a canal on a 10-mile-wide strip of land across the Isthmus of Panama. **302**

Hay-Herrán Treaty (1903) Agreement with Colombia that would have given the United States a 99-year lease on a five-mile-wide strip of land across the Isthmus of Panama; rejected by the Colombian senate. **302**

Haymarket Riot (1886) Incident in which a bomb exploded during a labor protest held in Haymarket Square in Chicago, killing several police officers. **197**

Highway Act (1956) An act that provided money to create a national interstate highway system. **547**

hippies Members of the 1960s counterculture who experimented with different ways of living and behaving. **584**

Ho Chi Minh Trail A network of paths, small roads, and tunnels that led from North Vietnam, through Laos and Cambodia, to South Vietnam; the major supply route of the Vietcong. **628**

Holocaust Adolf Hitler's carefully planned extermination of about 6 million European Jews. **498**

Homestead Act (1862) Law passed by Congress to encourage settlement in the West by giving government-owned land to small farmers. **170**

Homestead Strike (1892) Strike at Andrew Carnegie's Homestead Steel factory in Pennsylvania that erupted in violence between strikers and private detectives. **198**

Hoovervilles Camps built outside of major cities by people who had lost their homes during the Great Depression; called Hoovervilles because the people blamed President Herbert Hoover for their situation. **426**

horizontal integration Ownership of all businesses in a particular field. **191**

House of Burgesses Colonial Virginia's elected assembly. **19**

House Un-American Activities Committee (HUAC) Congressional committee created in 1938 to investigate U.S. citizens accused of communist activities. **527**

Hull House Settlement house founded by Jane Addams and Ellen Gates Starr in Chicago in 1889. **221**

Hundred Days Special session of Congress in 1933 during which the bulk of New Deal programs was passed. **432**

hydrogen bomb A type of nuclear bomb. **540**

Immigration and Nationality Act (1965) Legislation that established new quotas for immigrants; limits did not apply to those who had relatives in the United States. **581**

Immigration Reform and Control Act (1986) Legislation that granted legal status to illegal aliens, or noncitizens, who could prove they had lived continuously in the United States since before January 1, 1982. **718**

Immigration Restriction League Organization formed in 1894 by nativists who wanted to reduce immigration; called for a new law requiring immigrants to prove that they were able to read and write before they could enter the United States. **214**

impeach To bring charges against. **40**

imperialism The practice of extending a nation's power by gaining territories for a colonial empire. **288**

imports Items that a country purchases from other countries. **19**

independent counsel Special prosecutor appointed to investigate claims against government officials. **710**

Indian Citizenship Act (1924) Legislation that granted all American Indians the legal protections and voting privileges of U.S. citizenship. **391**

Indian Removal Act (1830) Congressional act that authorized the removal of American Indians from east of the Mississippi River to Indian Territory. **93**

Indian Reorganization Act (IRA) (1934) Legislation that ended land allotment to individual American Indians and allowed some land to be returned to tribal ownership. **455**

indict To formally accuse a person of a crime. **67**

Industrial Revolution Period of rapid growth in the use of machines in manufacturing and production that began in Britain in the mid-1700s and later spread to the United States. **94**

Industrial Workers of the World (IWW) Socialist organization formed in 1905 to bring all workers into one large union. **251**

Information Revolution Rapid growth in the availability and transfer of information that took place in the 1990s; made possible by the increased use of computers. **722**

initiative Law enabling voters to propose a new law by collecting signatures on a petition. **243**

installment plan A program for purchasing goods in which the customer makes a small initial payment and then continues to make monthly payments with interest until the item is paid for. **371**

Intermediate-Range Nuclear Forces Treaty (INF) (1987) Treaty signed by President Ronald Reagan and Soviet leader Mikhail Gorbachev that eliminated all medium-range nuclear weapons from Europe. **691**

Internal Security Act (1950) Law that required suspected communist organizations to register with the federal government and that gave the government the right to arrest people suspected of treasonous activities. **528**

Internet Worldwide system of computer networks. **722**

internment   Forced relocation and imprisonment of people. **483**

Interstate Commerce Act (1887)   Law that provided uniform national regulations for trade between the states. **201**

Interstate Commerce Commission (ICC) (1887)   Commission created by the Interstate Commerce Act to ensure that railroads charged fair rates and treated all shipping customers fairly. **201**

Intolerable Acts (1774)   Four laws passed by Parliament to punish colonists for the Boston Tea Party; closed Boston Harbor and canceled the Massachusetts colony's charter. **22**

Iran-contra affair   Name given to the 1986 scandal in which the U.S. government secretly sold weapons to Iran and then used the profits to fund the contras in Nicaragua. **689**

Iran hostage crisis   Situation that began in 1979 in which 53 Americans were taken hostage in the U.S. Embassy in Tehran, Iran, and were held for 444 days. **670**

Iroquois League   A political confederation of five northeastern tribes—the Cayuga, Mohawk, Oneida, Onondaga, and Seneca—developed by the Iroquois. **8**

island-hopping   World War II strategy of conquering only certain Pacific islands that were important to the Allied advance toward Japan. **492**

isolationism   National policy of avoiding involvement in other nations' affairs. **288**

Jazz Age   A term for the 1920s; so called because of jazz music's popularity during the decade. **400**

Jim Crow laws   Laws that enforced segregation in the southern states. **140**

judicial branch   Division of the federal government that is made up of the national courts; interprets laws, punishes criminals, and settles disputes between states. **32**

judicial review   Principle that gives the Supreme Court the right to declare an act of Congress unconstitutional. **88**

Judiciary Act (1789)   Legislation passed by Congress that created a federal court system. **84**

kamikaze   World War II tactic used by Japanese pilots of crashing planes filled with explosives into Allied ships. **494**

Kansas-Nebraska Act (1854)   Law that created the territories of Kansas and Nebraska and allowed voters there to choose whether to allow slavery. **106**

Keating-Owen Child Labor Act (1916)   Legislation that prohibited companies from shipping their products across state lines if they employed children under 14; was overturned by the Supreme Court in 1918. **283**

Kellogg-Briand Pact (1928)   Pact signed by the United States and 14 other nations that outlawed war. **366**

Khmer Rouge   Cambodian communist army. **637**

Knights of Labor   The first national labor union in the United States; organized in 1869 and included workers of different races, gender, and skills. **196**

Kristallnacht   "Night of broken glass," November 9, 1938; night when Nazis killed or injured many Jews and destroyed many Jewish properties. **465**

Ku Klux Klan   Secret society created by white southerners in 1866 that used terror and violence to keep African Americans from obtaining their civil rights. **138**

La Raza Unida Party (LRUP)   The "United People's Party"; organized in 1970 to increase Hispanic political power. **608**

League of Nations   International congress of nations formed in 1919 that was designed to settle disputes and protect democracy. **345**

League of United Latin American Citizens   Hispanic civil rights organization formed in 1929. **604**

legislative branch   Division of the government that proposes bills and passes them into laws. **32**

Lend-Lease Act (1941)   Law that allowed the United States to loan weapons and other war supplies to Britain, and later to the Soviet Union, to fight against the Axis Powers in World War II. **478**

Levittown   Early example of a preplanned and massproduced housing development; created by William Levitt on Long Island in New York. **548**

Liberty bonds   U.S. bonds sold during World War I to raise money for loans to the Allies. **337**

Limited Nuclear Test Ban Treaty (1963)   Agreement signed by U.S. president John F. Kennedy and Soviet leader Nikita Khrushchev to ban above-ground testing of new nuclear weapons. **577**

Little Rock Nine   African American students who first integrated Central High School in Little Rock, Arkansas, in 1957. **556**

Long March (1934)   Year-long retreat of Chinese Communists to escape a Chinese Nationalist army attack. **522**

Long Walk (1864)   Three-hundred-mile march made by Navajo captives to a reservation in Bosque Redondo, New Mexico, that led to the deaths of hundreds of Navajo. **155**

loose construction   Way of interpreting the Constitution that allows the federal government to take reasonable actions that the Constitution does not specifically forbid it from taking. **84**

Los Angeles Riots (1992)   Riots that erupted after the verdict in the Rodney King case, in which police officers were found not guilty of using excessive force against an African American motorist. **719**

Lost Generation   A group of writers who reacted to the death and destruction of World War I by criticizing postwar society. **402**

Louisiana Purchase (1803)   Purchase of French land between the Mississippi River and the Rocky Mountains that doubled the size of the United States. **89**

Lusitania   British passenger liner sunk by a German U-boat in May 1915; the deaths of 128 Americans on board contributed to U.S. entry into World War I. **333**

Maginot Line   Fortified wall that France built along its border with Germany after World War I. **476**

mandate   Public support. **571**

Manhattan Project   Secret Allied project begun in 1942 to develop an atomic bomb. **496**

manifest destiny Belief shared by many Americans in the mid-1800s that the United States should expand across the continent to the Pacific Ocean. **103**

Marshall Plan U.S. program of giving aid to European countries to help them rebuild their economies after World War II. **514**

Massacre at Wounded Knee (1890) U.S. Army's killing of approximately 150 Sioux at Wounded Knee Creek in South Dakota; ended U.S.-Indian wars on the Great Plains. **157**

mass culture Leisure and cultural activities shared by large numbers of people. **222**

massive retaliation The strategy of threatening to use nuclear weapons in order to stop communist aggression. **540**

mass transit Public transportation. **217**

Mayflower Compact (1620) Legal contract written by the Pilgrims to specify basic laws and social rules for their colony. **15**

McCarthyism Method of making vicious accusations without offering proof; named after Senator Joseph McCarthy. **529**

McKinley Tariff (1890) Law that allowed all countries to ship sugar duty-free to the United States; a serious blow to Hawaiian sugar producers. **289**

Medicaid (1965) Federal health insurance program for people with low incomes. **581**

Medicare (1965) Federal health care program for people over the age of 65. **581**

Mexican American Youth Organization (MAYO) Group formed in 1967 by José Angel Gutiérrez to help fight discrimination. **608**

Mexican Cession Land that Mexico ceded to the United States after the Mexican War through the Treaty of Guadalupe Hidalgo; included present-day California, Nevada, and Utah, most of Arizona and New Mexico, and parts of Colorado, Texas, and Wyoming. **104**

Mexican Revolution Revolution begun in 1910 by Francisco Madero against Mexican dictator Porfirio Díaz. **308**

MIAs Soldiers who are missing in action. **640**

Middle Ages Period of European history that lasted from the late 400s until around 1350. **8**

Middle Passage Voyage that brought enslaved Africans across the Atlantic Ocean to North America and the West Indies. **19**

migration Movement of people from one region to another. **6**

militarism Policy of aggressive military preparedness. **326**

Missouri Compromise (1820) Agreement proposed by Henry Clay that allowed Missouri to enter the Union as a slave state, Maine to enter as a free state, and outlawed slavery in any territories or states formed north of the 36°30' line. **91**

mobilize Prepare a military force for war. **327**

Model T Car created by Henry Ford in 1908 that was priced low enough that many Americans could afford to buy it; also known as the Tin Lizzie. **367**

monopoly Sole economic control of a business or product. **10**

Monroe Doctrine (1823) President James Monroe's statement warning European nations not to colonize or interfere in the Americas. **91**

Montgomery bus boycott (1955–56) African American boycott of the city buses in Montgomery, Alabama, that led to the changing of discriminatory bus rules. **558**

Montgomery Improvement Association Organization formed by African Americans in Montgomery, Alabama, in 1956 to strengthen the bus boycott and to coordinate the protest efforts of African Americans; led by Martin Luther King Jr. **558**

Morrill Act (1862) Federal law that gave land to western states to encourage them to build colleges. **170**

Motown Records First major record label owned by an African American; founded by businessman Berry Gordy in 1959. **586**

muckrakers Journalists who wrote about corruption in business and politics in order to bring about reform. **242**

mugwumps Algonquian word for "big chiefs"; referred to Republican reformers in the 1880s who supported Democrat Grover Cleveland in the presidential election of 1884. **239**

Munich Conference (1938) Meeting between British, French, and German leaders in which Germany was given control of the Sudetenland in exchange for German leader Adolf Hitler's promise to make no more claims on European territory. **476**

National Aeronautics and Space Administration (NASA) Agency established by Congress in 1958 to conduct space research. **540**

National American Woman Suffrage Association (NAWSA) Group formed in 1890 by Elizabeth Cady Stanton and Susan B. Anthony to win the vote for women. **256**

National Association for the Advancement of Colored People (NAACP) Group formed by W. E. B. Du Bois and others in 1909 to pursue the goals of economic, educational, and social equality for African Americans; inspired by the Niagara Movement. **259**

National Association of Colored Women Group led by Mary Church Terrell that supported political reforms for African Americans, including women's suffrage and protecting the voting rights of black men in the South. **260**

National Grange Social and educational organization founded in 1867 to gain more political representation for farmers and to improve their living standards. **201**

National Industrial Recovery Act (NIRA) (1933) Federal law to encourage economic growth by suspending antitrust laws and eliminating unfair competition among employers; declared unconstitutional in 1935. **434**

nationalism The feeling that a specific nation, language, or culture is superior to others. **326**

National Labor Relations Act (NLRA) (1935) Federal law that made unions and collective bargaining legal; also known as the Wagner-Connery Act. **448**

National Liberation Front (NLF) Organization formed to fight Ngo Dinh Diem's government in South Vietnam. **626**

National Organization for Women (NOW) Group formed in 1966 by Betty Friedan and other feminists to increase women's political power. **611**

National Origins Act (1924) Law that reduced immigration, gave preference to northern and western European immigrants, and banned Japanese immigrants. **388**

National Park Service Federal organization created in 1916 to supervise U.S. parks and monuments. **271**

National Traffic and Motor Vehicle Safety Act (1966) Law that required the federal government to enact safety standards for all cars sold in the United States. **591**

National War Labor Board   Agency created by President Woodrow Wilson in 1918 to settle disputes between workers and management. **338**

National Woman's Party (NWP)   Organization founded by Alice Paul in 1913 that used controversial methods to help women win the vote. **257**

nativists   U.S. citizens who opposed immigration because they were suspicious of immigrants and feared losing jobs to them. **95**

Nat Turner's Rebellion (1831)   Rebellion in which Nat Turner and a group of Virginia slaves killed local planter families in an unsuccessful attempt to overthrow slavery. **98**

naturalization   Legal process by which a foreign-born person becomes a U.S. citizen. **70**

Navigation Acts (1650–96)   A series of English laws that regulated trade in the American colonies in order to increase England's profits. **19**

Nazis   National Socialist Party; political group led by Adolf Hitler that rose to power in Germany during the 1930s. **464**

Neutrality Acts   Four laws passed in the late 1930s that were designed to keep the United States out of international incidents. **467**

New Deal   President Franklin D. Roosevelt's programs for helping the U.S. economy during the Great Depression. **431**

New Federalism   A system of revenue sharing proposed by President Richard Nixon that had the federal government give money to the states to use as they saw fit. **656**

New Freedom   Woodrow Wilson's program during the presidential campaign of 1912 that called for government action against monopolies to ensure free competition. **276**

New Frontier   A set of domestic and foreign-policy proposals announced by President John F. Kennedy in his 1961 inaugural address. **571**

new immigrants   Immigrants who came to the United States during and after the 1880s; most were from southern and eastern Europe. **210**

New Nationalism   Theodore Roosevelt's plan for government that called for a strong executive, more active business regulation, and additional social welfare measures; Roosevelt ran on this platform in the 1912 presidential election. **275**

New Right   Conservative voters' groups that grew in strength during the 1980s. **682**

Niagara Movement   Group of African Americans, including W. E. B. Du Bois, formed in 1905 that demanded economic and educational equality, as well as an end to segregation and discrimination. **259**

nickelodeons   Early motion picture theaters; so called because admission was usually a nickel. **396**

Nineteenth Amendment (1920)   Constitutional amendment that gave women the vote. **257**

no-man's-land   Strip of land between the trenches of opposing armies along the western front during World War I. **330**

nonaggression pact (1939)   Secret agreement between German leader Adolf Hitler and Soviet leader Joseph Stalin not to attack one another and to divide Poland. **476**

North American Free Trade Agreement (NAFTA) (1993)   Trade agreement between the United States, Canada, and Mexico. **709**

North Atlantic Treaty Organization (NATO)   Military alliance formed in 1949 by the United States, Britain, and 10 other countries to help defend each other in case of attack. **517**

Northwest Passage   A waterway in North America that would allow ships to sail from the Atlantic to the Pacific Oceans; early explorers searched for but never found it. **12**

Nuremberg Trials (1945)   War crimes trials of high-ranking Nazi officials held by the International Military Tribunal in Nuremberg, Germany. **511**

Ohio Gang   Group of President Warren Harding's friends from Ohio, many of whom were involved in a series of government scandals. **363**

old immigrants   Immigrants who came to the United States before the 1880s; most were from northern Europe. **210**

Open Door Policy (1899)   Declaration made by Secretary of State John Hay that all nations should have equal access to trade with China. **293**

open range   Public land used by ranchers to graze herds. **165**

Operation Desert Fox (1998)   A series of joint U.S. and British air strikes against Iraq after the nation refused to allow United Nations weapons inspectors to perform their job. **716**

Operation Desert Storm (1991)   United Nations invasion led by the United States to make Iraq withdraw from Kuwait. **697**

Operation Restore Hope   A United Nations relief effort in the early to mid-1990s to help provide food to starving people in Somalia, where a civil war was taking place. **715**

Operation Rolling Thunder   A series of air strikes launched by the United States during the Vietnam War to destroy North Vietnam's war industries. **628**

Oregon Trail   A 2,000-mile trail stretching from western Missouri to Oregon Territory. **102**

Organization of Petroleum Exporting Countries (OPEC)   Alliance formed by five major oil-producing nations in 1960 to maintain high prices by controlling the production and sale of oil. **657**

pacification   Policy followed by U.S. and South Vietnamese officials of trying to protect villagers by creating civilian areas guarded by government troops. **629**

Pacific Railway Acts (1862, 1864)   Two laws passed by the federal government that gave loans and land grants to railroad companies to encourage them to build a transcontinental railroad. **160**

Paleo-Indians   The first Americans who crossed from Asia into North America sometime between 50,000 and 10,000 B.C. **6**

Palmer raids (1920)   Raids ordered by Attorney General A. Mitchell Palmer on suspected radical organizations. **360**

Panama Canal   Canal built across the Isthmus of Panama to link the Atlantic and Pacific Oceans; opened in 1914. **304**

Panama Canal treaties (1977) Agreement made between U.S. and Panamanian leaders to transfer control of the Panama Canal to Panama by the year 2000. **669**

Panic of 1873 A U.S. financial crisis; beginning of an economic downturn that weakened the Republican Party. **139**

Panic of 1929 Continued drop in stock prices following Black Tuesday. **421**

pardons Freedom from punishment. **41**

Paris Peace Accords (1973) Agreement made by leaders of the National Liberation Front, North Vietnam, South Vietnam, and the United States to end the Vietnam War; called for the removal of all U.S. troops from Vietnam, the return of American prisoners of war, and the establishment of a demilitarized buffer zone to separate North Vietnam and South Vietnam. **639**

Parliament The British legislature. **19**

patent Exclusive right to manufacture or sell an invention. **185**

Payne-Aldrich Tariff Act passed in 1909 that reduced some tariffs but raised others. **274**

Peace Corps President John F. Kennedy's program that sends American volunteers to assist developing nations with improvement projects. **574**

Pendleton Civil Service Act (1883) Act that established a merit system for awarding federal jobs. **240**

perestroika Soviet policy established in the 1980s that initiated political and economic reforms. **691**

petition A formal request. **66**

Platt Amendment (1902) Amendment to the Cuban constitution that gave the United States the right to become involved in Cuba's foreign and domestic affairs; was in effect until 1934. **300**

Plessy v. Ferguson (1896) Supreme Court case that established the separate-but-equal doctrine for public facilities. **141**

political action committees (PACs) Organizations that collect money to contribute to candidates who support the same issues as the contributors. **73**

political machines Political organizations that used legal and illegal methods to ensure that their candidates won elections. **238**

political parties Groups of people who organize to help elect government officials and influence government policies. **86**

poll tax A special tax that a person had to pay in order to vote. **140**

Pontiac's Rebellion (1763) Unsuccessful attack by Ottawa chief Pontiac and his allies against British forts on the northwestern frontier in an attempt to drive out European settlers. **21**

Pony Express A system of messengers on horseback established in 1860 to carry mail across the United States. **160**

pop art Art movement that challenged the values of traditional art by using popular, commonplace images and objects. **585**

Populist Party National political party formed in 1891 that supported free coinage of silver, labor reforms, immigration restrictions, and government ownership of railroads and the telegraph and telephone systems. **203**

Potsdam Conference (1945) Meeting of U.S. president Harry S Truman, British prime minister Winston Churchill, and Soviet leader Joseph Stalin after Germany's surrender in World War II, at which they divided Germany and Austria into four zones of occupation. **510**

progressives Group of reformers who worked to improve social and political problems, beginning in the late 1800s. **241**

prohibition The banning of the manufacture, sale, and transportation of alcohol. **383**

Protestant Reformation Religious movement begun by Martin Luther and others in 1517 to reform the Catholic Church. **13**

public works Building projects such as hospitals, roads, and schools funded by federal money. **429**

Pullman Strike (1894) Railroad strike by workers at Pullman's Palace Car Company that stopped traffic on many railroad lines until federal courts ordered the workers to return to their jobs. **199**

Pure Food and Drug Act (1906) Legislation that prohibited the manufacture, sale, or transportation of mislabeled or contaminated food and drugs through interstate commerce. **268**

Radical Republicans Members of Congress who felt that southern states needed to make great social changes before they could be readmitted into the Union. **131**

range rights Rights to water sources on the Great Plains; ranchers bought these rights to give them exclusive control of both the water and the land around it. **165**

range wars Battles among large ranchers, small ranchers, and farmers on the Great Plains for use of the open range. **168**

realism A writing style that became popular during the late 1800s that concentrates on presenting accurate images of American society. **225**

realpolitik German word meaning "practical politics"; policy developed by Henry Kissinger and implemented by President Richard Nixon that put American interests, rather than political or moral ideals, first in foreign-policy decisions. **658**

recall Measure allowing voters to remove an official from office before his or her term is over. **243**

Reconstruction (1865–77) Period following the Civil War during which the U.S. government worked to rebuild the southern states and reunite the nation. **125**

Reconstruction Acts (1867–68) Laws that put the southern states under military control and required them to draft new constitutions upholding the Fourteenth Amendment. **133**

Reconstruction Finance Corporation (RFC) (1932) Organization established by President Herbert Hoover to loan money to businesses and banks to help them keep operating. **429**

Redeemers Group of southern Democrats that helped return the Democratic Party to political power in the South during Reconstruction and tried to limit the civil rights of African Americans. **140**

Red Scare A wave of anticommunist fear that swept the United States after World War I. **359**

referendum Measure allowing citizens to vote on proposed laws. **243**

regionalists Painters during the 1930s who sought inspiration from regional customs and folk themes. **458**

relief Food, clothing, shelter, and money provided to people in need. **427**

reparations Payments for damages and expenses brought on by war. **346**

representative democracy   Government by elected representatives of the people. **38**

Republican Party   Political party formed in 1854 to stop the spread of slavery to the West. **106**

Republic of Texas   Independent nation of Texas that existed from 1836 to 1845, when Texas was annexed by the United States. **102**

reservations   Federal lands set aside for American Indians. **152**

reserved powers   Powers retained by the state governments or by citizens. **38**

rock 'n' roll   Musical style developed in the 1950s that drew heavily from African American rhythm and blues and used new instruments such as electric guitars. **553**

Roosevelt Corollary (1904)   President Theodore Roosevelt's addition to the Monroe Doctrine; declared that the United States would police affairs in the Western Hemisphere to keep Europeans from intervening in the region. **306**

roundup   Act of driving cattle together and collecting them in a herd. **166**

Rural Electrification Administration   Organization established during the Second New Deal that extended electrical power lines into isolated rural areas. **439**

sanctions   Economic penalties. **670**

Sand Creek Massacre (1864)   Surprise attack led by Colonel John M. Chivington in which some 200 peaceful Cheyenne in southeastern Colorado were killed. **153**

Sandinistas   Revolutionary political party in Nicaragua that overthrew a pro-American dictator in 1979. **688**

Saturday Night Massacre   Name given to the series of events that included the firing of a special prosecutor investigating Watergate and the resignations of the U.S. attorney general and his next in command for refusing to fire the prosecutor. **662**

scalawags   Name that southern Democrats gave to white southern Republicans during Reconstruction; means "liars and cheats." **136**

Scopes trial (1925)   Trial of John T. Scopes, a high school science teacher who was arrested in Dayton, Tennessee, and tried for teaching Darwin's theory of evolution. **386**

search-and-destroy missions   U.S. strategy in the Vietnam War in which U.S. patrols searched for hidden enemy camps and supplies and destroyed them with massive firepower and air raids. **629**

search warrant   A judge's order authorizing the search of a person's home or property to look for evidence relating to a crime. **67**

Second Battle of the Marne (1918)   Last offensive launched by the Germans during World War I and a turning point of the war for the Allies. **341**

Second Great Awakening   A period of religious evangelism that began in the 1790s and became widespread in the United States by the 1830s. **98**

Second Industrial Revolution   A period of explosive growth in manufacturing and industry in the late 1800s. **184**

Second New Deal   New program of reforms proposed by President Franklin D. Roosevelt's administration in 1935. **438**

segregation   Forced separation of people of different races in public places. **140**

Selective Service Act (1917)   Law that required men between the ages of 21 and 30 to register for the draft into the armed forces. **336**

Selective Training and Service Act (1940)   First peacetime draft in U.S. history. **481**

self-determination   Right of people to decide their own political status. **345**

Seneca Falls Convention (1848)   National women's rights convention; site at which the Declaration of Sentiments was written. **99**

settlement houses   Neighborhood centers that arose in the late 1800s to offer education, recreation, and social activities to immigrants and poor people. **221**

Seventeenth Amendment (1913)   Constitutional amendment allowing American voters to directly elect U.S. senators. **243**

sharecropping   System used on southern farms after the Civil War in which sharecroppers worked land owned by someone else in return for a small share of the crops. **142**

Share-Our-Wealth   Plan organized in 1934 by U.S. senator Huey Long that called for the federal government to limit the size of all personal fortunes so that every family would be guaranteed a minimum income of $2,500 a year. **438**

Sherman Antitrust Act (1890)   Law that made it illegal to create monopolies or trusts that restrained trade. **194**

Sherman Silver Purchase Act (1890)   Law that increased the amount of silver purchased by the U.S. government for coinage. **203**

silent generation   Name given to teenagers and college students in the 1950s because many of them seemed to conform to social expectations without protest. **551**

Silent Majority   President Richard Nixon's term for a large group of conservative voters who disliked the changes that took place in the 1960s. **656**

Silk Road   Overland trade route from China as far west as the Black Sea. **9**

sit-down strike   Type of strike in which striking workers refuse to work or to leave the factories so that owners cannot replace them. **448**

sit-in   Demonstration in which protesters sit down in a location and refuse to leave. **596**

Sixteenth Amendment (1913)   Constitutional amendment that allowed the federal government to pass direct taxes, such as an income tax. **279**

Smoot-Hawley Tariff (1930)   Legislation that raised U.S. duties on imports to all-time highs; caused foreign governments to raise their own trade restrictions. **424**

socialism   Economic system in which the government or the workers own and operate the means of production. **251**

Social Security Act (1935)   Law that created Social Security, which provides retirement pensions and unemployment insurance to U.S. workers. **438**

societies   Groups of people who live together and share a culture. **6**

Society of American Indians   Group founded in 1911 by several American Indians to assist Indians living on reservations. **260**

sodbusters   Name given to both the Plains farmers and the plows they used to break up the region's tough sod. **173**

Southern Christian Leadership Conference   Group founded by Martin Luther King Jr. and other ministers that helped lead the struggle for civil rights. **559**

southern strategy   The Republican Party's attempt to win the support of southern Democrats and others who opposed civil rights reform by limiting further civil rights legislation. **656**

Southern Tenant Farmers' Union (STFU)   Group formed by tenants, sharecroppers, and farm laborers in 1934 to bring attention to the problems these groups faced. **449**

Spanish Armada   Large Spanish naval fleet defeated by England in 1588. **13**

speakeasies   Secret, illegal clubs that served alcohol during prohibition. **384**

speculation   The investing of money in a high-risk venture in hopes of making a profit. **420**

spheres of influence   Areas of a country, particularly in China during the late 1800s, where foreign nations control much of the trade and natural resources. **292**

Sputnik (1957)   The world's first artificial satellite; launched by the Soviet Union. **540**

Square Deal   Political program designed by President Theodore Roosevelt to treat every citizen fairly; approach was applied to resolving disputes between labor and management in business. **267**

stagflation   Economic situation characterized by both high inflation and high unemployment. **656**

stalemate   Situation in which neither side of a conflict can win a decisive victory. **330**

Stamp Act (1765)   Law passed by Parliament that raised tax money by requiring colonists to pay for an official stamp whenever they bought paper items, such as newspapers, licenses, and legal documents. **22**

states' rights   Belief that the power of the states should be greater than the power of the federal government. **92**

steerage   Area in a ship's lower levels; many immigrants who came to the United States traveled in this less-expensive space. **210**

Strategic Arms Limitation Talks (SALT) (1972)   Talks between U.S. president Richard Nixon and Soviet leader Leonid Brezhnev that led to a treaty limiting the numbers and types of long-range nuclear missiles each country could have. **659**

Strategic Defense Initiative (SDI)   A plan for a space-based defense system to protect the United States from Soviet missiles. **690**

strict construction   Way of interpreting the Constitution that allows the federal government to take only the actions the Constitution specifically says it can take. **84**

Student Nonviolent Coordinating Committee (SNCC)   Student organization formed in 1960 to coordinate civil rights demonstrations and provide training for protesters. **596**

Students for a Democratic Society (SDS)   Student group that actively protested discrimination, rigid college rules, and the growing U.S. presence in Vietnam. **584**

subsidy   Bonus payment. **290**

suburbs   Residential neighborhoods outside a city. **217**

Suez Canal crisis   International crisis that began in 1956 when Britain, France, and Israel invaded the Suez Canal region in Egypt. **542**

Sun Belt   States in the South and Southwest that attracted many new people and businesses in the 1950s because of low tax rates, a warm climate, and job opportunities. **546**

supply-side economics   Economic theory stating that government tax cuts would lead to increased economic activity, increased tax revenues, and a balanced budget. **683**

Sussex **pledge** (1916)   Promise issued by German leaders during World War I not to sink merchant vessels without warning. **333**

swing   New style of jazz developed by big-band leaders during the 1930s. **459**

synthetic   Artificial. **374**

Taft-Hartley Act (1947)   Law that gave the federal government greater authority to end strikes and required union leaders to take an oath stating that they were not Communists. **520**

talkies   Movies with sound or dialogue. **396**

Teapot Dome scandal   Scandal during President Warren Harding's administration involving Secretary of the Interior Albert Fall's leasing of oil reserves in return for personal gifts and loans. **364**

Teller Amendment (1898)   Amendment to a U.S. resolution declaring that the United States did not intend to take over and annex an independent Cuba. **296**

temperance movement   A social reform effort begun in the mid-1800s to encourage people to limit their alcohol consumption. **100**

tenements   Poorly built, overcrowded housing where many immigrants lived. **211**

Tennessee Valley Authority (TVA) (1933)   New Deal program that built dams to provide hydroelectric power and flood control to the Tennessee River valley. **436**

terrorism   Use of violent attacks by individuals or small groups to advance political goals. **710**

Tet Offensive (1968)   Attack by North Vietnamese and Vietcong troops against South Vietnam during the Vietnam War; took place during Tet (the Vietnamese New Year) and demonstrated that the North Vietnamese were still militarily strong. **633**

Texas longhorn   Hardy breed of cow raised by ranchers throughout western Texas. **164**

Thirteenth Amendment (1865)   Constitutional amendment that outlawed slavery. **126**

38th parallel   Line of latitude that divides North Korea and South Korea. **523**

Three-Fifths Compromise (1787)   Agreement worked out at the Constitutional Convention stating that three fifths of the slaves in each state would be counted as part of the state's population for determining representation in the lower house of Congress. **32**

Tonkin Gulf Resolution (1964)   Congressional measure that gave President Lyndon B. Johnson the authority to wage war in Vietnam. **627**

totalitarianism   Political system in which the government controls every aspect of citizens' lives. **463**

town meetings   Political meetings, first started in New England, at which people make decisions on local issues. **16**

Townshend Acts (1767)   Laws passed by Parliament placing duties on certain items imported by the colonists. **22**

trade deficit   An imbalance in which a nation imports more than it exports. **664**

transcontinental railroad   A railroad that crossed the continental United States, connecting the East to the West. **160**

Transportation Revolution   Rapid growth in the speed and convenience of transportation; began in the United States in the early 1800s. **95**

Treaty of Brest-Litovsk (1918)   Peace agreement between the Central Powers and Russia that removed Russia from World War I. **340**

Treaty of Ghent (1814)   Treaty between the United States and Britain that ended the War of 1812. **91**

Treaty of Guadalupe Hidalgo (1848)   Treaty that ended the Mexican War and ceded much of Mexico's northern territory to the United States. **104**

Treaty of Medicine Lodge (1867)   Agreement between the U.S. government and southern Plains Indians in which most of the tribes agreed to live on reservations. **154**

Treaty of Paris of 1783   Peace agreement that officially ended the Revolutionary War and established British recognition of the United States. **25**

Treaty of Versailles (1919)   Treaty ending World War I that required Germany to pay billions of dollars of war costs and established the League of Nations. **347**

trench warfare   World War I military strategy of defending a position by fighting from the protection of deep ditches. **329**

Triangle Shirtwaist Factory Fire   Accident at a New York City factory in which 146 workers died after a fire broke out in the building; helped spur legislation to improve factory safety standards. **248**

Triple Alliance   Military alliance formed by Austria-Hungary, Germany, and Italy in the late 1800s. **326**

Triple Entente   Military alliance formed by Britain, France, and Russia in 1907. **326**

Truman Doctrine (1947)   President Harry S Truman's policy stating that the United States would provide economic aid to any country fighting against communism. **514**

trust   Legal arrangement grouping several companies under one board of directors to eliminate competition and to regulate production. **191**

Twelfth Amendment (1804)   Constitutional amendment that created a separate ballot for president and vice president. **87**

Twenty-first Amendment (1933)   Constitutional amendment that ended national prohibition by repealing the Eighteenth Amendment. **385**

Twenty-sixth Amendment (1971)   Constitutional amendment that lowered the federal voting age from 21 to 18. **638**

U-boats   German submarines. **330**

Underwood Tariff Act (1913)   Act that significantly lowered U.S. tariff rates and introduced the first modern personal income tax. **279**

United Farm Workers (UFW)   Union formed by César Chávez to improve pay and working conditions for migrant farm-workers. **606**

United Mine Workers (UMW)   Union of coal mine workers that went on strike in 1946. **520**

United Nations (UN)   International organization chartered in 1945 to promote world peace and resolve conflicts between nations. **510**

Universal Negro Improvement Association (UNIA)   Association founded by Marcus Garvey in 1914 to end imperialism in Africa and discrimination in the United States. **389**

University of California v. Bakke (1978)   Supreme Court case that ruled that a white applicant had been unfairly denied admission to medical school because the university followed a quota system based on race. **601**

urban renewal   Program launched by the federal government to improve life in U.S. cities through better public services and new housing projects. **549**

U-2 incident (1960)   Event in which the Soviets shot down a U.S. U-2 spy plane over the Soviet Union. **543**

vaqueros   Mexican cowboys in the West who tended cattle and horses. **166**

vertical integration   Ownership of businesses involved in each step of a manufacturing process. **191**

veto   To cancel legislation. **40**

Vietcong   Communist guerrilla force that functioned as the National Liberation Front's army and began fighting against Ngo Dinh Diem's government in South Vietnam in the 1950s. **626**

Vietminh   Group of Vietnamese nationalists organized in the 1940s by Ho Chi Minh to drive the Japanese out of Vietnam; also known as the League for the Independence of Vietnam. **624**

Vietnamization   Policy followed by the Nixon administration of gradually turning over all the fighting in the Vietnam War to the South Vietnamese Army. **636**

Vietnam Veterans Memorial   Memorial in Washington, D.C., dedicated in 1982 to honor Americans who died in or went missing in the Vietnam War. **641**

Volstead Act (1919)   Legislation that established federal penalties for the manufacture and sale of alcohol during prohibition. **383**

Voting Rights Act of 1965   Law that protected all citizens' right to vote. **599**

Voting Rights Act of 1975   Legislation that required areas with large immigrant populations to provide ballots in the voters' preferred language. **609**

War Industries Board (WIB)   Agency created by President Woodrow Wilson during World War I to oversee the production and distribution of goods manufactured by the nation's war industries. **337**

War on Drugs   President George Bush's organized effort to end the trade and use of illegal drugs both in the United States and abroad. **693**

War on Poverty   President Lyndon B. Johnson's programs to help poor Americans. **580**

War Powers Act (1973)   Legislation that required the president to get congressional approval before committing U.S. troops to an armed struggle. **641**

War Production Board (WPB)   World War II agency that oversaw the conversion of factories to war production. **481**

Warren Commission   Special group appointed by President Lyndon B. Johnson to investigate the assassination of President John F. Kennedy. **579**

Washington Conference (1921)   Meeting among the United States and the world's major nations to discuss disarmament. **365**

Watergate   Scandal in which President Richard Nixon authorized a cover-up of a break-in at the Democratic National Committee headquarters; led to Nixon's resignation in 1974. **660**

welfare state   System of government institutions that provides for basic needs of citizens. **443**

Whiskey Rebellion (1794)   Protest by small farmers in Pennsylvania against new taxes on whiskey and other alcohol. **85**

Wisconsin Idea   Governor Robert La Follette's program of reforms for Wisconsin in the early 1900s; became a model for other state governments. **244**

Woman's Christian Temperance Union   Women's reform organization founded in 1874 to fight alcohol abuse. **255**

Woodstock (1969)   Concert that took place near Woodstock, New York; became a symbol of the counter-culture's idealistic spirit. **587**

Works Progress Administration (WPA) (1935)   New Deal agency created to put American men and women to work repairing bridges, roads, buildings, and parks. **439**

xenophobia   Fear and hatred of foreigners. **360**

XYZ affair (1797)   Incident in which French agents attempted to get a bribe from U.S. diplomats in exchange for discussions on French-U.S. relations; led to an undeclared naval war between the United States and France. **87**

Yalta Conference (1945)   Meeting of U.S. president Franklin D. Roosevelt, British prime minister Winston Churchill, and Soviet leader Joseph Stalin during World War II to plan for the postwar world. **510**

yellow journalism   The use of sensational, often exaggerated stories in newspapers or other publications to attract readers. **295**

Zimmerman Note   Telegram sent by Germany's foreign minister to Mexico during World War I proposing an alliance between the two countries. **334**

zoot-suit riots (1943)   Attacks by U.S. sailors against Mexican Americans in Los Angeles. **483**

Index

p511; rise to power in Germany, 464–65, *p464. See also* World War II

Nebraska, *mxx,* 376, *c743;* American Indians in, 152; cattle towns and, 165; date of admission to Union, *m79;* railroads and, 160, *c163;* pioneers in, 171; territory of, 106

Negro National League, 397

Neighborhood Watch, 75

Netherlands, 477; early interest in exploration, 13; global possessions in 1914, *m316*

Neutrality Acts, 467

Neutrality Proclamation, 85

Nevada, *mxx, c743;* American Indian reservations in, *m153;* Comstock Lode and, 158; date of admission to Union, *m79;* Mexican Cession and, 104

New Amsterdam, 18, *m35*

New Deal: African Americans and, 455–56, *p456;* agricultural reforms of, 452; aid to farmers, 435–36; American Indians and, 454–55, *p455;* arts programs of the, 440, *p440,* 458; criticisms of, 437–38, 443; Eisenhower and, 544; end of, 442; evaluation of, 443, *f473;* federal spending during, *f473, m473;* labor programs, 434, 439–40, 448; recovery programs, 434–35; relief programs, 429, 434–35, 439–40, *c441;* Second New Deal, 438–40; Social Security and, 438, *f439;* supporters of, 443; U.S. Supreme Court and, 435, 436, 441–42; unemployment and, 434–35, *p434,* 436, 438–40, *f439, p439, c441,* 442, 443, *f473;* women and, *p439,* 454; work relief and, 429, *p434,* 435, 436, 439–40, *p439, p440, c441,* 458. *See also* Franklin D. Roosevelt

New Democrat, 708

New England: colonial, 16–17, *m16;* colonial economy in, 20; Dominion of, 19; Great Awakening in, 20; textile mills in, 94–95; town meetings in, 16

New Federalism, 656. *See also* Richard Nixon

New France, 13

New Freedom, 276. *See also* Woodrow Wilson

New Frontier, 571–72. *See also* John F. Kennedy

New Hampshire, *mxx, c743;* date ratified U.S. constitution, *m79;* establishment of colony, 16, *m16*

new immigrants, 210–14, *c210, p210;* Ellis Island and, 211, *p211;* daily life of, 211–12, *p211, p212, f212;* labor and, 212–13, *p213;* opposition to, 213–14, *p214. See also* old immigrants

New Jersey, *mxx, c743;* date ratified U.S. constitution, *m79;* Edison's research laboratory in, 185, *f186, p186;* establishment of colony, *m16,* 18; labor strike in, *p358;* motion picture industry in, 396; Revolutionary War and, 24; *War of the Worlds* broadcast and, 460

New Mexico, *mxx, c743;* American Indian reservations in, *m153;* Compromise of 1850 and, 106; date of admission to Union, *m79;* Gadsden Purchase, 104; land grant rights for Mexican Americans and, 606; Mexican Cession and, 104; Mexican War and, 104; Santa Fe Trail in, 102, *m103;* territory of, *m103, m153;* testing of atomic bomb in, 510

New Nationalism, 275, 276. *See also* Theodore Roosevelt

New Netherland, 13, 18. *See also* New York

New Orleans, Louisiana: Battle of, 91; birthplace of jazz, 400; Civil War and, 110; 1866 riot in, 133; Freedom Rides and, 596, *m597;* jazz in, 400; Louisiana Purchase and, 89; Pinckney's Treaty and, 8; southern literature about, 145; "The Star-Spangled Banner" and, *f90;* War of 1812 and, 91

New Right, 682, *p682. See also* Moral Majority, Ronald Reagan

newspapers, 224–25; advertising in 1920s and, 372; African American, 390; antislavery, 98; muckraker articles in, 268; yellow journalism and, 295, *p296. See also* names of individual newspapers

New South movement, 144, *p144*

New Sweden, 13

Newton, Huey, 600

New York, *mxx, c743;* colonial boycott of British goods, 22; colonial economy of, 20; Erie Canal in, 91; establishment of colony, *m16,* 18; energy consumption in, *f731;* late 1800s high society in, 193; motion picture industry in, 396; Revolutionary War and, 24; stock market and, 190, 373, 420, *p420*

New York City, New York: Armory Show in, 403; bombing of World Trade Center, 710; colonial economy of, 20; Coney Island in, 223, *p223;* date ratified U.S. constitution, *m79;* design of Central Park, 217, *f218, m218;* Edison's power plant in, *f186,* 187; Harlem, 400–01, *m401;* immigrants in, 211, *p211;* jazz and, 400; Mormon Church founding in, 102; Panic of 1929 and, *p422;* philanthropy and, 217; Seneca Falls Convention in, 99; skyline of, *p374;* skyscrapers in, 216, 405; stock market in, 190, 373, 420, *p420;* subways in, 217; Tammany Hall in, 238, *p238;* tenement housing in, 263; Triangle Shirtwaist Factory Fire, 248, *p249*

New York Journal, 295, *p296*

New York State Tenement House Law, 243

New York Stock Exchange, 190, 373, 420, *p420*

New York World, 295

Nez Percé, *m7, m153,* 155–56; Chief Joseph and, 155–56, *f155, p155*

Ngo Dinh Diem, 625–26

Niagara Movement, 259

Nicaragua, *mxxvi, m305,* 306, 688–89, *m688, p689*

Nicholas II (Russia), 327

Nichols, Terry, 710

nickelodeons, 396. *See also* motion pictures

Nimitz, Chester, 491, 492

Niña (ship), 11

Nine-Power Treaty, 365

Nineteenth Amendment, *f59, f81,* 257, 391

Ninth Amendment, *f56,* 69

Nixon, E. D., 558

Nixon, Pat, 658

Nixon, Richard, 40, 543, 635, *f637, p742;* Checkers speech, 525; and civil rights, 656; and the economy, 656–57, *p656;* as Eisenhower's running mate (1952), 525; election of 1960, 570–71, *m570;* election of 1968, 656; election of 1972, 638; energy crisis and, 657, *c658;* foreign policy of, 658–59, *p659;* New

Federalism and, 656; pardoning of, 663; resignation of, 662–63, *p663;* SALT treaty and, 659; Silent Majority and, 656; U.S. Supreme Court and, 656; Vietnam War and, 636–41; visit to China, 654, *p654,* 658; Watergate scandal and, 660–63, *p660, p661, p662*

no-man's-land, 330

nominating conventions, 92

nonaggression pact, 476

Non-Intercourse Act, 90

nonviolent resistance: César Chávez and, 605; civil rights and, 595–99, *p596, m597, f598, p598;* Martin Luther King Jr. and, *f598;* student movement and, 583–85, *p583, p584;* Student Nonviolent Coordinating Committee (SNCC), 596–97, 599, 612

Noriega, Manuel, 693

Normandy, France, 487–89

Norris, Frank, 200, 225

North, Oliver, 689

North, the: African Americans in, 389, *c410, f410–11;* American Indians in, 390–91; Civil War and, 107–11; Great Migration and, 389, *c410;* growth of transportation in 95, *f96,* 96, 184–85, *p185;* industry in, 94–95, 184, *c184,* 185; manufacturing and, 94–95; Mexican Americans in, *f409, m409;* migration to, *c410; f408–11, p410*

North Africa: OPEC member nation, *m657;* World War II and, 484, 485

North America, *mxxvi;* Columbian Exchange and, 12, Dutch colonies in, 13; early cultures of, 6, *m7,* 8; early European colonization in, 12–13, *m12;* English colonies in, 13, 14–20; first migration to, 6; French colonies in, 13; naming of, 12; Native American culture areas of, 6, *m7,* 8; major resources in, *m316;* political map of, *mxxvi;* Swedish colonies in, 13

North American Defense System (NORAD), *m537*

North American Free Trade Agreement (NAFTA), 709, *p709*

North Atlantic Treaty Organization (NATO), 517, *p517, p717;* air strikes on Serbia, 717; Cold War and, *f534–35, m534–35;* 50th anniversary of, *p717;* war in Balkans and, 716—17; war in Kosovo and, 717

North Carolina, *mxx, c743;* Civil War and, 108; date ratified U.S. constitution, *m79;* establishment of colony, *m16,* 18; proposed state of Franklin and, *f79;* readmission to Union, 134; Reconstruction and, *m134;* secession and, 108; Wright brothers' flight tests in, 188, *p188*

North Dakota, *mxx, c743;* American Indian reservations in, *m153;* date of admission to Union, *m79;* farming in, 173–74

North Korea: Korean War and 524–25, 526, *f536, m537;* 38th parallel and, 523. *See also* Korea, Korean War

North Vietnam, *f644, m644;* Ho Chi Minh Trail and, *m644;* support for Vietcong, *f644. See also* South Vietnam, Vietnam War

Northwest Ordinance of 1787, 31, *f78–79, c78, m78, m79*

Northwest Passage, 12–13

public transportation and, 557–59, *p559*; sit-ins and, 595, 596; Supreme Court rulings, 555, 556; post–World War II, 554–55, *p554, p555*

Seguín, Juan, 102

Selassie, Haile, 464

Selective Service Act, 336

Selective Training and Service Act, 481

self-determination, 345

Selma, Alabama: civil rights movement and, 599

Seminole, *m7*, 93, *m153*

Senate, U.S., 32, 38–40, *f45*, 709; powers of, 40, *f46–49, f53*; checks and balances, 32–33; elections for, *f46*; filling vacancies in, *f59*; impeachment cases and, 40, *f46, p133*, 133–34, *c662*, 663, 712; role of vice president in, 39, *f46*; separations of powers, 32–33, *c63*; standing committees in, 39–40; terms of office, 38, *f45, f46, f59–60, c80*; U.S. Constitution on, *f45–49*; Watergate hearings, 661–62, *p661. See also* Congress

Seneca, 8

Seneca Falls Convention, 99, *f99*

separation of powers, 38, *c63*

Separatists, 15

Serbia: war in the Balkans and, 716–17, *p716*; Dayton peace accords and, 717; NATO air strikes on, 717

Servicemen's Readjustment Act. *See* GI Bill of Rights

settlement houses, *f220*, 221, 241, *p241*, 245

Seven Days Battles, 108

Seventeenth Amendment, *f59*, 243

Seventh Amendment, *f56*, 67, 68

7th Calvary, U.S. Army, 154, *p154*

Seward, William, 288

Seward's Folly, 288

Seymour, Horatio, 134

shah of Iran. *See* Mohammad Reza Pahlavi

Shame of the Cities, The (Lincoln Steffens), 242

sharecropping, 142–43

Share-Our-Wealth, 438. *See also* Huey Long

Shawnee, 90

Shays, Daniel, 31

Shays's Rebellion, 31

Shepard, Alan, Jr., 589

Sherman, John, 194

Sherman, William Tecumseh, 111, 125, *m126*, 153

Sherman Antitrust Act, 194, 199, 249, 267–68, 281

Sherman Silver Purchase Act, 203

Shoshoni, *m7*, 89, *m153*

Shuttlesworth, Fred, 597

Siberia, 463

silent generation, 551

Silent Majority, 656

Silent Spring (Rachel Carson), 591

Silk Road, 9

Silliman, Benjamin, Jr., 185

silver, 158; free coinage of, 202–03, 204–05; mining of, 158, 159–60, *f178, m178*

Simmons, William J., 388

Sinclair, Upton, 268, *f269*

Singapore, *mxxix*, 490

Singleton, Benjamin, 171

Sioux, *m7, m103*, 150, 152, *p152*, 153–54, *m153, p154*, 260; Ghost Dance and, 156–57; Massacre at Wounded Knee and, 156–57. *See also* names of individual Sioux

Sirhan, Sirhan, 634

Sister Carrie (Theodore Dreiser), 225–26

sit-down strike, 448–49, *p448*

sit-in, 596

Sitting Bull, 154, 156; on American Indian culture, 260

Sixteenth Amendment, *f58*, 279

Sixth Amendment, *f55–56*, 67, 68, 72

skyscrapers, 216, 219; design in the 1920s, 405, *p405*

Slater, Samuel, 94

slavery: abolishment of, *f57*, 126; abolition movement and, 98–99; in colonial America, 15, 18, 19, 20; Compromise of 1850, 106; culture of, 97–98, *p97*; as divisive issue, 106; *Dred Scott* decision, 107; Emancipation Proclamation, 109, *f112–13*; free African Americans and, 97, 98, *p98*; Fugitive Slave Act, 106; global, 10, 12; Kansas-Nebraska Act, 106, 107; labor of, 97; Lincoln on, 107; Mexican Cession and, 106; Missouri Compromise and, 91, 106, 107; opposition to, 98–99; revolts of, 98; slave codes, 20, 97, 98; slave trade, 10, 19, 20, 98; in the South, 97; in Spanish America, 12; in Texas, 101; Three-Fifths Compromise and, 31–32; Underground Railroad and, 98–99; westward expansion of, 101, 106. *See also* African Americans, freedpeople, slaves

slaves: aid for freedpeople, *m126*; apportionment and, 31–32; culture of, 97–98, *p97*; in early America, 15; early trade of, 10, 19, 20; emancipation of, 109, *f112–13*; Fugitive Slave Act, 106; Middle Passage and, 19; religion and, 98; revolts of, 98; Underground Railroad, 98–99. *See also* African Americans, freedpeople, indentured servants, slavery

Sloat, John Drake, 104

Slovenia: war in the Balkans and, 716–17

Smith, Alfred E., 366

Smith, Bessie, 400, *p400*

Smith, John, 14, *f15, p15*

Smith, Joseph, 102

Smith, Mamie, 400

Smith, Moe, 384

Smith, Sophia, 252

Smoot-Hawley Tariff, 424

Social Darwinism, 192

socialism, 251

Socialist Party, 276, *p276, m277*, 359, 363; Palmer raids and, 360

social reform. *See* progressives, reform

Social Security Act, 438, *f439, c441*, 544

societies, 6

Society of American Indians, 260, *p260*

Society of Friends, The. *See* Quakers

sodbusters, 173

Soil Conservation Act of 1935, 1952

Sojourner (space rover), 725

Somalia, *mxxx*, 714–715

Somme River (France): battle at the, 330

sonar technology, 484

Songhay Empire, 9

Sons of Liberty, 22

Sosa, Sammy, 720

Soto, de Hernando, 12

soul music, 586–87

Souls of Black Folk, The (W. E. B. Du Bois), 259

Sound and the Fury, The (William Faulkner), 457

Souter, David, 694

South, the: abolition and, 98–99; agriculture of, 142–43, *c144*; balance of power and, 91, 106, 107, *c107*; Black Codes, 130–31, *p131*; canals in, *m138*; in the Civil War, 107–11; Confederate States of America, 107; congressional representation, *c107*; cotton in, 97, *c97*, 143, *p143, c144*; education in, *f127*, 137, *m138*, 140, *m149*; farming in, 97, 142–43, *p142*; free African Americans in, 97, 124–25, *m126*; Great Depression and, *f472*; Great Migration and, *f410*; impact of Civil War on, 123, 124–25; industrial growth in, 140, 144–45; Jim Crow laws, 140; Ku Klux Klan in, 138–39, 388–89, *p389*; literature of, 145, *p145, f146*; migration out of, *f408–11*; mill life in, 145; music of, 98, *p145*, 146–47, *p147*, 399–400; New South, 144, *p144*; post–Civil War, 123, 124–25, *p124, m138*; Reconstruction and, 125–44, *m134, m138, c143, c144*; secession of, 107; sharecropping, 142–43; slavery in, 97–98, *p98*, 106

South Africa, *mxxx*; apartheid and, 670, 714, *p714*; Nelson Mandela and, 714

South America, *mxxvii*; early civilizations in, 6; European exploration of, 12; major resources in, *m316*; political map of, *mxxvii*; impact of global depression on, *m471*

South Carolina, *mxx, c743*; after Civil War, 123; in Civil War, 107; date ratified U.S. constitution, *m79*; establishment of colony, *m16*, 18; freedpeople in, 125, *m126*; labor in, *f472*; nullification crisis and, 92–93; readmitted to Union, 134; during Reconstruction, *m134*; secession and, 107

South Dakota, *mxx, c743*; American Indian reservations in, *m153*; date of admission to Union, *m79*

Southeast Asia: and consequences of Vietnam War, 639–40; imperialism in, 288

Southern Christian Leadership Conference (SCLC), 597, 599

southern colonies (English), *m16*, 17–18; economy in, 19–20

southern strategy, 656

Southern Tenant Farmers' Union (STFU), 449, *p449*

South Korea: Korean War and 524–25, 526; 38th parallel and, 523. *See also* Korea, Korean War

South Vietnam, *f644, m644*; Ho Chi Minh Trail and, *m644*; soldiers, *p645*; Vietcong, *c645, p645. See also* North Vietnam, Vietnam War

Southwest: American Indians and reservations in, 6, *m7*, 8, *m153*, 155, *f155, p155*, 156, *p156*; Gadsden Purchase and, 104; Mexican cession and, 104; Mexican immigration to, *f408–09*; Mexican Americans in, *m409*; migrant farming in, *p409*; migration out of, *f408–09*; Native American cultures in, 6, *m7*; ranching in, 164–66, *p166*;

For permission to reprint copyrighted material, grateful acknowledgment is made to the following sources:

American Heritage Publishing Company: From "Abandon Ship! Abandon Ship!" by Stephen Bower Young from *World War II: The Best of American Heritage,* edited by Stephen W. Sears. Copyright © 1991 by American Heritage Publishing Company.

Arte Público Press: "Brindis: For the Barrio" from *Arise, Chicano! and Other Poems* by Angela de Hoyos. Copyright © 1975 by Angela de Hoyos and Mireya Robles. Published by M & A Editions, San Antonio.

Bantam, a division of Bantam Doubleday Dell Publishing Group, Inc.: Quote by Alexander Taffel from *The Sixties: Years of Hope, Days of Rage* by Todd Gitlin. Copyright © 1987 by Todd Gitlin.

Rodolfo Gonzales: From *I Am Joaquín/Yo Soy Joaquín: An Epic Poem* by Rodolfo Gonzales. Copyright © 1967 by Rodolfo Gonzales.

HarperCollins Publishers Ltd.: From "Stalingrad: December 1942, A German Infantryman's View" from *In Their Shallow Graves* by Benno Zieser, translated by Alec Brown. Copyright © 1956 by Elek Books.

Henry Holt and Company, Inc.: From *A Rumor of War* by Philip Caputo. Copyright © 1977, 1997 by Philip Caputo.

The Heirs to the Estate of Martin Luther King, Jr., c/o Writers House, Inc. as agent for the proprietor: From "I Have a Dream" by Martin Luther King, Jr. Copyright © 1963 by Martin Luther King, Jr.; copyright renewed © 1991 by Coretta Scott King. From *Stride Towards Freedom* by Martin Luther King, Jr. Copyright 1958 by Martin Luther King, Jr.; copyright renewed © 1986 by Coretta Scott King.

Alfred A. Knopf, Inc.: "I Too Sing America" from *Collected Poems* by Langston Hughes. Copyright © 1994 by the Estate of Langston Hughes.

G. P. Putnam's Sons, a division of Penguin Putnam Inc.: Quote by Winona Espinosa from *The Homefront: America During World War II* by Mark Jonathan Harris, Franklin D. Mitchell, and Steven J. Schechter. Copyright © 1984 by Putnam Publishing Group.

Random House, Inc.: From "On the Pulse of Morning" from *On the Pulse of Morning* by Maya Angelou. Copyright © 1993 by Maya Angelou.

Scribner, a division of Simon & Schuster, Inc.: From *The Great Gatsby* (Authorized Text) by F. Scott Fitzgerald. Copyright 1925 by Charles Scribner's Sons; copyright renewed 1953 by Frances Scott Fitzgerald Lanahan. Copyright © 1991, 1992 by Eleanor Lanahan, Matthew J. Bruccoli, and Samuel J. Lanahan as Trustees under Agreement dated 7/3/75 created by Frances Scott Fitzgerald Smith.

Special Rider Music: From lyrics from "Blowin' in the Wind" by Bob Dylan. Copyright © 1962 by Warner Bros. Music; copyright renewed © 1990 by Special Rider Music. All rights reserved. International copyright secured. From lyrics from "The Times They Are A-Changin'" by Bob Dylan. Copyright © 1963, 1964 by Warner Bros. Music; copyright renewed © 1991 by Special Rider Music. All rights reserved. International copyright secured.

Amy Tan and Sandra Dijkstra Literary Agency: From "Mother Tongue" by Amy Tan. Copyright © 1990 by Amy Tan. First published in *The Threepenny Review.*

Texas A&M University Press: From *With a Black Platoon in Combat: A Year in Korea* by Lyle Rishell. Copyright © 1993 by Lyle Rishell.

Viking Penguin, a division of Penguin Putnam Inc.: From *The Crucible* by Arthur Miller. Copyright 1952, 1953, 1954 and renewed © 1980, 1981, 1982 by Arthur Miller. From *The Grapes of Wrath* by John Steinbeck. Copyright 1939 and renewed © 1967 by John Steinbeck.

Sources Cited

From *A Kid on the Comstock: Reminiscences of a Virginia City Childhood* by John Taylor Waldorf. Published by American West Publishing Company, Palo Alto, 1970.

From Severita Lara interview by Jesús Treviño, January 31, 1992; from Lionel Steinberg interview by Sylvia Morales, December 7, 1994; and from Reies López Tijerina interview by Luis Torres, December 29, 1989, from *Chicano!* by F. Arturo Rosales. Published by Arte Público Press, Houston, TX, 1996.

Quote by Gale Kaplan from "Just a Housewife" from *A History of Women in America* by Carol Hymowitz and Michaele Weissman. Published by Bantam Books, 1978.

Quote by Diane Nash from "Inside the Sit-ins and Freedom Rides: Testimony of a Southern Student" from *The New Negro,* edited by Mathew H. Ahmann. Published by Biblo and Tannen, New York, 1969.

Quote by Sgt. Dave Richardson from "Battle above the Solomons" from *Yank: The Story of World War II as Written by the Soldiers* by the Staff of *Yank,* the Army Weekly. Published by Brassey's, Inc., McLean, VA, 1984.

From "A Preliminary New York to Buffalo Tour" by S. W. Rushmore from *Motoring in America: The Early Years,* edited by Frank Oppel. Published by Castle Books, New Jersey, 1989.

Quote by John Cash from "Howard University Becomes 'Hot Pick'" by Jonathan P. Decker from *Christian Science Monitor,* June 2, 1997, Philadelphia.

From "That Everyone's American Dream Would Come True" by Dan Helfrich from *Ordinary Americans,* edited by Linda R. Monk. Published by Close Up Publishing, 1994.

From *If I Die in a Combat Zone, Box Me Up and Ship Me Home* by Tim O'Brien. Copyright © 1973 by Tim O'Brien. Published by Delacorte Press/Seymour Lawrence, New York, 1973.

Quote by a Pittsburgh man from *America's History,* edited by James A. Henretta et al. Published by The Dorsey Press, Chicago, 1987.

Quotes by an assistant to Oliver North, an English visitor to the Berlin Olympic Games, a German woman, a Peace Corps volunteer, Gus Rodriguez, Barry Rosen, and a Wall street broker from *The Century* by Peter Jennings and Todd Brewster. Published by Doubleday, New York, 1998.

From *When Heaven and Earth Changed Places: A Vietnamese Woman's Journey from War to Peace* by Le Ly Hayslip. Published by Doubleday, 1989.

Quote by Christa McAuliffe from *No Downlink: A Dramatic Narrative about the Challenger Accident and Our Time* by Claus Jensen, translated by Barbara Haveland. Published by Farrar, Straus & Giroux, New York, 1996.

Quotes by Harvey Frommer and Michael Mitchell from *American Decades, 1980–1989,* edited by Victor Bondi. Published by Gale Research Inc., Detroit, 1996.

From "The Mexican Problem" from *North from Mexico: The Spanish-Speaking People of the United States* by Carey McWilliams. Published by Greenwood Press, New York, 1948.

Quotes by Dan Carpenter, Elton Fax, Selma Hannish, and Richard Nugent from *You Must Remember This: An Oral History of Manhattan from the 1890s to World War II* by Jeff Kisseloff. Published by Harcourt Brace & Company, San Diego, 1989.

Quote by Guy Owen from *The Private Side of American History: Readings in Everyday Life,* edited by Thomas R. Frazier. Published by Harcourt Brace, Orlando, FL, 1983.

Quotes by an Air Force colonel's son and an Army sergeant's daughter from *Military Brats: Legacies of Childhood Inside the Fortress* by Mary Edwards Wertsch. Copyright © 1991 by Mary Edwards Wertsch. Published by Harmony Books, New York, 1991.

From *Their Eyes Were Watching God* by Zora Neale Hurston. Published by HarperCollins Publishers, Inc., New York, 1937.

From *Georgia O'Keeffe* by Roxanna Robinson. Published by HarperCollins Publishers, Inc., New York.

From *The Long Winter* by Laura Ingalls Wilder. Published by HarperCollins Publishers, Inc., New York, 1940.

From *Yesterday: A Memoir of a Russian Jewish Family* by Miriam Shomer Zunser, edited by Emily Wortis Leider. Published by HarperCollins Publishers, New York, 1978.

Quote by a Hungarian immigrant from *This Was America* by Oscar Handlin. Published by Harvard University Press, Cambridge, Mass., 1949.

From "Fighting to Survive, A History of Survival" by Alison Ligon from the *Herald-Sun.* Available on the World Wide Web at http://www.herald-sun.com/hbcu/docs/history.html, February 10, 1998.

Quote by Ten Bears of the Vamparika Comanche from *Bury My Heart at Wounded Knee: An Indian History of the American West* by Dee Brown. Published by Henry Holt and Company, New York, 1971.

Quotes by a draft resister, Dr. Harold Bloomfield, John Osborne, and Claude Summers from *It Seemed Like Nothing Happened: The Tragedy and Promise of America in the 1970s* by Peter N. Carroll. Published by Henry Holt and Company, Inc., New York, 1982.

Quotes from "The Final Armistice" and from "The Collapse of the Central Powers" from *The First World War: A Complete History* by Martin Gilbert. Published by Henry Holt and Company, New York, 1994.

Quotes from *My People the Sioux* by Luther Standing Bear. Published by Houghton Mifflin Company, Boston, 1928.

From *A Place Called Chinese America* by Diane Mei Lin Mark and Ginger Chih. Published by Hunt Publishing Company, Dubuque, IA, 1985.

Quote by Mitsuo Fuchida from "Five Fatal Minutes: Japanese Carriers Crippled, Battle of Midway, 4 June 1942" from *Midway: The Battle That Doomed Japan* by Mitsuo Fuchida with Masataka Okumiya. Published by Hutchinson, 1957.

Quote by Mary Smith from "The Woman Worker Speaks" by Ruth Young and Catherine Filene Shouse from *Independent Woman,* vol. 24, October 1945.

Quote by C. D. Jackson from "Tokens Left at the Wall" by Arnold Abrams, May 24, 1996, from *Newsday.com: The Vietnam Memorial.*

From "Interview with Nguyen Huu Tho" by Christine Pelzer White from *Journal of Contemporary Asia,* vol. 11, no. 1, 1981.

Quote by a Garden City, Kansas, woman from *Kansas City Times,* March 1935.

Quote by Juan Chanax from *Strangers among Us* by Roberto Suro. Published by Alfred A. Knopf, Inc., New York, 1998.

From *Remembering America: A Voice from the Sixties* by Richard N. Goodwin. Published by Little, Brown and Company, Boston, 1988.

Quotes by Jerome Franks, Virginia Lewis MacInnes, and Sylvia Van Hazinga from *Ticket to Paradise: American Movie Theaters and How We Had Fun* by John Margolies and Emily Gwathmey. Published by Little, Brown and Company, Boston, 1991.

Quote by Gordon Parks from *The Great Depression: America in the 1930s* by T. H. Watkins. Published by Little, Brown and Company, Boston, 1993.

From "About Women" from *Los Angeles Times,* May 12, 1974.

Quote from *LULAC News,* Houston, TX, 1946.

Quote by Sam Rayburn from *Sam Johnson's Boy: A Close-up of the President from Texas* by Alfred Steinberg. Published by Macmillan, New York, 1968.

Quote by Jessie Lee Brown Foveaux from *The Manhattan (Kansas) Mercury,* March 1, 1998.

From quotes by Meryl Streep from *MAQ.* Available on the World Wide Web at http://www.geocities.com/Hollywood/Hills/2844/MSQ.html.

Quote by a rancher from Cut Bank, Montana, to David Houston and Florence Harrison from *America Enters the World: A People's History of the Progressive Era and World War I* by Page Smith. Published by McGraw-Hill Book Company, 1985.

From the "Memories of Max Mannheimer: Theresienstadt-Auschwitz-Warsah-Dachau, 10 November 1938" from "Night of Broken Glass." Published online at http://www.hagalil.com. English translation by Holt, Rinehart and Winston.

Quote by Juanita "Skeeter" Maxey from *America Goes to the Movies: 100 Years of Motion Picture Exhibition* by Barbara Stones. Published by the National Association of Theatre Owners, North Hollywood, 1993.

Quote by Sarah Gavit from "Tribe in Utah Fights for Nuclear Waste Dump" by Matthew L. Wald from *The New York Times,* April 18, 1999.

Quotes by a Reagan supporter and Earl B. Dunckel from *Sleepwalking through History: America in the Reagan Years* by Haynes Johnson. Published by W. W. Norton & Company, Inc., New York, 1991.

From "Vaudeville at Angelus Temple" by Sheldon Bissell from *The Outlook*, CXLIX, May 23, 1928.

Quotes by Stella Boone and Ethel Stringer from *From Ballots to Breadlines: American Women, 1920–1940* by Sarah Jane Deutsch. Published by Oxford University Press, New York , 1994.

From "The Reagan Years" from *The Unfinished Journey: America since World War II* by William H. Chafe. Published by Oxford University Press, New York, 1991.

Quote about Kermit Johnson and by an assembly-line worker from *Who Built America?* vol. 2, *From the Gilded Age to the Present*, edited by Joshua Freeman et al. Published by Pantheon Books, 1992.

Quote from *By Any Means Necessary: Speeches, Interviews, and a Letter* by Malcolm X. Published by Pathfinder, New York, 1970.

Quotes by Charles Houston on segregation and by Joseph McNeil from "Down Freedom's Main Line: The Movement's Next Generation" from *Eyes on the Prize: America's Civil Rights Years, 1954–1965* by Juan Williams. Published by Penguin Books, 1987.

Quote by Malcolm Cowley from *Poetry*, LII, July 1938.

Quotes by Florence Ausburn and George Robinson from *Listening to Radio, 1920–1950* by Ray Barfield. Published by Praeger Publishers, Westport, CT, 1996.

From letter by Mary McLeod Bethune to Charles H. Houston, April 10, 1939, from *Farewell to the Party of Lincoln* by Nancy J. Weiss. Published by Princeton University Press, Princeton, NJ, 1983.

Quote by Mary Jane Owen from *No Pity: People with Disabilities Forging a New Civil Rights Movement* by Joseph P. Shapiro. Published by Random House, Inc., New York, 1993.

Quote by Gutzon Borglum from *F.D.R., My Boss* by Grace Tully. Published by Scribner, New York, 1949.

From *The Spirit of St. Louis* by Charles Lindbergh. Published by Scribner's Sons, New York, 1953.

From *A Farewell to Arms* by Ernest Hemingway. Published by Scribner's Sons, New York, 1957.

Quote by Ethel Noland, friend of Harry Truman, from *Oral History Transcripts* from *Truman* by David McCullough. Published by Simon & Schuster, New York, 1992.

Quotes by Esther Clark, Mary Lyon, and Mary Roberts from *Pioneer Women: Voices from the Kansas Frontier* by Joanna L. Stratton. Published by Simon & Schuster, Inc., New York, 1981.

From "An Emigrant's Farewell" from "Songs of the Mexican Migration" from *Puro Mexicano*, edited by J. Frank Dobie. Published by Southern Methodist University Press, Dallas, 1969.

Quote by a baseball fan from "Record Smasher" by Tom Verducci from *Sports Illustrated*, April 22, 1999. Available on the World Wide Web at http://www.cnnsi.com/features/1998/weekly/980914/record.html.

Quote by Linda Bloodworth-Thomason from *A Century of Women*, based on a documentary script by Jacoba Atlas with Heidi Schulman and Kyra Thompson. Published by TBS Books, Atlanta, GA, 1994.

From *Over There: A Marine in the Great War* by Carl Andrew Brannen. Published by Texas A&M University Press, College Station, TX, 1996.

From interview with Barbara Baisley from "Man and Woman of the Year: Middle Americans" from *Time*, January 5, 1970. Published by Time, Inc., New York.

Quote by Nevada Dove from "Don't Mess Around with The Toxic Crusaders" by Deborah Elder Brown" from *Time*, May 3, 1999. Available on the World Wide Web at http://cgi.pathfinder.com/time/reports/environment/heroes/heroesgallery/.

Quote by Barbara Langsam from "Letters to the Editor" from *Time*, March 27, 1992. Published by Time, Inc., New York.

Quote by Eloina Ortega from "The Nation" section from *Time*, July 5, 1976. Published by Time, Inc., New York.

Quote by Gail S. Shaffer from "Letters to the Editor" from *Time*, July 20, 1998. Published by Time, Inc., New York.

Quote by Russell Baker's Aunt Pat from *The Great Depression: America, 1929–1941* by Robert S. McElvaine. Published by Times Books, New York, 1984.

Quote by a Victorio follower from *In the Days of Victorio: Recollections of a Warm Springs Apache* by Eve Ball. Published by University of Arizona Press, Tucson, 1970.

Quote by Chester Copeland and from an interview with Paul and Pauline Griffith from *Like a Family: The Making of a Southern Cotton Mill World* by Jacquelyn Dowd Hall et al. Published by the University of North Carolina Press, 1987.

From interview with Madge Alford from Indian-Pioneer Papers, University of Oklahoma, Norman.

Quote by Josia Reams from *Class and Tennessee's Confederate Generation* by Fred Arthur Bailey. Published by University of South Carolina Press, Chapel Hill, 1987.

From the film *The Plow That Broke the Plains* by Pare Lorentz. Published by the U.S. Resettlement Administration, 1936.

From "Students and the Movement: An Interview with Diane Nash" from *Eyes on the Prize: America's Civil Rights Years* by Juan Williams. Published by Viking Penguin, New York, 1987.

Quote by John Howard Lawson from *Thirty Years of Treason: Excerpts from Hearing Before the House Committee on Un-American Activities*, edited by Eric Bentley. Published by Viking Press, New York, 1971.

Quote about Richard Nixon and quote by Leona Marshall Libby from *The Fifties* by David Halberstam. Published by Villard Books, 1993.

Quote by Michiko Yamaoka, interviewed by Mitsuru Ohba, from "Voices of A-Bomb Survivors" Web site, October 13, 1998. Available on the World Wide Web at http://www.csi.ad.jp/ABOMB/Hibakusha/h03.html.

Quote by Moritz Vegh from *The Boys* by Martin Gilbert. Published by Weidenfeld & Nicolson, London, 1996.

From "Marian Wright Edelman" from *Current Biography Yearbook, 1992*. Published by H. W. Wilson Company, New York, 1992.

From *Fifty Years on the Old Frontier* by James H. Cook. Published by Yale University Press, 1994.

Photography Credits

Table of Contents and Front Matter: Page iv, Independence National Historical Park Collection; v (t) From The Civil War: Forward to Richmond. Photograph by Al Freni, © 1983 Time-Life Books, Inc. Courtesy, Troiani Collection; v (b) North Wind Picture Archives; vi (t) Frank Driggs Collection; vi (b) The Granger Collection, New York; vii (t) Corbis-Bettmann, vii (b) Culver Pictures, Inc.; viii (b) SuperStock; viii (t) The Granger Collection, New York; ix Library of Congress, FSA/OWI Collection; x (b) Woodfin Camp & Associates, Inc.; xi (t) AP/Wide World Photos; xi (b) Novosti/SIPA Press; xii AP/Wide World Photos; xiv (b) Image copyright © 2000 PhotoDisc, Inc./HRW; xiv (t) Image copyright © 2000 PhotoDisc, Inc./HRW; xiv (c) National Portrait Gallery, Smithsonian Institution/Art Resource, NY; xv (tl) Image copyright © 2000 PhotoDisc, Inc./HRW; xv (extreme l coin) Sam Dudgeon/HRW Photo; xv (bc) Sam Dudgeon/HRW Photo/The Nokia phone is a registered trademark of Nokia Corporation and/or one of its affiliates.; xv (tr) Image copyright © 2000 PhotoDisc, Inc./HRW; xv (b) The Granger Collection, New York; xv (cl coin) Sam Dudgeon/HRW Photo; xv (extreme r coin) Sam Dudgeon/HRW Photo.

Themes in American History: Page xvi-xvii (border), National Archives; xvi (t) Image copyright © 2000 PhotoDisc, Inc./HRW; (tl-poster) Peter Newark's Western Americana; (tl-rider/horse) The Granger Collection, New York; (cl) Michael Holford; (cr) Paul S. Conklin; (b) FSA/OWI Collection, photo by Alfred Palmer, May 1942, Library of Congress/HRW Photo Research Library; xvii, Courtesy Charlotte Luongo/HRW Photo by Victoria Smith; (tr) Sam Dudgeon/HRW Photo/The Nokia phone is a registered trademark of Nokia Corporation and/or one of its affiliates.; (c) The Granger Collection, New York; (r) © Catherine Karnow/Woodfin Camp/PNI; (s) Sam Dudgeon/HRW Photo.

Critical Thinking: Page xviii-xix (border), National Archives; xviii (cl) Corbis/Dave Bartruff; (crt) Victoria Smith/HRW Photo; (crb) Archive Photos; (t) Image copyright © 2000 PhotoDisc, Inc./HRW; (tl-poster) Peter Newark's Western Americana; (tl-rider/horse) The Granger Collection, New York; (b) FSA/OWI Collection, photo by Alfred Palmer, May 1942, Library of Congress/HRW Photo Research Library; xix (t) Courtesy Charlotte Luongo/HRW Photo by Victoria Smith; (c) The Granger Collection, New York; (tr) Sam Dudgeon/HRW Photo/The Nokia phone is a registered trademark of Nokia Corporation and/or one of its affiliates.; (r) © Catherine Karnow/Woodfin Camp/PNI; (b) Sam Dudgeon/HRW Photo.

Unit One: Page 0, Washington University Gallery of Art, St. Louis, MO/SuperStock; 1 (c) Culver Pictures, Inc.; 2 (tl & tr) The Granger Collection, New York; (bl) J. Brain/Peabody Museum, Harvard/Anthro-Photo File; (b) © Bill Bachmann/PhotoEdit; (c) Sistine Chapel, Vatican, Rome, Italy/SuperStock; (tr) The Granger Collection, New York; 3 (tc) Independence National Historical Park Collection; (cl) Corbis/Burnstein Collection; (bl) Corbis/copyright Werner Forman; (bc) Altar Cross from Peter I's Turning Shop, St. Petersburg, c.1720/Hermitage, St. Petersburg, Russia/Bridgeman Art Library; (br) D. Donne Bryant. **Chapter One:** Page 4, The Granger Collection, New York; 5 George Lepp/Tony Stone Images; 6 (t) Michael Holford; 6 (b) Rich Buzzelli/Tom Stack & Associates; 8 Musee Conde, Chantilly/Giraudon; 9 E.T. Archive; 10 British Library/E.T. Archive; 11 The Metropolitan Museum of Art, Gift of J. Pierpont Morgan, 1900. (00.18.2) Photograph copyright 1979 The Metropolitan Museum of Art; 12 Henry E. Huntington Library & Art Gallery; 13 Corbis-Bettmann; 14 Rare Books and Manuscripts Division, The New York Public Library, Astor, Lenox and Tilden Foundations; 15 The Granger Collection, New York; 16 Peabody Essex Museum, Salem, Massachusetts; 17 Culver Pictures, Inc.; 18 The Granger Collection, New York; 19 (t) State Capitol, Commonwealth of Virginia, Courtesy Library of Virginia, image altered; 19 (b) The Granger Collection, New York; 20 Courtesy of the Free Library Of Philadelphia; 21 The Granger Collection, New York; 22 Peter Newark's American Pictures; 23 Collection of the New-York Historical Society; 24 Art Resource, NY; 26 (b) Image copyright © 2000 PhotoDisc, Inc./HRW; 26 (t) HRW Photo Research Library; 26–29 (border) Sam Dudgeon/HRW photo; 30 Independence National Historical Park Collection; 31 Detail of "Washington Addressing the Constitutional Convention." Virginia Museum of Fine Arts, Richmond, VA. Gift of Edgar William and Bernice Chrysler Garbisch. Photo: Ron Jennings, © 2000 Virginia Museum of Fine Arts.; 33 Library of Congress. **Chapter Two:** Page 36, Paul S. Conklin; 37 The Granger Collection, New York; 38 (l) Paul S. Conklin; 38 (r) Jay Mallin Photos; 40 from THE HERBLOCK GALLERY (Simon & Schuster, 1968); 42 Collection, the Supreme Court of the United States, courtesy The Supreme Court Historical Society; 43 Paul Conklin; 44 Independence National Historical Park Collection; 44–63 (border) HRW Photo by Sam Dudgeon; 64 Independence National Historical Park Collection; 65 The Granger Collection, New York; 66 (t) AP/Wide World Photos; 66 (b) Jeffrey Brown/Liaison Agency; 67 (t) Bob Daemmrich Photo, Inc.; 69 Louie Psihoyos/Woodfin Camp & Associates, Inc.; 70 Sandra Baker/Liaison Agency; 71 Paul Sakuma/AP/Wide World Photos; 72 (l) David Young Wolff/PhotoEdit; 72 (r) Spencer Grant/PhotoEdit; 73 Jeff Greenberg/PhotoEdit; 74 (t) Joe Marquette/AP/Wide World Photos; 74 (b) Bob Daemmrich/Stock, Boston; 75 Chris Gardner/AP/Wide World Photos; 78 (t, c, & b) Image copyright © 2000 PhotoDisc, Inc./HRW; 79 H. Abernathy/H. Armstrong Roberts; 80 (t) Image copyright © 2000 PhotoDisc, Inc./HRW; 80 (b) Corbis-Bettmann; 81 (br, tr, cr, & bl) HRW Photo by Lance Schriner; 81 (b) Image copyright © 1998 PhotoDisc, Inc./HRW; 81 (tl) Peter Van Steen/HRW Photo. **Chapter Three:** Page 82, Albert Bierstadt, "Emigrants Crossing the Plains," 1867, Oil on Canvas, A.011.1T: National Cowboy Hall of Fame, Oklahoma City, OK.; 83 Courtesy of the John Carter Brown Library at Brown University; 84 (b) Corbis-Bettmann; 84 (t) Larry Stevens/Nawrocki Stock Photo; 85 (b) The Granger Collection, New York; 85 (t) © Laurie Platt Winfrey Inc./Woodfin Camp & Associates, Inc.; 86 (border) Sam Dudgeon/HRW photo; 86 (t) HRW Photo Research Library; 87 Sally Anderson-Bruce/The Museum of American Political Life, University of Hartford, West Hartford,CT; 88 Collection of the American Numismatic Society, New York; 89 North Wind Picture Archives; 90 (c) & 91 The Granger Collection, New York; 92 (border) Sam Dudgeon/HRW photo; 92 (t) HRW Photo Research Library; 93 National Portrait Gallery, Smithsonian Institution, Gift of the Swedish Colonial Society through Mrs. William Hacker/Art Resource, NY; 94 Archive Photos; 95 Corbis-Bettmann; 97 (t) Smithsonian Institution neg. #75-2984; 97 (b) Image copyright © 1997 PhotoDisc, Inc./HRW; 98 (t) Kennedy Galleries; 98 (b) UPI/Corbis-Bettmann; 99 (border) Sam Dudgeon/HRW photo; 99 (t) HRW Photo Research Library; 100 Archive Photos; 101 Alamo Collection, photograph courtesy the Daughters of the Republic of Texas Library, CT97.23; 102 (b) Archives Division-Texas State Library, Photographer, Eric Beggs; 102 (t) Harcourt Brace Photo; 105 Colorado Historical Society; 106 & 107 The Granger Collection, New York; 108 (b) Virginia Historical Society; 108 (t) from THE CIVIL WAR: FORWARD TO RICHMOND, Photograph by Al Freni, © 1983 Time-Life Books, Inc. Courtesy, Troiani Collection; 110 State Museum of Pennsylvania; 111 National Geographic Image Collection; 112–113 (border) Sam Dudgeon/HRW photo; 112, 113 (t) HRW Photo Research Library; 117 © Frank Siteman/Stock Boston.

Unit Two: Page 118 & 119 (c), The Granger Collection, New York; 120 (tl, & bl) The Granger Collection, New York; (tr) Corbis; (bc) National Maritime Museum, Greenwich, London; (br) Giraudon/Art Resource, NY; 121 (tl, & tc) The Granger Collection, New York; (tr) Photography by Karen Yamauchi for Chermayeff & Geismar Inc./Metaform Inc.; (bl) Corbis/Craig Aurness; (cbl & cbr) IOC/Olympic Museum Collections; (br) Spode three handled cup commemorating the South African War, 19th century/Spode Cotehele House, Cornwall, UK/Bridgeman Art Library. **Chapter Four:** Page 122, North Wind Picture Archives; 123 The Museum of the Confederacy Richmond, Virginia, Katherine Wetzel Photographer; 124 The Valentine Museum; 125 (t) Library of Congress; 125 (borders) HRW Photo by Sam Dudgeon; 125 (rc) HRW Photo Research Library 127 (c) The Stock Market/© William Taufic; 127 (trb) Sam Dudgeon/HRW Photo; 128 SuperStock; 129 Corbis-Bettmann; 130 Stock Montage, Inc.; 131 (b) Corbis-Bettmann; 131 (t), 132, & 133 (b) The Granger Collection, New York; 133 (t) Louisiana Collection, Howard Tilton Memorial Library, New Orleans, LA 70118; 134 The Granger Collection, New York; 135 Library of Congress; 136 Courtesy of South Caroliniana Library, University of South Carolina, Columbia.; 137 The Granger Collection, New York; 139 North Wind Picture Archives; 140 (t) U.S. Senate Collection; 140 (b) The Granger Collection, New York; 141 H. Armstrong Roberts; 142 Corbis-Bettmann; 143 & 144 The Granger Collection, New York; 145 (t) Archive Photos; 145 (b) North Wind Picture Archives; 146 (c) The Granger Collection, New York; 147 Courtesy of Fisk University Library, Special Collections.

Chapter Five: Page 150, Peter Newark's Western Americana; 151 The Granger Collection, New York; 152 (t) Werner Forman Archive, Pohrt Collection, Plains Indian Museum, BBHC, Cody Wyoming, USA/Art Resource, NY; 152 (b) Corbis-Bettmann; 154 The Granger Collection, New York; 155 (c) & 156 Corbis-Bettmann; 157 The Granger Collection, New York; 158 E.R. Degginger/Color-Pic, Inc.; 159 National Archives (NARA) 160 (l) Colorado Historical Society; 160 (r) Peter Newark's Western Americana; 161 (c) Hulton Deutsch Collection/Tony Stone Images; 162 (t) Peter Newark's Western Americana; 162 (b) Peter Newark's American Pictures; 163 (l) Peter Newark's Western Americana; 163 (r) Union Pacific Museum Collection; 164 Boltin Picture Library; 165 (t) Peter Newark's Western Americana; 165 (b) Montana Historical Society, Helena; 166 (t) Peter Newark's Western Americana; 166 (b) Solomon D. Butcher Collection, Library of Congress; 167 (l) Buffalo Bill Historic Center, Cody, Wyoming; 167 (r) Peter Newark's Western Americana; 169 The Granger Collection, New York; 170 Peter Newark's Western Americana; 171 (t) AKG London; 171 (b) S.D. Butcher/Denver Public Library, Western History Collection; 173 Courtesy of the California History Room, California State Library, Sacramento, California; 174 (b) Peter Newark's Western Americana; 174 (bkgd) © PI/Photo © David Hardwood/Panoramic Images, Chicago 1998; 174 (tl) Peter Newark's Western Americana; 174 (tr) The Granger Collection, New York; 175 Library of Congress; 178 (tl, tr, & b) & 179 Image copyright © 2000 PhotoDisc, Inc./HRW; 178 (c) Colorado Historical Society; 180 National Archives (NARA); 181 Image copyright © 2000 PhotoDisc, Inc./HRW. **Chapter Six:** Page 182, The Granger Collection, New York; 183 Archive Photos; 185 (tl & br) The Granger Collection, New York; 185 (bl) Science Museum, London, UK/Bridgeman Art Library, London/New York; 186 (c) & 187 The Granger Collection, New York; 188 Stock Montage, Inc.; 189 From the Conwellana-Templana Collection of the Temple University Libraries; 190 (t) Culver Pictures, Inc.; 191 Carnegie Library of Pittsburg; 192 Courtesy of the Rockefeller Archive Center, photograph by Charles Uht. John D. Rockefeller, painted by Eastman Johnson, 1895; 192 (b) Sam Dudgeon/HRW photo; 192 HRW Photo Research Library; 193 (c) The Granger Collection, New York; 194 & 195 Corbis-Bettmann; 196 The Granger Collection, New York; 197 Corbis-Bettmann; 199 The Granger Collection, New York; 200 Corbis-Bettmann; 201 The Granger Collection, New York; 202 J.R. Holland/Stock, Boston; 203 (t) The Granger Collection, New York; 203 (b) Library of Congress; 204 The Granger Collection, New York; 205 Corbis-Bettmann; 207 The Granger Collection, New York. **Chapter Seven:** Page 208, Library of Congress #LCUSZC4-4637 DLC Detroit Publishing Co. Photo Collection; 209 The Granger Collection, New York; 210 Photography by Karen Yamauchi for Chermayeff & Geismar Inc./Metaform Inc.; 211 (t) Frank Driggs Collection; 211 (b) FPG International; 212 Culver Pictures, Inc.; 213 & 214 The Granger Collection, New York; 215 Photography by Karen Yamauchi for Chermayeff & Geismar Inc./Metaform Inc.; 217 (t) The Granger Collection, New York; 217 (b) Photo courtesy of Illinois Railway Museum; 218 (c) The Granger Collection, New York; 219 (b) Corbis/Hulton-Deutsch Collection; 219 (t) 1901 Autumn Announcement reprinted courtesy of the Marshall Field's Archive, Chicago, IL; 220 (b) The Granger Collection, New York; 220 (t) National Gallery of Art, Washington, D.C./SuperStock; 221 Corbis; 222 David Spindel/SuperStock; 223 (l) Everett Collection; 223 (r) National Baseball Hall of Fame Library & Archive, Milo Stewart, Jr., Cooperstown, N.Y.; 224 (tr) Corbis; 224 (bl) Corbis-Bettmann; 225 KJA Dime Novels, Rare Books and Manuscripts Division, The New York Public Library, Astor, Lenox and Tilden Foundations; 226 (b) Museum of Fine Arts, Boston, Massachusetts/SuperStock; 226 (t) Giraudon/Art Resource, NY; 227 (r) Corbis/Paul Almasy; 227 (l) The Granger Collection, New York; 231 © Jonathan Nourok/PhotoEdit.

Unit Three: Page 232, SuperStock; 233 (c) Corbis-Bettmann; 234 (tl) The Granger Collection, New York; (c) Christie's Images; (tc) Sam Dudgeon/HRW Photo/Courtesy The European Influence, Austin, Texas.; (b & tr) SuperStock; 235 (t & tr) The Granger Collection, New York; (bl) Stock Montage/SuperStock; (br) Archive Photos; (tc) Barbara Puorro Galasso/Courtesy George Eastman House; (bc) SuperStock. **Chapter Eight:** Page 236, (t) The Granger Collection, New York; 237 Stock Montage, Inc.; 238-240 The Granger Collection, New York; 241 Brown Brothers; 242 (bl) Corbis-Bettmann; 242 (br) Culver Pictures, Inc.; 242 (tl) Everett/CSU Archives; 242 (t) SuperStock; 242 (tr) Corbis; 243 Corbis-Bettmann; 244 (tr) Courtesy of the Rosenberg Library, Galveston, Texas; 244 (b) Library of Congress; 245 The Granger Collection, New York; 246 (t) Corbis-Bettmann; 246 (r) Brown Brothers; 247 The Granger Collection, New York; 248 Corbis-Bettmann; 249 (tr) UPI/Corbis-Bettmann; 249 (tl) The Granger Collection, New York; 250 AP/Wide World Photos; 251 Library of Congress; 252 Library of Congress; 253 (c) © Mary Cassatt/Wood River Gallery/PNI; 254 & 255 Corbis-Bettmann; 256 National Portrait Gallery, Smithsonian Institution/Art Resource, NY; 258 Library of Congress; 259 (b) The Granger Collection, New York; 259 (t) Corbis-Bettmann; 260 (t) Courtesy of Rio Grande Press; 260 (b) Corbis; 261 Keystone-Mast Collection, UCR/CALIFORNIA MUSEUM OF

PHOTOGRAPHY, University of California, Riverside. **Chapter Nine:** Page 264, The Granger Collection, New York; 265 Library of Congress; 266 (b) The Granger Collection, New York; 266 (t) The National Museum of American History by Shirley Abbott. Published by Harry N. Abrams, Inc., New York; 267 Theodore Roosevelt Collection, Harvard College Library; 268 Corbis-Bettmann; 269 (c) © Laurie Platt Winfrey, Inc./Woodfin Camp & Associates, Inc.; 271 Corbis-Bettmann; 272 The Granger Collection, New York; 273 Archive Photos; 274 (t) Stock Montage, Inc.; 274 (b) The Granger Collection, New York; 275 (b) Corbis-Bettmann; 275 (t) Tacoma Tribune/Forest History Society; 276 (b) Theodore Roosevelt Collection, Harvard College Library; 276 (t) The Granger Collection, New York; 278 Bridgeman Art Library, London/New York; 279 (t) Corbis-Bettmann; 279 (b) © Spencer Grant/Stock, Boston/PNI; 280 (c) Bob Daemmrich Photography; 281 Stock Montage, Inc.; 282 Courtesy of the Crisis Publishing Co., the publisher of the magazine of the National Association for the Advancement of Colored People. General Research and Reference Division; Schomburg Center for Research in Black Culture; The New York Public Library; Astor, Lenox and Tilden Foundations; 283 The Granger Collection, New York; 285 Stock Montage, Inc. **Chapter Ten:** Page 286, Library of Congress; 287 Stock Montage, Inc.; 288 The Granger Collection, New York; 289 (t) Anchorage Museum of History and Art, Gift of Mr. and Mrs. John M. Sorenson; 289 (b) Library of Congress; 290 UPI/Corbis-Bettmann; 291 (c) Bishop Museum, The State Museum of Natural and Cultural History; 292 Peabody Essex Museum, Salem, Massachusetts; 293 Snark International/Art Resource, NY; 294 Brown Brothers; 296 (b) © Laurie Platt Winfrey Inc./Woodfin Camp & Associates, Inc.; 296 (t) & 298 (c) The Granger Collection, New York; 299 Library of Congress; 300 Keystone-Mast Collection #X6637, UCR/University of California at Riverside/California Museum of Photography ; 301 U.S. Naval Institute Photo Archives; 302 & 304 (t) The Granger Collection, New York; 304 (b) Brown Brothers; 306 The Granger Collection, New York; 307 Corbis-Bettmann; 308 & 309 (b) The Granger Collection, New York; 309 (t) Library of Congress; 311 & 313 The Granger Collection, New York; 314 (br) Davies & Starr Inc./Tony Stone Images; 314 (c) © Burke; Triolo/FoodPix/PNI; 314 (t) Stock Montage/SuperStock; 314 (bl) Image copyright © 1998 PhotoDisc, Inc./HRW; 315 National Archives/HRW Photo Library; 316 Courtesy of © The Mariners' Museum, Newport News, Virginia; 317 (t) SuperStock; 317 (b) Image copyright © 1998 PhotoDisc, Inc./HRW; 319 Michelle Bridwell/Frontera Fotos.

Unit Four: Page 320, National Archives (NARA); 321 (c) The Granger Collection, New York; 322 (tl) The Granger Collection, New York; (tc & tr) Photo by Sam Dudgeon/Courtesy The Neon Radio, Lockhart, Texas, www.neonradio.com; (br) SuperStock; (bl) Sam Dudgeon/HRW Photo/The Detroit News; 323 (t) Corbis/Bettmann; (bc) Mary Evans Photo Library, England; (br) The Granger Collection, New York; (bl) AKG Photo, London; (tl) © Tribune Media Services, Inc. All Rights Reserved. Reprinted with permission.; (tr) SuperStock. **Chapter Eleven:** Page 324, Culver Pictures, Inc.; 325 Liaison Agency; 326 Nawrocki Stock Photo; 327 (t) The Granger Collection, New York; 327 (b) Archive Photos; 328 Corbis-Bettmann; 329 Lunch at Chatillon camp for the 8th Battalion, August 1918 (oil on canvas) by Joseph Felix Bouchor (1853–1937), Musee Franco-Americaine, Blerancourt, Chauny, France/Roger-Viollet, Paris/Bridgeman Art Library, London/New York; 330 (l) Trustees of the Imperial War Museum, London; 330 (r) Culver Pictures, Inc.; 333 (b) Woodfin Camp & Associates, Inc.; 333 (br) Stock Montage, Inc.; 333 (t) & 334 The Granger Collection, New York; 335 Sam Dudgeon/HRW photo; 336 © Archive Photos/PNI; 337 The Granger Collection, New York; 338 Archive Photos; 339 The Granger Collection, New York; 340 Eric Beggs/HRW Photo; 341 (t) Liaison Agency; 341 (b) Corbis-Bettmann; 343 (l) Archive Photos; 343 (r) © Dorling Kindersley Ltd./Courtesy of Spink & Son Ltd., London.; 344 UPI/Corbis-Bettmann; 345 Corbis-Bettmann; 346 (t) Trustees of the Imperial War Museum, London; 346 (b) © Laurent Van Der Stockt/Liaison Agency; 348 (bkgd) Corbis-Bettmann; 348 (r, & l) HRW Photo by Eric E. Beggs; 349 Corbis-Bettmann; 350 (c) HRW Photo Research Library; 350 (t & b) HRW Photo by Sam Dudgeon; 351 (c) The Granger Collection, New York; 351 (t & b) HRW Photo by Sam Dudgeon. **Chapter Twelve:** Page 354, Laurie Platt Winfrey Inc./Woodfin Camp & Associates, Inc.; 355 National Archives (NARA); 356 The Granger Collection, New York; 357 (c) Brown Brothers; 358 (t) Corbis/Pemco-Webster & Stevens Collection; Museum of History & Industry, Seattle; 358 (c) Corbis-Bettmann; 359 Stock Montage, Inc.; 360 (b) The Museum of Modern Art, New York. Gift of Abby Aldrich Rockefeller. Photograph © 1997 The Museum of Modern Art, New York. © 1997 Estate of Ben Shahn/Licensed by VAGA, New York, NY; 360 (t) & 361 UPI/Corbis-Bettmann; 362 HRW Photo by Lance Schriner; 363 Corbis-Bettmann; 364 The Granger Collection, New York; 365 (b) The Granger Collection, New York; 365 (t) Steven Laschever/The Museum of American Political Life, University of Hartford, West Hartford,CT; 366 Herbert Hoover Presidential Library/Corbis; 367 Archive Photos; 368 (b) The Granger Collection, New York; 368 (t) From the Collections of Henry Ford Museum and Greenfield Village; 369 Detail, Mural: Detroit Industry, South Wall, by Diego M. Rivera, Gift of Edsel B. Ford, Photograph © 1994, The Detroit Institute of Arts; 370 (t) Stock Montage, Inc.; 370 (b) & 371 (b) The Granger Collection, New York; 371 (t) Sam Dudgeon/HRW photo; 372 Culver Pictures, Inc.; 373 & 374 (bl) The Granger Collection, New York; 374 (tl) Christie's Images; 374 (br) ©Lionel Green/Archive Photos/PNI; 375 (c) Christie's Images; 376 Corbis/Pemco-Webster & Stevens Collection; Museum of History & Industry, Seattle; 379 Image copyright © 2000 PhotoDisc, Inc./HRW. **Chapter Thirteen:** Page 380, (l) The Granger Collection, New York; 380 (r) John Held Jr., LIFE Magazine, © TIME Inc./Courtesy of the general libraries, The University of Texas at Austin/HRW photo by Victoria Smith; 381 SuperStock; 382 (b) Brown Brothers; 382 (t) SuperStock; 383 ED Archive, London/SuperStock; 384 © Collection of the New-York Historical Society; 385 (l) Woodfin Camp & Associates, Inc.; 385 (r) Culver Pictures, Inc.; 386 The Granger Collection, New York; 387 & 388 (t) Photography by Karen Yamauchi for Chermayeff & Geismar Inc./Metaform Inc.; 388 (b) The Granger Collection, New York; 389 (t) Photography by Karen Yamauchi for Chermayeff & Geismar Inc./Metaform Inc.; 389 (b) Archive Photos; 390 (t) Arte Publico Press, University of Houston, 1991; 390 (b) Corbis-Bettmann; 390 (cl) Courtesy of Rosie & Henry Montalvo/HRW Photo by Victoria Smith; 391 APA/Archive Photos; 393 (t) AP/Wide World Photos; 393 (b) Courtesy of Karen Sherrod, Austin, TX/HRW Photo by Victoria Smith; 394 Courtesy of Texas Highways Magazine; 395 (c) Walt Disney Pict./Shooting Star International; 396 (l) SuperStock; 396 (r) Walt Disney Pict./Shooting Star International; 397 (b) Corbis-Bettmann; 397 (t) & 398 The Granger Collection, New York; 399 & 400 Archive Photos; 400 (b) Ed Carlin/Archive Photos; 400 (tr) © Hulton Getty/Woodfin Camp & Associates, Inc.; 402 National Portrait Gallery, Smithsonian Institution/Art Resource, NY; 403 (t) Addison Gallery of American

Art, Phillips Academy; 403 (b) Corbis/Ansel Adams Publishing Rights Trust; 404 (c) © 1999 The Georgia O'Keeffe Foundation/Artists Rights Society (ARS), New York. The Metropolitan Museum of Art, Alfred Stieglitz Collection, 1952. (52.203) Photograph © 1994 The Metropolitan Museum of Art; 405 © Catherine Karnow/Woodfin Camp/PNI; 407 (b) The Phillips Collection, Washington, D.C.; 408 (t, c, bl, & b-chart) Image copyright © 2000 PhotoDisc, Inc./HRW; 408 (t-chart) Digital Stock Corp./HRW; 409 Library of Congress/Corbis; 410 (l) Photographs & Prints Division, Schomburg Center for Research in Black Culture, The New York Public Library, Astor, Lenox and Tilden Foundations; 410 (t) & 411 (r) Image copyright © 2000 PhotoDisc, Inc./HRW; 411 (l) Brown Brothers; 412 The Granger Collection, New York; 413 © William Hart/PhotoEdit.

Unit Five: Page 414, American Red Cross; 415 (c) The Granger Collection, New York; 416 (tl) O. J. Jordan/Time Magazine; (tc) Texas Ranger Hall of Fame and Museum, Waco, Texas. Sam Dudgeon/HRW Photo ; (cl) SIPA Press; (cr) Wood River Gallery/PNI; (b) National Maritime Museum, Greenwich, London; (tr) Corbis/Richard A. Cooke; 417 (tc) Courtesy Charlotte Luongo/Victoria Smith/HRW photo; (bc) Courtesy of Jed Collectibles, Pemberton, New Jersey/© 1943 renewed 1971 by Harcourt Inc. /HRW Photo by Sam Dudgeon; (bl) Smithsonian Institute; (tr) Archive Photos; (br) Jodi Cobb/National Geographic Society Image Collection; (tl) Culver Pictures, Inc. **Chapter Fourteen:** Page 418, The Granger Collection, New York; 419 HRW Photo by Sam Dudgeon; 420 (br) Archive Photos; 420 (cr) FPG International; 420 (tl) John Held Jr., LIFE Magazine, © TIME Inc./Courtesy of the general libraries, The University of Texas at Austin/HRW photo by Victoria Smith; 421 & 422 (t) The Granger Collection, New York; 422 (b) Brown Brothers; 423 AP/Wide World Photos; 424 © Cindy Lewis 1997; 425 AP/Wide World Photos; 426 (br) National Museum of American Art, Smithsonian Institution, Washington, D.C./Art Resource, NY; 426 (t) Brown Brothers; 427 (c) Harry Ransom Humanities Research Center The University of Texas at Austin; 428 The Granger Collection, New York; 429 Brown Brothers; 430 Archive Photos; 431 The Granger Collection, New York; 432 (t) Franklin D. Roosevelt Library; 432 (b) FPG International; 433 (border) Sam Dudgeon/HRW Photo; 433 (c) HRW Photo Research Library 434 (tl) National Portrait Gallery, Smithsonian Institution/Art Resource, NY; 434 (br) Corbis-Bettmann; 435 (tc) Culver Pictures, Inc.; 435 (br) AP/Wide World Photos; 437 Library of Congress; 438 UPI/Corbis-Bettmann; 439 (c) Lawrence Migdale/Stock Boston; 439 (tc) The Granger Collection, New York; 440 (b) Albro, Maxine: California Agriculture (detail). Coit Tower, San Francisco, 1934. Photo by Lito, courtesy Masha Zakheim; 440 (t) Franklin D. Roosevelt Library; 442 & 443 The Granger Collection, New York. **Chapter Fifteen:** Page 446, Dallas Museum of Art, Dallas Art Association Purchase; 447 Lambert/Archive Photos; 448 (cl, cr, & t) Sam Dudgeon/HRW Photo; 448 (b) Corbis-Bettmann; 449 Southern Historical Collection, University of North Carolina, Photo by Louise Boyle; 450 Franklin D. Roosevelt Library; 451 (c) The Granger Collection, New York. From THE GRAPES OF WRATH by John Steinbeck. Copyright 1939 renewed © 1967 by John Steinbeck. Used by permission of Viking Penguin, a division of Penguin Putnam, Inc.; 452 Library of Congress; 453 & 454 Brown Brothers; 455 UPI/Corbis-Bettmann; 456 National Archives (NARA); 457 Archive Photos; 458 (b) Art Institute of Chicago/SuperStock; 458 (tl) & 459 (b) The Granger Collection, New York; 459 (t) Archive Photos; 460 (tc) Courtesy of Ruth Sugeno from the Kerbey Lane Doll Shoppe, Austin, TX. Sam Dudgeon/HRW Photo; 460 (l) Jay Mallin Photos; 460 (b) Everett Collection; 461 Corbis/Bettman; 462 HRW Photo by Sam Dudgeon; 463 (tl & tc) David King Collection; 463 (b) Culver Pictures, Inc; 464 Nawrocki Stock Photo; 465 Arnold Kramer, United States Holocaust Memorial Museum; 467 The Granger Collection, New York; 470 (t) Classic PIO Partners; 470 (c, br, & bl) Image copyright © 2000 PhotoDisc, Inc./HRW; 471 Hulton-Deutsch Collection/Corbis; 472 (b) FPG International; 472 (t & c) Image copyright © 2000 PhotoDisc, Inc./HRW; 473 (t) Charles Apple; 473 (bl) Brown Brothers; 473 (br) Image copyright © 1998 PhotoDisc, Inc./HRW. **Chapter Sixteen:** Page 474, The Granger Collection, New York; 475 Library of Congress/Corbis; 476 (t) Archive Photos; 476 (b) National Gallery of Canada, Ottawa, Gift of the Massey Collection of English Painting, 1946.; 478 Brown Brothers; 479 Archive Photos; 480 HRW Photo by Sam Dudgeon, stamps courtesy Kristen Darby; 481 (b) UPI/Corbis-Bettmann; 481 (t) The Granger Collection, New York; 482 (c) Archive Photos; 483 Library of Congress, FSA/OWI Collection; 484 Hulton-Deutsch Collection/Corbis; 485 (bl) AKG Photo; 485 (tr) Courtesy Sen. Daniel Inouye; 486 (b) Ria-Novosti/Sovfoto; 486 (t) Archive Photos; 488 (c) AKG Photo; 489 Library of Congress, FSA/OWI Collection; 490 Archive Photos; 491 (t) Nawrocki Stock Photo; 491 (b) United States Marine Corps; 492 AKG Photo; 494 AP Photo/Joe Rosenthal/Wide World Photos; 495 Photri; 496 (t) AKG Photo; 496 (bl) AP/Wide World Photos; 496 (br) Phillip Jones-Griffiths/Magnum Photos; 497 (c) Archive Photos; 498 Nawrocki Stock Photo; 499 Corbis-Bettmann; 502 Sam Dudgeon/HRW photo/Courtesy Victoria Smith and Blas Cantú; 503 © Robin L. Sachs/PhotoEdit.

Unit Six: Page 504, © Willinger/FPG International; 505 (c) Photofest; 506 (cl) Everett Collection; (tc) 1999 Jay Mallin; (tr) Ken Eward/Science Source/Photo Researchers, Inc.; (tl) Classic PIO Partners; (b) SuperStock; 507 (tl & br) SuperStock; (bc) © Colorsport; (tc) Everett Collection; (tr) J. David Andrews/Masterfile; (bl) Royal Geographic Society.

Chapter Seventeen: Page 508, Franklin D. Roosevelt Library; 509 Copyright © 1945 by The New York Times Co. Reprinted by Permission; 510 (t) UPI/Corbis-Bettmann; 510 (b) SuperStock; 511 (b) Archive Photos; 511 (t) UPI/Corbis-Bettmann; 512 Editorial cartoon by Tom Little, 1948; courtesy of the Nashville Tennessean; 513 HRW Photo by Sam Dudgeon/U.S. Postal Service; 514 (border) Sam Dudgeon/HRW photo; 514 (c) HRW Photo Research Library; 515 Woodfin Camp & Associates, Inc.; 516 (c) © Andres Hernandez/Liaison Agency; 517 Victoria Smith/HRW Photo; 518 Alfred Eisenstaedt, LIFE Magazine, © TIME Inc.; 519 (t) The White House, Courtesy Harry S. Truman Library; 519 (b) Veterans Administration Photo; 520 Corbis-Bettmann; 521 The White House Collection, copyright White House Historical Association and The National Archives and Records Administration; 522 & 523 (t) The Granger Collection, New York; 523 (b) Corbis-Bettmann; 525 (l) Archive Photos; 525 (r) Corbis-Bettmann; 526 AP/Wide World Photos; 527 Michael Barson/Archive Photos; 528 (r) Syracuse University Library Department of Special Collections. Syracuse, New York; 529 (l) Archive Photos; 529 (r) UPI/Corbis-Bettmann; 530 (l) Everett Collection; 531 Archive Photos; 534 (t & b) Image copyright © 2000 PhotoDisc, Inc./HRW; 534 (c) UPI/Corbis-Bettmann; 535 Library of Congress/Corbis; 536 (l) Archive Photos; 536 (r) Image copyright © 2000 PhotoDisc, Inc./HRW; 537 (l) © N/A/Chicago Historical Society/PNI; 537 (r) Image copyright © 1998 PhotoDisc, Inc./HRW. **Chapter Eighteen:** Page 538, Ewing Galloway; 539 Corbis-Bettmann; 540 (r) © Sovfoto/Eastfoto; 540 (l) Reuters/HO/Archive Photos; 542 (c) FPG International; 543 Lockheed Martin Corporation; 544 The

Power of Positive Thinking © 1952, 1978 by Prentice-Hall, Inc. Courtesy the Norman Vincent Peale Center for Christian Living. HRW photo by Sam Dudgeon.; 546 (t) © Cindy Lewis; 546 (b) © 1954/TIME Inc. Reprinted by Permission; 548 (t) © The New Yorker Collection 1954 Robert Day from cartoonbank.com. All Rights Reserved; 548 (b) Archive Photos; 550 Hake's Americana, York, PA; 551 (t) © L.P. Winfrey/Woodfin Camp & Associates, Inc.; 551 (b) Everett Collection; 552 (c) © 1999 Pollock-Krasner Foundation/Artists Rights Society (ARS) New York. Musee National d'Art Moderne, Paris, France/Giraudon/Art Resource, NY; 553 Corbis; 554 Corbis-Bettmann; 555 UPI/Bettmann Newsphotos; 556 Black Star; 557 UPI/Corbis-Bettmann Newsphotos; 558 (t) AP/Wide World Photos; 558 (b) Brown Brothers; 559 UPI/Corbis-Bettmann Newsphoto; 562 Victoria Smith/HRW Photo, Courtesy Cynthia H. Luongo; 563 Sam Dudgeon/HRW Photo.

Unit Seven: Page 564, NASA/HRW Photo Research Library; 565 (c) Arnie Sachs, © 1994 Consolidated News Pictures; 566 (c & tl) Everett Collection; (tr) Courtesy of VISTA/Peace Corps; (tc) Christie's Images; (b) Corbis/Jeremy Horner; 567 (tcr & tcl) Reprinted by permission of Ms. Magazine © 1972/Courtesy of the general libraries, The University of Texas at Austin/Sam Dudgeon/HRW Photo; (tl) SuperStock; (br) Lyle Leduc/Liaison Agency; (bl) Corbis/Christopher Cormack; (tr) © 1999 Jay Mallin All rights reserved. **Chapter Nineteen:** Page 568, AP/Wide World Photos; 569 (t) HRW Photo by Victoria Smith; 569 (b) Victoria Smith/HRW Photo; 570 Corbis; 571 (l) AP/Wide World Photos; 571 (r) Owen/Black Star; 572 Photri; 573 ©1961 Newsweek, Inc. All rights reserved. Reprinted by permission. Courtesy of the general libraries, The University of Texas at Austin/HRW Photo by Victoria Smith; 574 (c) © Bob Daemmrich/The Image Works; 575 UPI/Corbis-Bettmann; 577 Sovfoto; 578 Carlos A. Hedstrom, Jr. Collection/The Sixth Floor Museum at Dealey Plaza; 579 (t) Arnold Newman/Lyndon Baines Johnson Library Collection; 579 (b) AP/Wide World Photos; 580 (b) Lyndon Baines Johnson Library Collection/Photo by Victoria Smith; 580 (t) Ralph Morse LIFE Magazine, © TIME Inc.; 581 (b) Lyndon Baines Johnson Library Collection; 581 (t) Reprinted with permission from the Atlanta Journal and the Atlanta Constitution/Lyndon Baines Johnson Library Collection; 582 Charles Moore/Black Star; 583 Ted Cowell/Black Star; 584 (t) AP/Wide World Photos; 584 (b) Henry Diltz/Corbis; 585 (c) © 1999 The Andy Warhol Foundation for the Visual Arts /ARS, New York, Corbis-Bettmann; 586 (t) AP/Wide World Photos; 586 (bl, bc, & br) Archive Photos; 587 Jacques Chenet/Woodfin Camp & Associates, Inc.; 588 Smithsonian Institute; 589 L. P. Winfrey/Woodfin Camp & Associates, Inc.; 591 Alfred Eisenstaedt/Life Magazine © Time Inc.; 593 Rauschenberg, Robert, Estate, 1963, Philadelphia Museum of Art: Gift of the Friends of the Philadelphia Museum of Art. **Chapter Twenty:** Page 594, UPI/Corbis-Bettmann; 595 © 1976 Bill Pogue c/o MIRA; 596 AP/Wide World Photos; 598 UPI/Corbis-Bettmann; 599 UPI/Corbis-Bettmann; 600 (bl) AP/Wide World Photos; 600 (t) © 1998 John Launois/Black Star; 600 (br), 601, 602 & 603 (border) Sam Dudgeon/HRW Photo; 603 (c) Woodfin Camp & Associates, Inc.; 604 Dr. Hector P. Garcia Papers, Special Collections & Archives, Texas A&M University-Corpus Christi Bell Library; 605 (tc) Archive Photos; 605 (bl & br) Image copyright © 2001 PhotoDisc, Inc.; 606 (t) J.R. Eyerman/Time Magazine; 606 (b) Sally Andersen-Bruce, Museum of American Political Life; 607 (c) From Mexican American Literature; 608 Woodfin Camp & Associates, Inc.; 609 Courtesy of Elizabeth Martinez; 610 Associated Press AP/Wide World Photos; 611 (r) The Schlesinger Library, Radcliffe College/From THE FEMININE MYSTIQUE by Betty Friedan. Copyright ©1983, 1974, 1973, 1963 by Betty Friedan. Reprinted by permission of W. W. Norton & Company, Inc.; 611 (l) Corbis-Bettmann; 612 (t) Corbis/Reuters; 612 (b) AP/Wide World Photos; 613 (c) Corbis/AFP; 614 (t) AP/Wide World Photos; 614 (b) Richard Pasely/Stock Boston; 615 (r) © Martin A. Levick; 615 (l) Victoria Smith/HRW Photo; 616 © Chris Arend/AllStock/PNI; 617 (t) Dennis Brack/Black Star; 617 (b) AP/Wide World Photos; 618 © David Burnett/Contact Press Images/PNI; 619 Corbis-Bettmann. **Chapter Twenty-One:** Page 622, Arthur Grace/Sygma; 623 © Harlingue-Viollet/Liaison Agency; 624 Woodfin Camp & Associates, Inc.; 625 (t) Michigan State University Archives & Historical Collections; 625 (b) UPI/Corbis-Bettmann; 626 AP/Wide World Photos; 627 Max Scheler/Black Star; 629 (t) Archive Photos; 629 (b) AP/Jeff Widener/Wide World Photos; 630 Larry Burrows, LIFE Magazine © TIME Warner Inc.; 631 Sara Matthews/Swarthmore College Peace Collection; 632 (t) CBS News; 632 (b) AP/Wide World Photos; 634 (b) Jack Kightlinger/Lyndon Baines Johnson Library Collection; 634 (b) Archive Photos; 635 Roger Lubin/Jerobam 1972; 636 AP/Wide World Photos; 637 (t) Corbis-Bettmann; 637 (b) & 638 UPI/Corbis-Bettmann; 639 (t) Jean Claude Fracolon/Liaison Agency; 639 (b) Sam Dudgeon/HRW Photo, Courtesy Gene Rumann; 640 (c) AP/Wide World Photos; 641 UPI/Corbis-Bettmann; 644 (c) Corbis/Tim Page; 644 (t) Corbis/Nik Wheeler; 644 (b) Image copyright © 1998 PhotoDisc/HRW; 645 Corbis/Wolfgang Kaehler; 646 (b) Photri; 646 (t) Lyle Leduc/Liaison Agency; 646 (c) Digital Stock Corp./HRW; 647 (bl) © Charles Bonnay/Black Star/PNI; 647 (t) Victoria Smith/HRW Photo; 647 (c) Law/The Image Works; 647 (br) Image copyright © 1998 PhotoDisc, Inc./HRW; 649 Andy Sacks/Tony Stone Images.

Unit Eight: Page 650, R. Krubner/H. Armstrong Roberts; 651 © Stephen Frisch/Stock Boston; 652 (tl) National Archives/HRW Photo Research Library; (tc) Bill Pierce/Woodfin Camp & Associates, Inc.; (c) Corbis/Wally McNamee; (tr) Dennis Brack/Black Star/PNI; (bl) SuperStock; (br) Copyright T.S.M./Woodfin Camp & Associates, Inc.; 653 (tr) © 1999 Jay Mallin; (bl) AP/Wide World Photos; (br) Stephen Alvarez/National Geographic Image Collection; (tl) Wally McNamee/Woodfin Camp & Associates, Inc.; (c) JPL/NASA. **Chapter Twenty-Two:** Page 654 & 655, AP/Wide World Photos; 656 (t) Archive Photos; 656 (b) © John Barr/Liaison Agency; 658 (bkgd) Image copyright © 2000 PhotoDisc, Inc./HRW; 658 (r-car) Digital Stock Corp./HRW; 658 (l-gas pumps) Richard Haynes/HRW Photo; 659 Liaison Agency; 660 ©1999 Dennis Brack/Black Star; 661 AP/Wide World Photos; 662 (t) Margulies/Rothco; 662 (b) The Granger Collection, New York; 663 UPI/Corbis-Bettmann; 664 (b) © 1976 Dirck Halstead/Liaison Agency; 664 (t) Corbis-Bettmann; 665 Photri; 666 Ted Hardin/Black Star; 667 (b) Wally McNamee/Woodfin Camp & Associates, Inc.; 667 (t) Corbis-Bettmann; 668 (c) Jeff Greenberg/PhotoEdit; 669 UPI/Corbis-Bettmann; 670 © Alain Mingham/Liaison Agency; 671 Sam Dudgeon/HRW Photo; 673 (t) Paul Barton/The Stock Market; 673 (b) Jason Laure/Woodfin Camp & Associates, Inc.; 674 Corbis/Galen Rowell; 675 (t) Image copyright © 2000 PhotoDisc, Inc./HRW; 675 (c) Jim Pozarik/Liaison Agency; 676 (t) Photo courtesy of Apple Computer, Inc.; 676 (b) © 1997 Lucasfilm Ltd./Photofest; 677 © Ned Matura/Liaison Agency; 679 Draper Hill/© 1974 The Commercial Appeal, Memphis. **Chapter Twenty-Three:** Page 680, Novosti/SIPA Press; 681 © Michael Evans/Sygma; 682 (t) Sygma; 682 (b) Wally McNamee/Woodfin Camp & Associates, Inc.; 683 (t)